Commercial Law

Second Edition

Edited by:

Professor Michael Furmston
Singapore Management University and Emeritus Professor, University of Bristol

Professor Jason Chuah
Head of Academic Law, City University London

With contributions from:

James Devenney, Professor of Commercial Law and Head of the School of Law, University of Exeter

Susan Hawker, Principal Lecturer, London Metropolitan University

Howard Johnson, LLM Tutor Cardiff University

Louise Merrett, Senior Lecturer in Law, University of Cambridge

Martin Morgan-Taylor, Principal Lecturer, De Montfort University

Jo Reddy, Adjunct Lecturer, The University of Hong Kong

Chris Willett, Professor in Commercial Law, University of Essex

PEARSON

Harlow, England • London • New York • Boston • San Francisco • Toronto • Sydney
Auckland • Singapore • Hong Kong • Tokyo • Seoul • Taipei • New Delhi
Cape Town • São Paulo • Mexico City • Madrid • Amsterdam • Munich • Paris • Milan

Pearson Education Limited
Edinburgh Gate
Harlow CM20 2JE
United Kingdom
Tel: +44 (0)1279 623623
Web: www.pearson.com/uk

First published 2010 (print)
Second edition published 2013 (print and electronic)

The rights of Michael Furmston and Jason Chuah to be identified as authors of this work have been asserted by them in accordance with the Copyright, Designs and Patents Act 1988.

ISBN: 978-1-4479-0447-2 (print)
    978-1-4479-0448-9 (PDF)
    978-1-2920-0342-9 (eText)

Library of Congress Cataloging-in-Publication Data
Commercial law/edited by Professor Michael Furmston, Singapore Management University and Emeritus Professor, University of Bristol; Professor Jason Chuah, Head of Academic Law, City University London; with contributions from Chris Willett, Professor in Commercial Law, University of Essex [and seven others]. — Second Edition.
    pages cm
  ISBN 978-1-4479-0447-2 (pbk.)
  1. Commercial law—Great Britain.   2. Consumer protection—Law and legislation—Great Britain.
  3. Dispute resolution (Law)—Great Britain.   I. Furmston, M. P.   II. Chuah, Jason.   III. Willett, Chris.
    KD1629.F87 2013
    346.4107—dc23

                                                                                          2013005950

10 9 8 7 6 5 4 3 2 1
17 16 15 14 13

Print edition typeset in 9/12.5pt Giovanni by 35

NOTE THAT ANY PAGE CROSS-REFERENCES REFER TO THE PRINT EDITION

Brief contents

Contents

8   Consumer credit law and regulation

by Howard Johnson

9   Commercial mediation, conciliation and arbitration

by Jason Chuah

Companion Website

For open-access **student resources** specifically written
to complement this textbook and support your learning,
please visit **www.pearsoned.co.uk/legalupdates**

Guided tour

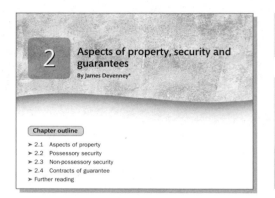

Chapter outlines are located at the start of each chapter and highlight the main topics that will be explored in the chapter.

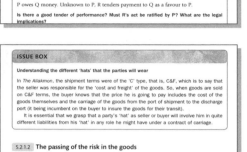

Debate and issues boxes highlight particularly contentious areas of the law and help you refine your critical analysis skills necessary for gaining those top marks in exams.

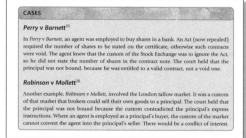

Case boxes provide summaries of the facts and key legal principles from the essential cases that you will need to refer to in your studies.

POINT OF INTEREST

The law of agency is based on the Latin maxim '*Qui facit per alium, facit per se*', which means 'he who acts through another is deemed in law to do it himself'.

An agency agreement is usually established with consent, that is, the principal agrees to the agent acting on his behalf and the agent agrees to do so. However, an agency agreement does not necessarily arise under contract. The agency can be gratuitous. For example, in *Chaudhry v Prabhakar*,[1] a woman had just passed her driving test. She wanted to buy a secondhand car and asked her friend to find one for her. She told her friend that the car must not have been the subject of an accident. Her friend found a car offered for sale by a car repairer. He noticed that the bonnet had been repaired but did not ask the repairer for information. When her friend recommended her to buy the car, she asked if the car had been in an accident before. He answered in the negative. After buying the car, the woman discovered that the car had been involved in an accident and proved unroadworthy. The woman sued her friend for breach of his duty of care. The Court of Appeal held that a gratuitous agent owes a duty of care and there was a breach here.

Point of interest boxes highlight interesting facts surrounding the subject.

LEGISLATIVE PROVISION

Regulation 2(1)

'commercial agent' means a self-employed intermediary who has continuing authority to negotiate the sale or purchase of goods on behalf of another person (the 'principal'), or to negotiate and conclude the sale or purchase of goods on behalf of and in the name of that principal . . .

Note that an agent must be self-employed in order to fall within the Regulations. This means he cannot be an employee or a company officer, although a company or partnership can be a commercial agent as long as it acts as an independent contractor. Where an agent buys and

Further reading

Brindle, M. and Cox, R. W., *Law of Bank Payments* (4th edn, Sweet and Maxwell, London, 2010).

Cresswell, Blair, Hill, Wood, et al., *Encyclopaedia of Banking Law* (Looseleaf from 1996) (Butterworths Lexisnexis, London).

Ellinger, E. P., Lomnicka, E. and Hare, C., *Ellinger's Modern Banking Law* (5th edn, Oxford University Press, Oxford, 2010).

Elliott, N., Odgers, R. and Phillips, J. M., *Byles on Bills of Exchange and Cheques* (28th edn, Sweet and Maxwell, London, 2007).

Enonchong, N., *The Independence Principle of Letters of Credit and Demand Guarantees* (Oxford University Press, Oxford, 2011).

Legislative provision boxes highlight the key sections of important legislation that you will need to draw upon when answering problem or essay questions.

Further reading lists at the end of all chapters point you to relevant academic articles enabling you to delve deeper into the academic debates surrounding the subject.

Preface to the second edition

Much has been said already and much might yet be said about the best method of approaching the study of commercial law for students. The subject is so vast that one of the major challenges for us was ascertaining the 'right' content matter. There will be some areas which some scholars consider significant to the study of commercial law which have necessarily been omitted. The other challenge which we hope we had done rather better at overcoming is ensuring that the wide-ranging areas we have chosen to cover are given appropriate expert airing. We are therefore most grateful to our panel of specialist contributors for their help in assembling this second edition without compromising on the latest developments in the law and its readability.

We would also to like to thank the reviewers of our first edition for their helpful comments. We have tried to incorporate some of these suggestions whilst ensuring that the book continues to satisfy the mainstream commercial syllabi on an undergraduate English Law programme. We have also been drawn to the fact that some schools use the book for their postgraduate students. We have therefore grown the lists of further reading to ensure that the book offers more for the student seeking to engage in wider and deeper research into English commercial law.

This second edition maintains the pedagogic features in the first edition which our readers have found useful. These features include debate boxes, issues for further thought, relevant case studies, diagrams to aid understanding, footnotes and reading lists, etc. As before, we have tried not to compromise when it comes to the intellectual facets of the law. This is not a practice manual; students are often challenged to question the rationale and logic of the law. We believe that the text makes a good balance between the practical and analytical aspects of the law.

We hope our colleagues skilled in the fine art of teaching and our discerning students will continue to find this volume useful.

Michael Furmston
Jason Chuah
September 2012

Contributors

Jason Chuah is Professor of Commercial Law and Head of the Academic Law Department at the City Law School, City University London. He has taught and published extensively in commercial law, banking law, international trade law and shipping law for many years.

James Devenney is Professor of Commercial Law and Head of the School of Law at the University of Exeter. His research and teaching interests are in the fields of commercial law and contract law.

Michael Furmston is Professor of Law at Singapore Management University's School of Law, an Emeritus Professor at the University of Bristol and a Bencher of Gray's Inn since 1989.

Susan Hawker is a Principal Lecturer in International Trade and Shipping Law at London Metropolitan University and Course Director of the Postgraduate Diploma in Maritime Law.

Howard Johnson is an LLM Tutor at Cardiff University. He has extensive teaching and research interests in the area of consumer law and, in particular, consumer credit. He is on the Editorial Board of the *Financial and Credit Law* journal.

Louise Merrett is a Barrister and Senior Lecturer in Law at Cambridge University and a Fellow of Trinity College. Her main areas of teaching and research are commercial law and the conflict of laws.

Martin Morgan-Taylor is a Principal Lecturer at De Montfort University in Leicester, where he teaches and researches consumer, e-commerce and commercial law, and the law relating to light pollution.

Jo Reddy is a Barrister and Adjunct Lecturer at The University of Hong Kong and has been lecturing to students in the UK and overseas in contract and commercial law since 1985.

Chris Willett is Professor of Commercial Law at the University of Essex. He teaches, researches and publishes widely in consumer, commercial and contract law; in particular, on unfair contract terms and practices, product and service quality, financial services and services of general interest.

Table of cases

Table of statutes

1 What is commercial law?

By Michael Furmston

Chapter outline

➤ 1.1   What is commercial law?

1.1   What is commercial law?

1.1.1 Introduction

The primary meaning given to the word 'commerce' in the *Oxford English Dictionary* is:

> Exchange between men of the products of nature or art; buying and selling together; trading; exchange of merchandise, esp. as conducted on a large scale between different countries or districts; including the whole of the transactions; arrangements, etc., therein involved.

The central activity may be said to be the buying and selling of goods, particularly on a large scale.

The central meaning of 'commercial law' would, on this basis, be the rules which control and facilitate the buying and selling of goods. In this sense commercial law has existed for thousands of years, at least from soon after money was invented as a convenient means of exchange. Certainly many of the problems which we deal with today in the law of sales were familiar to the great Roman jurists of the second and third century AD: the concepts of property and risk; the extent to which the seller is liable for defects in the goods.

So any book on commercial law in any system is very likely to have at its centre an account of the law of sale of goods. There is one major qualification to this. In common law systems it is usual to write on and teach the law of contract separately. This is a matter of culture and not of logic. Many transactions involving the sale of goods are solved in common law systems by applying the rules of the general law of contract and in others by applying the law of sale of goods, but only the latter rules are discussed fully in books on commercial law.[1]

In the earliest sales the buyer will simply have paid in cash. Of course many buyers will still pay in cash but over the centuries many different forms of payment have evolved from

---

[1] See Chapters 4 and 5.

the early modern forms by bill of exchange to the most modern forms by electronic transfer. Study of methods of payment is clearly a central feature of commercial law.[2]

The various ways by which the parties can be represented are also important features. A high proportion of modern commercial contracts are made by agents on one or both sides. The law regulating agency is therefore a central part of commercial law.[3]

1.1.2 What do commercial people want from commercial law?

The traditional view is that commercial people want rules which are clear. The primary reason for this is that if the rules are clear it is possible to steer around them. So many of the rules in sale of goods are 'default rules', that is rules which apply only if the parties have not provided an answer for themselves.[4] Much commercial law is heavily influenced by the contracts which commercial individuals make or which are designed for them by commercial lawyers. These contracts are themselves heavily influenced by what has happened in the past and often by the desire to avoid it.

A good example is the invention of the contract of hire purchase. This arose because in the 1870s and 1880s goods started for almost the first time to be sold into the homes of the increasingly affluent working class on credit. An example would be a piano. Some purchasers found it difficult to keep up payments and sold the piano for cash to a neighbour. The supplier was still entitled to payment from his customer but in the nature of things the customers often had no cash and therefore the supplier sought to recover the piano from the person who bought it. They soon discovered that even if the contract of sale provided that the goods did not belong to the buyer until all the payments had been made, the rules of sale meant that the buyer would be able to transfer ownership to someone who bought from him in good faith.[5]

In response to this some bright lawyer invented the contract of hire purchase. In this contract the customer hires the goods for a period of, say, three years and pays monthly for doing so. At the end of the three years he has an option to buy the goods, typically for a trivial sum. The House of Lords was persuaded that in such a transaction the customer was not a buyer unless and until he exercised the option.[6] The result was that if he sold before then he did not pass a good title to the person to whom he sold. So although a credit sale and a hire purchase have the same economic objectives they have substantially different legal results.

A similar development is the banker's letter of credit. This is used all over the world as a means of facilitating international sales by giving the seller adequate assurance that he will be paid, but at the same time not requiring the buyer to pay until he has adequate control of the goods.[7]

---

[2] See Chapter 6.
[3] See Chapter 3.
[4] A good example is the rules for the passing of property and risk, nearly all of which can be changed by the parties if they want to.
[5] These rules are discussed in section 4.6.4.5.
[6] *Helby v Mathews* [1895] AC 471.
[7] See discussion in Chapters 5 and 6.

1.1.3 How did commercial law develop?

By the early 17th century something which looks recognisably like the modern law of contract had emerged. Informal exchanges of promises were generally enforceable and the doctrine of consideration had become established.[8] The reader will probably have encountered a few cases from this period.[9]

Major steps in the development of commercial law took place during the 18th century. The judgment of Holt CJ in *Coggs v Bernard*[10] is still the starting point for the analysis of bailment.[11] In 1756 Lord Mansfield became Chief Justice of the King's Bench, a position he held until 1788. He has strong claims to be regarded as the most important English (though he was Scots) commercial law judge.[12] During his tenure major developments were made in the law of insurance,[13] of bills of exchange[14] and of bills of lading.[15] By this time, too, England had become the most important commercial nation in Europe.

From this period on commercial law developed continuously. There was interactive pressure between what was happening in commerce and the legal system. Both were also subject to increasingly rapid technological change. The development of post and the railways, followed by telegraphic communication and steamships that could carry cargo on a reliable and predictable basis, transformed communication and made new kinds of transaction possible. During the latter part of the 19th century it became, for a period, fashionable to codify areas of commercial law, that is to state the rules which had been developed through the cases in statutory form in the Bills of Exchange Act 1882, the Sale of Goods Act 1893 and the Marine Insurance Act 1906.

The codifying statutes sought to make the law more accessible. In principle it looks easier to read the statutes than to plough through lots of cases. This would not be true if the statutes were written as statutes of the UK Parliament are normally written, in a language and style from which the meaning can only be wrung out with great difficulty. The codifying statutes are undoubtedly much easier to understand than this. Compare for this purpose the Sale of Goods Act 1893 with the Consumer Credit Act 1974.

Nevertheless, codifying statutes do have difficulties of their own. One is that although they dispose of pre-Act cases, they inevitably develop a body of case law of their own concerned with their interpretation. More seriously, they slow down the pace of change. This can be seen by comparing the law of contract in 1893 and 2009 and the law of sale of goods for the same period. Undoubtedly the law of contract changed much more. It is easier for a case law system to evolve to meet changing business practice and views of what is fair and sensible than for a statute-based system.

---

[8] A good account is that by Brian Simpson in Chapter 1 of M. P. Furmston, *Cheshire, Fifoot and Furmston's Law of Contract* (16th edn, Oxford University Press, Oxford, 2012).

[9] *Pinnel's* case (1602) 5 Co Rep 117a; *Lampleigh v Braithwait* (1615) Hob 105.

[10] (1703) 2 Lord Raym 908.

[11] D. Ibbetson in C. Mitchell and P. Mitchell (eds), *Landmark Cases in the Law of Contract* (Hart Publishing, Oxford, 2008) Chapter 1.

[12] No fewer than three chapters in *Landmark Cases in the Law of Contract* (ibid.) are devoted to his decisions in *Pillans v Van Mierop* (1765) 3 Burr 1663 (Gerard McMeel), *Carter v Boehm* (1766) 3 Burr 1905 (Stephen Watterson) and *Da Costa v Jones* (1778) 2 Cowp 729 (Warren Swain).

[13] *Carter v Boehm* (see above n. 12).

[14] *Pierson v Dunlop* (1777) 2 Cowp 577.

[15] *Lickbarrow v Mason* (1787) 2 Term Rep 63.

1.1.4 **The rise of the consumer**

Both life and business practices evolved very substantially in the 20th and early years of the 21st centuries. Perhaps the most striking example in this context is the recognition of the consumer as a separate interest. As has been shown very clearly in the past two years, modern capitalist societies are heavily dependent on purchases by consumers of goods and services and of the willingness of consumers to incur substantial debts in order to make these purchases. It is not at all easy to get the balance right.

The rise of the consumer has been followed by legislation to protect the consumer by giving him special treatment in relation to the procurement of goods and services[16] and in relation to the provision of credit.[17]

1.1.5 **Other meanings of 'commercial'**

The discussion above goes far to explain the content of a book on commercial law but it should be recognised that the word 'commercial' has other shades of meaning. An English barrister who said that he had a commercial practice might well mean that he spent much of his time in the Commercial Court, a part of the Queen's Bench Division, which specialises particularly in international sales and shipping disputes. An English solicitor who said that he had a commercial practice might well be interested in a much wider range of topics.

Companion Website

For open-access **student resources** specifically written to complement this textbook and support your learning, please visit **www.pearsoned.co.uk/legalupdates**

ON THE WEBSITE

---

[16] See Chapter 8.
[17] See Chapter 9.

2 Aspects of property, security and guarantees

By James Devenney*

Chapter outline

➤ 2.1   Aspects of property
➤ 2.2   Possessory security
➤ 2.3   Non-possessory security
➤ 2.4   Contracts of guarantee
➤ Further reading

2.1   Aspects of property

2.1.1 Introduction

The concept of 'property' is fundamental to commercial law for, at least, two reasons. First, 'property' forms the subject matter of many commercial transactions.[1] Secondly, 'property' – or the whereabouts of property – may have some highly significant consequences in commercial law. For example, as we shall see below,[2] the whereabouts of property in relation to contracts of sale of goods is highly significant for the following (non-exhaustive) reasons:[3]

- it impacts on whether the seller or buyer bears the risk of loss of, or damage to, the goods;[4]
- it impacts on whether a contract of sale of goods can be frustrated;[5]
- it impacts on a seller's ability to claim the price of the goods;[6]
- it has real ramifications should either the seller or the buyer become insolvent.[7]

*Professor of Commercial Law and Head of School, Exeter University Law School. I am indebted to Professor Mel Kenny (De Montfort University) and Professor Lorna Fox O'Mahony (Durham University) for the work we have completed on this area of law.
[1] See, generally, E. McKendrick, *Goode on Commercial Law* (4th edn, Butterworths, London, 2010) Chapter 2.
[2] See Chapter 4.
[3] See, generally, I. Brown, *Commercial Law* (Butterworths, London, 2001) at pp. 302–304.
[4] See s. 20, Sale of Goods Act 1979 although note, in particular, s. 20(4), Sale of Goods Act 1979.
[5] *Cf.* s. 7, Sale of Goods Act 1979 and *Kursell* v *Timber Operators and Contractors* [1927] 1 KB 298.
[6] *Cf.* s. 49, Sale of Goods Act 1979.
[7] See, generally, R. M. Goode, 'Ownership and Obligation in Commercial Transactions' (1987) 103 *LQR* 433.

In this section we shall examine some aspects of the concept of property.

2.1.2 Real property and personal property[8]

It is customary to distinguish *real property* (or *realty*) from *personal property* (or *personalty*). Essentially realty refers to land[9] whereas personalty is a residual category of 'things' other than land.[10] In this section we shall focus on personalty (although much of what will be said could apply equally to realty).

Personalty consists of *chattels real* and *chattels personal*. In general terms chattels real refers to leasehold interests in land whereas chattels personal is a residual category of personalty not amounting to chattels real. Chattels personal may be tangible or intangible. An example of the former is goods. Examples of the latter are debts and copyright.

2.1.3 General principles of personal property law

In everyday parlance it is common for the word 'property' to be used as a reference to a 'thing'.[11] Thus – *in this sense* – a car is property, a table is property, a kettle is property, etc. Yet lawyers use the word 'property' in a different way. More specifically, lawyers use the word 'property' to refer to the *relationship* (and associated rights) between an individual (or individuals) and a 'thing'.[12]

---

[8] See, generally, E. L. G. Tyler and N. E. Palmer, *Crossley Vaines' Personal Property* (5th edn, Butterworths, London, 1973) Chapters 1–3.

[9] *Cf.* chattels real, below.

[10] See S. Worthington, *Personal Property Law: Text and Materials* (Hart Publishing, Oxford, 2000) at p. 4.

[11] *Ibid.* at p. 3.

[12] See, for example, S. Worthington, *Equity* (2nd edn, Clarendon, Oxford, 2006) at pp. 51–53. Although it should be noted that property rights do not exist in relation to some 'things': *cf.* L. Skene, 'Proprietary Rights in Human Bodies, Body Parts and Tissue: Regulatory Contexts and Proposals for New Laws' (2002) 22 LS 102 and *Yearworth v Bristol NHS Trust* [2009] EWCA Civ 37 at [45] *per* Lord Judge CJ: '(a) In this jurisdiction developments in medical science now require a re-analysis of the common law's treatment of and approach to the issue of ownership of parts or products of a living human body, whether for present purposes (viz. an action in negligence) or otherwise . . . (b) The present claims relate to products of a living human body intended for use by the persons whose bodies have generated them . . . (c) For us the easiest course would be to uphold the claims of the men to have had ownership of the sperm for present purposes by reference to the principle first identified in *Doodeward* [*Doodeward v Spence* (1908) 6 CLR 406]. We would have no difficulty in concluding that the unit's storage of the sperm in liquid nitrogen at minus 196°C was an application to the sperm of work and skill which conferred on it a substantially different attribute, namely the arrest of its swift perishability. We would regard *Kelly* [*R v Kelly (Anthony Noel)* [1999] QB 621] as entirely consistent with such an analysis and Dobson as a claim which failed for a different reason, namely that the pathologist never undertook to the claimants, and was not otherwise obliged, to continue to preserve the brain . . . (d) However, as foreshadowed by Rose LJ in *Kelly*, we are not content to see the common law in this area founded upon the principle in *Doodeward*, which was devised as an exception to a principle, itself of exceptional character, relating to the ownership of a human corpse. Such ancestry does not commend it as a solid foundation. Moreover a distinction between the capacity to own body parts or products which have, and which have not, been subject to the exercise of work or skill is not entirely logical. Why, for example, should the surgeon presented with a part of the body, for example, a finger which has been amputated in a factory accident, with a view to re-attaching it to the injured hand, but who carelessly damages it before starting the necessary medical procedures, be able to escape liability on the footing that the body part had not been subject to the exercise of work or skill which had changed its attributes? . . . (e) So we prefer to rest our conclusions on a broader basis . . . (f) In our judgment, for the purposes of their claims in negligence, the men had ownership of the sperm which they ejaculated . . .'

Furthermore, the word 'property' is also used to refer to the impact of that relationship on other individuals.[13]

ISSUE BOX

As we have seen (in section 2.1.2) it is customary to make a distinction between real property and personal property. In what sense is the word 'property' being used in that context?[14]

A number of important points need to be made about the legal concept of property.

1. It is often stated that property rights bind the world[15] (which may be extremely significant in an insolvency scenario).[16] Yet care must be taken with any such statement.[17] In the first instance, property rights (for example, equitable property rights) will not always bind third parties.[18] Moreover, in relation to some forms of personal property such a statement seems scarcely apposite.[19] Conversely, there may be situations where so-called personal rights bind third parties.[20]

2. Ownership has been defined as the 'greatest possible interest in a thing which a mature system of law recognises'.[21] Yet, as is implicitly recognised in this quotation, more than one individual may have an interest in a particular 'thing'. For example – as we shall see below[22] – where the owner of goods pledges those goods, the pledgee acquires a 'special property' in the pledged goods.[23] Nevertheless, in such circumstances, the pledgor retains the 'general' property in the pledged goods.[24] Accordingly, particularly in such circumstances, it is helpful to think of ownership in terms of residual rights.[25]

3. In general terms, ownership and possession are not synonymous concepts.[26] Nevertheless, as we shall see throughout this text, the concept of possession is vitally important in

---

[13] See M. Bridge, *Personal Property Law* (3rd edn, Clarendon, Oxford, 2002) at p. 12.

[14] *Cf.* S. Worthington, *Personal Property Law* at p. 3.

[15] See A. P. Bell, *Modern Law of Personal Property in England and Ireland* (Butterworths, London, 1989) at pp. 6–13.

[16] See, generally, R. M. Goode, 'Ownership and Obligation in Commercial Transactions', *op. cit.*

[17] See A. P. Bell, *op. cit.*

[18] See M. Bridge, *op. cit.*

[19] See A. P. Bell, *op. cit.* at p. 8. See also S. Worthington, *Equity, op. cit.* at p. 62 who states (in relation to the assignment of a debt from A to C):

> ... if B becomes insolvent, then A's (or C's) claim to £100 will abate along with the claims of all of B's general creditors. The debt does not afford A (or C) any protection on B's insolvency ... The chose in action has the attribute of transferability, but not the attribute of excludability and its associated insolvency protection. This is why debts are commonly described as 'personal' rights, not proprietary rights ... But in another sense debts *are* property, and more complicated transfer options can deliver a degree of insolvency protection to third parties ...

[20] See the excellent discussion in L. S. Sealy and R. J. A. Hooley, *Commercial Law: Text, Cases and Materials* (4th edn, Oxford University Press, Oxford, 2008) at pp. 66–68.

[21] A. M. Honoré, 'Ownership', in A. G. Guest (ed.), *Oxford Essays in Jurisprudence* (Oxford University Press, Oxford, 1961) at p. 107.

[22] See section 2.2.2.

[23] See M. Bridge, *op. cit.* at p. 176.

[24] *Cf.* R. Bradgate, *Commercial Law* (3rd edn, Butterworths, London, 2000) at p. 510.

[25] See A. M. Honoré, *op. cit.* at p. 126 *ff.*

[26] *Cf.* R. Bradgate, *op. cit.* at p. 365.

commercial law.[27] For example,[28] the concept of possession is central to the creation of a pledgee's 'special interest' in the pledged goods[29] and it is also pivotal in relation to a number of the exceptions to the principle of *nemo dat quod non habet*.[30]

4. It is important to note that ownership can be legal or equitable. Moreover, through equity the number of limited interests (such as charges)[31] that can exist in relation to personal property has been much increased.[32]

2.1.4 Security

In sections 2.2 and 2.3 we are going to explore *security* in relation to debts and other obligations. A useful starting point when exploring security is *Bristol Airport PLC v Powdrill*[33] where Browne-Wilkinson V-C stated:

> Security is created where a person ('the creditor') to whom an obligation is owed by another ('the debtor') by statute or contract, in addition to the personal promise of the debtor to discharge the obligation, obtains rights exercisable against some property in which the debtor has an interest in order to enforce the discharge of the debtor's obligation to the creditor.[34]

In general terms security, therefore, consists of a right of recourse against another's asset or assets should that other fail to perform a relevant obligation (and this brings with it certain advantages should that other become insolvent).[35]

In *Re Cosslett (Contractors) Ltd*[36] Millett LJ stated:

> There are only four kinds of consensual security known to English law: (i) pledge; (ii) contractual lien; (iii) equitable charge and (iv) mortgage. A pledge and a contractual lien both depend on the delivery of possession to the creditor. The difference between them is that in the case of a pledge the owner delivers possession to the creditor as security, whereas in the case of a lien the creditor retains possession of goods previously delivered to him for some other purpose. Neither a mortgage nor charge depends on the delivery of possession. The difference between them is that a mortgage involves a transfer of legal or equitable ownership to the creditor, whereas an equitable charge does not.[37]

In this chapter we will focus on consensual securities but we shall also consider some securities which arise by operation of law (such as equitable liens).[38] One final point: *security* needs to be distinguished from *quasi-security*. In general terms quasi-securities are functionally similar to securities but, for one reason or another,[39] are not technically securities. For

---

[27] See R. Goode, *Commercial Law* (4th edn, Penguin, London, 2012) at p. 34.
[28] See, generally, L. S. Sealy and R. J. A. Hooley, *op. cit.* at pp. 77–78.
[29] As we shall see below, a pledgee is a bailee. On the different types of bailment, see *Coggs v Bernard* (1703) 2 Lord Raym 909. Cf. *TRM Copy Centres (UK) Ltd v Lanwell Services Ltd* [2009] UKHL 35.
[30] See Chapter 4.
[31] On which, see section 2.3.3.
[32] See, generally, S. Worthington, *Equity, op. cit.*, Chapter 3.
[33] [1990] Ch 744.
[34] *Ibid.* at 760.
[35] See, generally, R. M. Goode, 'Ownership and Obligation in Commercial Transactions', *op. cit.*
[36] [1998] Ch 495.
[37] *Ibid.* at 508.
[38] See section 2.3.4.
[39] *Cf.* R. Bradgate, *op. cit.* at p. 489.

example, a retention of title clause[40] is a common type of quasi-security. A retention of title clause is not classified as a security as it involves the seller (the 'creditor') retaining property rather than the buyer (the 'debtor') granting the creditor a means of recourse against the debtor's assets.[41]

2.2 Possessory security

2.2.1 Introduction

In this section we will explore possessory securities. More specifically, we will examine pledges and some types of lien.

2.2.2 Pledges[42]

Classically, and in general terms, a pledge arises where one party (the pledgor) delivers goods (or documents of title[43]) to another party (the pledgee) as security for a debt (or other obligation).[44] This (short) description of a pledge raises a number of points. First, as delivery is central to the concept of a pledge, it has been held that it is not possible to pledge purely intangible property.[45]

Secondly, delivery can be actual, constructive or symbolic[46] (although the precise relationship between actual, constructive and symbolic delivery is debatable). Thus, depending on the precise circumstances,[47] delivery might be achieved where the pledgor's goods are stored in a particular room, or building, and the pledgor gives the pledgee the only key[48] to that room (along with a right to access that room).[49] Alternatively, where the pledgor's goods are being held by a third-party bailee, delivery might be achieved by the pledgor directing the bailee to hold the goods for the pledgee and the bailee attorning to the pledgee.[50] Indeed, where the goods are in the possession of the pledgor, delivery might be achieved through the pledgor attorning to the pledgee.[51]

---

[40] See Chapter 4.

[41] See, generally, L. S. Sealy and R. J. A. Hooley, *op. cit.* at pp. 1082–1083.

[42] On the application of the Consumer Credit Act 1974, see generally Chapter 8.

[43] *Cf. Official Assignee of Madras* v *Mercantile Bank of India Ltd* [1935] AC 53.

[44] See *Halliday* v *Holgate* (1868) LR 3 Exch 299.

[45] See *Harrold* v *Plenty* [1901] 2 Ch 314. *Cf.* the position of negotiable instruments in *Carter* v *Wake* (1877) 4 Ch D 605. See also *Enviroco Ltd* v *Farstad Supply* [2009] EWHC 906 at [11]; [2009] EWCA Civ 1399 (CA); [2011] UKSC 16 particularly at [62] (SC).

[46] See L. S. Sealy and R. J. A. Hooley, *op. cit.* at p. 1094.

[47] *Cf. Dublin City Distillery Ltd* v *Doherty* [1914] AC 823.

[48] Where the pledgor retains a key, there may still be sufficient delivery if the pledgor's access is subordinated to the control of the pledge: see *Hilton* v *Tucker* (1888) 39 Ch D 669. *Cf. Dublin City Distillery Ltd* v *Doherty* [1914] AC 823.

[49] See *Wrightson* v *McArthur & Hutchinson (1919) Ltd* [1921] 2 KB 807.

[50] See *Dublin City Distillery Ltd* v *Doherty* [1914] AC 823.

[51] *Ibid.* Such an arrangement may be caught by the Bills of Sale Acts: see R. Bradgate, *op. cit.* at pp. 508–509.

ISSUE BOX

What problems may arise where a pledgor attorns to a pledgee in respect of an undivided part of a bulk?[52]

Thirdly, despite the comments of Lord Mersey in *The Odessa*,[53] it is generally accepted that a pledgee acquires a 'special property' in the pledged goods.[54]

Finally, it should be remembered that a pledge is a form of bailment.[55]

2.2.2.1 Remedies of the pledgee

Subject to any statutory restrictions,[56] a pledgee may sell the pledged property if the pledgor fails to pay the debt (or perform another relevant obligation) in a timely fashion.[57] In so doing, the pledgee 'must take care that the sale is a provident sale'.[58] Furthermore, where the pledgee realises more than is necessary to settle the debt, the pledgee must account to the pledgor for the surplus.[59] Conversely, where the sale does not generate enough to settle the debt, the pledgee can bring a personal action against the pledgor in respect of the balance.[60]

2.2.2.2 Termination of a pledge

A pledge might, depending on the circumstances, be terminated in the following ways:

- satisfaction of the secured debt (or other obligation);
- waiver;
- by redelivery of the pledged property to the pledgor;[61]
- breach of certain terms of the agreement.[62]

2.2.3 Liens

It is almost customary[63] to begin an examination of liens by reference to *Hammonds* v *Barclay*[64] where Grose J famously stated:

---

[52] *Cf. Maynegrain Pty Ltd* v *Compafina Bank* [1982] 2 NSWLR 141. See also Chapter 4.
[53] [1916] 1 AC 145 at 158.
[54] See M. Bridge, *op. cit.* at p. 176.
[55] See *Coggs* v *Bernard* (1703) 2 Lord Raym 909.
[56] *Cf.* Chapter 8.
[57] See *Re Hardwick* (1886) 17 QBD 690.
[58] See *The Odessa* [1916] 1 AC 145 at 152 *per* Lord Mersey.
[59] *Cf. Mathew* v *TM Sutton Ltd* [1994] 4 All ER 793.
[60] See *Jones* v *Marshall* (1889) 24 QBD 269.
[61] *Cf. Reeves* v *Capper* (1838) 5 Bing NC 136 (where the terms of the redelivery meant that the pledge survived).
[62] See, for example, *Cooke* v *Hadden* where the pledgee consumed the pledged champagne. *Cf. Donald* v *Suckling* (1866) LR 1 QB 585.
[63] See, for example, R. Bradgate, *op. cit.* at p. 512 and L. S. Sealy and R. J. A. Hooley, *op. cit.* at p. 1106.
[64] (1802) 2 East 227.

A lien is a right in one man to retain that which is in his possession belonging to another, till certain demands of him the person in possession are satisfied.[65]

Yet it must be stressed that there are a number of different types of lien and not all of them are possessory in nature. The main types of lien might be classified as follows:

- common law liens;
- contractual liens;
- statutory liens;
- equitable liens; and
- maritime liens.

Equitable liens and maritime liens are non-possessory in nature and so will be dealt with below at section 2.3.4. Contractual liens and statutory liens[66] are shaped, respectively, by the relevant contract or statute. In this section we will focus on common law liens.

2.2.3.1 Common law liens – an introduction

Common law liens are possessory in nature. Classically, and in general terms, a common law lien provides the lienee with a personal right[67] to retain possession of the lienor's goods or documents[68] (such goods or documents already being in the possession of the lienee for a different purpose)[69] until a certain demand is met (such as payment of a debt).[70] As we have seen, one of the differences between a common law lien and a pledge is that:

> . . . in the case of a pledge the owner delivers possession to the creditor as security, whereas in the case of a lien the creditor retains possession of goods previously delivered to him for some other purpose.[71]

Common law liens arise by operation of law in certain reasonably well-known situations.[72] Nevertheless, as we shall see in section 2.2.3.3, a common law lien can be enhanced by contract. Alternatively, a contract may prevent a common law lien from arising.[73]

---

[65] See also *Tappenden v Artus* [1964] 2 QB 185 at 194, where Diplock LJ stated that a lien is a self-help remedy.
[66] An example of a statutory lien is an unpaid seller's lien over goods under the Sale of Goods Act 1979, ss. 41–43. See further, Chapter 4 below. For an unsuccessful claim that a fleet lien under the Civil Aviation Act 1982 was contrary to the European Convention on Human Rights 1950, Protocol 1, Art. 1 see *Global Knafaim Leasing Ltd v Civil Aviation Authority* [2012] EWHC 1348.
[67] Although *cf.* the discussion in L. S. Sealy and R. J. A. Hooley, *op. cit.* at p. 1106.
[68] See M. Bridge, *op. cit.* at p. 170.
[69] *Cf. Bernal v Pirn* (1835) 1 Gale 17.
[70] The lienee holds the goods or documents as a bailee.
[71] See *Re Cosslett (Contractors) Ltd* [1998] Ch 495 at 508 *per* Millett LJ.
[72] On the creation of common law liens, see generally *Tappenden v Artus* [1964] 2 QB 185.
[73] See, for example, *Forth v Simpson* (1849) 13 QB 680 (where a common law lien was prevented from arising in favour of a horse trainer as a result of the owner's contractual right to take possession of the horses at will). See also *Wilson v Lombank Ltd* [1963] 1 WLR 1294 and *George Wimpey Manchester Ltd v Valley & Vale Properties Ltd (in administration)* [2012] EWCA Civ 233. *Cf.* also s. 246(2), Insolvency Act 1986.

2.2.3.2 Types of common law lien

Common law liens may be *general* or *particular*.[74] A particular lien entitles the lienee to retain, for example, the lienor's goods until a debt *which is connected to those goods*[75] is satisfied. Examples of such liens include a repairer's lien over the repaired goods[76] and an innkeeper's lien over some of a guest's belongings.[77] By contrast, a general lien entitles the lienee to retain, for example, the lienor's goods until *any* debt is satisfied. Examples of such liens include a solicitor's lien[78] and a stockbroker's lien[79] over papers belonging to a client.

2.2.3.3 Remedies of the common law lienee

Common law liens are not automatically coupled with a power of sale.[80] Nevertheless, a lienor may be able to apply to court for an order for the sale of the relevant property.[81] Moreover, a power of sale may be attached to a common law lien by contract[82] and/or statute.[83]

2.2.3.4 Termination of common law liens

As common law liens are possessory in nature, they will *generally* terminate when the lienee loses possession of the relevant goods or documents.[84] A common law lien may also be terminated through waiver,[85] by the lienor meeting the lienee's demand[86] or through a wrongful act by the lienee.[87]

2.3 Non-possessory security

2.3.1 Introduction

In this section we will explore non-possessory securities. More specifically, we will examine (i) mortgages, (ii) charges and (iii) equitable and maritime liens.

[74] Although the courts are not fond of general liens: see *Rushforth v Hadfield* (1806) 7 East 224.
[75] See generally M. Bridge, *op. cit.* at p. 172.
[76] See *Albermarle Supply Co Ltd v Hind & Co* [1928] 1 KB 307. See also *Spencer v S Franses Ltd* [2011] EWHC 1269 (establishing the medieval provenance of certain embroideries). Cf. *R (on the application of Malik Law Chambers Solicitors) v Legal Complaints Service* [2010] EWHC 981 (on reasonableness of exercise of lien).
[77] See *Mulliner v Florence* (1878) 3 QBD 484.
[78] See *Stevenson v Blakelock* (1813) 1 M S 535.
[79] See *Re London & Globe Finance Corporation* [1902] 2 Ch 416.
[80] See *Somes v British Empire Shipping Co.* (1859) 28 LJQB 220.
[81] See, generally, L. S. Sealy and R. J. A. Hooley, *op. cit.* at p. 1118.
[82] See, for example, *Marcq v Christie Manson & Woods Ltd (t/a Christies)* [2003] EWCA Civ 731.
[83] See, for example, s. 1, Innkeepers Act 1878 and ss. 12–13, Torts (Interference with Goods) Act 1977.
[84] See *Pennington v Reliance Motor Works Ltd* [1923] 1 KB 127. Cf. *Albermarle Supply Co Ltd v Hind & Co* [1928] 1 KB 307 where the goods were released 'in pawn' and so the lien was not lost.
[85] Cf. R. Bradgate, *op. cit.* at p. 517.
[86] *Ibid.*
[87] See *Mulliner v Florence* (1878) 3 QBD 484.

> **ISSUE BOX**
>
> Do non-possessory securities create dangers for third parties who subsequently deal with the chargor?[88]

2.3.2 Mortgages

A useful starting point for an examination of mortgages[89] is *Downsview Nominees Ltd* v *First City Corpn Ltd*[90] where Lord Templeman stated:

> A mortgage, whether legal or equitable, is security for repayment of a debt. The security may be constituted by a conveyance, assignment or demise or by a charge on any interest in real or personal property. An equitable mortgage is a contract which creates a charge on property but does not pass a legal estate to the creditor. Its operation is that of an executory assurance, which, as between the parties, and so far as equitable rights and remedies are concerned, is equivalent to an actual assurance, and is enforceable under the equitable jurisdiction of the court.[91]

A number of points can be made in connection with this statement. First, in general terms the concept of a mortgage is built around the idea of a transfer of property to the mortgagee as security for a debt (or, indeed, other obligation); and the transfer is made on the basis that it will be reversed once the debt is paid (or other obligation fulfilled). Once the debt is paid (or other obligation fulfilled), the property is said to be redeemed.[92]

Secondly, and depending on the precise circumstances, a mortgagor will often have the right (an 'equity of redemption') to redeem the mortgaged property despite the fact that the day for payment of the debt (or performance of the other obligation) has passed.[93]

Thirdly, as Lord Templeman noted, it is possible to mortgage both real and personal property.

Fourthly, the form of a mortgage will be affected by the type of property to be mortgaged and by the type of mortgage. Thus, for example, a legal mortgage of land must usually be created by means of a legal charge. By contrast, a legal mortgage of a debt is often created by written assignment and the associated formalities.

Finally, as Lord Templeman also noted, a mortgage can be legal or equitable. For example, a mortgage of an equitable interest will be an equitable mortgage.[94] In addition, an equitable mortgage may arise out of an ineffective attempt to create a legal mortgage (such as where the necessary formalities have not been adhered to).[95]

---

[88] *Cf.* section 2.3.5 below.

[89] See generally L. S. Sealy and R. J. A. Hooley, *op. cit.* at p. 1123.

[90] [1993] AC 295.

[91] *Ibid.* at 311.

[92] See *Santley* v *Wilde* [1899] 2 Ch 474.

[93] See *G and C Kreglinger* v *New Patagonia Meat and Cold Storage Co Ltd* [1914] AC 25. See also J. Devenney, 'A Pack of Unruly Dogs: Unconscionable Bargains, Lawful Act (Economic) Duress and Clogs on the Equity of Redemption' [2002] JBL 539. See also Companies Act 2006, s.739.

[94] See M. Bridge, *op. cit.* at p. 180.

[95] *Ibid.*

2.3.2.1 Remedies

Mortgages have been described as 'highly potent security'[96] on account of the potential remedies available to a mortgagee where the mortgagor is in default. Yet it must be remembered that the precise remedies available to a mortgagee will be shaped by the terms of the mortgage agreement, any statutory requirements and, possibly, whether the mortgage is legal or equitable.[97] Subject to this qualification, the *in rem* remedies available to a mortgagee against a mortgagor in default often include the following.

(a) Foreclosure

Where a mortgagor is in default a mortgagee might apply to court for an order of foreclosure. Essentially, where an order of foreclosure is granted, the mortgagor loses their right to redeem the mortgaged property and the mortgaged property is (fully) vested in the mortgagee. Furthermore, an order of foreclosure extinguishes the debt secured by the mortgage (even if the mortgaged property is worth *less* than the debt secured by the mortgage).[98] Moreover, where the mortgaged property is worth *more* than the debt secured by the mortgage, the mortgagee is not liable to account for the difference.[99]

The remedy of foreclosure has been likened to forfeiture[100] and, therefore, is subject to various procedural safeguards. As a result, foreclosure proceedings are rather cumbersome and not common in practice.[101]

(b) Possession

Where a mortgagor is in default, a mortgagee will often have the right, subject to any statutory restrictions, to take possession of the subject matter of the mortgage.[102] Possession can, however, be burdensome.[103]

(c) Appointment of a receiver

Where a mortgagor is in default, a mortgagee will also often have the right to appoint a receiver with, for example, the power to realise the mortgaged property.

(d) Power of sale

Where a mortgagor is in default, a mortgagee will also often have the right to sell the mortgaged property. In selling the property, the mortgagee should take reasonable care to obtain a reasonable price.[104] Once sold, and in contrast to an order of foreclosure, the mortgagor remains liable for any shortfall;[105] and the mortgagee is liable to account to the mortgagor for any surplus.

---

[96] R. Bradgate, *op. cit.* at p. 518.
[97] See R. Goode, *Commercial Law, op. cit.* at pp. 680–684.
[98] See R. Goode, *Commercial Law, op. cit.* at p. 684.
[99] *Ibid.*
[100] See M. Bridge, *op. cit.* at p. 186.
[101] See *Palk* v *Mortgage Services Funding PLC* [1993] Ch 330 at 336 *per* Sir Donald Nicholls VC.
[102] See generally *Re London Pressed Hinge Co Ltd* [1905] 1 Ch 576.
[103] See R. Goode, *Commercial Law, op. cit.* at p. 680 and *cf. Chaplin* v *Young (No 1)* (1864) 33 Beav 330 at 337–338.
[104] *Cf. Cuckmere Brick Co Ltd* v *Mutual Finance Ltd* [1971] Ch 949.
[105] See, for example, *Gordon Grant and Co. Ltd* v *Boos* [1926] AC 781.

2.3.3 Charges

2.3.3.1 Introduction

In *Re Charge Card Services Ltd*[106] Millett J, as he then was, described the essence of an (equitable)[107] charge in the following terms:

> ... the essence of an equitable charge is that, without any conveyance or assignment to the chargee, specific property of the chargor is expressly or constructively appropriated to or made answerable for the payment of a debt, and the chargee is given the right to resort to the property for the purpose of having it realised and applied in or towards payment of the debt.[108]

Subsequently, in *Re Cosslett (Contractors) Ltd*[109] Millett LJ, as he had become, stated:

> It is of the essence of a charge that a particular asset or class of assets is appropriated to the satisfaction of a debt or other obligation of the chargor or a third party, so that the chargee is entitled to look to the asset and its proceeds for the discharge of the liability.[110]

A charge is a flexible device. Thus, for example, a charge can relate to *real* or *personal* property,[111] it can be *fixed* or *floating*,[112] and it can relate to future property.[113] Moreover, it *may* be possible to create a charge by means of a purely oral contract.[114] In general terms, once a charge becomes exercisable the chargee may ask a court to appoint a receiver or order a sale of the charged property; it has also been common for charge contracts to grant a chargee an independent right to appoint a receiver and an independent power of sale.[115]

ISSUE BOX

What is the difference between a charge and a mortgage?[116]

2.3.3.2 Fixed charges

In general terms, a fixed (or specific) charge is a charge over an asset (or assets) which prohibits the chargor from dealing with the asset (or assets) without the permission of the

---

[106] [1987] Ch 150.

[107] A charge may also be created through statute: see ss. 85–87, Law of Property Act 1925.

[108] [1987] Ch 150 at 176.

[109] [1998] Ch 495.

[110] *Ibid.* at p. 508. See also *Swiss Bank Corpn v Lloyd's Bank Ltd* [1982] AC 584 at 595.

[111] See generally R. Bradgate, *op. cit.* at p. 522.

[112] See sections 2.3.3.2–2.3.3.3. Note, however, that as a result of the Bills of Sale Acts 1878 and 1882 an individual generally cannot grant a floating charge.

[113] *Cf. Holroyd v Marshall* (1862) 10 HL Cas 191.

[114] See L. S. Sealy and R. J. A. Hooley, *op. cit.* at p. 1132.

[115] See generally S. Mayson, D. French and C. Ryan, *Company Law* (28th edn, Oxford University Press, Oxford, 2011) at pp. 314–321. Note also the curtailment, by virtue of s. 72A, Insolvency Act 1986, of the ability of a chargee under a floating charge to appoint an administrative receiver.

[116] *Cf. Re Bond Worth Ltd* [1980] Ch 228 at 250 where Slade J observed: 'The technical difference between a "mortgage" or "charge", though in practice the phrases are often used interchangeably, is that a mortgage involves a conveyance of property subject to a right of redemption, whereas a charge conveys nothing and merely gives the chargee certain rights over the property as security for the loan.'

chargee. Such a charge, therefore, might be given over a particular piece of machinery which the chargor needs to retain for use in its business.[117] The essence of a fixed charge was captured by Vaughan Williams LJ in *Re Yorkshire Woolcombers Ltd*:[118]

> I do not think that for a 'specific security' you need have a security of a subject matter which is then in existence. I mean by 'then' at the time of the execution of the security; but what you do require to make a specific security is that the security whenever it has once come into existence, and been identified or appropriated as a security, shall never thereafter at the will of the mortgagor cease to be a security. If at the will of the mortgagor he can dispose of it and prevent its being any longer a security, although something else may be substituted more or less for it, this is not a specific security.[119]

ISSUE BOX

What is the position where a chargor purports to transfer to a third party an asset which is subject to a fixed charge?[120]

2.3.3.3 Floating charges

As we shall see below,[121] the essence of the distinction between fixed charges and floating charges is that under a floating charge the chargor is permitted to deal with the charged assets in the normal course of its business whereas under a fixed charge the chargor is not, as we have seen,[122] so permitted. Accordingly, a floating charge can be granted over a class of assets, the composition of which changes over time. For example, a company might need to grant security in the form of a charge over its stock but it may also need to sell and buy stock as part of its business; in such circumstances the company might offer a floating charge.

A useful insight into floating charges was given by Lord Macnaghten in *Illingworth v Houldsworth*:[123]

> . . . a floating charge . . . is ambulatory and shifting in its nature, hovering over and so to speak floating with the property which it is intended to affect until some event occurs or some act is done which causes it to settle and fasten on the subject of the charge within its reach and grasp.[124]

As this quote suggests, a floating charge hovers over the charged class of assets until the charge 'crystallises'.[125] On crystallisation the floating charge is transformed into a fixed charge over the then assets of the chargor which fall within the class or classes of assets charged.[126]

---

[117] See R. Bradgate, *op. cit.* at p. 526.
[118] [1903] 2 Ch 284.
[119] *Ibid.* at 294. See also *Re Harmony Care Homes* [2009] EWHC 1961 at [26].
[120] *Cf.* section 2.3.3.7 below.
[121] See section 2.3.3.5.
[122] See section 2.3.3.2.
[123] [1904] AC 355.
[124] *Ibid.* at 358.
[125] On which see section 2.3.3.4.
[126] See *Re Griffin Hotel Co Ltd* [1941] Ch 129 and *George Barker (Transport) Ltd v Eynon* [1974] 1 WLR 462. It may also attach to future property: see L. S. Sealy and R. J. A. Hooley, *op. cit.* at p. 1138.

Thereafter, the chargor is no longer permitted to deal with the charged assets without the consent of the chargee.[127]

The fact that, prior to crystallisation, a chargor under a floating charge is permitted to deal with the charged assets in the normal course of its business raises a number of interesting questions. First, what is the jurisprudential basis of floating charges? This is an issue on which there are differing opinions.[128] One view is that, essentially, a floating charge is a charge over each of the assets charged with a licence enabling the chargor to deal with the charged assets in the normal course of its business. However, such a view was not well received in *Evans* v *Rival Granite Quarries Ltd*[129] and so the issue remains open to debate.[130]

The second question raised by the fact that, prior to crystallisation, a chargor under a floating charge is permitted to deal with the charged assets in the normal course of its business is whether or not such a chargor can thereby grant another charge over the charged assets *ranking in priority*[131] to the earlier charge. It seems that such a chargor may be able to create a fixed charge over such assets with priority over the earlier floating charge.[132] By contrast, it seems that a chargor cannot, generally, create a floating charge over entirely the same assets as the earlier floating charge with priority over the earlier floating charge.[133] On the other hand, it seems that it may be possible for a chargor to create a floating charge over *some* of the same class of assets as the earlier floating charge with priority over the earlier floating charge.[134] Moreover in *Griffiths* v *Yorkshire Bank PLC*[135] Morritt J very controversially held that a subsequent floating charge may gain priority over an earlier floating charge by crystallising before the earlier floating charge.[136]

Accordingly, there are circumstances where a chargor under a floating charge can grant another charge over the charged assets *ranking in priority* to the earlier charge. As a result floating charges often include 'negative-pledge' clauses. Essentially a negative pledge clause provides that the chargor will not grant another charge over the charged assets *ranking in priority* to that charge. Such a clause may prevent a subsequent charge gaining priority over the earlier charge if the subsequent chargee has *actual* notice of the 'negative-pledge' clause.[137] Yet where the subsequent chargee does not have *actual* notice of the 'negative-pledge' clause, the utility of such a clause is much less clear. In particular, it *seems* that mere registration of the earlier floating charge under the Companies Act 2006[138] will not give a subsequent

---

[127] *Cf.* R. Goode, *Commercial Law, op. cit.* at p.734.

[128] See generally S. Mayson, D. French and C. Ryan, *op. cit.* at pp. 328–329.

[129] [1910] 2 KB 979.

[130] *Cf.* S. Worthington, 'Floating Charges: An Alternative Theory' [1994] *CLJ* 81.

[131] See generally section 2.3.3.7.

[132] See *Wheatley* v *Silkstone and Haigh Moor Coal Co* (1885) 29 Ch D 715.

[133] See *Re Benjamin Cope & Sons Ltd* [1914] 1 Ch 800.

[134] See *Re Automatic Bottle Makers Ltd* [1926] Ch 412. Although the precise scope of this decision is debatable: see R. Goode, *Commercial Law op. cit.* at p. 733.

[135] [1994] 1 WLR 1427.

[136] See A. Walters, 'Priority of the Floating Charge in Corporate Insolvency: *Griffiths* v *Yorkshire Bank PLC*' (1995) 16 *Co Law* 291.

[137] See *English & Scottish Mercantile Investment Co Ltd* v *Bunton* [1892] 2 QB 700.

[138] On which see section 2.3.5. As will be discussed below, at the time of writing the Department for Business, Innovation and Skills were consulting on amending the charge registration scheme in the Companies Act 2006. Under the (draft) Companies Act 2006 (Amendment of Part 25) Regulations 2012 a new s. 859D would be inserted into the Companies Act 2006. The new s. 859D would provide:

'(1) A statement of particulars relating to a charge created by a company complies with this section if it contains the following particulars:

chargee constructive notice of the *terms* of the earlier charge.[139] Thus in *G and T Earle Ltd* v *Hemsworth Rural District Council*[140] Wright J stated:

> . . . having been registered . . . the plaintiffs, like all the world, are deemed to have constructive notice of the fact that there are debentures. But it has never been held that the mere fact that persons in the position of the plaintiffs have constructive notice of the existence of the debentures also affects them with constructive notice of the actual terms of the debentures or that the debentures are subject to the restrictive condition to which these debentures were subject. No doubt it is quite common for debentures to be subject to this limiting condition as to further charges, but that fact is not enough in itself to operate as constructive notice of the actual terms of any particular set of debentures.[141]

However, there is *some* authority to support the proposition that if a subsequent chargee has *actual* notice of the existence of a prior charge, the subsequent chargee will have constructive notice of the terms of that prior charge on the basis that, in such circumstances, a reasonable (subsequent) chargee would investigate the terms of that prior charge.[142]

2.3.3.4 Crystallisation of floating charges

As noted above,[143] on crystallisation a floating charge is transformed into a fixed charge over the then assets of the chargor which fall within the class or classes of assets

(a) the registered name and number of the company;

(b) the date of creation of the charge and (if the charge is one to which section 859C applies) the date of acquisition of the property or undertaking concerned;

(c) where the charge is created or evidenced by an instrument, the particulars listed in subsection (2);

(d) where the charge is not created or evidenced by an instrument, the particulars listed in subsection (3).

(2) The particulars referred to in subsection (1)(c) are –

(a) any of the following –

   (i) the names of each of the persons in whose favour the charge has been created or of the security agents or trustees holding the charge for the benefit of one or more persons; or,

   (ii) where there are more than four such persons, security agents or trustees, the names of any four such persons, security agents or trustees listed in the charge instrument, and a statement that there are other such persons, security agents or trustees;

(b) whether the charge is expressed to be a floating charge and, if so, whether it is expressed to cover all the property and undertaking of the company;

(c) whether any of the terms of the charge prohibit or restrict the company from creating any further security that will rank equally with or ahead of the charge;

(d) whether (and if so, a short description of) any land, ship, aircraft or intellectual property that is registered or required to be registered in the United Kingdom, is subject to a charge (which is not a floating charge) or fixed security included in the instrument;

(e) whether the instrument includes a charge (which is not a floating charge) or fixed security over –

   (i) any tangible or corporeal property, or

   (ii) any intangible or incorporeal property,

not described in paragraph (d).'

This is supplemented by a proposed new s. 859R: '(1) A person taking a charge over a company's property shall be taken to have notice of any matter requiring registration and disclosed on the register at the time the charge is created.'

[139] *Cf. Siebe Gorman & Co Ltd* v *Barclays Bank Ltd* [1979] 2 Lloyd's Rep 142.

[140] (1928) 44 TLR 605. On which see S. Mayson, D. French and C. Ryan, *op. cit.* at p. 336.

[141] *Ibid.* at p. 608. See also *Wilson* v *Kelland* [1910] 2 Ch 306.

[142] *Ian Chisholm Textiles Ltd* v *Griffiths* [1994] 2 BCLC 291. This case is helpfully discussed in S. Mayson, D. French and C. Ryan, *op. cit.* at p. 336.

[143] See section 2.3.3.3.

charged.[144] So what events crystallise a floating charge? Since *Re Brightlife Ltd*[145] there has been more emphasis on the terms of the floating charge in determining the events which may crystallise a floating charge. More specifically *Re Brightlife* recognised the validity of 'automatic crystallisation clauses'. An automatic crystallisation clause is a clause which provides for the automatic crystallisation of a floating charge in particular circumstances (such as the failure of the chargor to act in a particular way).[146]

Notwithstanding the foregoing, a floating charge will often crystallise in the following circumstances:

- where the chargee appoints a receiver;
- where the chargor goes into liquidation;[147]
- where the chargor ceases business;[148]
- where the chargee gives the chargor notice of crystallisation.[149]

2.3.3.5 Distinguishing fixed charges from floating charges

In determining whether a particular charge is a fixed charge or a floating charge, the courts look at the essence of the charge.[150] A useful starting point is in the judgment of Romer LJ in *Re Yorkshire Woolcombers Association Ltd*[151] where the learned judge stated:

> I certainly do not intend to attempt to give an exact definition of the term 'floating charge', nor am I prepared to say that there will not be a floating charge within the meaning of the Act, which does not contain all the three characteristics that I am about to mention, but I certainly think that if a charge has the three characteristics that I am about to mention it is a floating charge. (1) If it is a charge on a class of assets of a company present and future; (2) if that class is one which, in the ordinary course of the business of the company, would be changing from time to time; and (3) if you find that by the charge it is contemplated that, until some future step is taken by or on behalf of those interested in the charge, the company may carry on its business in the ordinary way as far as concerns the particular class of assets I am dealing with.[152]

Nevertheless, in recent years there has been a tendency to focus on the third characteristic identified by Romer LJ. Thus in *Agnew* v *Commissioner of Inland Revenue*[153] Lord Millett stated:

> This was offered as a description and not a definition. The first two characteristics are typical of a floating charge but they are not distinctive of it, since they are not necessarily inconsistent with a fixed charge. It is the third characteristic which is the hallmark of a floating charge and serves to distinguish it from a fixed charge. Since the existence of a fixed charge would make it impossible for the company to carry on business in the ordinary way without the consent of the charge holder, it follows that its ability to do so without such consent is inconsistent with the fixed nature of the charge.[154]

---

[144] See *Re Griffin Hotel Co Ltd* [1941] Ch 129 and *George Barker (Transport) Ltd* v *Eynon* [1974] 1 WLR 462.
[145] [1987] Ch 200.
[146] See generally S. Mayson, D. French and C. Ryan, *op. cit.* at p. 325.
[147] *Re Panama, New Zealand and Australian Royal Mail Co.* (1870) LR 5 Ch App 318.
[148] *Re Woodroffes (Musical Instruments) Ltd* [1986] Ch 366.
[149] *Re Brightlife Ltd* [1987] Ch 200.
[150] See *Re ASRS Establishment Ltd* [2000] 2 BCLC 631.
[151] [1903] 2 Ch 284.
[152] *Ibid.* at 295.
[153] [2001] UKPC 28.
[154] *Ibid.* at [13].

> **CASE**
>
> ### *National Westminster Bank PLC v Spectrum Plus Ltd*[155]
>
> Similarly in National Westminster Bank PLC v Spectrum Plus Ltd Lord Scott stated:
>
> > . . . the essential feature of a floating charge, the characteristic that distinguishes it from a fixed charge, is that the asset subject to the charge is not finally appropriated as a security for the payment of the debt until the occurrence of some future event. In the meantime the chargor is left free to use the charged asset and to remove it from the security.[156]
>
> *National Westminster Bank PLC v Spectrum Plus Ltd* concerned the vexed issue of the circumstances in which a charge over book debts could constitute a fixed charge. In that case, the House of Lords held that the chargor's freedom to use the proceeds of collected debts was inconsistent with the charge being a fixed charge.[157]

As a final point, and as Sealy and Hooley note, 'freedom is a relative rather than absolute concept, and some degree of restriction is not incompatible with a charge being a floating charge'.[158]

2.3.3.6 Significance of the distinction between fixed charges and floating charges

As noted above,[159] one advantage of a floating charge is that it allows a chargor to grant security over assets which it also needs to be able to deal with in the normal course of business. Equally, from a chargee's point of view, the ability of the chargor to deal with the charged assets in the normal course of business *may*, depending on the circumstances, increase the risk that the security will not meet the obligation secured.

In evaluating the advantages and disadvantages of fixed and floating charges, one should also consider the following points.

- Traditionally the holder of a floating charge was often able to appoint an administrative receiver once the charge became enforceable. This had the advantage, *inter alia*, from the chargee's point of view, of preventing the chargor entering into administration.[160] However, as noted above,[161] the ability of a holder of a floating charge (which was created on or after 15 September 2003) to appoint an administrative receiver has been severely curtailed.[162]

---

[155] [2005] UKHL 41.

[156] *Ibid.* at [111].

[157] The House of Lords overruled *Siebe Gorman and Co Ltd* v *Barclays Bank Ltd* [1979] 2 Lloyd's Rep 142 and *Re New Bullas Trading Ltd* [1994] 1 BCLC 485. *Cf Re Harmony Care Homes* [2009] EWHC 1961 with *Gray* v *G-T-P Group Ltd* [2010] EWHC 1772.

[158] See L. S. Sealy and R. J. A. Hooley, *op. cit.* at p. 1134.

[159] See section 2.3.3.3.

[160] See generally R. Bradgate, *op. cit.* at p. 529.

[161] See section 2.3.1.

[162] See s. 72A, Insolvency Act 1986 and *cf.* ss. 72B–72H, Insolvency Act 1986. *Cf.* also *In the Matter of Dairy Farmers of Britain Ltd* [2009] EWHC 1389.

- As we will see below,[163] all floating charges are registrable under the Companies Act 2006 whereas not all fixed charges are registrable under the Companies Act 2006.[164]

- The claim of a chargee under a floating charge may be subordinated to the claims of the chargor's preferential creditors.[165]

- The claim of a chargee under a floating charge will be subordinated to the expenses of liquidation.[166]

- In certain circumstances, a prescribed percentage of realised assets under floating charges must be set aside for the chargor's unsecured creditors.[167]

- In certain circumstances, a floating charge, but not a fixed charge, can be challenged under s. 245, Insolvency Act 1986.

2.3.3.7 Priorities between charges

Sometimes a dispute will arise about the order of priority to be given to competing charges. The starting point for dealing with such disputes are the general rules of priority.[168] Accordingly, for example, a legal charge[169] will usually take priority over an equitable charge, and an earlier equitable charge will usually take priority over a later equitable charge. However, the following considerations should also be borne in mind:

- registration regimes,[170] and particularly a failure to register a registrable charge, may impact on the question of priority;[171]

- chargees are free to agree a different order of priority for charges;[172]

- as we have seen,[173] a chargor may be able to create a fixed charge over particular assets with priority over the earlier floating charge;[174]

- as we have seen,[175] it seems that it may be possible for a chargor to create a floating charge over *some* of the same class of assets as an earlier floating charge with priority over the earlier floating charge;[176]

- if *Griffiths v Yorkshire Bank PLC*[177] is correct a subsequent floating charge may gain priority over an earlier floating charge by crystallising before the earlier floating charge.

---

[163] See section 2.3.5.
[164] See also L. S. Sealy and R. J. A. Hooley, *op. cit.* at p. 1136.
[165] See ss. 40 and 175(2)(b), Insolvency Act 1986.
[166] See s. 176ZA, Insolvency Act 1986.
[167] See s. 176A, Insolvency Act 1986 and *cf. Thorniley v Revenue & Customs Commissioners* [2008] EWHC 124.
[168] For a masterful survey of which, see R. Goode, *Commercial Law, op. cit.* at pp. 697–701.
[169] Although *cf.* M. Bridge, *op. cit.* at p. 182.
[170] *Cf.* Bills of Sale Act 1878, s. 10.
[171] See section 2.3.5.
[172] *Cf.*, for example, *Cheah Theam Swee v Equiticorp Finance Group Ltd* [1992] 1 AC 472.
[173] See section 2.3.3.3.
[174] *Wheatley v Silkstone and Haigh Moor Coal Co* (1885) 29 Ch D 715.
[175] See section 2.3.3.3.
[176] *Re Automatic Bottle Makers Ltd* [1926] Ch 412.
[177] [1994] 1 WLR 1427.

2.3.4 Equitable liens and maritime liens[178]

An equitable lien is a form of non-possessory security which is similar in effect to an equitable charge[179] and which arises by operation of law.[180] Such a lien may be conferred on an unpaid seller of land as security for the purchase price.[181] The precise scope of application of equitable liens is not very clear.[182]

A maritime lien is also a form of non-possessory security which arises by operation of law. In general terms a maritime lien is granted over a ship, and its cargo, as security in relation to, for example, salvage costs, wages etc.[183]

2.3.5 Registration requirements

2.3.5.1 Introduction

Certain non-possessory securities may be registrable under one or more registration regime.[184] For example, Sch. 1 to the Merchant Shipping Act 1995 makes provision for the registration of mortgages on particular ships. In this section we will focus on two registration regimes: the registration regime under the bills of sale legislation and the registration regime under Part 25 of the Companies Act 2006.[185]

2.3.5.2 Registration under the bills of sale legislation

Certain non-possessory securities created[186] by individuals[187] over 'personal chattels'[188] may be registrable under the Bills of Sale legislation (*viz.* the Bills of Sale Act 1878 and the Bills of Sale Act (1878) Amendment Act 1882).[189] The Bills of Sale legislation is notoriously complex.[190] A useful starting point for an examination of the Bills of Sale legislation is the definition of a 'bill of sale':

---

[178] *Cf. Dornoch Ltd* v *Westminster International BV* [2009] EWHC 889 (Admlty).

[179] See M. Bridge, *op. cit.* at p. 194.

[180] *Ibid.*

[181] See *Re Birmingham* [1959] Ch 523.

[182] *Cf.* J. Phillips, 'Equitable Liens: A Search for a Unifying Principle', in N. Palmer and E. McKendrick (eds), *Interests in Goods* (2nd edn, LLP, London, 1998) Chapter 39.

[183] See R. Goode, *Commercial Law, op. cit.* at p. 662.

[184] For a masterful survey of which, see R. Goode, *Commercial Law, ibid.* at pp. 701–713.

[185] At the time of writing the Department for Business, Innovation and Skills is consulting on draft regulations to amend Part 25 of the Companies Act 2006 (the (draft) Companies Act 2006 (Amendment of Part 25) Regulations 2012). At the same time the Secured Transactions Law Reform Project, under the directorship of Professor Sir Roy Goode QC, is considering wider reform.

[186] As opposed to non-possessory securities arising by operation of law: see L. S. Sealy and R. J. A. Hooley, *op. cit.* at p. 1140.

[187] The Bills of Sale legislation does not apply to non-possessory securities granted by companies: see Bills of Sale Act (1878) Amendment Act 1882, s. 17. See also *Online Catering Ltd* v *Acton* [2010] EWCA Civ 58.

[188] Defined in Bills of Sale Act 1878, s. 4. See also *Chapman* v *Wilson* [2010] EWHC 1746 (future property).

[189] As amended by the Bills of Sale Act 1890 and the Bills of Sale Act 1891.

[190] See R. Bradgate, *op. cit.*, p. 496. The Department for Business, Innovation and Skills consulted on banning bills of sale for consumer lending in 2009 (see www.bis.gov.uk/Consultations/ban-use-of-bills-of-sale-for-consumer-lending?cat=closedwithresponse).

The expression 'bill of sale' shall include bills of sale, assignments, transfers, declarations of trust without transfer, inventories of goods with receipt thereto attached, or receipts for purchase moneys of goods, and other assurances of personal chattels, and also powers of attorney, authorities, or licenses to take possession of personal chattels as security for any debt, and also any agreement, whether intended or not to be followed by the execution of any other instrument, by which a right in equity to any personal chattels, or to any charge or security thereon, shall be conferred, but shall not include . . .[191]

A number of points need to be made about this definition and the scope of the Bills of Sale legislation. First, somewhat counterintuitively, purely oral agreements are outside of the scope of the Bills of Sale legislation.[192]

Secondly, possessory securities are also generally outside of the scope of the Bills of Sale legislation.[193]

Thirdly, a distinction needs to be made between 'absolute bills of sale' and 'security bills of sale'. In essence a 'security bill of sale' is a bill of sale given as security for the payment of money whereas an 'absolute bill of sale' is not given as security for the payment of money.[194] All bills of sale, duly adhering to the relevant formalities,[195] must be attested and registered with the relevant registrar,[196] normally within seven days of its execution.[197] If a 'security bill of sale' is not registered in a timely fashion it will be void.[198]

ISSUE BOX

What is/are the purposes behind the Bills of Sale legislation?

2.3.5.3 Registration under Part 25 of the Companies Act 2006

Part 25 of the Companies Act 2006 contains a registration regime for certain charges *created* by companies over its property (as opposed to charges created by operation of law).[199] The charges which are registrable under Part 25 of the Companies Act are set out in s. 860 of that Act.[200]

---

[191] Bills of Sale Act 1878, s. 4. *Cf.* Bills of Sale Act (1878) Amendment Act 1882, s. 3.

[192] See *Newlove* v *Shrewsbury* (1888) 21 QBD 41.

[193] See *Charlesworth* v *Mills* [1892] AC 231 although *cf. Dublin City Distillery Ltd* v *Doherty* [1914] AC 823 at 854.

[194] *Cf.* Bills of Sale Act (1878) Amendment Act 1882, s. 3.

[195] See, for example, Bills of Sale Act (1878) Amendment Act 1882, s. 4.

[196] *Cf.* Bills of Sale Act 1878, s. 13.

[197] Bills of Sale Act 1878, s. 8.

[198] Bills of Sale Act (1878) Amendment Act 1882, s. 8.

[199] See, generally, S. Mayson, D. French and C. Ryan, *op. cit.* at pp. 333–340.

[200] The (draft) Companies Act 2006 (Amendment of Part 25) Regulations 2012 propose that all charges are registrable unless excluded by the new s. 859A.

LEGISLATIVE PROVISION

COMPANIES ACT 2006

Section 860

(1) A company that creates a charge to which this section applies must deliver the prescribed particulars of the charge, together with the instrument (if any) by which the charge is created or evidenced, to the registrar for registration before the end of the period allowed for registration.

. . .

(7) This section applies to the following charges—

(a) a charge on land or any interest in land, other than a charge for any rent or other periodical sum issuing out of land,

(b) a charge created or evidenced by an instrument which, if executed by an individual, would require registration as a bill of sale,

(c) a charge for the purposes of securing any issue of debentures,

(d) a charge on uncalled share capital of the company,

(e) a charge on calls made but not paid,

(f) a charge on book debts of the company,

(g) a floating charge on the company's property or undertaking,

(h) a charge on a ship or aircraft, or any share in a ship,

(i) a charge on goodwill or on any intellectual property.

Charges are defined so as to *include* mortgages.[201] Yet the parameters of the concept of a 'charge' can be debatable (as can be demonstrated by reference to (extended) retention of title clauses[202]).[203]

The period allowed for registration is normally '21 days beginning with the day after the day on which the charge is created'.[204] Failure to register in a timely fashion is an offence.[205] Moreover, s. 874(1) provides that if a company creates a s. 860 charge, the charge ('so far as any security on the company's property or undertaking is conferred') will be void against the company's liquidator, administrator or creditor unless s. 860 has been complied with.[206] This is supplemented by s. 874(3) which provides that s. 874(1) is 'without prejudice to any contract or obligation for repayment of the money secured by the charge; and when a charge becomes void under this section, the money secured by it immediately becomes payable'.

---

[201] Companies Act 2006, s. 861(5).

[202] See Chapter 4.

[203] *Cf.* also R. Bradgate, *op. cit.* at p. 499.

[204] Companies Act 2006, s. 870(1) although note the other provisions of that section and s. 873. See also G. McCormack, 'Extension of Time for Registration of Company Charges' [1986] *JBL* 282.

[205] See s. 860(4)–(5). The (draft) Companies Act 2006 (Amendment of Part 25) Regulations 2012 propose that criminal liability is removed.

[206] See also *Smith v Bridgend County Borough Council* [2001] UKHL 58.

2.3.6 **Reform?**

2.4 **Contracts of guarantee**

2.4.1 **The nature of contracts of guarantee**

2.4.1.1 **Introduction**

A party to a contract (A) may seek a measure of security in relation to the other party's (B's) performance of the contract by obtaining a guarantee from a third party (C). In essence, a contract of guarantee is a contract under which the guarantor (C) agrees to be answerable for the contractual default of B.[207] Such a contract may be illustrated by a simple example. B (often referred to as the 'principal debtor') wishes to borrow money from A (often referred to as the 'creditor'). A is unwilling to lend money to B unless the debt is guaranteed by C (a guarantor). If C agrees to guarantee repayment of the loan by B, and the money is advanced to B, then *if* B defaults in repaying the loan C is *prima facie* answerable to A.

In many cases there will be two contracts in such situations: a loan contract between A and B, and a contract of guarantee between A and C (a *bipartite* guarantee).[208] Accordingly we will focus on such situations although it is important to appreciate that there may be variations on this model. For example, there may also be a contract between B and C. Alternatively all three parties may be party to the contract of guarantee (a *tripartite* guarantee).[209]

2.4.1.2 **Key features of contracts of guarantee**

At the outset, it is necessary to identify a number of key features of contracts of guarantee. First, a guarantor undertakes *secondary liability*. In other words the guarantor's liability is

---

[207] See R. Bradgate, *op. cit.* at p. 538 and R. Goode, *Commercial Law, op. cit.* at p. 878.
[208] See L. S. Sealy and R. J. A. Hooley, *op. cit.* at p. 1157.
[209] *Ibid.*

dependent on the default of the principal debtor.[210] Secondly, a contract of guarantee is an *accessory contract*; in general terms a contract of guarantee is dependent on the existence of a principal obligation between the creditor and principal debtor.[211] This leads to the principle that the liability of the guarantor is *normally*[212] *co-extensive* with the liability of the principal debtor.[213] Thus if the liability of the principal debtor is reduced, the liability of the guarantor is normally reduced *pro tanto*. Moreover, if the principal obligation is void or unenforceable, there will usually be no liability on the part of the guarantor.[214]

2.4.1.3 Types of guarantee

We have already made a distinction between bipartite and tripartite guarantees.[215] Contracts of guarantee may also be classified in the following ways.

- A guarantor may merely assume *personal liability* or a guarantor may assume personal liability supported by *real security*. Alternatively, a guarantor may merely provide real security.[216]

- A guarantee may be a *discrete guarantee* or it may be a *continuing guarantee*.[217] A discrete guarantee might be used to secure a specific debt whereas a continuing guarantee might be used to secure running account credit (for example, an overdraft).[218]

- A guarantee might be *limited* to a specified amount. Alternatively, or in addition, a guarantee might be limited in duration.[219] Equally a guarantee might be *unlimited*.

2.4.1.4 Formation of contracts of guarantee[220]

Contracts of guarantee can take the form of either a *bilateral contract* or a *unilateral contract*. The essential difference between bilateral and unilateral contracts is that in the case of the former both parties have obligations under the contract whereas in the case of the latter only one party has an obligation under the contract. Thus, for example, where the creditor *promises* the guarantor that it will lend money to the principal debtor, and the guarantor *promises* in return to guarantee repayment by the principal debtor, the contract will be bilateral. By contrast, where, for example, the guarantor promises to guarantee the principal debtor's repayment of a sum of money *if* the creditor advances such sum of money to the principal debtor (the creditor being under no obligation to advance the said sum of money), the contract will be unilateral.[221]

---

[210] See R. Goode, *Commercial Law, op. cit.* at p. 878. See also *Vossloh AG v Alpha Trains (UK) Ltd* [2010] EWHC 2443 (Ch).
[211] See L. S. Sealy and R. J. A. Hooley, *op. cit.* at p. 1150.
[212] *Ibid.,* although *cf. Moschi v Lep Air Services Ltd* [1973] AC 331 at 349 *per* Lord Diplock.
[213] See *Moschi v Lep Air Services Ltd* [1973] AC 331.
[214] See, for example, *Coutts & Co v Browne-Lecky* [1947] KB 104.
[215] See above at section 2.4.1.1.
[216] See *Smith v Wood* [1929] 1 Ch 14 and *Re Conley* [1938] 2 All ER 127.
[217] On revocation, see *Close Brothers Ltd v Pearce* [2011] EWHC 298.
[218] See R. Bradgate, *op. cit.* at p. 542.
[219] See, generally, L. S. Sealy and R. J. A. Hooley, *op. cit.* at p. 1159.
[220] On formation see *Investec Bank (UK) Ltd v Zulman* [2010] EWCA Civ 536 and *Destiny 1 Ltd v Lloyds TSB Bank PLC* [2011] EWCA Civ 831.
[221] *Cf. Offord v Davies* (1862) 12 CBNS 748.

2.4.1.5 Formalities[222]

Contracts of guarantee are subject to s. 4, Statute of Frauds 1677.

LEGISLATIVE PROVISION

STATUTE OF FRAUDS 1677

Section 4

. . . noe Action shall be brought . . . whereby to charge the Defendant upon any special promise to answere for the debt default or miscarriages of another person . . . unlesse the Agreement upon which such Action shall be brought or some Memorandum or Note thereof shall be in Writeing and signed by the partie to be charged therewith or some other person there unto by him lawfully authorized.[223]

Certain formalities may also be required of contracts of guarantee by the Consumer Credit Act 1974.[224]

2.4.1.6 Principles of construction

Principles of construction will be discussed below at section 2.4.2.3.

2.4.1.7 The distinction between contracts of guarantee and contracts of indemnity

A contract of guarantee should be distinguished from a contract of indemnity. A useful starting point is the judgment of Holroyd Pearce LJ in *Yeoman Credit Ltd* v *Latter*.[225] In that case Holroyd Pearce LJ stated:

---

[222] See, generally, *Actionstrength Ltd* v *International Glass Engineering In. Gl. En. SpA* [2003] UKHL 17. On the use of e-mails see *Golden Ocean Group Ltd* v *Salgaocar Mining Industries Pvt Ltd* [2012] EWCA Civ 265 at [22] and [32]: 'The conclusion of commercial contracts, particularly charterparties, by an exchange of emails, once telexes or faxes, in which the terms agreed early on are not repeated verbatim later in the exchanges, is entirely commonplace. It causes no difficulty whatever in the parties knowing at exactly what point they have undertaken a binding obligation and upon what terms . . . Subject to the requirement of signature to which I shall return, I can see no objection in principle to reference to a sequence of negotiating emails or other documents of the sort which is commonplace in ship chartering and ship sale and purchase. Whether the pattern of contract negotiation and formation habitually adopted in other areas of commercial life presents difficulty in adoption of the same approach must await examination when the problem arises. Nothing I have said is intended to discourage the obviously sensible practice of incorporating a guarantee either in a readily identifiable self-standing document or otherwise providing for it as part of the terms of a formally executed document. The Statute must however, if possible, be construed in a manner which accommodates accepted contemporary business practice . . . It was common ground both before the judge and before us that an electronic signature is sufficient and that a first name, initials, or perhaps a nickname will suffice.'

[223] See also s. 3, Mercantile Law Amendment Act 1856, which states: 'No special promise to be made by any person . . . to answer for the debt, default, or miscarriage of another person, being in writing, and signed by the party to be charged therewith, or some other person by him thereunto lawfully authorised, shall be deemed invalid to support an action, suit, or other proceeding to charge the person by whom such promise shall have been made, by reason only that the consideration for such promise does not appear in writing, or by necessary inference from a written document.' On the possibility of rectification see *Fairstate Ltd* v *General Enterprise and Management Ltd* [2010] EWHC 3072 at [75]–[76].

[224] See Chapter 8.

[225] [1961] 1 WLR 828.

An indemnity is a contract by one party to keep the other harmless against loss, but a contract of guarantee is a contract to answer for the debt, default or miscarriage of another who is to be primarily liable to the promise.[226]

Essentially an indemnifier assumes liability which is *primary* and *independent* of the contract between, in the situation outlined in section 2.4.1.1, A and B. This is significant for the following (non-exhaustive) reasons:

- contracts of indemnity are not subject to s. 4, Statute of Frauds 1677;
- as contracts of indemnity are independent of the contract between A and B, an indemnifier will normally remain liable even if the underlying contract is invalid.[227]

However, it is not always easy to determine whether a particular contract is a contract of guarantee or a contract of indemnity.[228] Thus in *Yeoman Credit Ltd* v *Latter*[229] Harman LJ noted that the distinction between contracts of guarantee and contracts of indemnity has:

. . . raised many hair-splitting distinctions of exactly the kind which brings the law into hatred, ridicule and contempt by the public.[230]

In determining whether a particular contract is a contract of guarantee or a contract of indemnity, a court will look at the *essence* of the agreement.[231] Thus in *Yeoman Credit Ltd* v *Latter*[232] Holroyd Pearce LJ stated:

. . . we must have regard to its essential nature in order to decide whether or not it is really no more than a guarantee.[233]

Thus, a 'principal debtor' clause does not necessarily mean that the contract is one of indemnity.[234]

2.4.2 The protection of guarantors

2.4.2.1 Introduction

A guarantor, particularly a non-professional guarantor, may occupy a vulnerable position.[235] For example, a guarantor may be in a weak bargaining position with the creditor. Moreover,

---

[226] *Ibid.* at 830–831.

[227] For further discussion see L. S. Sealy and R. J. A. Hooley, *op. cit.* at p. 1151.

[228] *Cf.*, generally, *Pitts* v *Jones* [2007] EWCA Civ 1301; *Van Der Merwe* v *ILG Capital LLC* [2008] 2 Lloyd's Rep 187; *Associated British Ports* v *Ferryways NV* [2009] EWCA Civ 189 and *Wuhan Guoyu Logistics Group Co* v *Emporiki Bank of Commerce SA* [2012] EWHC 1715. See also P. McGrath, 'The Nature of Modern Guarantees' (2009) 1 *CRI* 10.

[229] [1961] 1 WLR 828.

[230] *Ibid.* at 835.

[231] See, for example, *Harburg India Rubber Comb Co* v *Martin* [1902] 1 KB 778 at 784–785 *per* Vaughan Williams LJ. *Cf. Marubeni Hong Kong and South China Ltd* v *Mongolian Government* [2005] EWCA Civ 395. See also *Meritz Fire & Marine Insurance Co Ltd* v *Jan de Nul NV* [2010] EWHC 3362 and [2011] EWCA Civ 827.

[232] [1961] 1 WLR 828.

[233] *Ibid.* at 831.

[234] See *Heald* v *O'Connor* [1971] 1 WLR 497 and *General Produce Co* v *United Bank Ltd* [1979] 2 Lloyd's Rep 255. See also *McGuinness* v *Norwich & Peterborough Building Society* [2010] EWHC 2989 and [2011] EWCA Civ 1286.

[235] See J. Devenney, L. Fox O'Mahony and M. Kenny, 'Standing Surety in England and Wales: The Sphinx of Procedural Protection' (2008) *Lloyd's Maritime and Commercial Law Quarterly* 513 at 514, R. Parry, 'The Position of Family Sureties within the Framework of Protection for Consumer Debtors in European Member States' (2005) 13 *ERPL* 357 and R. Goode, *Commercial Law*, *op. cit.* at p. 798.

the guarantor may be in an unenviable position in relation to the principal debtor;[236] for example, in a number of cases which we shall discuss below, the guarantor was subjected to considerable pressure from the principal debtor to execute the guarantee. These factors, and other factors,[237] may result in a situation where the guarantor is exposed to liability which is out of all proportion to the guarantor's resources and may result in the guarantor being subject to an indefinite obligation.[238]

In this section we shall explore the protection which the law of England and Wales affords to guarantors. In so doing, it is important not to lose sight of the following three general considerations. First, guarantee transactions are poly-contextual in nature.[239] In other words, such agreements transcend traditional legal boundaries.[240] Therefore, the protection afforded to guarantors in a particular jurisdiction often involves a complex blend of various legal fields and concepts including (aspects of) specific guarantees law, contract law, property law, consumer law and family law.[241] Moreover, although a detailed consideration of such provisions is beyond the scope of this chapter, insolvency and social welfare provisions also impact on the overall level of guarantor protection in a particular jurisdiction.[242] Secondly, the level of guarantor protection in any particular jurisdiction often involves balancing the interests of the guarantor and the creditor.[243] Thirdly, the precise balance between the interests of the guarantor and the interests of the creditor may have wider social and economic consequences. For example, in *Royal Bank of Scotland* v *Etridge (No 2)*[244] Lord Nicholls reflected, in the context of guarantees given by non-professional parties, on the importance of such transactions in the following terms:

> The problem . . . raised by the present appeals is of comparatively recent origin. It arises out of the substantial growth in home ownership over the last 30 or 40 years . . . More than two-thirds of householders in the United Kingdom now own their own homes. For most home-owning couples, their homes are their most valuable asset. They must surely be free, if they so wish, to use this asset as a means of raising money, whether for the purpose of the husband's business or for any other purpose . . . Bank finance is in fact by far the most important source of external capital for small businesses with fewer than ten employees. These businesses comprise about 95 per cent of all businesses in the country, responsible for nearly one-third of all employment . . . If the freedom of home-owners to make economic use of their homes is not to be frustrated, a bank must be able to have confidence that a wife's signature of the necessary guarantee and charge will be as binding upon her as is the signature of anyone else on documents which he or she may sign. Otherwise banks will not be willing to lend money on the security of a jointly owned house or flat.[245]

---

[236] See J. Devenney, L. Fox O'Mahony and M. Kenny, *op. cit.*

[237] *Ibid.*

[238] *Ibid.*

[239] See M. Kenny, 'Standing Surety in Europe: Common Core or Tower of Babel' (2007) *MLR* 175 and M. Kenny and J. Devenney, 'The Fallacy of the Common Core: Polycontextualism in Surety Protection: A Hard Case in Harmonisation Discourse', in M. Andenæs and C. Andersen (eds), *The Theory and Practice of Harmonisation* (Edward Elgar Publishing, Cheltenham, 2012).

[240] *Ibid.*

[241] *Ibid.*

[242] See Parry, *op. cit.*, at 358. See further J. Devenney, L. Fox O'Mahony and M. Kenny, *op. cit.*, and L. Fox O'Mahony, *Conceptualising Home: Theories, Laws and Policies* (Hart Publishing, Oxford, 2006) at pp. 220–228.

[243] See, for example, *Royal Bank of Scotland* v *Etridge (No 2)* [2001] UKHL 44 at [34]–[37].

[244] [2001] UKHL 44.

[245] At [34]–[35].

2.4.2.2 The protection afforded to guarantors during the negotiation of contracts of guarantee

It is, of course, clear that the Law of England and Wales does not impose a general duty to negotiate contracts in good faith.[246] Indeed it is far from clear what such a duty would entail.[247] Nevertheless, the negotiation phase of contracts of guarantees, like other contracts, is regulated by a series of vitiating factors.[248] Thus where the guarantor and creditor enter into the contract of guarantee under a sufficiently fundamental common mistake, the 'contract' may, under general principles, be void under the doctrine of common mistake.[249] Indeed, as has been argued elsewhere,[250] these vitiating factors form an important pillar to the protection provided to guarantors (particularly non-professional guarantors) in England and Wales and, as such, they will be explored in some detail in this section.

(a) Non-disclosure

A creditor may be aware of information which is, for example, relevant to the risk assumed by the guarantor. Yet, as contracts of guarantee are not contracts *uberrimae fidei*,[251] the creditor is not under a general duty of disclosure. Nevertheless, a guarantor may be able to, in effect, claim a remedy for non-disclosure if they can successfully forge an argument that the non-disclosure amounts to an implied misrepresentation; thus in *London General Omnibus Co Ltd v Holloway*[252] Vaughan Williams LJ stated:

> . . . a creditor must reveal to the surety every fact which under the circumstances the surety would expect not to exist, for the omission to mention that such a fact does exist is an implied representation that it does not.[253]

In addition, there is a growing body of case law[254] which recognises that there may be a duty on a creditor to disclose *unusual* features of the transaction[255] although the parameters and implications of this (limited) duty are still being hammered out.[256]

---

[246] See *Interfoto Picture Library Ltd v Stilletto Visual Programmes Ltd* [1989] 1 QB 433 at 439 *per* Bingham LJ.

[247] See J. Devenney, M. Kenny and L. Fox O'Mahony, 'England and Wales', in A. Columbi-Ciacchi and S. Weatherill (eds), *Regulating Unfair Banking Practices in Europe: The Case of Personal Suretyships* (Oxford University Press, Oxford, 2010) and *cf.* R. Brownsword, *Contract Law: Themes for the Twenty-first Century* (2nd edn, Oxford University Press, Oxford, 2006) Chapter 6.

[248] On which see J. Cartwright, *Unequal Bargaining: A Study of Vitiating Factors in the Formation of Contracts* (Clarendon, Oxford, 1991).

[249] See, for example, *Associated Japanese Bank (International) Ltd v Crédit du Nord SA* [1989] 1 WLR 255. The situations where relief will be granted for common mistakes have narrowed as a result of the disfavour into which *Solle v Butcher* [1950] 1 KB 671 has fallen since *Great Peace Shipping Ltd v Tsavliris* [2002] EWCA Civ 1407. See, generally, A. Chandler, J. Devenney and J. Poole, 'Common Mistake: Theoretical Justification and Remedial Inflexibility' [2004] *JBL* 34. On the possibility of a claim of *non est factum* see *Beardsley Theobald's Retirement Benefit Scheme Trustees v Yardley* [2011] EWHC 1380.

[250] See J. Devenney, L. Fox O'Mahony and M. Kenny, 'Standing Surety in England and Wales, *op. cit.*

[251] Confirmed by the House of Lords in *Royal Bank of Scotland v Etridge (No 2)* [2001] UKHL 44 particularly at [112] *per* Lord Hobhouse.

[252] [1912] 2 KB 72.

[253] *Ibid.* at 78. See *North Shore Ventures Ltd v Anstead Holdings Inc* [2011] EWCA Civ 230.

[254] See J. Devenney, M. Kenny and L. Fox O'Mahony, 'England and Wales', *op. cit.*

[255] *Levett v Barclays Bank PLC* [1995] 1 WLR 1260, *Crédit Lyonnais Bank Nederland v Export Credit Guarantee Department* [1996] 1 Lloyd's Rep 200, and *Royal Bank of Scotland v Etridge (No 2)* [2001] UKHL 44.

[256] *Royal Bank of Scotland v Etridge (No 2)* [2001] UKHL 44 at [81] *per* Lord Nicholls.

(b) Misrepresentation

Alternatively a creditor may induce[257] a guarantor to enter into the guarantee by an express or implied misrepresentation. In such situations, the guarantor may, subject to the general bars on the remedy of rescission and (possibly) s. 2(2) of the Misrepresentation Act 1967, have the transaction set aside.[258] Moreover, if the misrepresentation was made either fraudulently or negligently, the guarantor may have a right to damages for any loss suffered.[259]

More difficulty arises where the principal debtor induces, by means of misrepresentation, the guarantor to enter into a contract of guarantee with the creditor. In such circumstances the contract will *usually* only be set aside if the creditor had notice of the principal debtor's misrepresentation.[260] As the principles of notice are closely associated with undue influence, they will be discussed below.[261]

(c) Inappropriate pressure – an introduction

As noted elsewhere,[262] in recent years a recurring complaint from guarantors, particularly non-professional guarantors, has been that the transaction was induced by pressure.[263] Of course, not all types of pressure are objectionable.[264] Nevertheless, the law of England and Wales regulates the types of pressure which may be legitimately employed in the contracting process; and it does so largely through the doctrine of duress and the doctrine of undue influence.[265]

Although there appears to be a significant degree of overlap between the doctrine of duress and the doctrine of undue influence,[266] it is customary – given their different origins – to consider each separately.

---

[257] The misrepresentation does not, of course, need to be the sole or the main reason why the guarantor chose to enter the transaction: *Edgington* v *Fitzmaurice* (1885) 29 Ch D 459.

[258] See, generally, J. Poole and A. Keyser, 'Justifying Partial Rescission in English Law' (2005) 121 *LQR* 273.

[259] The measure of damages will depend, to a certain extent, on whether the misrepresentation was fraudulent or negligent. If the misrepresentation can be shown to have been fraudulent, damages can be claimed in the tort of deceit. In such cases the complainant can recover for all loss directly flowing from the fraudulent misrepresentation: see *Doyle* v *Olby (Ironmongers) Ltd* [1969] 2 QB 158 at 167 per Lord Denning MR and *Smith New Court Securities Ltd* v *Scrimgeour Vickers (Asset Management) Ltd* [1997] AC 254. Furthermore, after some uncertainty, it now seems that exemplary damages may be awarded in cases of fraudulent misrepresentation: see *Banks* v *Cox* [2002] EWHC 2166 at [13] and *Parabola Investments Ltd* v *Browallia Cal Ltd* [2009] EWHC 901 (Comm) at [205] (*cf.* [2010] EWCA Civ 486). On the other hand, if the misrepresentation was negligent, damages can be claimed either under the Misrepresentation Act 1967, s. 2(1) or, possibly, through the tort of negligence. The Misrepresentation Act 1967, s. 2(1), somewhat surprisingly, adopts the same measure of damages as under the tort of deceit: see *Royscot Trust Ltd* v *Rogerson* [1991] 2 QB 297. By contrast, the measure of damages under the tort of negligence may be more limited: see, generally, J. Poole and J. Devenney, 'Reforming Damages for Misrepresentation: the Case for Coherent Aims and Principles' [2007] *JBL* 269.

[260] See *Barclays Bank PLC* v *O' Brien* [1994] 1 AC 180 and *Royal Bank of Scotland* v *Etridge (No 2)* [2001] UKHL 44.

[261] See pp. 36–37.

[262] See J. Devenney, M. Kenny and L. Fox O'Mahony, 'England and Wales', *op. cit.*

[263] See, for example, M. Pawlowski and J. Brown, *Undue Influence and the Family Home* (Cavendish, London, 2001) and N. Enonchong, *Duress, Undue Influence and Unconscionable Dealing* (Sweet and Maxwell, London, 2006), Part IV.

[264] See, for example, *Allcard* v *Skinner* (1887) 36 ChD 145 at 157 *per* Kekewich J.

[265] See J. Devenney, M. Kenny and L. Fox O'Mahony, 'England and Wales', *op. cit.*

[266] See *Williams* v *Bayley* (1866) LR 1 HL 200, *Osbaldiston* v *Simpson* (1843) 13 Sim 513, *Dewar* v *Elliott* (1824) 2 LJ os Ch 178, *Collins* v *Hare* (1828) 1 Dow fcl 139, *Seear* v *Cohen* 45 LT 589, *Kaufman* v *Gerson* [1904] 1 KB 591, *Mutual Finance Ltd* v *John Wetton & Sons Ltd* [1937] 2 KB 389 and *Davies* v *London & Provincial Marine Insurance Co* 8 Ch D 469. See also M. Cope, *Duress, Undue Influence and Unconscientious Bargains* (The Law Book Company Ltd, Sydney, 1985) para. 125; P. Birks and Y. Chin, 'On the Nature of Undue Influence', in J. Beatson and D. Friedmann (eds), *Good Faith and Fault in Contract Law* (Clarendon, Oxford, 1995) at pp. 63–64; and J. Devenney and A. Chandler, 'Unconscionability and the Taxonomy of Undue Influence' [2007] *JBL* 541 especially 552–553.

(d) Duress

Over the years, the theoretical basis of the doctrine of duress has generated much discussion.[267] However, it is now clear that a successful plea of duress requires two fundamental elements. First, the pressure in question must, usually,[268] have left the person subject to the pressure with no practical choice but to enter into the transaction.[269] Secondly, the pressure must be 'illegitimate'[270] although the concept of 'illegitimacy' is difficult to map;[271] nevertheless threats of unlawful force to the person and some forms of economic pressure are 'illegitimate'.[272] Indeed, as noted elsewhere,[273] there is some evidence that the concept of 'illegitimacy' is still developing.[274]

Nevertheless, in the context of guarantee transactions, inappropriate pressure claims tend to be formulated in terms of the doctrine of undue influence.[275]

(e) Undue influence – an introduction

As argued elsewhere,[276] a central pillar of the *overall* protection afforded to guarantors in England and Wales is the equitable doctrine of undue influence.[277] Accordingly, at this juncture it would seem pertinent to explore two issues. First, what is the scope of the protection afforded to guarantors by the doctrine of undue influence? Secondly, what is the position where, as is more common, the contract of guarantee has been induced by the undue influence of the principal debtor rather than by the undue influence of the creditor?

(f) Mapping the doctrine of undue influence

It is not easy to map the doctrine of undue influence for, as Lindley LJ famously noted in *Allcard* v *Skinner*,[278] '. . . no Court has ever attempted to define undue influence'.[279] Indeed, in

[267] See, for example, P. S. Atiyah, 'Economic Duress and the Overborne Will' (1982) 98 *LQR* 197, J. Beatson, 'Duress as a Vitiating Factor in Contract' [1974] *CLJ* 97, J. P. Dawson, 'Economic Duress: An Essay in Perspective' (1947) 45 *Michigan Law Review* 253 and A. M. Honoré, 'A Theory of Coercion' (1990) 10 *OJLS* 94 and R. Bigwood, *Exploitative Contracts* (Oxford University Press, Oxford, 2003) at pp. 285ff.

[268] In cases where the pressure is in the form of unlawful force to the person, or threats of such force, the pressure only needs to be *a* reason why the person subject to the pressure entered into the transaction: *Barton* v *Armstrong* [1976] AC 104, *cf. Huyton SA* v *Peter Cremer GmbH & Co* [1999] CLC 230.

[269] *B & S Contracts* v *Victor Green* [1984] ICR 419, *Atlas Express Lord* v *Kafco (Importers and Distributors) Ltd* [1989] 1 All ER 641 and *The Evia Luck* [1991] 4 All ER 871.

[270] See, for example, *Universe Tankships Inc of Monrovia* v *International Transport Workers' Federation* [1983] 1 AC 366 although *cf.* S. Smith, 'Contracting Under Pressure: A Theory of Duress' (1997) *CLJ* 343.

[271] See, for example, J. Devenney, 'A Pack of Unruly Dogs', *op. cit.*

[272] *The Siboen and The Sibotre* [1976] 1 Lloyd's Rep 293 and *Pao On* v *Lau Yiu Long* [1980] AC 614.

[273] See J. Devenney, M. Kenny and L. Fox O'Mahony, 'England and Wales', *op. cit.*

[274] See, for example, 'R' v *HM Attorney General for England and Wales* [2003] UKPC 22; [2003] EMLR 499 but note A. Phang, 'Undue Influence Methodology, Sources and Linkages' [1995] *JBL* 552 at 569.

[275] See, generally, B. Fehlberg, *Sexually Transmitted Debt* (Clarendon, Oxford, 1997).

[276] See J. Devenney, L. Fox O'Mahony and M. Kenny, 'Standing Surety in England and Wales', *op. cit.*

[277] See, generally, B. Fehlberg, *op. cit.*

[278] (1887) 36 Ch D 145.

[279] *Ibid.* at 183. Lindley LJ did, however, also note (at 181) that undue influence involved '. . . some unfair and improper conduct, some coercion from outside, some overreaching, some form of cheating and generally, though not always, some personal advantage obtained by a donee placed in some close and confidential relation to the donor'. See also *Niersmans* v *Pesticcio* [2004] EWCA Civ 372 at [2] where Mummery LJ stated: 'The striking feature of this appeal is that fundamental misconceptions [relating to the doctrine of undue influence] persist, even though the doctrine is over 200 years old and its basis and scope were examined by the House of Lords in depth . . . less than 3 years ago in the well known case of *Royal Bank of Scotland PLC* v *Etridge (No 2)* [2002] 2 AC 773. The continuing confusions matter. Aspects of the instant case demonstrate the need for a wider understanding, both in and outside the legal profession, of the circumstances in which the court will intervene to protect the dependant and the vulnerable in dealings with their property.' See further *Bank of Scotland* v *Bennett* [1997] 3 FCR 193 at 216 *per* James Mumby QC, sitting as a Deputy Judge of the High Court.

recent years there has been much debate about the jurisprudential basis of the doctrine of undue influence.[280] Thus, Professors Birks and Chin argued that undue influence was essentially about the impairment of consent and that it was 'not necessary for the party claiming relief to point to fraud or unconscionable behaviour on the part of the other'.[281] Yet, whilst such a view has gained *some* support in the case law,[282] Birks and Chin's overall thesis is not unproblematic.[283] For example, it *may* adopt a pathological view of 'trust',[284] as well as taking an unduly restrictive, capacity driven, view of undue influence.[285] Furthermore, their view does not sit easily with the language employed by the House of Lords in *National Westminster Bank PLC v Morgan*,[286] *Barclays Bank PLC v O'Brien*[287] and *Royal Bank of Scotland v Etridge (No 2)*,[288] nor with more recent opinions of the Judicial Committee of the Privy Council,[289] all of which adopt an unconscionability-based approach to undue influence.[290] Thus in *Royal Bank of Scotland v Etridge (No 2)* Lord Nicholls[291] stated:

> Undue influence is one of the grounds of relief developed by courts of equity *as a court of conscience*. The objective is to ensure that the influence of one person over another is *not abused*. In everyday life people constantly seek to influence the decisions of others . . . The law has set *limits to the means properly employable for this purpose* . . . Equity extended the reach of the law to other *unacceptable forms of persuasion*.[292]

---

[280] See, for example, R. Bigwood, 'Undue Influence: "Impaired Consent" or "Wicked Exploitation"' (1996) 16 *OJLS* 503, D. Capper, 'Undue Influence and Unconscionability: A Rationalisation' (1998) 114 *LQR* 479, M. Chen-Wishart, 'The O'Brien Principle and Substantive Unfairness' [1997] *CLJ* 60, B. Fehlberg, *op. cit.* at pp. 24–25, L. McMurtry, 'Unconscionability and Undue Influence: An Interaction?' [2000] 64 *Conv* 573, M. Oldham, '"Neither Borrower Nor Lender Be": the Life of O'Brien' (1995) *Child and Family Law Quarterly* 104, at 108–109, J. O'Sullivan, 'Undue Influence and Misrepresentation after O'Brien: Making Security Secure', in F. Rose (ed.), *Restitution and Banking Law* (Mansfield Press, Oxford, 1998) at pp. 42–69, M. Pawlowski and J. Brown, *Undue Influence and the Family Home* (Cavendish, London, 2001) pp. 7–17, 27–30 and 205–212, N. S. Price, 'Undue Influence: *finis litium*' (1999) 115 *LQR* 8, S. Smith and P. S. Atiyah, *Atiyah's Introduction to the Law of Contract* (6th edn, Clarendon, Oxford, 2002) at pp. 288–291. This debate is reflected in the relevant case law: *Dunbar Bank PLC v Nadeem* [1998] 3 All ER 876, *Crédit Lyonnais Bank Nederland NV v Burch* [1997] 1 All ER 144, *Hammond v Osborn* [2002] EWCA Civ 885, *Portman Building Society v Dusangh* [2000] 2 All ER (Comm) 221 at 233 *per* Ward LJ, *Royal Bank of Scotland v Etridge (No 2)* [2001] EWCA Civ 1466, *Irvani v Irvani* [2000] 1 Lloyd's Rep 412 and *Barclays Bank PLC v Goff* [2001] EWCA Civ 635.

[281] P. Birks and Y. Chin, 'On the Nature of Undue Influence', in J. Beatson and D. Friedmann (eds), *Good Faith and Fault in Contract Law* (Clarendon, Oxford, 1995) at p. 61, although contrast P. Birks, 'Undue Influence as Wrongful Exploitation' (2004) 120 *LQR* 34.

[282] See, for example, *Hammond v Osborn* [2004] EWCA Civ 885, *Turkey v Awadh* [2005] EWCA Civ 382 and *Jennings v Cairns* [2003] EWCA 1935.

[283] See L. Fox O'Mahony and J. Devenney, 'The Elderly, Their Homes and the Unconscionable Bargain Doctrine', in M. Dixon (ed.), *Modern Studies in Property Law* (Vol. 5, Hart Publishing, Oxford, 2009).

[284] See M. Chen-Wishart, 'Undue Influence: Beyond Impaired Consent and Wrongdoing Towards a Relational Analysis', in A. Burrows and A. Rodger (eds), *Mapping the Law: Essays in Memory of Peter Birks* (Oxford University Press, Oxford, 2006) at p. 208.

[285] *Ibid.*

[286] [1985] AC 686.

[287] [1994] AC 180.

[288] [2001] UKHL 44.

[289] See *R v Attorney-General for England and Wales* [2003] UKPC 22 and *National Commercial Bank (Jamaica) Ltd v Hew's Executors* [2003] UKPC 51. The late Professor Birks acknowledged the difficulties that these decisions created for his thesis (P. Birks, 'Undue Influence as Wrongful Exploitation', *op. cit.*).

[290] See further J. Devenney and A. Chandler, 'Unconscionability and the Taxonomy of Undue Influence', *op. cit.* at 541–542.

[291] [2001] UKHL 44.

[292] *Ibid.* at [6–7] (emphasis added). Lord Hobhouse added, at [103], that undue influence 'is an equitable wrong committed by the dominant party against the other which makes it unconscionable for the dominant party to enforce his legal rights against the other'. Lord Bingham agreed with Lord Nicholls.

Yet, perhaps the most troublesome aspect of Birks and Chin's view of undue influence is their conceptualisation of unconscionability.[293] More specifically, Birks and Chin link the concept of unconscionability to a notion of 'wicked exploitation'. As has been argued elsewhere,[294] unconscionability can be a much more subtle and delicate concept and, accordingly, it can be argued that undue influence is based on a notion of unconscionability with clear parallels to the unconscionable bargain doctrine[295] (a doctrine which will be discussed later in this chapter).

Whatever the true jurisprudential basis of undue influence, it is clear that an important dimension of the doctrine of undue influence is its ability to regulate relational pressures.[296]

It is often said that relational undue influence can take many forms[297] and, therefore, it would be fruitless to attempt to list all instances of undue influence.[298] Nevertheless it is possible to identify familiar scenarios.[299] Thus at one end of the spectrum are cases where one person relinquishes their will to another. For example, in *Bank of Montreal* v *Stuart*[300] Mrs Stuart:

> ... had no will of her own. Nor had she any means of forming an independent judgment even if she had desired to do so. She was ready to sign anything her husband asked her to sign and do anything he told her to do.[301]

---

[293] See J. Devenney and A. Chandler, 'Unconscionability and the Taxonomy of Undue Influence', *op. cit.* at 541.

[294] *Ibid.*

[295] *Ibid.*

[296] See *Royal Bank of Scotland* v *Etridge (No 2)* [2001] UKHL 44 at [8]. See also *Bainbridge* v *Browne* (1881) Ch D 188 (parent and child), *Allcard* v *Skinner* (1887) 36 Ch D 145 (spiritual advisor and advisee), *Avon Finance* v *Bridger* [1985] 2 All ER 281 (co-habiting couple), *Crédit Lyonnais Bank Nederland NV* v *Burch* [1997] 1 All ER 144 (employer and employee), *Barclays Bank PLC* v *O'Brien* [1994] 1 AC 180 (husband and wife) and *Grosvenor* v *Sherratt* (1860) 28 Beav 659 (uncle and niece).

[297] See, for example, *Allcard* v *Skinner* (1887) 36 Ch D 145 at 183 *per* Lindley LJ.

[298] An interesting and not uncontroversial more recent case of undue influence arose in *Hewett* v *First Plus Financial Group PLC* [2010] EWCA Civ 312, where Briggs J stated at [31]–[33]: 'The second question is whether the fact that Mr Hewett was having an affair was something which his obligation of fairness and candour towards his wife required him to disclose, in connection with his request that she charge her interest in the Property as security for his debts. Mr Lightfoot for First Plus submitted that it depended upon whether that was a material fact, a question which he invited the court to decide in the negative. I consider that it was plainly a material fact calling for disclosure ... The horrible decision (as the Judge correctly put it) facing Mrs Hewett may be summarised as follows. Should she accede to her husband's proposal, in the hope of saving her family's home from her husband's creditors, as the basis for the continuation of a stable family life to which both she and her husband would contribute, taking the grave risk that his tendency towards financial irresponsibility would lead to the loss of both his and her beneficial interests in the Property? Or should she, by refusing his proposal, preserve her significant beneficial interest in the Property from the claims of his creditors as, in effect, a plank in the shipwreck? Central to that decision was a balancing of the reliability of her husband's promise to support the family in the future by making sure that the increased mortgage instalments were duly paid, against the risk that a failure on his part would lead to the loss not merely of his, but also of her, beneficial interest in the Property ... It is evident that Mrs Hewett's decision to accede to her husband's request was based upon an assumption on her part that he was as committed as she was to the marriage, to the family and to the preservation of their home life in the future. The truth was that he had already embarked upon an affair which, although by no means a certainty, carried with it the serious risk that it would lead in due course to Mr Hewett's departure from the family and withdrawal of both emotional and financial support, as eventually occurred. On that analysis of the decision facing Mrs Hewett, I consider that Mr Hewett's affair cried out for disclosure.'

[299] See J. Devenney and A. Chandler, 'Unconscionability and the Taxonomy of Undue Influence', *op. cit.* at 541.

[300] [1911] AC 120.

[301] *Ibid.* at 136–137 *per* Lord Macnaughten.

By contrast, at the other end of the spectrum are cases where relational dynamics in a pre-existing relationship either make one person more susceptible to pressure from the other[302] or where the pressure is only objectionable in the context of the pre-existing relationship.[303]

In between these two extremes are a myriad of situations where there is no 'routine dependence or submissiveness . . .'[304] nor 'unpleasantness'[305] but it can be shown that:

> . . . (a) the other party to the transaction (or someone who induced the transaction for his own benefit) had the capacity to influence the complainant; (b) the influence was exercised; (c) its exercise was undue; (d) its exercise brought about the transaction.[306]

At this point it is useful to note that it has become commonplace to make a distinction between actual undue influence and presumed undue influence. Broadly speaking, actual undue influence refers to situations where undue influence can be affirmatively proven.[307] By contrast, the concept of presumed undue influence was much more mysterious.[308] Nevertheless, following *Barclays Bank PLC v O'Brien*,[309] it seemed that undue influence would be presumed where (i) there was a relationship of trust and confidence between the parties,[310] and (ii) the parties entered into a transaction which was manifestly disadvantageous to the party seeking relief.[311]

As regards the requirement that there was a relationship of trust and confidence between the parties, some relationships were, as a matter of law, *deemed* to be relationships of trust and confidence. Obviously, in such cases, it was easier to raise a presumption of undue influence. Such relationships were known as '2A relationships',[312] examples of which included the relationship between a parent and an unemancipated child,[313] and the relationship between a medical advisor and advisee.[314] However, the relationship between a husband and a wife[315] was not a '2A relationship'. If a particular relationship was not a '2A relationship' then the party seeking relief had to demonstrate a *de facto* relationship of trust and confidence (a so-called 2B relationship).

In *Royal Bank of Scotland v Etridge*[316] Lord Nicholls[317] framed the so-called presumption of undue influence in terms of an *inference* of undue influence. In other words, if the relevant requirements are satisfied, the complainant establishes a *prima facie* case of undue influence which transfers the evidential burden to the other party to convince the court that the transaction was not procured by undue influence. As has been argued elsewhere, on such an analysis,

---

[302] See *Wingrove v Wingrove* 11 PD 81, *Scott v Sebright* 12 PD 21 and *Hampson v Guy* 64 LT 778.

[303] See *CTN Cash & Carry Ltd v Gallaher* [1994] 4 All ER 714 at 719d *per* Steyn LJ.

[304] P. Birks and Y. Chin, 'On the Nature of Undue Influence', in J. Beatson and D. Friedmann (eds), *op. cit.* at p. 78.

[305] *Ibid.*

[306] *Bank of Credit and Commerce International S.A. v Aboody* [1990] 1 QB 923 at 963 *per* Slade LJ (giving the judgment of the Court).

[307] *Barclays Bank PLC v O'Brien* [1994] 1 AC 180 at 196.

[308] J. Devenney, L. Fox O'Mahony and M. Kenny, 'Standing Surety in England and Wales', *op. cit.* at 516.

[309] [1994] AC 180.

[310] Although this phrase is not apt to cover all of the relationships where a presumption of undue influence may arise: see, for example, *Re Craig (decd)* [1970] 2 All ER 390.

[311] J. Devenney, L. Fox O'Mahony and M. Kenny, 'Standing Surety in England and Wales', *op. cit.* at 516.

[312] J. Devenney and A. Chandler, 'Unconscionability and the Taxonomy of Undue Influence', *op. cit.* at 541.

[313] *Bainbridge v Browne* (1881) Ch D 188.

[314] *Huguenin v Baseley* (1807) 14 Ves 273.

[315] *Barclays Bank v O'Brien* [1994] 1 AC 180.

[316] [2001] UKHL 44.

[317] *Ibid.* at [16] (Lords Bingham and Clyde expressly agreed with Lord Nicholls).

the *precise* nature of the relationship between the parties seems to be of pivotal importance.[318] Yet, disappointingly, none of their Lordships really engaged with the question of why some relationships are automatically deemed to be relationships of trust and confidence (formerly referred to as 2A relationships).[319]

The notion of a manifestly disadvantageous transaction has also been particularly problematic in the context of contracts of guarantee.[320] More specifically, in a number of cases the courts had to consider the situation where a wife had agreed to act as guarantor for her husband's business debts. In a sense, such a transaction is manifestly disadvantageous to the wife; she is guaranteeing the debts of another, often without direct benefit.[321] On the other hand, the wife *may* be getting a very real indirect benefit *if* the fortunes of the husband and wife are intertwined.[322] The difficulties are multiplied where, for example, the wife has a shareholding in the business which the husband runs.[323]

In *Royal Bank of Scotland* v *Etridge*[324] the House of Lords felt that the phrase 'manifest disadvantage' was apt to mislead. However, Their Lordships distanced themselves from suggestions (notably in *Barclays Bank PLC* v *Coleman*)[325] that this requirement should be completely abandoned. Instead they held that this requirement should be refined: in the future the second ingredient necessary for a presumption/inference of undue influence would be whether the transaction, failing proof to the contrary, was only explicable on the basis of undue influence.[326] Significantly for present purposes, Lord Nicholls did not think that a wife acting as guarantor for her husband's debts would *normally* satisfy this requirement.[327]

(g) Undue influence by the principal debtor

In cases where a contract of guarantee is induced by the undue influence of the *creditor*, the guarantor will, subject to certain bars, be entitled to have the contract rescinded. However, a more common complaint is that the contract of guarantee was procured not by the undue influence of the *creditor* but by the undue influence of the *debtor*. In such cases it is more difficult to argue that the contract of guarantee should, automatically, be voidable. More specifically, in such cases the courts must balance both the interests of the guarantor and the creditor in the light of any public interest.[328]

In *Barclays Bank PLC* v *O'Brien*[329] the House of Lords sought to balance these competing interests through an innovative use of the doctrine of notice. More specifically, where a contract of guarantee had been procured by the undue influence of the *debtor*, the guarantor would, subject to certain bars, only be entitled to have that transaction set aside if the creditor

---

[318] See J. Devenney, L. Fox O'Mahony and M. Kenny, 'Standing Surety in England and Wales', *op. cit.* at 517.
[319] *Ibid.*
[320] See J. Devenney, M. Kenny and L. Fox O'Mahony, 'England and Wales', *op. cit.* and B. Fehlberg, 'The Husband, the Bank, the Wife and Her Signature – The Sequel' (1996) 59 *MLR* 675, particularly at 677.
[321] See J. Devenney, L. Fox O'Mahony and M. Kenny, 'Standing Surety in England and Wales', *op. cit.* at 517.
[322] *Ibid.*
[323] *Ibid.* B. Fehlberg, *op. cit.* See also *Goode Durant Administration* v *Biddulph* [1994] 2 FLR.
[324] [2001] UKHL 44.
[325] [2000] 1 All ER 385 at 397–399.
[326] [2001] UKHL 44 at [29].
[327] [2001] UKHL 44 at [30].
[328] [2001] UKHL 44 at [34]–[37]. See also J. Devenney, L. Fox O'Mahony and M. Kenny, 'Standing Surety in England and Wales', *op. cit.* at 518.
[329] [1994] 1 AC 180.

had notice of the debtor's misconduct. Significantly, notice could be either actual or constructive. Constructive notice, of course, refers to situations where a creditor is *deemed* to have notice by virtue of a failure to take certain steps, whether or not the creditor in fact has knowledge of the debtor's misconduct.[330] A creditor will, on pain of being fixed with constructive notice, be required to take certain steps in this context if they have been 'put on notice'. In *Barclays Bank PLC* v *O'Brien* Lord Browne-Wilkinson stated:

> . . . in my judgment a creditor is put on inquiry when a wife offers to stand surety for her husband's debts by the combination of two factors: (a) the transaction is on its face not to the financial advantage of the wife; and (b) there is a substantial risk in transactions of that kind that, in procuring the wife to act as surety, the husband has committed a legal or equitable wrong that entitles the wife to set aside the transaction.[331]

Subsequently there was some debate as to the correct application of these principles. In particular, in one line of authority there was some confusion as to whether or not a creditor was only put on notice where it knew that the relationship between the husband and wife was one of trust and confidence. Moreover, there was some uncertainty in relation to how these principles applied to other types of relationship. However, in *Royal Bank of Scotland* v *Etridge*[332] Lord Nicholls stated that a creditor is always put on enquiry where the relationship between the principal debtor and the guarantor is non-commercial and this is known to the bank.

As noted above, once a creditor is put on enquiry it must, on pain of being fixed with constructive notice, take steps to minimise the risk of undue influence. So what steps must a creditor take in such circumstances? In *Royal Bank of Scotland* v *Etridge*[333] the House of Lords laid down a procedure for future surety transactions, requiring that creditors obtain from the surety's solicitor confirmation that the guarantor had understood the documentation.[334] In such situations a creditor would normally be obliged to supply the guarantor's solicitor with information on the underlying loan and the principal debtor's indebtedness to enable the solicitor to properly advise the guarantor.[335] Moreover specific criteria applying to both creditors and their legal advisers in all non-business, third-party security cases have emerged from *Etridge* onward.[336]

ISSUE BOX

Are the steps which a creditor must take in order to avoid being fixed with constructive notice insufficiently demanding? Or do these steps encourage a creditor to be proactive from an early stage?[337]

---

[330] See J. Devenney, M. Kenny and L. Fox O'Mahony, 'England and Wales', *op. cit.*
[331] [1994] 1 AC 180 at 196.
[332] [2001] UKHL 44.
[333] [2001] UKHL 44.
[334] See J. Devenney, L. Fox O'Mahony and M. Kenny, 'Standing Surety in England and Wales', *op. cit.* at 518.
[335] [2001] UKHL 44 at [79] *per* Lord Nicholls. *Cf.* also D. Morris, 'Surety Wives in the House of Lords: Time for Solicitors to "Get Real"?' (2003) 11 *Feminist LS* 57.
[336] See J. Devenney, L. Fox O'Mahony and M. Kenny, 'Standing Surety in England and Wales', *op. cit.* at 518. See also *Kapoor* v *National Westminster Bank PLC* [2010] EWHC 2986.
[337] *Ibid.*

(h) Unconscionability[338]

In some cases a guarantor may be able to successfully argue that the contract of guarantee should be set aside on the ground of unconscionability.[339] Such an argument might be formulated in, at least, two ways. Thus a guarantor might be able to argue that the contract of guarantee is *directly* vitiated by unconscionability.[340] Alternatively, a guarantor may be able to argue that a contract of guarantee is *indirectly* vitiated by unconscionability; more specifically a guarantor may be able to argue that their dealings with the principal debtor were coloured by unconscionability and the creditor was fixed with notice of this fact on *O'Brien/Etridge* principles.[341]

However, it is not easy to map the concept of unconscionability in this context[342] and, perhaps unsurprisingly, the relevant cases often frame the enquiry in terms of whether or not the transaction offends the conscience of the court.[343] Nevertheless, although each case should be assessed in a holistic manner,[344] some guidance can be gleaned from the judgment of Peter Millett QC in *Alec Lobb (Garages) Ltd v Total Oil GB Ltd.*[345] In that case the learned judge stated:

> . . . if the cases are examined, it will be seen that three elements have almost invariably been present before the court has interfered. First, one party has been at a serious disadvantage to the other, whether through poverty or ignorance, or lack of advice, or otherwise, so that circumstances existed of which unfair advantage could be taken . . . Secondly, this weakness of the one party has been exploited by the other in some morally culpable manner . . . And third, the resulting transaction has been, not merely hard or improvident, but overreaching and oppressive. In short, there must, in my judgment, be some impropriety, both in the conduct of the stronger party and in the terms of the transaction itself . . . which in the traditional phrase 'shocks the conscience of the court' . . .[346]

---

[338] N. Bamforth, 'Unconscionability as a Vitiating Factor' [1987] *LMCLQ* 538; R. Bigwood, *Exploitative Contracts, op. cit.*; D. Capper, 'Unconscionable Bargains and Unconscionable Gifts' [1996] 60 *Conv* 308; J. Cartwright, 'An Unconscionable Bargain' (1993) 109 *LQR* 530; M. Chen-Wishart, *Unconscionable Bargains* (Butterworths, Sydney, 1989); J. Devenney 'A Pack of Unruly Dogs', *op. cit.* at 539; R. Hooley and J. O'Sullivan, 'Undue Influence and Unconscionable Bargains' [1997] *LMCLQ* 17; and L. McMurty, 'Unconscionability and Undue Influence: An Interaction?' [2000] 64 *Conv.* 573.

[339] In some ways, the unconscionable bargain doctrine has been overtaken by the doctrine of undue influence in England and Wales. Nevertheless, the former doctrine does continue to be a ground for relief: see *Cresswell v Potter* [1978] WLR 258n; *Portman Building Society v Dusangh* [2000] 2 All ER (Comm) 221 at 233; *Crédit Lyonnais Bank Nederland NV v Burch* [1997] 1 All ER 144; *Royal Bank of Scotland v Etridge (No 2)* [2001] EWCA Civ 1466; *Irvani v Irvani* [2000] 1 Lloyd's Rep 412; *Barclays Bank PLC v Goff* [2001] EWCA Civ 635; and *Jones v Morgan* [2002] EWCA Civ 565. By contrast the unconscionable bargain doctrine has undergone a renaissance in Australia and New Zealand: D. Capper, 'Undue Influence and Unconscionability: A Rationalisation' (1998) 114 *LQR* 479; A. Finlay, 'Can We See the Chancellor's Footprint?' (1999) 14 *JCL* 265 and I. J. Hardingham, 'The High Court of Australia and Unconscionable Dealing' (1984) 4 *OJLS* 275.

[340] See, for example, *Portman Building Society v Dusangh* [2000] 2 All ER (Comm) 221.

[341] See, for example, *Crédit Lyonnais Bank Nederland NV v Burch* [1997] 1 All ER 144. See also H. Tijo, 'O'Brien and Unconscionability' (1997) 113 *LQR* 129.

[342] See, for example, L. Fox O'Mahony and J. Devenney, 'The Elderly, Their Homes and the Unconscionable Bargain Doctrine', *op. cit.*

[343] See, for example, *Crédit Lyonnais Bank Nederland NV v Burch* [1997] 1 All ER 144.

[344] See D. Capper, 'Undue Influence and Unconscionability: A Rationalisation' (1998) 114 *LQR* 479 at 496, which was approved by the Court of Appeal in *Portman Building Society v Dusangh* [2000] 2 All ER (Comm) 221.

[345] [1983] 1 All ER 944.

[346] *Ibid.* at 961.

As this passage suggests, a key ingredient to an unconscionability claim in this context is the concept of a 'special disadvantage'.[347] Yet the concept of a 'special disadvantage' is amorphous.[348] Nevertheless, in the past particular instances of necessity,[349] mental deficiency[350] and drunkenness[351] have all contributed to a finding of unconscionability in this context. Moreover, as has been argued elsewhere,[352] socio-economic disadvantages may sometimes amount to a 'special disadvantage' for these purposes. For example, in *Fry* v *Lane*[353] Kay J felt able to synthesise previous case law in the following terms:

> [W]here a purchase is made from a poor and ignorant man at a considerable undervalue, the vendor having no independent advice, a Court of Equity will set aside the transaction. This will be done even in the case of property in possession and *a fortiori* if the interest is reversionary.[354]

Moreover, in *Cresswell* v *Potter*[355] Megarry J sought to update this summary in the following terms:

> . . . the euphemisms of the 20th century may require the word 'poor' to be replaced by 'member of the lower income group' or the like, and the word 'ignorant' by less highly educated.[356]

Returning to *Alec Lobb (Garages) Ltd* v *Total Oil GB Ltd*, it seems that Peter Millett QC was also of the opinion that essential to a finding of unconscionability in this context was the presence of a significant imbalance in the disputed contract[357] to the detriment of the party seeking relief. Yet, even if such a view is correct,[358] the application of such a requirement to contracts of guarantee is intriguing. More specifically, it might be argued that the nature of contracts of guarantee is such that they will usually be significantly disadvantageous to the guarantor. Nevertheless, it seems that the courts will not adopt such a strict stance.[359] Indeed, as has been argued elsewhere, the courts have engaged in difficult socio-culturally charged evaluations of the acceptability of particular contracts in particular contexts.[360] Thus, in *Portman Building Society* v *Dusangh*[361] – a case in which an old, illiterate father mortgaged his home in support

---

[347] See L. A. Sheridan and G. Keeton, *Fraud and Unconscionable Bargains* (Barry Rose, Chichester, 1985) pp. 9–10 and *Clarion Limited* v *National Provident Institution* [2002] 1 WLR 1888 at 1913 *per* Rimer J; *cf. Boustany* v *Pigott* (1993) 69 P&CR 298 where relief was granted without an *express* identification of a 'special disadvantage'.

[348] See J. Devenney and A. Chandler, 'Unconscionability and the Taxonomy of Undue Influence', *op. cit.* 541 at 543.

[349] See *Wood* v *Abrey* (1818) 3 Madd 417 and *Miller* v *Cook* (1870) 10 LR Eq 641.

[350] See *Price* v *Berrington* (1851) 3 Mac&G 486, *Niell* v *Morely* (1804) 9 Ves 478, *Montgomery* v *Montgomery* (1879) 14 ILTR 1 and *Hart* v *O'Connor* [1985] 2 All ER 880. Contracts of guarantee are also, of course, subject to the normal contractual rules governing capacity (J. O'Donovan and J. Phillips, *The Modern Contract of Guarantee* (Sweet and Maxwell, London, 2003) at pp. 56–64).

[351] See *Dunnage* v *White* (1818) 1 Swan 137 and *Cory* v *Cory* (1747) 1 Ves Sen 19; *cf. also Irvani* v *Irvani* [2000] 1 Lloyd's Rep 412.

[352] See L. Fox O'Mahony and J. Devenney, 'The Elderly, Their Homes and The Unconscionable Bargain Doctrine', *op. cit.*

[353] (1888) 40 Ch D 312.

[354] *Ibid.* at 322.

[355] [1978] 1 WLR 255n. See also *Mountford* v *Callaghan* (unreported, 29 September 1999, QBD) and *Growden* v *Bean* (unreported, 26 July 1982, QBD).

[356] *Ibid.*

[357] So-called 'substantive unconscionability'.

[358] *Cf. Cooke* v *Clayworth* (1811) Ves 12; 34 ER 222.

[359] See, for example, *Portman Building Society* v *Dusangh* [2000] 2 All ER (Comm) 221.

[360] See J. Devenney, L. Fox O'Mahony and M. Kenny, 'Standing Surety in England and Wales', *op. cit.* at 521.

[361] [2000] 2 All ER (Comm) 221.

of the business ventures of his son – the Court of Appeal rejected a claim that the transaction was coloured by unconscionability primarily on the ground that such a transaction was not to the manifest disadvantage of the father.[362] In support of such a view, Simon Brown LJ stated:

> . . . it was not manifestly disadvantageous to this appellant that he should be able to raise money by way of re-mortgage so as to benefit his son . . . I would agree . . . that the transaction was an improvident one, necessarily dependent for its success upon the son's ability to make the monthly repayments . . . Undoubtedly, therefore, it placed the property at risk. But I simply cannot accept that building societies are required to police transactions of this nature to ensure that parents (even poor and ignorant ones) are wise in seeking to assist their children . . . In short, the conscience of the court is not shocked.[363]

Such a view was echoed by Ward LJ:[364]

> So it was a case of father coming to the assistance of the son. True it is that it was a financially unwise venture because, absent good profit from the business, there was never likely to be the income to service the borrowing and the father's home was at risk. But there was nothing, absolutely nothing, which comes close to morally reprehensible conduct or impropriety. No unconscientious advantage has been taken of the father's . . . paternal generosity . . . The family wanted to raise money: the building society was prepared to lend it. One shakes one's head, but with sadness and with the incredulity at the folly of it all, alas not with moral outrage.[365]

Portman Building Society v *Dusangh* can be contrasted with *Crédit Lyonnais Bank Nederland NV* v *Burch*.[366] In the latter case, a junior employee acted as surety for her employer and the Court of Appeal[367] were clearly of the opinion that the transaction could have been set aside for unconscionability if it had been pleaded before the court.[368] As Millett LJ stated:

> This transaction cannot possibly stand . . . An eighteenth-century Lord Chancellor would have contented himself with saying as much . . . The transaction was not merely to the manifest disadvantage of the respondent; it was one which, in the traditional phrase, 'shocks the conscience of the court'. The respondent committed herself to a personal liability far beyond her slender means, risking the loss of her home and personal bankruptcy, and obtained nothing in return beyond a relatively small and possibly temporary increase in the overdraft facility available to her employer, a company in which she had no financial interest.[369]

The precise nature, and extent, of the protection afforded to guarantors by the concept of unconscionability is, of course, linked to the theoretical framework within which the foregoing elements operate.[370] However, the theoretical basis of unconscionability in this context is debatable.[371] As we have seen, in *Alec Lobb (Garages) Ltd* v *Total Oil GB Ltd* Peter Millett QC was of the view that the stronger party must act in a 'morally culpable manner'. Yet this does little to clarify the matter. For example, it could be argued that some form of active trickery

---

[362] See J. Devenney, L. Fox O'Mahony and M. Kenny, 'Standing Surety in England and Wales', *op. cit.* at 521.
[363] *Ibid.* at 228–230.
[364] Sedley LJ agreed with Simon Brown and Nourse LJJ.
[365] [2000] 2 All ER (Comm) 221 at 234.
[366] [1997] 1 All ER 144.
[367] *Ibid.* at 151 *per* Nourse LJ and 153 *per* Millett LJ.
[368] See J. Devenney, L. Fox O'Mahony and M. Kenny, 'Standing Surety in England and Wales', *op. cit.* at 521.
[369] [1997] 1 All ER 144 at 152.
[370] See L. Fox O'Mahony and J. Devenney, 'The Elderly, Their Homes and The Unconscionable Bargain Doctrine', *op. cit.*
[371] J. Devenney and A. Chandler, 'Unconscionability and the Taxonomy of Undue Influence', *op. cit.* at 541.

by the stronger party is required.[372] Equally, such a view contrasts uneasily with many of the seminal decisions on unconscionability as a vitiating factor.[373] For example, in *Baker v Monk*[374] Turner LJ gave the following, illuminating insight into the doctrine:

> *I say nothing about improper conduct on the part of the Appellant; I do not wish to enter into the question of conduct.* In cases of this description there is usually exaggeration on both sides, and I am content to believe that in this case there has been no actual moral fraud on the part of the Appellant in the transaction: but, for all that, in my judgment an improvident contract has been entered into.[375]

Such a view also seems[376] to find resonance in the idea of 'passive acceptance' which can be found in the Opinion of the Judicial Committee of the Privy Council in *Hart v O'Connor*.[377] However, even on this wider view of unconscionability, intriguing issues remain. For example, many of the cases contemplate that there must be a causal connection between the guarantor's special disadvantage and the resultant contract of guarantee.[378] Yet, other cases appear to shun such an approach.[379] Thus, as has been argued elsewhere,[380] there is a line of authority which seems, somewhat controversially, to support a jurisdiction to relieve certain sections of society from unwise bargains regardless of whether or not there is a causal connection between the resultant bargain and the alleged 'special disadvantage'.[381]

2.4.2.3 Policing the terms of the guarantee

The traditional view is, of course, that the law of England and Wales is generally unconcerned with the fairness or otherwise of the terms of a contract.[382] Nevertheless, as we shall see below, statute now makes provision for the review of particular contractual terms in a number of circumstances. Additionally, as has been argued elsewhere,[383] there are a number of ways in which the courts may have *some* scope to covertly regulate the terms of contracts. For example, in the past the courts have, to a certain extent, been able to influence the scope of contractual obligations through adopting a particular approach to the construction of those obligations.[384] Thus, in the context of contracts of guarantee, the courts have traditionally

---

[372] *Ibid.*

[373] *Ibid.*

[374] (1864) 4 De GJ&S 388; 46 ER 968.

[375] *Ibid.* at 425 (emphasis added).

[376] J. Devenney and A. Chandler, 'Unconscionability and the Taxonomy of Undue Influence', *op. cit.* at 541.

[377] [1985] 2 WLR 944.

[378] J. Devenney, 'An Analytical Deconstruction of the Unconscionable Bargain Doctrine in England and Wales' (University of Wales unpublished PhD thesis, Cardiff, 2003) at pp. 1–7.

[379] J. Devenney and A. Chandler, 'Unconscionability and the Taxonomy of Undue Influence', *op. cit.* at 541 and 549.

[380] *Ibid.*

[381] See *Evans v Llewellin* (1787) 1 Cox CC 333 at 349; 29 ER 1191 at 1194, and *Cresswell v Potter* [1978] 1 WLR 255n.

[382] See, for example, *Maynard v Moseley* (1676) 3 Swans 651; *Wood v Fenwick* (1702) Pr Ch 206; *Floyer v Sherard* (1743) Amb 18; *Lukey v O'Donnel* (1805) 2 Sch&L 395; *Longmate v Ledger* (1860) 2 Giff 157; *Burmah Oil Co. Ltd v Governor of Bank of England* (1981) 125 SJ 528; and *Hart v O'Connor* [1985] 2 All ER 880 at 887 *per* Lord Brightman. See also S. M. Waddams, 'Protection of Weaker Parties in English Law', in M. Kenny, J. Devenney and L. Fox O'Mahony, *Unconscionability in European Private Law Financial Transactions* (Cambridge University Press, Cambridge, 2010), *cf.* C. Barton, 'The Enforcement of Hard Bargains' (1987) 103 *MLR* 118 and S. Smith, 'In Defence of Substantive Fairness' (1996) 112 *LQR* 138.

[383] J. Devenney, L. Fox O'Mahony and M. Kenny, 'Standing Surety in England and Wales', *op. cit* at 522.

[384] See, for example, the judgment of Lord Denning MR in *George Mitchell v Finney Lock Seeds* [1983] QB 284.

taken a strict approach to determining the extent of the surety's liability.[385] Similarly the courts have traditionally adopted a strict interpretation of clauses which attempt to exclude a guarantor's right to be discharged in circumstances where a guarantor would otherwise be discharged.[386] Of course the courts may have to reflect carefully on such approaches in the light of more modern general approaches to the construction of contracts.[387] Nevertheless, in *Liberty Mutual Insurance Co (UK) Ltd v HSBC Bank PLC* Rix LJ stated that:

> . . . the reasonable man does not expect fundamental principles of law, equity and justice, such as rights of set-off or of subrogation to be excluded unless the contract clearly says so.[388]

Furthermore, despite the views of the House of Lords in *CIBC Mortgages PLC v Pitt*,[389] transactional outcomes appear relevant to both a finding of undue influence[390] and to a finding of unconscionability.[391] Thus, as is illustrated by *Dunbar Bank PLC v Nadeem*,[392] a court may have to carefully review the terms of the contract of guarantee where it is claimed that this contract has been procured by undue influence or unconscionability.

(a) Unfair Contract Terms Act 1977 and Misrepresentation Act 1967

The Unfair Contract Terms Act 1977 and the Misrepresentation Act 1967[393] will police terms which purport to exclude or limit a *creditor's liability*. Thus any attempt to exclude or limit a creditor's liability for negligence would be subject to UCTA 1977, s. 2(2).[394] On the other hand, UCTA 1977:

> seems inapt to fit . . . clauses [which] do not purport to exclude the liability of a creditor for breaches of contract but rather . . . preserve the liability of the guarantor in circumstances where the guarantor would otherwise be discharged.[395]

(b) Unfair Terms in Consumer Contracts Regulations 1999

As is well known, the Unfair Terms in Consumer Contract Regulations 1999[396] attempt to implement the EC Council Directive on Unfair Terms in Consumer Contracts.[397] These

---

[385] See, for example, *Blest v Brown* (1862) 4 De GF&J 367.

[386] *Trafalgar House Construction (Regions) Ltd v General Surety & Guarantee Co Ltd* [1996] 1 AC 199.

[387] In particular, *Investors Compensation Scheme Ltd v West Bromwich Building Society* [1998] 1 WLR 896 at 913 where Lord Hoffmann famously stated: 'The meaning which a document (or any other utterance) would convey to a reasonable man is not the same thing as the meaning of its words. The meaning of words is a matter of dictionaries and grammars; the meaning of the document is what the parties using those words against the relevant background would reasonably have been understood to mean.' See also *Fairstate Ltd v General Enterprise & Management Ltd* [2010] EWHC 3072 and *Rainy Sky SA v Kookmin Bank* [2011] UKSC 50.

[388] [2002] EWCA Civ 691 at [56]. See also *Static Control Components (Europe) Ltd v Egan* [2004] EWCA Civ 392.

[389] [1994] 1 AC 200, *cf.* J. Spanogle, 'Analyzing Unconscionability Problems' (1969) 117 *U Pa L Rev* 931.

[390] See M. Chen-Wishart, 'Undue Influence: Beyond Impaired Consent and Wrongdoing Towards a Relational Analysis', *op. cit.* at p. 212 and J. Devenney and A. Chandler, 'Unconscionability and the Taxonomy of Undue Influence', *op. cit.* 541 at 564–566.

[391] See L. Fox O'Mahony and J. Devenney, 'The Elderly, Their Homes and The Unconscionable Bargain Doctrine', *op. cit.*

[392] [1998] 3 All ER 876.

[393] Section 3.

[394] *Cf.* G. McCormack, 'Protection of Surety Guarantors in England: Prophylactics and Procedure', in A. Colombi Ciacchi (ed.), *Protection of Non-professional Sureties in Europe: Formal and Substantive Disparity* (Nomos, Germany, 2007), at pp. 166–171.

[395] G. McCormack, *op. cit.* at p. 171.

[396] SI 1999/2083.

[397] 93/13/EEC, OJ L95/221. See further H. Beale, 'Legislative Control of Fairness: The Directive on Unfair Terms in Consumer Contracts', in J. Beatson and D. Friedmann (eds), *Good Faith and Fault in Contract Law* (Clarendon Press, Oxford, 1995) and Chapter 7 below.

Regulations are primarily concerned with 'unfair terms in contracts concluded between a *seller or a supplier* and a *consumer*'.[398] Regulation 5(1) defines an 'unfair term' as follows:

> A contractual term which has not been individually negotiated shall be regarded as unfair if, contrary to the requirement of good faith, it causes a significant imbalance in the parties' rights and obligations arising under the contract, to the detriment of the consumer.

Regulation 5(1) is supplemented by Sch. 2 to the Regulations which contains a non-exhaustive list of terms which might be regarded as unfair.[399] By virtue of Regulation 8, a term which is found to be 'unfair' under the Regulations is not binding on the consumer.

If the Regulations apply to contracts of guarantee, a guarantor may be able to challenge a number of clauses which are common in guarantee transactions[400] provided, of course, that the guarantor is a consumer for the purposes of the Regulations.[401] For example, it has been argued that some clauses which exclude a guarantor's right to be discharged on the happening of certain events[402] may be vulnerable if the Regulations apply to such contracts.[403] Yet there is much uncertainty surrounding the issue of whether or not the Regulations apply to contracts of guarantee.[404] At the heart of the debate are the definitions of a 'consumer' and a 'seller/supplier' under the Regulations. A consumer is defined as 'any natural person who . . . is acting for purposes which are outside his trade, business or profession' whereas a seller/supplier is defined as 'any natural or legal person who . . . is acting for purposes relating to his trade, business or profession'.[405] The difficulty for a guarantor is that *even if* they are acting for purposes which are outside their trade, business or profession (a 'consumer'), *they* supply the service. By contrast, the creditor, who is usually acting in the course of business (a 'seller or supplier'), *receives* the service.[406] As such, this debate is part of the wider debate on whether or not, for the purposes of the Regulations, the consumer must be the recipient of goods or services.[407]

In *Bank of Scotland* v *Singh*[408] Judge Kershaw QC held that the Regulations were not applicable to contracts of guarantee and his view has subsequently been endorsed as both

---

[398] Regulation 4 (emphasis added). The scope of the Regulations is curtailed by Regulation 5(2). However, after some debate, it is now accepted that the Regulations may apply to contracts concerning land: see *London Borough of Newham* v *Khatun* [2004] EWCA Civ 55.

[399] See Chapter 7 below.

[400] See G. Andrews and R. Millett, *The Law of Guarantees* (4th edn, Sweet and Maxwell, London, 2005), who argued, at p. 85, that: 'If the regulations are applied to bank guarantees, it will be seen that there is considerable scope for an interventionist judiciary to redress the balance between creditor and surety significantly.'

[401] On the difficulties surrounding the definition of a consumer for the purpose of the Regulations, see, for example, *Standard Bank Ltd* v *Apostolakis* [2000] ILPr 766, *Heifer International Inc* v *Christiansen* [2007] EWHC 3015, and *Evans* v *Cherry Tree Finance Ltd* [2008] EWCA Civ 331. For cases specifically dealing with this issue in areas related to the current context see *Bank of Scotland* v *Singh* (QBD, unreported, 17 June 2005) and *Barclays Bank PLC* v *Kufner* [2008] EWHC 2319 (Comm). See further, H. Schulte-Nölke, *EC Consumer Law Compendium – Comparative Analysis* (2008) at p. 730 (at: http://ec.europa.eu/consumers/rights/docs/consumer_law_compendium_comparative_analysis_en_final.pdf).

[402] See below at section 4.2.5.

[403] See H. Beale, *Chitty on Contracts* (30th edn, Sweet and Maxwell, London, 2010) at para. 44–134.

[404] See G. McCormack, 'Protection of Surety Guarantors in England: Prophylactics and Procedure', *op. cit.* at pp. 172–173 and J. Devenney and M. Kenny, 'Unfair Terms, Surety Transactions and European Harmonisation: A Crucible of Europeanised Private Law?' [2009] *Conv* 295.

[405] Regulation 3.

[406] See also J. O'Donovan and J. Phillips, *op. cit.* p. 223.

[407] *Cf. Chitty on Contracts, op. cit.* at para. 15-032 and J. Devenney and M. Kenny, 'Unfair Terms, Surety Transactions and European Harmonisation', *op. cit.*

[408] (QBD, unreported, 17 June 2005.) Discussed in J. Devenney and M. Kenny, 'Unfair Terms, Surety Transactions and European Harmonisation', *op. cit.*

'convincing'[409] and 'compelling'.[410] Nevertheless, in *Barclays Bank PLC v Kufner*[411] Field J expressly disagreed with these views and held that the Regulations were capable of applying to contracts of guarantee. *Barclays Bank PLC v Kufner* centred around a bank loan made to a company ('Kel') which was beneficially owned by the defendant. The loan – which was to assist with the purchase of a motor yacht – was secured by a mortgage over the yacht and the defendant provided a guarantee. Thereafter, Kel took steps to sell the yacht to another company ('Paelten') and it was agreed that the bank would assist by making a loan to Paelten. The second loan would be secured by a mortgage over the yacht and would also be guaranteed by the defendant. Moreover, as a result, the loan to Kel, along with the defendant's liability under the first guarantee, would be discharged.

However, this plan encountered a technical difficulty: the Paelten mortgage (which was to be registered in Madeira) could not be registered until the Kel mortgage had been discharged. Accordingly the bank discharged the Kel mortgage. The bank then attempted to register the Paelten mortgage but the Madeira Shipping Registry declined to register this mortgage. Thereafter the facts become a little hazy but it seems that the yacht was sold and its whereabouts became almost impossible to ascertain.

Subsequently the bank sought to enforce the defendant's Kell guarantee and the defendant sought to defend this claim on the ground, *inter alia*, that the bank was in breach of an 'equitable duty' not to release any security for the principal debt.[412] The difficulty for the defendant was that the contract of guarantee included, as is – it seems – commonplace,[413] a clause which purported to allow the bank to release securities for the principal debt. Accordingly the defendant sought to argue that such a clause was not binding on him as a result of the Regulations.[414]

As we have already noted, Field J accepted that the Regulations apply to contracts of guarantee. In so doing, he relied almost exclusively on the judgment of the European Court of Justice in *Bayerische Hypotheken und Wechselbank v Dietzinger*.[415]

CASE

Bayerische Hypotheken und Wechselbank v Dietzinger[416]

Bayerische Hypotheken und Wechselbank v Dietzinger considered the applicability of Council Directive 85/577/EEC (on contracts negotiated away from business premises) to guarantees. Directive 85/577/EEC applies to certain situations where 'a trader supplies

---

[409] *Williamson v Governor of the Bank of Scotland* [2006] EWHC 1289 at [46] *per* George Bompas QC, sitting as a Deputy Judge.

[410] *Manches LLP v Carl Freer* [2006] EWHC 991 at [25] *per* Judge Philip Price QC.

[411] [2008] EWHC 2319 (Comm). Discussed in detail in J. Devenney and M. Kenny, 'Unfair Terms, Surety Transactions and European Harmonisation', *op. cit*. See also *Royal Bank of Scotland PLC v Chandra* [2010] EWHC 105& [2011] EWCA Civ 192.

[412] See *Skipton Building Ltd v Stott* [2001] QB 261. See further below at section 4.2.5.

[413] See *Kufner* at [16].

[414] See J. Devenney and M. Kenny, 'Unfair Terms, Surety Transactions and European Harmonisation', *op. cit*.

[415] Case C-45/96, [1998] ECR I-1199.

[416] *Ibid*.

goods or services to a consumer'[417] and in a somewhat tentative judgment,[418] the European Court of Justice stated that:

> ... it is apparent from the wording of Art. 1 of Directive 85/577 and from the ancillary nature of guarantees that the directive covers only a guarantee ancillary to a contract whereby, in the context of 'doorstep selling', a consumer assumes obligations towards the trader with a view to obtaining goods or services from him. Furthermore, since the directive is designed to protect only consumers, a guarantee comes within the scope of the directive only where, in accordance with the first indent of Art. 2, the guarantor has entered into a commitment for a purpose which can be regarded as unconnected with his trade or profession.[419]
>
> In reaching this conclusion the European Court of Justice held, not without controversy, that nothing in the directive required 'the person concluding the contract under which goods or services are to be supplied to be the person to whom they are supplied'[420] and that guarantees are merely ancillary to the main contract.[421]

Such an ingenious, if strained,[422] interpretation of the Council Directive on Unfair Terms in Consumer Contracts may be welcomed by some on the grounds of the (perceived) benefits of harmonisation in creating a single market in financial transactions.[423] Yet there are a number of counter-arguments.

First, as is demonstrated by the debates on the scope of the new Consumer Credit Directive, there has not been a rush for the harmonisation of this particular area of private law.[424]

Secondly, the harmonisation of this area of private law is fraught with danger.[425] As noted above, guarantee transactions are poly-contextual. Thus the protection afforded to guarantors may be located in a number of different legal fields. Indeed, whilst most EU Member States

---

[417] Article 1.

[418] See M. Kenny, 'Standing Surety in Europe: Common Core or Tower of Babel', *op. cit.*, 175 at 180.

[419] *Supra* at [20].

[420] *Supra* at [19].

[421] *Supra* at [18]. See J. Devenney and M. Kenny, 'Unfair Terms, Surety Transactions and European Harmonisation', *op. cit.*

[422] Indeed it is arguable that such an interpretation is *even* more strained in the context of the Council Directive on Unfair Terms in Consumer Contracts than it is in the context of Directive 85/577/EEC on contracts negotiated away from business premises; the former directive provides a framework for addressing terms which cause a significant imbalance in the contract and such an interpretation opens that directive to contracts in which, almost by definition, the benefit flows one way (guarantees): see J. Devenney and M. Kenny, 'Unfair Terms, Surety Transactions and European Harmonisation', *op. cit.* and *Manches LLP v Carl Freer* [2006] EWHC 991 at [25] *per* Judge Philip Price QC. *Cf.* also *Berliner Kindl Brauerei AG v Andreas Siepert* [2000] ECR 1-1741 at [25]–[26] where the ECJ, in considering Council Directive 87/102/EEC for the approximation of the laws, regulations and administrative provisions of the Member States concerning consumer credit, stated: '... the scope of the Directive cannot be widened to cover contracts of guarantee solely on the ground that such agreements are ancillary to the principal agreement whose performance they underwrite, since there is no support for such an interpretation in the wording of the Directive ... or in its scheme and aims.'

[423] *Cf. Chitty on Contracts, op. cit.* at para. 44–136.

[424] See G. McCormack, *op. cit.* at pp. 172–173 and J. Devenney and M. Kenny, 'Unfair Terms, Surety Transactions and European Harmonisation', *op. cit.*

[425] See M. Kenny and J. Devenney, 'The Fallacy of the Common Core', *op. cit.*

have sought to increase the protection afforded to particular guarantors, there is much diversity in the nature of the protection so afforded.[426] Moreover, as has been argued elsewhere, the protection afforded to guarantors in individual EU Member States often involves different, complex, orchestrations of various legal fields, concepts and mechanisms.[427] Thus to tinker with just one aspect of these orchestrations – particularly one as fundamental as the policing of unfair terms – could be dangerous and could have unintended consequences.[428] Certainly the application of the Regulations to contracts of guarantee *may* significantly alter the balance of interests between the guarantor and the creditor,[429] and this may result in such transactions becoming less attractive to banks[430] with the consequence that access to credit is narrowed.[431]

Thirdly, the extent to which such a strained interpretation actually contributes to the harmonisation of this area is debatable.[432] The EC Directive on Unfair Terms in Consumer Contracts is a minimum harmonisation directive which only sought 'to fix in a general way the criteria for assessing the unfair character of contract terms'.[433] The test for unfairness in Regulation 5 was explored in *Director General of Fair Trading* v *First National Bank PLC*[434] where Lord Bingham stated:

> Good faith in this context is not an artificial or technical concept; nor, since Lord Mansfield was its champion, is it a concept wholly unfamiliar to British lawyers. *It looks to good standards of commercial morality and practice.*[435]

Such an approach appears to be dependent on the normative assumptions operating in a particular jurisdiction[436] and, as has been argued elsewhere,[437] there are clear differences in such assumptions throughout the EU. Thus one might refer to, for example, the significant differences in the operation of the doctrine of undue influence in the Republic of Ireland when compared with England and Wales.[438] Thus it has been argued that different Member States use:

> different benchmarks . . . when reviewing contractual terms . . . Accordingly, traders cannot use a contractual clause which is valid across the EU, but must instead formulate different clauses for each member state. Hence, considerable obstacles to the functioning of the internal market exist. Providers can only perform pre-formulated contracts across borders with considerable transaction costs.[439]

---

[426] See A. Colombi Ciacchi, 'Non-legislative Harmonisation of Private Law under the European Constitution: The Case of Unfair Suretyships' (2005) 13 *ERPL* 297 and J. Devenney and M. Kenny, 'Unfair Terms, Surety Transactions and European Harmonisation', *op. cit.*

[427] M. Kenny and J. Devenney, 'The Fallacy of the Common Core', *op. cit.*

[428] See J. Devenney and M. Kenny, 'Unfair Terms, Surety Transactions and European Harmonisation', *op. cit.*

[429] *Cf.* G. Andrews and R. Millett, *op. cit.* at p. 85.

[430] See M. Kenny, 'Standing Surety in Europe: Common Core or Tower of Babel', *op. cit.*, 175 at 195–196.

[431] See J. Devenney and M. Kenny, 'Unfair Terms, Surety Transactions and European Harmonisation', *op. cit.*

[432] *Ibid.*

[433] Recital 15.

[434] [2002] UKHL 52.

[435] *Ibid.* at [17].

[436] See J. Devenney and M. Kenny, 'Unfair Terms, Surety Transactions and European Harmonisation', *op. cit.*

[437] M. Kenny and J. Devenney, 'The Fallacy of the Common Core', *op. cit.*

[438] See P. O'Callaghan, 'Protection from Unfair Suretyships in Ireland', in A. Colombi Ciacchi (ed.), *op. cit.*; J. Mee, 'Undue Influence and Bank Guarantees' [2002] 37 *Irish Jurist* 292.

[439] H. Schulte-Nölke, *op. cit.* at p. 348.

Nor does it appear that such differences are being superseded by a real EU jurisprudence on unfair terms.[440]

2.4.2.4 Formative regulation of contracts of guarantee

As noted above, the Statute of Frauds 1677, s. 4, renders contracts of guarantee unenforceable '. . . unlesse the Agreement upon which such Action shall be brought or some Memorandum or Note thereof shall be in Writeing and signed by the partie to be charged therewith or some other person thereunto by him lawfully authorized'. Furthermore, the Consumer Credit Act 1974, ss. 105–106, specifies certain formalities and requires the provision of certain information in respect of securities provided in relation to regulated agreements.[441] Such requirements *may* provide a measure of protection for guarantors for, as Judge Pelling QC stated in *J. Pereira Fernandes SA* v *Mehta*, the purpose of such provisions:

> is to protect people from being held liable on informal communications because they may be made without sufficient consideration or expressed ambiguously or because such communication might be fraudulently alleged against the party to be charged.[442]

ISSUE BOX

Should the same formative requirements be extended to all classes of guarantors?

See *Actionstrength Ltd* v *International Glass Engineering In. Gl. En. SpA* [2003] UKHL 17.

2.4.2.5 Protection extended to guarantors during the life of the guarantee transaction

We now move on to consider *some* of the principles which extend a measure of protection to guarantors during the life of the guarantee transaction. At the outset it is necessary to make a number of points. First, we have already considered some of the principles which may extend a measure of protection to guarantors during the life of the guarantee transaction. For example,

---

[440] See, for example, the European Commission's *Report on Directive 93/13/EEC on Unfair Terms in Consumer Contracts* [Com (2000) 248 final] at p. 32 noted that: 'An analysis of CLAB shows that already 4.4% of the judgments handed down by national courts in the field covered by the Directive refer to the Community text. At the current stage of European construction this is a figure to be proud of and reflects the progressive impact of Community law on the national legal orders.' At p. 34 it noted that: 'National courts could have referred many cases to the Court of Justice for a preliminary ruling and it would have been very useful if the judgments of the Court of Justice had been able to cast light on the scope of some of the Directive's more obscure provisions. Indeed the doctrine reveals the reluctance of the national courts to refer cases to the Court of Justice in this legal field.' At p. 30 it noted: 'the application of the same general criterion in two Member States may give rise to very different decisions, as a result of the divergences between the rules of substantive law that apply to different contracts. Hence harmonisation under the Directive is more apparent than real.' See also *Freiburger Kommunalbauten GmbH Baugesellschaft and Co KG* v *Hofstetter* [2004] ECR-I 3403 at [22] where the European Court of Justice noted that it 'may interpret general criteria used by the Community legislation in order to define the concept of unfair terms. However, it should not rule on the application of these general criteria to a particular term'.

[441] J. Devenney, L. Fox O'Mahony and M. Kenny, 'Standing Surety in England and Wales', *op. cit.* at 522.

[442] [2006] EWHC 813 (Ch) at [16].

in section 2.4.1.2 we explored the secondary and accessory nature of a guarantor's liability,[443] and this may provide *some* protection to guarantors.[444] Secondly, the courts have resisted attempts to impose a general duty of care on creditors to look after the economic interests of the guarantor.[445] Thirdly, there is, it seems, no *general* principle that requires a creditor not to act in a way that is prejudicial to the guarantor.[446]

(a) Material alteration of guarantee transaction by creditor

In section 2.4.1.5 we noted that certain formalities are required of contracts of guarantee (notably those required by the Statute of Frauds 1677, s. 4). Thereafter, if a creditor, without the consent of the guarantor, *materially* alters the instrument which created the guarantee, the guarantor is discharged from liability.[447] It seems that this rule is based on a policy of deterring and punishing fraud.[448]

(b) Where the creditor is in breach of the guarantee transaction

Where a creditor is in breach of the guarantee contract the guarantor may be discharged of liability. Much will depend on whether or not the creditor's breach of the guarantee contract is repudiatory in nature. Where the creditor's breach of the guarantee contract is repudiatory in nature and the repudiation is accepted by the guarantor, the guarantor will be discharged.[449] The position will be otherwise where the creditor's breach is not repudiatory in nature.[450]

(c) Situations where the creditor is in breach of the principal contract[451]

As noted elsewhere,[452] where a creditor is in breach of the principal contract the guarantor may be discharged of liability. In the first instance much will depend on whether or not the creditor's breach of the principal contract is repudiatory in nature. Where the creditor's breach of the principal contract *is* repudiatory in nature *and* the repudiation is accepted by the principal debtor, the debtor and the guarantor will both be discharged.[453] By contrast, where the creditor's breach of the principal contract *is not* repudiatory in nature, *prima facie* neither the debtor nor the guarantor will be discharged.[454] Nevertheless in *National Westminster Bank PLC v Riley*[455] May LJ stated:

---

[443] See *Moschi v Lep Air Services Ltd* [1973] AC 331, *Western Credit Ltd v Alberry* [1964] 1 WLR 945 and *Walker v British Guarantee Association* (1852) 18 QB 277.

[444] On the possibility of some form of 'set-off' see L. S. Sealy and R. J. A. Hooley, *op. cit.* at p. 1181.

[445] *Cf. China and South Sea Bank Ltd v Tan Soon Gin* [1990] 1 AC 536 and see J. Devenney, L. Fox O'Mahony and M. Kenny, 'Standing Surety in England and Wales', *op. cit.* at 523. *Cf. Dubai Islamic Bank PJSC v PSI Energy Holding Co BSc* [2011] EWHC 2718.

[446] *Cf. Bank of India v Trans Continental Commodity Merchants Ltd* [1983] 2 Lloyd's Rep 298 and see J. Devenney, L. Fox O'Mahony and M. Kenny, 'Standing Surety in England and Wales', *op. cit.* at 523.

[447] See *Pigot's Case* (1614) 11 Co Rep 26b, *Suffell v Bank of England* [1882] 9 QBD 555, *Raffeisen Zentralbank Oesterreich v Crosseas Shipping Ltd* [2000] 1 WLR 1135 and *Bank of Scotland v Butcher* [2003] EWCA Civ 67.

[448] See *Co-operative Bank v Tipper* [1996] 4 All ER 366 at 372.

[449] *Cf. Skipton Building Society v Stott* [2001] QB 261.

[450] *Cf. Chitty on Contracts, op. cit.* at para. 44–103.

[451] That is, a contract between the creditor and the principal debtor.

[452] See J. Devenney, M. Kenny and L. Fox O'Mahony, 'England and Wales', *op. cit.*

[453] *Watts v Shuttleworth* (1861) 7 H&N 353; 158 ER 510.

[454] *Cf. Chitty on Contracts, op. cit.* at para. 44–086.

[455] [1986] BCLC 268.

I do not think that a non-repudiatory breach of the principal contract will, with nothing more, discharge a surety who has guaranteed that contract. A repudiatory breach, if accepted, will certainly do so, but a non-repudiatory breach will not unless it can be shown in fact to amount to a 'departure' from a term of the principal contract which has been 'embodied' in the contract of guarantee . . . See in particular *Blest v Brown* [1862], 4 de GF&J 367 and *Holme v Brunskill* [1878], LR 3 QBD 455.[456]

It seems that in such cases the guarantor is discharged on the ground of variation.[457]

(d) Material alterations of the principal contract

Under normal circumstances a guarantor will be discharged of liability where the creditor and principal debtor alter, without the consent of the guarantor,[458] the principal contract.[459] This principle will not apply where it is strikingly clear that the alteration definitely would not prejudice the guarantor.[460]

(e) Agreement extending time for the principal debtor

As a result of the foregoing, a guarantor will usually be discharged where the creditor enters into a binding agreement[461] allowing the principal debtor more time to meet its obligations.[462]

(f) Loss or release of securities[463]

Where a creditor holds securities in respect of the principal debt, the release (or loss)[464] of such securities by the creditor may discharge the guarantor.[465] Furthermore,[466] a guarantor's liability may be reduced, or even discharged, by the creditor's negligent realisation of such securities;[467] although this principle does not affect a creditor's discretion as to when, or indeed if, to realise a security.[468]

2.4.2.6 Protection extended to guarantors *after* the life of the guarantee transaction

A guarantor who satisfies his or her liability under the contract of guarantee, usually has a right to be indemnified by the principal debtor.[469] Moreover, the guarantor may be entitled to any security held by the creditor in respect of the principal obligation by the process of

---

[456] *Ibid.*, at 275–276. This statement should be read in the light of the manner in which the case was argued and, in particular, the argument in the case about the proper interpretation of *Vavasseur Trust Co. Ltd v Ashmore* (unreported, 2 April 1976).

[457] See *Chitty on Contracts, op. cit.* at para. 44–086. See further below.

[458] *Cf. Crédit Suisse v Allerdale Borough Council* [1995] 1 Lloyd's Rep 315.

[459] See *Whitcher v Hall* (1826) 5 B&C 269 and *Holme v Brunskill* (1878) 3 QBD 495. *Cf.* A. Berg, *Suretyship: Holme v Brunskill and Related Rules* (2006) 122 LQR 42.

[460] See *Holme v Brunskill* [1878] 3 QBD 495.

[461] *Cf.* G. McCormack, 'Protection of Surety Guarantors in England: Prophylactics and Procedure', *op. cit.* at p. 165.

[462] See *Polak v Everett* (1876) 1 QBD 669.

[463] See J. Devenney, M. Kenny and L. Fox O'Mahony, 'England and Wales', *op. cit.*

[464] *Wulff v Jay* (1872) LR 7 QB 756.

[465] See *Re Darwen & Pearce* [1927] 1 Ch 176, but *cf. Carter v White* (1883) 25 Ch D 666.

[466] See J. Devenney, M. Kenny and L. Fox O'Mahony, 'England and Wales', *op. cit.*

[467] *Mutual Loan Association v Sudlow* (1858) 5 CB(NS) 449.

[468] See J. Devenney, M. Kenny and L. Fox O'Mahony, 'England and Wales', *op. cit.*

[469] See generally L. S. Sealy and R. J. A. Hooley, *op. cit.* at pp. 1184–1185.

subrogation.[470] Finally, a guarantor may be entitled to a contribution from any co-guarantor if the first-mentioned guarantor has borne a disproportionate amount of the liability for the principal debtor's default.[471]

ISSUE BOX

To what extent, if at all, is the law relating to guarantees a default law?

See *Moschi* v *Lep Air Services Ltd* [1973] AC 331.

Further reading

Andrews, G. and Millett, R., *The Law of Guarantees* (4th edn, Sweet and Maxwell, London, 2005).

Beale, H., Bridge, M., Gullifer, L. and Lomnicka, E., *The Law of Security and Title-based Financing* (2nd edn, Oxford University Press, Oxford, 2012).

Bell, A. P., *Modern Law of Personal Property in England and Ireland* (Butterworths, London, 1989).

Bridge, M., *Personal Property Law* (3rd edn, Oxford University Press, Oxford, 2002).

Devenney, J. and Chandler, A., 'Unconscionability and the Taxonomy of Undue Influence' [2007] *JBL* 541.

Devenney, J., Fox O'Mahony, L. and Kenny, M., 'Standing Surety in England and Wales: The Sphinx of Procedural Protection' (2008) *LMCLQ* 527.

Devenney, J. and Kenny, M., *Consumer Credit, Debt and Investment in Europe* (Cambridge University Press, Cambridge, 2012).

Devenney, J. and Kenny, M., 'Unfair Terms, Surety Transactions and European Harmonisation: A Crucible of Europeanised Private Law?' [2009], Conv. 295.

Devenney, J., Kenny, M. and Fox O'Mahony, L., 'England and Wales', in A. Columbi-Ciacchi and S. Weatherill (eds), *Regulating Unfair Banking Practices in Europe: The Case of Personal Suretyships* (Oxford University Press, Oxford, 2010).

Diamond, A. L., *A Review of Security Interests in Property* (DTI, London 1989).

Fox O'Mahony, L. and Devenney, J., 'The Elderly, Their Homes and the Unconscionable Bargain Doctrine', in M. Dixon (ed.), *Modern Studies in Property Law* (Vol. 5, Hart Publishing, Oxford, 2009).

Goode, R. M., 'Removing the Obstacles to Commercial Law Reform' (2007) 123 *LQR* 602.

Goode, R., 'Ownership and Obligation in Commercial Transactions' (1987) 103 *LQR* 433.

Kenny, M., 'Standing Surety in Europe: Common Core or Tower of Babel' (2007) *MLR* 175.

---

[470] *Ibid.*
[471] *Ibid.*

Kenny, M. and Devenney, J., 'The Fallacy of the Common Core: Polycontextualism in Surety Protection: A Hard Case in Harmonisation Discourse', in Andenæs, M. and Andersen, C. (eds), *The Theory and Practice of Harmonisation* (Edward Elgar Publishing, Cheltenham, 2012).

Kenny, M., Devenney, J. and Fox O'Mahony, L., *Unconscionability in European Private Law Financial Transactions* (Cambridge University Press, Cambridge, 2010).

Law Commission, *Company Security Interests* (Law Com No 295, 2005).

Mayson, S., French, D. and Ryan, C., Company Law (28th edn, Oxford University Press, Oxford, 2011).

McBain, G., 'Modernising and Codifying the Law of Bailment' [2008] *JBL* 1.

McCormack, G., 'Protection of Surety Guarantors in England: Prophylactics and Procedure', in A. Colombi Ciacchi (ed.), *Protection of Non-professional Sureties in Europe: Formal and Substantive Disparity* (Nomos, Germany, 2007).

McKendrick, E., *Goode on Commercial Law* (4th edn, Butterworths, London, 2010).

O'Donovan, J. and Phillips, J., *The Modern Contract of Guarantee* (Sweet and Maxwell, London, 2003).

Sealy, L. S. and Hooley, R. J. A., *Commercial Law: Text, Cases and Materials* (4th edn, Oxford University Press, Oxford, 2008).

Sheehan, D., *The Principles of Personal Property Law* (Hart Publishing, Oxford, 2011).

Tyler, E. L. G. and Palmer, N. E., *Crossley Vaines' Personal Property* (5th edn, Butterworths, London, 1973).

Waddams, S. M., 'Protection of Weaker Parties in English Law', in M. Kenny, J. Devenney and L. Fox O'Mahony, *Unconscionability in European Private Law Financial Transactions* (Cambridge University Press, Cambridge, 2010).

Worthington, S. *Personal Property Law: Text and Materials* (Hart Publishing, Oxford, 2000).

Worthington, S. 'Floating Charges: An Alternative Theory' [1994] *CLJ* 81.

Worthington, S. *Equity* (2nd edn, Oxford University Press, Oxford, 2006) Chapter 3.

Companion Website

For open-access **student resources** specifically written to complement this textbook and support your learning, please visit **www.pearsoned.co.uk/legalupdates**

ON THE WEBSITE

3 Agency

By Jo Reddy

Chapter outline

3.1   Introduction

Agency is a special relationship whereby one person, called the principal, authorises another, called the agent, to act on their behalf. The most important effect of this relationship is that an agent can affect the principal's legal position in respect of third parties by the making of contracts or the disposition of property.

An agency agreement is usually established with consent, that is, the principal agrees to the agent acting on his behalf and the agent agrees to do so. However, an agency agreement does not necessarily arise under contract. The agency can be gratuitous. For example, in *Chaudhry v Prabhakar*,[1] a woman had just passed her driving test. She wanted to buy a secondhand car and asked her friend to find one for her. She told her friend that the car must not have been the subject of an accident. Her friend found a car offered for sale by a car repairer. He noticed that the bonnet had been repaired but did not ask the repairer for information. When her friend recommended her to buy the car, she asked if the car had been in an accident before. He answered in the negative. After buying the car, the woman discovered that the car had been involved in an accident and proved unroadworthy. The woman sued her friend for breach of his duty of care. The Court of Appeal held that a gratuitous agent owes a duty of care and there was a breach here.

In *Chaudhry*, the agency was non-contractual, so that there need not be any consideration for the relationship to arise and the agent's right to indemnity arises by operation of law, that is, under principles of unjust enrichment whereby the agent has a restitutionary right to reimbursement of expenses.[2] On the other hand, if the agency agreement is contractual, there necessarily needs to be consideration. Furthermore, the agent also has the right to an indemnity if it was an express or implied term of the contract.[3] The contractual agent is under a contractual obligation to carry out his duties (if he is a commercial agent, he needs to be more proactive)[4] and he does have a contractual right to remuneration.

An agency agreement need not be in writing of course. Just as any contract, it can be made orally, in writing or by conduct.[5]

An agency agreement is a consensual relationship. This consent can be implied from conduct. An example of when the principal consents is this: if the principal appoints a person to a position which is usually an agency position, for example, if the principal appoints a solicitor, he will have, by implication, consented to the solicitor acting as his agent.[6] An agent consents if the agent actually tries to act on behalf of the principal. However, just because the agent does what the principal asks does not invariably mean he consented to the agency relationship. It must be absolutely clear that what the agent does amounts to consenting to act as his agent.

The consent theory to an agency agreement is not absolute. An agency relationship can exist even though there is no consent of the principal; for example, it is possible to argue that

---

[1] [1989] 1 WLR 29.
[2] *Mohammed v Alaga* [2000] 1 WLR 1815; *AG v Blake* [2001] 1 AC 268.
[3] Sometimes, the right to an indemnity is excluded either expressly or impliedly. For example, estate agents generally cannot claim reimbursement for the cost of advertisements, since the commission payable is normally inclusive of such expenses.
[4] See section 3.11.1 below.
[5] There are some exceptions to this, for example, under the Law of Property Act.
[6] Consent will not, however, be presumed merely from a principal's silence, unless there are special circumstances.

agency can arise out of apparent authority irrespective of the wishes of the parties.[7] There is also no consent where the agency arises by operation of law, for example, agency by necessity. Neither party consents to act, but consent is deemed by operation of law because it would otherwise be unfair to third parties not to do so.[8]

3.2 Theories

There are three main theories that seek to define and explain the legal nature of agency; they are interlinked.

3.2.1 Power-liability theory

The theory is simply this: where the principal grants legal powers (that is, legal ability) to his agent to act on his behalf, this creates liabilities and obligations between the principal and the third party. In other words, the agent possesses the power to affect the principal's legal position and the principal is under a correlative liability to have his legal position altered by his agent. So the power conferred by law on the agent is a facsimile of the principal's own power. The natural conclusion is that the contract with the third party is that of the principal (not that of the agent), which is why, *prima facie*, at common law, the only person who may sue is the principal, and the only person who can be sued is the principal.[9]

The power-liability theory focuses on the external relationship between the principal and the third party. It ignores the internal relationship between the principal and his agent. It is the appearance of the principal's consent to the agent acting for him that is important. Courts will take an *objective* approach. It does not matter what the principal's actual intention is; what is important is what does the principal's intention look like to the third party. Often of course, the principal's actual intention and the appearance of his intention are the same. This is certainly true whenever the agent acts in accordance with his actual authority.

Under this theory, once the principal grants power to his agent to alter his (the principal's) legal relations with a third party, the law recognises these powers. There is no need to consider the principal's consent. The agency relationship is thus a matter of law. There are criticisms of the theory. One is that the power-liability theory excludes many who are commonly called agents. Estate agents, for example, introduce buyers to sellers without usually having the power to bind either party. But estate agents are subject to fiduciary duties in the same way as narrowly defined agents. Some major cases in agency law concern estate agents. It seems odd for the theory to exclude them from definition. Furthermore, although courts will take an objective approach about the principal's intentions when conferring power on his agent, this does not always hold true. Courts sometimes take an subjective approach, especially in cases of apparent authority. We shall consider what apparent authority is in section 3.4.1

---

[7] See section 3.4.1 below.
[8] See section 3.4.3 below.
[9] *Montgomerie v UK Mutual SS Association Ltd* [1981] 1 QB 370 at 371 *per* Wright J. There are a number of exceptions to this rule and these are discussed at section 3.10.1.

below.[10] Essentially, apparent authority focuses on the external relationship, that is, as far as the third party is concerned, did this agent appear to have authority to transact on behalf of the principal? So far, apparent authority aligns with the power-liability theory. But as we shall see later, in order for a third party to be able to rely on the appearance of authority to bind the principal, the third party must have been unaware that the agent had no (or exceeded) his authority. Courts therefore take a subjective approach. So, if a third party knew the agent did not have authority (even if the agent appeared to have authority), the third party cannot rely on the appearance of authority to bind the principal to the transaction.[11] Thus, the power-liability theory of the appearance of the principal's consent does not always hold true; the objective approach to consent does not always hold.

In fact, power-theorists believe that consent is not necessary anyway. They say that the principal only needs to have the power to confer power on his agent. The case often held to support this view is *Boardman v Phipps*.[12] Whilst it is certainly true that there was no consent in *Boardman*, that case was not concerned with the principal's liability to the third party. The case focuses on the agent's liability to his principal for breach of his fiduciary duties. The basic premise of the power-liability theory is that the focus is on the external relationship, that is, between the principal and the third party, so the power-theorists, belief is ill-founded.

3.2.2 Consent theory

The consent theory is not totally opposite to the power-liability theory; they are interlinked. The consent theory is this: if the principal consents to the agent acting on his behalf, the principal is bound. After all, one of the main purposes of commercial law is to facilitate and recognise agreements between two parties. So, if one party consents to another to act on his behalf, this further promotes his freedom to do more. If the principal therefore consents to himself entering into the transaction, he can consent to his agent doing it for him.

The consent theory focuses on the internal relationship between the principal and his agent.[13] Where the principal places trust and confidence in his agent, this gives rise to a fiduciary relationship. The theory largely ignores the external relationship between the principal and the third party.

There are criticisms of this theory. As we shall see later,[14] sometimes, agency will arise by operation of law. For example, agency of necessity is created without the consent of the principal.

What is certainly true is that the consent theory focuses on the fiduciary relationship between the principal and his agent. The US Restatement (Third) of Agency (Tentative Draft No 2) (2003), § 1.01 defines agency as:

... the fiduciary relationship that arises when one person (a 'principal') manifests assent to another person (an 'agent') that the agent shall act on the principal's behalf and subject to the principal's control, and the agent manifests assent or otherwise consents to act.

---

[10] This is also referred to as ostensible authority or agency by estoppel.
[11] *Armagas v Mundogas* [1986] AC 717.
[12] [1967] 2 AC 46.
[13] This therefore deals with one of the criticisms of the power-liability theory.
[14] See section 3.4.3 below.

This statement reinforces the fact that agency is a fiduciary relationship and the relationship is in most cases consensual (and very often contractual). It is also true that the agent's role is to act on behalf of the principal. Although the theory claims that consent lies at the heart of agency, not all agency relationships arise as a result of prior consent given by the principal. The concept of ratification[15] operates to create an agency relationship retrospectively and affects the legal consequences of actions with third parties which have already taken place as well as affecting the relationship between the principal and the agent.

As Lord Pearson said in *Garnac Grain* v *HMF Faure & Fairclough and Bunge*:[16]

> The relationship of principal and agent can only be established by the consent of the principal and the agent. They will be held to have consented if they have agreed to what amounts in law to such a relationship, even if they do not recognise it themselves and even if they have professed to disclaim it.

Whether or not the principal and agent consented to the creation of agency is determined by taking an objective approach. Would a reasonable person think an agency existed? Agency may exist where the principal represents to a third party by actions or words that an agent has authority to act as agent, and the third acted on the representation.

3.2.3 Qualified consent theory

This combines the consent theory with the protection of 'misplaced reliance'. If the principal consents to the agent acting for him and the third party has relied on the objective appearance of consent, the law will protect the third party if his reliance was misplaced, that is, if his reliance resulted in loss.

3.2.4 Capacity

As long as the principal has the capacity to contract, the agent's capacity is irrelevant. Thus, a principal can appoint an agent to do anything which he, the principal, can himself do. This is true even if the agent cannot in his own right do it. For example, if the agent is a minor,[17] the minor can bind his principal to a third party, whereas contracts with minors are generally void or voidable.[18] If a minor is employed as an agent, the minor agent can bind the principal to a third party. The other side of the coin is that if the principal cannot do something (for example, the principal is an alien enemy at a time of war), he cannot appoint an agent who is not an alien enemy to do it.

---

[15] See section 3.5 below.
[16] [1968] AC 1130 at 1137.
[17] Under 18 years of age.
[18] *Mercantile Union* v *Ball* [1937] 2 KB 498. On the other hand, if a minor can lawfully bind themselves to a particular contract because it is for their benefit, they can lawfully appoint an agent to do it for them (*Doyle* v *White City Stadium* [1935] 1 KB 110).

3.3 Types of authority

There are basically two types of agency:

1. with actual agreement;

2. without actual agreement.

We shall look at each in turn. Remember the agent must have some form of authority, otherwise the principal is not bound to the contract with the third party. Once the principal is bound, the principal is generally liable for all the agent's failings, including his agent's misrepresentations and fraud. Courts are reluctant to allow the exclusion of negligent liability. Courts are even more reluctant to allow a party to exclude liability for his own fraudulent conduct on grounds of public policy. By definition, fraud involves dishonesty. Thus, a principal is liable for his agent's fraud even if the principal did not himself act fraudulently. However, in this 'inherited' fraud situation, there are fewer policy objections against allowing a principal to exclude his liability for his agent's fraud. If exclusion of such responsibility is in theory possible, Lord Bingham in *HIH* v *Chase Manhattan Bank*[19] emphasised that such intention must be expressed in very clear and unmistakable terms on the face of the contract.

So, as soon as there is some authority for the agent to act on his behalf, the principal is bound to the third party and liable to the third party for his agent's acts.

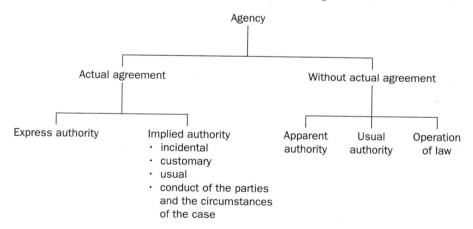

3.3.1 Agency with actual agreement

An agent has actual authority when what he does was previously authorised by his principal (expressly or impliedly). Whether an agent has authority is a question of fact. Working out

---

[19] [2003] UKHL 6.

the scope of an agent's actual authority is important, because only if an agent acts within the scope of his actual authority is he entitled to be paid and receive an indemnity from his principal. If an agent acts outside his actual authority, he may be liable to his principal for breach of contract or he may be liable to the third party for breach of implied warranty of authority. If an agent exceeds an express limitation on his authority or when he does something expressly prohibited by the principal, the agent does not have actual authority (subject of course to the principal's ratification, that is, the principal may decide to accept his agent's unauthorised act).

Actual authority can be either express authority or implied authority.

3.3.2 Actual express authority

Express authority is the authority the principal expressly gives to his agent. As with any contract, no particular formalities are required for an agency agreement to come into existence. The extent of an agent's express authority depends on the construction of words of appointment. If the instructions are vague or ambiguous, the principal is bound if the agent in good faith interprets them differently (*Weigall v Runciman*).[20] Of course, in the modern world, if the principal's instructions are not clear, the agent would be expected to seek clarification from the principal. If it is reasonable to expect the agent to seek clarification but he does not, the agent may not be able to rely on his own mistaken interpretation of his instructions (*European Asian Bank v Punjab & Sind Bank (No 2)*).[21]

3.3.3 Actual implied authority

3.3.3.1 Incidental authority

If an agent is appointed for a particular purpose, he has implied incidental authority to do everything necessary to achieve that purpose. Note, however, when an agent is appointed to sell goods on behalf of the principal, he generally has no authority to receive payment for it (*Mynn v Jolliffe*),[22] so that the third party needs to pay the principal direct.[23]

3.3.3.2 Customary authority

The principal impliedly authorises his agent to act in accordance with the custom of the market. The principal is bound even if he does not know of it,[24] subject to the requirement that the custom must not contradict the express agreement between the principal and his agent.

---

[20] (1916) 85 LJKB 1187. A principal instructed his agent to 'fix' a steamer, meaning the agent was to let the steamer. The agent instead hired a steamer. The court held that the principal was bound to the contract with the third party.

[21] [1983] 2 All ER 508.

[22] (1834) 1 Mood & R 326.

[23] See section 3.6.1 below.

[24] *Baycliffe v Butterworth* (1847) 17 LJ Ex 78.

> **CASES**
>
> ## Perry v Barnett[25]
>
> In *Perry* v *Barnett*, an agent was employed to buy shares in a bank. An Act (now repealed) required the number of shares to be stated on the certificate, otherwise such contracts were void. The agent knew that the custom of the Stock Exchange was to ignore the Act, so he did not state the number of shares in the contract note. The court held that the principal was not bound, because he was entitled to a valid contract, not a void one.
>
> ## Robinson v Mollett[26]
>
> Another example, *Robinson* v *Mollett*, involved the London tallow market. It was a custom of that market that brokers could sell their own goods to a principal. The court held that the principal was not bound because the custom contradicted the principal's express instructions. Where an agent is employed as a principal's buyer, the custom of the market cannot convert the agent into the principal's seller. There would be a conflict of interest.

So, the principle is clear: a principal is bound by customary authority unless the custom contradicts the principal's express instructions.

There are two other 'types' of implied actual authority. Some authors consider this as one type, that is, 'usual' authority, sections 3.3.3.3 and 3.3.3.4 below combined. It is preferable to deal with them separately.

3.3.3.3 Usual authority

An agent may have usual authority of someone in that agent's position, trade, business or profession. The test is what authority would a reasonable person in the agent's position believe they possessed. For example, if an agent is appointed as managing director of a company, it is implied that the managing director has the usual authority that managing directors have. Another example is, if an agent is appointed as an estate agent, the agent does not have authority to sell property because this is not what estate agents usually have authority to do. However, estate agents have authority to make representations about property because that is what estate agents usually have authority to do.

3.3.3.4 Authority is implied because of the conduct of the parties and the circumstances of the case

Sometimes, even if the agent does not have 'usual' authority, but because of the principal's conduct and what happened on the facts, the agent has actual implied authority. In *Hely-Hutchinson* v *Brayhead*,[27] the agent was chairman of a company (the principal). The company's

---

[25] (1885) 15 QBD 388.
[26] (1875) LR 7 HL 802.
[27] [1968] 1 QB 549.

board of directors allowed the agent to act as *de facto* managing director. To encourage a third party to invest funds in a sister company, the managing director wrote on the principal company's headed paper, agreeing for the principal company to indemnify the third party in the event the third party suffered any loss. After the third party invested funds, the sister company went into liquidation. The third party sought to enforce the indemnity against the principal. The Court of Appeal held that the agent, as chairman, had no 'usual' authority to bind the principal to the third party. But, because the company's board of directors allowed him to act as *de facto* managing director, the agent's authority was implied by the conduct of the parties and the circumstances of the case. As we said before, if an agent exceeds the express limitation on his authority or if he does something expressly prohibited by his principal, the agent does not have actual authority. The agent is in breach of their contract with the principal. This does not mean, however, that the principal is not bound to the third party. The principal will be bound if:

(a) those acts fall within the authority which an agent of that type would usually possess (section 3.3.3.3 above) or because of the principal's conduct and what happened on the facts; and

(b) the third party dealing with the agent is not aware of the restrictions which the principal placed on the agent's authority.

(c) In this situation, the agent's usual authority is not a form of actual implied authority (because of the restriction on his authority). It in fact goes to invest the agent with 'apparent' authority (*First Energy* v *Hungarian International Bank*).[28] What is a little confusing is that the phrase 'usual authority' can be used in two very different ways:

   (i) referring to actual implied authority between a principal and their agent (section 3.3.3.3); and

   (ii) referring to apparent authority between a principal and a third party.

If, of course, *Watteau* v *Fenwick* remains good law, it is arguable that there is a third 'type' of usual authority. We shall deal with this point later.

As a reminder: if the principal has given actual authority to an agent and the agent's act falls within the scope of that authority, all the agent's acts will bind the principal. This is true even if the agent acts fraudulently (*HIH* v *Chase Manhattan Bank*).

3.4 Agency without actual agreement

This section deals with agency where there is no actual agreement between the principal and his agent. This does not mean the agent has no authority at all. It means that, in some circumstances, even if a principal has not actually conferred authority on an agent, an agent can bind his principal to a third party.

---

[28] [1993] 2 Lloyd's Rep 194.

3.4.1 Apparent authority[29]

A third party hardly ever relies on an agent's 'actual' authority. This is because 'actual' authority is the authority which the principal specifically places on the agent. This does, of course, carry some implied authorities but a third party can only know what those implied authorities are if he knows what the express authority is. Since a third party does not normally know what the principal has expressly authorised the agent to do or the extent of that authority, the third party needs to rely on the perception as to the authority of the agent.

For example, if I appoint a solicitor, the solicitor has actual express authority to act on my behalf. The solicitor has actual implied usual authority to do what solicitors do. Suppose I say, 'Do not settle the claim'; if my solicitor settles, he does not have actual authority to do so. Nevertheless I, as principal, will be bound to the third party.

Apparent authority is often called agency by estoppel. As Lord Denning said in *Central London Properties v High Trees*,[30] where a person makes a promise, intending the promise to be relied on and the promisee does rely, the promisor is estopped from going back on the promise. Thus, if a principal puts his agent in a position where it is reasonable for a third party to assume the agent has authority, the principal cannot go back on his representation of authority. Apparent authority is 'the authority as it appears to others', *per* Lord Denning in *Hely-Hutchinson v Brayhead*.[31]

Apparent authority often coincides with actual authority. An agent may have both actual implied authority (sections 3.3.3.3 and 3.3.3.4) and apparent authority to do all the things within the usual scope of an agent of that character as between the principal and the third party.

In *Hely-Hutchinson*, the chairman had no express authority to enter into the indemnity agreement on behalf of the principal company. No authority could be implied from the fact that he was chairman. But, by allowing the chairman to act as *de facto* managing director, the chairman had authority implied from the conduct of the parties and the circumstances of the case (actual implied authority).

What is clear is that apparent authority can exceed actual authority. For example, suppose a company board of directors appoints a managing director, and the managing director is expressly instructed not to purchase goods worth more than £10,000 without the board's prior approval. In this situation, the managing director's 'actual' authority is subject to the £10,000 limitation. However, the managing director's 'apparent' authority includes all the usual authority of a managing director and the principal company will be bound to third parties who are unaware of the restriction on the agent's authority. So, if the managing director agrees to purchase goods worth £20,000 and does so as managing director for and on behalf of the company, the principal is bound because the third party is not aware of the restriction. The point is that a third party hardly ever knows what the agent's actual authority is because that is invariably only known between the principal and his agent.

Thus, whenever an agent acts within the scope of his apparent authority, the principal is bound as if he actually authorised the transaction. This is true even if an agent's agreement

---

[29] This is also referred to as ostensible authority or agency by estoppel.
[30] [1956] 1 All ER 256.
[31] [1968] 1 QB 549 at 583.

with his principal has ended. In *Summers* v *Solomon*,[32] the principal owned a jeweller's shop. He employed a manager to run it for him and regularly paid for jewellery ordered by the manager from a third party to sell in the shop. The manager left the principal's employment, ordered jewellery in the principal's name and absconded. The third party sued for the price of the unpaid jewellery. The court held that the principal was liable to pay for the jewellery. The agent had no actual authority to purchase jewellery from the third party once his employment had been terminated. However, because of the previous course of dealings, the third party was entitled to rely on the apparent authority of the manager and the third party was not given actual notice of the termination of the agency agreement.

An important point of this case is that notice must actually reach the third party – constructive notice will not be sufficient.

Apparent authority cannot be created out of nothing. In *Summers* v *Solomon*, there had been a previous course of dealings. The requirements were laid down in *Freeman & Lockyer* v *Buckhurst Park Properties*.[33] In this case, the company's board of directors had the power to appoint a managing director. They did appoint a managing director but did not do so under the procedures as required under the company's articles of association. They nevertheless allowed the managing director to enter into a contract with a third party firm of architects to apply for planning permission to develop a large piece of land. The question for the court was whether the managing director had the apparent authority to bind the principal company. The House of Lords held that the managing director did have apparent authority and the principal company was bound to the contract with the architects. The board of directors knew the managing director was employing architects and permitted him to do so. Thus, by conduct, the board represented that the managing director had the authority to enter into contracts of the type managing directors would normally have authority so to do on behalf of the company.[34] Lord Diplock said:[35]

> . . . apparent authority . . . is a legal relationship between the principal and the contractor created by a representation made by the principal to the contractor, intended to be and in fact acted upon by the contractor, that the agent has authority to enter on behalf of the principal into a contract of a kind within the scope of the apparent authority so as to render the principal liable to perform any obligations imposed upon him by such a contract.

Apparent authority thus acts as an estoppel, that is, the principal is estopped from denying that his agent had the authority to do what he did.

As we said, apparent authority cannot be created out of nothing. There are two distinct requirements, as follows.

3.4.1.1 There must be a representation of authority made by the principal to the third party

The representation can be made in several ways: expressly (orally or in writing); impliedly (for example, through previous course of dealings); or by placing an agent in a specific

---

[32] (1857) 7 E & B 879.
[33] [1964] 2 QB 480.
[34] Like *Hely-Hutchison*, the agent's authority is implied from the conduct of the parties and the circumstances of the case.
[35] [1964] 2 QB 480 at 503.

position which carries usual authority (for example, by appointing a person as managing director).[36]

The representation must be made by the principal.[37] It is not sufficient for an agent to say he has authority. In *AG for Ceylon* v *Silva*,[38] Crown agents falsely told the buyers they had authority to sell steel plates which were Crown property. The Privy Council held that the Crown was not bound by the sale, because the agent had no actual authority and the principal did not represent that the agent had apparent authority.

Lord Diplock in *Freeman & Lockyer* said that the representation needs to be made by a principal who had actual authority, but of course, this is quite a tricky situation. Companies can only operate through agents. It cannot by itself do any act, and it cannot make representations. In *Freeman & Lockyer*, the principal was a company. If companies can only act via agents, then the representation of authority has to come from one of its agents. Thus, if one agent (A1) represents that another agent (A2) has authority, Lord Diplock is essentially saying that A1 must have 'actual' authority in order to invoke apparent authority. On the other hand, if A1 represents A1 has authority, the principal is not bound. In *Armagas* v *Mundogas*,[39] the vice-president of a company said he had authority to agree the deal for the sale and leaseback of a ship. The third party knew the agent did not have actual authority because it was unusual. The third party nevertheless sought to enforce the agreement against the principal on grounds that the vice-president had the apparent authority to enter into the contract. The House of Lords held that the company was not bound because the principal company made no such representation. It was not usual in the company's business that vice-presidents agreed to the sale and leaseback of ships and the third party knew this.

The position is not without difficulty. There is nothing to prevent a principal from authorising an agent to make representations about the agent's own authority to act on behalf of the principal. Thus, it is possible for A1 (who has actual authority) to tell A2 that A2 has authority to make representations that he (A2) has authority. In this situation, the representation is made by the principal. In *First Energy* v *Hungarian International Bank*,[40] a senior bank manager did not have actual authority to agree credit facilities. The third party knew this but asked the bank manager for credit facilities nevertheless. After several meetings, the bank manager wrote to the third party saying he had obtained approval from head office to go ahead. The Court of Appeal held that the bank was bound by the agreement.

Although the agent did not have apparent authority to enter into the transaction, it was reasonable for the third party to believe the agent had apparent authority to communicate that the transaction had been approved. This is because it would be unreasonable to expect a third party to check in this situation to see if the bank's head office had in fact given approval to the transaction. Bank managers usually have authority to sign and send letters on behalf of a bank, but, if a third party knows that it is not usual, he cannot rely on apparent authority to bind the principal.

---

[36] It also seems clear from the facts of *Freeman & Lockyer* that representation can include representation by omission, that is, where the principal fails to intervene when he knew that his agent was acting in a particular way is deemed to constitute representation to the third parties that the actions are authorised.

[37] The principal cannot therefore be an undisclosed principal. Such an idea is logically inconsistent with the requirement of a representation by a principal.

[38] [1953] AC 461.

[39] [1986] AC 717.

[40] [1993] 2 Lloyd's Rep 194.

In *British Bank of the Middle East* v *Sun Life*,[41] a branch manager of an insurance company had no usual authority to authorise policy pay-outs. It was well known that only the head office could do this. The House of Lords held that the third party cannot rely on the apparent authority of the branch manager.

It seems, therefore, that if an agent represents that he has authority, the principal is not bound unless it was reasonable in the circumstances for the third party to believe that the agent had authority to make representations about their own authority on behalf of the principal.

First Energy should perhaps be treated as an exceptional case, decided on its own facts. Although the bank manager did not have actual authority to make the decision, his position as senior bank manager armed him with apparent authority to communicate his principal head office's decision to a third party. In *Armagas*, the vice-president was not in a position that would lead a reasonable third party to believe that the vice-president had such authority. Furthermore, not only must the principal make the representation of authority in order to bind him on grounds of apparent authority, the principal must make the representation to the third party. Thus, if the third party knew that the representation was not intended for him or for the whole world, he cannot succeed.

3.4.1.2 The third party must have relied on the representation

Apparent authority cannot help a third party unless he relied on the principal's express or implied representation that the agent had authority. So, if the third party knew or ought to have known the agent did not have actual authority, he cannot bind the principal on grounds of apparent authority.[42] In *Overbrooke Estates* v *Glencombe Properties*,[43] the auction sales catalogue stated that the auctioneer did not have the seller's authority to make representations about the sale property. Before the sale, the auctioneer told the buyer that the local authority had no plans regarding the property. The buyer bought the property and found that the auctioneer's statement was untrue – the local authority was intending to include the property in a slum clearance programme. The court found that the buyer knew (or certainly ought to have known) of the terms in the sales catalogue, so the buyer knew the auctioneer did not have the seller's actual authority to make representations. Therefore, the buyer could not have relied on the apparent authority of the agent.

Can silence amount to a representation that the agent had apparent authority? The answer must necessarily be no. However, in *Spiro* v *Lantern*,[44] the wife contracted to sell her husband's house. She did not have actual authority and the third-party buyer thought he was dealing with the wife as principal.[45] After the contract had been entered into, the husband said nothing to the third party and did nothing to discourage the third party from incurring expenses trying to conclude the purchase of the house. The husband refused to sell and the third party brought an action asking for specific performance. The Court of Appeal held that the husband was estopped from denying that his wife had authority to sell the house on his behalf. The husband was under a duty to inform the third party of the non-existence of authority.

Remember that not only must the principal have made the representation but also the third party must have relied on that representation. Reliance is normally evidenced by the

[41] [1983] 2 Lloyd's Rep 9.
[42] In *Armagas* v *Mundogas* [1986] 2 All ER 385, the third party knew the vice-president did not have authority.
[43] [1974] 3 All ER 511.
[44] [1973] 3 All ER 319.
[45] The third party cannot therefore argue apparent authority.

third party entering into the contract.[46] Note however, in *Spiro*, both the principal's represen-tation and the third party's reliance occurred after the contract was concluded.

3.4.1.3 Does reliance need to be detrimental?

Some argue that the third party's reliance must have resulted in detriment to the third party. There are cases either way. Lord Diplock in *Freeman & Lockyer v Buckhurst Park Properties*[47] considered a change of position as sufficient. In *Farquharson Bros v King*,[48] a timber company owned timber kept at a third party warehouse. The company told the warehouse that they would receive instructions from one of the company's clerks about where to deliver the timber. The company's clerk was a rogue. He told the warehouse that the timber was to be held on account of a man called Brown (the rogue's alias). In the name of Brown, the rogue sold the timber to a third party. The question for the court was who was the rightful owner of the timber. The House of Lords held that the timber belonged to the timber company. The representation made by the timber company was to the warehouse. That representation did not mislead the third party because the third party was not aware of it.[49] No representation was made to the third party, thus there was no reliance by the third party. The House held that not only must the third party rely on the representation, but also the third party needed to suffer detriment.

Of course, the strict requirements of estoppel means there does need to be detriment, but the modern approach to apparent authority seems to be that the only detriment that needs to be shown is the entering into a contract.[50]

3.4.1.4 Summary

Apparent authority is very wide. It can operate to enlarge an agent's actual authority;[51] to extend an agent's authority beyond the termination of the agency relationship;[52] and to arm an agent with authority in a situation where he would normally have actual authority but for a restriction placed on that authority by his principal and where the third party is not aware of the restriction.[53]

---

[46] That is, based on the principal's representation that the agent had authority, the third party entered into the contract.

[47] [1964] 2 QB 480.

[48] [1902] AC 325.

[49] Thus, the estoppel exception to the *nemo dat non quod habet* principle did not apply.

[50] *The Tatra* [1990] 2 Lloyd's Rep 51.

[51] For example, in *First Energy*, the bank manager did not have actual authority to give credit but he did have apparent authority to convey head office approval.

[52] We have already seen the case of *Summers v Soloman*. In *Drew v Nunn* (1879) 4 QBD 661, the husband represented to third-party tradesmen that his wife had his authority to carry out some redecoration works. The husband became insane (which meant the agent's actual authority automatically terminated) but the third party was not aware of this and carried on dealing with the wife. The third party sued the husband on the unpaid invoice. The court held that the husband was liable for the amount because he had held his wife out to tradesmen as his agent, thus his wife had his apparent authority which extended beyond the termina-tion of her actual authority.

[53] As we have said, actual authority often coincides with apparent authority. In *Manchester Trust v Furness* [1895] 2 QB 539, the owner of a ship instructed the shipmaster to sign the bill of lading as agent of the charterers (and not as agents of the owner which was the usual situation). The shipmaster thus did not have actual authority because of restriction but nevertheless signed the bill of lading as agent of the owner. The court held that the owner was liable to the third-party holder of the bill of lading because the third party was not aware of the restriction placed on the shipmaster's actual authority.

Apparent authority is a form of estoppel. The rationale for the doctrine of estoppel of course is that it is unfair for someone to back out of his promise. It would be unconscionable for someone to make a promise, have that promise relied on, and then allow the promissor to go back on that promise. Thus, if a principal represents that his agent has his authority, it is unconscionable for the principal to go back on his representation. Of course, a principal's representation to a third party can be an artificial one, especially where the representation amounts to no more than putting someone in a position which carries usual authority for an agent of that type, but it is not 'real' authority. The principal cannot sue a third party unless he ratifies his agent's unauthorised act. That is why it is not 'real' authority. If it was, then the principal can sue and be sued. Estoppel may be used as a shield and not a sword.[54] Apparent authority does not of itself allow a principal to enforce a contract against a third party.[55]

Apparent authority merely creates the appearance of authority which, for policy reasons, the law recognises as giving the agent power to affect the legal relations of his principal. Apparent authority arguably arises by operation of law, because the concept relies on the perception of authority by a third party.

3.4.2 Usual authority

It has been argued that this type of authority is no more than 'actual usual' or 'apparent' authority. The leading case, and one which has been severely criticised, is *Watteau v Fenwick*.[56] The agent owned a hotel. He sold it to a principal who kept the agent as the manager of the hotel. The licence to run the hotel remained in the agent's name and the sign on the front door stating this was kept. The principal told the agent not to buy cigars on credit. Contrary to his instructions, the agent bought cigars from a third party on credit. The third party thought the agent was still the hotel owner. When he found out that this was not the case, the third party sued the principal for the unpaid cigars. The court held the principal liable on the grounds that the third party was not aware of the restriction on the agent's authority. Wills J said '. . . the principal is liable for all the acts of the agent which are within the authority usually confided to an agent of that character, notwithstanding limitations, as between the principal and agent, put upon that authority'.[57]

It had been argued in court that this position should only be tenable where the principal was a disclosed principal, that is, where the third party knows that the agent is an agent. If a third party relies on the fact that the agent is an agent, the principal is bound if the third party is not aware of any restriction placed on the agent's authority.[58] Wills J rejected this argument. He said that if that argument was correct, it would mean that every time the principal was an undisclosed principal, the third party would necessarily lose out, that is, the secret limitation of authority would always take priority. Certainly Wills J's conclusion is correct, that is, the third party would lose out, because if in fact this is 'apparent' authority, the principal never made a representation. He was undisclosed.

---

[54] *Combe v Combe* [1951] 2 KB 215; *Baird Textiles v Marks & Spencer* [2002] 1 All ER (Comm) 737, CA.
[55] The concept exists primarily to protect the third party. It does not create an agency relationship between the principal and their agent. Thus the relationship does not create any rights for the principal.
[56] [1893] 1 QB 346.
[57] [1893] 1 QB 346 at 348.
[58] It was argued therefore that this type of authority is like apparent authority and there is no need for a separate category of 'usual' authority.

This decision has been severely criticised but it has never been overruled in English courts. One problem with the decision is that a third party who is not relying on the fact that the agent is an agent, may nevertheless bind the principal. The third party was not even aware of the existence of a principal.

One of the main problems with *Watteau* is that it flies against the fundamental principle in commercial law that there is mutuality in parties' rights and liabilities, that is, a party should have the right to both sue and be sued. We will see later in this chapter that the doctrine of the undisclosed principal does not help because the undisclosed principal rules only apply where an agent has actual authority. An agent in the *Watteau* situation has no actual authority because of the restriction. We shall also see that an undisclosed principal cannot ratify an agent's unauthorised act. This, in essence, means that a principal cannot sue a third party in a *Watteau* situation. If a principal cannot sue a third party when the principal is undisclosed when the agent enters into the contract with the third party, why should the third party be permitted to sue the principal when the third party later finds out that there is a principal? When a third party enters into a contract with an agent, if he was not aware of the existence of a principal, the third party did not rely on the fact that the agent had authority. It seems unjust that a principal should have liability without the right of action, especially when the principal never authorised the contract in the first place (either because the agent exceeded authority or acted contrary to his instructions).

Those in favour of Wills J have argued that the *Watteau* decision is similar in effect to the *nemo dat quod non habet* exceptions, that is, even though the owner of goods does not authorise a rogue to sell the goods to a third party, when the *bona fides* purchaser for value buys from the rogue, the owner is undisclosed, nevertheless the *nemo dat* exceptions dictate that the owner is bound to transfer title to the third party. This argument is wrong. The *nemo dat* exceptions do not mean that the owner is contractually bound to transfer title to a third party. The owner does not end up in a contractual relationship with the third party. The only effect of the *nemo dat* exceptions is that the owner is prevented from arguing that the third party is now the owner. This does not create contract liability between the original owner and the *bona fide* purchaser for value.[59]

In fact, the *Watteau* situation is not real agency at all. The true position is that an agent is left to contract with third parties as if he were the principal, in circumstances where the agent has to account to his principal in his dealings. It has been suggested that *Watteau* is an example of estoppel by conduct – not estoppel by agency. This would mean that *Watteau* is not really concerned with agency at all.

What the principal represented in *Watteau* by leaving his agent in charge is not that the agent is the principal's agent but that the agent and the owner of the hotel are one and the same person. By putting someone in charge of the principal's business in such a way that the agent appeared to be the owner of it, the principal gave the third party the impression that the agent was the owner of the hotel and the same person the third party did business with.

If *Watteau* represents good law, it means that principals run very dangerous risks by employing an agent. The principal's liability would be almost limitless. Thus, if a principal employs an agent but does not disclose that the agent is an agent, the principal is liable for anything the agent does if it is within the principal's business activity. Although this protects third parties, it is a great risk for the principal.

---

[59] For example, if the goods were a car which was found to be defective after sale the *bona fide* purchaser cannot sue the original owner, whereas if it were a true agency situation, the third party could sue.

Watteau has been severely criticised by almost all English court decisions but it has not been overruled. The decision has certainly been overruled in Canada. The Canadian Court of Appeal had no hesitation about declaring *Watteau* to be not good law. As Woods JA said in *Sign-O-Lite Plastics* v *Metropolitan Life*:[60]

> It is astonishing that after all these years, an authority of such doubtful origin, and of such unanimously unfavoured reputation, should still be exhibiting signs of life and disturbing the peace of mind of trial judges. It is surely time to end any uncertainty which may linger as to its proper place in the law of agency. I have no difficulty in concluding that it is not part of the law of this province.

Note that the third party must not know of the restriction placed on an agent's authority. Of course, if the third party knew or ought to have known of the restriction placed on the agent's authority, the third party cannot rely on usual authority.[61]

3.4.3 Authority by operation of law – necessity

This is where the common law deems a person to be the agent of another. In these situations, the agency relationship arises irrespective of consent or the intentions of the parties. The leading example is where an agent's authority arises out of an emergency. For example, if during a ship's voyage the ship was severely damaged, the shipmaster would have the authority to discard some cargo to save the rest of the cargo on board.[62] Authority by operation of law is based on the principle of unjust enrichment. There is no need for an agreement to exist between the principal and the agent. The agreement is not even consensual. It arises by operation of law.

It is arguable that apparent authority arises out of operation of law, because it is the law that dictates that it is unconscionable for a principal to back out of his representation that the agent had his authority to enter into the transaction. However, remember that the principal's representation need not be expressed – merely placing an agent in a specific position which carries usual authority is sufficient.

Agency of necessity only arises if there is a genuine emergency. It must have been impossible or impractical to communicate with the owner for instructions or the owner failed to give instructions. With modern telecommunication systems, this requirement is likely to limit the scope for agency of necessity to arise. Furthermore, the agent must act reasonably and in good faith for the benefit of the principal. What the agent does must have been commercially necessary (and not, for instance, to avoid an inconvenience).[63]

3.5 Ratification

Ratification is a powerful concept. If an agent does an unauthorised act, a principal can ratify that act. The concept of ratification can also operate to create agency in relation to a person who is not an agent at all. It acts retrospectively and affects the legal consequences of actions

---

[60] [1990] 73 DLR 541 at 548.
[61] *Kinahan* v *Parry* [1911] 1 KB 459.
[62] *The Winson* [1982] AC 939; *Great Northern Railway* v *Swaffield* (1874) LR 9 Exch 132.
[63] *Sachs* v *Miklos* [1948] 2 KB 23.

with third parties which have already taken place as well as affecting the relationship between the principal and the agent. Thus, the concept of ratification is subject to three limitations.

3.5.1 An agent must purport to act for a disclosed principal

A person who performs the act, whether or not he is an agent, must either expressly or impliedly indicate that he is acting on behalf of someone else. It follows, therefore, that an undisclosed principal cannot ratify. In *Keighley, Maxsted v Durant*,[64] a principal instructed his agent to buy corn at 44s 3d a quarter. The agent could not buy at this price but bought at 44s 6d a quarter. The agent used his own name and did not disclose he was acting for a principal. The principal ratified the purchase and then changed his mind and refused to accept delivery. The third party sued on the contract. The House of Lords held that ratification was not possible in the circumstances and the principal was not liable, because an undisclosed principal cannot ratify.

The doctrine of privity dictates that only parties to the agreement can sue and be sued. Agency is an exception to the doctrine of privity. The Contracts (Rights of Third Parties) Act 1999 does allow a third party to sue in some circumstances. In essence, the Act creates a third party rule: a third party can enforce a contract where the contracting parties so intend. One limitation is that the third party must be identified or identifiable at the time the contract was made: (s. 1(3)). If a principal is undisclosed, then he is not identified in the contract, so the 1999 Act cannot help him to enforce the contract which his agent entered into with a third party, that is, an undisclosed principal cannot ratify.[65]

If an agent forges his principal's signature, can the principal ratify? The answer is no, because the agent was not purporting to act on the principal's behalf. By forging the principal's signature, the agent is purporting to be the principal. He was not purporting to act on the principal's behalf. This is because the doctrine of ratification presupposes that the unauthorised transaction ratified is valid except for the agent's lack of authority. When the principal ratifies the transaction, the defect in authority is removed and becomes authorised. If the transaction suffers from other defects, the principal may not be able to remove them by ratification. Forgery is one such example; a forged document thus cannot be ratified by the principal.

3.5.2 The principal must have been in existence when the transaction was entered into

In *Kelner v Baxter*,[66] before a hotel company was formed, the directors entered into contracts to purchase wine on behalf of this not-yet-formed company. When the company was incorporated, the company wanted to ratify the purchases. The court held that the company may not do so because it was not yet in existence at the time the contracts were made on its behalf. It did not yet exist, so nothing can be done on behalf of a non-existent company.

[64] [1901] AC 240.
[65] As we said before, *Watteau v Fenwick* has been severely criticised. One reason is because Wills J allowed the undisclosed principal to be bound to the third party, though the principal cannot ratify. The principal therefore has liabilities but no rights under the contract his agent entered into with the third party.
[66] (1886) LR 2 CP 174.

Under s. 51 of the Companies Act 2006, once a company is formed, the contract is binding between the agent promoter and the third party, but the Companies Act is not satisfactory, because there is no direct link between the third party and the principal company. The Contracts (Rights of Third Parties) Act 1999 does not help either because although the principal company was identified or identifiable at the time the contract was entered into, the company would have rights but probably no liabilities. *Kelner* v *Baxter* has been criticised and it is likely that it will be repealed by future Companies Acts.

There are other ways around this limitation to the principal's ability to ratify his agent's unauthorised transaction. For example, in equity, courts might permit a principal company to enforce the contract with a third party because the agent acted as trustee for the principal company.

3.5.3 The principal must ratify in time

If time is fixed for performance, the principal must ratify[67] before performance. If no time is fixed for performance, the principal must ratify within a reasonable time. In *Bolton Partners* v *Lambert*,[68] a third party offered to sell property to the managing director of a company who accepted without authority on behalf of the company. The third party withdrew the offer and told the company of this. The company then ratified the managing director's unauthorised acceptance. The court held that the principal did ratify in time. It was a valid contract for the purchase of the property. Ratification relates back to the time of the unauthorised act and the third party's withdrawal of the offer was ineffective.

The effect of ratification is that an unauthorised contract made by an agent becomes an authorised contract from when it was entered into. Ratification is retrospective.

One limitation to this rule is that the principal must be able to enter into the contract at the time it was made and remains able to enter into the contract at the time it sought to ratify it. For example, if the principal did not yet exist at the time of the unauthorised transaction, the principal cannot ratify (*Kelner* v *Baxter*). If the principal did exist at the time of the unauthorised transaction, the principal must be able to enter into the same transaction at the time it sought to ratify. In *Grover & Grover* v *Matthews*,[69] an agent took out an insurance policy on his principal's property. He had no authority to do so. When the principal's property was destroyed, the principal wanted to ratify the insurance policy contract. The court held that the principal cannot ratify because at the time it sought to ratify, the principal could not have taken out the insurance contract. If the principal could not have entered into the contract with the third party himself, then he cannot circumvent this by allowing the agent to do so on his behalf.[70]

The rule in *Bolton* v *Lambert* has been criticised, because it allows the principal a choice – the principal can ratify or not. If he does not ratify, the principal washes his hands clean of the contract, whereas if he does ratify, the principal takes the benefit of the contract. It is somewhat unfair on a third party not to know whether or not the principal is bound to the

---

[67] In the same way that the general law of contract requires no formalities, none attach to ratification (except that ratification of the execution of a deed needs to be done by deed).

[68] (1889) 41 Ch D 295.

[69] [1910] 2 KB 401.

[70] There are exceptions to this rule, for example, marine insurance.

contract. Of course, if the principal ratifies, the third party has a valid contract with the principal, one that the third party had wished for, whereas if the principal does not ratify, although the principal has no rights and obligations under the contract, the third party has rights against the agent and can sue the agent for breach of implied warranty of authority.[71] The only harshness is the third party is kept in suspense. If the principal wants to ratify, he must do so within a reasonable time. If the principal intimates to the third party that he does not intend to ratify, he cannot later change his mind and ratify.

Suppose, however, in *Bolton Partners* v *Lambert*, the agent had told the third party that he accepts the offer on the company's behalf 'subject to ratification'. In this situation, the third party is able to withdraw the offer because, until the company ratifies the agent's acceptance, an offeror is entitled to withdraw an offer at any time up to ratification.[72]

3.6 Agency relationships

Now we must look at the rights and liabilities of the parties involved in agency.

3.6.1 Principal and third party

A distinction must be made between a disclosed principal (that is, the third party knows of the existence of a principal) and an undisclosed principal (that is, the third party is not aware of a principal).

3.6.1.1 Disclosed principal

The general rule is that a disclosed principal can sue and be sued by a third party.

If a third party owes the principal contract monies, his liability to pay is not discharged if the third party pays the agent, unless the agent had authority to receive payment (*Mynn* v *Jolliffe*). Of course, one needs to look at the contract between the principal and the third party. If a contract term stipulates for payment to be made via the agent or through previous course of dealings, then this payment method will prevail.

Where the principal is disclosed, a third party cannot set off against the principal any of the agent's debts.

3.6.1.2 Undisclosed principal

The general rule is that an undisclosed principal can also sue and be sued by a third party.

The situation we are looking at here is where the existence of agency is not disclosed. The third party thinks he is contracting with the agent and he is unaware that the agent is acting for a principal. Nevertheless, the general rule remains that the principal can intervene and enforce the contract. This is an exception to the doctrine of privity under the common law. It is not an exception under the Contracts (Rights of Third Parties) Act 1999, because an

---

[71] See section 3.10.3 below.
[72] *Payne* v *Cave* (1789) 3 Term Rep 148; *Byrne & Co* v *Leon Van Tien Hoven & Co* (1880) LR 5 CPD 344.

undisclosed principal is not identified or identifiable at the time of the contract, so the Act does not apply. The undisclosed principal rules have been established in the interests of commercial convenience.

It is important to bear in mind that the contract is made between the agent and the third party and the undisclosed principal intervenes in an existing contract. There is no requirement that an agency be disclosed, but one might think that if an agency is not disclosed, that might affect the relationship between the parties. Not necessarily so.

A fundamental principle of contract is agreement between the parties, but with an undisclosed principal, a third party enters into a contract with another party, and then finds out that that party is in fact an agent and the contract is with someone else, the principal. Where is the agreement *between* the parties?

The justification for the doctrine of the undisclosed principal has been the subject of much discussion by academic writers. It is generally accepted that, although it runs against the fundamental principles of privity of contract (that is, there must be agreement between the parties), the doctrine is justified on grounds of commercial convenience. In the commercial world, there are many reasons why a principal might wish to be undisclosed. For example, not wanting to alert rivals of his buying/selling activity or not wanting his identity to affect the price. Similarly, an agent might wish to keep the identity of his principal undisclosed. For example, to prevent a third party from dealing directly with the principal. The undisclosed principal situation is often used in practice.

Generally, in commercial law, we assume that buyers and sellers are willing to buy/sell to anyone. Contracts are not personal and businesspeople are generally not concerned about the identity of the other contracting party. As Lord Lindley in *Keighley, Maxsted v Durant* said: '. . . in the great mass of contracts it is a matter of indifference to either party whether there is an undisclosed principal or not.'[73]

In commercial contracts, the presumption is that the third party is willing to contract with anyone, unless there are special circumstances. As Lord Diplock in *Teheran-Europe v ST Belton* put it: 'In the case of an ordinary commercial contract such willingness of the other party may be assumed by the agent unless either the other party manifests his unwillingness or there are other circumstances which should lead the agent to realise that the other party is not willing.'[74]

An example of the special circumstances can be seen in the case of *Greer v Downs Supply*.[75] This case involved an undisclosed principal. A third party bought timber from the agent. One reason for this was because the agent owed the third party money from a previous transaction and the agent agreed to set off the debt against the purchase price. The undisclosed principal sought to intervene. The Court of Appeal held that the principal may not intervene. The third party intended to contract only with the agent because they specifically agreed that the third party could set off the agent's debt against the purchase price. No other party can intervene in this situation.

Many theories have been advanced to explain the doctrine of the undisclosed principal. For example, trust lawyers argue that the agent acts as trustee for the undisclosed principal, but this has been rejected by the courts (for example, Ungoed-Thomas in *Pople v Evans*).[76]

---

[73] [1901] AC 240.
[74] [1968] 2 QB 545.
[75] [1927] 2 KB 28.
[76] [1969] 2 Ch 255.

Another argument is based on assignment, that is, the contract made between the agent and the third party is automatically assigned to the undisclosed principal, but this is not a perfect analogy. Assignment generally transfers rights. The undisclosed principal doctrine transfers rights and liabilities. The assignment theory has been rejected by the courts (for example, the Privy Council in *Siu Yin Kwan v Eastern Insurance*).[77]

There is no watertight explanation of the undisclosed principal doctrine but courts have nevertheless applied the doctrine and are prepared to justify it on grounds of commercial convenience.

Lord Lloyd in (*Siu Yin Kwan v Eastern Insurance*)[78] summarised the law.

1. An undisclosed principal can sue and be sued on a contract made by an agent on his behalf, if it is within the scope of the agent's actual authority.[79]

2. The agent of an undisclosed principal may also sue and be sued on the contract (that is, because the initial contract is between the agent and the third party).

3. The agent must have intended to act on his principal's behalf.

4. Any defence which a third party has against the agent is available against his principal.

5. The terms of the contract may expressly or impliedly exclude the principal's right to sue and his liability to be sued.

3.7 Limitations

There are limitations to the undisclosed principal doctrine. There needs to be because it might be unfair to a third party who thought he was dealing only with the other party to then find out that that other party was in fact the agent of a principal.

3.7.1 Personal considerations

The general rule is that an undisclosed principal cannot intervene if the agent's contract is of a personal nature, that is, where the third party relied on the skill, solvency or other personal characteristics of the agent and which cannot be vicariously performed. For example, if the third party and the agent enter into a contract whereby the agent is to paint the third party's portrait, the principal cannot intervene. This is because the third party is relying on the agent's positive attributes. These attributes need not be personal skills. These attributes could be the agent's solvency or where the agent owes the third party money.[80]

Difficulty has been caused by cases where the third party is not relying on the agent's positive attributes but is objecting to the undisclosed principal's negative attributes.

---

[77] [1994] 2 AC 199.
[78] [1994] 2 AC 199 at 207.
[79] If the agent has no actual authority, the undisclosed principal cannot sue or be sued on contract. Can the principal ratify? No, because an undisclosed principal cannot ratify.
[80] We have already seen the case of *Greer v Downs Supply* [1927] 2 KB 28.

> ## CASE
>
> ### Said v Butt[81]
>
> This case involved a theatre critic who wanted tickets to attend the first night of a play. He knew the theatre owners would not sell him a ticket, because he had written an unfavourable review on a previous occasion. He asked a friend to obtain tickets for him. When the critic arrived at the theatre, the manager would not permit him entry. The critic sued the manager for breach of contract. The court held that there was no contract between the theatre and the critic, because the theatre had reserved the right to sell first night tickets to selected persons and the critic was not a selected person. McCardie J said that the critic could not assert the right as an undisclosed principal because he knew the theatre was not willing to contract with him.
>
> *Said v Butt* has been severely criticised. Whether an undisclosed principal should be allowed to intervene ought to depend on whether the third party felt the agent was the only person he wanted to deal with, that is, the agent has some positive attribute important to the third party. The *Said v Butt* decision would seem to permit a third party to argue that although the agent's identity does not matter, the undisclosed principal's personality is detrimental.
>
> The court in *Said v Butt* clearly felt that the first night performance at the theatre was a special case. Whatever happened on the first night would more or less determine the success or failure of the play, so the theatre had special reasons to restrict the audience to people who could influence the outcome of the first night in their favour. So the theatre would not wish to permit entry to antagonistic theatre critics.

The general rule is that the undisclosed principal can intervene unless the third party can show he only wanted to deal with the agent because the agent has some positive attribute. However, the rule could potentially be extended to suggest that an undisclosed principal can intervene unless the third party can show he only wanted to deal with the agent or he did not want to deal with the principal. Is such an extension justifiable? Given that the doctrine of the undisclosed principal is already a controversial rule as it seems to fly in the face of the requirement that there is agreement between the parties, it is preferable to keep the doctrine within strict boundaries. It is justified on purely commercial convenience grounds.[82]

The result in *Dyster v Randall*[83] is preferred. A developer wanted to buy land from the owner, but he knew the owner mistrusted him. He therefore employed X to buy in X's name. The developer then said he intervened as an undisclosed principal. Specific performance was granted. The court held that there was a contract between the third party and the principal. Lawrence J agreed with some of what McCardie J said in *Said v Butt*. Perhaps the first night of a theatre performance was special, but in *Dyster*, the undisclosed principal could intervene because the third party did not rely on the personal attributes of the agent. It was a simple

---

[81] [1920] 3 KB 497.

[82] Remember Lord Lindley's statement in *Keighley, Maxsted v Durant* [1901] AC 240 – parties do not usually care about the identity of the other contracting party.

[83] [1926] Ch 932.

agreement for the sale of land. The benefit of such agreements is assignable and the assignee can enforce specific performance.

There was no direct misrepresentation in *Dyster*. The third party did not ask the agent whether he was buying for an undisclosed principal and the agent said nothing. Silence does not amount to misrepresentation (*BCCI* v *Ali* (1999)), not even if the agent knew that if he told the third party who the principal was that third party would not have entered into the contract. There is no duty to disclose in English law. Certainly, if misrepresentation was involved, the undisclosed principal cannot intervene (*Archer* v *Stone*).[84]

Courts favour this approach, particularly where commercial parties are involved. In *Nash* v *Dix*,[85] a Committee of Roman Catholics wanted to buy a chapel from the owner to turn it into a Roman Catholic place of worship. The owner refused to deal with the Committee. The owner sold to X but repudiated the contract when he found out that X was going to resell to the Committee. The court held that there was a contract between X and the owner. The owner was bound to sell, because X was not an agent. He was in fact acting as principal. X had simply bought to resell at a profit. There was no misrepresentation by X.

Lawrence J (in *Dyster*) mentioned the *Nash* v *Dix* case. Although the *Nash* v *Dix* court decided that X was not an agent, Lawrence J thought that even if the agent was an agent of an undisclosed principal, the court would have come to the same conclusion in any event, that is, it was a simple matter of the sale of land.

So, the principle seems clear: an undisclosed principal can intervene even if the third party would not have dealt with the agent if he had known the agent was an agent of the principal. The decision in *Said* v *Butt* is out on a limb, that is, the limitation on the undisclosed principal's right to intervene should only relate to the agent's personal attributes and not to the principal's negative attributes.

Returning to *Said* v *Butt*, suppose the critic goes to the theatre and said he was not buying the ticket for himself but for Mr X (a disclosed and named principal). Can the critic later reveal himself as the real principal and not Mr X? Probably not. In *The Remco*,[86] an agent said he was acting for a named principal. He chartered a ship. Later, he said he was in fact the principal. The court held that the agent cannot enforce the contract because the third party relied on the identity of the principal as material (for example, because the charterer is responsible for paying freight). So, it may well be that the critic cannot reveal himself as the principal if the third party was relying on Mr X's attributes.

Imagine another situation: the critic goes to the theatre and says he is buying for someone else but does not say for whom (a disclosed and unnamed principal). Can the critic take the benefit of the contract? The cases are unclear on this point. Some would argue yes because the third party was not relying on the principal's attributes (he was disclosed but unnamed). If *Said* v *Butt* is good law, the critic would not be able to intervene because the principal's negative attributes are taken into account. There have been cases where if an agent acts for an unnamed principal, and later reveals himself as the principal, the agent can enforce the contract, but there are criticisms of this approach.[87]

---

[84] (1898) 78 LT 34.
[85] (1898) 78 LT 445.
[86] [1984] 2 Lloyd's Rep 205.
[87] See section 3.7.2 below.

3.7.2 Exclusion by the terms of the contract

The doctrine of the undisclosed principal can be excluded by the terms of the contract. In *Humble v Hunter*,[88] an agent chartered a ship. He signed the charterparty as 'owner'. His mother was in fact the owner. His mother then revealed herself as the undisclosed principal and wanted to enforce the contract. The court held that the undisclosed principal cannot intervene. The description of the agent as 'owner' in the charterparty contract was inconsistent with the terms of that contract. It was a term of the contract that the agent was contracting as the owner of property. He cannot then show that someone else is in fact the owner. The agent impliedly contracted that there is no principal behind him.[89] This is not a question of agency – it is one of property law.[90]

Humble v Hunter has been criticised and it is unlikely to be followed. For example, in *Fred Drughorn v Rederiaktiebolaget Trans-Atlantic*,[91] the agent signed a charterparty as 'charterer'. The House of Lords held that the undisclosed principal can intervene in the contract. A charterparty is essentially a contract for the hire or use of a ship. It was a custom of the trade that charterers often contract as agents for undisclosed principals. *Humble v Hunter* was distinguished.

Only in exceptional cases will an undisclosed principal not be permitted to intervene on the grounds that it is inconsistent with the terms of the contract. Possibly the only situation would be if the agent signed as 'owner' or 'proprietor'. In *Siu Yin Kwan v Eastern Insurance*,[92] an employer's liability insurance policy was taken out covering the crew on a ship. The agent's name was stated as the employer. In fact, the employers were the owners of the ship. The owners were negligent and the ship sank in a typhoon. Two crew members died. Because the owners were insolvent, the relatives of dead crew members sued the insurers. The question was whether or not they could do so. The answer depended on whether the owners could themselves have enforced the policy. The insurers argued that the insurance policy included a term that benefits under the policy could not be assigned, so the undisclosed principal cannot intervene. The Privy Council held that the undisclosed principal (who were the true employers) can intervene. It was of no consequence to the insurance company who the employers were because all the information required was the same and thus there was nothing material to risk. The relatives were entitled to recover against the insurers.

As Lord Lloyd said in *Siu Yin Kwan*[93]:

> If courts are too ready to construe written contracts as contradicting the right of the undisclosed principal to intervene, it would go far to destroy the beneficial assumption in commercial cases . . .

---

[88] (1848) 12 QB 310.

[89] If an agent gives an express undertaking that there is no principal involved and that the agent is the real and only principal, then there is no question at all – the undisclosed principal cannot intervene.

[90] Similarly, in *Formby v Formby* [1910] WN 48, the term 'proprietor' was treated in the same way as 'owner', that is, proprietor means proprietor. The undisclosed principal was precluded from arguing that the agent was acting on his behalf at the time of the transaction.

[91] [1919] AC 203.

[92] [1994] 2 AC 199.

[93] [1994] 2 AC 199 at 210.

3.7.3 **Set offs**

If the principal is disclosed at the time the contract is entered into, the third party cannot set off the agent's debts against the principal. However, where an undisclosed principal is involved, the third party thought he was dealing with the agent only and thus is able to set off previous debts. The general rule where the principal is undisclosed is that a third party can set off against the principal any defences accrued against the agent up to the point the principal intervenes.

On the other hand, if the third party did not consider the other contracting party's identity as relevant or did not believe he was dealing with an agent (that is, the third party thought there might be an undisclosed principal involved), the third party cannot set off the agent's debts against the principal. In *Cooke* v *Eshelby*,[94] the agents were cotton brokers. It was the practice of the Liverpool cotton market that brokers sometimes dealt on their own account and sometimes as agents. The agents sold cotton to a third party on behalf of an undisclosed principal. The third party did not enquire whether this transaction was on their own account or for an undisclosed principal. The third party had not paid when the undisclosed principal went into liquidation. The trustee in bankruptcy claimed the price from the third party. The third party argued that they should be allowed to set off what the agent owed them on a previous occasion. The House of Lords held that the third party had no right of set off. If it had really mattered to the third party that they dealt with the brokers on their own account (so they could set off previous debts), they should have enquired. The third party knew that the agents were either dealing on their own account or for an undisclosed principal. This was sufficient to put the third party on notice of the possible existence of a principal.

There are some difficulties with *Cooke* v *Eshelby*. The result appears reasonable but Lord Watson went on to say that, in order for a third party to be able to set off, an undisclosed principal must have misled the third party by allowing the agent to appear as principal. There are two main problems with this estoppel approach. First, how can a third party rely on a representation by a person who is undisclosed? The fact that the principal is undisclosed means necessarily that there is no representation other than from the agent. Secondly, the whole point about the undisclosed principal in the first place is that the agent always appears to be the principal, so it is difficult to see just how an undisclosed principal can ever mislead a third party.

The better approach is to say that a third party can set off an agent's debts whenever an undisclosed principal is involved. This might seem unfair on the principal but then it is not the fault of the third party that the agent has disobeyed the principal's instructions. By choosing to deal through an agent, the principal necessarily takes the risk that his agent might exceed his authority or disobey his instructions and act as though he were principal.

3.7.4 **Money paid**

If an undisclosed principal gives money to his agent to pay a third party but the agent fails to do so, does the principal remain liable to the third party? According to *Armstrong* v *Stokes*,[95]

---

[94] (1887) 12 App Cas 271.
[95] (1872) LR 7 QB 598.

the answer is no. This case involved agents who were brokers. They dealt sometimes on their own account and sometimes they acted for principals. The third party dealt with these agents many times. They never asked if the agents were acting for themselves or for principals. The agents bought shirts from the third party on behalf of an undisclosed principal. The shirts were delivered to the agents on credit. The principal paid the price of the shirts to the agent but the agent did not pay the third party. When the third party discovered the existence of a principal, the third party sued the principal for the unpaid shirts. The court held that the third party was not entitled to be paid. The principal had already made payment via its agents.

This case has been severely criticised. The question here is whether a principal needs to pay twice to discharge one debt. It sounds unfair that a principal has to pay twice, hence the *Armstrong* decision that the principal does not have to pay again, but of course, this is unfair on the third party who does not get paid at all (just because the undisclosed principal had passed monies to his agent). However, it is not quite as unfair to the third party at first sight because, if the principal was undisclosed at the time of the contract, the third party cannot rely on the principal's creditworthiness. The third party thought they were dealing with an agent as principal (who subsequently turns out to be a rogue).

Armstrong has been severely criticised and the Court of Appeal in *Irvine* v *Watson*[96] suggested that *Armstrong* will probably not be followed.

CASE

Irvine v *Watson*[97]

In *Irvine*, a principal employed an agent to buy oil. The agent bought from a third party on payment terms 'cash on delivery'. The third party knew the agent was buying for a principal but the principal was unnamed. The third party delivered the oil to the agent without asking for cash payment. The principal was not aware that the agent had not yet paid the third party in accordance with the contract terms, and the principal paid the agent. The agent did not pass on the monies to the third party who now sued the principal for the price. The Court of Appeal held that the principal must pay the third party.

The principal can only avoid liability if the third party induced the principal to settle with the agent. The principal in *Irvine* argued that the contract term stipulated for cash on delivery, and thus the third party induced the principal into thinking the agent had paid the third party, and the principal was merely reimbursing the agent. Bramwell LJ disagreed. Just because a third party did not insist on cash against delivery as they could have done under the contract is not by itself sufficient to say that the third party induced the principal into thinking that the agent had paid the third party. It was the custom of the market that such clauses were invariably written into contracts but not always enforced.

The result of *Irvine* appears fair. After all, the agent is the principal's agent, and the principal has a better opportunity of assessing the agent's creditworthiness. Note, however, that

[96] (1880) 5 QBD 414.
[97] *Ibid*.

Armstrong involved an undisclosed principal. *Irvine* involved a disclosed but unnamed principal. It seems wrong that an undisclosed principal is in a better position (*Armstrong*) than a disclosed but unnamed principal (*Irvine*). In *Armstrong*, the undisclosed principal did not have to pay twice. In *Irvine*, the disclosed but unnamed principal must pay twice unless somehow the third party represented that the agent had paid the third party.

The *Armstrong* decision is wrong. *Irvine* said as much. While the doctrine of the undisclosed principal exists for commercial convenience, it is important to protect the third party. In a situation where an agent fails to pass payment to the third party, either the principal or the third party will lose out. It is surely fairer to place the loss on the principal. It is submitted therefore that the better position is this: an undisclosed principal who pays his agent but his agent does not pass the payment on to the third party, remains liable to the third party. This should be the general rule regardless of whether an undisclosed, disclosed and unnamed or disclosed and named principal is involved.

3.8 Election

Remember that, in an undisclosed principal situation, the initial contract is between the agent and the third party, which is why Lord Lloyd in *Siu Yin Kwan* said that an agent can sue and be sued on the contract. Once the undisclosed principal intervenes, the agent loses his rights of action against the third party. The agent nevertheless remains liable to the third party until the third party elects whether to hold the principal or the agent liable.

In two situations, a third party can sue the principal or the agent. The third party has a choice: whenever the principal is undisclosed and where the agent incurs personal responsibilities under the contract made on behalf of a disclosed principal (*The Swan*).[98] The third party cannot sue both, because the third party only makes one contract with one person, that is, there is only one obligation. So, the right to sue the agent and the right to sue the principal are in the alternative. The third party may lose his right to sue one of them if he has 'elected' to hold the other liable. The third party cannot change his mind who to sue once he has elected. So, what amounts to an election? The principal in *Clarkson, Booker v Andjel*[99] was a travel agency. They instructed an agent to buy tickets from a third party. The agent did not disclose he was acting as an agent. The third party was not paid and when they discovered that the agent was acting for a principal, they threatened to sue both the agent and the principal. Proceedings commenced against the principal. Shortly after, the principal became insolvent. The third party brought the action against the agent. The agent argued that the third party had elected to sue the principal and thus lost the right to sue them as agent. The Court of Appeal held that the action against the principal was *prima facie* evidence of election but it did not amount to final election, so the third party could sue the agent.

Thus, commencing proceedings constitutes evidence of election but this is not conclusive. It seems clear that it is not necessary to obtain judgment before election is deemed complete, but the issuing of a writ is itself not sufficient.[100]

---

[98] See section 3.10.1 below.
[99] [1964] 2 QB 775.
[100] It is arguable that election is based on estoppel, that is, if a third party sues one party, he is then estopped from suing the other.

3.9 Merger

If judgment is obtained against one party, this amounts to a merger (that is, the third party's cause of action against the principal or the agent has 'merged'). This precludes later action against the other party. This is not the same as election because the third party may not have full knowledge of the relevant facts. The third party may have obtained judgment in ignorance of the existence of a principal and therefore cannot have elected.

3.10 Agent and the third party

3.10.1 Rights and liabilities under the contract

The general rule is that an agent has no rights and is not liable under the contract which he makes on behalf of his principal. This is because the purpose of agency is to facilitate some aspect of the legal relationship between the principal and a third party. Thus, where the agent carries out his instructions satisfactorily, the agent and third party have no legal rights and liabilities towards each other. The agent simply disappears from view. There are, however, several exceptions to this rule.

3.10.1.1 Where the agent contracts personally

Suppose a written contract is signed by an agent without any mention that a principal is involved, is the agent contracting personally? Probably yes, so the agent can enforce and is liable under the contract. If the agent adds 'pp', 'per pro',[101] is this a personal contract or is the agent acting as agent? Probably acting as agent, but this is not conclusive. It depends on the circumstances of each case. For example, *The Swan*[102] involved a one-man company. The director authorised repairs to be carried out on a boat which he owned but the company hired it from him. He gave instructions on the company's notepaper and signed it as 'Director'. The company went into liquidation. The repairers sued the director personally on the unpaid invoice. The court held that the director was personally liable because he was the owner of the boat. This meant he had a personal interest in the repair works in addition to his interest as the director of the company. The director had not done enough to make clear to the repairers that he was only acting as an agent. It was therefore reasonable for the repairers to assume that the director was acting both as agent and in his personal capacity. So, although *prima facie* he was an agent, because the boat belonged to the director, it was reasonable in the circumstances to conclude he was personally liable.[103]

---

[101] *Per procurationem.*
[102] [1968] 1 Lloyd's Rep 5.
[103] The court considered it relevant that the repair works were extensive and on completion would greatly increase the value of the boat.

We have already discussed the possibility that a third party can sue either the principal or the agent in one of two circumstances. Where the agent incurs personal responsibility is one of those circumstances. Furthermore, an agent may incur personal liability if it were the custom of a particular trade.[104]

3.10.1.2 When the principal is undisclosed

The general rule is that the agent is liable under the contract and entitled to enforce it.[105]

3.10.1.3 The agent is in fact the principal

If an agent acts for a named principal, the agent can enforce the contract after giving notice to the third party that he acted on his own behalf. This is true as long as this would not prejudice the third party. For example, it may be that the third party relied on the solvency of the named principal and so the agent cannot enforce the contract. In *The Remco*,[106] the agent declared that he was acting for a named principal when he chartered a ship. He later informed the third party that he was in fact the principal. The court held that the agent cannot enforce the contract because the third party regarded the identity of the principal as material.[107]

Where an agent acts for an unnamed principal and later reveals himself as principal, there have been cases suggesting the agent can enforce the contract, but there are criticisms of this approach. As we discussed earlier,[108] when a third party is unwilling to contract with the agent for personal reasons, for example, as in *Said v Butt*, the agent may not enforce the contract.

3.10.2 Under collateral contract

There might be rights and liabilities between the agent and the third party under a collateral contract. In *Andrews v Hopkinson*,[109] a car dealer told the customer: 'It's a good little bus. I would stake my life on it.' The customer entered into a contract with the finance company, arranged through the dealer, to acquire the car on hire purchase. The court held that there was a collateral contract between the dealer and the customer for the defective goods.

3.10.3 Implied warranty of authority

If an agent purports to act for a principal knowing he has no authority to do so, he is liable to the third party for impliedly warranting he had such authority. This is true even if the agent believed his principal would ratify (*Polhill v Walter*).[110] It is not clear, however, on what basis

---

[104] *Kelner v Baxter* (1866) LR 2 CP 174.
[105] Lord Lloyd in *Siu Yin Kwan v Eastern Insurance* [1994] 2 AC 199.
[106] [1984] 2 Lloyd's Rep 205.
[107] Because, for example, the charterer is responsible for paying the freight.
[108] See the limitations to the undisclosed principal doctrine, section 3.7.
[109] [1957] 1 QB 229.
[110] (1832) 3 B & Ad 114.

the agent is liable. It is generally thought that liability is based on breach of a collateral contract, in which event, the *Hadley* v *Baxendale*[111] rules as regards damages would follow, but, if fraud or negligent misrepresentation by the agent is involved, the third party may seek tort damages.

If an agent thought he had authority when in fact he had none, he remains liable to the third party.[112] *Yonge* v *Toynbee*[113] involved a solicitor who was conducting litigation on behalf of a client. The client became insane but the solicitor did not know this and continued with the litigation. The third party sued the solicitor for the costs they incurred on the basis that the solicitor's actual authority came to an end when the client became insane and so the solicitor was in breach of an implied warranty of authority. The Court of Appeal permitted the third party to recover costs, because the solicitor had no actual authority to continue with the litigation after the client went insane. It made no difference that the solicitor had acted in good faith and with due diligence.[114]

The rule seems harsh on the agent because it makes no difference if an agent acted in good faith or not, but the agent's liability is strict. One exception to this is where the principal is liable to the third party on the grounds of apparent or usual authority. In *Rainbow* v *Howkins*,[115] an auctioneer had the authority to sell a horse with a reserve price. Contrary to his instructions, he sold it without reserve. The court held that the auctioneer was not liable for breach of implied warranty, because the buyer could enforce the contract against the seller on the grounds that the auctioneer had the apparent authority to sell without reserve. Note that some academics disagree. It is arguable that the agent remains liable because what the agent represents is that he had actual authority from his principal at the time he entered into the transaction on his principal's behalf. The agent does not represent that he has apparent authority (which as we said is somewhat artificial – almost akin to operation of law to help third parties).[116] The essential point is that these rules exist for the protection of a third party. So, as long as either the principal or the agent is liable to the third party, then either argument provides sufficient protection.

If an agent does an unauthorised act but the principal ratifies that act, the third party cannot sue the agent for breach of implied warranty of authority. Once the principal ratifies, the transaction is treated as though it was entered into by the agent with actual authority. Ratification relates back to the time of the transaction.[117] Although at the time the agent enters into the transaction the agent is, technically, in breach of implied warranty of authority, there is no real loss to the third party if the principal ratifies.

3.10.3.1 Damages for breach of warranty of authority

As stated, it is not clear on what basis an agent is liable, but it is generally thought that the action lies for breach of a collateral contract. Thus, the measure of damages is the contract

---

[111] (1854) 23 LJ Ex 179.
[112] There are statutory exceptions to this rule, for example, under the Powers of Attorney Act 1971 and the Bankruptcy Act 1914.
[113] [1910] 1 KB 215.
[114] We have also seen the case of *Drew* v *Nunn* (1879) 4 QBD 661.
[115] [1904] 2 KB 322.
[116] See above, section 3.4.1.
[117] See *Bolton Partners* v *Lambert* (1889) 41 Ch D 295.

measure of damages, that is, as if the contract had been fully performed, subject to the remoteness rules.[118] The general rule is that damages are assessed at the date of breach, but this is not an absolute rule. A court could assess damages at some other date if it thought it just to do so.

CASE

Habton Farms v Nimmo[119]

An agent purported to act as agent for a certain racehorse owner. He agreed to buy a horse from the seller for £70,000. He had no authority to do so and the principal refused to take delivery of the horse. The seller did not accept the principal's 'repudiation'. The seller did nothing; he made no effort to sell the horse. Four weeks after the delivery date agreed with the agent, the horse contracted a disease and died. The seller sued the agent for breach of warranty of authority. He claimed £70,000 in damages. The agent argued that damages should be zero because on the day of the contract (that is, the date of breach of warranty of authority), there was no difference between the contract price agreed for the horse and the market price for it. The Court of Appeal held that the agent was liable for the full £70,000. Damages is the contract measure of damages. If the contract had been fully performed, the seller would have divested himself of the ownership, possession and risk of the horse in return for the price four weeks before the horse died.

The result would have been different if the seller had sold the horse and merely sold at a lower price. In that case, the seller would be entitled to the difference in value between the contract price and the market price. The seller would not be entitled to claim more than his actual loss.[120]

3.11 The principal and the agent – duties of an agent

3.11.1 To carry out his instructions, that is, he must obey

One of the central duties of an agent is to obey his principal's instructions. If an agent does not do what he was instructed to do, he is liable for breach of contract with his principal. This only applies to agents who are operating under contract. A gratuitous agent will not be liable simply for failure to perform.

---

[118] *Hadley v Baxendale* (1854) 9 Ex 341.
[119] [2003] 1 All ER 1136.
[120] *Bence Graphics v Fasson* [1997] QB 87; *The Golden Victory* [2007] UKHL 12.

3.11.2 **To act with due care and skill**

We have discussed *Chaudhry* v *Prabhakar*[121] – even a gratuitous agent is accountable to his principal (though the standard of care may be different from that owed by a contractual agent). 'Due care and skill' means that the agent must act with such care as is reasonable in all the circumstances. The duty is not restricted to purely contractual liability. In *Hedley Byrne* v *Heller*,[122] before extending credit to Easipower, Hedley Byrne questioned Easipower's bankers (Heller) regarding the creditworthiness of its customer. In reliance on Heller's statement in the positive, Hedley Byrne extended a loan to Easipower. When Easipower were unable to repay the loan, Hedley Byrne sued Heller for negligent misrepresentation. The House of Lords held that Heller had been negligent because where a representor owes a duty of care, he ought to have realised that a representee may rely on his advice.[123]

If an agent is paid for special skills, then a greater degree of care and skill is expected of him.

3.11.3 **Owes a fiduciary duty**

An agent is not a trustee, but he owes a fiduciary duty because of the nature of agency. An agent has the power to affect the legal relations between his principal and a third party. This means an agent is placed in a position of trust and confidence. Equity will therefore intervene and impose fiduciary duties on the agent to protect his principal from an abuse of trust. Because fiduciary duties arise in equity, it is owed whether or not the agent is paid, that is, the same rules will apply whether the agent is to be paid or he acts gratuitously.[124] There are two major consequences of this.

3.11.3.1 **Conflict of interest and duty**

This is a paramount duty. An agent must not put himself in a situation where his interest and duty conflict. The burden of proof rests on the agent, that is, the agent has to prove that there was no conflict of interest in such a situation. This fiduciary duty of good faith has been applied very strictly. *Boardman* v *Phipps*[125] involved a solicitor who was acting as agent for trustees of an estate. He attended the annual general meeting of a company in which the estate held a minority shareholding. The solicitor received information on the value of the shares and he considered them undervalued. The trustees of the estate declined the opportunity to purchase more shares. The solicitor, in good faith, used his own money to purchase a controlling interest in the company. The company prospered and the solicitor made a large profit from his shares. The estate also benefited because it retained a minority shareholding. Nevertheless, the House of Lords held that the solicitor must pay his personal profit to the estate because the information acquired by the solicitor belonged to the estate.

---

[121] [1989] 1 WLR 29, see above, section 3.1.
[122] [1964] AC 465.
[123] However, because of an effective exemption clause, Hedley Byrne were not entitled to damages.
[124] Note that fiduciary duties dictate what the agent must not do. They do not require the agent to act proactively.
[125] [1967] 2 AC 46.

It was irrelevant that the agent had acted in good faith or indeed produced a benefit for his principal. In the Court of Appeal, Lord Denning said:[126]

> It is quite clear that if an agent uses property with which he has been entrusted by his principal so as to make a profit for himself out of it without his principal's consent, then he is accountable for it to his principal . . . So also if he uses a position of authority to which he has been appointed by his principal so as to gain money for himself, then he is also accountable to his principal for it . . . Likewise with information or knowledge which he has been employed by his principal to collect or discover or which he has otherwise acquired for the use of his principal, then again if he turns it to his own use so as to make a profit by means of it for himself, he is accountable.

There will be a conflict of interest where, for example, a principal instructs his agent to buy goods on his behalf and where the agent sells his own goods to the principal. *Robinson v Mollett*[127] involved the London tallow market. It was a custom of the trade that brokers could sell their own goods to principals. Nevertheless, the court held that the principal was not bound by the transaction because the custom of the trade contradicted the principal's express instructions. It is not possible to convert an agent employed as the principal's buyer into the principal's seller.

If a contract is made in breach of this fiduciary duty, the contract is voidable at the option of the principal, that is, the principal can rescind the contract. The principal's right to rescind lasts until the breach is discovered.[128] This does not depend on whether or not the principal suffers loss. That is because an agent's breach of fiduciary duties *bites at the very heart of the agency relationship*. In cases of 'ordinary' breach of contract, remedies are awarded but the contract often continues. An agent who is in breach of his fiduciary duties *offends equity*, so an injured principal can *avoid the tainted relationship*. The relationship is *not* void *ab initio*. The principal has the choice whether or not to avoid it.

CASE

Imageview Management Ltd v Kelvin Jack[129]

Jack was (and still is) a professional football player from Trinidad & Tobago. He appointed an agent to negotiate a contract for him to play with a UK club. The terms of the agency contract included a fixed two-year period and a commission of 10 per cent of the player's monthly salary; the agent was to advise and promote the principal. Everyone knew that Jack would require a work permit which he was not expected to pay for. Dundee Football Club offered Jack a contract and asked Jack's agent to obtain the necessary work permit, agreeing to pay the agent £3,000 for this (although the usual cost of obtaining such a permit was in the region of £750). The agent did not inform Jack of this arrangement, and when Jack found out, he refused to pay the agent any commission.

---

[126] [1965] Ch 992 at 1018.
[127] (1875) LR 7 HL 802.
[128] Assuming that none of the bars to rescission apply. In *Oliver v Court* (1820) Dan 301, the principal was able to rescind the transaction after 13 years.
[129] [2009] EWCA Civ 6.

The agent sued Jack. The Court of Appeal decided unanimously to find against the agent; Jack was entitled to be repaid all fees paid to the agent including the £3,000 as a secret profit.

Like *Boardman*, *Imageview* v *Kelvin Jack* is a harsh decision. The principal did not suffer any loss. The principal was not expected to pay for the work permit and he was not asked to pay, but the message from the courts is clear: an agent must not breach his fiduciary duties. As Lord Justice Jacob stressed, the law imposes high standards on agents. An agent's own personal interests came:

> . . . entirely second to the interest of his client. If you undertake to act for a man you must act 100% body and soul, for him. You must act as if you were him. You must not allow your own interests to get in the way without telling him.[130]

Even where an agent honestly believes that what he is doing is legal, this makes no difference: the remedy of repayment of all commission remains the standard remedy. As Lord Atkin said in *Rhodes* v *Macalister*:[131]

> The complete remedy is disclosure, and if an agent wishes to receive any kind of remuneration from the other side and wishes to test whether it is honest or not, he has simply to disclose the matter to his own employer and rest upon the consequences of that. If his employer consents to it, then he has performed everything that is required of an upright and responsible agent.

Thus, had the agent in *Imageview* v *Kelvin Jack* disclosed the payment of £3,000 to Jack, and Jack had consented to this, the agent would have been able to retain it.

In the commercial world, institutions are so enormous nowadays that it is sometimes difficult to entirely avoid a conflict of interest. For example, in a banking institution, often one department is advising the owner-seller of a business and another department of the same bank may be advising the potential buyer. The bank, as agent, may be in breach of the duty of confidentiality. Of course, there are strict rules regarding banks in this position. Regarding a 'normal' agent, all the agent can do is try and manage conflicts of interest as reasonably as he can. An agent could of course try to exclude or limit his liability to the principal if there is a conflict but such exemptions need to be reasonable under the Unfair Contract Terms Act 1977.[132]

Whether or not an agent is entitled to commission if there is a breach of fiduciary duties depends on whether or not the agent's breach of duty goes to the root of his obligations. If it does, the agent loses his right to commission, even if he acted honestly.[133]

3.11.3.2 Bribes and secret profits

An agent must not make a secret profit or take a bribe. He cannot accept commission from a third party. It is irrelevant that the agent acted in good faith or the principal suffered no loss.

---

[130] At para. 6.
[131] (1923) 29 Com Cas 19 at 29.
[132] A clause excluding for fraud is unlikely to be reasonable (*HIH* v *Chase Manhattan* [2003] UKHL 6).
[133] See *Hippisley* v *Knee* below, section 3.11.3.2.

In *Hippisley* v *Knee*,[134] an agent was employed to sell his principal's goods. It was agreed that the agent would be reimbursed his expenses. The agent sold the goods and claimed expenses for the cost of advertising. The agent claimed the full cost of the advertisements, though he received a discount. The agent had acted honestly because it was a trade custom for discounts to be given to agents (though the principal did not know this). The Court of Appeal held that the agent was in breach of his duty. He must account for the discount as a secret profit.

The court in *Hippisley* nevertheless allowed the agent to keep his agency commission because he had acted in good faith. His breach of the duty was incidental to the sale of goods itself. Similarly, in *Boardman* v *Phipps*, although the solicitor must pay his profit over to the principal as a secret profit, the court allowed the solicitor to retain some moneys for his time spent and expenses in producing the profit. The solicitor had acted in good faith and his breach of duty did not go to the root of his obligations.

If the secret profit does not amount to a bribe, the agent is under no criminal or tortious liability. So, for example, if an agent were given a trade discount, the agent is not criminally liable but he must account for the payment to the principal. In *Regier* v *Campbell-Stuart*,[135] a principal instructed his agent to buy a house on his behalf. The agent bought the house for £2,000 in the name of a nominee and then bought from the nominee for £4,500. The agent then resold the house to his principal for £5,000. The court held that the agent was liable to account to the principal not only for £500 profit made but also for £2,500 profit on the previous transaction.

A secret profit amounts to a bribe if the third party at the time of paying it knew the agent was an agent of another and this payment is not disclosed to the principal. Once a bribe is established, it is conclusively presumed against the third party that his motive was corrupt and the agent was affected and influenced by the payment. It is irrelevant whether or not the bribe induced the contract between the principal and the third party. That motive is corrupt is conclusive. A bribed agent cannot be expected to put the interests of his principal first.

Where a bribe is involved, the principal has available very powerful remedies. The agent can be summarily dismissed even if he was appointed for a fixed period of time and the agent loses his right to commission on that transaction. The agent must pay the bribe over to his principal whether or not the principal has suffered loss (including any profits made from the bribe, for example, if the bribe money had been invested and that investment produced a profit)[136] or, instead of claiming the bribe, the principal may claim damages from the agent and the third party for the loss suffered as a result of the bribe. This loss may be calculated in terms of any gain acquired by the third party. The principal can recover the bribe from the third party even though the agent cannot. Whether or not the principal chooses to set aside the transaction, he may keep the bribe. In *Logicrose* v *Southend United Football Club*,[137] the chairman of the football club was bribed £70,000 to grant a stall licence. The court held that the principal could recover the bribe whether or not it chose to avoid the contract with the third party. Furthermore, the agent and the third party may incur criminal liability.[138]

[134] [1905] 1 KB 1.
[135] [1939] 1 Ch 766.
[136] *Attorney General for Hong Kong* v *Reid* [1994] 1 AC 324.
[137] [1988] 1 WLR 1256.
[138] Under the Bribery Act 2010; see *R v Patel* [2012] EWCA Crim 1243.

There are some exceptions – the full force of the fiduciary duties will not apply to all contracts, for example, in estate agents' contracts.

3.11.4 Not to delegate his duties

The general rule is that an agent cannot delegate his authority to another person nor appoint a sub-agent unless the agent has the express or implied consent of his principal. This is because the relationship between principal and agent is personal. Even if the appointment of a sub-agent has been authorised by the principal, this does not necessarily mean there is privity between the principal and the sub-agent. When a principal employs an agent to do a thing, the agent undertakes responsibility for the whole transaction and the agent is responsible for any negligence in carrying it out, even if the negligence is that of the sub-agent. This is true even if the appointment of the sub-agent was authorised by the principal.

If a principal consents to the appointment of a sub-agent, does the sub-agent owe the principal the 'normal' duties of an agent, for example, to act with due care and skill, and does the full force of the fiduciary duties apply? It is necessary to compare two cases.

CASES

De Bussche v Alt[139]

In *De Bussche v Alt*, a shipowner employed an agent to sell a ship in India, China or Japan. The agent was not able to sell the ship himself but appointed (with the principal's consent) a sub-agent in Japan. The principal contacted the sub-agent with detailed instructions. Subsequently, the sub-agent bought the ship himself and then resold it to a third party for profit. The Court of Appeal held that the sub-agent must account to the shipowner for his profit. There was privity between the principal and the sub-agent.

Calico v Barclays Bank[140]

In *Calico v Barclays Bank*, a principal sold cotton to a buyer in Beirut. He instructed Barclays Bank to insure the cotton if the buyer did not accept the consignment. Barclays Bank did not have an office in Beirut. With knowledge of the principal, Barclays Bank appointed the Anglo-Palestine Bank in Beirut to act as its agents. Barclays Bank instructed the Anglo-Palestine Bank to insure the goods if the consignment of cotton was not accepted. Contrary to its instructions, Anglo-Palestine Bank did not insure the goods and the cotton was destroyed by fire. The principal sued Barclays Bank and Anglo-Palestine Bank for negligence. The court held that the Anglo-Palestine Bank was not liable because there was no privity of contract between them and the principal. Barclays Bank was held liable because the general rule is that an agent has responsibility for the whole transaction.[141]

---

[139] (1878) 8 Ch D 286.
[140] [1931] All ER Rep 350.
[141] However, because Barclays Bank was able to rely on an effective exclusion of liability clause, the principal lost out on this occasion.

The difference between *De Bussche* and *Calico* is that, in the former case, the principal ship-owner had contacted the Japanese sub-agent directly and corresponded with them and given specific instructions. That created privity. In *Calico*, the principal's only contact was with Barclays Bank and, as agent, it undertook full responsibility for the transaction.

Both these cases involved a principal who gave express consent to the appointment of a sub-agent. A principal can give his consent impliedly, for example, because it is the trade custom or in an emergency. In that situation, the sub-agent owes the same duties to the principal as if he had been appointed by the principal himself.

If the delegation to a sub-agent is unauthorised, the principal is not liable to the sub-agent for commission (unless, of course, the principal ratifies the sub-delegation). Note that if a sub-delegation is unauthorised, a principal may nevertheless be bound to the third party for the sub-agent's acts if the third party can show that the agent had the apparent authority to delegate, for example, through previous course of dealings (*Summers* v *Soloman*).[142]

3.11.5 Indemnity

It is an implied term in an agency agreement that if losses result from the agent's negligence or misconduct, the agent must indemnify the principal.

3.12 Rights of the agent

3.12.1 Remuneration

An agent's remuneration is based on the terms of his agency agreement. If the agency agreement is silent as to the amount of remuneration, courts will generally infer an agreement to pay on a *quantum meruit* basis, that is, a reasonable amount,[143] especially if the agency involved a commercial relationship. The agent is entitled to be paid when he has done what he was supposed to have done under his contract. The agent must, however, be the direct or effective cause of the transaction, because if something breaks the chain of causation, the agent will not be entitled to payment. In *Coles* v *Enoch*,[144] an agent was employed to find a tenant for his principal's property. A third party overheard the conversation between the agent and someone else. Although the agent only gave a general description of the property, the third party found the property himself and made an offer directly to the principal, which was accepted. The court held that the agent was not entitled to commission because his actions had not been the direct cause of the third party's agreement with the principal.

---

[142] (1857) 7 E & B 879.
[143] *Foley* v *Classique Coaches* [1934] 2 KB 1.
[144] [1939] 3 All ER 327.

Difficulties have arisen from estate agency[145] fees. In *Luxor* v *Cooper*,[146] a principal wanted to sell two cinemas. He agreed with the estate agents that he would pay commission 'on completion of sale'. The estate agents introduced a third party who wanted to buy the cinemas, but the principal changed his mind and refused to sell. The estate agents sued the principal for commission. The action failed. The House of Lords held that the estate agents were not entitled to commission because there was no sale.

In fact, the commission under the agency agreement in *Luxor* was £10,000. That was over 60 years ago, so amounted to a substantial sum. The House clearly felt that perhaps the estate agents had taken the risk of all or nothing, that is, the owner might change his mind.[147]

If the principal willfully breaks the contract which the agent concluded with the third party, the agent is entitled to commission. In *Alpha Trading* v *Dunnshaw-Patten*,[148] an agent introduced a third-party buyer of cement. The principal accepted the deal and contracted with the buyer. Then, because the market price of cement was rising and there was the possibility of a lucrative contract elsewhere, the principal did not perform the contract of sale with the third party. The agent claimed damages for lost commission. The Court of Appeal held that the agent was entitled to commission. It was an implied term of the agency contract that a principal would not deprive the agent of commission by willfully breaking the contract with the third party.

There is no implied term in an agency contract that a principal must give the agent a chance to earn commission. The court in *Luxor* would not imply such a term because to do otherwise would restrict the principal's freedom to deal with his own property, that is, the owner had to keep cinemas on the market just to give the estate agents an opportunity to earn commission.

Even though an agent has no opportunity to earn commission, compensation may be payable.

CASE

Turner v Goldsmith[149]

In this case, the principal was a manufacturer of shirts. He employed the agent as a sales representative on commission for a period of five years. The factory burnt down and the principal argued that the agency agreement was terminated, and thus no commission was payable. The court agreed that the agency agreement was terminated but the agent was entitled to be compensated by way of a reasonable sum, representing what the agent was likely to have earned.

---

[145] Estate agents do not fit easily into the concept of legal agency because, in general, estate agents do not have the power to bind their principal to a third party. Nevertheless, estate agents are regarded as being governed by the general rules applicable to other agents, particularly in relation to payment of commission.

[146] [1941] AC 108.

[147] Similarly, in *Cutter* v *Powell* (1795) 6 Term Rep 320, the widow could not recover her deceased husband's wages because his was an entire contract and Cutter had not performed the whole contract. The contract rate for the work was 30 guineas which was four times the usual rate. The court felt that Cutter had taken the risk of all or nothing. Thus his widow was not able to recover any part of the wages.

[148] [1981] QB 290.

[149] [1891] 1 QB 544.

3.12.2 Indemnity

A principal must indemnify his agent against all liabilities reasonably incurred in the execution of his authority. This not only refers to contractual liability but also tortious liability. Where the agency is contractual, the agent's right to an indemnity is based on an implied term and the agent's action will be in contract. Where the agent acts gratuitously, the agent can claim a restitutionary right to reimbursement of expenses on the basis of unjust enrichment.

3.12.3 Lien

In some circumstances, an agent may be able to claim a lien over his principal's property. There are two types of liens. The particular lien is where an agent has a lien over his principal's property which comes into his possession in the course of the agency. In this situation, the agent may hold the property (though not dispose of it) until his principal satisfies his obligation to pay the agent his commission or indemnifies the agent in accordance with the agency contract. The general lien is where an agent has a lien over property in his possession until his principal satisfies *all* claims of the agent. Agents usually have particular liens. In practice, courts are reluctant to find that a general lien exists, although, because of trade custom or the inclusion of specific terms in the agency contract (such as an 'all monies clause'), agents such as bankers and solicitors have a general lien.

3.13 Termination of agency

Just as an agency agreement can be created by agreement between the agent and his principal, the agreement may also be terminated by agreement. Where the agency agreement is stated to be for a fixed period of time, the agreement automatically ends at the end of that period. If there is no fixed period of time, the agreement ends after reasonable notice is given by either party. An agency agreement may also be terminated if there is a serious breach of the agency agreement, for example, where the agent accepts a bribe from a third party, he can be summarily dismissed even if he was appointed for a fixed period of time.[150] The agency agreement is automatically terminated in the event of a frustrating event, such as illegality. Death or bankruptcy of the principal or the agent will terminate the agency agreement. However, where a power of attorney is given to the agent and this is stated to be irrevocable to secure the agent's interest, the power of attorney is irrevocable whilst the agent's interest remains. This is so despite the principal's death or bankruptcy.[151]

Insanity of the principal will terminate the agency agreement. However, in this instance, although the agency agreement is terminated between the principal and agent, the termination only affects the agent's actual authority (expressed or implied). Insanity of the principal does not necessarily terminate the agent's apparent or usual authority, unless the third party is aware of the principal's insanity or notice is given to the third party.[152]

[150] See agent's duties, section 3.11.3.2.
[151] Section 4 of the Powers of Attorney Act 1971.
[152] We already looked at the case of *Drew* v *Nunn*, section 3.4.1.3.

3.14 Commercial Agents (Council Directive) Regulations 1993

These Regulations only apply to 'commercial agents' and only affect the relations between 'commercial agents' and their principals; they do not affect the third party. In general, an agent covered by the regulations is better protected than one who is not. Parties cannot contract out of the regulations. Even if the law chosen to govern the agency agreement is stated to be outside English law, the Regulations override such a choice of law regarding the activities of the commercial agent carried out in the UK. So, if a company in Hong Kong appoints an agent in the UK to sell its products or source goods under an agreement which states that Hong Kong law is to be applied to its terms, the agent is covered by the Regulations.

The object of the Regulations is expressed in the EU directive from which the Regulations are derived. The Preamble to the directive refers to the need to remove:

> the differences in national laws concerning commercial representation [which] substantially affect the conditions of competition and the carrying-on of that activity within the Community and are detrimental both to the protection available to commercial agents vis-à-vis their principals and to the security of commercial transactions.

The lack of harmonisation was also perceived as capable of substantially inhibiting 'the conclusion and operation of commercial representation contracts where principal and commercial agents are established in different Member States'.

The Regulations only apply to a particular type of agent.

LEGISLATIVE PROVISION

Regulation 2(1)

'commercial agent' means a self-employed intermediary who has continuing authority to negotiate the sale or purchase of goods on behalf of another person (the 'principal'), or to negotiate and conclude the sale or purchase of goods on behalf of and in the name of that principal . . .

Note that an agent must be self-employed in order to fall within the Regulations. This means he cannot be an employee or a company officer, although a company or partnership can be a commercial agent as long as it acts as an independent contractor. Where an agent buys and sells goods in his own right rather than having authority to negotiate or contract on the principal's behalf, he is not a commercial agent but in fact a distributor and thus not protected under the Regulations. Thus, in *Raoul Sagal (t/a Bunz UK)* v *Atelier Bunz GmbH*,[153] a jewellery trader who invoiced customers in his own name was held not to be a commercial agent even though his supplier dispatched the goods directly to the customers, insured the goods until they reached the customers and the trader's resale price was fixed at a 30 per cent mark-up against the supplier's price to the trader. The Court of Appeal expressed the view where

[153] [2009] EWCA Civ 700.

an agent represents an undisclosed principal, he cannot be an agent within the meaning of the Regulations since the Regulations require an agent to have 'continuing authority to negotiate the sale or purchase of goods on behalf of another person (the "principal") or to negotiate and conclude the sale or purchase of goods on behalf of and in the name of that principal'. So, if an agent for an undisclosed principal contracts in his own name (and not in the name of the principal), such agents do not fall within the 1993 Regulations.

The agent must also have the continuing authority to negotiate on behalf of the principal. The Regulations are thus concerned with relationships which have the potential of being developed over time. So, if an agent is appointed for a one-off transaction, the agency agreement falls outside the Regulations. 'Continuing authority' is not hard to prove, as was shown in *Nigel Fryer Joinery Services v Ian Firth Hardware*,[154] where it was held that all that was needed was that the agent negotiated, persuaded customers to buy, dealt with and managed sales. The power to negotiate is sufficient. The agent does not have to have the authority to conclude contracts in order to be a commercial agent.

Furthermore, the regulations only apply if the continuing authority relates to the sale or purchase of goods contracts. The Regulations do not therefore apply to the sale or purchase of services. This means that an agent who sells services is not entitled to the substantial rights and protections contained in the Regulations. Finally, the Regulations do not apply to unpaid agents.[155] If the Regulations do not apply, the agency agreement is governed by the common law rules.

3.14.1 Duties of an agent

LEGISLATIVE PROVISION

Regulation 3

(1) In performing his activities a commercial agent must look after the interests of his principal and act dutifully and in good faith.

(2) In particular, a commercial agent must:

(a) make proper efforts to negotiate and, where appropriate, conclude the transactions he is instructed to take care of;

(b) communicate to his principal all the necessary information available to him;

(c) comply with reasonable instructions given by his principal.

This is much the same as an agent's common law duties, that is, to follow his instructions and to comply with an agent's fiduciary obligations. However, there are two specific duties imposed under the Regulations which seem to go a little further. First, the agent is to 'make

---

[154] [2008] EWHC 767 (Ch).
[155] Regulation 2(2).

proper efforts' to negotiate and conclude transactions. This seems to amount to a duty of due diligence, expecting an agent to be more proactive than the common law requires. Secondly, the commercial agent is to communicate 'all necessary information' to his principal. There is no equivalent under the common law. The commercial agent is thus expected to be more proactive in providing information, rather than the common law approach of prohibiting the concealment of relevant information (for example, as regards secret profits).

3.14.2 **Duties of the principal**

LEGISLATIVE PROVISION

Regulation 4(1)

In his relations with his commercial agent a principal must act dutifully and in good faith.

Under the Regulations, the principal has a duty to provide certain information to his agent. In particular, the principal should provide his agent with information and supply relevant documents necessary for the performance of the agency contract.[156] For example, if an agent has been instructed to sell cars for his principal, the principal needs to provide his agent with the relevant documents to conclude the transactions, such as the logbooks of the cars. Furthermore, the principal must keep his agent informed regarding transactions arranged by the agent. For example, the agent must be told whether the principal has accepted or refused the transaction, or whether or not it has been executed. The agent needs to know because it affects the agent's right to remuneration. The principal does not have such obligations under the common law.

Furthermore, both the agent and the principal are entitled, on request, to receive from each other a signed written document setting out the terms of the agency contract.[157] This does not mean that the agency contract needs to be made in writing, merely that a record of its terms can be asked for.

3.14.3 **Remuneration**

Remuneration depends on the contract terms agreed between the principal and the agent. If the contract is silent, the regulations state that the agent is to be paid a 'reasonable remuneration'. This is similar to the common law position. Note, however, if an agent is to be unpaid, the Regulations do not apply, and the agent is a mere gratuitous agent under the common law.

A commercial agent is entitled to his commission when the transaction is concluded as a result of the agent's action.[158] This is much the same as 'direct or effective cause' under the

---

[156] This is similar to the common law business efficacy test (*The Moorcock* (1889) LR 14 PD 64).
[157] Regulation 13.
[158] Regulation 7.

common law.[159] Even if a transaction is not concluded as the result of an agent's action, the agent is entitled to commission for as long as the agency contract subsists in two situations. First, if the transaction is concluded with a third party previously acquired by the agent for transactions of the same kind. Secondly, where the agent has exclusive rights in a geographical area, or with a specific group of customers, and contracts are made with any of those.

Under reg. 8, even if the agency agreement is terminated, an agent may still be entitled to commission where the transaction is mainly attributable to his efforts during the period covered by the agency contract and if the transaction was entered into within a reasonable period after that contract terminated; or the order of the third party reached the principal or the commercial agent before the agency contract terminated.

The agent is entitled to his commission when the principal's contract with the third party is executed.[160] However, no commission is payable if the contract between the principal and the third party is not executed through no fault of the principal (for example, because of a frustrating event or the third party withdraws from the transaction).[161]

Note, however, the Regulations do not say that an agent loses his right to commission if the agent acts contrary to his instructions, even where he acts in bad faith. The agent will, of course, be in breach of his duty of good faith and, if this results in loss to the principal, compensation could be sought, but it does not appear that the agent's commission can be withheld. For example, suppose a principal instructs his agent not to deal with XYZ Ltd. The agent in fact deals with XYZ Ltd. Although the agent has no actual authority, the principal may be bound to the contract with the third party on grounds of apparent authority.[162] In this situation, it appears that the agent is entitled to be paid his commission. Of course, if the principal suffers loss because of the agent's breach (that is, not acting in accordance with his instructions), the principal may claim compensation or an indemnity from his agent, but the Regulations are silent as to whether or not the principal may withhold the agent's commission.

3.14.4 Termination of the agency agreement

The Regulations specify a minimum period of notice. Depending on the duration of the agency contract, the notice period is somewhere between one and three months.[163] Failure to give proper notice does terminate the agency contract, but it means that the termination was wrongful. In exceptional circumstances or where one party fails to carry out his obligations under the contract, the agency contract may be terminated immediately without the notice periods specified in reg. 15.[164]

Under reg. 17, an agent has the right to an indemnity or compensation on the termination of an agency agreement if the agent makes such a claim within one year of termination. However, note the exceptions under reg. 18.

---

[159] *Coles v Enoch* [1939] 3 All ER 327, see section 3.12.1.
[160] Regulation 10.
[161] Regulation 11.
[162] See section 3.4.1.
[163] Regulation 15.
[164] Regulation 16.

LEGISLATIVE PROVISION

Regulation 18

The compensation . . . shall not be payable to the commercial agent where:

(a) the principal has terminated the agency contract because of default attributable to the commercial agent which would justify immediate termination of the agency contract . . . ; or

(b) the commercial agent has himself terminated the agency contract, unless such termination is justified:

(i) by circumstances attributable to the principal; or

(ii) on grounds of the age, infirmity or illness of the commercial agent in consequence of which he cannot reasonably be required to continue his activities; . . .

So, not surprisingly, if the agent commits a repudiatory breach of the agency contract which his principal accepts, the agent is not entitled to make a claim under reg. 17.[165] Furthermore, if the agent initiates the termination of the agency contract, this will generally remove his entitlement to an indemnity or compensation.

If the situation does not fall under the reg. 18 exceptions, the agent must make his claim for an indemnity or compensation within one year of the termination of his agency agreement, otherwise that entitlement is lost.[166] Usually, the termination date of an agency is established from the terms of the agency contract, but the problem sometimes arises when it is not clear and it is only once the termination has happened that the one year for giving notice starts to run. This matter was considered in *Claramoda v Zoomphase Ltd*.[167] The case involved an agent who sold a range of fashion garments and had been told by her principal that the Spring/Summer 2007 season was to be the last season she would act as commercial agent. The commercial activities relating to the fashion seasons took place well in advance, such that the Spring/Summer 2007 season came to an end in October 2006, but the agent continued dealing with customer queries regarding orders, discrepancies over paperwork and chased payments from customers until January 2007. The agent served notice in November 2007 (that is, more than a year after the end of the Spring/Summer fashion season, but less than a year after the follow-up commercial activities came to an end in January 2007).

The principal argued that the agent's 'authority to negotiate sales', which is a requirement of being a commercial agent, came to an end when the Spring/Fashion 2007 season ended in October 2006, that is, the commercial agency ended on that date. The court disagreed. The commercial activity which took place after the end of the fashion season was indistinguishable from the earlier activity, and therefore the agent remained a commercial agent until January 2007, so her notice was within time. One issue to note from this case is that an agency agreement does not necessarily end when the agent no longer takes orders. If the agent

---

[165] In *Fryer Joinery Services v Ian Firth Hardware* [2008] EWHC 767 (Ch), the High Court held that the agent's persistent and continued failure to provide the required weekly reports, despite numerous requests and warnings from the principal, was a repudiatory breach of the agreement sufficiently serious to justify the termination of the agency.

[166] Regulation 17(9).

[167] [2009] EWHC 2857 (Comm).

continues to carry out other duties (such as dealing with customer queries), that demonstrates that the agent had authority to negotiate sales and so the agent fell within the definition of a 'commercial agent'.

Under reg. 17, if the agency contract term specifies that the agent is entitled to an indemnity, then in money terms, this is calculated as one year's commission. If the agency contract does not say whether an indemnity or compensation is payable, reg. 17 provides that an agent has the right to compensation. However, the regulations do not give any guidance as to how much compensation is payable. For years, courts have been grappling with this. Bearing in mind that the reasoning behind the Council Directive is to protect commercial agents, the European Commission published a report recommending the French approach, which is that two years' gross commission (based on the average earnings of preceding years) be paid. Scottish courts have followed this French approach and although the decisions are not binding on English courts, some English cases have awarded agents compensation under reg. 17 of two years' gross commission. The House of Lords has now made the English position much clearer. In *Lonsdale v Howard & Hallam*,[168] Mr Lonsdale was a commercial agent selling ladies' shoes for 13 years. The principal company's business declined, so it sold its brand name to a competitor. The new company employed most of the principal's agents but not Mr Lonsdale. Instead, Mr Lonsdale was offered £7,500 compensation under reg. 17. Lonsdale argued the two-year approach and said that he had earned approximately £12,000 per year. No expert valuation was given in court. The court awarded £5,000 in compensation (indeed, less than what Mr Lonsdale had been offered). Mr Lonsdale appealed. The House of Lords dismissed the appeal, because, on termination, an agent suffers loss of goodwill attaching to the agency business, which the court had valued at £5,000.

Goodwill can be traded (in the same way as businesses are sold). In *Lonsdale*, the court said that compensation under reg. 17 should be based on the value of the agency business, that is, the value of goodwill at the date of termination. The value is whatever a notional buyer might pay for the agency business. In *Lonsdale*, since the principal's business was in financial difficulty and was thus terminating the agent's contract, the value of the agency business to a notional buyer was small because the commission-earning power was small. The result of *Lonsdale* is a more flexible approach to the calculation of compensation under reg. 17. Of course, parties will need to seek accountants' advice as to the value of an agency business, but this would be less rigid than the French approach of two years' gross commission. The two-year rule is such an arbitrary approach. It is surely better for the court to take into account the facts of an individual case.

Potentially significant is the more recent High Court decision in *Michael McQuillan, Lorna McQuillan v Darren McCormick, Wizzeweb Ltd, Pandora Jewelry Ltd*.[169] When the agency was terminated, the agents claimed for compensation under reg. 17. Each party instructed its own expert and the experts ultimately agreed that the valuation of the business was some £342,895.

Judge Behrens declined to adopt this figure on the basis that the agency was terminable on one year's notice on either side. He held that it was unlikely that any potential purchaser would pay more than one year's income stream for it. The experts had determined that the annual income stream was £149,000, so the judge awarded reg. 17 compensation of

[168] [2007] UKHL 32.
[169] [2010] EWHL 1112 (QB).

£150,000. The judge clearly based his decision on the notice period on which the agency could be terminated. This is not a factor that was identified either in the *Lonsdale* case or in the Regulations themselves.

Although *McQuillan* is a High Court decision and thus does not have binding authority, it will be of persuasive value. This decision is perhaps more in keeping with the general approach of the English courts to determining loss-based compensation. If followed, it could represent a shift in the balance of protection offered to agents on termination. It would mean that the compensation under reg. 17 could be capped by the termination notice period of the agency agreement. Where there is no express provision for notice periods, as we said above, the regulations specify a minimum period of notice. Depending on the duration of the agency contract, the notice period is somewhere between one and three months. Thus, an agent whose agency is terminated on, say, three months' notice might find his compensation under reg. 17 capped at a sum equivalent to only three months' net profit.[170]

As we said before, under reg. 17, if the agency contract term specifies that the agent is entitled to an indemnity, this is calculated as one year's commission. If the agency contract does not say whether an indemnity or compensation is payable, reg. 17 provides that an agent has the right to compensation. Previously, it was often thought that providing an indemnity on termination would produce a more certain outcome for the principal. The impact of *McQuillan* may be that principals will prefer the compensation option combined with the minimum notice period under reg. 15. It will be interesting to see how the *McQuillan* principle is applied.

Further reading

Beale, H. (ed.), *Chitty on Contracts* Vol. 2, (31st edn, Sweet and Maxwell, London, 2012).

Watts, G., *Bowstead and Reynolds on Agency* (19th edn and 1st supp., Sweet and Maxwell, London, 2012).

Companion Website

For open-access **student resources** specifically written to complement this textbook and support your learning, please visit **www.pearsoned.co.uk/legalupdates**

ON THE WEBSITE

---

[170] Had the notice period in *McQuillan* been three months, on this basis, the compensation would have been only £37,500.

4 Sale of goods

By Michael Furmston

Chapter outline

4.1   Introduction

4.1.1 The origins of sales law

This chapter gives an account of the law which governs the various ways in which goods may be supplied. Goods are usually, though not always, supplied under a contract. The law of sale of goods is, exceptionally for English law, to be found in a single statutory code. In 1893, Parliament passed the Sale of Goods Act. This Act was designed to codify the common law on sale of goods, that is, to state the effects of the decisions of the courts in a succinct statutory form. The draftsman of the Act, Sir MacKenzie Chalmers, was not trying to change the law but to state it clearly and accurately, though it does appear that in a few cases he anticipated developments which the courts had not yet made.

Judges have repeatedly said that, in deciding the meaning of a codifying statute like the Sale of Goods Act 1893, the cases on which it was based should not normally be consulted. The most famous statement is that of Lord Herschell in *Bank of England* v *Vagliano Brothers*[1] (a case decided in reference to the Bills of Exchange Act 1882, another codifying statute), where he said that:

> . . . the purpose of such a statute surely was that on any point specifically dealt with by it, the law should be ascertained by interpreting the language used instead of, as before, by roaming over a vast number of authorities in order to discover what the law was, extracting it by a minute critical examination of the prior decisions.

So, as a rule, reference to pre-1893 cases should not be necessary, but there have been many cases since then and now it is often only possible to discover the accepted meaning of sections in the 1893 Act by careful examination of those cases. In addition, the 1893 Act was amended a number of times and, in 1979, Parliament passed a new Sale of Goods Act. This was a consolidating measure which simply brought together in a tidy form the 1893 Act as it had been amended between 1893 and 1979 and made no changes in the law. Indeed, with only a couple of exceptions, the section numbers of the 1893 and 1979 Acts are identical.

The law of sale of goods is for the most part, therefore, an exposition of the effect of the Sale of Goods Act 1979 but it is probably not the case that all the answers are to be found in the Act.

A further difficulty is that although sale is by far the most important contract under which goods are supplied, it is not the only one. There are, in fact, many ways in which goods may be supplied and in some cases the boundaries between them may have legal consequences. These problems are discussed below.[2]

4.1.2 **The borderline between contract law and sales law**

Not all the legal problems which arise in relation to a contract for the sale of goods are part of the law of sale of goods. Many must be solved by applying the general law of contract. So, for instance, the question of whether or not there is a contract at all is primarily a matter for the general law of contract. Although all lawyers would agree that this distinction between the general law of contract and the special law of the sale of goods exists, there would be many different answers as to where precisely the boundary lies. In practice, however, legal rules do not exist in watertight compartments, and from time to time it will not be possible to explain the legal position without discussing the general law of contract. Indeed, the draftsman of the Sale of Goods Act had the same problem. A number of the provisions of the Act, for instance those governing damages, appear to be simply applications of general contract principles to the specific case of the sale of goods. Most of the time, the distinction between general contract law and special sales law has no more importance than this. Occasionally, however, the relationship between general and special rules assumes practical significance. An example is *Cehave* v *Bremer, The Hansa Nord*.[3] This case concerned the buyer's right to reject defective goods.

---

[1] [1891] AC 107.
[2] See section 4.2.
[3] [1976] QB 44.

> **CASE**
>
> ### The Hansa Nord
>
> The contract was for the sale of citrus pulp pellets, which were to be used for feeding animals. It was an express term of the contract that the goods should be shipped in good condition. It was accepted that the goods shipped were not in good condition (though the defects were relatively minor) and the pellets were in fact eventually used for cattle feed. The buyer claimed to be entitled to reject the goods. His principal argument was that all terms in a contract of sale of goods are either conditions or warranties and that the buyer is entitled to reject the goods if the term broken by the seller is a condition; breach of the term that the goods be shipped in good condition would often be serious, and it should therefore be classified as a condition. This argument appeared to derive a good deal of support from the Sale of Goods Act 1893 since, in that Act, all the terms which are classified are classified as either conditions or warranties. Indeed, between 1893 and 1962, it was widely thought to be a general principle of contract law that all terms of a contract were either conditions or warranties. However, the Court of Appeal rejected the argument. Instead, it argued that under general contract law there were three categories of terms: conditions, warranties and innominate terms; that *Cehave* v *Bremer* was governed by general contract law, and that the relevant rules must be the same for sale as for other contracts.

This complex and difficult technical question will be discussed in more detail below.[4] The important point to emphasise for present purposes is that the Court of Appeal was able to reach the result it desired by classifying the matter in dispute as one of general contract law.

4.1.3 Is the Sale of Goods Act a complete code?

It seems likely that Sir MacKenzie Chalmers intended the Sale of Goods Act 1893 to contain all the special rules about the sale of goods. He was certainly well aware of the problems discussed in the last section and dealt with them by providing in s. 62(2) that:

> . . . the rules of the common law[5] including the law merchant, save in so far as they are inconsistent with the provisions of this Act, and in particular the rules relating to the law of principal and agent and the effect of fraud, misrepresentation, duress or coercion, mistake or other invalidating cause, apply to contracts for the sale of goods.

In *Re Wait*,[6] Atkin LJ clearly took the view that where a matter was dealt with by the Act, the treatment was intended to be exhaustive. He said: 'The total sum of legal relations . . . arising out of the contract for the sale of goods may well be regarded as defined by the code.' The question in that case was whether the buyer could obtain specific performance of the contract.

---

[4] See section 4.10.2.

[5] It is not completely clear here whether 'common law', in this context, is opposed to statute law or to equity. See M. Bridge, *Sale of Goods* (2nd edn, Oxford University Press, Oxford, 2009) pp. 8–10. See, also, *Riddiford* v *Warren* (1901) 20 NZLR 572; *cf. Graham v Freer* (1980) 35 SASR 424.

[6] [1927] 1 Ch 606.

Section 52 of the Sale of Goods Act provides that a buyer may obtain specific performance of a contract for the sale of specific or ascertained goods. (These terms are explained below.)[7]

The Act does not expressly say that specific performance cannot be obtained where the goods are not specific or ascertained, but Atkin LJ thought that s. 52 should be treated as a complete statement of the circumstances in which specific performance should be granted for a contract of sale of goods. However, in the more recent case of *Sky Petroleum Ltd v VIP Petroleum Ltd*[8] Goulding J held that he had jurisdiction to grant specific performance in such a case, though the views of Atkin LJ do not appear to have been drawn to his attention.

The problem was discussed again, though not decided, in *Leigh and Sillivan Ltd v Aliakmon Shipping Co Ltd*[9] where Lord Brandon of Oakbrook stated that his provisional view accorded with that expressed by Atkin LJ in *Re Wait*.

4.1.4 Domestic and international sales

Most of the cases discussed in this book will concern domestic sales, that is, sales where the buyer, the seller and the goods are all present in England and Wales. Obviously, there are many international sales which have no connection at all with English law. However, there are many international sales which are governed by English law, either because English law is the law most closely connected with the transaction or because the parties have chosen English law as the governing law. It is, in fact, common for parties expressly to choose English law because of a desire to have the transaction governed by English law or for disputes to be litigated or arbitrated in England. So, many transactions in the grain or sugar trades will be subject to English law by reason of the parties' choice, although neither the seller nor the buyer nor the goods ever come near England.

In general, where an international sale transaction is subject to English law, it will be subject to the provisions of the Sale of Goods Act. However, in practice, a solution which makes good commercial sense for domestic sales may make much less sense for international sales and of course vice versa. So, although the Act specifies that risk *prima facie* passes with property, a rule which is often applied in domestic sales, in practice, it is extremely common in international sales for risk and property to pass at different moments. Furthermore, most international sales involve use of documents, particularly of the bill of lading, and often involve payment by letter of credit, which is virtually unknown in domestic sales. The rules set out in this text should, therefore, be applied with great caution in the context of international sales.[10]

4.1.5 Commercial and consumer sales

The Sale of Goods Act 1893 was predominantly based on Chalmers' careful reading of the 19th-century cases on sales. These cases are almost entirely concerned with commercial transactions, particularly relatively small-scale commodity *sales*. Few consumer transactions,

---

[7] See section 4.3.3.
[8] [1974] 1 All ER 954; [1974] 1 WLR 576.
[9] [1986] 1 All ER 146; [1986] 1 AC 785.
[10] For international sales see Chapter 5.

except perhaps sales of horses, figure in this body of case law. It is true that the 1893 Act has some provisions which only apply where the seller is selling in the course of a business, but these provisions do not discriminate according to whether the buyer is buying as a business or as a consumer. For the most part, this is still true, although the modern consumer movement has meant that we now have a number of statutory provisions which are designed to protect consumers in circumstances where it is assumed either that businesspeople can protect themselves or that they need less by way of protection. These developments are particularly important in relation to defective goods and to exemption clauses.[11]

4.2 Types of transaction

This section considers the different ways in which the act of supplying goods may take place. It is largely descriptive, but some legal consequences flow from the choice of transaction, and these are pointed out.

4.2.1 Non-contractual supply

Usually, where goods are supplied there will be a contract between the supplier and the receiver of the goods. Most of this chapter is taken up with considering the various kinds of contract which can be involved, but it should be noted first that a contract is not essential.

The most obvious case where there is no contract is where there is a gift. In English law, promises to make gifts in the future are not binding unless they are made under seal (for example, covenants in favour of charities) but a gift, once executed, will be effective to transfer ownership from donor to donee provided that the appropriate form has been used. So, in principle, effective gifts of goods require physical handing over though, no doubt, in the case of a bulky object like a car, it would be sufficient to hand over the keys as the effective means of control. A major difference between gifts and other forms of supply is that the legal responsibility of the donor for the condition of the goods is relatively slight. Most suppliers of goods make implied undertakings about the quality of the goods but, in the case of a gift, the donor's liability is probably limited to warning of known dangerous defects in the goods. So, if I give away my car, I ought to warn the donee if I know that the brakes do not work, but I shall not be liable if the engine seizes up after 200 miles.

In some cases, a donee may have an action against the manufacturers. So, if I give my wife a hairdryer for her birthday and it burns her hair because it has been badly wired, she will not have an action against me except in the unlikely case that I knew of the defect. In most cases, the retail shop which supplies the goods would be in breach of their contract with me but I would not have suffered the loss, whereas my wife, who has suffered the loss, has no contract with them. However, she could sue the manufacturer if she could prove that the hairdryer had been negligently manufactured. It is a curious feature of the present law that my wife would legally be much better off if I had I given her the money to buy the hairdryer for herself.

---

[11] The whole topic of consumer protection receives extensive discussion in Chapter 7.

CASE

Esso Petroleum v Customs and Excise[12]

It can be surprisingly difficult to decide whether or not a transaction is a gift. Many promotional schemes make use of so-called gifts; can customers complain if they do not receive the gift? Often, the answer seems to be yes. The question was examined by the House of Lords in this case.

Esso had devised a marketing scheme which was linked to the England football squad for the 1970 World Cup in Mexico. Coins were provided, each of which bore the head and shoulders of a member of the squad. Prominent signs were placed in Esso filling stations stating that those who bought four gallons of petrol would receive a coin and books were given away in which sets of coins could be collected. The legal analysis of this scheme arose in an unexpected way. Customs and Excise claimed that the coins were subject to purchase tax. This tax (effectively the predecessor of VAT) was due if the coins were produced for the purpose of being sold. The scheme had been so successful that, although each coin was of minimal value, over £100,000 would have been due if Customs and Excise had won the case. Esso argued that because the coins were being given away, the customer who bought four gallons would have no legal right to a coin. In the House of Lords, this argument failed, though only by three votes to two. The majority view was that the customer would have a legitimate expectation of receiving a coin, but in practice it was very unlikely that a disappointed customer would go to court and pursue a claim. However, Esso succeeded with a second line of argument. Of the three judges who held that the coins were supplied under contract, two were persuaded that the transaction involved was more than one contract. According to this analysis, the customer bought the petrol under a conventional contract of sale, and there was a separate contract under which the filling station owner undertook to transfer a coin for every four gallons bought. The legal point of this was that this second contract was not a contract of sale since the coin was not being bought for money and purchase tax was only due if the coins were being produced for the purpose of being sold.

Even where it is clear that money will change hands, the transaction is not necessarily contractual. An important example is the supply of prescribed drugs under the National Health Service. Although for many patients there is now a substantial charge, the House of Lords held in *Pfizer Corp v Minister of Health*[13] that there is no contract between patient and pharmacist. The basic reason for this is that a contract depends on agreement, although the element of agreement is often somewhat attenuated in practice. The patient's right to the drugs and the pharmacist's duty to dispense do not depend on agreement but on statute. Similar reasoning applies to public utilities, such as suppliers of water (*Read v Croydon Corporation*).[14]

---

[12] [1976] 1 All ER 117; [1976] 1 WLR 1.
[13] [1965] AC 512.
[14] [1938] 4 All ER 632.

4.2.2 Sale of goods/sale of land

Section 2 of the Sale of Goods Act 1979 defines a contract of sale of goods as a contract by which the seller transfers or agrees to transfer the property in goods to the buyer for a money consideration called the price. It follows that this is essentially a transaction in which one side promises to transfer the ownership of goods and the other pays the price in money. Therefore, cases where there is no money price and situations where the object of the sale is not goods but land or intangible property, that is, property interests which cannot be physically possessed, such as shares, patents and copyrights (discussed further below),[15] are not contracts for the sale of goods.

It is one of the features of English law that quite different regimes apply to contracts for the sale of land and the sale of goods. So, for instance, while sellers of goods are under extensive implied liability as to the quality of these goods, sellers of land are liable only for their express undertakings as to quality. Usually, of course, there is no difficulty in deciding whether the contract is one for the sale of land or for the sale of goods, but there are some borderline problems in relation to growing crops or minerals under the land. Under s. 61(1) of the Sale of Goods Act 1979, a contract for crops or minerals is a contract for the sale of goods if they are to be severed from the land either before the sale or under the contract of sale.[16] On the other hand, a contract for the sale of a farm would normally be treated as a contract for the sale of land even though there were growing crops.

In some cases, however, the court might treat the transaction as two contracts, one for the sale of the farm and the other for the sale of the crops. In *English Hop Growers v Dering*[17] the defendant (the owner of a hop farm) had agreed to sell hops only to the plaintiff. The defendant sold the farm when the hop crop was nearing maturity and the court analysed this transaction as being two contracts, one for the sale of the farm and the other for the sale of the hops. The practical result was that the defendant was in breach of the contract with the plaintiff. If the transaction had been treated as a single contract, the result would have been different for the defendant had not promised not to sell the farm.

4.2.3 Exchange

The requirement in s. 2 of the 1979 Act that there must be a money price in a sale means that an exchange of a cow for a horse is not a sale. For most purposes, this makes no great practical difference because the courts are likely to apply rules similar to the Sale of Goods Act by analogy. Between 1677 and 1954, contracts for the sale of goods worth £10 or more were required to be evidenced in writing. This requirement was never applied to exchanges, so many of the older cases arose in this context. Straightforward exchange or barter does not appear to be very common in domestic trade, though it is increasingly common in international trade where one of the parties is short of hard currency. On the other hand, part exchange is very common, particularly in relation to motor cars. This raises the question of

---

[15] See section 4.3.1.
[16] For fuller discussion, see M. Bridge, *op cit.* pp. 37–41.
[17] [1928] 2 KB 174.

the correct classification of, for example, an agreement to exchange a new car for an old one plus a payment of £2,000.

In practice, this is often solved by the way that the parties write up the contract. In many cases they will price each car so that the natural analysis is that there are two sales with an agreement to pay the balance in cash. This was how the transaction was approached in *Aldridge* v *Johnson*[18] where 32 bullocks valued at £192 were to be transferred by one party and 100 quarters of barley valued at £215 were to be transferred by the other.

Many 'new for old' car trades would be susceptible to this two contract approach. An alternative approach would be to say that the new car was being sold but that the customer was given the option of tendering the old car in part payment rather than paying the whole price in cash. Customary practices as to part exchange prices would usually make this a more attractive option to the buyer. Sales where the buyer has the option to do or deliver something in partial substitution for the price are by no means unusual. Such an option does not convert the transaction from a sale to an exchange.

Where the component elements of the deal are not separately priced, it is obviously difficult to adopt this analysis. So, if, in *Aldridge* v *Johnson*, the agreement had simply been one for 32 bullocks and £23 to be transferred by one party and 100 quarters of barley by the other, the transaction would have been properly classified as an exchange. It is possible that if the money element in the exchange was predominant and the goods element a makeweight, the transaction should be regarded as a sale, but this situation seems never to have been litigated in England.

Exchange is usually discussed in relation to transfer of goods by each party, but the same principles would seem to apply where goods are transferred in exchange for services.

4.2.4 Contracts for work and materials

Many contracts which are undoubtedly contracts of sale include an element of service. So, if I go to a tailor and buy a suit off the peg, the tailor may agree to raise one of the shoulders since one of my shoulders is higher than the other. The contract would still be one of sale. Conversely, if I take my car to the garage for a service, the garage may fit some new parts, but such a transaction would not normally be regarded as a sale. Of course, in both these cases, the parties could, if they wished, divide the transaction up into two contracts, one of which would be a contract of sale and the other a contract of services, but in practice this is not usually done.

It is clear that there are many contracts in which goods are supplied as part of a package which also includes the provision of services. Some are treated as contracts of sale; others are treated as a separate category called contracts for work and materials. Again, this distinction was important between 1677 and 1954 because contracts of sale over £10 were required to be evidenced in writing, whereas contracts for work and materials were not. Since 1954, the distinction is less important because, although the Sale of Goods Act does not apply to contracts for work and materials, similar rules are usually applied by analogy. This is perhaps as well, since it is far from clear where the line between a sale and work and materials is to be drawn.

---

[18] (1857) 7 E&B 855.

In some cases, it is possible to say that the property transfer element is so predominant that the contract is clearly one of sale; in others, the work element is so large that it is obviously one of work and materials. This approach seems to work with the off-the-peg suit (sale) and car service (work and materials) examples above, but what is the position where there is a substantial element of both property transfer and work?

Unfortunately, in the two leading cases, the courts adopted different tests. In *Lee v Griffen*,[19] a contract by a dentist to make and fit dentures for a patient was said to be a contract of sale on the ground that at the end of the day there was a discernible article which was to be transferred from the dentist to the patient. On the other hand, in *Robinson v Graves*[20] it was said that a contract to paint a portrait was one for work and materials because 'the substance of the contract is the skill and experience of the artist in producing a picture'. These tests appear to be irreconcilable.

The way in which the parties have set up the transaction may sometimes solve the problem of classification. If I select a length of cloth from my tailor, pay for it and then ask for a suit to be made up from it, a court is very likely to say that there are two contracts, one to buy the cloth and the other to make the suit. In commercial life, it is quite common for the customer to provide the materials from which goods are produced. The 'free issue of materials' is discussed below.

Where the contract is classified as one for work and materials, the supplier's obligations as to the quality of the goods will be virtually identical to those of the seller, since the terms to be implied under the Supply of Goods and Services Act 1982 are the same as those to be implied under the Sale of Goods Act 1979. It is worth explaining, however, that the supplier's obligation as to the quality of the work will often be substantially different from that concerning the quality of the materials. This can be simply illustrated with the everyday case of taking a car to a garage for a service. Let us suppose that, during the service the garage supplies and fits a new tyre to the car. As far as the fitting is concerned, the garage's obligation is to ensure that the tyre is fitted with reasonable care and skill. However, it may be that the tyre, though fitted carefully, contains a defect of manufacture not apparent to visual inspection which leads to a blow-out when the car is being driven at speed on the motorway. The garage will be liable for this defect because the tyre was not satisfactory or reasonably fit for its purpose, and this liability is quite independent of any fault on the part of the garage.

In other situations, contracts for work and materials may be treated differently from contracts of sale. In *Hyundai Heavy Industries Co Ltd v Papadopoulos*[21] and *Stocznia Gdanska SA v Latvian Shipping Co*[22] the House of Lords held that, in a shipbuilding contract which was terminated after work had started but before delivery, there was no total failure of consideration. The result would certainly have been different if the transaction had been treated as a sale.

4.2.5 Construction contracts

In most respects, a contract with a builder to build a house is very like a contract with a tailor to make a suit. In both cases, property in the raw materials will pass but the skills deployed

[19] (1861) 1 B&S 272.
[20] [1935] 1 KB 579.
[21] [1980] 2 All ER 29.
[22] [1998] 1 All ER 883.

in converting the raw materials into the finished product appear to make up the greater part of the transaction. There is one obvious difference, however. A contract to buy a ready-made suit is clearly a contract for the sale of goods, but a contract for a house already built is a contract for the sale of land. This has meant that the seller of a house does not normally undertake the implied obligations as to the quality of the product which are undertaken by the seller of goods. It is perhaps doubtful whether this distinction is sensible, since it seems to be based on historical factors rather than on any underlying policy reasons. In modern practice, the purchaser of a new house will often be offered an express guarantee as, for instance, under the National Housebuilders Council (NHBC) scheme, and the prudent purchaser of a secondhand house will have it surveyed, although this will not protect against defects which the reasonably competent surveyor could not be expected to discover.

However, although English law treats sales of off-the-peg suits and houses quite differently, it treats the contract to make suits and build houses very similarly since it will imply into a contract to build a house terms as to the quality of the materials and workmanship. So, in *Young and Marten Ltd* v *McManus Childs Ltd*,[23] a contract for the erection of a building required the builders to use 'Somerset 13' tiles on the roof. They obtained a supply of these tiles (which were only made by one manufacturer) and fixed them with reasonable skill. Unfortunately, the batch of tiles proved to be faulty and let in the rain. The House of Lords held that the builders were in breach of their implied obligations as to fitness for purpose.

4.2.6 Free issue of materials

Tailors who make suits to measure tend to have lengths of suitable cloth in stock. However, not everyone who is in the business of making up something will find it convenient to hold stocks of materials. It may be commercially more satisfactory for the customer to provide the material. This leads to the phenomenon often called 'free issue of materials'. For example, a customer may collect supplies of steel from a stockholder and deliver them to a fabricator for making up according to a specification.

On the face of it, this transaction does not involve any changes in ownership since the steel already belongs to the customer when it is handed to the fabricator. Such a contract would, therefore, be one for the fabricator's services.

The position might be different where the raw materials were invoiced to the supplier and the finished product then invoiced back to the customer. This will often support an inference that the customer had sold the raw materials and was buying the finished product. The most difficult case is perhaps when the finished product is made up partly from materials supplied by the maker and partly from those supplied by the customer. The solution appears to lie in deciding which are the principal materials.

4.2.7 Hire purchase

It seems likely that buyers have always been keener to get the goods than to pay for them, but undoubtedly one of the features of the modern consumer society is the extent of the credit

---

[23] [1969] 1 AC 454.

explosion fuelled by a deliberate decision by suppliers to encourage consumers to acquire goods on credit rather than for cash. This leads to all sorts of problems which are discussed in other chapters,[24] but it is necessary to notice the effect on the range of possible transactions.

One of the risks that a seller who supplies on credit runs is that the customer will fail to pay. A natural response to this is to provide that, if the buyer does not keep up the payments, the seller can repossess the goods. It is not necessarily sufficient, however, to rely on a contractual right to repossess, since a customer who is a bad payer may have other financial problems and could become insolvent leading to any asset being divided up amongst all the creditors. In order to guard against this possibility, a seller may provide that the goods are to remain his or her property until the buyer has paid for them in full and to a large extent this will protect against the buyer's insolvency. (This is discussed more fully below.)[25]

A buyer who is hard up may not simply fail to keep up the payments but may sell the goods in order to raise some cash. Although a buyer who has not yet become the owner should not do this, such a sale will often be effective to transfer ownership to the sub-buyer. In the 1890s, ingenious lawyers were seeking a way to prevent the seller's rights being defeated in this way and invented the contract of hire purchase.

Under this contract, the customer agrees to hire the goods for a period (usually two or three years) and has an option to buy them at the end of this period, usually for a nominal additional sum. The economic expectation of the parties is that the customer will exercise this option and, indeed, the rate charged for hire will be calculated on the basis of the cash price of the goods plus a handsome rate of interest and not on the market rate for hiring them. Nevertheless, the customer does not actually contract to buy the goods, and the House of Lords held in *Helby* v *Matthews*[26] that the contract was not one of sale, and that a sale by the hirer before all the instalments had been paid did not operate to transfer ownership to the sub-buyer. The effect of this decision was that, although economically and commercially a contract of hire purchase had the same objectives as a credit sale, its legal effect was fundamentally different.

A further oddity of hire purchase is that, particularly in the case of motor cars, the finance does not actually come from the supplier but from a finance company, that is, a body whose commercial purpose is to lend money, not to supply goods. The position may be represented diagrammatically in the following figure.

The customer may often think that the goods are being bought on credit from the supplier, whereas, in fact, they are being acquired on hire purchase from the finance company. Typically, the supplier will have the finance company's standard forms which will be completed for the customer to sign. These will usually amount to an offer to sell the car to the finance

[24] See Chapter 7 (Consumer protection) and Chapter 8 (Consumer credit law and regulation).
[25] See section 4.6.3.2.
[26] [1895] AC 471. For a modern example of a case which was treated as a conditional sale although labelled hire purchase, see *Forthright Finance Ltd* v *Carlyle Finance Ltd* [1997] 4 All ER 90, where the contract required the customer to pay all the instalments making up the price of the car.

company and an offer by the customer to take the car on hire purchase terms. Both contracts will come into existence when the finance company decides to adopt the transaction. In the standard situation, there is indeed no contract between the supplier and the customer, though courts have been willing to discover such a contract with relative ease. For instance, in *Andrews v Hopkinson*[27] a car dealer said to a customer: 'It is a good little bus; I would stake my life on it.' This was held to be a contractually binding warranty. In that case, the contract between dealer and customer was what lawyers call a 'collateral' contract, that is, one dependent on the main contract between the finance company and customer. Implicitly, the dealer is treated as saying: 'If you take this car on hire purchase terms from the finance company, I will guarantee it.'

Instead of taking the car on hire purchase terms, the customer might go to a bank for a personal loan in order to buy the car for cash. In substance, this would be a very similar transaction; the interest charged would be comparable and, indeed, many of the finance companies are owned by banks. It will be seen, however, that the legal form is very different. This artificiality has been the source of many difficulties.

From the 1890s onwards, hire purchase became a very popular technique for supplying goods on credit. It has been widely used in consumer transactions but is by no means unknown in commercial ones. It has always co-existed with conditional sales, that is, transactions where the supplier delivers goods but on condition that the ownership shall remain in the seller until all instalments have been paid. The modern tendency embodied in the comprehensive and complex Consumer Credit Act 1974 is to treat all forms of instalment credit in the same way.

4.2.8 Hire

In practice, whether the contract is one for sale, exchange, work and materials or hire purchase, the customer will end up as the owner of the goods. However, the customer may be more concerned with the use than the ownership of the goods. One reason for this could be that only short-term use is intended, for example, a car which is hired for a week's holiday, but there may be other reasons. Many British families choose to rent rather than buy a television, despite countless articles demonstrating that, if the television lasts for more than three years, it is cheaper to buy it than to rent it. Perhaps the most plausible reason for this is the belief that rental companies offer better service than sellers or independent repairers.

A contract in which goods are transferred from the owner to a user for a time, with the intention that they will be returned later, is a contract of hire. It is an essential part of such a contract that the possession of the goods is transferred. So, a number of transactions which would colloquially be described as 'hire' are not accurately so called. For instance, one might well talk of hiring a bus for a school outing but this would not strictly be correct if, as would usually be the case, the bus came with a driver. In that case, the owner would remain in possession through the driver and the contract would be simply one for use of the bus. The position is the same in a commercial context, where a piece of plant, such as a bulldozer or a crane, is supplied with an operator (except where, as is often the case, the operator is transferred with the equipment and becomes for the time being the employee of the hirer). In this latter case, it would be accurate to describe the transaction as hire.

---

[27] [1957] 1 QB 229.

4.2.9 Leases

In recent years, it has been common for contracts for the use of goods to be made and described as 'leases'. So, a car may be 'leased' rather than bought, as may major items of office equipment or computers. There can be a number of advantages in this from the customer's point of view. One is that such transactions appear to be of an income rather than a capital nature, so they will not show up in the company's balance sheet as a capital purchase. This can be attractive as it may make the company's financial position look better. Nor is this necessarily a cosmetic benefit since there can be perfectly good business reasons for wishing to avoid tying up capital in equipment, particularly where it has to be borrowed at high rates of interest. Apart from these financial advantages, there may also be tax benefits for a business in leasing equipment rather than buying it.

Although the term 'lease' is very commonly used to describe such transactions, there is at present no separate legal category of leases of goods, unlike leases of land which have been recognised from the 12th century. Therefore, in law, most leases will simply be contracts of hire. In some cases, however, there may be an understanding that at the end of the period of the lease the customer may or will buy the goods. This may amount to no more than a non-binding arrangement, in which case it will have no effect on the legal nature of the transaction. If, however, the customer has an option to buy the goods at the end of the lease, the transaction will in substance be one of hire purchase. If the customer has agreed to buy the goods at the end of the lease, then it would seem that the contract is actually one of sale.

It is worth noting that, in many 'leases', the 'lessor' is not the supplier but a bank or finance house. In such cases, the supplier sells the goods to a bank which then leases them to the customer. This produces a triangular relationship similar to that in a hire purchase contract, shown diagrammatically in section 4.2.7. This rather artificial arrangement can give rise to difficulties, particularly when the goods turn out to be defective. It is natural to assume that the supplier is the person primarily responsible for the quality of the goods, but the fact that there is usually no contract between the supplier and the customer makes it difficult to give effect to this assumption. The lessor would be under implied obligations as to the quality of the goods, but is likely to have attempted in its standard form of lease to escape from these obligations. The confusion between supplier and lessor is accentuated by the practice, apparently common in the photocopier leasing trade, of the finance house adopting a name confusingly similar to that of the supplier.[28]

4.2.10 Practical significance of these distinctions

Many readers may feel that this quite elaborate catalogue of different transactions is a typical example of the passion of lawyers for making things more complicated. The practical difficulty is the predominance of statute law in this area. Each of the statutes deals with a particular contract and each is therefore peculiar to that contract. This is particularly so with the Sale of Goods Act 1979, which applies only to contracts for the sale of goods strictly defined and which is much the most important statute in the field.

---

[28] See *Lease Management Services v Purnell Secretarial Services* [1994] 13 Tr LR 337.

Judges have reduced these difficulties in practice by being willing, in some cases, to apply the rules of the Sale of Goods Act by analogy with other contracts. This was particularly true in relation to implied undertakings as to the ownership and quality of the goods, and Parliament adopted this approach in 1982 when it passed the Supply of Goods and Services Act. This provided for implied terms as to ownership and quality in contracts of exchange and work and materials, which were in identical terms to those contained in the Sale of Goods Act.

Nevertheless, the 1982 Act only dealt with these problems and, important as they are, they make up only a proportion of the whole. No doubt, in some other areas, judges will solve problems by applying the Sale of Goods Act 1979 by analogy. This technique works best where the solution can, at least in theory, be explained as turning on the implied understanding of the parties, but there are some provisions in the Sale of Goods Act which cannot possibly be explained in such a way (see particularly the rules discussed in s. 6).

4.3 Meaning and types of goods

This section deals with some basic definitions. This is not very exciting but it is essential in order to understand what follows.

4.3.1 The definition of goods

LEGISLATIVE PROVISION

Section 61(1) of the Sale of Goods Act 1979 states that 'goods':

> Includes all personal chattels other than things in action and money, [and, in Scotland, all corporeal moveables except money] and, in particular, 'goods' includes emblements, industrial growing crops, and things attached to or forming part of the land which are agreed to be severed before sale or under the contract of sale.

The words in brackets reflect the different legal terminology of Scotland and may be ignored for present purposes. The remainder of the text uses some unfamiliar language and requires further explanation.

Historically, English lawyers have divided property into 'real property' (basically, land) and 'personal property' (all forms of wealth other than land). This terminology has found its way into ordinary usage. In origin, real property was property which could be recovered by a real action, that is, an action which leads to the recovery of property *in specie* and not to damages for its non-return. Unfortunately, when this distinction was first drawn (in the 12th century), only freehold estates could be recovered by real action. Purists therefore took the view that leasehold estates were not real property. By the 15th century, leasehold interests were as effectively protected by the courts as freehold interests, but the terminology survived and leasehold interests were called 'chattels real'. This terminology is now archaic, but it survived long enough to influence the definition in 1893, and the 1979 Act simply repeats the wording of the 1893 Act.

POINT OF INTEREST

Etymologically, the words 'chattel' and 'cattle' appear to be different spellings of the same old Norman French word, which meant property, but, over the centuries, 'cattle' has been narrowed to its modem meaning of livestock while the word 'chattel' has retained its wider meaning. So, 'personal chattels' would mean all forms of property other than 'real property' (freehold interests in land) and 'chattels real' (leasehold interests in land). The Act goes on specifically to exclude 'things in action' and 'money'. 'Things in action' are those forms of property which cannot be physically possessed so that they can only be enjoyed by bringing an action. This includes such things as shares, patents, copyrights, trademarks, rights under bills of exchange and policies of insurance. The exclusion of 'money' presumably means that a contract to purchase foreign exchange is not a sale of goods. On the other hand, a contract to purchase banknotes issued by the Confederate States of America probably is a contract for the sale of goods, since the notes will have been bought for their historic interest and are no longer usable as currency.

The second half of the definition deals with the case of the sale of growing crops, etc, which has already been discussed.

A problem of great practical importance is whether computer software is goods. Where it is supplied on a disk, it would seem that the disk is goods but, in practice, software suppliers often simply install the system on the customer's computer(s) and go away. In this case, there is no physical object which is transferred and the software supplier will often retain owner-ship of the program, simply giving the customer a licence. In the Court of Appeal, in *St Albans City and District Council* v *International Computers Ltd*[29] Sir Iain Glidewell took the position, *obiter*, that, if not goods, software should be treated like goods for the purpose of the implied terms as to quality. It must, however, be arguable that the software supplier is providing a service rather than goods and is, therefore, only under a duty of care.

4.3.2 Existing and future goods

The Sale of Goods Act 1979 contains two explicit sets of subdivisions of goods. One is existing and future goods and the other specific and unascertained goods (discussed in 'Specific and unascertained goods', below).

---

[29] [1996] 4 All ER 481.

LEGISLATIVE PROVISION

Section 5(1) says that:

> The goods which form the subject of a contract of sale may be either existing goods, owned or possessed by the seller, or goods to be manufactured or acquired by him after the making of the contract of sale, in this Act called future goods.

Future goods are also defined by s. 61(1) as:

> . . . goods to be manufactured or acquired by the seller after the making of the contract of sale. It will be seen that goods which are in existence may be future goods, as where the seller has agreed to sell goods which at the time of the contract are owned by someone else. A typical example of future goods would arise where the seller was to make the goods, but the category would appear also to include things which will come into existence naturally, as where a dog breeder agrees to sell a puppy from the litter of a pregnant bitch. In such a case, there is an element of risk that things will not turn out as the parties hope; for instance, that all the puppies die or that the buyer had contracted for a dog puppy and all the puppies are bitches. In such a case, the court will have to analyse the agreement to see whether the seller's agreement was conditional on there being a live puppy or a puppy of the right sex.

4.3.3 Specific and unascertained goods

Section 61(1) defines 'specific goods' as 'goods identified and agreed on at the time a contract of sale is made'.

Unascertained goods are not defined by the Act but it is clear that goods which are not specific are unascertained. It is important to emphasise that the distinction relates to the position at the time the contract of sale is made. Later events will not make the goods specific but they may, and often will, make them ascertained.

As we shall see the distinction between specific and unascertained goods is of particular importance in the passing of property between seller and buyer. It may prove helpful, therefore, to explain further that unascertained goods may be of at least three different kinds.

One possibility is that the goods are to be manufactured by the seller. Here, they will usually become ascertained as a result of the process of manufacture, although, if the seller is making similar goods for two or more buyers, some further acts may be necessary to make it clear which goods have been appropriated to which buyer.

The second possibility is that the goods are sold by a generic description, such as '500 tons Western White Wheat'. In such a case, the seller could perform the contract by delivering any 500 tons of Western White Wheat (provided that it was of satisfactory quality, etc). If the seller was a trader in wheat, they might well have more than 500 tons of wheat but would not be bound to use that wheat to perform the contract; they could and often would choose to buy further wheat on the market to fulfil the order. Where there is an active market, sellers and buyers may be entering into a complex series of sales and purchases according to their perception of how the market is moving and leaving who gets what wheat to be sorted out later. This is obviously particularly likely where the sales are for delivery at some future date rather than for immediate despatch. In this situation, the seller may form plans to use a parcel of wheat to deliver to buyer A and another parcel to buyer B. Usually, the forming of these plans will not make the goods ascertained until the seller makes some act of appropriation which prevents a change of mind.

A third, and perhaps less obvious, possibility is that the goods may be part of an undivided bulk. So, if the seller has 1,000 tons of Western White Wheat on board the SS Challenger and sells 500 tons to A and 500 tons to B, these are sales of unascertained goods, since it is not possible to tell which 500 tons has been sold to which purchaser. Important practical consequences flow from this rule: in this situation, the goods become ascertained only when it can be established which part of the cargo is appropriated to which contract. So, in *Karlhamns Oljefabriker* v *Eastport Navigation*[30] 22,000 tons of copra were loaded on board a ship in the Philippines, of which 6,000 tons were sold to a Swedish buyer. At this stage, of course, the goods were unascertained. The ship called at Rotterdam and at Hamburg on its way to Sweden and 16,000 tons were offloaded at these two ports. It was held that the goods became ascertained on the completion of discharge in Hamburg, as it was then possible to say with certainty that the remainder of the cargo was destined for the purchaser. This rule was significantly modified by the Sale of Goods (Amendment) Act 1995. Under the terms of this Act, if a seller sells part of an undivided bulk, the buyer may become a tenant in common of a proportional share of the whole bulk (see section 4.6).

4.3.4 Sales and agreements to sell

LEGISLATIVE PROVISION

Section 2 of the Sale of Goods Act 1979 draws a distinction between sales and agreements to sell. Section 2(4) provides:

> Where under a contract of sale the property in the goods is transferred from the seller to the buyer, the contract is called a sale.

Section 2(5) states:

> Where under a contract of sale the transfer of the property in the goods is to take place at a future time or subject to some condition later to be fulfilled, the contract is called an agreement to sell.

The reason for this distinction arises from an ambiguity in the word 'sale' which may refer either to the contract between buyer and seller or to the transfer of ownership from seller to buyer which is the object of the agreement. In English law, it is possible, in principle, for ownership to pass from seller to buyer simply by agreement, without either delivery of the goods or payment of the price.

---

[30] [1982] 1 All ER 208.

ISSUE BOX

1. In what ways will studying sales law be different from studying contract law?
2. I go to a tailor who agrees to make a suit for me out of material which I choose from his store. What kind of contract is this? Why might it matter?
3. I take my car to a garage for a service. During the service they fit a new tyre. On the way home the tyre explodes and the car crashes. In what circumstances will the garage be liable?
4. When do goods become ascertained?

4.4 Price

4.4.1 Introduction

In a contract of sale, the irreducible minimum of obligations is for the seller to deliver the goods and the buyer to pay the price. This section considers the rules about the ascertainment of the price, and section 4.5 describes the rules about payment of the price and delivery of the goods.

LEGISLATIVE PROVISION

Sections 8 and 9 of the Sale of Goods Act 1979 deal with the price. Section 8 provides:

(1) The price in a contract of sale may be fixed by the contract, or may be left to be fixed in a manner agreed by the contract, or may be determined by the course of dealings between the parties.

(2) Where the price is not determined as mentioned in subs (1) above, the buyer must pay a reasonable price.

(3) What is a reasonable price is a question of fact dependent on the circumstances of each particular case.

Section 9 states:

(1) Where there is an agreement to sell goods on the terms that the price is to be fixed by the valuation of a third party, and he cannot or does not make the valuation, the agreement is avoided; but if the goods or any part of them have been delivered to and appropriated by the buyer, he must pay a reasonable price for them.

(2) Where the third party is prevented from making the valuation by the fault of the seller or buyer, the party not at fault may maintain an action for damages against the party at fault.

These sections do not appear in fact to cover all the difficulties that can arise, and in practice resort is also made to the general principles of contract law.

4.4.2 The parties say nothing about the price

The fact that no price has been agreed might be good evidence that the parties had not completed a contract but it is clear that in practice people often make binding contracts without having agreed on the payment terms. Many people will ask a solicitor to handle the buying or selling of their house without agreeing or even asking about the cost, though the practice of asking for an estimate and 'shopping around' is becoming more widespread. Similarly, a customer may ring up an established supplier and ask for certain specified goods to be sent round without asking the price. In such a case, it is clear that there is a contract to buy at a reasonable price (s. 8(2)).

Section 8(3) of the Sale of Goods Act 1979 provides that what is a reasonable price is a question of fact. If the seller is in business, evidence of his or her usual prices will be good evidence of what is a reasonable price but, in theory at least, it is not decisive. Undoubtedly, however, the scope for arguing that the seller's usual prices are not reasonable must be limited in some cases. If a Chelsea housewife telephones an order to Harrods Food Hall, it may be doubted whether she can resist paying their standard charges on the ground that she could have bought the goods more cheaply at a supermarket. No doubt, one reason for this is that a court would be entitled to take into account the size, location and expense of the seller's premises and the quality of service offered in deciding what was reasonable. Another different argument pointing to the same result would be that it is the universal practice of English grocers to price the goods on their shelves so that customers may reasonably expect that all goods will be sold at marked prices, no more and no less.

Obviously, however, there are sales where the seller is not in business or is not in the business of selling goods of the kind sold. In such cases, there will be no seller's standard price to appeal to and the court will have to do the best it can with such evidence as the parties present to it.

4.4.3 The parties fix the price in the contract

This is the simplest and probably most common situation. Obviously, the parties may fix the price in a number of different ways. I may sell my car for £3,000 but, if I take the car to the filling station, I would ask for as much petrol as was needed to fill the tank at 105p per litre; in the first case, a global price and, in the second, a unit price. It may make sense in some cases to fix a price in relation to some objective external measure, for example, 1,000 barrels of oil delivered on 1 December at the best price quoted that day on the Rotterdam spot market.

POINT OF INTEREST

An important point often overlooked in practice is what the prices include. Retail sellers are usually obliged to quote VAT inclusive prices but, in most other cases, prices are VAT exclusive unless otherwise agreed. It may be important to know whether the price covers packing and delivery. Such matters are covered in well-drafted conditions of sale and purchase but are otherwise often forgotten.

4.4.4 The price is left to be fixed in a manner agreed by the contract

Section 8(1) of the Sale of Goods Act 1979 clearly contemplates that the contract may leave the prices to be fixed later in an agreed manner. One such manner would be third-party valuation, but this is expressly dealt with by s. 9 and is discussed separately below. The Act is silent on other methods of price fixing and the matter is not free from difficulties.

One possibility is that the contract may provide for the price to be fixed by the seller (or the buyer). At first sight, it seems strange for one party to agree that the price is to be fixed by the other, but such contracts are in fact quite common. A classic example is the contracts made by oil companies to supply petrol to filling stations. These are nearly all on a long-term basis because the companies are anxious to have guaranteed outlets. Typically, therefore, filling station operators agree to take all their supplies of petrol from a particular company for a period of five years. Obviously, it is not possible to make such a contract at a fixed price since no one knows what the price of oil will be next month, let alone over the next five years. It would be legally permissible to provide for price indexation but, in practice, very difficult to find a sufficiently flexible and comprehensive index. Often, the problem is solved by providing that the price is to be the list price at the date of delivery. There have been at least 20 litigated cases arising out of such contracts over the last 50 years, since owners of filling stations are often anxious to escape from one petrol company into the arms of another, but in none of these cases has it been argued that the price agreement is invalid.

One explanation for this would be that the buyer is protected in such cases by the requirement to pay the list price since this is the price that is being charged to all filling stations tied to that particular company and, if a company were to treat all of its outlets badly, then those which were approaching renewal date would switch to another supplier. If this is right, then a seller who agrees to sell at list price at date of delivery and who does not in fact have a price list may be in a different position. It would be possible to say that unilateral price fixing is only adequately certain where it contains some objective element.

However, in *May and Butcher Ltd v R*[31] Lord Dunedin said:

> With regard to price, it is a perfectly good contract to say that the price is to be settled by the buyer.

In *Lombard Tricity Finance Ltd v Paton*[32] this was assumed to be correct by the Court of Appeal and was applied to a contract which entitled a lender to change the interest rate unilaterally, but in *Paragon Finance PLC v Staunton*[33] the Court of Appeal held that such variations should not be dishonest, capricious or arbitrary.

Rather than leave the price to be fixed by one party, the parties may agree that the price shall be fixed by agreement between them later. This is a common but potentially dangerous course. There is no problem if the parties do agree on a price but difficulties arise if they do not. It might be thought that, in that case, s. 8(2) would apply and a reasonable price would be due. However, in *May and Butcher v R*[34] the House of Lords held otherwise. In that case,

---

[31] [1934] 2 KB 17n.
[32] [1989] 1 All ER 918. See also *Shell UK Ltd v Lostock Garage* [1976] 1 WLR 1187, where the question went by default.
[33] [2001] EWCA Civ 1466; [2002] 2 All ER 248.
[34] [1934] 2 KB 17n.

there was a contract for the sale of tentage at a price to be agreed between the parties. The parties failed to agree and the House of Lords held that there was no contract. The argument which was accepted was that s. 8(2) only applied where there was no agreement as to the price so that its operation was excluded where the parties had provided a mechanism for fixing a price which had not worked. This decision has never been overruled and is still, in theory, binding. Nevertheless, the courts have not always followed it.

In *Foley v Classique Coaches*[35] the plaintiffs sold land to the defendants who agreed, as part of the same contract, to buy all their petrol from the plaintiffs 'at a price to be agreed between the parties in writing and from time to time'. The transfer of the land was completed and the defendants later argued that the agreement to buy the petrol was not binding as the price was uncertain. This argument was rejected by the Court of Appeal. One can see a number of possible factors influencing this decision. The agreement to buy the petrol was only part, and a relatively small part, of the whole agreement; the rest of the agreement had been performed; the defendants had got the land; and it is reasonable to think that their undertaking to buy petrol made them more attractive purchasers to the plaintiff so that they got a better price. The court also attached importance to a clause in the contract providing for disputes to be referred to arbitration, though the general principle is that an arbitrator ought to reach exactly the same decision as the judge.

These two cases reflect a tension which exists throughout the law of contract. On the one hand, judges feel that the parties should take care in the formulation of their agreements, employ competent lawyers and leave no loose ends; on the other hand, there is a feeling that the law should seek to serve the realities of commercial life and, if there is a deal, there should be a contract. Probably, no judge holds in its extreme form either view, but some clearly lean more to one side than to the other. Two recent cases from the general law of contract suggest that, at the moment at least, the pendulum has swung in favour of the second view. In *Beer v Bowden*[36] there was a lease for 14 years. The lease provided that the rent should be £1,250 a year for the first five years and thereafter:

> . . . such rent as shall be agreed between the landlords and the tenant . . . and in any case . . . not less than the yearly rental of £1,250.

The contract provided no machinery for fixing the rent if the parties did not agree after the first five years and the tenant argued that he was entitled to stay for the full term at £1,250 a year. The Court of Appeal rejected this argument. It said that the purpose of the minimum rent provision was to cover the situation where rents generally fell and that it did not indicate that if there was no agreement the rent should stay at £1,250. The court considered that the parties had intended to agree that the rent should be a reasonable one. (It is important to note that, in this case, the tenant did not argue that the whole contract was invalid for uncertainty since the last thing he wished to do was to abandon the lease.)

The case suggests that the provision of defective machinery for reaching agreement is not inconsistent with an inference that the parties intend a reasonable price. This view is strongly reinforced by the decision of the House of Lords in *Sudbrook Trading Estate v Eggleton*.[37] In that case, there was a lease with an option for the tenant to buy the landlord's interest at a price

---

[35] [1934] 2 KB 1.
[36] [1981] 1 WLR 522; [1981] 1 All ER 1071.
[37] [1982] 3 All ER 1; [1983] 1 AC 444.

to be agreed. The lease, which was clearly professionally drawn up, contained a provision that, if the parties did not agree on the price, it was to be fixed by two valuers, one to be appointed by either side. The lease did not provide for what was to happen if the valuers were not appointed. The tenant sought to exercise the option; the landlord by this time did not wish to sell, refused to appoint its valuer and argued that there was no binding contract. There was an unbroken series of cases for over 100 years accepting this argument but the House of Lords rejected it. Their view was that in substance the parties clearly intended to agree on a reasonable price. This was reinforced by the provision for the appointment of valuers, since they are professional people who would be bound to apply professional, and therefore reasonable, standards. It followed that the agreement was clear and should not fail simply because the parties had provided defective machinery for carrying it out. If necessary, the court could provide a means for discovering a reasonable price. There is, therefore, a good chance that a court will hold where the parties do not agree that they intended the price to be a reasonable one. This is particularly likely where the goods have actually been delivered and accepted by the buyer. Nevertheless, it remains imprudent for the parties to make such an agreement granted that courts sometimes hold such agreements to be inadequately certain. These dangers can be avoided entirely by providing machinery for dealing with those cases where later agreement proves impossible or by simply providing that the price 'shall be such as the parties may later agree or in default of agreement of a reasonable price'.

4.4.5 Fixing the price by third-party valuation

This is dealt with by s. 9 of the Sale of Goods Act 1979, which is set out above. The provisions are reasonably straightforward. Price fixing by third-party valuation is valid but dependent on the third party actually undertaking the valuation. If one party prevents the valuation, he or she is said to be liable to an action. Presumably, it would be the seller who would usually prevent the valuation by not making the goods available. It is worth noting that the result of such obstruction by the seller is not a contract to sell at a reasonable price as is the case where the goods are delivered and no valuation takes place, but an action for damages. This may not make much difference in practice, since what the buyer has been deprived of is the chance to purchase the goods at the price the valuer would have fixed and a court would almost certainly hold this to be the same as a reasonable price. (In many cases, the buyer will not in fact recover substantial damages. This will become clearer after reading section 4.10.)

An important question is what, if anything, sellers can do if they think the valuation too low, or what buyers can do if they think it is too high. No doubt, the valuation is not binding if it can be shown that the valuer was fraudulently acting in concert with the other party. Apart from this case, it would seem that it is binding, as between seller and buyer. However, the party who is disappointed with the valuation will have an action against the valuer if it can be shown that the valuation was negligent. This was clearly accepted by the House of Lords in *Arenson v Casson*,[38] a case involving the sale of shares in a private company at a price fixed by valuation. In order to show that a valuation was negligent, it is not sufficient to show that other valuers would have reached a different figure. It must be shown that the figure produced was not one that could have been arrived at by a reasonably competent valuer.

[38] [1977] AC 747.

4.4.6 **Price fluctuations**

If the contract is to run over a long period, a price which appears sensible at the time the contract is made may come to seem quite inappropriate later on. Two questions arise in this context. The first concerns the steps the parties can take to provide for economic or market fluctuations; the second is whether the law will intervene to relieve a party who has entered into a fixed-price contract which has been overtaken by massive inflation (or indeed deflation).

We have already seen that the parties may, at least in some cases, deal with price fluctuations by allowing one party to vary the price, but clearly, in many cases, such an arrangement will not be acceptable to the other party involved. The parties may agree to renegotiate prices from time to time but, apart from the difficulties which have already been pointed out, an endless cycle of renegotiation may not be commercially sensible. It may, therefore, be desirable to provide a more structured solution, either by linking the price to an index or by providing a formula for measuring increases or decreases in costs. At one time, it was thought, because of some remarks by Denning LJ in *Treseder-Griffin* v *Cooperative Insurance Society Ltd*,[39] that such attempts might be contrary to public policy. The argument was that resistance to inflation demanded unwavering allegiance to nominalism; the principle that a pound is a pound is a pound. It is true that many economists think that systems in which all wages are indexed to the cost of living fuel inflation, since wage increases filter fairly quickly back into the cost of living so that the increases feed on themselves and multiply. However, it is quite a different matter to forbid individuals to recognise the realities of inflation and guard against it, and this was recognised in the case of *Multiservice Bookbinding* v *Marden*[40] where an English mortgage in which the capital repayments and interest were tied to the Swiss franc was held to be valid.

Granted that provision against cost fluctuations in a long-term contract is permissible, how should it best be done? The most extensive experience is in relation to construction contracts where two systems have emerged. One is to take a baseline price and permit additions (and reductions) because of prescribed increases (or decreases) in cost. In principle, this should produce a fair result, but there are serious practical difficulties in defining which cost increases can be passed on and to what extent, especially as material and labour costs are not spread evenly over the life of the contract. This solution tends to produce complex formulae and much scope for dispute.

The other system is for the basic price to be indexed. In the building industry, there are appropriate indices which are independent and regularly published. This produces a simple calculation and it may be assumed that, in the long run, occasional minor roughnesses even themselves out. However, this system does depend on the existence of an appropriate index. It would not be sensible, for example, to link sales of oil to the Retail Price Index since that may be going up when the price of oil is coming down. It would probably not make sense to tie petrol prices at the pump to OPEC-posted prices or prices on the Rotterdam spot market, since the first may be too stable and the latter too volatile to produce a sensible result. To pursue the index solution therefore requires the most careful examination of whether or not the index under consideration is appropriate.

---

[39] [1956] 2 QB 127.
[40] [1979] Ch 84.

Earlier, a question was proposed as to whether or not English law would relieve a party who had entered into a fixed-price contract which was overtaken by later events. In general, the answer is that it will not and indeed there is only one case which contradicts that rule. This was the decision of the Court of Appeal in the striking case of *Staffordshire Area Health Authority v South Staffordshire Waterworks*.[41] In this case, the defendant entered into a contract in 1929 to supply water to the plaintiffs. The contract provided that 'at all times hereafter' the hospital was to receive 5,000 gallons of water a day free and all the additional water it required at the rate of 7 old pence (2.9 new pence) per 1,000 gallons. (This rate was about 70 per cent of the then market rate.) By 1975, the market rate was 45p per 1,000 gallons. The Court of Appeal held that the defendants were entitled to give notice to terminate the agreement.

A number of observations may be made about the case. First, the termination came 46 years after the contract was made and the market price was then some 16 times the contract price (depending on what arithmetical allowance is made for the free gallons). In any view, therefore, the facts were strong and are unlikely to recur often. Secondly, only one of the judges (Lord Denning MR) explicitly based his decision on the effects of inflation; the other two judges purported to decide the case by reading the words 'at all times hereafter' as controlling the price only so long as the agreement continued and not as referring to its duration. It is difficult to believe, however, that they ignored the actual situation in arriving at this somewhat strange construction of the agreement.

4.5   Delivery and payment

4.5.1 Introduction

LEGISLATIVE PROVISION

Section 27 of the Sale of Goods Act 1979 provides:

> It is the duty of the seller to deliver the goods and of the buyer to accept and pay for them in accordance with the terms of the contract of sale.

Section 28 states:

> Unless otherwise agreed, delivery of the goods and payment of the price are concurrent conditions, that is to say, the seller must be ready and willing to give possession of the goods to the buyer in exchange for the price and the buyer must be ready and willing to pay the price in exchange for possession of the goods.

This section considers the legal problems arising from the duty of the seller to deliver the goods and of the buyer to accept and pay for them. It will discuss, first, the problems relating to payment and the relationship between payment and delivery, then, the rules about delivery and finally, the buyer's duty of acceptance.

[41] [1978] 3 All ER 769; [1968] 1 WLR 1387.

4.5.2 **Payment**

Section 28 states that, unless otherwise agreed, payment and delivery are concurrent conditions. This means that they should take place at the same time. Obviously, the parties may have agreed expressly or by implication that payment is to precede delivery or the other way round and this is extremely common. In practice, payment and delivery cannot take place simultaneously without the willing cooperation of both parties and this means, as the second half of s. 28 makes clear, that the seller who complains that the buyer has not paid must show that he or she was ready and willing to deliver and, conversely, a buyer who complains of the seller's failure to deliver must show that he or she was ready and willing to pay the price. In practice, this is often done by tendering the goods or the price respectively.

It is worth examining in a little more detail the position where the parties agree that payment is to precede delivery or vice versa. In commercial sales, it is often agreed that goods will be delivered on usual trade terms, such as payment within 30 days or payment within 30 days of receipt of invoice. The effect of such an agreement is that the seller must deliver first and cannot subsequently have a change of mind and insist on payment on delivery. This would be so even if there were grounds for thinking that the buyer might not be able to pay. (It is arguably a defect in English law that, unlike some other systems, once the contract is under way, there is no right to require convincing assurances that the other party can and will perform.)[42] A seller in this position has, in effect, to gamble on whether or not any information about the buyer's inability to pay turns out to be true, since the loss from delivering goods to a buyer who cannot pay for them will usually be greater than any liability in damages that might be incurred for non-delivery.

For the same reason, a seller cannot refuse to deliver because the buyer has been late in paying on an earlier contract. Sellers often think they are entitled to do this and frequently do, but it is clear that this is wrong. In *Total Oil v Thompson*[43] a petrol company entered into a typical contract to supply petrol to a filling station. The contract provided for delivery on credit terms, but the filling station owner turned out to be a bad payer and the petrol company attempted to change to a cash on delivery basis. It was held that they were not entitled to do this. A seller is, of course, entitled to change the payment terms in respect of future contracts.

It may be agreed that the buyer is to pay in advance. This often happens in international sales where the buyer agrees to pay by banker's letter of credit. In this case, it is clear that the seller's obligation to deliver is conditional on the buyer having opened a letter of credit which complies with the terms of the contract. So, in *Alan Co Ltd v El Nasr Export and Import Co*,[44] there was a contract for the sale of coffee beans and the buyer agreed to open a credit in Kenyan shillings. In fact, the credit opened was in pounds sterling, though for the correct amount at the then prevailing rate of exchange. It was held that the seller's obligation to deliver (indeed, to ship) the goods was conditional on the buyer opening a credit in Kenyan shillings.

Questions may arise about the form of payment. The starting point is that, in the absence of contrary agreement, the seller is entitled to be paid in cash but, of course, the parties are free to make other agreements.

[42] *Cf.* Uniform Commercial Code 2.609.
[43] [1972] 1 QB 318.
[44] [1972] 2 QB 189.

Twenty years ago the main alternative to cash would have been payment by cheque. Now cheques are much less used and many payments are made by debit or credit card or by electronic transfers between bank accounts. The possibilities are more fully discussed in Chapter 7. In many cases it will be easy to infer that a seller has agreed to accept payment by one or more of these methods. Express statements are common. A seller may for instance stipulate for a slightly larger payment if he is to be paid by credit card (this is because the credit card company will levy a charge on him.) Questions may arise where the chosen method of payment fails.

In international sales, the price may be expressed in a foreign currency. In this situation, it is vital to distinguish between the money of account and the money of payment. The money of account is the currency which measures the extent of the buyer's obligation; the money of payment is the currency in which payment is actually to be made. The two may be, but need not be, the same. The distinction is, of course, crucial in the case of fluctuations in currency value between the date of the contract and the date of payment. So, it is the practice of the Rotterdam spot market in oil for all transactions to be in US dollars even though, as will often be the case, neither buyer nor seller is American. In such a market, which is highly international, there are powerful arguments of convenience for all transactions being measured in a single currency.[45]

4.5.3 Delivery

The first thing to say about 'delivery' is that the word bears a meaning in the Sale of Goods Act 1979 quite different from its colloquial meaning. If I say that a grocer will deliver, this would usually be taken to mean that the groceries will be brought to the house of a customer. In the Sale of Goods Act, the word does not have any necessary connotation of taking the goods to the customer and refers simply to the seller's obligation to hand the goods over. In the basic case, the seller performs his or her obligations by making the goods available to the buyer at his or her (the seller's) place of business. It is undoubtedly prudent for the parties to spend some time thinking about delivery, and well-drafted conditions of sale or purchase contain provisions which deal with such questions as whether the customer is to collect the goods 'ex works' and, if so, whether the goods will be packed and whether labour will be available to help with loading. In many cases, sellers may quote a price which includes carriage and, in this event, it is desirable to fix the destination and whether or not the price includes unloading and positioning or installation. The Act provides an answer to some of these questions, which applies in the absence of contrary agreement. In other cases, the parties may use shorthand expressions like 'FOB Felixstowe' or 'CIF Hamburg' to which the courts have attached a body of meaning arising out of scores of litigated cases.

4.5.3.1 The meaning of delivery, s. 61(1) of the Sale of Goods Act 1979

Section 61(1) states that 'delivery' means 'voluntary transfer of possession from one person to another'. This is slightly misleading, as it suggests that delivery necessarily involves the

---

[45] See L. Collins (general ed.), *Dicey, Morris and Collins: The Conflict of Laws* (14th edn, Sweet and Maxwell, London, 2006) pp. 1975–1983.

seller handing the goods to the buyer. Although the typical case is undoubtedly that of the seller making the goods available to the buyer at the place and time set out in the contract, there are many cases where this does not happen.

In some cases, the buyer will already have been in possession of the goods. A typical example would be where goods were being acquired on hire purchase and the customer exercised an option to buy the goods at the end of the period of hire. It would be absurd to require formal delivery and redelivery of the goods. They are sufficiently delivered to the buyer in this case because there is a change in the capacity in which the goods are possessed. Conversely, the goods may be delivered even though the seller stays in possession, if the capacity in which he or she is in possession changes. An example would be the practical position of the dealer in the standard hire purchase car triangle (see section 4.2). The dealer sells the car to the finance company but the car is never physically transferred to the finance company. It goes straight from dealer to customer. Physical transfer to the customer is a sufficient delivery to the finance company because the customer has only received possession because of a contract which recognises that the finance company is the owner of the car.[46]

In some cases, it may be sufficient to transfer the means of control. So, delivery of a car may be made by transfer of the keys, and delivery of goods in a warehouse in the same way. This last example is very old and was discussed by Roman lawyers. It is sometimes called a symbolic delivery but, at least for classical Roman law, delivery of the key at the warehouse was required and this strongly suggests that control was the test.[47]

CASE

Albright and Wilson UK Ltd v Biochem Ltd[48]

In this case Biochem Ltd, a chemical producer, had two different plants (A and B) on the same site. It placed two different orders with two different suppliers P and Q, one of which was to go to plant A and the other to plant B. By an unfortunate mischance both suppliers employed the same carrier and the driver was confused as to what he was doing. The result was that the goods from supplier P which should have gone to plant A went to plant B but with a delivery order appearing to show that it was what plant B was expecting. This led to the mixture of 23 tons of sodium chlorate with existing stocks of EPI and to an explosion. The House of Lords held that this amounted to a purported delivery by supplier Q which was a breach of contract.

Section 29(4) of the Sale of Goods Act 1979 deals with the case of goods which are in the possession of a third party. It provides:

Where the goods at the time of sale are in the possession of a third person, there is no delivery by seller to buyer unless and until the third person acknowledges to the buyer that he holds the

---

[46] This is easy enough to say in the standard situation where there are no complications. It has caused considerable difficulty where the underlying transactions are illegal (*Belvoir Finance Co Ltd* v *Stapleton* [1971] 1 QB 210; [1970] 3 All ER 664).

[47] See De Zulueta, *Digest* 41, 1 and 2, p. 54, discussing D41-1-9.6.

[48] [2002] 2 All ER (Comm) 753.

goods on his behalf; nothing in this section affects the operation of the issue or transfer of any document of title to the goods.

The most common example of this would be where the seller had put the goods into the hands of someone whose business it is to store other people's goods, such as a warehouseman. Obviously, the seller could tell the warehouseman to deliver the goods to the buyer but the buyer might wish to leave the goods in the hands of the warehouseman. Again, it would be absurd to require a formal delivery and redelivery, but here agreement between seller and buyer will not be sufficient to effect delivery. The common practice is for the seller to give the buyer a delivery order, that is, a document instructing the warehouseman to deliver to the buyer. The buyer can present this to the warehouseman and ask that the goods be kept on his (the buyer's) behalf. Delivery takes place when the warehouseman recognises that the buyer is the person now entitled to the goods (this is technically known as an 'attornment').

This rule does not apply, as s. 29(4) of the 1979 Act states, where there is a document of title involved. The notion of a document of title is quite a difficult one and can best be explained by considering the most important example, a bill of lading. A bill of lading is the document issued by the master of a ship to a person who puts goods on board the ship for carriage. The bill has a number of functions. It operates as evidence of the terms on which the goods are to be carried and also as a receipt for the goods. In the days of sail, goods might be put on board a ship for carriage and the bill of lading sent ahead by a faster ship. The practice of dealing in the bills of lading grew up and, by the late 18th century, the courts had come to recognise the bill of lading as having a third function of being a document of title to the goods on board ship. So, if the owners of goods put them on a ship and received a bill of lading made out to themselves or 'to order', they could endorse the bill by writing on its face a direction to deliver the goods to someone else and that would transfer to that person the right to receive them from the ship's master. In other words, the shipowner is required to deliver to whoever holds a bill of lading properly endorsed. In the case of commodity cargoes where trading is very active, the goods may be transferred many times while they are on the high seas.

The principal difference between the warehouseman and the ship's master is that, because the bill of lading is a document of title, the transfer is effective at once without the need for any attornment. In some cases, it is not possible to transfer the bill of lading, for instance, because only part of the goods covered by the bill of lading is being sold. In this situation, the seller may issue a delivery order addressed to the master but, since the delivery order is not a document of title, delivery will not be effective until the master attorns.

Finally, delivery to a carrier may be a delivery to the buyer. This is dealt with by s. 32.

LEGISLATIVE PROVISION

Section 32 provides:

> (1) Where, in pursuance of a contract of sale, the seller is authorised or required to send the goods to the buyer, delivery of the goods to a carrier (whether named by the buyer or not) for the purpose of transmission to the buyer is *prima facie* deemed to be a delivery of the goods to the buyer.

(2) Unless otherwise authorised by the buyer, the seller must make such contract with the carrier on behalf of the buyer as may be reasonable having regard to the nature of the goods and the other circumstances of the case; and, if the seller omits to do so, and the goods are lost or damaged in the course of transit, the buyer may decline to treat the delivery to the carrier as a delivery to himself or may hold the seller responsible in damages.

(3) Unless otherwise agreed, where goods are sent by the seller to the buyer by a route involving sea transit, under circumstances in which it is usual to insure, the seller must give such notice to the buyer as may enable him to insure during their sea transit; and, if the seller fails to do so, the goods are at his risk during such sea transit.

It should be emphasised that the rule that delivery to the carrier is delivery to the buyer is only a *prima facie* rule and can be rebutted by evidence of a contrary intention. So, in the case of sea carriage, if the seller takes the bill of lading to his own order, as would usually be the case (so as to reserve a right of disposal, see section 4.6), this is evidence of a contrary intention. Further, if the seller sends the goods off in his or her own lorry, this will not be delivery to a carrier for this purpose, nor probably if the carrier is an associated company.

One of the consequences of the rule that delivery to the carrier is delivery to the buyer may be that, as between seller and buyer, the 'risk' of accidental damage to the goods in transit will fall on the buyer. (This is discussed more fully in section 4.7.) However, this possibility is qualified by s. 32(2) and (3) since, if the seller fails to make a reasonable contract of carriage or, in the case of sea carriage, fails to give notice enabling the buyer to insure, the risk will fall back on him or her. (In CIF contracts, the most important form of export sale, it is part of the seller's obligations to insure.)

In *Young* v *Hobson*[49] electrical engines were sold on FOR terms (that is, 'free on rail' – the seller's price covers the cost of getting the goods 'on rail'). The seller made a contract with the railway under which the goods were carried at the owner's risk when he could have made a contract for them to be carried at the carrier's risk at the same price, subject to an inspection by the railway. This was held not to have been a reasonable contract to have made.

LEGISLATIVE PROVISION

The Sale and Supply of Goods to Consumers Regulations 2002 adds an additional subsection to s. 32 which provides:

(4) In a case where the buyer deals as consumer or, in Scotland, where there is a consumer contract in which the buyer is a consumer, subsections (1) to (3) above must be ignored, but if in pursuance of a contract of sale the seller is authorised or required to send the goods to the buyer, delivery of the goods to the carrier is not delivery of the goods to the buyer.

4.5.3.2 Place of delivery

In many cases, the parties will expressly agree the place of delivery or it will be a reasonable inference from the rest of their agreement that they must have intended a particular place.

If there is no express or implied agreement, then the position is governed by s. 29(2).

[49] (1949) 65 TLR 365.

LEGISLATIVE PROVISION

Section 29(2) provides:

> The place of delivery is the seller's place of business if he has one, and if not, his residence; except that, if the contract is for the sale of specific goods, which to the knowledge of the parties when the contract is made are in some other place, then that place is the place of delivery.

This reflects the general position that in the absence of contrary agreement it is for the buyer to collect the goods, but the language is very much that of 1893 rather than 1979, reflecting the fact that the 1979 Act was simply a tidying up operation. The language assumes that the seller has only one place of business which will very often not be the case today. Presumably, where the seller has several places of business, the court will look at all the surrounding circumstances to see which of the seller's places of business is most appropriate.

4.5.3.3 Time of delivery

It is very common, particularly in commercial contracts, for the parties expressly to agree the date for delivery. This may be done either by selecting a particular calendar date, for example, 1 May 2009, or by reference to a length of time, such as six weeks from receipt of order. In this respect, it is worth noting that the law has a number of presumptions about the meaning of various time expressions, so that a year *prima facie* means any period of 12 consecutive months; a month means a calendar month; a week means a period of seven consecutive days and a day means the period from midnight to midnight (the law in general taking no account of parts of a day).

The parties might agree that delivery is to be on request. This could happen, for instance, where the buyer can see the need for considerable volume over a period of time and does not wish to risk having to buy at short notice. If the buyer lacks storage facilities, he or she may leave the goods with the seller and call them up as required. A typical example might be a builder who is working on a housing estate and can see how many bricks, doors, stairs, etc., will be needed but does not want to store them for long periods on site. In this situation, the seller must deliver within a reasonable time from receiving the request and, since the goods should have been set on one side, a reasonable time would be short.

The parties may completely fail to fix a date. The position will then be governed by s. 29(3) of the Sale of Goods Act 1979.

LEGISLATIVE PROVISION

Section 29(3) provides:

> Where under the contract of sale the seller is bound to send the goods to the buyer, but no time for sending them is fixed, the seller is bound to send them within a reasonable time.

Although this sub-section only deals expressly with the case where the seller is bound to send the goods to the buyer, it is assumed that the same rule applies where the seller has to make the goods available for collection by the buyer. What is a reasonable time clearly depends on all the relevant circumstances. If the goods are in stock, delivery should usually be possible within a few days; clearly, if goods have to be made up to special requirements or ordered from another supplier or the manufacturer, a longer period will be reasonable.

4.5.3.4 Effect of late delivery

It is normally a breach of contract for the seller to deliver late.[50] The major exception to this rule would be where the contract gives some excuse for late delivery such as a *force majeure* clause. The buyer is entitled to damages to compensate for the loss suffered due to late delivery (see section 4.10). In many cases, however, the buyer will not be able to show that any significant loss has been suffered as a result of the delay and the damages will thus only be nominal. In some cases, the buyer will be entitled to reject on late delivery, depending on whether 'time is of the essence' or not. This is one of those legal expressions which are widely known and frequently misunderstood. As far as the recovery of damages is concerned, it does not matter at all if time is of the essence, though curiously enough the House of Lords did not finally decide this until *Raineri v Miles* (1981).[51] For this purpose, the only question is whether or not late performance was a breach of contract. However, if, but only if, time is of the essence, a late delivery can be rejected. Time can be of the essence for three reasons.

The first is that the contract expressly says so. In practice, it often contains a statement that time is (or alternatively is not) of the essence. Indeed, one would expect well-drafted conditions of purchase to make time of delivery of the essence while standard conditions of sale often say that the seller will do his best to deliver on time but do not give a guarantee to do so.

The second is that the court characterises the contract as one where time is inherently of the essence. This is essentially a two-stage process. In the first stage, the court will consider whether the contract is of a kind where prompt performance is usually essential. So, for instance, prompt completion of a building contract is not usually imperative and indeed seems seldom to be achieved. The second stage is to consider if there are particular circumstances which justify departure from the usual classification. So, if the contract is to build a stadium for the next Olympics, it would probably be easy to persuade the court that it was important to complete the stadium before the beginning of the Games. Applying this approach, the courts have consistently held that the time of delivery is normally of the essence in commercial sales.

The third possibility is that, although time is not initially of the essence, the buyer may 'make' time of the essence. What this slightly misleading expression means is that, if the seller does not deliver on time, a buyer may call on him to deliver within a reasonable time, on pain of having the goods rejected if this does not happen. Provided the court later agrees with the buyer's assessment of what was a reasonable further time of delivery, such a notice will be effective.

---

[50] It may also be a breach of contract to tender delivery early. See *Bowes v Shand* (1877) 2 App Cas 455 where the contract called for rice shipped during the months of March and/or April. The seller tendered rice shipped in February and the buyer was held entitled to reject in cases of this kind; the date of shipment is treated as part of the 'description' of the goods (see section 4.8).

[51] [1981] AC 1050.

It is important to emphasise that, if time is of the essence, buyers can reject late delivery without any proof that in the particular case any real loss has been suffered. So, in a commercial contract of sale, if delivery is due on 1 January, buyers would usually be entitled to reject delivery on 2 January. This means that, if the buyers no longer want the goods, for instance, because the market has moved against them, they can escape from the contract.

Buyers are not, of course, obliged to reject late delivery and, indeed, will often have little commercial alternative but to accept the goods because they are needed and are not readily obtainable elsewhere. There is an important practical difference here between a buyer who purchases goods for resale and one who purchases goods for use. A buyer who accepts late delivery of the goods waives any right to reject for late delivery but does not waive the right to damages.

It may happen that the seller tells the buyer that the goods are going to be late but underestimates the extent of the delay. The difficulties that this may produce are well illustrated by the case of *Charles Rickards Ltd* v *Oppenheim*.[52] In this case, the plaintiff agreed to supply a Rolls-Royce chassis for the defendant, to be made by 20 March 1948. It was not ready by 20 March but the defendant continued to press for delivery. By June, the defendant had lost patience with the plaintiff and on 29 June said that the delivery could not be accepted after 25 July. The plaintiff did not tender delivery until 18 October and sued for damages for non-acceptance. The action failed. The correct analysis of this would seem to be that time was originally of the essence, that the defendant waived the right to reject by continuing to call for delivery but made time of the essence once more by the notice of 29 June.

4.5.3.5 Rules as to quantity delivered

Section 30 of the Sale of Goods Act 1979 contains a number of rules which arise where the seller delivers the wrong quantity. The basic rule is that the buyer is entitled to reject if the seller fails to deliver exactly the right quantity.

LEGISLATIVE PROVISION

Section 30(1) deals with the simplest case and provides:

> Where the seller delivers to the buyer a quantity of goods less than he contracted, to sell, the buyer may reject them, but, if the buyer accepts the goods so delivered, he must pay for them at the contract rate.

At first sight, it seems obvious that the buyer is not bound to accept short delivery, but there is an important practical consequence of this rule and the rule that the seller cannot deliver in instalments unless the contract expressly provides for delivery in that manner. It follows that if the seller delivers part of the goods and says that the balance is following, the buyer is entitled to reject. What happens in this situation if the buyer accepts the part delivery? It is probable that he or she has waived the right to reject but waiver is conditional on the seller honouring the undertaking to deliver the balance. If the seller fails to do so, it seems probable

[52] [1950] 1 KB 616.

that the buyer can reject after all. Of course, if he or she has meanwhile sold or consumed that part delivery, it will not be possible to reject, since rejection depends on returning the goods.

When the seller tenders a partial delivery, the buyer has a choice between rejecting the consignment and accepting the whole of the delivery of the contract quantity. It is not possible to accept part of the delivery and reject the balance. Section 30(2) and (3) deals with delivery of too much and provides that:

> (2) when the seller delivers to the buyer a quantity of goods larger than he contracted to sell, the buyer may accept the goods included in the contract and reject the rest, or he may reject the whole;

> (3) where the seller delivers to the buyer a quantity of goods larger than he contracted to sell and the buyer accepts the whole of the goods so delivered, he must pay for them at the contract rate.

It will be seen that buyers are entitled to reject not only if sellers deliver too little but also if they deliver too much. This may appear surprising but it has the important practical consequence that a seller cannot force the buyer to select the right amount out of an excess and this would be important in a case where the separation of the correct amount would be difficult and expensive. In this case, therefore, buyers have three alternatives: they may reject the whole delivery; they may accept the contract amount and reject the balance; or they may accept the whole delivery and pay *pro rata*.

LEGISLATIVE PROVISION

Section 30(4) of the Sale of Goods Act 1979 provides:

> Where the seller delivers to the buyer the goods he contracted to sell mixed with goods of a different description not included in the contract, the buyer may accept the goods which are in accordance with the contract and reject the rest, or he may reject the whole.

A good example of this rule in practice is the pre-Act case of *Levy* v *Green*,[53] where the buyer ordered crockery and the seller delivered the correct amount of the crockery ordered, together with some more crockery of a different pattern. In this case, the buyer again had three choices:

(a) to reject the whole delivery;

(b) to accept the contract delivery and reject the balance; or

(c) to accept the whole delivery.

It will be seen that this is very similar to the case of delivering too much; the only difference being that, if the excess is accepted, it must be paid for at a reasonable price rather than at the contract rate (since there is no contract rate for non-contract goods). Many commentators have thought that s. 30(4) was only aimed at the case of a delivery in full with an admixture of other goods. However, the courts have also applied it to a mixture of a short delivery of the contract goods together with other goods. So, in *Ebrahim Dawood Ltd* v *Heath Ltd*,[54] there was a contract for the delivery of 50 tons of steel sheets of five different sizes 'equal tonnage

---

[53] (1859) 1 E&E 969.
[54] [1961] 2 Lloyd's Rep 512.

per size'. Instead of delivering 10 tons of each of the five sizes the seller delivered 50 tons of one size. This was treated as being a mixture of 10 tons of the right size and 40 tons of the wrong size so that the buyer was entitled to accept the 10 tons and reject the balance.

It will be seen that the rules stated in s. 30(1)–(4) of the Sale of Goods Act 1979 impose a very strict duty on the seller to deliver the correct quantity of goods. It is, of course, open to the parties to modify this and this is expressly recognised by s. 30(5) which provides:

> This section is subject to any usage of trade, special agreement, or course of dealing between the parties.

So, a seller may be able to show that there is a settled practice between the parties that the buyer always accepts what is delivered or that there is a usage in the trade to that effect. That would require proof of previous dealings between the parties or of the practices of the particular trade to which the parties belong respectively.

It is clearly open to the parties to deal with the matter by the contract. There are a number of ways in which this might be done. It is common in commodity contracts for there to be an express tolerance, for example, 1,000 tons Western White Wheat, 5 per cent more or less at the seller's option. In such a case, any amount between 950 tons and 1,050 tons would be a contract amount but the rules in s. 30 would apply to deliveries of 949 or 1,051 tons. Another possibility would be that the contract was for the sale of a particular bulk, say 'all the sugar in my warehouse in Bristol, thought to be about 500 tons'. In this case, there would be a binding contract even if there were 400 tons or 600 tons in the warehouse, though, if the figure of 500 had not been an honest estimate, the seller might be liable for misrepresentation.

LEGISLATIVE PROVISION

Section 30 is amended by s. 4 of the Sale and Supply of Goods Act 1994 which adds a new sub-section (2A), providing that:

> (2A) A buyer who does not deal as a consumer may not:
>
> (a) where the seller delivers a quantity of goods less than he contracted to sell, reject the goods under subs (1) above; or
>
> (b) where the seller delivers a quantity of goods larger than he contracted to sell, reject the whole under subs (2) above . . .
>
> if the shortfall or, as the case may be, excess is so slight that it would be unreasonable for him to do so.

So, the buyer's right of rejection is now qualified in the case of non-consumer sales, where the shortfall or excess is so slight that it would be unreasonable for the buyer to reject. It seems that there are two stages: first, the court decides that the shortfall (or excess) is slight; secondly, it decides that, in the circumstances, it would be unreasonable to allow the buyer to reject.

Apart from this, the only other qualification of the strictness of the rules in s. 30 occurs where it is possible to invoke the legal maxim *de minimis non curat lex*, which may be roughly translated as 'the law takes no account of very small matters'. Undoubtedly, this principle can apply, but for this purpose, very small means very, very small. One of the few examples is

Shipton Anderson v *Weil Brothers*,[55] where the contract was to sell 4,950 tons of wheat and the seller delivered an excess of 55 pounds. It was held that the buyer was not entitled to reject. The discrepancy in this case was of the order of 0.0005 per cent, which is certainly very small. All systems of measurement contain some margin of error and it seems safe to say that a buyer cannot reject for a discrepancy which is within the margin of error of the appropriate system. This seems especially so where it is clear that if there is an error it is in the buyer's favour (assuming, as would usually be the case in such situations, the seller is claiming no more than the contract price). However, it also seems clear that the scope for applying the *de minimis* principle in this area is very limited.

4.5.3.6 Delivery by instalments

LEGISLATIVE PROVISION

Section 31(1) of the Sale of Goods Act 1979 provides that:

Unless otherwise agreed, the buyer of goods is not bound to accept delivery of them by instalments.

The Act does not expressly say so but it must surely also be the case that the buyer is not entitled to call on the seller to deliver by instalments, unless otherwise agreed.

Of course, delivery by instalment is in practice very common and, indeed, many contracts of sale could not be performed in any other way.

ISSUE BOX

The Act does not define 'instalment' and there would be scope for argument as to whether or not a delivery was by instalment. Let us suppose, for instance, that a contractor building a motorway makes a contract for 1,000 tons of precoated chippings for immediate delivery and that there is no lorry which can be legally driven on the roads capable of carrying more than 100 tons. It will be implicit in the contract that at least 10 lorry loads will be necessary. If 10 lorries arrive simultaneously, is that a delivery by instalments? One suspects that the answer is in the negative, but, if that is right, what is the position if one of the lorries breaks down on the way to the site? It is thought that this is covered by s. 30(1) (see section 4.5.3.5, above) rather than by s. 31(1).

Where the parties decide on delivery by instalments, there are a number of practical questions which ideally they ought to answer in the contract. A basic question is whether to opt for a fixed schedule of instalments or allow the seller or the buyer options as to the timing and number of instalments. If there are to be fixed instalments, then the number and intervals need to be fixed and the contract should say whether or not they are to be of equal size.

[55] [1912] 1 KB 574.

It seems desirable to say something here about defective performance of instalment contracts. (Remedies in general are more fully discussed in section 4.10.) Either party can, of course, bring an action for damages for loss resulting from a defective performance in relation to one instalment. The critical question is whether faulty performance in relation to one instalment entitles a party to terminate the contract. In other words, can a seller refuse to deliver a second instalment because the buyer has not paid for the first one or, conversely, can the buyer treat the contract as at an end because the goods delivered under one instalment are faulty?

As has been stated, where there are a series of separate contracts, it is not possible to refuse to perform a second contract because the other party failed to perform the first. This rule does not apply to a single contract performable in instalments, even where the contract provides 'each delivery a separate contract', since the House of Lords held in *Smyth* v *Bailey*[56] that these words did not actually operate to divide the contract up.

In the case of instalment contracts, it is undoubtedly open to the parties explicitly to provide that defective performance by one party in relation to any one instalment entitles the other party either to terminate or at least to withhold performance until that defect is remedied. Even if the parties do not explicitly so provide, defective performance in relation to one instalment may still have this effect because of s. 31(2) of the Sale of Goods Act 1979, which provides:

> Where there is a contract for the sale of goods to be delivered by stated instalments, which are to be separately paid for, and the seller makes defective deliveries in respect of one or more deliveries, or the buyer neglects or refuses to take delivery of or pay for one or more instalments, it is a question in each case depending on the terms of the contract and the circumstances of the case whether the breach of contract is a repudiation of the whole contract or whether it is a severable breach giving rise to a claim for compensation but not to treat the whole contract as repudiated.

This sub-section does not expressly cover all the things which may go wrong with instalment contractors. For instance, it does not cover the case where the seller fails to make a delivery at all rather than making a defective delivery, nor does it cover the case where the instalments are not 'stated' but are at the buyer's or seller's option. Nevertheless, these situations seem also to be covered by the test laid down which is that everything turns on whether or not the conduct of the party in breach amounts to a repudiation by that party of his obligations under the contract. This concept is considered in more detail in section 4.10 below but, for present purposes, it can be said that it must be shown either that the contract breaker has expressly or implicitly stated that he or she does not intend to fulfil the contract or that the innocent party has been substantially deprived of what was contracted for. In practice, the courts are very reluctant to treat defective performance in relation to a single instalment as passing this test. An accumulation of defects over several instalments may do so, as in *Munro* v *Meyer*[57] where there was a contract to buy 1,500 tons of meat and bone meal, delivery at the rate of 125 tons a month. After more than half had been delivered, the meal was discovered to be defective. It was held that the buyer was entitled to terminate and reject future deliveries. On the other hand, in *Maple Flock Co Ltd* v *Universal Furniture Products (Wembley) Ltd*,[58] it was held that the fact that the first of 19 deliveries were defective could not be treated as a repudiation because the chances of the breach being repeated were practically negligible.

[56] [1940] 3 All ER 60.
[57] [1930] 2 KB 312.
[58] [1934] 1 KB 148.

CASE

Regent OHG Aisenstadt v Francesco of Jermyn Street[59]

This case revealed that there is a conflict between s. 30(1) and s. 31(2) of the 1979 Act. In this case, the sellers were manufacturers of high-class men's suits who contracted to sell 62 suits to the buyers who had an expensive retail outlet. Delivery was to be in instalments at the seller's option. The sellers in fact tendered the suits in five instalments. For reasons which had nothing to do with this contract, the parties fell out and the buyers refused to accept delivery of any of the instalments. This was clearly a repudiation, and the sellers would have been entitled to terminate. In fact, the sellers did not do so and continued to tender the suits. Shortly before tendering the fourth instalment, the sellers told the buyers that, because a particular cloth was not available, the delivery would be one suit short. This shortfall was not made up in the fifth and final delivery so that the sellers ended up by tendering 61 suits instead of 62. It was clear that, if the contract had been for a single delivery of 62 suits, the case would have been governed by s. 30(1) and the buyer would have been entitled to reject delivery which was one suit short. Equally clearly, however, the seller's conduct did not amount to repudiation within the test laid down by s. 31(2) for delivery by instalments. It was held that, in so far as there was a conflict between ss. 30(1) and 31(2), the latter must prevail and that the buyer was accordingly not entitled to reject.

4.5.4 Acceptance

Section 27 of the Sale of Goods Act 1979, quoted above, concerns the seller's duty to deliver the goods and the buyer's duty to accept. At first sight, one might think that the buyer's duty to accept is the converse of the seller's duty to deliver, that is, the duty to take delivery. However, it is quite clear that, although acceptance and taking delivery are connected, they are not the same thing. In fact, 'acceptance' is a sophisticated and difficult notion.

LEGISLATIVE PROVISION

According to s. 35, the buyer is deemed to have accepted the goods when he does one of three things:

(a) intimates to the seller that he has accepted them;

(b) after delivery, he does any act in relation to the goods which is inconsistent with the ownership of the seller; or

(c) after lapse of a reasonable length of time, he retains the goods without intimating to the seller that he rejects them.

---

[59] [1981] 3 All ER 327; [1988] 1 WLR 321.

This section does not so much define acceptance, as explain when it happens. It is implicit in the section that acceptance 'is the abandonment by the buyer of any right to reject the goods. (This by no means involves the abandonment of any right to damages.) The buyer may be entitled to reject goods for a number of different reasons, for instance (as we have already seen) because the seller delivers too many or too few goods or, sometimes, delivers them late. Other grounds for rejection, such as defects in the goods, will be dealt with later.

Section 35 of the Act tells us that buyers can abandon the right to reject the goods, that is, they can 'accept' them in a number of different ways. Before examining these, it is worth noting that buyers cannot be under a duty to accept in this sense since they would be perfectly entitled to reject the goods in such cases. Buyers can only be under a duty to accept when they have no right to reject. In s. 27, therefore, the word 'accept' must mean something different from what it means in s. 35, that is, something much closer to a duty to take delivery.

The reason for the elaboration of s. 35 is that in this area the law of sale appears to be slightly different from the general law of contract. The buyer's right of rejection is analogous to the right of an innocent party to terminate in certain circumstances for the other party's breach of contract. Under the general law of contract, it is not usually possible to argue that a party has waived the right to terminate unless it can be shown that he knew the relevant facts which so entitled him[60] but, in the law of sale, the buyer may lose the right to reject before knowing he or she had it. This is no doubt hard on the buyer, but is probably justified on balance by the desirability of not allowing commercial transactions to be upset too readily. So the buyer loses the right to reject not only by expressly accepting but also by failing to reject within a reasonable time or by doing an act which is inconsistent with the ownership of the seller, such as sub-selling.

A key question here is, what is a 'reasonable time'?

CASE

Bernstein v Pamson Motors Ltd[61]

In this case the plaintiff sought to reject a new motor car the engine of which seized up after he had owned it for three weeks and driven it only 140 miles. Rougier J held that the car was not of merchantable quality but that a reasonable time had elapsed and the right to reject had been lost. He took the view that the reasonableness of the time did not turn on whether the defect was quickly discoverable but on:

> What is a reasonable practical interval in commercial terms between a buyer receiving the goods and his ability to send them back, taking into consideration from his point of view the nature of the goods and their function, and from the point of view of the seller the commercial desirability of being able to close his ledger reasonably soon after the transaction is complete.[62]

---

[60] It is usual to qualify this statement by reference to the mysterious decision in *Panchaud Frères SA v ETS General Grain Co* [1970] 1 Lloyd's Rep 53, but, in *Glencore Grain Rotterdam BV v Lebanese Organisation for International Commerce* [1994] 4 All ER 514, *Panchaud* was explained as a decision on acceptance.

[61] [1987] 2 All ER 220.

[62] This result can reasonably be described as less than self-evident and it was widely criticised by consumer groups. There are many Canadian cases on the meaning of this section and some at least are perceptibly more generous to buyers. See M. Bridge, *Sale of Goods, op. cit.*, p. 639.

LEGISLATIVE PROVISION

Since *Bernstein*, s. 35 and its partner, s. 34, have been amended by the Sale and Supply of Goods Act 1994. The amendments enhance the opportunity of the buyer to be able to check the goods to see if they comply with the contract. These two sections now read:

34(1) Unless otherwise agreed when the seller tenders goods to the buyer, he is bound on request to afford the buyer a reasonable opportunity of examining the goods for the purpose of ascertaining whether they are in conformity with the contract and, in the case of a contract for sale by sample, of comparing the bulk with the sample.

35(1) The buyer is deemed to have accepted the goods subject to sub-s. (2) below:

(a) when he intimates to the seller that he has accepted them;

(b) when the goods have been delivered to him and he does any act in relation to them which is inconsistent with the ownership of the seller.

(2) Where goods are delivered to the buyer, and he has not previously examined them, he is not deemed to have accepted them under sub-s. (1) above until he has had a reasonable opportunity of examining them for the purpose:

(a) of ascertaining whether they are in conformity with the contract; and

(b) in the case of a contract for sale by sample, of comparing the bulk with the sample.

(3) Where the buyer deals as consumer or (in Scotland) the contract of sale is a consumer contract, the buyer cannot lose his right to rely on sub-s. (2) above by agreement, waiver or otherwise.

(4) The buyer is also deemed to have accepted the goods when after the lapse of a reasonable time he retains the goods without intimating to the seller that he has rejected them.

(5) The questions that are material in determining for the purposes of sub-s. (4) above whether a reasonable time has elapsed include whether the buyer has had a reasonable opportunity of examining the goods for the purpose mentioned in sub-s. (2) above.

(6) The buyer is not by virtue of this section deemed to have accepted the goods merely because:

(a) he asks for, or agrees to, their repair by or under an arrangement with the seller; or

(b) the goods are delivered to another under a sub-sale or other disposition.

(7) Where the contract is for the sale of goods making one or more commercial units, deemed to have accepted all the goods making the unit; and in this sub-section 'commercial unit' means a unit division of which would materially impair the value of the goods or the character of the unit.

(8) Paragraph 10 of Sched 1 below applies in relation to a contract made before 22 April 1967 or (in the application of this Act to Northern Ireland) 28 July 1967.

Under this new version, all three of the grounds for acceptance are subject to the buyer's right to examine the goods. So, even if the buyer tells the seller that he has accepted the goods, this is not binding until he has had a reasonable opportunity of examining them. Similarly, a buyer does not lose the right to reject by failing to do so within a reasonable time or by doing acts inconsistent with the seller's ownership if he or she has not had a reasonable opportunity of examination. Suppose, for instance, that A sells goods to B, and B sub-sells the same goods to C, and that B tells A to deliver the goods direct to C. The goods delivered by A are defective and C rejects them. B can reject in this situation because there has not been a reasonable opportunity to examine the goods. Of course, B will not be able to reject unless C has rejected since otherwise he or she will not be able to return the goods, but it is precisely C's rejection which is the event which will make B wish to reject.

The amendments made by the 1994 Act introduced some new features. Thus, s. 35(3), a new provision, is important in view of the widespread practice of asking consumer buyers to sign acceptance notes. A consumer buyer will not lose his right to rely on his not having had a reasonable opportunity to examine the goods because the delivery man got him to sign a note of acceptance. It should be noted that it is the right to examine which cannot be lost by 'agreement, waiver or otherwise'. This does not mean that the right to reject cannot be lost by 'agreement, waiver or otherwise' once the right to examine has been exercised. So, if defective goods are delivered to a consumer buyer, who examines them, decides that they are defective but decides to keep them, he will not later be able to say that he has not accepted them. Section 35(6), however, is another new provision which recognises that a reasonable buyer will often wish to give the seller a chance to make the goods work. A disincentive to doing this was that one might be advised that giving the seller a chance to repair was an acceptance, thereby preventing a later rejection of the goods if the repair was ineffective. This is now not the case.

CASE

JH Ritchie Ltd v Lloyd Ltd[63]

In this case the buyers bought a combination steel drill and power harrow from the sellers. They used the equipment for the first time on 26 April 1999. On 27 April vibration was noticed coming from part of the drive chain of the harrow. On 28 April, the vibration continuing, the buyers stopped using the harrow. After discussion with the sellers, the harrow was taken away for inspection and, if possible, repair. It appeared that the defect was that bearings were missing from two of the rotors. The bearings were obtained and fitted and the harrow returned. The buyers asked what was wrong with the harrow and the sellers refused to say. The buyers rejected. The House of Lords held that in the circumstances a term should be implied into the arrangement for inspection and possible repair that the sellers would provide the buyers with information about the defect. The harrow was a complex piece of agricultural equipment. The buyers could not make a properly informed judgment as to what to do without the information they asked for.

Has *Bernstein* v *Pamson Motors Ltd* been reversed by the 1994 Act? Section 35(4) is now qualified by another new provision, s. 35(5), and it may be argued that this has had the effect of altering the notion of a reasonable time.

---

[63] [2007] 1 WLR 670.

> **CASE**
>
> ## *Clegg* v *Olle Anderson*[64]
>
> The decision of the Court of Appeal in *Clegg* v *Olle Anderson* provides support for the demise of *Bernstein*. In this case the buyer agreed in 1999 to buy a new yacht from the seller for £236,000. The seller was buying the yacht from the manufacturer. The contract provided that the keel 'would be in accordance with the manufacturer's standard specification'. On delivery the seller indicated that the keel was in fact substantially heavier but promised to make reasonable modifications. The evidence at trial was that the keel did not affect the safety of the yacht but would shorten the life of the rigging and that the changes could be made at a reasonably modest price (about £1,680). The buyer rejected some three weeks after delivery and the Court of Appeal held that he had not accepted. Nothing in the discussion of possible remedies for the keel amounted to an acceptance.

Instead of waiting for the seller to tender delivery and then refusing to accept, the buyer may announce in advance that he or she will not take the goods. Usually, this will amount to an 'anticipatory breach' (discussed more fully in section 4.10) and will entitle the seller to terminate the contract though he or she may choose instead to continue to tender the goods in the hope that the buyer will have a change of mind and take them.

A difficult problem arises where buyers announce in advance that they will not take the goods and later seek to argue that they would have been entitled to reject the goods in any case because they were defective. The general rule in the law of contract is that a party who purports to terminate for a bad reason can usually justify the termination later by relying on a good reason which has only just been discovered. Of course, the buyer will often have great practical problems in establishing that the goods which the seller would have delivered would have been defective. This is probably the explanation of the difficult and controversial case of *British and Benningtons* v *NW Cachar Tea*,[65] where the buyer had contracted to buy tea to be delivered to a bonded warehouse in London. There was no express date for delivery and delivery was therefore due within a reasonable time. Before a reasonable time had elapsed, the buyers said that they would not accept delivery. The ships carrying the tea had been diverted by the shipping controller and the buyers seem to have thought that this would prevent delivery within a reasonable time. (The buyer and the court took different views of what time would be reasonable.) The House of Lords held that the buyer had committed an anticipatory breach and that the seller could recover damages. The best explanation of this result seems to be that, at the time of the buyer's rejection, the seller had not broken the contract and, although he could not prove that he would certainly have delivered within a reasonable time, the buyer could not prove that the seller would not have delivered within a reasonable time. The position would be different if the seller had committed a breach of contract so that it could be said for certain that he would not be able to deliver within a reasonable time.

---

[64] [2003] 1 All ER (Comm) 721; [2003] EWCA Civ 320; *Reynolds* (2003) 119 LQR 544. See also *Jones* v *Gallagher* [2005] 1 Lloyd's Rep 377; *Truk (UK) Ltd* v *Tokmakidis GmbH* [2000] 1 Lloyd's Rep 543.

[65] [1923] AC 48.

> **ISSUE BOX**
>
> 1. In a contract between a seller and a buyer what rules apply if the contract says that the price is:
>   (a) to be fixed by the buyer;
>   (b) to be fixed by X?
> 2. What does it mean to say that payment of the price and delivery of the goods are concurrent conditions?
> 3. A contracts to sell to B 50 tons of coffee beans to be delivered on 1 May. What is the position if:
>   (a) A delivers 60 tons; or
>   (b) A delivers on 2 May?

4.6 Ownership

4.6.1 Introduction

The primary purpose of a contract for the sale of goods is to transfer ownership of the goods from the seller to the buyer. This section deals with a series of problems which arise in this connection. The first involves the nature of the seller's obligations as to the transfer of ownership; the second concerns the moment at which ownership is transferred; and the third, the circumstances in which a buyer may become the owner of the goods, even though the seller was not the owner.

It is necessary, first of all, to say something about terminology.[66] The Sale of Goods Act 1979 does not in general talk about ownership. It does talk a good deal about 'property' and 'title'. Both of these words can, for present purposes, be regarded as synonyms for ownership. The Act uses the word 'property' when dealing with the first two questions above and 'title' when dealing with the third. This is because the first two questions involve disputes between sellers and buyers, whereas the third question involves a dispute between an owner, who was not the seller, and the buyer. We shall also encounter the expression 'reservation of the right of disposal' which, despite appearances, also turns out to be another expression effectively meaning ownership. A distinction is sometimes drawn between the 'general property' and the 'special property'. Here, the words 'general property' are being used to describe ownership and the words 'special property' to describe possession, that is, physical control without the rights of ownership. So, if I rent a television set for use in my home, the rental company has the general property (ownership) and I have the special property (possession).

---

[66] G. Battersby and A. D. Preston, 'The Concepts of "Property", "Title" and "Owner" Used in the Sale of Goods Act 1893' (1972) 35 *MLR* 268.

4.6.2 **The seller's duties as to the transfer of ownership**

The seller's duties are set out in s. 12 of the Act.

> **LEGISLATIVE PROVISION**
>
> Section 12 provides:
>
> (1) In a contract of sale, other than one to which sub-s. (3) below applies, there is an implied condition on the part of the seller that, in the case of a sale, he has the right to sell the goods, and in the case of an agreement to sell he will have such a right at the time when the property is to pass.
>
> (2) In a contract of sale, other than one to which sub-s. (3) below applies, there is also an implied warranty that:
>
> (a) the goods are free, and will remain free until the time when the property is to pass, from any charge or encumbrance not disclosed or known to the buyer before the contract is made; and
>
> (b) the buyer will enjoy quiet possession of the goods except so far as it may be disturbed by the owner or other person entitled to the benefit of any charge or encumbrance so disclosed or known.

It will be seen that these two sub-sections set out three separate obligations. Of these, by far the most important is that set out in s. 12(1), under which the seller undertakes that he or she has the right to sell the goods. It is important to note that the seller is in breach of this obligation, even if he or she believes that he or she is entitled to sell the goods and even though the buyer's enjoyment of the goods is never disturbed. Suppose, for instance, that X's goods are stolen by A, who sells them to B, who sells them to C, who sells them to D. In this situation, X can claim the goods or their value from A, B, C or D. Obviously, he cannot recover more than once but he has a completely free choice as to whom to sue. In practice, he would usually not sue the thief A because he has disappeared or spent the money. He is more likely to sue D, who still has the goods, unless B or C for some reason appear more attractive defendants (for example, because D has left the country). However, so far as the rights of the parties to the individual contracts of sale are concerned, it makes no difference who X sues or even that he sues no one. A is still in breach of his contract with B; B is in breach of his contract with C and C is in breach of his contract with D. What X has done may affect the amount of money, if any, that can be recovered in any of these actions, but not the existence of the obligation. Section 12(1) concerns the right to sell, it does not cover the transfer of ownership. There are cases where the seller has no right to sell, but does transfer ownership because it is one of the exceptional cases where a non-owner seller can make the buyer the owner. In such cases, the seller will be in breach of s. 12(1). In most cases, the seller will be entitled to sell, either because he or she is the owner or agent of the owner, or because he or she will be able to acquire ownership before property is to pass (as will be the case with future goods). Perhaps surprisingly, it has been held that even though the seller is the owner, he or she may, in exceptional circumstances, not have a right to sell the goods. This is illustrated by the leading case of *Niblett v Confectioner's Materials*,[67] where the plaintiffs bought tins of

[67] [1921] 3 KB 387.

milk from the defendants. Some of the tins of milk were delivered bearing 'Nissly brand' labels, which infringed the trademark of another manufacturer. That manufacturer persuaded Customs and Excise to impound the tins and the plaintiffs had to remove and destroy the labels, before they could get the tins back. It was held that the defendants were in breach of s. 12(1) because they did not have the right to sell the tins in the condition in which they were, even though they owned them. This was clearly reasonable, as the plaintiffs had been left with a supply of unlabelled tins which would be difficult to dispose of.

4.6.2.1 To what remedy is the buyer entitled if the seller breaks his or her obligation under s. 12(1)?

The buyer can certainly recover, by way of damages, any loss which he or she has suffered because of the breach. Further, the seller's obligation is stated to be a condition and, as we shall see (in section 4.10), the buyer is generally entitled to reject the goods when there is a breach of condition. In practice, however, it will very seldom be possible to use this remedy because the buyer will not usually know until well after the goods have been delivered, that the seller has no right to sell.

CASE

Rowland v Divall[68]

In this case, the Court of Appeal held that the buyer had a more extensive remedy. In that case, the defendant honestly bought a stolen car from the thief and sold it to the plaintiff, who was a car dealer, for £334. The plaintiff sold the car for £400. In due course, some four months after the sale by the defendant to the plaintiff, the car was repossessed by the police and returned to its true owner. Clearly, on these facts, there was a breach of s. 12(1) and the plaintiff could have maintained a damages action, but in such an action it would have been necessary to take account not only of the plaintiff's loss but also of any benefit he and his sub-buyer had received by having use of the car. The Court of Appeal held, however, that the plaintiff was not restricted to an action for damages, but could sue to recover the whole of the price. This was on the basis that there was a total failure of consideration; that is, the buyer had received none of the benefit for which he had entered the contract, since the whole object of the transaction was that he should become the owner of the car.[69]

It is important to note that the reasoning in *Rowland v Divall* turns on the view that the whole object of the transaction is that the buyer becomes the owner of the goods. Accordingly, it does not matter that the buyer has never been dispossessed. Of course, he or she cannot have the price back and keep the goods if he or she has them, but the situation may arise where the buyer does not have the goods, but has never been dispossessed by the true owner. Suppose, for instance, that A steals a case of wine from X and sells it to B, who sells it to C, who drinks all the wine before the theft becomes apparent. It appears that C can recover the

---

[68] [1923] 2 KB 500.
[69] In *Barber v NWS Bank* [1996] 1 All ER 906, it was held to be an express term of a conditional sale agreement that the seller was owner at the time of the contract. The buyer recovered all the sums paid during the currency of the contract.

price in full from B, even though he has drunk the wine. This would not be so surprising if C had been sued by X, but as we have seen, X can, if he chooses, sue B. So, on these facts, B, who may be entirely innocent and honest, can be sued by both X and by C. Obviously, this does not appear to be a fair result.

No English case has presented these facts, but *Rowland v Divall* was carried a stage further in *Butterworth v Kingsway Motors*.[70] Here, X, who was in possession of a car under a hire purchase agreement, sold it to Y before he had paid all the instalments. Y sold the car to Z, who sold it to the defendant, who sold it to the plaintiff. X meanwhile continued to pay the instalments. Several months later, the plaintiff discovered that the car was subject to a hire purchase agreement and demanded the return of the price from the defendant. Eight days later, X paid the last instalment and exercised his option under the hire purchase contract to buy the car. The result of this was that the ownership of the car passed from the finance company to X and so on down the line to the plaintiff. It followed that the plaintiff was no longer at risk of being dispossessed, but it was, nevertheless, held that he could recover the price. Later developments did not expunge the breach of s. 12(1), since the defendant had not had the right to sell at the time of the sale. It will be seen that the plaintiff, who had suffered no real loss, in effect received a windfall since his use of the car was entirely free.

It is interesting to ask what the position would have been if the plaintiff had demanded return of the price nine days later, that is, after X had paid the last instalment. In the Northern Ireland case of *West v McBlain* (1950)[71] Sheil J thought that the buyer would still have been entitled to demand return of the price. This is logical, but it may be thought that it pushes logic one step too far. Certainly, that was the view expressed by Pearson J in *Butterworth v Kingsway Motors* in considering this possibility.

A statutory exception to *Rowland v Divall* has been created by s. 6(3) of the Torts (Interference with Goods) Act 1977. This deals with the situation where the goods have been improved by an innocent non-owner. If, on the facts of *Butterworth v Kingsway Motors*, one of the parties in the chain had replaced the engine, then the plaintiff would have had to give credit for this enhancement of the car's value in his action for the price. It would not matter for this purpose whether the new engine was fitted by the defendant or by one of the previous owners, provided that the engine was fitted by someone who, at the time of fitting, believed that he was the owner.

4.6.2.2 Subsidiary obligations

In most cases, the buyer's protection against a seller who has a defective title to the goods will be under s. 12(1). Section 12(2) provides two subsidiary obligations which cover situations that might not be covered by s. 12(1). Section 12(2)(a) deals with the case where the seller owns the goods but has charged them in a way not disclosed to the buyer. A possible example would be if I were to sell you my watch which, unknown to you, is at the pawnbroker's. This is not likely to happen very often because most forms of borrowing against goods, in English practice, involve transferring ownership to the lender and will therefore fall, if at all, under s. 12(1).

A good example of the operation of the warranty of quiet possession under s. 12(2)(b) is *Microbeads v Vinhurst Road Markings*.[72] In this case, the buyer found himself subject to a claim

---

[70] [1954] 1 WLR 1286; [1954] 2 All ER 694.
[71] [1950] NI 144.
[72] [1975] 1 All ER 529; [1975] 1 WLR 218.

by a patentee of a patent affecting the goods. The patent had not in fact existed at the time the goods were sold and there was, accordingly, no breach of s. 12(1). The Court of Appeal held, however, that s. 12(2) covered the case where the patent was issued after the sale. Section 12(2) states that the obligations contained in it are warranties, and it follows that the buyer's only remedy, in the event of breach, is an action for damages.

4.6.2.3 Can the seller exclude his or her liability under s. 12?

In its 1893 version, s. 12 of the Sale of Goods Act contained after the words 'in a contract of sale' the words 'unless the circumstances of the contract are such as to show a different intention'. This strongly suggested that the draftsman contemplated the possibility that the contract might contain a clause excluding or qualifying the seller's duties under the section. Some commentators argued, on the other hand, that if transfer of ownership were, as held in *Rowland* v *Divall*, the whole object of the transaction, it could not be permissible to exclude this obligation. No English case ever squarely presented this problem and the matter was resolved by Parliament in 1973, when, in the Supply of Goods (Implied Terms) Act (re-enacted as s. 6 of the Unfair Contract Terms Act 1977), provision was made that a seller could never exclude or limit his or her obligations under s. 12(1) and (2). (The topic of excluding and limiting clauses is considered in more detail in section 4.9.)

However, the seller is permitted to contract on the basis that he or she only undertakes to transfer whatever title he or she actually has. In other words, the seller may say, 'I do not know whether I am owner or not, but if I am, I will transfer ownership to you'. Of course, the seller cannot do this if he or she knows he or she is not the owner, and one would normally expect that the buyer would demand a significant reduction in price for taking this risk.

LEGISLATIVE PROVISION

This possibility is governed by s. 12(3)–(5) which provides that:

12(3) This sub-section applies to a contract of sale in the case of which there appears from the contract or is to be inferred from its circumstances an intention that the seller should transfer only such title as he or a third person may have.

(4) In a contract to which sub-s. (3) above applies there is an implied warranty that all charges or encumbrances known to the seller and not known to the buyer have been disclosed to the buyer before the contract is made.

(5) In a contract to which sub-s. (3) above applies there is also an implied warranty that none of the following will disturb the buyer's quiet possession of the goods, namely:

(a) the seller;

(b) in a case where the parties to the contract intend that the seller should transfer only such title as a third person may have, that person;

(c) anyone claiming through or under the seller or that third person otherwise than under a charge or encumbrance disclosed or known to the buyer before the contract is made.

It will be seen that s. 12(3) envisages the possibility that it may be inferred from the circumstances that the seller is only contracting to sell whatever title he or she has. This would obviously be unusual, but an example which is often given is that of a sale by a sheriff after he has executed a judgment debt. If, for instance, the sheriff takes possession of the television set in the judgment debtor's house and sells it, he will usually have no idea whether it belongs to the judgment debtor or is subject to a hire purchase or rental agreement. It will be seen that s. 12(4) and (5) contains modified versions of the obligations which are usually implied under s. 12(2).

4.6.3 The passing of property

This section deals with the rules of English law which decide when ownership is to pass from seller to buyer. It is worth asking first why this question is important, since it is safe to say that as a rule, the buyer is much more concerned with delivery of the goods and the seller with payment of the price. There are two main reasons. The first is that as a matter of technique, English law makes some other questions turn on the answer to this question. So, as a rule, the passing of risk (discussed in section 4.7) is linked to the passing of property, as is the seller's right to sue for the price, under s. 49(1) (as opposed to maintaining an action for damages for non-payment of the price, which is discussed in section 4.10). There is nothing essential about this link. Other systems of law have developed rules about the passing of risk which are wholly divorced from their rules about the passing of property. The principal advantage of the English system is perhaps a certain economy of effort in dealing with two questions at the same time. The disadvantage is that the separate questions which are thus linked together may, in fact, demand a more sophisticated range of answers than can be provided by a single concept.

The second reason is that the question of who owns the goods usually becomes important if either buyer or seller becomes insolvent. Sellers, for instance, often offer credit to their customers; that is, they deliver the goods before they have been paid for. Inevitably, some buyers, having received the goods, are unable to pay for them because they have become insolvent. If, on the one hand, the buyer has not only received the goods but also becomes the owner of them, the seller's only remedy will be to prove in the liquidation and usually this will mean that he will not be paid in full and, indeed, often not at all. On the other hand, if the seller still owns the goods, he will usually be entitled to recover possession of them, which will be a much more satisfactory remedy. This desire to improve the position of the seller in the buyer's insolvency has become so commercially important that it has led to widespread use of 'retention of title clauses', which are discussed more fully below.

The basic rules as to the passing of property are set out in ss. 16 and 17 of the Sale of Goods Act.

LEGISLATIVE PROVISION

Section 16

Where there is a contract for the sale of unascertained goods, no property in the goods is transferred to the buyer unless and until the goods are ascertained.

Section 17

(1) Where there is a contract for the sale of specific or ascertained goods, the property in them is transferred to the buyer at such time as the parties to the contract intend it to be transferred.

(2) For the purpose of ascertaining the intention of the parties, regard shall be had to the terms of the contract, the conduct of the parties and the circumstances of the case.

So, the first rule is that property cannot pass if the goods are unascertained. This makes the distinction between specific and unascertained goods (which was explained in section 4.3) fundamental, since the second rule is that if the goods are specific or ascertained, the parties are free to make whatever agreement they like about when property is to pass. This second rule was adopted by English law in relation to sale of goods at a very early stage and is in marked distinction both to the sale of land, where a formal act of conveyance is needed for an effective transfer of ownership, and to gifts of goods, where an effective physical delivery is necessary to such a transfer. This means that where the goods are specific or ascertained, transfer of property under a sale is completely separate from questions of delivery or payment. It is a typical feature of English contract law to make results depend on the intentions of parties. This is sometimes criticised on the ground that the parties may well have formed no relevant intention. Like many such criticisms, this is true only in part. The advantage of a rule based on intention is that it provides great flexibility to parties who know what they are doing. Where, as will often be the case, a contract is subject to standard conditions of sale or purchase, one would certainly expect to find a provision expressly dealing with the passing of property. In other cases, the transaction will be set against a commercial background, which provides determinative clues to the parties' intentions. So, in international sales, the parties will often provide that payment is to be 'cash against documents' and this will usually mean that property is to pass when the buyer takes up the documents and pays against them.

Nevertheless, it is undoubtedly true that there will be many cases, particularly perhaps consumer transactions, where the parties do not direct their thoughts to this question. Assistance is then provided by s. 18, which provides rules for ascertaining the intention of the parties 'unless a different intention appears'. Rules 1, 2 and 3 deal with sales of specific goods.

LEGISLATIVE PROVISION

Section 18

Unless a different intention appears, the following are rules for ascertaining the intention of the parties as to the time at which the property in the goods is to pass to the buyer.

Rule 1 Where there is an unconditional contract for the sale of specific goods in a deliverable state, the property in the goods passes to the buyer when the contract is made, and it is immaterial whether the time of payment or the time of delivery, or both, be postponed.

Rule 2 Where there is a contract for the sale of specific goods and the seller is bound to do something to the goods for the purpose of putting them into a deliverable state, the property does not pass until the thing is done and the buyer has notice that it has been done.

Rule 3 Where there is a contract for the sale of specific goods in a deliverable state but the seller is bound to weigh, measure, test, or do some other act or thing with reference to the goods for the purpose of ascertaining the price, the property does not pass until the act or thing is done and the buyer has notice that it has been done.

It will be noted that rule 1 contemplates that in the case of specific goods property may pass at the moment the contract is made. However, this will not in practice be very common, since in *RV Ward v Bignall*[73] it was said that in modern conditions it would not require much material to support the inference that property was to pass at a later stage. So, if I select an article in a shop and hand it to the cashier, there would be a contract as soon as the cashier had signified acceptance of my offer, but a court might well hold that the property did not pass until I had paid. Rule 1 only applies where the contract is 'unconditional' and the goods are in a 'deliverable state'. In contract and sales law, the word 'condition' bears many different meanings. In the present context, it is usually taken to mean that the contract does not contain any term which suspends the passing of property until some later event. The words 'deliverable state' are defined by s. 61(5) which provides that: 'Goods are in a deliverable state within the meaning of this Act when they are in such a state that the buyer would under the contract be bound to take delivery of them.'

This definition is potentially very wide, since there are many possible defects in the goods which would entitle the buyer to refuse to accept delivery. (This is discussed more fully in sections 4.8 and 4.10.) It would seem that if the goods are actually delivered to the buyer, rule 1 would not prevent property passing. So, if A sells a car to B and delivers a car containing a latent defect which would have justified rejection if B had known of it, it seems that property probably passes to B on delivery. It is probable that, in formulating rule 1, the draftsman had principally in mind the situation covered by rule 2, where the goods are not defective, but need something doing to them before the buyer is required to accept delivery. An example would be when there is a sale of a ton of coffee beans and the seller agrees to bag the beans before delivery.

LEGISLATIVE PROVISION

Rule 4 deals with sale or return and provides that:

> When goods are delivered to the buyer on approval or on sale or return or other similar terms the property in goods passes to the buyer:
>
> (a) when he signifies his approval or acceptance to the seller or does any other act adopting the transaction;
>
> (b) if he does not signify his approval or acceptance to the seller but retains the goods without giving notice of rejection, then, if a time has been fixed for the return of the goods, on the expiration of that time, and, if no time has been fixed, on the expiration of a reasonable time.

The principal difficulty here is to determine exactly what is meant by 'sale or return'. There are many transactions in which there is an excellent chance in practice that the seller, if asked, will accept a return of goods and give a cash refund. Many retail shops will do this and equally publishers usually accept returns from retail booksellers. Such transactions are usually not contracts of sale or return in the strict sense, since the buyer does not have a contractual

---

[73] [1967] 1 QB 534.

option to accept or reject the goods, but simply a commercial expectation that he or she will be able to return the goods if he or she wishes to do so.

If the transaction is one of sale or return, the buyer loses the right to return the goods if he or she approves or accepts them or otherwise adopts the transaction. This means that if the buyer does something which an honest person would not do unless he intended to adopt, he will be treated as having adopted. So, in *Kirkham* v *Attenborough*[74] the buyer borrowed money from a pawnbroker on the security of the goods and this was treated as an adoption. Alternatively, property may pass to the buyer under rule 4(b) because he has failed to reject in time.

Sale or return contracts were considered by the Court of Appeal in *Atari Corp (UK) Ltd* v *Electronic Boutique Stores (UK)*.[75] The plaintiffs were manufacturers of computer games; the defendants owned a large number of retail outlets. The defendants wanted to test the market for the plaintiff's games. They took a large number on the basis that they were given until 31 January 1996 to return them. On 19 January 1996, they gave notice that sales were unsatisfactory and that they were arranging for the unsold games to be brought to a central location for return. This was held to be an effective notice, even though the games to be returned were not specifically identified or ready for immediate return.

LEGISLATIVE PROVISION

Rule 5 deals with unascertained goods and provides:

Rule 5

(1) Where there is a contract for the sale of unascertained or future goods by description, and goods of that description and in a deliverable state are unconditionally appropriated to the contract, either by the seller with the assent of the buyer or by the buyer with the assent of the seller, the property in the goods then passes to the buyer; and the assent may be express or implied, and may be given either before or after the appropriation is made.

(2) Where, in pursuance of the contract, the seller delivers the goods to the buyer or to a carrier or other bailee or custodier (whether named by the buyer or not) for the purpose of transmission to the buyer, and does not reserve the right of disposal, he is to be taken to have unconditionally appropriated the goods to the contract.

In practice, this is the most important of the rules. We have already seen that, in the sale of unascertained goods, property cannot pass until the goods are ascertained, even if the parties were to try to agree otherwise. This basic principle was recently reaffirmed by the Privy Council in *Re Goldcorp Exchange Ltd*.[76] In this case, a New Zealand company dealt in gold and sold to customers on the basis that the company would store and insure the gold free of charge. They issued certificates to the customers. No specific gold was set aside for any specific customer though there were assurances (which were not kept) that a sufficient supply of gold would be held at all times to meet orders for delivery by customers. In fact, the company

---

[74] [1897] 1 QB 201.
[75] [1998] 1 All ER 1010.
[76] [1994] 2 All ER 806. The earlier Court of Appeal decision in *Re Wait* [1927] 1 Ch 606 is also very instructive in this context.

became hopelessly insolvent and had inadequate supplies of gold. The Privy Council held that it was elementary that property had not passed from the sellers to the buyers.

This case can be usefully contrasted with *Re Stapylton Fletcher Ltd*.[77]

CASE

Re Stapylton Fletcher Ltd

In this case, wine merchants bought and sold wine and also sold it on the basis that they would store it for customers until it was fit to drink. On one hand, the wine merchant kept the boxes of wine which they were holding for customers in a separate unit. This unit contained nothing but wine which was being stored for customers and, at all times, the right quantities of vintages were in stock and the total was in strict compliance with the customers' storage records. On the other hand, the wine merchant did not mark individual cases of wine with the customers' names, since where, as was usually the case, there was more than one case of a particular vintage, it was convenient to supply customers off the top of the pile which necessarily meant that individual cases were not allocated. The wine merchants became insolvent. In this case, it was held that the wine was sufficiently ascertained for the customers to become tenants in common of the stock in the proportion that their goods bore to the total in store for the time being. This decision is very important because it shows that the ascertainment rule does not prevent two or more owning goods in common where there is an undivided bulk. Once the goods are ascertained, the property will pass at the time agreed by the parties. Where the parties have reached no express agreement, rule 5 propounds a test based on appropriation.

In some cases, ascertainment and appropriation may take place at the same time. This was so in *Karlhamns Oljefabriker* v *Eastport Navigation*[78] (discussed in section 4.3.3). This is quite likely to be the case where the goods are appropriated by delivery to a carrier, as happens particularly in international sales (though in such sales there are often express agreements as to the passing of property). So, if the seller contracts to sell 1,000 tons Western White Wheat CIF Avonmouth and puts 1,000 tons of Western White Wheat aboard a ship bound for Avonmouth, this may both ascertain and appropriate the goods. In many such cases, however, the seller will load 2,000 tons having sold 1,000 tons to A, and 1,000 tons to B. In such a case, the goods will not be ascertained until the first 1,000 tons are unloaded at the destination. Even where the seller puts only 1,000 tons on board, this will not necessarily constitute appropriation because he may not at that stage have committed himself to using *that* 1,000 tons to perform *that* contract.

This example brings out the special meaning of appropriation in this context. Suppose a wine merchant has 100 cases of Meursault 1985 in his cellars and advertises it to his customers at £15 per bottle or £175 per case. Not surprisingly, he quickly receives orders for the 100 cases and, as a first step, labels each of the cases with the name of the customer for whom it is intended. In a sense, he has clearly appropriated the cases to the contracts but not for the

---

[77] [1995] 1 All ER 192.
[78] [1982] 1 All ER 208.

purposes of rule 5. This was clearly decided in *Carlos Federspiel* v *Twigg*,[79] where the seller had agreed to sell a number of bicycles to the buyer. The seller had packed the bicycles, marked them with the buyer's name and told the buyer the shipping marks. The seller then became insolvent. The buyer argued that the bicycles had been appropriated to its contract and that property had passed to it. This argument was rejected on the grounds that the seller could properly have had a change of mind and appropriated new bicycles to the contract.

It is essential that there is a degree of irrevocability in the appropriation. It is this which makes delivery to the carrier often the effective act of appropriation.

4.6.3.1 The Sale of Goods (Amendment) Act 1995

This Act makes a limited but important amendment to the basic doctrine of unascertained goods in relation to the problem of a sale of a part of an undivided bulk.

LEGISLATIVE PROVISION

Additional words are added to s. 18 rule 5, as follows:

(3) Where there is a contract for the sale of a specified quantity of unascertained goods in a deliverable state forming part of a bulk which is identified either in the contract or by subsequent agreement between the parties and the bulk is reduced to (or to less than) that quantity, then, if the buyer under that contract is the only buyer to whom goods are then due out of the bulk:

(a) the remaining goods are to be taken as appropriated to that contract at the time when the bulk is so reduced; and

(b) the property in those goods then passes to that buyer.

(4) Paragraph (3) above applies also (with the necessary modifications) where a bulk is reduced to (or to less than) the aggregate of the quantities due to a single buyer under separate contracts relating to that bulk and he is the only buyer to whom goods are then due out of that bulk.

This has the effect of providing statutory confirmation of the decision in *Karlhamns Oljefabriker* v *Eastport Navigation*, above.

LEGISLATIVE PROVISION

The main change consists in the addition of ss. 20A and 20B to s. 20. These sections provide as follows:

Undivided shares in goods forming part of a bulk
20A–(1) This section applies to a contract for the sale of a specified quantity of unascertained goods if the following conditions are met:

(a) the goods or some of them form part of a bulk which is identified either in the contract or by subsequent agreement between the parties; and

---

[79] [1957] 1 Lloyd's Rep 240.

(b) the buyer has paid the price for some or all of the goods which are the subject of the contract and which form part of the bulk.

(2) Where this section applies, then (unless the parties agree otherwise), as soon as the conditions specified in paras. (a) and (b) of sub-s. (1) above are met or at such later time as the parties may agree:

(a) property in an undivided share in the bulk is transferred to the buyer; and

(b) the buyer becomes an owner in common of the bulk.

(3) Subject to sub-s. (4) below, for the purposes of this section, the undivided share of a buyer in a bulk at any time shall be such share as the quantity of goods paid for and due to the buyer out of the bulk bears to the quantity of goods in the bulk at that time.

(4) Where the aggregate of the undivided shares of bulk in a bulk determined under sub-s. (3) above would at any time exceed the whole of the bulk at that time, the undivided share in the bulk of each buyer shall be reduced proportionately so that the aggregate of the undivided shares is equal to the whole bulk.

(5) Where a buyer has paid the price for only some of the goods due to him out of a bulk, any delivery to the buyer out of the bulk shall, for the purposes of this section, be ascribed in the first place to the goods in respect of which payment has been made.

(6) For the purposes of this section, payment of part of the price for any goods shall be treated as payment for a corresponding part of the goods.

Deemed consent by co-owner to dealings in bulk goods
20B–(1) A person who has become an owner in common of a bulk by virtue of s. 20A above shall be deemed to have consented to:

(a) any delivery of goods out of the bulk to any other owner in common of the bulk, being goods which are due to him under his contract;

(b) any dealing with or removal, delivery or disposal of goods in the bulk by any other person who is an owner in common of the bulk in so far as the goods fall within that co-owner's undivided share in the bulk at the time of the dealing, removal, delivery or disposal.

(2) No cause of action shall accrue to anyone against a person by reason of that person having acted in accordance with para. (a) or (b) of sub-s. (1) above in reliance on any consent deemed to have been given under that sub-section.

(3) Nothing in this section or s. 10A above shall:

(a) impose an obligation on a buyer of goods out of a bulk to compensate any other buyer of goods out of that bulk for any shortfall in the goods received by that other buyer;

(b) affect any contractual arrangement between buyers of goods out of a bulk for adjustments between themselves; or

(c) affect the rights of any buyer under his contract.

This makes one major and a number of minor changes. The major change is that it has become possible for property to pass in an individual bulk provided that:

(a) the bulk of which the unascertained goods form part is identified; and

(b) the buyer has paid the price; and

(c) the parties have agreed.

It will be seen that this is the only place where the Act makes the passing of property turn on payment of the price. This underlines that the main purpose of the change is to improve the position of the buyer who has paid in advance when the seller becomes insolvent.

The minor changes are that:

(a) the buyer's share of the bulk is proportionate and if the bulk becomes less than the total of shares created all shares are reduced proportionately;

(b) the buyer's share is proportional to what he has paid, so, if there is a bulk of 1,000 tons and the buyer buys 500 tons but only pays the price of 250 tons, he is entitled to a quarter of the bulk.

If we take the case where A has 1,000 tons of Western White Wheat on board the SS Chocolate Kisses and sells 200 tons to X who pays, the wheat will now be owned 80 per cent by A and 20 per cent by X. It might now be argued that the consent of X is needed for further dealing with the goods. In practice, this would often be inconvenient because A's dealings with the goods will be continuous and it will often be chance which buyer pays first. This is dealt with by s. 20B, under which buyers in the position of X will be deemed to have given their consent to such dealings.

4.6.3.2 Retention of title clauses[80]

We have seen in the previous section that, subject to the goods being ascertained, the parties may make whatever agreement they like about when property is to pass. So, property may pass even though the goods have not been delivered and the price not yet paid. Conversely, the parties may agree that the property is not to pass even though the goods have been delivered and paid for. It is very likely that a seller who employs standard conditions of sale and normally gives his or her customers credit will wish to provide that property does not pass simply on delivery but only at some later stage, such as when payment is made. This possibility is clearly implicit in ss. 17 and 18. It is, however, explicitly stated in s. 19.

LEGISLATIVE PROVISION

Section 19

(1) Where there is a contract for the sale of specific goods or where goods are subsequently appropriated to the contract, the seller may, by the terms of the contract or appropriation, reserve the right of disposal of the goods until certain conditions are fulfilled; and in such a case, notwithstanding the delivery of the goods to the buyer, or to a carrier or other bailee or custodier for the purpose of transmission to the buyer, the property in the goods does not pass to the buyer until the conditions imposed by the seller are fulfilled.

---

[80] This topic appears to have produced more books than the rest of sales law put together. See I. Davies, *Effective Retention of Title* (Fourmat Publishing, London, 1991); G. McCormack, *Reservation of Title* (Sweet and Maxwell, London, 1990) and J. Parris, *Effective Retention of Title Clauses* (WileyBlackwell, Oxford, 1986). S. Wheeler, *Reservation of Title Clauses: Impact and Implications* (Oxford University Press, Oxford, 1991), is not an exposition of the law but rather an examination of how effective such clauses are to protect sellers in practice. See also N. Palmer, 'Reservation of Title' (1992) 5 *JCL* 175; G. McCormack, 'Reservation of Title in England and New Zealand' (1992) 12 *LS* 195.

(2) Where goods are shipped, and by the bill of lading the goods are deliverable to the order of the seller or his agent, the seller is *prima facie* to be taken to reserve the right of disposal.

(3) Where the seller of goods draws on the buyer for the price, and transmits the bill of exchange and bill of lading to the buyer together to secure acceptance or payment of the bill of exchange, the buyer is bound to return the bill of lading if he does not honour the bill of exchange, and if he wrongfully retains the bill of lading the property in the goods does not pass to him.

It will be seen that s. 19 talks about the seller reserving 'the right of disposal of the goods'. This, despite appearances, is effectively another synonym for ownership. The expression has been of longstanding use in relation to export sales and bills of lading and it is worth spending a moment explaining the operation of the bill of lading as it gives an excellent example of the reservation of the right of disposal. Before the invention of the aeroplane, all export sales in this country involved the use of sea carriage and this is still the predominant way of moving goods. Most sellers do not have ships of their own and therefore performance of the contract of sale will normally involve entrusting the goods to a sea carrier. In the classical arrangement, the seller would put the goods on board a ship having made arrangements for them to be carried to a seaport in the buyer's country. The seller would usually receive from the sea carrier a bill of lading. The bill of lading fulfils three distinct functions. It acts as a receipt so as to show the goods have been loaded on board the ship, it acts as evidence of the contract between the seller and the sea carrier for the carriage of the goods to their destination, and it operates as a 'document of title'. It is this third role which concerns us here.

Since the 18th century, it has been recognised that someone who has put goods on board a ship and received a bill of lading has control of the goods in a way which enables him or her to transfer that control to another person by a transfer of the bill of lading. This is because by mercantile custom the captain of the ship would deliver the cargo to the holder of the bill of lading provided it had been suitably endorsed. This meant, for instance, that the seller could put goods on board the ship not yet having sold them and, while they were on the high seas, dispose of them. Buyers would often pay for the goods against the bill of lading and other documents knowing that when the ship arrived they would be able to get the cargo from the master. So, the bill of lading provided a means of disposal of the goods. The seller could have sold the goods and property could have passed to the buyer without any dealings with the bill of lading. The buyer would then, however, have had difficulty in getting the goods off the ship. In practice, a buyer who knows that the goods are on board the ship is very unlikely to want to pay in cash unless he or she receives the bill of lading or some other equivalent document. In some commodity trades, there may be several sales and sub-sales of the goods while they are on the high seas, each effected by transferring the bill of lading against payment. Section 19(1) expressly recognises this general possibility and s. 19(2) expressly recognises the specific possibility that the seller will take the bill of lading to his or her own order and that this will normally show that he is reserving the right of disposal.[81] Because commercial custom recognises the effectiveness of transfers of bills of lading made in the proper form, the seller can dispose of the bill of lading and the goods by endorsing it

---

[81] Even where the buyer has paid 80 per cent of the price before shipment: *Mitsui& Co v Flota Mercante Grancolombirma* [1988] 1 WLR 1145.

to the buyer (that is, by writing across the face of the bill of lading an instruction to deliver to the buyer).

In the context of export/import sales, this has long been well recognised as standard practice. It has also, no doubt, long been standard practice for sellers supplying goods on credit in domestic sales to have simple clauses saying that the goods are theirs until they are paid for. No problem arises with such clauses. This should always have been clear, but some deviant decisions in Scotland required it to be reaffirmed. In *Armour* v *Thyssen Edelstahlwerke AG*,[82] the House of Lords overturned decisions of the Scottish courts treating a simple reservation of title as creating a charge. Lord Keith of Kinkel, delivering the principal speech, said:

> I am, however, unable to regard a provision reserving title to the seller until payment of all debts due to him by the buyer as amounting to the creation by the buyer of a right to security in favour of the seller. Such a provision does, in a sense, give the seller security for the unpaid debts of the buyer. But, it does so by way of a legitimate retention of title, not by virtue of any right over his own property conferred by the buyer.[83]

However, in the last 30 years, much more elaborate and complex clauses have begun regularly to be used. The starting point of modern discussion is the decision of the Court of Appeal in *Aluminium Industrie* v *Romalpa*.[84] This case has been so influential that the sort of complex clauses which are used are quite often referred to as Romalpa clauses (or alternatively as retention or reservation of title clauses). In the *Romalpa* case, the plaintiff was a Dutch company which sold aluminium foil to the defendant, an English company. The plaintiff had elaborate standard conditions of sale which provided, among other things:

(a) that ownership of the foil was to be transferred only when the buyer had met all that was owing to the seller;

(b) required the buyer to store the foil in such a way that it was clearly the property of the seller until it had been paid for;

(c) that articles manufactured from the foil were to become the property of the seller as security for payment and that until such payment had been made the buyer was to keep the articles manufactured as 'fiduciary owner' for the seller and if required to store them separately so that they could be recognised.

The buyer was permitted to sell finished products to third parties on condition that, if requested, he or she would hand over to the seller any claims which he or she might have against said buyers.

It is important to note the breadth of the basic clause about transfer of ownership. The goods were being supplied regularly on credit terms. In such a situation, it is perfectly possible, even though the goods are being punctiliously paid for on time, that there is always money outstanding to the seller so that property never passes at all. So, if the standard credit terms of the trade are to pay 28 days after delivery of the invoice and there are deliveries of goods every 21 days, there will nearly always be money owing to the seller, even though the buyer is paying on time. In the *Romalpa* case itself, the buyer eventually became insolvent, owing the plaintiff over £120,000. The buyer had some £50,000 worth of foil and also had, in a separate bank account, some £35,000 which represented the proceeds of foil which the plaintiff

---

[82] [1990] 3 All ER 481; [1991] 2 AC 339.

[83] In this case, the clause retaining property in the seller until money due was paid. This is very important where there is a series of transactions between seller and buyer.

[84] [1976] 2 All ER 552; [1976] 1 WLR 676.

had supplied to the defendant and which the defendant had then sub-sold. The Court of Appeal held that the plaintiff was entitled both to recover the foil and also the £35,000 which was in the separate account.

This case illustrates in a dramatic way the practical importance of these retention of title clauses. They are basically a device to protect the seller against the buyer's insolvency. If the buyer remains solvent, the retention of title clause does little more than involve it in some tiresome extra paperwork. This is because, although the buyer may in theory be holding substantial quantities of goods which belong to the seller, it will not, so long as it is solvent, be liable to redeliver the goods to the seller, unless it commits some major breach of contract which entitles the seller to bring the contract to an end. However, if the buyer becomes insolvent, a seller who has a valid retention of title clause will be in a significantly improved position. Small businesses become insolvent every day and large businesses not infrequently. What usually happens in such cases is that nearly all of the assets fall into the hands of the HM Revenue & Customs who have preferential claims and into the hands of the bank, which will have taken a mortgage over the company's premises and a floating charge over the company's other assets. Arguably, the English insolvency law regime favours the tax authorities and the banks too much at the expense of ordinary trade creditors. Retention of title clauses can be seen as an attempt to redress the balance. Such a step is perfectly effective if all that is done is to use the power of s. 19 to delay the passing of ownership from seller to buyer.

However, many sellers, like the one in *Romalpa*, have much more elaborate clauses. Since 1976, these clauses have been the subject of a number of litigated cases, and in many of them the courts have held that the clause is ineffective. This is partly because these decisions have turned on the particular wording of specific clauses and partly on a perception by the judges that the sellers, in seeking to do too much, have overreached themselves. The general problem which lies behind the cases is that, whatever the abstract legal analysis, the seller's practical objective is to create a form of security interest in the goods. The companies legislation provides a limited number of possibilities for the creation of security interests in the property of companies (in practice the buyer has always been a company in the litigated cases; if the buyer were not a company, these difficulties would disappear). In particular, in a number of cases, the other creditors of the buyer have successfully argued that the retention of title clause is invalid because it amounts to an unregistered charge over the company's assets. This argument does not succeed if all that the seller has done is to have a straightforward s. 19 clause providing that ownership remains with it until it has been paid (*Clough Mill v Martin*).[85] This reasoning extends a step further where there are a series of sales and the seller has drafted the clause so as to retain ownership so long as any money is outstanding from any sale. This is permissible even if the seller retains ownership over goods which have been paid for, because such ownership would be subject to an implied term that the seller could only deal with the goods to the extent needed to discharge the balance of the outstanding debts.

So, retention of title clauses work perfectly satisfactorily if the buyer intends to keep the goods in its hands unaltered. However, buyers often intend either to resell the goods or to incorporate the goods in a larger product, or to use the goods as raw materials for the manufacture of goods. In an attempt to secure rights in cases of this kind, sellers have often adopted elaborate clauses of the kind mentioned in the discussion above of the *Romalpa* case. It is necessary, therefore, to say something about these more complex clauses.

[85] [1984] 3 All ER 982; [1985] 1 WLR 111.

In some cases, the contract has provided that the buyer is to have legal ownership of the goods but that 'equitable and beneficial' ownership is to remain in the seller. Such a clause was considered in *Re Bond Worth*[86] where the goods supplied were raw materials used by the buyer for the manufacture of carpets. Slade J held that the clause was invalid as being an attempt to create an unregistered charge. It seems, therefore, that in general the seller must attempt to retain legal ownership. However, this will not work where the goods are being incorporated into larger goods unless the goods remain identifiable. An interesting case in this respect is *Hendy Lennox v Grahame Puttick Ltd*[87] where the goods were diesel engines which were being used by the buyer for incorporation into diesel generating sets. The engines remained readily identifiable because all the engines were those provided by the seller and each engine had a serial number. Furthermore, the engines could, with relative ease, have been disconnected and removed from the generating sets. It was held that, in such a situation, the seller could continue to assert rights of ownership even after the engines had been incorporated into the generators.

In other cases, the goods are incorporated into finished products in a way in which it would be impossible to unscramble the omelette and separate out the constituent eggs. Sellers have sometimes sought to provide in this situation that they retain ownership in the raw materials or that the finished product is to be treated as theirs. This would probably present no problems if the seller had supplied all the ingredients for the finished products but in practice this has never been the facts of a reported case. One might envisage a case in which the finished product is made up partly of goods supplied by seller A and partly of goods supplied by seller B, each of whom has provided that the finished product is to belong to him. Such a case too has never been reported. The cases which have arisen have been those in which one of the ingredients in the finished product has been provided by a seller who employed a retention of title clause and the other ingredients by sellers who did not. In practice, in all of these cases the courts have held that the seller does not in fact retain a valid interest in the finished product. So, in *Borden v Scottish Timber Products*[88] a seller who supplied resin to a buyer who used it to manufacture chipboard obtained no property interest in the chipboard and, in *Re Peachdart*[89] a seller who supplied leather for the making of handbags failed successfully to assert a claim against the handbags. It is not clear whether the seller could improve on these cases by more sophisticated drafting. Suppose a seller on the facts of *Re Peachdart* had provided in the contract that the handbags were to be the joint property of the seller and the manufacturer. It is at least possible that this would create rights which the court would protect.[90] In New Zealand, it has been held that a seller of trees could retain ownership rights after the trees have been converted into logs by the buyer.[91]

The buyer may have bought the goods intending to resell them. Normally, the retention of title clause will not be effective to prevent the sub-buyer acquiring a good title for reasons which will become clearer after the reading of the next section (see *Four Point Garage v Carter*).[92] However, a seller may insert a clause in the contract providing that the buyer is to

---

[86] [1979] 3 All ER 919; [1980] 1 Ch 228.
[87] [1984] 2 All ER 152; [1984] 1 WLR 485.
[88] [1981] Ch 25.
[89] [1984] Ch 131.
[90] See *Coleman v Harvey* [1989] 1 NZLR 723; *Hudson* [1991] LMCLQ 23.
[91] *New Zealand Forest Products v Pongakawa Sawmill* [1991] 3 NZLR 112.
[92] [1985] 3 All ER 12.

have permission to sub-sell the goods but that the proceeds of such sub-sale are to be put into a separate bank account which is to be held on trust for the seller. If the buyer in fact opens such an account and pays the proceeds into it, this would be an effective clause. In practice, a buyer who is having financial problems and is approaching insolvency is very likely to find ways of paying the proceeds of sub-sales into an account with which he or she can deal so that such a clause will not provide complete practical protection for the seller.

4.6.4 Transfer of title where the seller is not the owner

In this section, we consider cases where the seller was not in fact the owner nor the authorised agent of the owner at the time of the sale. This situation may arise in a range of cases, running from the situation where the seller has stolen the goods all the way to a case where the seller honestly believes that he is the owner of the goods but has himself been misled by a previous seller. In this type of case, there is a conflict of interest between that of the original owner of the goods who is seeking to recover them or their value, and the ultimate buyer who has paid good money for goods which he believed the seller to be entitled to sell to him. In general, it is desirable to protect the interests both of the owners of property and of honest buyers who pay a fair price. In the case of transactions in land, the choice comes down unhesitatingly in favour of protecting the interests of owners. This is possible because transferring ownership of land is a highly formal act normally carried out by lawyers. In practice, therefore, it is extremely difficult for an honest buyer who employs a competent lawyer not to discover that the seller is not entitled to sell. In practice, it would be extremely difficult to apply this technique to transactions in goods. Some legal systems have therefore decided that the primary interest is to protect the honest buyer who pays a fair price and has no ground for suspecting that his seller is not the owner. English law has not chosen this option, however. Instead, it has started from the position that the seller cannot normally transfer any better rights than he himself has. This is often put in the form of the Latin maxim *nemo dat quod non habet* (roughly, no one can transfer what he does not have). Lawyers often talk in shorthand about the *nemo dat* rule. However, although it is clear that this is the basic rule, it is equally clear that it is subject to a substantial number of exceptions. Most of the exceptions are set out in ss. 21–26 of the Sale of Goods Act 1979, and we will discuss each exception in turn.

4.6.4.1 Estoppel

LEGISLATIVE PROVISION

SALE OF GOODS ACT 1979

Section 21(1)

Subject to this Act, where goods are sold by a person who is not their owner, and who does not sell them under the authority or with the consent of the owner, the buyer acquires no better title to the goods than the seller had, unless the owner of the goods is by his conduct precluded from denying the seller's authority to sell.

For present purposes, the sting of this section lies in its tail which is an application of the general legal doctrine of estoppel. The operation of the doctrine is to prevent (estop) a party from advancing an argument which he or she would otherwise be entitled to put forward. So, for instance, a party may be prevented from putting forward an argument because it has been the subject matter of a previous judicial decision on the same facts which is binding on him or her. An example of the operation of the doctrine in the present context is *Eastern Distributors Ltd* v *Goldring*.[93] In this case, the owner of a van wished to raise money on it and for this purpose entered into an arrangement with a car dealer which involved the deception of a finance company. The scheme was that the dealer would pretend to have bought the van and to be letting it to the owner on hire purchase terms. The owner signed in blank one of the finance company's hire purchase agreements, together with a delivery note stating that he had taken delivery of the van. The dealer then completed a further form purporting to offer to sell the van to the finance company. The result was that the finance company paid the dealer. On these facts, it could perhaps have been argued that the owner had actually authorised the dealer to sell his van to the finance company. However, the case was decided on the basis that the owner had not authorised the dealer to sell the van to the finance company and that he was estopped from so arguing. This was on the basis that, by signing the forms in the way he had, he had made it easy for the dealer to deceive the finance company as to who was the true owner of the van.

It is common in analysing the operation of estoppel in this area to distinguish between estoppel by representation, which arises where it could be said that the true owner has represented that someone else has authority to sell the goods, and estoppel by negligence, which arises where the true owner has behaved carelessly in respect of the goods in such a way as to enable the goods to be dealt with in a way which causes loss to a third party. However, in practice, the courts have been very cautious in applying either limb of the doctrine. In particular, it is clear that it does not, by the mere act of the owner putting his or her goods into the hands of someone else, represent that that person has authority to sell them, nor is it negligent to do so unless it is possible to analyse the transaction in such a way as to support the argument that the true owner owed a duty of care in respect of the goods to the party who has been deceived.

CASE

Moorgate Mercantile v *Twitchings*[94]

The narrow scope of both estoppel by representation and estoppel by negligence is shown by *Moorgate Mercantile* v *Twitchings* (1977), in which the majority of the House of Lords rejected the application of both doctrines. This case concerned a car which had been let on hire purchase terms. It is so common for parties who have taken cars on hire purchase to sell them for cash before they have completed the hire purchase contract that the hire purchase companies set up an organisation called Hire Purchase Information (HPI), which acts as a central registry of hire purchase transactions in relation to motor

---

[93] [1957] 2 QB 600.
[94] [1977] AC 890.

cars. Membership of the organisation is not compulsory, but most finance companies belong to it and many car dealers are affiliated to it so that they are able to obtain information. The normal practice is for finance companies which are members to notify all credit transactions involving cars. Then, if the car is offered to another dealer or finance company, they can check with HPI as to whether or not there is an existing credit agreement in relation to the car. This system obviously makes it much more difficult for a car subject to a credit agreement to be disposed of without the agreement being revealed. (Obviously, it does not prevent direct sale to another member of the public.) In the present case, the plaintiff finance company let a car on hire purchase to A. The plaintiff was a member of HPI and normally registered all its agreements with it. For some reason, which was never explained, the particular transaction with A was not registered and a few months later he offered the car for sale to the defendant. A told the defendant he was the owner of the car and when the defendant contacted HPI he was told that the car was not registered with them. The defendant bought the car from A and, in due course, sold it to B. Later, the plaintiff discovered that the car had been sold and brought an action against the defendant. The defendant argued that there was estoppel both by representation and by negligence. These arguments, though successful in the Court of Appeal, were rejected by a majority of three to two in the House of Lords. The majority view was that there was no estoppel by representation since no representation had been made by the plaintiff; any representation which had been made had been made by HPI but it had simply said, which was true, that the car was not registered with it. HPI was not in any case the agent of the plaintiff for the purpose of making any representation about the car. One ground for rejecting arguments based on estoppel by negligence was that it had not been proved that failure to register was the plaintiff's fault. (It was never proved how the failure had taken place.) However, the majority in the House of Lords would have rejected the argument based on estoppel by negligence even if it could have been shown that the plaintiff had failed to register this particular transaction. This was on the basis that the plaintiff owed no duty of care to other finance companies or to dealers to register the transaction. In coming to this conclusion, great weight was attached to the fact that the whole scheme was voluntary and not mandatory. This case demonstrates very clearly the policy issues involved and the cautious way in which the courts have in practice decided to apply the doctrine of estoppel.

Another restriction of the scope of s. 21(1) was revealed by the decision in *Shaw* v *Commissioner of Police*.[95] In this case, the claimant, Mr Natalegawa, a student from Indonesia, owned a red Porsche. He advertised it for sale in a newspaper and received a call from a gentleman calling himself Jonathan London who said he was a car dealer and was interested in buying the car on behalf of a client. The claimant allowed London to take delivery of the car and gave him a letter saying that he had sold the car to London and disclaiming further legal responsibility for it. In return, he received a cheque for £17,250 which in due course proved worthless. London agreed to sell the car to the plaintiff for £11,500, £10,000 to be paid by banker's draft. When London presented the draft, the bank refused to cash it and

[95] [1987] 3 All ER 305; [1987] 1 WLR 1332.

London disappeared. In due course, the police took possession of the car and both the plaintiff and the claimant sought possession of it. The Court of Appeal held that, as far as s. 21 was concerned, the case would have fallen within its scope if the sale by London to the plaintiff had been completed. It was clear, however, that, as far as the contract between the plaintiff and London was concerned, property in the car (if London had had it) was only to pass when London was paid. Since London had never been paid, the transaction was an agreement to sell and not a sale. This is logical because on the facts the plaintiff would not have become the owner of the car even if London had been an owner or an authorised agent. It would be paradoxical if the plaintiff were to be in a better position because London was a dishonest man.

4.6.4.2 Sale in market overt

> **LEGISLATIVE PROVISION**
>
> **SALE OF GOODS ACT 1979**
>
> **Section 22(1)**
>
> Where goods are sold in market overt, according to the usage of the market, the buyer acquires a good title to the goods, provided he buys them in good faith and without notice of any defect or want of title on the part of the seller.

As the language suggests, this was a very old, indeed the oldest, exception to the general rule. It started from the perception that a dishonest person is less likely to sell goods that he does not own in an open market than in a private sale. This rule reflects the supervision given to markets in the Middle Ages and may well have been historically true. This rationale has little place in modern business conditions and the exception has been removed by the Sale of Goods (Amendment) Act 1994.

4.6.4.3 Sale under a voidable title

> **LEGISLATIVE PROVISION**
>
> **SALE OF GOODS ACT 1979**
>
> **Section 23**
>
> When the seller of goods has a voidable title to them, but his title has not been avoided at the time of the sale, the buyer acquires a good title to the goods, provided he buys them in good faith and without notice of the seller's defect of title.

This exception is much more important in practice. It applies where the seller, instead of having no title at all, has a title which is liable to be avoided. The most obvious example would be where the seller had obtained possession of the goods by fraud. Where a contract is induced by one party's fraud, the result is not that the contract is void but that it is voidable, that is, liable to be set aside by the deceived party. Where an owner of goods has parted with them to a fraudulent buyer, he or she is entitled to set aside the contract and, if he acts in time, can recover the goods. However, if the fraudulent person has meanwhile sold the goods on to an innocent buyer, that innocent buyer will obtain a title which is better than that of the original owner. This is the point of s. 23.

A critical question, therefore, is what does the original owner have to do to set aside the voidable contract? Telling the fraudulent person or taking the goods from him would certainly do but in practice the fraudulent person and the goods have usually disappeared. In *Car and Universal Finance Ltd* v *Caldwell*,[96] the Court of Appeal held that it was possible to avoid the contract without either telling the fraudulent person or retaking possession of the goods. In that case, the owner had sold his car to a rogue and received a worthless cheque in return. The next morning, the owner presented the cheque at the bank and discovered that it was worthless. He immediately informed the police and the motoring organisations. It was held that the sale had been effectively avoided on the grounds that it is sufficient to do all that can in practice be done to set the transaction aside. Many commentators were surprised at this decision and indeed the opposing view was taken in Scotland on virtually identical facts in *McLeod* v *Kerr*.[97]

In practice, however, whether right or wrong, the decision in the *Caldwell* case is not as important as it appears at first sight because similar facts will usually fall within the scope of another exception (discussed in section 4.6.4.5): buyer in possession after sale.

4.6.4.4 Seller in possession after sale

LEGISLATIVE PROVISION

Section 24 of the Sale of Goods Act 1979 provides:

> Where a person having sold goods continues or is in possession of the goods, or of the documents of title to the goods, the delivery or transfer by that person, or by a mercantile agent acting for him, of the goods or documents of title under any sale, pledge, or disposition thereof, to any person receiving the same in good faith and without notice of the previous sale, has the same effect as if the person making the delivery or transfer were expressly authorised by the owner of goods to make the same.

It is easy to apply this section to the case where the seller simply sells goods to A and then, without ever having delivered them to A, sells the same goods to B.

Difficulties have arisen, however, because the section talks of the seller who continues or is in possession of the goods. Suppose that a car dealer sells a car to A who pays for it and takes it away, and then the following day brings it back for some small defect to be rectified.

---

[96] [1965] 1 QB 525.
[97] [1965] SC 253.

While the car is at the dealer's premises, the dealer sells it to B. It would be possible to read the section as giving B's rights precedence over those of A but it is quite clear that if A had taken his car to any other dealer who had sold it to B, A's rights would have prevailed over those of B. It would be very odd to make the positions of A and B depend on whether A takes his car for a service to the person from whom he has bought it or to someone else. In fact, the courts have not read the section in this way but they have given different explanations for not doing so.

In *Staffordshire Motor Guarantee* v *British Wagon*[98] a dealer sold a lorry to a finance company who then hired it back to him under a hire purchase agreement. The dealer then, in breach of the hire purchase agreement, sold the lorry to another buyer. It was held that the rights of the finance company prevailed over those of the second buyer. The explanation given was that for s. 24 to apply the seller must continue in possession 'as a seller'. However, this view was later rejected by the Privy Council on appeal from Australia in *Pacific Motor Auctions* v *Motor Credits*[99] and by the Court of Appeal in *Worcester Works Finance* v *Cooden Engineering*.[100] In these cases, it was said that the crucial question was whether the seller's possession was physically continuous. If it was, as in the *Staffordshire Motor Guarantee* case, then s. 24 applied.

If there has been a break in possession so that the buyer has, even for a short time, had the goods in his hands although he has later redelivered them to the seller, then s. 24 does not apply. This obviously covers the case of the buyer who takes the car back to be serviced the following day, but it means that s. 24 also applies to the rather common commercial case where a motor dealer transfers ownership to a finance company or a bank but remains in possession. This is a common means of financing the stock which the dealer has on his floor and enables more stock to be carried than if the dealer had to carry the full cash cost of the cars. It is, in effect, a form of security for the lender against the dealer's stock. This form of transaction may well give the lender adequate security in the case of the insolvency of the dealer, but s. 24 will prevent it giving the lender adequate protection against the dishonest dealer who sells the cars and disappears with the proceeds.

In order to take advantage of this exception there must be delivery to a buyer who takes in good faith. An important decision on the scope of this is *Michael Gerson (Leasing) Ltd* v *Wilkinson*.[101] In this case X wished to raise money by a sale and lease back of its plant and machinery to A. X did not keep up the agreed payments but remained in possession. Six months later X sold and leased back some of the goods (the parcel) to B but again did not keep up the payments. B terminated the contract and sold the parcel to C. Later A terminated the first lease and purported to sell all the goods to D who resold them to E. The Court of Appeal held that C had become the owner of the parcel. In this case both A and B were finance companies which were in the business of financing companies by sale and lease back transactions. The Court of Appeal analysed such transactions as involving constructive delivery to the finance company and redelivery to the seller as bailee.

---

[98] [1934] 2 KB 304.
[99] [1965] AC 867.
[100] [1972] 1 QB 210.
[101] [2001] QB 514; [2001] 1 All ER 148.

4.6.4.5 Buyer in possession after sale

> **LEGISLATIVE PROVISION**
>
> SALE OF GOODS ACT 1979
>
> **Section 25**
>
> (1) Where a person having bought or agreed to buy goods obtains, with the consent of the seller, possession of the goods or the documents of title to the goods, the delivery or transfer by that person, or by a mercantile agent acting for him, of the goods or documents of title, under any sale, pledge, or other disposition thereof, to any person receiving the same in good faith and without notice of any lien or other right of the original seller in respect of the goods, has the same effect as if the person making the delivery or transfer were a mercantile agent in possession of the goods or documents of title with the consent of the owner.
>
> (2) For the purposes of sub-s. (1) above:
>
> (a) the buyer under a conditional sale agreement is to be taken not to be a person who has bought or agreed to buy goods; and
>
> (b) 'conditional sale agreement' means an agreement for the sale of goods which is a consumer credit agreement within the meaning of the Consumer Credit Act 1974 under which the purchase price or any part of it is payable by instalments, and the property in the goods is to remain in the seller (notwithstanding that the buyer is to be in possession of the goods) until such conditions as to the payment of instalments or otherwise as may be specified in the agreement are fulfilled.

It will be seen that this section is in a sense the reverse of s. 24 since it deals with the situation where possession of the goods has passed to the buyer before ownership has passed to him and permits such a buyer to transfer ownership to a sub-buyer. The wording talks of 'a person having bought or agreed to buy goods'. Normally, if the buyer has bought the goods, there would be a complete contract of sale and property would have passed to him. In that case, of course, he would be in a position to transfer ownership to a sub-buyer without any question of s. 25 arising. The section is concerned with the situation where the buyer has obtained possession of the goods (or the documents of title to the goods) with the consent of the seller but without becoming the owner.

The section does not apply where someone has obtained goods without having agreed to buy them. So, in *Shaw v Commissioner of Police*[102] a car had been obtained from the owner on the basis that the person obtaining it might have a client who might be willing to buy it. It was held that he was not a buyer within the meaning of s. 25 and was not therefore in a position to transfer ownership to a sub-buyer. In the same way, on one hand, a customer under a hire purchase agreement is not a buyer for the purpose of s. 25 because in such a case the customer

---

[102] [1987] 3 All ER 305.

has only agreed to hire the goods and is given an option to buy the goods which he is not legally obliged to exercise even though commercially it is extremely likely that he will (see the discussion in section 4.2). On the other hand, a customer who has agreed to buy the goods but has been given credit is a buyer within s. 25, even though the agreement provides that he is not to become the owner until he has paid for the goods. Section 25(2) contains a statutory modification of this rule in the case where the buyer has taken under a 'conditional sale agreement' as defined in s. 25(2)(b), that is where the price is to be paid by instalments and falls within the scope of the Consumer Credit Act 1974. The reason for this exception is to make the law about conditional sale agreements within the Consumer Credit Act the same as for hire purchase agreements within the Act.

Section 25 has important effects on the reasoning contained in *Car and Universal Finance v Caldwell*,[103] discussed above. In some cases of this kind, although the buyer's voidable title would have been avoided, he would still be a buyer in possession within s. 25. This was shown in *Newtons of Wembley Ltd v Williams*,[104] where the plaintiff agreed to sell a car to A on the basis that the property was not to pass until the whole purchase price had been paid or a cheque had been honoured. A issued a cheque and was given possession of the car but in due course his cheque bounced. The plaintiff took immediate steps to avoid the contract as in the *Caldwell* case and, after he had done this, A sold the car to B in a London street market and B then sold the car to the defendant. The Court of Appeal held that, although the plaintiff had avoided A's title, A was still a buyer in possession of the car and that B had therefore obtained a good title from A when he bought from him in good faith and had taken possession of the car. It was an important part of the Court of Appeal's reasoning that the sale by A to B had taken place in the ordinary course of business of a mercantile agent.

4.6.4.6 Agents and mercantile agents

In practice, most sales are made by agents since most sellers are companies and employ agents to carry on their business. This presents no problem where, as would usually be the case, agents make contracts which they are authorised to make. Furthermore, under general contract law, agents bind the principal not only when they do things which they are actually authorised to do, but also when they do things which they *appear* to be authorised to do. The common law concerning principal and agent is expressly preserved in the Sale of Goods Act by s. 62.

However, it is clear that the law of sale has developed by use of a concept of 'mercantile agents' which is wider than that of agency in the general law of contract. This concept developed because of a limitation which was imposed on the general law of agency. If I put my car into the hands of a car dealer to sell on my behalf, I will normally be bound by the contract which he makes even though he goes outside my authority, for instance by accepting a lower price than I have agreed.[105] However, if instead of selling the car, the dealer pledges it as security for a loan, he would not under general contract law be treated

---

[103] [1965] 1 QB 525.
[104] [1965] 1 QB 560.
[105] *Lloyds and Scottish Finance Ltd v Williamson* [1965] 1 All ER 641; [1965] 1 WLR 404.

as having apparent authority to do so. This is so, even though, from the point of view of a third party dealing with the dealer, his relationship to the car looks quite the same whether he is selling it or pledging it.

The pledging of goods and documents of title is a very important part of financing commercial transactions in some trades. So, people importing large amounts of commodities, such as grain or coffee, may very likely pledge the goods or documents of title to the goods, in order to borrow money against them. It was felt unsatisfactory, therefore, to have this distinction between the agent who sells and the agent who pledges and this was the subject of statutory amendment by a series of Factors Acts starting in 1823 and culminating in the Factors Act 1889, which effectively removes the distinction.

LEGISLATIVE PROVISION

The Factors Act 1889 continues in force after the passage of the Sale of Goods Act 1893 and 1979. Section 21(2) of the Sale of Goods Act provides that:

. . . nothing in this Act affects:

(a) the provisions of the Factors Acts or any enactment enabling the apparent owner of goods to dispose of them as if he were their true owner.

Sections 8 and 9 of the Factors Act provide:

(8) Where a person, having sold goods, continues, or is in possession of the goods or of the documents of title to the goods, the delivery or transfer by that person, or by a mercantile agent acting for him, of the goods or documents of title under any sale, pledge, or other disposition thereof, *or under any agreement for sale, pledge, or other disposition thereof*, to any person receiving the same in good faith and without notice of the previous sale, shall have the same effect as if the person making the delivery or transfer were expressly authorised by the owner of the goods to make the same.

(9) Where a person, having bought or agreed to buy goods, obtains with the consent of the seller possession of the goods or the documents of title to the goods, the delivery or transfer, by that person or by a mercantile agent acting for him, of the goods or documents of title, under any sale, pledge, or other disposition thereof, *or under any agreement for sale, pledge, or other disposition thereof*, to any person receiving the same in good faith and without notice of any lien or other right of the original seller in respect of the goods, shall have the same effect as if the person making the delivery or transfer were a mercantile agent in possession of the goods or documents of title with the consent of the owner [emphasis added].

It will be seen that these provisions are very similar to the provisions of ss. 24 and 25 of the Sale of Goods Act. The difference is the presence of the words in italics in the text above. A key question is clearly what is meant by a 'mercantile agent'. This is defined by s. 1(1) of the Factors Act as meaning 'a mercantile agent having in the customary course of his business as such agent authority either to sell goods, or to consign goods for the purpose of sale, or to buy goods, or to raise money on the security of goods'. The effect of dealings by mercantile agents is set out in s. 2 of the Factors Act.

LEGISLATIVE PROVISION

FACTORS ACT 1889

Section 2(1)

Where a mercantile agent is, with the consent of the owner, in possession of goods or of the documents of title to goods, any sale, pledge, or other disposition of the goods, made by him when acting in the ordinary course of business of a mercantile agent, shall, subject to the provisions of this Act, be as valid as if he were expressly authorised by the owner of the goods to make the same; provided that the person taking under the disposition acts in good faith, and has not at the time of the disposition notice that the person making the disposition has not authority to make the same.

(2) Where a mercantile agent has, with the consent of the owner, been in possession of goods or of the documents of title to goods, any sale, pledge, or other disposition, which would have been valid if the consent had continued, shall be valid notwithstanding the determination of the consent: provided that the person taking under the disposition has not at the time thereof notice that the consent has been determined.

(3) Where a mercantile agent has obtained possession of any documents of title to goods by reason of his being or having been, with the consent of the owner, in possession of the goods represented thereby, or of any other documents of title to the goods, his possession of the first-mentioned documents shall, for the purposes of this Act, be deemed to be with the consent of the owner.

(4) For the purposes of this Act, the consent of the owner shall be presumed in the absence of evidence to the contrary.

The most important limitation on the wide-ranging power given by s. 2 is that in order for the mercantile agent to be able to pass title he or she must not only be in possession with the owner's consent, but must be in possession as a *mercantile agent* with the owner's consent. So, for instance, a car dealer who has both a showroom and a servicing facility is clearly a mercantile agent and has the consent of his or her service customers to have possession of their cars for servicing, but if he were to put one of these cars into the show room and sell it, this would not be a transaction protected by the Factors Acts because he would not have had possession of the car as a mercantile agent, but rather as a repairer.

An interesting case in this connection is *Pearson* v *Rose and Young*.[106] Here, the plaintiff delivered his car to a mercantile agent in order to obtain offers, but gave no authority to sell it. The agent succeeded in obtaining the logbook by a trick, in circumstances where it was clear that the owner had not consented to the dealer having possession of the logbook. Having got both the logbook and the car, the dealer then dishonestly sold it. The Court of Appeal held that this was not a transaction protected by the Factors Act. The reason was that although the dealer had possession of the car with the owner's consent, he did not have possession of the logbook with the owner's consent. He could, of course, have sold the car

---

[106] [1951] 1 KB 275.

without the logbook, but the court held that this would not have been a sale in the ordinary course of business of a mercantile agent and therefore the sale without the logbook would have been outside the Factors Acts; it followed that the sale with the logbook, where the logbook had been obtained without the owner's consent, was also outside the Act.

CASE

National Employer's Insurance v Jones[107]

An important decision on s. 9 of the Factors Act and s. 25(1) of the Sale of Goods Act 1979 is *National Employer's Insurance v Jones*. In that case, a car was stolen and sold to A, who sold it to B, who in turn sold it to a car dealer C. C sold it to another car dealer D, and it was then sold to the defendant who bought it in good faith. It had been assumed in many previous transactions that in such circumstances the defendant was not protected, since the original invalidity arising from the theft was not cured by any of the subsequent sales. However, in this case, the defendant argued that the transaction fell within the literal scope of s. 9 because D had obtained possession of the goods with the consent of the dealer who had sold the goods to him and who was certainly a mercantile agent. It is true that both s. 9 and s. 25 refer to consent of the seller and not consent of the owner, and Sir Denys Buckley in the Court of Appeal dissented from the majority view and held that the transaction was covered by ss. 9 and 25. However, a unanimous House of Lords took the opposite view. They held that the word 'seller' in ss. 9 and 25 must be given a special meaning and could not cover a seller whose possession could be traced back (through however many transactions) to the unlawful possession of a thief. This must be correct, since otherwise the sale by the thief to the first purchaser would not be protected, but the sale by that purchaser to the second purchaser would be.

4.6.4.7 Part III of the Hire Purchase Act 1964

It will be seen that in modern times, the vast majority of cases which involve the operation of the *nemo dat* principle involve a dishonest handling of motor cars. This is no doubt because:

(a) a car is by nature easily moved; and

(b) cars command a ready cash price on the secondhand market and can, in practice, often be traced by the original owner.

One of the most common forms of dishonesty is for a person to acquire a car on hire purchase terms and then to dispose of it for cash before he has completed the hire purchase contract. In practice he will find it difficult to dispose of the car for cash to an honest dealer because the existence of the hire purchase transaction would normally be discovered by reference by the dealer to HPI, as discussed earlier. However, it is very easy for a person who has acquired a car on hire purchase to sell it for cash on the secondhand

---

[107] [1990] AC 24.

market by advertising, and equally very difficult for someone buying from him to know that the seller is not in fact the owner of the goods. Such transactions are not protected by s. 25 because someone acquiring goods on hire purchase is not a buyer, nor is he protected by the Factors Act, because the seller is not a mercantile agent.

In order to deal with this situation, the Hire Purchase Act 1964 created a new exception to the *nemo dat* rule by providing that if a car which was subject to a hire purchase or credit sale agreement was sold to a private purchaser, that purchaser would acquire a good title if he bought it in good faith and without notice of the hire purchase or credit sale agreement.

This protection is accorded only to private purchasers and does not apply to dealers.[108] However, the private purchaser does not need to be the person who actually buys and makes the initial purchase of the goods from the person who is dishonestly disposing of goods. So, if X has a car on hire purchase terms and dishonestly sells it to a dealer B, who then sells it to C who buys it in good faith, unconscious of the defects in A's or B's title, C will obtain a good title, even though he has bought from B (the dealer) and not from A (the original hirer) and even though B himself did not obtain a good title.

It is obviously very important, therefore, to know who is a 'private purchaser'. Private purchasers are those who are not 'trade or finance purchasers', and a trade or finance purchaser is one who at the time of the disposition carried on a business which consisted wholly or partly of either:

(a) purchasing motor vehicles for the purpose of offering or exposing them for sale; or

(b) providing finance by purchasing motor vehicles for the purpose of letting them under hire purchase agreements or agreeing to sell them under conditional sale agreements.

It is perfectly possible to carry on either of these activities part time, so that someone who buys and sells cars as a sideline will be a trade purchaser, if he is doing so as a business, that is, with a view to making a profit. On the other hand, a company which is not in the motor trade or the financing of motor purchase business will be a private purchaser for the purpose of Part III of the 1964 Act.

In *GE Capital Bank Ltd* v *Rushton*[109] the bank provided finance for a dealer to buy seven cars on its behalf. In January 2004 the dealer sold the cars to R who was not a dealer. In February 2004 the bank terminated the plan and the next day R sold one of the cars to J. The Court of Appeal held that J was protected by Part III of the Act but that R was not because although not a dealer he was involved in the transaction as a business venture.

In *Rohit Kulkarni* v *Manor Credit (Davenham) Ltd*[110] a Mercedes was bought by Manor Credit, which hire purchased it to Gwent Fleet Management Ltd, which agreed to let on hire purchase terms to retail customers. In fact Gwent purported to sell it to Dr Kulkarni. All of these transactions took place in a week in March 2008. Gwent went into liquidation and Manor Credit claimed that the car was still theirs. They sought to argue that Gwent had sold the car to Dr Kulkarni before they had entered into the hire purchase agreement and that therefore the statute did not apply. The Court of Appeal side-stepped this difficulty by holding

---

[108] In *Barber v NWS Bank* [1996] 1 All ER 906, the buyer arguably acquired ownership under the Act, but the Court of Appeal pointed out that s. 27(6) said that this did not exonerate the seller from civil or criminal liability.
[109] [2006] 3 All ER 865; [2005] EWCA Civ 1556.
[110] [2010] EWCA Civ 69; [2010] 2 All ER (Comm) 1017.

that the effective date of the sale was that of delivery of the car, which was clearly after Manor Credit and Gwent had entered into the hire purchase agreement.

4.6.4.8 Other statutory provisions

There is, of course, no limit to the power of Parliament to create further exceptions to the *nemo dat* principle. In *Bulbruin Ltd* v *Romanyszyn*,[111] a local authority sold an abandoned vehicle to the defendant under powers conferred on it by the Road Traffic Regulation Act 1984 and the Removal and Disposal of Vehicles Regulations 1986. It turned out that, before coming into the hands of the local authority, the vehicle had been stolen from the plaintiff and fitted with false number plates. The Court of Appeal held that the defendant had acquired good title.

4.7   Non-existent goods, risk and frustration

Suppose that the goods which are the subject of the contract never existed or once existed and have now ceased to exist or that the goods, although they exist, have been damaged or that goods of this kind are no longer available on the market. How does this affect the rights of the parties? There are two separate doctrines which are used to answer questions such as this. These are the doctrines of risk and of frustration. Before we examine these doctrines, however, we must consider the special case of goods which never existed at all or which, having once existed, have perished.

4.7.1 Non-existent goods

LEGISLATIVE PROVISION

Section 6 of the Sale of Goods Act 1979 provides:

> Where there is a contract for the sale of specific goods and the goods without the knowledge of the seller have perished at the time when the contract was made, the contract is void.

This section is commonly assumed to have been an attempt by the draftsman of the 1893 Act to state the effect of the famous pre-Act case of *Couturier* v *Hastie*.[112] In that case, the contract was for the sale of a specific cargo of corn which was on board a named ship sailing from Salonica to London. In fact, at the time the contract was made, the cargo of corn had been sold by the master of the ship in Tunis because it was fermenting owing to storm damage.

---

[111] [1994] RTR 273.
[112] (1856) 5 HLC 673.

(The master of the ship was of course the servant of the ship's owners and not of the seller.) One might have expected that if, on these facts, litigation took place at all, it would arise by the buyer suing the seller for non-delivery of the goods. In fact, however, the seller sued the buyer, claiming that he was entitled to the price even though he had no goods to deliver. At first sight, this seems an absurd argument, since normally the buyer's obligation to pay the price is conditional on the seller's being able to deliver the goods. The seller's argument was that, in a contract of this kind, the buyer had agreed to pay against delivery of the shipping documents, which would have given him rights against the carriers and against the insurers of the goods. As we shall see, this argument would sometimes succeed because of the rules about the passing of risk where the goods perished after the contract was made. Indeed, in some cases of international sales, it would even succeed where the goods were damaged (as opposed to having perished) after shipment, but before the contract was made, because of the possibility that risk might retrospectively go back to the date of shipment. However, the Court of Exchequer Chamber and the House of Lords were agreed that in this case the seller's action failed.

Couturier v *Hastie* has been extensively discussed, not only in relation to the law of sales, but also in relation to the general law of contract. It has been taken by some as an example of a general principle that, if the parties' agreement is based on some shared fundamental mistake, then the contract is void. Other writers have treated it as an example of an overlapping but rather narrower principle that if, unknown to the parties, the subject matter of the contract does not exist or has ceased to exist, the contract is void. The controversy as to whether either or both of these principles is part of the general law of contract has not been finally resolved and cannot be pursued in detail here. It is important to note, however, that s. 6 of the Sale of Goods Act 1979 does not turn on either of these principles.

In order to apply s. 6, one needs to know what is meant by the goods having perished. It is clear that in *Couturier* v *Hastie*, the corn may still have existed at the time of the contract. There is no evidence in the report of the case of what happened to the corn after it was sold in Tunis. It seems clear that it was treated as having perished because, as a commercial entity, the cargo had ceased to exist. In *Barrow, Lane and Ballard Ltd* v *Philip Phillips Co Ltd*,[113] there was a contract for 700 bags of ground nuts which were believed to be in a warehouse. In fact, unbeknown to the parties, 109 bags had been stolen before the contract was made. It was held that s. 6 applied and the contract was void. It will be seen that only some 15 per cent of the contract parcel had been stolen, but this was treated as sufficient to destroy the parcel as a whole. Clearly, whether this will be so in other cases will depend very much on the particular facts of the case and precisely what it is the seller has contracted to deliver. It was probably also relevant in the above case that there was no realistic chance of recovering the stolen bags.

On the one hand, goods will not be treated as having perished merely because they have been damaged. On the other hand, there may be damage so extensive as effectively to deprive the goods of the commercial character under which they were sold. So, in *Asfar & Co Ltd* v *Blundell*[114] the contract was for a sale of a cargo of dates. The dates had become contaminated with sewage and had begun to ferment. Although all the dates were still available, the cargo was treated as commercially perished.

---

[113] [1929] 1 KB 574.
[114] [1896] 1 QB 123.

It will be seen that s. 6 applies only to the sale of specific goods and only where the goods have perished 'without the knowledge of the seller'. A seller who knows that the goods have perished will therefore normally be liable for breach of contract and might, in some cases, alternatively be liable for fraud. A difficult question is what the position would be if the seller ought to have known that the goods had perished. In 1856, communications between Tunis and London were no doubt not such as to make it easy for the seller to have discovered quickly what had happened to the cargo. This would not be the case today. The literal wording of s. 6 suggests that, if the seller does not know that the goods have perished, even though he or she could easily have discovered it, the contract is void. It does not follow, however, that the buyer would be without a remedy, since in some such cases the seller would be liable for having represented negligently that the goods did exist. This is one of the possible explanations of the famous Australian decision of *McRae v Commonwealth Disposals Commission*[115] although this was actually a case where the goods had never existed rather than one where the goods had once existed and had perished. In *McRae*, the Commonwealth Disposals Commission sold to the plaintiff the wreck of a ship which was said to be on a named reef off the coast of New Guinea. The plaintiff mounted an expedition to salvage the ship, only to find that the ship, and indeed the named reef, did not exist. It is easy to see that simply to hold that there was no contract on these facts would have been very unfair on the plaintiff who had wasted much time and money searching for a ship which did not exist. It was not surprising, therefore, that the High Court of Australia held that the plaintiff could recover this lost expenditure although they did not recover the profit they might have made if the ship had been there and had been successfully salvaged.

There has been much discussion over whether an English court would reach the same result. The Australian court took the view that s. 6 did not apply to the facts since it dealt only with goods which had once existed and had perished, not with goods that had never existed at all. Some commentators in England, however, have taken the view that s. 6 is simply a partial statement of the common law rule and that the common law rule applies not only to goods which are perished but also to goods which have never existed. It would be possible to accept this view but to hold that a seller could be sued for misrepresentation whether the goods perished or had never existed, if it could be shown either that he or she knew that the goods no longer existed or that he or she ought to have known this. In *McRae*, the High Court of Australia would have held the sellers negligent but, in 1951, it was widely believed that there was no liability to pay damages for loss caused by negligent misrepresentation; this is now clearly no longer the case since the decision of the House of Lords in *Hedley Byrne & Co Ltd v Heller & Partners Ltd*.[116]

An alternative approach would be to say that, except for those cases which are covered by the express words of s. 6, there is no rigid rule that simply because the goods do not exist there is no contract. Obviously, in many cases, the rational inference will be that the parties' agreement is conditional upon the goods existing. In other cases (and this was the reasoning of the High Court of Australia in *McRae*), the seller may reasonably be treated as having contracted that the goods do exist. Yet a third possibility is that the buyer may have contracted on the basis that he would take the risk that the goods did exist (this was in effect the

---

[115] (1951) 84 CLR 377.
[116] [1964] AC 465.

argument of the sellers in *Couturier* v *Hastie*, rejected on the facts of that case but not necessarily to be rejected in other cases).

4.7.2 **The doctrine of risk**[117]

The previous section was concerned with problems which arise where the goods have 'perished' before the contract is made. Obviously, the goods may be destroyed or damaged after the contract is made. The principal tool used to allocate the loss which arises where the goods are damaged or destroyed after the contract is made is the doctrine of risk. This is a special doctrine developed for the law of sale, unlike the doctrine of frustration which is a general doctrine of the law of contract and will be discussed in the next section.

4.7.2.1 **What is the effect of the passing of risk?**

It is important to emphasise that the doctrine of risk does not operate to bring the contract of sale to an end. It may, however, release one party from his or her obligations under the contract. So if, for instance, the goods are at the seller's risk and they are damaged or destroyed, this would, in effect, release the buyer from his or her obligation to accept the goods, but it would not release the seller from the obligation to deliver them. Conversely, if the goods are at the buyer's risk and are damaged or destroyed, he or she may still be liable to pay the price even though the seller is no longer liable for failing to deliver the goods. In some cases where the goods are damaged, this would be the fault of a third party and that third party may be liable to be sued. This is particularly likely to be the case where the goods are being carried, because experience shows that goods in transit are particularly vulnerable to accidents. However, a very important practical consideration to take into account here is that a party will not necessarily have a tort action for damage to the goods simply because the risk as between buyer and seller has been placed on it.[118] This is because tort actions for damage to goods by third parties are usually only available to those who either own the goods or are in possession of them at the time that the damage is caused. So, if the goods are in the hands of the carrier in a situation where they still belong to the seller but risk has been transferred to the buyer, and the carrier carelessly damages the goods, the buyer will not normally have an action against the carrier. This is what happened to the buyer in *Leigh and Sillivan* v *Aliakmon Shipping Co Ltd*.[119]

It follows from this, of course, that a very important practical consequence of the passing of risk is to determine which party needs to insure. If the parties are making a special agreement about risk, it will obviously be sensible to make an agreement which naturally fits in with the parties' standard insurance arrangements. So, if goods are delivered to the buyer on terms that the buyer is not to become the owner until he has paid for them, it may still be sensible for the parties to agree that the risk is to pass to the buyer on delivery to it since, once the goods are in the buyer's hands, they will fall within the scope of the contents insurance of the buyer for its house, factory or office. A trap for the unwary here, however, may be that

---

[117] L. S. Sealy [1972B] *CLJ* 225.
[118] In certain circumstances, a buyer who receives the bill of lading will have a contract action against the carrier.
[119] [1986] 2 WLR 902.

the contents insurance only covers those goods which are owned by the insured. Such provisions are quite common in insurance policies, and the prudent insured should take steps to make certain that goods which are in their possession, but which they do not yet own, are insured.

4.7.2.2 When does risk pass?

LEGISLATIVE PROVISION

The basic rule is set out in s. 20 of the Sale of Goods Act 1979, which provides:

(1) Unless otherwise agreed, the goods remain at the seller's risk until the property in them is transferred to the buyer, but when the property in them is transferred to the buyer the goods are at the buyer's risk whether delivery has been made or not.

(2) But, where delivery has been delayed through the fault of either buyer or seller, the goods are at the risk of the party at fault as regards any loss which might not have occurred but for such fault.

(3) Nothing in this section affects the duties or liabilities of either seller or buyer as a bailee or custodier of the goods of the other party.

It will be seen that English law has adopted the basic rule that risk is to pass at the same time as property. This is perhaps the most important example of the general principle, discussed in section 4.6, that the passing of property is most significant, not in itself, but for the consequences which flow from it. The basic rule automatically takes care of all the problems just discussed of who can sue a third party who negligently damages the goods and of insuring goods which one does not own.

Nevertheless, it is quite clear that the parties can, and frequently do, separate the passing of risk and property. So, in standard conditions of sale, the seller will often provide that risk is to pass on delivery but that property is not to pass until the goods have been paid for. This is because the seller does not wish to be bothered with insuring the goods once he or she has delivered them, but is anxious to retain ownership of the goods as security against not being paid in full.

In the same way, the basic rule may be modified by commercial practice. So, in the most common form of international sale of goods, the CIF contract (cost, insurance, freight), the usual understanding will be that risk is to pass as from the date of shipment of the goods, but commonly property will not pass until the seller has tendered the documents (usually the bill of lading, invoice and policy of insurance) and been paid.

This is because the most common practice is for the seller to retain the shipping documents (and, indeed, to take the bill of lading to his own order) to ensure that he gets paid. The rule that the risk passes as from shipment means that the buyer has to look in respect of damage after shipment to his rights under the policy of insurance or against the carrier.

In the normal case, the buyer will be protected as against the carrier because he will receive the bill of lading, and in most cases the transfer of the bill transfers the seller's contract rights against the carrier under the bill of lading to the buyer. This did not happen in *Leigh and Sillivan v Aliakmon*, above, because in that case the parties had made special arrangements which did not involve the transfer of the bill of lading and had not adequately addressed their minds in making these arrangements to the problems of suing the carrier. We may also note in passing that in a CIF contract, risk may, and quite often does, pass before the contract has been made because of the presumption that risk passes as from shipment. This means that, if the goods are sold while they are on the high seas, the risk of damage between shipment and the date of contract will pass to the buyer. This rule did not apply in *Couturier v Hastie* because the goods in that case had not simply been damaged but had totally perished.[120]

These cases can no doubt be explained on the basis of an implied agreement between the parties. The risk is to pass in accordance with what is commercially usual. There seem, however, to be at least two kinds of cases where risk may pass at a different time from property even though there is no expressed or implied agreement. The first arises in the case of sales of unascertained goods. As we have seen, property cannot pass in such a case until the goods are ascertained. However, there may be cases where property is not ascertained because the goods form part of an unascertained bulk, but nevertheless fairness requires that risk should pass. The classic example is *Sterns v Vickers*.[121]

CASE

Sterns v Vickers

In this case, the sellers had some 200,000 gallons of white spirit in a tank belonging to a storage company. They sold to the buyers some 120,000 gallons of the spirit and gave the buyers a delivery warrant. The effect of the delivery warrant was that the storage company undertook to deliver the white spirit to the buyers or as the buyers might order. In fact, the buyers sub-sold, but the sub-purchaser did not wish to take possession of the spirit at once and arranged with the storage company to store it on his behalf, paying rent for the storage. Clearly, although there had been a sale and a sub-sale, ownership was still in the hands of the original sellers since the goods were still unascertained. While the bulk was unseparated, the spirit deteriorated. The Court of Appeal held that, although there was no agreement between the parties, the risk had passed as between the original seller and buyer to the buyer. The reason for this was that, as soon as the buyers had the delivery warrant, they were immediately able to obtain delivery of the spirit and therefore risk should pass to them, even though they chose not to take immediate possession of the goods.

The facts of *Sterns v Vickers* are rather special, since the reason why property did not pass to the buyer was a deliberate decision by the buyer. It does not always follow that risk will pass

---

[120] See *Groom (C) v Barber* [1915] 1 KB 316; *Manbre Saccharine Co Ltd v Corn Products Co Ltd* [1919] 1 KB 198.
[121] [1923] 1 KB 78.

before the goods are ascertained; indeed, the usual rule must be to the contrary. In *Healy* v *Howlett*[122] the plaintiff was an Irish fish exporter. He consigned 190 boxes of mackerel to an Irish railway to be sent to England, in order to perform three contracts. The plaintiff had sold 20 boxes to the defendant, a Billingsgate fish merchant, and sent a telegram to Holyhead telling the railway officials to deliver 20 of the boxes to the defendant and the other boxes to the other buyers. No specific box was appropriated to any specific sale. Unfortunately, the train was delayed and the fish deteriorated before they reached Holyhead. It was held that as property had not passed to the buyer since the goods were not ascertained, equally, risk had not passed to the buyer, because there was circumstance to justify departure from the *prima facie* rule that risk passes at the same time as property.

The passing of the Sale of Goods (Amendment) Act 1995, which is discussed in section 4.6, made it possible in the circumstances defined by the Act for property in an undivided bulk to pass. The 1995 Act contains no provision as to risk. At first sight, therefore, it would seem that risk will pass with property. It should be noted, however, that most of the cases affected by the Act are likely to be international sales where, in practice, the passing of risk and property are usually separated.[123]

The second situation where it is usually assumed that risk does not pass though property may have passed, is illustrated by the pre-Act case of *Head* v *Tattersall*,[124] which it is generally assumed would be decided in the same way after the Act.

In this case, the plaintiff bought a horse from the defendant who warranted that it had been hunted with the Bicester hounds. The contract provided that the horse might be returned by a certain day if it appeared that it had not in fact hunted with the hounds, and the plaintiff chose to return it before the agreed date. On the face of it the plaintiff was clearly entitled to do this, but before the horse had been returned, it had been injured while in the plaintiff's possession, although without any fault on his part. The defendant argued that the correct way to analyse the situation was to treat the property as having passed from the defendant to the plaintiff subject to an agreement that it might revest in the defendant at a later stage, but subject to a proviso that the horse was at the plaintiff's risk while it was in his hands. The court held, however, that the plaintiff was entitled to return the horse. Cleasby B expressly stated that property had passed to the plaintiff and then revested in the defendant. The same conclusion is implicit in the other two judgments. Of course, on these facts, the plaintiff would have had an alternative remedy on the warranty, but that is clearly not the basis of the decision. This can only be on the basis that the agreement that the horse might be returned was an agreement which was substantially unqualified, but it would often be the case that it would be a more sensible interpretation of an agreement of this kind that the goods should be returned only if they were in substantially the same condition when returned as when originally delivered.

The general rule stated in s. 20(1) of the Sale of Goods Act 1979 is subject to the qualifications contained in sub-ss. (2) and (3). Sub-section (2) states that if the seller is late in making the delivery or the buyer is late in accepting delivery, the incidence of risk may be different from what it would otherwise have been. This would be so, however, only if the loss is one

---

[122] [1917] 1 KB 337.
[123] See p. 166.
[124] (1870) LR 7 Ex 7.

which might not have occurred if delivery had not been delayed. However, the onus will be on one party who is in delay to show that the loss would have happened in any event.[125] Sub-section (3) is really no more than a specific example of the general principle that the passing of risk concerns the allocation of the risk of damage which is not the fault of either party. The most important example of this is where the risk is on one party, but the other party is in possession of the goods and fails to take good care of them.

A substantial change to s. 20 has been made by the Sale and Supply of Goods to Consumers Regulations 2002 which introduces a new sub-section (4) which provides:

> (4) In a case where the buyer deals as consumer or, in Scotland, where there is a consumer contract in which the buyer is a consumer, subsections (1) to (3) above must be ignored and the goods remain at the seller's risk until they are delivered to the consumer.

It will be seen that this means that where the buyer is a consumer the risk will be on the seller until the goods are delivered.

We should also note s. 33 of the Sale of Goods Act 1979, which provides:

> Where the seller of goods agrees to deliver them at his own risk at a place other than that where they are when sold, the buyer must nevertheless (unless otherwise agreed) take any risk of deterioration in the goods necessarily incident to the course of transit.

Practical examples of the application of this section are very hard to find. It seems probable that the draftsman had in mind a pre-Act case, in which goods were sent by canal barge and the court held that some risk of splashing by water was a necessary incident of this form of transit. So s. 33 would not apply to a case where the goods deteriorated because they were not fit to undertake the journey which had been contracted for. Therefore, in *Mash and Murrell* v *Joseph I Emanuel Ltd*[126] potatoes were consigned from Cyprus to Liverpool and it was held that not only must the potatoes be sound when loaded, but they were also impliedly warranted sound enough to survive the ordinary risks of sea carriage from Cyprus to Liverpool. The result would be different if the potatoes had gone off because they had been inadequately ventilated during the voyage, as that would be a risk which was on the buyer (although of course the buyer might have a claim against the carrier).

4.7.3 The doctrine of frustration

The doctrine of frustration is part of the general law of contract. It provides that, in certain exceptional circumstances, events which take place after the contract may be so cataclysmic in effect that it is appropriate to treat them as bringing the contract to an end. In practice the operation of the doctrine is limited to events which make it physically or legally impossible to perform the contract or changes of circumstance so great that in effect the continued performance of the contract would be to require the performance of what is commercially a fundamentally different contract. It is quite clear that the mere fact that the changes of circumstances made it more difficult or more expensive for one of the parties to perform

---

[125] See *Demby Hamilton Ltd* v *Barden* [1949] 1 All ER 435.
[126] [1961] 1 All ER 485; [1962] 1 All ER 77.

the contract is not enough. In principle, there can be no doubt that this doctrine applies to contracts for the sale of goods like any other contract.

4.7.3.1 When does the doctrine of frustration apply?

LEGISLATIVE PROVISION

Section 7 of the Act contains a provision which deals expressly with frustration, which provides:

> Where there is an agreement to sell specific goods and subsequently the goods, without any fault on the part of the seller or buyer, perish before the risk passes to the buyer, the agreement is avoided.

This section is clearly a very incomplete statement of the doctrine of frustration as applied to contracts of sale. It deals only with specific goods which perish, whereas frustration may involve many other events than the destruction of the goods. For instance, where goods are sold internationally, there is often a requirement to obtain an export or import licence. Failure to obtain such a licence would not normally be a frustrating event because the parties would know at the time of the contract that the licence was required and the contract would often expressly or impliedly require one of the parties to obtain (or, at least, to use his or her best endeavours to obtain) the licence. However, it might be that after the contract was made, a government introduced a wholly new export or import licensing system which was unforeseen. There might be plausible arguments in such a case that the contract was frustrated.

It is also possible to argue that a contract for the sale of unascertained goods is frustrated, but of course such goods cannot usually perish (except for the special case of sale of part of the bulk, as discussed below). In practice, the courts, although admitting the possibility that sales of unascertained goods can be frustrated, have been very slow in fact to hold them frustrated. Two examples of unsuccessful arguments will perhaps illustrate this point. In *Blackburn Bobbin Ltd v TW Allen Ltd*[127] there was a contract for the sale of 70 standards of Finland birch timber. Unknown to the buyer, the seller intended to load the timber in Finland for shipment to England. This was the usual trade practice at the time of the contract. In fact, before delivery began, the 1914 war broke out and shipment became impossible. It was held that the contract was not frustrated. It will be seen that, although the contract called for timber from Finland, it did not contain any provision that the timber was in Finland at the time of the contract. This illustrates the fundamental point that whether frustration applies or not always depends on the precise nature of the contractual obligations undertaken and the precise nature of the calamity which has overtaken them.

---

[127] [1918] KB 540; [1918] 2 KB 467.

> ## CASE
>
> ### *Tsakiroglou & Co Ltd v Noblee and Thorl*[128]
>
> A second case is *Tsakiroglou & Co Ltd v Noblee and Thorl*. This was one of a number of contracts in which Sudanese ground nuts had been sold CIF European ports. At the time of the contract, the seller, whose duty it is under a CIF contract to arrange and pay for the sea carriage to the port of destination, intended to put the goods on a ship going through the Suez Canal. By the time the date for shipment arrived, the canal was closed because of the 1956 Suez Crisis. In order to perform the contract, therefore, the seller needed to put the ground nuts on a ship coming to Europe via the Cape of Good Hope. This was perfectly possible, since the cargo was not perishable but involved the seller in significant extra expenditure partly because the route via the Cape was much longer and partly because the closure of the Canal had in any event greatly increased world freight rates by altering the balance between supply and demand for shipping space. The seller argued that the changes were so dramatic as to frustrate the contract. This was not at all an implausible argument and one experienced judge, McNair J, in a case on virtually identical facts, did hold that the contract was frustrated. However, the House of Lords in this case held that the contract was not frustrated. The principal reason for this decision seems to be that, in a CIF contract, the seller includes the cost of carriage as an integral part of the agreement. The seller therefore takes the risk of freight rates going down. The shipping market is volatile and freight rates go up and down all the time. What had happened was simply an extreme example of price fluctuation, but that itself was not enough to bring the contract to an end.

Perhaps the most interesting cases are two examples where farmers sold in advance the product of a harvest and then suffered an unforeseen bad harvest which produced a crop much less than anticipated.

In *Howell* v *Coupland*[129] a farmer sold in March, for delivery upon harvesting the following autumn, 200 tons of potatoes to come from his farm. In fact, only 80 tons were harvested. The buyer accepted delivery of the 80 tons and brought an action for damages for non-delivery of the balance of 120 tons. It was held that the unforeseen potato blight which had affected the crop released the seller from his obligation to deliver any more than had in fact been grown. It should be noted that the buyer was perfectly happy to accept and pay for the 80 tons; it was certainly arguable that, if the potato blight released the seller, it also released the buyer from any obligation to take the potatoes at all. Obviously, there could be commercial situations in which, if the buyer could not obtain the full 200 tons from one source, it was perfectly reasonable of him to refuse to accept any delivery at all. The case does not decide that a buyer could not elect to do this. (Section 7 of the Sale of Goods Act is usually thought to be an attempt by the draftsman to state the effects of *Howell* v *Coupland*, but it is usually held that s. 7 does not, in fact, cover the case, since the goods in *Howell* v *Coupland* were not specific, but, rather, future goods. Nevertheless, it is usually assumed that *Howell* v *Coupland* was correctly decided and would be decided in the same way today.)

---

[128] [1962] AC 93.
[129] (1876) 1 QBD 258.

In the modern case of *HR & S Sainsbury Ltd* v *Street*,[130] the farmer contracted to sell to a corn merchant 275 tons of barley to be grown on his farm. In this case, there was a generally poor harvest and only 140 tons were harvested on the defendant's farm. The defendant argued that the contract was frustrated and sold the 140 tons to another merchant. (The reason no doubt being that because of the generally poor harvest, barley prices were higher than expected and the defendant was then able to get a better price from another merchant.) McKenna J held that the farmer was in breach of contract by not delivering the 140 tons which had actually been harvested, although the bad harvest did relieve him of any obligation to deliver the balance of 135 tons. Again, it should be noted that in this case the buyer was willing and indeed anxious to take the 140 tons and the case does not therefore decide that the buyer in such a case was bound to take the 140 tons, although the doctrine of frustration where it operates, does normally operate to release both parties from future performance of the contract.

In the case above, the farmer appears to have sold his crop in advance to a single merchant. Obviously, a farmer might expect to harvest 200 tons and agree to sell 100 tons off his farm to each of two different merchants. Suppose in such a case he had a crop of only 150 tons. It is unclear what the effect of this would be. Commentators have usually argued that in this case the fair result would be that each of the buyers should have 75 tons, but it is unclear whether this result can be reached. A similar problem arises where a seller has a bulk cargo, say, 1,000 tons of wheat on board a known ship and sells 500 tons to A and 500 tons to B, only for it to be discovered on arrival that 100 tons of the cargo are damaged without any fault on the part of the seller.

4.7.3.2 The effect of frustration

If a frustrating event takes place, its effect is to bring the contract to an end at once and relieve both parties from any further obligation to perform the contract. This is so even though the frustrating event usually only makes it impossible for one party to perform. So, the fact that the seller is unable to deliver the goods does not mean that the buyer is unable to pay the price, but the seller's inability to deliver the goods relieves the buyer of the obligation to pay the price. This rule is easy to apply where the contract is frustrated before either party has done anything to perform it, but the contract is often frustrated after some acts of performance have taken place. This has proved a surprisingly difficult question to resolve.

At common law, it was eventually held in the leading case of *Fibrosa* v *Fairbairn*[131] that, if a buyer had paid in advance for the goods, he could recover the advance payment in full if no goods at all had been delivered before the contract was frustrated. However, that decision is based on a finding that there had been a 'total failure of consideration'; that is, that the buyer had received no part of what it expected to receive under the contract. If there was a partial failure of consideration, that is, if the buyer had received some of the goods, then it would not have been able to recover an advance payment of the price even though the advance payment was significantly greater than the value of the goods which it had received. This obviously appears unfair to the buyer. The decision in the *Fibrosa* case was also potentially unfair to the seller. Even though the seller has not delivered any goods before the contract is frustrated, it may well have incurred expenditure where the goods have to be

---

[130] [1972] 1 WLR 834; [1972] 3 All ER 1127.
[131] [1943] AC 32.

manufactured for the buyer's requirements and some or perhaps even all of this expenditure may be wasted if the goods cannot easily be resold because the buyer's requirements are special. These defects in the law were largely remedied by the Law Reform (Frustrated Contracts) Act 1943, which gave the court a wide discretion to order repayment of prices which had been paid in advance or to award compensation to a seller who had incurred wasted expenditure before the contract was frustrated.

LEGISLATIVE PROVISION

Section 2(5)(c) of the 1943 Act provides that the Act shall not apply to:

> Any contract to which s. 7 of the Sale of Goods Act . . . applies or . . . any other contract for the sale, or for the sale and delivery, of specific goods, where the contract is frustrated by reason of the fact that the goods have perished.

So, the 1943 Act does not apply to cases where the contract is frustrated either under s. 7 of the Sale of Goods Act or in other cases where it is frustrated by the goods perishing. (It should be mentioned here that it is not at all clear whether it is possible for the contract to be frustrated by perishing of the goods other than under s. 7. Some commentators have strongly argued for this view, but it has been doubted by others and the question has never been tested in litigation.) On the other hand, the 1943 Act does apply where the contract is frustrated by any event other than the perishing of the goods. It is really quite unclear why Parliament drew this distinction, but the effect is that, if the contract of sale is frustrated by the destruction of the goods, then the effects of frustration are determined by the common law before the 1943 Act with the results described above.

4.7.3.3 *Force majeure* clauses[132]

The English law doctrine of frustration is rather narrow in its scope and the parties may often wish, therefore, to provide for unexpected contingencies which do not or may not fall within the doctrine of frustration. Such clauses in commercial contracts are very common. They are often referred to as *force majeure* clauses, *force majeure* being the equivalent, though rather wider, French doctrine akin to frustration. There is no doubt that the parties are free to widen the effect of unexpected events in this way. Indeed, the rationale commonly put forward for the narrow scope of the doctrine of frustration is exactly that the parties can widen their provision if they choose to do so. It is not possible here to consider all the clauses which might possibly be found, which would justify a book in itself. Sometimes, clauses are found which simply say that the contract is subject to *force majeure*, but this is probably a bad practice since it is far from certain exactly what an English court will hold *force majeure* to mean. More sophisticated clauses usually, therefore, set out what is meant either by a list of events, such as strikes, lockouts, bad weather and so on, or by a general provision that the events must be unforeseen and outside the control of the parties, or by some combination of these. A typical

---

[132] See E. McKendrick (ed.), *Force Majeure and Frustration of Contract* (2nd edn, LLP, London, 1995) especially chapters 1, 2, 3, 4, 5, 10 and 13; and G. H. Treitel, *Frustration and Force Majeure* (Sweet and Maxwell, London, 2004).

clause will also frequently require the party (usually the seller) who claims that there has been *force majeure*, to give prompt notice to the buyer. Whereas the doctrine of frustration brings the contract to an end, *force majeure* clauses often opt for less drastic consequences. So, it may be provided that, if there is a strike which affects delivery, the seller is to be given extra time, though the clause may go on to say that, if the interruption is sufficiently extended, the seller is to be relieved altogether.

ISSUE BOX

1. What are the seller's obligations as to the transfer of ownership to the buyer? To what extent can he limit them?

2. What is the connection between the transfer of property and the transfer of risk?

3. A is a manufacturer of sofas. A sells them to retailers who sell them to members of the public. A would like to guard against the retailers becoming insolvent before they have paid for the sofas. Advise A.

4. A, a car dealer, sells the same car to B and C. Who will become the owner?

4.8 Defective goods

4.8.1 Introduction

This section is concerned with the legal problems which arise where the goods are 'defective'. (The word 'defective' is put in quotation marks because what we mean by that word is itself one of the central questions to be discussed.)[133] It may be safely suggested that complaints about the quality of the goods far exceed in number any of the other complaints which may be made where goods are bought, so the topic is of great practical importance. It is also of some considerable theoretical complexity because of the way in which the rules have developed.

Liability for defective goods may be contractual, tortious or criminal. The main part of this section will be devoted to considering the situations in which the buyer has a contractual remedy against the seller on the grounds that the goods are not as the seller contracted. However, liability for defective goods may also be based on the law of tort. Since 1932, it has been clear that in most cases there will be liability in tort where someone suffers personal injury or damage to his or her property arising from the defendant having negligently put goods into circulation. This liability does not depend on there being any contract between plaintiff and defendant, though the possibility of such a claim is not excluded by the fact that there is a contract between plaintiff and defendant. So, a buyer of a motor car might

---

[133] The word will not necessarily have the same meaning throughout the section, nor will it necessarily bear its lay meaning. So, if a seller contracts to sell a red car and delivers a blue car, the buyer may be entitled to reject it though the man in the street would hardly call it 'defective'.

formulate the claim against the seller in this way on the basis that the seller had negligently carried out the predelivery inspection. In practice, the buyer would usually be better off pursuing his contractual rights against the seller but this will not always be so. A major development in tort liability has taken place since the adoption in 1985 by the European Community of a directive on product liability, enacted into English law by Part I of the Consumer Protection Act 1987. This Act is aimed at imposing liability for defective products on producers of products, but sellers may be producers either where their distribution is vertically integrated so that the same company is manufacturing, marketing and distributing the goods retail or where, although they are not manufacturing the goods, they sell them as if they were their own (as in the case of major stores which sell 'own brand' goods).[134]

A seller may also come under criminal liability. A typical and all too common example is the secondhand car dealer who turns back the odometer so as to make it appear that the secondhand car has covered fewer miles than is in fact the case. This is a criminal offence under the Trade Descriptions Act 1968. The notion of using the criminal law to regulate the activities of dishonest sellers is very old and goes back to the medieval imposition of standard weights and measures. However, the modern development of an effective consumer lobby has greatly increased the scope of criminal law in this area. In many cases, where there is criminal liability, there would also be civil liability either in contract or in tort. So, the buyer of the secondhand car with the odometer fraudulently turned back would, in virtually all cases, have a civil claim either on the basis that the seller had contracted that the mileage was genuine or on the basis that the seller had fraudulently or negligently represented that it was genuine. Many buyers, however, would find that seeking to enforce this remedy would be a forbidding task because of the expense and trauma involved. The great advantage of enforcement through criminal law is that it is in the hands of local authority officials (commonly called Trading Standards Officers) whose job it is to enforce the criminal law in this area and the cost of whose time falls upon the general body of taxpayers and not upon individual victims of undesirable trading practices. (The disadvantage is that the criminal law primarily operates by punishing the guilty rather than by ordering them to compensate the victim.)[135]

Two other preliminary points may be made. The first is that a seller may seek to exclude or limit his or her liability by inserting appropriate words into the contract of sale. Historically, this has been an extremely common practice and indeed it still is. However, the modern tendency has been to regard such clauses with considerable hostility and, particularly in consumer transactions, they are now very likely to be ineffective. The rules relating to exclusion clauses are discussed in section 4.9. The second point is that this section is concerned to set out the duties of the seller and manufacturer. In practice, the duties of the seller are intimately connected with the remedies of the buyer. In particular it is of critical importance whether failure by the seller to deliver goods of the right quality entitles the buyer to reject the goods (that is, to refuse to accept them) or simply to give him or her a right to damages. In practice, the rules about the seller's obligations and the buyer's remedies interact, because sometimes courts are reluctant to hold that goods are defective where the result would be to entitle the buyer to reject them even though they would be content for the buyer to have a less drastic remedy by way of damages. The remedies of the parties are considered more fully in section 4.10.

---

[134] This is discussed more fully in Chapter 7 on consumer protection.
[135] This is also discussed more fully in Chapter 7 on consumer protection.

4.8.2 Liability in contract: express terms

Two hundred years ago, English law in this area was more or less accurately represented by the maxim *caveat emptor* ('let the buyer beware'). Under this regime, the seller was only liable in so far as he or she had expressly made undertakings about the goods. As we shall see, this is quite clearly no longer the case and English law has come to impose quite extensive liabilities on the seller even where he or she makes no express undertakings by holding that the contract is subject to the implied terms discussed later. Nevertheless, the possibility of express terms is still very important. In any complex commercial contract where goods are being procured for the buyer's specific requirements, the buyer would be well advised to formulate very carefully the express undertakings which he or she wishes the seller to make. Even in commercial dealings, however, where goods have been bought 'off the shelf', not much may be said by way of express undertakings.

CASE

Oscar Chess v Williams[136]

It might be thought that it is a relatively simple task to decide whether or not a seller has made express undertakings about the goods. In fact, this is not the case, and English law has managed to make this a much more difficult question than it would appear at first sight. The problems can be illustrated by the decision of the Court of Appeal in *Oscar Chess v Williams*. In this case, the seller wished to trade in his existing car in part-exchange for a newer car. The buyer, who was a dealer, asked him how old the car was, and the seller described it as a 1948 Morris. In fact, the car was a 1939 Morris but the 1939 and 1948 models were identical and the log book had been altered by a previous owner so as to make the car appear to be a 1948 model. At this time, 1948 cars commanded a higher trade-in price than 1939 cars and the dealer allowed the seller a price in the 1948 range. In due course, the dealer became suspicious and checked the cylinder block number with Cowley, which showed that the car was a 1939 car. There was no doubt on the evidence that the seller had stated that the car was a 1948 model, but the majority of the Court of Appeal held that he had not contracted that it was a 1948 model.

Why did the court reach this decision? The theoretical test is usually formulated by asking what the parties intended. How did the Court of Appeal discover what the parties had intended? Of course, if the parties had said what they intended, this test would be easy to apply, but more often than not, the parties do not say what they intend. In practice, if the parties express no intention, the court is in effect substituting its own view of what the parties, as reasonable people, probably intended. This is necessarily a vague and flexible test. Over the years a number of factors have been taken into account. One argument would be that the statement was of a trivial commendatory nature such that no one should be expected to treat it as meant to be contractually binding. Classic examples would be the house described by an

[136] [1957] 1 All ER 325; [1957] 1 WLR 370.

estate agent as 'a desirable residence' or an obviously secondhand car described by a car dealer as 'as good as new'. It is probably fair to say that modern courts are less willing to accept this classification in marginal cases, particularly where the buyer is a consumer. So, in *Andrews v Hopkinson*,[137] a car dealer said of a secondhand car: 'It's a good little bus. I would stake my life on it.' This was held to be contractually binding and not merely a commendatory statement. (In fact, the car when sold had a badly defective steering mechanism, and a week after being delivered suddenly swerved into a lorry.)

The statement in *Oscar Chess v Williams* as to the age of the car was clearly not in the blandly commendatory category. It was obviously an important statement and affected the price that was offered for the car. In the circumstances one would normally expect such statements to be contractually binding. The most important factor in the decision was probably that the seller was a consumer and the buyer was a dealer, a kind of reverse consumerism. It is very plausible to think that if the facts had been reversed and the seller had been a dealer, the result would have been different. This analysis is supported by the later decision of the Court of Appeal in *Bentley v Harold Smith Motors*.[138] In this case, the sellers, who were dealers, claimed to be experts in tracing the history of secondhand Bentley motor cars and assured the prospective buyer that a particular car had only done 20,000 miles since it had been fitted with a replacement engine and gearbox. It was held that this statement was contractually binding. Another factor which distinguishes the *Oscar Chess* and *Bentley* cases is that in the *Bentley* case the sellers had held themselves out as capable of discovering the truth, and probably were, whereas in the *Oscar Chess* case, the seller was clearly not at fault since he had not unreasonably relied on the statement in the log book. It is quite clear, however, that the mere fact that a seller is not at fault does not mean that his or her statements are not contractually binding.

Another factor would be whether there was a significant time lag between the making of the statement and the completion of the contract. In *Routledge v McKay*[139] both buyer and seller were private persons and the seller stated that a motorcycle he was offering was a 1942 model, again relying on a statement in the logbook which had been fraudulently altered by an earlier owner. The parties did not actually complete the contract until a week later, and it was held by the Court of Appeal that the statement as to the age of the motorcycle was not a contractual term. On the other hand, in the case of *Schawel v Reade*,[140] a potential buyer who was looking at a horse which he wished to buy for stud purposes, started to examine it and was told by the seller: 'You need not look for anything: the horse is perfectly sound.' The buyer stopped his examination and some three weeks later bought the horse which turned out to be unfit for stud purposes. In this case it was held that the statement as to the soundness of the horse was a term of the contract.

In the cases so far discussed, the contract was concluded by oral negotiations. Of course, the parties often render the contract into writing. Obviously, if they incorporate everything that is said in negotiations into the written contract, it will be clear that they intend it to be legally binding. But, suppose an important statement is made in negotiations and is left out of the written contract. At one time, it was believed that the so-called parol evidence

---

[137] [1957] 1 QB 229.
[138] [1965] 2 All ER 65; [1965] 1 WLR 623.
[139] [1954] 1 All ER 855; [1954] 1 WLR 615.
[140] [1913] 2 IR 81.

rule meant that such statements did not form part of the contract. It is undoubtedly the law that the parties cannot give evidence of what was said in the negotiations for the purpose of helping the court interpret the contract they have actually made. (Of course, the history of negotiations may be relevant to decide whether or not there was a contract at all.) This rule often surprises laypeople and at first sight seems odd. Certainly, many other legal systems do not have the same rule. However, it is clear that, if the parties have agreed on a written contract as a complete statement of what they intend, the exclusion of the earlier negotiations is perfectly rational because it is of the essence of negotiations that there is give and take and the parties change their position. Accordingly, what parties have said as a negotiating position earlier cannot be taken to be a safe guide as to what they intended in the complete written statement.

The above rule is well established but its scope is, in practice, quite seriously restricted because courts are quite willing to entertain arguments that what looks like a complete written contract is not in fact a complete contract at all, but simply a partial statement of the contract. In fact, the courts have recognised two different analyses here, though their practical effect is often the same. One analysis is to say that there is a contract partly in writing and partly oral; the other analysis is to say that there are two contracts, one in writing and one oral. The practical effect in both cases is to permit evidence to be given of oral statements which qualify, add to, or even contradict what is contained in the written contract. An excellent example of this is the case of *Evans v Andrea Merzario*.[141] In this case, the plaintiff was an engineering firm which commonly imported machinery from Italy. For this purpose, it used the defendant as forwarding agent (that is, as a firm which organised the carriage of the goods, although it did not carry the goods itself). The transactions were carried out using the defendant's standard conditions which were based on the standard conditions of the forwarding trade. In 1967, the defendant decided to switch over to use of containers and a representative of the defendant called on the plaintiff to discuss this change. The plaintiff had always attached great importance to its goods being carried below deck because of the risk of corrosion by sea-spray while crossing the Channel. In conventional carriage of the kind used before 1967, goods would normally be in the hold and therefore clearly below the deck line. In a container ship, many of the goods are carried above the deck line because of the way the containers are stacked in the middle of the ship. This switch to containers therefore carried with it a greatly increased chance that the goods would be above deck and would be affected by spray. The defendant's representative assured the plaintiff that the goods would always be carried below deck. Several transactions followed, all of which were again on the defendant's standard conditions which purported to permit carriage above deck. On one particular voyage, a container carrying goods belonging to the plaintiff and being well above deck, fell overboard and was lost. The plaintiff may have had an action against the carrier but this action would probably have been subject to limitations in the carrier's standard terms. The plaintiff therefore elected to sue the defendant which claimed that it was protected by the clause in its standard conditions that it could arrange for carriage of the containers above deck. The Court of Appeal was clear, however, that the defendant was not so protected. Two members of the Court of Appeal held that there was a single contract, partly in writing, partly oral; the third member held that there were in fact two contracts (this difference in analysis

---

[141] [1976] 1 All ER 930; [1976] 1 WLR 1078.

only seems to matter where there is some legal requirement that the contract should be in writing or where there have been attempts to transfer the rights of one of the parties and it may be arguable that the rights under the written contract may be transferred independently of a separate collateral contract).

It can be seen that the decision in the *Evans* v *Andrea Merzario* case is very far-reaching. In effect, all the transactions between the parties were subject to the oral undertaking given by the representative in his 1967 visit, even years later when all the relevant personnel in the two companies concerned might well have changed. From the point of view of the defendants, this is not at all an attractive result. In practice, modern standard written contracts often contain clauses designed to reduce the possibility of this kind of reasoning by providing expressly that the written contract is the whole of the contract between the parties and that all previous negotiations are not binding unless expressly incorporated into the contract. Such 'merger' or 'whole contract' clauses are very common, but their legal effect is not wholly clear.[142] It would probably be imprudent of sellers to assume that the presence of such a clause in their standard written terms would always prevent them from being bound by an oral statement made by one of their sales representatives.

4.8.3 Liability for misrepresentation

Where the seller has made statements about the goods but the court has held that these statements are not terms of the contract, it might be thought that this was the end of the matter. However, it is quite clear that this is not the case. Some such statements will give rise to liability in misrepresentation.

4.8.3.1 What is a misrepresentation?

Basically, a misrepresentation is a statement of a fact made by one party to the contract to the other party before the contract is made which induces that other party to enter into the contract. So, the statement in *Oscar Chess* v *Williams* that the car was a 1948 Morris was, even if it was not a term of the contract, undoubtedly a misrepresentation.

It should be noted, however, that not all of the terms of a contract are concerned with making statements of fact. Many terms contain promises as to future conduct, for example that we will deliver the goods next week. In principle a promise to deliver goods next week is not capable of being a misrepresentation because it is not a statement of fact. For such a promise to give rise to liability, it must be a term of the contract. This principle is well established but it is subject to one very important qualification. Hidden within many statements which look like statements of intention or opinion or undertakings as to the future, there may be a statement of fact. This is because, as was said by Bowen LJ in *Edgington* v *Fitzmaurice*,[143] 'the state of a man's mind is as much a fact as the state of his digestion'. The application of this famous aphorism is well illustrated by the case in which a company issued a prospectus inviting members of the public to lend money to it and stating that the money

---

[142] See M. P. Furmston (ed.), *The Law of Contract* (4th edn, Butterworths, London, 2010) para. 3.7, for a full discussion.
[143] (1885) 29 Ch D 459.

would be employed so as to improve the building and extend the business. In fact, the directors intended to spend the loan on discharging certain existing liabilities. It was held that the company had not contracted to spend the money on improving the buildings and extending the business but there had been a misrepresentation of fact because what the intention of the company was at the time of the prospectus was a question of fact. If the director had in fact intended to spend the money on improving the buildings and extending the business and had later changed their minds, then there would have been no liability in misrepresentation since there would have been no misstatement about the intention of the company at the time of the loan. On the other hand, of course, if the directors had contracted that the money would be spent in this way, they would have broken the contract if they had later changed their minds.

In the same way, a statement of opinion is a statement of fact about what one's opinion currently is. So, if, in *Oscar* v *Williams*, the seller had said that he thought that the car was a 1948 Morris, he would not have been misrepresenting his state of mind since he did indeed think that it was. But, if this had not in fact been his opinion, then he would have been liable. So a car salesperson who is asked how many miles a car does to the gallon and says: 'I don't know but I think about 40' when he believes the mileage per gallon to be no better than 30, is guilty of misrepresenting his state of mind. Furthermore, courts have been prepared to hold that where people who state an opinion look as if they know what they are talking about, they may implicitly represent not only that they hold the opinion but that they know some facts upon which the opinion could reasonably be based. So, even if the car salesperson believes that the car will do 40 miles this may be a misrepresentation if he has never read any investigations. This is certainly the case where sales representatives are selling a particular brand of new car about which the customer could reasonably expect them to be well informed.

Sales representatives have a tendency to make eulogistic statements about the goods which they are trying to sell. Historically, English law has recognised that not all such eulogistic statements should be treated as giving rise to liability on the grounds that no reasonable person would take them seriously. It is probably fair to say, however, that standards have risen in this area and the courts are significantly more likely today to hold that a statement is either a term or a misrepresentation. This will certainly be the case with eulogistic statements which purport to be backed up by facts and figures.

In order to create liability, it is necessary to show not only that there has been a misrepresentation but that the other party to the contract entered into the contract because of the misrepresentation. So, in a number of 19th-century cases concerning flotation of companies, it was shown that there were fraudulent statements in the prospectus but it was also shown that some people bought shares in the company without ever having seen the prospectus and were ignorant of its contents. It was held that such a person could not rely on the undoubted misrepresentation in the prospectus. Even where one party knows there is misrepresentation, he may not have entered into the contract because of it but may have relied on his own judgement or indeed known that the statement was untrue. Equally, it is not necessary to show that the misrepresentation was the only reason for entering into the contract. It would be sufficient to show that the misrepresentation was a significant reason for entering into the contract. Of course, people often enter into contracts for a combination of reasons and provided that one of the reasons is the misrepresentation this will be quite sufficient.

4.8.3.2 Types of misrepresentation

Originally, misrepresentation created liability only where it was fraudulent; that is, where the person making the statement did not honestly believe that it was true. During the 19th century there was some vacillation of judicial opinion about the precise definition of fraud, which was promoted by a significantly wider definition of fraud adopted by the Court of Chancery. The narrow common law definition was applied by the House of Lords in the famous case of *Derry* v *Peek*.[144] In this case, a company applied for a special Act of Parliament authorising it to run trams in Plymouth. The Act passed provided that the trams might be animal powered or, if the consent of the Board of Trade was obtained, steam or mechanically powered. The directors persuaded themselves that, since earlier plans had been shown to the Board of Trade without apparent objection, the requirement of the Board of consent was a formality and issued a prospectus saying that the company had the right to use steam power. In fact, the Board of Trade refused to give consent and the company was, in due course, wound up. The plaintiff, who had bought shares in the company, and of course suffered a loss, alleged that the directors had been fraudulent. The statement that the company was authorised to use steam power was clearly untrue but the House of Lords held that the directors were not fraudulent because they honestly believed the statement to be true. It is clear that on the facts this was a rather indulgent view since it might well had been said that the directors knew that what they said was untrue but hoped and believed that it would soon become true. However, on the basis that the directors, however foolishly and carelessly, believed their statement, the House of Lords had no difficulty in affirming that they could not be liable for fraud. To establish liability in fraud, it had to be shown that the person making the statement knew that it was untrue or at least did not care whether it was true or false.

Derry v *Peek* is still a leading decision as a definition of fraud. However, for 75 years after the decision, it was treated not only as deciding that the directors were not fraudulent but that no liability at all should attach to circumstances of this kind. In fact, there was an immediate statutory amendment to the decision but it was limited to the special case of share prospectuses and it was not until the decision of the House of Lords in 1963 in *Hedley Byrne* v *Heller*[145] that it was possible for a careless statement made by one person and relied on by another, causing that other to suffer financial loss, to give rise to liability. The precise limits of the decision in *Hedley Byrne* are still being worked out by the courts and it is clear that the statement has to be not only careless but made in circumstances in which the defendant owed a duty of care to the plaintiff. This involves consideration of such factors as whether or not the defendant should have contemplated that the plaintiff would have relied on him or her; and if the plaintiff did in fact rely on the defendant, and if in normal circumstances it was reasonable for him or her to have done so. What is clear is that there may be a duty of care between one contracting party and another where, in the run-up to the contract, it is reasonable for that party to rely on advice which is given the other. So, in *Esso Petroleum* v *Mardon*,[146] the plaintiff let a filling station to the defendant on a three-year lease. In the negotiations representatives of the plaintiff had expressed the opinion that the filling station might be expected to sell 200,000 gallons a year. In fact, this was a careless

---

[144] (1889) 14 App Cas 337.
[145] [1964] AC 465.
[146] [1976] QB 801.

overestimate which did not take into account the rather curious configuration of the pumps that was imposed by local planning restrictions. The defendant had no previous experience running a filling station, though he was an experienced businessman, and reasonably relied on the plaintiff's representatives who had many years' experience in the marketing of petrol. It was held that, although the lease, not surprisingly, contained no mention of the forecast, the plaintiff did owe a duty of care to the defendant because it knew that the defendant was relying on its expertise and the defendant was reasonable in so doing. So, the defendant's counter claim to the plaintiff's action for arrears of rent, that he should recover damages for negligent misrepresentation, was upheld. It should be emphasised that not every contract will give rise to liability in this way but there will be many contracts in which one party reasonably relies on the other's expertise and will have a damages action if the other party gives careless advice.

During the 1950s, it increasingly became felt that the combination of the rules about terms of the contract and misrepresentation was unsatisfactory. The question was referred to the Law Reform Committee and in its tenth report in 1962 that Committee recommended a change in the law so that damages could be given for negligent misrepresentation. This proposal was made before the decision of the House of Lords in *Hedley Byrne* v *Heller* and indeed implicitly assumed that the law would not be changed in the way that it was by that decision. In a rational world it would have been appropriate to reconsider the Committee's report in light of the decision in *Hedley Byrne* v *Heller* but instead the Committee's report was made the basis of the Misrepresentation Act 1967.

LEGISLATIVE PROVISION

MISREPRESENTATION ACT 1967

Section 2(1)

Where a person has entered into a contract after a misrepresentation has been made to him by another party thereto and as a result thereof he has suffered loss, then, if the person making the misrepresentation would be liable to damages in respect thereof had misrepresentation been made fraudulently, that person shall be so liable notwithstanding that the misrepresentation is not made fraudulently, unless he proves that he had reasonable ground to believe and did believe up to the time the contract was made that the facts represented were true.

The rule enacted by this sub-section overlaps with the common law rule laid down in *Hedley Byrne* v *Heller* but it is not the same rule. The *Hedley Byrne* rule is wider-ranging in that it applies whether or not there is a contract between plaintiff and defendant. Indeed, many of the cases under *Hedley Byrne* are of this kind. On the other hand, the Misrepresentation Act only applies where the result of the misrepresentation is that a contract is entered into between the person making the representation and the person to whom it is made. However, where the Act applies, it is more favourable to the plaintiff because, in effect, it provides for recovery of damages for negligent misrepresentation and puts on the person making the misrepresentation the burden of proving that it was not negligent. Furthermore, the statutory provision establishes liability for negligent misrepresentation in relation to all contracts, whereas the rule in *Hedley Byrne* would only apply to those contracts where one contracting party owes the other a duty of care in relation to statements made during negotiations, as in *Esso* v *Mardon*.

Of course, there will remain cases in which the person making the misrepresentation is neither fraudulent nor negligent in the *Hedley Byrne* sense and can succeed in rebutting the presumption of negligence implicit in the 1967 Act. The seller in *Oscar Chess* v *Williams* would be an example of such a case. Such a case may be described as one of innocent misrepresentation (though we should note that, before 1963, that term was commonly applied to all cases of misrepresentation which were not fraudulent in the *Derry* v *Peek* sense).

4.8.3.3 Remedies for misrepresentation

A plaintiff who has entered into a contract as a result of a misrepresentation by the defendant can recover damages either by showing that the defendant was fraudulent as in *Derry* v *Peek*, or by showing that the defendant owed a duty of care and was in breach of that duty as in *Esso* v *Mardon* or if the defendant is unable to show that it was not negligent in making the misrepresentation. A plaintiff, if he or she wishes, can rely on all three of these theories. In practice, prudent plaintiffs do not usually make allegations of fraud unless they have a very strong case since English courts traditionally are reluctant to stigmatise defendants as fraudulent.

The possibility of recovering damages for negligent as well as fraudulent misrepresentation substantially reduces the importance of deciding whether the statement of fact is a contractual term or a misrepresentation although it does not totally remove the significance of this distinction. It should be noted, however, that it does not follow that the same amount of damages can be recovered in a contract action as in an action for misrepresentation. The possible distinctions can perhaps best be illustrated by adopting the facts of the well-known case of *Leaf* v *International Galleries*.[147] In this case, the plaintiff bought a painting from the defendant which the defendant incorrectly stated to have been painted by Constable. The plaintiff might have argued on these facts that it was a term of the contract that the painting was by Constable. If he could establish this, the plaintiff could have recovered whatever sum of money was necessary to enable him to obtain what he should have obtained under the contract, that is a genuine Constable. On the other hand, in an action for misrepresentation, which would be substantially a tortious action, he would recover sufficient damages to enable him to be restored to his original position before the contract. If the price which was paid was a standard market price for a painting by Constable of that kind, the two tests would reach substantially the same result. If, however, there was a significant gap between the price paid and the open market price it would make a difference which is adopted.

So, in *Leaf*, the plaintiff had only paid £80 for the painting and his maximum recovery in tort would therefore be £80, even assuming that the painting actually had no value at all. On the other hand, it is likely that the open market price for the Constable, even in 1945, was several thousand pounds and in a contract action the plaintiff could expect to recover the difference between this and the value, if any, of the painting he actually received. This is of course a dramatic difference on the figures of the case. In practice, it is difficult to believe that someone who buys a painting for £80 can actually believe that the other party is contracting that it is a Constable because, at least in a sale by a dealer where he was contracting that the

---

[147] [1950] 2 KB 86.

painting was by Constable, he would be asking a price at the market level of guaranteed Constables.

Alternatively, the plaintiff may seek to rescind the contract on the grounds of the defendant's misrepresentation. During the course of the 19th century, it became established in the Court of Chancery that rescission was available as a general remedy to parties who had entered into contracts as a result of misrepresentation, even if the misrepresentation was entirely innocent. This is still the case. However, although rescission is a remedy easily granted where the contract has been made but not performed, it can have dramatic results where the contract has been carried out because it involves unscrambling the omelette. Section 2(2) of the Misrepresentation Act 1967 has, therefore, conferred on the court a general power to award damages instead of allowing rescission. The right to rescission may also be lost by the operation of what are often called the bars to rescission. This, again, is a reflection of the fact that rescission is a potentially drastic remedy and so plaintiffs have a choice whether to rescind or not and if they choose not to rescind then they are said to affirm the contract and thereby to lose the right. There is some theoretical discussion as to whether or not one could lose this right simply by doing nothing. The practical answer is that plaintiffs who know they have the right to rescind are very ill advised not to make a prompt decision. Rescission is also impossible where the plaintiff cannot restore in substance what he or she has received under the contract as the subject matter of the contract has been consumed or used, so that the court may say that it is impossible to unscramble the omelette. Courts sometimes take a broad view on this question, particularly where the defendant is fraudulent. So, if the defendant sells a business to the plaintiff on the basis of fraudulent representations as to the value of the business, the defendant may well not be able to resist rescission by arguing that the business being offered back is not the one that he sold. To require exact restoration in such cases would obviously be impractical. The principle that the contract is capable of being affirmed and is not rescinded until the plaintiff chooses to do so is often expressed by saying that the contract is voidable. This means that the contract is capable of having legal effects up to the moment that it is avoided. A very important consequence of this is that rights may be conferred on third parties and that the recognition of those rights prevent rescission. Classic examples are in the case of fraudulent buyers. Suppose a buyer obtains goods from a seller by a fraudulent representation, for instance, that his cheque is of value, and then sells the goods on to a third party before the seller discovers the fraud. This can undoubtedly create rights in the third party which cannot be defeated by rescission. (This matter has already been considered in section 4.6.)

4.8.4 Implied terms

The implied terms laid down for contracts of sale of goods are contained in ss. 13, 14 and 15 of the Sale of Goods Act 1979. These provisions are undoubtedly of central importance and they are amongst the most commonly quoted and relied on provisions in the whole Act. Similar provisions have been laid down by statute for contracts of hire purchase starting with the Hire Purchase Act 1938. Much more recently, general provisions applying to all contracts under which property in goods is transferred other than contracts of sale and hire purchase have been laid down by the Supply of Goods and Services Act 1982. This Act also lays down very similar provisions in relation to contracts of hire. So we may now say that in any contract under which property or possession in goods is transferred there will be a core of basic obligations, subject only to the ability of the seller to qualify or exclude his liability (which will be discussed in section 4.9).

4.8.4.1 Obligations of the seller as to description

LEGISLATIVE PROVISION

SALE OF GOODS ACT 1979

Section 13

(1) Where there is a contract for the sale of goods by description, there is an implied term that the goods will correspond with the description.

(1A) As regards England and Wales and Northern Ireland, the term implied by sub-s. (1) above is a condition.

(2) If the sale is by sample as well as by description, it is not sufficient that the bulk of the goods corresponds with the sample if the goods do not also correspond with the description.

(3) A sale of goods is not prevented from being a sale by description by reason only that, being exposed for sale or hire, they are selected by the buyer.

The first thing to note about s. 13 is that, unlike s. 14, it applies to contracts for the sale of goods of all kinds and is not limited to the case of the seller who sells goods in the course of a business. So, even a private seller is bound by this section. Secondly, we should note that the section involves a paradox. If one contracts to sell a horse and delivers a cow, one might say that the cow does not fit the description of the horse contained in the contract and s. 13 applies. However, one might also say that the failure to deliver a horse is a breach of an express term of the contract. This was recognised in *Andrews Brothers* v *Singer*.[148] In this case, the seller contracted to deliver a new Singer car under a standard printed form in which the seller sought to exclude liability for implied terms. The effectiveness of such an exclusion raises important questions (which are discussed in section 4.9). The important point for present purposes is to note that the Court of Appeal said that in any case the exclusion of implied terms was ineffective to exclude the seller's obligation to deliver a 'new Singer car' because that was an express term of the contract. The section obviously assumes that there will be cases in which a description is attached to the goods which is an express term but becomes an implied condition by virtue of s. 3(1). This raises two central questions. The first is, what *is a sale by description, and the second is, what words are to be treated as forming part of the description.*

What is a sale by description? The Act contains no definition of a sale by description. In the 19th century, it was often assumed that sales by description were to be contrasted with sales of specific goods. However, this distinction has not been maintained in the post-Act law. In *Varley* v *Whipp*,[149] it was held that a contract to buy a specific secondhand reaping machine

[148] [1934] 1 KB 17.
[149] [1900] 1 QB 513.

which was said to have been new the previous year and very little used was a sale by description. In that case, though the goods were specific, they were not present before the parties at the time that the contract was made; however, in *Grant v Australian Knitting Mills*[150] the Privy Council treated the woollen undergarments which were the subject of the action as having been sold by description, even though they were before the parties at the time of the contract. At the time of that case, what is now s. 13(3) of the Act was not a part of the Act but it clearly assumes that a contract can be a sale by description despite being a contract in which the goods are specific and effectively chosen by the buyer. So, in a modern supermarket, most of the goods have words of description on the packaging and such contracts are clearly sales by description. The effect of this development is that virtually all contracts of sale are contracts for sale by description except for the very limited group of cases where the contract is not only for the sale of specific goods but also no words of description are attached to the goods.

This makes the second question, what is the description, very important. It might be the law that if the contract is one of sale by description and words of description are used then they inevitably form part of the description. This would have dramatic practical effects. It would mean that the decision in *Oscar Chess v Williams* was wrong because the statement that the car was a 1948 Morris should have been treated as part of the description of the car. Indeed, this was precisely the result reached in a rather similar case, *Beale v Taylor*,[151] where the seller advertised that he had a 1961 Triumph Herald for sale. In fact, the car was an amalgam of two Triumph Heralds, the front and back of which had been put together. Only half of the car was of the 1961 vintage and it was held that the seller was liable because the car did not correspond with the description (the seller in this case was a private and not a commercial seller and so was not bound by s. 14 of the Act but, as noted above, was subject to s. 13).

However, it is clear that not all words which could be regarded as words of description will be treated as part of the description of the goods for the purpose of s. 13. An important case is *Ashington Piggeries v Christopher Hill*.[152] In this case, the plaintiff was in the business of compounding animal foodstuffs according to formulae provided by its customers. It was invited by the defendant to compound a vitamin-fortified mink food in accordance with a formula produced by the defendant. The plaintiff made it clear that it was not expert in feeding mink but suggested substitution of herring meal for one of the ingredients in the defendant's formula. Business continued on this footing for about 12 months and the plaintiff then began to use herring meal which it bought from a supplier under a contract which stated that it was 'fair average quality of the season' and was to be taken 'with all faults and defects . . . at a valuation'. In fact, unknown to any of the parties, this meal contained a chemical produced by chemical reaction which was potentially harmful to all animals and particularly to mink. These facts raised the questions of whether the plaintiff was liable to the defendant and whether the supplier was liable to the plaintiff. The House of Lords held that as between the plaintiff and defendant it was not part of the description that the goods should be suitable for feeding mink. As between the plaintiff and its supplier, the House of Lords held that the goods did comply with the description 'Norwegian herring meal' which was part of the description but it was not part of the description that the goods should be 'fair average quality of the season'. Of course, the goods could not have been correctly described

---

[150] [1936] AC 85.
[151] [1967] 3 All ER 253; [1967] 1 WLR 1193.
[152] [1972] AC 441.

as 'meal' if there was no animal to which they could be safely fed. Why were the words 'fair average quality of the season' not part of the contractual description? The answer given by the House of Lords was that these words were not needed to identify the goods.

> ## CASE
>
> ### *Harlingdon and Leinster Enterprises* v *Christopher Hull Fine Art*[153]
>
> In this case both the defendant and the plaintiff were art dealers. In 1984, the defendant was asked to sell two oil paintings which had been described in a 1980 auction catalogue as being by Gabriele Munter, an artist of the German expressionist school. The defendant contacted the plaintiff amongst others and an employee of the plaintiff visited the defendant's gallery. Mr Hull, for the seller, made it clear that he was not an expert in German expressionist paintings. The plaintiffs bought one of the paintings for £6,000 without making any more detailed enquiries about it. The invoice described the painting as being by Munter. In due course, it was discovered to be a forgery. The majority of the Court of Appeal held that it had not been a sale by description. The principal test relied on by the Court of Appeal was that of reliance. It was pointed out that paintings are often sold accompanied by views as to their provenance. These statements may run the whole gamut of possibilities from a binding undertaking that the painting is by a particular artist to statements that the painting is in a particular style. Successful artists are of course often copied by contemporaries, associates and pupils. It would be odd if the legal effect of every statement about the identity of the artist was treated in the same way. This is certainly not how business is done since much higher prices are paid where the seller is guaranteeing the attribution and the Court of Appeal therefore argued that it makes much better sense to ask whether the buyer has relied on the seller's statement before deciding to treat the statement as a part of the description. On any view, this case is very close to the line. It appears plausibly arguable that the majority did not give enough weight to the wording of the invoice or to the fact that the buyers appear to have paid a warranted Munter price. It should be noted that the buyers did not argue, as they might have done, that it was an express term of the contract that the painting was by Munter.

In this last case, as the attribution to Munter was the only piece of potentially descriptive labelling attached to the painting, the Court of Appeal held that it was not a sale by description. In other cases, such as the *Ashington Piggeries* case, whilst it may be clear that some of the words attached are words of description, it may be held that other words are not. Whether one is asking the question as to whether there is a sale by description or the question what is a description, the questions whether the words are used to identify the goods and whether they are relied on by the buyer will be highly relevant factors. Where there has been a sale by description, the court then has to decide whether or not the goods correspond with the description. In a number of cases, courts have taken very strict views on this question. An extreme example is *Re Moore and Landauer*.[154] That was a contract for the purchase of Australian canned fruit. It was stated that the cans were in cases containing 30 tins each. The

---

[153] [1991] 1 QB 64; [1990] 1 All ER 737.
[154] (1921) 2 KB 519.

seller delivered the right number of cans but in cases which contained only 24 tins. It was not suggested that there was anything wrong with the fruit or that it made any significant difference whether the fruit was in cases of 30 or 24 cans. Nevertheless, it was held that the goods delivered did not correspond with the contract description. Similarly, in *Arcos v Ronaasen*,[155] the contract was for a quantity of staves half an inch thick. In fact, only some 5 per cent of the staves delivered were half an inch thick, though nearly all were less than $^9/_{16}$th of an inch thick. The evidence was that the staves were perfectly satisfactory for the purpose for which the buyer had bought them – that is, the making of cement barrels – but the House of Lords held that the goods did not correspond with the description. The buyer is unlikely to take a point of this kind unless he or she is anxious to escape from the contract, for example, because the price of tinned food or wooden staves has fallen and it is possible to buy more cheaply on the market elsewhere.

CASE

Reardon Smith v Hansen-Tangen[156]

It may be thought that some of these decisions lean somewhat too much to the side of the buyer. In this case Lord Wilberforce said that these decisions were excessively technical. There was a series of transactions to charter and sub-charter a ship, as yet unbuilt. The size and dimensions of the ship were set out in the contract and the ship was described as 'motor tank vessel called yard number 354 Osaka Zosen'. The ship which was tendered when built complied with the technical specification but had been built at a different yard and therefore had the yard number Oshima 004. The tanker market having collapsed, the charterers sought to escape by saying that the ship did not comply with the description. The House of Lords rejected this argument. The technical reason for doing so was that the yard number did not form part of the description but, in reaching this conclusion, the House of Lords were clearly influenced by the underlying commercial realities of this situation. Since these cases, the Sale of Goods Act has been amended by the Sale and Supply of Goods Act 1994. One effect of those amendments was to remove the right to reject goods where the breach is so slight that to reject goods would be unreasonable. This new restriction on the right to reject applies to breaches of the conditions in ss. 13–15, but does not apply to a buyer who is a consumer (see s. 15A, section 4.10.2).

4.8.4.2 **Satisfactory quality**

From the time the original Sale of Goods Act (of 1893) was passed, until 1994, there was a statutory implied condition that the goods supplied be of 'merchantable quality'. In 1994, s. 14 was amended to make it a condition that the goods supplied 'are of satisfactory quality'. The amendments were made by the Sale and Supply of Goods Act 1994, which also removed the definition of 'merchantable' quality and produced a definition of 'satisfactory' quality.

[155] [1933] 1 AC 470.
[156] [1976] 1 WLR 989; [1976] 3 All ER 570 for a full discussion see M. Bridge, 'Reardon Smith Lines Ltd v Yngvar Hansen-Tangen, The Diana Prosperity (1976)', in C. Mitchell and P. Mitchell, *Landmark Cases in the Law of Contract* (Hart Publishing, Oxford, 2008) Chapter 11.

The thinking behind this change was that the expression 'merchantable quality' is not used anywhere, either in English law or colloquial English, except in the context of the Sale of Goods Act. It is, therefore, an expression which is understood only by lawyers specialising in sale of goods law. It was thought that buyers and sellers who were told that the goods must be of merchantable quality would not get much guidance from this statement. This may be agreed, but the problem was to find an appropriate substitute. The 1994 Act was based on a Law Commission Report of 1987 in which it had been suggested that 'merchantable quality' should become 'acceptable quality'. It may perhaps be thought to matter relatively little which of these words is used. Although 'acceptable' and 'satisfactory' are both words which are used every day and which most people will understand, they do not by themselves help buyers and sellers to know at all clearly where the line is to be drawn between acceptable and unacceptable and satisfactory and unsatisfactory goods. So, this change by itself is really almost entirely cosmetic.

LEGISLATIVE PROVISION

The relevant parts of s. 14, as it now is, read as follows:

(1) Except as provided by this section and s. 15 below and subject to any other enactment, there is no implied condition or warranty about the quality or fitness for any particular purpose of goods supplied under a contract of sale.

(2) Where the seller sells goods in the course of a business, there is an implied term that the goods supplied under the contract, are of satisfactory quality.

(2A) For the purposes of this Act, goods are of satisfactory quality if they meet the standard that a reasonable person would regard as satisfactory, taking account of any description of the goods, the price (if relevant) and all other relevant circumstances.

(2B) For the purposes of this Act, the quality of goods includes their state and condition, and the following (among others) are in appropriate cases aspects of the quality of goods:

(a) fitness for all the purposes for which goods of the kind in question are commonly supplied;

(b) appearance and finish;

(c) freedom from minor defects;

(d) safety; and

(e) durability.

(2C) The term implied by sub-s. (2) above does not extend to any matter making the quality of goods unsatisfactory:

(a) which is specifically drawn to the buyer's attention before the contract is made;

(b) where the buyer examines the goods before the contract is made which that examination ought to reveal; or

(c) in the case of a contract for sale by sample, which would have been apparent on a reasonable examination of the sample.

The implied conditions as to satisfactory quality, like the parallel obligation as to fitness for purpose, which will be considered shortly, applies only to a seller who sells goods in the course of a business. Section 61(1) says that 'business' includes a profession and the activities of any government department (including a Northern Ireland department) or local or public authority. This is obviously not a definition of business but an extension of it to include activities by bodies which would not fall within the natural meaning of the word 'business'. It should be noted that the Act does not say that the seller must be in the business of selling goods of that kind and, indeed, members of professions or central or local government will not normally be in the business of selling goods of a particular kind but may be within the scope of s. 14. Under the original 1893 version of the section, the implied obligation as to merchantable quality applied only where the goods were 'bought by description from a seller who deals in goods of that description'. The current wording 'where the seller sells in the course of business' dates from an amendment to the original Sale of Goods Act in 1973, and it was clearly intended to broaden significantly the scope of the section. There will be relatively few cases which are outside it, except that of the private seller who is, for instance, disposing of his car.[157] Even a private seller may be caught where he or she employs a business to sell on his or her behalf because of the provisions of s. 14(5) which provides:

> The preceding provisions of this section apply to a sale by a person who in the course of a business is acting as agent for another as they apply to a sale by a principal in the course of a business, except where that other is not selling in the course of a business and either the buyer knows that fact or reasonable steps are taken to bring it to the notice of the buyer before the contract is made.

This sub-section was considered by the House of Lords in *Boyter* v *Thomson*.[158] In this case, a private seller instructed a business to sell a cabin cruiser on his behalf. The buyer purchased the boat thinking that it was being sold by the business and that it was owned by the business. It was agreed that the boat was not of merchantable quality. The buyer did not know that the owner of the cabin cruiser was a private person and no reasonable steps had been taken to bring that to the buyer's notice. The House of Lords held that the effect of s. 14(5) was, in the circumstances, that both the principal and the agent were liable to the buyer.

It will be noted that the obligation that the goods shall be of satisfactory quality applies to 'goods supplied under the contract' and not to the goods which are sold. Obviously, the goods which are sold would usually be the goods which are supplied under the contract but this will not always be the case. A good example is *Wilson* v *Rickett Cockerell*[159] where there was a contract for the sale of Coalite. A consignment of Coalite was delivered but included a piece of explosive which had been accidentally mixed with the Coalite and which exploded when put on the fire. This case predated the current version of the Act, but the Court of Appeal held that the obligation that the goods should be of merchantable quality applied to all the goods which were supplied under the contract and, of course, it followed that the delivery was defective. The current version of the Act refers to 'goods supplied under the contract', and clearly confirms the correctness of this decision.

In the original Sale of Goods Act 1893, there was no statutory definition of 'merchantable quality'. In 1973, a definition was introduced which reflected the case law prior to that date. In 1994, a new definition, now of 'satisfactory quality', was introduced. This new definition, in s. 14(2A) and (2B), introduces a number of factors (in sub-s. (2B)) not expressly set out in the earlier definition (of merchantable quality). The factors of description and the price spelt out in sub-s. (2A) were, however, part of the earlier definition, and thus the earlier case law on them

---

[157] See *Stevenson* v *Rogers* [1999] 1 All ER 613, distinguishing *R and B Customs Brokers* v *United Dominions Trust* [1988] 1 All ER 847; see section 4.9.3.3.

[158] [1995] 3 All ER 135.

[159] [1954] 1 QB 598.

remains relevant. Turning to the matter of price, no doubt there are some goods which are so defective that nobody would buy them whatever the price. In other cases, whether a buyer would buy goods knowing their condition depends upon the price. So, in *BS Brown v Craiks*,[160] the buyer ordered a quantity of cloth which was to be used for making dresses. The cloth delivered was unsuitable for making dresses though it would have been suitable for industrial purposes. The buyer had not told the seller for what purpose the cloth was required. The contract price was 36.25d per yard which was higher, but not much higher, than the going rate for industrial cloth. The House of Lords held that the goods were of merchantable quality. The buyer had paid a high price in the industrial range but had not paid a 'dress price'. If the facts had been exactly the same except that the price had been 50d per yard, the result would presumably have been different, since in such a case there would have been an irresistible argument that the seller was charging a dress price and therefore had to supply goods of dress quality.

Turning to the factor of description, it is not clear that the law, after the introduction of sub-s. (2B), is exactly the same as before. In the earlier case of *Kendall v Lillico*[161] the plaintiffs bought animal food stuff for pheasants which was contaminated with a substance contained in Brazilian ground nut extraction which was one of the ingredients which made up the food stuff. The defendant settled the claim of the plaintiffs and claimed over against the suppliers. Although the suppliers had supplied Brazilian ground nut extraction which was contaminated, they were not supplying goods of unmerchantable quality because the Brazilian ground nut extraction was perfectly suitable as a basis for food stuff for poultry. The purpose for which the goods are bought and used is of critical importance in relation to s. 14(3), as we shall see below. It is also important, however, as to s. 14(2). If the extraction had been sold as poultry feed, it would not have been merchantable because feed which is poisonous to poultry cannot be sold as poultry feed. If sold as animal food, it would be a completely different matter since the extraction was perfectly suitable for feeding to many, though not to all, animals. From this case, it seemed that if the goods as described in the contract had a number of potential purposes, they would be of merchantable quality if they could be used for one of the purposes for which goods of that description were commonly used. Consistent with that was the decision in *Aswan Engineering v Lupdine*,[162] where the Court of Appeal rejected an argument that the then wording of s. 14 meant that goods were not of merchantable quality unless they were fit for all the purposes for which goods of that kind were commonly bought. The definition of 'satisfactory quality', however, refers in s. 14(2B)(a) to a list of factors including, 'in appropriate cases . . . the fitness of the goods for the purposes for which goods of the kind in question are commonly applied. This appears to *reverse* the decision in *Aswan Engineering v Lupdine*.

This might appear a rather technical change but, in fact, it is of considerable practical importance. It substantially reduces the need to rely on s. 14(3) and show that the seller knows the buyer's purpose in buying the goods. Where goods are bought for one of a number of common purposes, the buyer will be able to rely on s. 14(2) if they are not fit for all those purposes, even, it would appear, if they are fit for all purposes for which the buyer requires them. Of course, if they are fit for the purpose for which the buyer actually requires them, the buyer will usually suffer no loss but it is likely that, sooner or later, a case will occur where the buyer tries

---

[160] [1970] 1 All ER 823; [1970] 1 WLR 752.
[161] [1969] 2 AC 31.
[162] [1987] 1 All ER 135; [1987] 1 WLR 1.

to get out of the contract because of some movement in the market and uses this as an excuse. Suppose, for instance, that the buyer is a dairy farmer who buys the goods for purposes of feeding to cows and that the same material is commonly fed to pigs but that the particular batch, though perfectly suitable for feeding cows, will not do for pigs. It would appear that, if the buyer realises this at the time of delivery, he could probably reject under the present wording.

Other factors appearing in the definition of satisfactory quality which did not appear in the definition of merchantable quality are those contained in s. 14(2)(B)(c), (d) and (e). These add further detail to the definition. There were very few reported cases which involved consideration of whether these issues fell within the statutory definition of merchantable quality. It was said that there were a large number of small cases coming before county courts or the arbitration process in small claims courts where different judges were taking different views as to where to draw the line. This is obviously a matter of particular importance to consumers. Is a consumer who buys a new washing machine and finds it has a major scratch across the paintwork bound to accept it? Is a consumer whose washing machine stops and is unrepairable after 13 months' use entitled to complain that he expected to get three to five years' repairable use out of the washing machine? Is a combination of minor defects on your new motor car sufficient to make it unsatisfactory? The wording of the new section must make an affirmative answer to these questions much more likely.

CASE

Bernstein v Pamson Motors[163] *and Rogers v Parish*

There were, however, a number of cases under the old law (relating to merchantable quality) which involved complaints about new cars. Much of this case law is equally applicable to the definition of satisfactory quality. It is extremely probable that a new car will have some defects. Normally, the buyer will in fact expect to get these defects put right under the manufacturer's warranty. This does not affect the seller's obligation to deliver a car of satisfactory quality. In *Bemstein v Pamson Motors* the plaintiff bought a new car and some three weeks later when it had done only 140 miles, it broke down because the engine completely seized up. It was held that this made the car unmerchantable. Similarly, in *Rogers v Parish*, a new Range Rover had, during its first six months of life, a whole series of defects as to the engine, gear box, body and oil seals. The defects did not make the car unsafe or unroadworthy and each of them was put right but the Court of Appeal held that there was a breach of the requirement of merchantable quality. The Court of Appeal held that the manufacturer's obligations under the guarantee were irrelevant to the legal position of buyer and seller. Any argument that the buyer must expect some defects in a new car could hardly apply on the facts of either of these cases because no buyer would expect his or her car to seize up after 140 miles or to require a replacement engine or gear box in the first six months of its life. These principles are equally applicable in principle to secondhand cars (or indeed other secondhand goods), though obviously the reasonable expectations of a buyer of secondhand goods will not be identical with the reasonable expectations of the buyer of new goods.

[163] [1987] 2 All ER 220.

In *Shine* v *General Guarantee Corporation*[164] the subject of the sale was a 1981 Fiat X1-9 sports car which was offered for sale secondhand in August 1982 at £4,595. The evidence was that this was the going rate for such a car in good condition. In fact, for some 24 hours in January 1982, the car had been totally submerged in water and had been written off by the insurance company. The Court of Appeal held that the car was not of merchantable quality since no one would have bought the car knowing of its condition without at least a substantial reduction of the price. It will be seen that this reason in effect, in a case of this kind, requires the seller either to lower the price or to draw the buyer's attention to the relevant defect.

In *Keith and Ann Lowe* v *W Machell Joinery Ltd*[165] The claimants were converting a barn into a house. They bought from the defendants a bespoke modern staircase made of oak. The staircase was of the dimensions and quality requested but it appeared that, as made, it did not comply with the building regulations though this defect could be cured easily and cheaply. It was held that the staircase was unfit for purpose and not of satisfactory quality.

By sub-s. (2C), the obligation to supply goods of satisfactory quality is excluded:

(a) as regards a defect which is specifically drawn to the buyer's attention before the contract is made;

(b) where the buyer examines the goods before the contract is made, as regards defects which that examination ought to have revealed;

(c) in the case of a sale by sample, as regards any defect which would have been apparent on an examination of the sample.

The second of these requires a further word of comment. Of course, examination does not exclude liability for defects which would not have been revealed by careful examination. Many of the defects discussed in this chapter are of this kind. Furthermore, this section does not require the buyer to examine the goods so he is not prevented from complaining when he or she does not examine at all the defects which a reasonable examination would have revealed. The practical effect of this is that the buyer ought either to carry out a careful examination or no examination at all. To carry out a cursory examination is likely to produce the worst of both worlds.

In *Bramhill* v *Edwards*[166] the seller sold to the buyer for £61,000 a secondhand American motor home. The motor home was 102 inches wide and the evidence was that this exceeded the maximum width of 100 inches permitted by reg. 8 of the Road Vehicles (Construction and Use) Regulation 1986. The Court of Appeal held that the home was of satisfactory quality because the reasonable buyer would know that 'a significant number of vehicles of greater width than permitted were in use on its roads and . . . The authorities were turning a blind eye to that illegal use'.[167]

---

[164] (1988) 1 All ER 911.
[165] [2011] EWCA Civ 794; [2012] 1 All ER (Comm) 153
[166] [2004] 2 Lloyd's Rep 653.
[167] [2004] 2 Lloyd's Rep at 660 *per* Auld LJ.

LEGISLATIVE PROVISION

Section 14(2) is further amended by the Sale and Supply of Goods to Consumers Regulations 2002 which introduce the additional sub-sections:

(2D) If the buyer deals as consumer or, in Scotland, if a contract of sale is a consumer contract, the relevant circumstances mentioned in sub-section (2A) above include any public statements on the specific characteristics of the goods made about them by the seller, the producer or his representative, particularly in advertising or on labelling.

(2E) A public statement is not by virtue of sub-section (2D) above a relevant circumstance for the purposes of sub-section (2A) above in the case of a contract of sale, if the seller shows that:

(a) at the time the contract was made, he was not, and could not reasonably have been, aware of the statement;

(b) before the contract was made, the statement had been withdrawn in public or, to the extent that it contained anything which was incorrect or misleading, it had been corrected in public; or

(c) the decision to buy the goods could not have been influenced by the statement.

(2F) Sub-sections (2D) and (2E) above do not prevent any public statement from being a relevant circumstance for the purposes of sub-section (2A) above (whether or not the buyer deals as consumer or, in Scotland, whether or not the contract of sale is a consumer contract) if the statement would have been such a circumstance apart from those sub-sections.

This enables the court in deciding whether or not the goods are satisfactory to take into account public statements. Such statements include statements made not only by the seller but also those made by the producer. In the case of manufactured goods the manufacturer will often make statements about them over which the seller will have no control. In principle the seller can escape by showing that he was not aware and could not reasonably have been aware of the statement but one may suspect that it will not be easy to do this.

4.8.4.3 Fitness for purpose

LEGISLATIVE PROVISION

SALE OF GOODS ACT 1979

Section 14(3)

Where the seller sells goods in the course of a business and the buyer, expressly or by implication, makes known:

(a) to the seller; or

(b) where the purchase price or part of it is payable by instalments and the goods were previously sold by a credit-broker to the seller, to that credit-broker;

any particular purpose for which the goods are being bought, there is an implied condition that the goods supplied under the contract are reasonably fit for that purpose, whether or not that is a purpose for which such goods are commonly supplied, except where the circumstances show that the buyer does not rely, or that it is unreasonable for him to rely, on the skill or judgement of the seller or credit-broker.

It should perhaps be noted that, in the 1893 version of the Act, the implied term about fitness for purpose was s. 14(1) and the implied term about merchantable quality was s. 14(2). This change in the order may reflect a change in view as to which of the obligations is primary and which is secondary. It should be emphasised that, in practice, buyers who complain of the goods being defective very commonly rely on both implied conditions and that there is a significant degree of overlap. Indeed, the buyer may rely also on arguments about description and again there will be overlap between ss. 13 and 14(2) because whether or not the goods are of satisfactory quality will often turn on the description under which they are sold. The two major differences between s. 14(2) and s. 14(3) are that the buyer may have a better *chance* of succeeding under s. 14(3) if he or she has disclosed a particular purpose for which he or she requires the goods to the seller; however, there is no liability under s. 14(3) if it is shown that the buyer did not rely on the skill and judgement of the seller. There is no such qualification in relation to the obligation of satisfactory quality under s. 14(2).

A layperson reading s. 14(3) for the first time might be forgiven for thinking that, in order to be able to rely on it, the buyer must do something to draw to the seller's attention the purpose for which he requires the goods. However, this is not the way in which the section has been construed. Where goods are produced for a single purpose, the court will easily infer that the goods are being bought for that purpose even though all that the buyer does is to ask for goods of that kind. So, it has been held that to buy beer or milk makes it clear that one is buying it for drinking; that to buy tinned salmon makes it clear that it has been bought for the purpose of being eaten; that to buy a hot water bottle makes it clear that it has been bought for the purpose of being filled with very hot water and put in a bed; and to buy a catapult makes it clear that it has been bought for the purpose of catapulting stones. In other words, if there is a single purpose, it is easy to infer that goods must be fit for that purpose and if the seller is a seller of goods of that kind it will be inferred that the buyer is relying on the seller's skill and judgement, unless it is shown otherwise.

The position is different where goods have more than one purpose. We may distinguish at least two variants on this possibility. One is where goods are used for a purpose which is a specialised and more demanding version of the standard purpose. Suppose that a buyer is buying pig food to feed to a herd of pigs which have super-sensitive stomachs. Suppose further that he or she orders a pig food from a supplier who supplies pig food which would be entirely suitable for pigs with normally robust digestive systems. In that case, if that is all that has happened, the supplier will not be in breach of contract since although what has happened has revealed the ordinary purpose for which the goods were required, it does not reveal the extraordinary requirements of the buyer. In order to be able to complain that the pig food was not suitable for the pigs, the buyer would need to have made it clear to the supplier more precisely what his or her requirements were.[168]

Alternatively, the goods may be capable of being used for a range of purposes which are different, as in *Kendall v Lillico*, where the goods were suitable for feeding cattle but not suitable for feeding poultry. A buyer could recover on these facts if, but only if he or she had made it clear to the seller that the purpose was to buy food for feeding poultry. In fact, in that case, it was held that the seller did have a sufficient knowledge of the buyer's purpose to make

---

[168] *Slater v Finnin Ltd* [1996] 3 All ER 398 is a good example of such a case. See, also, *Rotherham Metropolitan Borough Council v Frank Haslam Milan* [1996] 59 Con LR 33 for a case where the buyer did not rely on the seller's skill and judgement.

him liable, and this case is therefore an example of goods which were of merchantable quality as cattle feed but which were not fit for the buyer's purpose.[169] Similarly, in *Ashington Piggeries* v *Christopher Hill*, the goods did comply with the contract description so that there was no liability under s. 13 but it was held that the buyer had adequately disclosed to the seller his intention to feed the compound to mink and therefore to found liability on s. 14(3). Finally, it should be emphasised that liability under this sub-section, as indeed under s. 14(2), turns on the goods not being of satisfactory quality or fitness for purpose respectively. It is no defence for the seller to show that he or she did all that could possibly have been done to ensure that the goods were fit for the purpose or were of satisfactory quality if in fact they are not.

CASE

Jewson Ltd v *Leanne Teresa Boyhan*[170] *and Balmoral Group* v *Borealis (UK) Ltd*[171]

In this case the buyer, Mr Kelly, had bought a former convent school building for conversion into 13 self-contained flats. He wanted to install individual heating systems in each flat and asked the claimants whether there were any electric boilers on the market which could be used for the development. The claimants found a company called Amptec which manufactured small electric boilers. There was a meeting at the property attended by Mr Kelly and representatives of the claimants and Amptec at which Amptec made statements about ease of installation, safety and cost. Mr Kelly bought the boilers from the claimants. The boilers worked satisfactorily but Mr Kelly refused to pay for them on the ground that the flats were given a low SAP (Standard Assessments Procedure) rating for home energy which put off potential purchasers. The Court of Appeal held that there was no breach of s. 14(3). Mr Kelly had not given the claimants sufficient information as to the SAP rating nor had he relied on the seller's skill and judgement as to the suitability of the boilers for the particular flats.

It will be seen that in this case the buyer had multifaceted purposes. He wanted the boilers to heat the flats, which they did, but he also wanted boilers which would make the flats saleable. He had not established reliance on Jewson for this purpose. Rather similar problems arise in *Balmoral Group* v *Borealis (UK) Ltd*. Balmoral manufactured storage tanks for oil and kerosene which were sold to the public by distributors. The tanks were made of plastic by a process known as rotomoulding. Between 1997 and 2002 Balmoral bought from Borealis for this purpose large quantities of polyethylene which had been manufactured using a polymer known as Borecene. Within a short time many of the tanks split. It was accepted that this was because of environmental stress cracking, which occurred when the chemical environment of a material caused premature brittle failure. The effect on Balmoral's oil tank business was disastrous.

---

[169] It is doubtful, however, that the goods would now be found to be of satisfactory quality; see the discussion in section 4.8.4.2.
[170] [2004] 1 Lloyd's Rep 505.
[171] [2006] 2 Lloyd's Rep 629.

> In this situation Christopher Clarke J held it was necessary to decide why the tanks failed. Borealis would be liable if with Borecene satisfactory green oil tanks could not be made despite an adequate design of tank. However, the design of the tanks was Balmoral's responsibility. A competent rotomoulder would know that different raw materials had different properties and would design accordingly. After an exhaustive consideration of the expert evidence the judge concluded that Borecene was not shown to be unsuitable for the purposes of making green oil tanks by remoulding.

4.8.4.4 Sales by sample

LEGISLATIVE PROVISION

SALE OF GOODS ACT 1979

Section 15

(1) A contract of sale is a contract for sale by sample where there is an express or implied term to that effect in the contract.

(2) In the case of a contract for sale by sample, there is an implied term:

(a) that the bulk will correspond with the sample in quality;

(b) [repealed];

(c) that the goods will be free from any defect, making their quality unsatisfactory, which would not be apparent on reasonable examination of the sample.

(3) As regards England and Wales and Northern Ireland, the *term* implied by sub-s. (2) above is a condition.

The Act contains no definition of what is a sale by sample other than the wholly unhelpful statement in s. 15(1) which leaves in the air the question of where there is an implied term that the sale is by sample. It is easy enough to see what is the central transaction to which this section applies. Sales by sample are common in the sale of bulk commodities because a seller can display to the buyer a sample of what he or she has and the buyer can agree that he will take so many pounds or tons. The sample here in effect largely replaces the need for any description by words of the goods and it is therefore natural to imply, as in s. 15(2)(a), a term that the bulk will correspond with the sample in quality.

However, there are other transactions of a quite different kind which could be regarded as sales by sample. So, for instance, a fleet manager of a large company may be deciding what car to buy for the company's representatives. He or she might very well be shown an example of a particular car and as a result place an order for 200. Would it follow that the 200 cars should be identical in quality with the one which he or she was shown?

4.8.4.5 Other implied terms

The terms set out in ss. 13, 14 and 15 of the Sale of Goods Act 1979 are the basic implied terms which will be incorporated into every contract of sale subject to the possibility of the seller successfully seeking to exclude them in the contract. However, there is nothing in the Act to say that this list is complete. In principle, there seems to be no reason why the general principles about implication of terms in the general law of contract should not apply. So, if a contract of sale is made against a background of a particular trade or local custom, it will be open for one party to seek to show that the custom exists, is reasonable and that contracts of sale made in this particular context are regarded by those in the trade or living in the locality as subject to this implied term.

Similarly, there is no reason why a party should not seek to show that in a particular contract a term is to be implied in order to give business efficacy to the contract. Perhaps the best example of an implied term which is not explicitly set out in the Act but which has been recognised is shown in *Mash and Murrell* v *Joseph I Emmanuel*.[172] In this case, there was a contract for the sale of Cyprus potatoes CIF Liverpool. On arrival in Liverpool, the potatoes were found to be inedible but the evidence was that they had been edible on loading in Limassol. Diplock J said that liability turned on the reason why the potatoes were inedible. There were various possible reasons such as bad stowage or inadequate ventilation during the voyage. These would not have been the seller's fault and the risk of these possibilities would pass to the buyer on shipment, leaving the buyer to an action against the carrier. However, one possibility was that the potatoes, although edible when shipped, had not been in a fit state to withstand a normal voyage from Cyprus to Liverpool. Diplock J said that it was an implied term of the contract in the circumstances that the goods would be fit to withstand an ordinary journey. The Court of Appeal differed from the conclusion that Diplock J reached but not with his analysis of this point.

In *KG Bominflot* v *Petroplus Marketing*[173] the defendants sold to the claimants 38,500 mt gasoil FOB Antwerp. The gasoil was inspected at Antwerp prior to loading and found to be within specification. The claimants wished to complain that the gasoil was outside specification when it was unloaded at El Ferrol four days later. The Court of Appeal refused to imply a term to cover the condition of the oil after loading.

4.8.4.6 Rights and remedies

The Law Commission produced a consultative document in 1983 and a full report in 1987. The report shows that there is a tension between the definition of the seller's obligations which we have just discussed and the buyer's remedies for breach of those obligations which is discussed in section 4.10. Under the existing framework of the Sale of Goods Act, each of the implied obligations in ss. 13, 14 and 15 is said to be a condition and, as will be explained in section 4.10, this is taken to mean that, if there is any breach of the obligation, the buyer is entitled to reject the goods. Courts have sometimes thought that, although the goods were defective, the defects were not of a kind which ought to have entitled the buyer to reject the goods. The leading example of this is *Cehave* v *Bremer*.[174] That was a contract for the sale of citrus pulp pellets which were intended by the buyer to be used for animal feed. There was damage to the goods and the buyer purported to reject them. There was then a forced sale by the Admiralty Court in Holland at which the buyer rebought the goods at a much lower price

---

[172] [1961] 1 All ER 485; [1962] 1 All ER 77.
[173] [2010] EWCA Civ 1145; [2011] 2 All ER (Comm) 522.
[174] [1976] QB 44.

and used them for feeding cattle. In these circumstances, the Court of Appeal was looking for a good reason to find that the buyer was not entitled to reject. What it did was to hold that the defect in the goods did not make them unmerchantable though it clearly reduced their value somewhat. The problem with this approach is that although it may be perfectly reasonable to restrict the buyer's right to reject the goods, it does not usually follow from this that the buyer should be left without any remedy at all. Often, the buyer ought to have a remedy at least in money terms to reflect the difference in value between what he contracted for and what he has received. There is also an important difference as far as rejection is concerned between consumers and those who buy goods commercially, particularly those who buy goods for resale. It is often perfectly reasonable to say to such buyers that they ought to put up with the goods and be satisfied with a reduction in price; it is much less commonly reasonable to say this to a consumer. This perception underlies further changes made by the Sale and Supply of Goods Act 1994 (which are discussed in section 4.10).

4.8.5 Liability in tort

Completeness requires some mention of claims which the buyer may have against other people, especially the manufacturer. In some circumstances, the buyer may have a contract claim against the manufacturer. Sometimes, indeed, the manufacturer and seller are the same person and in that case, of course, no problem arises. In other cases, although the manufacturer and seller are not the same person, the manufacturer may have entered into a separate contract with the buyer. The most obvious way in which such a contract might come about is by the operation of the manufacturer's guarantee. Most consumer durables are now issued accompanied by a guarantee in which the manufacturer typically promises to repair or replace the goods if they do not work within a period, generally a year.

Curiously enough, there is surprisingly little authority in English law on whether manufacturers' guarantees give rise to a contract between manufacturer and customer. The leading case is the classic one of *Carlill* v *Carbolic Smokeball Co* (1893).[175] In this case, the plaintiff, Mrs Carlill, bought a smokeball manufactured by the defendant from a retail chemist, relying on elaborate advertising by the defendant in which it offered to pay £100 to anyone who used the smokeball according to the directions and then caught flu. The plaintiff used the ball as directed, and then caught flu. The manufacturer was held liable to pay the £100, under a contract between it and the plaintiff. This is a rather special case because the claims made by the manufacturer were very explicit and specific. Typically, modern manufacturers' advertising tends to be couched in much less contractual language. The technical problem with giving contractual force to the manufacturer's guarantee is that often the customer will not know of the guarantee until after he or she has bought the goods and further he or she will often not have done anything in exchange for the guarantee. So there may be difficulty in satisfying the technical requirement of the English law of contract that promises are only binding if they are supported by consideration. On the other hand, it is reasonable to assume that a reputable manufacturer would be very reluctant to go back on the guarantee because of the very bad adverse publicity which would be attracted. This no doubt accounts for the absence of reported cases on the subject. Nevertheless, the situation is not wholly satisfactory especially

---

[175] [1893] 1 QB 256.

as many guarantees are couched in somewhat evasive language or impose onerous restrictions such as that the goods should be returned in the original packaging if they fail to work. The practice of consumer guarantees was the subject of a report issued by the Director General of Fair Trading in June 1986, urging higher standards on those who issue guarantees and hinting at the possibility of legislation in the long run. The whole question of consumer guarantees is now the subject of a European Directive. To some extent, this replicates existing English law, but it also involves substantial changes, particularly as to remedies.[176]

Of course, the manufacturer will often be liable in contract to the person to whom it has supplied the goods and the buyer may therefore be able to start off a chain of actions in which the buyer sues the retailer, the retailer sues the wholesaler and the wholesaler sues the manufacturer. By this means, if the fault in the goods is due to the manufacturer, liability can often be shunted back to it by a series of actions. However, this would not always be possible. The manufacturer may in fact be outside the country and difficult to sue; someone may have successfully sold the goods subject to an exclusion or limitation clause which prevents liability being passed up the chain or it may be that the chain breaks down in some other way. For instance, in *Lambert v Lewis*,[177] the buyer complained of a defective towing hook which had been fitted to his Land Rover. The buyer knew who had fitted the towing hook and it was clear who the manufacturer was, but the garage which had supplied the towing hook did not know from which of a number of possible wholesalers it had bought the towing hook. In these circumstances, the garage which had supplied the towing hook could not pass liability back because it could not identify the other party to the contract and it was not allowed to jump over this chasm and sue the manufacturer direct.

The question arises whether the buyer can sue the manufacturer direct in tort. Before 1932, it was widely believed that the answer to this question was no, and that the only actions in respect of defective goods were contractual actions. This was clearly revealed to be wrong by the majority decision of the House of Lords in *Donoghue v Stevenson*.[178] In this case, two ladies entered a café in Paisley and one bought for both of them ice-cream and ginger beer. When the second lady poured part of the ginger beer on her ice-cream, a snail came out of the bottle. On these facts, the plaintiff had no contract with anyone because she had not bought the ginger beer and, of course, her friend was not liable in contract since she had given it to her. The majority of the House of Lords held that, on such facts, the plaintiff could sue the manufacturer on the basis that the manufacturer owed her a duty of care to prepare the product with reasonable care; that a reasonably careful manufacturer of ginger beer would not allow snails to get into the bottle; that, since the bottle was opaque, there was no reasonable possibility of intermediate examination which might detect the snail before it reached the plaintiff and that the plaintiff reasonably foreseeably suffered physical injury as a result. It has never since been seriously doubted that this decision is correct and many decisions have followed and built upon it.

Although it is common to talk of liability in terms of manufacturers, liability in fact rests upon any person who produces or handles goods in circumstances where it is reasonably foreseeable that carelessness in the handling of the goods will cause physical injury or property damage and there is in fact carelessness. So, in appropriate cases, liability can attach to

---

[176] This is discussed more fully in Chapter 7.
[177] [1982] AC 225.
[178] [1932] AC 562.

wholesalers, repairers, those who service goods and indeed to sellers. So, for instance, a seller of a motor car would normally do a detailed check on the car before delivering it in order to discover defects. The seller who failed to do this would be liable in tort not only to the buyer (who has, in any case, an action in contract) but also to anyone else foreseeably injured, for example, a member of the buyer's family (who would, of course, have no contract action).

The defendant will not be liable in such an action unless he can be shown to have been negligent. This is a fundamental difference between tort actions and actions for breach of the implied terms in ss. 13–15 of the Sale of Goods Act. The latter do not require any proof of negligence. In a case such as *Donoghue v Stevenson*, the requirement of negligence was not a serious limitation on the plaintiff's chances of success, since, in practice, a court is likely, very easily, to infer that bottling should exclude the possibility of snails getting into the bottle. In practice, the manufacturer in such a case has to lead evidence of his or her system and is likely to be impaled on one limb or other of a dilemma. Either he shows that the system is usually foolproof, in which case it is likely to be inferred that it must have broken down in the particular case or he shows the system is vulnerable in which case he is negligent for not having a foolproof system. Malfunctions in the production system of this kind are reasonably easy for plaintiffs to contend with. Plaintiffs have much more difficulty when they wish to argue that all specimens of a particular product are defective. This was the problem which confronted the victims of the drug thalidomide who had to show not only that the drug was harmful to foetuses but also that the manufacturers and distributors were negligent not to have realised this. In practice, in a contested action, a plaintiff has very serious difficulty in doing this. It is this, amongst other things, which has led to the introduction of a regime of product liability (see below).

There is another major limit on liability in tort. As the law is currently understood, it seems that plaintiffs can recover only where they have suffered either physical injury or property damage. So, if a manufacturer of a motor car negligently installs a braking system and the plaintiff has an accident and is injured, the plaintiff should be able to recover but if the plaintiff discovers that the braking system is defective and stops driving the car before having an accident, he or she will not be able to recover in tort against the manufacturer for the loss of value of the car because it is not as good a car as it was thought to be. To put it another way, actions for shoddy goods lie in contract and not in tort.

The difficulty of proving negligence in certain types of defective product have led to calls for the adoption of a regime in which the liability of the manufacturer is strict, that is, liability should depend solely on the establishment that the goods were defective and not on a requirement to prove that the manufacturer was at fault. Such a system was adopted in the United States by judicial development, but it was always assumed that in this country the change would require legislation. Both the Law Commission (in 1977) and the Royal Commission on Civil Liability and Compensation for Death or Personal Injury, usually called the Pearson Commission (in March 1978), recommended statutory change to introduce such a regime. It appeared that this advice had fallen on deaf ears until, in July 1985, the European Community adopted a product liability directive, and the British Parliament enacted Part I of the Consumer Protection Act 1987. This Act does not remove any of the existing remedies which somebody damaged by defective goods may have. What it does is to introduce an additional set of remedies. In practice, it is likely that plaintiffs injured by defective goods after 1 March 1988 will seek to argue for liability both in contract or negligence under the old law, and also under the Consumer Protection Act. Although, where the

Act applies, the plaintiffs would usually be better off suing under the Act than in an action in negligence, they would often still be better off pursuing a contract action, if they have one.[179]

4.8.6 **Criminal liability**

Many of the changes which have taken place in the law discussed in this chapter in recent years have been driven by consumerism, that is, the development of consumers as an organised group able to lobby for laws which protect their interests. One of the major problems with protecting the consumer is that changes in the substantive law of contract and tort do not help very much if the sums at issue are small and the cost of using lawyers is large. One way of dealing with this has been to provide special systems for trying small consumer cases in county courts from which lawyers are excluded. Another important development has been the building up of criminal law in the field of consumer protection. The great advantage of this from the consumer's point of view is that it has no cost, since the operation of the criminal law is a service provided by the State. The disadvantage is that usually one does not receive financial compensation for one's own particular loss, though the courts have been given power in the course of criminal proceedings to make compensation orders for those who have been injured by criminal behaviour. Nevertheless, at the prevention level, it is clear that the criminal law is of fundamental importance. Dishonest secondhand car dealers are much more likely to refrain from turning back the odometers of cars they sell because of the fear that they may be caught and prosecuted than because of the fear that a customer to whom they sell a car will sue.

The notion that criminal law had a role to play in the fair regulation of the market is very old since it goes back to rules designed to produce fair weights and measures which have existed since medieval times. Again, it is not possible to do more here than pick out a few salient points.

The most important Act in practice is the Trade Descriptions Act 1968 which gives rise to over 30,000 prosecutions a year. This makes it a criminal offence to apply a false trade description to goods in the course of a trade or business or to offer to supply any goods to which a false trade description is applied. The concept of trade description is very wide-ranging and has been treated as embracing eulogistic statements such as describing a car as a beautiful car or in 'immaculate condition' which would probably be regarded as not giving rise to liability in contract at all. Section 11 contains elaborate provisions about false or misleading indications as to the price of goods which have been replaced by Part III of the Consumer Protection Act 1987. Section 20(1) of that Act introduces a general offence of giving misleading price information and establishes a code of practice.

Another important step is to have the power to prevent certain kinds of dangerous goods coming on the market at all. Extensive powers were granted to ministers to make orders under the Consumer Protection Act 1961 and the Consumer Safety Act 1978. These have been used to regulate such matters as unsafe electric blankets and flammable nightwear. These powers now exist under Part II of the Consumer Protection Act 1987.

---

[179] This Act is discussed more fully in Chapter 7 on consumer protection. The leading case so far is *A v National Blood Authority* [2001] 3 All ER 289. The statute being based on the directive, its construction may involve questions of European Law: *O'Byrne v Sanofi Pasteur* [2006] 1 WLR 1606.

> **LEGISLATIVE PROVISION**
>
> This part of the 1987 Act also introduced a general safety requirement which in s. 10(1) creates an offence if a person:
>
> (a) supplies any consumer goods which fail to comply with the general safety requirements;
>
> (b) offers or agrees to offer to supply any such goods; or
>
> (c) exposes or possesses any such goods for supply.

A similar offence was subsequently created by the General Product Safety Regulations 1994, which is now the primary piece of legislation on this matter.

Under the Fair Trading Act 1973, the Director General of Fair Trading has important powers to promote fair trading practices. An important example of secondary legislation arising out of this Act is the Consumer Transactions (Restrictions on Statements) Order 1976 which prohibits traders from putting up notices which purport to exclude liability. These developments are discussed more fully in Chapter 7 on consumer protection.

4.9 Exemption and limitation clauses

4.9.1 Introduction

During the last 150 years, English law has come, principally by means of developing the implied terms discussed in section 4.8, to impose substantial obligations on the seller, particularly as to the quality of the goods. A natural response of sellers is to seek to qualify these obligations by inserting into the contract terms which seek to exclude, reduce or limit liability. Over the last 50 years, English law has come to impose very considerable restrictions on the ability of the seller to do this, even where he can persuade the buyer to agree to a contract which contains such a clause or clauses. This section will be concerned with explaining the devices which have been developed for this purpose.

It is important, however, to start by emphasising that such clauses are remarkably heterogeneous in form. It would be a mistake to assume that the underlying policy questions in relation to all types of clause are identical. Most clauses operate so as to qualify the results of the seller breaking the contract. This may be done in a wide variety of ways:

(a) the contract may provide that none of the implied terms set out in section 4.8 shall be implied;

(b) the contract may provide that, if the seller breaks the contract, its liability should be limited to a particular sum, say £100;

(c) the contract may provide that, if the seller breaks the contract, it should only be liable to replace or repair the goods;

(d) the contract may provide that the seller shall not be liable for particular kinds of loss; for instance, contracts often provide that the seller is not liable for consequential loss so that, if it fails to deliver the goods, it will not be liable for loss of profit which the buyer suffers through not having the goods;

(e) the contract may provide that if the buyer wishes to complain he must do so within, say, 14 days;

(f) the contract may provide that if the buyer wishes to complain he must do so by means of arbitration;

(g) the contract may provide that, if the goods are defective, the buyer is not to be entitled to reject them but only to have the price reduced, and so on.

However, a clause may operate to define what it is that the seller is agreeing to do. Suppose an auctioneer of horses says that one of the horses which is up for sale is 'warranted sound except for hunting'. This could be regarded as excluding liability if the horse would not hunt but it is more properly regarded as making it clear that the seller is not assuming any liability for the soundness of the horse as a hunter though it is warranting that the horse is sound in other respects. This distinction is fundamental since there is a great difference between saying from the outset that one does not assume an obligation and accepting an obligation and then seeking to qualify it. This distinction was recognised in a different context in *Renton v Palmyra*[180] where the contract provided for timber to be carried from British Columbia to London but contained a clause permitting the master of the ship, in the event of industrial disputes in London, to discharge at the port of loading or any other convenient port. Because of a dock strike in London, the master delivered the goods in Hamburg. The House of Lords held that in the circumstances delivery in Hamburg was a performance of the contract because, properly construed, the contract provided alternative means of performance and not an excuse for non-performance. This was important because the contract was subject to the Hague Rules which forbid most forms of contractual limitation on liability. It must be admitted that much more commonly courts have chosen to ignore this distinction and to assume that all clauses operate by way of defence, so as first of all to consider what the rest of the contract says and then to consider whether the clause is effective to qualify that obligation. The difference in approach is not merely technical because it colours the whole flavour of the process of interpretation.

Common law and statute have developed rules which control the ability of the parties to exclude or qualify liability. Although, as regards contracts of sale, the statutory regime is much more extensive and important, it is convenient to consider the common law position first, both because it provides the historical context in which the statutory regime exists and because in order to be valid a contractual exclusion clause must survive both the common law and statutory tests.

4.9.2 The position at common law

4.9.2.1 Is the excluding clause part of the contract?

This question is assumed to be easy to answer where there exists a contractual document which has been signed by the parties. In this position, the basic rule is that the parties can be

[180] [1957] AC 149.

taken to have agreed to what the contract means, even though they have never read it and would not understand it if they had. Some commentators have criticised this rule on the grounds that, in many cases, the agreement on which it based is wholly artificial. It is no doubt true that those who sign a contract embrace a range from those who can understand nothing up to those who are perfectly familiar with the contract and understand precisely its legal effects. It is probably not sensible, however, to make the binding force of the contract turn on where on the spectrum particular contracting parties stand. To enquire into these questions on a regular basis would be to consume vast amounts of judicial time without any obvious benefit.

More difficult questions arise where there is no signed contract but it is argued that excluding terms have been incorporated into the contract by notices or the delivery of non-contractual documents like tickets. There is no doubt that, in certain circumstances, one can incorporate terms into a contract by displaying a notice at the point at which the contract is made or, as on the railway, by handing over a ticket which contains references to the contractual conditions. These conditions need not be set out in the ticket provided they are sufficiently identified. So, almost ever since the railways began, tickets have borne on the front the words, 'For conditions see back' and on the back a reference to the company's timetable. In principle, this is perfectly acceptable. Similarly, there is no reason why one of the parties should not say by notice or ticket that all the contracts it makes are subject to the rules of a particular trade association. The critical test was that laid down in *Parker v South Eastern Railway*,[181] that is, whether or not in the circumstances the delivery of the ticket is sufficient notice of the terms referred to on it. In principle, it appears that the standard of reasonable notice is variable, so that, the more surprising the term, the greater the notice required. So, in *Thornton v Shoe Lane Parking*,[182] the plaintiff wished to park his car in the defendant's multi-storey car park. Outside the park was a notice stating, 'All cars parked at owner's risk'. The ticket he received contained references to terms displayed inside. Inside the car park, there were notices which purported to exclude not only liability for damage to cars but also liability for damage to drivers. This is a much less common clause and the Court of Appeal held that, in the circumstances, the plaintiff was not bound by it because he had not been given adequate notice so that he could make a real choice whether to park his car in that car park or somewhere else. It was obviously an important part of this reasoning that, whereas car parks very commonly carry notices excluding liability for damaged cars, it is much less usual for them to carry notices excluding liability for damage to drivers. In the later case of *Interfoto Picture Library v Stiletto Visual Programmes*,[183] the Court of Appeal stated it as a general proposition that, where contracts were made by processes which involved the delivery by one side to the other of standard printed terms, the author of the terms was under a general duty to draw to the attention of the other side any terms which were unusual. Of course, it follows that in a contested case it may be necessary to produce evidence of what terms are usual in a particular profession, trade or industry.[184]

---

[181] (1877) 2 CPD 416.
[182] [1971] 2 QB 163.
[183] [1988] 1 All ER 348; [1989] QB 433.
[184] Cases will arise where both buyer and seller have standard terms. In such cases a careful historical analysis of the facts may be necessary to see on whose terms, objectively speaking, the contract has been made. See *Balmoral Group Ltd v Borealis UK Ltd* [2006] 2 Lloyd's Rep 629.

4.9.2.2 Limitations imposed by the common law on the effectiveness of exemption clauses

The principal tool used by common law to control exemption clauses has been the process of construction, that is, the process by which the court construes (decides the meaning of) the contract. Courts have traditionally approached this process of construction by making a number of assumptions. These assumptions may often overlap but are probably analytically distinct. So, it is assumed that it is unlikely for one party to agree that the other party shall not be liable even where he or she is negligent; similarly, it is thought that the more serious a breach of contract has been committed by one party, the less likely the other party will have agreed in advance that such a serious breach does not matter.[185] Indeed, it was thought during much of the 1960s and 1970s that if the breach was sufficiently fundamental, even the clearest words could not exclude liability for it, but this was eventually decided by the House of Lords to be a heresy. The thrust of both of these assumptions is that, if one party wishes to exclude its liability for negligence or a serious breach of the contract, it needs to say so in clear terms. Of course, in practice, what that party wants to do is to make expansive promises in the big print and cut them down by 'weasel words' in the small print. Few car parks would think it good business to put a large sign over the entrance saying, 'Abandon hope all ye who enter here'; it is quite a different matter to put a wide-ranging exclusion clause in small print on the back of the ticket. A third assumption which overlaps with these two but may have separate application is the *contra proferentem* principle which says that, if one party has drafted or is responsible for the drafting of a document and the document is ambiguous, then any ambiguities should be resolved in favour of the other party. All three of these assumptions are perfectly sensible within their proper limits. Undoubtedly, courts have, from time to time, gone over the top and used the devices to reject the effect of excluding clauses, not because they were not clearly drafted but because the court did not like them. More recent decisions have suggested that now that there is the statutory regime described below it is much less appropriate than it was in the past to take these techniques beyond their proper limits. It has also been suggested by the House of Lords that the force of the presumptions does depend very considerably on the type of clause which is employed. So, clauses which impose financial limits on liability should not be treated with the same degree of hostility as clauses which exclude liability altogether. (Of course, this distinction can hardly apply where the financial limit is so low as in effect to exclude liability altogether.)

It has also been said that where one party has only entered into the contract because he or she has been misled by the other about the effect of the exclusion clauses then the exclusion clauses are without effect. This principle would obviously apply where the misrepresentation was fraudulent but it seems to apply even if misrepresentation was entirely innocent. So, in *Curtis* v *Chemical Cleaning and Dyeing Co*,[186] the plaintiff took a wedding dress to the defendant for cleaning. Usually at a dry cleaner one would simply receive some kind of ticket by way of receipt but this particular cleaner had documents headed 'receipt' which it was the practice to ask the customer to sign. The plaintiff asked that assistant what was in the document and was told that it excluded liability for certain risks, for instance, damage to the beads and sequins which were on the wedding dress. In fact, the receipt contained the clause, 'The Company is not liable for any damage, however caused'. The dress was in fact stained while

---

[185] *KG Bominflot v Petroplus* [2010] EWCA Civ 1145; [2011] 2 All ER (Comm) 522.
[186] [1951] 1 KB 805.

being cleaned and the defendant sought to rely on the clause as a defence. The Court of Appeal held that it could not do so because of the misstatement by the shop assistant about the effect of the document. There was no evidence in the case as to the assistant's understating of the document and it is obviously entirely possible that the assistant understood it no better than the customer. This does not appear to matter.

It is not clear whether or not the principle that surprising clauses should be specifically drawn to the attention of the other party applies where the document is signed. The cases in which it has arisen have not been cases of signed documents but the underlying rationale would seem to be equally applicable in such a case.

4.9.3 Statutory control of exemption and limitation clauses

There is a history of statutory control of exemption clauses going back to the middle of the 19th century when there were controls over the terms on which carriers of goods could seek to exclude liability. It is only much more recently, however, that general statutory regulation of such clauses has become accepted as an appropriate technique. A major step was the Supply of Goods (Implied Terms) Act 1973 which made major changes in the possibility of excluding clauses in the fields of sale and hire purchase. These changes were re-enacted but with major additions in the Unfair Contract Terms Act 1977. This Act has provisions dealing specifically with contracts for the supply of goods and also provisions of general application which may affect contracts for the supply of goods.

4.9.3.1 Sections 6 and 7 of the Unfair Contract Terms Act

Section 6 of the Act applies to contracts of sale and hire purchase. Section 7 of the Act applies to other contracts under which ownership or possession of goods passes. Both sections deal with clauses which seek to exclude liability for failure to transfer ownership and this has already been discussed in section 4.6. The main thrust of the sections is in the implied terms as to the quality of the goods. Section 6 lays down the same rule for contracts of hire purchase as for contracts of sale. Section 7 lays down the same rules for other contracts under which ownership or possession is to pass. For simplicity of exposition, the rest of this account talks of contracts of sale but there is a uniform regime for all of these contracts.

Section 6 divides contracts into two groups; those where the buyer is dealing as a consumer and those where the buyer is not. Where the buyer is dealing as a consumer, ss. 13, 14 and 15 cannot be excluded. If the buyer is not dealing as a consumer, ss. 13, 14 and 15 can be excluded if the term satisfies the requirement of reasonableness. In effect, therefore, the implied terms become mandatory in consumer sales[187] and, even in commercial sales, the seller will only be able to exclude them if he or she is able to satisfy a court that the term excluding or limiting liability was, in all the circumstances, reasonable. The operation of this scheme obviously involves two questions.

(a) Who is a consumer?

(b) What is reasonable in this context?

The answer to the first question is to be found in s. 12.

---

[187] The effect on consumers is discussed more fully in Chapter 7 on consumer protection.

LEGISLATIVE PROVISION

Section 12

(1) A party to a contract 'deals as consumer' in relation to another party if:

(a) he neither makes the contract in the course of a business nor holds himself out as doing so; and

(b) the other party does make the contract in the course of a business; and

(c) in the case of a contract governed by the Law of Sale of Goods or Hire Purchase, or by s. 7 of this Act, the goods passing under or in pursuance of the contract are of a type ordinarily supplied for private use or consumption.

(2) But, on a sale by auction or by competitive tender, the buyer is not in any circumstances to be regarded as dealing as consumer.

Setting aside then the special cases of auction and competitive tender which can never be consumer sales, we see that a consumer sale requires three elements: a consumer buyer, a non-consumer seller and consumer goods. So, a sale by one consumer to another is not for this purpose a consumer sale. In any case a consumer seller does not attract liability under s. 14 of the Sale of Goods Act 1979. It is thought, however, that a consumer seller who seeks to exclude liability under s. 13 of the Sale of Goods Act would be subject to the test of reasonableness. There is no definition of consumer goods and there are obvious marginal cases – for example, someone who buys a van intending to use it as his or her means of family transport. It is thought that courts will take a broad view of consumer goods for this purpose. The most difficult question is whether the buyer is making the contract in the course of a business or holding himself or herself out as doing so. There are many cases where a buyer buys goods partly for business and partly for non-business use. A typical example is the purchase of a car by a self-employed person. It is very likely that such a person would use the car substantially for family and social purposes but it is also very likely that for tax reasons it would be bought through the business. Many commentators had assumed that this would have made the transaction a non-consumer transaction but the contrary view was taken by the Court of Appeal in *R and B Customs Brokers* v *United Dominions Trust*.[188] In this case, the plaintiff was a limited company, owned and controlled by Mr and Mrs Bell. The company conducted the business of shipping brokers and freight forwarding agents. It decided to acquire a Colt Shogun four-wheel drive vehicle which turned out to be defective. The question was whether or not the transaction was a consumer transaction, in which case the exclusion clauses in the defendant's standard printed form would be totally ineffective. The defendant argued that the transaction must be a business transaction because companies only exist for the purpose of doing business. (This is obviously a stronger case on this point than if the plaintiffs had not incorporated themselves but had simply done business as a partnership having no separate legal personality.) The Court of Appeal held, however, that the company was a consumer and not a business for the purpose of s. 12. The principal reason for this decision was that the company was not in the business of buying cars. This decision has attracted a good deal of

---

[188] [1988] 1 All ER 847.

criticism since it appears to fly in the face of the wording of the Act (in particular, it is difficult to see what effect can be given with this approach to the words 'nor holds himself out as doing so'). It is also very difficult to see how the regularity with which the plaintiffs bought cars was relevant to the character of the plaintiffs as consumers or non-consumers.[189] Nevertheless, sellers would be prudent to assume that the decision is likely to be followed and its effect is clearly significantly to broaden the notion of what is a consumer for this purpose.

LEGISLATIVE PROVISION

The second question is, what is reasonable? Section 11(1) says that whether or not the term is reasonable depends on:

Having regard to the circumstances which were, or ought reasonably to have been, known to or in the contemplation of the parties when the contract was made.

At the time when the Act was passed, there was a debate about whether reasonableness should be determined at the time the contract was made or at the time the dispute arose. The Act adopts the former solution but in practice, of course, the question will not arise until there has been a breach of contract and a dispute. The court will, in practice, be able to approach the question in the context which has actually arisen. This provision is less important in practice than it is in theory.

LEGISLATIVE PROVISION

Section 11(4)

Where by reference to a contract term or notice a person seeks to restrict liability to a specified sum of money, and the question arises (under this or any other Act) whether the term or notice satisfies the requirement of reasonableness, regard shall be had in particular (but without prejudice to sub-s. (2) above in the case of contract terms) to:

(a) the resources which he could expect to be available to him for the purpose of meeting the liability should it arise; and

(b) how far it was open to him to cover himself by insurance.

This provision gives statutory force to the general notion that a clause limiting liability has a better chance of being treated as reasonable than a clause which seeks to exclude liability altogether. This is only the case under s. 11(4) if the seller can show that the limit of liability is reasonably related to the resources which he has available. In other words, a small business can more readily defend a low limit of liability than a large one. However, many liabilities are, of course, insured and it is therefore relevant to consider whether the seller can cover himself or herself by insurance. In general, it is difficult for sellers effectively to insure against the cost of replacing the goods but they can insure against the possibility of

---

[189] The reasoning is also hard to reconcile with that of the Court of Appeal as to 'course of business' under s. 14 of the SGA in *Stevenson* v *Rogers* [1999] 1 All ER 613.

having to pay damages for loss caused by defective goods. However, such insurance is commonly written with a premium which is calculated in relation to the maximum which the insurer will cover. It would seem that it is probably open to a seller to show that it was not economically possible for him or her to insure for liability for more than, say, £100,000 for any one claim. This would be relevant to the decision as to whether or not limitation of liability was reasonable under s. 11(4).

LEGISLATIVE PROVISION

The court is also required to have regard to five guidelines which are set out in Sch. 2 of the Act:

(a) the strength of the bargaining positions of the parties relative to each other, taking into account (among other things) alternative means by which the customer's requirements could have been met;

(b) whether the customer received an inducement to agree to the term or in accepting it had an opportunity of entering into a similar contract with other persons, but without having to accept a similar term;

(c) whether the customer knew or ought reasonably to have known of the existence and extent of the term (having regard, among other things, to any custom of the trade and any previous course of dealing between the parties);

(d) where the term excludes or restricts any relevant liability if some condition is not complied with, whether it was reasonable at the time of the contract to expect that compliance with that condition could be practicable;

(e) whether the goods were manufactured, processed or adapted to the special order of the customer.

Some comments may be offered on the guidelines. Obviously, as far as (a) is concerned, the more equal the bargaining position of the parties the more likely it is that the court could be persuaded that the clause is reasonable. Similarly, if one party is in a monopoly position it is likely to have considerable difficulty in persuading the court that the terms are reasonable, whereas, if there is a wide range of possible suppliers, this is likely to point in the other direction and particularly if some of them offer more favourable terms. There is an overlap here with (b), so that, if a buyer has a choice of paying a higher price and getting a contract without exclusion clauses, whether that is from the same seller or different sellers, the buyer who chooses the lower price may find that the clause is regarded as reasonable.

Guideline (c) calls for some comment. If the term is incorporated in the contract it must, in some sense, be the case that the buyer knows or has the opportunity of knowing it. It seems clear that more is required for the guideline to apply. It is thought that what is envisaged here is the case of an experienced buyer who knows the terms common in a particular trade and is not taken by surprise by them. (The reasoning in the *Stiletto* case above is obviously relevant here.) An example of the application of guideline (d) would be where the contract requires the buyer to complain of defects in the goods within a short period. Such a requirement might well be held reasonable in regard to defects which are obvious on delivery, particularly if the goods are to be delivered by a third-party carrier, since notice may enable the seller to claim against the carrier. On the other hand, such a clause would usually not be reasonable if the defect was not immediately obvious.[190]

CASE

George Mitchell (Chester Hall) Ltd v Finney Lock Seeds Ltd[191]

The guidelines do not exhaust the factors which may be taken into account in deciding on what is reasonable. The leading decision is *George Mitchell (Chester Hall) Ltd v Finney Lock Seeds Ltd*. In this case, the defendant was a firm of seed merchants which agreed to supply the plaintiff, a farming concern, with 30 pounds of Dutch winter cabbage seed for £192. The contract was treated as subject to an invoice which contained a clause purporting to limit liability if the seed was defective to a replacement of the seed or refund of the price and to exclude:

> All liability for any loss or damage arising from the use of any seeds or plants supplied by us and for any consequential loss or damage arising out of such use . . . or for any other loss or damage whatsoever.

In fact, the seed delivered was not winter cabbage seed and was also defective. The plaintiff's crop was therefore a total failure. The plaintiff claimed that the cash value of the crop would have been some £63,000. The defendant claimed to be liable only to repay £192. If one looks at the guidelines in such a case, guidelines (b), (d) and (e) have little or no impact; there is probably not much to choose in the bargaining strength of the parties and clauses of this kind are well known in the seed trade so that it is unlikely that the reasonable farmer would be taken by surprise. On the other hand, it might be difficult to find a seed merchant who would supply seed on substantially different terms.

The House of Lords held that the clause was unreasonable. The principal factor relied on by the House of Lords was that the defendant had led evidence that, in practice in such cases, it commonly made *ex gratia* payments. The purpose of leading this evidence was to show that the defendant was reasonable. Instead, the House of Lords took it as evidence that even the defendant did not regard its own clause as reasonable. These rather special circumstances are perhaps unlikely to arise again because in future sellers will not be so incautious as to lead such evidence. Other factors to which significant weight was attached included the fact that the breach by the sellers was a particularly clear and substantial one and that there was evidence that it was easier for sellers to insure against losses of this kind than for buyers. Undoubtedly, which parties can most economically and efficiently insure is often a critical factor in deciding whether a clause is reasonable. So, if a seller could show that a particular loss was of a kind against which buyers commonly insure, this would significantly increase his or her chances of persuading a court that the clause was reasonable.[192] Similarly, if the task being undertaken is relatively simple and its consequences fall within a modest compass, it will be less easily shown to be reasonable to seek to exclude liability.[193]

---

[190] *RW Green Ltd v Cade Bros Farm* [1978] 1 Lloyd's Rep 602.
[191] [1983] 1 All ER 10; [1983] 2 AC 803.
[192] *Smith v Eric S Bush* [1990] 1 AC 831; [1989] 2 All ER 514.
[193] *Ibid.*

Another interesting case which is worth mentioning is *Walker v Boyle*,[194] where Dillon J held that neither the fact that the contract (for the sale of land) was on standard nationally used terms, nor the fact that the parties were represented by solicitors throughout, prevented the use being unreasonable. This was because the clause in question sought to shift from seller to buyer the risk of the seller giving an inaccurate answer to questions, the answers to which were entirely within the seller's control.

4.9.3.2 Section 2 of the Unfair Contract Terms Act

LEGISLATIVE PROVISION

Section 2

(1) A person cannot by reference to any contract term or to a notice given to persons generally or to particular persons exclude or restrict his liability for death or personal injury resulting from negligence.

(2) In the case of other loss or damage, a person cannot so exclude or restrict his liability for negligence except in so far as the term or notice satisfies the requirement of reasonableness.

(3) Where a contract term or notice purports to exclude or restrict liability for negligence, a person's agreement to or awareness of it is not of itself to be taken as indicating his voluntary acceptance of any risk.

Although this section is aimed at liability in negligence it is capable of applying to sellers and other suppliers of goods because, in some cases, the buyer may be able to formulate a claim against them as based on negligence. For instance, where the seller has negligently given precontract advice or, as discussed above, has carried out a negligent predelivery inspection of a motor car. It will be seen that s. 2 forbids contracting out of liability when negligence causes death or personal injury and subjects contracting out for negligence which causes other forms of loss to the test of reasonableness. What is said above about reasonableness will apply here also. Strictly speaking, the Act provides that the guidelines should only be taken into account in respect of ss. 6 or 7 of the Act. However, in practice, it seems that the courts have had regard to guidelines whenever questions of reasonableness arise. It would really be absurd to try to operate two different tests of reasonableness under the same Act.[195]

---

[194] [1982] 1 All ER 634; [1982] 1 WLR 495. This was a case on the Misrepresentation Act 1967, but it is thought that the reasoning applies equally to the Unfair Contract Terms Act. See also *Britvic Soft Drinks Ltd v Messer UK Ltd* [2002] 2 All ER (Comm) 321, *Bacardi-Martini Beverages Ltd v Thomas Hardy Packaging Ltd* [2002] 2 All ER (Comm) 335.

[195] *Flamar Interocean Ltd v Denmac Ltd* [1990] 1 Lloyd's Rep 434 at 439.

4.9.3.3 Section 3 of the Unfair Contract Terms Act

> **LEGISLATIVE PROVISION**
>
> **Section 3**
>
> (1) This section applies as between contracting parties where one of them deals as consumer or on the other's written standard terms of business.
>
> (2) As against that party, the other cannot by reference to any contract term:
>
> (a) when himself in breach of contract, exclude or restrict any liability of his in respect of the breach; or
>
> (b) claim to be entitled:
>
> (i) to render a contractual performance substantially different from that which was reasonably expected of him; or
>
> (ii) in respect of the whole or any part of his contractual obligation, to render no performance at all except in so far as (in any of the cases mentioned above in this sub-section) the contract term satisfies the requirement of reasonableness.

This provision is of very general scope. It will be seen that it applies either where one of the contracting parties is a consumer or where the contract is on one party's written standard terms of business. Obviously, there will be very many contracts of sale where the buyer is a consumer and many, both commercial and consumer contracts, where the contract is on the seller's standard written terms of business. So, many contracts of sale will be subject to s. 3. This section is therefore very important in relation to obligations under contracts of sale other than those covered by the implied terms in ss. 13, 14 and 15. It would apply, for instance, to the questions of when the seller is to deliver the goods. Many sellers state in their written standard terms of business that the dates of delivery are estimates only and so on. It would certainly be open to a court to enquire if such a provision was reasonable. In practice it is very difficult to see that it can be reasonable simply to have a blanket excuse for being late in delivery. It would be a different matter if the seller inserted a clause excusing failure to deliver on time for specified events which were outside the seller's control. Such clauses are, of course, very common and in principle they would appear reasonable.

It should be noted that the scope of s. 3 is potentially very wide-ranging because it covers not only attempts to exclude liability for breach of contract but also attempts to provide in the contract to be able to deliver a contractual performance substantially different from that which was reasonably expected or to render no performance at all. A careful draftsman might seek to formulate the contract so as to give the seller the right to offer an alternative performance or in certain circumstances not to perform at all without these acts being breaches, but it seems that such clauses would still be subject to the test of reasonableness. If one applied this literally, it would mean that a clause, providing that the seller need not deliver the goods until the buyer had paid for them in advance, was subject to the test of reasonableness. In practice, it is unlikely that a court would be at all anxious to construe the words in this sense and in any case it would usually hold that such a clause was reasonable.

4.9.3.4 Unfair Terms in Consumer Contracts Regulations 1999

The Directive on Unfair Terms in Consumer Contracts was adopted by the Council of Ministers on 5 April 1993. Member States were required to implement its provisions by 31 December 1994. The Directive was not mandatory as to its precise terms; it laid down a minimum standard which Member States must reach for protection of consumers against unfair terms in consumer contracts. The effect of the Regulations which seek to give effect to the Directive is considered in Chapter 7 on consumer protection.

4.10 Remedies

4.10.1 General principles

This section is intended to discuss what remedies may be available to either the buyer or the seller if the other party breaks the contract. The positions of buyer and seller in a contract of sale are not, of course, symmetrical; the seller's obligation is to deliver the goods and the buyer's obligation is to pay the price. The failure of the seller to deliver the goods or to deliver goods of the right quality and so on will have different results from the failure of the buyer to pay the price, and may call for some difference in remedies. Nevertheless, the remedies available to the parties do derive very largely from the general law of contract and it seems more convenient, therefore, to approach the problem first by considering the general principles and then by considering how the position of the buyer and seller may differ.

It is important to make clear from the beginning that there will be a number of cases in which the injured party has no effective remedy for the other party's breach. This is because the most usual remedy is damages to compensate for the financial loss flowing from the breach and it will quite often be the case that little or no financial loss has flowed. Suppose, for instance, that a seller has contracted to deliver 1,000 tons of coffee beans at £525 per ton on 1 January and fails to deliver them. The buyer's remedy, as we shall see, is primarily measured in terms of what it would cost the buyer to buy substitute goods on the market on that date. It may be, however, that the price has fallen and, in that case, the buyer will actually profit from the seller's failure to perform, though, of course, the buyer does not have to account to the seller for the profit! Even if the price remains steady, the buyer will only have lost the cost of going out to the market to buy substitute goods which will often not amount to much. So the buyer will be entitled to an action for nominal damages but perhaps not much more.

Let us consider in turn what the possible remedies are. One party may be entitled to withhold performance until the other has performed. So, if the seller has agreed to give the buyer credit, the buyer is not obliged to pay until the seller has delivered the goods. In a sense, the right to withhold performance is a right rather than a remedy but it is also often the most effective way of concentrating the mind of the other party. In certain circumstances, one party will be entitled not only to withhold performance but also to bring the contract to an end – to terminate it. A particular and very important example of this is the buyer's right to reject the goods, though the right to reject the goods is not exactly the same as the right to terminate and is not subject to exactly the same rules. Withholding performance, termination and rejection are discussed more fully later.

In certain circumstances, one party may be entitled to get the contract specifically enforced. This is the standard remedy for contracts for the sale of land because, from an early time, English courts have taken the view that each parcel of land is unique and a disappointed buyer cannot simply be compensated by damages since they cannot go out and buy an identical parcel of land elsewhere. This explanation is no doubt stretched when confronted by a typical English modern housing development, but it appears to remain intact. A buyer may be able to obtain specific performance of a contract for the sale of goods but this is very much an exceptional remedy. The Sale of Goods Act 1979 does not contemplate an action for specific performance brought by the seller, but it does provide that, in certain circumstances, the seller may bring an action for the price and though this action is historically different from the action for specific performance it produces, from the seller's point of view, many of the same consequences. Specific performance and the action for the price are discussed later under 'Specific enforcement'. In practice, the most common remedy for breach of a contract of sale of goods will be an action for damages. If the contract has been broken by one party, the other party will always have an action for damages, though, as pointed out above, the damages may only be nominal in amount. The critical question is how much can be recovered by a buyer or seller in an action for damages. This will be considered in detail later in section 4.10.4.

The remedies we have discussed so far are what we may call the standard remedies provided by the general law. However, the law permits the parties to make further provisions about remedies. We have already seen, in section 4.9, the rules which have developed where the contract seeks to limit the remedies which would normally be available. It is possible, however, to seek to extend the range of remedies. So, the contract may provide that if the seller is late in delivering he or she shall pay so much a day by way of liquidated damages for each day of delay. Conversely, the contract may provide that the buyer is to pay a deposit or that he is to pay part of the price in advance. Some of these possibilities are so common that substantial bodies of rules have been developed about them. These will be discussed more fully later in section 4.10.5. Section 4.10.6, discusses certain special remedies which the seller has against the goods where the buyer is insolvent. In practice, the seller's most effective remedy is to have retained ownership, which we have already discussed in section 4.6.

4.10.2 Withholding performance, termination and the buyer's right to reject

Withholding performance and termination are analytically separate but in practice there is a major degree of overlap. This is because the factual situations which lead one party to wish to withhold performance or to terminate are very similar. In practice, the threat by one party to withhold performance will either lead the other party to attend to his or her performance, in which case the contract will go on, or not, in which the case the innocent party would usually have to decide a little later whether to terminate or not. So, litigation is much more commonly about termination but no doubt withholding performance takes place very often in practice and has the desired result.

> ## LEGISLATIVE PROVISION
>
> A critical question in deciding whether or not one party is entitled to withhold performance is to consider what the contract says or implies about the order of performance. So, for example, s. 28 of the 1979 Act says:
>
> > Unless otherwise agreed, delivery of the goods and payment of the price are concurrent conditions, that is to say, the seller must be ready and willing to give possession of the goods to the buyer in exchange for the price and the buyer must be ready and willing to pay the price in exchange for possession of the goods.

So, in this standard case, neither the seller nor the buyer can withhold performance; each must be ready and willing to perform his or her side if he or she is to call on the other side to perform. In practice, however, other arrangements about payment and delivery are often made. The buyer may agree, and commonly does in an international sale, to open a banker's letter of credit and it has commonly been held that in such a situation the seller's obligation to ship the goods is conditional upon the buyer having opened the letter of credit for the right amount and the right currency with the right payment periods and so on. So, if the buyer fails to do this, the seller can withhold performance.[196] Conversely, the seller may have agreed to give the buyer credit. Suppose an oil company agrees to supply a filling station with all its requirements for oil for three years, payment to be made seven days after delivery. It is not open to the oil company unilaterally to change the terms and insist on payment in cash, even if the buyer has broken the contract by not always paying within the seven-day limit (*Total Oil (Great Britain) Ltd v Thompson Garages (Biggin Hill) Ltd*).[197]

These results can be expressed by saying that the buyer's obligation to pay is conditional on the seller having delivered the goods or that the seller's obligation to ship the goods is conditional on the buyer having opened a letter of credit. The parties need not necessarily have explicitly said what the order of performance is to be; in these cases, the courts have effectively inferred the order of performance from the commercial setting. So, in the case of the banker's letter of credit, it is unreasonable to expect the seller to expose itself to the risks of shipping the goods if the letter of credit has not been opened.

If we turn to consider the circumstances in which one party may terminate the contract, general contract law uses two principal approaches. One, which has been heavily used in relation to the sale of goods, is to proceed in terms of classifying the term of the contract which has been broken. This approach postulates that there are certain terms of the contract, commonly called conditions, which are so important that any breach of them should entitle the other party to terminate the contract. It is for this reason that a buyer can reject goods for breach of description, even though the breach appears in commercial terms to be quite trivial, as in *Arcos v Ronaasen* and *Re Moore and Landauer*, discussed above in section 4.8. Many of the obligations which we have discussed in the preceding chapters are expressed as being conditions and so attract the operation of this rule. In addition, there seems to be no reason why the parties may not agree that other express terms of the contract are to be treated as conditions. Unfortunately, the word 'condition' is used by lawyers in so many different

---

[196] *WJ Alan & Co Ltd v El Nasr Export and Import Co* [1972] 2 QB 189; [1972] 2 All ER 127.
[197] [1972] 1 QB 318.

senses that it is not absolutely certain that a court will construe a statement that a particular obligation is a condition as producing this result, as is shown by the decision of the House of Lords in *Schuler* v *Wickman*,[198] where it was said to be a condition of the agreement that Wickman should visit each of the six largest UK motor manufacturers at least once every week for the purposes of soliciting orders on behalf of Schuler. The House of Lords held by a majority, Lord Wilberforce dissenting, that this was not intended to produce the result that Schuler could terminate the contract because of Wickman's failure to make one visit in one week to one of the manufacturers. One suspects that, in fact, that was exactly what it was intended to do but that the majority of the House of Lords regarded this as such a draconian remedy that it chose to read the contract differently. Nevertheless, in a document clearly drafted by a lawyer, it must usually be the case that, if it says that a particular obligation is a condition, breach of it will be treated as giving rise to a right to terminate.

A second way of approaching the problem of termination is to ask how serious a breach of contract committed by the defendant is. Basically, there are two principal possibilities. One is that one party has behaved in such a way as to make it clear that it is repudiating its obligations under the contract. A party can do this either by explicitly repudiating or by doing something which is inconsistent with any continuing intention to perform the contract. A classic example, given the context, is the old case of *Frost* v *Knight*[199] where the defendant, having agreed to marry the plaintiff upon the death of his father, broke off the engagement during the father's lifetime. It was held that the lady could sue for damages at once, even though the date for performance of the contract might be many years off because it was clear to a reasonable man that the defendant would not perform (actions for breach of promise of marriage were abolished in 1970, but the principle of the case is still of general application).

Of course, deciding whether a particular course of conduct amounts to an implicit repudiation of a party's obligations may raise difficult questions of judgement. This is particularly the case where a party does something which turns out to be a breach of the contract but which it claims it was contractually entitled to do. The difficulties can be seen by contrasting two decisions of the House of Lords. In *Federal Commerce and Navigation* v *Molena Alpha*[200] there were disputes between a shipowner and time charterer. The owner, acting on legal advice, instructed the master not to issue freight prepaid bills of lading and to require the bills of lading to be endorsed with charter party terms. They told the charterer that they had given these instructions. It was eventually decided that although the owner believed it was entitled to take these steps, it was in fact not entitled to do so. The House of Lords held that the owner's statement that it was going to take these steps was, in the circumstances, a repudiation. On the other hand, in *Woodar Investment Development* v *Wimpey Construction*,[201] Woodar agreed to sell 14 acres of land to Wimpey, completion to be two months after the granting of outline planning permission or on 21 February 1980, whichever was earlier. Because of developments in the land market, Wimpey was anxious to escape from the contract if it could. It claimed to be entitled to do so on the basis of a right to rescind which was in the contract but which was eventually held not to cover the circumstances which in fact existed. In this case, the House of Lords held, though only by a majority of three to two, that this conduct was not repudiatory. It will be seen that in both cases one party claimed to be

[198] [1973] 2 All ER 39; [1974] AC 235.
[199] (1872) 7 Exch 111.
[200] [1979] AC 757.
[201] [1980] 1 All ER 571; [1980] 1 WLR 277.

entitled to do something under the contract which in fact it was subsequently held not to be entitled to do. In the first case, this conduct was treated as repudiatory and in the second, it was not. The fact that two Lords of Appeal dissented in the second case shows, as will be apparent to the reader, that the cases are not easy to distinguish. The principal difference probably lies in the fact that in the *Federal Commerce* case the behaviour of the shipowner was immediately coercive of the charterer whereas in the *Woodar* case, Wimpey had perhaps said no more than it would not perform when the time came and there was plenty of time to resolve the question of whether or not Wimpey was in fact correct in its view of the contract without bringing the contract to an end.

A second class of case in which one party is entitled to terminate is where the other party has performed in such a defective way as effectively not to have performed at all. Of course, some defective performances may be treated as evidence of an intention to repudiate. The thrust of this argument, however, is that one party, although he or she is doing his or her best, is doing it so badly that the other party is entitled to treat the contract as at an end. Such a breach is often called a fundamental breach though, in fact, many other metaphors have been used to describe the quality of defective performance which produces this effect. What is quite clear is that, if one is talking of defective performance, a serious defect is involved so that the other party is deprived of an essential part of what he or she entered the contract to obtain.

Whether one is talking in terms of breach of condition or in terms of repudiatory or funda- mental breach, it is clear that the contract does not come to an end simply because one of these events takes place. In each case, the innocent party has a choice. It can treat the breach of condition, the repudiatory breach or the fundamental breach, as bringing the contract to an end or it can continue to call for performance of the contract. Of course, in practice, it will often become clear that the contract breaker cannot or will not perform and persistence in this course will inevitably lead the innocent party, in the end, to bring the contract to an end but, as a matter of legal theory, the contract comes to an end as a result of the innocent party's decision to terminate, not as a result of the guilty party's breach. The most obvious practical importance of this is that the innocent party's decision not to terminate will often give the other party a second chance to perform his side of the contract properly. Where the innocent party does elect to terminate the contract, the contract is not treated as never having existed but as terminated from that moment so that existing contractual rights and duties are not expunged. It follows that the innocent party can terminate and also claim damages for breach of contract if damage has been suffered.

There are special rules about late performance. Although the rules are similar to those in relation to other forms of breach in that they distinguish between important late performance and cases where late performance, although in breach of contract, is relatively unimportant, they have developed in a slightly different way because this was an area where equity inter- vened so as, in certain circumstances, to grant specific performance of the contract to one party even though he or she was late in performing.

The modern position may be stated as follows. A late performance is always a breach of contract and will give rise to an action for damages for any loss which actually follows from the late performance (in practice, it is often very difficult to show any loss resulting from late performance). However, whether or not the contract can be terminated for late performance depends on whether or not 'time is of the essence of the contract'. Time may be of the essence of the contract either because the contract expressly says so (and many contracts do expressly say that time is or is not of the essence of the contract) or because the contract is of a kind in which the courts treat timely performance as being essential. In general, courts have treated timely performance of the obligation to deliver the goods by the seller as of the essence of the contract, at least in a commercial context, unless the contract expressly says that time is not of the essence. However, the buyer's obligation to pay the price is not treated as an obligation where time is of the essence unless the contract expressly says so.

Where time is not of the essence but one party is late in performing, the other party is said to be able to 'make time of the essence'. What this means is that the innocent party may say to the late performer that, if performance is not completed within a reasonable time, he or she will bring the contract to an end. It is fundamental to this possibility that the further time given for the performance is reasonable in all the circumstances and a party choosing to do this would be well advised to err on the side of generosity.

We saw above that the parties may agree in the contract that a particular obligation is to be treated as a condition. Alternatively, the parties may provide in the contract that one party is to be entitled to terminate. Such provisions are, in fact, very common. Sometimes, the event which gives rise to the right to terminate may be a breach of contract which would not have entitled the party to terminate. Such provisions are, in fact, very common. Sometimes, the event which gives rise to the right to terminate may be a breach of contract which depends on one party paying periodically. It is common to provide that failure to pay promptly entitles the other party to terminate, although a court would not usually hold that a single failure to pay promptly was either a repudiatory breach or a fundamental breach. In some cases, a party may contract for the right to terminate without there being any breach of contract by the other side. So, if the government places an order for a new fighter aeroplane, it may provide in the contract that the whole project can be cancelled if at a later stage defence policy changes. This would be a perfectly rational contractual arrangement to make. One would expect such a contract to contain provisions that the supplier was to be paid for the work which he or she had actually done up to the time of cancellation but the contract might well exclude the profit which the supplier would have made if the contract had been carried forward to completion. Obviously, clauses of this kind require careful negotiation and drafting.

Where the contract contains provisions for termination for events which are not in fact breaches of contract justifying termination on general principles, it may be important whether the contract makes the obligation essential or simply gives rise to a right to terminate. This is illustrated by the important case of *Lombard North Central* v *Butterworth*.[202]

CASE

Lombard North Central v *Butterworth*

In this case, the plaintiff had leased a computer to the defendant for a period of five years and the defendant had agreed to pay an initial sum of £584.05 and subsequent quarterly payments of the same sum. As is usual in such agreements, there was a clause giving the plaintiff the right to terminate the agreement if the instalments were not punctually paid. The defendant made two punctual payments and four late payments and the plaintiff then terminated the agreement, recovered possession of the computer and sold it for

[202] [1987] 1 All ER 267; [1987] QB 527.

£172.88. It was clear that the plaintiff was entitled to do this. The question was to what further damages he was entitled. In a number of earlier decisions, of which the most important was *Financings v Baldock*,[203] it had been held that, in such circumstances, the plaintiff could not recover damages for loss of the interest payments which would have been earned if the contract had run to its end because the termination of the contract arose out of the plaintiff's decision to exercise his contractual right to terminate and not out of the defendant's breach of contract. However, in the present case, the contract, although very similar to earlier contracts, contained an extra provision which stated that 'punctual payment of each instalment was of the essence of the agreement'. The Court of Appeal held that this made a fundamental difference, since its effect was that each failure to pay promptly was not only an event entitling the plaintiff to terminate but was also a breach of condition. It was said to follow that the termination of the contract flowed not from the plaintiff's decision to exercise its rights but from the defendant having committed a fundamental breach of contract so that all the plaintiff's loss flowed from this. This case shows that large results can flow from small variations in the wording of the contract.

The buyer's right to reject the goods is, in a sense, simply an example of the right to withhold performance or to terminate. It may be only the withholding of performance because in a few cases the seller will be able to make a second tender of the goods. This would usually only be where he or she can make a second tender within the contractually permitted time for delivery. Suppose the contract calls for delivery in January and the seller makes a defective tender on 1 January; he or she may well be able to make an effective tender later in the month. Where, as will often be the case, the contract calls for delivery on a particular day and time is of the essence, this possibility will, in practice, not exist and then rejection of the goods will effectively terminate the contract. Since many of the seller's obligations are expressed to be conditions, the buyer will have the right to reject the goods for breach of condition in a wide variety of circumstances. These include:

(a) a delivery of less or more than the contract quantity or of other goods mixed with the contract goods, as discussed in section 4.5;

(b) failure by the seller to perform their obligations as to title as discussed in section 4.6; or

(c) failure by the seller to carry out their obligations as to the quality of the goods as discussed in section 4.8.

The buyer will also often be able to reject the goods because delivery is late, as discussed above. There is a major difference, however, between the rules governing the buyer's right to reject goods for breach of condition and the general law about termination. Usually, an innocent party cannot lose the right to terminate the contract until it has discovered that it has got it. However, it is clear that in some circumstances the buyer may lose the right to reject for breach of condition through acceptance even though it does not know that it has the right to reject because it has not yet discovered the defect which gives rise to this right. This is because the buyer loses the right to reject the goods by acceptance and it is possible for acceptance to take place before the buyer discovers the defect in the goods. This is because, under s. 35(1),

---

[203] [1963] 1 All ER 443; [1963] 2 QB 104.

one of the ways in which the buyer can accept the goods is to retain them after the lapse of a reasonable time and a reasonable time is held to run from delivery and not from discovering that the goods are defective. This is discussed more fully above, under 'Acceptance' (s. 5).

LEGISLATIVE PROVISION

The right of rejection is modified by two provisions which are incorporated by virtue of s. 4 of the Sale and Supply of Goods Act 1994. The first of these is a new s. 15A which provides:

(1) Where in the case of a contract of sale:

(a) the buyer would, apart from this sub-section, have the right to reject goods by reason of a breach on the part of the seller of a term implied by ss. 13, 14 or 15 above; but

(b) the breach is so slight that it would be unreasonable for him to reject them, then, if the buyer does not deal as a consumer, the breach is not to be treated as a breach of condition but may be treated as a breach of warranty.

(2) This section applies unless a contrary intention appears in, or is to be implied from, the contract.

(3) It is for the seller to show that a breach fell within sub-s. (1)(b) above.

(4) This section does not apply to Scotland.

On the one hand, it is assumed that, for a consumer buyer, the right of rejection is of particular importance. The great attraction of rejection, from the consumer's point of view, is that it avoids any need to resort to litigation and forces the seller to decide whether it is worthwhile litigating. It can be assumed that, in respect of all goods except cars, consumers will be extremely reluctant to litigate, whatever the defects. The right of rejection is therefore particularly important. It is assumed, on the other hand, that, in the case of commercial sales, a reduction in price will, more often than not, satisfy the buyer's legitimate demands, unless the defect is a serious one. It is open to a commercial buyer to bargain for s. 15A to be excluded. It must be noted that it will require some cases to be sure what exactly will count as a slight breach and when it will be unreasonable to reject the goods because of such a breach. There is a twofold test here. The seller must show both that the breach is slight and that it is unreasonable to reject. It is not to be assumed that, simply because the breach is slight, it will be unreasonable to reject.

LEGISLATIVE PROVISION

Finally, the buyer is given slightly greater rights of rejection by a new s. 35A which provides:

(1) If the buyer:

(a) has the right to reject the goods by reason of a breach on the part of the seller that affects some or all of them; but

(b) accepts some of the goods, including, where there are any goods unaffected by the breach, all such goods,

he does not by accepting them lose his right to reject the rest.

(2) In the case of a buyer having the right to reject an instalment of goods, sub-s. (1) above applies as if references to the goods were references to the goods comprised in the instalment.

(3) For the purposes of sub-s. (1) above, goods are affected by a breach if by reason of the breach they are not in conformity with the contract.

(4) This section applies unless a contrary intention appears in, or is to be implied from, the contract.

By virtue of this new section, the buyer does not lose the right to reject some goods as part of a parcel of goods which are defective because he has accepted other goods in the parcel which are not defective. Under the previous law, the buyer who had 1,000 tons of wheat delivered to him, of which 400 tons were defective and 600 tons all right, had the choices of either rejecting the whole 1,000 tons or accepting the whole 1,000 tons (in either case, he might claim damages). Under s. 35A, he will now have the option, if he wishes, to reject 400 tons and keep the 600 tons which are of good quality. This seems an entirely sensible change.

4.10.3 Specific enforcement

LEGISLATIVE PROVISION

SALE OF GOODS ACT 1979

Section 52

(1) In any action for breach of contract to deliver specific or ascertained goods the court may, if it thinks fit, on the plaintiff's application, by its judgment or decree direct that the contract shall be performed specifically, without giving the defendant the option of retaining the goods on payment of damages.

(2) The plaintiff's application may be made at any time before judgment or decree.

(3) The judgment or decree may be unconditional, or on such terms and conditions as to damages, payment of the price and otherwise as seem just to the court.

It will be seen that this section talks only of specific or ascertained goods and the question of whether or not specific performance can be given for unascertained goods is considered below. As far as specific or ascertained goods are concerned, the section is in very broad terms. However, in practice, the courts have been very slow to exercise the broad powers given by the section. The reason for this is they have usually taken the view that in a contract for sale of goods damages will be an adequate remedy, since usually the buyer can go out and buy substitute goods and be adequately compensated by a money payment. So, in *Cohen v Roche*[204] the court refused specific performance of a contract for what was described as 'ordinary Hepplewhite

---

[204] [1927] 1 KB 169.

furniture'. Today, there is perhaps not such a market for 'ordinary Hepplewhite furniture' that one can easily go out and buy substitutes and such a case would perhaps be close to the line. It was perhaps an important factor in the case that the buyer was buying the goods for resale. This greatly strengthened the argument that damages were an adequate remedy. A leading case in which specific performance was granted was *Behnke* v *Bede Shipping*[205] in which the subject matter of the contract was a ship. It cannot be assumed, however, that specific performance would routinely be given even of a contract for the sale of a ship. So, in *CN Marine* v *Stena Line*,[206] specific performance was refused of such a contract. A court would want to inquire, in any decision whether to grant specific performance or not, into all the circumstances, in particular, on any hardship which would be caused to one party or the other by giving or refusing specific performance or the conduct of the parties leading up to the contract. This reflects a combination of two policies: the general feeling that specific performance is usually not necessary in the case of goods and the general equitable principle that specific perform- ance is not to be granted mechanically and that all the circumstances are to be considered. Another recent case which illustrates the reluctance of the court to grant specific performance is the *Bronx Engineering* case[207] where the subject matter of the contract was a machine weighing over 220 tons, costing £270,000 and only buyable with a nine-month delivery date.

As we said above, s. 52 only talks in terms of 'specific or ascertained goods'. This leaves in the air the question of whether or not specific performance can ever be granted of unascertained goods. One view, which was discussed in section 4.1, is that the Sale of Goods Act contains an exhaustive code of the remedies available. This view was expressed in relation to specific performance in *Re Wait*.[208] However, in the leading modern case where the question arose, the judge did, in fact, grant specific performance of a contract for unascertained goods though he did not refer to s. 52 or consider the theoretical question of whether he had jurisdiction or not. This was in *Sky Petroleum* v *VIP Petroleum*.[209] In this case, there was a contract for the supply of petrol to a filling station and the seller refused to deliver. Normally, no question of specific performance would arise on such facts because the filling station could go and buy petrol on the market and be compensated adequately by damages. However, at the time of the case, the Yom Kippur war had recently disrupted supplies of petrol so that alternative supplies were not available to the buyer. In the circumstances, specific performance was a uniquely desirable and effective remedy. The decision of the judge that he should give specific performance seems entirely sensible though it is perhaps unfortunate that he did not con- sider the theoretical question of whether or not he had power to do so.

Section 52 talks of plaintiffs and defendants and not of buyers and sellers. So it may be that, in theory, a seller can sue for specific performance. However, this is not likely to be a practical question except in the most extraordinary circumstances, since a seller will nearly always be able to sell the goods elsewhere and recover compensation by way of damages for any loss that he or she suffer. There will be cases, however, where the seller would wish, if possible, to sue for the price rather than to sue for damages. This is principally because, in the English system, actions for defined sums of money are much easier, quicker and, there- fore, cheaper than actions for damages.

---

[205] [1927] 1 KB 649.
[206] [1982] 2 Lloyd's Rep 336.
[207] [1975] 1 Lloyd's Rep 465.
[208] [1972] 1 Ch 606.
[209] [1974] 1 All ER 954.

LEGISLATIVE PROVISION

Section 49 of the 1979 Act provides:

(1) Where, under a contract of sale, the property in the goods has passed to the buyer and he wrongfully neglects or refuses to pay for the goods according to the terms of the contract, the seller may maintain an action against him for the price of the goods.

(2) Where, under a contract of sale, the price is payable on a day certain irrespective of delivery and the buyer wrongfully neglects or refuses to pay such price, the seller may maintain an action for the price, although the property in the goods has not passed and the goods have not been appropriated to the contract.

Although the action for the price is in a sense the seller's equivalent of the buyer's action for specific performance, the two remedies should be kept clearly distinct. This is for historical reasons. The action for specific performance arises historically from the jurisdiction of the Court of Chancery to grant specific performance which was always said to be discretionary and to turn on taking into account all the relevant circumstances. The action for the price was not an equitable action but basically a common law action for debt. This means that, where sellers are entitled to sue for the price, they do not have to show that they have suffered any loss; they do not have to take steps to mitigate the loss as they do in a damages action and the action is not subject to any general discretion in the court. However, the seller does not have an action for the price simply because the buyer's obligation to pay the price has crystallised and the buyer has failed to pay. The seller has to bring the case within one or other of the two limbs of s. 49. It will be seen that s. 49(1) links the right to sue for the price to the passing of property. This is another example of the point discussed in section 4.6 that the passing of property in the English system is largely important because of the other consequences which are made dependent on it. It will be remembered that whether or not property has passed is quite independent of delivery. So, in principle, a seller may be able to sue for the price because property has passed even though he still has the goods in his hands. Conversely, a seller who has delivered the goods but has provided that property is not to pass until he has been paid, as is of course common under retention of title clauses, cannot sue for the price under s. 49(1).

Section 49(2) provides an alternative basis for an action for the price where the price is payable 'on a day certain irrespective of delivery'. This clearly covers the simple case where the contract says that the price is payable on 1 January. It certainly does not cover the rather common case where the price is payable on delivery, even where the contractual date for delivery is agreed, because it can then be held that that is not a day certain irrespective of delivery; *Stein Forbes* v *County Tailoring*.[210] What about the cases which fall in between these two extremes? It certainly seems that it will do if the parties agree a date, even though, at the time of the agreement, neither of them knows when it is, such as on Derby Day 2013 or probably on some date which will become certain but is outside their control, such as the date of the next General Election. (These are no doubt not very likely practical examples!) An important practical test arose over *Workman Clark* v *Lloyd Brazileno*.[211] This was a

---

[210] (1916) 86 LJ KB 448.
[211] [1908] 1 KB 968.

ship-building contract under which it was agreed that the price was to be paid in instalments which were linked to the completion of various stages of the ship. Such provisions are extremely common in shipbuilding contracts for obvious cash flow reasons. So, a shipbuilding contract may well provide that 20 per cent of the price is to be paid on the laying of the keel. Obviously, at the time of the contract, no one will know exactly when the keel will in fact be laid, even if the contract contains provisions as to when it should be laid. Nevertheless, in the *Workman Clark* case, it was held that such provisions were for payment on a day certain because when the duty to pay arose, the day on which it fell due was certain. So, it would seem that in general it is sufficient that the day of payment is certain when payment falls due, provided that it is not delivery which makes it certain.

A question which has not been tested in litigation is whether or not the parties may extend the scope of s. 49 by agreement. A seller, for instance, might well wish to provide that property was not to pass until he or she had been paid but that he or she could sue for the price once the goods had been delivered. There does not seem to be any obvious reason why the parties should not be able to make an agreement to this effect.

4.10.4 Actions for damages

LEGISLATIVE PROVISION

The 1979 Act contains three sections which deal with damages. These are:

50 (1) Where the buyer wrongfully neglects or refuses to accept and pay for the goods, the seller may maintain an action against him for damages for non-acceptance.

(2) The measure of damages is the estimated loss directly and naturally resulting, in the ordinary course of events, from the buyer's breach of contract.

(3) Where there is an available market for the goods in question the measure of damages is *prima facie* to be ascertained by the difference between the contract price and the market or current price at the time or times when the goods ought to have been accepted or (if no time was fixed for acceptance) at the time of the refusal to accept.

51 (1) Where the seller wrongfully neglects or refuses to deliver the goods to the buyer, the buyer may maintain an action against the seller for damages for non-delivery.

(2) The measure of damages is the estimated loss directly and naturally resulting, in the ordinary course of events, from the seller's breach of contract.

(3) Where there is an available market for the goods in question the measure of damages is *prima facie* to be ascertained by the difference between the contract price and the market or current price of the goods at the time or times when they ought to have been delivered or (if no time was fixed) at the time of the refusal to deliver.

53 (1) Where there is a breach of warranty by the seller, or where the buyer elects (or is compelled) to treat any breach of a condition on the part of the seller as a breach of warranty, the buyer is not by reason only of such breach of warranty entitled to reject the goods, but he may:

(a) set up against the seller the breach of warranty in diminution or extinction of the price; or

(b) maintain an action against the seller for damages for the breach of warranty.

> (2) The measure of damages for breach of warranty is the estimated loss directly and naturally resulting, in the ordinary course of events, from the breach of warranty.
>
> (3) In the case of breach of warranty of quality, such loss is *prima facie* the difference between the value of the goods at the time of delivery to the buyer and the value they would have had if they had fulfilled the warranty.
>
> (4) The fact that the buyer has set up the breach of warranty in diminution or extinction of the price does not prevent him from maintaining an action for the same breach of warranty if he has suffered further damage.

In practice, these provisions do not add a great deal to the general law of contract and many cases are decided without reference to them. It is more satisfactory, therefore, to start by setting out some general contractual principles about damages. For this purpose, it is useful to start by considering what kinds of loss a buyer or seller may suffer as a result of the other party breaking the contract. In order to do this, English commentators have now largely adopted a distinction first drawn in a famous *American Law Review* article in 1936 between expectation loss, reliance loss and restitution loss.[212] This terminology is now beginning to be recognised by the English courts.[213]

Expectation loss is the loss of what the injured party expected to recover if the contract was carried out. The great feature of the law of contract is that on the whole it is designed to protect people's expectations and a plaintiff should therefore normally be able to get damages which will carry him or her forward into the position which he or she hoped and expected to reach. So, in principle, if I order goods which I intend to use in my business for the purpose of making a profit, I should be able to recover damages for non-delivery of the goods which will compensate me for not having made the profit. Needless to say, this broad general principle is subject to qualifications which will appear later. Cases may arise, however, in which it is very difficult for the plaintiff to prove, in any way which would be acceptable to a court, what his or her expectation loss would be but where it is clear that the plaintiff has suffered loss as a result of the contract having been broken, the plaintiff may seek to argue that he or she has suffered what is called reliance loss, that is, loss arising out of having relied on the defendant honouring the contract. A good example is the case of *McRae v Commonwealth Disposals Commission* (discussed above in section 4.7). In this case, the plaintiff did not recover his expectation loss, that is, the profit he would have made from recovering the tanker if it had existed, because this was too speculative to be established but he did recover his reliance loss, that is, the cost of mounting the expedition to look for the tanker.

The general principle appears to be that the plaintiff has a free choice whether or not to formulate the claim in terms of expectation loss or reliance loss unless the defendant can prove that the bargain that the plaintiff had made was such a bad one from the plaintiff's point of view that it would not even have recouped the reliance loss if the contract had been performed (*CCC Films v Impact Quadrant Films*).[214]

A third form of loss which the plaintiff may have suffered is that he or she may have paid over money to the defendant in pursuance of a contract which has gone off, as for example

---

[212] L. L. Fuller and W. R. Purdue Jr, 'The Reliance Interest in Contract Damages' (1936) 46 *Yale LJ* 52.
[213] *CCC Films (London) Ltd v Impact Quadrant Films Ltd* [1985] QB 16; [1984] 3 All ER 298.
[214] [1984] 3 All ER 298.

where the purchaser has paid part of the price in advance and the seller has then failed to deliver the goods. In certain circumstances, the plaintiff will be able to sue simply to recover the money but this would not be part of a damages action but a separate action of a restitutionary kind.

The law does not say, whether the plaintiff is formulating the claim for expectation loss or for reliance loss; it can recover all its loss. The courts have said that some loss is too remote. It is at this question that ss. 50(2) and 51(2) are aimed. It will be seen that those sections lay down the same test which is that the measure of damages is the estimated loss directly and naturally resulting, in the ordinary course of events, from the breach of contract. This is the draftsman's attempt to state the general contract law in the context of a failure by the seller to deliver the goods or by the buyer to accept them respectively. This rule is contained, for general contract law, in a series of cases of which *Hadley v Baxendale*[215] is the earliest and still most famous and the *Heron II*[216] is perhaps the most important modern example. Both of those cases were concerned with delay in delivery by carriers but they lay down principles of general application. They do provide both an endorsement and a substantial addition to the test laid down in ss. 50(2) and 51(2). They provide an endorsement because, indeed, a plaintiff can normally recover any loss which directly and naturally results, in the ordinary course of events. However, a plaintiff may also be able to recover loss which does not directly and naturally result provided that he or she has adequately informed the defendant before the contract is made of the circumstances which in the particular case made the loss a consequence of the defendant's breach of contract. It follows that a defendant cannot say that the loss is too remote if it flows either from the ordinary course of events or from circumstances which the defendant adequately knew about at the time the contract was made. It follows that, in principle, the more the defendant knows about the plaintiff's business, the greater the possibility that the plaintiff will be able to recover compensation for loss which flows from the defendant's breach of contract. In some cases, judges have described these results by using the language of foreseeability, though, in the *Heron II*, the House of Lords deprecated the use of that word which they thought more appropriate to the law of tort and suggested alternative formulations such as 'contemplated as a not unlikely result'.

It is important to make clear, however, that what the parties have to contemplate is the kind of loss which will be suffered and not its extent. So, if a seller fails to deliver, it is foreseeable that the buyer will have to go out and buy substitute goods. One of the ways of calculating the buyer's loss is to compare the contract price and the price that the buyer has actually had to pay. This is readily within the contemplation of the parties. It would make no difference that the price had gone up in a way which nobody could have contemplated at the time of the contract (*Wroth v Tyler*).[217]

It is often said that the plaintiff must mitigate his damages. This is, strictly speaking, an inaccurate way of putting the point. The plaintiff can do what he likes but would only be able to recover damages which result from reasonable behaviour after the contract is broken. This is really an application of the general principle that the plaintiff can only recover what arises in the ordinary course of events and in the ordinary course of events those who suffer breaches of contract respond in a reasonable way (or at least the law treats them as if they will). This

[215] (1854) 9 Exch 341.
[216] [1969] 3 All ER 686.
[217] [1974] Ch 30.

principle can be an important limitation on the amount that the plaintiff recovers. This is illustrated by the case of *Payzu v Saunders* (1919)[218] where the defendant had agreed to sell to the plaintiffs a quantity of silk, payment to be made a month after delivery. The defendant, in breach of contract, refused to make further deliveries except for cash and the plaintiff treated this as being a repudiation and elected to terminate the contract. This they were certainly entitled to do. They then sued for damages on the basis that the market price of silk had risen and that they could claim the difference between the contract price and the market price at the date of the buyers' repudiation. This argument was rejected on the grounds that, the market having risen, it would have been cheaper for the buyers to accept the seller's offer to deliver against cash at the contract price. Of course, it will often be difficult for the plaintiff to know immediately after the contract what is the best course. In principle, if the plaintiff acts reasonably, it should be able to recover its financial loss even though, with the wisdom of hindsight, it appears that the plaintiff could have minimised the loss by doing something different (*Gebruder Metelmann v NBR (London)*).[219]

How do we apply these general principles to the specific case of a contract for the sale of goods? One answer is given by ss. 50(3) and 51(3) which, it will be seen, are in very similar terms. This states the market rule to which several references have already been made. English litigation in the field of sale of goods has been dominated by commodity contracts where there is a national or international market and it is possible to say with precision what the market price is during the hours when the market was open. In such a situation, it is assumed that if the seller refuses to deliver, the buyer will buy against the seller in the market or that if the buyer refuses to accept, the seller will sell against the buyer in the market and that the starting point for inquiry is the difference between the contract price and the market price. This is basically a very simple rule to apply and it is a useful example of the application of the general principle. The fact that it is the only specific case actually discussed in the Act perhaps, however, gives it more prominence than it really deserves. It should be emphasised that the rule does not apply where there is no 'available market' and even where there is an available market, the rule will not necessarily apply.[220]

Whether the market rule is the right rule to apply will depend, amongst other things, on the nature of the loss suffered by the plaintiff.[221] This is shown by the case of *Thompson v Robinson* (1955).[222] In that case, the plaintiff was a car dealer which contracted to sell a Standard Vanguard car to the defendant who wrongfully refused to take delivery. At this time, there was effective resale price maintenance for new cars so that there was no difference between the contract price and the market price and the buyer argued that the plaintiff had suffered no loss. However, the plaintiff showed that in fact there was a surplus of Standard Vanguard cars and that it had therefore lost its profit on the deal which could not be replaced by selling the car to someone else since it had more cars than it could sell. In this case, the plaintiff's loss was the loss of the retail mark-up, that is, the difference between the price at

---

[218] [1919] 2 KB 581.
[219] [1984] 1 Lloyd's Rep 614.
[220] There may be a market for goods of the contract description but not of the contract amount. For a solution of the consequential problems, see *Shearson Lehman v Maclaine Watson* [1990] 3 All ER 723. For discussion of available market see *Coastal (Bermuda) Petroleum Ltd v VVT Vulcan Petroleum SA (No 2)* [1994] 2 Lloyd's Rep 629.
[221] *Sealace Shipping Co v Oceanvoice, The Alecos* [1991] Lloyd's Rep 120.
[222] [1955] 1 All ER 154; [1955] Ch 177.

which the car was bought from the manufacturer and the price at which it could be sold. Of course, if the dealer could sell as many cars as it could obtain, then it would not effectively have lost this sum, as was held in the later case of *Charter* v *Sullivan*.[223]

DEBATE BOX

From the buyer's point of view, a most important question arises where it wishes to argue that what has been lost is a particularly valuable sub-sale. Suppose A has contracted to sell to B for £100 and B has contracted to sell to C for £150. Suppose, further, that A fails to deliver in circumstances where B cannot buy substitute goods in time to perform his contract with C and loses his profit on the transaction. Can he recover the profit? If we were applying the standard rules, this would appear to turn either on whether this was a loss in the usual course of things, which it might well be if the buyer was a dealer since the sub-sale would then appear to be entirely usual, or where the buyer had told the seller of the sub-sale. In practice, the courts have been reluctant to go so far. The leading case is *Re Hall and Pims Arbitration*.[224] In this case, the contract was for the sale of a specific cargo of corn in a specific ship. The contract price was 51s 9d per quarter and the buyer resold at 56s 9d per quarter. The seller failed to deliver and, at the date when the delivery should have taken place, the market price was 53s 9d per quarter. Clearly, the buyer was entitled at least to the difference between 51s 9d and 53s 9d per quarter but claimed to be entitled to the difference between 51s 9d and 56s 9d, the price at which it had agreed to resell. It was held by the House of Lords that this was right. However, this was a very strong case for two reasons. The first was that both the sale and the sub-sale were of the specific cargo so that there would be no question of the buyer going into the market to buy substitute goods. The second was that the contract of sale between plaintiff and defendant expressly provided for resale by the buyer.

Section 50 is concerned with the case where the buyer refuses to accept the goods and s. 51 with the case of the seller who fails to deliver. Of course, the seller can break the contract not only by failing to deliver but also by delivering late or making a defective delivery. This is dealt with by s. 53 which was set out above. It will be seen that again this sets out reliance on the market rule. It is clear, however, that there are many other forms of loss which may arise in the usual course of things. So defective goods may cause damage to persons or property before their defects are discovered. Late delivery may cause loss of profit where the goods were to be used to make profits. An interesting case on s. 53 is *Bence Graphics International Ltd* v *Fasson UK Ltd*.[225] In this case, the sellers sold to the buyers large quantities of cast vinyl film which was to be used by the buyers and resold as decals for the container industry. It was an express term that the film should last in a usable form for five years but, in fact, it degraded much sooner. The trial judge took the view that the film was valueless in its delivered form and that the buyer could therefore recover the whole of the price, some £500,000. The

---

[223] [1957] 2 QB 117.
[224] (1928) 139 LT 50.
[225] [1997] 4 All ER 979.

majority of the Court of Appeal disagreed. The buyer could only recover its proven loss. This included a small amount of unusable film left on its hands and potential liabilities to sub-buyers, but, in fact, very few of these sub-buyers had asked for their money back. If this state of affairs continued, it would endure to the seller's advantage.

A major problem with all of these rules about damages is the extent to which the plaintiff is seeking to recover his or her actual loss or what one might call his or her notional loss. In general, for instance, when one is applying the market rule, it does not seem to matter whether the buyer has gone into the market and bought substitute goods or not. The buyer can recover the difference between the contract price and the market price even though he does not buy against the seller; conversely, the buyer cannot recover more than this where he has stayed out of the market until later and then had to buy back at a higher price. However, it seems that sometimes courts will look to see what actually happens. An important and difficult case is *Wertheim v Chicoutimi*[226] where the seller delivered late. At the time when the goods ought to have been delivered, the market price was 70s a ton but by the time the goods were actually delivered, the market price was 42s 6d a ton. On the principles set out above, it would seem to follow that the buyer should have been able to recover the difference between 70s and 42s 6d for every ton he had contracted to buy. In fact, the buyer had managed to resell the goods at the remarkably good price in the circumstances of 65s a ton. It was held that he could only recover the difference between 70s and 65s for each ton bought. At first sight, this looks reasonable since it might be said that this was the only loss which the buyer had actually suffered. On the other hand, the reasoning deprives the buyer of the profit to which his commercial astuteness at selling well over the market price would normally have entitled him. It is not surprising, therefore, that the correctness of this decision has been much debated.

4.10.5 Party provided remedies

It seems, within broad limits, that parties have freedom to add on by contract additional remedies. So, we have already seen earlier that the right to terminate may be extended by contract. Two other important additional remedies which should be mentioned are liquidated damages and deposits. Many contracts of sale provide that, in the event of certain breaches, typically late delivery by the seller, he or she shall pay damages at a rate laid down in the contract, for instance £X for every day by which delivery is delayed. Such provisions have important practical advantages because, as noted above, it is very much easier to bring actions for defined sums of money. However, the parties do not have complete freedom as to what may be agreed in this area. Since the 17th century, the courts have distinguished between liquidated damages which are enforceable and penalties which are not. The distinction turns on whether the sum agreed is a reasonable pre-estimate as at the time of the contract of the amount of loss which is liable to flow from the contract being broken in the way contemplated. If the sum agreed is a reasonable pre-estimate, then it is classified as liquidated damages and is recoverable. If it is more than the reasonable pre-estimate then it is classified as a penalty and is not recoverable, leaving the plaintiff to recover such unliquidated damages

---

[226] [1911] AC 301.

as he can in fact establish. It is important to emphasise that the test is not the plaintiff's actual loss but the plaintiff's contemplated loss as at the time of the contract. So liquidated damages can be recovered even though there is no actual loss or less actual loss than the agreed sum, provided the pre-estimate was reasonable.

A contract may provide for the payment in advance by the buyer of sums of money. Here, the law has drawn a distinction between deposits and advance payments. In certain types of contract, it is common for the payment to be made in stages, tied to the achievement of particular stages of work. So, as we saw above, in a shipbuilding contract, it would be common for there to be a payment of part of the price when the keel is laid. The purpose of these schemes is to help the seller with cash flow. It typically occurs in major capital contracts when the seller or supplier has to spend considerable sums of money on acquiring components and on fitting them together. Suppliers, typically, are unwilling to finance the whole of the cost of this and stipulate for payment in instalments tied, as we have said, to particular stages of completion.

Alternatively, the buyer may have paid a deposit so as to give the seller a guarantee that the buyer will in fact go through with the contract. So, the buyer may have gone into the seller's shop and picked some goods and said that he would like to buy them and would come back tomorrow to collect them. In certain trades, it would be very common for the seller to take a deposit because sellers know from experience that many buyers do not return and they may lose the opportunity of selling the goods elsewhere.

The importance of the distinction is this. If, having paid money in advance, the buyer then breaks the contract, he or she will of course be liable to damages and, if the damages exceed what has been paid in advance, then it will simply be a question of the seller recovering the balance. However, the seller's damages may be less than the deposit or advance payment. In this situation, the courts have said that the seller can keep the deposit even if the deposit is greater than the seller's actual loss whereas, if there has been an advance payment which is greater than the seller's actual loss, the seller can only keep the actual loss and must return the balance.

The amount of the deposit may be not only greater than the seller's actual loss but than any loss to the seller greater than was reasonably foreseeable at the time of the contract. In such a case, it might plausibly be argued that the deposit is in fact a penalty. In practice, however, courts have tended to keep the rules about penalties and deposits in watertight compartments. A marked change of attitude was revealed in the case of *Workers' Trust and Merchant Bank Ltd* v *Dojap Investments Ltd*,[227] where the Privy Council was prepared to treat a deposit in a contract for the sale of land as penal where it exceeded the going rate (10 per cent) (of course even a deposit of 10 per cent might exceed any likely loss but it was effectively held that it was too late to question the taking of deposits at the going rate).

4.10.6 Seller remedies against the goods

The seller's principal concern is to ensure that he is paid for the goods. The most effective and common way of doing this is for the seller to retain ownership of the goods as long

---

[227] [1993] 2 All ER 370. See also *Amble Assets LLP* v *Longbenton Foods Ltd* [2011] EWHC 3774; [2012] 1 All ER (Comm) 764.

as possible. We have already discussed this in section 4.6. The Act does, however, give the unpaid seller further rights in relation to the goods as well as his right to sue the buyer for the price or damages. The provisions which are contained in ss. 38–48 of the Act are complex but do not appear to be of much practical importance in modern situations. The central provision is s. 39 which says:

(1) Subject to this and any other Act, notwithstanding that the property in the goods may have passed to the buyer, the unpaid seller of goods, as such, has by implication of law:

(a) a lien on the goods or right to retain them for the price while he is in possession of them;

(b) in case of the insolvency of the buyer, a right of stopping the goods in transit after he has parted with the possession of them;

(c) a right of resale as limited by this Act.

. . .

(3) Where the property in goods has not passed to the buyer, the unpaid seller has (in addition to his other remedies) a right of withholding delivery similar to and co-extensive with his rights of lien or retention and stoppage in transit where the property has passed to the buyer. It will be seen that, subject to the conditions set out in the other relevant sections, the seller has the possibility of exercising a lien on the goods, that is of retaining possession of them until he or she is paid, of reselling them or of stopping them in transit, that is, by giving notice to the carrier not to deliver to an insolvent buyer.

4.10.7 Additional remedies of consumer buyer

The Sale and Supply of Goods to Consumer Regulations 2002 adds additional remedies to consumer buyers by adding new s. 48A to 48F.[228]

ISSUE BOX

1. A sells to B a painting for $500,000. Before the sale A says that the painting is by Picasso. In what circumstances will A be liable if the painting is not by Picassso?

2. A is a housebuilder who decides to use some new and very heavy slates for the roofs of the houses he is building. He wants to make sure that the timbers under the roofs will support the tiles. Advise him as to what he should say to his suppliers.

3. Two weeks ago A bought a brand new car with a manufacturer's guarantee. This morning the engine appears to have seized up. Advise him.

4. Discuss the ways in which consumer buyers are better protected than commercial buyers. Is this fair to small businesses?

5. A contracts to sell 500 tons of coffee beans to B at $50 a ton, with delivery on 1 June. On 1 June, A fails to deliver and the market price is $55. B does nothing until 5 June when he buys in the market at $45. Advise B.

[228] These are discussed in Chapter 7 on consumer protection.

Further reading

There are a number of excellent textbooks on the sale of goods. See in particular:

Adams, J. and MacQueen, H., *Atiyah's Sale of Goods* (12th edn, Pearson Longman, Harlow, 2010).

Bridge, M., *The Sale of Goods* (2nd edn, Oxford University Press, Oxford, 2009).

An account which looks at the problems specifically from a consumer standpoint is:

Macleod, J. K., *Consumer Sales Law* (2nd edn, Routledge-Cavendish, Oxford, 2007).

The classic practitioner's text is A. G. Gnest (gen. ed.), *Benjamin's Sale of Goods* (7th rev. edn, Sweet and Maxwell, 2006). **Judah P. Benjamin** was a leading figure in the Confederate State of America (the South). After the South lost the civil war he fled to England and went to the bar. He wrote the first edition to help start his practice and it has remained a classic ever since.

For section 4.6 on ownership

Battersby, G. and Preston, A. D., 'The Concepts of "Property", "Title" and "Owner" Used in the Sale of Goods Act 1893' (1972) 35 *MLR* 268.

Bradgate, R. and White, F., 'Sale of Goods Forming Part of a Bulk: Proposals for Reform' [1994] *LMCLQ* 315.

Burns T., 'Better Late than Never: The Reform of the Law on the Sale of Goods Forming Part of a Bulk' [1996] *MLR* 260.

Davies, I., *Effective Retention of Title* (Fourmat Publishing, London, 1991).

Lawson, F. H., 'The Passing of Property and Risk in Sale of Goods: A Comparative Study' (1949) 65 *LQR* 352.

McCormack, G., *Reservation of Title* (Sweet and Maxwell, London, 1990).

McCormack, G., 'Reservation of Title in England and New Zealand' (1992) 12 *LS* 195.

Palmer, N., 'Reservation of Title' (1992) 5 *JCL* 175.

Parris, J., *Effective Retention of Title Clauses* (WileyBlackwell, Oxford, 1986).

Wheeler, S., *Reservation of Title Clauses: Impact and Implications* (Oxford University Press, Oxford, 1991).

For section 4.7 on non-existent goods, risk and frustration

McKendrick, E. (ed.), *Force Majeure and Frustration of Contract* (2nd edn, LLP, London, 1995).

Sealy, L. S., 'Risk in the Law of Sale' [1972B] *CLJ* 225.

Treitel, G. H., *Frustration and Force Majeure* (Sweet and Maxwell, London, 2004).

For section 4.10 on remedies

Saidov, D. and Cunnington, R. (eds), *Contract Damages: Domestic and International Perspectives* (Hart Publishing, Oxford, 2008) especially Chapters 14 (McGregor, H.), 17 (Furmston, M.) and 18 (Bridge, M.).

Companion Website

For open-access **student resources** specifically written to complement this textbook and support your learning, please visit **www.pearsoned.co.uk/legalupdates**

ON THE WEBSITE

5 International sale of goods

By Susan Hawker

5.1 Introduction

5.1.1 What is an international sale contract?

A contract of sale is usually regarded as an 'international' contract of sale where the sale contract requires either the seller or the buyer to contract for the transportation of the goods from one country to another. From this point of view, the international element is not if the seller and buyer are in the same state, but that the goods are moved from one state to another. This is what Goode refers to as an 'export' sale,[1] and it is the type of arrangement most usually referred to when thinking about international sales. A typical example of such a contract would be one for the sale of Thai rice under terms requiring the seller to have the rice put on board a vessel to be carried from the port of loading to a destination port designated by the buyer. Under this contract of sale it is part of the seller's obligations to arrange (or 'fix', as is said in the trade) the contract of carriage.

[1] R. Goode, *Commercial Law* (3rd edn, Penguin, London, 2004) p. 863.

A contract of sale can also be regarded as 'international' where the sale is entered into between parties who are situated in different states, irrespective of the places from and to where the goods are to be transported.[2] A typical example of such a contract is where the seller (in one state) agrees with the buyer (in a different state) to supply marine fuel for the running of a vessel being used by the buyer (this operation is known as 'bunkering', and marine fuels are referred to as 'bunkers').[3] In this international sale contract, either the buyer or seller will, as in the above type of international sale contract, have the obligation to transport the bunkers to the vessel. The obligation to transport the bunkers from bunker barge or lorry or pipeline or hose to the receiving vessel will be within one state, that is, at the port where the vessel is to be bunkered, rather than from one state to another. Nonetheless, as the seller and buyer are in different states, this comes within the definition of an international sale contract.

Under either type of international sale contract there will be obligations upon either the buyer or the seller to organise some element of transportation of the goods, as in the example above where the seller of the Thai rice is obliged to fix the carriage of the goods. These obligations are known as the 'shipment' terms of the sale contract. There are many different ways in which the buyer and seller can apportion the liabilities for carriage, insurance and risk of the goods during transportation, and there is an extensive range of shipment terms available to the parties to accommodate such apportionment. We will look at these shipment terms later in the chapter.

It has been suggested that the second type of contract referred to above raises 'no international issues', in the sense that these contracts are, in effect, domestic sale contracts notwithstanding that the parties are contracting from different states.[4] One can see why such contracts would more likely be thought of as being, or more akin to being, 'domestic'; for example, we could say that if a buyer in France contracts with, say, a London wine shop for the purchase of a bottle of wine, and then comes to London to collect that purchase, and pays in sterling, undoubtedly we would consider this to be national domestic sale, governed by English law. We saw in the bunkers contract example above, offered as an illustration of the second type of international sale contract, a similarity to the example of the national sale contract for the bottle of wine. In the bunker contract the buyer contracts with the seller and then sends the vessel he is trading to the port where he is to receive the bunkers. Some contention might well, then, arise in referring to this second category of contract as being 'international'. Caution must, however, be counselled before excluding the bunker type of contract from being considered within the ambit of international sales, as in 'culture' they are far removed from national domestic sales. The parties to such contracts are both operating on a commercial basis, and have a more robust attitude than modern consumers to their contractual relationships, in that they are particularly aware of the vagaries of trade and the factors which influence the framework in which their contract will be negotiated and performed. The parties to these contracts also, critically, expect far less legal regulation of their contracts than

---

[2] This is the definition of an 'international' sale contract under the Vienna Sales Convention 1980 (see Art. I).

[3] When steamships took over commercial shipping from sail, the fuel (coal) was stored in 'bunkers'. 'Bunkers' became the name used for marine fuel and the space used to store it on board. The first ships to burn fuel oil appeared in the 1900s, and by 1960 coal-burning vessels were almost gone. For further information about the bunkering industry see N. Draffin, *An Introduction to Bunkering* (Petrospot, Adderbury, 2008).

[4] For example, by P. Todd, *Cases and Materials on International Trade Law* (Thomson Sweet and Maxwell, London, 2003), at p. 3, para. 1-001. Todd raises this in explanation of focusing on those contracts which do involve inter-sale responsibility for the transportation of the goods from one *state* to another (i.e. export sales).

do consumers.[5] Thus, the approach by the Vienna Sales Convention 1980 in regarding these type of commercial sale contracts as 'international' appears to be a sensible reflection of the expectations of the international trade world, and, thus, we should remember that the concept of 'international sales' is not confined to export sales.

This chapter, however, focuses in depth on two export sale contracts: the 'FOB terms' as in *Sinochem v Mobil*,[6] where the parties contracted for the sale of a quantity of crude oil; and the 'CIF terms' as in *Lewis Emanuel & Son v Sammut*,[7] where the parties contracted for the sale of a quantity of potatoes. These abbreviations indicate the particular shipment contracts used, and have been established by trade practice. They indicate what is included in the price of the goods and define the parties' obligations under the contract. Whilst there is a wide range of shipment terms, the two most common upon which goods are sold are 'FOB' and 'CIF'. 'FOB' means 'free on board', and puts the parties to the sale on notice that the contract price of the goods requires the seller to put the goods on board the vessel which the buyer would ordinarily have contracted for the carriage of the goods.[8] The goods go on board 'free' of any carriage or insurance, the cost for which are the responsibility of the buyer. 'CIF' means 'cost, insurance and freight', and puts the parties to the sale contract on notice that the contract price for the goods requires the seller to put the goods on board the vessel that he has contracted for the carriage of the goods. The price of the goods, then, is inclusive of their carriage and their insurance.[9]

5.1.2 The 'culture' of international sales

The motivating force that underlies international sale contracts is trade and one should not think of the law relating to these contracts as existing in a vacuum away from trade practice. Neither should one think of international sales contracts as existing as an autonomous contract; the shipment terms of the sale contract 'marry' the sale contract to a carriage contract, which in itself may be part of a 'matrix' of shipping contracts.[10] The documents issued under the international sale contract may well be used to support finance arrangements involving third parties (for example, a bank) and additional obligations. We must understand, then, that the international sale contract exists only as part of the bigger picture of international trade.

---

[5] This expectation is endorsed by Parliament: for example the requirement under the Unfair Contract Terms Act 1977 that exclusion clauses be reasonable is in fact excluded from the 'international sale and supply contracts': s. 26 (an excellent consideration of when the requirements of s. 26 will be satisfied can be found in the judgment of Cooke J, in *Air Transworld Ltd v Bombardier Inc* [2012] EWHC 243 (Comm)); there is no statutory regulation of 'unfair' terms in commercial sales (as there is in consumer sales under the Unfair Terms in Consumer Contracts Regulations 1999), and no statutory requirement that any concept of good faith apply to the interpretation of terms or dealings in commercial sales.

[6] [2000] 1 Lloyd's Rep 339.

[7] [1959] 2 Lloyd's Rep 692.

[8] Where a party contracts for the carriage of goods, we say that the contract is 'fixed', i.e. then, in an FOB contract the buyer has 'fixed' the vessel. The trade vernacular for this arrangement is to say that the 'freight has been fixed'.

[9] 'C&F', otherwise referred to as 'CRF', means 'cost and freight', which puts the buyer on notice that he must insure the goods during their carriage by sea.

[10] For example, the carriage contract negotiated in compliance with the sale contract's shipment terms might be on a sub-charter from a charterer, who has in turn either chartered the vessel from the owner or sub-chartered it in turn from another charterer. The charterer who charters the vessel from the owner is known as the 'head charterer'.

This is the backdrop against which we should view international sales, and in doing so we should understand that the trade and the law should be seen as going 'hand in hand', rather than as being two distinct and polarised elements. It would be useful when first coming to international sales to think in terms of bringing the 'law to the traders' and the 'trade to the lawyers', in the sense that the law and trade practice go 'hand in hand'. The commercial backdrop against which international sales exists appears highly influential in the way that English courts determine disputes, adopting an approach that generally appears to 'keep trade moving' in a 'commercially sensible' way.

In *The Hansa Nord*,[11] buyers of citrus pulp pellets under a CIF sale contract purported to reject the entire quantity of goods sold, on the basis that some of the goods had not been 'shipped in good condition' such as required by the contract.[12] The matter went to arbitration in accordance with the contract, where the arbitrator found that the buyers were not entitled to reject. The buyers appealed to the Board of Appeal under the arbitration rules of the contract. The Board of Appeal held that the buyers were entitled to reject the goods as the sellers were in breach of (i) the express obligation to ship the goods in 'good condition', and (ii) the implied obligation as to merchantability in s. 14(2) of the Sale of Goods Act (1893). This was upheld by the court of first instance, and the sellers appealed to the Court of Appeal, which unanimously allowed their appeal.

In reality, the buyers' rejection was driven purely by a fall in the market rate for the goods rather than any inability to use the goods for the usual and intended use of cattle feed. Having purported to reject as against the sellers, the buyers then, however, proceeded to repurchase all the goods at the lower market rate, and then use them for the originally intended purpose, in the manufacture of cattle feed. The buyers concealed the entirety of their actions in doing this from the Board of Appeal, which recorded it in its award that it 'was not satisfied that we have been presented with the full account of how the goods were disposed of in Rotterdam after rejection of the Buyers'. Lord Denning MR thought this to be a 'devastating comment',[13] and was clearly unimpressed by the conduct of the buyers, making the somewhat salutary point that the fall in the market rate 'may give an explanation' for what happened subsequent to the goods arriving in Rotterdam.

His Lordship was of the view that 'the fair' way to determine the issue was to ask a commercial man what 'merchantable quality' meant and whether a breach of the obligation would entitle a buyer to reject. He noted that the Board of Appeal had found that whilst the goods might not be of 'merchantable quality' within the meaning of the phrase used in the Sale of Goods Act, they were, notwithstanding the damage, 'merchantable' in a commercial sense.[14] His Lordship held that the Board of Appeal had been incorrectly advised to interpret the meaning of 'merchantable quality' within the statutory sense as being different from the commercial sense. His Lordship's opinion was that as the statute used the words 'merchantable quality' in a commercial sense the Board of Appeal should not have been persuaded to

---

[11] *Cehave NV v Bremer Handels GmbH* [1975] 2 Lloyd's Rep 445.

[12] Clause 7 of the form 100 of the forms of the then London Cattle Food Trade Association (established in 1906), which merged in 1971 with the London Corn Trade Association (established in 1878) to form the Grain & Feed Trade Association ('Gafta'). Gafta is one of the major trade associations in England today.

[13] *Supra* n. 11 at p. 448.

[14] His Lordship also noted that the Board of Appeal had not found any breach of the implied condition of fitness for purpose under s. 14(1) of the Act, which was not surprising given that all of the pellets had in fact been used for their originally intended purpose!

give them some other 'statutory sense'. Thus, in his Lordship's view, no breach of the implied condition under s. 14(2) had occurred. This, of course, meant that the buyers could not reject the goods on the basis of breach of this obligation.

In his Lordship's view, the separate obligation to ship the goods in 'good condition' was an intermediate stipulation, that is, an innominate term, giving no right to reject unless the breach went to the root of the contract. His Lordship was of the view that as a 'matter of good sense', the buyer should accept the goods unless there was a serious and substantial breach fairly attributable to the seller. On the facts, this was not the type of breach that had occurred here: the breach did not go to the root of the contract and the buyers were not entitled to reject. Put simply, the buyers had got what they originally contracted for, but now wanted them at the subsequent much lower price.

To look at the case from a commercially pragmatic view, that the market rate had fallen sharply, was not fairly attributable to the sellers, and should not, therefore, be the propelling force behind the interpretation of the law.[15] It is clear from the critical tone in Lord Denning's language that his Lordship clearly thought that the buyers had acted 'sharply' and without regard to commercial expectation and awareness of the risks thrown up by this relationship, such as a changing market rate. That there was this risk would not have been unknown to the parties when they entered into the contract. In the absence of any term in the contract apportioning the effect of a rising or falling market, the Court's approach here was to allow the risk to lie where it fell, that is, at the buyers' feet, so to speak.

International sales frequently involve a highly volatile and fast-changing market. Mustill J (as he then was) observed, in *Gebruder Metelmann GmbH & Co KG v BR (London) Ltd*, the extreme volatility of the futures sugar market, noting that prices might 'change by tens of dollars within a single day, so that the quoted price may bear only a distant relation to the price at which bargains are being struck even in the same market, later in the same day.'[16]

One might think that in contemplating the possibility of such risk against the involvement of what may likely be large amounts of money (in the *Gebruder Metelmann* contract, for example, the contract was for 2,000 tons of sugar at US$803 per tonne), the parties would ensure that such contracts be drafted in the tightest possible legal terms, to reduce as far as possible the impact of risk. This is not, however, generally the case, a more usual trade response to concerns about risk being, 'But this is world trade for you'.[17] Roskill LJ alluded to this in making the point in *The Hansa Nord* that the contents of the standard form contract relied on by the parties contained much that was inappropriate to the sale of citrus pulp pellets.[18] The reality of this relationship is likely to have been that the parties were used to contracting on these terms and, in the interests of getting the business done, saw no reason to spend time amending or adding to the standard terms, because to do so would have fettered a business opportunity and would *not* be 'world trade for you'.

---

[15] Lord Denning MR commented that the market rate had fallen 'greatly' (at p. 447). The contract price for the goods in September 1970 was £100,000 for 3,400 tons, whereas the Rotterdam price in May 1971 (when the goods arrived at the discharge port) was, for sound goods of this quantity, only £86,000.

[16] (1983) 133 NLJ 642. The facts and Mustill J's judgment are set out in full in the Court of Appeal report at [1984] 1 Lloyd's Rep 614.

[17] As firmly said by Dennis Lysemose Anderson (Global Risk Management Ltd) at Lloyd's Maritime Academy Bunker Schools (June 2009), in response to concerns about the risk of hedge funding in the purchase of bunker contracts.

[18] The contracts being designed for bulk feed stuffs and including a quality clause with provisions wholly irrelevant to the purposes of these sales.

It is this attitude that provides an insight into the expectations of parties to these contracts. These expectations take account of the risks which the parties will likely be facing, and against which they will negotiate. Many of the contracts or terms relied upon in international sales will, as in *The Hansa Nord*, have been drafted by international trade associations and business organisations, and are the drafting of commercial men rather than lawyers. Such contracts are, then, more concerned with trade practice and commercial expectations rather than what may amount to formal imperfection.[19] Indeed, in the *Gebruder Metelmann* contract, one of the issues before Mustill J was the assessment of the quantum (measure) of damages, an exercise which, his Lordship said, could not be 'embarked upon with any pretence of precision'. The volatility of the sugar market is such that the price at which goods are sold might depend upon the hour as well as the day of trading, a fact well known to the parties when entering into the contract.[20] Breach by one party is always a foreseeable occurrence of such contracts given the continuing fluctuations of trade influences. It would not be unreasonable, therefore, to think that some appropriately drafted precise quantum clause would have been a sensible inclusion into the contract. Of course, an argument *against* the inclusion of such a clause could well rest upon the volatility of the market, on the basis that neither party would want, at the time of entering into the contract, to agree to a definitive assessment of damages. This less legalistic approach reflects a trade preference towards a less fettered business environment. Devlin has suggested that it is this preference for such trade drafting that keeps commercial law 'in tune with the ideas of business men', and that in pursuing 'their way undeterred in the drafting of their own contracts commercial men have ensured that 'the ideas of the lawyers are ultimately controlled by the laymen'.[21] The corollary of this is that the trade is prevented from becoming stifled by regulation in which the law, rather than commercial expectation, could emerge as the dominant driving force of international sales. Certainly this would support the view that trade contracts engender a less fettered commercial experience, in which, it might be argued, business can be done. This was the view of a witness before Lord Devlin, who, on being asked why he had not written to the other side so as to reach some agreement upon which conditions should prevail, answered, 'We should never get any business done if we did *that* sort of thing,' adding, 'besides, we haven't got time for it.'[22]

A less legalistic approach to the contract also affords a greater element of flexibility within the relationship, affording more scope for acceptable compromise should performance difficulties arise. The willingness to negotiate towards compromise might be motivated by the prevailing need in international trade generally to preserve a good reputation.[23] In *The Aliakmon*,[24] it was noted by Sir John Donaldson MR in the Court of Appeal that the

---

[19] For example, Gafta (*supra* n. 12) and the International Chamber of Commerce (the ICC). These are mentioned here purely as two *ad hoc* examples, coming to mind quickly given their presence in the trade. There is no intention at all to suggest that their excellent contracts and other regulatory provisions are lacking in clarity or sophistication, nor that their contracts and other provisions have 'formal imperfections'!

[20] At the time of entering into this contract the sellers, Metelmann, were one of the largest sugar dealers in the German Federal Republic, exporting more than 800,000 tons of sugar per year. Bernard Metelmann, who took over the company's business management after the death of its founder, Herbert Metelmann, in 1977, was chairman of ASSUC, the European Association of Sugar Traders, for more than eight years.

[21] P. Devlin, 'Relation Between Commercial Law and Commercial Practice' [1951] *MLR* 249, at p. 253.

[22] *Ibid.*, at p. 252.

[23] The Institute of Chartered Shipbrokers' motto is 'My word is my bond', and this attitude seems to be a forceful dynamic within the shipping and international trade industry generally.

[24] [1986] AC 785.

buyers, who could not pay for a consignment of steel coils under the terms of a C&F contract,[25] were 'a substantial and respectable concern and were greatly embarrassed at the situation which had arisen'.[26]

The sellers were equally substantial, and the parties got together in an attempt to resolve the problem. They agreed that the goods would be held 'to the order of' or 'at the disposal of' the sellers, whose approval would be obtained before the goods were resold. His Lordship 'fully accepted' that the parties were not concerned with the legal analysis of their new bargain, but with the need to convert the goods into money as quickly as possible.[27] To this end, the sellers had offered to do their best to help the buyers resell the goods. This is by no means an untypical example of the commercially driven approach in international trade relationships, and serves well to illustrate the culture against which the law is applied.

In thinking about the culture of international sales, we should keep in mind that overall the risks in international sales are greater than in domestic sales and are not solely confined to a changing market rate. On the physical side, there are greater risks associated with transit, especially when goods are carried by sea. Additionally, there are increased difficulties in checking the reliability or credit standing of an overseas party. Various influences determine the viability of any international sale contract and include:

- *the supply of the goods*: taking into account such factors as production, international pricing policies, production costs, depletion and new avenues of particular products (for example oil);

- *geopolitics*;

- *legislation*: governing, for example, the sale of goods contract *per se*, international transport, imports and exports, developing environmental and consumer protection concerns;

- *demand for goods*: taking into account such factors as financial markets, seasonality and weather phenomena, consumer trends.

5.1.3 English common law and international sales

Some mention should be made about the application of English law to international sales. All contracts must be governed by some national law, that is, by some domestic private law, there being no 'international' law to govern such relationships.[28] Our international sale contract must, then, be governed by one national law, which is referred to as the 'applicable law'

---

[25] The market rate having fallen.

[26] [1985] 1 Lloyd's Rep 119 at 201.

[27] This lack of legal analysis could be argued to have been certainly the buyers' mistake. It is clear that the parties were not interested in who owned the goods, nor the legal consequence of the buyers having neither the legal property nor, in their own name, an immediate possessory interest in the goods. The legal consequence of their renegotiations resulted in the buyers, as consignees of the goods, having no action against the carriers for loss and damage caused to the goods by poor stowage.

[28] Whether one law or another will apply may be the subject of contention between the parties to any dispute, as may be the question of where the parties will bring their claim, i.e. in which jurisdiction. This is the law of 'conflicts', which is dealt with in Chapter 10. Our discussion in this chapter is based on the premise that the parties have chosen English law as the applicable law, and the English courts' jurisdiction, thus obviating this conflicts issue. What we are asking here is not *what* law governs the contract, but *why* English law is the predominate choice of law in international sale and carriage contracts.

of the contract. This could be, for example, French law, or the law of New York State or any national law. The concept of a contract as a relationship of obligations, under any system of law, is, as suggested by Schmitthoff, 'founded on two fundamental notions: the autonomy of the parties' will and the principal of the sanctity of contracts, expressed in the maxim *pacta sunt servanda* (agreements are binding)'.[29] The parties to an international sale contract will, then, likely choose an applicable law from a system that they think will best support their intentions.

It appears that English law is a (if not *the*) most popular choice of law in international sale contracts: it is the law incorporated into international sale contracts used by the big international trade associations such as Gafta and the Federation of Oils, Seeds and Fats Associations ('Fosfa'), and is the law incorporated into many charterparty and bill of lading contracts. Given that English law is a common law system of law, more subject to policy considerations by the courts than one would find in codified systems of law, one might ask, 'Why English law?' There is no one definitive answer, but commentators suggest that it is the lack of 'mandatory' law that distinguishes English commercial law from that of civil law jurisdictions.[30]

This lack of mandatory law, which is based on principles (that is, being broad statements that apply to a range of acts) rather than codified rules, allows for greater party autonomy than one might achieve under a civil jurisdiction. It is certainly arguable that the needs within the *culture* of international trade are met by the approach taken by English law. Schmitthoff points out that the autonomy of the parties' will in the law of contract may be regarded as a foundation on which an autonomous law of international trade is developed by those parties.[31] Later, in distinguishing between interventionist legislation, which he called 'economic law', and commercial law, he went on to say that:

> The basis of commercial law is the contractual principal of autonomy of the parties' will. Subject to the ultimate reservation of public policy, the parties are free to arrange their affairs as they like.[32]

In his article 'Contract law: Fulfilling the Expectations of Honest Men',[33] Lord Steyn observed:

> The commercial advantage of the English approach is that it promotes certainty and predictability in the resolution of contractual disputes. And, as a matter of principle, it is not unfair to impute to contracting parties the intention that in the event of a dispute a neutral judge should decide the case applying an objective standard of reasonableness. That is then the context in which in English law one should interpret the proposition that effect must be given to reasonable expectations of honest men.

What can be seen is that this 'certainty' and 'predictability', is visible in the *attitude* of the English courts, an approach enabled by dealing with principles rather than legal rules. Legal principles within a common law jurisdiction are developed as broad statements that lend themselves more readily to being applied to a range of acts than do specific rules. Some

[29] C. M. Schmitthoff, *Select Essays on International Trade Law* (Nijhoff, Graham and Trotman, London, 1988) p. 256.

[30] R. Goode, *Commercial Law in the Next Millennium* (Sweet and Maxwell, London, 1998) p. 10. Professor Goode suggests that a lawyer from a civil law jurisdiction might find 'truly astounding' the extent to which such out-of-court rights and remedies are so freely available in English law.

[31] C. M. Schmitthoff, *Commercial Law in a Changing Economic Climate* (2nd edn, Sweet and Maxwell, London, 1981) pp. 1 and 22.

[32] C. M. Schmitthoff, 'The Concept of Economic Law in England' [1966] *JBL* 309, at p. 315.

[33] [1997] *LQR* 433.

commentators have suggested that the application and development of principles are not as dependant on 'creative compliance' as are rules.[34] International sales are complex relationships, and certainly the approach by the English judiciary to disputes arising therefrom does show a more reachable balance between 'piecemeal' determination within a constant 'cohesive flow' than may be afforded by the application of set rules.

This is not to say that there is no statutory regulation under the English law of sale contracts, and international sale of goods, like other sale contracts governed by English law, are, as we will see, today subject to the Sale of Goods Act 1979 as amended.

5.2 The matrix of contracts in international trade

Whilst the sale of goods contract lies at the heart of international trade, as has been suggested above, the wider international trade picture is one of many contracts, linked to each other by virtue of the sale contract having been formed. The international sale contract is at the heart of what was referred to above as a 'matrix' of contracts in the bigger international trade picture. It is helpful, therefore, to look at this bigger picture at this stage, so that we can see how the obligations created in one contract may give rise to the existence of other contracts, and so that we can understand how the balance of risk, delay and damage is spread between the contracts. An overview of the entire picture will help us to understand the policy issues that frequently arise in English commercial law. Examination of the wider picture shows that allowing or restricting liability in any one particular contractual relationship will have a 'domino-like' effect on international trade as a whole. The important point is that none of these individual relationships exists in a vacuum. Liability imposed in one area may upset the delicate balance of risk and price in international transactions. This is a great concern of the English courts and explains the reasoning in many of the more 'difficult' decisions. In looking at the matrix of contracts at this stage, we shall not be dealing in depth with the many legal issues that arise, but provide an introductory overview at the particular features of each contract which cause that contract to be linked to others within the matrix.

Examination of the wider picture will show that breach of the contract of sale will produce a 'domino effect' – it will affect the ability of those who have made related contracts to perform their obligations. The composite nature of international sale arrangements means that a party who breaches an international contract of sale may face not only contractual liability to the other party, but also liability to others in tort or bailment. Therefore, although we are concerned in this chapter with the international sale contract itself and the rights and liabilities arising thereunder, we must keep in mind that this contract does not exist in a vacuum.

It is also useful at this stage to gain an understanding of international trade language. The terminology used in the world of international trade can be confusing initially, because certain words are often used in a way that is quite distinct from both everyday usage and general commercial usage. It is important to refer to a party by his correct name within a particular relationship, and it should be remembered that a party to one contract within the

[34] D. McBarnet and C. Whelan, 'The Elusive Spirit of the Law: Formalism and the Struggle for Legal Control' [1991] *MLR* 848.

international trade matrix may, under a different 'hat', also be a party to one of the other contracts. This means, for example, that in one capacity as a contractual party (that is, wearing one of his 'hats') he may have liability in respect of delay or damage to the goods, whilst in another capacity he will not. A firm grasp of the language used to describe him, according to which 'hat' he is wearing, helps us to avoid confusion – it enables us to describe accurately the particular role (or roles) which the party is playing within the contractual matrix at any one time, so that we can clearly identify his rights and obligations. This overview will, hopefully, bring an understanding of the trade language to us as lawyers.

5.2.1 **The international sale contract**

CASE

The Aliakmon[35]

We have already looked at this case, but a consideration of the various 'hats' which the parties wore will help us to understand the matrix of contracts and the importance of keeping a firm distinction between the roles that the parties to an international sale contract might play within the wider trade picture. As we saw, in this case the sellers sold a quantity of steel coils to the buyer on C&F ('cost and freight') shipment terms. This meant that the seller was responsible for arranging for the carriage of the goods from the port of loading (the 'shipment' port) on a vessel destined for the buyers' nominated discharge port. The goods were shipped on the defendant shipowners' vessel, *The Aliakmon*, in Korea, and carried to Immingham (UK). As a result of bad stowage, the goods were damaged. The buyers could not pay the sale contract price, and it was agreed between the sellers and buyers that the goods should remain at the sellers' disposal and that sales of the goods by the buyers should be notified to the sellers. When the goods were discharged from the vessel in Immingham, they were stored in a warehouse by the buyers acting as agents for the sellers. The buyers brought an action in negligence against the defendants for £120,487.52, that being the difference between the sound value of the steel and the damaged value (and various other expenses incurred). The action failed, the House of Lords holding unanimously that the defendants owed no duty to the claimants, the claimants being neither the legal owners of the goods nor having any possessory title in their own name at the time the goods were damaged.

5.2.1.1 **Sale contracts on 'shipment terms'**

The important feature of this contract is that it will be on 'shipment terms', which set out, as between seller and buyer, which one of them has the contractual obligation to provide transport of the goods. As soon as we have a contract of sale on shipment terms, we know that at

---

[35] *Supra* n. 24.

the very least we shall also have a contract for the carriage of those goods, possibly together with a cargo insurance contract. It should be noted that the phrase 'shipment terms' relates only to the contract of *sale* – contracts of *carriage*, therefore, cannot be described as being on shipment terms (which may seem strange to people who are unfamiliar with the language of international trade). The terms 'seller' and 'buyer' are only ever used to describe the parties *in their capacity as parties to the contract of sale*.

ISSUE BOX

Understanding the different 'hats' that the parties will wear

In *The Aliakmon*, the shipment terms were of the 'C' type, that is, C&F, which is to say that the seller was responsible for the 'cost and freight' of the goods. So, when goods are sold on C&F terms, the buyer knows that the price he is going to pay includes the cost of the goods themselves and the carriage of the goods from the port of shipment to the discharge port (it being incumbent on the buyer to insure the goods for their transit).

It is essential that we grasp that a party's 'hat' as seller or buyer will involve him in quite different liabilities from his 'hat' in any role he might have under a contract of carriage.

5.2.1.2 The passing of the risk in the goods

This is an issue of utmost importance in sale of goods, whether the sale be an international or domestic sale contract. By the 'risk in the goods' we mean the liability for any damage that occurs to the goods which are the subject matter of the sale. Thus, where a person is bound to bear the accidental loss of, or damage to, goods, they are said to be 'at his risk'. In many cases it will be obvious when the risk has passed to the buyer.

Section 20 of the Sale of Goods Act 1979 lays down a presumption (which scarcely ever applies in international sale contracts) that the risk will pass with the property in the goods:

(1) Unless otherwise agreed, the goods remain at the seller's risk until the property in them is transferred to the buyer, but when the property in them is transferred to the buyer the goods are at the buyer's risk whether delivery has been made or not.

(2) But where delivery has been delayed through the fault of either buyer or seller the goods are at the risk of the party at fault as regards any loss which might not have occurred but for such fault.

(3) Nothing in this section affects the duties or liabilities of either seller or buyer as a bailee or custodier of the goods of the other party.

In many commercial sale contracts, however, the risk and the property do *not* pass at the same time, as we have already seen from our consideration of *The Aliakmon*.[36]

It should be noted that when we speak of the 'risk in the goods', we are talking about the risk in goods *that conform with the contract of sale*. If, when the buyer takes physical possession of the goods, he discovers that they do not conform with the contract, he will have an action

---

[36] *Supra* n. 24.

for damages against the seller and may, if the breach is fundamental, repudiate the contract, that is, reject the goods. So, by 'bearing the risk in the goods', we do not mean that the buyer bears the risk that the goods will not conform with the contract. Where the goods do not conform, the buyer has an action against the seller for breach of contract. This is the point at which he may either 'accept' the goods or reject them for failing to be of the requisite quality.

As soon as the buyer notifies the seller of his intention to reject the goods, then, provided the buyer does not wrongly reject the goods,[37] the risk passes back to the seller.

In the international trade picture, the goods will not necessarily be in the possession of the buyer when they are 'delivered' to him, but in the possession of a third party, namely the carrier. International trade would not be well served by the presumption that the goods remain at the seller's risk until the buyer receives them. It is frequently the case that goods which have been the subject of an international sale contract will then be sold on by the buyer to a sub-buyer, who in turn may sell to a further sub-buyer, etc. If the risk remained with the original seller, rather than passing to each buyer in turn, the original seller would be unable to say with certainty when his liabilities in respect of the goods had come to an end, that is, when he was 'free' from the risk in the goods. To facilitate international trade, it is necessary that the seller is regarded as having fulfilled his obligations as soon as possible – this leaves him free to organise his business affairs without the constant threat of future litigation. In international sale contracts the risk will generally pass to the buyer long before he actually receives the goods.

5.2.1.3 The delivery of the goods

Although the buyer may not have actually received the goods in physical terms, it is likely that at law the goods are taken to have been 'delivered' to him. The seller is responsible for delivering the goods to the place of delivery. The seller may undertake to hold the goods for the buyer to collect, or he may agree to deliver the goods to the buyer's premises, or, as is most likely in the context of international commercial sales, he may agree to deliver the goods to a third person such as a carrier. There is no provision in the Sale of Goods Act requiring the seller to deliver the goods to the buyer. Section 29 of the Act provides:

> (1) Whether it is for the buyer to take possession of the goods or for the seller to send them to the buyer is a question depending in each case on the contract, express or implied, between the parties.
>
> (2) Apart from any such contract, express or implied, the place of delivery is the seller's place of business if he has one, and if not, his residence; except that, if the contract is for the sale of specific goods, which to the knowledge of the parties when the contract is made are in some other place, then that is the place of delivery.

It can be seen that the legal meaning of 'delivery' is rather different from the popular meaning. It does not mean actual transfer to the buyer, but the 'voluntary transfer of possession', which can be to a third party.

---

[37] It may be that a commercial buyer does not have a general right to repudiate if the goods are not of the requisite quality: (a) the contract may well specifically provide a margin for error or a limited range of circumstances in which the buyer may repudiate or (b) s. 15(A) of the Sale of Goods Act 1979 may be raised by the seller against the buyer in defence regarding repudiation.

This is critical and forms the basis of many international sale contracts. In the 'C' shipment terms contracts, the goods are delivered to the buyer when they are shipped on board, that is, when they cross the ship's rails. In the 'C' contracts, this is the point at which the risk of subsequent loss and damage will pass to the buyer unless the contract expressly provides otherwise.[38] In *The Aliakmon*, the risk passed to the buyer on delivery, that is, on shipment of the goods. So, under the terms of the sale contract, the seller has at this point discharged his obligations and has, so to speak, 'fallen out of the picture'.

5.2.2 The relationship between the sale contract and the carriage contract

It is at this point that we become concerned about the relationship between the sale and the carriage contracts. Once the goods have been delivered and the risk has passed to the buyer, he will be unable to sue the seller for any damage that occurs to the goods during their transport. Obviously, the law would not serve international traders very well if it said that the buyer, who was not yet in possession of the goods, must bear full liability for goods which become damaged before he receives them, so it allows the buyer to sue the carrier in respect of damage caused to the goods during their transit. It now becomes important to examine the roles that the buyer and seller have *under the contract of carriage*.

5.2.2.1 'Shippers', 'carriers' and 'consignees'

The purpose of 'shipment terms' in an international contract of sale is to show, as between buyer and seller, who is responsible for organising the contract of carriage. The party who has this responsibility will negotiate with a carrier for the carriage of the goods. The person who negotiates for the carriage of the goods – who might be either the seller or the buyer – is always called 'the shipper'. There are two parties to the contract of carriage – the shipper (who will pay the freight in return for the carriage) and the carrier (who will carry the goods in return for the freight). The person to whom the goods are carried is known as the 'consignee'. Both the shipper and the consignee have an interest in the carriage of the goods and are therefore known as 'cargo interests'.

5.2.2.2 CIF sale contracts

Under a CIF sale contract, the seller is responsible for arranging the contract of carriage. Thus, the seller becomes the shipper under the carriage contract. The seller now has two roles in two

---

[38] The parties to such contracts frequently do agree this, but the buyer will, of course, usually pay a higher contract price for such terms. For example, in Gafta contracts, a sale on 'tale quale terms' provides that the buyer of a parcel must accept it in whatever condition it is at the time of delivery, the seller only having given an undertaking that the goods were in good condition on shipment, for example, cl. 5 of Gafta 100 2007 Contract for Shipment of Feedingstuffs in Bulk *Tale Quale*. When grain is bought on 'rye terms', however, the seller guarantees the condition on discharge (that is, the risk passes on discharge), for example, cl. 17 of Gafta 101 2007 Contract for Shipment of Feedingstuffs in Bulk *Rye Terms*. Clause 17 provides that the condition of the goods as shipped is guaranteed on arrival, that is, at discharge.

separate contracts: he is the seller under the sale contract and the shipper under the carriage contract. (Note that once we start discussing the seller's relationship with the carrier under the contract of carriage we must refer to him as the shipper – there are no sellers in carriage contracts.) So, we now have two completely separate contracts which are linked to each other by virtue of the seller being obliged, under one contract, to become the shipper in the other. The sale and the carriage contracts are at the heart of the matrix. The goods have, of course, been shipped for the benefit of the buyer – they are to be carried to his named port of destination. The buyer, therefore, is the 'consignee' of the goods. The seller will have been given a receipt for the goods by the carrier. This will name the consignee as entitled to collect the goods and will show the condition in which the goods were shipped. Where the goods are shipped in a good condition, we say that this receipt is 'clean'. In general English common law terms, the buyer/consignee is not privy to the contract of carriage between the shipper and the carrier. This raises the question of what cause of action he has against the carrier, an issue we explore below.

5.2.2.3 FOB sale contracts

Although there are three variants of FOB contracts, we can say in general terms that the buyer is responsible for the contract of carriage, so here it is the buyer who will become the shipper under the carriage contract. Again, we have two completely separate contracts which are linked to each other by virtue of the fact that the buyer is, under one contract, obliged to become the shipper in the other. Again, it is the buyer who is interested in collecting the goods, and to whom the goods are likely to have been consigned (although, of course, our FOB buyer could in turn have sold on CIF terms to a sub-buyer). When the goods are loaded, a clean receipt will be given which shows that the goods have been shipped in good condition according to the contract of sale. In this type of contract, then, we can see that the buyer is both shipper and (normally) the consignee of the goods. As shipper, of course, he is privy to the contract of carriage with the carrier and will be able to sue the carrier on this contract in respect of damage to the goods.

5.2.3 The contract of carriage

5.2.3.1 Bills of lading

When goods are shipped, the shipper will be given a 'clean receipt', by the 'ship's master' – the 'captain' of the ship. More needs to be said about this 'receipt'.

- First, it enables the consignee to know that the goods were shipped in good condition, so if the goods arrive damaged, the damage must have occurred during their transit.

- Second, this receipt will be a 'bill of lading', which is regarded as a negotiable document capable of transferring the right to sue the carrier on the contract of carriage to the 'lawful holder' of the bill of lading – under the Carriage of Goods by Sea Act 1992. The bill of lading itself (that is, the actual document) is regarded as *actually being the contract of carriage* when it is put in the hands of a consignee or subsequent 'indorsee' (a subsequent buyer to whom the bill of lading will be indorsed by the consignee).

We know that where the contract of sale is on FOB terms, the buyer negotiates the contract of carriage as shipper, but here, even if he is also the consignee of the goods, he does not take the bill of lading issued in respect of the goods as his contract of carriage. The bill of lading only becomes a contract once it has been put into the hands of a consignee or indorsee who did not negotiate the contract of carriage as shipper. This is an important point, as the negotiated contract of carriage may in fact contain different terms from those in the bill of lading.

CASE

The Ardennes[39]

Here, the plaintiff exporter wished to ship a consignment of Mandarin oranges from Spain to London, and was anxious that the goods should arrive before 1 December, in order to avoid a threatened rise in import duty. The contract of carriage contained an express clause that the vessel would sail direct to London. In fact, however, the vessel on which the oranges were shipped already had a cargo on board destined for Antwerp. The bill of lading which had been issued in respect of the oranges contained a 'liberty to deviate' clause, entitling the vessel to call at intermediate ports on the voyage to London – so there was a difference in terms between the carriage contract and the bill of lading. As a result of calling in at Antwerp, the vessel did not reach London until 4 December, by which time there had been an increase in import duty and a considerable fall in the market price of oranges due to an influx of other cargoes.

The plaintiff succeeded in an action against the carrier for damages for breach of the express provision in the contract not to deviate.

The position would have been very different if the plaintiff had, while the goods were in transit, sold the goods on to a buyer and had transferred to this buyer as consignee the bill of lading. The bill of lading contract would have contained the 'liberty to deviate' clause.

5.2.3.2 The bill of lading as evidence of the contract of carriage

Since the bill of lading will only constitute the contract of carriage where it is in the hands of a consignee or indorsee who has not negotiated for the carriage, we can draw a distinction between two functions of the bill of lading – it may be *evidence of the contract of carriage* or it may actually *be* the contract of carriage. As between the shipper and the carrier, the bill of lading can only ever be *evidence* of the contract. It is admissible in court to prove the terms of the contract, but it is not the contract itself. The contract itself is formed by the mutual exchange of promises between the shipper and the carrier. Since the parties will negotiate the space in the vessel and the freight rate before the goods are put on board, this exchange of promises will take place before the bill of lading is issued. This point was made by Lord Goddard, in *The Ardennes*:

[39] [1951] 1 KB 55.

The contract has come into existence before the bill of lading is signed. The bill of lading is signed by one party only and handed by him to the shipper, usually after the goods have been put on board. No doubt if the shipper finds that it contains terms with which he is not content, or that it does not contain some term for which he has stipulated, he might, if there were time, demand his goods back, but he is not in my opinion thereby prevented from giving evidence that there was a contract which was made before the bill of lading was signed and that it was different from that which is found in the document or contained some additional term.[40]

In *The Aliakmon*, the bill of lading would have been evidence of the contract between the shipper and his carrier.[41] We will see below that in fact the shipper's carrier might well be a different entity from the consignee's, as was the case in *The Aliakmon*. This happens where the carrier who negotiates with the shipper has chartered the vessel from either the owner or another charterer 'in the chain'. We consider this issue below, when we look at carriers, ship-owners and charterers in section 5.2.3.4.

5.2.3.3 The bill of lading as the contract of carriage

Once the bill of lading has been transferred or indorsed to the consignee or indorsee, it becomes the contract of carriage itself. In *Leduc v Ward*,[42] a cargo of rapeseed was to be shipped on *The Austria* to Dunkirk. There was a 'liberty clause' in the original carriage contract, enabling the shipowner 'to call at any ports in any order'. Instead of sailing directly to Dunkirk the ship called at Glasgow. By sailing to Glasgow, the ship encountered bad weather and was lost as a result. It was alleged that the indorsee should be bound by an agreement between the shipper and carrier that the ship should proceed first to Glasgow (even though the bill of lading made no mention of this). Lord Esher MR rejected this suggestion, saying that, as far as the indorsee was concerned, the contract of carriage had been reduced into writing and that:

> ... then the general doctrine of law is applicable, by which, where the contract has been reduced into writing which is intended to constitute the contract, parol evidence to alter or qualify the effect of such writing is not admissible, and the writing is the only evidence of the contract, except where there is some usage so well-established and generally known that it must be taken to be incorporated with the contract.[43]

In the hands of the consignee the bill of lading is a contract with the person for whom the master signs the bill of lading. This is typically the owner of the vessel,[44] but it can also be a charterer (typically a time charterer).[45]

---

[40] *Ibid.*, at p. 59.
[41] It is important to understand that the bill of lading's role as evidence of the contract of carriage in the shipper's hands is only the case where the shipper does not charter the vessel to carry the goods. Where this happens, then the contract is contained in the charter, and the bill has no contractual status whatsoever in the shipper's hands (see *Rodocanachi, Sons & Co v Milburn* (1886) 18 QBD 67 (CA)).
[42] (1888) 20 QBD 475.
[43] *Ibid.*, at p. 480.
[44] See *The Rewia* [1991] 2 Lloyd's Rep 325.
[45] See *The Starsin* [2003] 1 Lloyd's Rep 571.

ISSUE BOX

It might well at this point be wondered why in *The Aliakmon* the buyer, as consignee, did not take the bill of lading as a contract of carriage. Whilst this is an issue we consider below, it is helpful now to ask ourselves the following questions.

- **How, under English law, would the consignee of the goods (who is the CIF buyer) have a contract with the carrier?**

He will not have 'mutually exchanged his promises' with the carrier, as required by English common law formalities for contract formation, and neither today would the Contracts (Rights of Third Parties) Act 1999 help, as this Act expressly excludes for this purpose bill of lading contracts from its ambit.[46] We need, therefore, some *statutory* creation of such a contract: this was the Bills of Lading Act 1855, now repealed and replaced by the Carriage of Goods by Sea Act 1992.

- **Why do we need to allow this consignee to be able to sue the carrier in contract?**

The answer to this question lies in an appreciation of 'how trade works': the seller wishes to 'fall out of the sale picture' as quickly as possible, which is why the risk in the goods will generally pass to the buyer on shipment (that is, on delivery). The buyer would not buy goods on this basis without being able to claim against someone for loss and damage sustained during their carriage. The carrier wishes to be sued in contract so that they can take advantage of the exclusions and limitations incorporated into that contract.

- **Why can we not just say that the consignee is privy as a third party to the original contract as negotiated by the shipper (the CIF seller)?**

There are several answers to this question.

(a) The shipper may have chartered the vessel, either from the shipowner or a charterer who then sub-charters to our shipper. There may be a long chain of charters. There is no way in which our consignee, who simply buys a bill of lading, can easily or at all find out with whom their shipper has contracted: the bill of lading that they buy will not contain these details and he has no right to investigate his shipper's contracts with third parties. Thus, who then would be our consignee's carrier?

(b) The bill of lading is the shipping document received by the consignee. It will show for whom the bill was signed, that is, on behalf of either the owner or a charterer in the chain. If we say that the bill is the consignee's contract, then he has immediate notice of his carrier.

(c) If we were to say that the consignee had right of suit on the shipper's contract, then likely we would also have to recognise that contracts formed under English law are based on a *quid pro quo* basis, such that the party who can sue can also be sued.[47] If the consignee were privy to the shipper's contract, he might expose himself to untold liability under that contract, of the sort that no CIF buyer would want to assume.[48]

---

[46] Section 6(5).

[47] The Contracts (Rights of Third Parties) Act 1999 confers no such *quid pro quo* rights.

[48] Typically such liabilities would be those incurred by a charterer under a voyage charter.

(d) The bill of lading has a much more limited range of carriage liabilities to which a consignee may be liable: unpaid freight,[49] general average[50] and liability for loss and damage sustained by the carrier from non-declared dangerous goods.[51] It is considered appropriate, in the overall division of liabilities arising in international carriage, that the consignee takes the bill of lading on this *quid quo pro* basis.

(e) Contracts contained in bills of lading are almost invariably governed by one of the international carriage regimes, which impose a minimum level of liability upon carriers.[52]

5.2.3.4 'Carriers', 'shipowners' and 'charterers'

We have consistently referred to the person who contracts with the shipper for the carriage of the goods as the 'carrier'. We have not referred to him as the 'shipowner'. It is important to be precise in our terminology. Just as shippers and sellers are quite distinct (as in fact are buyers and consignees), so it is with 'carriers' and 'shipowners'. The person who contracts with the shipper is the 'carrier', because he agrees to carry the goods to a named destination in return for freight (payment). This carrier may not in fact own the ship – he may have hired the vessel for a period of time (under a time charter in return for the payment of 'hire') or he may have commanded the entire space in the vessel for a particular voyage or consecutive voyages (under a voyage or consecutive voyage charter in return for the payment of freight) from the shipowner. In this case, the carrier also wears the hat of 'charterer' and his charter contract will be quite separate from the carriage contract he has with the shipper. Thus, the carrier is the person who agrees to carry the goods in return for freight, and the charterer is the person who either charters the ship for a period of time or for a voyage. The shipowner is the person who owns the ship.[53]

Where the shipper of the goods charters the vessel to carry the goods, he now wears two hats – he is the shipper of the goods and the charterer of the vessel (which was not the case in *The Aliakmon*: here, our seller only wore the hat of shipper in the carriage relationship). The person from whom he charters the vessel also wears two hats – carrier of the goods and

---

[49] A trade-savvy buyer would be advised in his sale negotiations to demand a 'freight pre-paid' bill from his seller.

[50] The term 'general average' means a sharing of losses caused to cargo owners and the ship in the face of uncommon danger by the intentional sacrifice of the cargo or any part of the ship or by any extraordinary expenditure by one or other of those interested in the cargo and ship.

[51] It is not that dangerous goods may not be carried. Rather, the liability, which is absolute strict liability, is to fully inform the carrier of the nature of the goods. The meaning of the term 'dangerous goods' is not to be narrowly construed: *The Giannis NK* [1988] 1 Lloyd's Rep 337.

[52] There are currently three such regimes: the Hague Rules, the Hague-Visby Rules and the Hamburg Rules. The two most popular regimes are the Hague and Hague-Visby regimes (the latter of which became effective in the UK on 23 June 1977, incorporated as an attached schedule to the Carriage of Goods by Sea Act 1971). A fourth regime is on the horizon: the United Nations Commission on International Trade Law (UNCITRAL) Convention on Contracts for the International Carriage of Goods Wholly or Partly by Sea (the 'Rotterdam Rules') was adopted by the General Assembly of the United Nations on 11 December 2008. The Convention was opened for signature at Rotterdam on 23 September 2009. The ratification/adoption of 20 states is required before the Rules can become law.

[53] The term 'shipowner' may be used to describe *either* the person who actually has the legal title in the ship *or* the person who, under a demise or bareboat charter, 'owns' the ship during the charter period for the purposes of liabilities to all who are involved with the use of the ship or injured by her use (i.e. the 'adventures' of the vessel).

shipowner.[54] Where the parties enter into a charterparty, the actual charter document itself is regarded as the contract. This means that no other evidence is admissible to prove that there were any other terms in this contract. Thus, when the bill of lading is issued in respect of the goods, it cannot evidence the charter contract between the shipper/charterer and carrier/ owner. (It is, of course, a receipt showing condition of the goods when they were put on board and is admissible to show what condition the goods were in when they were shipped.) However, once this bill of lading is transferred to the consignee, it becomes, in his hands, the actual contract of carriage.

In *The Aliakmon*, the sellers as shippers contracted with the time charters of the vessel, who wore the 'hat' of time charterers in their relationship with the owners of the vessel and of carriers in the contract with the shippers. The buyers, then, wearing their 'hat' as consignees, brought an action against the defendant shipowners (and not the time charterers) as the master of the vessel had signed the bill of lading for the owners.

ISSUE BOX

Why did the buyer in *The Aliakmon* sue the carrier in negligence instead of for breach of contract on the bill of lading contract?

The answer requires an understanding of the development of this area of law.

5.2.3.5 The Bills of Lading Act 1855

As the common law developed, it did recognise the transferability of the bill of lading as a document of title: *Lickbarrow* v *Mason*.[55] The common law did not, however, recognise that transfer as an assignment of the bill of lading as a contract of carriage. The problem was that the doctrine of privity in English common law did not allow the transferee of the bill of lading (such as the CIF buyer) to sue in contract on that bill of lading. English common law requires that consideration must move from a party entitled to sue on a contract: *Tweddle* v *Atkinson*.[56] This is known as the doctrine of privity. In *Dunlop Pneumatic Tyre Co Ltd* v *Selfridge & Co*,[57] Viscount Haldane LC, in describing the doctrine of privity, said:

> My Lords, in the law of England certain principles are fundamental. One is that only a person who is party to a contract can sue on it . . . A second principle is that if a person with whom a contract not under seal has been made is to be able to enforce it consideration must have been given by him to the promisor or to some other person at the promisor's request. These two principles are not recognised in the same fashion by the jurisprudence of certain Continental countries or of Scotland, but here they are well established.[58]

---

[54] Where there is a chain of charters, a charterer who sub-charters is said to be a 'disponent owner' for his charterer. This is a term used by the shipping industry to mean the party who has liability as owner under the charter, but who does not bear all liabilities of owner *vis-à-vis* the world for the adventures of the vessel. So, where the O (being the owner) charters to TC (being the time charter) and TC sub-charters to VC (being the voyage charterer), TC is the disponent owner under the voyage charter with VC.

[55] (1974) 5 TR 683.

[56] (1861) 1 B & S 393.

[57] [1915] AC 847.

[58] *Supra* n. 57, at p. 853.

The Bills of Lading Act 1855 was passed to remedy this problem. Section 1 provided that where the bill of lading *and the property in the goods* were transferred to the consignee, then the right to sue the carrier on the bill of lading as a contract would also be transferred to him. This Act was in force when the relationships in *The Aliakmon* were formed. As the buyer did not have the property in the goods (although, as we have seen, he held the bill of lading and had the risk in the goods) s. 1 of the Act was not satisfied. The buyer could not, therefore, sue the carrier in contract. The buyer of unascertained goods was also in this difficult position: *The Elafi*.[59] With the growth of the bulk carrier, CIF sales of unascertained goods became more common and it was recognised that the law on this point no longer gave effect to reasonable commercial expectations. In 1985, the Law Commission was invited to consider this area of the law with a view to possible reform of the problems created by the Bills of Lading Act 1855.[60]

5.2.3.6 The Carriage of Goods by Sea Act 1992

The approach favoured by the Law Commission was to allow the lawful holder of a bill of lading to sue the carrier in contract, irrespective of whether or not the property in the goods had passed to him and regardless of whether or not the holder was at risk at the time of the loss. This approach follows the practice in the USA and in a number of European countries. As a consequence of the Law Commission's recommendations, the Carriage of Goods by Sea Act 1992 was enacted to give effect to this approach to rights of suit in respect of the carriage of goods by sea. The Act came into force on 16 September 1992, and the Bills of Lading Act was repealed. The Act extends the right of suit in contract against the carrier to the lawful holder of a sea waybill and to the lawful holder of a ship's delivery order.[61]

Today, therefore, the claimant in such a case as *The Aliakmon*, being the 'lawful holder' of the bill of lading (s. 2(1)(a) of the 1992 Act), would now be able to sue the carrier on the contract of carriage contained in the bill of lading.

---

[59] [1982] 1 All ER 208. The property in unascertained goods cannot pass to the buyer: s. 16 SGA 1979. Thus, the buyer can be in the position of having the risk in the goods and having paid for them against presentation of the documents without 'owning' them at law. Although the issue in *The Aliakmon* was a 'one off' and to this extent not of especial interest within the international trade context, it very well highlights the position of the buyer of part of a bulk sale. This does, of course, put the buyer at additional risk of the seller's bankruptcy, as, under English law, notwithstanding that the buyer had paid for the goods, the goods were still within the ownership of the seller. This meant that the seller's trustee in bankruptcy would have a better interest in the goods than the buyer, who would have to join the other creditors against the seller. Amendments to the SGA in 1995 remedied this difficulty, under s. 20(A), which provides that the buyer of unascertained goods becomes an owner in common with the seller of the bulk upon payment of the price. He can now call for those goods as against a trustee in bankruptcy.

[60] The Law Commission's Report (Law Com No 196) on the rights of suit of those concerned with contracts of goods by sea makes interesting reading. The Law Commission was approached by Gafta, following a Gafta arbitration case called *The Gosforth* (S en s 1985 Nr 91). This case might be regarded as the 'high water mark' of trade tension about this issue.

[61] Some mention should be made of the Contracts (Rights of Third Parties) Act 1999, which came into force in English law on 11 May 2000. The Act has a somewhat modest reform on the doctrine of privity (see s. 1). It suffices here to say that the Act has no impact on the holder of a bill of lading's right to sue the carrier on that bill of lading (nor on the holder of a sea waybill or corresponding electronic transaction, nor on the holder of a ship's delivery order): s. 6(5)(a) and (b), which excludes such 'contracts for the carriage of goods by sea' from the ambit of the Act (except that a third party may avail himself of an exclusion or limitation of liability clause in such a contract: s. 6(5)).

5.3 The international sale contract

5.3.1 What the contract involves

Essentially, then, a contract of sale on shipment terms will involve the parties deciding who is responsible for the mode of shipment and delivery of the goods. The type of shipment terms used will indicate the parties' intentions as to who is to assume responsibility for shipment and delivery. Typically, an international sale contract will also set out the parties' intentions in respect of the following matters:

- arranging payment for the goods and setting up any documentary credits to support the payment;
- arranging insurance cover for the goods whilst they are in transit;
- ensuring that the packaging of the goods is sufficient to meet the requirements of the policy under which the goods are insured;
- the delivery date of the goods;
- the law of which state should govern the contract;
- the state in which any dispute should be determined (a forum clause);
- whether any dispute which arises is to be determined by arbitration;
- responsibility for obtaining export licences;
- ensuring that the packaging of the goods conforms to any import regulations in force in the country of destination;
- responsibility for any pre-shipment inspection (PSI) certificates;
- ensuring that customs documentation is obtained and customs clearance requirements are met.

5.3.2 The passing of risk: the seller's or carrier's liability?

We can see from the discussion above about the matrix of contracts in international trade that this is one of the most important questions that we must ask. The traditional international trade transaction is one where the goods are sold on shipment terms to be carried by sea, so this type of transaction will be the focus of our study. Contracts for the carriage of goods by air, road or rail raise very similar issues in respect of the sale contract under which those goods are to be carried. Particular difficulties may arise when goods are the subject of multi-modal transport and/or transhipment. Again, however, the issues which arise in respect of the contract of sale will be very similar to those which arise in the context of sea carriage.

Two fundamental questions always arise if the goods arrive damaged.

- Under the contract of sale, had the risk in the goods passed to the buyer by the time the goods were damaged?
- If so, can the buyer (in the context of carriage relationships as the consignee or indorsee) sue the carrier on the contract of carriage?

Whatever the mode of carriage, the same difficulties under English law will arise if the consignee or indorsee cannot sue on the contract of carriage and is forced instead to sue in tort.

In this chapter we are concerned with obligations of buyer and seller under the contract of sale. We will come to see why the documents representing the goods are so crucial in international sales. In order to appreciate this and to consider the parties' respective sale obligations properly, however, we must understand where the sale obligations start and end. We must, then, have a clear idea of where the sale contract 'fits' in the bigger picture. A key issue in sale contracts is the point at which the risk of loss and damage to the goods has passed to the buyer. Once this has occurred, any claim by the buyer in respect of loss or damage to the goods (for example, during the carriage of the goods to the buyer's destination) must be brought against the carrier rather than against the seller. In other words, if the seller has complied with his obligations under the contract of sale, then he will, so to speak, have 'fallen out of the picture'. Where this has happened, we would turn away from the contract of sale and would look instead at the carriage relationships. For the purposes of this chapter we are looking at the obligations and liabilities between the buyer and the seller *before* the risk in the goods passes to the buyer, that is to say, before the seller has 'fallen out of the picture'.

The point at which the risk passes is determined by the contract of sale itself. Thus, where the buyer has accepted the risk in the goods under the contract of sale, he must, as consignee/indorsee, sue the carrier in respect of their damage. Understanding this requires us to understand a document called a 'bill of lading' and the concept of the buyer receiving a 'clean' bill of lading.

The bill of lading is the receipt given by the carrier when the goods are put on board the vessel. If the goods are shipped in order, that is, if they conform to the specifications of the contract of sale,[62] the bill is 'clean'. It is subsequently transferred to the buyer. This is his evidence against the carrier that the goods were damaged during transit. If the bill of lading is clean, then the buyer can seek a remedy against the carrier. On the other hand, if the bill of lading is 'claused', the buyer will be entitled to reject it as against the seller. Either way, the buyer is shown to have a remedy.

5.3.3 The bill of lading

Provided that the documents are accurate and that they have not been falsified, it is possible to use the bill of lading as evidence of who has liability for the defects in the goods. It is important to recognise, however, that there are certain situations where a defect in the goods cannot be reflected in the bill of lading, simply because the defect in question will not become apparent until the goods have been discharged and collected by the buyer. There may be an inherent fault in the goods which the bill of lading could not identify (for example, pages missing from books, snails in a consignment of bottles of wine).

---

[62] As far as the bill can show. It is often the case that the master of the vessel (who is usually responsible for overseeing the loading and stowage of the goods and for signing the bill of lading) will not be able to tell if the goods do in fact match the specifications of the sale contract or that the goods are being shipped in good condition, for example, where goods are packed in boxes, pallets or, especially, in containers. The bill is likely, then, to be signed: 'Said to contain . . .' or 'Said by the shipper to . . .'.

The buyer does not take the risk of inherent defects in the goods. In *Mash and Murrell v Joseph I Emmanuel*,[63] the seller in Cyprus sold potatoes CIF Liverpool.[64] The potatoes, which were sound when loaded, had rotted by the time the ship arrived. It was held by Diplock J that the sellers were liable on the basis that in such a contract the goods must be loaded in such a state that they could withstand the rigours of a normal journey and be in a merchantable condition on arrival. (This case was in fact reversed on appeal, but only on its facts. It was followed in *The Rio Sun*.[65])

Despite doubts being cast on Diplock J's decision in some later cases, the House of Lords – approving a speech delivered by the then Lord Diplock! – unanimously affirmed that the implied condition in respect of quality and reasonable fitness for purpose is a continuing warranty that the goods will be fit for a reasonable time: *Lambert v Lewis*.[66]

This line of thinking clearly suggests that the seller cannot simply absolve himself of all liability in respect of providing conforming goods by the production of a clean bill of lading. We might also, in considering this issue, usefully have regard to the recent case of *KG Bominflot Bunkergesellschaft Für Mineralöle mbh & Co KG v Petroplus Marketing AG*,[67] where the Commercial Court, in taking this approach, was minded that the implied term as to 'satisfactory quality' in s. 14(2) of the Sale of Goods Act 1979 makes 'durability' an aspect of 'satisfactory quality'.[68] In that case, Field J stressed that reasonable time is dependent on the time taken to complete a normal voyage to the destination in question. Where the destination has not been specified, it would not be appropriate to adopt the concept of a 'normal voyage' as the measure of what is a reasonable time. What is a reasonable time will depend on the circumstances of the contract in question – including the sort of carriage envisaged, nature of the goods and whether the seller knows that the buyer is buying for resale or own use.

5.3.4 The main 'shipping documents' that support international sales

Our consideration of the role of a clean bill of lading in international sales leads us on to a consideration of the main documents that support international sales. These are generally known as the 'shipping documents' and are of fundamental importance in international trade. These documents represent, and are evidence of, the rights and liabilities that the parties have under the contract of sale. Because of the time which it takes for goods to travel by sea, the documents are particularly important in ensuring that trade relationships run smoothly while the goods are on board ship. They often have an important role in enabling the parties to finance their ongoing transactions by providing evidence that the goods have been shipped and by giving security over the goods to their respective banks. Moreover, the buyer of goods may wish to sell the goods whilst they are being carried, and the only evidence he will have of there being any goods which he is entitled to sell is the documentary proof.

---

[63] [1961] 1 All ER 485.
[64] [1961] 1 All ER 485.
[65] [1985] 1 Lloyd's Rep 350.
[66] [1982] AC 225.
[67] [2009] EWHC 1088 (Comm).
[68] Section 14(2B)(e).

Thus, the documents relating to international sales on shipment terms have a symbolic importance.

The contract of sale will require specific documents to be presented by the seller to the buyer. The buyer is entitled to reject documents which do not conform with the contract and repudiate the contract. In the 'C' contracts, the buyer may refuse to take up documents which are not in order and may treat out-of-order documents as a repudiatory breach of the contract of sale by the seller. In all three variants of the FOB sale, the buyer may reject non-conforming documents, leaving the seller the opportunity to tender fresh documents which conform with the contract if there is time to do so. If the seller cannot tender new conforming documents, then the buyer is entitled to treat this as a repudiatory breach of the contract of sale by the seller.

As we have seen above, in a rapidly changing market, where the price of goods can rise or fall significantly after the contract of sale has been formed, either party may have his eye very firmly on the possibility of releasing himself from the contract by claiming a repudiatory breach by the other party. Indeed, it is not uncommon in international trade for a party to repudiate, when the market has fallen, and then to suggest renegotiating what is in fact the very same contract he has repudiated, but on more favourable terms (as we saw in *The Hansa Nord*)! The courts are well aware of this practice in international trade and have, by the development and application of the innominate term, found a way of preventing a party from repudiating a contract merely because it has become commercially unattractive to him. The courts are unwilling to allow a party to escape from what has simply become to him 'an unwelcome bargain' (*per* Lord Mustill in *The Gregos*).[69] Amendments to the Sale of Goods Act, in 1994, gave what might be argued as being statutory effect to this judicial approach. It should be remembered, of course, the 'guilty party' (the defendant) does not decide if the contract is to be treated as repudiated – this is a matter for the party affected by the breach. Thus, even where one party is in repudiatory breach, the other may well wish the contract to continue.

The principal documents in respect of shipment contracts are discussed below.

5.3.4.1 The bill of lading

Whether or not the seller can tender a 'clean' bill of lading is of crucial importance between buyer and seller. The seller is under a duty to tender documents which conform to the contract. The buyer is under a duty to accept these documents. The bill of lading should acknowledge the fact that the goods have been received and loaded in apparent good order and condition (that is, that they are apparently of satisfactory quality as required by s. 14(2) of the Sale of Goods Act 1979, as amended). If this is not the case, then the defect is noted on the bill of lading and the bill is 'claused'. The buyer is not obliged to accept a 'claused' bill of lading. Where the bill of lading is clean, and under the contract of sale the risk in the goods has passed to the buyer on shipment, the buyer must sue the carrier rather than the seller for any damage which occurs to the goods. If the buyer is not privy to the original contract of carriage, then he will sue the carrier on the contract of carriage contained in the bill of lading (under the Carriage of Goods by Sea Act 1992). Delivery of the goods at their destination must normally be made only to the named consignee/indorsee upon production of the bill of lading.

---

[69] [1995] 1 Lloyd's Rep 1.

5.3.4.2 The commercial invoice

This is an invoice describing the goods sold and describing them in such a way that it is possible to identify them as the contract goods or as answering the description of the contract goods.

5.3.4.3 The policy of marine insurance

The contract of sale may require that the goods which are the subject of the contract be covered to the extent indicated in the contract by a policy of marine insurance. This policy must be expressed in such a way as to make it clear that it covers the goods specified in the two documents above for the whole of the voyage covered by the bill of lading. Where the bill of lading is transferred from one person to another, the policy of insurance will be assigned at the same time.

Other documents which the contract of sale may require the seller to submit to the buyer include a certificate of origin, a certificate of quality (for example, a PSI certificate, as mentioned above),[70] and export and/or import licences.

ISSUE BOX

The use of electronic bills of lading

Developments in information technology, and in particular in data encryption, have made it possible for a paper bill of lading to be replaced by an electronic substitute. There has been much discussion of the need for the shipping industry to take a proactive role in the use of electronic commerce, and certainly there have been energetically promoted commercial electronic document interchange ('EDI') schemes to replace paper bills of lading with electronic bills. These schemes include the following.

- The International Comité Maritime (the 'CMI') Rules on electronic bills of lading (1990). This has been a somewhat doomed initiative as many traders and carriers do not regard it as secure. The Rules only apply if contractually adopted by the parties, which has generally not happened.

- The 'SeaDocs' project (the Seaborne Trade Documentation System), the first serious attempt to introduce computerised bills of lading trading, was instigated in the bulk oil trade in 1983 by the Chase Manhattan Bank and the International Association of Independent Tanker Owners ('Intertanko'). This has been another doomed project as, apart from the initial pilot project, SeaDocs was never operational.

- Incoterms 1990 introduced recognition of electronic documentation.[71]

- The 'Bolero' project (the Bills of Lading in Europe), which was the initiative of the ICC in 1999, replaces the paper bill of lading with the 'Bolero Bill' and provides a system where every 'indorsement' of the bill is recorded and monitored. Hence, every time title in the

---

[70] Certificates of quality will frequently provide for the time at which the quality and condition of the goods are to be taken as final and binding. This is a somewhat tense issue, as can be seen in the recent appeal to the Commercial Court from Gafta arbitration, in *RG Grain Trade LLP* v *Feed Factors International Ltd* [2011] 2 Lloyd's Rep 432.

[71] Incoterms are the ICC's standard shipment terms, and are discussed in section 5.4.4.

goods changes hands, an appropriate electronic record will be put on the database so that every new owner will be properly recognised electronically. This electronic indorsement replaces the physical delivery of the bill of lading in the conventional transaction. It is a joint venture between the Society for Worldwide Interbank Financial Telecommunictions ('SWIFT') and the Through Transport Club ('TTC'),[72] which enables users to exchange electronic messages and trade documents via the Internet.[73]

Much has been written about electronic bills, the big question being, 'Will they catch on?' It may be thought that there is some hope that they will; Bolero has enjoyed success, and technology constantly develops. The Carriage of Goods by Sea Act 1992 allows the Secretary of State, by regulations, to provide for the application of the Act to electronic documentation, and the use of electronic documents under the Rotterdam Rules, should they come into force, is recognised. It may, however, be argued that not only must infrastructure requirements increase to support trading by electronic documentation, but also a fundamental shift in commercial practice, which does not appear to be on the immediate horizon.

5.3.5 The development of the sale of goods legislation

Before looking at international contracts of sale, we should consider the development of the legislation that governs sales of goods in English law.

The development of sales law through the common law led to a complex, and sometimes conflicting, mass of case law, explaining why in the 19th century there was a call for rationalisation of the law and codification. This process was achieved not by an all-embracing commercial code, but through the codification of certain specific areas of commercial law. In 1888, the celebrated statutory draftsman, Sir Mackenzie Chalmers – who had already drafted the Bills of Exchange Act 1882 – was commissioned to prepare Bills for the codification of the law relating to sale of goods. The Sale of Goods Act 1893 was the result of his labours. Although there has been criticism of this Act, mainly because it did not, as originally drafted, provide wholly satisfactory remedies for the buyer in consumer contracts, the codification was a great success as a merchants' code.

It was not until 1973, in the Supply of Goods (Implied Terms) Act 1973 (an Act mainly concerned with consumer transactions), that significant changes were made to any part of the 1893 Act. Following the 1973 amendments, and some further changes made by the Unfair Contract Terms Act 1977, the Act of 1893 was consolidated and re-enacted as the Sale of

---

[72] TTC is a P&I Club. P&I (Protection and Indemnity) cover is available from mutual insurers (known generally as P&I Clubs or Associations) and from fixed premium underwriters. The majority of world tonnage is covered by P&I Clubs. P&I cover is provided to vessels and shipowners in respect of liabilities for claims by third parties. A P&I Club is an association of shipowners who have grouped together to insure each other for their third-party liabilities on a mutual non-profitmaking basis, as recognised by s. 85 of the Marine Insurance Act 1906. By 'mutual' we mean that there is an equitable division or sharing of all of the potential risks and liabilities of the owners and vessels (known as 'members' and 'entered' vessels respectively) by the members of the association. As far as possible, all of the members are of equal status and should not impose a greater burden on some members than any other members. It is an important feature of mutual P&I insurance to ensure that one shipowner member neither subsidises the operations of another shipowner member, nor is himself subsidised by those other shipowner members.

[73] See www.bolero.net

Goods Act 1979. This is now the principal source of the law. The 1979 Act has, however, been amended by the Sale and Supply of Goods Act 1994, the Sale of Goods (Amendment) Act 1994 and the Sale of Goods (Amendment) Act 1995. All references in this chapter are to the 1979 Act, as amended, unless otherwise stated.

Some mention should be made here of the United Nations Convention on Contracts for the International Sale of Goods, otherwise known as the Vienna Sales Convention 1980. In 1966, the United Nations constituted the United Nations Commission on International Trade Law (UNCITRAL), which became operative on 1 January 1986. The objective of UNCITRAL is to further the progressive harmonisation and unification of the law of international trade. The Vienna Sales Convention is one of the most important UNCITRAL texts. It was adopted by the United Nations in April 1980, at Vienna, and came into operation on 1 January 1988, after the required number of ratifications and successions were received. It is intended to supersede the two Hague Conventions on the Uniform Laws on International Sales of 1964. The Vienna Convention has not yet been given effect in the UK.[74]

The Hague Conventions on the Uniform Laws on International Sales of 1964 (the Uniform Laws) have, however, been adopted into the law of the UK, under the Uniform Laws on International Sales Act 1967 (which came into force on 18 August 1972). Under the 1967 Act the Uniform Laws only apply if the parties expressly provide for their application, that is, if the parties 'contract in' (if the Vienna Convention comes into English law, parties who do not wish it to apply will have to 'contract out'). Professor Goode suggests that although the Uniform Laws were a major step towards the unification of international sales law, they suffered 'serious deficiencies' which limited their utility.[75]

5.4 Standard form contracts and shipment terms

5.4.1 The nature of standard form contracts

It is important to understand the nature of standard form contracts. In complex contracts, such as international sale contracts, the difficulty is often to determine exactly what obligations the terms of the contract create. This difficulty is not usually apparent in negotiating the contract, but becomes apparent when there is a dispute in which the parties argue that the terms in question have different meanings. Merchant traders do not necessarily have fine legal semantics in mind when negotiating their contracts, but they are, of course, subject to the niceties of the law in fixing their rights and obligations. Standard form contracts have been developed in international trade practice with the aim of clarifying and firmly setting out the parties' respective liabilities. Such contracts have the two-fold advantage of satisfying trade requirements of certainty as to potential liability and of avoiding subsequent legal analysis of what the parties must have intended. This latter issue is particularly important because what the court may think the parties intended, on the basis of the legal analysis, may in fact not reflect the ideas that the merchants had when conducting their negotiations. The

[74] www.uncitral.org/uncitral/en/uncitral_texts/sale_goods/1980CISG_status.html
[75] *Supra* n. 1, at p. 914.

approach is objective rather than subjective. Mercantile contract terms present particular difficulties because they are sometimes agreed by commercial parties without the benefit of legal advice. Legal imperfections will, therefore, inevitably appear. Often, the court may have to reconcile an imprecision in a contractual term using legal arguments with which the term was never intended to be overlaid.

Standard form contracts developed during an age of freedom of contract, otherwise known as the *laissez-faire* era in English common law. The notion of standard trading contracts as a bargaining process arose at the same time as the doctrine of *laissez-faire* and is a consequence of a free enterprise system. Thus, the *laissez-faire* attitude has remained central to the way that the law approaches standard form contracts. Judicial and legislative tolerance of the standard form contract is dependent upon the parties to those contracts being on an equal bargaining level.[76]

5.4.2 The role of standard form contracts

The main concern in Anglo-American jurisprudence in respect of standard form contracts is whether or not they can be said to reflect sufficient negotiation to allow them to be treated as enforceable contracts. As Leff has argued, if a contract, by definition, requires a certain amount of dealing or haggling, a form offered on a take-it-or-leave-it basis does not look very much like a contract.[77] Rakoff suggests that such a contract could be construed as a contract of adhesion.[78] This suggestion leads to the argument that the courts should scrutinise the reasonableness of contract terms offered in a standard form.[79] The classic view in English law on standard contracts comes from the judgment of Lord Diplock in *Schroeder v Macauley*.[80] His Lordship said that standard form contracts are of two kinds. The first, of early origin, are widely used in commercial transactions and are the result of extensive prior negotiations by the parties and are adopted because they 'facilitate the conduct of trade'.[81] Examples cited of this type of standard contract were bills of lading, charter parties, insurance policies and contracts of sales in the commodity markets. Here, his Lordship said, there is a strong presumption that the terms of these contracts are fair and reasonable because they are used by the parties where 'this bargaining power is fairly matched'.[82]

It is not surprising that the courts, on both sides of the Atlantic, give effect to the standard form contracts generally used in international trade. They are taken as facilitating trade and

---

[76] L. A. Kornhauser, 'Unconscionability in Standard Forms' (1976) 64(5) Sept., *California Law Review* 1152–1179.

[77] A. A. Leff, 'Contract as a Thing' (2006) 19 *American University Law Review*, pp. 131–157.

[78] T. D. Rakoff, 'Contracts of Adhesion: An Essay in Reconstruction' (1983) 96 *Harvard Law Review*, pp. 1176–1180.

[79] Kornhauser argues that, especially in today's mass economy, there is nothing inherently virtuous about individualised bargaining and nothing inherently suspicious about refusing to bargain: *supra* at n. 75.

[80] [1974] 1 WLR 1308 at 1316.

[81] The second class of standard form contracts (essentially consumer-type transactions) led Lord Diplock to presume that the same approach would not apply. These were said to be of comparatively modern origin and are 'the result of the concentration of particular kinds of business in relatively few hands'. *Ibid.*

[82] Nonetheless, there are at times tensions between the freedom of contract paradigm and the situation of exploitation assumed by some to be created by standard form contracts. It could be argued that there is no such thing as real freedom of contract and that a party may be 'forced' into a trade association's standard form contract by market pressure, which may be considered as one of the 'soft law' means of establishing international uniformity in international trade.

most international sale and carriage contracts are on some kind of recognised standard form.[83] It should be remembered that international trade – encompassing international sales and shipping contracts – was going on long before the common law as we know it today came into existence. Forms of mercantile contracts were already in use in the mercantile courts by the time the common law started to develop, and were certainly recognised by the *lex mercatoria*. The *lex mercatoria*, or merchant law, existed as a distinct course of law for hundreds of years and was administered by its own courts, before being vanquished by the courts of common law. Disputes in the mercantile courts were determined according to principles based on mercantile codes and customs, reflecting international trade and commercial practices. Eventually, however, the application of the *lex mercatoria* by the merchant courts declined, as a result of the acquisition by the common law courts of most of the country's commercial litigation. Much of this decline can be attributed to Sir Edward Coke in the mid-17th century, who had a passionate devotion to the common law and the common law courts and a fierce hostility to all competing courts, including the merchant and Admiralty courts.

The decline of the *lex mercatoria* and the emergence of the common law were gradual and overlapping; there was never one moment when the *lex mercatoria* was 'out' and the common law was 'in'. Although it is debatable how far the common law courts applied and absorbed the law merchant,[84] it is inevitable that there was some overlap of the application of the *lex mercatoria* and the common law aims, especially given that the first common law courts were keen to attract business from the merchant courts. Thus, it seems safe to assume that the early common law courts were compelled to modify their own principles and practices in respect of commercial litigation in order to accommodate the needs of the mercantile community. It is likely that the common law courts achieved this by 'borrowing' principles from the *lex mercatoria*, whilst in the main applying concepts of the common law. In this way those applying to the common law courts would get as good a service as they had received from the merchant courts. Without this approach, the common law courts would not have captured what mercantile business they did. As we have seen, a study of modern English commercial law evidences that this is still very much the approach of the Commercial Court today; it attempts to develop and apply the law according to the needs and practices of traders.

The early common law cases can likely be taken then to at least reflect an acceptance of how the *lex mercatoria* had been applied, despite authorities from the *lex mercatoria* and very early common law cases being scant.[85] Certainly sales cases do not appear other than in isolated instances until the beginning of the 18th century. Despite the efforts of Lord Mansfield[86] by the empanelling of special juries to acknowledge mercantile custom, sales law did not develop much in his courts, but was instead dealt with in the unrecorded proceedings of arbitrations and private settlements. This, as it is today, would have been the expected manner of dispute resolution for many traders: in 1895, Bateson commented that arbitration was 'almost invariably dealt with' in the various trade associations' mercantile forms, which were commonly used for international sale contracts.[87] Bateson went on to describe the four forms

---

[83] For example, the ICC's Incoterms.

[84] See R. Goode, *Commercial Law in the Next Millennium* (Sweet and Maxwell, London, 1998).

[85] The first printed English law book appears to have been Littleton's *Tenures* (1481) – see J. H. Baker, *An Introduction to English Legal History* (3rd edn, Butterworths, London, 1990).

[86] Chief Justice 1756–1788.

[87] H. D. Bateson, 'Forms of Mercantile Contracts' [1895] *LQR* 266.

in common use at the time, which related to the parties to the contract[88] and which were all in writing. He also described the four forms which related to the position of the goods sold: these were 'spot' contracts, 'arrival' contracts, 'FOB' contracts and 'CIF' contracts.[89] He concluded his article by saying that 'with these eight forms of mercantile contracts it will not be difficult to frame or follow other forms'. In this he was correctly prophesying what has in fact happened – we have seen the growth of associations' standard form contracts, sampling and analysis procedures and arbitration rules. Indeed, currently, Gafta has just over 200 sale forms,[90] each tailored to accommodate the sale of particular goods (often from a particular country of origin) and the varying contractual requirements that parties will have. There are also rules for arbitration under Gafta and guidelines for the negotiation of insurance and letters of credit.

Whilst it is true that many commercial disputes are dealt with by arbitration, which affords for a 'trade analysis' of what the terms must have meant, it is now a fact that commercial parties are inclined to be more litigious than in the past. They are likely to engage legal representatives to argue the law, rather than to rely solely on dispute resolution using trade methodology – such as the 'scratch and sniff' approach, which might be used in arbitrations by Gafta to determine, for example, if grain is of satisfactory quality as required by the contract.[91] The increasing resort to litigation is indicative of a sophisticated modern trading environment, in which the quantities of goods sold can be enormous, as they are often carried in bulk shipments. Hence, the potential liabilities of the parties are magnified in terms of cost and this may explain the more legally robust attitude adopted by traders.

5.4.3 Standard international sale terms

Certain trade terms have become widely recognised in international trade. These terms will be specifically referred to by the parties in negotiating their contract. The trade terms are intended to define the responsibilities in respect of the delivery of the goods, and the extent to which the seller is responsible for the goods whilst they are in transit. The particular trade terms used will show what is included in the price which the buyer is paying for the goods.

---

[88] (1) Where both the seller, issuing a sold note, and the buyer, issuing a bought note (the two documents together constituting the contract), contracted as principals. (2) Where the sold note and the bought note were negotiated by the selling broker and the buying broker, who would both be named in the notes. In such a case the broker(s) would either copy out the contract on to a contract form or would enter the agreement in his contract book. If no entry was made in the broker's contract book then disputes could arise if the two notes did not correspond exactly. Bateson (*supra* n. 86) was of the opinion (at p. 271) that: 'Such experience as I have had leads me to believe that in the press of business in modern times the broker's contract book is going out of fashion, and the true record of the contract of sale is to be found in the sold note and bought note.' (3) Where the selling and buying brokers guaranteed their respective principals and charged a *del credere* or guarantee commission. These details would be set out in the sold and bought notes. (4) Where the rights of the buyer and seller, if not disclosed on the fact of the contract, were excluded.

[89] Respectively: a sale of goods for immediate delivery; a sale for the goods to arrive at the port stipulated; 'free on board' where the seller must place the goods on board a ship named by the buyer; 'cost, insurance and freight' where the seller insures and ships the goods.

[90] The latest revision being April 2012.

[91] It is in fact debatable to what extent this procedure is today relied upon, the parties now often relying on more sophisticated methods of quality assessment. The 'scratch and sniff' approach is, however, it appears, still very much relied upon in the coffee beans trade.

As has been said, in contracts of sale on shipment terms for the carriage of goods by sea, the two most common trade terms are FOB and CIF. These two terms will be considered in some detail below. At this point, an overview of the most commonly used terms in international trade may be useful.

Abbreviation	EXW
Full name	Ex works (. . . named place)
Duties	The buyer or his agent has to collect the goods from the seller's factory or warehouse. Thus, the seller has fulfilled his obligations to deliver when he has made the goods available at his premises (that is, works, factory, warehouse, etc.) to the buyer.
Abbreviation	FCA
Full name	Free carrier (. . . named place)
Duties	The seller fulfils his obligation to deliver when he has handed over the goods, cleared for export, into the charge of the carrier named by the buyer at the named place or point.
Abbreviation	FAS
Full name	Free alongside (. . . named port of shipment)
Duties	The seller is responsible for delivering the goods alongside the ship so that they can be loaded by the buyer or his agent. This means that the buyer must bear all the cost and risk of loss or damage to the goods from the moment they are so delivered, that is, even before the goods crossed the ship's rail. This term requires the buyer to clear the goods for export. It should not, therefore, be used when the buyer cannot carry out directly or indirectly any export formalities.
Abbreviation	FOB
Full name	Free on board (. . . port of shipment)
Duties	The seller is responsible for placing the goods on board the ship and for paying all charges up to the point that the goods are loaded over the ship's rail. The buyer bears the risk of loss or damage to the goods from this point and the cost of the carriage. This term requires the seller to clear the goods for export. We will look at FOB contracts in more detail in section 5.6 below.
Abbreviation	CFR
Full name	Cost and freight (. . . port of discharge)
Duties	The seller is to arrange and pay for the contract of carriage (the freight) of the goods to the destination port. The seller must also provide an effective notice of shipment to the buyer in order that the buyer can arrange appropriate insurance for the goods. The seller is also responsible for the issue of a sales invoice and a clean bill of lading. The seller must clear the goods for export.
Abbreviation	CIF
Full name	Cost, insurance and freight (. . . port of discharge)

Duties	The seller is to arrange and pay for both the contract of carriage (the freight) and insurance for the goods. He must produce a sales invoice, an insurance policy and a clean bill of lading. The seller must clear the goods for export.
Abbreviation	CPT
Full name	Carriage paid to (. . . named place of destination)
Duties	'Carriage paid to' means that the seller pays the freight for the carriage of the goods to the named destination. The risk of loss or damage to the goods, as well as any additional costs due to events occurring after the time the goods have been delivered to the carrier, is transferred from the seller to the buyer when the goods have been delivered into the custody of the carrier. This term requires the seller to clear the goods for export.
Abbreviation	DAF
Full name	Delivered at frontier (. . . named place)
Duties	This term requires the seller to make the goods available, cleared for export, at the named point and place at the frontier, but before the customs controls of the adjoining country.
Abbreviation	DES
Full name	Delivered ex ship (. . . named port of destination)
Duties	This term means that the seller has fulfilled his obligation to deliver the goods when they have been made available to the buyer on board the ship, cleared for import, at the port of destination. The seller has to bear all costs and risks involved in bringing the goods to the named port of destination.
Abbreviation	DEQ
Full name	Delivered ex quay (duty paid) (. . . named port of destination)
Duties	Under this term, the seller will have fulfilled his obligation to deliver when he has made the goods available to the buyer on the quay (wharf) at the named port of destination, clear for import. The seller has to bear all risks and costs including duties, taxes and other charges of delivering the goods thereto. This term should not be used if the seller is unable directly or indirectly to obtain the import licence.
Abbreviation	DDU
Full name	Delivered duty unpaid (. . . named port of destination)
Duties	Under this term, the seller will have fulfilled his obligation to deliver the goods when they have been made available at the named place in the country of importation. The seller has to bear the costs and risks involved in bringing the goods to this named place *excluding* duties, taxes and other official charges payable upon importation, as well as the costs and risks of carrying out customs formalities. The buyer has to pay these additional costs and bear any risks caused by his failure to clear the goods for import in time.
Abbreviation	DDP
Full name	Delivered duty paid (. . . named place of destination)

Duties   Under this term, the seller will have fulfilled his obligation to deliver when the goods have been made available to the buyer at the named place in the country of importation. The seller has to bear the risks and costs, including duties, taxes and other charges of delivering the goods clear for importation. Whilst the 'EXW' term represents the minimum obligation for the seller, this term represents the maximum obligation. This term should not be used if the seller is unable directly or indirectly to obtain the import licence.

5.4.4 Incoterms

5.4.4.1 What are 'Incoterms'?

'Incoterms' (the International Rules for the Interpretation of Trade Terms) are a set of additional standard terms which *interpret* the international shipment terms used in international sale contracts. These interpretation terms were introduced by the International Chamber of Commerce (ICC) to simplify and clarify the international trade terms. Incoterms may, in fact, have customary or even statutory force in some jurisdictions, but will be applied in English law only if chosen by the parties. Thus, a party can trade on CIF terms, for example by using one of the Gafta CIF forms (which expressly exclude the incorporation of Incoterms)[92] or on Incoterms CIF.[93] In view of the changes made to Incoterms from time to time, it is important to ensure that where the parties intend to incorporate Incoterms into their contract of sale, an express reference is always made to the current version of Incoterms. A failure to refer to the current version may result in disputes as to whether the parties intended to incorporate that version or an earlier version into their contract. Merchants wishing to use the new Incoterms 2010 should, therefore, specify clearly that their contract is governed by 'Incoterms 2010'.

Incoterms make a valuable contribution to international uniformity in the interpretation of contractual terms. The purpose of Incoterms is to provide a set of international rules for the interpretation of the most commonly used trade terms in foreign trade. Thus, the uncertainties of different interpretations of such terms in different countries can be avoided or at least reduced to a considerable degree. Frequently, parties to a contract are unaware of the different trading practices in their respective countries. This can give rise to misunderstandings, disputes and litigation, with all the waste of time and money that this entails. In order to remedy this problem, the ICC first published Incoterms in 1936. Amendments and additions were later made in 1953, 1967, 1976, 1980, 1990, 2000 and lastly in 2010, in order to bring the rules into line with current international trade practices. During the process of revision leading to a new edition, the ICC invites views and responses to successive drafts of the proposed revisions, from a wide-ranging spectrum of world traders, through the medium of various national trade organisations to which those traders belonged.

---

[92] It is not unusual for standard form sale contracts under trade associations/federations to exclude Incoterms. These specialised contracts are sufficiently comprehensive as to the parties' respective obligations so as to render the reliance of Incoterms as, at best, superfluous, and, at worst, verbose to the point of being muddled. For example, Gafta and Fosfa contracts all expressly exclude Incoterms (although to do so is superfluous, as under English law, Incoterms do not apply unless expressly incorporated *into* the contract!).

[93] It might usefully be noted that Incoterms use uppercase letters for abbreviating the standard form terminology.

5.4.4.2 The scope of Incoterms

It should be stressed that the scope of Incoterms is limited to matters relating to the rights and obligations of the parties to the contract of sale with respect to the delivery of the goods sold. ('Goods', in this sense, are confined to 'tangibles'; they do not include 'intangibles'.) It must also be very firmly kept in mind that Incoterms do not relate to the contract of carriage; they are sale contract terms. It is a common misconception that Incoterms apply to contracts of carriage. Obviously, however, the parties' agreement to use particular Incoterms will necessarily have implications for the other contracts which are part of the matrix. For example, a seller, having agreed to an Incoterms CIF contract, cannot perform such a contract by any other mode of transport but carriage by sea, because under Incoterms CIF he must present a bill of lading or other maritime document to the buyer – this is simply not possible if another mode of transport is used.

It is also sometimes wrongly assumed that Incoterms provide for all the duties which the parties may wish to include in their contract of sale, but Incoterms deal only with the relation between sellers and buyers in very distinct respects. Incoterms deal with a number of identified obligations imposed on the parties, such as the seller's obligation to place the goods at the disposal of the buyer or to hand them over for carriage or to deliver them at their destination. Incoterms provide for the distribution of risk between the parties in these cases. Further, they deal with the obligations to clear goods for export and import, the packing of the goods and the buyer's obligation to take delivery, as well as the obligation to provide proof that the respective obligations have been duly fulfilled.

Although Incoterms are extremely useful in implementing international contracts of sale, a number of problems which may arise in such contracts are not dealt with at all, for example, transfer of ownership and other property rights, breaches of contract, the consequences flowing from such breaches and exclusions of liability in certain situations. Incoterms are not intended to *replace*, but to *supplement*, the traditional contractual terms which are needed for a complete contract of sale. Thus, the parties will contract on a standard form contract subject to particular Incoterms or will negotiate their own contract incorporating the relevant Incoterms.

In practice, it frequently happens that the parties themselves, by adding words to an Incoterm, seek further protection than the term offers. It should be emphasised that Incoterms give no guidance whatsoever for such additions. Thus, if the parties cannot rely on a well-established custom of the trade for the interpretation of such additions, they may encounter serious problems when no consistent understanding of the addition can be proved. The container trade (where goods are stowed – or 'stuffed', to use the trade term – into a container before being carried by road, rail or sea or a combination of modes of transport) has developed a variety of trade terms, for example:

- FCL (full container load);
- LCL (less than full container load);
- Free Carrier (broadly equivalent to FOB);
- Freight Carriage Paid (equivalent to CFR); and
- Freight Carriage and Insurance Paid (equivalent to CIF).

The preambles to certain of the terms do alert parties to the need for special provisions if they wish to go beyond the stipulated Incoterms.

One important difficulty (which might be said to be meat and drink to lawyers!) is raised by the use that Incoterms make of the phrases:

- 'usual terms';
- 'normally used';
- 'usual route'; and
- 'customary manner'.

The word 'usual' is sufficiently vague, in legal terms, to allow for trade practices to be taken into account when considering the obligations imposed by these terms. The concept of what is 'usual' is quite different from the objective legal concept of what is 'reasonable'. These phrases, employed in the Incoterms, are rather bland, so that they throw back on to the buyer and the seller the burden of setting out in their contract exactly what, in particular circumstances, they expect. The message from any legally minded adviser must be that the parties should specifically state their expectations in their contract rather than leave the meaning of these phrases to be determined once litigation has started.

The ICC launched Incoterms 2010 in mid-September 2010 and they came into effect on 1 January 2011. Their aim is to reflect the changes in international trade since the 2000 version was published and to create greater clarity about their intended use.[94]

5.5 CIF contracts

5.5.1 The nature of CIF contracts

Having now considered the overall 'picture' in which our international sale contract exists, we can now turn our attention to the first of our export contracts to be looked at in depth: the CIF contract.[95]

5.5.1.1 The parties' duties

The CIF contract is one of the two 'classic' export sale contracts. As we have already seen, the letters 'CIF' stand for 'cost, insurance and freight'. In a CIF contract, the buyer looks to the seller to make the whole of the shipping arrangements, including those relating to insurance, and the buyer takes delivery of the goods symbolically by taking over the shipping

---

[94] For example, under Incoterms 2010 the FOB contract is stated as being only applicable to sea and inland waterway transport. Goods carried in containers are commonly today carried on 'multimodal' terms, under one contract involving two or more modes of carriage, with the seller (as shipper) typically contracting with one head carrier for the entire transport, each individual mode being sub-contracted by the head carrier (again, in each sub-contract, as shipper). Under this arrangement, the seller will usually receive a multimodal bill which he then endorses over to his buyer. Generally, FOB is regarded as a monomodal term, it having no application in road, rail or air transport. It may be that CPT ('carriage paid to') is a more appropriate term for the container trade and it is certainly hoped that the new edition of Incoterms will better provide for multimodal contracts.

[95] For a consideration of the historical development of FOB (and CIF) contracts, see D. M. Sassoon, 'The Origin of FOB and CIF Terms and the Factors Influencing their Choice' [1967] JBL 32.

documents relating to the consignment. These documents will include, at least, the bill of lading, the commercial invoice and the insurance policy. What the buyer bargains for is not so much to acquire the goods in a physical sense as to take over the whole commercial venture.

In contrast with the FOB contract, which specifies the port of loading, the CIF contract specifies the port of arrival, or one of a number of ports, from which the buyer will nominate one at some stage after the contract is concluded. Of the CIF contract, Lord Wright said, in *Ross T Smyth & Co Ltd* v *T D Bailey, Sons & Co*:

> The contract in question here is of a type familiar in commerce, and is described as a CIF contract. The initials indicate that the price is to include cost, insurance and freight. It is a type of contract which is more widely and more frequently in use than any other contract used for purposes of sea borne commerce. An enormous number of transactions, in value amounting to untold sums, are carried out every year under CIF contracts. The essential characteristics of this contract have often been described. The seller has to ship or acquire after that shipment the contract goods, as to which, if unascertained, he is generally required to give a notice of appropriation. On or after shipment, he has to obtain proper bills of lading and proper policies of insurance. He fulfils his contract by transferring the bills of lading and the policies to the buyer. As a general rule, he does so only against payment of the price, less the freight, which the buyer has to pay. In the invoice which accompanies the tender of the documents on the 'prompt' – that is, the date fixed for payment – the freight is deducted, for this reason. In this course of business, the general property in the goods remains in the seller until he transfers the bills of lading. These rules, which are simple enough to state in general terms, are of the utmost importance in commercial transactions. I have dwelt upon them perhaps unnecessarily, because the judgment of the Court of Appeal might seem to throw doubt on one of their most essential aspects. The property which the seller retains while he or his agent, or the banker to whom he has pledged the documents, retains the bills of lading is the general property and not a special property by way of security. In general, however, the importance of the retention of the property is not only to secure payment from the buyer but for purposes of finance. The general course of international commerce involves the practice of raising money on the documents so as to bridge the period between shipment and the time of obtaining payment against documents. These credit facilities, which are of the first importance, would be completely unsettled if the incidence of the property were made a matter of doubt. By mercantile law, the bills of lading are the symbols of the goods. The general property in the goods must be in the seller if he is to be able to pledge them. The whole system of commercial credits depends on the seller's ability to give a charge on the goods and the policies of insurance. A mere unpaid seller's lien would, for obvious reasons, be inadequate and unsatisfactory.[96]

Some comment here should be made about Lord Wright's reference to the 'notice of appropriation'. A notice of appropriation is not part of the shipping documents. It is a communication from the seller to the buyer (which is invariably required by the trade to be in writing) informing the buyer that the goods have been shipped. It is a preliminary communication that the buyer will receive before he receives the shipping documents. This advance statement gives particulars of the shipment, such as when and, importantly, on what vessel the goods have been shipped, so that the buyer can begin to negotiate sub-contracts knowing that he will be able to perform them. The seller cannot revoke the notice unless the contract of sale allows for this, nor can he substitute other goods or deliver the goods on another ship: *Grain Union SA* v *Hans Larsen*.[97] Although a notice of appropriation is not required under common law, many of the trade associations require such notices under their CIF standard form

---

[96] [1940] 3 All ER 60 (House of Lords) at 67.
[97] [1993] All ER Rep 342.

contracts. The meaning of appropriation within the context of the notice of appropriation should not be confused with the meaning of appropriation under s. 18 (rule 5) of the Sale of Goods Act 1979.[98] The notice of appropriation referred to by Lord Wright does not bring rule 5 into play. The property in the goods under a CIF sale will normally pass when the shipping documents are handed over in exchange for the purchase price. This is a later stage than when the notice of appropriation is given. The notice of appropriation is thus the communication which informs the buyer that those goods carried on the ship referred to in the notice answer to his contract with the seller. The notice of appropriation may be given in respect of specific or ascertained goods (the notice turning the latter into specific goods) or unascertained goods.

It is important to grasp the fact that the documents are of fundamental importance to the buyer in a CIF sale. The aim of the contract is to obtain the documents and, therefore, the right to dispose of the goods, as quickly as possible, so that they can be sold on the market. Because the documents are such a key feature of the CIF contract, it might be said that a CIF contract is a 'two-tier' contract: a sale of the documents as well as a sale of the goods. As Devlin J noted in *Kwei Tek Chao v British Traders*:

> A CIF contract puts a number of obligations upon the seller, some of which are in relation to the goods and some of which are in relation to the documents. So far as the goods are concerned, he must put on board at the port of shipment goods in conformity with the contract description, but he must also send forward documents, and those documents must comply with the contract. If he commits a breach the breaches may in one sense overlap, in that they flow from the same act. If there is a late shipment . . . the seller has not put on board goods which conform to the contract description and, therefore, he has broken that obligation. He has also made it impossible to send forward a bill of lading which at once conforms with the contract and states accurately the date of shipment. Thus, the same act can cause two breaches of two independent obligations.[99]

5.5.1.2 A sale of documents or a sale of goods?

In the CIF contract, therefore, emphasis is on the symbolic delivery of goods, using the documents which embody the title to those goods. It is a 'cash against documents' contract. The buyer cannot refuse the documents and ask for the actual goods; nor can the seller withhold the documents and tender the goods they represent: *Manbré Saccharin Co v Corn Products*.[100] The nature of the CIF contract was explained well by Lord Porter in *The Julia*:

> . . . the obligations imposed upon a seller under a CIF contract are well known, and in the ordinary case include the tender of a bill of lading covering the goods contracted to be sold and no others, coupled with an insurance policy in the normal form and accompanied by an invoice which shows the price . . . Against tender of these documents the purchaser must pay the price. In such a case the property may pass either on shipment or on tender, the risk generally passes on shipment or as from shipment, but possession does not pass until the documents which represent the goods are handed over in exchange for the price. In the result the buyer after receipt of the documents can claim against the ship for breach of the contract of carriage and against the underwriter for any loss covered by the policy.[101]

---

[98] Section 18 deals with the rules relating to the passing of the property in the goods, and rule 5 relates to the passing of property when unascertained goods have been appropriated in favour of the buyer, which is when the goods are set aside for the buyer – unconditionally appropriated.

[99] [1954] 2 QB 459 at 480–481.

[100] [1919] 1 KB 198.

[101] [1949] AC 293 at 309.

In *The Julia*, the seller had reserved the right to substitute for the bill of lading a delivery order served on the buyer's agent at the port of destination. The House of Lords held that the buyer's payment in respect of the tendered documents was not made against all the 'shipping documents' as required by a CIF contract. Rather, it was an advance payment for a contract to be performed later. This was not a true CIF contract, despite the parties referring to it as such. In reality it was an ex ship contract for the delivery of the goods at Antwerp (an arrival contract), not when they were shipped on board, as under a true CIF contract.[102] Lord Porter was of the opinion that:

> ... the strict form of CIF contract may, however, be modified ... Not every contract which is expressed to be a CIF contract is such. Sometimes ... terms are introduced into contracts so described which conflict with CIF provisions ... the true effect of all its terms must be taken into account, though, of course, the description CIF must not be neglected.[103]

This is a salutary warning to parties who purport to contract on a recognised standard form and who include their own variants of its terms to the extent that they cease to contract on a standard form as they originally intended. The importance of ascertaining the contract upon which the parties are proceeding is shown by the questions which arise as to the allocation of obligations between the buyer and the seller.[104] The more complex the contract, the more difficult it may be to determine exactly what obligations variant terms have created.[105] Thus, lack of attention to detail when drafting the contract may result in an essential question having to be determined by the court (which, of course, is costly in terms of time and money).[106]

CASE

The Red Sea[107]

The contract in question was for the sale of 22,500 tons minimum to 25,000 tons maximum of jet aviation fuel. The contract provided *inter alia* that any terms not specifically covered were to be governed by Incoterms 1990 plus amendments. The relevant Incoterms (A5 and B5) together provided for the risk of loss and damage to pass from the seller to the buyer on shipment. Additional terms in the contract as amended related to the product, and its quality and origin, and included a fuel specification, intended, *inter alia*, to provide a code for use. A products clause required the sellers to make 'best endeavours' to have a static dissipator additive (the 'SDA') placed on board the vessel in drums, to be added to the fuel after shipment. At the time of shipment no SDA had been

---

[102] The goods could not be delivered in Antwerp as Belgium was occupied by the Germans whilst the vessel was at sea, and the sellers as charterers of the vessel ordered her to Lisbon, at which point the cargo was discharged. Thus, under the terms of the contract as it was construed by their Lordships, the sellers were in breach of their obligation to deliver the goods.

[103] *Supra*, n. 102, again at 309.

[104] Dispute about such allocation and the intention of the parties regarding their substantive obligations may well lead to costly 'conflicts' litigation (in *Scottish & Newcastle International Ltd v Othon Ghalanos Ltd* [2008] 1 Lloyd's Rep 462).

[105] Incoterms 2000 expressly warns about this problem in its introduction.

[106] It may also lead to expensive private international law or 'conflicts' issues: see *Scottish & Newcastle International Ltd v Othon Ghalanos Ltd* [2008] 1 Lloyd's Rep 462.

[107] [1997] 1 Lloyd's Rep 610.

added to the fuel. Following shipment too much SDA was added. The fuel was, therefore, outside the specification at the time of shipment and after admixture.

Rix J (as he was then) had to determine, as preliminary issues, whether or not the contract was in fact on CIF terms and, if so, whether or not it was subject to Incoterms 1990 CIF clause B5, the crux of the issue focusing on whether the risk of the post-shipment SDA fell on the seller or the buyer. Whether or not it could be said that there was any 'contractual description' of the goods, what the sellers' obligations in relation to the additive were and if the sellers were in breach of any terms of the contract also fell to be considered. In looking at both the sellers' and buyers' understanding of the fuel specification, his Lordship commented that he was 'faced essentially by a choice between two constructions, neither of which is wholly satisfactory, and both of which have difficulties'.

A more careful drafting of this contract would have obviated the need for the Commercial Court to have to deal with these preliminary issues, instead leaving the parties free to spend their time and money on determining the substantive issue of whether or not the sellers were in breach of the products clause. Of course, had the contract been clear, then it is not at all unlikely that the parties would have had no need to proceed to court, both being aware of their duties and where the risk of damage lay.

There has been a tendency for judicial and academic opinion to assume that CIF contracts are contracts for the sale of documents rather than goods. This is unfortunate, but understandable in the light of the importance that is attached to the documentary duties under the CIF contract. Scrutton J's judgment on this point in *Karberg (Arnhold) & Co v Blythe Green, Jourdain & Co* has become famous:

> I am strongly of the opinion that the key to many of the difficulties arising in CIF contracts is to keep firmly in mind the cardinal distinction that a CIF sale is not a sale of goods, but a sale of documents relating to goods. It is not a contract that goods shall arrive, but a contract to ship goods complying with the contract of sale, to obtain, unless the contract otherwise provides, the ordinary contract of carriage to the place of destination, and the ordinary contract of insurance of the goods on that voyage, and to tender these documents against payment of the contract price. The buyer then has the right to claim the fulfilment of the contract of carriage, or, if the goods are lost or damaged, such indemnity for the loss as he can claim under the contract of insurance. He buys the documents, not the goods, and it may be that under the terms of the contracts of insurance and affreightment he buys no indemnity for the damage that has happened to the goods. This depends on what documents he is entitled to under the contract of sale. In my view, therefore, the relevant question will generally be not 'what at the time of declaration or tender of documents is the condition of the goods?' . . . but 'what, at the time of tender of documents, was the condition of those documents as to compliance with the contract of sale?'[108]

Despite the fact that the appeal against Scrutton J's judgment in *Karberg v Blythe* was disallowed, there was some dissent in the Court of Appeal as to the correctness of his Lordship's view. Nonetheless, it has survived. In *Van der Zijden Wildlander (PV) NV v Tucker and Cross Ltd*, Donaldson J said:

> The contract called for Chinese rabbits, CIF. [The sellers'] obligation was, therefore, to tender documents, not to tender the rabbits themselves. If there were any Chinese rabbits afloat, they could have bought them, and it is for the sellers to show that no such rabbits were available.[109]

[108] [1915] 2 KB 379 at 388.
[109] [1975] 2 Lloyd's Rep 240 at 242.

It is common sense that a seller cannot tender documents relating to goods which either never existed in the first place or were never shipped. In *Couturier* v *Hastie*,[110] it was held that one cannot tender documents relating to lost or damaged specific goods. In *Johnson* v *Taylor Brothers Co Ltd*,[111] a Swedish seller was unable to tender documents to an English buyer because he never shipped the goods in the first place. It was held that goods must exist and must have been shipped before the seller can tender documents relating to them. Of Scrutton J's view in *Karberg* v *Blythe*, Warrington LJ said, in the Court of Appeal:

> . . . it seems to me that it is not in accordance with the facts relating to these contracts. The contracts are contracts for the sale and purchase of goods, but they are contracts which may be performed . . . by:
>
> - first, placing [the goods] on board ship; and
> - secondly, by transferring to the purchaser the shipping documents.[112]

The buyer is bound to accept documents tendered by the seller if those documents are tendered strictly in conformity with the contract. It must be apparent from the documents themselves that everything is in order. The commercial invoice, the bill of lading and the insurance policy must describe the goods in exactly the same terms as does the contract:

- the quantities must tally;
- the contract of carriage must be consistent with the contract as regards date of shipment, route, etc.; and
- the policy of insurance must accurately reflect the details of the voyage contemplated by the contract and risks which the contract stipulates that it must cover.

The buyer is entitled to insist on 'continuous documentary cover', which means that the contract of carriage must cover the whole period during which the goods are in transit, and the insurance policy must likewise cover all the normal risks that may befall the goods during the whole period from shipment to arrival. If the buyer rejects documents which are consistent with the contract (that is, conforming documents), then the seller may elect to treat this as a repudiatory breach on the part of the buyer. The seller will then be relieved from the duty of delivering the goods themselves: *Berger & Co Inc* v *Gill & Duffus SA*.[113] In this case the Court of Appeal held that the buyers were entitled to justify a wrongful rejection of the documents on the basis that the goods that finally arrived were not in conformity. The House of Lords overruled this approach as being a total contradiction of the essence of a CIF contract. The fact that the goods delivered could have been rejected on the basis of non-conformity did not, and could not retrospectively, validate a wrongful rejection of the goods. The duties in respect of acceptance of the documents and acceptance of the goods are distinct and separate.

The buyer under a CIF contract has two rights of rejection, which, as Devlin J noted in *Kwei Tek Chao*, are distinct and separate rights:

> The right to reject the documents arises when the documents are tendered and the right to reject the goods arises when they are landed and when after examination they are not found to be in conformity with the contract.[114]

---

[110] (1856) 5 HL Cas 673.
[111] [1920] AC 144.
[112] [1916] 1 KB 495 at 514.
[113] [1984] AC 382 (House of Lords).
[114] *Supra*, n. 100 at 481.

Where the defect in the documents is discovered before taking delivery of the goods the buyer is entitled to reject the consignment even though the goods had been paid for and the property in them had passed to the buyer. In *Kwei Tek Chao*, the contract of sale required delivery of the goods to be made in Hong Kong. Property in the goods passed to the buyer when he paid for them against the bills of lading. It was later discovered by the buyer that the goods had been shipped outside the shipment period. The bills of lading had been forged without the seller's complicity. Devlin J held that the buyer was entitled to reject the goods, title to which was defeasible. The argument that the buyer, when reselling the bill of lading, intended to transfer the title in the goods to the sub-purchaser was rejected by Devlin J on the basis that the buyer only had conditional property in the goods – conditional on the goods being in conformity with the contract and that, therefore, he could not have transferred more than conditional property. His Lordship also dealt with the question of whether, by dealing with the documents, the buyer had done an act inconsistent with the seller's ownership in the goods. Under s. 35 of the Sale of Goods Act, the buyer is deemed to have accepted the goods when he intimates to the seller that he has accepted them or when he does any act to the goods delivered to him that is inconsistent with the ownership of the seller. The question did not, in fact, arise in the case, but Devlin J addressed it in the interest of 'those who may be concerned'. His Lordship observed that so long as the buyer was merely dealing with the documents, he did not commit an act inconsistent with the seller's ownership in the goods and that he retained the right to reject the goods if, upon examining them after their arrival, they were found not to conform to the contract.

In *Finlay v Kwik Hoo Tong*,[115] the sellers failed to perform two specific duties:

(i)   to ship goods that matched the contract of sale; and

(ii) to tender conforming and genuine documents.

The bill of lading in fact stated inaccurately (but without fraud) that shipment had taken place within the shipment period. The buyers had accepted the documents without notice of this fact. On the strength of the documents the buyers had resold the goods to sub-purchasers, who refused to take delivery of the goods on the basis that the goods did not meet their contractual description. If the original buyers had known of the defect in the documents, they would have rejected them and avoided the falling market price in the goods. They sued the sellers to recover damages for this loss. The Court of Appeal found for the buyers. The sellers had failed to tender conforming documents and had deprived the buyers of the ability to reject them, which they would have done given the falling market rate. The buyers were awarded damages which reflected the difference between the contract price and the market price. It was also held that the computation of damages may take into account the commercial morality of a seller's conduct and a buyer's business reputation.

It should be noted that the buyer's own conduct may prevent him from rejecting either the documents or the goods. In *Panchaud Frères SA v Etablissements General Grain Co*, the issue for the Court of Appeal was if the buyer, by taking up the documents and paying against them, should be prevented from later complaining of late shipment or a defect in the documents which was apparent when the buyer accepted them. Here, shipment was to be June/July 1965. The bill of lading stated that shipment had taken place on 31 July 1965, but the certificate of quality suggested that the goods had been shipped in August. Lord Denning

---

[115] [1929] 1 KB 400.

MR was of the view that if a buyer who is entitled to reject acts in a way that leads the seller to believe that he will not rely on that breach, he cannot afterwards set it up as a ground of rejection. The court was of the opinion that the buyer should have examined the documents carefully before accepting the goods afterwards. It was held that if a buyer accepts the documents he will only be able to reject the goods for such non-conformity as would entitle a buyer to reject the goods that was not apparent on the face of the documents. If the defect was apparent on the face of the documents – as here – then the buyer would be taken to have waived his right to reject the goods for that defect. Thus, in this case the buyer was unable to reject the goods and was only entitled to claim nominal damages.

POINT OF INTEREST

Ademuni-Odeke[116] rightly makes the point that this line of thinking loses sight of a crucial fact in respect of CIF contracts, namely that it is only as a result of the risk in the goods passing to the buyer, and the bill of lading and insurance policy giving him an action against either the carrier or the policy's underwriters, that the documents assume such importance. The documents are vital only because they represent the goods.

5.5.2 The passing of property and risk

5.5.2.1 The passing of property

The property in the goods will pass when the parties intend: s. 17 of the Sale of Goods Act. We have seen that the property in unascertained goods cannot pass (s. 16) but that the buyer does now become an owner in common with the other owners: s. 20A. Once unascertained goods become ascertained (either by separation or by exhaustion), then the property passes according to the presumed intention of the parties.[117] Section 18 provides assistance in determining the parties' intention.

It will generally be unnecessary to invoke the presumptions in s. 18 when dealing with CIF sales (or international sales on other shipment terms), because the intention of the parties is usually very clear. As Chuah points out,[118] the presumed intention behind CIF contracts is that the seller is entitled to be paid if he presents conforming documents to the buyer. Thus, the presumed intention is that the property in the goods will pass upon the transfer of the documents in exchange for payment of the contract price: *Mistui & Co Ltd* v *Flota Mercante Grancolumbiana SA (The Ciudad de Pasto)*.[119] There may, however, be cases in which the courts will find that this is not the presumed intention, as, for example, in *The Albazero*.[120] In this case the sale agreement was between two companies within the same corporate group. The

---

[116] Ademuni-Odeke, *Law of International Trade* (Blackstone Press, London, 1999).
[117] Section 17 SGA 1979.
[118] J. Chuah, *Law of International Trade: Cross-Border Commercial Transactions* (4th edn, Sweet and Maxwell, London, 2009) p. 144.
[119] [1988] 2 Lloyd's Rep 208.
[120] [1977] AC 774.

issue was which company had the *locus standi* (a place of standing – the right to be heard in court or other proceeding) as owners to take action following the loss of the goods. It was held that the property in the goods had passed when the bill of lading was posted. As the sale was between allied firms, there was no serious issue as to the property passing upon payment for the goods.

It should be noted that it is not the taking out of the bill of lading in the buyer's name that indicates the seller's intention of passing the property to the buyer, but the actual transfer of that document to the buyer. Where the bill is delivered to the buyer or his agent, then the courts will presume that this is the point at which the property is to pass to the buyer, unless there is firm evidence (by, for example, a reservation of title clause) that the seller intended otherwise. In general trade practice there is an intention of reciprocity – where payment is made against the documents, then property will pass.

There may be exceptional cases where the seller releases the goods to the buyer before handing over the bill of lading to him, for example by giving the buyer a delivery order in respect of the goods being shipped.[121] This deliberate retention of the bill of lading may indicate an intention of the parties that property is not to pass on such delivery of the goods, but later when payment is made. The point should further be made that the fundamental principle should not be overlooked that the retention of title to the goods is regarded as 'security' for payment of the price. If this 'security' is furnished in another way, for example by the provision of a standby letter of credit by a reputable bank, it may well be that the court would find that the intention of the parties here is that the property is to pass when the bank issues the credit: *The Filiatra Legacy*.[122]

Where the buyer has paid against the documents but later rejects the goods, as in *Kwei Tek Chao* (above), the property in the goods returns to the seller.

5.5.2.2 The passing of risk

Section 20 of the Sale of Goods Act 1979 lays down a presumption that the risk will pass with the property in the goods. It is important to remember that s. 20 scarcely ever applies in international sale contracts. The passing of risk will, unless the parties have agreed otherwise, pass upon shipment of the goods. Thus, the risk in the goods may pass to the buyer before the property in the goods.

An important issue stems from the above: if the goods are shipped and a clean bill of lading is issued and the seller makes a correct tender of the documents, the buyer must pay the purchase price even if the goods have, subsequent to the clean bill of lading having been signed, become lost or damaged: *Manbré Saccharine Co v Corn Products Co*.[123] The buyer now bears the risk of this damage to the goods and must claim against the insurance for the goods, or claim against the carrier on the bill of lading contract. We saw above in section 5.2 in looking at the matrix of contracts, that the bill of lading becomes a contract of carriage when it is transferred to the CIF buyer, who thus becomes the consignee in carriage terms. The bill of lading is his contract of carriage.

---

[121] C. Murray, G. Dixon, D. Holloway and D. Timson-Hunt, *Schmitthoff: Export Trade: The Law and Practice of International Trade* (11th edn, Sweet and Maxwell, London, 2007).
[122] [1991] 2 Lloyd's Rep 337.
[123] [1919] 1 KB 465.

It can be seen from the above that the CIF buyer may bear the risk in the goods even though he does not have the property. Where the seller reserves the title in the goods (s. 19 of the Sale of Goods Act) the buyer will have no proprietary interest in the goods: s. 20A of the Act only applies to unascertained goods. This will mean that the buyer will be unable to bring an action in the tort of negligence against anyone who damages the goods (for example, stevedores during the discharge of the goods) before he has received possession of them.

5.6 FOB contracts

5.6.1 The nature of FOB contracts

The FOB contract is the second of the two 'classic' export-sale contracts. Where the seller sells 'free on board', he undertakes to place the goods on board a ship that has been named to him by the buyer and that is berthed at the agreed port of shipment. All charges incurred up to and including the delivery of the goods on board ship have to be borne by the seller. The buyer has to pay all subsequent charges, such as the stowage of the goods in or on board ship, freight and marine insurance, as well as unloading charges, import duties, consular fees and other incidental charges due on arrival of the consignment in the port of destination.

There are three types of FOB contract, which were described by Devlin J in *Pyrene Co Ltd* v *Scindia Navigation Co Ltd* as follows:

> The FOB contract has become a flexible instrument. In . . . the classic type . . . the buyer's duty is to nominate the ship, and the seller's to put the goods on board for account of the buyer and procure a bill of lading in terms usual in the trade. In such a case the seller is directly a party to the contract of carriage at least until he takes out the bill of lading in the buyer's name. Probably the classic type is based on the assumption that the ship nominated will be willing to load any goods brought down to the berth or at least those of which she is notified. Under present conditions, when space often has to be booked well in advance, the contract of carriage comes into existence at an earlier point of time. Sometimes the seller is asked to make the necessary arrangements; and the contract may then provide for his taking the bill of lading in his own name and obtaining payment against the transfer, as in a CIF contract. Sometimes the buyer engages his own forwarding agent at the port of loading to book space and to procure the bill of lading; if freight has to be paid in advance this method may be the most convenient. In such a case the seller discharges his duty by putting the goods on board, getting the mate's receipt and handing it to the forwarding agent to enable him to obtain the bill of lading. The present case belongs to this third type; and it is only in this type, I think, that any doubt can arise about the seller being a party to the contract.[124]

The variant of FOB contract which was used in *Pyrene* v *Scindia* is generally referred to as the 'strict' FOB. The seller in this case had no function in the making of the contract of carriage, whether as agent for the buyer or as principal. The buyer nominated the ship. Devlin J held, however, that although the seller was not party to the contract of carriage, he did 'participate' in this contract so far as it affected him. Thus, his Lordship held that the seller was able to sue the carriers in respect of damage to the goods caused by the carrier before the goods

---

[124] [1954] 2 QB 402 at 424.

crossed the ship's rail. Devlin J's view that the sellers 'participated' in the contract of carriage is difficult to understand, since it was clear that his Lordship did not consider that he was bound by all of its terms – his 'participation' in the contract was partial, and it is hard to see what consideration could have passed from the seller to the carrier. Sealy and Hooley suggest an alternative form of reasoning which may be easier to accept, *viz* that the seller's participation was in fact along the lines of a collateral contract to the carriage contract.[125]

His Lordship found it to be an 'irresistible' conclusion that it was the intention of all parties that the seller should participate in the contract of affreightment so far as it affected him. The key to understanding his Lordship's view is probably this: if one manages to argue that the seller was part of the contract of carriage, and could, therefore, sue the carrier on that contract, it goes without saying that the carrier would then be able to limit his liability by reliance upon a limitation clause in the contract of carriage. This, in effect, leaves everyone happy. The seller now has a remedy against someone in contract, and the defendant under that contract has the ability to limit his liability. This helps to 'spread' liabilities and to keep international freight rates down. Time and again, this idea of 'loss spreading' reveals itself as an underlying policy concern of the courts. This concern, for example, was expressed strongly by Lord Denning in his dissenting judgment in *Scrutton Ltd* v *Midlands Silicones Ltd*.[126]

5.6.2 The three variants of the FOB contract

5.6.2.1 The 'classic' FOB

The first variant of the FOB contract identified by Devlin J in *Pyrene* v *Scindia* is the 'classic' FOB. Here, the seller puts the goods on board a ship nominated by the buyer. The seller is considered as being directly a party to the contract of carriage, at least until he indorses the bill of lading in favour of the buyer. The seller, on behalf of the buyer, receives the bill of lading from the carrier. The bill of lading may show the seller as consignee – enabling him at this point to sue on the contract of carriage. This bill of lading will be to the seller's 'order' (which means that it can be indorsed in favour of another party). The seller will then indorse the bill of lading in favour of the buyer.

Prima facie, the seller who procures a bill of lading by which the goods are deliverable to himself is deemed to have reserved the title in those goods, under s. 19(2) of the Sale of Goods Act. Whether or not the seller did intend to reserve the title in the goods is a question of intention. Did the seller, by taking the bill of lading in his own favour, intend to leave himself free to allocate the goods to another contract or did he intend to retain constructive possession of the goods (as if he still had possession, notwithstanding that the carrier has actual possession), allowing property to pass but subject to the seller's right of lien and stoppage in transit (see section 5.7.1.1)? The presumption under s. 19(2) can be rebutted by the seller sending to the buyer a notice of appropriation pursuant to the contract of sale. Alternatively, the bill of lading may be made out to the buyer, with the seller shown as the consignor. In this case, s. 19(2) does not apply. Where the seller is named as consignor,

---

[125] L. S. Sealy and R. J. A. Hooley, *Commercial Law: Text, Cases and Materials* (4th edn, Oxford University Press, Oxford, 2008).
[126] [1962] AC 466.

he 'participates' in the contract of carriage at least until he transfers the bill of lading to the buyer.

- The duties of the classic FOB seller:
  - to ensure that goods which in all respects match the requirements of the contract of sale are available at the port of loading, and to ship those goods free on board;
  - to pay all handling and transport charges in connection with delivering the goods to the port of loading for shipment across the ship's rail;
  - to complete all declarations required by HM Revenue & Customs.
- The duties of the classic FOB buyer:
  - to decide the date within the agreed shipment period when the goods are to be loaded;
  - to obtain space on a vessel that is fit to carry the contract goods;
  - to allow the seller enough time to get the goods to port by issuing a valid nomination of the vessel and the date when the vessel will be ready to collect;
  - to make a second nomination substituting the original vessel if there is sufficient time for loading and the seller is given reasonable notice.

5.6.2.2 The 'extended' FOB

The second variant is the FOB contract with additional services. Here, the seller is asked to make the necessary arrangements for the shipment of the goods and, in this sense, he acts as shipper. The contract made between the seller and the buyer may provide for the seller to take the bill of lading in his own name. In this case, the buyer is named as consignee. The seller then transfers the bill of lading (together with the other shipping documents) to the buyer and obtains payment against transfer, as in a CIF contract. Whether in booking space the seller acts as principal or as the buyer's agent depends upon the contract. However, it is important to understand that in neither case is the seller himself necessarily responsible for the freight. If he is not and the carrier refuses to accept the goods until freight has been paid, the seller need not proceed to load the goods until he is put in funds by the buyer. Whether or not the seller is responsible for the freight will depend upon the terms of the contract. Where the seller acts as the agent of the buyer, the buyer is always privy to the contract of carriage, notwithstanding that the seller may be named as the shipper/consignor of the goods. In this latter case, the seller 'participates' in the contract of carriage at least until he transfers the bill of lading to the buyer.

Another name for this variant is the 'extended' FOB. It differs from the classic FOB in two essential respects.

- First, where the seller makes the contract of carriage as principal, the buyer is not a party to that contract unless he becomes so by operation of the Carriage of Goods by Sea Act 1992 (that is, if and when the buyer is the 'lawful holder' of the bill of lading).
- Second, it is the seller who nominates the ship. The extension of the seller's duty may include an obligation to procure insurance (under a separate invoice). As we have seen, the seller may also be responsible for the freight. In such cases, the difference between this type of FOB contract and a CIF contract will simply be in the computation of the price.

5.6.2.3 The 'strict' FOB

The third variant is the 'strict' FOB contract (as used in *Pyrene v Scindia*, above). Here, the shipping arrangements are made by the buyer or the buyer's forwarding agent. The buyer books space on a particular ship. The seller discharges his duty under the contract of sale by putting the goods on board, getting the mate's receipt, shipping certificate or standard shipping note and handing it to the forwarding agent to enable him to obtain the bill of lading. In a strict FOB, as the seller does not contract to arrange for the carriage of the goods, he fulfils his contractual obligation if he furnishes some document other than a bill of lading – for example, some document, such as a mate's receipt, shipping receipt or standard shipping note, that enables the buyer to obtain a bill of lading. The seller 'participates' in the carriage contract until he hands over the shipping document to the buyer.

Devlin J's division of the FOB contract into the three variants above was approved by the Court of Appeal in *The El Amria and The El Minia*.[127] Devlin J's ability to find that the seller 'participated' in the contract of carriage was also approved. Donaldson LJ was of the opinion that in 'this latter type the buyer is a party to the contract of carriage *ab initio*'.[128]

Although the courts are quite clear that the above variants do exist and appear happy to use the above classifications, there does seem to be some confusion in their use of terminology. In *The Al Hofuf*,[129] an FOB clause used in the oil trade was in issue. Mocatta J referred to the clause as being of the 'classic' type, but it is more likely that in fact the clause fell into the category of 'strict' FOB contracts described above. (Schmitthoff uses the classifications of 'strict' and 'classic' synonymously and, in describing what is generally considered to be a 'strict' FOB, uses a novel classification, namely 'fob contract (buyer contracting with carrier)'.[130]) We should perhaps approach FOB contracts with a flexible attitude and, like the courts and academics, not be too concerned about their precise classification – it should be remembered that Devlin's real aim in setting out the FOB variants was to justify circumventing the privity rule so that the seller could be construed as being in the contract of carriage. In international trade terms, it is considered essential that this approach is taken – if the seller is not part of the contract, the carrier will not be able to rely upon the limitation clauses in that contract. All jurisdictions recognise the importance of carrier limitation: it is very difficult for a claimant to 'break' limitation because the courts take the view that without limitation the balance of international trade will be distorted. It is considered better that all parties to the shipping adventure bear some of the risk, in financial terms (hence the importance of proper insurance!) One could say that international trade is really as much about risk management as the law. Being aware of this may help to understand some of the difficult judicial decisions that arise in international trade law. The law is often applied or developed creatively in order to allow the courts to come to a decision that facilitates trade. In *Pyrene v Scindia*, the seller in fact attempted to sue the carrier in negligence, saying that he was not privy to the contract of carriage and that, therefore, the carrier could not rely upon the limitation clauses in the contract. Devlin rejected this argument finding, as we know, that the seller had 'participated' in the contract.

---

[127] [1982] 2 Lloyd's Rep 28.
[128] *Ibid.*, at 32.
[129] [1981] 1 Lloyd's Rep 81.
[130] *Supra* n. 122 at 20.

> **ISSUE BOX**
>
> We should be careful to examine when Devlin J's 'three variants' of the FOB contract will be either a relevant or necessary consideration. To be clear when the issue is relevant we should examine Devlin's desired outcome from his analysis of this type of contract: to ensure that the carrier will be in a *bill of lading contract* with the shipper, so as to justify an outcome of that contract being governed by the Hague (or, today, the Hague-Visby) Rules and affording the carrier a known limitation and the cargo interest a minimum level of protection by the carrier's carelessness.
>
> That the carrier should be able to avail himself of a limitation of liability regime seems a consistent thread running through post-Hague Rules cases: that the carrier in *The Aliakmon* may not have been able to limit if sued in negligence does appear to have influenced Lord Brandon, as shown by his concern that this claim might arise outside the protection normally afforded to shipping contracts by the Hague regimes.[131]

Unless the contract says otherwise, it will generally be assumed that the FOB contract in question is the 'strict' one. The common law 'strict' FOB is certainly the type of FOB contract envisaged in Incoterms. Thus, under the FOB buyer's obligations in Incoterms 2000, clause B3 provides quite clearly that the buyer must contract at his own expense for all of the carriage of the goods from the named port of shipment. A further common variant is to add words such as:

- 'stowed' (FOBS);
- 'trimmed' (FOBT); or
- 'stowed and trimmed' (FOBST).

These extend the seller's obligations beyond the point of putting the goods over the ship's rail. These terms are price terms in that the seller has to perform the additional duties at his own expense.

What is apparent is that the FOB contract is inherently flexible, making it suitable for variants. Where the contract is governed by English law, common to all three variants are the general duties imposed by the Sale of Goods Act 1979, subject to the expressed terms of the contract. Hence, the seller must deliver to the buyer goods which conform with the contract description and with the implied terms as to the quality, fitness and (if relevant) sample. He must make his delivery within the time specified and must comply with all other obligations imposed by the contract within the time specified or, if no time is specified, within a reasonable time. The buyer must accept the goods at the point of delivery and pay the price in the manner required by the contract at the time stated.

5.6.3 The passing of property and risk

As under a CIF contract, where an FOB contract is used, the property in the goods will pass in accordance with the intention of the parties. The passing of property is a general sales law

---

[131] This suggestion is made notwithstanding the recognition that his Lordship was undoubtedly also concerned in this case to rein in the liberal approach adopted towards claims in negligence for pure economic loss in *Junior Books v Veitchi* [1983] 1 AC 520.

issue and has no special relevance in the context of international sales contracts. As Staughton LJ explained in *The Ciudad de Pasto*:

> The expression FOB determines how the goods shall be delivered, how much of the expense shall be borne by the sellers, and when risk of loss or damage shall pass to the buyers. It does not necessarily decide when property is to pass.[132]

In an FOB contract, it will generally be presumed that the parties intend the property in the goods to pass when the buyer makes payment against conforming documents.

The general rule in relation to the passing of risk is that risk of damage to or loss of the goods will normally pass to the buyer on shipment of the goods. The risk will remain with the seller, however, if he has not complied with the requirements of s. 32(3) of the Sale of Goods Act 1979, which provides:

> Unless otherwise agreed, where goods are sent by the seller to the buyer by a route involving sea transit, under circumstances in which it is usual to insure, the seller must give such notice to the buyer as may enable him to insure them during their sea transit, and if the seller fails to do so, the goods are at his risk during sea transit.

There has been some speculation as to whether or not it might be said that in fact the risk in goods under an FOB contract passes not at the point when the goods cross the ship's rail, but when they have been deposited safely on board and the loading operation is complete. Some authority for this argument might be found in Devlin J's judgment in *Pyrene* v *Scindia*, where he expressed the view that to consider the risk passing at the precise moment that the goods crossed the ship's rail was outdated. His Lordship said:

> . . . the division of loading into two parts is suited to more antiquated methods of loading than are now generally adopted and the ship's rail has lost much of its nineteenth-century significance. Only the most enthusiastic lawyer could watch with satisfaction the spectacle of liabilities shifting uneasily as the cargo sways at the end of a derrick across a notional perpendicular projecting from the ship's rail.[133]

With respect, this argument is hard to justify. The notion of the 'ship's rail' is very much alive in the international trade world. It is a concept to which traders very frequently refer. Also, if we look at the buyer's obligations in Incoterms 2000 in respect of the transfer of risks (clause B5), we will see that the risk will pass, in the absence of any other express stipulation in the contract, when the goods cross the ship's rail. B5 provides:

> The buyer must bear all risks of loss or damage to the goods from the time they have passed the ship's rail at the named port of shipment.

5.7 Remedies

In this penultimate section we consider the remedies available to the parties where a breach of an international sale contract occurs.

---

[132] *Supra*, n. 120 at 213.
[133] *Supra*, n. 125 at 419.

5.7.1 Remedies available to the seller

There are two types of remedy available to sellers in international sale contracts:

1. 'real' remedies;
2. 'personal' remedies.

5.7.1.1 Real remedies

Where the buyer defaults in his primary obligation, that is, in payment of the price, the seller can, of course, sue for damages, that is, the seller can bring a personal claim on the contract. In complex mercantile arrangements, however, this may not always be appropriate and the seller's right to do so may not provide him with the best remedy. The law, therefore, has developed a number of what are termed 'real' rights and remedies, under which the seller can look to the *goods* as a kind of security for payment of the price. These rights and remedies are considered in turn below.

Lien for the price and right of resale

The unpaid seller's right of *lien* is his right, if he is in possession of the goods, to *retain possession of them until the price is paid*: s. 41(1) of the Sale of Goods Act 1979. This right arises under s. 41(1) where:

- the goods have been sold without any stipulation as to credit; or
- the goods have been sold on credit but the term of credit has expired; or
- the buyer has become insolvent.

The lien will come to an end (that is, the unpaid seller will lose the right to retain the goods) if he delivers the goods to, *inter alia*, a carrier, unless he has specifically reserved to himself the right to dispose of the goods: s. 43(1).

The seller's right of lien is merely a right to retain the goods until the purchase price is paid – it is *not* a right to sell them. The Sale of Goods Act 1979 does, however, under s. 48(3), give the unpaid seller the right to resell the goods where:

- the goods are of a perishable nature; or
- the goods are not perishable, but the unpaid seller gives notice to the buyer of his intention to resell and the buyer does not within a reasonable time pay or tender the price.

Where the unpaid seller does resell the goods under s. 48(3), he may still recover damages from the buyer for any outstanding loss occasioned by the buyer's breach.

Stoppage in transit

Sections 44 to 46 of the Sale of Goods Act 1979 set out the right of the unpaid seller to stop the goods while they are in transit to the buyer, before they have actually reached the buyer. (It should be noted that the Latin phrase *in transitu* was used in the Sale of Goods Act 1893, because it was a term understood in the trade at that time. The anglicised terminology was introduced in the 1979 Act.)

Section 44 provides that the seller may exercise this remedy where the buyer 'becomes insolvent'. Section 61 of the Act deems the buyer to be 'insolvent' for these purposes if he has either ceased to pay his debts in the ordinary course of business or he cannot pay his debts as they become due. The right of stoppage is of much greater practical value to the seller than the right of lien, particularly since the provisions of ss. 44 to 46 have usually been interpreted by the courts favourably for the seller.

The stoppage in transit operates as if the seller had simply reached out to the goods on the carrying vessel and taken them back. The right of stoppage can only be used when the goods are in transit. The seller may assume possession of the goods which are in transit by giving notice to the carrier. The unpaid seller has the right to resell the goods and will pass a good title to the new buyer, subject, of course, to s. 47(2). However, if, under s. 48(1), the buyer is entitled to tender the money after the goods have been stopped in transit (before the seller has resold them) and order that the goods be delivered to him, it might be more sensible to think of the goods as being the 'buyer's' goods, that is, to suppose that the buyer has retained the property throughout the relevant period.

Confusingly, *both* views are correct. The seller can resell the goods and pass on a good title to the new buyer *and* the buyer, before the seller resells the goods, can pay up and demand the goods. It might well be observed that, in developing the remedy of stoppage in transit, the legal niceties of property law appear to have been entirely dispensed with for the convenience of commerce!

A 'retention of title' clause

Section 19 of the Sale of Goods Act 1979 allows the seller to reserve the title in the goods until certain conditions are fulfilled by the buyer. A retention of title clause is commonly known as a 'Romalpa clause', because of the case from which the clause takes its name: *Aluminium Industrie Vaassen BV v Romalpa Aluminium Ltd.*[134] Such a clause must, of course, be incorporated into the parties' contract by the seller at the time when the contract is made. Thus, the retention of title clause might be thought of as a 'risk prevention' measure by the seller, rather than as a remedy which the law makes available upon breach by the buyer.

The simple retention of title clause must be distinguished from a security agreement, which is not subject to the rules of sale of goods and must be registered under the Companies Acts where the transaction involves a company. The House of Lords addressed this issue in *Armour v Thyssen Edelstahlwerk AG,*[135] here it was argued that the retention of title clause was in reality a right to security in the form of a security agreement (or charge) over the buyer's property. Had this argument succeeded, the clause would have been ineffective. The House of Lords rejected the argument, however, on the basis that a simple provision reserving title to the seller until all payments and debts due to him were forthcoming did not amount to a charge. In this case, the German sellers successfully claimed to have retained title to steel sold and delivered to a Scottish company. It was held that a retention of title clause in standard form was effective (in respect of the goods in question, which were identifiable) in Scottish law.

[134] [1976] 2 All ER 552.
[135] [1991] 2 AC 339.

5.7.1.2 **Personal remedies**

The seller's personal remedies are the actions he may bring against the buyer for financial compensation. There are two such actions: an action for the price of the goods sold and an action for damages for non-acceptance, both of which are discussed below. The distinction between an action for the price and an action for damages is of considerable importance. In purely monetary terms, there will usually be a substantial difference between the price of the goods and damages for non-acceptance.

Mitigation

The general rule under English law is that the injured party must mitigate the loss that he will suffer as a result of the other party's breach of contract. The doctrine of mitigation places a duty on the victim of a breach of contract to attempt to secure an alternative performance of the obligations owed to him by the defendant under the contract. The innocent party is, thus, under a duty to take all reasonable steps to mitigate the damage. This principle applies to all contracts governed by English law and it applies equally whether the innocent party is the buyer or the seller. In practice, breach of contract often leads to some attempt between the parties of a negotiation of a settlement or a finding of some alternative way of performance of the contract. The doctrine of mitigation generally requires the innocent party to accept reasonable offers of alternative performance or negotiation of settlement. If he does not, then the amount of damages that he can recover may be reduced. In *The Solholt*, the defendants breached a contract to build and deliver a ship by delivering late.[136] The claimants refused late delivery at the contract price. They sued the defendants but recovered no damages because the court held that it would have been reasonable for them to mitigate their loss by accepting late delivery as offered by the defendants at the contract price.

It can be seen that the doctrine of mitigation restricts the innocent party's scope for opportunistic behaviour if the contract is breached. The doctrine does, therefore, effectively protect the position of the defendant, by forcing the innocent party to secure the next best alternative on the open market.

In the context of the sale of goods, it is important to note that if the property in the goods has passed to the buyer and the seller is entitled to sue for the price, the established view is that the seller is under no obligation to mitigate his loss by attempting to resell the goods to another party, where this option is possible. In legal terms, it is as if the seller refuses to repudiate the contract because of the buyer's breach and simply carries on with the contract, that is, by seeking the price rather than the return of the goods. This analysis is in line with the leading House of Lords' case of *White & Carter (Councils) Ltd* v *McGregor*, that the innocent claimant's right to repudiate or to treat the contract as intact prevails over his duty to mitigate. Reaction to this decision has been mixed.[137] Indeed, in the case itself, Lord Keith gave one of two dissenting judgments, saying that such a result was not:

> . . . in my opinion, in accordance with principal authority, and cuts across the rule that where one party is in breach of contract the other must take steps to minimise the loss sustained by the breach.[138]

---

[136] [1983] 1 Lloyd's Rep 605.
[137] [1962] AC 413.
[138] *Ibid.* at 442.

White & Carter has subsequently been distinguished, unsurprisingly in 'shipping contract' cases where the Commercial Court and the Court of Appeal seem intent upon arriving at 'commercially just' decisions. In *Attica Sea Carriers* v *Ferrostaal* (a case concerning a demise charter, that is, a contract between a shipowner and a charterer, under which the charterer takes over the entire management of the ship), Lord Denning was of the opinion that *White & Carter* should not be followed except in a case which was on all fours with it.[139] His Lordship said that *White & Carter*:

> ... has no application whatever in a case where the plaintiff ought in all reason to accept the repudiation and sue for damages – provided that damages would provide an adequate remedy for any loss suffered by him.[140]

An important departure from *White & Carter* can be seen by the judgment of Lloyd J in *The Alaskan Trader* (another charterparty dispute). Lloyd J said:

> ... there comes a point at which the court will cease, on general equitable principles, to allow the innocent party to enforce his contract according to its strict legal terms. How one defines that point is obviously a matter of some difficulty for it involves drawing a line between conduct which is merely unreasonable ... and conduct which is *wholly* unreasonable ... But however difficult it may be to define the point, that there *is* such a point seems to me to have been accepted ...[141]

We cannot, however, be certain that any one particular court will adopt this approach in *The Odenfeld* (yet another charterparty dispute!). Kerr J distinguished *Attica Sea Carriers* and considered that only in such extreme cases would *White & Carter* not apply.[142]

Interestingly, in the United States, under s. 2-709(1)(b) of the Uniform Commercial Code, the seller of goods may only recover their price if he is:

> ... unable after reasonable effort to resell them at a reasonable price or the circumstances reasonably indicate that such effort will be unavailing.

An action for the price

The seller's right to bring an action for the price is provided for in s. 49 of the Sale of Goods Act 1979. This right arises in two specified situations:

1. where, under the contract, the property in the goods has passed to the buyer and he wrongfully neglects or refuses to pay for the goods according to the terms of the contract (s. 49(1)); and

2. where, under the contract, the price is payable on a certain day irrespective of delivery, and the buyer wrongfully neglects or refuses to pay the price (s. 49(2)).

Damages for non-acceptance

The seller may bring an action against the buyer for damages for non-acceptance when the buyer has wrongfully neglected to accept and pay for the goods: s. 50(1) of the Sale of Goods Act 1979. The measure of damages is the estimated loss arising directly and naturally, in the ordinary course of events, from the buyer's breach. This can be recognised as the rule

---

[139] [1976] 1 Lloyd's Rep 250.
[140] *Ibid.* at 651.
[141] [1983] 2 Lloyd's Rep 654 at 651.
[142] [1978] 2 Lloyd's Rep 357.

of 'remoteness', deriving from the well-known case of *Hadley v Baxendale*.[143] It is embodied in s. 50(2).

Section 50 goes on to set out a formula for the assessment of damages, known as the 'market price' rule. Section 50(3) provides:

> Where there is an available market for the goods in question the measure of damages is *prima facie* to be ascertained by the difference between the contract price and the market or current price at the time or times when the goods ought to have been accepted or (if no time was fixed for acceptance) at the time of the refusal to accept.

Section 50(3) will apply only if there is an 'available market' for the goods in question. Jenkins LJ suggested a definition for the term 'market' in *Charter v Sullivan*:

> I doubt if there can be an available market for particular goods in any sense relevant to s. 50(3) of the Sale of Goods Act, 1893, unless those goods are available for sale in the market at the market or current price in the sense of the price, whatever it may be, fixed by reference to supply and demand as the price at which a purchaser for the goods in question can be found, be it greater or less than or equal to the contract price.[144]

Section 50(3) makes it clear that the relevant market price is that available at the time of the failure or refusal to accept. The case law shows that the courts will use as a benchmark the price prevailing on the market at a relevant *place*. Thus, in *Muller, MacLean & Co v Leslie & Anderson*, damages were awarded to the seller based on the market price in India at the time of the ship's arrival.[145] In this case, the contract was for a consignment of padlocks FOB New York, to be shipped to India. The buyers wrongly refused to accept the shipping documents after the goods had been shipped.

Where there is an *anticipatory repudiation* of the contract by the buyer (for example, the buyer, before the time when he is due to accept the goods, informs the seller that he does not intend to do so) and where this anticipatory repudiation is accepted by the seller, damages are *prima facie* to be assessed by reference to the market price at the time when the goods ought to have been accepted, that is, at the time fixed for delivery by the contract: see s. 50(3). The seller's duty to mitigate his loss, however, may well place him under an obligation to resell the goods as soon as possible after he has accepted the buyer's repudiation. This will certainly happen, for example, where the buyer's repudiation occurs against the background of a falling market. Of course, the seller is not obliged to accept the repudiation and where he does not, he will be under no duty to mitigate until the actual breach occurs (that is, at the time when the buyer ought to have accepted the goods): *Tredegar Iron & Coal Co Ltd v Hawthorn Bros & Co.*[146]

5.7.2 Remedies available to the buyer

5.7.2.1 Goods which do not correspond to description or quality

If the seller delivers or tenders goods which do not conform with the contract description, whether as regards quantity or quality, it is likely that the buyer will be able to reject them.

---

[143] (1854) 9 Exch 341.
[144] [1957] 2 QB 117 at 128.
[145] (1921) 8 Lloyd's Rep 328.
[146] (1902) 18 TLR 716.

As we noted earlier, however, s. 15A of the Sale of Goods Act 1979 has modified the buyer's right to repudiate for breach of the seller's obligations under ss. 13, 14 or 15.

5.7.2.2 Goods delivered in the wrong quantity

Where the seller has delivered goods in the wrong quantity, the buyer has a choice of remedies, as set out in s. 30 of the Sale of Goods Act 1979:

(1) in the case of a short delivery, the buyer may reject the goods or accept them and pay at the contract rate (s. 30(1)) (that is, pay for the goods according to the contract price *pro rata* for the quantity actually delivered);

(2) in the case of an excessive delivery, the buyer may reject all of the goods, or accept the contract quantity and reject the rest, or accept all the goods and pay for the excess at the contract rate.

In the same way that s. 15A modifies the buyer's right to repudiate for a breach of the implied conditions under the Sale of Goods Act 1979, s. 30(2A) (which was also introduced by the Sale and Supply of Goods Act 1994) provides for similar modifications of the right of a buyer, in a non-consumer contract, to reject goods delivered in the wrong quantity. Thus, where the shortfall or the excess is so slight that it would be unreasonable for the buyer to reject, he will not be entitled to do so. Under s. 30(2B) it is for the seller to show that a shortfall or excess falls within sub-s. (2A).

5.7.2.3 Restrictions on the buyer's right to reject the goods

We have already noted the limitations on the right to reject imposed by s. 15A and s. 30(2A). Here, it should be noted that the buyer must be careful when accepting the documents, lest he act in any way which disentitles him to later reject the goods. If the buyer accepts documents which contain an apparent defect, then he will be taken to have waived his right to reject the goods which do not conform to the contract of sale, by virtue of the defect apparent in the documents. In such a case, the buyer will only be able to reject the goods for non-conformity if the defect in the goods was not apparent on the face of the documents: *Panchaud Frères* v *Etablissements General Grain Co.*[147]

5.7.2.4 The seller's right to 'cure' a defective tender of goods

A seller will normally have the right to 'cure' a defective tender of goods, if this can be done within the time allowed by the contract and if this is not otherwise inconsistent with the contract. The seller will not, of course, be able to 'cure' the defective tender if the goods were specific goods or if they have been 'unconditionally appropriated' to the contract by a notice of appropriation communicated to the buyer.

In *Borrowman Phillips & Co* v *Free & Hollis*, the buyers contracted to buy a cargo of American maize, to be shipped between 15 May and 30 June.[148] The sellers attempted to deliver maize which was on the *Charles Platt*, but were unable to secure documents relating to the goods. Following an arbitrator's finding that the tender was not acceptable, the sellers made a second tender of goods on board the *Maria D* and of the documents relating to that consignment.

[147] [1970] 1 Lloyd's Rep 53.
[148] (1878) 4 QBD 500.

The buyers rejected the second tender on the ground that the sellers were not entitled, under the contract, to substitute other goods for those represented by the first tender. The Court of Appeal, however, held that the sellers were entitled to make a second tender of documents and goods meeting the contract description, so long as time permitted and so long as the second tender was not inconsistent with the contract – the contract did not bind the sellers to deliver goods on board the *Charles Platt*. The buyers, therefore, had to pay damages for non-acceptance of the goods and documents. The crucial point in this case, as pointed out by Brett LJ, was that the sellers had not insisted upon the first tender (that is, they had not insisted that the buyers must accept it), which left them free to make a corrective tender so long as there was time to do so.

5.7.2.5 Instalment contracts

Under s. 31, the buyer is not bound to accept delivery of the goods by instalments unless the contract specifically provides for instalments: Sale of Goods Act 1979, s. 31(1).

Where the contract is for goods to be delivered by stated instalments, which are to be separately paid for, and the seller makes defective deliveries in respect of one or more of these instalments – or if the buyer neglects or refuses to take delivery of or pay for one or more instalments – it is a question in each case, depending on the terms of the contract and the circumstances of the case, whether the breach of contract entitles the buyer to repudiate the whole contract or it is a 'severable breach' which will entitle the buyer only to claim compensation but not to treat the contract as a whole as being at an end: s. 30(2).

5.7.2.6 The buyer's action for non-delivery

The buyer's right to sue the seller for damages for non-delivery closely parallels the seller's action for damages for non-acceptance. Section 51 of the Sale of Goods Act 1979 provides:

(1) Where the seller wrongfully neglects or refuses to deliver the goods to the buyer, the buyer may maintain an action against the seller for damages for non-delivery.

(2) The measure of damages is the estimated loss directly and actually resulting, in the ordinary course of events, from the seller's breach of contract.

(3) Where there is an available market for the goods in question the measure of damages is *prima facie* to be ascertained by the difference between the contract price and the market or current price of the goods at the time or times when they ought to have been delivered or (if no time was fixed) at the time of the refusal to deliver.

5.7.2.7 The buyer's action for late delivery

This issue has to be determined by ordinary contractual principles, as the Act makes no provision relating to the assessment of damages when the seller fails to deliver the goods on the due date, but the buyer accepts them when they are actually delivered.

5.7.2.8 Specific performance

Section 52(1) empowers the court, in an action by a buyer for breach of contract for failure to deliver *specific or ascertained goods*, to order that the contract be specifically performed. This deprives the seller of the option of retaining the goods on payment of damages. It should be noted that although the Act provides statutory authority for the remedy of specific performance, this remedy is an equitable remedy and can only be granted if the court is of the opinion that in all the circumstances of the case it is just and fair to do so. Indeed, s. 52(1) provides for this discretion on the part of the court, stating that the court may award specific performance 'if it thinks fit'. The court will not generally exercise its discretion under s. 52 if the contract is concerned with goods of ordinary description which the buyer intends to resell, nor where damages would enable substitutes to be bought on the market. In *Howard Perry Ltd* v *British Railways Board*, the court, when making an interlocutory order for delivery up (an analogous interim order to that of specific performance) of 500 tons of steel, appeared to accept that procuring substitute goods would have been difficult and would have caused such delay that the plaintiff's business would have been seriously disrupted.[149]

Will specific performance be ordered in respect of 'commercially unique' goods? This appears to be a term coined by Treitel.[150] It is interesting that in *Cohen* v *Roche*, the court refused to award the remedy of delivery up in relation to a sale for 'eight genuine Hepplewhite chairs'.[151] One would have thought these to be 'commercially unique', especially in the eyes of the buyer! Until recently, no case could be cited confidently in support of specific performance being ordered on this ground, although in *Behnke* v *Bede Shipping Co Ltd*, the court did order specific performance of a contract to sell a ship.[152] Wright J appeared to regard it as relevant that the buyer needed it immediately for the purposes of his business and that the ship was of 'peculiar and practically unique value to the plaintiff'.

Commercial uniqueness as a ground for specific performance was controversially accepted in *Sky Petroleum Ltd* v *VIP Petroleum Ltd*.[153] Here, an interim injunction amounting to temporary specific performance was granted to enforce the supply of petrol to the plaintiffs' filling stations at a time when the petrol market was in such an unusual state that the plaintiffs would be unlikely to find an alternative supply and as a result would be forced to stop trading. The decision was particularly radical because petrol is not even 'specific or ascertained' goods within s. 52 of the Sale of Goods Act 1979. Goulding J did indicate, in awarding the injunction, that he was departing from the 'general rule' in order to preserve the position under the contract until a later date.

It is noteworthy here that the United States' Uniform Commercial Code, in para. 2-716(1), has sought to encourage acceptance of the notion of 'commercial uniqueness' in relation to goods that are not specific or ascertained.

5.7.2.9 Damages for breach of warranty

Section 53 sets out a series of propositions about the buyer's remedies where there has been a breach of warranty by the seller or where the buyer has elected (or is compelled) to treat a breach of condition as a breach of warranty.

The test for the measure of damages again echoes the rule in *Hadley* v *Baxendale*, that is, the damages will be the estimated loss directly and naturally arising, in the ordinary course of events, from the breach of warranty (s. 53(2)).

---

[149] [1980] 1 WLR 1375.
[150] H. G. Treitel, 'Specific Performance in the Sale of Goods' [1966] *JBL* 21 at p. 215.
[151] [1927] 1 KB 169.
[152] [1927] 1 KB 649.
[153] [1974] 1 WLR 576.

Where there is an available market, the measure of damages for breach of a warranty of quality is *prima facie* the difference between the value of the goods at the time they were delivered to the buyer and the value they would have had if they had fulfilled the warranty (s. 53(3)).

Consequential losses for breach of warranty are assessed on ordinary contractual principles: see *H Parson (Livestock) Ltd* v *Uttley Ingham & Co Ltd*.[154]

5.7.2.10 Claims for special loss

In addition to the seller's right to sue for the price, or for damages for non-acceptance, he may also have the right to claim 'special damages'. Section 54 provides that:

> Nothing in this Act affects the right of the buyer or the seller to recover interest or special damages in any case where by law interest or special damages may be recoverable . . .

We have seen when discussing the issue of damages, that the Sale of Goods Act echoes the rule in *Hadley* v *Baxendale*, that is, the damages will be the estimated loss directly and naturally arising, in the ordinary course of events, from the breach of contract. This is sometimes referred to as the 'first limb' of the rule in *Hadley* v *Baxendale*. The 'second limb' deals with 'special damages'. In *Victoria Laundry* v *Newman*, the Court of Appeal held that special damages or loss related to that loss which ought reasonably to have been in the contemplation of both parties, when they entered into the contract, as the probable result of the breach of that contract.[155]

In difficult cases involving the question of assessment of damages, the courts will have regard to 'well-established trading patterns' when calculating damages. The court will also have regard to the level of the parties' sophistication and may well hold that a party to a contract in a specialised field should be taken as knowing about the arrangements that the other must make in order to be able to perform his part of the contract.

This issue will be of particular importance where the court is asked to determine whether the claimants can claim only the normal measure of damages applied to breaches of the kind or 'special loss' encompassing consequential damages. In a contract for the sale of crude oil such as in *Addax* v *Arcadia*, the difference can be significant; here it was US$816,550.85![156]

The claimants had sold barrels of crude oil FOB to the defendants and it was a condition of the contract that delivery of one lot would take place during the period 22 or 23 May 1998, at a Nigerian terminal. In breach of this condition loading did not take place until 30 May 1998 and was completed on 31 May 1998, when a bill of lading was issued. The price paid was to be paid by reference to the date when delivery was effected.

In order to supply the defendants, the claimants had entered into a contract with NPCC, the State-owned oil company, under which they had a number of options as to price arrangement. The defendants argued that damages should be restricted to the difference between the price the sellers actually received and what they would have received had the contract been performed on time. Any other loss arising in respect of the claimants' contract with NPCC must be ignored. This was on the basis that as they had not known about the claimants' arrangements in relation to buying the oil for onward sale to them, part of the claim was

---

[154] [1978] QB 791.
[155] [1949] 2 KB 538.
[156] [2000] 1 Lloyd's Rep 493.

too remote in law or, alternatively, was indirect or consequential. Morrison J rejected this argument. This was a commercial contract to be looked at on its own and the loss was recoverable as 'special loss'. The sale and purchase of crude oil was part of a well-established trading pattern, where the slightest movement of price could make a significant difference to profitability on a deal. There was a multitude of transactions available. The parties were sophisticated oil traders and the defendants would have known that the claimants would be entering into a contract to buy the oil for onward sale to them and of the options open to them. Thus, in Morrison J's view, the defendants' assessment of the claimants' damages was wrong in principle and had no commercial merit.

5.7.3 Liquidated damages

The parties to a contract may make an assessment of the quantum of damages that are likely to result from either one's breach and may include in the contract a stipulation that a stated sum of money is to be paid by the party in breach. This is known as liquidated damages. Such a clause enables the parties to estimate their liability in advance. A liquidated damages clause will be effective in the case of a breach and the claimant will recover the sum stated, not damages under the *Hadley* v *Baxendale* principle. No action for unliquidated damages will be allowed. The Privy Council in *Philips Hong Kong Ltd* v *Attorney-General of Hong Kong* expressed the view that liquidated penalty clauses should be incorporated into commercial contracts wherever possible, as such clauses lead to certainty.[157]

If, however, the clause is not a genuine assessment of losses, but is punitive in its aim, then it will be construed as a penalty clause and will be void. Where the clause is a penalty clause it will be ignored by the court in an action for breach of contract and the claimant will recover the whole of his loss: *Wall* v *Rederiaktiebolaget Luggude*[158] and, more recently, *Jobson* v *Jobson*.[159]

The parties may be in dispute over whether a clause is a penalty clause or a liquidated damages clause. The fact that the clause may be called a 'penalty' or 'liquidated damages' clause is not in itself decisive. The court will look at the construction of the clause and at the contract. In *Dunlop Pneumatic Tyre Co* v *New Garage*,[160] Lord Dunedin stated the 'various propositions' which he felt were 'deducible' from the decisions which he acknowledged ranked as authoritative:[161]

1. Though the parties to a contract who use the words 'penalty' or 'liquidated damages' may *prima facie* be supposed to mean what they say, yet the expression used is not conclusive. The court must find out whether the payment stipulated is in truth a penalty or liquidated damages. This doctrine may be said to be found *passim* in nearly every case.

2. The essence of a penalty is a payment of money stipulated as *in terrorem* of the offending part; the essence of liquidated damages is a genuine covenanted pre-estimate of damage (*Clydebank Engineering and Shipbuilding Co* v *Don Jose Ramos Yzquierdo y Castaneda*).[162]

[157] (1993) *The Times*, 15 February 1993.
[158] [1915] 3 KB 66.
[159] [1989] 1 WLR 1026.
[160] [1915] AC 79.
[161] *Ibid.* at p. 86.
[162] [1905] AC 6.

3. The question in relation to whether a sum stipulated is a penalty or liquidated damages is a one of construction to be decided as to the terms and inherent circumstances of each particular contract, judged at the time of the making of the contract, not the time of the breach (*Public Works Commissioner* v *Hills*,[163] and *Webster* v *Bosanquet*).[164]

4. To assist this task of construction various tests have been suggested, which if applicable to the case under consideration may prove helpful or even conclusive. Such are:

   (a) it will be held to be a penalty if the sum stipulated is extravagant and unconscionable in amount in comparison with the greater loss that could conceivably be proved to have followed from the breach . . . ;

   (b) it will be held to be a penalty if the breach consists only in not paying a sum of money, and the sum stipulated is a sum greater than the sum which ought to have been paid . . . ;

   (c) there is a presumption (but no more) that it is a penalty when 'a single lump sum is made payable by way of compensation, on the occurrence of one or more or all of several events, some of which may occasion serious and others but trifling damages'.[165]

   Alternatively:

   (d) it is no obstacle to the sum stipulated being a genuine pre-estimate of damage, that the consequences of the breach are such as to make precise pre-estimation almost an impossibility; on the contrary, that is just the situation when it is probable that pre-estimated damage was the true bargain between the parties . . .

The Court of Appeal has recently held that liquidated damages clauses should be construed so as to avoid, if possible, the finding that breaches of contract resulting in minor losses would be covered by such a clause: *Cenargo Ltd* v *Empresa Nacional Bazán de Construcciones Navales*.[166] The court held that to construe a liquidated damages clause otherwise would be to jeopardise that clause as, 'if a liquidated damages clause is held to apply to trifling breaches of contract or breaches of contract which result in a trifling loss, the whole clause might be struck down as a penalty clause'. This approach to the construction of liquidated damages clauses was in line with the Privy Council's in *Webster* v *Bosanquet*.[167] In *Cenargo*, the Court of Appeal held that the courts should do their best to avoid the result that a liquidated damages clause would become due on a trifling breach by construing the clause so as to make the sum payable only on major breaches, for which the clause is a valid pre-estimate.

Some contracts stipulate for payment of a particular sum on the happening of certain events other than breach of the contract itself. These payments are not liquidated damages and the distinction between liquidated damages and penalties is inapplicable.

5.7.4 Repudiation

If either party wrongfully refuses or fails to perform one or more of his obligations under the contract, the question of whether or not the seller can repudiate the contract will arise. This

---

[163] [1906] AC 368.
[164] [1912] AC 394.
[165] Citing Lord Watson in *Lord Elphinstone* v *Monkland Iron and Coal Co* (1886) LR 11 App Cas 332 at 342.
[166] [2002] EWCA Civ 524.
[167] [1912] AC 395 PC (Cey).

is a difficult issue in today's judicial climate. It is clear that in determining the effect of a breach by one party, the courts are hesitant to regard repudiation as an obvious step to be taken by the other. We have seen that the classification of the term which has been breached as an 'innominate term' allows the courts to consider the impact the particular breach in question has on the actual parties to the case. This approach arguably enables the court to imply, to some extent, a duty of good faith into commercial dealings.

Such an approach, however, may lead to the creation of 'judicial jurisprudence' and, as was recognised by Lord Diplock in *The Scaptrade*,[168] there are practical reasons of commercial policy for declining, in effect, to create 'new law' out of sympathy for the particular parties in the case. In a common law system, creation of 'new law', by extending the reasoning of previous authority, tends to make the law more complex and can lead to uncertainty. It is of utmost importance in commercial dealings, however, that each party knows where he stands – traders need to ascertain their legal positions quickly so that they can act accordingly and respond to changes in the market. Thus, Lord Bridge, in *The Chikuma*, was firmly of the opinion that the ideal for which the courts should strive is to produce a result such that in any given situation both parties seeking legal advice as to their rights and obligations can expect the same clear and confident answer and neither will be tempted to embark upon lengthy and expensive litigation in the belief that victory depends on the 'sympathy' of the court.[169]

This line of thinking, therefore, explains why, since the *Hong Kong Fir Shipping* case,[170] it has undoubtedly been a fact that, in commercial cases, the courts have tended to construe terms in commercial contracts as innominate, rather than as conditions. Indeed, in *The Gregos*, Lord Mustill was of the firm view that although some terms were clearly established as conditions, the courts should not seek to construe other terms as conditions.[171] This is not the first time that this view has been put forward by the courts: consider our discussion above, when looking at the culture of international trade law, of *The Hansa Nord*.[172] Equally, in *Bunge Corporation v Tradax Export SA*, Lord Wilberforce was clearly of the view that in what he called 'suitable cases' the courts should not be reluctant to hold that an obligation had the force of a condition.[173] His Lordship did refer with approval to Roskill LJ's judgment in *The Hansa Nord*, agreeing that the courts should not be 'too ready' to interpret contractual clauses as conditions. Indeed, he recognised that he himself had commended, and continued to commend, the greater flexibility in the law of contract to which the decision in the *Hong Kong Fir Shipping* case had given rise. In respect of certain clauses in mercantile contracts, however, his Lordship took the view that to apply the 'gravity of the breach' test propounded in *Hong Kong Fir* would be unsuitable. His Lordship thought that an obligation as to a time clause in an international sale contract must always be construed as a condition. In *Bunge v Tradax*, the buyer was required by a term of the contract to provide a vessel and give the seller at least 15 days' notice of the readiness of the vessel, so that it could be loaded. They were four days late in doing so. It was held that the provision as to time was a condition, breach of which entitled the seller to repudiate the contract.

---

[168] [1983] 2 AC 694.
[169] [1981] 1 WLR 314.
[170] [1962] 2 QB 26.
[171] [1995] 1 Lloyd's Rep 1.
[172] [1976] 1 QB 44 (Court of Appeal).
[173] [1981] 2 Lloyd's Rep 1.

It is important to understand the effect of a repudiatory breach on the contract. When a party breaches a condition or is in fundamental breach of an innominate term, the innocent party may repudiate (that is, push away or reject) *any future* obligations that he may have under the contract. Thus, for example, where the seller is in fundamental breach of any of ss. 13–15 (and the seller cannot, as against a commercial buyer, prove that the breach was not fundamental to this buyer under s. 15A), then the buyer may reject acceptance of the goods.

The repudiatory breach does not, however, affect outstanding obligations or the effectiveness of any exclusion or limitation clauses. This was firmly laid down by the House of Lords in *Photo Production Ltd* v *Securicor Transport Ltd*, in which their Lordships unanimously held that the question of whether or not such a clause was applicable where there was a fundamental breach of contract was one of the true construction of the contract.[174]

In *Harbutt's Plasticine Ltd* v *Wayne Tank and Pump Co Ltd*, the Court of Appeal had held that the effect of a fundamental breach was to avoid the contract *ab initio* (from the beginning).[175] If the contract came to an end as a result of the breach, the effect was to avoid any exclusion clause (and, by analogy, any limitation clause or any obligation that the innocent party might already have under the contract) *ab initio*. (Of course, the contract would remain 'alive for the awarding of damages either for previous breaches, or for the breach which constitutes the repudiation', *per* Lord Wright in *Heyman* v *Darwins*.[176]) This approach was in fact inconsistent with the earlier case of *Suisse Atlantique Société D'Armement Maritime SA* v *NV Rotterdamsche Kolen Central*, in which the House of Lords had held that a demurrage clause in a voyage charter was applicable, notwithstanding a fundamental breach by the shipowners.[177] The charterers had argued that the demurrage provisions could not apply in the light of the owners' repudiatory breach. The charterers contended that if the delays for which the owners were responsible were such as to entitle the charterers to treat the charterparty as repudiated, the demurrage provisions did not apply and that they were, therefore, entitled to recover the full loss that they had suffered. In rejecting this argument, Lord Wilberforce said that whether or not a clause would survive a fundamental breach of contract was a matter of construction of the contract. On a consideration of the main purpose of this contract, his Lordship was of the opinion that the demurrage clause was not put to an end by the owners' fundamental breach.

Harbutt's Plasticine was overruled by their Lordships in *Photo Production* v *Securicor*. In considering the approach to the doctrine of fundamental breach taken by the Court of Appeal in *Harbutt's Plasticine*, Lord Wilberforce said:

> I have, indeed, been unable to understand how the doctrine can be reconciled with the well-accepted principle of law, stated by the highest modern authority, that when in the context of contract one speaks of termination, what is meant is no more than that the innocent party or, in some cases, both parties, are excused from further performance.[178]

An example of the *Photo Production* approach can be seen in the case of *The Dominique*, in which the owners' fundamental breach of a voyage charter did not affect the charterers' obligation to pay outstanding freight under the charter.[179] The freight had become due before the owners' breach occurred and the charterers, were, therefore, liable to pay it. (Their

---

[174] [1980] AC 827.
[175] [1970] 1 QB 447.
[176] [1942] AC 356 at 379.
[177] [1967] 1 AC 361.
[178] *Supra* n. 175 at p. 844.
[179] [1989] 1 Lloyd's Rep 431.

Lordships also held in this case that the owners' repudiatory breach was incapable of giving rise to a defence of equitable set off in favour of the charterers.)

The concept of repudiation should not be confused with the equitable remedy of rescission of contract. As we have seen, repudiation is the action that an injured party may take in respect of a fundamental breach by the other party. The remedy of rescission is where the court will put the parties back (if it is possible to do so and it is just and equitable to do so) into a pre-contractual position. At times, the courts have unfortunately used the two terms interchangeably. This is incorrect and should be avoided. Lord Wilberforce made this point in *Photo Production* when he said:

> A vast number of expressions are used to describe situations where a breach has been committed by one party of such a character as to entitle the other party to refuse further performance: discharge, rescission, termination, the contract is at an end, or dead, or displaced; clauses cannot survive, or simply go. I have come to think that some of these difficulties can be avoided; in particular the use of rescission, even if distinguished from rescission *ab initio*, as an equivalent for discharge, though justifiable in some contexts (see *Johnson* v *Agnew*)[180] may lead to confusion in others. To plead for complete uniformity may be to cry for the moon. But what can and ought to be avoided is to make use of these confusions in order to produce a concealed and unreasoned legal innovation: to pass, for example, from saying that a party, victim of a breach of contract, is entitled to refuse further performance, to saying that he may treat the contract as at an end, or as rescinded, and to draw from this the proposition, which is not analytical but one of policy, that all (or arbitrarily) some of the clauses in the contract lose, automatically, their force, regardless of intention.[181]

His Lordship went on to approve of the following words of Lord Porter in *Heyman* v *Darwin*:[182]

> To say that the contract is rescinded or has come to an end or has ceased to exist may in individual cases convey the truth with sufficient accuracy, but the fuller expression that the injured party is thereby absolved from future performance of his obligations under the contract is a more exact description of the position. Strictly speaking, to say that on acceptance of the renunciation of a contract the contract is rescinded is incorrect. In such a case the injured party may accept the renunciation as a breach going to the root of the whole of the consideration. By acceptance he is discharged from further performance and may bring an action for damages, but the contract itself is not rescinded.[183]

5.8 Conclusion

Some questions may be raised in readers' minds as to why, in a chapter on international sales, more has not been made of the Sale of Goods Act 1979. Much has been made of the culture of international sales law, of reliance on standard form contracts and trade terms, with less being made of legislation than one might initially expect. Our conclusion to this chapter is, then, to consider the actual impact of the Act on this area of trade and to question the extent to which in reality such contracts are 'regulated' by its provisions.

---

[180] [1980] AC 367.
[181] *Supra* n. 175 at 844.
[182] *Ibid.*, again at 844.
[183] [1942] AC 356 at 399.

In examining the relevance of the current Act to international sales, it is useful to reflect again briefly on the chronological history of English sales law. The Sale of Goods Act 1893 was the first codification of English sales law. The aim of this codification was to give legal clarity and certainty in commercial disputes, being drafted to reflect the sales law that had started to acquire its modern shape through a series of cases spanning the first three-quarters of the 19th century.[184] It should, of course, be remembered that international trade is not a creation of the modern common law era, and the merchant law, or *lex mercatoria*, was the focus of commercial dispute resolution long before the common law was 'born'.[185]

What we should keep in mind when considering the impact of sales legislation on international sales cases is that the trade, and thus the disputes, were the precursors of the law. The emerging common law, then, had to accommodate established trade practice, rather than a modern means of doing business developing against a framework of established law.

The success of the adaptation of the common law to the requirements of merchants was brought about by two outstanding commercial lawyers, Chief Justice Holt and, as mentioned above, Lord Mansfield. During his time as Chief Justice, from 1689 to 1710, Holt laid the foundations of the law relating to negotiable instruments, bailment and agency. Building upon these efforts Lord Mansfield, as Chief Justice from 1756 to 1788, went on to organise the vast mass of case law on commercial disputes into an ordered structure. In the 19th century, the formulation of the principles of commercial law in all its major aspects was further developed and refined by outstanding commercial lawyers, such as Benjamin, Story and Chalmers, Charlesworth and Smith, Palmer and Byles. The close of the 19th century was highlighted by the statutory drafting by Sir MacKenzie Chalmers of the Bills of Exchange Act 1882 and the Sale of Goods Act 1893 which were adopted almost verbatim throughout the Commonwealth. We can see, then, that it was the common law courts, especially from the 18th century onwards, that developed the body of principles and rules that make up modern English commercial law, rather than the original merchant courts.

The Sale of Goods Act 1893 was, then, predominately a commercial code. The cases on which the Act was based were generally commercial disputes between organisations and traders. The perceived need for a more consumer-driven code did not arise until much later, reflected in the repeal of the 1893 Act for the Sale of Goods Act 1979, which in turn has been the subject of predominately consumer-orientated amendments.[186] Atiyah suggests that the 1979 Act has 'not been one of the more successful pieces of codification undertaken by Parliament towards the end of the nineteenth century'.[187] This is attributed to the fact that more cases dealt with under the 1979 Act today involve consumers, whereas the 1979 Act follows its predecessor in being based on the more commercial sales trading. The subsequent amendments to the 1979 Act are a somewhat piecemeal attempt to introduce the level of consumer protection that we have now come to expect from the law. It might well be argued that a complete overhaul of sales legislation is required, with two separate codes being drafted, one specifically for modern trade.

---

[184] M. G. Bridge, 'The Evolution of Modern Sales Law' [1991] *LMCLQ* 52.

[185] For an excellent discussion on the *lex mercatoria* see L. E. Trackman, 'The Evolution of the Law Merchant: Our Commercial Heritage' [1980] 12(1) *JML&C* 1.

[186] For example, the term 'merchantable' quality was amended in 1994 to 'satisfactory' quality (see the Law Commission Report, *Sale and Supply of Goods* (Law Com No 160, 1987).

[187] P. S. Atiyah, J. Adams and H. MacQueen, *The Sale of Goods* (11th edn, Longman, Harlow, 2005) p. 6.

On reflection, however, this raises a danger of over-regulation, which appears to be anathema to those engaged in international trade. In looking at the cases one can see that in international sales the Act appears to be regarded as a supportive framework of guidance, rather than as a mandatory regulating code. This view would certainly accord with the aim of the 1893 Act, which, it will be recalled, was to codify what was happening in sales law. So, the 1979 Act makes no attempt to codify the general principles of common law contract, leaving the substantive formation of the sale contract and its co-existence with other relationships to the common law.[188] This can be argued as militating towards supporting what we have seen is a culture in English law towards international sales, in which freedom of contract is the basis of trade. Thus, our consideration in this chapter has been to introduce how English law approaches international sales law, in which statutory regulation is perceived as a safety net in the absence of the parties' clear intent, rather than as a consideration of statutory provisions prescribing on a mandatory basis how those parties should conduct their business.

Further reading

Bridge, M., *The International Sale of Goods: Law and Practice* (2nd edn, Oxford University Press, Oxford, 2007).

Chuah, J., *Law of International Trade: Cross-border Commercial Transactions* (4th edn, Sweet and Maxwell, London, 2009).

Cohun, M. M., 'International sales of Bulk Liquids on Mortified cif Terms: Overcoming The Problems' [2012] *LMCLQ* 606.

Goode, R., *Commercial Law* (4th edn, Penguin, London, 2012).

Lorenzon, F., 'International Trade and Shipping Documents' in Y. Baatz, *Maritime Law Southampton on Shipping Law* (formerly Sweet and Maxwell, London, 2011).

Murray, C., Dixon, G., Holloway, D. and Timon-Hunt, D., *Schmitthoff: Export Trade: The Law and Practice of International Trade* (11th edn, Sweet and Maxwell, London, 2007).

Debattista, C., 'Legislative Techniques in International Trade: Madness of Method?' [2002] *JBL* 626.

Takahashi, K., 'Right to Terminate (Avoid) International Sales of Commodities' [2003] *JBL* 102.

Companion Website

For open-access **student resources** specifically written to complement this textbook and support your learning, please visit **www.pearsoned.co.uk/legalupdates**

ON THE WEBSITE

---

[188] See s. 62(2).

6 Payment and payment instruments

By Jason Chuah

6.1   Introduction

This chapter deals with the very important subject of money and payments. It begins with an examination of the legal concept of payment followed by a consideration of the different forms of payment. These forms of payment include money or legal tender, payment cards, funds transfers and negotiable instruments. The subject of negotiable instruments is discussed with particular reference to bills of exchange and cheques. The chapter then concludes with an explanation of the payment methods used in commercial transactions.

6.1.1 Tender of payment

Commerce is ultimately about making money. Goods and services are supplied in exchange for a price. Suppliers quite rightly expect to be paid. Payment must therefore be made by the buyer in a manner which is acceptable to the supplier. Payment is considered by law to be effective when it is made by or with the authority of the debtor and accepted as effective by the creditor or his authorised agent and any condition precedents have been satisfied or waived by the debtor. Payment is complete when the payment order has become irrevocable;[1] in other words, the placing of the money unreservedly at the disposal of the creditor is payment. In *PT Berlian Laju Tanker TBK v Nuse Shipping Ltd (The Aktor)*,[2] a case concerning the payment for a new ship, Christopher Clarke J said:

> whether or not payment has occurred will depend on whether funds have been transferred by 'any commercially recognised method of transferring funds, the result of which is to give the transferee the unconditional right to the immediate use of the funds transferred'.

On the same basis, the transmission of an electronic payment is deemed only to have been complete when it is received not when it is initiated electronically (*West v Revenue and Customs Commissioners*[3]).

It would thus follow that a money obligation can be discharged in a number of ways:

(a) the delivery of physical cash (but this is not convenient or safe where large amounts are involved);

(b) the delivery of goods or services in a system of barter or counter-trade; the goods or services may be delivered to some third party who the creditor has consented to;

(c) the transfer of funds using the banking system from one account to that of the creditor;

(d) the forging of a new contractual relationship with the same creditor or another third party by the debtor (novation); an example is where A enters into a new contract of sale as consideration of B agreeing to treat the old contract as having been discharged;

(e) liabilities between the parties being set off under a payment or settlement netting arrangement.

When payment is due, the debtor should make a tender of performance. This is important because if payment is refused, the debtor could argue that he had attempted to perform his part of the contract by tendering payment. If the debtor had attempted to perform but was prevented from doing so by the creditor, the creditor will bear the risk of the contract being frustrated by supervening events. However, the tender of money must be valid. It must comply with the terms of the contract as regards time of payment, mode of payment, place of payment, etc. In particular, it must be unconditional. The following questions are especially relevant in ascertaining whether or not a tender of money is valid.

(a) Was the exact and correct amount tendered?

(b) Was the tender made to the creditor or his authorised agent?

(c) Was the tender a continuing tender? (That is, was the debtor always in a position to pay the sum due?)

A tender of legal tender[4] is always acceptable but a tender in kind of cheques or other negotiable instrument is only a valid tender if such forms of payment have been pre-agreed

---

[1] Where the clearing system is involved, a payment is complete when the bank holding the funds accepts the person to whom payment is to be made as its creditor.
[2] [2008] EWHC 1330 (Comm).
[3] [2010] UKFTT 443 (TC).
[4] See section 6.2.1.

between the parties. This is equally the case with bank accounts – a bank customer has the right to demand payment in cash, even including cases where the withdrawal is for large sums of money. A bank is therefore not allowed to charge customers for providing cash.[5]

As far as the place of payment is concerned, unless this has been agreed, the debtor is required to seek out the creditor at his place of residence or business (*Robey & Co v Snaefell Mining Co Ltd*).[6] In *Thompson v Palmer*[7] an English company based in Newcastle had constructed a dock for the defendants in Spain. Lord Esher MR stated:

> I think the implication is that they (the payments) were to be made at Newcastle, where the plaintiff generally carried on business, and where the necessary plans and calculations for the works would be made.

The court thus rejected the suggestion that the defendants could tender the amount due in any part of the world where the plaintiff might be, because the plaintiff would not have the means of ascertaining the correctness or otherwise of the amount tendered. Although that reasoning is much less compelling in the light of modern communications, the legal position seems to remain that the payment is to be made where the claimant generally carries on business.[8] It would appear that this is the case even where the creditor is abroad provided that when the debt was made, he was abroad (*Fessard v Mugnier*).[9]

There is, however, a slight variation in the case of bank accounts. The bank's obligation to repay the customer only arises if the customer makes a demand and that obligation is therefore to be performed at the place or branch where the account is maintained.[10]

The time for payment will naturally depend on the terms of the contract. Those terms may be implied or express. In *Mardorf Peach & Co v Attica Sea Carriers (The Laconia)*,[11] for example, it was assumed that where payment falls due on a day when the bank is closed, payment should be made by the last working day before the nominal due date. For example, if the payment is required to be made on 12 June and 12 June happens to fall on a Sunday, payment should be made on Friday 10 June (assuming that Saturday is a day when the bank is closed).

In *The Brimnes*,[12] the charterparty provided that the ship could be withdrawn by the shipowners if payment was not made on time. On 2 April 1970 at 10.53 BST the charterers instructed the shipowner's bank to transfer the hire into the shipowner's account. However, as a result of the difference in time in New York and because of the bank's internal procedures, the credit was not effected until 18.07 BST on 2 April. Meanwhile at 17.45 BST on the same day, the shipowners telexed the charterers withdrawing the ship. As to when payment was actually made, the Court of Appeal held that 'payment' was not to be made until 'the process has reached the stage at which the creditor has received cash or that which he is prepared to treat as the equivalent of cash or has a credit available on which, in the normal course of business or banking practice, he can draw, if he wishes, in the form of cash'.

[5] *Libyan Arab Foreign Bank* v *Bankers Trust Co* [1989] QB 728.
[6] (1887) 20 QBD 152.
[7] [1893] 2 QB 80 at 84.
[8] See also the Northern Irish case of *ICS Computing Ltd, Fargell Ltd* v *Capital One Services Inc* (2002) NIQB 2.
[9] (1865) 18 CBNS 286.
[10] *Clare & Co* v *Dresdner Bank* [1915] 2 KB 576; *Woodland* v *Fear* (1857) 7 E&B 519; *Frankman* v *Anglo-Prague Credit Bank* [1948] 2 All ER 1025.
[11] [1977] AC 850.
[12] [1975] QB 929; see also *The Chikuma* [1981] 1 WLR 314. There is some uncertainty as to the correctness of this decision with reference to bank transfers (see *The Afovos* [1983] 1 WLR 195) especially where the payment order is irrevocable. See discussion below in section 6.4.3.

Therefore, the mere receipt of the order at 10.53 BST was not payment. Payment only took place when the shipowners had an unconditional right to the amount in the account. The dispatch and receipt of the telex message were merely a part of the process which led towards the making of payments. Receipt by the bank of the order to make the transfer was really only the start of the payment process, not the payment itself. The charterers could not be said, as far as the Court of Appeal was concerned, to have done enough to effect a complete and effective tender of performance.

Where payment is made 'under reserve', there is no unconditional tender of performance (*Banque de l'Indochine et de Suez v JH Rayner (Mincing Lane) Ltd*).[13] Naturally, if funds are deposited but the payee is not allowed to withdraw or dispose of them until some event occurs, there is also no unconditional tender of performance (*The Chikuma*).[14]

DEBATE BOX

P owes Q money. Unknown to P, R tenders payment to Q as a favour to P.

Is there a good tender of performance? Must R's act be ratified by P? What are the legal implications?

Consider the following references:

Birks and Beatson (1976) 92 LQR 188

Chase Manhattan Bank v Israel-British Bank [1981] Ch 105

Secured Residential Funding PLC v Douglas Goldberg Hendeles [2000] NPC 47

British Bank of the Middle East v Sun Life Assurance of Canada [1983] 2 Lloyd's Rep 9

The Chikuma [1981] 1 All ER 652

The presumption is that time of payment is not of the essence. That means a delay in making payment will not of itself bring the contract to an end.[15] As far as the sale of goods is concerned, s. 10(1) Sale of Goods Act 1979 makes it plain that stipulations as to time of payment shall not be of the essence of the contract. Clear terms making time of the essence need to be used. Although there has been some support for making time of the essence in mercantile contracts (where s. 10(1) Sale of Goods Act 1979 does not apply),[16] it is not usually applied to payment obligations.[17] The House of Lords has clarified in *United Scientific Holdings Ltd v Burnley Borough Council*[18] that whilst time of payment is not usually of the essence in commercial contracts, it will be so if:

(a) the parties specifically made it so; or

(b) the factual matrix is such that it should be of the essence.

---

[13] [1983] 1 All ER 1137.

[14] [1981] 1 WLR 314.

[15] A. G. Guest, *Chitty on Contracts* (30th edn, Sweet and Maxwell, London, 2009) para. 21–013.

[16] *Bunge Corp v Tradax SA* [1981] 2 All ER 513.

[17] C. Proctor, *Goode on Payment Obligations in Commercial and Financial Transactions* (2nd rev. edn, Sweet and Maxwell, 2009) para. 3–26.

[18] [1976] Ch 128.

Where payment is on demand, the court will allow some reasonable time between the time of demand and the time of actual payment. In *Bank of Baroda* v *Panessar*[19] this is what Walton J has to say:

> Money payable 'on demand' is repayable immediately on demand being made . . . Nevertheless, it is physically impossible in most cases for a person to keep the money required to discharge the debt about his person. He may in a simple case keep it in a box under his bed; it may be at the bank or with a bailee. The debtor is therefore not in default in making the payment demanded unless and until he has had a reasonable opportunity of implementing whatever reasonable mechanics of payment he may need to discharge the debt. Of course, this is limited to the time necessary for the mechanics of payment. It does not extend to any time to raise the money if it is not there to be paid.[20]

There is some debate as to whether or not it is fair to adopt such a strict rule. It has been argued that the so-called 'mechanics of payment' test should perhaps yield to a more relaxed approach whereby the debtor is given time not only to implement the mechanics of payment but actually to raise the finance if he does not have ready access to funds. That was however rejected by the Court of Appeal in *Lloyd's Bank* v *Lampert*,[21] preferring the element of certainty in the mechanics of payment test. In the area of high finance, the rule in *Panesar*, by ensuring that the period of time between the demand and actual payment is as narrow as possible, is especially helpful to maintain a high degree of certainty given the constant fluctuations in prices which are all too common in high finance. What is reasonable will always be a matter of the context – in high finance, for example, a couple of days may be unreasonable. It is of course open to the parties to prescribe the maximum period permitted.[22]

The mechanics of payment test is likely to apply to cases where time for payment, though stipulated, is not made of the essence. It should, however, also be noted that it is possible for the innocent party to make time of the essence by giving reasonable notice in cases where time of payment was not originally of the essence. The notice must be clear and unequivocal (*Chaitlal* v *Ramlal*).[23] It is, however, not fully resolved whether the creditor must allow some reasonable time to elapse (so as to allow the mechanics of payment test to be applied) before serving notice or not. It seems naturally strange that the creditor should allow two periods of reasonable time to elapse before he is entitled to his money. Nevertheless, there is case law which seems to suggest this. *Green* v *Sevin*[24] is frequently relied on as the authority[25] for the requirement that the creditor should allow two periods of reasonable time. In *Green* v *Sevin*, payment had not been made after a delay of two years. The creditor then gave notice requiring payment be made within three weeks of the notice. Fry J held that that was not permitted, stating:

> That which is not of the essence of the original contract is not to be made so by the volition of one of the parties, unless the other has done something which gives a right to the other to make

[19] [1987] Ch 335.
[20] *Ibid.* at 348.
[21] [1999] 1 All ER (Comm) 161. In that case, the court also ruled that there was no inconsistency between a term requiring repayment of the loan on demand and a term making available a loan facility to the debtor for a specified period of time.
[22] See *Sucden Financial Ltd* v *Fluxo-Cane Overseas Ltd* [2010] EWHC 2133 (Comm).
[23] [2004] 1 P & CR 1 (PC).
[24] (1879) 13 Ch D 589.
[25] See, for example, *Smith* v *Hamilton* [1951] Ch 174; *Babacomp Ltd* v *Rightside Properties Ltd* [1973] 3 All ER 873; *Woods* v *Mackenzie Hill Ltd* [1975] 1 WLR 613.

it so. You cannot make a new contract at the will of one of the contracting parties. There must have been such improper conduct on the part of the other as to justify the rescission of the contract *sub modo*, that is, if a reasonable notice be not complied with.

However, it should be observed that *Green v Sevin* was concerned with an open-ended payment obligation – no time for completion of performance was actually specified. Indeed, the date for the completion of the purchase of the property in the case was not even a firm contractual date. It was an aspiration; a mere target date for completion. On that basis, it is not entirely appropriate to rely on Fry J's dicta in *Green v Sevin* as the authority for requiring the creditor first to give reasonable time for payment and then also to give reasonable time for payment when giving the notice making time of the essence (*British & Commonwealth Holdings PLC v Quadrex Holdings Inc*).[26]

6.1.2 A receipt as evidence of payment

A receipt is usually accepted as evidence of payment but, in law, it is not conclusive evidence (*Stratton v Rastall*).[27] The contract may, however, provide that where a receipt is given (usually with a signature) this will constitute conclusive evidence of payment but where the receipt was given under a unilateral mistake of which the other party was aware, it would be set aside (*Hurst Stores v ML Europe Property*).[28] Rectification will be made even if no actual knowledge is present (*Commission for the New Towns v Cooper (Great Britain) Ltd*).[29]

6.1.3 Payment made under a mistake

Where a payment is made under a mistaken belief as to the facts or law, as a matter of restitution, that payment could be recovered from the payee. The old legal position was that only payments made under a mistake of fact could be recovered.[30] In *Kleinwort Benson v Lincoln City Council*[31] the House of Lords endorsed the Law Commission's criticisms[32] of the old rule and changed the law.

Those criticisms are:

- the rule is unfair as it allows the payee to retain monies which, but for the mistake, he would not otherwise have received.

- the distinction between mistakes of fact and law leads to capricious results; Lord Goff compares two examples: in one case, an insurer paid out even though he did not have to

---

[26] [1989] QB 842; see also *Raineri v Miles* [1981] AC 1050; C. Proctor, *op. cit.*, para. 3–30; C. T. Emery 'The Date Fixed for Completion' [1978] *Conv* 144 and A. Sydenham, 'Unreasonable Delay: Something of a Long-stop on the Failure of a Notice to Complete?' (1980) 44 *Conv* 19.

[27] (1788) 2 Term Rep 366; see also *Foster v Dawber* (1851) 6 Exch 839.

[28] [2004] EWCA Civ 490.

[29] [1995] Ch 259.

[30] *Bilbie v Lumley* (1802) 2 East 469.

[31] [1999] 2 AC 349.

[32] Law Commission, *Restitution: Mistakes of Law and* Ultra Vires *Public Authority Receipts and Payments* (Law Com No 227, 1994).

as a matter of law (because the insured had failed to make proper disclosure); in the second, the insurer paid out even though he did not have to because the insured had not paid his premium – it seems capricious that in the first (mistake of law), the insurer cannot get his money back whilst in the second (mistake of fact) he could;

● it is not always clear distinguishing between mistakes of law and fact.

Although the House of Lords all agreed that the old rule should be abrogated, three law lords went further and held that where a payment was made based on a settled understanding of the law and that understanding of the law is subsequently changed by a judicial decision, the payment should also be recoverable on the basis of a mistake of law. The minority thought that as that was a settled understanding, there could not have been a mistake.[33]

There is no defence in saying that the payee had received the money in good faith and honestly.[34] The money paid is recoverable because one party has been unjustly enriched.[35] It would also follow that payments made under a void contract could be recovered because the mistake is one of law – a mistake as to the validity of the contract. However, the majority went so far as to state that such a payment would be recoverable even though the void contract had been fully performed. That seems a little unfair given that the payer had actually received a benefit, despite the contract being invalid.[36] After all, as a claim for restitution, the following four tests must be satisfied (*Banque Financière de la Cité* v *Parc (Battersea) Ltd*),[37] namely:

(a) the defendant has benefited or enriched as a result of the payment;

(b) the enrichment was at the claimant's expense;

(c) the enrichment was unjust;

(d) there are no defences for the enrichment.

It is also important to note that the payment must have been made under a mistake – where the debtor pays 'to be on the safe side' because he is unsure about the necessity of the payment or the existence of the debt, that may not be a mistaken payment.[38]

6.1.4 Appropriation of payment

What happens when the debtor tenders payment which is unable to settle all his debts owing to the creditor? In general, the debtor can specify which debt the tender was intended to satisfy. This is called appropriation of payments. Appropriation of payments can be express or implied. For example, A has two debts outstanding with B, one for £100 and the other for £80.10. If he drew a cheque to the sum of £80.10, the highly specific figure would suggest that the cheque was intended to pay off the £80.10 debt. The position is less clear if he drew

---

[33] See L. Smith, 'Threeparty . . . for mistake of law (*Kleinwort Benson* v *Lincoln CC*)' [1999] RLR 148.

[34] Contrast the views of the Australian judge, Brennan J, in *David Securities* v *Commonwealth Bank of Australia* (1991–92) 175 CLR 353.

[35] The concept of unjust enrichment was first recognised by the House of Lords in *Lipkin Gorman* v *Karpnale* [1991] 2 AC 548; see also *Westdeutsche Landesbank* v *Islington London Borough Council* [1996] AC 669.

[36] Supra, n. 32.

[37] [1999] 1 AC 221 at 227A–B.

[38] *Re Kaupthing Singer & Friedlander Ltd (in administration)* [2010] EWCA Civ 561.

a cheque for £70. Of course he is always entitled to state expressly which debt the cheque was intended to meet.

Where the debtor failed to appropriate payment to the debts, the creditor would thus be entitled to do so. In the second example above, the creditor would therefore be allowed to appropriate the £70 to either of the debts. The law on appropriation of payments though does not change the general contract law rule that part payment of a debt is not a full discharge of the debt.

Time when the debts were incurred is generally immaterial. However, in the case of current accounts this is especially relevant. The rule in *Clayton's* case[39] states that where no appropriation of payment has been made (by either the debtor or creditor), the money paid in will be applied to pay the earliest outstanding debt. The rule is only a rebuttable presumption, a rule of convenience. It can certainly be displaced by the circumstances of the case which indicate a presumed intention to the contrary (*Commerzbank Aktiengesellschaft v IMB Morgan PLC*).[40] In *IMB Morgan*, a rogue had caused funds from various innocent individuals to be put into a bank account which the authorities managed to freeze. The problem for the court was how the funds which had become intermingled were to be distributed as the claims exceeded the available funds. According to the rule in *Clayton's* case payments out of an account are attributed to payments into the account in the order in which payments were made in. The first payment out is attributed to the first payment in, and so on. This rule can, however, cause injustice when applied to cases where tracing claims, such as *IMB Morgan*. In *Barlow Clowes International Ltd (in liquidaton) v Vaughan*[41] Woolf LJ commented:

> The rule need only be applied when it is convenient to do so and when its application can be said to do broad justice having regard to the nature of the competing claims.

It would not be applied when there was a better alternative. Indeed, it has been suggested that the rule in *Clayton's* case is not appropriate for those who had the common misfortune of falling victim to a large-scale fraud.[42]

DEBATE BOX

Prepayment

Prepayments are defined by the Office of Fair Trading as 'any advance payment made by a consumer to a trader for goods and services which are not to be supplied immediately' (*Farepak: review of the regulatory framework. Advice from the Office of Fair Trading*, December 2006).

Farepak Food and Gifts Ltd

Farepak operated a Christmas savings club. Members would pay money into a 'pot' which Farepack would exchange for gift vouchers just before Christmas. It went into liquidation before the vouchers were sent out to consumers leaving 120,000 members,

---

[39] *Devaynes v Noble* (1816) 1 Mer 572.
[40] [2004] EWHC 2771 (Ch).
[41] [1992] 4 All ER 22.
[42] *El Ajou v Dollar Land Holdings PLC (No. 2)* [1995] 2 All ER 213.

who were mainly on low incomes, without any redress. From the liquidation, they would only receive 5 pence for every pound the company owed them.

Current protection may lie in the following.

- Payments made with a credit card towards items costing more than £100 are guaranteed under consumer credit legislation (s. 75, Consumer Credit Act 1974).

- Insolvency law allows the realised assets of an insolvent business to be distributed to creditors (s. 214, Insolvency Act 1986).

- Laws which seek to deter misuse of consumer prepayments by imposing penalties on company directors.

- Laws relating to certain services (such as package holidays, funerals, etc.) by requiring the ring-fencing of customers' monies or mandatory insurance.

- Voluntary measures taken by certain industries, for example, by placing requirements on their trade association members to subscribe to codes of practice.

'English law does not offer sufficient legal protection for consumers who make prepayments.' Discuss.

Further reading

www.consumerfocus.org.uk/news/the-truth-about-paying-upfront

Although payment may be made in kind or other contractual devices, the most common forms of payment are:

(a) money;

(b) payment cards;

(c) funds transfers;

(d) negotiable instruments.

POINT OF INTEREST

Cheque volumes reached a peak in 1990 but usage has fallen since then, mainly owing to increased use of plastic cards and direct debits by personal customers. However, cheques remain popular in the business sector for paying suppliers. Overall cheque volumes are expected to continue to fall from a level of 2.8 billion in 1999 to about 1.7 billion by 2009.

(Source: UK Payments Administration Ltd (UKPA, at: www.ukpayments.org.uk)

The use of cash and cheques has been declining gradually and plastic money or funds transfer are becoming more popular. That said, the use of cash and cheques remains useful in the mix of payment forms and accordingly each of the four forms of payment will be considered in turn. In international trade, a further payment method is often used that involves banks, namely the documentary credit.

6.2 Money

6.2.1 Legal tender

We often take the concept of money for granted; we have an idea of what it is and why it matters. As a matter of economics, the function of money is to enable trading to occur without the so-called double coincidence of barter[43] or the mere exchange of goods/services. Money is thus considered in economics as anything which the community forming the market would accept as a means of payment, would qualify as 'money'. Thus, in the past, we have seen cowrie shells in India, silver ingots in China, whales' teeth in Fiji, the tally sticks of Henry I, and decorative metal objects called 'manilla' in West Africa being used as a means of payment.

However, as a matter of law, money takes on a slightly more complicated complexion. Professor Mann, who wrote the highly authoritative text, *The Legal Aspect of Money*,[44] said:

> . . . the quality of money is to be attributed to all chattels which, issued by the authority of the law and denominated with reference to a unit of account, are meant to serve as universal means of exchange in the State of issue.

In law, money is thus what the law of the land defines as 'legal tender'. Two Acts are particularly relevant in defining legal tender – the Coinage Act 1971 and the Currency and Bank Notes Act 1954.

LEGISLATIVE PROVISION

Section 2 of the Coinage Act 1971 states that the following will be legal tender:

(a) gold coins under the Coinage Act 1971 are legal tender for payment of any amount, provided that they are of the required weight;

(b) cupro-nickel or silver coins of denominations of more than 10 pence are legal tender for payment of any amount not exceeding £10;

(c) cupro-nickel or silver coins of denominations of not more than 10 pence are legal tender for payment of any amount not exceeding £5;

(d) bronze coins are legal tender for payment of any amount not exceeding 20 pence;

(e) any other coins which have been proclaimed by the Government as constituting legal tender.

---

[43] An example might be used to explain this. Assume that X has made ten cakes. Her family can only eat two. She wants to trade eight cakes for a pair of shoes but Y, who makes shoes, lives ten miles away. In the time taken by X to travel to Y's home, the cakes would have become stale. X might therefore trade her cakes for a chair made by Z. She knows that Y would like to have a chair. She then exchanges the chair with Y for the shoes. You can see how inconvenient, costly and time-consuming all this is.

[44] C. Proctor, *Mann on the Legal Aspect of Money* (6th edn, Oxford University Press, Oxford, 2005) paras 1.15–1.19.

As far as paper money goes, under the Currency and Bank Notes Act 1954 (ss. 1(1) and (2)), bank notes are legal tender for payment of any amount. Section 1(3) states bank notes shall be payable only at the head office of the Bank of England, unless expressly made payable at some other place. Section 1(4) goes on to state that the holder of bank notes shall be entitled, on demand made by him during office hours at the head office of the Bank of England, to receive in exchange for the notes bank notes of such lower denominations being bank notes which for the time being are legal tender in the UK or in England and Wales, as he may specify. Prior to 1931, bank notes could be exchanged for gold. The law, however, now allows for bank notes to be exchanged only for other bank notes.

The fact that an instrument is legal tender means that in law it will be fully negotiable. Whoever is in possession of it will have full and complete property in it. No action for specific recovery of 'money' can be brought against a person who has given value for it in good faith. In *Wookey* v *Pole*,[45] Best J explained that the title was complete not because the 'loser' cannot identify his money again but because the right to money is inseparable from the possession of it. Incidental to this principle is the presumption that payment in money will normally be an absolute (rather than a conditional) discharge of a payment obligation. Naturally, as legal tender, the creditor may not refuse to accept money as payment of a money debt owed to him without prior agreement. However, legal tender and money are not exactly the same. Money may or may not constitute legal tender, whilst legal tender is always money.

Another important implication of the concept of legal tender is that money cannot be bought or sold. Legal tender could be lent or received as a gift or in discharge of a money obligation, but it could not in itself be the subject of a payment. Where money is made the commodity of exchange rather than legal tender the law will treat it accordingly. An example may be the sale of money as a collector's item rather than as a means of payment. In such cases a failure to deliver the money will result in a breach of contract and not create a debt.[46] A serious, though rare, difficulty is establishing that the transaction in issue is for the delivery of money as commodity or legal tender.

POINT OF INTEREST

Are Scottish bank notes legal tender?

Scottish bank notes are not legal tender; not in England, Wales, Northern Ireland and even, in Scotland. They were legal tender for a brief term in 1939 but by 1946, that status was removed. Bank notes were not used in Scotland until the founding of the Bank of Scotland in 1695. Even then, the bank did not issue Scottish but sterling notes. However, by the 18th century, Scottish currency denominated notes were issued by banks, private companies and wealthy individuals. This messy state of affairs led to the passing of the Bank Notes (Scotland) Act 1765. Although the Act did not prohibit individuals and entities from issuing notes, it required that the notes issued must be payable on demand 'in lawful money of Great Britain and without reserving any power or option of delaying

---

[45] (1820) 4 B & Ald 1.

[46] *Camdex International Ltd* v *Bank of Zambia* [1997] 6 Bank LR 44; also *In Re British American Continental Bank Ltd, Lisser & Rosenkranz's Claim* [1923] Ch 276.

payment'. It also rendered all notes which were then still in circulation to be payable on demand. The Act also provided that no bank note should be issued for a sum less than 20 shillings *sterling* (note emphasis). In 1845, a new Act followed. The Bank Notes (Scotland) Act 1845 provided that bank notes issued in Scotland should not be for fractions of a pound and that bank notes for a sum less than £1 were void. Penalties were also introduced for anyone other than a banker who issued a note payable on demand for less than £5. As far as Bank of England notes are concerned, the Currency and Bank Notes Act 1954 provides that English bank notes of denominations less than £5 are legal tender. That means that English bank notes of £5 and more are not legal tender in Scotland. It followed, thus, with the removal of the Bank of England £1 note, that no Bank of England note is legal tender in Scotland. Effectively, therefore, Scotland has no legal tender. However, as we have seen, the absence of a legal tender does not necessarily mean the absence of money – money is anything the market considers to be an acceptable means of payment. Indeed, as s. 1(1) of the 1954 Act states, any bank notes issued by the Bank of England (though not legal tender) may be put into circulation in Scotland and Northern Ireland as well as in England and Wales. This is what the Bank of England says about Scottish bank notes, not being legal tender:

> The term legal tender does not in itself govern the acceptability of banknotes in transactions. Whether or not notes have legal tender status, their acceptability as a means of payment is essentially a matter for agreement between the parties involved. Legal tender has a very narrow technical meaning in relation to the settlement of debt. If a debtor pays in legal tender the exact amount he owes under the terms of a contract, he has good defence in law if he is subsequently sued for non-payment of the debt. In ordinary everyday transactions, the term 'legal tender' has very little practical application.[47]

Further reading

Malcolm, C. A., *The Bank of Scotland 1695–1945* (1948)

Munro, N., *The History of the Royal Bank of Scotland* (1927)

6.2.2 Foreign currency

Where the contract expresses a payment in foreign currency, this can cause problems for the trader. Picture this – a trader in the UK agrees to buy goods at US$1 per kg for delivery in a month's time and payment will follow delivery. At the time of contract, the exchange rate is US$ 1 to GB€ 0.5 but at the time of delivery the pound has devalued to a rate of US$ 1 to GB€ 0.6. The trader will now have to find more to pay for the goods which are priced in US$. The currency expressed by the contract in the price is generally known as the *money of payment*. The actual amount payable (in our example, the GBP used to make up the final USD equivalent) is called the *money of account*. The principle of fixing the value of a debt obligation despite fluctuations in the money's buying power or exchange rate is known as the principle of nominalism. The principle places the risk of unfavourable foreign exchange fluctuations on the trader who has agreed to money of account being expressed in a particular currency.[48]

[47] www.bankofengland.co.uk/banknotes/about/faqs.htm
[48] *Woodhouse AC Israel Cocoa Ltd SA v Nigerian Produce Marketing Co Ltd* [1971] 2 QB 23.

When a money obligation is expressed in a currency of a foreign country, that country's laws will be referred to for a definition as to what constitutes a unit of that currency (*Pyrmont v Schott*).[49] Thus, if the contract called for payment in Japanese currency, Japanese law will be referred to as to what constitutes legal units of that currency.

An English court has the power to give judgment in a foreign currency or its equivalent in sterling as at the time of payment to enforce a contractual money obligation expressed in a foreign currency (*Miliangos v George Frank (Textiles) Ltd*).[50] The amount entered in a foreign currency must however be converted into sterling when the judgment is executed.[51]

CASE

Camdex International Ltd v Bank of Zambia[52]

The problem there was if a transaction involving foreign currency (that is to say, the foreign currency is the subject matter of the transaction) is one of commodities or money. A Zambian company was compelled by Zambian law to pay any foreign currency earnings to the Bank of Zambia which would in turn credit the company with an official equivalent in Zambian kwacha. In an action brought against the Bank of Zambia for unpaid kwacha, the court was asked if the claim was for a debt or merely for damages. If the transaction was a commodity exchange (that is, the currency being treated as commodity), the action would be merely for damages but if it was a money transaction, then the matter would be one for debt.

The Court of Appeal held that as the obligation in question was the payment of a stipulated sum in a stipulated currency, then it was an obligation properly described as one of debt. It was immaterial that that obligation arose from a loan, sale or other transaction.

6.2.3 Electronic money

The notion of electronic money is new. The trend to 'dematerialise' physical money is not new – the use of money equivalents such as negotiable instruments, etc., has long been established. Physical money easily lends itself to theft, loss or damage and is not always convenient to use when large amounts are payable. Hence the need to rely on alternatives.

When PayPal first introduced its concept of digital cash, the plan was for people to beam money from one Palm Pilot (an early handheld device with limited technology) to another.

---

[49] [1939] AC 145.

[50] [1976] AC 443; see also *The Despina R and The Folias* [1979] AC 685 and *Jean Kraut AG v Albany Ltd* [1977] QB 182.

[51] For the purposes of proving a debt incurred or payable in a currency other than sterling in the event of insolvency, reg. 2.86 of the Insolvency Rules 1986 provides that 'the amount of the debt shall be converted into sterling at the official exchange rate prevailing on the date when the company entered administration or, if the administration was immediately preceded by a winding up, on the date that the company went into liquidation.' 'The official exchange rate' is defined in reg. 2.86(2) as 'the middle exchange rate on the London Foreign Exchange Market at the close of business, as published for the date in question'. In the absence of any such published rate, it is such rate as the court determines.

[52] [1997] 6 Bank LR 44.

The idea did not take off as people were really not keen to beam money to someone standing in front them. However, there was serious demand for something to enable payments to be made over the Internet to people who are at a distance and who might be complete strangers. PayPal is now arguably one of the world's largest 'banks', with over 100 million account holders. It provides users with a virtual wallet which can be used to pay for goods and services over a computer Internet connection or, indeed, in face-to-face transactions using a smartphone. In some shop trials in the USA, users have even been able to pay at the till of a 'bricks-and-mortar' shop simply by typing in their phone numbers and a secret password. The complete dematerialisation of the wallet seems to be underway.

It might be said that electronic money is any means of payment which relies on electronic records of monetary value accessible by the user and acceptable to the debtor as a payment method. A legal construction is found in the Directive 2009/110/EC (the Electronic Money Directive) and the UK Electronic Money Regulations 2011 which has transposed the directive into UK law. Article 2(2) of the directive (and reg. 2(1) of the UK Regulations) defines electronic money as 'electronically, including magnetically, stored monetary value as represented by a claim on the issuer which is issued on receipt of funds for the purpose of making payment transactions, and which is accepted by a natural or legal person *other than the electronic money issuer*' (emphasis added). The Commission makes it clear that the definition should cover electronic money held on a payment device in the electronic moneyholder's possession or stored remotely at a server and managed by the electronic moneyholder through a specific account.

There are two types of electronic money applications envisaged – card-based or device-stored applications and network-based applications. Card-based or device-stored electronic money applications are sometimes called electronic purses. The purpose is to facilitate small value retail (and usually face-to-face) payments. The electronic money provider will, in exchange for money from the user, incorporate digitised data in a device issued to the user. That data will represent the monetary value the issuer has received from the user. When the user employs the device to make a purchase, the seller will use a device at the point of sale to record the transaction and reduce the monetary value stored on the device. The seller will then subsequently submit the record of the transaction to the issuer and receive money payment from the issuer. Network-based applications are monetary value stored as software in the user's computer for purchases made over networks such as the Internet (such as services provided by Moneybookers, PayPal, etc.). They are usually called digital cash and it is managed and held in an account which the customer can access remotely by telephone or computer.

Regulation 3(a) excludes monetary value stored on instruments that can be used to acquire goods or services only:

(i) in or on the electronic money issuer's premises; or

(ii) under a commercial agreement with the electronic money issuer, either within a limited network of service providers or for a limited range of goods or services.

This provision will exclude from the definition of electronic money a large number of store cards, petrol cards, travel cards, employee cards, meal vouchers, membership cards, etc. A 'limited network' exists if the device can be used only either for the purchase of goods and services in a specific store or chain of stores or for a limited range of goods or services, regardless of the geographical location of the point of sale.[53]

---

[53] Recital 7, Preamble to Directive 2009/110/EC.

DEBATE BOX

The Oyster card, issued by London Underground, can be used to pay for journeys made on the services provided by London Underground, other rail companies and some shops associated with London Underground. Under the old Electronic Money Directive (2000/46/EC), it would count as electronic money and, as such, London Underground would have been treated as an electronic money issuer. However, under the new law, reg. 3 makes it clear that the device will not be deemed electronic money if it can only be used within a 'limited network'. Such devices and their issuers will be regulated by the Payment Services Regulations. On the other hand, if the card could be extended to wider range of suppliers and providers of services and goods, it might be argued that the device is no longer constrained within a limited network. It is immediately obvious that the difficulty with reg. 3(a) is the definition of 'limited network'.

In *Smart Voucher Ltd v Revenue and Customs Commissioners*,[54] S sold to customers a voucher which contained a number which could be used to authorise online transactions. S contracted with a network of merchants all of whom agreed to accept the vouchers as payment for products and services. S made its profits from charging the merchants a commission. Merchants using the system had to integrate their own websites with S's software system. Does the voucher constitute electronic money?

Regulation 3(b) also excludes from the definition of electronic money, 'monetary value that is used to make payment transactions executed by means of any telecommunication, digital or IT device, where the goods or services purchased are delivered to and are to be used through a telecommunication, digital or IT device, provided that the telecommunication, digital or IT operator does not act only as an intermediary between the payment service user and the supplier of the goods and services'. An example of this is the purchase of 'apps' using a monetary value credited to the customer by the provider and the provider is not merely an intermediary. The 'app' is bought by means of the IT device and is delivered to the device and, importantly, the provider is not merely a conduit for the delivery of the 'app'. A typical situation might be where a mobile phone subscriber pays the network operator directly for the 'app'.[55]

Electronic money clearly does not qualify as legal tender. As such, electronic money applications can never be absolute payment for the discharge of payment obligations. The creditor cannot be compelled to accept electronic money as payment as a matter of law. It is for the parties' contract to specify that electronic money will be acceptable to them.

The growth in the use of electronic money in the EU has been slower than hoped or anticipated by the EU. Only relatively few electronic money institution licences have been given. In 2009 there were only seven electronic money issuers in the EU – four in the UK, one in Germany, one in the Netherlands, and one in Norway. Some blame might be laid on the old Electronic Money Directive (Directive 2000/46/EC) which prevented an issuer from engaging in non-electronic money activities. Whilst the rationale to prevent the issuer from failing because of its non-electronic money activities is understandable, it does prevent well-known, financially stable non-electronic money undertakings (such as mobile telephony

---

[54] [2009] UKFTT 169 (TC).
[55] See para. 6 of the Preamble to Directive 2009/110.

companies, television companies, etc.) from entering the electronic money market. This, it has been said, had caused the EU to lag behind developing countries in using mobile telephony as a platform for banking.

There was also criticism that the capital requirements, though simplified under the Electronic Money Directive, are nevertheless still too high. Capital requirements are generally the assets the undertaking (firm) should hold to protect the customer from losing out if the undertaking becomes bankrupt. The new Payment Services Directive 2007/64/EC[56] appears to have learnt these lessons. It sets different (lower) capital requirements for firms which offer payment services but are not conventional credit institutions (banks or other financial institutions).

6.2.3.1 Regulatory regime

Under the new Electronic Money Directive, only electronic money issuers recognised and authorised by the Member States may issue electronic money (Art. 10). In the UK, the new Electronic Money Regulations provide that applications to be registered must be made to the Financial Services Authority (FSA). The FSA will then consider if the applicant satisfies the conditions laid down in reg. 6, including the existence of a robust system and honest and competent officers for ensuring that customers' funds would be properly protected. The FSA will need to satisfy itself that the applicant (who has to be a 'body corporate') has a sound business plan, an initial capital of at least €350,000, financial information to show that it will be able to maintain adequate capital on an ongoing basis and a robust governance and risk management plan (see the FSA Guidance on the scope of the Electronic Money Regulations 2011 (PERG 3A)).

Under the regime, the issuer will be required to inform the FSA of any material developments from time to time. This is in addition to the regular reporting duties on the issuer.

6.2.3.2 How the business of issuing of electronic money should be conducted?

Regulation 39 requires electronic money issuers to issue e-money at par value. That means that the e-money issued must be for the same amount as the funds received. The customer is entitled to receive £10 worth if they had handed over £10 to the issuer. The issuing of the electronic money should be made without delay following receiving funds from the customer. It is important to recognise that if the issuer's agent receives funds, the funds are considered to have been received by the issuer itself. It is not, therefore, acceptable for an electronic money issuer to delay in enabling the customer to begin spending the e-money because the issuer is waiting to receive funds from its agent.[57]

Electronic money issuers are not allowed to grant interest or any other benefits related to the length of time the electronic money is held (reg. 45). A question which might be asked is if the issuer may offer benefits to customers for maintaining certain spending thresholds – for example, an issuer may promise to reward a customer with special discounts who spends a minimum £100 every month. As far as the FSA is concerned, that would not be in

---

[56] The Payment Services Directive has been implemented into UK law by the Payment Services Regulations 2009 (see below, section 6.5).
[57] See Chapter 8 of the FSA document 'The FSA's role under the Electronic Money Regulations 2011 Our approach – March 2011'.

breach of reg. 45.[58] It is less clear if reg. 45 would be breached if the issuer offered a reward to a customer who spends a minimum of £100 per month for at least one year.

The contract between the issuer and customer should make clear what the conditions for redemption are. Redemption means the right to exchange the electronic money to cash. Under the old law, the issuer did not have to redeem electronic money if it was worth less than €10 as long as this was made clear in the contract. Additionally, if the contract stipulates it, the electronic money could become irredeemable after a specified period (of not less than one year). The new Regulations have changed that. The electronic money can be redeemed at any time and at par value (reg. 39). Though there is some uncertainty about the precise scope of reg. 39, the FSA takes the view that it would not be acceptable to have a term in the contract which causes the customer's right to redeem to expire after a specified period of validity. That said, this does not affect the issuer's right to prevent the customer from using the electronic money after a specified period of time – the lapse of the right of use however does not mean the lapse of the right of redemption.[59]

Fees may be charged (reg. 41) but these must be specified in the contract and are reasonable and proportionate. Moreover, fees could only be charged where:

- redemption is requested before termination of the contract;
- the customer terminates the contract before any agreed termination date; or
- redemption is requested more than one year after the date of termination of the contract.

6.3 Payment cards

Payment cards are convenient to use as a cash alternative. However, they are creatures of contract and, as such, their use must be consistent with the terms of the contract. Also, some cards are regulated as credit instruments. This makes using them subject to complexities not usually associated with cash.

This chapter will discuss the following payment cards:

(a) cheque guarantee cards;

(b) debit cards and cash cards;

(c) credit cards and charge cards.

There is, of course, a fourth type of payment card – the digital smart card. That has already been mentioned in the context of electronic money above.

6.3.1 Cheque guarantee cards

A cheque guarantee card is a card issued by a bank or building society which promises payment of the amount stated on the cheque to the recipient as long as the amount is not in

---

[58] Paragraph 8.14, FSA Document 'The FSA's Role under the Electronic Money Regulations 2011: Our Approach – March 2011'.

[59] Paragraph 8.7, FSA Document 'The FSA's Role under the Electronic Money Regulations 2011: Our Approach – March 2011'.

excess of the pre-agreed guarantee limit. The cheque guarantee may be issued as a standalone card or part of a multifunctional card. Lord Diplock in *Metropolitan Police Commissioner v Charles*[60] described the card as a representation given to the payee by the bank that the cheque supported by the card will be paid by the issuer on presentation, but always provided that the use of the card by the drawer to bind the issuer to pay the cheque is within the actual or ostensible authority conferred on them by the issuer. There will also be other conditions attached to the use of the card, including:

- the maximum amount guaranteed;
- the cheque must carry a signature which matches the card's;
- the name of the drawer of the cheque should match that of the cardholder;
- an expiry date of the card;
- the cheque should be drawn only in the UK;
- the card number should be written on the back of the cheque;
- the card has not been defaced or altered.

The guarantee supported by the card cannot be countermanded once the cheque has been handed over. The guarantee is autonomous of the underlying transaction. The bank will thus not make any enquiry into the transaction which induced the drawing and delivering of the cheque. The cardholder or account holder thus gives up their right in common law to countermand a payment instruction. This relinquishment of their common law right will be implied, as a matter of business efficacy, into the customer–banker relationship even if there is no express term to that effect.

It would appear that the cheque guarantee card does not constitute a credit token under s. 14, Consumer Credit Act 1974.

LEGISLATIVE PROVISION

Section 14

(1) A credit-token is a card, cheque, voucher, coupon, stamp, form, booklet or other document or thing given to an individual by a person carrying on a consumer credit business, who undertakes:

(a) that on the production of it (whether or not some other action is also required) he will supply cash, goods and services (or any of them) on credit; or

(b) that where, on the production of it to a third party (whether or not any other action is also required), the third party supplies cash, goods and services (or any of them), he will pay the third party for them (whether or not deducting any discount or commission), in return for payment to him by the individual.

(2) A credit-token agreement is a regulated agreement for the provision of credit in connection with the use of a credit-token . . .

---

[60] [1977] AC 177.

As such, it is not likely to be regulated by that Act, especially its provisions on connected lender liability (s. 56) and the customer's limited liability for card misuse (s. 83). The principal point of reference is therefore the contract subject to any test of unfairness required by the Unfair Contract Terms Act 1977 and/or the Unfair Terms in Consumer Contract Regulations 1999.[61] As far as the contract is concerned, subject to these criteria, the bank customer who does not inform the bank if the card is lost or misused may find themselves liable to the full extent of the guaranteed amount.

Another important aspect of the use of the cheque guarantee card is that which Lord Diplock referred to in *Metropolitan Police Commissioner* v *Charles*. The card will only be effective if the circumstances show that there was actual or ostensible authority by the cardholder to sign the cheque. In *First Sport Ltd* v *Barclays Bank PLC*,[62] the recipient had accepted a cheque drawn with the support of a cheque card in good faith. The cheque was signed in his presence but the signature was a forgery. A 2:1 majority in the Court of Appeal held that the payee was entitled to payment from the card issuer although the signature had been forged. The card stated that it 'may only be used by the authorised signatory'. The bank's position was that they were not liable to pay because the signatory was not authorised. Unfortunately for the bank, Evans LJ held that whilst there was no actual authority, the fraudster had ostensible authority to bind the bank. It is interesting to note that Kennedy LJ's dissenting view was that ostensible authority could only be relied on if the bank had conducted itself in such a manner as to be estopped from denying it. On the facts, the bank had clearly not done anything to give the impression that the signatory had ostensible authority.

It was of no surprise that following this decision, banks quickly introduced in their standard terms and conditions that the guarantee will only be honoured if the cheque has actually been signed by the bank customer himself.

6.3.2 Debit cards and cash cards

A debit card is a card which enables payment to be made directly from the cardholder's bank account. In some cases, such as the 'Solo' or 'Electron' cards, the bank account is checked at the point of sale and if there are sufficient funds, the transaction will go through. In the case of 'Switch', 'Visa' or 'Delta' debit cards, the account is not checked at the point of sale and the transaction could thus be processed despite the lack of funds. However, this would result in the account being overdrawn and charges for an overdrawn account will be payable. The card can also be used to withdraw cash from an automated teller machine (ATM) or a merchant who is prepared to offer 'cashback' services. Where the card is used to obtain cash, it operates as a cash card.

It is also not obvious whether debit and cash cards are 'credit tokens' for the purposes of s. 14 Consumer Credit Act 1974 but s. 187(3A) of the CCA 1974 (as amended by s. 89 of the Banking Act 1987) does make it clear that, unlike credit cards and charge cards, debit cards and cash cards are *not* within the scope of s. 56 or s. 75 of the CCA 1974 (the provisions giving rise to 'connected lender liability').[63]

---

[61] SI 1999/2083.
[62] [1993] 3 All ER 789.
[63] See section 8.12.

The debit and cash card, like the cheque guarantee card, must be used subject to the express terms of the contract. Unlike the cheque guarantee card, though, there are usually at least two contracts – one between the cardholder and the issuer, and one between the merchant and the issuer. As between the cardholder and the bank, the master agreement will normally specify that the bank's own records will be conclusive proof of the transactions made by the card. It remains to be seen, however, whether such a strict encumbrance could satisfy the test of unfairness in the Unfair Terms in Consumer Contracts Regulations[64] (and/or the Unfair Contract Terms Act 1977).[65] As a matter of law, the debit card and cash card will be subject to the rules on card misuse in the Payment Services Regulations 2009.[66]

6.3.3 Credit cards and charge cards

The UK Banking Code 2008 (now defunct[67]), in its Glossary, had defined a credit card in the following 'customer-friendly' terms:

> A card which allows you to make purchases and withdraw cash up to an arranged credit limit. You can pay off the credit we grant you in full or in part by a set date. Interest is usually charged on the amount of any balance you still owe. In the case of cash withdrawals, interest is normally charged from the transaction date. You may also have to pay an annual fee.

Although the Banking Code has now been repealed, it did offer us a workable definition given the lack of a proper definition in the current regulatory regime.

A charge card is also a card which allows the debtor to buy goods and withdraw cash up to an arranged credit limit but unlike the credit card, the debtor must pay the balance *in full* at the end of a set period. An example of the charge card is the American Express card. There is no interest payable because the balance must be paid in full but if the customer is late in paying the balance, a severe late fee (which can sometimes be up to 5 per cent of the balance) is imposed. The customer may also risk having the card cancelled and/or future use of the card being restricted. The charge card is useful for businesses wanting to ensure that no credit is received and to keep track of expenses on a month-by-month basis. With the reduced cost of credit, the charge card has been largely overtaken by the credit card as far as consumers are concerned.

The contractual structure for the credit card is by far the most complicated amongst the different payment cards systems.[68] Credit cards with logos such as Visa and MasterCard are issued by financial institutions under licence from Visa or MasterCard. The cards would only be acceptable for payments to merchants belonging to the relevant scheme. Merchants have to pay a fee to be a member of the scheme. Some financial institutions may act as 'merchant

---

[64] Regulations 5, 6.

[65] Section 11.

[66] SI 2009/209. See section 6.5.

[67] The voluntary code was replaced by non-voluntary and legally binding rules published by the FSA called *Banking: Conduct of Business Sourcebook (BCOBS)* from November 2009. Under the new rules, there is a general duty on banks to act fairly towards their customers but the BCOBS will only apply to firms taking or accepting deposits from customers. Non-deposit-taking activities will be excluded – including overdrafts, unsecured credits and credit cards.

[68] For an account of how complicated the structure can become, see *Household Global Funding Incorporated v British Gas Trading* [2001] EWCA 1156. In *Lancore Services Ltd v Barclays Bank PLC* [2010] 1 All ER 763 Rimer LJ gave a helpful summary of the system for processing credit card payments.

acquirers' by signing up merchants to the relevant schemes and processing transactions involving their merchants and the cardholders. They will also provide card verification services to the merchants.

As such, there can be four parties to the credit card transaction – the cardholder, the merchant, the issuing bank and the acquiring bank. As far as the issuing and the acquiring banks are concerned, they are likely to have a contractual relationship with Visa or MasterCard.

In a typical credit card transaction, the merchant will obtain authorisation from the cardholder's issuing bank at point of sale. As soon as the authorisation is granted, the merchant will generate what is known in the industry as 'paper' requesting payment from the acquiring bank. The acquiring bank will pay the merchant the purchase price deducting a commission as payment for the service. The acquiring bank will then turn to the issuing bank for payment. The issuer will pay the merchant acquirer the retail price minus a fee, called an *interchange fee*.[69] The issuing bank will debit the cardholder's account. How soon and how much the cardholder should pay will be a matter for the credit agreement between the cardholder and the issuing bank.

What if the goods are defective and the cardholder seeks to enforce his rights against the merchant under sales law? In such an event, the issuing bank will reverse the debit on the cardholder's account and charge back the sum to the acquiring bank. The acquiring bank will then recoup that from the merchant. It is therefore the acquiring bank that will bear the risk of the merchant becoming insolvent.

6.3.3.1 Relationship between cardholder and issuer

The relationship between the cardholder and the issuing bank is that of a credit arrangement. Also, in many cases it would be a consumer contract. As such, two sets of laws are immediately relevant – consumer credit law and the law governing unfair terms in consumer contracts. As to the latter, the good faith requirements which qualify the adoption of standard terms and exclusions will apply.[70] On the former, the Consumer Credit Act 1974 renders the credit card agreement a regulated credit agreement (s. 15) and the credit card itself is a credit token (s. 14). This means that subject to various restrictions, the panoply of the Act will offer the consumer certain safeguards in his dealings with the credit provider.

In *Elliott v DG of Fair Trading*,[71] the consumer was offered a provisional credit card. The question was whether that constituted a credit token under the Act. The court held that it did even though no final decision had been taken to issue a fully fledged card to the consumer.

---

[69] Interchange fees are either agreed bilaterally, between issuing and acquiring banks, or multilaterally, by means of a decision binding all banks participating in a payment card scheme. The industry refers to these as multilateral interchange fees. The interchange fee is actually what the issuer will need to pay to Visa or MasterCard where the card is issued carrying those logos. Interchange fees are very controversial because as there are effectively only two dominant providers of credit card schemes (namely, Visa and MasterCard), the propensity for price fixing and unfair charging is significant. See for example, the UK Office of Fair Trading's investigations into unfair interchange fees. (www.oft.gov.uk/oft_at_work/markets/services/mastercard-visa). The EU Commission had taken action against Visa and MasterCard compelling the publication of their fees. Concerns were also expressed as to the fact that these fees are frequently not cost-based (therefore not justified in terms of competition law). For more information, see http://ec.europa.eu/competition/sectors/financial_services/inquiries/index.html. See also *Visa Europe Ltd v European Commission* Case T-461/07 [2011] 5 CMLR 3.

[70] Regulation 5, Sch. 2 to the Unfair Terms in Consumer Contracts Regulations 1999.

[71] [1980] 1 WLR 977.

That was despite the fact that a card could not be operational until the applicant had disclosed his personal financial details and signed the agreement. The court held that a card which contained a statement that upon its production cash and goods would be available on credit was a credit token whether or not the statement was true. The issuer was thus convicted of issuing unsolicited credit tokens contrary to s. 51, CCA 1974.

In contrast, a charge card would not be caught by s. 14. This is because the card issuer is not a person who carries on a 'consumer credit business'. Article 3(1)(a)(ii)(bb), Consumer Credit (Exempt Agreements) Order 1989[72] makes the charge card agreement an 'exempt agreement' under the Consumer Credit Act 1974. The card issuer could not thus be deemed to be a person who carries on a 'consumer credit business' because the agreement he makes with the consumer is not a regulated credit agreement. Indeed, it is logical not to treat an arrangement as a credit agreement whereby the cardholder is required to pay off the full amount at the end of the stipulated period.

Card misuse is a serious problem and it is not unnatural for issuers to seek recompense from the card user. However, in this respect, it is not simply for the issuer to stipulate what the parties' liabilities are in the contract between the cardholder and itself. The Consumer Credit Act 1974 protects the consumer from unduly strict terms on liability for card misuse. Section 83(1) provides that 'the debtor under a regulated consumer credit agreement shall not be liable to the creditor for any loss arising from use of the credit facility by another person not acting, or to be treated as acting, as the debtor's agent'. The term 'credit facility' is clearly wide-ranging enough to encompass 'credit tokens' (such as a credit card).

Despite the general rule in s. 83(1), the card issuer may require the cardholder to assume some risk of card misuse. Section 84(1) imposes liability on the cardholder for up to £50 or the credit limit (if lower) for loss arising from the use of the card when the card was not in his possession. The cardholder would also be liable for any loss caused by the misuse of the card if the person who misused the card had obtained possession of the card with the cardholder's consent. If the cardholder had informed the issuer as to the likelihood of misuse, the cardholder would no longer be liable for the £50 under ss. 84(3). That communication may be done orally or in writing; the contract may specify though that an oral communication be confirmed in writing (s. 84(5)). The consumer would also not be liable if his card had been misused in connection with a distance contract[73] (such as when a rogue uses the card for Internet transactions) (ss. 84(3A) and (3B)). The consumer should also be informed of his rights and liabilities in the case of card misuse.[74] The consumer's liability for misuse should also be read in conjunction with the Payment Services Regulations 2009.[75] Regulation 57 of the 2009 Regulations states that the user must use the payment instrument (the card) in accordance with the terms of its issue and notify the service provider without undue delay any loss, theft, misappropriation or unauthorised use of the payment instrument. He must also take reasonable steps to keep the personalised security features of the payment

---

[72] SI 1989/869.

[73] A distance contract is defined in reg. 2 of the Consumer Protection (Distance Selling) Regulations 2000, SI 2000/2334 as 'any contract concerning goods or services concluded between a supplier and a consumer under an organised distance sales or service provision scheme run by the supplier who, for the purpose of the contract, makes exclusive use of one or more means of distance communication up to and including the moment at which the contract is concluded'.

[74] See Consumer Credit (Agreements and Cancellation Notices and Copies of Documents) (Amendment) Regulations 1988, SI 1988/2047.

[75] See section 6.5.

instrument safe (reg. 57(2)). Consistent with the Consumer Credit Act 1974, reg. 62 limits the user's liability to card misuse to a ceiling of £50. Regulation 62(3)(c) supports the exception made to unauthorised use of payment cards in Internet transactions.

It should also be stressed that the cardholder would not be liable unless he had actually accepted the credit card. Section 66(1) of the Consumer Credit Act 1974 states quite unequivocally that 'the debtor not be liable under a credit-token agreement for use made of the credit-token by any person unless the debtor had previously accepted the credit-token, or the use constituted an acceptance of it by him'. This would thus imply that the issuer will bear the risk of the card going astray *en route* to the debtor.

The Consumer Credit Act 1974, however, is silent as to the liability for misuse by the cardholder himself. The above discussion relates to card misuse by an unauthorised third party. Liability for personal misuse by the cardholder is, however, provided for in the Payment Services Regulations 2009. Regulation 62 makes a user, who had acted fraudulently or with intent or gross negligence as to the use of the card, liable for all losses incurred as a result of the card misuse. Where the misuse also amounts to criminal conduct, naturally, the criminal law will be relevant.

As far as the charge card is concerned, the cardholder's liability for card misuse is largely subject to the 2009 Regulations and the terms of the agreement. In *Re a Debtor (No 78 of 2000)*,[76] the debtor was required to pay the issuer even though the goods bought using the charge card had not been received because she had allowed her husband to use her card which was in direct contravention of the terms of her contract with the issuer. The contract had also required her to question any doubtful payments in a reasonable time. She only questioned the payment three years after it was made. She had therefore not complied with the terms of her agreement and as such, had to bear the risk of the card misuse. As regards the 2009 Regulations, regs 57 and 62 would apply to the misuse of a charge card.[77]

A subject of much significance is the concept of connected lender liability. Section 75(1) of the Consumer Credit Act 1974 states:

> If the debtor under a debtor-creditor-supplier agreement . . . has, in relation to a transaction financed by the agreement, any claim against the supplier in respect of a misrepresentation or breach of contract, he shall have a like claim against the creditor, who, with the supplier, shall accordingly be jointly and severally liable to the debtor.

That means, if the goods supplied by the merchant are defective, the card issuer will be liable to compensate the cardholder for the breach of the sale contract regardless of whether or not the cardholder decides to claim against the merchant. Liability under s. 75 only arises where the cash price of the supply is over £100 but not more than £30,000 (s. 75(3)). It applies, however, even if the credit only relates to part of the price (for example, where the consumer pays part in cash or by cheque).

The rationale behind the concept of connected lender liability is that the card issuer is 'much better placed than the cardholder to secure redress from the offending supplier' and agreements between issuers and merchants would usually impose an express obligation on the merchant to deal promptly with legitimate complaints by cardholders.[78]

---

[76] Unreported, 13 July 2001.
[77] See section 6.5.5 below.
[78] Crowther Report (Cmnd 4596) para. 6.12.10.

The House of Lords has confirmed in *OFT* v *Lloyd's TSB*[79] that s. 75 would apply not only to domestic transactions but also to transactions made abroad (and on the Internet).[80] As to the argument by the issuer that it should not be compelled to be liable for over 29 million merchants worldwide, Lord Mance held that there was nothing in the legislation that limited its scope to domestic transactions. Additionally, the principal theme of the Crowther Report was that creditors would have a strong contractual and commercial influence over their merchants and that, where resort could not be had to such merchants, losses were better borne by creditors. Creditors are better able to spread their losses and risks over the public at large.

6.3.3.2 Relationship between merchant and bank/merchant acquirer

There is usually a so-called 'master agreement' between merchant acquirer and merchant. That agreement will also incorporate the so-called by-laws of the Visa and MasterCard schemes, if the cards concerned are those issued with those logos respectively. In order to be paid, the merchant is required by the master agreement to check that the PIN[81] (where the card is supported by chip and PIN technology) has been properly validated and approved before proceeding with the sale or, where a signature is required, to check that the signature matches that on the back of the card. The merchant is also required to verify that the card-holder is actually entitled to make a purchase exceeding a prescribed limit (the floor figure). In certain types of transactions, the merchant is also duty bound to adopt specific security and fraud prevention measures.[82] A commission or fee is deducted from the sale price as we have observed. So why do merchants accept card payments? Lord Rodger in *Union Bank of Jamaica* v *Yap*[83] commented:

The merchants taking part in the Visa and MasterCard schemes benefit from the business that they attract because their customers can pay by credit card. The acquiring banks therefore provide a valuable service to the merchants in processing the transactions. Equally, the fees that the banks can charge for this service can make it potentially profitable for them to have processing arrangements with large numbers of merchants.

It should, however, also be noted that although the immediate contract is between the bank and the merchant, the merchant will have to bear the cost of the interchange fee imposed on the merchant acquirer by the issuer (where applicable, the issuer in turn has to settle the fee with the scheme in question, Visa, MasterCard or some other undertaking).

The card issuer is usually entitled under the contract to terminate the facility at specified intervals – it is likely to do so if the merchant attracts a high level of chargeback. Chargeback occurs when the cardholder disputes or challenges the quality of the goods or services provided and a refund is processed through the credit card. In *NSB* v *Worldpay*[84] N provided a service for reuniting pet owners with their lost pets. Pet owners could purchase the service on an annual basis or for the lifetime of the pet. W was a merchant acquirer which provided credit and debit card payment processing services to merchants. W gave notice to terminate the agreement and claimed to be entitled to retain a substantial sum under the contract on

---

[79] [2008] 1 AC 316.
[80] See [2008] *LMCLQ* 333–352; *Finance & Credit Law* (2007), Nov/Dec, 4–5.
[81] Personal Identification Number.
[82] See, for example, *Union Bank of Jamaica* v *Yap* [2002] UKPC 26.
[83] *Ibid*.
[84] [2012] EWHC 927 (Comm).

the basis that it considered in good faith that there was a high risk of chargebacks. The court agreed with W that it was acting in good faith on the basis of a review by an independent firm of accountants which showed that there was a high risk of chargebacks.

The bank acting as merchant acquirer would clearly have a claim against a fraudulent merchant. It is tempting for merchants, knowing that the bank will usually honour a payment by credit card, if the merchant has no means of knowing that the card presented for payment has been misappropriated from the true cardholder. In *Do-Buy 925 Ltd* v *National Westminster Bank PLC*[85] D, a jewellery trader, had accepted debit card payment from a customer (X) for goods totalling £359,000. After the sale had been effected, it transpired that X was not the true holder of the card, having obtained it by fraud. D was unable to prove that the sale transaction actually took place. That meant, as far as the court was concerned, that there was no genuine transaction for which the payment should be covered by the merchant acquirer. The contract between the merchant acquirer and the merchant will usually stipulate that it is the merchant's responsibility 'to prove that the debit of a cardholder's account was authorised by the genuine cardholder'.

The merchant should also be careful not to process card payments for other third-party suppliers; the agreement usually makes it clear that the right to be reimbursed is confined to transactions between itself and its customers. In *Lancore Services Ltd* v *Barclays Bank PLC*[86] it was held that the merchant acquirer was entitled to withhold payments to the merchant and to terminate the contract between them when the merchant had used the facilities to process illegal sales made by third parties who dealt in online pornography and pharmaceuticals. That, however, does not mean that, as between the cardholder and the card issuer, the transaction is unauthorised – the consumer is not required to enquire into any lack of authority. Hence, in *Bank of Scotland* v *Alfred Truman*[87] X had processed credit card payments on behalf of Y in sales made by Y to customers. Although there may be an issue as to whether or not X had the authority under his agreement with the merchant acquirer to process payments for a third party (Y), the court held that the merchant acquirer was liable to the customers under s. 75 CCA 1974 for the non-delivery of the goods sold by Y. The judge ruled that X's contractual arrangements with Y gave rise to an indirect relationship between Y and the card issuer which was sufficient to constitute a pre-existing arrangement within the meaning of s. 12(b) of the 1974 Act.

6.3.3.3 Relationship between cardholder and merchant

This is obviously a sale or supply of services transaction. Questions about payment will thus be resolved according to the terms of the sale or supply contract. However, what is the legal position of the supplier who is unable to secure payment from the card issuer? For example, what if the card issuer has become insolvent?

As far as the charge card is concerned, the Court of Appeal has confirmed in *Re Charge Card Services*[88] that where the supplier had accepted payment by charge card, he cannot subsequently pursue the cardholder for payment if the issuer is insolvent or, for some other reason, unable to pay. Payment by charge card is presumed to be absolute or unconditional. Millett J, whose judgment was affirmed by the Court of Appeal, said:

[85] [2010] EWHC 2862 (QB).
[86] [2009] EWCA Civ 752.
[87] [2005] EWHC 583 (QB).
[88] [1989] Ch 497.

. . . the terms on which the supplier is entitled to payment from the card-issuing company are quite different from those on which the supplier would be entitled to payment from the customer if he were subject to any residual liability not discharged by the use of the card. The card-issuing company is liable to pay the supplier very shortly after the receipt of the sales vouchers and claim form, but is entitled to deduct its commission; while the customer is liable to pay the full value of the voucher, but is entitled to much longer credit. If the customer is liable to pay the supplier on the failure or default of the card-issuing company, it is on terms more onerous than either, for he must be liable to make immediate payment of the full face value of the voucher. It is difficult to find any justification for imputing to the customer an intention to undertake any such liability.

It would seem to follow that there are no special reasons why the rule should not also extend to credit cards.

POINT OF INTEREST

The payment made is to the merchant. The question has arisen in recent times as to whether or not, if the customer adds an amount to the bill to be paid by credit or charge card intended to be passed on to a third party by the merchant, the merchant is under any duty to pass it on. This frequently happens in restaurants. A customer decides to add a tip intended for the waiter/waitress but the restaurateur keeps the entire sum for himself. It was held in *Nerva and Others* v *RL & G Ltd*[89] that the tips made out in the credit card slip belonged to the restaurateur. It was subsequently also confirmed by the European Court on Human Rights that there was no breach of the freedom to enjoy one's possessions (Art. 1 Protocol 1) because the credit card vouchers were made out in the name of the restaurateur and the waiters did not have a possessory right to the tips. That of course is not to say that they did not have a contractual right to the tips, but key to the claim that Art. 1 Protocol 1 had been breached is possession.

Do you think it makes a difference if you specifically ask the restaurant to pass the tips (which you have included in your credit card payment) on to the waiting staff?

6.4 Funds transfers

Modern commercial payments almost invariably entail some kind of electronic transfer of funds. These funds transfers may occur either as a credit or debit transfer. A credit transfer takes place when the payer's account is debited whilst the payee's account is credited. A credit transfer may be arranged as a one-off payment (a direct CHAPS[90] or BACS[91] transfer) or on a recurring basis (for example, a standing order). A debit transfer occurs when the payer authorises his bank to pay on the presentation of a debit instrument (such as a cheque) or

---

[89] [1995] IRLR 2000 (HC); [1996] IRLR 461 (Court of Appeal); *Nerva and Others* v *United Kingdom* [2002] IRLR 815 (European Court of Human Rights).
[90] Clearing House Automated Payment System.
[91] Bankers' Automated Clearing Services.

a debit instruction (such as a direct debit mandate) by the payee. Much of the credit and debit is carried out by a process of adjusting the balances on the accounts of the payer and payee. It is therefore a bit misleading to call this a funds transfer because there is no actual transfer of money involved. There is also no assignment by the payer of his debt to his bank to the payee; as Staughton J said in *Libyan Arab Foreign Bank* v *Bankers Trust*:[92]

> An account transfer means the process by which some other person or institution comes to owe money to the Libyan Bank or their nominee, and the obligation of Bankers Trust is extinguished or reduced *pro tanto*. 'Transfer' may be a somewhat misleading word, since the original obligation is not assigned (notwithstanding *dicta* in one American case which speak of assignment); a new obligation by a new debtor is created.

In an electronic funds transfer, the originating bank is committed to the receiving bank at the time the receiving bank receives the payment message. Where the funds transfer is performed by the delivery of paper instruments, the originating bank is committed as soon as the paper has been delivered. The debtor will not be able to revoke or countermand his payment order as soon as the originating bank (his bank) is committed to the funds transfer.

The adjusting of balances of accounts can occur in one of three contexts:

(a) between branches of the same bank (in-house payment);

(b) between banks in the same country (domestic payment);

(c) between banks in different jurisdictions (complex payment).

6.4.1 In-house payment

This occurs when the payer and payee both hold accounts with the same bank. The adjusting of balances in their accounts could thus be made by the bank's own in-house clearing room. This should be fairly straightforward and simple because the bank alone will control and manage the entire process. In-house payment does not imply that the accounts must be with the same branch.

In an in-house transfer, the payment and the commitment to pay will usually coincide. Payment becomes complete as soon as the relevant book entries are made reflecting the credit and debit. Since both creditor and debtor have accounts in the same bank, the transfer occurs when the bank unconditionally recognises the payee as having taken the payer's place as its creditor. It was held in *Momm* v *Barclays Bank International Ltd*[93] that as there was strong evidence that the bank had given the transfer unconditional recognition, the transfer was deemed to be complete. In that case, Barclays Bank as instructed by Herstatt Bank credited the claimant's account. Both Herstatt and the claimant held accounts with Barclays (that is, it was an in-house payment). However, Herstatt's account did not have an adequate credit balance. The following day Herstatt Bank collapsed. Barclays reversed the claimant's credit entry. Kerr J held that Barclays was wrong to do that because the payment was completed as soon as the bank initiated the electronic process which credited the claimant's account.

That said, if the bank had credited an account when the creditor was not expecting any credit transfer to take place, the payment would not be complete until the creditor expressed his consent to the credit transfer.

[92] [1989] QB 728 at 750.
[93] [1977] QB 790.

It is clearly open to the bank to reverse an entry if it had not unconditionally recognised the payee as having taken over the place of the payer as its debtor. Entries made in the bank's books are therefore not conclusive as to the question of whether or not there had been a decision to pay by the debtor. The posting of credits and debits is not a final act unless, as in *Momm*, there is unconditional recognition of the payee's new status as the bank's debtor.[94]

6.4.2 Domestic payment

A domestic payment is made when the movement on accounts is made in the local currency between different banks. When the payer's bank receives the payment instructions, it will debit the payer's account and request the payee's bank to credit the payee's account. The two banks will then need to settle as between themselves the money 'transferred'. The two banks can settle either on a bilateral or multilateral basis. In order to understand bilateral and multilateral settlement, consider the example below.

EXAMPLE

Payer banks with Bank A. Payee banks with Bank B. Payer pays payee £10,000. A debits payer's account and then instructs B to credit payee's account. A now owes B £10,000. If A has an account in B, B will adjust that account so that B will receive £10,000. This is bilateral settlement and the two banks (where one has an account with the other) are called correspondents. More usually, though, both A and B will have accounts with a third bank, *viz* the central bank. The two accounts will be adjusted with a credit and debit entry by the central bank. This is called multilateral settlement.

The settlement of the banks' accounts can take place in real time where real-time gross settlement (RTGS) is available or at periodic intervals where only net settlement is available. Gross settlement occurs when the parties settle each payment separately through the central bank without taking into account other obligations flowing between them. Where it takes place in real time, it is called real-time gross settlement. Net settlement means the banks will settle a number of transfers (either as payer or payee) accumulated over a period of time (for example, at the end of the working day or the following day) and only the net balance is paid. Net settlement therefore has the cost advantage because the banks do not need to engage with the settlement process continually but only periodically. Liquidity is always maintained – it is not easily threatened by a large transfer, for example. However, the risk of net settlement is that the debtor bank may become unable to pay (as a result of insolvency, for example) at the appointed time of settlement.

6.4.3 Complex payment

The movement of funds across borders and using a foreign currency is called a complex payment. Several banks may be involved. Where a credit transfer is instructed, the payer's bank

---

[94] See also *Sutherland v Royal Bank of Scotland PLC* 1997 SLT 329.

will transmit a payment message to its correspondent in the country of the payee's bank. The correspondent bank will in turn pass the message on to the payee's bank and the two banks (both being in the same country) will then settle by making payment across the books of the central bank in that country. As between the correspondent bank and the payer's bank (known as the originating bank), settlement will be made according to the terms of their contract. In the case of a debit transfer, the payee's bank will convey the debit instrument to its correspondent (in the country where the payer's bank is based) to collect payment in the local jurisdiction. It is also common for debit instructions requiring the correspondent bank to obtain payment using the local settlement system.

The payment chain is thus complicated. See the example in the following figure.

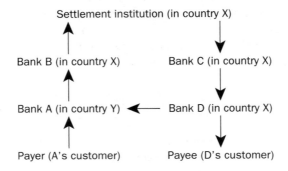

Bank A is known as a second-tier bank, that is, one which is not a direct participant in the payment system of country X. In order for the 'money' to reach the payee, the payment process involves debiting the payer's account with Bank A, Bank A's account with Bank B and Bank B's account with the settlement institution. It will also require crediting Bank C's account with the settlement institution and the payee's account with Bank C.

The settlement institution is likely to be the central bank in X; the settlement between direct participants (B and C) takes place there using X's currency. However, there are also settlements between A and B, and C and D. As the several settlements in our example may not necessarily all adopt the same settlement system (some might be RTGS, others net), this can cause uncertainty and a lack of finality. Although most parties will provide contractually as to who bears the risk, etc., the payee will remain exposed to the risk of non-payment even though the payer has transmitted the payment instruction. This explains why the rule in *The Brimnes*,[95] where applied to funds transfers, may lead to what some might consider to be unfairness.

6.4.4 **Risks**

There are essentially two major risks in international funds transfers – the Herstatt risk and sovereign risk. The Herstatt risk, which takes its name from the collapse of the German bank Bankhaus ID Herstatt KGaA in 1974, affects most foreign exchange transactions. Where a

---

[95] [1975] QB 929. See section 6.1.1 above.

transaction involves foreign exchange, there are two credit transfers. Assuming that the transaction is for the transfer of money by Bank A from the UK to Bank B in the USA. A will deliver sterling to B whilst B, upon receipt, will pass on the same amount in dollars to the payee. The intention is that both these transfers occur at the same time. However, there is often some delay between them. The first bank to complete its payment obligation would thus run the risk of the latter bank failing to meet its obligation to deliver after receiving the funds.[96]

Sovereign risk is the risk of the foreign government deciding to prohibit the withdrawal or transfer of funds held in an account in its territory. In such a case, the contract for payment is likely to be treated as frustrated because of a foreign illegality.

The intervention of foreign government action also may include the intervention of foreign insolvency laws preventing the movement of funds following the collapse of a participant in the payment chain (whether an intermediary or the payer). In England and Wales, insolvency law requires that the assets of an insolvent bank (or company) be distributed in equal proportion to all its creditors (this is known as the *pari passu* principle).[97] However, rule 4.90, Insolvency Rules 1986 provides that where before the company goes into liquidation there have been mutual credits, mutual debts or other mutual dealings between the company and a creditor, account shall be taken of what is due from each party to the other and the sums due from one party shall be set off against the sums due from the other. This exception, however, only applies to cases involving bilateral netting or where mutual obligations are being set off. It does not apply where multilateral netting is involved (*Re Bank of Credit & Commerce International SA (No 8)*).[98] Bilateral netting, as we have seen, is where the settlement or netting is between two parties. Multilateral netting is where the debits and credits between several parties are adjusted collectively.

The EU Directive on Settlement Finality in Payment and Securities Settlement Systems as implemented by the Financial Markets and Insolvency (Settlement Finality) Regulations 1999[99] tries to cut the risks of insolvency laws defeating a properly executed funds transfer in both domestic and complex payments. Part III of the Regulations provide that transfer orders and netting are legally enforceable and binding on third parties, even in the event of insolvency proceedings, provided the transfer orders were entered into the system before the moment of opening of such insolvency proceedings. However, the protection will only apply to those systems which have been specifically classed as 'designated systems' by the Bank of England (Part II of the Regulations). In exceptional cases, the protection will also apply to transfer orders made very soon after insolvency proceedings have commenced but on the same day, and it is for the clearing house, central counterparty or settlement agent to prove that they were not aware of the opening of insolvency proceedings (reg. 20).

---

[96] See R. Dale, 'Controlling Foreign Settlement Risks' (1999) 14 *BFLR* 329 on how these risks might be managed.

[97] Section 107, Insolvency Act 1986.

[98] [1998] AC 214; Lord Hoffmann made it plain that 'there can be no set off of claims by third parties, even with their consent. To do so would be to allow parties by agreement to subvert the fundamental principle of *pari passu* distribution of the insolvent company's assets' (at 223). Multilateral netting naturally and necessarily involves third parties. See also *British Eagle International Airlines Ltd* v *Compagnie Nationale Air France* [1975] 1 WLR 758.

[99] SI 1999/2979; it should also be noted that there are special rules on bank insolvencies in the new Banking Act 2009. See also the Banking Act (Parts 2 and 3 Consequential Amendments) Order 2009, SI 2009/317 for new terminologies relevant to finality and settlement post bank insolvency.

6.5 Regulation of payment services

In 2009, the many different forms of payment services were brought within a single set of regulations to ensure that the organisations and financial institutions offering these services might be better regulated to provide the consumer with enhanced protection and to ensure that within the EU payment movements are properly harmonised to support free movement and pro-competition principles. The Payment Services Regulations 2009 were introduced to implement into UK law the EU Directive on Payment Services in the Internal Market.[100] The Regulations came into force on 1 November 2009.

The UK Treasury, when tabling the Regulations, expressed the objectives of the new regime in these terms.[101]

- To establish a prudential authorisation regime for non-credit or non-electronic money (e-money) institutions, known under the Directive as 'payment institutions'. Payment institutions which obtain authorisation in one EU Member State will be able to 'passport' their business and operate in other Member States without having to comply with further licensing requirements in other Member States. Smaller providers operating below a certain threshold will also be able to be registered providing they do not intend to operate in other Member States;

- To harmonise conduct of business rules covering information requirements and rights and obligations for payment providers and end-users. These rules will apply to all payment service providers, including credit institutions, electronic money institutions and payment institutions and will include provisions that are expected to support the industry-led Single Euro Payments Area initiative;

- To ensure that the rules governing access to payment systems are non-discriminatory. This is aimed at encouraging competition among payment service providers.

6.5.1 Scope of application of the payment services regulations

It cannot be stressed enough that the regulations apply to most forms of payment services, not only funds or credit transfers. Part 1 of Schedule 1 of the Regulations gives a full list of services which the law considers to be 'payment services'. In general, they include any services which enable payments to be made through a payment account or some other source. They do not include services which deal with the transfer or collection of physical cash or other paper-based payment instruments. Part 2 provides thus that the following activities do not constitute payment services:

(a) payment transactions executed wholly in cash and directly between the payer and the payee, without any intermediary intervention;

(b) payment transactions between the payer and the payee through a commercial agent authorised to negotiate or conclude the sale or purchase of goods or services on behalf of the payer or the payee;

[100] Directive 2007/64 which replaces the Directive on Cross-border Credit Transfers (Directive 97/5).
[101] www.opsi.gov.uk/si/si2009/em/uksiem_20090209_en.pdf

(c) the professional physical transport of banknotes and coins, including their collection, processing and delivery;

(d) payment transactions consisting of non-professional cash collection and delivery as part of a not-for-profit or charitable activity;

. . .

(f) money exchange business consisting of cash-to-cash operations where the funds are not held on a payment account;

(g) payment transactions based on any of the following documents drawn on the payment service provider with a view to placing funds at the disposal of the payee –

    (i) paper cheques of any kind, including travellers' cheques;

    (ii) bankers' drafts;

    (iii) paper-based vouchers;

    (iv) paper postal orders;

(h) payment transactions carried out within a payment or securities settlement system between payment service providers and settlement agents, central counterparties, clearing houses, central banks or other participants in the system . . .

The Financial Services Authority gives the following table as a guide to what is covered by 'payment services'.[102]

Payment service	Example
Services enabling cash to be placed on a payment account and all of the operations required for operating a payment account	• Payments of cash into a payment account over the counter and through an ATM. Services enabling cash withdrawals from a payment account and all of the operations required for operating a payment account
Services enabling cash withdrawals from a payment account and all of the operations required for operating a payment account	• Withdrawals of cash from payment accounts, for example through an ATM or over the counter
Execution of the following types of payment transaction: • direct debits, including one-off direct debits • payment transactions executed through a payment card or a similar device • credit transfers, including standing orders	• Transfers of funds with the user's payment service provider or with another payment service provider • Direct debits (including one-off direct debits). N.B.: Acting as a direct debit originator would not, of itself, constitute the provision of a payment service • Transferring e-money • Credit transfers, such as standing orders, BACS or CHAPS payments
Execution of the following types of payment transaction where the funds are covered by a credit line for a payment service user: • direct debits, including one-off direct debits • payment transactions through a payment card or a similar device • credit transfers, including standing orders	• Direct debits using overdraft facilities • Card payments • Credit transfers using overdraft facilities

---

[102] 'The FSA's role under the Payment Services Regulations 2009: Our approach' (May 2012) p. 12.

Payment service	Example
Issuing payment instruments or acquiring payment transactions	● Card-issuing (other than mere technical service providers who do not come into possession of funds being transferred) and card merchant-acquiring services (rather than merchants themselves)
Money remittance	● Money transfer/remittances that do not involve payment accounts
Execution of payment transactions where the consent of the payer to execute a payment transaction is given by means of any telecommunication, digital or IT device and the payment is made to the telecommunication, IT system or network operator, acting only as an intermediary between the payment service user and the supplier of the goods and services	● Mobile or fixed phone payments, where the payment is made from the phone itself rather than the phone being used as an authentication tool to send a payment order to another payment service provider ● Payments made from handheld devices (for example, BlackBerry)

6.5.2 Authorisation regime

Parts 2 to 4 of the Regulations set up an authorisation regime for certain providers of payment services. These are those providers who are not already regulated elsewhere such as credit institutions or electronic money institutions. Providers of payment services not already regulated might include a mobile telephone operator or a firm offering money transfer services. This part of the Regulations tries to plug the gap in existing banking regulation which relates only to credit institutions (and electronic money institutions are deemed to be credit institutions under the Electronic Money Directive). Payment service providers will be registered either as authorised payment institutions (regs 5–11) or as small payment institutions (regs 12–15) depending on the value of the payment transactions they execute and whether they are seeking to establish a branch or provide services in another Member State. In order to be registered or authorised, providers must meet capital requirements (reg. 18 and Sch. 3) and prove that they are able to protect the users' funds (reg. 19). They must also keep proper records and provide information to the Financial Services Authority (FSA) about accounts and outsourcing (regs 20–22). The register of payment service providers will be maintained by the FSA.

6.5.3 Duty to provide information

Parts 5 and 6 are perhaps the more important section for the reader. Part 5 applies to *all* payment service providers – not only those registered under the regulations. This means all providers – credit institutions, electronic money institutions, authorised payment institutions and small payment institutions – must meet the requirements in Part 5 which relate to the provision of appropriate information to payment service users. There are separate provisions for single payment service contracts (regs 36–39) and framework contracts (regs 40–46). In the former, prior to the contract being made, the service provider must inform the user as to:

- the information or unique identifier (such as the payee's name, address, bank details, etc.) which the user should provide to execute the payment order;[103]
- the maximum time in which the payment order will be executed;
- charges payable to the provider by the user and, where applicable, a breakdown of these charges;[104]
- any relevant exchange rate to be applied, where applicable;[105]
- detailed information (possibly in the small print) as to the parties' rights and liabilities, the identity of the provider, a description of the actual payment service, the applicable law of the contract, etc. (Sch. 4).

As far as framework contracts are concerned, the payee too is entitled to similar information from his service provider once the payer's payment order has been executed. Simplified requirements will however apply where the payment order is for small sums. Regulation 35 refers to these as instruments which:

(a) can be used only to execute individual payment transactions of €30 or less, or in relation to payment transactions executed wholly within the UK, €60 or less;

(b) have a spending limit of €150, or where payment transactions must be executed wholly within the UK, €300; or

(c) store funds that do not exceed €500 at any time.

6.5.4 **Payment instrument**

What is a payment instrument?

LEGISLATIVE PROVISION

Regulation 2

'Payment instrument' means any:

(a) personalised device; or

(b) personalised set of procedures agreed between the payment service user and the payment service provider;

used by the payment service user in order to initiate a payment order . . .

---

[103] This is to ensure that the service will not be delayed – it is not for the user to know what is required to facilitate the prompt execution of the payment order, hence, the onus in reg. 36 is on the provider to ask for such information from the user. If the payer having received such information is unable to supply the correct information, the service provider is within its rights to charge the user for the failure.

[104] One criticism might be that whilst the charges borne by the user are to be set out clearly, the charges to be borne by the payee are not explained to the user.

[105] Naturally, where the payment is to be made within borders, this is quite unnecessary.

It would seem therefore that debit cards, cash cards, cash deposits, cash withdrawals, money remittance payments, charge cards and credit cards would all fall within this definition. The position of the cheque guarantee card is less clear. It is difficult to argue that the cheque guarantee card actually initiates payment. In this connection, it is also useful to note that the Regulations apply only to providers of payment services. Payment services are set out in Parts 1 and 2 of Sch. 1.

Regulation 37 provides that, after receipt of the payment order, the service provider should inform the user as to when the order was received, the amount transferred and in what currency and in what exchange rate, and any charges (and breakdown, where applicable) payable or paid. The provider should also give the user a reference by which the user could identify the payment transaction (reg. 37(2)(a)).

In the case of a framework contract[106] (one where the payment services are executed on a running basis), the service provider is required to provide the information listed in Sch. 4 in good time before the payment service user is bound by the framework contract (reg. 40(1)(a)). Where the contract is concluded at the payment service user's request using a means of distance communication which does not enable provision of such information in accordance with reg. 40(1)(a), this should be immediately after the conclusion of the contract (reg. 40(1)(b)).

These provisions on information cannot be contracted out of where the service user is a consumer, a micro-enterprise (such as a teashop owner, sandwich seller or market trader) or a charity (reg. 33(4)). Service providers are not allowed to charge for the provision of the information referred to in the regulations (regs 47–50).

6.5.5 Substantive rights and obligations in the provision of payment services

Part 6 of the Regulations provides for the rights and obligations relating to the provision of payment services. It makes provision for matters including charges (reg. 54), consent to payment transactions (reg. 55), unauthorised or incorrectly executed payment transactions, liability for unauthorised payment transactions (regs 59–62), refunds, execution of payment transactions, execution time and the liability of payment service providers (regs 63–79). These provisions cannot be contracted out of where the user is a consumer, micro-enterprise or charity. These provisions will also only have limited effect on small-scale payments covered by framework contracts (reg. 53). Small-scale payment instruments are those which:

(a) can be used only to execute individual payment transactions of €30 or less or in relation to payment transactions executed wholly within the UK, €60 or less;

(b) have a spending limit of €150 or where payment transactions must be executed wholly within the UK, €300; or

(c) store funds that do not exceed €500 at any time.

Regulation 54 provides that all the charges must be those adumbrated in the contract and must correspond reasonably to the actual costs of the service. This latter limb is naturally

---

[106] The Regulations define this as a 'contract for payment services which governs the future execution of individual and successive payment transactions and which may contain the obligation and conditions for setting up a payment account' (reg. 2).

controversial because the law is effectively a price-setting measure. The payee and its payment service provider may agree for the payment service provider to deduct its charges from the amount transferred before crediting it to the payee provided that the full amount of the payment transaction and the amount of the charges are clearly stated in the information provided to the payee (reg. 68(2)).

The provider must ensure that proper consent to the transfer has been obtained from the user (reg. 55). In general, the user cannot revoke the order once it has been received by the payer's service provider (reg. 67(1)) unless this is agreed to by the service provider. In the case of a payment transaction initiated by or through the payee, the payer may not revoke the payment order after transmitting the payment order or giving consent to execute the payment transaction to the payee (reg. 67(2)). As for direct debits, the payer may not revoke the payment order after the end of the business day preceding the day agreed for debiting the funds (reg. 67(3)). The burden of proof of consent is on the provider (reg. 60). In the event an execution was made without proper consent, the provider must refund those funds and, where applicable, restore the debited payment account to the state it would have been in had the unauthorised transaction not taken place (reg. 61(b)).

As to the rights and liabilities on use of the payment instrument, other than the terms in the contract between the parties, the regulations impose certain duties on the user and provider which cannot be varied by contract. Regulation 56 permits the provider to stop the payment if it suspects that security has been compromised or that, if a credit line is exceeded by the payment, the payer would be unable to fulfil its financial obligations. If payment is stopped or interrupted by the provider, it should inform the payer not only of its intention to stop payment but also the reasons why it is seeking to do so (reg. 56(3)). The provision, however, does not specify how detailed the reasons should be. As a matter of commercial practicality, it may be quite legitimate for the provider simply to give perfunctory reasons but the law in this connection is silent. Regulation 57 requires the payer, who is in possession of a payment instrument (such as a payment card), to use it according to the terms and guidance given by the issuer, especially the personalised security features. If the instrument is stolen or misappropriated or misused, he should inform the issuer without undue delay. As for the service provider, it must ensure that it performs its business operations properly so as not to compromise the security of the payment instrument given to the user and to stop payment upon being informed of misuse by the user (reg. 58). The provider is also prohibited from sending unsolicited payment instruments to the user, unless, of course, an already issued payment instrument needs to be renewed or replaced (reg. 58(1)(b)).

In the case of misuse of the payment instrument, the user will be liable to a maximum of £50 but where there is fraud or intent or gross negligence, he will be liable for all losses incurred as a result of misuse (reg. 62). Where the user had informed the provider of the misuse, he will not be liable for any loss arising thereafter (reg. 62(3)(a)). Also, if the provider failed to provide for an appropriate means whereby the user could notify them, it would appear that the provider will be liable for the loss to the full amount (reg. 62(3)(b)). Where the payment instrument was misused by a third party in a distance contract (say, an unauthorised Internet transaction), the user shall not be held liable (reg. 62(3)(c)).

The providers are also liable for any incorrect execution of the payment order (regs 75 and 76). Disputes often arise, however, as to the precise meaning of the payment order. The courts, when interpreting the terms of the payment order, will give proper regard to the terminology and practices in the relevant industry (*Winnetka Trading* v *Julius Baer*

International Ltd.[107]) It should be noted that the provider has no duty to warn the user as to whether or not the payment order is sensible and advisable.[108]

Where the liability of a payment service provider ('the first provider') is attributable to another payment service provider or an intermediary, reg. 78 states that the other payment service provider or intermediary must compensate the first provider for any losses incurred or sums paid.

A general defence is available where a breach of the Regulations was the result of abnormal and unforeseeable circumstances beyond the person's control and where the consequences would have been unavoidable despite all efforts to the contrary (reg. 79).

An improvement in the Payment Services Regulations is reducing the time when the payee's account is put in credit. In payment transactions to a payment account, reg. 70(1) provides that the payee's service provider's account[109] is credited by the end of the business day following the time of receipt of the payment order. In the case of cheques or other paper instruments, the service provider's account should be credited by the end of the second business day following the time of receipt of the order (reg. 70(3)(a)). In more complex cases not involving euro, sterling or only one foreign currency conversion between euro and sterling, the service providers will have up to four business days to credit the payee's service provider's account (reg. 70(4)). Cases not falling within reg. 70 will be a matter of the relevant contracts.

Regulation 73 also requires that the credit value date on the payee's account must not be any later than the business day on which the service provider's account has been credited. The payee's payment service provider must also ensure that the amount of the payment transaction is at the payee's disposal immediately after that amount has been credited to that payment service provider's account.

It should be noted that in the case of credit cards or other payment on credit instruments, a service provider must meet not only the requirements of the Payment Services Regulations 2009 but also the provisions of any relevant consumer credit legislation.

6.6 Negotiable instruments

6.6.1 Concept of negotiability

Many payments are made using negotiable instruments. Negotiable instruments are particularly important in commerce because the person in possession could sue for payment on the instrument itself without needing to rely on any underlying contractual payment obligation. For example, if A pays B for goods sold using a cheque, B can sue on the cheque if the cheque is dishonoured because A finds the goods not to be of satisfactory quality. B does not need to rely on his performance of the sale contract to seek payment due under the cheque. The cheque (negotiable instrument) is thus autonomous and is not dependent on an underlying sale contract.

---

[107] [2011] EWHC 2030 (Ch).

[108] *Ibid.*

[109] Readers should note that this does NOT refer to the payee's personal bank account; this refers to the account of the payee's bank into which funds are first transferred.

The rights of payment under a negotiable instrument are also not subject to any set offs. For example, X owes Y £10 whilst Y owes X £5. If X draws a cheque for £10 in Y's favour, when Y tenders the cheque for payment, X's bank must pay the full amount on the face of the cheque, namely, £10. The bank will not make the deduction of Y's £5 debt.

As such, the holder of a dishonoured negotiable instrument is generally entitled to obtain judgment on the negotiable instrument without having to go to full trial in court. He would normally be entitled to obtain summary judgment.[110]

There is no statutory definition of the term 'negotiable instrument'. An instrument at common law normally connotes a document which physically embodies the payment obligation. A payment obligation is a commitment to pay a sum of money to a person at a specified time or an order to a third party to pay a sum of money to the other person at a specified time. It is usually a matter of construction whether the document carried as its principal object a payment obligation. In *Claydon* v *Bradley*[111] a document stated: 'Received from Mr. and Mrs. T. Claydon the sum of £10,000 (ten thousand pounds) as a loan to be paid back in full by 1 July 1983 with an interest rate of 20% (twenty per cent) per annum.' The Court of Appeal held that it was a mere receipt and not a payment instrument. Although there was a commitment to repay the debt, it was not intended to be a payment instrument.

A payment instrument is a documentary intangible, that is to say, it is the embodiment of the payment obligation whereby money has to be paid with its possession being the best evidence of the right to that money.

An instrument is also a chattel in law. That means the person who owns the instrument has all the rights to use and dispose of it an owner would have in relation to his goods. The owner can pass title in the instrument by delivering the instrument to another person. A person who comes into possession of the instrument may be exposed to the risk of a claim in conversion by the true owner if he had not provided good consideration for the instrument.[112]

An instrument can be negotiable or non-negotiable. Negotiability was defined by Blackburn J in *Crouch* v *Crédit Foncier of England*:[113]

It [is] a safe rule that where an instrument is by the custom of trade transferable, like cash, by delivery, and is also capable of being sued upon by the person holding it *pro tempore,* then it is entitled to the name negotiable instrument, and the property in it passes to a *bona fide* transferee for value, though the transfer may not have taken place in market overt.

The negotiable instrument has two characteristics:

(a) it is transferable by mere delivery; all rights contained in the instrument will pass to the transferee;

(b) the transferee, who is a *bona fide* holder for value, can actually acquire a better title to it than the transferor.

An instrument may acquire the character of negotiability through course of custom. In *Goodwin* v *Robarts*[114] it was held that the custom being asserted must be demonstrated with sufficient clarity and notoriety, and should not contradict any established legal principle. It

---

[110] Part 24, Civil Procedure Rules 1998.
[111] [1987] 1 WLR 521; see also *Akbar Khan* v *Attar Singh* [1936] 2 All ER 545.
[112] *Marfani Co Ltd* v *Midland Bank* [1968] 1 WLR 956; *Dextra Bank & Trust* v *Bank of Jamaica* [2001] UKPC 50.
[113] (1873) LR 8 QB 374.
[114] (1875) LR 10 Ex 337.

must also be a general custom, not a mere local or particular custom. There should not be any expressions on the face of the instrument actually rendering the document non-negotiable – for example, words like 'not negotiable'. Foreign instruments may be recognised as negotiable instruments provided they too satisfy these conditions.[115] In *Goodwin*, it was held by the House of Lords that the scrip[116] of a foreign government, issued by it on negotiating a loan, is by the custom of all the stock markets of Europe a negotiable instrument. The rights in the scrip could therefore pass by mere delivery to a *bona fide* holder for value. English law would recognise the universal custom. Therefore, any person taking it in good faith would obtain a title to it independent of the title of the person from whom he took it.

This suggests that the categories of payment instruments which could be taken as a negotiable instrument are not closed. However, in conventional commercial practice, the main negotiable instruments are bills of exchange, promissory notes, cheques and certificates of deposit.

6.6.2 Main types of negotiable instrument

6.6.2.1 Bill of exchange

Modern forms of bills of exchange were used in the fairs in Europe in the 12th and 13th centuries.[117] In English law, the first reported case on a bill of exchange was in 1602[118] which involved a bill of exchange used to pay a foreign debt. The international aspect has always been important, particularly relevant in the use of bills of exchange. It was used to facilitate the payment of international trade in the seller's currency, but without the inconvenience and perils of carrying physical cash. Professional money exchangers would work with each other to enable the collection and payment of funds in the different countries. The buyer will pay a local money exchanger a sum of money (the purchase price plus commission). A bill would then be drawn by the money exchanger on his foreign correspondent in the seller's country requiring the drawee (the foreign correspondent) to pay the seller. The bill would then be sent by the drawer to the seller. The seller then presents the bill to the correspondent who would pay him. The drawer will reimburse the correspondent. Credit could also be provided. The bill of exchange soon also found favour with domestic traders in England around the 15th century.

In modern sales (especially international sales), on the other hand, the seller (drawer) will draw up a bill of exchange on the buyer or the buyer's bank (drawee). The bill of exchange will then be presented to the buyer or his bank when the goods have been delivered. The drawee will either pay at sight of the bill or at a future time, depending on the terms of the bill of exchange. The drawee signifies his undertaking to pay by accepting the bill. Where the bill is to be payable at a future predetermined time and it has been accepted, the payee could either wait until the bill matures before collecting payment or, more usually, discount

---

[115] *Gorgier* v *Mieville* (1824) 3 B & C 45.

[116] It promises to give to the bearer, after all instalments have been duly paid, a bond for the amount paid, with interest.

[117] See J. W. Daniel, *A Treatise on the Law of Negotiable Instruments* (1933) Chapter 1; W. E. Britton, *Handbook on the Law of Bills and Notes* (1943) pp. 2–22.

[118] *Martin* v *Boure* (1603) Cro Jac 6.

or negotiate the bill to a third party for value before the bill matures. This would naturally improve the seller's liquidity.

The following specimen form of a bill of exchange might help us understand how it works.

BILL OF EXCHANGE		
Drawer's name and address (A)		Maturity (B)
	Date of issue (C)	Drawer's ref. (D)
Drawee's name and address (E)	Pay against this bill of exchange to (F)	Payable with (G)
Amount in words and currency (H)	Amount and currency in figures (I)	Place of payment (J)
Additional information (K)	Accepted by (L)	Drawer's signature (M)

Legend:

(A) Drawer's name – the drawer is the person who is completing this bill of exchange.

(B) The maturity date of the bill of exchange. If immediate payment is needed, the drawer should write 'at sight' in this box. Where payment is to be made at a pre-agreed date, he should write 'maturity yyyy-mm-dd' or if payment is to be at a predetermined time, words such as '60 days after bill of lading date' or '60 days after date of issue', etc. would be fine.

(C) Date of issue – the date of the issuance of the bill of exchange.

(D) The drawer may wish to insert a reference number here.

(E) The drawee is the person to whom payment is due. This would be the seller in a sale of goods transaction.

(F) Payee – the party receiving payment at maturity. If the drawer is the intended payee, which is usually the case with a sale, the drawer will write in this box 'ourselves'. The payee of the bill of exchange may make an indorsement on the reverse of the bill of exchange if he wishes to negotiate (discount or sell) the bill for value. The indorsement is made using the firm's stamp, etc. and signed by an authorised person.

(G) The bill could be payable at the premises of a third party, for example, a bank, the address of which should be stated here.

(H) The amount expressed in words.

(I) The amount expressed in figures.

(J) Place of payment is normally where the drawee is located. It is possible for this to be some other place; if this is the case, box J should be completed accordingly.

(K) The drawer may wish to refer to other information related to the bill such as a letter of credit and its reference number, etc.

(L) When the drawee accepts the bill of exchange, he is called the acceptor. He indicates his acceptance of the bill by signing in this box.

(M) The drawer's company stamp and authorised signature should appear here. A bill which is not signed is not acceptable.

6.6.2.2 Promissory note

A promissory note is usually a document in writing carrying a promise to pay, unconditionally, a certain sum of money to a particular person or bearer. In early times, it was questioned whether promissory notes were merely contractual and therefore not actually negotiable.[119] However, the Promissory Notes Act 1704 settled the matter by confirming the negotiability of promissory notes.

---

[119] *Clerke v Martin* (1702) 2 Lord Raym 757.

6.6.2.3 Certificates of deposit

A certificate of deposit is a debt instrument or receipt issued by a bank or financial institution. It attests to the fact that a certain sum of money has been deposited with the bank. It may also state the duration of the deposit and any interest to be payable. The interest rate may either be fixed or floating. If the certificates relate to a sum in sterling, they are called sterling certificates. They are treated as negotiable instruments because they are usually drawn as 'payable to bearer or to order'. They were first issued in the 1960s but in recent times whilst they are widely used in the secondary money markets, paper versions are becoming less commonplace. Certificates of deposit tend to be held and transferred in an electronic format. A useful working definition might be had from s. 55(3), Finance Act 1968 (a provision which now has been repealed):

> 'certificate of deposit' means a document relating to money, in any currency, which has been deposited with the issuer or some other person, being a document which recognises an obligation to pay a stated amount to bearer or to order, with or without interest, and being a document by the delivery of which, with or without indorsement, the right to receive that stated amount, with or without interest, is transferable.[120]

6.6.2.4 Cheques

Most students will be familiar with the cheque. It was developed out of the deposit receipt issued by goldsmiths to depositors of funds in their safety deposit boxes in medieval times. The practice of allowing third parties to obtain payments from those funds, using the cheque, began to grow. The receipt was also transferable or negotiated. It thus came to be recognised as a negotiable instrument. The Bills of Exchange Act 1882 (s. 73) deems a cheque to be a bill of exchange drawn on a banker which was payable on demand. The use of cheques has been decreasing year on year with the advent of funds transfers and it is now quite rare for the cheque to be negotiated. It is almost solely used as a payment order instructing the bank to pay money into the account of a payee. Hence, although through custom the cheque had become a negotiable instrument, for fear of fraud it is seldom now used as such.

6.7 Bills of exchange

6.7.1 Introduction

Bills of exchange are governed by the Bills of Exchange Act 1882 and the common law rules on negotiable instruments. The subject is vast and in this book we shall confine our consideration to some of the more significant rules.

The Bills of Exchange Act 1882 is a code. This means, as Lord Herschell made clear in *Bank of England* v *Vagliano*,[121] the approach to its construction should be:

---

[120] For more on certificates of deposit, see Crenwell, Blair, Hill, Wood, et al. *Encyclopaedia of Banking Law* (Looseleaff from 1996) (Butterworths, Lexisnesis, London 1982–) at paras F112–132.
[121] [1891] AC 107.

in the first instance to examine the language of the statute and to ask what is its natural meaning, uninfluenced by any considerations derived from the previous state of the law and not to start with enquiring how the law previously stood and then assuming that it was probably intended to leave it unaltered, to see if the words of the enactment will bear an interpretation in conformity with this view.

Although it is a code, it does not mean that no reference should be made to the common law. The Bills of Exchange Act 1882 deals primarily with the bill of exchange as a negotiable instrument; on matters such as its role as a chattel, English property and tort law would be relevant. Hence, s. 97(2), recognising this necessity, states that 'the rules of common law including the law merchant, save in so far as they are inconsistent with the express provisions of this Act, shall continue to apply to bills of exchange, promissory notes and cheques'.

A bill of exchange is defined in s. 3 of the Act as an unconditional order in writing, addressed by one person to another signed by the person giving it, requiring the person to whom it is addressed to pay on demand or at a fixed or determinable future time a sum certain in money to or to the order of a specified person or to the bearer. Section 3(2) adds that an instrument which does not comply with these conditions, or which orders any act to be done in addition to the payment of money, is not a bill of exchange. If a document is not a promissory note but merely a contract or evidence of a debt, the claimant will not be able to rely on the law on negotiable instruments to enforce it.[122]

6.7.2 **The formal requirements**

1. The requirement that it should be in *writing* includes pre-printed words (s. 2). Although the written requirement might well extend to electronic forms, the provisions of the 1882 Act, understandably, do not easily lend themselves to a dematerialised bill of exchange. For example, the Act has specific rules on material alteration of a bill, indorsement in blank, inchoate bills, etc., which would be very difficult to apply where the bill is not a physical document.

2. A bill of exchange is an *order*, not a request. Therefore, a document which is expressed in the terms, 'We hereby authorise you to pay on our account to the order of A £6,000', is not a bill of exchange (*Hamilton v Spottiswoode*).[123]

3. It must be *unconditional*. Therefore, an instrument which says, 'Pay £100 if the goods are of satisfactory quality', would not qualify as a bill of exchange. This is a matter of construction in many cases. In *Bavins v London and South Western Bank*,[124] the instrument stated: 'provided the receipt form at foot hereof is signed.' It was held not to be a bill of exchange. On the other hand, in *Thairlwall v Great Northern Ry*[125] the words used were, 'This warrant will not be honoured after three months from date unless specially indorsed by the secretary'. The court said that was not a condition. The words merely informed the payee as to what the drawer considered to be a reasonable time for presenting the warrant. There is some doubt though as to whether a bill containing terms such as, 'Documents against

---

[122] *The Belize Bank Ltd v The Association of Concerned Belizeans* [2011] UKPC 35 – there a 'loan note' was held to be a promissory note.
[123] (1894) 4 Ex 200.
[124] [1900] 1 QB 270.
[125] [1910] 2 KB 509.

Acceptance', used quite widely in international commerce, would be treated as an uncon-ditional bill.[126] An order for payment out of a particular fund is not unconditional, but an unqualified order which is coupled with an indication of a fund from which the drawee is to refund himself, or a statement of the transaction which gives rise to the bill, is uncon-ditional (s. 3(3)).

4. It must be *addressed by one person (drawer) to another person (drawee)*.

5. It must be *signed by the drawer*.

6. Payment is to be made in *a sum certain in money*. Section 9(1) provides that a sum pay-able with interest, by instalment or according to an indicated foreign exchange rate will be considered to be 'certain in money'. For example, in *Belize Bank Ltd v Association of Concerned Belizeans*,[127] the promissory note could be expressed in these terms 'FOR VALUE RECEIVED, THE GOVERNMENT OF BELIZE . . . hereby unconditionally promises to pay to the holder of this Note for the time being, being on the date of this Note . . . the prin-cipal sum of . . . BZ\$33,545,820 together with interest thereon accruing daily from and including the date of issue of this Loan Note and compounded monthly at the rate of interest of . . . 13% per annum.'

7. The bill must be *payable on demand or at a fixed or determinable future time*. If no time for payment is stipulated, s. 10(1) provides that the bill will be deemed to be payable on demand. The future time for payment must be capable of determination. Therefore, if it states, 'pay 90 days after acceptance of the bill of exchange' or '60 days after sight of the bill', that is a determinable future time[128] but where it says 'payable on or before 31 December 1956', it is not sufficiently certain.[129] A bill payable on demand is called a demand bill. A bill payable at a fixed future time is called a fixed bill, whilst one payable at a determinable future time is called a time or usance bill.

8. The bill has to be *payable to or to the order of a specified person*. That person can include the drawer or drawee. It can also be made *payable to bearer*. Therefore a cheque which is drawn 'cash or order' is not a bill of exchange.[130] If there is a latent ambiguity as to the payee's identity, extrinsic evidence may be adduced to show who is the intended payee. Equally, extrinsic evidence will not be admissible to explain a patent ambiguity. In the latter case, the instrument would not satisfy the definition of a bill of exchange in s. 3. Therefore, if a bill is drawn, 'pay Mohammed Khan' and there are two persons called Mohammed Khan in the company, extrinsic evidence may be adduced to show which of the two Mohammed Khans is the intended payee. However, extrinsic evidence could not be adduced to explain that the drawer actually intended to pay 'Tariq Khan' and not some-one called 'Mohammed Khan'. If the payee is a fictitious or non-existent person, the bill may be treated as payable to bearer (s. 7(3)). If the bill names a real person but it was

---

[126] *Korea Exchange Bank v Debenhams (Central Buying) Ltd* [1979] 1 Lloyd's Rep 548; *Rosenhain v Commonwealth Bank of Australia* (1922) 31 CLR 46.

[127] [2011] UKPC 35.

[128] *Korea Exchange Bank v Debenhams (Central Buying) Ltd ibid*; it is usually a matter of construction as to whether there is sufficient certainty in the words on the bill to warrant a finding of fixed or determinable future time. In *Korea Exchange Bank*, it would appear that the court would take a strict approach and refuse to read words into the bill of exchange which seemingly have been omitted.

[129] *Williamson v Rider* [1963] 1 QB 89.

[130] *Orbit Mining and Trading v Westminster Bank Ltd* [1963] 1 QB 794.

never intended by the drawer for that person to be the payee, that bill may be treated as one made out to a fictitious person. In *Bank of England* v *Vagliano*,[131] G, VB's employee, had forged Z's signature on a bill drawn in favour of P, an existing person with whom VB did business. VB, deceived by G, accepted the forged bill. G then forged P's indorsement and presented the bill for payment to VB's bank. The bank paid. VB sought to recover from the bank the sum paid. The House of Lords held that as P was never intended by G to take under the bill, he was a fictitious person. The bill was thus a bearer bill. As the bank had paid the bearer, VB's claim failed. Lord Herschell said:

> I do not think that the word 'fictitious' is exclusively used to qualify that which has no real existence. When we speak of a fictitious entry in a book of accounts, we do not mean that the entry has no real existence, but only that it purports to be that which it is not – that it is an entry made for the purpose of pretending that the transaction took place which is repre-sented by it . . . I have arrived at the conclusion that, whenever the name inserted as that of the payee is so inserted by way of pretence/merely, without any intention that payment shall only be made in conformity therewith, the payee is a fictitious person . . .

Equally, where the drawer intends the payee to take under the bill, the payee is not fictitious even though the drawer's conduct had been induced by illegal means (such as duress, unconscionable conduct, deception). In *North and South Wales Bank Ltd* v *Macbeth*,[132] A was induced by B's misrepresentation to make out a cheque in C's favour. B then forged C's indorsement and paid the cheque into his own account. A claimed the amount from C's bank. The court held that the cheque was not a bearer cheque because the payee was not fictitious. A therefore succeeded in getting his money back. In the case where the payee is actually non-existent rather than fictitious, intention becomes irrelevant (*Clutton* v *Attenborough & Son*).[133]

6.7.2.1 Dates

A bill is not defective simply because it does not carry a date on its face (s. 3(4)(a)). It can also be ante-dated or post-dated (s. 13(2)). That does not mean the date, especially the date of acceptance, if provided, is not relevant. Section 45(1), for example, states that where a bill is not payable on demand, presentment for payment must be made on the date the bill falls due. The date of the bill and its acceptance is pivotal in calculating when the bill will mature. It is therefore not surprising that s. 12 allows the holder of a bill payable after date or sight to insert the date of issue or acceptance where it has been left out.

6.7.2.2 Inchoate instruments

It is possible for a document which is not a bill of exchange to be converted into a bill of exchange. Such a document may, for example, be a signed document delivered by the signer to the intended payee who would then complete the document making it into a bill of

---

[131] [1891] AC 107.
[132] [1908] AC 137; see, too, *Vinden* v *Hughes* [1905] 1 KB 795.
[133] [1897] AC 90; in that case A had been deceived by B into believing that he owed C some money. He then drew a cheque naming C as payee. B then indorsed the cheque in C's name and negotiated it for value to D. The House of Lords held that the cheque was a bearer cheque because C is a non-existent person. Additionally, as A did not know that C did not exist, there was no question as to intention.

exchange. A blank cheque is often cited as an example of such an inchoate instrument. Section 20 provides that such a document will give the person in possession *prima facie* authority to fill it in as a bill of exchange and therefore enforce it against the signer. The holder must complete the inchoate instrument within a reasonable time and must act according to the authority given to him (s. 20(2)). What is a reasonable time is a question of fact. It is open to the person refusing to honour the bill to show that the holder had not acted with authority and/or within reasonable time but once the bill has been transferred to a holder in due course, the bill becomes fully indefeasible. The signer may naturally make the inchoate instrument not negotiable thereby preventing a holder in due course from acquiring any rights on the instrument. In *Wilson and Meeson v Pickering*,[134] P gave Q, his secretary, a blank cheque marked 'not negotiable', with instructions that Q should complete the cheque in favour of the Inland Revenue as the payee. Q fraudulently made the cheque out to R. P sought to recover the money from R. The Court of Appeal held that the words 'not negotiable' meant that R could not obtain a better title to the cheque than Q (s. 81). P was therefore allowed to recover from R.

6.7.2.3 Lost bills

Where a bill is lost, s. 69 provides that the holder of a bill lost before it is overdue can require the drawer to give him a duplicate. An indemnity may be required by the drawer from the holder, in case the lost bill is found and misused.

6.7.3 Negotiation of the bill of exchange

A bill of exchange is presumed, unless the contrary is proved, to be negotiable (s. 8). Section 8(4) asserts that a bill is payable to order when it is expressed to be payable to order; or is expressed to be payable to a particular person and does not contain words prohibiting transfer or indicating an intention that it should not be transferable. A bill which stipulates, 'pay A £50', is therefore a negotiable bill. It is payable either to A or to his order. Contrast it with a bill which says, 'pay A only £50'. Such a bill would be non-negotiable. Naturally if the words 'not negotiable' are used, the bill loses its negotiability. In *Hibernian Bank Ltd v Gysin and Hanson*,[135] for example, a bill of exchange was drawn 'pay to the order of the Irish Casing Co Ltd only the sum of £500 effective value received' and crossed 'not negotiable'. Such a bill was simply not transferable and did not constitute an order bill.

A bill of exchange is negotiated when it is transferred by one person to another in such a manner as to constitute the transferee the holder of the bill (s. 31(1)). Negotiation enables the transferee to become a party to the bill of exchange and to enforce it in his own name. Section 31(2) provides that a bearer bill is negotiated by delivery whilst an order bill is negotiated by indorsement of the payee or where the bill has already been indorsed to a specified indorsee, by the latter's indorsement, together with delivery of the bill (s. 31(3)).

---

[134] [1946] 2 KB 422.
[135] [1939] 1 KB 483.

6.7.3.1 Indorsement

'Indorsement' means the writing of the name of the transferor on the bill, completed by delivery;[136] usually all the indorser (transferor) has to do is sign the bill. Section 34 provides that an indorsement can be either 'in blank' or 'special'. An indorsement in blank requires merely the signature of the transferor. No transferee needs to be specified. Such a bill is treated as payable to bearer. A special indorsement, however, will explicitly name the transferee. If the holder of a bill payable to his order transfers it for value without indorsing it, the transfer gives the transferee such title as the transferor had in the bill, and the transferee in addition acquires the right to have the indorsement of the transferor (s. 31(4)). However, unless the indorsement of the transferor is actually obtained, the transferee remains no more than an assignee of the rights on the bill and does not acquire more rights than the transferor (*Whistler* v *Forster*).[137]

An indorsement must not transfer to the indorsee only a part of the amount payable or to two or more indorsees severally; it must be the indorsement of the entire bill (s. 32(2)).

Of course, where the bill has been made non-negotiable, it could not be negotiated. A negotiable bill could also be rendered non-negotiable by the indorser. Where the indorser writes on the bill, 'Pay D only' or 'Pay D for the account of X' or 'Pay D or order for collection', this would prevent further negotiation of the bill. Such an act is called a restrictive indorsement (s. 35(1)).

6.7.4 Securing payment using a bill of exchange – holders of the bill of exchange

Persons entitled to receive payment under the bill of exchange must usually be in possession of the bill of exchange. The person in possession of the bill is called a holder. There are several types of holders and their rights over the bill vary. The concept of the holder is central to the Bills of Exchange Act 1882. There are essentially three types of holders under the Act:

(a) mere holder;

(b) holder for value;

(c) holder in due course.

6.7.4.1 Mere holder

A *mere holder*, as the person having possession of the bill, has some basic rights in respect of the bill. Section 2 defines a holder as the payee or indorsee of a bill or note who is in possession of it or (in the case of a bearer bill) the bearer thereof. Under s. 38(1) any holder of a bill may sue in his own name and payment to the holder will discharge the bill.[138] He could thus negotiate the bill, seek payment from the persons liable to pay under the bill,[139] and if the bill is dishonoured, sue on the bill in his own name.

---

[136] Section 32(1).
[137] (1863) 14 CB(NS) 248.
[138] Discharge of the bill is subject to the conditions in s. 59(1).
[139] See section 6.7.5.

6.7.4.2 Holder for value

A *holder for value* is one who has given value for the bill. Valuable consideration is defined in s. 27 as:

(a) any consideration sufficient to support a simple contract;

(b) an antecedent debt or liability.

Such a debt or liability is deemed valuable consideration whether the bill is payable on demand or at a future time. Section 27(2) further provides that where value has at any time been given for a bill the holder is deemed to be a holder for value as regards the acceptor and all parties to the bill who became parties prior to such time.

In *Oliver* v *Davis*,[140] W paid a debt on behalf of her sister's fiancé. When W later found out that her sister and her fiancé had broken up, she stopped the cheque. The creditor sued W on the cheque. The Court of Appeal held that the antecedent debt or liability referred to in s. 27 is 'an antecedent debt or liability of the . . . *drawer* . . . and [is] intended to get over what would otherwise have been prima facie the result that at common law the giving of a cheque for an amount for which you are already indebted imports no consideration, since the obligation is past and has been already incurred' (emphasis added). The Court of Appeal thus held that the antecedent debt or liability must be either that of the promisor or drawer of a bill or, if of a third party, then at least there must be some relationship between the receipt of the bill and the antecedent debt or liability such as forbearance or a promise to forbear, express or implied, on the part of the recipient in regard to the third party's debt or liability. When W gave the cheque to the creditor, he gave her no promise, express or implied, to forbear in respect of any remedy he might have against the sister's fiancé, nor, as a result of her cheque, had he changed his position in any way to his detriment in regard to his claim on the fiancé. The court thus gave judgment for W.

It should also be noted that although s. 27(1) accepts past consideration, it does not alter the principle that consideration must flow from the promisee.[141]

It is for the drawer to prove the lack of consideration if payment is resisted.[142] That burden is not light. Section 21(3) provides, for instance, that where a bill is no longer in the possession of a party who has signed it as drawer, a valid and unconditional delivery by him is presumed until the contrary is proved. Furthermore, under s. 27(2) a holder can claim to be a holder for value as against a third party (as opposed to an immediate party) even though he himself has not provided consideration. Section 27(2) provides that where value has at any time been given for a bill the holder is deemed to be a holder for value as regards the acceptor and all the parties to the bill who became parties prior to such time. In *MK International Development Co Ltd* v *The Housing Bank*,[143] the bank was instructed by its customer to draw a cheque payable to 'MK or bearer' after debiting the customer's account. The bill was then delivered to the customer who passed it on to MK. It was contended by the bank that MK had not given consideration to them for the promise to pay. The Court of Appeal agreed that s. 27(2) required that the holders should themselves have provided consideration.

---

[140] [1949] 2 KB 727.
[141] *Ibid.*
[142] *Diamond* v *Graham* [1968] 1 WLR 1061.
[143] [1991] 1 Bank LR 74; see also (1991) (4) *LMCLQ* 463–469.

However, since the cheque had first passed to the customer instead of directly to MK, the correct question was whether or not the customer had provided consideration. As he had, MK as holder in due course should be able to rely on the consideration provided by the bank's customer under s. 27(2).

6.7.4.3 Holder in due course

A holder in due course takes the bill relieved of any defects of title of earlier parties in the chain, including any personal defences which a prior party might have against another prior party (s. 38(2), s. 29(2)). As Sir Eric Sachs said in *Ceborra SNC v SIP (Industrial Products) Ltd*, 'save in truly exceptional circumstances', the holder of a bill of exchange on maturity can have it treated as cash. Section 29 defines a holder in due course as:

a holder who has taken a bill, complete and regular on the face of it, under the following conditions; namely:

(a) that he became the holder of it before it was overdue, and without notice that it had been previously dishonoured, if such was the fact;

(b) that he took the bill in good faith and for value, and that at the time the bill was negotiated to him he had no notice of any defect in the title of the person who negotiated it.

In particular the title of a person who negotiates a bill is defective within the meaning of this Act when he obtained the bill, or the acceptance thereof, by fraud, duress, or force and fear, or other unlawful means, or for an illegal consideration, or when he negotiates it in breach of faith, or under such circumstances as amount to a fraud.

Professors Sealy and Hooley[144] suggest that the following would constitute the exceptional circumstances which would defeat the title of the holder in due course:

(a) real or absolute defences arising from the invalidity of the bill itself or the invalidity of the defendant's apparent contract on the bill (such as contractual incapacity, forged signature, *non est factum*);

(b) when the holder in due course sues as agent or trustee for another person or when he sues for another person, any defence or set off available against that person would also be available *pro tanto* against the holder;

(c) when the holder in due course does not comply with his duties as to presentment for acceptance and/or payment or when he fails to comply with the proper procedure on dishonour.

Section 30(2) provides that every holder of a bill is *prima facie* deemed to be a holder in due course and that if in an action on a bill it is admitted or proved that the acceptance, issue or subsequent negotiation of the bill is tainted by fraud, duress, force, fear or illegality, the burden of proof then falls on the holder to prove that value has been given for the bill in good faith. This does not however extend to the original payee. Section 29(1) makes it quite clear that the holder in due course is a person to whom the bill has been negotiated. Thus, the original payee of the bill of exchange could not be a holder in due course. He might be

---

[144] L. S. Sealy and R. J. A. Hooley, *Commercial Law: Text, Cases and Materials* (4th edn, Oxford University Press, Oxford, 2008) pp. 528–529.

a holder for value because he may have given consideration for the bill, but because the bill was not negotiated to him, he is not a holder in due course. That said, the payee could acquire the rights of the holder in due course. Section 29(3) provides that a mere holder who derives his title to a bill through a holder in due course will receive all the rights of that holder as regards the acceptor and all parties to the bill prior to that holder. The proviso is that he must not have been a party to any fraud or illegality affecting the bill.

CASE

Jade International Steel Stahl und Eisen GmbH and Co KG v Robert Nicholas (Steels) Ltd[145]

A problematic situation arose in *Jade International Steel Stahl und Eisen GmbH and Co KG v Robert Nicholas (Steels) Ltd.* J had drawn a bill of exchange payable to themselves or order on N. J indorsed and discounted the bill to Bank G. G then discounted it to Bank M. N refused to honour the bill on the basis that the goods paid for by the bill were defective. M Bank then indorsed the bill in blank and as each bank exercised its rights of recourse the bill was passed back down to J. The question thus arose as to whether or not J was entitled to the rights of a holder in due course under s. 29(3).

The Court of Appeal held that when J initially discounted the bill, they lost their capacity as drawers/payees and when the bill returned to their possession, they were deemed to be holders for the purposes of s. 29(3). It seems unjust to deprive M of the contractual rights they had initially possessed before they discounted the bill simply because the dishonoured bill had returned to J. It also does not make good commercial sense to defeat the object of the practice of bill discounting. Bill discounting is, after all, an important element in the finance of trade.

Returning to the definition of a holder in due course, under s. 29 the bill must be complete and regular on the face of it. A bill is 'incomplete' if any material detail is missing, for example, where the name of the payee or the sum payable has been omitted.[146] What does the law mean by 'regular'? In *Arab Bank Ltd v Ross,*[147] the bills named as payees 'Fathi and Faysal Nabulsy Company'. The firm then indorsed the bills 'Fathi and Faysal Nabulsy' but left out inadvertently the word 'Company'. The Court of Appeal ruled that the bills were not regular on their face. The indorsement must adhere to the terms of the bill. The word 'Company' was part of the name of the payee. There is a distinction between what is regular and what is valid. A bill of exchange could very well appear regular on its face but in fact be invalid. For example, a forged indorsement is clearly invalid but it will be regular because on the face of the bill of exchange, there is nothing on it which would put the transferee on inquiry.

---

[145] [1978] QB 917.

[146] The absence of a date, however, as we have seen above, does not make the bill incomplete (s. 3(4)(a)). Neither is the place where it is drawn or the place where it is payable (s. 3(4)(c)).

[147] [1952] 2 QB 216.

> **ISSUE BOX**
>
> What if the amount in writing does not match the amount in figures on the bill? Its validity is not affected since s. 9(2) provides that the amount in writing shall prevail over the one in figures. However, is the bill regular on its face? What if there is a discrepancy between the currency used, for example, with one reference made to 'lira' and another to 'sterling' on the bill? See *Banco di Roma* v *Orru* [1973] 2 Lloyd's Rep 505.

There is also a distinction to be made between regularity and liability. A person might have made an irregular indorsement but he would be held liable on the bill despite that irregularity. For example, if a payee, who is wrongly described on the bill, indorses it in his own true name, the indorsement is irregular, but he is liable to any subsequent holder and cannot set up the irregularity as a defence. On the other hand, a regular indorsement will not impose liability on the innocent party, if the indorsement was forged or unauthorised. In *Kirk* v *Blurton*,[148] for example, the intended payee was a firm of two partners, 'JB and CH'. The bill named as payee 'JB'. CH then indorsed the bill. The court held that the indorsement could not bind JB. CH had not implied authority in law to bind his co-partners by so doing.

It is also imperative that the holder in due course had acted in good faith and without knowledge of fraud when taking the bill. In *Jones* v *Gordon*,[149] G drew a bill on S and S did the same on G. They were both aware of each other's impending bankruptcy. J then bought the bills drawn by S which were accepted by G even though he was aware that G was in financial difficulties. He also declined to make inquiries into G's affairs when buying the bills. When G was made a bankrupt, J tried to prove against G's estate for the amount due under those bills. The House of Lords held that J was not a *bona fide* purchaser as he was deemed to have known of the fraud. J had paid only £200 for the bills which carried a nominal value of £1,727. Lord Blackburn said, 'it is an important element in considering whether the man who gave the undervalue was acting *bona fide*, in ignorance and error, or was assisting in committing a fraud, and avoided making inquiries because they might be injurious to him'. Hence, it would appear some element of dishonesty or sharp conduct is required. If J had failed to make inquiries simply because he was an honest blunderer or a stupid man, he could be said to be a *bona fide* holder. Indeed, s. 90 states that a thing is done in good faith where it is done honestly.

Section 29(1)(b) provides that the holder must have taken the bill for value. The question is whether or not this means that he must personally have provided consideration. The view that consideration does not need to flow from him personally might be supported by s. 27(2) which refers only to value having been given for the bill instead of value having been given by the holder. The question is whether or not s. 27(2) could be relied on by a holder seeking to qualify as a holder in due course under s. 29. In *Clifford Chance* v *Silver*[150] the Court of Appeal thought that he could. However, *Clifford Chance* does fly in the face of the long-established

---

[148] (1841) 9 M&W 284.
[149] (1877) 2 App Cas 616.
[150] [1992] 2 Bank LR 11; see also commentary of the case in [1993] 11 *JBL* 571.

view to the contrary[151] that whilst s. 27(2) could be relied on by a holder for value, it did not apply to holders in due course. Also, the absence of any authority being relied on in *Clifford Chance* does not readily make it an entirely persuasive decision. Clarification of the conflicting provisions in the Bills of Exchange Act 1882 is required.

6.7.5 Liability on the bill of exchange

The persons usually liable on the bill of exchange would be the drawer, the drawee/acceptor and any indorser. However, that assumes that they had the capacity to contract because the liability created by the bill of exchange is contractual. Section 22(1) states that the capacity to incur liability as a party to a bill is to be determined by reference to general law. In the context of natural persons, a minor or a mentally incapacitated person will not be able to assume liability on the bill. In the case of corporate entities, with the abolition of the *ultra vires* rule by the Companies Act 1989,[152] it will be most unusual for a company not to be held liable on the bill as drawer, drawee, acceptor or indorser as the case may be.

6.7.5.1 Complete and irrevocable contract

The contract on the bill is important – it must be complete and irrevocable in order to give rise to liability. Section 21(1) presumes that every contract on the bill is incomplete and revocable until delivery of the bill. Delivery is the transfer of possession, actual or constructive, from one person to another. However, if an acceptance is written on the bill and the drawee gives notice to or according to the directions of the person entitled to the bill that he has accepted it, acceptance becomes complete and irrevocable. If the bill is held by a holder in due course, a valid delivery of the bill by all the parties prior to him so as to make them liable to him will be conclusively presumed (s. 21(2)). Where the bill is no longer in the possession of the person who signed it as drawer, acceptor or indorser, the rebuttable presumption is that a valid and unconditional delivery by them has been made (s. 21(3)).

6.7.5.2 Signature and name

The liability of the drawer, acceptor or indorser also depends on if there exists a valid signature (s. 23). A valid signature is one which is either signed by the person concerned or under his authority (s. 91). Where a person signs a bill in a trade or assumed name, he will be held liable thereon as if he had signed it in his own name (s. 23(1)). The signature of a firm's name is equivalent to the signature by the person so signing of the names of all persons liable as partners in that firm.[153] A signature by procuration[154] (where an agent signs 'per

---

[151] W. Hedley, *Bills of Exchange and Bankers' Documentary Credits* (2nd edn, LLP, London, 1994) p. 66; A. G. Guest, *Chalmers and Guest on Bills of Exchange, Cheques and Promissory Notes* (14th edn, Sweet and Maxwell, London, 1991) p. 274; R. Goode, *Commercial Law* (2nd edn, Penguin, London) p. 543.

[152] Section 108 (see amended s. 35(1)(4) Companies Act 1985 subsequently replaced by s. 39 companies Act 2006); under the old *ultra vires* rule, a company had capacity to contract only in matters which are provided for in its memorandum and articles of association (see *Ashbury Railway Carriage and Dron Co Ltd* v *Riche (1875)* LR 7 HL 653).

[153] See *Kirk* v *Blurton* (section 6.7.4.3 above).

[154] The term in Latin is *procurare,* meaning 'to take care of'. 'Procuration' means the delegation of authority or power to a procurator or agent.

procurationem', *'per pro'* or *'pp'*) operates as notice that the agent has only a limited authority to sign the bill. Under those circumstances, the principal is only liable if the agent acted within their actual authority.[155] From *Morison* v *London County & Westminster Bank Ltd*[156] it would appear that even a holder in due course would be held to such a notice.

Where a bill is a company bill, s. 91(2) provides that it is sufficient that the bill is sealed with the corporate seal. The signature can be dispensed with. However, in many cases, a signature will be provided for the creditor to be assured that the bill is properly authorised. Section 52 of the Companies Act 2006 provides that a bill of exchange or promissory note is deemed to have been made, accepted or indorsed on behalf of a company if made, accepted or indorsed in the name of, or by or on behalf or on account of, the company by a person acting under its authority. It would therefore follow that the person signing on behalf of the company will bind the company but not himself personally. Personal liability however will attach if he does not indicate that he signs for and on behalf of the company. If he merely describes himself as an agent or representative of a company, that alone would not be enough. It is usually a case of construction of the document as a whole.

In *Bondina Ltd* v *Rollaway Shower Blinds Ltd*,[157] W, a company director, signed a cheque below the preprinted name of the company. The cheque was one printed with the company's account number. It was argued that W (other than the company) was also therefore liable on the cheque. The court rejected that argument. It held that when W signed the cheque he must be said to have adopted all the printing and writing on it, including the printing of the company's name and the company's account number. The bill showed that the drawer of the cheque was the company and not W.

Section 26(2) states that when determining whether a signature is that of the principal or of the agent, the construction most favourable to the validity of the instrument shall be adopted. The full extent of this provision is not entirely clear; there is no reported decision on the section.[158] The intention of the signatory appears to be relevant as to whether he signed as principal or agent. To that end, extrinsic evidence may be admitted. In *Rolfe Lubell & Co* v *Keith*,[159] for example, a bill was drawn by a company for the payment of certain goods. The seller, fearing that the bill might be dishonoured by the company, insisted the managing director personally indorsed it. The director indorsed the bills by entering his name in a rubber-stamped box on the back of the bills bearing the printed words 'for and on behalf of [the company]'. Kilner-Brown J held that extrinsic and oral evidence of the director's agreement to undertake personal liability was admissible. The judge also added that it was unlikely that the managing director could have intended to indorse the bills merely on behalf of the company since such an indorsement would have achieved nothing, the company being liable on the bills already in its role as drawee. The managing director was thus jointly and severally liable on the bill.

There are also certain conditions a company bill should satisfy under the Companies Act 2006.

---

[155] Section 25.
[156] [1914] 3 KB 356.
[157] [1986] 1 All ER 564.
[158] Case searches were made on 17 February 2013 on Westlaw and LexisNexis.
[159] [1979] 1 All ER 860.

LEGISLATIVE PROVISION

The Companies (Trading Disclosures) Regulations 2008/495 made pursuant to the 2006 Act provide in reg. 6 that a company shall disclose its registered name on:

(a) its business letters, notices and other official publications;

(b) *its bills of exchange, promissory notes, endorsements and order forms;*

(c) *cheques purporting to be signed by or on behalf of the company;*

(d) orders for money, goods or services purporting to be signed by or on behalf of the company;

(e) its bills of parcels, invoices and other demands for payment, receipts and letters of credit;

(f) its applications for licences to carry on a trade or activity; and

(g) all other forms of its business correspondence and documentation. (Emphasis added.)

The registered name for a public limited company must end with 'Public Limited Company' or 'PLC' (s. 58, Companies Act 2006) and for a private limited company must end with 'Limited' or 'Ltd' (s. 59, Companies Act 2006).

The failure to comply may result in criminal prosecution of the directors (s. 84 Companies Act 2006; reg. 10, Companies (Trading Disclosures) Regulations 2008/495).

Under s. 83 of the Companies Act 2006, an action brought by a company to enforce a contract which was made in breach of the name disclosure regulations will be dismissed if the defendant shows:

(a) that he has a claim against the claimant arising out of the contract that he has been unable to pursue by reason of the latter's breach of the regulations; or

(b) that he has suffered some financial loss in connection with the contract by reason of the claimant's breach of the regulations;

unless the court before which the proceedings are brought is satisfied that it is just and equitable to permit the proceedings to continue.

Regulation 6, Companies (Trading Disclosures) Regulations 2008/495 replaces s. 349(1) of the old Companies Act 1985. Section 349(1) provided that the name of the company shall be mentioned in legible characters in all bills purporting to be signed by or on behalf of the company. The requirement of s. 349(1) was strictly construed. Case law shows that where the word 'Limited' (or 'Ltd') has been omitted from the name written or printed on a cheque drawn by a company, that would be a breach of s. 349(1).[160] It is likely that the same approach would be adopted in respect of reg. 6, at least as far as the criminal law implications are concerned. However, the provisions dealing with civil consequences are a little more textured.

Under s. 349(4) of the old Companies Act 1985, a person who signs or authorises to be signed on behalf of the company a bill on which the company name is not so mentioned, incurs personal liability on it unless the bill is paid by the company. In *Lindholst & Co A/S* v

---

[160] *Fiorentino Comm Giuseppe Srl v Farnesi* [2005] EWHC 160 (Ch); *Lindholst & Co A/S v Fowler* [1988] BCLC 166 and *British Airways Board v Parish* [1979] Lloyd's Rep 361.

Fowler,[161] the signer was held personally liable for a company bill which had described the company as 'Corby Chicken Co' instead of 'Corby Chicken Co Ltd'. That said, the strictness of the rule is subject to the law on estoppel as we see in *Durham Fancy Goods* v *Michael Jackson Fancy Goods*.[162] In that case, the drawer had drawn a bill requiring the drawee firm to accept the bill. The drawer created a space on the bill for the drawee's company secretary to sign. The drawer had typed in the space, 'for and on behalf of M. Jackson'. The correct name was 'Michael Jackson (Fancy Goods) Ltd'. The company secretary did not check the correctness of the name and duly signed the bill accepting it. As to whether he was personally liable or not, Donaldson J held that as the error was first generated by the drawer, they would be estopped from enforcing the liability in the Companies Act[163] against the company secretary. Whether there is an estoppel is highly fact dependent[164] and or not, since *Durham Fancy Goods*, the move seems to be to place an onus on the signer to check the bill before signing.[165] In this connection, the Company Law Review when reviewing the Companies Act 1985 observed that the rule in s. 349(4) could operate quite harshly on company employees, especially junior employees who may not be conversant with the law, in the event the company becomes insolvent.[166] The recommendation was for the abrogation of s. 349(4), which was duly carried out in the 2006 Act.

The new ss. 83 and 84 refer specifically to the imposition of civil and criminal liability only on officers. Officers include directors, company secretaries and shadow directors, in general. Those new sections do not provide for personal liability on bills signed without using the correct company name. Section 83, in particular, places the onus on the defendant resisting a claim brought by the company on an instrument or contract where the correct name had not been used to show that he had been unable to claim arising from that contract which he had been unable to pursue or that he had suffered financial loss in connection with that contract as a result of the incorrect name being used.[167]

A forged signature is totally incapable of transferring title to an indorsee. In criminal law, a forged instrument is defined in s. 1, Forgery and Counterfeiting Act 1981, as a false instrument[168] made with the intent to induce another person to accept it as genuine so that that other person might, 'by reason of so accepting it to do or not to do some act to his own or any other person's prejudice'. Section 24 provides that where a signature is forged or unauthorised[169] it is wholly inoperative and no right to retain the bill or give a discharge therefore or to enforce payment thereof against any party thereto can be acquired through or under that signature. A signature made in excess of authority may however be ratified by the principal but a forgery cannot be ratified. Where a bank has collected a bill of exchange carrying a forged or unauthorised indorsement, it could therefore be liable in conversion to the true

---

[161] [1988] BCLC 166.

[162] [1968] 2 All ER 987.

[163] The case predated the Companies Act 1985. It concerned s. 108, Companies Act 1948, which has some similarities to s. 349(4).

[164] *Hellas* v *Kumar Bros International* [1998] All ER (D) 130.

[165] See also *Maxform SpA* v *Mariani & Goodville Ltd* [1981] 2 Lloyd's Rep 54.

[166] Paragraph 24, Company Law Review Steering Group Report on Trading Disclosures (Oct 2000, at: www.berr.gov.uk/files/file23241.pdf).

[167] This sanction is similar to that in s. 5, Business Names Act 1985 (which has now been repealed).

[168] A false instrument is defined by s. 9(1)(d) of the 1981 Act in these terms: 'if it purports to have been made . . . on the authority of a person who did not in fact authorise its making in those terms'.

[169] On the difference between forged and unauthorised signatures, see *Morison* v *London County and Westminster Bank* [1914] 3 KB 356.

owner even though it may not have acted in negligence or malice. It should however be said that an exception is made for cheques under s. 4 of the Cheques Act 1957. More on this will be considered later.

Although a forged or unauthorised signature has no validity, it does not mean that the bill itself is rendered totally ineffective. For example, where there are a number of indorsements on the bill and only one is forged, the holder will be able to enforce payment from those who indorsed the bill after the forged signature. He will of course not be able to enforce liability of those who indorsed it (including the drawer) prior to the forgery.

There is an important exception to the rule that the forged or unauthorised signature is wholly inoperative. Where one person has led another to believe that the signature is in order, he would be estopped from denying the validity of the signature. In a very sad case, *Greenwood v Martins Bank*,[170] the wife had been forging the husband's signature on cheques[171] drawn on the bank. The husband found out but the wife pleaded with him not to inform the bank. She lied to him saying that the money was to help her sister. Eight months later he finally found out the truth and informed the bank. On his return from the bank, the wife shot herself. The House of Lords held that as he had a duty to inform the bank as soon as he discovered the forged signatures and he did not do so, he was estopped from denying their validity. He could not therefore recover the amounts paid out by the bank to the wife. Mere silence or inaction however cannot amount to an estoppel unless there is a duty to disclose or act. In *Tai Hing Cotton Mill Ltd v Liu Chong Hing Bank Ltd*,[172] the Privy Council noted that a current account holder merely owed to his bank, in the absence of express agreement:

- a duty to exercise due care in drawing cheques so as not to facilitate fraud or forgery, and;
- a duty to notify the bank immediately of any unauthorised cheques of which he became aware.

There is no wider duty to take reasonable precautions in his business to prevent forged cheques from being presented to the bank or to check his bank statement to identify any discrepant payments of which he should notify the bank. The bank's customer is not under any implied duty to help prevent fraud being perpetrated on the bank. There being no such duty, the customer would not be estopped from asserting the payments or bills were not authorised (or forged).

Another exception to the general rule that a forged or unauthorised signature is inoperative lies in ss. 54(2) and 55(2). These, it should be said, involve very specific signatories. In s. 54(2), the acceptor is precluded from denying to a holder in due course the genuineness of the drawer's signature. Similarly, s. 55(2) precludes the indorser from denying to a holder in due course the genuineness and regularity in all respects of the drawer's signature and all previous indorsements.

It might also be recalled that where the payee is a fictitious or non-existent person, the bill may be treated as payable to bearer (s. 7(3)).[173] The consequence of this is that title in the bill can pass even though the indorsement is forged.

---

[170] [1933] AC 51.

[171] It should of course be remembered that *Greenwood*'s case predated the Cheques Act 1957 – the principle in relation to cheques has therefore changed but the principle in *Greenwood*'s case remains relevant to our consideration of bills of exchange generally.

[172] [1986] AC 80.

[173] See *Bank of England v Vagliano* [1891] AC 107.

6.7.6 Acceptance

LEGISLATIVE PROVISION

Section 17

(1) The acceptance of a bill is the signification by the drawee of his assent to the order of the drawer.

(2) An acceptance is invalid unless it complies with the following conditions, namely:

(a) it must be written on the bill and be signed by the drawee, the mere signature of the drawee without additional words is sufficient;

(b) it must not express that the drawee will perform his promise by any other means than the payment of money.

When the acceptor accepts the bill, he becomes liable to pay the bill according to the terms of his acceptance (s. 54(1)). Such an acceptance is known as a general acceptance. However, acceptance may be qualified (s. 19). An acceptance is qualified if:

- it is conditional, that is to say, payment by the acceptor is dependent on the fulfilment of a condition stated on the bill; or
- it is partial, that is to say, the acceptor agrees only to pay part of the amount of the bill; or
- it is to pay only at a specific place or at a particular time;
- the acceptance relates to only some of the drawees.

It should be noted though that whilst qualified acceptance is provided for in the Act, s. 44(1) emphatically allows the holder to refuse to take a qualified acceptance and to treat it as non-acceptance and sue for dishonour. Equally, if the holder takes the qualified acceptance, the drawer and indorsers are released from their liability if they had not expressly or impliedly authorised the holder to take qualified acceptance (s. 44(2)). Therefore, a bank collecting a bill should not take a qualified acceptance without first obtaining consent from its customer.

6.7.6.1 Presentment for acceptance

Presentment for acceptance is not the same as presentment for payment. When a bill requires payment on demand, then presentment for acceptance and payment occurs at the same time. However, a time or usance bill is generally presented for acceptance immediately after being drawn (for example, in a sale contract, after the goods have been delivered) and when it is returned by the drawee to the drawer/payee is held by him until maturity or discounted to some third party (indorsee). Section 39(1) stresses that where a bill is payable after sight, presentment for acceptance is necessary to fix the maturity of the bill. Where the bill expressly requires presentment for acceptance, the holder must present it for acceptance (s. 39(2)). There is also an obligation to present for acceptance where the bill was drawn payable elsewhere than at the residence or place of business of the drawee (s. 39(2)). In all other cases, there is no need to present for acceptance under the Act (s. 39(3)). That is not to say that presentment for acceptance is commercially unimportant; indeed, it would be the rare case in international commerce that a bill is not presented for acceptance.

Only the named drawee can accept the bill. The exception to this rule is what the Act calls 'acceptance for honour'. This is when a stranger to the bill accepts the bill with the holder's consent *supra protest* for the honour of any party liable thereon following dishonour by non-acceptance. This kind of acceptance is made by a third party for the honour of the drawer or any of the indorsers, often without their knowledge. With the availability of a wide range of guarantee instruments in modern commerce, this practice is quite rare. Provisions dealing with the practice are found in ss. 65–68.

6.7.6.2 The liability of the drawer and indorser

Section 55(1)(a) states quite unequivocally that the drawer, by drawing the bill, 'engages that on due presentment it shall be accepted and paid according to its tenor and that if it be dishonoured he will compensate the holder or any indorser who is compelled to pay, provided that the requisite proceedings on dishonour be duly taken'. It may appear strange that the drawer is made ultimately liable to back the bill of exchange when in many sale contracts, the drawer is the payee, but it should not be forgotten that the bill of exchange can take many forms, including an order by the drawer to pay as payee a third party, instead of himself.

As far as the indorser is concerned, s. 55(2)(a) states that his act of indorsement 'engages that on due presentment it shall be accepted and paid according to its tenor and that if it be dishonoured he will compensate the holder or any subsequent indorser who is compelled to pay, provided that the requisite proceedings on dishonour be duly taken'. He is also precluded from denying to his immediate or subsequent indorser that the bill at the time he indorsed it was valid and that he had good title to it (s. 55(2)(c)).[174]

The drawer is not permitted to deny to the holder in due course the existence of the payee and his then capacity to indorse (s. 55(1)(b)). Similarly, the indorser is not allowed to deny to the holder in due course the genuineness and regularity of the drawer's signature and all prior indorsements (s. 55(2)(b)).

6.7.7 Presentment for payment

6.7.7.1 General rule

The general rule in s. 45 is that a bill must be duly presented for payment. If it is not presented, the drawer is discharged. A bill is only duly presented for payment if it is presented in accordance with the rules set out in s. 45. In particular, s. 45(1) provides that where the bill is not payable on demand, presentment must be made on the day it falls due. In *Yeoman Credit Ltd v Gregory*,[175] the claimants had drawn two bills of exchange on E and payable at N Bank. E accepted and indorsed them. One bill was payable on 9 December (a fixed bill) whilst the other was payable on 'demand'. Before the claimants presented the bills they were instructed by E to present them at a branch of M Bank. The claimants made a notation on the

---

[174] See *Ladup Ltd v Shaikh Nadeem* [1983] QB 225.
[175] [1963] 1 All ER 245.

bill to that effect. They presented them at M Bank on 9 December but the bank refused to pay. The bills were then presented to N Bank on 11 December. N Bank refused to pay because the date of 9 December had lapsed. That was late presentment. The court held that the bank was entitled to rely on the terms on the face of the bill. The pencil notation on it even if approved by E could not be binding on N Bank.

Section 45(2) provides that where the bill is payable on demand, then, subject to the provisions of the Act, presentment must be made within a reasonable time after its issue in order to render the drawer liable and within a reasonable time after its indorsement, in order to render the indorser liable.

6.7.7.2 Procedural requirements

Presentment is also governed by certain procedural rules. Presentment must be made at a reasonable hour on a business day to the payer or some other person authorised to make payment on his behalf (s. 45(3)). A bill is presented at the proper place, if it is presented:

- at the place of payment specified in the bill;
- where no place is specified, at the drawee or acceptor's address as stated on the bill;
- where neither of the above is present, at the acceptor's place of business, if known, and, if not known, at his ordinary place of residence, if known;
- in any other case, to the acceptor wherever he can be found or at his last known place of business or residence.

Presentation may be made through the post where that is agreed to or provided for by usage (s. 45(8)). Section 46(1) excuses the holder where any delay in presentment for payment was caused by circumstances beyond the holder's control provided presentment is then effected with reasonable diligence after the cause of the delay has ceased to operate. There are some situations where presentment for payment can be dispensed with (s. 46(2)):

(a) where, after the exercise of reasonable diligence presentment cannot be effected, but the fact that the holder has reason to believe that the bill will, on presentment, be dishonoured, does not dispense with the necessity for presentment;

(b) where the drawee is a fictitious person;

(c) as regards the drawer where the drawee or acceptor is not bound as between himself and the drawer, to accept or pay the bill, and the drawer has no reason to believe that the bill would be paid if presented;

(d) as regards an indorser, where the bill was accepted or made for the accommodation of that indorser and he has no reason to expect that the bill would be paid if presented;

(e) by waiver of presentment, express or implied.

The purpose of such dispensation is to avoid the need for presentation of a bill when it is not possible for good reason to present it (see paras (a) and (b)) or where the drawer himself does not require it, having waived it (see para. (e)) or where it would be pointless to present it because the drawer himself knows that the bill will not be paid if presented (see paras (c) and (d)) (*Fiorentino Comm Giuseppe Srl* v *Antonio Giancarlo Farnesi and Barry Liss*).[176] In *Farnesi*, the drawer had tendered three cheques in payment of a debt. However, as the word 'Limited'

---

[176] [2005] EWHC 160 (Ch).

had been omitted on the face of the cheques (in breach of s. 349(1) Companies Act 1985),[177] the first cheque was dishonoured when it was presented for payment. It was held that the remaining two cheques need not be presented because the creditor had good reason to believe that they (for the same defect) would be dishonoured if presented. Presentment was thus excused by s. 46(2)(c).

It should be noted that cheques, although bills of exchange, are governed by s. 74 of the Bills of Exchange Act 1882 and that section is applied to the exclusion of s. 45.[178] Section 74 gives the drawer of a cheque limited relief from liability where the cheque is not presented within a reasonable time.[179]

6.7.8 Dishonour of the bill

When a bill is presented for payment or if presentment had been excused and the bill is overdue and unpaid, it is deemed to have been dishonoured. A dishonoured bill will give the holder an automatic right or recourse against the drawer or indorser (s. 47). Although it is an automatic right, which means no other breaches or defaults need to be proved, the holder must give notice of dishonour to the drawer or indorser as the case may be. No action may be brought prior to the giving of notice of dishonour (s. 48).[180] The notice must be given by the holder to the last indorser and to any other person he wishes to claim against. If the holder merely serves notice on the last indorser, that indorser must give a similar notice to the other prior indorsers if he intends to claim against them on the bill. The prior indorsers must do likewise to the predecessors in the chain if they wish to pin liability on them.[181]

The Act does not, however, specify what form the notice of dishonour should take. That said, in substance and practice, it should refer to the bill in question and assert that the bill has been dishonoured. The notice may be given as soon as the bill is dishonoured and must be given in a reasonable time. In general, without any special circumstances, where the parties live in the same place, the notice must be given in time to reach the recipient on the day after the dishonour of the bill or, where the parties live in different places, the notice must be given on the day after the dishonour via post at a convenient hour on that day and if there is no such post on that day, then by the next post thereafter.[182]

---

[177] Now replaced by reg. 6, Companies (Trading Disclosures) Regulations 2008, SI 2008/495; see section 6.7.5.2.

[178] *King and Boyd* v *Porter* [1925] NILR 103 (CA).

[179] *Fiorentino Comm Giuseppe Srl* v *Farnesi* [2005] EWHC 160 (Ch).

[180] There are a number of instances when notice of dishonour can be dispensed with. For example, where the bill is dishonoured by non-acceptance (as against non-payment), the holder in due course who acquired his rights subsequent to the omission shall not be affected by the absence of the notice (s. 48(1)). Section 50(2) also contains a list of instances when the notice of dishonour could be dispensed with. These include cases where, despite reasonable diligence, the notice could not reach the drawer or indorser or where it has been waived. Notice is also dispensed with as regards the drawer (a) where the drawer and drawee are the same person, (b) where the drawee is a fictitious person or a person not having capacity to contract, (c) where the drawer is the person to whom the bill is presented for payment, (d) where the drawee or acceptor is as between himself and the drawer under no obligation to accept or pay the bill, or (e) where the drawer has countermanded payment. As regards (e), it follows that in the case of a simple unendorsed cheque, payment of which is countermanded by the drawer, notice of dishonour is not required (see *Barclays Bank Ltd* v *W J Simms Son & Cooke (Southern) Ltd* [1980] QB 677).

[181] See s. 49 generally.

[182] Section 49(12).

By and large, the Act anticipates that the notice of dishonour be given only after the dishonour of the bill (s. 48). However, in *Eaglehill Ltd v J Needham Builders Ltd*[183] the House of Lords explained that that only meant that the notice should not be *received* prior to the dishonour. The holder is nevertheless entitled to *send off* the notice prior to dishonour. Delay in giving notice of dishonour will only be excused if it is shown that that was caused by circumstances beyond the holder's (or indorser's) control and was not imputable to his misconduct or negligence. However as soon as the cause of delay has ceased to operate, notice must be given with reasonable diligence and promptness.[184]

6.7.9 Discharge of the bill

A bill of exchange is discharged in one of the following situations.

6.7.9.1 Payment in due course[185]

'Payment in due course' is defined in s. 59 as 'payment made at or after the date of maturity of the bill to the holder thereof in good faith and without notice that his title to the bill is defective'. The section clearly refer to payment. Hence, the holder is fully entitled to insist on payment in money. Sections 3(1) and 17(2)(b) support this proposition. Both these sections anticipate payment in money. It is of course permissible for the holder to agree to accept some other form of payment. If the acceptor or drawee claims this to be the case, the onus is on them to prove such assent.

6.7.9.2 The acceptor becoming the holder of the bill in his own right at or after maturity[186]

Section 61 provides that when the acceptor is or becomes a holder of the bill in his own right at or after the bill's maturity, the bill is discharged. This is redolent of the common law principle that a debt is cancelled out when the 'debtor' becomes also the 'creditor' (*Neale v Turton*).[187] In that case, the claimant had supplied goods to a firm of which he was a partner. He then drew bills on the firm. The bills may have looked something like this:

[Date]

Three months after date pay to me or my order the sum of £115, for value received.

William Henry Neale

Accepted, payable at the Bank of England per proprietors of the London Steam Washing Company,

Isaac Buxton

Company Secretary

---

[183] [1973] AC 992.
[184] Section 50.
[185] Section 59.
[186] Section 61.
[187] (1827) 4 Bing 149.

Best CJ held that the claimant could not recover on the bills against the company. His Lordship said:

> The bills are drawn on the directors of the company, and accepted for the directors. They are the agents of the company, and accept as agents of the company. The case therefore is that of one partner drawing on the whole firm, including himself. There is no principle by which a man can be at the same time Plaintiff and Defendant. We are clearly of opinion, that these bills being drawn on the directors are, in effect, drawn on the company of which the Plaintiff is himself a member. He cannot be at the same time drawer and acceptor.

In s. 61, while the principle in *Neale* is largely maintained, there are two qualifications. First, the acceptor must come to hold the bill in his own right, not merely as a collector without recourse or a representative. Secondly, his coming to hold it in his own right must occur either at or after maturity.

6.7.9.3 A waiver or renunciation in writing by the holder of his rights against the acceptor[188]

Section 62 provides that through an express waiver or renunciation by the holder of his rights on the bill, the bill will be discharged. There are however two important qualifications – the renunciation must be absolute and unconditional; and the renunciation must be in writing, unless the bill is delivered up to the acceptor. The rule in s. 62 is also a variant of a time-honoured common law rule. In *Foster v Dawber*,[189] a renunciation of a debt was held to be effective even though it was unsupported by consideration and not made by deed. Parke B said: 'The rule of law has been so often laid down and acted upon, although there is no case precisely on the point as between immediate parties, that the obligation on a bill of exchange may be discharged by express waiver, that it is too late now to question the propriety of that rule.' Although it might be unsupported by case law in 1851, the rule is now properly enshrined in the Bills of Exchange Act 1882.

The renunciation does not need to be made to the creditor directly; it can be made to a person nominated by the drawee or acceptor. In fairness, the renunciation should be made at or after maturity where the rights being renounced are those against the acceptor. As regards rights against other parties to the bill, it may be made at any time before, at or after maturity.

6.7.9.4 An intentional cancellation of the bill by the holder[190]

Where a bill is intentionally cancelled by the holder or his agent and that cancellation is apparent on the face of the bill, the bill is discharged. If the holder or his agent intentionally cancels the signature of any party liable on the bill, that act of cancellation will discharge that party's liability. A cancellation made unintentionally or under a mistake or without the authority of the holder is inoperative. The burden of proof is however on the person alleging that the cancellation was made unintentionally, by mistake or without authority.[191]

---

[188] Section 62.
[189] (1851) 6 Exch 839.
[190] Section 63.
[191] Section 63(3); see *Bank of Scotland v Dominion Bank (Toronto)* [1891] AC 592 for an example of a purported cancellation.

6.7.9.5 A material alteration of the bill without the assent of the parties liable on it, subject to certain conditions[192]

Where a bill or acceptance is materially altered without the assent of the parties liable on the bill, the bill is avoided except against a party who has himself made, authorised or assented to the alteration and subsequent indorsers. The liabilities in the bill are wiped out *ab initio*. The bill cannot be enforced at all, not even according to the original terms prior to the alteration. A material alteration, though not generally defined, is described in s. 64(2) as including any alteration of the date, the amount, the time and place of payment and, where a bill has been accepted generally, the addition of a place of payment without the acceptor's assent. This is of course not an exhaustive list but it constitutes a list of some of the more common occurrences. A more general test is found in Brett MR's judgment in *Suffell v Bank of England*.[193] According to His Lordship, a material alteration is one 'which would alter the business effect of the instrument if used for any ordinary business purpose for which such instrument or any part of it is used'.[194] A contrast however might be made of this business purpose test with the Court of Appeal's legal effect test in *Koch v Dicks*.[195] In *Koch*, the place of drawing[196] on the bill was changed from a place within, to a place outside, the British Isles. The bill thus changed from an inland bill to a foreign bill. The court thus concluded that it was a material alteration rendering the bill as having been discharged and of no effect. What is interesting was the test adopted by the Court of Appeal in that case. The court stated that a material alteration should be one which would affect the rights as between the parties to the bill, that is to say, one which would alter the legal nature or incidence of the instrument.[197] On that basis, as the rights of the parties of an inland bill are quite different from those of a foreign bill, there was a material alteration.

It has to be said that neither test is wholly satisfactory. The business purpose test is rather broad, tending perhaps to render void a larger proportion of bills than the legislature would have intended. The *Koch* test, on the other hand, might be too restrictive.

Section 64(1) talks about a materially altered bill being 'avoided'. As to what 'avoided' means, guidance might be had from *Smith & Hayward v Lloyd's TSB Bank Group PLC*.[198] In that case, A was sent a cheque by B payable to C in the sum of £127,240.30. The cheque was stolen and fraudulently altered so that the payee read, 'Joseph Smitherman'. It was then paid into an account in that name at Bank D. A sued D for the tort of conversion, alleging that D had converted the cheque by receiving £127,240.30 from the paying bank and claimed restitution of the cheque's face value. D averred that alteration of the payee's name was a material alteration which rendered the cheque void. The Court of Appeal affirmed Blofeld J's decision that the cheque was void when it came into the possession of the defendant bank and therefore the defendant bank was not liable in the tort of conversion for the face value of the

---

[192] Section 64.
[193] (1882) 9 QBD 555.
[194] At 568.
[195] [1933] 1 KB 307.
[196] Note this is not the place of payment – amending that would be a material alteration. On the other hand, there is some indication in *Foster v Driscoll* [1929] 1 KB 470 that changing the place of drawing from London to Lausanne did not constitute a material alteration.
[197] *Ibid.* at 324, *per* Greer LJ.
[198] [2001] 1 All ER 424; *cf. Slingsby v Westminster Bank* [1932] 2 KB 583.

cheque. The Court of Appeal held that the effect of the word 'avoided' in s. 64 was that a cheque or bill which had been materially altered by the fraud of a third party was no longer a cheque or bill representing a chosen action but a worthless piece of paper. In such a case, the face value of the cheque could not be recovered in a claim for conversion. Only nominal damages were recoverable since only a worthless piece of paper had been converted. It might be also noted that the Court of Appeal refused the claimants any recourse to equity to temper the impact of s. 64.[199]

There are some exceptions to the material alteration rule in s. 64. Where the alteration is not apparent and the bill is in the hands of a holder in due course, such holder may avail himself of the bill as if it had not been altered and enforce payment of the bill according to its *original* tenor.[200]

6.7.10 Post discharge liability

The question here is if, after the bill had been discharged, the acceptor or drawer might nevertheless remain liable if the discharged bill is transferred to a *bona fide* purchaser for value without notice of the discharge. In *Glasscock v Balls*,[201] A had borrowed money from B. He gave B a promissory note payable on demand to B's order and a mortgage on his assets as security. B transferred the mortgage to C and received an amount equal to the loan to A. B also then indorsed and delivered the promissory note to D. D took it in good faith and for value. The Court of Appeal held that the note, not having been paid or returned to A, was still current at the time of the indorsement, therefore D as a *bona fide* indorsee for value was entitled to recover on it. There was no general principle that the note would be treated as overdue merely because it was payable on demand and bore a date which has long since passed. Lord Esher MR added that if a negotiable instrument remained current, even though it had been paid, there would be nothing to prevent a person to whom it was indorsed for value, without knowledge that it had been paid, from claiming. In the present case, D's rights were even more potent because the bill had not yet been paid.

It should however not be forgotten that s. 29(1)(a) provides that if a bill is payable at a fixed date and the holder transfers it after maturity, the transferee could not become a holder in due course as the instrument had become overdue. The *Glasscock* issue thus would arise only in the case of demand, not fixed bills. Even then a demand bill can become overdue if they have been in circulation for an unreasonable period of time.[202]

Section 55(2)(c), it might be recalled, provides that if an order is indorsed and transferred after discharge the indorser may not deny to his immediate or subsequent indorsee that the bill was a valid and subsisting bill at the time of his indorsement. In the case of a bearer bill, if it is transferred after discharge the transferor will be liable to his transferee for value for breach of warranty under s. 58(3).

---

[199] See *Morison v London County and Westminster Bank* [1914] 3 KB 356.
[200] Section 64(1).
[201] [1890] LR 24 QBD 13.
[202] Section 36(3).

Cheques

This is an expansive subject but, for our purposes, we shall limit our discussion to those principles which relate to its role as a payment instrument.

6.8.1 Formalities and procedures

A cheque is a mandate from the customer to his bank to pay according to his instructions or order. A cheque is defined by s. 73 of the Bills of Exchange Act 1882 as 'a bill of exchange drawn on a banker payable on demand'. That section also makes clear that, 'except as otherwise provided in ss. 73–82, the provisions of the Act applicable to bills of exchange payable on demand apply also to cheques'. This is important because, whilst the Act stresses that the cheque is a bill of exchange and would normally be governed by the law on bills of exchange, there will be some variation in the applicable rules.

For a start, s. 73(1) read in conjunction with s. 3 implies that a cheque is an unconditional order in writing, drawn by one person on another person who is a bank, signed by the drawer, requiring the bank to pay on demand a sum certain in money, to or to the order of a specified person or to bearer. Although it must be payable on demand, the cheque does not need to state explicitly on its face that it is payable on demand, since this is presumed in the absence of an indicated date for payment.[203] It would seem to follow that a post-dated cheque is still payable on demand and therefore a valid cheque.[204] That said, it would be an obvious breach of mandate for the drawee bank to pay a post-dated cheque and debit its customer's account *before* the date of the issue.[205]

There is no stipulation in the Act as to the date on which the cheque is drawn. However, as a cheque can become stale if left unpaid after an unreasonable period of time,[206] an issue date would be useful to help ascertain if the cheque had been in circulation for an unduly long time. In *London and County Banking Co v Groome*,[207] Field J noted:

> Of course, even with regard to cheques, there is no doubt that in the ordinary course of business they are intended almost as cash, and for early if not prompt payment; and it is well-known law that, as between the maker and payee, although there is no absolute duty to present a cheque promptly, that duty exists to such an extent that exact rules have been laid down beyond which the payee may not delay presentment, if he wishes to avoid the consequence of any damage caused to the maker by the insolvency of the drawee, or otherwise.[208]

What constitutes an unreasonable length of time is a matter of fact.

---

[203] Section 10.
[204] *Royal Bank of Scotland v Tottenham* [1894] 2 QB 715; *Bank of Baroda Ltd v Punjab National Bank Ltd* [1944] AC 176; and *Hodgson & Lee Pty Ltd v Mardonius Pty Ltd* (1986) 5 NSWLR 496.
[205] *Morley v Culverwell* (1840) 7 M&W 174 at 178 (Parke B); *Pollock v Bank of New Zealand* (1901) 20 NZLR 174; *Hodgson & Lee Pty Ltd v Mardonius Pty Ltd*, ibid.
[206] Section 36(3).
[207] (1881) 8 QBD 288.
[208] At 293.

It is rare these days for cheques, despite being negotiable instruments, to be made transferable. Most cheques are preprinted with crossings[209] and the words 'a/c payee only'; as such most modern cheques are therefore not negotiable instruments. In law, though, whether or not a cheque is transferable depends on whether it is payable to a specific person's order or to the bearer. It is payable to the bearer if it is expressed to be so payable or if the last indorsement on it is executed in blank.[210] It is payable to order if it is expressed to be so payable or if it is expressed to be payable to a particular person but does not contain words prohibiting transfer or indicating an intention that it should not be transferable.[211]

In the case of a cheque payable to order, it must identify the payee with reasonable certainty.[212] In *Daun and Vallentin v Sherwood* [213] the payee's name had been omitted. As such the cheque or bill was deemed to be payable to the bearer. Be that as it may, as already noted, a bill (including a cheque) made out for 'cash or order' will not be treated as a bill of exchange.[214]

It should also be remembered that the provisions on signatures will also apply – especially in the case of company cheques. A private limited company must display clearly on the face of the cheque the words 'Limited' or 'Ltd' (reg. 6, Companies (Trading Disclosures) Regulations 2008/495). Failure to do so might result in the company being unable to pursue a claim in contract (to which the non-disclosure or misrepresentation of the company's registered name is related) against the relevant third party (s. 83, Companies Act 2006).

6.8.2 Payment and wrongful payment

As we have discussed earlier, a cheque needs to be cleared for payment to be made to the payee. When the payee takes the cheque, he will normally pass it to his bank (the collecting bank), which will in turn present it to the drawer's (payer's) bank through the cheque-clearing system for the appropriate account movement to occur. In the old days, the physical cheque had to travel from the collecting bank to paying bank or clearing bank. In modern times, the mere electronic transmission of the cheque's image or details would be enough. This is called cheque truncation. Cheque truncation was specifically provided for by the Deregulation (Bills of Exchange) Order 1996 which introduced ss. 74A–74C to the Bills of Exchange Act 1882.[215] Section 74B(1) provides that a banker may present a cheque for payment to the banker on whom it is drawn by notifying him of its essential features by electronic means or otherwise, instead of by presenting the cheque itself. Section 74B(2) then makes it plain that truncation can effectively replace physical delivery of the cheque for the purposes of presentment for payment.

When payment is made by cheque, it does not constitute unconditional or absolute payment. In this respect, the cheque does not operate like a debit or credit card[216] or, indeed,

---

[209] See section 6.8.3 below.
[210] Section 8(3).
[211] Section 8(4).
[212] Section 7(1).
[213] (1895) 11 TLR 211.
[214] See section 6.7.2 above.
[215] Prior to the 1996 Order, it was held in *Barclays Bank PLC v Bank of England* [1985] 1 All ER 385 that presentment must mean presentment of the actual cheque itself (s. 74, Bills of Exchange Act 1882).
[216] See, for example, *Re Charge Card Services* [1989] Ch 497.

cash. It does not discharge the underlying debt before clearance. If the cheque is dishonoured, the payer will remain liable to the payee for the original debt (plus interest, where applicable). However, as the cheque is a negotiable instrument,[217] if it is dishonoured, the payee can sue on the cheque itself (without needing to prove the underlying contract) using the court's summary judgment process, in general. In the absence of fraud, invalidity, illegality or total failure of consideration, the payer cannot set up a defence of set off.[218] This rule is often referred to as the 'cheque rule'.[219]

As we have seen, where the cheque has been forged, unauthorised or stolen,[220] the bank collecting it may be liable to the true owner for conversion. The bank may however rely on the following defences:

- s. 4(1), Cheques Act 1957;
- it has become a holder in due course;
- contributory negligence by the true owner;
- defence of illegality or public policy.

6.8.2.1 Section 4(1), Cheques Act 1957

Section 4(1) of the Cheques Act 1957 provides:

> where a banker, (a) in good faith and without negligence, receives payment for a customer of an instrument to which this section applies; or (b) having credited a customer's account with the amount of such an instrument, receives payment thereof for himself; and the customer has no title, or a defective title, to the instrument, the banker does not incur any liability to the true owner of the instrument by reason only of having received payment thereof.

Good faith is defined in s. 90 in terms of honesty, whether there is negligence or not. What constitutes negligence is highly fact-dependent.[221] A simple example of negligence would be the bank collecting a cheque marked 'a/c payee' for an account other than the named

---

[217] Though seldom used as one (see section 6.8.1 above).

[218] It is quite clear from *Fielding & Platt* v *Selim Najjar* [1969] 1 WLR 357 that these defences are not easy to raise. See, too, *Nova (Jersey) Knit Ltd* v *Kammgarn Spinnerei GmbH* [1977] 1 WLR 713.

[219] In *Esso Petroleum* v *Milton* [1997] 1 WLR 938, the cheque rule was extended by the Court of Appeal to direct debit mandates. Thorpe LJ and Sir John Balcombe considered that modern commercial practice was to treat payments by direct debit in the same way as payments by cheque and the equivalent of cash, therefore, in general, a payment for goods and services by direct debit should preclude a defence of equitable set off. The judges however recognised that the precise circumstances might require further consideration. The dissenting judge on this point, Simon Brown LJ, had a different understanding of the direct debit mandate. His Lordship said, 'many direct debit arrangements are nowadays entered into for the settlement of transactions effected on credit rather than in substitution for cash transactions. I may have a charge account at a store which routinely allows its customers 28 days' credit. Were I, for convenience, to enter into an agreement to pay my account by periodic direct debit payments, that surely ought not to deny me my basic credit entitlement nor limit the scope of such defences as would otherwise be available to me were some purchase to prove unsatisfactory' (at 948). See also (1991) (1) (Feb) LMCLQ 5–9 and (1997) (113) (Jul) LQR 374–377.

[220] Different rules apply for a cheque which has been materially altered. See section 6.7.9.5.

[221] For examples, see *Marfani & Co Ltd* v *Midland Bank Ltd* [1968] 2 All ER 573; *Lumsden & Co* v *London Trustee Savings Bank* [1971] 1 Lloyd's Rep 114; *Orbit Mining and Trading Co Ltd* v *Westminster Bank Ltd* [1963] 1 QB 794; *Baker* v *Barclays Bank Ltd* [1955] 2 All ER 571; *Honourable Society of the Middle Temple* v *Lloyd's Bank PLC* [1999] 1 All ER (Comm) 193. There are many cases on banks' negligence but these few should give a flavour of what considerations guide the courts.

account. The burden of proof is on the bank to show that it has acted in good faith and taken reasonable care (and/or that the facts do not give it cause for suspicion, thereby it had no duty to make enquiries).[222] It should also be noted that 'a bank cannot be held to be liable for negligence merely because they have not subjected an account to a microscopic examination'.[223] Therefore, the court will be reluctant to condemn as negligent a practice widely adopted by the banking industry. It should be slow to rely on the wisdom of hindsight.[224]

6.8.2.2 The bank becomes a holder in due course

Of course, where a collecting bank has become a holder in due course of a cheque, not only does it hold the cheque free from any defect of title of prior parties but it may enforce payment against all parties liable on the cheque (Bills of Exchange Act 1882, s. 38(2)).[225] The crucial issue is proof that the bank had given value.

If the bank has paid prior to the cheque clearing, it may be able to rely on s. 2, Cheques Act 1957. The section provides that 'a banker who gives value for, or has a lien on, a cheque payable to order which the holder delivers to him for collection without indorsing it, has such (if any) rights as he would have had if, upon delivery, the holder had indorsed it in blank'. What is pivotal is whether the bank has given value.[226] Lord Denning MR said in *Westminster Bank v Zang*[227] that it is not sufficient for the bank to show simply that they credited the account of the company at once before the cheque was cleared. That alone would not constitute valuable consideration. More must be shown – for example, that there was an express or implied agreement between banker and customer that the customer could draw against the cheques before they were cleared.[228] As Salmon LJ said: 'An obvious way of becoming a holder for value is to give value by honouring a cheque drawn against an uncleared cheque whether or not there is an antecedent contract to do so. Whether the bank has honoured a cheque drawn against uncleared effects or not is a matter of fact.'[229]

Valuable consideration is also deemed to exist where there is lien on the bill. Section 27(3), Bills of Exchange Act 1882, provides that where the holder of a bill has a lien on it arising either from contract or from implication of law, he is deemed to be a holder *for value* to the extent of the sum for which he has a lien. A bank will usually have a lien to the amount of any overdraft. When we talk about a lien on the cheque, we do not refer to a lien on the paper but the chose in action the cheque represents. That does not, however, mean that the physical cheque is unimportant. In *Westminster Bank Ltd v Zang*,[230] the bank was deemed to have lost its lien when it handed over the cheque to its customer so as to enable the customer to sue the drawer. Possession of the cheque is vital to the lien.

---

[222] *Architects of Wine Ltd* v *Barclays Bank PLC* [2007] EWCA Civ 239.
[223] *Per* Sankey J, *Lloyd's Bank Ltd* v *The Chartered Bank of India, Australia and China* [1929] 1 KB 40 at 73.
[224] *Architects of Wine Ltd* v *Barclays Bank PLC* [2007] EWCA Civ 239.
[225] *Midland Bank Ltd* v *Charles Simpson Motors* [1960] CLY 217; *Barclays Bank Ltd* v *Harding* [1962[CLY 1329; *Midland Bank Ltd* v *R V Harris Ltd* [1963] 2 All ER 685; *Barclay* v *Astley Industrial Trust Ltd* [1970] 2 QB 527.
[226] As to what is meant by 'value', see s. 27(2), Bills of Exchange Act 1882.
[227] [1966] AC 182 at 202.
[228] *AL Underwood Ltd* v *Bank of Liverpool and Martins* [1924] 1 KB 775.
[229] *Westminster Bank Ltd* v *Zang* [1966] AC 182 at 210.
[230] [1966] AC 182.

6.8.2.3 Contributory negligence by the true owner

If the true owner of the cheque had been negligent in allowing the cheque to be misused, the collecting bank may plead the defence of contributory negligence despite s. 11(1) Torts (Interference with Goods) Act 1977 which removes contributory negligence as a defence in a claim for conversion. Section 47 of the Banking Act 1979 provides: 'In any circumstances in which proof of absence of negligence on the part of a banker would be a defence in proceedings by reason of the Cheques Act 1957, s. 4, a defence of contributory negligence shall also be available to the banker notwithstanding the provisions of the Torts (Interference with Goods) Act 1977, s. 11(1).'

6.8.2.4 Illegality and public policy

Naturally, where to allow the claimant to recover the proceeds of the cheque would be to fly in the face of public policy, the court would not allow the claim for conversion. In *Thackwell v Barclays Bank PLC*[231] the claimant claimed damages from the bank for conversion of a cheque. However, the cheque was part of a fraudulent scheme, of which the claimant was aware. If the court were to order the bank to pay damages to the claimant for the conversion, that would amount to materialising the proceeds of the fraud.

If the collecting bank is found liable to pay damages for conversion arising out of the collection of a cheque for a customer, the bank is entitled to be indemnified by its customer.[232] After all, the bank is only acting as the customer's agent. The same applies where the bank is acting as a collecting agent for a foreign bank. The indemnity is lost however if the collecting bank has acted in bad faith or in a way which it knew to be unlawful or which was manifestly unlawful or has acted outside its authority.[233] The bank may also be able to seek contribution from any other party (for example, a paying bank or the collecting bank's own agent who collected the cheque) liable for the damage caused.[234]

This is but a limited discussion of the issue; interested readers are encouraged to consult a specialist banking law text.

6.8.3 Crossed cheques

A cheque is crossed to prevent payment in cash to the payee. When two parallel lines are drawn on the face of a cheque, the cheque is said to be crossed generally. Sometimes, in such a crossing, the words 'and company' or abbreviations thereof are added in the space between the two lines.[235] In such a case, it must be presented for payment through a bank account. The holder cannot present it in person for cash. A cheque is said to be 'crossed specially' if it bears across its face in addition the name of a banker, either with or without the words 'not

---

[231] [1986] 1 All ER 676.
[232] *Yeung Kai Yung* v *Hong Kong and Shanghai Banking Corp* [1981] AC 787.
[233] *Honourable Society of the Middle Temple* v *Lloyd's Bank PLC* [1999] 1 All ER (Comm) 193.
[234] Sections 1(1), 6(1), Civil Liability (Contribution) Act 1978; apportionment is based on what is fair and equitable (*Linklaters* v *HSBC* [2003] EWHC 1113 (Comm); *Middle Temple* v *Lloyds Bank PLC* [1999] 1 All ER 193).
[235] Section 76(1).

negotiable'.[236] There is no need to draw two parallel lines. A cheque crossed specially can only be presented for payment through the bank named in the cheque.

Section 77 of the Bills of Exchange Act 1882 provides that in general only the drawer and holder may cross a cheque. In the case of the cheque crossed specially, the named bank may cross it specially to another bank for collection. In the case of an uncrossed cheque or a cheque crossed generally which has been sent to a banker for collection, he may cross it specially to himself. A bank which ignores a crossing may be held liable to the true owner under s. 79(2). There is nevertheless an exception to this rule. Where the cheque on presentment for payment does not appear to be crossed or to have a crossing which has been obliterated or has been added to or altered in a way not authorised by the Act, the bank would not be held liable if it ignored the crossing, provided it pays the cheque in good faith and without negligence.[237]

However, following the passage of the Cheques Act 1992 and the introduction of 'a/c payee only' cheques, general and special crossings are no longer commonplace. That Act introduced into the Bills of Exchange Act 1882 a new section, s. 81A. Section 81A formalises the practice of crossing cheques 'account payee' or 'a/c payee'. It provides that a cheque crossed 'a/c payee' with or without the word 'only' is not transferable and is only valid as between the parties thereto. With the change in the law, most banks now issue cheques preprinted with 'a/c payee' as a measure to combat the theft of cheques in the post and subsequent fraudulent indorsement of the cheques to the thief or his accomplices. Prior to 1992, the words 'a/c payee' did not affect the transferability of the cheque. It was little more than a notice to the collecting bank that the cheque be collected only for the named payee's account.[238]

6.9 Banker's drafts, counter cheques and travellers' cheques

6.9.1 Banker's drafts

A banker's draft is not a bill of exchange, strictly speaking. This is because it is drawn by the bank on itself instead of being an order to pay made by one person to another as required in s. 3(1), Bills of Exchange Act 1882. However, s. 5(2) of the Bills of Exchange Act 1882 makes a special case for such instruments. Where the drawer and drawee are the same person, the holder may treat the instrument either as a bill of exchange or a promissory note. Under s. 5, Cheques Act 1957, the provisions of the Bills of Exchange Act 1882 relating to crossed cheques should also apply, with appropriate modifications, to bankers' drafts. Further, a bank

---

[236] Section 76(2).
[237] Section 79(2), Bills of Exchange Act 1882.
[238] *National Bank v Silke* [1891] 1 QB 435; *Importers Co Ltd v Westminster Bank Ltd* [1927] 2 KB 297; *Universal Guarantee Pty Ltd v National Bank of Australasia Ltd* [1965] 1 WLR 691.

collecting a banker's draft is protected by s. 4, Cheques Act 1957. If the banker's draft is stolen and the payee's name fraudulently altered, the draft will be invalid under s. 64.[239]

6.9.2 Counter cheque

A counter cheque or building society cheque is akin to a banker's draft. It is drawn by the building society on its own local branch account and is made payable to a person named by the customer. Section 5(2) would likewise apply. The customer's account will usually be debited with the amount of the counter cheque before the cheque is handed over to the customer or payee. Although in legal effect, the counter cheque is on par with the banker's draft, some building societies appear more prepared to dishonour a counter cheque when in similar circumstances, for commercial reasons, it would not consider dishonouring its own draft.[240] The payee who is in possession of the counter cheque is not a holder in due course because the counter cheque had never been negotiated to him (s. 29(2), Bills of Exchange Act 1882). As such, he is not entitled to the protection conferred by the Act on holders in due course.

A building society cheque can usually be stopped if it is lost or stolen. Conversely, a banker's draft is irrevocable.[241] Therefore, a payee who pays the building society cheque into his account assuming that it would be safe to spend the money could find himself having to repay the building society if it turns out that the cheque had been obtained by fraud or forgery. The Financial Ombudsman may offer advice and assistance to customers who complain about the building societies' failure to spot the fake when they pay it in or to warn them about the risks of accepting a payment of this type.[242]

6.9.3 Travellers' cheque

The travellers' cheque is effectively a promise by the issuer to pay the amount on the face of the cheque to the traveller or a person to whom the traveller has transferred the cheque, provided the instrument is countersigned with the specimen signature placed upon it by the traveller when he purchases it. It is therefore not a cheque for the purposes of s. 73, Bills of Exchange Act 1882 because it is not drawn on a banker payable on demand. Some commentators have argued that the travellers' cheque is likely to be a negotiable instrument as a matter of mercantile custom.[243] The rights and liabilities of the issuer, traveller and purchaser are subject to the terms of their contracts[244] and probably the Payment Services Regulations 2009. The use of travellers' cheques is in decline as modern customers prefer to use their payment cards to withdraw cash whilst travelling.

---

[239] See *Harvey Jones Ltd v Woolwich PLC* [2000] 2 All ER (Comm) 693 and *Smith v Lloyd's TSB Bank PLC* [2001] QB 541.

[240] See *Abbey National PLC v JSF Finance & Currency Exchange Co Ltd* [2006] EWCA Civ 328, para. 12.

[241] *Ibid.*, para. 54.

[242] www.financial-ombudsman.org.uk/publications/factsheets/cheques.pdf

[243] See, for example, E. P. Ellinger, 'Travellers' Cheques and the Law' (1969) 19 *Univ of Toronto LJ* 132; J. C. Stassen, 'The Legal Nature of Travellers' Cheques' (1978) 95 *South African Law Journal* 180 and Frohlich, 'Travellers' Cheques and the Law in Australia' (1980) 54 ALJ 388.

[244] See *Fellus v National Westminster Bank PLC* (1983) 133 NLJ 766; *Elawadi v Bank of Credit and Commerce International* [1989] 1 All ER 242; *Braithwaite v Thomas Cook Travellers Cheques Ltd* [1989] 1 All ER 235.

6.10 Trade finance

6.10.1 Documentary credit

As we have seen, the payment system exists to enable money to be paid by one party to another. This is particularly important in the context of a sale, but there is a further dynamic in play in this context. The seller will inevitably wish to be paid before he relinquishes control of ownership in the goods but the buyer will wish to ensure that the goods are actually on their way to him before paying the seller. There is thus an impasse. The situation is far more acute in international sales. The parties are less likely to know each other and so the lack of trust becomes more significant. Also, there is usually a risk of increased delay while the goods are in transit given the distances involved. Capital is thus tied up during this time. Finally, if things go wrong, the parties will find themselves faced with a cross-border dispute with all the attendant problems of ascertaining jurisdiction, choice of law and enforcing foreign awards.[245]

The documentary credit system was established to overcome these hurdles in international trade. It works like this.

(a) The buyer (applicant) will apply to his bank (issuing bank) to open a letter of credit in the seller's favour. What this means is that the issuing bank undertakes to pay the seller directly and as soon as the seller tenders relevant shipping documents showing that the goods have been shipped to the buyer. The issuing bank's commitment to pay is separate and distinct from that of the buyer so that even if the buyer becomes insolvent, the issuing bank has to pay the seller if the requisite documents are properly tendered by the seller.

(b) The issuing bank will then inform the seller that the letter of credit has been opened in his favour. Usually this is done through a nominated bank in the seller's country – the bank doing this is called the advising bank. The letter of credit may also be confirmed by the seller's own bank (a confirming bank) – this is the independent undertaking of the confirming bank to pay against conforming documents. If it pays, it will seek reimbursement from the issuing bank. However, its undertaking is separate from that of the issuing bank, so that if the issuing bank becomes insolvent, the confirming bank must still necessarily pay against conforming documents.

(c) The advice to the seller will specify the documents required (for example, a bill of lading, any insurance document relating to the goods, official certificates, licences, etc.), the time for presentment and the expiry date of the letter of credit.

(d) The seller ships the goods and in return is given shipping documents (usually the bill of lading) by the carrier. The seller will then assemble all the documents required under the letter of credit and tender them to the issuing bank or its nominated bank.

(e) If the documents are in order, that is to say, if they are consistent with the terms of the letter of credit, the relevant bank (issuing bank or confirming bank) must pay the seller.

---

[245] The importance of this issue is considered in Chapter 10.

(f) The confirming bank (where applicable) will then present the documents to the issuing bank for reimbursement. The issuing bank in turn will present the documents to the buyer for payment. The buyer pays and is given the documents. With the documents (especially the bill of lading), the buyer is able to meet the ship carrying the goods and demand delivery of the goods.

Most documentary credits are governed by a set of rules written by the International Chamber of Commerce (ICC) called the Uniform Customs and Practice for Documentary Credits Publication No 600 (2007). These rules are usually incorporated into the letter of credit by contract by a clause stating that the letter of credit is issued subject to the UCP 600. The parties are free to exclude or limit the provisions of the UCP 600 as they see fit (Art. 1, UCP 600).

Central to the workings of the letter of credit are two principles:

(a) the principle of autonomy;

(b) the principle of strict compliance.

6.10.1.1 Principle of autonomy

The principle of autonomy states that the letter of credit and the underlying sale contract are two distinct and separate arrangements. Article 4 articulates it in this way:

> A credit by its nature is a separate transaction from the sale or other contract on which it may be based. Banks are in no way concerned with or bound by such contract, even if any reference whatsoever to it is included in the credit. Consequently, the undertaking of a bank to honour, to negotiate or to fulfil any other obligation under the credit is not subject to claims or defences by the applicant resulting from its relationships with the issuing bank or the beneficiary. A beneficiary can in no case avail itself of the contractual relationships existing between banks or between the applicant and the issuing bank.

The practical effect of the principle is that the bank must pay according to the terms of the letter of credit and cannot refuse on the grounds that the contract of sale has not been properly performed. It cannot refuse payment, for example, on the ground that the goods are not of satisfactory quality.

A notable exception to the principle is the fraud exception. Although fraud is not provided for in the UCP 600, it is a principle of the common law that no person should be entitled to benefit from his act of fraud. In *United City Merchants (Investments) Ltd* v *Royal Bank of Canada*, Lord Diplock said:

> To this general statement of principle as to the contractual obligations of the confirming bank to the seller, there is one established exception: that is where the seller, for the purpose of drawing on the credit, fraudulently presents to the confirming bank documents that contain, expressly or by implication, material representations of fact that to his knowledge are untrue ... The exception for fraud on the part of the beneficiary seeking to avail himself of the credit is a clear application of the maxim *ex turpi causa non oritur actio* or, if plain English is to be preferred, 'fraud unravels all'. The courts will not allow their process to be used by a dishonest person to carry out a fraud.[246]

The fraud exception, however, will be given a narrow application because of the centrality of the principle of autonomy to international trade. The fraud, for example, must have been

---

[246] [1983] 1 AC 168 at 183.

perpetrated by the beneficiary (seller) and some third party for the letter of credit to be unravelled by the fraud. In *United City Merchants*, the bill of lading had been fraudulently misdated by the loading agent (not acting for the seller). The House of Lords ruled that the loading agent's fraud could not defeat the seller's claim for payment under the letter of credit. The seller was not privy to the fraud.

It might also be assumed that where the documents tendered are forgeries, that would constitute a full defence to payment by the banks. The assumption stems from the notion that where the documents are forgeries, they are therefore nullities. A null instrument is void *ab initio* and could not therefore create any rights. Indeed, this has been the position adopted by some commonwealth courts.[247] In English law, it was confirmed by Judge Raymond Jack QC in *Montrod Ltd v Grundkotter Fleishvertriebs-GmbH*[248] that that should not be the position given that the seller is innocent of the forgeries.[249] The matter is not fully laid to rest as *Montrod Ltd* is a High Court decision and could thus be challenged at a higher court. It is, however, submitted that the reasoning by Judge Raymond Jack QC is highly persuasive – the preservation of the autonomy principle should only be resiled from under very restrictive circumstances in the light of the importance of the principle in supporting international trade.

If the bank is aware of the fraud, it must not pay. If it does, it will be acting in breach of its mandate.[250] Where it has paid without knowledge of the fraud, it could nevertheless seek reimbursement from the buyer or the issuing bank (in the case of the confirming bank).[251] The problem, however, is where the bank has some suspicions but not actual knowledge of fraud and is not confident it can prove fraud. Should it pay? The general rule is that a bank could only refuse payment to the seller if it can prove fraud to the usual high standard.[252] Indeed as Kerr J said in *RD Harbottle* v *National Westminster Bank*:

> It is only *in exceptional cases* that the courts will interfere with the machinery of irrevocable obligations assumed by banks. They are the life-blood of international commerce. Such obligations are regarded as collateral to the underlying rights and obligations between the merchants at either end of the banking chain. *Except possibly in clear cases of fraud* of which the banks have notice, the courts will leave the merchants to settle their disputes under the contracts by litigation or arbitration as available to them or stipulated in the contracts. The courts are not concerned with their difficulties to enforce such claims; these are risks which the merchants take. In this case the plaintiffs took the risk of the unconditional wording of the guarantees. The machinery and commitments of banks are on a different level. They must be allowed to be honoured, free from interference by the courts. Otherwise, trust in international commerce could be irreparably damaged.[253]

Hence, the best approach would be for the bank to inform the buyer of its suspicions and leave it with the buyer to decide if a freezing order should be brought to restrain it from paying the seller. This is preferable to the bank simply refusing to pay because unlike the bank, the buyer can obtain an order against the seller freezing the proceeds from the letter of

---

[247] See the Singapore case of *Beam Technologies* v *Standard Chartered Bank* [2002] 2 SLR 155; affd [2003] 1 SLR 597.

[248] [2001] 1 All ER (Comm) 368; see also Lord Diplock's *obiter dicta* in *United City Merchants*.

[249] For academic commentaries of the rule, see R. J. A. Hooley, 'Fraud and Letters of Credit' [2002] *CLJ* 379; P. Todd, 'Non-genuine Shipping Documents and Nallities' [2008] *LMCLQ* 547; *cf.* K. Donnelly 'Nothing for Nothing: A Nullity Exception in Letters of Credit' [2008] *JBL* 316.

[250] *Czarnikow-Rionda* v *Standard Bank* [1999] 1 All ER (Comm) 890.

[251] *Gian Singh & Co Ltd* v *Banque de l'Indochine* [1974] 1 WLR 1234.

[252] *Society of Lloyd's* v *Canadian Imperial Bank of Commerce* [1993] 2 Lloyd's Rep 579.

[253] [1978] QB 146 at 155 and 156 (emphasis added).

credit. In such a case, the buyer needs to show a good, arguable case and a real risk of dissipation of the money occurring if payment is made.[254] This burden, though not easy to discharge, is less onerous than that imposed on a bank to prove fraud.[255]

It is also not usually advisable for the buyer to seek an injunction on the bank. Such an order would be seen as an interference with the letter of credit. The legal position is therefore that the buyer must be able to adduce 'strong corroborative evidence' such that 'the only reasonable inference to draw is that of fraud'.[256] The court, only upon being satisfied, on a balance of convenience, would make a freezing order restraining the bank from paying. However, as damages would in theory be an appropriate remedy in most cases, the balance of convenience is most difficult to satisfy.[257]

If the underlying contract is illegal or contrary to public policy, the courts are not likely to enforce payment under the letter of credit. To do so would be to enforce that illegal contract.[258]

Closely associated with the principle of autonomy is the principle that the banks are concerned only with documents and not the actual performance of the underlying contract. Article 5 provides that the banks 'deal with documents and not with goods, services or performance to which the documents may relate'. Article 14 goes on to provide that the bank must examine a presentation to determine, on the basis of the documents alone, whether or not the documents appear on their face to constitute a complying presentation. It has no more than five banking days to examine the presentation (Art. 14(b)).

ISSUE BOX

A letter of credit states that the issuing bank will pay only if the goods were shipped in July. This would constitute a non-documentary condition which the seller can choose to ignore. However, the letter of credit states that the bill of lading which evidences shipment of the goods should be dated in July (therefore signifying that the goods were shipped in July); that would be considered a documentary condition which the seller must comply with if he wishes to be paid. It is immediately obvious that the distinction between documentary and non-documentary conditions can sometimes be difficult to make.

Consider this: the letter of credit requires that the certificate of quality should be issued by 'an independent and qualified surveyor'. The seller tenders a certificate issued by 'Mr J. Smith' and no other information is provided. Should the bank pay? See Art. 2, UCP 600.

Only original documents are usually acceptable. Article 17(b) provides that 'a bank shall treat as an original any document bearing an apparently original signature, mark, stamp, or label of the issuer of the document, unless the document itself indicates that it is not an original'. Additionally, unless a document indicates otherwise, a document will be accepted as original if it:

---

[254] *Turkiye Is Bankasi v Bank of China* [1996] 2 Lloyd's Rep 611.
[255] *Czarnikow-Rionda v Standard Bank* [1999] 1 All ER (Comm) 890.
[256] *Bolivinter Oil SA v Chase Manhattan Bank* [1984] 1 WLR 392.
[257] *Harbottle (RD) (Mercantile) Ltd v National Westminster Bank Ltd* [1978] QB 146.
[258] *Group Josi Re v Walbrook Insurance* [1996] 1 Lloyd's Rep 345; where the illegality is a foreign illegality, see *Mahonia v JP Morgan Chase Bank* [2003] 2 Lloyd's Rep 911; see also J. Chuah, 'Documentary Credits and Illegality in the Underlying Transaction' [2003] 9 *JIML* 518.

1. appears to be written, typed, perforated or stamped by the document issuer's hand; or

2. appears to be on the document issuer's original stationery; or

3. states that it is original, unless the statement appears not to apply to the document presented.[259]

6.10.1.2 Principle of strict compliance

The centrality of documents means that, other than the documents, the banks have no way of ensuring that the beneficiary is entitled to payment. Hence, they insist that the documentary conditions are strictly performed by the beneficiary seller. The rule is thus that the documents tendered must strictly comply with those that have been called for in the documentary credit; 'there is no room for documents which are almost the same, or which will do just as well'.[260] In *JH Rayner & Co Ltd v Hambros Bank Ltd*[261] the bill of lading referred to 'machine-shelled groundnut kernels'. The letter of credit referred to 'coromandel groundnuts'. The latter was a well-known tradename for the former, but the Court of Appeal held that the bank was entitled to refuse to pay the seller on the basis of non-compliance because a bank should not be expected to know the customs and customary terms of the customer's trade. In another case, where the letter of credit refers to the goods as 'new trucks', a contractually required certificate which describes the goods as 'new, good trucks' would not satisfy Art. 14(d) because the certificate could not be said to refer to new trucks.[262] It should, however, be remembered that only documents required by the letter of credit are relevant. Documents not specifically mentioned in the letter of credit will be disregarded even if they have been tendered and are found to be inconsistent with the documents required.

The documents required by the letter of credit must be consistent with each other. However, this does not mean that they must use identical terms. Article 14(d) provides that 'data in a document, when read in context with the credit, the document itself and international standard banking practice, need not be identical to, but must not conflict with, data in that document, any other stipulated document or the credit'.

The apparent harshness of the strict compliance principle is tempered to some extent by the following:

(a) the buyer is always entitled to waive any documentary discrepancy;[263]

(b) the seller may be entitled to make a re-tender of documents under the letter of credit (provided the letter of credit has not yet expired);

(c) minor typographical errors can be excused;[264]

---

[259] Article 17(c).

[260] *Equitable Trust Co of New York v Dawson Partners Ltd* (1927) 27 Ll L Rep 49 at 52.

[261] [1943] 1 KB 37.

[262] *Bank of Melli Iran v Barclays Bank (Dominion, Colonial and Overseas)* [1951] 2 Lloyd's Rep 367.

[263] Article 16.

[264] *Forestal Minosa Ltd v Oriental Credit Ltd* [1986] 2 All ER 400; *Seaconsar Far East Ltd v Bank Markazi Jomhouri Islami Iran* [1993] 1 Lloyd's Rep 236; para. 25 of the ICC International Standard Banking Practice on Documentary Credits (2007) provides that 'misspellings or typing errors that do not affect the meaning of a word or the sentence in which it occurs, do not make a document discrepant. For example, a description of the merchandise as "mashine" instead of "machine", "fountan pen" instead of "fountain pen" or "modle" instead of "model" would not make the document discrepant. However, a description as "model 123" instead of "model 321" would not be regarded as a typing error and would constitute a discrepancy.'

(d) a tolerance of 5 per cent more and 5 per cent less in the quantity of the goods will be permitted (provided the letter of credit does not refer to the quantity in terms of a stipulated number of packing units or individual items).[265]

6.10.2 **Performance guarantees**[266]

A default undertaking is one where the surety (usually a bank) undertakes to pay a sum of money to the beneficiary following the failure of a party (usually the applicant) to perform the underlying contract. In a straightforward simple guarantee situation, the surety will pay the beneficiary if the beneficiary is able to prove that the applicant had failed to perform his part of the contract (between him and the beneficiary). For example, if A agrees to lend money to B and C promises to pay A if B defaults, C has given a default undertaking in the form of a simple guarantee to A.

A more powerful default undertaking is the demand guarantee. Here, the surety undertakes to pay the beneficiary a sum of money on the beneficiary's mere assertion of the applicant's default to perform the underlying contract. No proof of actual default is required.

For example, in *Edward Owen Engineering Ltd v Barclays Bank International Ltd*,[267] A agreed to erect some greenhouses for B. B agreed to open a letter of credit in A's favour. In return A agreed to provide a performance guarantee in B's favour for 10 per cent of the contract price. The guarantee or bond was issued 'on demand without proof or conditions'. B failed to open the letter of credit as agreed, so A terminated the contract and refused to supply the greenhouses. B then claimed on the demand guarantee asserting that A had not performed the contract. The court allowed the claim, and stated:

> All this leads to the conclusion that the performance guarantee stands on a similar footing to a letter of credit. A bank which gives a performance guarantee must honour that guarantee according to its terms. It is not concerned in the least with the relations between the supplier and the customer; nor with the question whether the supplier has performed his contracted obligation or not; nor with the question whether the supplier is in default or not. The bank must pay according to its guarantee, on demand, if so stipulated, without proof or conditions. The only exception is when there is a clear fraud of which the bank has notice.[268]

It is thus obvious that the demand guarantee is a very powerful weapon indeed. The surety must pay first, and any argument between the parties about the underlying contract should only take place *thereafter*.

Distinguishing the demand guarantee from a simple guarantee is a matter of construction but it is not always an easy task (*Trafalgar House Construction (Regions) Ltd v General Surety and Guarantee Co Ltd*).[269] Given the bluntness of the demand guarantee, courts are naturally slow to construe a guarantee as a demand guarantee without clear words to that effect[270]. In *Trafalgar House*, the bond in question stipulated that 'on default by the Sub-contractor the Surety shall satisfy and discharge the damages sustained'. The House of Lords held that the

---

[265] Article 30.
[266] On guarantees generally, see Chapter 2.
[267] [1978] QB 159.
[268] *Ibid.*, at 171.
[269] [1995] 3 All ER 737.
[270] See also *Vossloh AG v Alpha Trains (UK) Ltd* [2010] EWHC 2443 (Ch).

words 'damages sustained' indicated that proof of the actual loss was required. The instrument was therefore a simple guarantee and not a demand guarantee.

The authors of *Paget's Law of Banking* (11th edn) say that the following factors would strongly suggest that a particular instrument is a demand guarantee:

(i) it relates to an underlying transaction between parties in different jurisdictions;

(ii) it is issued by a bank;

(iii) it contains an undertaking to pay 'on demand';

(iv) it does not contain clauses excluding or limiting the defences available to a guarantor, which will almost always be construed as a demand guarantee.

These are, however, not determinative[271] – they merely assist in the construction process. On the construction process, the Supreme Court held in *Rainy Sky* v *Kookmin Bank*[272] that a court must take account of all the relevant surrounding circumstances when interpreting the commercial instrument. If there were two possible constructions, the court was entitled to prefer the construction which was consistent with business common sense and to reject the other. However it is obvious that there is a danger of the court substituting its own judgment of the commerciality of the transaction for that of the parties or, indeed, the industry.

To this extent, the demand guarantee is autonomous from the underlying contract. However, it is subject to the fraud exception and defence of illegality like the letter of credit. Whether or not strict compliance is required, there is some uncertainty. A number of cases[273] take the view that strict compliance applies to demand guarantees, like the letter of credit. In others, such as *Siporex Trade SA* v *Banque Indosuez*,[274] the High Court held that the doctrine of strict compliance was not to be applied in demand guarantees. The rationale was that, in letters of credit, banks are dealing with the documents, therefore strict compliance is essential. Conversely, in demand guarantees, the banks are dealing with no more than a statement in the form of a declaration to the effect that a certain event or default has occurred. Whatever the controversy, it is naturally open to the parties to make strict compliance a condition. As Staughton LJ said in *IE Contractors Ltd* v *Lloyd's Bank PLC*:

> . . . the degree of compliance required by a performance bond may be strict or not so strict. It is a question of construction of the bond. If that view of the law is unattractive to banks, their remedy lies in their own hands.[275]

Parties to a demand guarantee may sometimes wish for the guarantee to be governed by the ICC's rules, the Uniform Rules on Demand Guarantees Publication No 758 (2010) (which replaces the older Uniform Rules Publication No 458 (1992)). Article 15 of the URDG No 758 provides that:

> a demand under the guarantee shall be supported by such other documents as the guarantee specifies, and in any event by a statement, by the beneficiary, indicating in what respect the applicant is in breach of its obligations under the underlying relationship. This statement may be in the demand or in a separate signed document accompanying or identifying the demand.

---

[271] *Associated British Ports* v *Ferryways NV* [2009] 1 Lloyd's Rep 595; *WS Tankship II BV* v *Kwangju Bank Ltd* [2011] EWHC 3103 (Comm).

[272] [2011] UKSC 50.

[273] For example, *Ermis Skai Radio and Television* v *Banque Indosuez Europa SRL* (unreported, 26 February 1997).

[274] [1986] 2 Lloyd's Rep 146; also *Frans Maas* v *Habib Bank* [2001] Lloyd's Rep Bank 14.

[275] [1990] 2 Lloyd's Rep 496 at 501.

There is neither a requirement to state the amount of damages the beneficiary claims to have sustained nor an obligation to show a link between the damages claimed to have been sustained and the amount claimed under the demand guarantee. However, this is subject to what the contract specifies. The contract may require the beneficiary to state clearly the extent of the financial harm he has suffered, for example. It is for the surety to determine on the face of documents that the demand is consistent with the terms of the demand guarantee (art 19, URDG No 758).

6.10.3 Factoring

Prompt and expeditious payment is crucial to the success of any business. However, buyers are naturally inclined to taking as long as possible to pay to preserve capital liquidity. Whilst letters of credit clearly help, it is also possible for sellers to sell their invoices to a third party (called a factor) who will take over the invoices, process them and seek payment on them from the buyer. The pain of chasing for payment is left to the factor. In effect, the factor provides a debt collection and ledger management service. It could therefore not only improve the company's cashflow but also reduce the cost of administering the ledger and invoices. This is called debt factoring.

It is also possible for the merchant simply to discount their invoices to the factor. Invoice discounting allows for the merchant to draw money against his invoices. He remains in control of the sales ledger; the factor does not manage the ledger in invoice discounting. The seller thus remains responsible for collecting the debt. Invoice discounting only works well where the applicant sells goods or services on credit. The invoice discounting arrangement is usually for a long period of time and can therefore sometimes be unsuitable for small businesses. Invoice discounting may or may not be disclosed to the buyer.

In debt factoring, the seller will raise an invoice which may require the buyer to pay the factor directly. Under the debt factoring agreement, the factor will pay a percentage of the invoice to the seller. The factor will then seek to recover payment from the customer. If the buyer does not pay, depending on whether the factoring agreement is for recourse or non-recourse factoring, the factor may or may not be able to seek payment from the seller. Naturally, non-recourse factoring is more expensive than recourse factoring. With non-recourse factoring, the seller must assign[276] to the factor his contractual rights against the buyer so as to enable the factor successfully to seek payment from the buyer.

In both invoice discounting and debt factoring, a monthly or annual fee may also be payable.

---

[276] See J. Lumsden, 'Contracts (Rights of Third Parties) Act 1999: Its Impact on Financiers' Assignments of Contracts' [2000] *JIBL* 160; J. Verill, 'Unlocking Capital: Factoring and Invoice Discounting' (1997) 8(2) *PLC* 31.

Further reading

Brindle, M. and Cox, R. W., *Law of Bank Payments* (4th edn, Sweet and Maxwell, London, 2010).

Cresswell, Blair, Hill, Wood, et al., *Encyclopaedia of Banking Law* (Looseleaf from 1996) (Butterworths Lexisnexis, London).

Ellinger, E. P., Lomnicka, E. and Hare, C., *Ellinger's Modern Banking Law* (5th edn, Oxford University Press, Oxford, 2010).

Elliott, N., Odgers, R. and Phillips, J. M., *Byles on Bills of Exchange and Cheques* (28th edn, Sweet and Maxwell, London, 2007).

Enonchong, N., *The Independence Principle of Letters of Credit and Demand Guarantees* (Oxford University Press, Oxford, 2011).

Fox, D., *Property Rights in Money* (Oxford University Press, Oxford, 2008).

Guest, A. G., *Chalmers and Guest on Bills of Exchange, Cheques and Promissory Notes* (17th edn, Sweet and Maxwell, London, 2009).

Hedley, W., *Bills of Exchange and Bankers' Documentary Credits* (4th edn, LLP, London, 2001).

Howard, M., Masefield, R. and Chuah, J. (eds), *Butterworths' Banking Law Guide* (Butterworths, London, 2006).

Malek, A. and Quest, D., *Jack on Documentary Credits* (4th edn, Tottel, London, 2009).

Proctor, C., *Goode on Payment Obligations in Commercial and Financial Transactions* (2nd rev. edn, Sweet and Maxwell, London, 2009).

Proctor, C., *Mann on the Legal Aspect of Money* (6th edn, Oxford University Press, Oxford, 2005) Sections I–III.

Salinger, F. R., Davidson, N., Mills, S. and Ruddy, N., *Salinger on Factoring: The Law and Practice of Invoice Finance* (4th edn, Sweet and Maxwell, London, 2005).

Companion Website

For open-access **student resources** specifically written to complement this textbook and support your learning, please visit **www.pearsoned.co.uk/legalupdates**

ON THE WEBSITE

7 Consumer protection

By Chris Willett and Martin Morgan-Taylor

Chapter outline

- ➤ 7.1 How and why the law protects consumers
- ➤ 7.2 Information and cancellation rights
- ➤ 7.3 Performance Standards (1) – Implied terms as to goods
- ➤ 7.4 Performance Standards (2) – Implied terms as to services
- ➤ 7.5 Performance Standards (3) – Liability in tort for defective products
- ➤ 7.6 Performance Standards (4) – General product safety and food safety in public law
- ➤ 7.7 Unfair terms
- ➤ 7.8 Preventive and criminal law regulation of unfair practices
- ➤ 7.9 EU Regulation on a Common European Sales Law
- ➤ Further reading

7.1 How and why the law protects consumers

7.1.1 Introduction – the advent of the consumer society

The 'consumer society' is often portrayed as a phenomenon of the 20th and 21st centuries, but there is some historical support for the view that the first recognition of the idea of consumer protection may date back to the 18th century.[1] Indeed, there has long been regulation in respect of essential items such as bread, meat, ale and fuel. In particular, there was early regulation in relation to prices and the provision of short measures.[2] Whether or not these

---

[1] See, for example, P. Stearns, 'Stages of Consumerism: Recent Work on the Issues of Periodization' (1997) 69 *Journal of Modern History* 102.

[2] For examples, see the Merchandise Marks Acts 1887–1953 which were the forerunners of the Trade Descriptions Act 1968, which, in turn, has been replaced by the Consumer Protection from Unfair Trading Regulations 2008, SI 2008/1277; the Adulteration of Food and Drink Act 1860.

statutes should be properly regarded as consumer protection measures is doubtful, as much of the motivation for their enactment probably stemmed from a desire to protect honest traders from their dishonest counterparts. As such, much of the earlier legislation can be regarded as being directed towards 'fair trading' rather than 'consumer protection'.

Nevertheless, the majority of what can be seen as attempts at protecting consumers appear to have developed in the period following World War II, as society became more affluent.[3] This affluence led to the emergence of a mass 'middle class' which was more prepared to enter into market transactions, seemingly fed by the greater availability of credit[4] and a much wider choice of novel goods and services, the availability and features of which would be conveyed to consumers through the medium of advertising.

7.1.2 The major consumer concerns: trade practices, consumer information rights and performance standards – an overview

The issues that may arise in the context of the legal regulation of the relationship between a business and its consumers can be categorised in a number of different ways. For present purposes, it is proposed to organise these issues within the broad categories of trade practices, information rights and performance standards.

7.1.2.1 Trade practices

The phrase 'trade practice' describes the ways in which businesses actually behave towards others, including consumers. Many of these practices will be perfectly acceptable, but there may be others that involve deception or excessive pressure that require close regulation.

Trade practices can occur at different stages. For example, the consumer might be influenced by statements made in advertisements on billboards or aired on television or by other forms of promotion, persuasion or sales talk prior to the making of a contract. However, trade practices may also occur during the currency of an existing contractual relationship where a trader seeks to persuade the consumer to take new goods or services or to make a payment in respect of an amount alleged to be owed by the consumer. It will be seen below[5] that there are both private law rules and public law controls over misleading, aggressive and other unfair trade practices which may, for example, allow a consumer to rescind a contract or may permit intervention by an enforcement body to obtain an enforcement order to restrict the use of such practices. Furthermore, in appropriate cases, unfair trade practices may constitute the commission of a criminal offence in respect of which a prosecution may be brought.

7.1.2.2 Consumer information and cancellation rights

It will be seen below[6] that one of the primary reasons for legislative intervention in favour of consumers is that there may be information deficiencies that result in inefficient market

---

[3] See, for example, A. Offer, *The Challenge of Affluence: Self-control and Well-being in the United States and Britain since 1950* (Oxford University Press, Oxford, 2007) p. 1.

[4] See J. Benson, *The Rise of Consumer Society in Britain 1880–1980* (Longman, London, 1994) p. 5.

[5] See discussion of the Consumer Protection from Unfair Trading Regulations 2008, SI 2008/1277 implementing the EU Unfair Commercial Practices Directive (2005/29/EC) at section 7.8 below.

[6] See discussion of the theoretical reasons for consumer protection, at section 7.1.5 below.

failure. If a consumer is to be able to make an informed decision he should be in possession of the information to allow him to make a rational choice. As such, the law often requires that traders provide consumers with certain information; whether about the trader with whom he deals or the product or service that he provides even before any contract is entered into.[7] In other cases, the seriousness of the undertaking entered into by a consumer is such that it is considered appropriate to provide time for reflection in the form of a 'cooling off' period, even though the trader has done nothing wrong.[8] However, cooling off periods are only effective if the consumer is aware that they exist. Consequently there is often a legal requirement that consumers should be made aware of that right.

7.1.2.3 Performance standards

The performance standards that a trader should comply with are based, in part, on the express promises made under the contract. However, it is also important to bear in mind that the trader is also subject to implied terms and other legal rules that may impose a required standard of performance. Both the nature and level of these standards may differ according to the type of contract entered into. For example, the supplier of goods is taken to guarantee the quality and fitness of the goods he supplies and to supply goods that accord with any identifying description given of them ('guarantee', in the sense that the standards are strict liability).[9] By contrast, the provider of a service does not guarantee the success of his service, but is expected to provide the service through the exercise of reasonable care and skill.[10] While these implied terms only apply where there is a contractual relationship between a trader, normally a retailer, and a consumer, the law also requires producers of products to ensure that they meet minimum safety standards, based on the expectations of a reasonable person. The obligations owed by a producer of a defective product may give rise to liability in contract, but more usually, given the absence of a contractual relationship between the producer and the consumer, liability is likely to arise in tort or under the criminal law.[11]

7.1.3 The respective roles of private law, market regulation and trade self-regulation as instruments of consumer protection

7.1.3.1 Private law

Private law rules, particularly those of the law of contract and the law of tort, give a private right to bring an action for damages or seek other remedies where a civil wrong has been

---

[7] See discussion of the Package Travel, Package Holidays and Package Tours Regulations 1992, SI 1992/3288 at note 50 *ff.* and the Cancellation of Contracts made in a Consumer's Home or Place of Work etc. Regulations 2008, SI 2008/1816 at note 53 *ff.* The sort of information required may relate to details about the identity of a business, contact details, arrangements for performance, the rights of the parties and how disputes are resolved.

[8] See discussion of the Cancellation of Contracts made in a Consumer's Home or Place of Work etc. Regulations 2008, SI 2008/1816 at section 7.2.3. The right of cancellation is not the same as the right to *rescind* based on misrepresentation or duress as cancellation rights are not based on the trader having done anything 'wrong'.

[9] See discussion of the implied terms in supply of goods contracts and the remedies available to consumers in the event of a breach at section 7.3.

[10] See discussion of the implied terms in contracts for the supply of services at section 7.4.

[11] See discussion of producers' liability for unsafe products at section 7.5.

committed. Most of these rules are common law-based, but where the common law has proved incapable of addressing problems specific to consumers there has been some legislative intervention. So, for example, there are various legislative controls on the rights of traders to use exemption clauses and other unfair terms in contracts with consumers (stronger controls than those applying in contracts between two traders).[12] Another example of legislative intervention setting higher standards arises in tort. Tortious liability at common law is primarily concerned with 'wrongs' on the part of a defendant. Thus, in the context of manufacturers' liability, the tort of negligence requires proof that a manufacturer has failed to exercise reasonable care. However, this common law liability has been supplemented by legislation that imposes a stricter form of liability based upon reasonable expectations of safety.[13]

Consumer rights to precontract information, noted above,[14] are also contractual in the sense that the consumer is sometimes entitled to avoid being liable under the contract where this information has not been given. In addition, private law regulates trading practices, for example where it permits the rescission of contracts where traders have made a misrepresentation, exercised undue influence or applied duress and by providing a tortious remedy in damages under the Misrepresentation Act, s. 2(1).

There is more to consumer private law than traditional rules, however. For instance, many trade associations create codes of practice that members of the association agree to abide by. A common feature of these codes is that participating businesses are required to provide their customers with contractual rights in respect of the goods or services provided and may provide for remedies that can exceed what is required by law.[15] So, here, the performance standards have been agreed to in the traditional 'contract way' but they emanate from a trade association rather than an individual trader.

ISSUE BOX

A further difficulty faced by consumers is that, frequently, the value of any claim they might have could be so small that the pursuit of a legal right might be uneconomic. As a consequence, the enforcement of private law rights has moved away from being concentrated in the traditional courts and may be dealt with by more informal means. For example, it is not uncommon for larger businesses and trade associations to set up internal redress schemes so as to help the consumer to avoid the need to use courts to enforce their rights. Furthermore, particularly in the financial services sector, there are many 'Ombudsman' schemes under which an adjudicator decides on the case and makes an award without the consumer needing to go to the traditional courts.[16] These alternative redress mechanisms are still

---

[12] See discussion of the Unfair Contract Terms Act 1977 and the Unfair Terms in Consumer Contracts Regulations 1999, SI 1999/2083 at section 7.7.

[13] See discussion of product liability at section 7.5.

[14] See n. 7 and section 7.2.

[15] There is also a further incentive to sign up to such codes if they are approved by the Office of Fair Trading pursuant to a scheme set up under the Enterprise Act 2002, s. 8(2) to (6), as this approval can be used as a marketing tool.

[16] Similar schemes exist where services of general interest or 'utility services' such as gas, water, electricity, telecommunications, etc. are concerned. In particular, Consumer Focus has taken over the roles of Energywatch and Postwatch under the provisions of the Consumer, Estate Agents and Redress Act 2007, which also establishes the basis of a consumer complaint handling and redress scheme in Part II (ss. 42–52).

related to the private law in the sense that they relate to consumers, as individuals, seeking to enforce rights or pursue remedies against businesses whether under the law of contract or the law of tort. However, they avoid the costs associated with traditional litigation.

In the event that litigation is considered to be justified, the county court has a small claims track that reduces the formality and costs associated with legal proceedings. The scheme applies to any claim for damages below £5,000. The court is able to adopt any method of proceeding that is considered to be fair and it is stipulated that hearings will be informal and that the strict rules of evidence will not apply.[17] The court does not have to receive evidence on oath and can limit the right of cross-examination, but reasons for arriving at a decision have to be given.

7.1.3.2 Public law

Public law also plays an important role in regulating business and protecting consumers in four different ways.

First, public bodies often have licensing powers to prevent businesses operating in the first place or to close them down in the event of persistent malpractice. Thus public houses and restaurants serving alcohol are licensed to do so by local authorities and a business offering consumer credit services is licensed by the Office of Fair Trading.

Secondly, such bodies often have powers to inspect and test premises and products, in particular, food supplied for human consumption, for quality and safety.[18] Public bodies also have powers to examine and scrutinise the contract terms and practices of traders, including and going beyond advertising directed at consumers[19] to ensure that those terms and practices are not unfair and to give guidance on how to comply with legal requirements.

Thirdly, where such bodies cannot persuade traders to comply with the law, or at least to do what the body believes is required, they may have powers to seek a court injunction or enforcement order which will require the trader to do something. Thus local authority environmental health departments can apply for an order requiring food premises to be cleaned to a certain hygiene standard and the Office of Fair Trading or a local authority trading standards department may seek an order to prevent a business from using unfair contract terms[20] or unfair practices.[21] The most broadly based version of this sort of power is the power to seek an enforcement order against traders that are committing a 'Domestic infringement',

---

[17] Civil Procedure Rules 1998, SI 1998/3132, r. 27.

[18] Of particular importance are the powers of local authority trading standards and environmental health departments.

[19] Here the powers are with local authority trading standards authorities and also with the Office of Fair Trading (OFT), the consumer protection agency connected to central government; as well as with other bodies such as sector-specific utility regulators, Consumer Focus and the (private) Consumers' Association. See sections 7.6.3, 7.7.4.6, 7.8.7 and 7.8.9.

[20] See the Unfair Terms in Consumer Contracts Regulations 1999, SI 1999/2083, reg. 12; and the discussion at section 7.7.4.6.

[21] See the powers under the Enterprise Act 2002, ss. 211–12 allowing the OFT, local authority trading standards authorities and others to seek 'enforcement orders' against the use of unfair practices as defined in the Consumer Protection from Unfair Trading Regulations 2008, SI 2008/1277; and the discussion at section 7.8.7.

namely, a breach of either a private law or a criminal law standard originating in domestic law, or committing a 'Community infringement', namely, the breach of a standard of whatever type in a European Directive.[22] Also, where appropriate, orders can be applied for that will stop a business from trading altogether, until some hygiene problem, for example, is resolved.[23]

Fourthly, public bodies have the power and duty to prosecute a trader where he committed an act or omission that amounts to a regulatory criminal offence. So, for example, in some circumstances it is a criminal offence to engage in an unfair commercial practice,[24] or to offer or sell products or food that fail to reach certain safety requirements.[25]

7.1.3.3 Self-regulation

Apart from private and public law, there is also a form of business regulation in the form of self-regulation via trade association codes of practice. These codes are forms of regulation, as are the internal redress mechanisms they provide for. However, as we saw above, they may both alter and add to the legal rights and performance standards that exist in private law as well as provide alternative ways of enforcing private law.

Self-regulatory standards may be of a type that are not enforceable by consumers at all. So, for instance, the Advertising Standards Authority (ASA) is a private body funded by the advertising industry which regulates advertising. It sets its own standards. These are set out in the Code of Advertising Practice (CAP) and operate on the general principle that advertising should be 'legal, decent, honest, and truthful'. The ASA enforces these standards by sanctions it takes against its members when they break the CAP standards. Individual consumers do not have the right to make a claim for damages on the basis that they have suffered a loss as a result of a breach of the CAP.

Although this self-regulatory system is not enforceable privately by consumers, it does interact closely with public law and its enforcement. Since the introduction of the Control of Misleading Advertisements Regulations 1988,[26] the OFT has had powers to seek injunctions against misleading advertising as defined in the Regulations. However, the CAP rules cover misleading advertising and go beyond this to cover other matters, such as decency. Accepted practice is that a formal legal injunction will only be sought by the OFT where the ASA is unable to bring the advertiser into line under the CAP. Following the repeal of the Misleading Advertisements Regulations since the introduction of the Consumer Protection from Unfair Trading Regulations (CPUTR) 2008 which include advertisements as potential unfair commercial practices,[27] it seems likely that enforcement bodies will continue to take a similar approach to advertising under these new Regulations by leaving quite a lot of freedom to the ASA and their enforcement of the CAP, before becoming involved.

---

[22] See Enterprise Act 2002, s. 212.

[23] See Food Safety Act 1990, s. 11.

[24] Consumer Protection from Unfair Trading Regulations 2008 (CPUTR), regs 8–12.

[25] Food Safety Act 1990, ss. 7, 8 and 14 and the General Food Regulations 2004, art. 14 considered in section 7.6.4.

[26] Implementing the Directive on Misleading Advertising 1984, Dir 84/450/EEC.

[27] These Regulations implement the EC Directive on Unfair Commercial Practices (2005/29/EC) which, itself, repealed the Directive on Misleading Advertising.

7.1.3.4 European law

Before the 1980s the private and public law rules protecting consumers were all of purely domestic origin. Some of this was domestic case law, such as common law rules of contract and tort and some of it was in domestic legislation as in the case of the criminal offences relating to food safety and the old criminal offences of false trade descriptions.[28] However, since then there has been a series of important directives that have required national governments to adopt new rules reflecting the requirements of these directives. These rules have had an enormous impact, usually improving consumer protection, in relation to private law and public law. So, for instance, the most recent of these, the Unfair Commercial Practices Directive, required Member States to give powers to enforcement bodies to take action against unfair practices as defined in the Directive; and the new definition of unfairness is now contained in the Consumer Protection from Unfair Trading Regulations 2008. The power to seek enforcement orders against these practices is contained in the Enterprise Act 2002 which allows for such orders against so-called 'Community infringements'.[29] This Directive neither requires any rights to be given in private law in relation to the practices in question, nor does it require that they be criminalised. However, the government has chosen to apply the same standards in criminal law, so that practices covered by the 2008 Regulations may be forbidden through the use of enforcement orders and result in criminal prosecution, so that the ground covered by the old domestic legislation remains covered.

Many other directives have required the introduction of new *private law* rights. For example, in contracts made at a distance there is a right to receive certain precontractual information and to cancel a concluded contract within a short period after entering it.[30] In package holiday contracts there is also a right to receive certain precontractual information and to insist on 'proper performance' of the contract.[31] In consumer contracts for the supply of goods there are remedies of repair, replacement, price reduction and rescission should the goods prove to be defective.[32] Furthermore, there is also a right not to be bound by 'unfair' contract terms.[33] Beyond the realm of contractual liability, there is a right to seek compensation against producers for defective products that cause injury or damage to property without proof of negligence.[34] At the same time, European law also requires that Member States should take effective action to actually *prevent* traders acting in breach of these standards.[35] In other words, some public law control is required and it is for this reason that acting in breach of such standards is classified as a 'Community infringement' against which enforcement orders may be sought.[36]

---

[28] The Trade Descriptions Act 1968 has now been repealed and replaced by the new offences on unfair practices under the Consumer Protection from Unfair Trading Regulations 2008, regs 8–12.

[29] Section 212, Sch. 13, as amended by the Consumer Protection from Unfair Trading Regulations 2008, reg. 26.

[30] See the Distance Selling Directive 1997 implemented by the Consumer Protection (Distance Selling) Regulations 2000, SI 2000/2334, reg. 11(2).

[31] The Package Travel Directive 1990, implemented by The Package Travel, Package Holidays and Package Tours Regulations 1992, SI 1992/3288, regs 9 and 15.

[32] The Consumer Sales Directive 1999, implemented by amendments to the Sale of Goods Act 1979, made by the Sale and Supply of Goods to Consumers Regulations 2002, SI 2002/3045.

[33] The Directive on Unfair Terms in Consumer Contracts 1993, as implemented by the Unfair Terms in Consumer Contracts Regulations 1999, SI 1999/2083, reg. 8.

[34] The Product Liability Directive 1985, implemented by the Consumer Protection Act 1987, Part 1.

[35] See the Injunctions Directive 1998 generally, and see Unfair Terms Directive 1993, art. 7.

[36] See Enterprise Act 2002, s. 212.

7.1.4 **General roles and goals of the different types of law**

Many of the private and public law rules cover the same or similar issues. So, for example, the same statements that can amount to a misrepresentation in private law and give rise to a right to rescind a contract may also be a misleading practice constituting the commission of a criminal offence under the Consumer Protection from Unfair Trading Regulations 2008 and against which an enforcement order may be obtained under the Enterprise Act 2002. Furthermore, a producer of food that is unfit for human consumption or contaminated may commit a criminal offence under the Food Safety Act 1990 but an enforcement order can be issued to prevent such supply; a retailer who supplies that food may be in breach of the implied term as to satisfactory quality in contract law; and the producer may be liable in tort under the Consumer Protection Act 1987, Part I.

The reason for this duplication is that the different rules serve different purposes. Private law provides remedies for individual consumers in respect of loss or damage they may have suffered. Thus a buyer of defective goods can have those goods repaired or replaced and may seek compensation for any loss suffered. But this only closes the door after the horse has bolted. It helps individual consumers who have the time and money to take action, but it is too late as the damage has already been done. Furthermore, many losses suffered by consumers may not be worth pursuing in a court, so there may be large numbers of consumers who have suffered loss, but are not compensated. The role of private law rules is primarily compensatory, so that although the risk of suffering the cost of having to compensate consumers or provide some other remedy may serve as a sort of deterrent, it is unlikely to be a sufficient deterrent as traders will know that they will not always be sued.

In contrast, public law enforcement orders are there to *prevent* the supply of defective products and services or to deter the use of unfair practices in the first place, but they serve no compensatory purpose. The purpose served by a regulatory agency is to protect people like consumers and as an agency dedicated to that particular function it will have more time and resources to devote to taking action against traders than private consumers do.

Public law in the form of criminal law is there to encourage better trading practices and to provide a form of punishment for those who put consumers at risk, whether economically or physically, through the supply of defective products and services and through the use of unfair practices. It is the State's way of saying that a certain type of behaviour is seriously unacceptable. Criminal law is also supposed to add an extra element of deterrence, since traders will be aware that they run the risk of being sued by individual consumers and being prosecuted by a public authority and obtaining a criminal conviction.

7.1.5 **Theoretical justifications for consumer protection**

The rules considered in this chapter are specifically concerned with persons who can be defined as consumers. However, there is no single definition of this word, but in general terms legislation is concerned with those who buy for private purposes and not for business purposes.[37]

---

[37] See the Unfair Terms in Consumer Contracts Regulations 1999, reg. 3(1).

The reasons for this special treatment are best understood by considering particular examples of rules that protect consumers.

In contract law *any* contracting party who has been induced to enter a contract as a result of a misrepresentation, duress or undue influence may rescind the contract, so there is no special treatment for consumers in respect of such unfair practices. However, the rules allowing a public body to seek an enforcement order against or prosecute a trader who engages in an unfair commercial practice are only aimed at practices affecting consumers.[38] This indicates that it is particularly important to take preventive action where consumers are concerned rather than leave them to pursue their own interests as the consumers' lack of knowledge, experience and bargaining power make it more likely that they will be deceived by misleading practices, pressured by aggressive or coercive practices and will be less likely than business customers to be able to protect their interests. Moreover, the consequences of unfair practices are likely to hit consumers harder than business customers. For example, having been misled or forced into a purchase, consumers must find the money to pay for it. By contrast, business customers might be able to absorb that cost by small adjustments to profits or by insurance. Consumers could protect themselves by suing the trader who has engaged in an unfair practice, but (as suggested above) consumer complaints are often small in value and consumers are less likely to take private law action in order to recover their losses due to their limited resources and the formality of legal action.

The consumers' inexperience and the cost of legal action are factors of which traders are aware, so that trading behaviour is less likely to be affected by market forces and competition between rival traders. Moreover, as many consumer purchases are not made on a repeat basis, they are less likely to be aware of which businesses to avoid.

There is also a European dimension to the policies underlying consumer protection. As we have already seen, for example, the rules on unfair practices were introduced because of the European Directive on Unfair Commercial Practices, adopted under Art. 95 of the Treaty of Rome with the aim of establishing further the single European market. Such measures are supposed to aim at a 'high level of consumer protection'[39] and so can be assumed to be based on a rough awareness of the above problems facing consumers. Also as well as protecting consumers a further goal is consumer confidence so that they will buy across national borders and therefore play a part in further developing the single European market.[40]

Perhaps the most important reason for protecting consumers is that of lack of information. The rules on trading practices try to address this in one way by making it unfair to make a 'misleading omission', that is, to fail to give information needed by consumers to make an 'informed decision'.[41] This is not just an informed decision to purchase, but also includes information that will allow the consumer to ensure that the contract achieves the consumer's expectations of performance, such as travel details in a holiday contract and how to contact the trader, how to seek redress or make a complaint and any risks associated with the contract, such as if the cost of a holiday will increase due to fluctuations in the price of aircraft fuel.

---

[38] See powers under the Unfair Terms in Consumer Contracts Regulations 1999 or those under the Enterprise Act 2002.

[39] See Treaty of Rome, Art. 153 and the preambles to the various directives.

[40] See the preambles to the various directives.

[41] See Unfair Commercial Practices Directive 2005, Art. 7, implemented by the Consumer Protection from Unfair Trading Regulations 2008, reg. 6.

Where specific pieces of information are considered very important, legislation may provide that it must be given and that adverse consequences may follow if the trader fails to comply with this obligation. This departs from the traditional *caveat emptor* or 'let the buyer beware' approach that is a feature of the general law of contract under which the contracting parties are taken to be responsible for asking for whatever information they think they need. The rules recognise that it is unrealistic for consumers, given their lack of knowledge and resources, to seek that information so that consumers are able to make an informed choice, get value for money and have control over what happens to them.

In other cases consumers are given cancellation rights for a short period after the conclusion of a contract,[42] once more departing from the ideas of *caveat emptor* and freedom of contract. These cancellation rights appear to recognise that lack of information, pressure and other factors may have caused consumers not to fully reflect on a decision that has been taken and provide the consumer with such opportunity and to make a more informed choice after reflection.

In addition to providing information and encouraging competition between traders, further justifications for intervention in favour of consumers include concern for the perceived weaker bargaining position of consumers, the actual impact of unfair practices on consumers and the consumer's lack of practical access to justice. The Unfair Commercial Practices Directive addresses a number of information-related problems. Yet, even if a trader has acted transparently by making the necessary information available to consumers, another concern is not to allow traders to act in threatening ways that reduce the consumers' choices, for example, by requiring consumers to take burdensome or costly steps to enforce their rights. Such practices may be viewed as unfair by virtue of being aggressive, no matter how clear the trader is about the steps the consumers must take.

In relation to the quality of products and services, there appears to be a desire to guarantee a certain basic level of value for money and safety irrespective of the information provided to consumers. The standards of performance required for the basic product or service supplied can be reduced to an extent if traders give appropriate precontractual information to lower consumers' expectations and warn of risks. For example, sellers are not responsible for defects in goods that have been specifically brought to the attention of the buyer.[43] However, traders cannot use exemption clauses to avoid liability for poor-quality goods, no matter how clear the language used by the trader.[44] Where services are concerned, tests of fairness apply[45] and a total exclusion of liability or one that significantly reduces liability is likely to be found to be unfair and ineffective no matter how clear the clause is.

Another difficult issue is how to determine where the distinction between consumers and business customers is to be made in terms of the levels of protection available. Some businesses may have just as little information and bargaining power as consumers and may be just as vulnerable. This issue has arisen recently with the Law Commission recommending that business buyers should not only be protected from exemption clauses, but also from terms imposing unfair obligations or liabilities on the buyer.[46]

[42] For example, the Distance Selling Directive 1997 gives a seven-day cancellation right implemented by the Consumer Protection (Distance Selling) Regulations 2000, reg. 11(2).

[43] Sale of Goods Act 1979, s. 14(2C).

[44] Unfair Contract Terms Act 1977, s. 6(2).

[45] Unfair Contract Terms Act 1977, ss. 2(2) and 11 and Unfair Terms in Consumer Contracts Regulations 1999, reg. 5.

[46] See Law Commission Report, 292, 2005, Parts 4 and 5.

7.1.6 Making the law more 'user-friendly'

The government is currently considering introducing a new Consumer Rights Act (CRA). One of the things which this would do is to contain a major reform of the law on the sale of goods and services. These reforms will affect in particular the law on implied terms and remedies for defective goods and services and on unfair contract terms[47] and seek to consolidate and restate the law in much clearer terms. The underlying policy is to make the law more 'user-friendly' and accessible for the consumers and businesses affected by it.[48] This is an important new strand in consumer policy as it recognises that laws are of limited use in protecting consumers unless they are accessible and easy to use. (See also below section 7.2 on the use of the CRA to implement the changes on information and cancellation rights brought about by the new Consumer Rights Directive.)

7.2 Information and cancellation rights

7.2.1 Introduction

One of the reasons why the law seeks to protect consumers is that consumers may enter into transactions with a business without the necessary information required to make an informed, rational purchasing decision. Moreover, because of the many different external pressures affecting consumers, they may sometimes enter into a transaction without giving its seriousness the level of thought that ought to be applied. For these reasons the law may make it compulsory for traders to provide certain types of information and, where appropriate, may give consumers time for reflection on the seriousness of a contractual commitment by providing a short-term right to cancel the contract.

7.2.2 Information rights

Specific areas, amongst others, where there are compulsory information supply requirements include consumer credit transactions,[49] package travel contracts,[50] and distance selling contracts.[51] These distinct areas appear to have been selected for special treatment for slightly

---

[47] See sections 7.3, 7.4 and 7.7 below for more details.

[48] The user-friendly approach derives from the work of the Law Commissions on unfair contract terms and remedies for defective goods (Law Com 292, Scot Law Com 199 and Law Com 317, Scot Law Com 216 respectively); and a report for the Department of Business, Innovation and Skills (BIS): BIS, Consolidation and Simplification of UK Consumer Law (London: BIS, 2010).

[49] Regulated by the Consumer Credit Act 1974, the Consumer Credit Act 2006 and Regulations made under these statutes.

[50] Regulated by the Package Travel, Package Holidays and Package Tours Regulations 1992, SI 1992/3288 (hereafter PTR 1992) implementing the EC Package Travel Directive, 1990/314/EEC.

[51] Regulated by the Consumer Protection (Distance Selling) Regulations 2000, SI 2000/2334 implementing the EC Distance Selling Directive, Dir 97/7/EEC, but to be repealed by the planned Consumer Rights Act, implementing the Consumer Rights Directive 2011/83/EU, see section 7.1.6 above. The CRD contains updated rules on information provision in distance and off premises contracts as well as rules on information provision in consumer contracts generally (see further notes 64–72 and related text). It must be implemented by 13th December 2013.

different reasons. For example, credit transactions may involve the dissemination of some quite complex information that might be difficult to understand. In the case of distance selling, perhaps the most obvious danger is that consumers may not be aware of the identity and contact details of the person with whom they have contracted. In contrast, in package travel contracts there are issues relating to the precise content of the package that need to be set out clearly so that the consumer is aware of what is and what is not to be expected.[52]

LEGISLATIVE PROVISION

PACKAGE TRAVEL, PACKAGE HOLIDAYS AND PACKAGE TOURS REGULATIONS 1992

Regulation 9 Contents and form of contract

(1) The other party to the contract shall ensure that:

(a) depending on the nature of the package being purchased, the contract contains at least the elements specified in Sch. 2 to these Regulations;

(b) subject to para. (2) below, all the terms of the contract are set out in writing or such other form as is comprehensible and accessible to the consumer and are communicated to the consumer before the contract is made; and

(c) a written copy of these terms is supplied to the consumer.

(2) Paragraph (1)(b) above does not apply when the interval between the time when the consumer approaches the other party to the contract with a view to entering into a contract and the time of departure under the proposed contract is so short that it is impracticable to comply with the sub-paragraph.

(3) It is an implied condition (or, as regards Scotland, an implied term) of the contract that the other party to the contract complies with the provisions of para. (1).

In the case of package travel contracts the required information must be provided in writing both *before the contract is made*[53] and must also be included *in the contract*, except in the case of very late bookings to which the requirement would be impractical. The purpose served by reg. 9 is that a tour operator is prevented from springing a surprise on the consumer by claiming that terms contained in other documentation not seen by the consumer have been incorporated into the contract.

The effect of non-compliance with reg. 9 is that there is a breach of contract, but there is no indication of what the remedy should be, but presumably it will allow withdrawal from the contract.

Compliance with reg. 9 is not difficult in the case of pre-advertised holidays since the required information can be set out in brochures and on Internet websites. However, there may be problems of compliance where a holiday is booked by telephone and paid for by

---

[52] See PTR 1992 reg. 9 and Sch. 2, requiring details of destinations, means and time of travel, features of the accommodation, the itinerary, excursions included, identity of the organiser, the price, special requirements and complaints mechanism.

[53] PTR 1992, reg. 9(1)(b).

credit card which is subsequently confirmed by the consumer's signature at the counter in a travel agency. Arguably the contract is made over the telephone, but at that point the provision of written information is not possible. However, the most likely result is that the telephone conversation and the act of signing can be treated as part of the same transaction, thereby complying with the requirements of reg. 9, provided the existence of the terms was mentioned during the telephone conversation.[54]

Where consumer credit transactions are concerned, there are many obligations imposed on creditors and there has been a considerable degree of recent updating, especially so as to implement European Directives.[55] One key purpose served by the Consumer Credit Acts 1974 and 2006 and subsequent Regulations is to ensure that the debtor is given sufficient information about the proposed contract in advertisements[56] and quotations[57] before it becomes binding. Further, the lender is under a general duty to provide precontractual information.[58] Advertising and consumer information must clearly explain the total credit charge, including the annual percentage rate of charge (APR),[59] If a trader fails to comply with the information supply requirements, the agreement is regarded as improperly executed[60] with the result that it cannot be enforced against the debtor without a court order.[61]

The obvious advantage of compulsory information provision is that it facilitates the comparison of competing products and allows consumers to shop around. The use of standard figures such as the APR also allows for easier comparison. It is also argued that compulsory disclosure of the total cost of credit will cause credit providers to think about their own charges which in turn could lead to greater competition between rival traders. Statements about consumer rights such as those relating to early settlement and the creditor's liability for defects make consumers more aware of their rights if things go wrong and so-called 'wealth warnings' may have the effect of reducing the number of defaulting debtors if consumers think twice before incurring debt.

It is undeniable, however, that compliance with compulsory information requirements will increase the cost of credit, which will be passed on in the form of higher interest rates

---

[54] See *Williams* v *Thompson Tour Operators Ltd* (1997), unreported, Gloucester CC.

[55] See generally the requirements of the Consumer Credit (Agreements) Regulations 1983, SI 1983/1553; the Consumer Credit (Agreements) (Amendment) Regulations 2004, SI 2004/1482; the Consumer Credit (Disclosure of Information) Regulations 2004, SI 2004/1481 and Regulations implementing the Consumer Credit Directive 2008/48/EC – the Consumer Credit (EU Directive) Regulations 2010, SI 2010/1010 (the EU Directive Regulations); the Consumer Credit (Total Charge for Credit) Regulations 2010, SI 2010/1011 (the TCC Regulations); the Consumer Credit (Disclosure of Information) Regulations 2010, SI 2010/1013 (the Disclosure Regulations); the Consumer Credit (Agreements) Regulations 2010, SI 2010/1014 (the Agreements Regulations); the Consumer Credit (Amendment) Regulations 2010, SI 2010/1969 (the Amendment Regulations) and the Consumer Credit (Advertisements) Regulations 2010, SI 2010/1970 (the Advertisements Regulations) and Regulations implementing Directive 2011/90/EU on consumer credit. See also section 8.5.

[56] Consumer Credit Act 1974, s. 44 and the Consumer Credit (Advertisements) Regulations 2010, SI 2010/1970 (the Advertisements Regulations).

[57] *Ibid.*, s. 55, as amended by the Consumer Credit (EU Directive) Regulations 2010, SI 2010/1010.

[58] The Consumer Credit (Disclosure of Information) Regulations 2010, SI 2010/1013 (the Disclosure Regulations).

[59] The Consumer Credit (Total Charge for Credit) Regulations 2010, SI 2010/1011 (the TCC Regulations).

[60] Consumer Credit Act 1974, s. 55(2). See also section 8.6.

[61] *Ibid.*, s. 65. Treating the contract as a nullity was regarded as a permissible contravention of the European Convention on Human Rights, Arts 6 and 1 on public interest grounds in *Wilson* v *First County Trust Ltd* [2003] UKHL 40.

than might otherwise be the case. Where credit advertising is concerned, the more detailed an advertisement, the more information must be supplied, but this may encourage credit providers to give less information so as to reduce compliance costs. It may also be the case that consumers do not always take account of the information given to them, but may just consider the credit limit and the number of repayments required[62] or may not even understand some of the complex information provided.[63]

The information rights referred to above relate specifically to package travel, distance selling contracts and consumer credit transactions. The Consumer Rights Directive (CRD)[64] extends the consumer's right to be given certain information before the time of the conclusion of the contract, to all consumer contracts[65] (on the basis that an informed consumer is better able to make a rational decision);[66] and says that the the information supplied must be clear and comprehensible.[67]

Member States are required to ensure that adequate and effective means are available to ensure compliance with the information obligations in the CRD; and this certainly includes public enforcement mechanisms[68] However, it is less clear what private law remedy should be provided for, especially in a jurisdiction such as the UK which has no tradition of a duty of disclosure.[69] The remedy might be one of avoidance of the contract, but this does not address the situation in which consumers have developed an expectation that an obligation should be complied with. One such situation is addressed by the CRD where the omitted information relates to charges in respect of which there has not been full disclosure, in which case it is provided that the consumer does not have to pay the charge.[70]

A curiosity in the initial p-CRD was that disclosure of information relating to delivery, payment, performance and complaint-handling was only required if the arrangements fell

---

[62] See DTI, 'Fair Clear & Competitive: The Consumer Credit Market in the 21st Century', 2003, Cm 6040.

[63] OFT, *Credit Card Survey*, OFT 709, 2004 suggests that consumer reliance on statements of the APR allowed 43 per cent of consumers to pick the best-value product, so what of the other 57 per cent?

[64] 2011/83/EU (to be implemented by the proposed Consumer Rights Act – see above). The CRD updates the information and cancellation rights currently in the distance selling directive (n. 51 above) and replaces the doorstep selling directive (85/577/EEC). It must be implemented by December 13 2013 (Art. 28) and the government plans to do this in a 'Consumer Rights Act', which it begain consulting on in 2012 – see further section 7.1.6 above. For a detailed discussion of the information provisions in this proposed Directive see A. Nordhausen Scholes, 'Information Requirements', in G. Howells and R. Schultze, *Modernising and Harmonising Consumer Contract Law* (Sellier European Law Publishers, Munich, 2009) pp. 213–238.

[65] Article 5, for contracts other than distance or off-premises (doorstep), requires disclosure as to the main characteristics of the product, the identity and address of the trader, full price disclosure, details of payment, delivery, performance and complaint-handling undertakings, after-sales service, the duration of the contract and financial guarantees. See also Arts. 6, 7 and 8 which are specific to distance and off-premises contracts which require, additionally, information as to rights of withdrawal, any code of conduct applicable to the trader, dispute settlement procedures and that a copy of any order form will be supplied in a durable medium. Art. 10 extends the cooling off period to 12 months and 14 days if the consumer is not informed of the right of withdrawal.

[66] However, the amount of information should not be so great as to create information processing problems: see N. Reich, 'Crisis or Future of European Consumer Law' (2009) *Yearbook of Consumer Law* (Ashgate, Surrey, 2009), pp. 3–67.

[67] See CRD, Art. 5(1) and also see the rules at n. 55 above.

[68] CRD, Arts 23 and 24.

[69] See H. Beale, 'The Draft Directive on Consumer Rights and UK Consumer Law: Where Now?', in G. Howells, and R. Schultze (eds) *Modernising and Harmonising Consumer Contract Law* (Sellier European Law Publishers, Munich, 2009) pp. 297–298.

[70] See CRD, Art. 22.

below the standard of professional diligence,[71] but it is difficult to see what the trader's professional diligence should have to do with an information supply requirement and, in any case, it is unlikely that even the best-informed consumer would be aware of what is or is not professionally diligent.[72] This provision does not appear in the finally adopted CRD.

7.2.3 Cancellation rights

LEGISLATIVE PROVISION

CONSUMER CREDIT ACT 1974

Section 67 Cancellable Agreements

(1) Subject to sub-section (2) a regulated agreement may be cancelled by the debtor or hirer in accordance with this Part if the antecedent negotiations included oral representations made when in the presence of the debtor or hirer by an individual acting as, or on behalf of, the negotiator, unless:

(a) the agreement is secured on land, or is a restricted-use credit agreement to finance the purchase of land or is an agreement for a bridging loan in connection with the purchase of land; or

(b) the unexecuted agreement is signed by the debtor or hirer at premises at which any of the following is carrying on any business (whether on a permanent or temporary basis):

(i)   the creditor or owner;

(ii) any party to a linked transaction (other than the debtor or hirer or a relative of his);

(iii) the negotiator in any antecedent negotiations.

(2) This section does not apply where section 66A applies.

In certain circumstances, the consumer is given the right to cancel what would otherwise be a binding contractual arrangement. This right is conferred in certain types of consumer credit transaction negotiated away from trade premises and involving oral representations made to the debtor, or a relative of his, in the course of antecedent negotiations[73] which need to be material in the sense that they are capable of inducing the consumer to enter a contract.[74] The general effect of this provision is to strike at unsolicited 'door-to-door' sales techniques which may involve remarks made to a consumer in his own home.

---

[71] p-CRD, Art. 5(1)(d).
[72] See A. Nordhausen Scholes *op. cit.*, p. 220.
[73] Consumer Credit Act 1974, s. 67. These can include advertisements (s. 56(4)) and 'off the cuff' remarks. See also section 8.8.
[74] See *Moorgate Services Ltd v Kabir* (1995) *The Times*, 25 April (statement relating to the amount of credit provided was material).

For the same broad reason, consumers have also been given cancellation rights in respect of doorstep sales generally,[75] which over time have exhibited a wide range of especially bad practices.[76] Particular features of doorstep sales are that they tend to be prevalent in low-income areas; salespeople may effectively force their way into the consumer's house and continue to deliver their sales pitch for hours, often long into the evening, and this may contain materially misleading statements.[77]

The Contracts Made in a Consumer's Home or Place of Work etc. Regulations 2008 (which apply to both doorstep sales and consumer credit agreements and require notice of cancellation rights to be prominently stated) provide for the mechanics of the process of cancellation by giving a seven-day cooling off period during which the consumer can elect to cancel, in writing, a contract valued at greater than £35 which has been concluded as a result of a solicited or unsolicited visit to the consumer's home, place of work or during an excursion organised by the trader away from the trader's business premises.[78] The trader must also give the consumer legible notice of the right of cancellation, which is no less prominent than any other information in the contract or document[79] and it is a criminal offence to fail to provide the consumer with this cancellation notice.[80] In order to prevent the trader from arguing that the notice of cancellation did not arrive on time, a cancellation notice is deemed to be effective when posted.[81]

However, these regulations with respect to the cooling off period for doorstep sales, will be repealed with the implementation of the CRD. Art. 6 (1)(h) of the CRD requires the trader to inform the consumer of the existence of a right to withdraw, Art. 7(1) requires this information to be on paper or in another durable medium. Art. 9 extends the cooling off period for doorstep sales to 14 days, except where the trader fails to inform the consumer of the right to withdraw, in which case Art.10(1) increases this period to 12 months plus 14 days. However, the Consumer Rights Directive does not apply to consumer financial services, which will continue to be regulated under the dedicated consumer credit legislation as discussed.

A cancelled agreement and any linked transaction (for example, a contract to insure the subject matter of the cancelled agreement) is treated as if it had never been entered into.[82] Thus payments made by the debtor can be recovered and goods delivered to the debtor must be returned. The debtor's right of cancellation is only lost if he fails to deliver the required cancellation notice within the period specified in the Consumer Credit Act 1974, s. 68.

---

[75] The EC Doorstep Selling Directive, Dir. 85/577/EEC implemented in the UK by the Consumer Protection (Cancellation of Contracts Concluded away from Business Premises) Regulations 1987 (amended in 1988 and 1998). These Regulations have now been replaced by the Cancellation of Contracts made in a Consumer's Home or Place of Work etc. Regulations 2008, SI 2008/1816. (When the Consumer Rights Directive (2011/83/EU) is implemented, it will be necessary to repeal this legislation; as the CRD, arts. 6(1)(h), 9–11 contains its own provisions on withdrawal rights from doorstep sales.)

[76] See Moloney Committee Report on Consumer Protection, Cmnd 1781 (1962), paras 741–742.

[77] See OFT, *Doorstep Selling: A Report on the Market Study*, 2004, OFT 716.

[78] Cancellation of Contracts Made away from the Consumer's Home or Place of Work etc. Regulations 2008, SI 2008/1816, reg. 5.

[79] *Ibid.*, reg. 7(3).

[80] *Ibid.*, reg. 17.

[81] *Ibid.*, reg. 8(5).

[82] Consumer Credit Act 1974, s. 69(4); Cancellation of Contracts Made away from the Consumer's Home or Place of Work etc. Regulations 2008, reg. 8(2).

Any money paid by the debtor as part of the total charge for credit, for example, a deposit or interest payment, can be recovered[83] and he ceases to be responsible for sums of money due after cancellation.[84] As a general rule, the debtor's claim for repayment will be made to the person to whom it was paid.[85] Thus, if money has been paid to an agent of the creditor, the debtor will be able to recover what has been paid from the agent and leave him to sort out matters with the creditor.

The general effect of the cancellation provisions of the 1974 Act is that the parties should be returned to their position before entering the contract. Thus, goods in the possession of the debtor are returnable[86] and the debtor must take reasonable care of the goods while they are in his possession.[87] Goods given in part exchange by the debtor are returnable[88] and unless those goods are returned to the debtor within ten days of cancellation, the debtor is entitled to a cash equivalent of the cost of those goods.[89]

While the main reason for granting cancellation rights in relation to credit transactions and doorstep selling is the fear that the consumer may have been lulled into a false sense of security in his own home, the reason for allowing cancellation of distance selling contracts is that the consumer is unable to see what he has purchased at the time of contracting. Distance selling covers a range of different methods of selling at a distance including catalogue sales, telemarketing, television shopping and Internet sales. The EC Distance Selling Directive (DSD) provides for a cooling off period that terminates seven days from the receipt of goods or seven days from the date of the contract in the case of services.[90] However, the CRD increases this cooling off period to 14 days in line with other types of transactions.[91] Some types of contract are excluded from the scope of the Distance Selling Regulations, in particular time-shares and auction sales (for example, eBay contracts). Also excluded are contracts for the provision of accommodation, transport,[92] catering or leisure services where the supplier contracts to provide those services, etc. on a specific date or within a specified period.

Where a distance-selling contract is regulated there is a requirement that consumers should be provided with a written notice that cancellation is not possible once services have commenced,[93] which caused problems for the car rental sector where consumers booked on the Internet and wanted to take up use of the hire car immediately. While the car rental sector is now exempt, this is also a potential problem with other contracts for services entered into over the Internet.

---

[83] Consumer Credit Act 1974, s. 70(1)(a); Contracts Made in a Consumer's Home or Place of Work etc. Regulations 2008, reg. 10(1).

[84] *Ibid.*, s. 70(1)(b).

[85] *Ibid.*, s. 70(3) and see also the Contracts Made in a Consumer's Home or Place of Work etc. Regulations 2008, reg. 11(2).

[86] Consumer Credit Act 1974, s. 72; Contracts Made in a Consumers Home or Place of Work etc. Regulations 2008, reg. 13(1).

[87] *Ibid.*, s. 72(3); Contracts Made in a Consumers Home or Place of Work etc. Regulations 2008, reg. 13(1).

[88] *Ibid.*, s. 73 and reg. 14(1).

[89] Ibid., s. 73(2) and reg. 14(2).

[90] Dir 97/7/EC implemented in the UK by the Consumer Protection (Distance Selling) Regulations 2000, SI 2000/2334, as amended in 2005. See reg. 11(2) for the cooling off period with respect to goods, and reg. 12(2) for services.

[91] See CRD Art. 9. The time that the period runs from varies according to the type of contract under Art. 9(2).

[92] Which includes car rental agreements: *Easycar UK Ltd* v *Office of Fair Trading* (2005) Case C-336/03.

[93] Consumer Protection (Distance Selling) Regulations 2000, reg. 8(3).

Future developments in the area of cancellation rights are addressed in the new Consumer Rights Directive[94] which contains a number of provisions specific to distance and off-premises contracts. In particular, it is proposed that there should be a common 14-day cancellation period, regardless of the type of contract.[95] While a standard-length withdrawal period has its attractions, it should also be noted that the reasons for giving a right of withdrawal may be different according to the type of contract concerned, so there is a possibility that a standard 14-day period may be too long in some cases, but too short in others.[96]

The 14-day period will commence on different dates according to the type of contract entered into, so that in services contracts the period will run from the date the contract is made,[97] in goods contracts for single items from the date of receipt of the goods[98] and in contracts for the sale of multiple goods in one order to be separately delivered, on the day the last goods are delivered.[99] This does mean that there are confusingly different starting dates and this impacts, perhaps most seriously, on contracts for the supply of a service as time will start to run against the consumer before any work is done.[100] The CRD reduces the 30-day period of time that the trader has to refund the consumer's money (should the consumer withdraw), to 14 days[101]. The CRD also extends the right to withdraw to digital content (music or video downloads not supplied on a tangible medium such as a DVD) until the day of the contract, which is taken to mean when downloading begins (Art. 9(2)(c)).

7.2.4 Effects and limits of information and cancellation rights

The point of the above information and cancellation rights is to help consumers to make more informed decisions as to the goods and services on offer and for these informed decisions to place more competitive pressure on traders to improve standards.[102] However, there are serious questions as to how well this works in practice;[103] in particular because of the proven difficulties consumers have in making use of standardised information[104] This, of course, is one reason why other forms of protection are needed, imposing mandatory contractual quality standards for goods[105] and for services[106] and for mandatory safety standards in tort and in public law.[107]

---

[94] See n. 64 above. For a detailed discussion of the provisions in this proposed Directive, see M. Loos, 'Rights of Withdrawal', in G. Howells and R. Schultze (eds), *Modernising and Harmonising Consumer Contract Law* (Sellier European Law Publishers, Munich, 2009) pp. 239–280.

[95] CRD, Art. 9(1).

[96] See n. 64.

[97] CRD Art. 9(2)(a).

[98] Article 9(2)(b).

[99] Article 9(2)(b)(i).

[100] Generally, see Loos n. 94, above.

[101] Article 13 above.

[102] C. Willett, 'The Functions of Transparency in Regulating Contract Terms: UK and Australian Approaches' (2001) 60 *ICLQ* 355–385.

[103] *Ibid* and I. Ramsay, *Consumer Law and Policy: Text and Materials on Regulating Consumer Markets* (2nd edn, Hart Publishing, Oxford, 2007) pp. 71–85.

[104] *Ibid*.

[105] See section 7.3 below.

[106] Section 7.4 below.

[107] Sections 7.5 and 7.6 below.

7.3 Performance Standards (1) – Implied terms as to goods

7.3.1 Introduction to the Special Consumer Goods Rules

LEGISLATIVE PROVISION

SALE OF GOODS ACT 1979

13. – Sale by description.

(1) Where there is a contract for the sale of goods by description, there is an implied [condition] that the goods will correspond with the description.

. . .

14. – Implied terms about quality.

. . .

(2) Where the seller sells goods in the course of a business, there is an implied [condition] that the goods supplied under the contract are of satisfactory quality.

(2A) For the purposes of this Act, goods are of satisfactory quality if they meet the standard that a reasonable person would regard as satisfactory, taking account of any description of the goods, the price (if relevant) and all the other relevant circumstances.

(2B) For the purposes of this Act, the quality of goods includes their state and condition and the following (among others) are in appropriate cases aspects of the quality of goods:

(a) fitness for all the purposes for which goods of the kind in question are commonly supplied;

(b) appearance and finish;

(c) freedom from minor defects;

(d) safety; and

(e) durability.

On fitness for particular purpose see section 4.8.4.3 above.

In contracts for the sale and supply of goods to consumers the same implied terms as to description, quality and fitness for particular purpose are applicable as are in business-to-business sales.[108]

---

[108] Sections 13–14 of the Sale of Goods Act for sales and see the Supply of Goods (Implied Terms) Act 1973 and Supply of Goods and Services Act 1982 for other supply contracts.

The main discussion of these implied terms and the remedies for their breach is in Chapter 4. However, there are certain important differences in the way the law has developed (and may continue to develop) where consumer buyers are concerned and these are the focus of this section. The main source of the differences has been the EU Consumer Sales Directive (CSD).[109] This was implemented by the Sale and Supply of Goods to Consumers Regulations (SSGCR) 2002,[110] which made various amendments to the Sale of Goods Act (SGA) 1979 (and related legislation applicable to other supply of goods contracts) in cases where the buyer 'deals as a consumer'. These make certain public statements relevant to whether goods are regarded as being of satisfactory quality; provide for remedies of repair, replacement, price reduction and rescission (in addition to the pre-existing remedies of damages and the so called 'short-term right to reject'); and lay down various rules on guarantees. In addition to implementing the CSD, the SSGCR also amend the rules on passing of risk in their application to consumers.

More recently, the Law Commissions and BIS have carried out work that may lead to reforms in the possible future CRA that was mentioned above (at 7.1.6) and we will discuss these later in this section.

The following section considers the various rules and issues just described in greater detail.

7.3.2 Who is a consumer?

As we have seen, if a buyer is deemed to be dealing as a consumer then the various rules considered in this section will apply. For these purposes, 'consumer' is defined as:

> . . . any natural person who . . . is acting for purposes which are outside his trade, business or profession.[111]

The focus, then, is on whether the predominant purpose of the purchase is private or not. In most cases the issue will be straightforward, for example, where a buyer buys a family car or household item. However, there may be cases where the line is difficult to draw, for example, where a sole trader buys a computer or phone for mixed business and home/family use.

The question as to whether or not a buyer is treated as having 'consumer' status is also relevant to the rules on if the implied terms and remedies for their breach can be excluded by use of express contract terms (basically, they cannot where the buyer is a consumer). This is an issue to which we shall turn in section 7.7.3.1. However, matters are complicated by the fact that a different definition of 'consumer' is used in that context.

---

[109] 99/44/EC.
[110] SI 2002/3045.
[111] SSGCR, reg. 2.

7.3.3 **Public statements**

7.3.3.1 **The general rule**

The CSD sets a standard of 'conformity' for goods sold to consumers.[112] Largely, this reflects the sort of standards set by the implied terms in SGA, ss. 13–14 on description, quality and fitness for particular purpose. So, in general, these implied terms were viewed as an adequate implementation of the directive and were left unchanged by the SSGCR. However, the CSD did provide expressly that certain public statements made by sellers, producers and others should be taken into account in determining, in particular, whether goods showed a level of quality that was normal and was reasonable to expect (one of the requirements under the general conformity standard)[113] and it was considered that the implied term as to satisfactory quality in SGA, s. 14(2) should be amended to provide expressly for this.

We have seen above that s. 14(2) Sale of Goods Act 1979 provides that, in deciding if goods are of satisfactory quality, various criteria (including, for example, price, description, fitness for common purposes, durability, etc.) should be taken into account. In particular, there is a general reference in s. 14(2A) to 'all the relevant circumstances'. A new s. 14(2D) was added by the SSGCR to the effect that:

> If the buyer deals as a consumer . . . the relevant circumstances mentioned in sub-section (2A) above include any public statements on the specific characteristics of the goods made about them by the seller, the producer or his representative, particularly in advertising or on labelling.

It should be noted that the provision refers to statements as to the 'specific characteristics' of the goods. This seems to cover statements on any quality, fitness, performance, etc. matter, although not 'sales puffs', that is, statements that are not objectively verifiable.

It seems to cover such statements, whether or not there is an explicit promise that the goods have the characteristics in question (that is, there is no need for language such as 'We guarantee' or 'We promise') and there certainly is no need for the statement to be backed up by a further promise to repair, replace or pay a sum of money if the goods do not live up to the statement (as in the *Carlill* case).[114] So, it might cover such statements as 'Shatter-Proof Glass Windshield'[115] which 'will not fly or shatter under the hardest impact' or the statement that a towing hitch is 'Foolproof. Locks absolutely'.[116]

As far as the *source* of the relevant statements is concerned, what seems to be covered are (i) statements made solely by the seller in brochures, notices, labelling and general advertising; (ii) statements originally made by the producer or his representative (in brochures, notices, labelling and general advertising) but then passed on, displayed or otherwise conveyed to the consumer by the seller; (iii) statements made by the manufacturer or his representative in brochures, notices, labelling and general advertising which have not been passed on to the consumer by the seller, but, rather, conveyed directly to the consumer via the media, billboard advertising, direct mail, text messaging, etc.

---

[112] Art 2.
[113] Art 2(2)(d).
[114] *Carlill* v *Carbolic Smoke Ball Co* [1893] 1 QB 256.
[115] *Baxter* v *Ford Motor Co* 168 Wash 456, 12 P2d 409, 15 P2d 1118, 88 ALR 521.
[116] *Lambert* v *Lewis* [1980] 1 All ER 978, CA.

ISSUE BOX

The pre-existing satisfactory quality obligation already covered statements falling into categories (i) and (ii) above. However, the real significance of s. 14(2D) is that the statements in category (iii) above are now part of the quality obligation owed to the consumer (it being unlikely that they would have been considered relevant before).[117] This is an important recognition of the strong degree of reliance by consumers on statements by manufacturers. Before the change, consumers would traditionally have found great difficulty in obtaining redress in respect of such statements. The seller would probably not have been liable for them under s. 14. In addition, the courts were very reluctant to impose contractual or tortious liability on the manufacturer for such statements. The examples given above of the statements about the windscreen and the towing hitch would (certainly on existing authority) not be held to give rise to contractual or tortious liability resting on the manufacturer. It is also doubtful as to whether or not such a statement would give rise to such liability even if it were said that such characteristics were 'guaranteed' or 'promised' unless this was backed up by a further promise or guarantee of the *Carlill* type, that is, a promise or guarantee that certain action will be taken if the goods do not have these characteristics or cannot achieve these things.

Of course, it must be remembered that s. 14(2D) does not create 'freestanding' liability for public statements. They are simply relevant to the overall assessment of quality along with all other factors, including, for example, price, description, state and condition and fitness for common purposes.

However, they are probably intended to be taken as a fair degree of prominence in the analysis. A public statement should surely have a particularly strong influence on the scope of the sellers' obligation when it relates to important aspects of quality and where the consumer has (reasonably) placed a strong degree of reliance on the statement. Price may be particularly relevant in this context. Advertising statements may have a strong influence, persuading the consumer to buy expensive goods at the luxury end of the market. Taking into account all other factors, the goods may be 'borderline' in terms of quality. However, they may not live up to an advertising statement. This should surely weigh strongly in favour of a finding that the goods are not of satisfactory quality.

7.3.3.2 'Defences'

In certain circumstances public statements made about the goods by the seller, the producer or his representative *will not* be relevant to the satisfactory quality obligation.[118] This is where the seller shows that:

(a) at the time the contract was made, he (i.e. the seller) was not, and could not reasonably have been, aware of the statement;

---

[117] See discussion by C. Willett, A. Naidoo and M. Morgan-Taylor, 'The Sale and Supply of Goods to Consumers Regulations' (2004) *JBL* 94, at 96–100.

[118] SGA, s. 14(2E).

(b) before the contract was made, the statement had been withdrawn in public or, to the extent that it contained anything which was incorrect or misleading, it had been corrected in public; or

(c) the decision to buy the goods could not have been influenced by the statement.

The first point to make in relation to defence (a) is that the question is if the seller is, or could have been, aware of the statement at the time of the contract between him (the seller) and the consumer. It is, in other words, irrelevant that the seller did not know of the statement at some earlier stage, for example, when he bought the goods from the producer and the statement had, perhaps, not yet been made.

Defence (a) might apply where the statement formed part of an advertising campaign by the producer which was aimed at another part of the EU and which the seller in question would not have known about at the time when he sold the goods to the consumer.

Defence (b) refers to the statement being 'withdrawn' or 'corrected'. Presumably this can be done either by the seller or the producer. Presumably also the withdrawal or correction will need to refer clearly to the original statement and be clear about the fact that it is being withdrawn and/or the manner in which it is being corrected. Finally, it will surely be insufficient if the withdrawal or correction is in an obscure trade magazine; the publicity must be effective to alert consumers.

In routine cases, defence (c) will surely be very difficult for the seller to establish, given the reliance that consumers arguably place upon manufacturers' statements, which statements are of course intended to induce exactly such reliance. Of course, the defence might be possible, if, for example, the buyer has obtained a third-party expert opinion that has made it clear that the statement is inaccurate. Presumably also there will be no reliance for present purposes where the seller can show that the consumer could not have known of the statement, for example, because it was made in a publication that the consumer did not have access to, where there is clear evidence that the consumer disregarded the statement or where any reasonable consumer would have known that the statement should not be taken seriously, for example, where it has been posted on an Internet site and was obviously posted there by an employee as a joke or prank.

7.3.4 Passing of risk

The 2002 Regulations altered the rule on risk (for example, of loss, deterioration, etc.) for consumer sales; so that risk does not pass with ownership ('property'),[119] but with delivery, this not taking place on transfer of the goods to a carrier, but, effectively, on physical delivery of the goods to the consumer.[120] This means that the seller is liable for non-delivery if the goods are lost and liable for breach of the implied terms in the case of deterioration or damage. The CSD made no express provision on risk, so this change was a voluntary one, but it reflects what is required of Member States by the new CRD.[121]

---

[119] As generally in sales contracts, see section 4.6.3. For an analysis of both the old and the new law, see M. Morgan-Taylor and A. Naidoo, 'The Draft Regulations to Adopt the Directive on Certain Aspects of the Sale of Consumer Goods and Associated Guarantees: Problems of the Time of Conformity for the Quality Obligation' [2002] 3 WebJCLI, http://webjcli.ncl.ac.uk/2002/issue3/taylor3.html

[120] Regulation 4(2), amending SGA, s. 20 and s. 32 (creating a new s. 32(4)).

[121] 2011/83/EU, Art. 20.

7.3.5 **Traditional remedies**

7.3.5.1 **Introduction**

In Chapter 4 we saw that where there is a breach of the implied terms there is a right to reject the goods and terminate the contract (the so-called 'short-term right to reject'). There is also a right to claim damages for breach of contract. As indicated above in this section, these remedies are also available to consumer buyers. However, for consumer buyers, new remedies of repair, replacement, price reduction and rescission were added to the legislation by the SSGCR 2002. We will give a brief summary of consumer issues arising from the traditional remedies before turning to the new remedies.

7.3.5.2 **Short-term right to reject**

Where the buyer does not deal as a consumer, this right does not apply where the breach is so slight as to make rejection unreasonable.[122] This restriction does not apply where the buyer is a consumer.

However, in contracts of sale, as in the case of business buyers, consumers lose the right to reject if they are taken to have 'accepted' the goods within the meaning of SGA, s. 35. This, just as in non-consumer sales, can either be by express intimation of acceptance, the doing of an act inconsistent with the ownership of the seller or by the lapse of a reasonable time (the 'reasonable time' rule being why the right to reject is known as 'short term').

LEGISLATIVE PROVISION

SALE OF GOODS ACT 1979

35. – Acceptance

(1) The buyer is deemed to have accepted the goods subject to sub-section (2) below:

(a) when he intimates to the seller that he has accepted them; or

(b) when the goods have been delivered to him and he does any act in relation to them which is inconsistent with the ownership of the seller.

(2) Where goods are delivered to the buyer, and he has not previously examined them, he is not deemed to have accepted them under sub-section (1) above until he has had a reasonable opportunity of examining them for the purpose:

(a) of ascertaining whether they are in conformity with the contract; and

(b) in the case of a contract for sale by sample, of comparing the bulk with the sample.

(3) Where the buyer deals as consumer . . . the buyer cannot lose his right to rely on sub-section (2) above by agreement, waiver or otherwise.

---

[122] SGA, s. 15A.

(4) The buyer is also deemed to have accepted the goods when after the lapse of a reasonable time he retains the goods without intimating to the seller that he has rejected them.

(5) The questions that are material in determining for the purposes of sub-section (4) above whether a reasonable time has elapsed include whether the buyer has had a reasonable opportunity of examining the goods for the purpose mentioned in sub-section (2) above.

(6) The buyer is not by virtue of this section deemed to have accepted the goods merely because:

(a) he asks for, or agrees to, their repair by or under an arrangement with the seller; or

(b) the goods are delivered to another under a sub-sale or other disposition.

(7) Where the contract is for the sale of goods making one or more commercial units, a buyer accepting any goods included in a unit is deemed to have accepted all the goods making the unit, and in this sub-section 'commercial unit' means a unit division of which would materially impair the value of the goods or the character of the unit.

In relation to 'intimation of acceptance' the issue of an acceptance or delivery note is of particular relevance, one danger being that the note could constitute an acceptance and a loss of the right to reject without the buyer actually inspecting the goods. However, the buyer is to some extent protected from this. Under s. 35(2) the buyer cannot be deemed to have accepted the goods until there has been an opportunity for examination and, in the case of consumer buyers, sub-s. (3) says that the consumer cannot 'by agreement, waiver or otherwise' give up the right to rely on sub-s. (2). So, the consumer might sign a delivery note which says that he accepts the goods. It may say nothing of examination or it may say that the consumer has waived (or agreed not to take up) this right. However, the effect of sub-s. (2) and (3) is that this will not constitute acceptance by express intimation. The consumer has either had a reasonable opportunity to examine the goods or he has not. If he has not then he cannot accept by express intimation.

In relation to doing an act inconsistent with the ownership of the seller, there are no distinct statutory provisions only applicable to consumers and consumers should generally refer to section 4.5.4. However, it is worth mentioning here the *Clegg* v *Andersen* case in which it was held that registering a yacht in the buyer's name did not amount to an inconsistent act.[123]

As to lapse of a reasonable time, it is worth repeating that (as where the buyer is a business) this is a question of fact in each case[124] and it is extremely difficult to predict the outcome in any given case. In one case (which has always been regarded as harsh on the consumer buyer) a three-week delay was regarded as too long to reject a car.[125] In a more recent case a delay of 17 months was too long to reject kitchen units,[126] but

---

[123] *Clegg* v *Anderson* [2003] 2 Lloyd's Rep 32.
[124] SGA, s. 59.
[125] *Bernstein* v *Pamson Motors (Golders Green) Ltd* [1987] 2 All ER 220.
[126] *Jones* v *Callagher* [2004] EWCA 10.

7 months was not too long to reject a yacht[127] and 4 months was not too long to reject a taxi.[128]

These variations emphasise just how fact-specific the decisions are. The type of product is obviously relevant. On one hand, if goods are perishable then they will clearly have to be rejected very quickly. On the other hand, where non-perishable and highly complex goods are concerned, it is clear that a longer period will be necessary in order to try out the goods.[129] In this context it is important to note s. 35(5) which says that it is relevant to consider if the buyer has had a reasonable opportunity to examine the goods for conformity, although this is only a factor to be weighed in the scales and a reasonable time can still be held to have passed even though the buyer could not have discovered the defect.

The seriousness of the defect may also be relevant. The court is likely to be more sympathetic to the buyer the more serious the defect is.

The impact of attempts to repair the goods has been an issue in several recent cases. Section 35(6) makes it clear that agreeing to a repair does not in itself constitute acceptance; but this does not mean that the 'reasonable time clock' will necessarily stop running while the seller attempts repair. The courts are more likely to stop the clock where the buyer has behaved reasonably in all the circumstances and where he is waiting for information from the seller as to the nature of the problem and the prospects for resolving it.[130]

Section 11(4) of the Sale of Goods Act, and the acceptance rules therein, do not apply to other contracts for the supply of goods. In such contracts the right to reject the goods and terminate the contract depends upon general common law principles. The right to reject and terminate is lost by 'affirmation'. The buyer loses the right to reject and terminate when he 'affirms' the contract. In order to be held to have affirmed the contract, the buyer must first know of the breach of contract *and* of his legal right to reject the goods and terminate the contract. The buyer must then, by words or conduct, unequivocally indicate that he wishes to affirm the contract.[131] This means that a buyer may discover a defect after some time and still be entitled to reject the goods at this stage.[132]

7.3.5.3 Damages

Damages are available on general contractual principles (that is, subject to rules on remoteness, mitigation and causation). In many cases the consumer will not require a damages claim, because he will either have received a refund (under the short-term right to reject or the longer-term right to rescind to be discussed below) or he will be able to claim one of the other new remedies, that is, repair, replacement or price reduction. However, even where such remedies are available, damages may still be necessary. First of all, in cases where the buyer has rejected the goods or rescinded the contract, the cost of obtaining a replacement may be greater than the original cost of the goods. The difference can be claimed in damages.

---

[127] *Clegg v Anderson* [2003] 2 Lloyd's Rep 32.
[128] *Fiat Auto Financial Services v Connolly* 2007 SLT (Sh Ct) 111.
[129] *Bernstein v Pamson Motors (Golders Green) Ltd* [1987] 2 All ER 220 *per* Rougier J, at 230–1; *Public Utilities Commission of City of Waterloo v Burroughs Business Machines Ltd* (1974) 52 DLR (3d) 481 (Ont CA).
[130] *Clegg v Anderson* [2003] 2 Lloyd's Rep 32, *Jones v Callagher* [2004] EWCA 10 and *J & H Ritchie Ltd v Lloyd Ltd* [2007] UKHL 9; [2007] 1 WLR 670.
[131] *Peyman v Lanjani* [1985] Ch 457; [1985] 2 WLR 154.
[132] See *Farnworth Finance Facilities Ltd v Attryde* [1970] 2 All ER 774.

Secondly, the buyer may suffer losses while the goods are in his possession due to the defective condition of the goods and these can be claimed for as well. So, for example, damages can be claimed for personal injury, for example, where a defective catapult caused a child to lose his sight as in *Godley* v *Perry*.[133]

Damages can also be claimed for damage to property, for example, where a detonator in smokeless fuel caused damage to the buyer's property.[134] Similarly damages are also available for the cost of hiring temporary replacements for defective goods and for inconvenience, distress and minor expenses. *Bernstein* v *Pamson Motors (Golders Green) Ltd*[135] is a good illustration. As we saw earlier the consumer had lost the right to reject the car and so could not recover the price. In fact no damages were recovered for the car being worth less than it would have been if it had not been defective. This was because the necessary repairs were carried out free under the manufacturer's warranty. However, the consumer recovered damages to take account of the cost of returning home by taxi after the car had broken down, the loss of a full tank of petrol, the distress caused by a ruined day out and the inconvenience of five days' lost use of the car.

7.3.6 The 'new' remedies

7.3.6.1 Introduction and burden of proof

LEGISLATIVE PROVISION

SALE OF GOODS ACT 1979

48A Introductory

(1) This section applies if:

(a) the buyer deals as consumer . . . and

(b) the goods do not conform to the contract of sale at the time of delivery.

(2) If this section applies, the buyer has the right:

(a) under and in accordance with s. 48B below, to require the seller to repair or replace the goods; or

(b) under and in accordance with s. 48C below:

    (i) to require the seller to reduce the purchase price of the goods to the buyer by an appropriate amount; or

    (ii) to rescind the contract with regard to the goods in question.

---

[133] [1960] 1 WLR 9.

[134] *Wilson* v *Rickett, Cockerell & Co Ltd* [1954] 1 QB 598. On approaches to remoteness in such cases, see *Parsons (Livestock) Ltd* v *Uttley, Ingham & Co Ltd* [1978] QB 791.

[135] *Bernstein* v *Pamson Motors (Golders Green) Ltd* [1987] 2 All ER 220; and see also *Jackson* v *Chrysler Acceptances* [1978] RTR 474 (£75 damages for the distress of a spoilt holiday that the buyer had told the seller the car was wanted for) and *UCB Leasing* v *Holtom* [1987] RTR 362 (CA) (£500 for the distress of three complete electrical failures in a car in four months).

(3) For the purposes of sub-section (1)(b) above goods which do not conform to the contract of sale at any time within the period of six months starting with the date on which the goods were delivered to the buyer must be taken not to have so conformed at that date.

(4) Sub-section (3) above does not apply if:

(a) it is established that the goods did so conform at that date;

(b) its application is incompatible with the nature of the goods or the nature of the lack of conformity.

These (repair, replacement, price reduction and rescission) have actually now been in place since the 2002 SSGCR, but they are still new relative to the short-term right to reject and damages remedies. They are available for breach of express terms and for breach of the implied terms as to description, quality and fitness for purpose.[136]

Following the CSD, there is an important reversal of the burden of proof in relation to the new remedies. It is said that if goods do not conform to the contract at any time within the period of six months from the date of delivery they are to be taken not to have conformed at the date of delivery[137] and the new remedies then become available. However this does not apply where either (a) it is established that the goods did conform at the date of delivery or (b) application of this 'presumption' is incompatible with the nature of the goods or the nature of the lack of conformity.[138] The presumption would be inconsistent with the nature of the goods if the goods have a life expectancy of less than six months (for example, perishable items such as food) and the problem in question has not developed any more quickly than would generally be expected for these types of goods. Equally, the nature of the lack of conformity may be such as to suggest that it is more likely to have been caused by the consumer (for example, a dent in a car appearing after four months) and in such a case the nature of the lack of conformity may be inconsistent with the six-month presumption being applied.

This six-month presumption is to be welcomed from the point of view of consumer protection. There is more chance that sellers will have access to information which will help to establish that goods are in conformity than there is that consumers will have access to information needed to establish non-conformity at the time of sale.

7.3.6.2 Repair, replacement, price reduction and rescission

The basic scheme

The remedies operate in a hierarchical fashion. First the consumer can choose between asking for repair or replacement.

Repair or replacement must be done within a reasonable period of time and without significant inconvenience to the buyer.[139] In addition, the seller must bear the costs of repair

---

[136] SGA, s. 48A.
[137] SGA, s. 48A(3).
[138] SGA, s. 48A(4).
[139] SGA, s. 48B(2)(a); SGSA, s. 11N(2)(a).

or replacement (including, for example, labour, materials and postage costs).[140] The consumer is not entitled to repair or replacement where either of these remedies is impossible or disproportionate (that is, disproportionate in comparison with one another or disproportionate in comparison to the price reduction or rescission remedies).[141]

If the remedy in question is impossible or disproportionate or if it is not carried out within a reasonable period of time or without significant inconvenience to the consumer, the consumer can ask for a price reduction or rescission.[142]

Advantages of repair/replacement remedies

POINT OF INTEREST

It is true that before these remedies became available, sellers would often, in practice, offer a repair or replacement. However, the existence of a legal right of repair/replacement may make it easier for consumers where a seller is uncooperative; in particular, it should make it more difficult for sellers to suggest that repair/replacement is the responsibility of the producer.

Possibility and proportionality of repair/replacement

(a) Impossible

Replacement might be impossible, for example, where the goods are unique. This would certainly cover a work of art, but there is controversy over whether or not it should be taken to cover an item such as a secondhand car.[143] In the latter case, a vehicle of the same year, similar mileage and other features might be perfectly acceptable to the consumer and it would seem unfair to allow sellers to use impossibility as a defence in such a case. Repair would be impossible, for example, where the goods are beyond repair.

(b) Disproportionate

One remedy is disproportionate in comparison with another 'if it imposes costs on the seller which, in comparison to those imposed on him by the other, are unreasonable, taking into account: (a) the value which the goods would have if they conformed to the contract of sale, (b) the significance of the lack of conformity, and (c) whether the other remedy could be effected without significant inconvenience to the buyer'.[144]

Criterion (a) points to the possibility, for example, that where low-cost goods are concerned, high-cost repairs (especially where they approach or exceed the value of the goods)

---

[140] SGA, s. 48B(2)(b); SGSA, s. 11N(2)(b). Article 3(3) of the SCGD says that repair or replacement must be carried out free of charge. In Case C-404/06 (*Quelle AG v Bundesverband der Verbraucherzentralen und Verbraucherverbände*, 17 April 2008), the ECJ has held that this prevents any sum being required from the consumer to reflect prior use of the replaced goods. Note, of course, that a deduction for beneficial use of the goods *is* allowed where the consumer is exercising his right to rescission.

[141] SGA, s. 48B(3); SGSA, s. 11N(3).

[142] SGA, s. 48C(1) and (2); SGSA, s. 11P(1) and (2).

[143] See the discussion in C. Willett, A. Naidoo and M. Morgan-Taylor, *op. cit.*, at p. 113.

[144] Section 48B(4).

are potentially disproportionate by comparison with the relatively low cost of replacement, rescission or price reduction. By contrast it may be that where higher-value goods are concerned, replacement costs have the potential to be disproportionate by comparison with (what will often be) modest or average repair costs or the costs of price reduction. However, criteria (b) and (c) remind us that in all cases, the interests of the consumer are relevant – the greater the problem with the goods, the more the remedy argued for by the seller inconveniences the consumer, the less likely the seller is to succeed in showing that the remedy asked for is disproportionate.

Reasonable time and significant inconvenience

As indicated above, even if repair and replacement are possible and proportionate (and therefore must be carried out by the seller), the consumer can choose price reduction or rescission if repair or replacement are not carried out within a reasonable period of time or without significant inconvenience to the consumer. In determining what is a reasonable time or what counts as significant inconvenience, regard is to be had to the nature of the goods and the purpose for which they have been acquired.[145] Obviously, courts are more likely to look sympathetically at the position of the consumer where, for example, the goods are vital household items or a car that is needed for essential work or family purposes.

Price reduction and rescission – advantages and operation

> **ISSUE BOX**
>
> Price reduction could already be achieved under the existing damages rules in the SGA. Section 53(1) provides for a damages remedy but allows this to be exercised by the buyer setting up the breach of contract in diminution or extinction of the price. Might the provision assist the consumer now that the possibility of attaining a price reduction has been made more transparent in the legislation?

As already indicated, the pre-existing short-term right to reject can last anything from a few weeks to a good number of months. However, the key point is that there can be no certainty over the length of time and it will often be a matter of a couple of months. So the 'long-term right to reject' that is available under the auspices of the rescission remedy provides the consumer with a final 'escape route' where repair/replacement has failed, is taking too long or is causing significant inconvenience to the consumer. Such a long-term right to reject also recognises that defects may emerge some time after the purchase.

However, where the rescission/long-term right to reject is granted, the amount of the price which is returned to the consumer may be 'reduced to take account of the use [the consumer] has had of the goods since they were delivered to him'[146] and the court may approach this issue in such a way 'as it thinks just'.[147]

---

[145] SGA, s. 48B(5); SGSA, s. 11N(5).
[146] SGA, s. 48C(3); SGSA, s. 11P(3).
[147] SGA, s. 48E(6); SGSA, s. 11R(6).

ISSUE BOX

It would seem appropriate to calculate beneficial use in the context of the expected lifecycle of the goods. The issue should surely be how long the consumer could reasonably expect to have use of the goods and what quality of use would be expected during this period. So if the expected lifecycle of the goods is five years, then if the goods break down after one year, the *prima facie* reduction in the refund might be 20 per cent. However, it might be that the quality of use which can be expected in the first year of use is significantly greater than in later years, so that the 20 per cent figure should be adjusted upwards to take account of this. Further, in assessing the use that the consumer has had of the goods, it must be appropriate to take into account compromises on the consumer's beneficial use which have already been caused by the defects in question.

Enforcement

All of the above remedies are enforceable by way of specific performance[148] and any order made by the court may be made on 'such terms and conditions as to damages, payment of the price and otherwise as it thinks just'.[149]

7.3.6.3 Interaction between remedies

In cases where the consumer still retains the above described 'short-term right to reject' the goods (because the goods have not yet been 'accepted' or the contract not yet affirmed) there is provision for interaction between the pre-existing right to reject and terminate and the new remedies of repair and replacement. Essentially if the consumer asks for repair or replacement he cannot reject the goods and terminate the contract, until he has given the seller a reasonable time to repair or replace as the case may be.[150] There is also similar provision for the relationship between the repair and replacement remedies. It is provided that if the consumer asks for repair or replacement he cannot seek the other of these two alternatives until he has given the seller a reasonable time to repair or replace as the case may be.[151]

7.3.6.4 The Law Commissions

In 2008, the Law Commissions issued a Joint Consultation Paper, 'Consumer Remedies for Faulty Goods'.[152] The Law Commissions recommend:

- not introducing a two-year cut-off for claims in general, although giving consideration as to whether or not such a period would be appropriate in some cases,[153] nor refusing remedies where defects are 'minor';[154]

---

[148] SGA, s. 48E(2); SGSA, s. 11R(2).
[149] SGA, s. 48E(6); SGSA, s. 11R(6).
[150] SGA, s. 48D(1) and (2)(a); SGSA, ss. 11Q(1) and (2)(b).
[151] SGA, s. 48(1) and (2)(c); SGSA, ss. 11Q(1) and (2)(c).
[152] 'Consumer Remedies for Faulty Goods' (2008) (Law Com Consultation Paper 188 and Scot Law Com Discussion Paper No 139); and see also 'Consumer Remedies for Faulty Goods: A Summary of Responses to Consultation', May 2009 (which reveals a fair degree of support for the Law Commissions' proposals).
[153] *Ibid.*, 8.170–171.
[154] *Ibid.*, 8.91.

- retaining the short-term right to reject, but restricting it to a normal 30-day period, at the same time possibly reducing this period where the goods are perishable or the consumer should have discovered the defect before doing an act inconsistent with returning the goods and possibly increasing it where the need for a longer period was reasonably foreseeable at the time of sale, was later agreed, is required by personal circumstances of the consumer or is justified by the fundamental nature of the defects which would take time to discover;[155]

- clarifying the current position by providing that:

  (a) repair/rescission are possible after two failed repairs or one failed replacement or where the product is dangerous or the seller has behaved unreasonably;

  (b) rescission is allowed after one failed repair where the product is in daily use and immediately where the product is essential (unless the inconvenience has been adequately reduced, for example, by provision of a temporary replacement);

  (c) that 'best practice' repair and replacement guidance should be issued (whether at national or EU level);[156]

- that consideration should be given to the circumstances in which loss of earnings and distress, disappointment, loss of amenity damages should be recoverable.[157]

7.3.6.5 The short-term right to reject

> **DEBATE BOX**
>
> We have seen that the Law Commissions favour retention of the short-term right to reflect, albeit restricting it normally to a 30-day limit. It has been argued that it may not be needed at all as long as the *other* proposals of the Law Commissions (immediately above) were implemented as these would make it easier to move from having to accept repair/replacement to having the option of rescission (which amounts to rejection in any case).[158] There is certainly some merit in this argument. The Law Commissions' tests for moving from repair/replacement to rescission/price revaluation focus on the number of attempts at repair/replacement, the behaviour of the seller, if the product is dangerous. These tests do try to recognise many of the main reasons that consumers might lose confidence in the goods and/or the seller and legitimately wish to reject.[159] At the same time, the need to satisfy these conditions might in practice make the position

---

[155] *Ibid.*, 8.75–77; the Law Commissions are undecided as to whether or not the rules on work and materials and hire purchase should also be subject to this approach or continue to be subject to the 'affirmation' rule described above (8.104).

[156] *Ibid.*, 8.135–7.

[157] *Ibid.*, 8.186–7.

[158] P. Dobson, 'The Consumer's Right to Reject: A Sacred Cow?' (2009) SLR 57(1).

[159] Loss of confidence being a key reason that one might give for thinking it reasonable for the consumer to escape from the contract altogether and not be expected to give the seller chances to repair or replace. See Law Commissions, 'Consumer Remedies for Faulty Goods: A Summary of Responses to Consultation', May 2009, at p. 8; and C. Willett, A. Naidoo and M. Morgan-Taylor, *op. cit.*, at p. 109.

uncertain and off-putting for the consumer,[160] who might easily be put off by a seller who insists they do not apply (in contrast with the current position, where if the consumer acts quickly the only thing the seller can argue about is the state of the goods).

In addition, the existence of the right to reject may encourage consumers to try new brands or retailers, it may provide sellers with the incentive to exercise better quality control and carry out more effective repairs and it is a useful bargaining tool that may prevent consumers being trapped in a cycle of failed repairs.[161]

A further point is that it seems inconsistent for consumers to have the right to cancel contracts such as distance sales and doorstep sales within 14 days, even where there are no defects,[162] while not allowing a short-term right to reject when goods are actually in breach. Also, consumers reasonably expect a short-term right to reject, as this has been the law for a long time, and, indeed, it is the practice of many shops to provide a 30-day return right even where there are no defects. These points on existing practice also suggest that such a right to reject has not caused serious problems for sellers.

7.3.7 Consumer guarantees and extended warranties

7.3.7.1 Introduction

Promises as to the goods and/or as to remedies may appear in guarantees or 'extended warranty' contracts between the seller or supplier and the buyer or between the manufacturer and the buyer.[163] The SSGCR 2002 (following the CSD)[164] lays down a regime for guarantees. Currently, it covers:

> ... any undertaking to a consumer by a person acting in the course of a business, given without extra charge, to reimburse the price paid or to replace, repair or handle consumer goods in any way if they do not meet the specifications set out in the guarantee statement or in the relevant advertising.[165]

This would only include free of charge guarantees typically offered by manufacturers (but retailer free of charge guarantees – although less typical – are also covered as the guarantor need only be someone 'acting in the course of a business'). However, the definition in the CRD makes no reference to 'free of charge', so this would require the regime to be amended to cover extended warranties (typically offered by retailers) and paid for.

---

[160] More generally that the Law Commissions compare the ease with which both consumers and traders understand the basic nature of the right to reject, something that helps produce certainty (see 'Consumer Remedies for Faulty Goods: A Summary of Responses to Consultation', May 2009 (which reveals a fair degree of support for the Law Commissions' proposals, at p. 8).

[161] See Law Commissions, 'Consumer Remedies for Faulty Goods: A Summary of Responses to Consultation', May 2009, at 8; C. Willett, A. Naidoo and M. Morgan-Taylor, *op. cit.*, at p. 109.

[162] See section 7.2.3.

[163] Generally on guarantees see C. Twigg-Flesner, *Consumer Product Guarantees* (Ashgate, Surrey, 2003) and R. Bradgate and C. Twigg-Flesner, *Blackstone's Guide to Consumer Sales and Associated Guarantees* (Oxford University Press, Oxford, 2003).

[164] And Art. 29 of the CRD would repeat this with some changes, on which see the text following.

[165] Regulation 2.

The regime only applies to guarantees given to consumers and a consumer is defined as 'any natural person who, in contracts covered by these Regulations, is acting for purposes which are outside his trade, business or profession'.[166]

7.3.7.2 Enforceability

It is provided that:

> Where goods are sold or otherwise supplied to a consumer which are offered with a consumer guarantee, the consumer guarantee takes effect at the time the goods are delivered as a contractual obligation owed by the guarantor under the conditions set out in the guarantee statement and the associated advertising.[167]

ISSUE BOX

This avoids any questions that might arise in English law as to whether or not a consumer actually provides consideration for a guarantee provided by the manufacturer.[168] It may also allow some promises and statements in advertising (note the reference to 'associated advertising') to be treated as contractually binding as against the advertiser (whether a retailer or producer).[169] As indicated above in section 7.3.3.1, the courts have traditionally been reluctant to impose such liability on producers in contract or tort, despite the strong degree of reliance arguably placed on producers' advertising by consumers. Of course, there is now some seller responsibility for producer statements under the satisfactory quality implied term, but this only involves taking account of such statements as one aspect of determining satisfactory quality (see section 7.3.3.1) and it does not address the situation in which the seller is insolvent and cannot be sued.

Another question arising in relation to these provisions is as to who exactly can enforce the guarantee. In particular the question is if a guarantee can be enforced by a party receiving the goods as a gift or under a sub-sale from the consumer. Neither reg. 15(1) nor Art. 6 in the SCGD indicate to whom the contractual obligation is owed. However, the provisions do refer to the guarantee being enforceable 'under the conditions' in the guarantee. On this basis it seems that if the guarantee says that it is 'non-transferable' then it will only be enforceable by the party to whom the goods were sold or supplied, while if the guarantee refers to it being 'transferable' then it will be enforceable by a party to whom the goods are gifted or sold (it should be noted that there is no express requirement in the provisions to the effect that the party seeking to enforce the guarantee should be a party to whom the goods were sold or supplied by the seller, supplier or producer). Where the guarantee says nothing as to transferability then as long as the goods and guarantee were originally provided to a consumer (that is clearly required) it remains arguable that it could still be enforced by a subsequent

---

[166] Regulation 2.
[167] Regulation 15(1).
[168] See C. Willett, A. Naidoo and M. Morgan-Taylor, *op. cit.*, at p. 115.
[169] For a full discussion of the possibility of such liability, see C. Willett, 'Direct Producer Liability', in G. Howells and R. Schulze (eds), *op. cit.*, 189–209, at pp. 195–198.

transferee. This argument is strengthened by the fact that, as already indicated, there is no express indication that the guarantee is only enforceable by the original consumer.

7.3.7.3 Transparency

The guarantor (and any party supplying the goods that are the subject of the guarantee) must, on request by a consumer, provide in writing (or in another durable medium) a copy of the guarantee.[170] In addition, the guarantor must ensure (where the guarantee is offered in the UK) that it is written in English.[171] In all cases he must ensure that the contents of the guarantee and the essential particulars for making claims[172] are set out in 'plain intelligible language'.[173]

7.3.7.4 Special provisions on extended warranties

As indicated above, an extended warranty contract will normally be paid for separately by the buyer. The contract is often an insurance contract and will be made between the purchaser and either a wholly independent company or with the retailer or some business that is associated with the retailer. Of course, what must also be remembered about an extended warranty is that the word 'warranty' is the commercial name given to this type of contract and has no legal significance. The terms in extended warranty contracts, as with the main sale or supply contract or a guarantee contract, may be legally classified as conditions, warranties or innominate terms.

A key problem with extended warranty contracts is that they are often expensive and many of the rights they provide do not add anything to the rights available in law under the implied terms as to quality, fitness, etc. and the rights under the free guarantee offered by manufacturers and many retailers. As a consequence, there tends to be a relatively low volume of claims[174] so that warranty is often poor value for money.

POINT OF INTEREST

The Competition Commission reported on extended warranties in 2003 and took the view that there may be a restriction on competition as a result of the following factors: few consumers seek information about extended warranties prior to the point of sale; the warranty is then offered at the point of sale and the consumer has little chance to consider alternatives at this point; there is usually no information at the point of sale on the prices or terms offered by other providers of extended warranties or as to the reliability or likely repair costs of the goods or the likelihood of theft or accidental damage; and the warranties available at the point of sale are usually always from one provider.[175]

---

[170] Regulations 15(3)–(4).
[171] Regulation 15(5).
[172] Notably the duration and territorial scope of the guarantee as well as the name and address of the guarantor: reg. 15(2).
[173] Regulation 15(2).
[174] OFT, *Extended Warranties on Domestic Electrical Goods*, 2002b, OFT para. 4.31.
[175] Competition Commission report, 'Domestic Electrical Goods: A Report on the Supply of Extended Warranties on Domestic Electrical Goods within the UK' (section headed 'Extended Warranties, Pricing and Profitability').

The Competition Commission recommended two alternative reform packages, one of which has now been enacted in the Supply of Extended Warranties on Domestic Electrical Goods Order 2005.[176] This requires that retailers display the price of the extended warranty alongside the electrical goods, in the store and in their printed advertising material; provide information about statutory rights,[177] cancellation rights and details of the warranty, including whether or not the warranty provides financial protection in the event of insolvency and terminates if a claim is made;[178] give 45 days to cancel the extended warranty, followed up by a written reminder of this right and the right to cancel at any time and receive a refund; and offer any consumers, who do not wish to purchase a warranty immediately, quotations stating that the extended warranty remains available on the same terms for 30 days if the consumer chooses not to buy it at that time. Any discounts tied to the purchase of the extended warranty are also to be available for 30 days.

7.3.8 Future reform consolidation and simplification

A recent Department of Business Innovation and Skills (BIS) Report reviewed key aspects of the contract law rules applicable to the supply of goods and services to consumers (see section 7.1.6 above).[179] The point of the BIS Report was to consider how the law might be streamlined and simplified to make it more accessible and less costly for businesses and consumers.[180] A number of proposals were made for the substantive, structural and terminological reform of the implied terms and remedies in contracts for the supply of goods.[181] The government now plans a single piece of legislation (a Consumer Rights Act – CRA) which would implement many of the proposals in the BIS Report (along with the provisions of the recent Consumer Rights Directive).[182] It would possibly also contain other measures, including reforms to the law on services (see section 7.4 below) and a new regime on unfair contract terms (see section 7.7 below).[183] A BIS consultation, based broadly on the BIS report discussed above, was insued in July 2012 and the government plans to issue a Bill in 2013 and final legislation in 2014.[184]

In relation to defective goods and remedies, first of all, the new law would be likely to follow the Law Commission proposals to clarify the law (see above at section 7.3.6.4). More generally, following the the BIS Report, the new law is likely to simplify things by compressing the implied terms as to description, quality and fitness of goods into a single package

[176] Extended Warranties on Domestic Electrical Goods Order 2005 (URN No 05/1717).
[177] Which, as we saw above, would be required under the CRD in any case.
[178] Again, this would probably be required under the CRD, as it requires the contents and the conditions for making claims to be set out.
[179] BIS, 'Consolidation and Simplification of UK Consumer Law' (BIS, London, 2010).
[180] *Ibid.*, at pp. 2–3.
[181] *Ibid.*, at pp. 3–8 for a summary.
[182] House of Commons Library, Proposed Consumer Rights Bill (SN/HA/06076, 19 October 2011) and www.bis.gov.uk/policies/consumer-issues/consumer-rights. Consumer Rights Directive, 2011/83/EU and see section 7.1.6 above. See now Consultation Document, BIS, Enhancing Consumer Confidence by Clarifying Consumer Law, July 2012.
[183] House of Commons, *ibid.*, and BIS, *ibid.*
[184] Enhancing Consumer Confidence by Clarifying Consumer Law, BIS, July 2012.

applicable to all types of supply transaction.[185] (Currently, essentially the same implied terms are repeated in various different statutes, depending on the precise classification of the transaction as a sale, hire, HP, work and materials contract etc.[186])

The report also dealt with the remedies for defective goods. It highlighted the current confusing and unnecessary differences between the remedies that apply to sales and those that apply to other supply transactions and suggested removing such differences where possible.[187] (Currently, for instance, the right to reject goods is lost on 'acceptance' of the goods under the Sale of Goods Act (SGA), while common law 'affirmation' governs other supply contracts.) This is also likely to be a feature of the new CRA if it ultimately becomes law.

7.4 Performance Standards (2) – Implied terms as to services

7.4.1 Introduction

The services provided for consumption are numerous and complex in terms of the problems to which they may give rise. At one end of the market there are professional advisory services such as those provided by lawyers and accountants in which there is no material end product, but into which the service provider injects a substantial degree of skill. However, there are other types of service, often encountered in the home improvement sector, in which there is an element of work or skill and a material end product, such as the services provided by a plumber who agrees to install a bathroom suite, often referred to as contracts for work and materials. In such cases it can be important to distinguish between the supply of goods element and the services element since liability in respect of the latter is fault-based whereas liability for defective quality in the goods supplied is strict. In the case of professional advisory services and also in the case of many medical services, the outcome of the service is often clouded in uncertainty, so that an absolute guarantee of the quality of those services would be an unrealistic proposition. For example, it would be unrealistic to expect a lawyer to guarantee that every case (s)he took on would be successful or that every surgical procedure performed by a surgeon will succeed.

The law relating to the standard of performance of services is partly based on common law rules, although these have been supplemented by legislative intervention. Of particular importance here is the Supply of Goods and Services Act 1982, which sets out the implied terms to be found in contracts for the supply of services which include a duty to carry out the service through the exercise of reasonable care and skill,[188] a duty to perform the service by the time specified in the contract or, in the absence of any contractual provision, within a reasonable time[189] and to charge the amount specified in the contract or, in the absence of

---

[185] BIS, above, Chapters 2 and 6.
[186] See section 7.3.1 above.
[187] BIS, above, Chapter 5, and section 7.3.5.2 above.
[188] Supply of Goods and Services Act 1982, s. 13.
[189] *Ibid.*, s. 14.

any contractual provision, to charge no more than a reasonable amount.[190] In relation to contracts that involve a supply of goods together with a service element, there are also implied terms relating to the goods supplied that are very similar to those found in contracts for the sale of goods relating to correspondence with description, satisfactory quality and fitness for purpose.[191] In addition to the general duties of a service provider, it should also be noted that there are specific liability regimes in respect of particular types of service, for example package holidays, credit services and services of general interest that have been introduced in order to comply with the requirements of specific EU directives.

7.4.2 The general basis of private law liability for defective services

The three main performance concerns associated with the provision of consumer services relate to the issues of defective performance of the service, late commencement or completion of the service and the amount payable for the service. Each of these matters is, at least in part, addressed by implied terms to be found in the Supply of Goods and Services Act 1982.

7.4.2.1 Defective performance

The duty to exercise reasonable care and skill

The standard of performance expected of a service provider is that he should provide the service with reasonable care and skill. Accordingly, the basis of liability for service providers is fault-based and therefore different from that applicable to the retail supplier of qualitatively defective goods under the Sale of Goods Act 1979[192] and the producer of unsafe goods under the Consumer Protection Act 1987.[193]

A feature of the liability of sellers and producers is that the test of liability for a defective product is based on the expectations of persons generally as to the appropriate standard of quality or safety as the case might be, so that liability is strict. In contrast the supplier of a service is based upon the level of performance that he puts in to the supply of the service, so that liability is fault-based and the supplier will only be liable if his performance falls below the standard of the reasonably competent.

Since the liability of a service provider is based upon the standard of reasonable care and skill, it is the same standard of performance as is expected of persons generally under the tort of negligence arising out of the general principle in *Donoghue* v *Stevenson*.[194] This means that the provider of a service can be liable regardless of whether or not there is a contract to provide that service. However, if there is no contract, the general requirements of the tort of negligence will need to be established. So, in such cases, it will have to be shown that there is a duty of care, which means that any harm suffered by the consumer should be reasonably foreseeable, the relationship between the provider and the consumer should be sufficiently

---

[190] *Ibid.*, s. 15.
[191] *Ibid.*, ss. 3 (description) and 4 (satisfactory quality and fitness for purpose). These terms are drafted in language almost identical to that found in the Sale of Goods Act 1979, ss. 13 and 14.
[192] See section 7.3.
[193] See section 7.5.
[194] [1932] AC 562.

proximate and that it should be just and reasonable in the circumstances to impose a duty of care.[195] These criteria were considered to have been satisfied in *Smith v Eric S Bush (a firm)*[196] in which a surveyor acting on behalf of a building society had carelessly prepared a valuation report on a house, failing to notice a significant defect that seriously diminished the value of the house and realising that the buyer of the house would rely upon the report. Accordingly the loss suffered by the consumer was reasonably foreseeable, the relationship between the parties was proximate as the surveyor knew that the borrower would pay the building society for the valuation report and that payment was passed on to the surveyor by the building society. It was also considered to be just and reasonable to impose a duty of care as it was well known that consumer housebuyers at the lower end of the market were likely to rely on nothing but the building society valuation in deciding whether or not to purchase a house. This reasoning, however, suggests that others such as more affluent buyers or business purchasers might not have been owed a duty of care in such circumstances. In *Smith v Bush* the surveyor was indirectly paid for the service he provided, however, so long as the general requirements for a duty of care can be established a person who provides a service entirely gratuitously may still owe a duty of care.[197]

In the case of services provided pursuant to a contract, there is no need to establish a duty of care. As noted above, where there is a contract for the service, the Supply of Goods and Services Act 1982, s. 13 implies a term requiring the exercise of reasonable care and skill where the supplier acts in the course of a business.

Reasonable care and skill

Whether or not there is a contract, the service supplier is generally only responsible where it is shown that there has been a lack of reasonable care and skill (this representing either, as the case may be, a breach of the tortious duty of care or of the implied term as to reasonable care and skill). The relevant standard (often referred to as the '*Bolam*' test) is usually that of the reasonably competent person in the same line of business.[198] Thus, a jeweller who pierces the ear of a customer must reach the standard expected of a reasonable jeweller rather than the standard expected of a surgeon or other medical practitioner,[199] but a tradesman who leaves his work in an unsafe condition is likely to fall below the reasonable standards of his trade.[200]

Although the *Bolam* test suggests that the defendant may have a defence to liability if he can show that he has acted in the same way that others in his trade might also have acted, it has been held, subsequently, that a court can determine that a standard practice no longer satisfies the reasonable care standard.[201] It is therefore ultimately down to the court to determine if, in the particular circumstances, the defendant has acted with reasonable care.

Since the test applied to the service provider is objective, it is no defence for the service provider to argue that he has done his incompetent best. The supplier is judged by the standards of the reasonably competent provider of that kind of service so that a plumber with

---

[195] See *Caparo Industries PLC v Dickman* [1990] 1 All ER 568.
[196] [1989] 2 All ER 514.
[197] See *Chaudhry v Prabhakar* [1989] 1 WLR 29.
[198] *Bolam v Friern Hospital Management Committee* [1957] 1 WLR 582, at 586, *per* McNair J.
[199] *Phillips v William Whiteley Ltd* [1938] 1 All ER 556.
[200] See *Kimber v Willett* [1947] 1 All ER 361.
[201] See *Bolitho v City & Hackney Health Authority* [1997] 4 All ER 771.

15 years' experience of the trade and one who has only recently gone into business will be judged by the same standards.[202]

More onerous duties?

The Supply of Goods and Services Act 1982, s. 13 implies a term to the effect that the service provider will exercise reasonable care, but that does not preclude the possibility that a stricter standard of performance may derive either from an express term of the contract or by law[203] or be implied by a court based on the facts of the case.[204] While it is unlikely that a professional service provider such as a lawyer or medical practitioner will ever guarantee the success of the work undertaken on behalf of a client or patient[205] because of the future uncertainty associated with the type of work undertaken, it is possible that other types of service provider might be treated differently. This is most likely to be the case in 'Design and Build' contracts in which a contractor, such as an architect or civil engineer, is engaged to design and supply an end product such as part of a building or other structure based on detailed information supplied by the client specifying his particular requirements, in which case it may be possible to imply a term to the effect that the end product will be fit for the purpose specifically made known by the customer.[206]

Where the service provider contracts to do skilful work that also involves a supply of goods under the terms of a contract for work and materials, as will be the case with many consumer contracts for home improvements, there are often different performance standards applicable to the service element and to the goods supplied. In some cases the issue may relate purely to the service, for example, where a trader who is supplying and fitting goods damages the pre-existing fixtures or fittings in a house or where a mechanic servicing and fitting parts to a car damages the car or leaves it unlocked, allowing it to be stolen. In such cases, it is clear that the standard applicable is the reasonable care one under s. 13 SGSA, so that there will only be liability where a lack of reasonable care is shown to have occurred.

However, slightly more complicated issues arise where the actual goods being supplied are part of the problem. So far as the goods themselves are concerned, there are strict liability implied terms that the goods will correspond with any description given of them,[207] will be of satisfactory quality[208] and will be fit for any particular purpose expressly or impliedly made known to the supplier by the consumer, provided it is reasonable for the consumer to rely upon the supplier's skill and judgement in selecting suitable goods.[209] This certainly applies

---

[202] See *Nettleship* v *Weston* [1971] 2 QB 691.

[203] See Supply of Goods and Services Act 1982, s. 16(3)(a).

[204] *Ibid.*, s. 16(3)(b).

[205] See *Thake* v *Maurice* [1986] 1 All ER 497.

[206] See *Greaves & Co Ltd* v *Baynham Meikle* [1975] 3 All ER 99 (guarantee that a factory floor would be suited for use by fork-lift trucks); *IBA* v *EMI & BICC* (1980) 14 *Building LR* 1 (guarantee that a television relay mast could withstand the strength of the winds to which it would be exposed).

[207] Supply of Goods and Services Act 1982, s. 3(2), a term identical to that in the Sale of Goods Act 1979, s. 13 considered in section 4.8.4.1 above and see *Randall* v *Newson* (1877) 2 QBD 102.

[208] *Ibid.*, s. 4(2), a term identical to that in s. 14(2) of the Sale of Goods Act 1979, considered in section 4.8.4.2 above and see *Young & Marten Ltd* v *McManus Childs Ltd* [1969] 1 AC 454.

[209] *Ibid.*, ss. 4(4) and (5) implying a term equivalent to that in the Sale of Goods Act 1979, s. 14(3), **considered** in section 4.8.4.3 above and see *GH Myers & Co* v *Brent Cross Service Co* [1934] 1 KB 46, but if the consumer fails to communicate a specific requirement that he might have the implied term in s. 4(4) will be of no assistance as it is likely that the requirement of reasonable reliance will not be complied with: see *CRC Flooring Ltd* v *Heaton* (1984) 3 Tr LR 33 (failure to communicate that a carpet with a medallion-shaped pattern should be laid so as to allow each medallion to sit centrally on each stair).

to goods that were defective before any service element commenced. In such cases, there is strict liability for breach of these implied terms as to the goods, there being no need to establish a lack of reasonable care. If the contract is one of sale (because the service element is less significant than the goods element) it may also be that the same strict standards apply to goods that were initially fine, but which have been damaged by the service element, for example, by installation. This seems to be the case where the goods are not viewed as having been delivered until the service element is complete, for example, until any promised installation has taken place.[210] Such a result is probably in keeping with the Directive on Aspects of the Sale of Consumer Goods and Associated Guarantees[211] which deems consumer goods not to be in conformity with the contract of sale where they are defective as a result of incorrect installation carried out by the seller or under his responsibility.[212] This Directive may also apply in cases where the installation element is predominant and the contract is therefore one for work and materials.[213] However, the UK seems to have overlooked the fact that the Directive seems to impose a strict liability standard based on the finished state of the goods. In response to the Directive, the government chose to amend the SGSA by providing that in contracts for the transfer of goods (that is, non-sales contracts) where installation of the goods forms part of the contract, goods are treated as not being in conformity with the contract if they are installed in breach of the implied term as to reasonable care and skill in s. 13 of the SGSA.[214] The result of this provision seems to be that (whatever is intended by the Directive) a supplier who damages goods during installation in a work and materials contract is only liable where he is shown to have fallen below the reasonable care standard. This could mean, for example, that if, due to a reasonable and non-negligent misreading of the manufacturer's instructions,[215] the goods are incorrectly installed so that they do not work properly the consumer may be without a remedy.

7.4.2.2 Reform – a broadly applicable strict liability standard?

The recent BIS report (see above, section 7.3.8) proposes that such a result-based standard (strict liability) should become the general norm.[216] If accepted, this would be implemented in the proposed CRA (see above, section 7.3.8). The proposal in the BIS report was that this would be based on the one standard used in the Draft Common Frame of Reference (DCFR)[217] This provides that:

---

[210] *Philip Head & Sons Ltd* v *Showfronts Ltd* [1970] 1 Lloyd's Rep 140.

[211] Dir 1999/44/EC.

[212] *Ibid.*, Art. 2(5); and see See C. Willett and D. Oughton, 'Liability for Incorrect Installation and Other Services Associated with Consumer Goods', in G. Howells, A. Nordhausen, D. Parry and C. Twigg-Flesner (eds), *The Yearbook of Consumer Law 2007* (Ashgate, Surrey, 2007) pp. 229–276.

[213] See Willett and Oughton, *ibid.*

[214] See Supply of Goods and Services Act 1982, s. 13 and s. 115(1)(b) (inserted by the Sale and Supply of Goods to Consumers Regulations 2002).

[215] See R. Bradgate and C. Twigg-Flesner, *op. cit.*, p. 79.

[216] BIS, chapter 4. A key reason for the proposal is that the current law is confusing for consumers and businesses; being based on a mixture of fault standards and strict standards (see text above) and being different from the position for goods, where liability is strict.

[217] C. Von Bar and E. Clive, *Principles, Definitions and Model Rules of European Private Law: Draft Common Frame of Reference* (OUP/Sellier, Oxford, 2010). The DCFR is intended as a resource for future development of European private law; on which see S. Whittaker, 'A Framework of Principle for European Contract Law' (2009) 125 *LQR* 616.

(1) The supplier of a service must achieve the specific result stated or envisaged by the client at the time of the conclusion of the contract, provided that in the case of a result envisaged but not stated:

(a) the result envisaged was one which the client could reasonably be expected to have envisaged; and

(b) the client had no reason to believe that there was a substantial risk that the result would not be achieved by the service.[218]

The other possible standard is one based on the standards applicable to goods, that is, to provide that a service must be of satisfactory quality and reasonably fit for any particular purpose stated. This has the advantage of making the law very accessible (in that the standards for goods and services are expressed in the same way). At the same time, in only focusing on the quality and fitness of the service itself, there is a question as to whether or not it provides quite as much protection for consumers as the DCFR standard, which actually requires the *final result* of the service to be as envisaged or stated. See now Consultation Document, BIS, Enhancing Consumer Confidence by Clarifying Consumer Law, July 2012, which proposes something in between this and the DCFR approach; essentially suggesting that the outcome of the service should be of satisfactory quality.

7.4.2.3 Late performance

A common consumer complaint is that work undertaken by a service provider is not completed on time or not commenced at the time the consumer expected. If the contract provides for a start date, then failure to start by that date may be regarded as a breach of contract, but a pertinent legal issue may be if the time for performance is to be regarded as being of the essence of the contract, and therefore a condition, breach of which will allow termination of the contract. Generally, there are three circumstances in which a time stipulation will be treated as being of the essence of a contract.[219] First, where the parties have expressly stated this to be the case, secondly where the nature of the subject matter suggests that the term should have this status and finally, where a party has waived an earlier breach but has given notice requiring performance by a new date.[220]

The main problem with most consumer contracts is that the consumer often fails to make any provision for the time of performance. However, it is possible that the particular circumstances may suggest that performance by a particular date is required. Furthermore, time may be of the essence of the contract where the subject matter suggests this, for example, where a financial product has a sharply fluctuating value.

If the contract is totally silent on the matter of the time for performance, the service provider is expected to perform within a reasonable time.[221] (If he does not do so, then, again, it will need to be determined whether time is of the essence or not, giving the consumer the right to terminate.) What is regarded as a reasonable time will depend on the particular facts of each case.[222] In determining what is a reasonable time, it is necessary to consider how long it would have taken a reasonable person in the same line of business as the defendant to provide the service. What little case law there is suggests that the courts may be quite generous

---

[218] IV. C.-2:106.
[219] *United Scientific Holdings Ltd* v *Burnley Borough Council* [1978] AC 904.
[220] See, for example, *Charles Rickards Ltd* v *Oppenhaim* [1950] 1 KB 616.
[221] Supply of Goods and Services Act 1982, s. 14(1).
[222] *Ibid.*, s. 14(2).

to defendants, thus it has been held that a garage could be expected to complete repairs to an accident-damaged vehicle within a period of five weeks, so that where the work took eight weeks, the defendant was in breach of contract and liable accordingly.[223]

7.4.2.4 Payment for consumer services

The amount payable for a service will depend on the terms of the contract. If an amount is specified, no matter how much or how little, it will generally be enforced as there is a general principle to the effect that the law does not judge the adequacy of the consideration for a promise. Difficulties may arise over the interpretation of certain types of statement. For example, it is generally considered that a quotation is an offer that can be accepted and so becomes binding on the offeror. In contrast, an estimate may be little more than an invitation to treat which is not binding on the trader who gives the estimate. However, this is not always the case and there have been instances in which an estimate has been regarded as binding on the trader.[224] However, if the trader gives no more than an estimate and declines to give a firm price after commencing work, it is possible that by doing so he may be guilty of negligence and liable for any losses suffered by the customer.[225]

If the contract makes no provision at all for the charge to be made for a service, the consumer can insist on paying no more than a reasonable price,[226] but what is reasonable will depend on the particular facts,[227] which may include matters such as delays, material costs and the availability of labour.

7.4.3 Package holidays

7.4.3.1 Introduction

One of the more valuable service contracts entered into by consumers is a contract to take holiday services. The law relating to holiday services is common law-based, but is also subject to specific provision deriving from the Directive on Package Holidays[228] if the holiday qualifies under the definition of a package holiday. There is also an important trade association in the form of the Association of British Travel Agents (ABTA) which has developed a code of practice to which travel agents and tour operators that are members subscribe.

The Package Holidays Directive, given effect by the Package Travel etc. Regulations (PTR), only applies where the arrangements made amount to a package, which requires a pre-arranged combination of two elements of tourism, namely, travel,[229] accommodation[230] or

---

[223] See *Charnock* v *Liverpool Corporation* [1968] 3 All ER 473.

[224] See *Croshaw* v *Pritchard* (1899) 16 TLR 45 (estimate binding on the trader).

[225] See *J & JC Abrahams Ltd* v *Ancliffe* [1978] 2 NZLR 420.

[226] Supply of Goods and Services Act 1982, s. 15(1).

[227] *Ibid.*, s. 15(2).

[228] Dir 90/314; OJ L 158/59, 13/6/90 implemented in English law by the Package Travel, Package Holidays and Package Tours Regulations 1992, SI 1992/3288.

[229] This must be a significant element in the package, so that airport transfers may not be sufficient to amount to transport: see *Keppel-Palmer* v *Exus Travel Ltd* [2003] All ER (D) 183. Would the same reasoning apply to shuttle bus rides from a hotel into a city centre?

[230] This would appear to include hotels, caravans, tents, chalets, but not intercultural exchange arrangements under which schoolchildren stay with 'host' families free of charge in the country they visit: see *Administrative Proceedings Concerning AFS Intercultural Programmes* (Case C237/97) [2000] 1 CMLR 845; [1999] 1 ECR 825.

other tourist services,[231] for a period of at least 24 hours and at an inclusive price.[232] For these purposes, the tour operator cannot avoid the application of the Directive by submitting separate accounts for different elements of the package and the Directive can still be treated as 'pre-arranged' if organised at the customer's request and in accordance with his specific instructions.[233] The phrase 'pre-arranged' can give rise to difficulties of interpretation, but it appears to mean that the holiday package should be arranged before the contract is concluded.[234] However, what this interpretation means is that if an element of the holiday is left to be arranged after the consumer arrives at the holiday location, such as many excursions, it will not be regarded as part of the pre-arranged package,[235] so that only common law rules will apply.

7.4.3.2 Performance of the contract

Consumer complaints about holidays predominantly relate to unfulfilled expectations which may arise either if elements of the planned holiday are changed after departure or if the tour operator or someone providing tourist services on the organiser's behalf fails to reach the required standard of performance.

Post-departure alterations

It may be that the consumer has booked a package and either a significant proportion of the services contracted for is not provided or the organiser becomes aware that he will not be able to procure a significant proportion of the services to be provided. In such circumstances, the organiser is required to make suitable alternative arrangements, at no extra cost to the consumer, to allow the package to continue and, where appropriate, compensate the consumer for any difference in value.[236] Alternatively, if it is impossible to make alternative arrangements or the arrangements made are declined, for good reason, the organiser must make transport arrangements, agreed to by the consumer, and, where appropriate, compensate the consumer.[237]

A difficulty with these provisions is to determine what is meant by 'a significant proportion' of the package, as this will be a question of fact. It would appear that if the accommodation booked is not available this will mean that a significant proportion has not been provided. Another example might be the unavailability of some other element that is the primary reason for taking the package, for example, where a package of travel, accommodation and Wimbledon final tickets are sold and the tickets are not available.

Regulation 14 is primarily concerned with non-performance of the package, as opposed to reg. 15, considered below, which is concerned with 'improper' performance. If the breach can be regarded as non-performance, using reg. 14 has an advantage over reg. 15, to the extent that it does not give the organiser a *force majeure* excuse for improper performance, but it provides for the same levels of compensation as reg. 15, where appropriate.

---

[231] This appears to be confined to services provided for pleasure or leisure and, controversially, does not extend to educational services (see *Administrative Proceedings Concerning AFS Intercultural Programmes, ibid*).

[232] PTR 1992, reg. 2(1).

[233] *Ibid.*, reg. 2(1)(c)(i) and (ii).

[234] *Club Tour Viagens v Lobo Gonclaves Garrido*, ECJ C-4000/00 [2002] ITLJ 55.

[235] See *Gallacher v Airtours Holidays Ltd* (2001) 2 CLY 4280, unreported.

[236] PTR 1992, reg. 14(2).

[237] *Ibid.*, reg. 14(3).

Proper performance of the contract

Where something goes wrong during a holiday, it may raise the issue of improper performance of the contract. If the contract does not make specific provision for the improper performance, it will be necessary to determine what are the terms of the contract, including those that can be implied.

At common law, the standard approach to the performance of contracts to provide a service is adopted, so that it is unlikely that a court will apply anything more than a term to the effect that the tour operator will exercise reasonable care and skill, as this is all that is likely to be acceptable to both of the parties under the 'officious bystander' test.[238] The problem that arises in holiday contracts is that although the tour operator contracts to supply the holiday services he is dependent on the actions of others for the proper performance of the contract. The case law in this area points to the fact that, at common law, the courts have been reluctant to saddle tour operators with liability in respect of the actions of third parties, with the result that if a term is implied it is unlikely to be anything more than a requirement to exercise reasonable care.[239]

Although the reasonable care standard will apply at common law to the tour operator's liability in most cases, there is the possibility that a court might infer a stricter standard of performance in cases where the tour operator has taken overall responsibility for the performance of the contract.

CASE

Wong Mee Wan v Kwan Kin Travel Services[240]

In this case, the tour operator contracted with the plaintiff's daughter to provide a package tour to a lake in China. The brochure contained the terms of the contract and described the itinerary for the tour, which included transportation across the lake by ferry. When the group reached the lake the ferry had already departed and the tour guide informed the group that they would have to cross the lake by speedboat. The speedboat hit another vessel and the plaintiff's daughter was drowned. The driver was not employed by the tour operator.

The issue was whether in this particular contract the defendant's duty was simply that they would arrange for services to be provided by others as their agents (where the law would imply a term into the contract that they would use reasonable care and skill in selecting those other persons) or that they themselves had undertaken to supply the services when there would be implied into the contract a term that they would as suppliers carry out the services with reasonable care and skill.

The Privy Council held an implied term of the contract that the holiday services would be carried out with reasonable skill and care, including any service provided by others.

---

[238] See *Shirlaw* v *Southern Foundries Ltd* [1939] 2 KB 206.

[239] See *Wall* v *Silver Wing Surface Arrangements* (1981), unreported (no liability for injuries sustained due to a padlocked fire escape, as the act of locking was carried out by the hotel management after the most recent inspection of the hotel by the tour operator); *Wilson* v *Best Travel* [1993] 1 All ER 353 (no failure to exercise reasonable care if the hotel reaches minimum safety standards in the country in which the hotel is located).

[240] [1996] 1 WLR 38, JCPC.

The important point in *Wong Mee* is that the defendants were taken to have expressly assumed responsibility for the whole package as the brochure said, 'We will do ...' (this, that and the other). Accordingly the tour operator was taken to have undertaken to provide rather than merely arrange the holiday services comprising the package.

Since the implementation of the Package Tours etc. Directive by the Package Tours Regulations 1992, it is now a requirement that the tour operator or the travel agent[241] should accept responsibility for the proper performance of the contract, irrespective of whether the holiday services are provided by the organiser or others.[242]

For the purposes of reg. 15, it is necessary to determine what facilities form part of the package. It has been seen already that for a feature of the holiday to form part of the package it must have been 'pre-arranged', so that excursions, etc. that are booked after arrival at the resort are not to be treated as an element of the package provided. A further difficulty that might arise is if a natural feature of the holiday location, such as the sea or some other geographical feature can be regarded as part of the package. In *Jones* v *Sunworld*,[243] Field J considered that there was no reason why natural features could not form part of the package if it had been advertised in the holiday brochure as an advantage of the package being sold. Thus it is clear that holiday facilities do not stop at the hotel door.

The primary requirement of reg. 15 is that the tour operator is required to ensure proper performance of the contract, but this will require a construction of the contract to ascertain what has been promised. There may be circumstances in which the tour operator has given a guarantee that certain facilities will form part of the holiday package, but in other cases it may be that all that can be said is that the tour operator has undertaken to exercise reasonable care and skill in some respect.

The package holiday contract may contain a number of different types of term. In some instances the tour operator may have expressly assumed liability in some respect, such as the acceptance of responsibility for the acts of others.[244] The contract may also contain express supervisory terms, indicating that the tour operator will monitor the performance or accreditation of intermediate providers, which might have the effect of increasing the tour operator's liability, depending on how the term is interpreted. There are also descriptive terms, usually derived from holiday brochures or websites which have assumed importance due to PTR 1992, reg. 6 which deems particulars in holiday brochures to be warranties, unless there is a statement to the effect that the particulars are subject to change.[245] Since information of this kind is likely to be verifiably true or false, it is likely that descriptive terms will be strictly construed. Thus if the brochure states that hotel rooms will be air-conditioned and there is no air-conditioning, whether or not the tour operator is at fault, he will be taken to have given a guarantee that the stated facility is available. These descriptive statements may sometimes appear to be little more than trade puffery, particularly if they suggest that the holiday accommodation reaches gold or platinum standard or constitutes luxury accommodation. Descriptions of this type raise the question of what is meant by the use of such words, but the case law seems to suggest that they may increase consumer expectations of quality and that

---

[241] See, for example, *Hone* v *Going Places Leisure Travel Ltd* [2001] EWCA Civ 947.

[242] PTR 1992, reg. 15.

[243] [2003] EWHC 591.

[244] See, for example, *Wong Mee Wan* v *Kwan Kin Travel Services* [1996] 1 WLR 38.

[245] PTR 1992, reg. 6(2)(b).

if what is provided is of poor quality there may be a breach of contract.[246] In contrast, brochure statements may also reduce expectations. For example, if a holiday is described as 'hedonistic' the consumer can expect others taking the same holiday to behave in a wild and exciting way.[247]

Some descriptive terms may be implied in certain circumstances, for example, where an inference can be drawn from a photograph in a brochure or other promotional material.

There is some doubt over the precise nature of the obligation relating to the supply of food that is fit for human consumption. On the one hand there is a strong argument that where a package holiday involves the supply of food, that element of the contract consists of a contract for the transfer of goods under the Supply of Goods and Services Act 1982, s. 4, so that there is a strict obligation to supply food that is of satisfactory quality and fit for the purpose for which it is required.[248]

Lastly, there are terms that will be implied, irrespective of the PTR such as the implied terms that the consumer will be safe and that reasonable care will be exercised in providing the holiday services.[249] For the purposes of such terms, it will be necessary to determine if the tour operator has fallen below the standard of reasonable care and if that breach of duty is the cause of any loss or harm suffered by the consumer.

Factors that may be relevant to whether or not there has been a breach of duty will include whether or not the accommodation complies with regulatory standards in the country in which the holiday facilities are located.[250] Also relevant is if the event complained about has happened before, as this will suggest that there is more that could have been done to avert the risk of harm.[251]

There are certain defences to liability under reg. 15 where the improper performance is due to neither the fault of the tour operator nor the fault of the service provider. These are that the improper performance is attributable to the consumer[252] or a third party not connected with the provision of the services contracted for and is unforeseeable or unavoidable[253] or that the improper performance is due to unforeseeable circumstances beyond the control of the party pleading the exception, the consequences of which could not have been avoided, even if all due care had been exercised,[254] or an event which the other party to the contract or the supplier of services, even with all due care, could not foresee or forestall.[255]

It seems unlikely that these defences will be relevant where the alleged breach of duty on the part of the tour operator is based on a reasonable care standard, since if the consumer, a third party or a *force majeure* event is the cause of the improper performance, it seems unlikely that any breach of a duty of care on the part of the defendant will be the cause of the loss suffered by the consumer.

---

[246] See, for example, *Buhus-Orwin v Coata Smeralda Holidays* [2001] CLY 4279 (rat-infested property could not be described as luxury); *Coughlan v Thomson Holidays Ltd* (2001) CLY 4276 (gold standard implied a holiday experience better than normal).

[247] See, for example, *Williams v First Choice Holidays* (2001) 8 CL 437.

[248] See also *Lockett v A & M Charles Ltd* [1938] 4 All ER 170, cf. *Martin v Thompson Tour Operations Ltd* [1999] CLY 3831 (reasonable care standard applied where water supply was bacterially contaminated).

[249] See *Hone v Going Places Leisure Travel Ltd* [2001] EWCA Civ 947.

[250] See *Wilson v Best Travel* [1993] 1 All ER 353; *Logue v Flying Colours Ltd* (2001) 6 CL 454.

[251] See, for example, *Brannan v Airtours Ltd* (1999) The Times, 1 Feb, CA.

[252] PTR 1992, reg. 15(2)(a). For example, late check-in at an airport: *Hartley v Intasun* [1987] CLY 3831.

[253] *Ibid.*, reg. 15(2)(b). This is arguably applicable to *Hone v Going Places & Leisure Travel Ltd* [2001] EWCA Civ 947 (evacuation of aeroplane caused by a bomb scare).

[254] *Ibid.*, reg. 15(2)(c)(i).

[255] *Ibid.*, reg. 15(2)(c)(ii).

If the improper performance amounts to the breach of a strict liability duty, the defences will be of immediate relevance, if they apply. A difficulty raised by the act of a third person defence is that the person must be unconnected with the provision of any holiday service. The defence has been applied to local authority operations on sewerage facilities outside the consumer's hotel,[256] which seems to suggest that the third party must have no direct or indirect connection to the anticipated performance of the package. So perhaps air-traffic controllers and baggage handlers, etc., indirectly connected to the performance of aspects of the package ought not to be regarded as unconnected third parties for the purposes of this defence. The second requirement is that the third party action must be 'unforeseeable or unavoidable' which seems to cover criminal conduct.[257]

The *force majeure* defence in reg. 15(2)(c) requires circumstances to be unforeseeable or to be beyond the tour operator's control, the consequences of which could not have been avoided, even if all due care had been exercised. It would appear that adverse weather conditions might qualify for this exception[258] although there is an argument to the effect that some weather events occur in certain areas at certain times of year with such regularity that they ought to be foreseen, but more mundane events like burst pipes are unlikely to fall within the defence.[259] Regulation 15(2)(c) also excuses the tour operator where an event is one that could not be foreseen or forestalled. This part of the defence appears to relate to the event itself, rather than the first part of reg. 15(2)(c) which is concerned with the consequences of the event. Thus while a hurricane might be foreseeable and some of its consequences could be avoided if all due care was exercised, there is nothing that anyone can do to dissuade it from striking where it does, that is, there is nothing that can forestall the event.

7.5 Performance Standards (3) – Liability in tort for defective products

7.5.1 Introduction

We saw above that the general rule is that consumers only have a claim for breach of the implied terms as to description, quality and fitness against the party who actually sold them the goods under a contract of sale or supply. Normally, this is a retailer. On this general rule, there is no claim under the implied terms for those who did not buy the goods under any form of contract but were, for example, given the goods as a gift. Equally, there is no claim under the implied terms for those who did buy the goods from a retailer but who now find that this retailer (who would normally be liable to them for breach of the implied terms) has become insolvent. These categories of consumers may sometimes be able to make a claim based on the common law exceptions to the privity of contract rule or based on the Contracts (Rights of Third Parties) Act 1999. However, this will only be possible in limited circumstances.[260]

---

[256] *Griffiths* v *Flying Colours Holidays Ltd* (1999) CLY 5473.
[257] See *Beales* v *Airtours Ltd* (1996) ITLJ 167 (mugging by backstreet robbers).
[258] *Hayes* v *Airtours Ltd* (2001) 2 CL 436 (hurricane damage).
[259] *Jordan* v *Thompson Holidays Ltd* (1999) CLY 3828.
[260] See C. Willett, 'The Role of Contract Law in Product Liability', in G. Howells (ed.), *The Law of Product Liability* (2nd edn, Butterworths, London, 2007).

Such consumers will also be able to make a claim in the tort of negligence against the producer (or any other party responsible for the problem with the goods). However, a key problem here is the need to establish fault on the part of the defendant. This means showing that the defendant did not reach the standard of a reasonable person. The problem here (from the point of view of consumer protection) is that the focus is on the behaviour of the defendant rather than the state of the product as such. So, whether, for example, a producer is liable in negligence will involve considering what could be expected of the producer, taking into account such factors as the degree of risk posed by the production process and the product and the cost of taking greater steps to prevent production of defective products.[261] So, there may be cases in which the product is defective and a consumer is affected, but the conclusion is that (in the light of the factors mentioned) the producer is found not to be negligent.

This problem does not arise under the implied terms. There the standard is one of 'strict liability', in the sense that the sole focus is on whether or not the goods are satisfactory, fit for purpose, etc. (it being irrelevant whether the defendant is negligent or not), but, as mentioned above, the problem is that these implied terms often cannot be used against producers. This section considers the Consumer Protection Act, which gives a remedy against producers and also does not require proof of negligence. The core issue is whether the product is 'defective' or not and this certainly improves the position of consumers in general, although we shall see that it is sometimes difficult to say how far this moves from a negligence standard.

7.5.2 Introduction to the Consumer Protection Act 1987

This Act was passed in order to implement the Product Liability Directive of 1985.[262]

LEGISLATIVE PROVISION

CONSUMER PROTECTION ACT 1987

Section 2 (1) provides that:

> . . . where any damage is caused wholly or partly by a defect in a product, every person to whom sub-section (2) applies shall be liable for the damage.

This of course begs a number of questions: as to what is a 'product', a 'defect', 'damage' and who the persons are under sub-s. (2) that are liable. Further, we shall see that defences are available and that time limits apply. We shall deal with these issues in turn. First, however, it is important to emphasise that the issue of causation arises as it does in any tort action. We can see that s. 2(1) expressly says that the damage must be 'caused' by the defect. However, it must also be emphasised that the consumer is the one who must establish all of the above, that is, the defect, the damage and the causal relationship between these elements. So, in one case it was held that the failure of silicone breast implants had to be proved to have caused the injury complained of *because of their defectiveness* at the time of supply. It was not

---

[261] See, for example, *Bolam* v *Friern Hospital Management Committee* [1957] 1 WLR 582; *Bolton* v *Stone* [1951] AC 580; *Paris* v *Stepney BC* [1951] AC 367; and *Daniels* v *Tarbard* [1938] 4 All ER 258.
[262] 85/374/EEC.

sufficient simply to demonstrate the fact that the articles in question had failed.[263] This need to establish causation (and the difficulty of doing so in many cases) is one of the things that the CPA regime continues to share with the common law negligence regime.

7.5.3 Product

'Product' means any goods or electricity.[264] 'Goods' includes 'substances, growing crops and things comprised in land by virtue of being attached to it'.[265] This obviously covers all moveable property such as cars, TVs, computers, tables, etc. 'Substances' also catches things in liquid, gas or vapour form.[266] In relation to buildings and land, the position is that they are not goods as such, so that the builder, seller, etc. are not liable under the Act. However, component parts, such as bricks, being 'comprised in' the building do qualify as goods and the producer of these would be liable if all the other requirements for liability are satisfied.[267]

Goods (as we saw above) also includes 'crops' and this now extends to agricultural produce that has not undergone an industrial process; the previous exclusion of such products being lifted in 2000 after a review of the Directive.[268]

Difficult issues arise in relation to such things as computer software and the ideas and advice in such things as books and games. Are these 'products' for the purposes of the Act? There is no space to develop the arguments here, but for a fuller analysis see the work of Geraint Howells.[269]

7.5.4 Defect

The basic rule is that goods are defective if 'the safety of the product is not such as persons generally are entitled to expect'.[270] Thus the test is based on general expectations of safety in relation to the product, rather than on the way in which the producer has conducted himself.[271] This is the basic distinction from the negligence concept described above, where even if the product is defective, the conduct of the defendant may not amount to negligence.

What persons generally are entitled to expect has been held to be an objective question to be determined by the judge, acting as an informed representative of the public at large,[272] although it is clear, and has been emphasised by the courts, that in performing this task, they are strongly dependent on expert evidence.[273] Another important point to emphasise here is

---

[263] *Foster v Biosil* [2001] 59 BMLR 178 and see Art. 4 of the Directive.
[264] Section 1(2).
[265] Section 45(1).
[266] *Ibid.*
[267] See also s. 46.
[268] See Consumer Protection Act (Product Liability) (Modification) Order 2000.
[269] G. Howells, 'Strict Liability', in G. Howells (ed.), *The Law of Product Liability* (2nd edn, Butterworths, London, 2007) pp. 265–442, at 4.58–4.73.
[270] Section 3(1).
[271] See *Abouzaid v Mothercare (UK) Ltd* [2000] All ER (D) 2436, paras 27–29 *per* Pill LJ.
[272] *Abouzaid, ibid.*
[273] See the two unsuccessful claims in *X v Schering Health Care Ltd* [2002] EWHC 1420 (QB) (claim that an oral contraceptive had increased the risk of thrombosis) and *Richardson v LRC Products Ltd* [2000] PIQR 164, QBD (claim in relation to a contraceptive that burst during intercourse).

that the issue is not what people expect, but what they are 'entitled' to expect. So, in a claim involving a burst condom, it was said that while users may expect condoms not to fail, they are not really entitled to this expectation, as they do, in fact, suffer from 'inexplicable failures'.[274] Of course, if a particular defect in the condom had been able to be established, then there would have been a claim. This again emphasises the importance of the burden of proof issue and being able to produce evidence pointing to a particular defect.[275]

In determining what persons generally are entitled to expect s. 3(2) provides also that account be taken of:

- the manner of marketing the product, its get-up, the use of any mark in relation to the product and any instructions or warnings given with the product:
  - for example, food which is marketed to children may be defective if it is unsafe for their consumption, even if an ordinary adult would be able to consume that food with no ill effect;[276]
  - as to warnings, the point is as to their potential to affect what consumers generally expect about the product, so, the lack of a warning might make a product defective, while the inclusion of a warning might mean that it is not defective;[277]
- what might reasonably be expected to be done with or in relation to the product:
  - for example, suppose uncooked red kidney beans are supplied without any indication that they may be harmful unless cooked in a particular way – is this is a danger which people are expected to know about or would be wise for the producer to give clear instructions as to use?

CASE

B v McDonald's Restaurants[278]

In this case the defendants had sold cups of tea and coffee at temperatures between 75°C and 90°C in polystyrene cups with lids on. The claimants, mainly children, some of whom were aged four or under, alleged that these constituted defective products. In rejecting this argument, Field J held that persons, generally, expect tea or coffee to be hot and that these are drinks normally consumed by adults and older teenagers who should realise that care must be taken to avoid spilling these drinks. Accordingly persons generally would not expect these drinks to be served at a much lower temperature.

- the time of supply – The point here is that product designs are very often made safer with the passage of time and, as long as I have supplied a product generally conforming to the

---

[274] See the *Richardson* case, *ibid*.

[275] For a recent example see *Ide v ATB Sales Ltd* [2008] EWCA Civ 424 (QB), where sufficient evidence was led to persuade the court that a bike handlebar had fractured due to a defect rather than as a result of the claimant losing control of the bike.

[276] Generally, see *A v National Blood Authority* [2001] 3 All ER (D) 289 at para. 22 (Burton J.).

[277] See *Worsley v Tambrands Ltd* [2000] PIQR 95.

[278] [2002] EWHC 490.

accepted standards at the time of supply, then this will normally be enough, but if it is already clear that there is a safer way to do it when I supply, then this will be more likely to lead to the conclusion that the product is defective.

A key decision on defectiveness is *A v National Blood Authority*.[279] In this case, blood contaminated with Hepatitis C was held to be defective. A key issue in this case was that the blood in question was what was described as a 'non-standard' product, which was 'unsafe' by virtue of the harmful characteristics they had and which the standard products did not have.[280]

The court focused on the legitimate public expectation of blood that is free from infection,[281] there being no warnings to change this expectation and it not being relevant that the medical profession (which is not 'persons generally') was aware of the risks.

In particular, also, the court emphasised the distinction from a negligence standard by saying[282] that the following issues (which would certainly be relevant in a negligence action) were not relevant here:

- the fault of the producer;
- the steps that the producer could have taken to make the product safer (that is, avoidability);
- whether the particular producer could or could not have done the same as other producers of similar products;
- the benefit to society or the utility of the product, except to the extent that there may be cases where the public is fully aware of the risk and accepts it because of the social utility of the product, for example, motor cars can kill when driven at a certain speed, but we all accept the need for cars;
- the fact that the NBA was under a statutory obligation to supply blood, so that they had no choice but to supply the blood, contaminated or not.

7.5.5 Damage

It will be recalled that the defect must cause 'damage'. This is defined in s. 5. It covers death, personal injury and damage to property that is ordinarily intended for private use, occupation or consumption and intended by the person suffering the loss for his own private use, occupation or consumption.[283] However, in the case of such property damage, recovery lies where the total damage exceeds £275 (if it does exceed this sum then the whole amount is claimable).[284]

---

[279] [2001] 3 All ER 289.

[280] Burton J, at 36.

[281] In other words, the potential for contaminated blood could not be treated in the same way as a sharp knife (that is, a risk which everyone accepted).

[282] At 68; and for a criticism of the strict approach (and arguing for more of a cost–benefit, negligence-based standard in relation to medical products) see R. Goldberg, 'Paying for Bad Blood: Strict Product Liability After the Hepatitis C Litigation' [2002] *MLR* 165, at p. 178 in particular. Whether or not a more negligence-based approach was ruled out by the National Blood Authority decision (and if it should be) where 'standard' products are concerned (that is, where the problem is a 'design defect', all products of that type being made that way, but this having safety problems) is a very complex question. For full consideration see G. Howells, 'Strict Liability', in G. Howells (ed.), *The Law of Product Liability, op. cit.*, pp. 265–442, at 4.173–180.

[283] Sections 5(1) and (3).

[284] Section 5(4).

It is important to note, however, that the 'property' damage that can be claimed for is a reference to property other than the defective product itself. It is stated that there is no liability for loss or damage to the product itself or the whole or any part of any product supplied with the product in question comprised in it.[285]

EXAMPLE

So, if a car is defective and crashes into a garden wall, there is a claim for the garden wall, as long as the damage to the wall exceeds £275. However, there is no claim for the damage caused to the car itself (or for any component part of the car, for example, the tyres) that were supplied with the car. However, if the damaged component part was actually not supplied with the car (for example, where new tyres have been fitted since purchase of the car) then there is a claim for the component part (for example, the tyres) as long as the damage exceeds £275.

This exclusion of a claim for the product itself broadly reflects the approach in the law of negligence where so-called 'pure economic loss' is not generally recoverable.[286] Of course, where there has been no incident actually inflicting damage on the product itself, but the product is simply of defective quality, there is no claim either (in this case there is no death, injury or damage to other property and, indeed, there is usually not a 'defect' in the first place as 'defect' is defined in terms of a *safety* – not simply a quality – problem). (Again this reflects the general position in negligence where economic loss is not recoverable.)

The problem here for consumers is that those who cannot use the implied terms (due to not being the buyer or because the producer is insolvent – see section 7.5.1) are unable to make use of the CPA to obtain redress against the producer where the product simply does not work or where it damages itself further, for example, a faulty wiring system damages the rest of the car (or even where the defects are dangerous, but have not actually damaged *other* property). The costs of putting the car right, making it safe, etc. are simply not covered by the CPA.

7.5.6 **Persons liable**

The claim can be made against producers, 'own branders' and those who have imported the product in the EU.[287] In cases where there is a long chain of distribution it may be difficult for the consumer to actually identify such parties. To help in this regard it is provided that the claimant may ask the party who supplied it at any stage in the process (whether retailer, wholesaler or whoever) to identify the producer, own brander or importer (if the request is made within a reasonable time and it is not reasonably practicable for the claimant to identify such parties himself). If the supplier fails to provide the information within a reasonable time then he is treated as being liable as if he was one of these parties.[288]

---

[285] Section 5(2).
[286] See *Murphy v Brentwood DC* [1991] 1 AC 398, and general works on negligence.
[287] Section 2(a)–(c).
[288] Section 2(3).

7.5.7 **Defences**

The defendant has a defence in the following circumstances:

- the defect is attributable to compliance with a statutory or Community obligation;[289]

- that the defendant did not at any time supply the product,[290] for example, the injury took place while the product was still on the premises of the defendant or after it had been stolen from his premises;

- that the supply by the defendant was not in the course of a business,[291] for example, it was supplied as a gift between family or friends;

- that the defect did not exist at the relevant time,[292] for example, goods are not defective when supplied by the defendant, but deteriorate later during transit by a third party for whom the defendant is not responsible;

- that the state of scientific or technical knowledge at the relevant time (that is, when the product was supplied) was not such that a producer of products of the same description as the product in question might be expected to have discovered the defect if it had existed in his products when they were under his control[293] (this is the so-called 'development risks' defence, which in essence, gives a defence where scientific and technical knowledge[294] at the time of original supply was not such as to have alerted producers to the defects that are now apparent, but[295] it was not allowed in the *National Blood Authority* case (above) because the risk of contamination was known at the time of the supply, it not being relevant that the actual contamination was not detectable);[296]

- that the defect was one in a subsequent product of which the product in question was comprised and was wholly attributable to the design of this subsequent product or to compliance with instructions given by the producer of the subsequent product[297] (this would protect a component producer where the problem arises from the design or the instructions of the end producer);

- that there has been contributory negligence by the claimant,[298] although, as always with this defence, it merely serves to reduce the damages claimable in proportion to the degree of contributory negligence.

---

[289] Section 4(1)(a).
[290] Section 4(1)(b).
[291] Section 4(1)(c).
[292] Section 4(1)(d).
[293] Section 4(1)(e).
[294] This knowledge being the most advanced available to anyone at the time, not simply what was available to the producer in question; the issue also being what could be *expected* of producers generally, not necessarily simply what was industry practice at the time: see Burton J in the *National Blood Authority* case at 49.
[295] On differences between the wording of the defence in the Directive and in s. 4 see the ECJ case *EC v UK* [1997] All ER (EC) 481.
[296] See also the approach to the defence (where it was also rejected) in the *Abouzaid* case (also discussed in relation to defectiveness above) and the approach taken in the ECJ case (*ibid.*) by Tesauro A.-G. at 933–935.
[297] Section 4(1)(f).
[298] Section 6(1).

7.5.8 Time limits

Action must be commenced within three years of the damage occurring or (if later) being discovered. However, no proceedings can be taken more than ten years after the defendant in question supplied the product.[299] So, even if the three-year period has still not expired, this ten-year rule may come into play and time bar a claim.

7.6 Performance Standards (4) – General product safety and food safety in public law

7.6.1 Introduction

Until 1961 there was no specific regulation of consumer safety in the UK. The Consumer Protection Acts 1961 and 1971, the Consumer Safety Act 1978 and the Consumer Safety (Amendment) Act 1986 progressively introduced a number of measures and control mechanisms intended to provide for product safety and culminated in the Consumer Protection Act 1987 Part II, which is still in force, but must now be read in the light of the General Product Safety Regulations 2005,[300] which replaced the General Product Safety Regulations 1994.[301] Although the General Product Safety Regulations 2005 apply to food, they do so only where some other, more specific regulation is inapplicable. This means that use of the 2005 Regulations will be rare as most of the law relating to food safety is based on the provisions of the Food Safety Act 1990 and the General Food Regulations 2002.[302] Generally, the earlier legislation worked on a vertical basis by giving powers to create regulations to deal with specific types of product and identified safety risks, for example, neck cords on children's clothing, electrical appliances, flammable materials in furniture products, etc. However, it will be seen that more recent attempts at the regulation of product safety operate on an horizontal basis.

7.6.2 Reasons for regulating product safety

Regulating the safety of consumer goods is undoubtedly justified, but an important consideration is how far it should go. It would be possible to look for absolute safety, but that would impose burdens on business that some would regard as unwarranted.

Generally, the main reason for legislating in respect of unsafe consumer goods is information-related since if consumers are unaware of hidden or long-term risks there is a justification for protecting them from those risks. This is especially so where simple market pressures are not sufficient to compel producers to give consumers the necessary information. Generally,

---

[299] See Sch. 1 to the CPA, amending the Limitation Act 1980.
[300] SI 2005/1803, giving effect to the General Product Safety Directive, Dir 2001/95/EC.
[301] SI 1994/2328.
[302] EC 178/2002.

market pressures persuade manufacturers to highlight the positive aspects of their goods, but what manufacturer is going to voluntarily highlight the fact that there is a chance that consumers will be killed or seriously injured if they use a particular product? This may also be viewed as a paternalistic argument premised on the belief that consumers are not well positioned to assess risks and take steps to guard against them, so that State intervention is justified to guard against the risks posed by unsafe goods.

A further issue is that of externalities, namely, the potential that a product has to cause harm to persons other than the purchaser, for example, a defective car wheel may well result in injury to the owner of a car, but injury may also be sustained by other road users, including pedestrians. While a purchaser can claim the protection of his contract with the person who sold the vehicle, the same is not true of a mere bystander or even a relative of the purchaser.

Generally, the approach to consumer safety is based on an economic approach which suggests that consumer safety is desirable but only to the extent that the economic benefits of regulation do not outweigh the costs imposed by regulation. Accordingly, what is sought is not absolute safety, but instead a risk of harm that is reduced to the extent that is optimally efficient. However, there are those who are uncomfortable with the idea that death or physical injury should be subject to economic considerations along these lines.

On occasions, it also appears that there may be political considerations where consumer safety is concerned. For example, tragic safety errors can produce dramatic press headlines which may create political pressure to intervene in the form of new legislation. It is not difficult to see how tragedies connected to the drug Thalidomide or the BSE scare and its connection to its human form, Creutzfeldt–Jakob Disease, created sufficient political pressure to prompt legislative action to address the public concerns. This range of justificatory reasons for legislative intervention may suggest that consumer safety policy may not have developed on an entirely rational basis.

7.6.3 The General Product Safety Regulations 2005

In 1989 the EC Commission produced its Directive on General Product Safety, since there was a perceived imbalance between the approach to consumer safety adopted in different Member States. Some had horizontal legislation of sorts on the matter of safety, but other Member States had only specific vertical legislation. One of the problems associated with the introduction of a Community-wide horizontal safety requirement was how to dovetail existing domestic laws with the laws introduced to comply with the Directive. In the event, it was decided that any attempt at seeking to identify areas of overlap would be too difficult, with the result that the original General Product Safety Regulations 1994 and the Consumer Protection Act 1987 (CPA) are quite separate provisions, not in any way related to each other. However, there were definite areas of overlap between the two, with the result that a person could contravene both sets of rules. In other respects the two sets of rules differ with the result that a trader might comply with one set of rules but offend against another set. The revised 2005 Regulations go some way to rationalising the law further and may effectively mean that the provisions of the CPA are no longer of any use, and s. 10 has been deleted by GPSR 2005, reg. 46. Particular reference is then made to matters such as the presentation or labelling of the product and the category of consumers at risk when using the product.

LEGISLATIVE PROVISION

GENERAL PRODUCT SAFETY REGULATIONS

The key element of the GPSR 2005 is the General Safety requirement stated in reg. 5(1) which provides that: 'No producer shall place a product on the market unless the product is a safe product.'

For these purposes, reg. 2 defines a safe product as one which 'under normal or reasonably foreseeable conditions of use, including duration . . . does not present any risk or only the minimum risks compatible with the product's use, considered as acceptable and consistent with a high level of protection for the safety and health of persons . . .'

The term 'producer' is defined by reg. 2 to include manufacturers, if based in the EU, and own branders, and if the manufacturer is not based in the EU, the term includes any representative which is EU-based or, in all other cases, the importer into the EU.

The general liability of producers in reg. 5(1) not to place unsafe products on the market is augmented by reg. 7 which obliges producers, where appropriate, to supply information, such as warnings, concerning possible risks associated with a product. Further 'distributors' of products have an obligation to 'participate in monitoring the safety' of products placed on the market, for example, by keeping documentation necessary for tracing the origin of a product.

The Regulations do not seek to set a standard of absolute safety, since this would be economically inefficient. As with the 1987 Act, the aim is to reduce risks to an acceptable level compatible with the intended use of the product.

As regards products covered by the 2005 Regulations, reg. 2 defines a product as 'any product intended for consumers or likely to be used by consumers, supplied whether for consideration or not in the course of a commercial activity and whether new, used or reconditioned'. Since the supply must be in the course of a commercial activity, it is clear that private sales are not intended to be covered. Moreover, only consumer goods are included in the definition, so that an item of heavy lifting gear intended for use only by building contractors would fall outside the definition. The definition clearly includes secondhand goods, which are not covered by the Consumer Protection Act 1987. However, some secondhand goods are excluded by reg. 4 which states that the regulations do not apply to products supplied for repair or reconditioning before use. It is also important to note that the 1987 Act excluded a number of consumer goods by virtue of the fact that there was more detailed regulation elsewhere, such as food, medicines, water and gas. These products are not excluded from the scope of the 2005 Regulations, with the result that food may fall within this set of safety requirements. Although it is unlikely that the GPSR 2005 will need to be invoked in respect of food, there is the possibility that they might be relevant to safety and novel foods, namely, a substance used as a food where it was not previously so used.

Perhaps the most innovative feature of the 2005 Regulations are the new powers vested in 'enforcement authorities', consisting of suspension notices,[303] warning notices,[304] withdrawal

---

[303] GPSR 2005, reg. 11.
[304] *Ibid.*, reg. 13.

notices[305] and recall notices.[306] These largely replace as an enforcement 'code' the provisions in the CPA concerning *prohibition notices, notices to warn, suspension notices and forfeiture orders*. Much of the new law is self-explanatory. If a product is considered not to reach the required standard of safety, the continued supply of it can be prevented temporarily through an application for a suspension notice and if necessary the product or a range of products may be withdrawn from the market through the use of a withdrawal notice. Perhaps the most significant new provision is the 'recall notice' which had long been argued for. However, an order for recall of a line of products may only be sought where no other action would be sufficient to prevent the risk.[307] If loss is caused to a producer by the requirements of complying with either a withdrawal or a recall notice, the authority is liable to compensate the producer if the product was not in fact dangerous and the notice was not 'triggered' by any act or default on the part of the producer.[308]

7.6.4 Food safety

Food safety is regulated under the Food Safety Act 1990 and various regulations made thereunder in respect of specific food issues. The regulation of the safety of food, as a product, has two focal points, namely, whether food is unsafe or injurious to health, but there are also provisions relating to the quality of food and general consumer protection concerns. Wider concerns, such as food and food premises hygiene, food labelling and hazard and crisis management, are also addressed, but are beyond the scope of this chapter.

The Food Safety Act 1990 ss. 7–9 replicate the requirements of the EC General Food Safety Regulation,[309] Art. 14(1) to the effect that no food is to be placed on the market if it is unsafe to the extent that it is injurious to health or unfit for human consumption.[310]

Under the Food Safety Act 1990, s. 7 it is a criminal offence for a person to render food injurious to health by adding an article to food, using an article as an ingredient in food, abstracting a constituent element from food or subjecting food to a process with the intent that it shall be sold for human consumption. Section 7 is unusual to the extent that it does require proof of intent on the part of a food producer, as opposed to the majority of offences under the Food Safety Act 1990 which impose strict criminal liability. For the purposes of s. 7, it must be established that the food is, in fact, injurious to health, which requires a court to have regard to not only the probable immediate and short-term or long-term effects of the food on the health of a person consuming it, but also on subsequent generations, the probable toxic effects of the food and the particular health sensitivities of a specific category of consumers where the food is intended for that category.[311] What is clear is that the offence of rendering food injurious to health requires some form of positive conduct in adding or taking something away from food on the part of the person charged, so that the process of natural decomposition will not be covered. As deliberate contamination of food by producers

---

[305] *Ibid.*, reg. 14.
[306] *Ibid.*, reg. 15.
[307] *Ibid.*, reg. 15(4).
[308] *Ibid.*, reg. 16(5) and reg. 16(6).
[309] EC 178/2002, given effect in the UK by the General Food Regulations 2004, SI 2004/3279.
[310] General Food Safety Regulations 2004, Art. 14(2).
[311] Regulation 178/2002 EC, Art. 14(4).

is now comparatively rare, it seems likely that the offence will rarely be invoked as the most common form of deliberate contamination, namely acts of food terrorism, are covered by other specific provisions.[312]

The Food Safety Act 1990, s. 8 relating to the sale of food that fails to satisfy food safety requirements has been modified by the General Food Regulations 2004.[313] For these purposes, in determining if food is unsafe, regard should be paid to the normal conditions of use of the food by the consumer and at each stage of the production, processing and distribution and to the information provided to the consumer, including anything contained in a label and information available to consumers regarding the avoidance of adverse health risks.[314] The normal conditions of use are likely to include the process of cooking or processing so that there may be circumstances in which the process of cooking or other processing has the effect of rendering safe something that might have previously posed a risk in its natural state or the state in which it arrived in the UK.[315]

Under the Food Safety Act 1990, s. 8 originally used the phrase 'unfit for human consumption', which was interpreted to mean more than merely 'unsuitable' so that the food had to be 'putrid, diseased or unwholesome'[316] in order to offend against the section. However, this did mean that food that was not detrimental to health *per se* could nonetheless be unfit. How the ECJ interprets the phrase remains to be seen, as the new definition of the term 'unsafe' includes unacceptability for human consumption.[317] Section 8 also referred to 'contaminated' food in order to deal with cases in which food contained something harmless, but unacceptable, such as a piece of string in a loaf of bread.[318] However, this is no longer required as the concept of unfitness is defined in terms of unacceptability in Art. 14(5) of the European General Food Safety Regulation, which will cover such cases.

Unusually, the Food Safety Act 1990, s. 14 addresses the issue of food quality, a general consumer protection issue, through the use of a strict liability criminal offence. Section 14(1) provides that it is an offence for a person to sell, to the purchaser's prejudice, any food, intended for human consumption,[319] which is not of the nature, substance or quality demanded by the purchaser. Food which is not of the nature demanded appears to cover cases in which the thing supplied is not of the expected variety.[320] Food not of the substance demanded is a phrase intended to cover the presence of unwanted foreign objects.[321] However, this did not mean that in every case the presence of unwanted material resulted in the commission of an offence, since harmlessness is a factor that may be taken into account.[322] Food not of the quality demanded requires a court to consider if the required standard of commercial quality[323] has been met and means more than merely non-correspondence with a description,

---

[312] See Public Order Act 1986, s. 38.
[313] SI 2004/3279, implementing the General Food Safety Regulation EC 178/2002.
[314] *Ibid.*, EC General Food Safety Regulation 2002, Art. 14(3).
[315] See, for example, *R v Archer, ex p Barrow, Lane & Ballard Ltd* (1983) 147 JPR 503 (contaminated dates rendered wholesome by processing into brown sauce).
[316] See *David Greig Ltd v Goldfinch* (1961) 105 Sol Jo 367; *Miller v Battersea BC* [1956] 1 QB 43.
[317] EC General Food Safety Regulation 2002, Art. 14(5).
[318] *Turner & Sons Ltd v Owen* [1956] 1 QB 48.
[319] Food Safety Act 1990, s. 14(2).
[320] For example, *Meah v Roberts* [1978] 1 All ER 97 (caustic soda supplied as lemonade); *Shearer v Rowe* (1985) 149 JP 698 (minced beef containing pork and lamb) and indeed, the 2013 scandal of horsemeat found in mince beef products.
[321] See *Smedleys Ltd v Breed* [1974] AC 839 (caterpillar in a tin of peas).
[322] See *Edwards v Llaethdy Meirion Ltd* [1957] Crim LR 402.
[323] *Anness v Grivell* [1915] 3 KB 685.

so that if the consumer is given high-quality minced beef with a very high fat content[324] or a diet drink that contains excess quantities of sugar,[325] the food may not be of the quality demanded. The three elements in s. 14(1) do tend to overlap so that it is possible that the supplier may offend against more than one requirement and it is also possible that food may be both qualitatively defective and unsafe at the same time.

In order for an offence to have been committed under s. 14, the purchaser must have been prejudiced. This requirement is not restricted to cases of actual damage or pecuniary loss since a purchaser is prejudiced by asking for one thing and receiving another.[326] Finally, in order for s. 14 to apply, there must have been a demand on the part of the purchaser that the food should be of a particular nature, substance or quality. For these purposes, if there is a recognised statutory standard for a particular type of food, the consumer will be presumed to have demanded that standard. However, in most cases it will be necessary to discern from the circumstances what has been asked for. For example, if different qualities are available for sale at different prices, a cheaper price may indicate that a lower standard has been asked for.[327]

The offences under the Food Safety Act 1990 are all offences of strict liability, but a defendant can seek to avoid liability by raising the statutory due diligence defence under s. 21, which requires the defendant to set up a system designed to guard against the commission of the offence charged by taking all reasonable precautions. In addition, the mere existence of a system, on paper, will not be enough, as the defence also requires the defendant to act with due diligence in putting those reasonable precautions into effect. For example, a contractor engaging a third party pest control company, with a system to report back any action needed by the contractor, such as to fit bristles under doors, is not in itself enough; it must be a robust protocol and it must be followed by the contractor.[328]

7.7 Unfair terms

7.7.1 Introduction

In this section we will be considering the legal controls over unfair terms in contracts with consumers. The big problem here is that the terms are often in so-called 'standard form contracts' or standardised notices on walls, tickets, etc. This may result in:

(a) *lack of transparency*: terms may be in small print or unclear legal jargon; sentences and paragraphs may be badly structured and hard to follow; and there may be so many terms, dealing with different and complex issues (and so little time), that consumers would never be able to read them, so the consumer does not have a real chance of understanding what he is agreeing to;

(b) *lack of choice*: most traders may use the same terms and if the consumer wishes to buy the goods they may have little real choice;

[324] *TW Lawrence Ltd v Burleigh* (1981) 146 JP 134.
[325] *McDonald's Hamburgers Ltd v Windle* (1986) 151 JP 333.
[326] *Hoyle v Hitchman* (1879) 4 QBD 233.
[327] See *Goldup v John Manson Ltd* [1982] QB 161.
[328] *R (on the application of Tesco Stores Ltd) v City of London Corporation* [2010] EWHC 2920 (Admin).

(c) *inequality of bargaining power*: consumers in particular tend not to have the bargaining power to force the trader to change terms as they tend to be less skilled in bargaining and not to be sufficiently important as individual customers to be able to force the trader to alter the terms;

(d) *unfairness in substance*: the resulting terms may allow the trader to escape important responsibilities to the consumer (so-called 'exemption clauses') or impose unfair obligations or liabilities on the consumer (for example, terms allowing the price to be increased, requiring full payment in advance in building contracts or imposing unfair bank charges).

This section explains the rules that have developed to address these problems. Essentially the story is of common law rules that were very limited in addressing the problems, followed by statutory controls that have been much more successful.

7.7.2 **Common law**

Before proper statutory controls were introduced, judges did show an awareness of the unfairness problems caused by standard form contracts. In *Suisse Atlantique SA v Rotterdamsche Kolen Centrale*, Lord Reid recognised the procedural problems arising in standard form contracts. He said:

> In the ordinary way the customer has no time to read [the standard terms], and if he did read them he would probably not understand them. And if he did understand and object to any of them, he would generally be told he could take it or leave it. And if he went to another supplier the result would be the same. Freedom to contract must surely imply some choice or room for bargaining.[329]

The problem was that the common law rules were completely inadequate to address the problems. A basic common law requirement is that terms on notices, tickets or in any standardised form, have to be '*incorporated*' to even be part of the contract (and, obviously if they are not part of the contract they do not have any effect, so they cannot be relied upon by the business against the consumer in court).

However, generally, terms are incorporated as long as there is notice of them.[330] This only deals with one aspect of fairness, that is, transparency, and the actual standard of transparency required is low. Where unsigned documents are concerned, the general rule is that there should be reasonable notice.[331] However, this means simply that the consumer should be made aware of the *existence* of terms. It does not generally matter whether the terms are in plain language, decent-sized print, well-structured and cross-referenced, etc., if (given subject matter and complexity) there is time to read and understand them or if particularly onerous, unusual or important terms have been drawn to the attention of the consumer (all of the things that are now required under the good faith concept in the Unfair Terms in Consumer Contracts Regulations – see next section).

In the case of unsigned documents, there *is* a higher standard of transparency (that is, a requirement to highlight/give prominence to the term) where terms are 'particularly onerous or unusual'.[332] (If this highlighting does not take place the term is treated as not having been incorporated into the contract.) However, this only applies in fairly extreme cases. 'Particularly onerous' has tended to mean that the term excludes some particularly important liability

---

[329] [1967] 1 AC 361 at 406.
[330] *Parker v SE Ry Co* (1877) 2 CPD 416.
[331] *Ibid.*
[332] *Interfoto Picture Library Ltd v Stiletto Visual Programmes Ltd* [1989] QB 433 and see above, section 7.4.2.4.

(for example, implied terms as to quality, etc. or liability for death or injury)[333] or imposes an extremely onerous obligation or liability (for example, as in *Interfoto*, a charge of nearly £4,000 for late return of photographic transparencies).[334] This will not cover the vast majority of terms, for example, those excluding or limiting liability for late delivery, misrepresentation, negligence causing economic loss or damage to property, allowing traders to vary or terminate performance, imposing unfair charges, requiring full payment in advance and allowing for unfair forms of enforcement by the trader. 'Particularly unusual' means not typical in the sector in question (in *Interfoto* the charge was many times greater than was normal for other similar traders). Clearly most terms will not be covered by this, as many will be routinely used, so that they will not be 'particularly unusual'.

In addition, this highlighting rule does not apply at all (that is even where outrageous terms, like those excluding liability for death or injury, are concerned) in the case of signed documents. In the case of signed documents the rule is still that the consumer is bound by virtue of the signature,[335] irrespective of how outrageous terms are in what they provide for and regardless of how unclear the terms are, whether there is small print, etc.

There are various other instances in which terms will not be treated as incorporated. First of all the term must have been incorporated before or at the time the contract is made. The classic example is *Olley v Marlborough Court Hotel*[336] where the notice in the hotel room came too late, the contract having been concluded before the guest reached the room. In addition, the document containing the terms must be a 'contractual document', that is, one in which one would reasonably expect to find terms. A mere receipt has been held to fall foul of this test.[337] However, these do not address the general problem of lack of transparency. So long as traders ensure there is notice of terms at the time of the contract and that they are in a proper contractual document, they will be incorporated under the general test and it will be irrelevant that they lack transparency.

Another approach taken by the courts was under the rules on '*construction*' of terms. Basically this means interpretation. The approach was that courts would try to interpret the terms in ways that favoured the consumer. Exemption clauses are construed strictly. This means that, in deciding if the clause covers the obligation or liability in question, the court should ask if the 'intent is clear, unambiguous and incapable of misleading'.[338]

So a reference to exclusion or limitation of 'warranties' will not cover exclusion or limitation of conditions, and an exclusion or limitation of 'implied conditions and warranties' will not cover express terms.[339] Closely associated with strict construction is the *contra proferentem* rule, which interprets ambiguities against the interests of the party relying on the clause. It has been said that these rules should be applied less rigorously to limitation as opposed to outright exclusion clauses.[340] An exemption clause will also be constructed, where possible,

---

[333] *Spurling v Bradshaw* [1956] 1 WLR 461 and *Thornton v Shoe Lane Parking* [1971] 2 QB 163.
[334] *Interfoto Picture Library Ltd v Stiletto Visual Programmes Ltd* [1989] QB 433.
[335] See *L'Estrange v Graucob* [1934] 2 KB 394 and *Peninsula Business Services v Sweeney* [2004] IRLR 49.
[336] [1949] 1 KB 532.
[337] *Chapelton v Barry Urban DC* [1940] 1 KB 532.
[338] *Mannai Investment Co Ltd v Eagle Star Life Assurance Co Ltd* [1997] 3 All ER 352 at 377.
[339] *Wallis, Son and Wells v Pratt and Haynes* [1911] AC 394, and *White v John Warwick and Co Ltd* [1953] 1 WLR 1285.
[340] *Ailsa Craig Fishing Co Ltd v Malvern Fishing Co Ltd* [1983] 1 WLR 964, HL *per* Lord Fraser at 970 and approved by the House of Lords in *George Mitchell (Chesterhall) Ltd v Finney Lock Seeds Ltd* [1983] 2 AC 803 at 810, 813 and 817.

so as not to cover a fundamental breach of contract or so as to allow the main purpose of the contract to be defeated.[341]

Ultimately, these construction rules were ineffective at controlling unfair terms. The bottom line was that if the term was clear enough in terms of the effect it was trying to have, then there was nothing the courts could do but to give effect to it. So, construction rules might force businesses to express specific terms a bit more clearly. However, this would not mean that the terms were not still in small print and dealing with complex issues that consumers would not understand even if they read them.

Rules on incorporation and construction, therefore, do not properly address the problems of terms and contracts being unclear to consumers. In addition, of course, these rules did nothing to deal with the problems of lack of choice, inequality of bargaining power and unfairness in substance.

There are some other common law controls. Even if an exemption clause has been incorporated into the contract and, as a matter of construction, covers the obligation or liability in question, it cannot be relied upon if at the time of the contract the seller or supplier has misrepresented its effect to the buyer[342] or if the seller or supplier has made an oral promise which is inconsistent with the purported effect of the clause.[343] However, these only deal with exceptional cases and all the trader need do is to ensure that he does not mislead the consumer as to what is in the document.

7.7.3 Unfair Contract Terms Act 1977

The Unfair Contract Terms Act (UCTA) 1977 was passed after two Law Commission Reports had proposed statutory control over exemption clauses.[344] The Law Commission Reports could see that the common law controls were insufficient. In summary, UCTA makes some exemption clauses completely ineffective and makes others subject to a reasonableness test.

LEGISLATIVE PROVISION

KEY POINTS

Totally ineffective

- Excluding or restricting liability for negligence causing death or injury (s. 2(1)).
- Excluding or restricting liability for implied terms as to description, quality and fitness (ss. 6(2) and (3)).

Subject to reasonableness test

- Excluding various other liabilities (ss. 2(2), 8 and 3).

The reasonableness test itself

- Contained in s. 11.

---

[341] *Photo Production Ltd v Securicor Transport Ltd* [1980] AC 827 and *Glynn v Margetson & Co* [1893] AC 351.
[342] *Curtis v Chemical Cleaning and Dying Co Ltd* [1951] 1 KB 805.
[343] *J Evans & Son (Portsmouth) Ltd v Andrea Merzario Ltd* [1976] 1 WLR 1078.
[344] 'Exemption Clauses in Contracts, First Report' (1969) Law Com No 24 and 'Exemption Clauses in Contracts, Second Report' (1975) No 69.

7.7.3.1 Completely ineffective

(a) Excluding or restricting liability for negligence causing death or injury

Under the Unfair Contract Terms Act (UCTA) 1977, terms that exclude or restrict liability for negligently causing death or personal injury are wholly ineffective.[345] This would cover, for example, a term excluding liability for death or injury caused by the tort of negligence or by breach of the implied term as to reasonable care and skill in a service contract (a term implied by s. 13 of the Supply of Goods and Services Act 1982). Note such terms are ineffective whether the party affected by them is a consumer or is acting in the course of a business.

EXAMPLE

John is a builder and visits another builder's yard on business accompanied by his brother, Joe (who has no connection with the business). They are both injured by falling debris (caused by the negligence of the builder's yard). The builder's yard tries to escape liability on the basis of a very large notice that is displayed at the entrance to the yard, saying: THE PROPRIETORS ARE NOT RESPONSIBLE FOR LOSS OR INJURY, HOWSOEVER CAUSED.

This clause is ineffective under s. 2(1) against both John and Joe and they can both claim damages for negligence.

The idea of this ban seems to be that it is *always* wrong to allow a careless party to escape liability for such serious consequences (remember this is not allowed no matter how clear the term is or on any grounds at all – we will see below that some terms are subject to a reasonableness or fairness test, which means that they might be allowed depending on all the circumstances).

(b) Excluding or restricting liability for implied terms as to description, quality and fitness

Also completely ineffective are terms that exclude or restrict liability for breach of the implied terms as to description, quality, fitness, etc. *in consumer contracts.*[346]

EXAMPLE

When you buy a defective TV, car, computer, etc. for your private use there can be no restriction or exclusion of your right to any of the relevant remedies (for example, damages, repair, replacement, etc.). See Chapter 4 and section 5.7 for full details of the implied terms and the remedies.

The Law Commissions recommended these bans because they thought that the implied terms gave important 'social rights' that businesses should not be able to take away.[347] They also

---

[345] Section 2(1).
[346] Sections 6(2) and 7(2).
[347] Law Commission, 'Second Report on Exemption Clauses', 1975.

agreed with the view of the Molony Committee to the effect that the result of such exclusions was that 'heavy and irrecoverable loss may fall upon the consumer who is unlucky enough to get a defective article'.[348]

Note that this ban only applies to consumer contracts. The definition is contained in s. 12 of the Act and its consequences are as follows. First of all, the buyer must not be acting in the course of a business (or holding himself out as so doing).[349] The typical private buyer buying, for example, household goods, a vehicle, a holiday or insurance is clearly not making the contract in the course of a business. However, what if someone buys goods for both private and business use? The purchase is not 'in the course of a business' merely because of the element of business purpose – purpose is not really the issue. It has been held that the contract is not made 'in the course of a business' unless the purchase is an integral part of the business.[350] A purchase is clearly integral to the business if it involves the type of goods which that business would typically buy for resale. However, it has been held not to cover the sort of goods that would simply be stock in trade goods for use in the business (for example, vehicles bought by a shipping firm[351] or office chairs bought by a solicitor). Seemingly these are only bought in the course of a business if they are bought on a regular basis or if the purchase is a one-off venture with a view to making a profit.[352]

The second requirement is that the other party *does* make the contract in the course of a business,[353] which means that the seller, supplier or other party who is using the exemption clause must be acting in the course of a business. This covers any transaction that is integral to business activities, including sales which are regular and typical for the business and on-off trade ventures, and probably also sales of assets previously used in the business, even if the sale is only to get rid of old stock and the sale of such assets is not regular.[354]

Next, the goods must be of the type 'ordinarily supplied for private use or consumption' unless the party not acting in the course of a business is an individual, in which case even if the goods are not of this type the contract can still be a consumer one.[355] Even where the buyer is not an individual (for example, where a shipping firm buys a car – see the *R and B Customs* case below) there is no requirement that the goods be of a type that are ordinarily used *exclusively* for private use or consumption. Goods such as computers are ordinarily used privately and in business, and would still qualify.

Next, there will not be a consumer contract, if the consumer is an individual and the goods are secondhand goods sold at public auction at which individuals have the opportunity of attending the sale in person or, if he is not an individual and the goods are sold by auction or by competitive tender.[356]

Finally, it is for the party alleging that the other is not dealing as a consumer to prove this.[357]

---

[348] Law Commission, 'First Report on Exemption Clauses', para. 68.

[349] Section 12(1)(a).

[350] *R & B Customs Brokers Co Ltd* v *United Dominions Trust Ltd* [1988] 1 All ER 847 and *Feldaroll Foundry PLC* v *Hermes Leasing (London) Ltd* [2004] EWCA Civ 747; (2004) 101(24) LSG 32.

[351] *Ibid.*

[352] *Ibid.*

[353] Section 12(1)(b).

[354] *Stevenson* v *Rogers* [1999] QB 1028.

[355] Section 12(1)(c) and s. 12(1A).

[356] Section 12(2).

[357] Section 12(3).

7.7.3.2 The UCTA reasonableness test

Terms controlled

Other terms are subject to a test of 'reasonableness'. First of all, these include terms in non-consumer contracts excluding the implied terms as to description, quality and fitness in supply of goods contracts.[358] Then, applicable to consumer contracts (as well as, often, to businesses) the reasonableness test applies to terms excluding or restricting liability for:

- *negligence* causing losses other than death or injury, for example, loss or damage to property;[359]
- *misrepresentation*;[360]
- *breach of express promises*, for example, promises as to time or place of delivery.[361]

The test also applies to terms allowing the trader to *offer a contractual performance substantially different from that reasonably expected or no performance at all*.[362] This covers the sort of term that gives businesses discretion in how they perform. Such terms are used all the time by businesses such as gyms, mobile phone companies, Internet providers, etc. A classic example, used by a shipping company, is:

> Steamers, Sailing Dates, Rates and Itineraries are subject to change without notice.[363]

The test

LEGISLATIVE PROVISION

The general test is set out in s. 11(1) which says that:

> In relation to a contract term, the requirement of reasonableness . . . is that the term shall have been a fair and reasonable one to be included having regard to the circumstances which were or ought reasonably to have been known to or in the contemplation of the parties when the contract was made.

The first thing to point out is that the very nature of a 'reasonableness' test is that it looks at a range of matters and balances them against each other. This means that it is very difficult to predict what the result will be in any given case, as some things about the term might be reasonable and others not. In addition, the higher courts will be reluctant to set aside a decision of a lower court and will only do so where it has 'proceeded upon some erroneous principles or was plainly or obviously wrong'.[364]

---

[358] Sections 6(3) and 7(3).

[359] Section 2(2) (always applicable to both business-to-consumer and business-to-business contracts).

[360] Section 8 (always applicable to both business-to-consumer and business-to-business contracts).

[361] Section 3(2)(a) the reasonableness test only protects business customers where the term in question is in the 'written standard terms' of the business using it (see s. 3).

[362] Section 3(2)(b) (again, the test only applies to these terms in business-to-business contracts on written standard terms).

[363] From *Anglo-Continental Holidays* v *Typaldos (London) Ltd* [1967] 2 Lloyd's Rep 61, CA, 462, cited in the Law Commission Report, 1975.

[364] Lord Bridge in *George Mitchell (Chesterhall) Ltd* v *Finney Seeds Ltd* [1983] 2 AC 803 at 810.

First of all, the courts look at the *relative bargaining power* of the parties.[365] The average consumer will be viewed as being weak relative to the average business, and this criterion will usually count against the term in consumer cases.[366]

Then there is the question of the *choices or alternatives* which were (or were not) available. The courts have adopted this line of thinking: a term is more likely to be reasonable if the business in question or a competitor offered a reasonable alternative,[367] that is, a term that does not exclude as much, or any, liability, but perhaps meaning that the goods or services cost a bit more.[368]

Another factor which has been identified by the courts is *whether the task in respect of which liability is being excluded or restricted is a particularly difficult one.*[369] It might be that a seller or supplier has promised a certain level of quality or has promised to carry out a repair or replacement in certain defined circumstances. However, it may be that specialist workmanship is necessary to achieve the level of quality promised or to carry out the repair effectively or that the range of sources from which a replacement is available is very limited. In such circumstances a clause excluding or limiting liability for non-performance of the relevant promise is more likely to be reasonable. However, there appears to be a *general policy against allowing exclusion of liability for negligence* and this is likely to weigh strongly where the task in question is not particularly difficult.[370]

The courts also consider in a broad sense, the *'practical consequences'* of the decision on the question of reasonableness.[371] This involves looking at the *sums of money involved for both parties and the impact upon the parties of upholding or disallowing the clause.* Where consumers are concerned the large loss which may flow from the breach may tend to count against the term.[372]

In this context it is of particular relevance to consider the *possibilities for either party to have insured against the type of risk in question.*[373] This involves looking not only at the cost of insurance but also at its availability in the practical circumstances of the case. So it is relevant to consider if, for whatever reason, there was limited time for one or both parties to arrange insurance.[374]

The courts are also likely to consider *whether or not the buyer has received an inducement* (for example, a lower price) to agree to a term (see Sch. 2, para. (b)) and *if the term places an unreasonable condition on liability*, for example an unreasonable time limit on making a claim – 'all claims within 28 days' (see Sch. 2, para. (d)).

---

[365] *Smith* v *Eric S Bush* [1989] 2 All ER 514.

[366] *Ibid.,* at 531.

[367] *Ibid.*

[368] See *ibid.* and *George Mitchell (Chesterhall) Ltd* v *Finney Lockseeds Ltd* [1983] 2 AC 803 where there was no choice and compare with *RW Green Ltd* v *Cade Bros Farm* [1978] 1 Lloyd's Rep 602 where there was a choice.

[369] *Smith* v *Eric S Bush* [1989] 2 All ER 514 at 531.

[370] See *George Mitchell (Chesterhall) Ltd* v *Finney Lockseeds Ltd* [1983] 2 AC 803, *Smith* v *Eric S Bush* [1989] 2 All ER 514 and *Britvic Soft Drinks* v *Messer UK Ltd* [2002] 2 Lloyd's Rep 368 where there was negligence and compare with *RW Green Ltd* v *Cade Bros Farm* [1978] 1 Lloyd's Rep 602 where there was no negligence.

[371] *Smith* v *Eric S Bush* [1989] 2 All ER 514 at 531.

[372] *Ibid.,* at 514.

[373] *Ibid*; *Sonicare International Ltd* v *East Anglia Freight Terminal Ltd* [1997] 2 Lloyd's Rep 48 and *George Mitchell (Chesterhall) Ltd* v *Finney Lockseeds Ltd* [1983] 2 AC 803.

[374] *Phillips Products Ltd* v *Hyland* [1987] 2 All ER 620.

The courts will also follow Sch. 2 and consider whether the customer 'knew or ought reasonably to have known of the existence and extent of the term' (see para. (c)). This clearly involves consideration as to *how transparent the term is to the buyer*.[375] There has been some suggestion in a Scottish case that transparency may be a prerequisite of reasonableness.[376]

However, it is very important to note in this context that the extent of knowledge and understanding that might be expected here is likely to be greater than what would be expected under the common law incorporation principles discussed above. In *Britvic Soft Drinks* v *Messer*, para. 21, Mance LJ said that it is 'legitimate to consider and take into account the actual extent of knowledge of a party, however much he or it may, under ordinary contractual principles, have become contractually bound by the particular term(s)'.

So, terms that are in small print or unclear language might be incorporated under the common law rules but fail the UCTA test of reasonableness.

7.7.4 The Unfair Terms in Consumer Contracts Regulations 1999 (UTCCR)

7.7.4.1 Introduction and relationship with UCTA

These Regulations were passed in order to implement the EC Directive on Unfair Terms in Consumer Contracts of 1993 (93/13/EC). They do not actually ban any terms outright like UCTA, although the UCTA bans on these terms were kept in place by the government. Also, the UCTA reasonableness test still applies to the terms outlined above.

The UTCCR apply a test of unfairness; although this only applies to contracts where the buyer is a private consumer (consumer contracts).[377] So, basically, in consumer contracts, terms must pass both the UCTA reasonableness test *and* the test of fairness in the UTCCR. However, the UTCCR does not apply to business-to-business contracts, so at the moment the only control in such contracts is under UCTA.

The Law Commission reviewed this regime in a report in 2005.[378] A key recommendation was to unify the UCTA and UTCCR rules into a single regime, the idea being to reduce the complexity caused by having two overlapping regimes.[379] We shall turn to the Law Commission proposals below.

7.7.4.2 More terms than UCTA

Unlike UCTA, the UTCCR does not only cover exemption clauses (that is, where the trader is trying to avoid liability to the consumer). It also covers terms that *impose unfair obligations and*

---

[375] See *Stag Line Ltd* v *Tyne Repair Group Ltd ('The Zinnia')* [1984] 2 Lloyd's Rep 211 at 222.

[376] *Knight Machinery (Holding) Ltd* v *Rennie* 1995 SLT 166.

[377] In order to be a consumer one must be buying for purposes outside a business, trade or profession (reg. 2(1)); which may mean that a business buying something that is not integral to the business (e.g. the shipping firm buying the car in the *R and B* case above) is not a consumer under the UTCCR, because such a purchase is nevertheless for a business purpose.

[378] Unfair Terms in Contracts, Law Com No 292 and Scot Law Com No 199.

[379] *Ibid.*, Part 3.

liabilities on the consumer. As the House of Lords have put it, *'imposing on the consumer . . . a disadvantageous burden or risk or duty'.*[380]

EXAMPLE

So, for example, as well as covering the sort of exemption clauses that are also covered by UCTA, the UTCCR also covers:

- terms that allow traders to increase the price after the contract, but before performance (for example, before goods or services are actually delivered);[381]

- terms requiring the consumer to pay in full for building work before it even begins[382] (this can be unfair, because it means that the consumer is not in a position to withhold payment if the work turns out to be defective – or if it is not done at all and the trader has disappeared!);

- terms allowing very high fees or charges to be paid (fees and charges that are disproportionate to any loss or disadvantage suffered by the financial institution by what the consumer has done) so long as the terms allowing for these charges are not excluded price terms (see section 7.7.4.3).

The OFT has already persuaded a number of credit card companies that it is generally unfair to provide for default charges of more than £12.[383]

However, the banks are proving much more determined in protecting the enormous amounts of revenue they make from overdraft charges. One argument was that such charges were not covered by the test of unfairness on the basis that the test does not apply so as to test the 'adequacy of the price . . . as against the goods or services supplied in exchange' (as long as the term is in 'plain and intelligible language') (reg. 6(2)(b)). Initially it was held by the Court of Appeal[384] that this exclusion from the test of unfairness only applies to charges that arise in the due performance of the contract (that is, the main price being charged under the contract – in the case of a bank account, any standing charge and the interest charged) and not to bank charges which only occur in those cases where the consumer exceeds their limit. However, the Supreme Court decided that even these changes were excluded from the test of unfairness by reg. 6 (2)(b) (*OFT* v *Abbey National* [2009] UKSC 6).

7.7.4.3 **Excluded terms**

Price terms

As we saw above, one type of term that is not covered by the test of unfairness is the basic price.[385]

---

[380] *DGFT* v *First National Bank* [2001] 3 WLR 1297, at 1307.
[381] See UTCCR, Sch. 2, para. 1(l) and OFT Unfair Terms Guidance 2001, at 12.3.
[382] See OFT Bulletin 3, at 2.14.
[383] See OFT's 'Action on Credit Card Default Charges', OFT, 5 April 2006; and OFT Press Release 130/06, 7 September 2006.
[384] *Abbey National PLC* v *Office of Fair Trading* [2009] EWCA Civ 116.
[385] Regulation 6(2)(b).

> ## DEBATE BOX
>
> On the one hand exclusion from control of the basic price seems right because market forces usually control prices (while they do not control other terms as consumers are unlikely to be thinking about these other terms when they decide who to buy from). Presumably based on this sort of reasoning, the view of the Law Commissions is that core price terms will rarely be unfair (and so should continue to be excluded from the test of unfairness). Another reason for this view given by the Law Commissions is that testing such terms for unfairness is an undue interference with freedom of contract.[386]
>
> On the other hand, it might be argued that the courts should have the power to control prices where they are much higher than the market norm and advantage has been taken of a weak or needy consumer.[387]
>
> In any event, aside from the controversy in relation to bank charges (see section 7.7.4.2) the House of Lords said in an earlier case that the price exclusion should be interpreted 'restrictively'.[388]

Main subject matter terms

Another sort of term excluded from the test of unfairness (as long as it is in plain and intelligible language) is one that defines the 'main subject matter' of the contract.[389] This basically means terms describing the main features of the product or service being bought. There is nothing particularly controversial about this exclusion, as such terms are not likely to be unfair.

Individually negotiated terms

Another type of term excluded from the test of unfairness is one that has been 'individually negotiated',[390] the argument being that the real problem is terms drafted by the business in which the consumer has had no input. In other words, if the consumer has had an input then why would the term be unfair? However, one problem is that even if I have an input, I am still likely to be in a much weaker position than the business and the result might still be an unfair term. Also, there is some evidence that some businesses may carry out a kind of 'fake' negotiation with the end result always being the terms they always use.[391] Even if this would not stand up in court, it will often be enough to put the consumer off challenging. The Law Commission recommendation is that individually negotiated terms should be subject to control under any new regime.[392]

Mandatory, etc. terms

Finally, terms reflecting 'mandatory statutory or regulatory provisions' are not covered by the test of unfairness.[393] So, for instance, if a term simply reflects an implied term that would exist

---

[386] See Unfair Terms in Contracts, Law Com No 292 and Scot Law Com No 199, 2005, at para. 3.57.
[387] See C. Willett, *Fairness in Consumer Contracts: The Case of Unfair Terms* (Ashgate, Surrey, 2007) at 5.8.2.
[388] *Director General of Fair Trading v First National Bank* [2001] 3 WLR 1297, Lord Steyn at 1312.
[389] Regulation 6(2)(a).
[390] Regulation 5(1).
[391] See European Commission Report on the Unfair Terms Directive, 2000, at p. 14.
[392] Unfair Terms in Contracts, Law Com No 292 and Scot Law Com No 199, 2005, para. 3.55.
[393] Regulation 4(2)(a).

as a matter of law anyway, then it is not controlled. In general this is unproblematic as such terms will usually be fair.

7.7.4.4 Plain language

The UTCCR contain a rule of construction similar to the *contra proferentem* one applicable at common law. It provides that written terms must be in plain and intelligible language and that, if there is doubt as to the meaning of a term, the interpretation most favourable to the consumer will apply.[394]

7.7.4.5 The test of unfairness

LEGISLATIVE PROVISION

According to reg. 5(1) a term is unfair:

. . .

if, contrary to the requirement of good faith, it causes a significant imbalance in the parties' rights and obligations under the contract, to the detriment of the consumer.

The House of Lords seem to have taken the view that for a term to be unfair there would need to be a significant imbalance in rights and obligations to the detriment of the consumer *and* a violation of the requirement of good faith; these being separate, if connected, requirements.[395]

So, dealing first with significant imbalance/detriment, the House of Lords related this to the substantive features of the term, there being a significant imbalance where the term is 'so weighted in favour of the supplier as to tilt the parties' rights and obligations under the contract significantly in his favour'.[396] This would be the case where terms give unduly beneficial rights to the trader (for example, exemption clauses) or impose undue burdens on the consumer (for example, the price variation, full payment in advance and bank charges examples given above, section 7.7.4.2).

Lord Bingham said that:

> The requirement of significant imbalance is met if a term is so weighted in favour of the supplier as to tilt the parties' rights and obligations under the contract significantly in his favour. This may be by the granting to the supplier of a beneficial option or discretion or power, or by the imposing on the consumer of a disadvantageous burden or risk or duty.[397]

Regulation 5(5) refers to Sch. 2 in the Regulations which 'contains an indicative and non-exhaustive list of the terms which may be regarded as unfair' and Lord Bingham said that the indicative list of terms provided guidance as to unfairness in substance (that is, as the sort of

---

[394] Regulation 7.
[395] *DGFT v First National Bank* [2001] 3 WLR 1297, Lord Bingham at 1307–1308, Lord Steyn at 1313.
[396] [2001] 3 WLR 1297, Lord Bingham at 1307.
[397] *Ibid.*

terms that will typically be said to cause 'significant imbalance to the detriment of the consumer').[398]

We should note that this list contains both exemption clauses and terms imposing obligations and liabilities on the consumer. More specifically, it includes terms inappropriately excluding liability for breach (including, in particular where death or injury results);[399] binding the consumer, but not the trader;[400] requiring consumers to pay for goods or services not received;[401] allowing traders to retain deposits when consumers do not perform, without allowing for equivalent compensation for the consumer in the opposite situation;[402] imposing disproportionate compensation on consumers that are in breach;[403] allowing traders, but not consumers, to terminate at will;[404] allowing traders to terminate contracts of indeterminate duration without reasonable notice, except on serious grounds;[405] automatic extension of contracts where the deadline expressed for the consumer to express a desire not to extend is too early;[406] allowing for alteration of the terms or performance without valid reasons;[407] allowing the price to be fixed at the time of delivery or increased, without there being a corresponding consumer right to cancel if the final price is too high;[408] allowing the transfer of consumer rights (where this would reduce consumer rights) without consent;[409] allowing traders to deny responsibility for commitments undertaken by their agents;[410] and various obstructions to consumer access to justice.[411]

Lord Bingham also said that whether or not a term caused a significant imbalance to the detriment of the consumer was a question that involved looking not only at the term in question but also at the contract as a whole, that is at the other terms of the contract.[412]

Turning to good faith, Lord Bingham equated good faith with 'fair and open dealing'.[413] He said that 'openness' meant that terms should be 'expressed fully, clearly and legibly', not contain 'concealed pitfalls or traps' and be given 'appropriate prominence' where they might 'operate disadvantageously' to the consumer.[414] He said that fair dealing:

> requires that the supplier should not, whether deliberately or unconsciously, take advantage of the consumer's necessity, indigence, lack of experience, unfamiliarity with the subject matter of the contract [or] weak bargaining position . . .[415]

---

[398] *Ibid.*
[399] Paragraphs 1(a) and (b).
[400] Paragraphs 1(c) and (o).
[401] Paragraph 1(f).
[402] Paragraph 1(d).
[403] Paragraph 1(e).
[404] Paragraph 1(f).
[405] Paragraph 1(g).
[406] Paragraph 1(h).
[407] Paragraphs 1(j) and (k).
[408] Paragraph 1(l).
[409] Paragraph 1(p).
[410] Paragraph 1(n).
[411] Paragraph 1(q) (excluding or hindering the consumer's right to take legal action or exercise any other legal remedy, particularly by requiring the consumer to take disputes exclusively to arbitration not covered by legal provisions, unduly restricting the evidence available to him or imposing on him a burden of proof which, according to the applicable law, should lie with another party to the contract).
[412] [2001] 3 WLR 1297, Lord Bingham, at 1307.
[413] [2001] 3 WLR 1297, at 1308.
[414] *Ibid.*
[415] *Ibid.*

Lord Steyn considered that there was 'a large area of overlap' between the significant imbalance and good faith limbs of the test.[416] Indeed, he rejected the idea that good faith is primarily concerned with procedural matters, saying that: 'Any purely procedural or even predominantly procedural interpretation of the requirement of good faith must be rejected.'[417]

At the same time it seems clear that he did view procedural matters as being relevant to good faith. He approved Lord Bingham's statement that good faith was about 'fair and open dealing'.[418]

Taking all of this together it appears that if a term excludes or restricts liability or imposes obligations or liabilities that would not otherwise exist, it will often cause a significant imbalance to the detriment of the consumer. The question will then be if there has been a violation of good faith. This appears to involve a combined analysis of the degree of unfairness in substance and various aspects of procedural fairness (in particular the degree of transparency, but also if (as will usually be the case) the consumer is in a weaker bargaining position and appears to have been taken advantage of).

According to reg. 6(1) the overall assessment of unfairness is made 'taking into account the nature of the goods or services for which the contract was concluded and by referring, at the time of the conclusion of the contract, to all the circumstances attending the conclusion of the contract and to all the other terms of the contract or of another contract on which it is dependent'.

Having looked at the substance of the term and concluded that it causes imbalance and detriment, it seems then that reg. 6(1) provides a general guide to enable the court to conclude if there is, overall, a lack of good faith, and consequently unfairness. We can see from reg. 6(1) that, as with the reasonableness test under UCTA, the assessment takes place by reference to the point at which the contract was made. Most of the factors considered relevant under the UCTA test will be relevant here.

(a) *Relative bargaining strength*: We should recall that in the *First National Bank* case Lord Bingham referred to whether or not the seller or supplier takes advantage of the weaker bargaining position of the consumer. Of course, as under UCTA, if the seller or supplier has, this will normally count against a term where it has been imposed, given that the seller or supplier will normally be in a stronger bargaining position than the consumer. However, where the term has not actually been imposed by the seller or supplier but has emanated from the consumer side (for example, from the consumer's professional advisers) then this is likely to count in favour of the term.[419]

(b) *Whether the consumer had a choice of terms*: This is a factor generally recognised as being relevant to good faith in continental jurisprudence.[420]

(c) *The nature of the supply*: It is relevant to consider if the goods are being supplied specially for this consumer[421] and if this is costly for the seller or supplier or causes the fulfilment of commitments to be more difficult.

---

[416] [2001] 3 WLR 1297 at 1313.
[417] *Ibid*.
[418] *Ibid*.
[419] See *Picardi* v *Cuniberti* [2003] BLR 487.
[420] H. Micklitz, 'La Loi Allemand Relative au Régime Fundique des Conditions Générales des Contrats du 9 Decembre 1976' (1989) *Rev Int Droit Comparé* 101, at 109.
[421] See recital 16 to the Preamble to the Directive.

(d) *The sums of money at stake for both parties*: In general, given that reg. 6(1) makes it relevant to consider the nature of the goods, the financial risks that will be associated with such goods must surely be relevant. In addition, it must be appropriate to consider the amount that the consumer stands to lose if an exclusion is valid. This must surely go to the question as to whether or not the term can be said to be causing a significant imbalance and this, in turn, must be relevant to whether or not there is a violation of the good faith requirement.

(e) *If the consumer received an inducement to agree to the term*: Recital 16 to the Preamble to the Directive says expressly that this factor is relevant to good faith.

(f) *If the term was transparent at the time of making the contract*: We saw above that Lord Bingham regarded transparency as a fundamental element of good faith. So it will be relevant to ask in relation to the term, 'Was it available at the point of contract? Was there an opportunity to consider it? Was it in a clearly structured contract? Given its significance, was it given due prominence? Was it in decent-sized print and printed in a colour of ink which made it readable? Was it in plain and intelligible language?' These are all matters that have been given attention by the OFT in their enforcement work under the UTCCR – on which see more below.

It seems arguable that in some cases the degree of significant imbalance and detriment caused in this way will be sufficient in itself to lead to the conclusion that the requirement of good faith has not been complied with. (So, a term might be said to be so unfair in substance that it would violate the good faith requirement, even though it is transparent.) This was not confirmed by the House of Lords, although it was by the Court of Appeal[422] and the House of Lords did not express any view to the contrary. It may also have support from the ECJ.[423] This seems most likely to be the case where the indicative list of unfair terms is concerned.

7.7.4.6 Enforcement

Unfair terms are not binding on the consumer in a private law action between the parties.[424] However, what has been much more significant under the UTCCR is the fact that bodies such as the Office of Fair Trading (OFT), local authority trading standards authorities and other bodies[425] can obtain injunctions to actually prevent traders using unfair terms in the first place.[426] This is because controls of this type were required under Art. 7 of the Unfair Terms Directive. Short of seeking an injunction, traders can be asked to provide 'undertakings' that

---

[422] See the view of H. Beale, 'Legislative Control of Fairness: The Directive on Unfair Terms in Consumer Contracts', in J. Beatson and D. Friedmann (eds), *Good Faith and Fault in Contract Law* (Clarendon, Oxford, 1995) pp. 232, 245, cited with approval by the Court of Appeal at [2000] QB 672, at 686 [2000] 2 All ER 759 at 769.

[423] See *Freiburger Kommunalbauten* v *Hofstetter*, C-237/02; and see discussion in C. Willett, *Fairness in Consumer Contracts, op. cit.*, 3.5.4 and 6.5.

[424] Regulation 8.

[425] Schedule 1 – the Information Commissioner, the Gas and Electricity Markets Authority, the Director General of Electricity Supply for Northern Ireland, the Director General of Gas for Northern Ireland, the Office of Communications, the Director General of Water Services, the Office of Rail Regulation, every weights and measures authority in Great Britain, the Department of Enterprise, Trade and Investment in Northern Ireland, the Financial Services Authority and the Consumers Association.

[426] See regs 10–15.

they will remove or amend terms.[427] These various powers are backed up by the power to obtain documents and information from traders about their terms.[428]

The importance of these powers cannot be overemphasised. We talked above about terms being 'totally ineffective' under UCTA and others subject to the reasonableness test, but in reality this only meant that under UCTA they are not effective (or may not be effective) if relied on by a business in a private law claim. UCTA did not actually make it illegal to use the terms or say that businesses could in some way be prevented from using such terms (even if a term in our contract is held to be unfair and not binding, the court has no power then to say that the term cannot be used against others). So, in practice, thousands upon thousands of terms continued to be used and, in most cases, in practice, the result would be that the trader got to do what the term said he could do – partly, of course, because the vast majority of consumers would not know to challenge the terms, would not want to go to court, etc.[429]

The powers under the UTCCR have been a foundation for the OFT in particular to persuade traders to remove or amend large numbers of terms.[430] The OFT have also issued a considerable body of guidance on unfairness which has informed their approach to enforcement.[431] This has presumably aided traders and their advisers in understanding and complying with the law[432] and presumably also aided consumers and their advisers in recognising breaches of the law.

7.7.4.7 The *First National Bank* case

In *DGFT* v *First National Bank* that we have been referring to above, a particular type of term was held not to be unfair by the House of Lords. This was a term allowing banks to continue to add interest to the amount that a consumer has been ordered to pay by the court after having defaulted on their loan. This could be an indication that the House of Lords will not take a very 'consumer protectionist' approach in general. However, it is very hard to say until we see the test applied a few more times to different types of term (for example, bank charges).[433]

---

[427] Regulation 10(3).

[428] Regulation 13.

[429] Now, in fact, acting contrary to UCTA represents a 'domestic infringement', allowing bodies such as the OFT and local trading standards authorities to seek an enforcement order against the trader (see Enterprise Act 2002, s. 211 and Enterprise Act 2002 (Part 8 Domestic Infringements) Order 2003, SI 2003/1593) but this was obviously not in place during the period between 1977 (when UCTA was first passed) and 1994 (when the original version of the UTCCR was passed).

[430] See the Unfair Contract Terms Bulletins 1–29, covering cases dealt with from the passing of the initial 1994 Unfair Terms in Consumer Contracts Regulations until September 2004, and the lists of Unfair Terms Cases with Undertakings that replaced the bulletins and run from October 2004 (available on the consumer enforcement area of the OFT's website at: www.oft.gov.uk).

[431] The duty to issue such guidance is laid down in reg. 15. The most notable general guidelines are those contained in the OFT Guidance of 2001. There have also been guidelines for particular sectors, for example, consumer entertainment contracts (2003), care home contracts (2003), home improvement contracts (2005), holiday caravan contracts (2005) and package holiday contracts (2004).

[432] This is of particular importance given the traditional concerns as to the uncertainty caused by broad standards of fairness. Any such uncertainty may not only be a cost for businesses but may also make it more difficult for businesses to comply.

[433] For a discussion of the approach of the House of Lords in this case, see C. Willett, *Fairness in Consumer Contracts*, op. cit., 5.5.4.

7.7.4.8 The Law Commissions and the proposed new Consumer Rights Act (CRA)

ISSUE BOX

As indicated above, there are currently Law Commission proposals to unify the provisions of UCTA and the UTCCR. The proposed new legislation would retain the existing UCTA ban on exclusion or restriction of liability for breach of the implied terms as to description, quality and fitness in consumer contracts and exclusion of liability for negligently caused death or injury.[434] Other terms would be subject to a single 'fair and reasonable' test.[435] The same terms as currently excluded from the UTCCR test would continue to be excluded from the new test, except that individually negotiated terms would no longer be excluded.[436]

The new 'fair and reasonable' test (which the Law Commissions believe is broad enough to satisfy what is required by the significant imbalance/good faith test from the UTD)[437] would take account of transparency, the 'substance and effect of the term' and 'all the circumstance existing at the time it was agreed'.[438] There would then be guidelines as to these various matters.[439] These guidelines broadly reflect the factors that we have already outlined as being relevant under the existing UCTA and UTCCR tests, although it would obviously be useful to have these spelt out in the detail that is proposed.

The latest idea is that these Law Commission proposals would be implemented in the proposed new CRA that has been discussed at various points in this chapter (see above, sections 7.1.6 and 7.3.8, for example).

7.8 Preventive and criminal law regulation of unfair practices

7.8.1 Introduction

This section is concerned with the powers of bodies to seek enforcement orders against various unfair trade practices, that is, a court order that prevents the trader continuing to carry out the practice in question. It is also concerned with the circumstances in which certain practices represent criminal offences.

Powers to seek enforcement orders are contained in the Enterprise Act (EA) 2002. First of all, bodies such as the OFT and local authority trading standards authorities can seek

---

[434] Unfair Terms in Contracts, Law Com No 292 and Scot Law Com No 199, 2005, para. 3.47 and Draft Bill, ss. 1(1) and 5.
[435] *Ibid.*, para. 3.90 and Draft Bill, s. 4(1).
[436] See 3.50–3.72 and Draft Bill, reg. 4(2)–(6).
[437] See 3.84–3.89.
[438] See 3.96 and Draft Bill, s. 14(1).
[439] Draft Bill, ss. 14(3)–(4).

'enforcement orders' to prevent so-called 'domestic infringements', an enforcement order being a court order requiring that the trader discontinues the conduct in question. Essentially, 'domestic infringement' covers a variety of actions that represent breaches of contract, statutory duties, criminal offences and torts that harm 'the collective interests of consumers'.[440] The label 'domestic' infringement is used to indicate that the actions in question represent breaches of standards that have been set by domestic law, that is, they have not come from EU law. So, it would cover, for example, practices that amount to the criminal offence of harassment under the Protection from Harassment Act (PHA) 1997 and breaking contracts by not delivering promised goods or services.[441] So, quite apart from harassment representing a criminal offence and failure to deliver goods or services giving consumers the right to seek private law remedies for breach of contract, an enforcement order can be issued requiring such conduct to cease in future.

Enforcement orders can also be obtained against so-called 'Community infringements', that is, actions that represent breaches of standards contained in various EU directives.[442] This would cover, for example, failure to honour the various information obligations and cancellation rights that are discussed in section 7.2 and which are provided for in directives on package travel, consumer credit, doorstep selling and distance selling.[443] It also covers selling goods that do not meet the conformity standards in the Consumer Sales Directive (or failing to provide the remedies in the Consumer Sales Directive),[444] the use of terms that are unfair under the Unfair Contract Terms Directive[445] and breaches of the provisions of the Timeshare, Electronic Commerce and Television Broadcasting Directives.[446] It would also now cover engaging in 'misleading' or 'aggressive' practices or contravening the requirement of 'professional diligence', within the meaning of the Unfair Commercial Practices Directive (UCPD) of 2005 (these now also being classified as 'Community infringements').[447]

Misleading acts or omissions, acting aggressively towards consumers or acting contrary to professional diligence (within the meaning of the UCPD) can also amount to criminal offences under the Consumer Protection from Unfair Trading Regulations (CPUTR) 2008.[448] This new regime replaces the old Trade Descriptions Act (TDA) 1968 and Consumer Protection Act (CPA), Part III, which previously applied criminal sanctions to misleading statements as to goods, services and prices. The new regime sits alongside the PHA 1997, which makes certain forms of harassment criminal. It also sits alongside the rules on harassment of debtors in s. 40 of the Administration of Justice Act (AJA) 1970.

This section will concentrate on the new unfair practices concepts just discussed, that is, those deriving from the UCPD. It deals with the meaning of unfairness and the enforcement order and criminal sanctions just outlined. Of course, as mentioned, enforcement orders are also available against a range of other Domestic and Community infringements and there

---

[440] EA, ss. 211, 213(1)–(2) and 217(6).

[441] See EA, ss. 211(a)–(b), and the Enterprise Act 2002 (Domestic Infringements) Order 2003, SI 1593. Note that the Protection from Harassment Act is also solely of domestic origin, as is the general common law rule that failure to deliver goods or services promised under a contract represents a breach of contract.

[442] EA, s. 212, Sch. 13.

[443] Directives 90/314/EEC, 85/977/EEC, 87/102/EEC (as amended by 98/7/EC) and 97/7/EC respectively.

[444] 99/44/EC.

[445] 93/13/EEC.

[446] Directives 94/47/EC, 2000/31/EC and 89/552/EEC (as amended by 97/36/EC) respectively.

[447] 2005/29/EC; and see Consumer Protection from Unfair Trading Regulations 2008, reg. 26.

[448] CPUTR, regs 8–12.

are a number of pre-existing criminal law provisions still in place (for example, the PHA and the rules on harassment of debtors in s. 40 of the AJA 1970). However, the new unfairness concepts deserve the closest attention, because they are of much broader application than any of the other infringements and because many of the other infringements (for example, in relation to information, cancellation, sale of goods and unfair terms) are dealt with in other sections.[449]

Note that this section does not deal with cases where consumer safety is the concern – these are dealt with in section 7.6.

Of course, many of the above Domestic and Community infringements are regulated in private law as well. Focusing on Community infringements in the sense of unfair practices under the UCPD/CPUTR, for instance, a misleading practice (as defined in the UCPD/ CPUTR) may also be a misrepresentation and allow rescission of any resulting contract and damages, while an aggressive practice (as defined in the UCPD/CPUTR) might amount to duress at common law and allow for rescission of any resulting contract. However, such practices are also subject to control by the enforcement orders and criminal measures discussed in this section, *inter alia*, to seek to prevent them occurring in the first place.

Note that *private law rules themselves have not been changed at all by the CPUTR* (the UCPD – which the CPUTR implements – did not require Member States to make any changes to private law).[450] However, the government asked the Law Commissions to consider if private law rules should be brought into line with the standards in the CPUTR/UCPD and what, if any, reforms to remedies would be appropriate. The Law Commissions reported on this in late 2008 and then again in 2011, proposing private law remedies for certain breaches of the fairness standards deriving from the UCPD.[451]

7.8.2 Unfairness

7.8.2.1 Overview

Under the new regime a practice can be unfair either on the basis that it is a misleading action or omission, an aggressive practice, contravenes the requirements of professional diligence, or is on the list of practices always regarded as unfair.

For the purposes of enforcement orders, the definitions are those in the UCPD, Arts 5–9 (defining misleading and aggressive practices and those contrary to professional diligence) and Annex 1 (the list of practices that are always unfair),[452] while, for the purposes of criminal liability, the definitions are those in the CPUTR, regs 3–7 and Sch. 1.[453] These are essentially the same definitions. However, when it comes to criminal liability, there is a difference (i) in that there is a *mens rea* requirement for the professional diligence offence and (ii) in that (for

---

[449] See sections 7.2, 7.3 and 7.7.
[450] Article 3(4).
[451] See Law Commissions, *A Private Right of Redress for Unfair Commercial Practices* (Law Commission, London, 2008), Law Commissions, *Consumer Redress for Misleading and Aggressive Practices*, LCCP 199, April 2011, and Law Commissions, *Consumer Redress for Misleading and Aggressive Practices*, Law Com 332, Scot Law Com 226, 2012.
[452] CPUTR, reg. 26.
[453] CPUTR, regs 8–12.

misleading and aggressive practices) defences are available (traditional in criminal law fair trading rules) based on the default of another, due diligence and innocent publication of an advertisement.[454]

7.8.2.2 Scope and importance

The coverage of the unfairness concept is much broader than that of many other measures because there is no restriction (as there is in the case of rules, for example, on the sale of goods or package travel) to particular types of transaction. It applies to all types of trader–consumer transactions.[455]

The coverage is *also very broad by virtue of the sheer range of activities it regulates within any given transaction*. It catches 'business-to-consumer commercial practices'[456] which 'means any act, omission, course of conduct or representation, commercial communication including advertising and marketing, by a trader, directly connected with the promotion, sale or supply of a product to consumers'.[457] In addition, such a practice may be 'before, during or after' a transaction.[458] This makes it applicable to promotion, negotiation, conclusion, performance and enforcement of the contract. Such a regime covers practices such as advertising, promotion, persuasion and negotiation at the precontractual stage, postcontractual alterations or variations, performance, delivery, etc. by the trader, performance, payment, etc. by the consumer, complaint handling, after-sales service, and enforcement by either party.

It should be noted, also, that the reference to sale or supply of a 'product' includes both goods and services.[459]

A 'consumer' is an individual acting for purposes outside his trade, business or profession,[460] while a 'trader' is any person acting for purposes relating to his business (which includes trade, craft or profession).[461]

The rules allowing for enforcement orders are intended to implement the UCPD. This required Member States to introduce some such controls.[462] The rules relating to criminal liability were probably not needed for this purpose, so the requirements of the UCPD are not relevant with regard to them. As for the rules allowing for enforcement orders, *as with the provisions implementing any directive*, the unfairness concept must be interpreted in such a way as to give as high a level of protection as the European Court of Justice (ECJ) believes was intended, that is, *it sets a minimum 'floor' of protection that Member States cannot go below*. However, there is a distinctive element to the UCPD which gives a particular potency to the impact of this new European unfairness concept on domestic law. This comes in the shape of the internal market clause (Art. 4).

---

[454] CPUTR, regs 16–18.

[455] There need only be a commercial transaction in relation to 'any goods or service including immovable property, rights and obligations', CPUTR, reg. 2 (UCPD Art. 3(1)), CPUTR, reg. 2 (UCPD Art. 2(c)).

[456] Article 3(1).

[457] Regulation 2 (Art. 2(d)).

[458] Regulation 2 (Art. 3(1)).

[459] Regulation 2(1) (Art. 2(c)).

[460] Regulation 2(1) (Art. 2(a), extending to natural persons).

[461] Regulation 2(1) (Art. 2(b)).

[462] Article 11(1).

> ### LEGISLATIVE PROVISION
>
> **Article 4**
>
> Member States shall neither restrict the freedom to provide services nor restrict the free movement of goods for reasons falling within the field approximated by this Directive.

This means that, within the scope of the Directive, the concept of unfairness *provides the ceiling as well as the floor for Member States in terms of the level of protection,*[463] so (in interpreting the unfairness concept and in relation to other proposed action falling within the scope of the Directive) Member States will be tied to any limits on the level of fairness that are provided for in the Directive. Indeed, ECJ case law has already emphasised that Member States can only ban practices on the basis that they fail to meet the fairness standards laid down in the UCPD (not on any other ground).[464] Having said this, the ECJ may be reluctant to interfere with the actual application (by national courts and regulators) of the unfairness concept to any given practice,[465] which may mean that, as long as the concepts from the UCPD are applied, there is a reasonable degree of flexibility in terms of how they are applied.

7.8.3 Misleading actions

7.8.3.1 The general test and types of information potentially covered

A commercial practice counts as a misleading action where:

> it contains false information and is therefore untruthful . . . or if it or its overall presentation, deceives or is likely to deceive the average consumer, even if the information is factually correct; and . . . it causes or is likely to cause him to take a transactional decision that he would not have taken otherwise.[466]

First it must be established that the information relates to one of the matters listed in the UCPD/CPUTR. This covers the vast majority of information that one can imagine being relevant in relation to the existence and basic nature of the product or service, its history, its composition, quantity, fitness, performance, benefits, risks, availability and delivery, sponsorship and approval of the product or service, the motives for the practice and the nature of the sales process, the price, the need for a service, replacement or repair, trader obligations in general and in relation to after-sales service and complaint handling in particular, the nature, attributes and rights of the trader or his agent and the rights of the consumer.[467]

---

[463] Subject to the fact that the internal market clause does not apply to financial services (Art. 3(9)).
[464] C-261/07.
[465] See C-237/02, where it was held that the unfairness test under the Unfair Contract Terms Directive should normally be applied by the national courts within the national legal context (not by the ECJ).
[466] Regulation 5(2)(a) and (b) and UCPD Art. 6(1).
[467] Regulation 5(4) (Art. 6(1)).

It must then, of course, be established that information is untruthful or deceives or is likely to deceive the average consumer and that it causes or is likely to cause him to take a transactional decision that he would not have taken otherwise.[468] We will deal below with whether or not information is likely to deceive and affect transactional decisionmaking, but first, what *is* a transactional decision?

A 'transactional decision':

means any decision taken by a consumer, whether it is to act or to refrain from acting, concerning:

(a) whether, how and on what terms to purchase, make payment in whole or in part for, retain or dispose of a product; or

(b) whether, how and on what terms to exercise a contractual right in relation to a product.[469]

The above outline shows that the misleading action concept covers precontractual advertising and sales promotion statements (for example statements as to the nature, history or price, which might affect consumer decisions as to 'whether to purchase' goods or services). These would have been covered by pre-existing rules (that is, the Trade Descriptions Act and the Control of Misleading Advertisements Regulations (CMAR)). However, these pre-existing rules tended not to cover statements made during the performance or enforcement of a contract. The TDA was focused on statements about the goods or services as such, while the CMAR applied to statements used to 'promote' (that is, to induce initial purchase of) the goods or services.[470] By contrast, statements made in the context of performance or enforcement are covered by the new regime. For example, the above outline shows that it covers statements as to the rights of consumers which might influence consumer decisions as to whether or not 'to exercise a contractual right' (possibly covering statements that deceive consumers as to their rights being likely to cause them to make the decision not to enforce these rights). Note also that the information as to the rights of the trader is covered. So, during enforcement of a contract, a trader might deceive a consumer as to the rights he has against the consumer, possibly causing the consumer to decide to pay something the trader claims is owed. This would be covered as the 'transactional decision' definition applies to decisions as to whether or not 'to make payment'.

7.8.3.2 What fails the test?

From the above definition, we can see that the information must be untruthful or deceive or be likely to deceive the average consumer and cause or be likely to cause the average consumer to take a transactional decision that he would not have taken otherwise.

---

[468] In cases where practices cause confusion with the products of a competitor or where a trader has given a firm and verifiable commitment to be bound to a code of practice, but not adhered to this code, there is a misleading practice without the need to satisfy the general test – all that needs to be established is that the likely result would be to cause the average consumer to take a transactional decision they would not have taken otherwise (reg. 5(2)/Art. 6(3)).

[469] Regulation 2(1) (Art. 2(k)).

[470] Control of Misleading Advertisement Regulations 1988, SI 1988/915, reg. 2(1).

> ## EXAMPLE
>
> Obviously, there will be many straightforward untruths where this test will easily establish this, for example, where there are straightforward false statements of fact – significant inaccuracy as to the mileage, service history or year of a car, the memory of a computer or camera, the make of a product, the material used in a product, etc.
>
> However, just as in misrepresentation in private law and under the old TDA, CPA and CMAR rules, there are always difficult lines to draw, for example, as to when a statement should be treated merely as puff, when opinions should be actionable and, more generally, how likely it is that consumers would be influenced by the statement. Although this new regime must certainly be approached squarely on the basis of the test it uses, there is likely to be some use made of decisions and examples under these other provisions for general guidance and inspiration.

Key to the new regime is the notion of the 'average consumer' – this is who must be deceived (or be likely to be deceived) and who must be likely to be caused to make a transactional decision he would not have made otherwise. The UCPD/CPUTR refer to this 'average consumer' as being 'reasonably well informed, reasonably observant and circumspect'.[471] There are several ECJ cases on this test.[472] So, for example, it has been held that where there was a marking on a Mars Bar indicating a 10 per cent increase in size from previously, the average consumer would not believe that the increase was larger than 10 per cent just because the actual size of the marking took up more than ten per cent of the size of the bar.[473] However, just because a consumer is not thought to be misled by this does not necessarily mean that it cannot be found that he will be misled by other practices. After all, the size of a Mars Bar is fairly easy for consumers to work out for themselves. The same cannot necessarily be said about matters that are either less likely to be given a great deal of attention and/or about which the consumer might find it more difficult to make a rational judgement (for example, as to the fitness or qualities of the goods or service, benefits and risks, sponsorship, trader obligations, etc.).

The case, *OFT v Purely Creative*[474] seems to recognise these limits in terms of what consumers are likely to read. It dealt with whether or not various 'scratchcard' and personalised letter promotions violated *inter alia* the general clauses on misleading actions and omissions. On the facts, it was held that some did and some did not. However, the key point for our purposes is that the High Court recognised that the 'average consumer' will not necessarily read all information provided.

This suggests that courts should focus on the main information provided (or *not* provided, where omissions are concerned) when deciding if the average consumer is likely to be

---

[471] Regulation 2(2) (Recital 18 to the Preamble of the UCPD).

[472] See, for example, Case C-210/96 (para. 37); C-470/93; C-220/98 and S. Weatherill, 'Who is the "Average Consumer?"', in U. Bernitz and S. Weatherill (eds), *The Regulation of Unfair Commercial Practices Under EC Directive 2005/29: New Rules and New Techniques* (Hart Publishing, Oxford, 2007), for a review of the cases.

[473] C-470/93.

[474] [2011] EWHC 106 (Ch). See M. Morgan-Taylor, 'Preventing Distribution of Promotions to Consumers Involving Unfair Practices – OFT application for Order Under Enterprise Act 2002: OFT v Purely Creative Ltd et al.', (2011) 16(3) *Communications Law* 115–117.

misled and caused to take a transactional decision that would not otherwise be taken. This core information (or lack of it) is what should determine if there has been a misleading action or omission rather than information provided in supplementary form, small print, etc.

7.8.3.3 Special tests

Although normally whether or not an action is misleading (or aggressive or contrary to professional diligence) depends on the likely impact on the 'average' consumer, this benchmark is varied either (i) to fit the average member of a 'clearly identifiable group' that is 'particularly vulnerable to the practice or the underlying product because of their mental or physical infirmity, age or credulity in a way which the trader could reasonably be expected to foresee' or (ii) the average member of a particular group at which a practice is directed.[475]

So, for example, there might be a practice that is not likely to mislead the average consumer. However, if a trader could reasonably foresee that children are likely to be misled by it or if it is directed specifically at children and they are likely to be misled by it, then it will be a misleading practice.

7.8.3.4 The 'always misleading' practices

As well as being able to be unfair on the basis of the misleading actions test, practices are *always* misleading (and therefore unfair) if they are one of those listed in the Annex to the Directive (set out in Sch. 1 to the Regulations).[476]

In broad terms the *misleading* actions described on the Schedule involve (i) suggesting that the product, service or trader can be relied on based on false claims as to commitment (and adherence) to codes of practice[477] or as to third-party endorsement,[478] (ii) including in marketing material an invoice or similar document seeking payment giving the consumer the impression he has already ordered the goods or services when he has not,[479] (iii) promoting a product similar to one made by a particular manufacturer so as deliberately to give the impression the product is made by that manufacturer when it is not,[480] (iv) false claims about if[481] or for how long[482] goods or services are available[483] or about broader market conditions,[484] (v) certain false claims as to after sales service,[485](vi) false claims about certain legal and status

---

[475] Regulations 2(3)–(5) (Arts 5(3) and 5(2)(b)).

[476] See reg. 3(4)(d) and Sch. 1 and UCPD, Art. 5(5) and Annex 1.

[477] Paragraphs 1 and 3.

[478] Paragraphs 2 and 4 and see the practice of promoting a product or service with media editorial comment, without making it clear that this is being paid for by the party whose products or services are on offer (para. 11).

[479] See para. 21.

[480] See para. 13.

[481] See para. 5 on 'baiting' consumers with unavailable goods or services and also para. 6 describing 'bait and switch', that is, offering certain goods or services with the real intention of promoting others.

[482] See para. 7 on false claims as to the time for which goods or services are available (whether at all or on certain terms) so as to induce an immediate (and uninformed) decision.

[483] See also, here, false claims that the trader is about to cease trading or move premises (para. 15).

[484] See para. 18 on giving materially inaccurate information as to market conditions or the possibility of finding the goods or services with the intention of inducing the consumer to acquire the product on conditions less favourable than normal market conditions.

[485] See para. 8 on a trader located in state X not fulfilling a promise to provide after-sales service in a language other than an official language of state X and para. 23 on falsely claiming after-sales service to be available in other Member States.

issues,[486] (vii) certain false claims as to the benefits of the goods or services, (viii) creating the false impression that the consumer has or will win a prize,[487] as well as other matters.[488]

OFT v *Purely Creative*[489] dealt with whether or not 'scratchcard' or personalised letter promotions breached para. 31(b) by giving the false impression that the consumer had won a prize which involved the consumer paying money or incurring a cost. In this case consumers were given a variety of options for claiming, involving different costs. These included prominently displayed premium-rate telephone call/text message modes, where the bulk of the charge went to the defendants, which when coupled with another charge for postage and insurance, cost more than the value of the most common 'prize'. However, there was a much cheaper postal mode of claiming costing no more than the price of a couple of stamps, which was given much less prominence in the promotional material. The High Court accepted that whilst a *de minimis* cost in proportion to the value of the prize was permissible, it held that the charges in this case were not *de minimis*. It also held that one of the modes of claiming was so expensive as to falsify the notion of winning a prize; the consumer was buying something, not winning it.[490]

The defendants appealed to the Court of Appeal, who referred the case to the court of Justice of the European Union to determine the scope of Paragraph 31. The five questions referred explore whether Paragraph 31 prohibits traders from telling consumers that they have won a prize if the consumer incurrs any charge in claiming using any of a variety of methods, even a *de minimis* charge, what is actually meant by *de minimis*, and whether a 'false impression' of winning a prize depends on the relative value of the prize when compared with the cost of claiming it. The court of Justice of the European Union held that a practise is banned if it involves the consumer incurring any cost whatsoever in claiming the item. Even if the cost of claiming the prize is *de minimis*, (such as the cost of a stamp), compared to the value of the item, whose the trader receives no benefit from the charge, or where one of a variety of means offered in order to claim the item is free.[491]

The fact that the general misleading action test does not apply to these practices introduces a greater degree of certainty. However, although there is no formal need to apply the general misleading practice test to these practices, the Schedule is not actually as far removed from this general test criteria in Art. 6 as might first be imagined. Some of the examples on the Schedule (dealing with misleading practices) require that the information be 'false',[492] while others refer to saying something which is 'materially inaccurate'.[493] The point is that this clearly calls for some form of evaluation as to falsity/material inaccuracy. This seems to mean that, in reality, even under the Schedule we will often need to ask a very similar question as is asked in the first part of the general test, that is, as to the truthfulness or capacity for

---

[486] That is, falsely indicating that a product can be legally sold (para. 9) or that the trader is distinctive in granting certain rights when in fact these rights derive from the law. See also false claims that the trader is not acting in a business capacity (para. 22).

[487] See para. 31.

[488] The Schedule also includes false indications that goods or services provide security (para. 12), cure illness (para. 17), are 'free' (para. 20), that prizes are available but not awarding the prizes (para. 19) and any claim that purchase will facilitate winning in a game of chance (para. 16).

[489] *Supra*, n. 474.

[490] See Morgan-Taylor, *supra*, n. 474, at 114–115.

[491] *Ibid.*, at 115–116 and Judgement in case c-428/11 *Purely Creative and others* v *Office of Fair Trading*.

[492] For example, para. 7 on 'false' claims as to the time for which goods or services are available.

[493] Paragraph 18 on giving 'materially inaccurate' information as to market conditions or the possibility of finding the goods or services.

deception of the statement. This would mean that the real difference under the Schedule is that we do not need to establish the second part of the general test, that is, that a transactional decision has resulted or is likely to result.

7.8.4 Misleading omissions

There is a misleading omission where the trader hides or omits or provides in an unclear, unintelligible, ambiguous or untimely manner 'material information' and, as a result, it causes or is likely to cause the average consumer to take a transactional decision he would not have taken otherwise.[494]

'Material information' is:

> information which the average consumer needs, according to the context, to take an informed transactional decision.[495]

Where invitations to purchase are concerned, particular types of information are deemed (expressly) to be 'material' and therefore needed for an informed decision. This is information as to the identity and address of the trader;[496] main characteristics of the product or service;[497] the price and various other charges (including how the price is calculated if it cannot be calculated in advance),[498] 'arrangements' for payment, delivery, performance or complaint handling, if they 'depart from the requirements of professional diligence',[499] and any cancellation right that exists.[500]

There were similar requirements to disclose this sort of information in the pre-existing regimes applicable to various specific types of contracts,[501] so that what is new, now, is that this sort of information needs to be provided in invitations to purchase preceding *all* types of contract.

However, beyond these specific types of information, what information is it that the average consumer 'needs' in order to make an 'informed transactional decision'?

ISSUE BOX

The first point to be made about this test is that it moves closer to a general duty of disclosure than has been the case in UK law previously. The old rules under the TDA, CPA and CMAR have all been focused on actual statements or representations. It is true that there might sometimes have been said to be a false or misleading statement or representation where only a 'half truth' had been told.[502] However, the question now is simply whether or not the consumer 'needs' the information, even if the trader has said nothing at all about the issue.

---

[494] Regulation 6(1) (Art. 7(1)).
[495] Regulation 6(3)(a) (Art. 7(1)).
[496] Regulations 6(4)(b) and (c) (Art. 7(4)(b)).
[497] Regulation 6(4)(a) (Art. 7(4)(a)).
[498] Regulation 6(4)(d)–(e) (Art. 7(4)(c)).
[499] Regulation 6(4)(f)(i)–(iv) (Art. 7(4)(d)).
[500] Regulation 6(4)(g) (Art. 7(4)(e)).
[501] See, for example the Financial Services (Distance Marketing) Regulations 2004, regs 7(1), 8(1) and Sch. 1.
[502] *R v Ford Motor Co* [1974] 1 WLR 1221.

EXAMPLE

It is very hard to predict what the 'needs' test might cover. However, it might be said that a consumer needs to know, for example, if he is 'tied in' to a contract for a minimum period or that the contract involves a commitment to future purchases.[503] He might also need to know about inherent risks of poor quality, limited fitness for purpose, injury, etc., where these are not obvious. So, for example, it is surely of importance for a consumer to know, for example, that a product such as a mobile phone is actually not new, but is reconditioned or secondhand or (given the introduction of digital reception) to know that a TV only has an analogue tuner.[504] Also, where this is not otherwise provided for, consumers might need ongoing information as to the progress of building work and information as to changes to terms and conditions.[505]

Finally, it should be noted that, as in the case of all unfair practices, the standard is varied where special consumer groups are concerned.[506] So, if the trader could reasonably foresee that particular types of consumer are likely to need information to make an informed decision or if the practice is directed specifically at particular consumers and they are likely to need this information, then it will be a misleading omission not to provide it (even although it would not be misleading in the case of the average consumer).

7.8.5 Aggressive practices

7.8.5.1 Introduction

LEGISLATIVE PROVISION

Regulation 7(1) [Art. 8]

A practice is aggressive if:

> . . . in its factual context, taking account of all its features and circumstances . . . it significantly impairs or is likely to impair the average consumer's freedom of choice or conduct in relation to the product concerned, through the use of harassment, coercion or undue influence; and . . . it thereby causes him or is likely to cause him to take a transactional decision that he would not have taken otherwise.

Regulation 7(2) [Art. 9]

In deciding whether or not a practice uses coercion, harassment or undue influence, account is to be taken of:

---

[503] These two examples are cited as possible misleading omissions by the OFT (OFT/BERR, 'Consumer Protection from Unfair Trading Regulations: Guidance on the UK Regulations' (OFT/BERR, London, 2008), at: www.oft.gov.uk/shared_oft/business_leaflets/cpregs/oft1008.pdf, at 7.18).

[504] *Ibid.*, OFT/BERR.

[505] *Ibid.* See also the Banking Code, section 6.

[506] Regulations 2(3)–(5) (Arts 5(3) and 5(2)(b)).

(a) its timing, location, nature or persistence;

(b) the use of threatening or abusive language or behaviour;

(c) the exploitation by the trader of any specific misfortune or circumstance of such gravity as to impair the consumer's judgment, of which the trader is aware, to influence the consumer's decision with regard to the product;

(d) any onerous or disproportionate non-contractual barrier imposed by the trader where a consumer wishes to exercise rights under the contract, including rights to terminate a contract or to switch to another product or another trader; and

(e) any threat to take any action which cannot legally be taken.

7.8.5.2 Undue influence

Although the above definition refers generally to whether or not undue influence (or coercion or harassment) restricts the 'freedom of choice' of the consumer, where undue influence is concerned, the restriction of choice that affects transactional decisionmaking cannot be just any restriction of choice. It must, specifically, be a restriction of choice that results from an information problem. We know this because undue influence is (separately) defined as:

> exploiting a position of power in relation to the consumer so as to apply pressure, even without using or threatening physical force, in a way which significantly limits the consumer's ability to make an informed decision.[507]

EXAMPLES

Undue influence may cover such things as:

- creating the need for a quick decision (for example, because the consumer is made to feel that otherwise he will not escape the attentions of the salesperson or because there are promised benefits only available to those making an early commitment);[508]

- an insurance salesperson exploiting concerns or emotions relating to risks that consumers or their families face, with the result that consumers do not properly reflect on the benefits and costs of the insurance;[509]

- when a consumer is struggling with existing commitments to the trader (and possibly to others), exploiting the consumer's concern over this to persuade him to take on further commitments that expose the consumer to the same or perhaps greater risks;[510]

- where the consumer is in default, threatening to take action that cannot legally be taken,[511] for example, to take criminal proceedings.[512]

---

[507] Regulation 7(3)(b) (Art. 2(j)).
[508] See guideline (a) above.
[509] See guideline (c) above.
[510] The OFT appear to view this scenario as one of undue influence. See OFT/BERR Guidance, n. 56, 8.4.
[511] See guideline (e) above.
[512] See Law Commission, n. 451, para. 2.77, where this is cited as a form of aggressive practice.

> **ISSUE BOX**
>
> The undue influence concept may cover a lot more than undue influence in private law.[513] It is not clear that the above examples would involve the type of relationship that is normally required for undue influence in private law. However, the last example above (that is, a threat to take criminal proceedings) was already covered under the harassment of debtor rules.[514]

7.8.5.3 Coercion and harassment

In the case of harassment and coercion, the question is if there is a restriction on 'freedom of choice or conduct'. This seems to go beyond cases where the problem is the lack of an informed decision. It arguably also covers cases in which the consumer can understand what his options are, but these options are simply unreasonable.

Obviously, there will be coercion where a physical threat is involved.[515] Apart from this there could be harassment or coercion in the following sorts of case:

- where the trader makes it unreasonably difficult for the consumer to enforce his (the consumer's) rights;[516]
- pressurising the consumer to perform, pay up, etc. by contacting him at unreasonable times and/or places (for example, late at night, at work, etc.);[517]
- requiring consumers to discuss debts by making contact on premium-rate telephone lines.[518]
- reporting consumers to a credit reference agency, where the claim that the consumer owes money is subject to dispute.[519]

> **ISSUE BOX**
>
> The coercion and harassment concepts may cover more than was caught by common law economic duress,[520] apart from anything else because they do not seem to require the sort of unlawful threat usually required for duress. However, the last two examples above (involving the pursuit of consumer debtors) would often already have been covered under the harassment of debtor rules.[521]

---

[513] See C. Willett, 'Unfairness under the Consumer Protection from Unfair Trading Regulations', in J. Devenney, L. Fox-O'Mahoney and M. Kenny, *Unconscionability in European Financial Transactions* (Cambridge University Press, Cambridge, 2010).
[514] Section 40, AJA 1970.
[515] See reg. 7(2)(Art. 9), guideline (b).
[516] See guideline (d).
[517] OFT/BERR, n. 59, para. 8.11.
[518] OFT/BERR, *ibid.*, n. 29.
[519] See *Office of Fair Trading* v *Ashbourne Management Services Ltd* [2011] EWHC 1237 (Ch).
[520] See Willett, *supra*, n. 513.
[521] Section 40, AJA 1970.

7.8.5.4 Average and other consumers

As in the case of all unfair practices, we can see from the above definition (section 7.8.5.1) that the question, in general, is if the transactional decisionmaking of the 'average consumer' would be affected by the practice. However, the standard is varied where special consumer groups are concerned. So, if the trader could reasonably foresee that particular types of consumer are likely to be unduly influenced, coerced or harassed by a practice, or if the practice is directed specifically at particular consumers and they are especially likely to be unduly influenced, coerced or harassed, then the practice will be deemed aggressive (even although it would not be aggressive in the case of the average consumer).[522]

7.8.5.5 Always aggressive practices

As well as being able to be unfair on the basis of the aggressive practices test, practices are *always aggressive* (and therefore unfair) if they are one of those listed in the Annex to the Directive (set out in Sch. 1 to the Regulations).[523]

The 'always aggressive' practices are:[524]

- creating the impression that the consumer cannot leave the premises until a contract is formed;

- conducting personal visits to the consumer's home, ignoring the consumer's request to leave or not to return except in circumstances and to the extent justified, under national law, to enforce a contractual obligation;

- making persistent and unwanted solicitations by telephone, fax, e-mail or other remote media except in circumstances and to the extent justified under national law to enforce a contractual obligation;

- requiring a consumer who wishes to claim on an insurance policy to produce documents which could not reasonably be considered relevant as to whether or not the claim was valid or failing systematically to respond to pertinent correspondence in order to dissuade a consumer from exercising his contractual rights;

- including in an advertisement a direct exhortation to children to buy advertised products or persuade their parents or other adults to buy advertised products for them (this provision is without prejudice to Art. 16 of Directive 89/552/EEC on television broadcasting);

- demanding immediate or deferred payment for or the return or safekeeping of products supplied by the trader, but not solicited by the consumer except where the product is a substitute supplied in conformity with Art. 7(3) of Directive 97/7/EC;

- explicitly informing a consumer that if he does not buy the product or service, the trader's job or livelihood will be in jeopardy;

- creating the false impression that the consumer has already won, will win or will, on doing a particular act, win a prize or other equivalent benefit, when in fact either:

---

[522] Regulations 2(3)–(5) (Arts 5(3) and 5(2)(b)).
[523] See reg. 3(4)(d) and Sch. 1 and UCPD, Art. 5(5) and Annex 1.
[524] They are contained in paras 24–31 of Sch. 1 (Annex 1).

- there is no prize or other equivalent benefit; or
- taking any action in relation to claiming the prize or other equivalent benefit is subject to the consumer paying money or incurring a cost.

7.8.6 Violation of professional diligence

LEGISLATIVE PROVISION

Regulation 3(3) [Art. 5(2)]

Even if a practice is not misleading or aggressive, it may be unfair if it 'contravenes the requirements of professional diligence' and thereby 'materially distorts' or is likely to 'materially distort' the economic behaviour of the average consumer.

Regulation 2(1) [Art. 2(e)]

'Material distortion' means that the consumer is not in a position to take an 'informed decision'.

Again, the standard is varied where special consumer groups are concerned. So, if the trader could reasonably foresee that the informed decisionmaking of particular types of consumer is likely to be affected by behaviour contrary to professional diligence or if the practice is directed specifically at particular consumers and informed decisionmaking is especially likely to be affected, then the practice will be unfair (even although it would not be unfair in the case of the average consumer).[525]

'Professional diligence' is defined as:

the standard of special skill or care which a trader may reasonably be expected to exercise towards consumers, commensurate with honest market practice and/or the general principle of good faith in the trader's field of activity.[526]

DEBATE BOX

This provision seems intended to catch new practices that are not covered by the other categories of unfairness. Nevertheless, it remains very unclear exactly what might be unfair under this heading that will not already be covered either as a misleading practice or omission or as undue influence. It is possible that it could cover abuse of the superior bargaining position of the trader. In such a case the consumer might be said to be unable to make an informed decision in the sense that he does not have the bargaining skill and experience to know how to protect his interests. This would again extend protection as there has been no pre-existing general power to act against abuse of superior bargaining power.

[525] Regulations 2(3)–(5) (Arts 5(3) and 5(2)(b)).
[526] Article 2(h).

7.8.7 Enforcement orders

As indicated in the introduction, practices falling into the above unfairness definitions are deemed to be 'Community infringements', meaning that enforcement orders can be obtained (in the High Court or county court in England, Wales or Northern Ireland or the Court of Session or Sheriff Court in Scotland) against a trader carrying out the practice or likely to carry out the practice.[527] These are available where the infringement harms the 'collective interests of consumers'.

Under EA, s. 213, enforcement orders can be sought by the Office of Fair Trading, local trading standards authorities and the Department of Enterprise, Trade and Investment in Northern Ireland (all deemed 'general enforcers'). They can also be sought by those designated as enforcers by the Secretary of State (thus far the Civil Aviation Authority, the Information Commissioner, the Rail Regulator, the Gas and Electricity Markets Authority and the Director Generals of Telecommunications, Water, Gas and Electricity for Northern Ireland).[528]

Enforcement orders can also be sought by those 'Community enforcers' listed in the Official Journal under Art. 4.3 of the Injunctions Directive[529] (bodies from other Member States).

Finally, they can be sought by Consumer Protection Co-operation Enforcers, such as the Civil Aviation Authority, the Financial Services Authority, Ofcom, PhonepayPlus (formerly ICSTIS) and the general enforcers mentioned above.[530] This is intended to facilitate cross-border cooperation in enforcement.

Under s. 214, the enforcer must consult the trader and the OFT to seek to ensure cessation of the practice. Normally this consultation period is 14 days, but 7 days is sufficient for an interim order, and, if the OFT considers it necessary, consultation can be dispensed with altogether. Under s. 219(4) an enforcer may accept an 'undertaking' that the practice will cease (and, therefore, not proceed to seek an enforcement order).

7.8.8 Criminal offences and defences

7.8.8.1 Offences

A trader commits an offence if he commits a misleading act or omission or an aggressive practice as defined above.[531] These are all strict liability offences, there being no *mens rea* requirement, although defences are available – see below.

A trader also commits an offence if he contravenes the requirement of professional diligence as defined in section 7.8.6.[532] It is important to note that in the case of professional diligence, the above definition *alone* applies for the purposes of obtaining enforcement orders against traders. However, for the trader to be criminally liable for breach of the professional diligence standard, there is *also* a *mens rea* requirement. The trader is only guilty of an offence

---

[527] EA, s. 212 and 217 and CPUTR, reg. 26.
[528] SI 2003/1399.
[529] 98/27/EC.
[530] EA, s. 215(5A), added by the Enterprise Act 2002 (Amendment) Regulations 2006, SI 2006/3363, in order to implement the EC Regulation on Consumer Protection Cooperation Regulations (EC) No 2006/2004, as amended by the UCPD).
[531] Regulations 9–11 and see regs 13 and 14 on penalties and time limits respectively.
[532] Regulation 8.

if he 'knowingly or recklessly [engages] in conduct' that is contrary to professional diligence and materially distorts or is likely to materially distort consumer behaviour.[533] It is important to stress here that the trader need only be 'knowing or reckless' as to his own behaviour. There is no need for him to know of (or be reckless as to) its actual or likely effects on consumers.

A trader also commits an offence if he engages in any practice set out in paras 1–10, 12–27 and 29–31 of the Schedule of practices that are always regarded as unfair.[534]

7.8.8.2 Defences

In the case of the misleading action and omission offences, the aggressive practice offence and the practices in Sch. 1, there are defences available. Such defences are not available in the case of the contravention of the professional diligence offence.

The defences are those that have long been used for trading standards offences in the UK, so that earlier case law under the TDA and other legislation may still prove helpful. The defences work as follows. First, there are the s. 17 defences, which require proof of at least one of a list of five things *and* the 'due diligence' element. Second, there is the s. 18 'innocent publication' defence. In general, defences are available partly because the offences are strict liability and it is thought that some form of escape route should be available where blame is minimal. The 'reasonable precautions and due diligence' requirement can also be viewed as a way of incentivising traders to manage their affairs so as to avoid the behaviour in question.

Section 17

To establish this defence, the defendant must first (under reg. 17(1)) prove that the commission of the offence is due to:

- a mistake, which must be a mistake by the person charged, rather than one of their employees;[535] or
- reliance on information supplied to him by another person (who the defendant must identify to the prosecution),[536] for example, information as to mileage from previous owners of a vehicle[537] or information on a product label placed there by the producer (and relied on by the retailer);[538] or
- the act or default of another person (who the defendant must identify to the prosecution)[539] who can be a party such as a sub-contractor or other party that is responsible for the activity in question, but can even be an employee,[540] for example, as in *Tesco v Nattrass*[541] where a supermarket manager who wrongly labelled washing powder counted as 'another person' for the purposes of the supermarket's defence; or
- an accident or another cause beyond his control, which may cover computer errors.[542]

---

[533] Regulation 8(1)(a).
[534] Regulation 12.
[535] *Birkenhead Co-operative Society* v *Roberts* [1970] 1 WLR 1497.
[536] Regulation 17(2).
[537] See *Simmons* v *Potter* [1975] RTR 347 (although the due diligence element was not established in this case – see below) and *Ealing LBC* v *Taylor* [1995] CLR 156 (where due diligence was established – see below).
[538] *Hurley* v *Martinez* [1991] CCLR 1.
[539] Regulation 17(2).
[540] So long as they are not so senior as to be an 'alter ego' of the company (e.g. members of the Board of Directors, managing director and other senior officers; see *Tesco v Nattrass* [1971] 2 All ER 127).
[541] *Ibid.*
[542] See *Berkshire CC* v *Olympic Holidays Ltd* (1994) 13 Trading LR 251.

Having established one of the above criteria, the defendant must then (under reg. 17(1)(b)) establish that he took all reasonable precautions *and* exercised all due diligence to avoid the commission of the offence by himself or any person under his control.

(i) Reasonable precautions

Whether or not there have been 'reasonable precautions' is a question of fact which will be affected by the circumstances of each particular case. Different precautions may be necessary according to whether the defendant is a manufacturer, a retailer or a supplier of services and according to the factual nature of the unfair commercial practice the defendant is alleged to have engaged in. Obviously, as the precautions must be taken to avoid the commission of an offence, the precautions must have been put in place before the offence is committed – what happens after the offence has been committed is relevant only in mitigation of a sentence.

In general, the key is that an appropriate system must be in place to prevent the practice taking place, for example, devising an adequate training programme for employees.[543] Another general point is that what is required may well vary according to whether the defendant is a large enterprise or a small corner shop.[544]

More specifically, whether or not there is a system for checking the reputability of the source of supply may be relevant, because this source may affect matters, for example, where labels on products supplied to a defendant from elsewhere are misleading. Further, although testing products (for example, to see if they comply with information on labels) may sometimes be required,[545] this is not always the case.[546] In the case of false mileage readings on cars, 'reasonable precautions' has often been held to require that the defendant has checked the history, for example, through the registration document and obtaining statements from previous owners,[547] although, even with some such checks, it has also been held that not enough had been done, and that a statement disclaiming knowledge as to whether or not the mileage was correct was required as a 'reasonable precaution' against customers being misled.[548]

(ii) Due diligence

The key here is that the system of reasonable precautions has actually been used in practice. If it has not, then there will be no due diligence and the defence will fail.[549]

Section 18

A further defence in relation to the offences under regs 9–12 (that is, the misleading action and omission offences, the aggressive practice offence and the practices in Sch. 1) is provided by reg. 18. There is a defence if the defendant can establish that it is his business to publish (or arrange for publication) of advertisements, he received the advertisement for publication

---

[543] See *Tesco v Nattrass*, above.

[544] See *Garrett v Boots the Chemist* (1980), 16 July 1980, unrep, D.C.

[545] *Amos v Melcon (Frozen Foods)* (1985) 149 JP 712, DC (insufficient evidence of sampling to check if meat labelled 'rump steak' was actually thus).

[546] *Hurley v Martinez* [1991] CCLR 1 (shop not expected to check to see if strength of wine was as described on label).

[547] See *Richmond upon Thames LBC v Motor Sales (Hounslow) Ltd* [1971] RTR 116; *Wandsworth LBC v Bentley* [1980] RTR 429 DC, and *Ealing LBC v Taylor* [1995] Crim LR 156.

[548] *Simmons v Potter* [1975] RTR 347.

[549] See *Turtington v United Co-operative Ltd* [1993] Crim LR 376 and the judgment of Lord Diplock in the *Tesco v Nattrass* case (above) for guidance on due diligence.

in the ordinary course of business and he did not know, and had no reason to suspect, that its publication would amount to an offence. This covers those (such as newspapers and magazines) who publish advertisements, as well as those (such as advertising agencies) who arrange for publication.

7.8.9 Enforcement body powers and duties

The foundation for enforcement orders and criminal prosecution is laid down by regs 19–25. In brief, reg. 19 imposes a duty on enforcement authorities to enforce the CPUTR. Regulations 20–22 give these authorities various powers to make test purchases and enter premises for the purposes of investigation, while reg. 23 deals with obstruction of authorised officers. Regulation 24 deals with duties to give notice to traders of test results and intended prosecution. Finally, reg. 25 provides for traders to receive compensation for loss or damage to goods that were seized or detained, where it turns out there has been no breach of the CPUTR and the exercise of the seizure or detention powers is not the result of any neglect or default by the trader.

7.9 EU Regulation on a Common European Sales Law

There is currently a proposal for an EU Regulation on a Common European Sales Law (CESL).[550] This will give sellers and consumers in cross-border sales a choice of law between the consumer's national law and the pan-EU regime in the CESL.[551] This would be applicable to the contractual relationship between the parties. It therefore includes rules on quality of goods, remedies and unfair terms etc. (see sections 7.3 and 7.7 above). However, it also contains rules on a much broader range of matters, offering a pan-EU alternative to national rules on contractual formation, information to be provided, defects in consent, prescription periods, etc.

Further reading

Atwood, B., Thompson, K. and Willett, C., *Food Law* (Bloomsbury Professional, London, 2009) Chapters 3, 5 and 8.

Beale, H., (1995), 'Legislative Control of Fairness: The Directive on Unfair Terms in Consumer Contracts', in J. Beatson and D. Friedmann (eds), *Good Faith and Fault in Contract Law* (Clarendon Press, Oxford, 1995) p. 231.

Beale, H., 'The Draft Directive on Consumer Rights and UK Consumer Law: Where Now?', in G. Howells and R. Schulze (eds), *Modernising and Harmonising Consumer Contract Law* (Sellier European Law Publishers, Munich, 2009) p. 289.

[550] COM (2011) 636 final.
[551] *Ibid.*, Art 3.

Bernitz, U. and Weatherill, S. (eds), *The Regulation of Unfair Commercial Practices Under EC Directive 2005/29: New Rules and New Techniques* (Clarendon Press, Oxford, 2007).

Bradgate, R. and Twigg-Flesner, C., *Blackstone's Guide to Consumer Sales and Associated Guarantees* (Oxford University Press, Oxford, 2003).

Bright, S., 'Winning the Battle Against Unfair Contract Terms' (2000) 20 *LS* 331.

Collins, H., (ed.), *The Forthcoming EC Directive on Unfair Commercial Practices: Contract, Consumer and Competition Law Implications* (Kluwer Law International, Oxford, 2004).

Goldberg, R., 'Paying for Bad Blood: Strict Product Liability After the Hepatitis C Litigation' (2002) *MLR* 165.

Grant, D. and Mason, S., *Holiday Law: The Law Relating to Travel and Tourism* (4th edn, Sweet and Maxwell, London, 2007).

Grant, D. and Urbanowicz, P., 'Tour Operators, Package Holiday Contracts and Strict Liability', (2001) *JBL* 253.

Howells, G., 'Strict Liability' in G. Howells (ed.), *The Law of Product Liability* (2nd edn, Butterworths, London, 2007) p. 265.

Howells, G., *Comparative Product Liability* (Dartmouth Publishing Company, Dartmouth, 1993).

Howells, G., Micklitz, H. and Wilhelmsson, T., *European Fair Trading Law: The Unfair Commercial Practices Directive* (Ashgate Publishing, Surrey, 2006).

Howells, G. and Weatherill, S., *Consumer Protection Law* (2nd edn, Ashgate Publishing, Surrey, 2005) Chapter 1.

Law Commission *Implied Terms in Contracts for the Supply of Services* (Law Com No 156, 1986).

Loos, M., 'Rights of Withdrawal', in G. Howells and R. Schultze, *Modernising and Harmonising Consumer Contract Law* (Sellier, European Law Publishers, Munich, 2009) pp. 239–280.

Macdonald, E., 'Unifying Unfair Terms Legislation' (2004) 67 *MLR* 69.

Macdonald, E., 'Bank Charges and the Core Exemption' (2008) 71 *MLR* 987.

Morgan-Taylor, M. and Naidoo, A., 'The Draft Regulations to Adopt the Directive on Certain Aspects of the Sale of Consumer Goods and Associated Guarantees: Problems of the Time of Conformity for the Quality Obligation' [2002] 3 *WebJCLI*.

Morgan-Taylor, M., 'Preventing Distribution of Promotions to Consumers Involving Unfair Practices: OFT Application for Order Under Enterprise Act 2002: OFT v Purely Creative Ltd et al.', *Communications Law* 16(3) 2011, 115–117.

Nebbia, P., *Unfair Contract Terms in European Law* (Hart Publishing, Oxford, 2007).

Newdick, C., 'The Development Risk Defence of the Consumer Protection Act 1987' (1988) 47 *CLJ* 455.

Nordhausen Scholes, A., 'Information Requirements', in G. Howells and R. Schultze (eds), *Modernising and Harmonising Consumer Contract Law* (Sellier, European Law Publishers, Munich, 2009) pp. 213–238.

Parry, D., 'Judicial Approaches to Due Diligence' (1995) *CLR* 695.

Ramsay, I., *Consumer Law and Policy: Text and Materials on Regulating Consumer Markets* (2nd edn, Hart Publishing, Oxford, 2007).

Saggerson, A., *Travel: Law and Litigation* (3rd edn, XPL Publishing, St Alloans, 2004).

Stapleton, J., *Product Liability* (Butterworths, London, 1994).

Stuyck, J., 'Unfair Terms', in G. Howells and R. Schulze (eds), *Modernising and Harmonising Consumer Contract Law* (Sellier European Law Publishers, Munich, 2009) p. 115.

Twigg-Flesner, C., *Consumer Product Guarantees* (Ashgate, Surrey, 2003).

Twigg-Flesner, C., Parry, D., Howells, G. and Nordhausen, A., *An Analysis of the Application and Scope of the UCP Directive* (DTI, London, 2005).

Twigg-Flesner, C., 'Fit for Purpose?: The Proposals on Sales', in G. Howells and R. Schulze (eds), *Modernising and Harmonising Consumer Contract Law* (Sellier European Law Publishers, Munich, 2009), p. 147.

Wilhelmsson, T. and Willett, C., 'Unfair Terms and Standard Form Contracts', in G. Howells, I. Ramsay and T. Wilhelmsson (eds), *Handbook of Research on International Consumer Law* (Edward Elgar Publishing, Cheltenham, 2010).

Willett, C., 'Implementation of the Unfair Terms Directive in the UK' (1997) *ERPL* 223.

Willett, C., *Fairness in Consumer Contracts: The Case of Unfair Terms* (Ashgate, Surrey, 2007).

Willett, C., 'The Role of Contract Law in Product Liability', in G. Howells (ed.), *The Law of Product Liability* (2nd edn, Butterworths, London, 2007).

Willett, C., 'Direct Producer Liability', in G. Howells and R. Schulze (eds), *Modernising and Harmonising Consumer Contract Law* (Sellier European Law Publishers, Munich, 2009) p. 189.

Willett, C., 'Unfairness under the Consumer Protection from Unfair Trading Regulations', in J. Devenney, L. Fox-O'Mahoney and M. Kenny (eds), *Unconscionability in European Financial Transactions* (Cambridge University Press, Cambridge, 2010).

Willett, C., 'Fairness and Consumer Decision Making Under the Unfair Commercial Practices Directive' (2010) 33 *Journal of Consumer Policy* 247–273.

Willett, C., 'The Functions of Transparency in Regulating Contract Terms: UK and Australian Approaches' (2011) 60 *ICLQ* 355–385.

Willett, C., 'General Clauses and Competing Ethics of European Consumer Law in the UK' (2012) 71(2) *CLJ* 412–440.

Willett, C. and Morgan-Taylor, M., 'Recognising the Limits of Transparency in EU Consumer Law', in J. Devenney and M. Kenny (eds), *European Consumer Protection, Theory and Practice* (Cambridge University Press, Cambridge, 2012).

Willett, C. and Oughton, D., 'Liability for Incorrect Installation and Other Services Associated with Consumer Goods', in G. Howells, A. Nordhausen, D. Parry and C. Twigg-Flesner (eds), *The Yearbook of Consumer Law 2007* (Ashgate, Surrey, 2007), pp. 229–276.

Willett, C., Naidoo, A. and Morgan-Taylor, M., 'The Sale and Supply of Goods to Consumers Regulations' (2004) *JBL* 94.

Companion Website

For open-access **student resources** specifically written to complement this textbook and support your learning, please visit **www.pearsoned.co.uk/legalupdates**

8 Consumer credit law and regulation

By Howard Johnson

8.1 Introduction

Consumer credit has increased enormously over the last half century or so. In the UK we have become a country increasingly dependent on debt, both as a country and as individual citizens. A massive change has taken place in respect of the use and perception of debt, both socially and culturally since the 1950s. Before World War II debt was regarded as being rather socially unacceptable and people proudly informed one that nothing in their house was 'bought on tick' (that is, on hire purchase), but post-war, with the development of the 'consumer society' and increased affluence, debt has become socially acceptable and now phrases like 'maxing the credit cards' are common and people commonly hold a wallet or handbag full of different credit and store cards. With increased affluence people have felt more confident about servicing higher levels of debt. The bursting of the asset and credit bubbles in the banking crisis of 2008–2009, the so-called 'credit crunch' and the following recession, has led to a slow down or decrease in the rise of debt but there is still considerable concern about levels of consumer over-indebtedness.[1] There has been increased regulatory focus on the issue of that minority of consumers who are seriously overindebted.[2] One must be very careful not to confuse the massive amounts outstanding in relation to property mortgages to buy houses and personal debt to buy things such as cars, items for a household such as televisions and services such as holidays, etc. – the latter is a relatively small proportion of consumer debt. Mortgage debt is largely secured by the value of the property though in times of following the recession such as the 2008–2009 'credit crunch' falls in property values can lead to negative equity where the value of the house is less than the outstanding mortgage. This chapter will focus more on personal consumer debt rather than on secured first mortgage lending from banks and building societies to consumers to acquire property (though the CCA regime does cover some second and subsequent charge mortgage lending).[3] High-cost credit for

[1] Household debt is monitored regularly by the Department for Business, Innovation and Skills (BIS) – see its Debt Monitoring Papers (at: http://webarchive.nationalarchiver.gov.uk+http://www.berr.gov.uk/files/file18559.pdf/). Figures published by the money advice charity Credit Action in February 2012 show unsecured debt at £208bn, down from £212bn in February 2011, and secured mortgage debt at £1.249 trillions, with average household debt (excluding mortgage debt) at £8,002 and, with mortgage debt, £56,016. Average consumer borrowing per UK adult was £4,235 in February 2012. Including mortgage debt this computes as the average UK adult owing £29,672, which is 123 per cent of average earnings. In 12 months to February 2012, £63.1bn, was estimated to have been paid in interest – that is £172m per day and an average of £2,427 per annum per household. However, £6.9bn of debt was written off in four quarters to end of 2011 (www.creditaction.org.uk/helpful-resources/debt-statistics.html, April 2012).

[2] BIS has focused considerable attention on overindebtness see: http://webarchive.nationalarchives.gov.uk/+http://www.berr.gov.uk/whatwedo/consumers/consumer-finance/over-indebtedness/index.htm) and more recently – CREDIT, DEBT AND FINANCIAL DIFFICULTY IN BRITAIN, 2011: A report using data from the YouGov DebtTrack survey, July 2012 https://www.gov.uk/government/uploads/system/uploads/attachment_data/file/36991/12-948-credit-debt-financial-difficulty-in-britain-2011.pdf. The UK Office of Budget Responsibility predicts household debt rising from £1.6 trillion in 2011 to £2.1 trillion in 2015 or from 160 per cent of disposable income to 175 per cent. However, households' net worth will exceed that, rising from £6.9 trillion to £7.55 trillion. The problem of course is much of that net worth is tied up in illiquid property assets and pension rights (http://budgetresponsibility.independent.gov.uk/wordpress/docs/household%20debt%20paper%20formatted.doc1.pdf, 21 April 2011).

[3] Recent research for the then Department for Business, Enterprise and Regulatory Reform (BERR) suggests that perhaps the problem of so–called 'overindebtedness' might be exaggerated and not quite the problem it is imagined to be (R. Disney, S. Bridges and J. Gathergood, *Drivers of Over-indebtedness*, Centre for Policy

vulnerable marginal or sub-prime borrowers who can often become involved with unlicensed illegal moneylenders[4] remains a significant concern nearly four decades after the modern consumer credit regime was introduced.[5] Vulnerable consumers raise two key problems: effective protection from unscrupulous lenders operating on the margins and providing them with affordable alternative sources of credit.[6] One of the regulatory challenges is that the credit market is very dynamic and constantly changing. The latest phenomena emerging is the growth of peer-to-peer lending through the operation of peer-to-peer sites such as Zopa, Funding Circle and Ratesetter – having an estimated turnover in June 2012 of some £250m.[7]

One risk with credit is that consumers will take on more than they can afford, whether through impulsiveness, bad planning or not fully understanding the extent of the commitment, etc.[8] To some extent this is addressed by the information and cancellation rights discussed in (see section 8.8), but, as discussed there, how effective these are is a matter of debate.[9] Certainly, these rights are (necessarily) only part of the picture of regulating consumer credit. This chapter deals with rules governing the regulation of consumer credit such as the rules on licensing, the advertising, marketing and canvassing of credit, customer

---

Evaluation, University of Nottingham, October 2008). Summary of the Report, para. 1: '. . . self-reported problems are not always associated with specific adverse financial circumstances or evidence of arrears, suggesting that trends in self-reported over-indebtedness are partly linked to perceptions fuelled by media coverage and to the household's own self-esteem and economic stability.'

[4] See 'OFT joins campaign to stop loan sharks', OFT PN 52/10, 24 May 2010, in which it was stated that an estimated 165,000 households in the UK were using illegal moneylenders, with half those in the most deprived areas of the country. Particular loan shark hotspots include Scotland, the North of England and the West Midlands.

[5] See OFT proposed reference of payday lenders to the competition commission – OFT acts against leading payday lenders and proposes to refer to competition commission. OFT Press Notice 20/13, 6 March 2013! http://www.off.gov.uk/news-and-updates/press/2013/20-13. For a general critique of payday loans, see 'Borrower beware', *Which?* June 2012, pp. 66–67.

[6] See two reports by Consumer Focus – 'Keeping the plates spinning: Perceptions of payday loans in Great Britain' Marie Burton, August 2010 (www.consumerfocus.org.uk/assets/1/files/2010/08/Keeping-the-plates-spinning.pdf) and 'Affordable credit: Lessons from Overseas', Personal Finance Research Centre (PFRC), University Bristol (www.consumerfocus.org.uk/files/2011/08/Affordable-credit-Lessons-from-overseas.pdf). These concerns, including criticism of what is seen as dilatoriness by the government in dealing with them, have been expressed by the House of Commons Business, Innovation and Skills Select Committee in its 14th Report (February 2012), on *Debt Management*, see Part III and Conclusions and Recommendations (www.publications.parliament.uk/pa/cm201012/cmselect/cmbis/1649/164902.htm).

[7] http://uk.zopa.com – some have called it the 'eBay of money'. The people who deposit their money in Zopa accounts do not benefit from the £85,000 account deposit protection scheme operated by the Financial Services Compensation Scheme (FSCS). However, suggestions by Andy Haldane, a director of the Bank of England, that the middlemen could eventually drop out would of course raise licensing issues under the CCA as such people would then be carrying on a consumer credit business.

[8] The Credit Services Association, a debt collection agency (DCA's) trade association in a press release of 27 April 2012 stated that, at the end of 2011, the total value of unpaid consumer debt held by CSA members for collection stood at £58 billion (£58.179bn), comprising £31 billion (£31.239bn) placed by creditors with DCAs to collect, and a further £27 billion (£26.940bn) of purchased debt owed to debt buyers. The total volume (that is, number) of consumer debts awaiting collection by CSA members now stands at, the CSA stated, a 'staggering' 32 million (32,130mn) as at the end of December 2011 – the equivalent of at least one significant debt for every UK household or £1,000 of uncollected debt owed by every man, woman and child in the country. However, this includes outsourced debts owed to government departments such as the Department for Work and Pensions (www.csa-uk.com/csa-news/63/unpaid-debts-revealed-in-new-industry-figures).

[9] See G. Howells, 'The Potential and Limits of Consumer Empowerment by Information' (2005) 32(3) *JLS* 2349–2370.

rights to end the agreement (other than under the cancellation rights mentioned in section 7.2), creditor liability for actions (such as breach of contract or misrepresentation) by a party that has supplied goods or services supported by the credit – so-called connected lender liability – and the various protections available to consumers when they are in default – the whole issue of dealing with consumer debt problems. In recent years – partly because of the pressures of the recession, claims management companies taking advantage of the complexity of the legislation to claim agreements are unenforceable and soliciting for business from debtors, the payment protection insurance-selling scandal and increased levels of consumer awareness, stimulated by a plethora of consumer affairs programmes on television and radio – there has been what has been described as a 'litigation explosion' in the area.[10]

It is worth noting that with the advent of the recession and the so-called 'credit crunch' in the summer of 2008 there have been increasing calls for the expansion and growth of cooperative self-help credit organisations, known as 'credit unions', which offer loans, usually of relatively small amounts at low or non-commercial rates. Credit unions, while quite extensive in some overseas countries and certain parts of the country such as Northern Ireland and the West of Scotland, have never caught on in a big way in the UK generally. Credit unions are subject to a special regime, which will not be discussed further in this chapter as it focuses on commercial business providers of credit and related services.[11]

In the light of the rapid expansion of the personal credit market and aggressive marketing by firms there is increased emphasis on requiring *responsible lending* and also encouraging the sharing of data by firms to ensure they have a good overview of the prospective debtor's finances.[12] These days most of us are familiar with someone who has multiple credit cards, often paying off the outstanding balance on one credit card by using another of their credit cards, resulting in the overall level of their debt rising relentlessly.

---

[10] See G. Howells, 'The Consumer Credit Litigation Explosion' (2010) 126 *LQR* 617–644.

[11] See N. Ryder, J. P. Devenney and G. Howells, 'The Credit Crunch: The Right Time for Credit Unions to Strike?' (2009) 29(1) *LS* 75–98 (on Westlaw) and also N. Ryder and J. Devenney, 'The Labour Government and Access to Affordable Credit: More Spin than Action?' (2005) 27(3–4) *Journal of Social Welfare and Family Law* 395. An earlier but still relevant perspective on use of welfare system loans is G. Howells, 'Social Fund Budgeting Loans, Social and Civil Justice?' (1990) *CJQ* 118. The government is seeking to enhance the role of credit unions, with the Department for Work and Pensions coordinating a feasibility study to examine the scope and the options for modernization and expansion of suitable credit unions, possibly through a link with the Post Office Network (www.dwp.gov.uk/other-specialists/the-growth-fund/latest-news). The government has been pursuing a deregulatory approach to permit expansion – see the Legislative Reform (Industrial and Provident Societies and Credit Unions) Order 2011, SI 2011/2687 and HM Treasury 'Legislative Reform Order', November 2009 (www.legislation.gov.uk/uksi/2011/2687/pdfs/uksiem_20112687_en.pdf).

[12] See *Consultation on the Removal of Barriers To The Sharing Of Non-Consensual Credit Data* (DTI URN 06/1357, 11/10/06) and see EU Internal Market Credit Histories (at: http://ec.europa.eu/internal_market/finservices-retail/credit/history_en.htm) and consultation document on how to share credit histories – *Consultation Document on Report of the Expert Group on Credit Histories*, 15/6/09 (at: http://ec.europa.eu/internal_market/consultations/2009/credit_histories_en.htm).

LEGISLATIVE PROVISION

Article 8.1 of the EU Consumer Credit Directive 2008/48/EC states:

> Member States shall ensure that, before the conclusion of a credit agreement, the creditor assesses the consumer's creditworthiness on the basis of sufficient information, where appropriate obtained from the consumer and, where necessary, on the basis of consultation of the relevant database. Member States whose legislation requires creditors to assess the creditworthiness of consumers on the basis of a consultation of the relevant database may retain this requirement.[13]

The OFT also regard 'irresponsible lending' as contravening the licensing provisions of the Act and issued new guidance, breach of which could lead to the revocation of a firm's licence for 'irresponsible lending'.[14]

A wider EU debate has also been initiated on this. A former EU Internal Market Commissioner, Charlie McCreevy, said:

> Responsible lending, where the credit products sold are appropriate for consumers' needs and are tailored to their ability to repay, and responsible borrowing, where consumers provide relevant, complete and accurate information on their financial conditions, are vital components in ensuring a stable and effective market.[15]

DEBATE BOX

Should debtors be relieved of paying back the whole or part of their debts where the creditor has been found to have engaged in 'irresponsible lending'?

Should consumers be encouraged to take greater responsibility for their lending decisions and bear the consequences?[16]

---

[13] Automatic updates of credit card limits should be a thing of the past by virtue of Art. 8(2) of the CCD and Art. 9 seeks to ensure cross-border accessing of databases to assist this assessment. Sharing of information causes tensions of course with consumer rights of privacy. For an earlier perspective on potential conflicts, see G. Howells, 'Data Protection, Confidentiality, Unfair Contract Terms, Consumer Protection and Credit Reference Agencies' (1995) *JBL* 343–359, and restrictions on disclosure of information by creditors when refusing to proceed with a prospective credit agreement at s. 157(2A).

[14] 'Irresponsible Lending: OFT guidance for creditors' (revised February 2011) OFT 1107 (at: www.oft.gov.uk/shared_oft/business_leaflets/general/oft1107.pdf).

[15] 'Responsible lending and borrowing in the EU', Press Release IP/09/922, 15/6/09 and see EU Internal Market webpage on responsible lending (at: http://ec.europa.eu/internal_market/finservices-retail/credit/responsible_lending_en.htm).

[16] A similar debate is going on in the investment industry on how far consumers should be responsible for their investment decisions – see *Consumer Responsibility*, FSA DP 08/05. The Financial Services Consumer Panel representing consumers' interests has reacted strongly against such a notion: 'The FSA's concentration on "consumer responsibility" is unrealistic and unhelpful in discussions about how to create an effective and efficient retail market that delivers real benefits to the consumer, the industry and to society. The regulator should focus its attention on the firms it authorises, not the consumers it is set up to protect', FSCP Press Release, 22 Jun 09, and full response, 'Consumer Responsibility' (at: www.fs-cp.org.uk/publications/pdf/dp0805_response.pdf).

Until 1974 credit was regulated by a number of piecemeal and fragmentary provisions, including the Bill of Sale Acts (1878–1882), Moneylenders Acts (1900–1927), Pawnbrokers Acts (1872–1960) and the Hire Purchase Act 1965. A much more comprehensive regime was introduced by the Consumer Credit Act 1974 (removing all of the above except the Bills of Sales Acts, which cover mortgages for personal property, known as chattel mortgages or Bills of Sale – something not caught by the 1974 Act).[17] There were inconsistent aims and principles, for example, very few restrictions on banks, say, advertising credit cards, but severe restrictions on what non-bank moneylenders could advertise. Under some legislation, such as the Moneylenders Acts 1900–1927, the slightest infraction of the agreement rules might render the loan agreement void and the loan irrecoverable, even where the consumer had suffered no prejudice, but in the case of hire purchase agreements, breach of the agreement rules could be dispensed with if the consumer had suffered no detriment. Sanctions varied wildly and there was no national enforcement body and patchy local enforcement.[18] However, the comprehensive nature of the 1974 Act was bought at the price of some complexity and technicality and even today many key issues have never been authoritatively resolved and both businesses and consumers find it a hard regime to understand.

Two key strands of credit had developed in the history of the provision of credit in England and Wales: *vendor credit* – essentially the supplying of goods on credit, such as hire purchase or conditional sale agreements – and *lender credit* – not necessarily linked to specific acquisitions of goods and services, such as bank loans, overdrafts and moneylending.

In 1968 a Royal Commission, the Crowther Commission (Crowther), was set up to look into the consumer credit market and its legal regulation. Its report formed the basis of the 1974 reforms.[19]

The 1974 Act remains the primary source of the law, with a large range of statutory instruments attached to it. However, following the White Paper, *Fair, Clear and Competitive: The Consumer Credit Market in the 21st Century*,[20] relevant reforms (for present purposes) were made by statutory instruments to the rules on advertising and early settlement calculations, while the Consumer Credit Act 2006 amended the 1974 Act[21] in relation to scope, financial

---

[17] The government of the day was not persuaded of the need for a reform of personal property law, which is a complex and technical area of law not pursued in this chapter. Chattel mortgages are unpopular because of the complexities of the Bills of Sales Acts 1878–1882, the slightest infraction of which can render the mortgage agreement void and the loan irrecoverable – a classic example of overkill in consumer protection legislation. See McBain, 'Repealing the Bills of Sale Acts' (2011) 5 *JBL* 475–512 and H. Johnson, 'Consumer Chattel Mortgages: To Ban or Not to Ban – Opportunity or Problem' (2011) *Durham Law Review* 26 November (at: http://durhamlawreview.co.uk/articles/24-consumer-chattel-mortgages-to-ban-or-not-to-ban-opportunity-or-problem.html). The government has opted for a voluntary code of practice to control potential abuses – see paras 37–49 and Annex C – Government Response to the Consultation on Proposals to Ban the Use of Bills of Sales for Consumer Lending' (BIS, January 2011).

[18] An excellent critique is contained in *Part Four – The Present State of Credit Law* of the Crowther Commission Report on Consumer Credit (1971) Cmnd 4596 (Crowther) – the Royal Commission on whose recommendations the CCA 1974 was largely based.

[19] Crowther set out proposals for two acts – one to deal with consumer credit transactions and a Lending and Security Act to deal with title to personal property and the taking of security over chattels. The latter proposal has never been acted on.

[20] The White Paper following a DTI/DWP Paper, *Tackling Over-indebtedness: Action Plan*, 2004 (at: http://webarchive.nationalarchives.gov.uk/+http://www.berr.gov.uk/files/file18559.pdf) and a related DTI Consultation Document – *Establishing a Transparent Market* (DTI Consultation Document, December 2003).

[21] This was done by amendment by incorporating the new provisions into the main Act so generally this chapter will refer to the CCA 1974 provisions, not to the CCA 2006 provisions amending the main Act. The changes were implemented over an 18-month period and are now in force.

limits, informational requirements, enforcement, licensing and unfair credit relationships. The implementation of the EU Consumer Credit Directive 2008/48/EC (CCD) has led to further reforms and an added layer of complexity with a series of parallel provisions covering areas outside previous domestic UK legislation but within the scope of the Directive (for example, s. 75A, CCA).[22]

Most recently, a number of new industry self-regulatory Codes of Practice governing areas such as use of bills of sale, store cards, credit card use and repayments and the 'payday loan' industry have been promoted by the Department for Business, Innovation and Skills with the threat of legislative intervention down the line if abuses are not corrected.[23]

8.2 Restructuring of the regulatory regime

A major restructuring of consumer credit regulation is being undertaken by the Coalition Government Act in the Financial Services provision for which provision is made in the ss 7(3)(5), 107 & 108, 2012. The proposed structure of the new regulatory regime is set out in 'High-level proposal for an FCA regirme for consumer credit' consultation paper CP 13/7 (March 2013): http://www.fsa.gov.uk/library/policy/cp/2013/13a/pdf. The main change will be the transference of responsibility from the shortly to be abolished Office of Fair Trading to the newly created Financial Conduct Authority, which in effect takes over the consumer protection and market regulation of financial products from the Financial Services Authority, which is to be abolished.[23a] For the first time the regulation of the entire credit market will be under one roof, so for example, all mortgage lending will be overseen by one body instead of, as is the case now, two – the FSA and the OFT.[23b] However, before the change takes place, the government is committed to designing a model of FCA regulation that reflects the particular characteristics of consumer credit and is proportionate for the different segments of the market according to the risk they pose to the consumer. The transfer will then be subject to approval by Parliament. Confirmation of the transfer of jurisdication has been made and the approval of Parliament will be sought in the summer of 2013 and the FCA finally taking over from the OFT in April 2014, if there is no legislative slippage. It is envisaged that some primary legislation will be able to be repealed and the new FCA will work like the FSA through a system of principles and conduct of business rules, enshrined in a more responsive and flexible handbook. Standards of conduct currently in the CCA, its statutory instruments and OFT Guidance Notices will be recast as FCA Rules and Guidance. There will be a greater

---

[22] The EU proposals have now been implemented and reference to the new sections of the revised Consumer Credit Act will be made but of course the final interpretation of whether or not this has been done appropriately lies with the Court of Justice of the European Communities. It is important to note that in *Martin Martin v EDP Editores SL* (C-227/08) [2010] 2 CMLR 27, the CJEU took the view that a judge could raise of their own volition infringement of EU consumer protection law in that case Directive 85/577 in relation to Contracts Negotiated Away from Business Premises even where the claimant had not pleaded the issue.

[23] See para 8.1B.

[23a] The FSA will formally cease to exist in April 2013 if the legislative schedule is kept to but already it has divided itself, as of April 2012, into two shadow bodies – the Shadow Prudential Regulatory Authority and the Shadow Financial Conduct Authority – in anticipation of the changes. The general proposals and rationale for them were set out in the Department for Business, Innovation and Skills Consultation Paper – *A New Approach to Financial Regulation: Consultation on Reforming the Consumer Credit Regime'* (December 2010 (at: www.hm-treasury.gov.uk/d/consult_consumer_credit211210.pdf).

[23b] The enabling powers are contained in sections 7 and 107 of the Financial Services Act 2012.

role for industry self-regulation and codes. New dimensions may include prudential require-ments such as minimum capital and/or professional indemnity insurance for licensees. Another crossover from investment and insurance areas would be an appointed representa-tives regime so that, for example, a car dealer would be an appointed representative of a finance company, which finance company would then be responsible for ensuring the car dealer's adherence to the new FCA credit regime. An example of how this might work is the £91,000 fine imposed on the UK Car Group Ltd (UKCG) for the failings of its appointed representative, CC Automotive Ltd – trading as Carcraft – in respect of the monitoring of payment protection insurance (PPI) sales. UKCG failed to deal appropriately with concerns raised in internal audits regarding sales of PPI by Carcraft, in particular to ensure the suit-ability of advice given to customers. There was not an adequate response to ongoing concerns over failure to record properly advice given to customers, issues of staff competence, monitor-ing of individual advisers and the provision of completed documentation to customers.[24] There is some concern about whether or not a regime devised for selling investments and insurance is suitable for a regime of lending money. The assumption, of course, is that the FCA will only have to licence major players such as banks and finance companies, leaving them in effect to police the smaller fry such as credit brokers and car dealers who will act as their appointed representatives. There are concerns that downgrading legislative provisions to rules in the FCA consumer credit handbook will only leave the expensive remedy of judi-cial review as a way of challenging these where there are concerns about their scope and proportionality. However, the government sees the significant advantage of a system that can respond to abuses in a dynamic and changing market more rapidly – this can be illustrated by the fact that almost from the date of passage there were criticisms of the CCA 1974 regime but major new primary legislation did not appear until 2006 and then took a further 18 months to roll out. The regime can also be fine tuned, aimed at practices of individual firms, with greater statutory discretion based on widely defined principles and broad rule-making powers.

8.3 Industry self-regulation

Reducing burdens on business and excessive red tape has been a repeated theme of recent UK governments and this has been reflected in the consumer credit area by the willingness of the Department for Business Innovation and Skills to utilise industry self-regulation and codes of good trading practice in the first instance to deal with problem areas. In recent times revised codes have been agreed in respect of store and credit cards,[25] the use of bills of sale or chattel mortgages as security for loans[26] and a revised code of practice for payday

---

[24] See 'FSA Fines Car Supermarket for PPI Sales Monitoring Failings', FSA/PN/047/2012, 3/5/12 (at: www.fsa.gov.uk/library/communication/pr/2012/047.shtml) and the final notice for UKCG Ltd (at: www.fsa.gov.uk/static/pubs/final/uk-car-group.pdf, 26/1/12 – breach of Principle 9, customers: relationship of trust) – the fine was reduced by 30 per cent for early settlement of the matter by UKCG Ltd.

[25] 'A Better Deal for Consumers: Review of the Regulation of Credit and Store Cards: Government Response to Consultation' involving five voluntary commitments on minimum payments, controlling credit limits, rights to information and right to compare costs with other providers (at: www.bis.gov.uk/assets/biscore/corporate/docs/c/10-768-consumer-credit-card-consultation-response.pdf).

[26] 'Government Response to the Consultation on Proposals to Ban the Use of Bills of Sale for Consumer Lending', January 2011, Code of Practice Annex C (at: www.gov.uk/government/uploads/system/uploads/attachment_data/file/31484/11-516-government-response-proposal-ban-bills-of-sale.pdf).

lenders.[27] Critics of this say it is soft law and will never effectively deal with the rogue fringe who do not subscribe to the code and such codes are rarely effectively enforced by trade associations with limited resources. Proponents point to flexibility, speedy implementation and the fact that non-compliance with the codes can be a reason for the OFT to issue a requirements notice or ultimately to revoke, suspend or vary a consumer credit licence.

8.4 Some key definitions and features

The Act creates its own complex definitional structure largely to guide a person around which parts of the Act apply to which type of agreement, but we still use the older common law and statutory terms such as 'hire purchase'. No one would dream of talking about a hire purchase agreement as 'a regulated consumer credit agreement which is a fixed sum, restricted-use, debtor-creditor-supplier agreement', which a hire purchase agreement is within the Act's definitions.

To help people navigate their way around the Act, Sch. 2 sets out a series of examples – but it is important to remember these are illustrative and not statutorily binding. On occasions courts have held that they are wrong, in the sense of not giving the correct legal position.[28]

8.4.1 'Individual'

In most other consumer legislation the protection is limited to those acting for non-business purposes.[29] Here the main rules (that is, on consumer credit and hire agreements) apply much more broadly to 'individuals'. This covers the typical private consumer, but also covers partnerships of up to three people as well as unincorporated bodies that are not partnerships and do not consist entirely of corporate bodies.[30] It should be noted that the new EU Consumer Credit Directive only applies to 'a natural person who, in transactions covered by this Directive, is acting for purposes which are outside his trade or profession' (Art. 3(a)).

[27] As from 25 July 2012 four main trade associations (Consumer Finance Association (CFA), Finance and Leasing Association (FLA), British Cheque and Credit Association (BCCA) and Consumer Credit Trade Association (CCTA)) agreed to increased requirements on information, transparency about charges and repayments, robust credit assessments and increased help for borrowers in difficulties. See BIS press release, 'Better Help for Consumers in Financial Difficulty from Payday Loans', 24 May 2012 (at: http://news.bis.gov.uk/Press-Releases/Better-help-for-consumers-in-financial-difficulty-from-payday-loans-67a77.aspx). The OFT gives payday lenders ultimatum about further legal action – see OFT Press Notice 20/1 & 3, 6 March 2013 http://www.oft.gov.uk/news-and-updates/press/2013/20-13.

[28] See *Heath v Southern Pacific Mortgage* (2009) 5 EG 107, where the judge agreed with the authoritative commentator on consumer credit law, Professor Roy Goode, that examples 16 and 18 on the elusive and difficult concept of 'multiple agreements' in s. 18 are wrong, and R. Carter 'Statutory Interpretation Using Legislated Examples: Bennion on Multiple Consumer Agreements' (2011) 32(2) *Stat LR* 86–115.

[29] For example, the Unfair Terms in Consumer Contracts Regulations 1999, SI 1999/2083 and the Consumer Protection from Unfair Trading Regulations 2008, SI 2008/1277, on which see, respectively, Chapter 4, section 4.9 and Chapter 7, section 7.7.

[30] Section 189(1), CCA 1974, as amended by s. 1 of the 2006 Act (narrowing the definition, which used to catch any size of partnership). It is also important to note that 'individual' can encompass unincorporated bodies such as social and sports clubs and even large trades unions such as the Transport and General Workers Union. Further, even corporate bodies may obtain some protections under the Act if they are one of a number of joint debtors who include individuals (see s. 185(5), CCA).

8.4.2 Credit, total charge for credit and financial limits

'Credit' is defined as 'a cash loan and any form of financial accommodation.'[31] Essentially, this is the sum being borrowed. It is important to note that the Act covers the giving or extending of the facility of credit – for example, if you enter an overdraft agreement it may be regulated, even though you never have to overdraw your bank account, or a credit card agreement must comply with the Act though it is never actually used by the consumer. The courts will look at the substance and not the form of the agreement to determine if credit has been granted. This is illustrated in the case of *McMillan Williams* v *Range*,[32] where a lady was employed as an assistant solicitor on a commission-only basis at the rate of a third of her client paid bill income. It was decided that she would be given an annual salary of £22,000 as an advance against these commission payments – everyone anticipating the commission would more than cover the advance. However, things went badly and her commission did not exceed her salary payments and she was required to repay some £18,300 overpaid 'commission'. She argued that the advances on her commission were credit, in effect a loan which she might have to pay back in whole or part, and there had been a failure to comply with the consumer credit agreement regulations and therefore the overpayments were irrecoverable. The Court of Appeal looking at the substance of the matter rejected this argument. In their view, where it was uncertain if the arrangements between the parties would give rise to a debt at all, there was no credit merely because the arrangements postponed any obligation to pay until such time as the future possible indebtedness had crystallised. Here, in substance, there was a contract of employment involving advance payment of remuneration in advance of the services to be provided and this did not involve the notion of credit.

'*Total charge for credit*', by contrast, is made up of the interest and any other charges (with certain exclusions, such as default, maintenance and variable bank charges) that it costs to borrow this sum (whether payable under the main agreement or associated agreements).[33] This charge for credit is converted into an annual percentage rate,[34] which has proved to be a

---

[31] 1974 Act, s. 9(1); and see *Dimond* v *Lovell* [2000] 2 WLR 1121 on this definition and *Black Horse Ltd* v *Hanson* [2009] EWCA Civ 73.

[32] [2004] 1 WLR 1858 – discussed in H. Johnson, 'The Concept of Credit' (2004) *F&CL* 4–5.

[33] See the Consumer Credit (Total Charge for Credit) Regulations 2010, SI 2010/1011 (as amended) and the Consumer Credit (Total Charge for Credit) Regulations 1980, SI 1980/51, as amended by the Consumer Credit (Total Charge for Credit, Agreement and Advertisement) (Amendment) Regulations 1999, SI 1999/3177, made under s. 20 of the 1974 Act and J. P. Devenney and N. Ryder, 'The Cartography of the Concept of "Total Charge for Credit" under the Consumer Credit Act 1974' [2006] *Conv* 475. Fact time given to pay part of total charge for credit does not convert the item into credit – see *Southern Pacific Personal Loans Ltd* v *Michael Walker* [2009] EWCA 218. The European Commission has issued a Staff Working Document explaining how the annual percentage rate of charge is to be worked out under the CCD – 'Guidelines on the Application of Directive 2008/48/EC (Consumer Credit Directive) in Relation to Costs and the Annual Percentage Rate of Charge', SWD (2012) 128 Final, 8/5/12 and amended the CCD in this area – Commission Directive 2011/90/EU, 14/11/2011 amending Part II of Annex 1 of the CCD in relation to assumptions to be made in relation to overdraft and open-ended credit agreements.

[34] The role of the APR and whether it should act as the 'driver' for other interest rates such as weekly or monthly rates were considered in *Sternlight* v *Barclays Bank* [2010] EWHC 1865 (QB), Judge Wakesman QC. The judge held that if the monthly and weekly rates were stated correctly as agreed in the contract there was no breach of consumer credit agreement – the APR not the 'driver' of these rates. The APR which had to be stated at the beginning of the agreement was a informational guide and not a prescribed term of the contract.

very complex exercise and, indeed, has led to criticism that the APR has not proved to be of a great use.[35] The complexity of interest rates and charges in relation to credit cards was the subject of a 'super-complaint' under s. 11, Enterprise Act 2002, which led to an agreement with the industry to clarify and make charges clearer for credit card users.[36]

It is important to note that the Act draws a strict demarcation line between the credit and the total charge for credit. In assessing if an agreement was within the scope of the Act, it was the amount of 'credit' advanced that was key to determining whether or not the agreement came within the scope of the current upper financial limit – latterly £25,000. This is less significant now that the upper limit has been abolished in the case of most regulated agreements, but may still be important in issues as to whether or not business lending to small partnerships exceeds £25,000 and, thus, is an exempt agreement or under £25,000 and regulated by the Act. It can also lead to complications with advertising and agreement regulations if an item is wrongly treated as credit rather than as part of the total charge for credit. Drawing the line between what is 'credit' and what is part of the total charge for credit has not always proved an easy task. The Supreme Court considered the matter in *Southern Pacific Securities 05-2 PLC v Walker*,[37] where they concluded that a broker administration fee was part of the charge for credit within s. 9(4) of the Act whether or not time was given for payment of it and whether or not the charge borne interest if payment was spread over a period.[38] Lord Clarke, delivering the judgment, stated:

> As the court sees it, the borrowers' case involves construing section 9(4) as if it read:
>
> > For the purposes of this Act, an item entering into the total charge for credit shall not be treated as credit even though time is allowed for payment (unless interest is charged, in which case it shall be treated as credit).
>
> > There is in our judgment no warrant for the addition of the words in italics. We agree with the conclusions of Mummery LJ at paras 34 and 35: in particular that the borrowers' submissions treat interest as a necessary feature or indicator of credit, which it is not, and that it was not the function of s. 9 to prohibit anything but rather to supply a special statutory meaning to the core concept of credit in the Act and to distinguish it from the charge for, or cost of, credit.[39]

Previously, s. 8(2) of the 1974 Act restricted its application to agreements where the total credit[40] did not exceed £25,000. This limit has been retained for agreements entered into predominantly for business purposes,[41] but abolished[42] for personal credit, that is, where private consumers are the borrowers, although it still applies to these latter agreements made before 5 April 2008. In calculating the total credit (to determine applicability of the regime to business agreements and pre-April 2008 private agreements) difficult decisions sometimes

---

[35] See Guidelines on the application of Directive 2008/48/EC (Consumer Credit Directive) in relation to costs and the Annual Percentage Rate of Charge, SWD (2012) 128 Final – on working the APR out under the CCD.

[36] See 'Response to the Super-complaint on Credit Card Interest Rate Calculation Methods by *Which?*', 26 June 2007, OFT935 (at: www.oft.gov.uk/shared_oft/reports/financial_products/oft935.pdf).

[37] [2010] 4 All ER 277.

[38] The fee and interest thereon were 'other charges' within the meaning of the Consumer Credit (Total Charge for Credit) Regulations 1980, reg. 4(b).

[39] At para. 23.

[40] That is, the sum being borrowed, not including interest or any other charges making up the total charge for the credit.

[41] New s. 16B, inserted by s. 4 of the 2006 Act.

[42] By amendment of s. 8(2) by s. 1 of the 2006 Act.

need to be made as to whether or not charges such as insurance premiums are part of the 'credit' (and therefore counting towards the sum subject to the financial limit) or part of the 'total charge for credit' (and, therefore not counting for these purposes).[43]

> **EXAMPLE**
>
> If £24,000 is borrowed by a small, three-person partnership, this is the 'credit', while the interest rate of, say, £2,000 is the 'total charge for credit'. Even though the total repayments involved amount to £26,000 the agreement would not be exempt because the credit advanced is only £24,000 and you do not count the £2,000 in the total charge for the credit.

Note that the 'total charge for credit' must be expressed as the so-called annual percentage rate, or, APR.[44]

The distinction between the credit and the total charge for credit is also important because if the credit figure in the agreement incorrectly includes an element that is part of the total charge for credit, the agreement may be unenforceable against the consumer.[45]

8.4.3 Types of agreement – regulated agreement

An agreement is a 'regulated' one where it is either a 'consumer credit agreement' or a 'consumer hire agreement' and it does not fall into one of the 'exempt' categories (to be considered below).

8.4.3.1 Consumer credit agreement

Section 8(2) defines a consumer credit agreement as one in which the creditor provides an individual (the debtor) with credit not exceeding the above financial limits. This includes credit card agreements, unsecured bank loans and overdrafts, loans secured by a mortgage over land and 'pledges'. Under a pledge the borrower passes possession in the goods to the creditor (as security), although he remains the owner (in contrast with a mortgage, where the borrower retains possession, but the creditor has a form of ownership).

A consumer credit agreement specifically includes the following.

---

[43] See, for example, the Court of Appeal decisions in *Humberclyde Finance Ltd* v *Thomson* [1997] CCLR 23 and *London North Securities Ltd* v *Meadows* [2005] EWCA Civ 956 (in both cases insurance premiums were part of the 'total charge for credit', not the credit itself, but in the *London North* case, money advanced to pay off arrears on a previous mortgage was held to be part of the credit). In the High Court decision in *Wilson* v *Robertson (London) Ltd* [2005] 3 All ER 873 (the documentation fee was part of total charge for credit, not the credit itself), the impact of these errors has been lessened since the repeal of s. 127(3)–(5) which mandated automatic unenforceability for certain types of omissions, errors or mistakes.

[44] Regulation 6, Consumer Credit (Total Charge for Credit) Regulations 1980, SI 1980/3177.

[45] See *Wilson* v *First County Trust (No 2)* [2001] 3 All ER 229, *Watchtower Investments Ltd* v *Payne* [2001] EWCA Civ 1159 and *McGinn* v *Grangewood Securities* [2002] EWCA Civ 522.

Hire purchase. This is where goods are hired[46] to the debtor (hirer) in return for periodical payments; property in the goods to pass to the debtor (hirer) on payment along with the exercise of an option to purchase by the debtor or the doing or happening of any specified event.[47] The key distinction from any form of sale (see below on these) is that the debtor/hirer in a hire purchase does not commit himself to buying under the contract, but merely has the option to purchase[48] (so long as the hire payments are made and any other relevant conditions satisfied).

Note that, whatever 'label' the parties put on the agreement, courts will decide, based on the substance of the agreement, whether it is a genuine hire purchase agreement or actually a conditional sale.[49]

Conditional and credit sales. In both cases, the key distinction between these and hire purchase is that the buyer commits to buy the goods from the outset. In a conditional sale all or part of the purchase price is payable in instalments, while the title is reserved to the seller until the conditions as to payment of instalments (or whatever else) are satisfied.[50] Under a credit sale the buyer is given time to pay, but there is no reservation of title – the ownership passes to him immediately.

Note that, in the case of hire purchase and conditional sales, the relationship may simply be with the dealer, that is, the dealer is supplying the goods and the credit facility to the consumer. However, in modern times, it is very common for the dealer to sell the goods for cash to a finance company, it being this finance company that actually enters in to the hire purchase or conditional sale agreement with the consumer.[51]

Note, finally, that the above types of consumer credit agreements are sub-classified depending on whether or not they are one of the following.

- *Running account or fixed sum credit.* These are defined in s. 10 of the Act and essentially the former covers, for instance, overdrafts and credit cards as they both involve the facility 'from time to time' of an advance up to a credit limit;[52] while the latter is 'any *other* facility' for credit and covers hire purchase, conditional sales, credit sales and bank loans.[53]

---

[46] Hire is technically a form of 'bailment', a contract under which possession, but not ownership, is given to another – the owner of the goods is the 'bailor', while the hirer is the 'bailee'.

[47] See definition in s. 189, CCA.

[48] *Helby* v *Matthews* [1895] AC 471, which can be contrasted with a conditional sale agreement, which fulfils the same economic effect and property will pass when the instalments have been paid, but the buyer has legally committed themselves to buy from the outset, as in *Lee* v *Butler* [1893] 2 QB 318. Not being a 'buyer' during the hire period has relevance in relation to the rules on transfer of title, on which see section 4.6 above.

[49] *Forthright Finance Ltd* v *Carlyle Finance Ltd* [1997] 4 All ER 90.

[50] *Carlyle Finance* v *Pallas Industrial Finance* [1999] 1 All ER (Comm) 659; *Forthright Finance Ltd* v *Caryle Finance Ltd* [1997] 4 All ER 90.

[51] The dealer must be careful about making any unauthorised representations or promises because in many circumstances they are deemed to be the statutory agent of the finance company under s. 56 of the CCA (see section 8.9.1).

[52] Section 10(1)(a) – see anti-avoidance provisions to stop parties setting artificially high and unrealistic credit limits to avoid the operation of the Act – s. 10(3), for example, a business credit agreement with a limit of £30,000 would be within the Act if the debtor could only use credit of £1,000 at any one time and would pay a higher interest rate if debit balance exceeded £20,000. In the context of the agreement it is unlikely the debtor would ever draw up to £30,000.

[53] Section 10(1)(b).

- *Restricted and unrestricted use credit.* These are defined in s. 11. The former covers credit (such as hire purchase, credit sales and conditional sales) that is intended solely to finance a transaction (or re-finance existing indebtedness) between the debtor and either the creditor or someone else (for example, the dealer).[54] The latter covers agreements (such as overdrafts) that are not restricted in this way.[55]

- *Debtor-creditor-supplier (D-C-S) and debtor-creditor (D-C) agreements.* These are defined in ss. 12 and 13. The former (D-C-S) covers two types of situation. First, there is the situation where the creditor and the supplier are the same person, for example, where the goods are supplied by a retailer under a hire purchase or conditional sale agreement financed by the retailer or where the goods (having been sold to a finance company by the retailer) are supplied by this finance company on some such basis. This is known as a 'two-party' debtor-creditor-supplier situation, it being 'two party' in the sense that there are only two parties, that is, the consumer and the supplier/creditor (who is the same person).

The second type of situation is where the creditor and supplier are different persons but have an 'arrangement',[56] for example, where retail sellers or suppliers agree to accept certain credit cards to finance purchases from their shops or where they have an arrangement with a finance company that the finance company will extend credit to finance purchases from those retailers. This is known as a 'three-party' debtor-creditor-supplier situation, it being 'three party' in the sense that there are three parties involved, that is, the consumer, the supplier of the goods and the party financing the transaction. In fact these days many D-C-S agreements are 'four-party' arrangements where you have a debtor (credit card holder), the creditor (bank issuing credit card), the supplier of the goods or services and a 'merchant acquirer' (usually a bank) who in effect operates the system processing payments for retailers and signing up retailers to the major networks such as Visa and MasterCard and making payments to the creditor – all of course for commissions or interchange fees (transactions entered into using a credit card processed through a merchant acquirer can still be a regulated D-C-S).[57]

Then there is a D-C agreement where there is no arrangement of the type described above, for example, a bank loan or overdraft that is not based on any relationship with the creditor and whoever the consumer may (or may not) choose to use the money to buy goods or services from. There is also a D-C agreement where the credit is to re-finance existing indebtedness, whether to the creditor or anyone else.

8.4.3.2 Consumer hire agreement

The Act also applies to consumer hire agreements. This category covers a bailment (hire) of goods to an individual who is not a hire purchase (that is, there is no option to purchase),

---

[54] Section 11(1)(a)–(c).
[55] Section 11(2)–(4). It is important to note that credit does not become restricted simply because certain uses would breach the contract, for example, an overdraft granted on the basis it is to be used by a student for living expenses would not be restricted simply because it would be a breach of contract to use it for gambling (s. 11(1)(3)).
[56] See s. 187. The concept is very wide and can include both pre-existing arrangements and future arrangements, for example, if you use a credit card at a dealer's who was not open when you entered the card agreement it will be a D-C-S agreement because it could be anticipated that new dealers would be constantly added to the approved list as new businesses opened.
[57] *Office of Fair Trading* v *Lloyds TSB Bank PLC* [2007] 1 QB 1 and see *Lancore Services Ltd* v *Barclays Bank PLC* [2008] EWHC 1264 (J. Chuah, 'Third-party Processing in Credit Card Arrangements' (2009) *F&C* 4–6).

where the agreement is capable of lasting more than three months. The payments required must be less than the £25,000 limit where the individual is acting for business purposes or (where a private consumer is concerned) the agreement was made before 5 April 2008. However, post-5 April 2008, where the individual is a private consumer, there is no upper limit. The concept of a regulated consumer hire agreement was recently considered by the House of Lords in *TRM Copy Centres (UK) Ltd* v *Lanwell Services Ltd*.[58] TRM leased photocopiers to businesses such as shops and sub-post offices in return for payments related to copy usage by the customers of the business. Under the location agreement the retailer agreed to the installation of the copier on his premises which was easily visible and accessible by customers. Both the retailer and his customers could use the machine for a fixed price per copy. The retailer undertook to collect the monies and account to TRM for it minus a commission which the retailer could keep. The retailer undertook to keep the copier operational and provide a clear, safe, accessible and orderly location for it. The retailer also undertook to use best efforts to maximise copy time, deal with refilling of supplies such as cartridges, paper, etc., remove jams and organise repairs where necessary. Lanwell supplied machines under a more traditional rental system and persuaded some of TRM's clients to use their equipment and remove TRM's. TRM sued them on the basis that their conduct amounted to the tort of inducing a breach of contract. Lanwell responded that TRM were entering into unlicensed regulated hire agreements and the resulting agreements were unenforceable under s. 40 of the CCA and thus no action in tort could lie if the retailers breached unenforceable agreements. The question was, therefore, was the definition in s. 15 satisfied?[59] The drafting of s. 15 complicates matters by defining hire as bailment and the two concepts are not synonymous. Their Lordships took the view that the agreement did not have the most obvious badge of a hire contract in that the retailer was under no obligation to make any payment if the retailer or their customers did not use the copier. The House of Lords focused on the commercial reality of the agreement and took the view that it was not hire. In reality, the payments were by the owner to the retailer, not the other way round, which is what one would expect in a hire agreement. The retailer kept back a certain percentage of the money, which was the owner of the copier's money, for which the retailer had to account.[60]

8.4.4 Types of agreement – partially regulated agreement

A 'non-commercial agreement' is one not made in the course of a business carried on by the creditor or owner;[61] covering, for example, loans made between friends or even by a business that is not generally in the business of extending credit.[62] Such agreements are excluded from a number of provisions of the Act, including those on formation and cancellation.[63]

---

[58] [2009] 1 WLR 1375.

[59] Scottish law would have recognised the contract as one of hiring (Lord Hope at para. 9) and so within s. 15.

[60] Baroness Hale was concerned at the exposure to abuse small businesses might face by this lacuna in the Act – see paras 21 and 22. From the start there has been concern that hire agreements do not fall very easily within the structure of the Act. See N. Palmer and D. Yates, 'The Application of the Consumer Credit Act 1974 to Consumer Hire Agreements' (1979) 38 *CLJ* 180.

[61] Section 189(1).

[62] *Hare* v *Schurek* [1993] CCLR 47.

[63] Section 74(1), CCA.

Also exempt from most of the provisions on formalities and cancellation are 'small agreements', these being regulated credit agreements (other than hire purchase or conditional sale) for credit up to £50 and regulated hire agreements involving payments up to £50.[64]

8.4.5 Types of agreements – exempt agreements

Sections 16, 16A and 16B of the 1974 Act along with the Consumer Credit (Exempt Agreements) Orders 1989 and 2007 exempt from the Act a number of agreements – though a number have had to be revised to comply with the EU CCD. These are the main ones.

- Agreements secured on land (that is, first mortgages) and made by local authorities as well as the vast majority of such agreements made by any other bodies.[65]

- D-C-S agreements to finance the purchase of land where the number of payments does not exceed four.

- D-C-S agreements (other than hire purchase and conditional sale) where the number of payments does not exceed four and the payments are to be made within 12 months of the date of the agreement.[66] This covers normal trade credit, for instance where a newsagent, garage or builder requires payment 'within 30 days of invoice'. This has been amended to comply with the CCD and this exemption will now only apply where the credit is granted free of interest, without any other charges and the credit has to be repaid by a limited number of payments (four or less) within a year beginning with the date of the agreement.[67]

- 'Running account' D-C-S agreements where the whole of the periodical payment is repayable by a single payment, for example, household newspaper and grocery accounts and charge cards, such as American Express.[68] Under the CCD this has been amended from 1 February 2011 to cover making payments in relation to specified periods not exceeding three months with one repayment of the whole credit and in relation to which no or insignificant charges are payable for the credit.

- D-C agreements only offered to a restricted class or classes of persons (for example, employees), where interest is the only component of the 'total charge for credit' and this interest does not exceed 1 per cent above the bank base rates.

- Consumer credit agreements, where the credit is to be used in connection with overseas trade and certain agreements with members of the armed forces of the USA, members of their families and an employee of the US army not habitually resident in the UK.

---

[64] Section 17, though, in one of those irritating parallel regimes which exist on the same topic (here cancellation rights), if a small credit agreement is covered the Consumer Protection (Cancellation of Contracts Concluded Away from Business Premises) Regulations 1987, SI 1987/2217, then the figure of £35 is substituted for £50 – s. 74[2A], CCA. This is just the type of thing that makes this regime disliked by many SMEs as a minefield of complexity.

[65] The control of first mortgage lending is the province of the Financial Services Authority operating under the Financial Services and Markets Act 2000.

[66] See cases such as *Zoan* v *Rouamba* [2000] 2 All ER 620, *Dimond* v *Lovell* [2000] 2 All ER 897, *Ketley* v *Gilbert* [2001] 1 WLR 986 and *Clark* v *Tull* [2003] QB 36 on complications in calculating this 12-month period.

[67] Consumer Credit (EU Directive) Regulations 2010, SI 2010/1010, reg. 66.

[68] This will not apply to charge cards where extended credit is allowed, that is, where the whole amount does not need to be paid off in a single payment.

- Hire agreements for the hire of metering equipment, for example, for water, electricity or gas.

- Agreements where the debtor is an Individual who makes a declaration[69] of willingness to forego protection under the Act and either the creditor, owner or an accountant declares that the debtor has a certain 'high net worth' (meaning a net income of at least £150,000 or assets with a total value of £500,000).[70] The CCD does not allow the UK to apply the 'high net worth' exemption to loans below £60,260 so this exemption now does not apply to loans below that figure, unless secured on land.[71]

- Credit agreements with an investment firm or credit institution in relation to the carrying out of transactions with that firm under the Market in Financial Instruments Directive 2004/39/EC.

- A D-C agreement where the creditor is a credit union and the rate of total charge for credit does not exceed 26.9 APR.

- Certain agreements relating to land mortgages in connection with investment property where the debtor or someone connected to them will use less than 40 per cent of the property in connection with a dwelling (s. 16C, CCA) – a court order will still be needed under s. 126 to enforce the mortgage despite the general exemption of these agreements from the rest of the Act (s. 16C(5), CCA).

- Agreements with business customers where, although the £25,000 limit is exceeded, the credit is wholly or predominantly for a business purpose. For example, a hire purchase agreement for a doctor's car that is only used occasionally for work would therefore not be exempt.[72]

Note that the business loan exemption does not apply where the 'unfair relationships' test is concerned, for example, a business loan to a small trader for £30,000 at an unfair rate of interest could be reopened by the court and this is the case in relation to most of the other exemptions, on which, see section 8.13.6.

8.4.6 Types of agreements – multiple agreements

One of the more elusive concepts in the Act is the concept of the multiple agreement – the idea is simple enough: it is an anti-avoidance provision to stop parties consolidating into one agreement what in reality are two separate agreements to avoid the operation of the Act, for example, a business loan to a small partnership where the credit advanced is £60,000. In principle this is outside the Act, but in reality it may be three separate agreements involving £20,000 put together to avoid the operation of the Act. The problem has been to apply the section in practice.

---

[69] In the form prescribed in Schs 1 and 2 to the Consumer Credit (Exempt Agreements) Order 2007.

[70] Section 16A.

[71] See Consumer Credit (EU Directive) Regulations 2010, SI 2010/1010, Pt 3, reg. 92 (as from 1 February 2011, subject to transitional provisions).

[72] Section 16B (and see above, section 8.4.3). It is worth noting that to avoid disputes the debtor can make a declaration that the agreement is being entered into wholly or predominantly for business purposes and this will create a rebuttable presumption to this effect. It will not apply if the debtor can show that the creditor or any person acting on his behalf knew or had reasonable cause to suspect that the agreement was not entered into for business purposes (ss. 16B(2)–(3), CCA).

Section 18 of the Act envisages four different situations, as follows.

1. An agreement the terms of which are to place it in two or more categories of agreement.

2. Part of it falls within one category and another part in another category.

3. Part of it is within one category of the Act and another part outside the Act.

4. An agreement where part of it falls within two or more categories.[73]

A good example of a multiple agreement is a credit card agreement. It is a D-C-S agreement when using the card to pay for goods from a dealer and D-C when using the card to take cash from an ATM machine, so the agreement must comply with any parts of the Act applying to D-C-S and to D-C.[74]

In the end the courts seem to look at the substance of matters and apply the section in an intuitively realistic way. In *Heath v Southern Pacific Mortgage Ltd*[75] a mortgage company had advanced some £28,400 to the borrower secured on her home. The sum of £19,000 was to be applied to pay off a pre-existing mortgage and the remainder was to be used by the borrower for her own purposes. The borrower in effect argued that there were two agreements which had not been correctly treated as separate agreements. The court took the view that, while the agreement fell within more than one definitional category in the Act (restricted use and unrestricted use), the agreement was a unitary one and not divided into parts when looking at the terms and the surrounding circumstances and, thus, at the time, as the credit advanced exceeded £25,000, the agreement fell entirely outside the Act and was unregulated.

8.4.7 Linked transactions

Various transactions linked to the main agreement are also covered by the complex notion of a 'linked transaction' in s. 19. Security transactions are not to be treated as linked.

A linked[76] transaction is created in a number of ways:

(a) it is entered into in compliance with a term of the principal agreement – for example, a compulsory Payment Protection Insurance policy or brokerage fee;

(b) the principal agreement is a D-C-S agreement and the transaction is to be financed by it – for example, the purchase of a car financed by a connected personal loan provided under arrangements between the car dealer and finance company;

---

[73] The problem is that the terms 'part' and 'category' are not statutorily defined. The drafting of the section has been robustly defended by the draftsman Francis Bennion, 'Multiple Agreements under the Consumer Credit Act 1974', in F. Bennion and P. Dobson, *Consumer Credit Control Encyclopedia*, Doc 1999.004 Release 49 (at: www.francisbennion.com). Others, including the judges, have struggled: see *National Westminster Bank v Story* [1999] Lloyd's Rep Bank 261, discussed by I. MacDonald, 'What's the Story with Multiple Agreements?' (1999) NLJ 962, and *Goshawk Dedicated (No 2) Ltd v Governor and Company of Bank of Scotland* [2006] 2 All ER 610 and R. Carter, 'Statutory Interpretation Using Legislated Examples: Bennion on Multiple Consumer Credit Agreements' (2011) 32(2) Stat LR 86–115.

[74] However, in relation to an overdraft which is a running account agreement, a variation arrangement allowing the overdraft to be exceeded by a fixed amount is not to be treated as a separate fixed sum agreement (s. 18(5)).

[75] [2009] EWHC 103 (Ch), affirmed *Heath v Southern Pacific Mortgages Ltd* [2009] EWCA Civ 1135 [2010] 1 All ER 748.

[76] 'Linked' is generally taken to mean subordinate or ancillary to the principal agreement. See *Citibank International PLC v Schleider* [2001] GCCR 2281.

(c) the creditor or certain associated parties initiate the transaction by suggesting it to the debtor or hirer with a view to getting them to enter into the principal agreement or for a purpose related to it or where the transaction is a restricted use agreement for a purpose relating to the financed transaction – for example, a travel agent suggests that a loan company will be more willing to lend money for a specific holiday if the debtor takes out holiday insurance with an associated company of the lender.

It is assumed the initiator of the alleged linked transaction was aware of the prospective principal agreement unless the initiator proves to the contrary.[77]

The fact that a transaction is linked is relevant for a number of reasons:

(a) it will generally not have effect until the principal transaction comes into effect;

(b) generally the linked transaction will be cancelled if the principal agreement is cancelled;

(c) rebates for early settlement may encompass monies paid or payable under linked transactions;

(d) when assessing the fairness of the principal transaction, sums payable to the creditor or any third party under a linked transaction can be taken into account in the overall assessment;[78]

(e) from the operation of s. 96(1), which provides that where a debtor or relative of theirs under a regulated consumer credit agreement is discharged before the time fixed by the agreement, they, and any relative of theirs, are discharged from any liability under a linked transaction other than in relation to debts already incurred.

In addition to a 'linked transaction' as defined in s. 19, there is also the concept of a 'linked credit transaction', introduced to implement s. 75A (secondary liability of the creditor for breaches of contract by the retailer), where the concept is defined in s. 75A(5):

In this section 'linked credit agreement' means a regulated consumer credit agreement which serves exclusively to finance an agreement for the supply of specific goods or the provision of a specific service and where:

(a) the creditor uses the services of the supplier in connection with the preparation or making of the credit agreement; or

(b) the specific goods or provision of a specific service are explicitly specified in the credit agreement.

8.5 Reform of consumer credit law – the Consumer Credit Directive 2008/48/EC

The Consumer Credit Act 1974 (CCA 1974) was subject to major revision by the Consumer Credit Act 2006 (CCA 2006) and further revised with the implementation of Directive

---

[77] Section 171(2), CCA.

[78] For practical and other business reasons, certain linked transactions are exempt from some of these effects, such as cancellation, for example, certain contracts of insurance, such as motor insurance, certain types of guarantee and extended warranties and transactions relating to the operation of savings, deposit or current accounts.

2008/48/EC, 23 April 2008[79] (CCD) which had to be implemented by 12 May 2010.[80] In a complex drafting exercise the UK government basically retained the current structure of domestic law where possible and bolted on new provisions to deal with the situation where the Directive covered areas not previously within the scope of the domestic legislation. The result has been to make the regime even more complicated with parallel regimes existing covering the 'new' EU-modified law and the 'old' domestic UK law not modified by the EU CCD.[81]

The CCD is concerned essentially with the formation of credit agreements, informational requirement, early repayment, the role of credit intermediaries and rights of cancellation and withdrawal. Creditors' remedies, consumer debt problems and enforcement generally are still left unharmonised and subject largely to national laws.

The UK government's approach was set out in 'Consultation on Proposals For Implementing the Consumer Credit Directive', April 2009 (BERR, 2009).

8.5.1 Exclusions

There are major exclusions from the scope of the CCD:

(i)   credit agreements secured by mortgages or other comparable instrument used, secured on property or by a right related to immoveable property (Art. 2(2)(a)) – the position broadly in the UK currently (the UK government intends to retain for the time being second charge mortgages within the scope of the CCA pending the results of a general review of their regulation);

(ii)   credit agreements, the purpose of which is to acquire or retain property rights in land or in an existing or projected building (for example, buy-to-let loans) – the UK does not intend to take advantage of this purpose test (BERR, 2009, p. 18);

(iii)   credit agreements of under €200 or more than €75,000 – the UK does not intend to apply the €200 *de minimis* rule but retain a light touch for agreements of under £50 and it does not intend to apply the €75,000 ceiling;[82]

(iv)   pure hire or leasing agreements where no obligation to purchase is laid down – it can be queried whether or not this exemption could apply to hire purchase agreements as there is no requirement to purchase in such agreements, only a bailment with an option to purchase, but, in any event, the UK government did not exempt hire purchase agreements (BERR, 2009, p. 18);

(v)   credit agreements for short-term overdrafts where credit has to be repaid within a month – the UK government did not take advantage of this exemption (BERR, 2009, p. 18);

---

[79] See OJ L133/66, 22/5/2008.

[80] Article 27, CCD.

[81] See webpages at http://webarchive.nationalarchives.gov.uk/+/http://www.berr.gov.uk/whatwedo/consumers/consumer-finance/ec-directives/page29927.html – Implementation was the responsibility of the 'new' Department for Business, Innovation and Skills (June 2009), formerly the Department for Business, Enterprise and Regulatory Reform (BERR) and, two years before that, the Department of Trade and Industry (DTI). In April 2009 the government published 'Consultation on Proposals for Implementing the Consumer Credit Directive' (at: http://www.bis.gov.uk/files/file50962.pdf).

[82] Converted into sterling on the adoption date, 20 May 2010, Art. 28, CCD.

(vi)   interest-free credit agreements with no other charges or short-term agreements which have to be repaid within three months but with only insignificant charges – the UK retained a modified version of the current rule of exemption where agreement is repaid within 12 months by not more than four instalments (BERR, 2009, p. 18);

(vii)   employee credit schemes where credit provided to an employee as a secondary activity and at rates lower than the prevailing market rate – the UK will take advantage of this exception (BERR, 2009, p. 18);

(viii)   credit agreements concluded with investment firms in certain circumstances for the investor to carry out authorised transactions – the UK will take advantage of this exemption (BERR, 2009, p. 18);

(ix)   credit agreements which are the outcome of a settlement reached in court or before another statutory authority – generally the UK did not take advantage of this exemption (BERR, 2009, p. 18);

(x)   pledge agreements – the UK did not take advantage of this exemption and pawn agreements will remain regulated subject to minor modifications in the current regime (BERR, 2009, p. 18);

(xi)   loans by statutory authorities to restricted groups at less than the market rate – the UK will take advantage of this exemption (BERR, 2009, pp. 18–19).

Overdrafts are subject to only parts of the Directive. Credit unions can be subject to either partial regulation or exclusion altogether on the basis that the credit agreements they enter into are insignificant in relation to the total value of all existing agreements and the total value of agreements entered by all such organisations is less than 1 per cent of all existing credit agreements in that Member State. Current account overdraft arrangements with a bank are subject to lighter touch regulation and not all parts of the CCD will apply to them.

Importantly, in the UK, business lending of up to £25,000 will be subject to the CCD provisions, subject to some key exceptions:

● advertising regulation (which UK legislation does not currently cover either);

● mandatory use of the Standard European Consumer Credit Information Document (set out in Annex II, CCD) and the informational requirements set out in Art. 10 of the CCD – however precontractual and some contractual information would still have to be provided;

● the requirement to provide amortisation tables on demand;

● the government is currently undecided as to whether or not adequate explanations will have to be provided to small businesses by creditors.

The UK government in general terms took the approach that, if a credit agreement was covered by existing UK legislation, the most practical solution would be to apply the CCA amended by the CCD equally to all credit agreements. However, it is not going to be rigid and intends to adopt a case-by-case approach as to whether or not to apply specific provisions within the CCD to out-of-scope agreements.

The new CCD takes a maximum harmonisation approach and is intended to harmonise key aspects of consumer credit legislation in Member States as part of the objective of creating a common credit market across the EU. At the same time, the Directive is also intended to maintain high levels of consumer protection. Unlike previous minimum harmonisation directives which permitted Member States to impose stricter non-discriminatory and proportional rules for the conduct of consumer credit activities in their Member State, this Directive will not permit such flexibility and may require the removal of some existing protections in Member States that currently exceed the agreed maximum harmonisation provision.

8.5.2 Key changes

In the main, UK law already meets most of the obligations set out in the CCD so most of the proposed changes to UK law will be of detail, but some significant changes listed below were required in the previous domestic UK law:

- a duty on the lender to provide adequate explanations about the credit on offer to the consumer (Art. 5(6), CCD), moving towards the notion prevalent in investment and insurance regulation of 'know your customer' and what is an appropriate product for them – currently UK law provides for disclosure but there is no requirement to ensure it is adequate for the needs of a particular consumer;[83]

- an obligation on the lender to check the overall creditworthiness of the prospective debtor, not merely that they have a good credit record with the particular credit company;

- more detailed regulation of credit reference databases and interaction with data protection law;

- a standard right for consumers to withdraw from a credit agreement within 14 days without giving a reason and regardless of whether the agreement was signed on or off trade premises;

- requirements to inform consumers when debts are sold on; and

- requirements for credit intermediaries to disclose fees and links to creditors.

The CCD will require some new terminology, such as the 'borrowing rate',[84] a new Annual Percentage Rate formula and a new early rebate settlement formula.[85] In relation to the waiving of its protections by a consumer debtor, the CCD is perhaps more expansively drafted than the CCA 1974: 'consumers may not waive the rights conferred on them' by the CCD, though s. 173(3) of the CCA still allows consumers to waive their rights where a court order or permission of OFT is required for the creditor to do something if the thing is done 'with that person's consent given at the time' and the section has not been amended with the implementation of the CDD. The Directive is mandatory in the EU and cannot be avoided by using a non-EU law as the law of the contract where the contract has a close link with a Member State (Art. 22(4), CCD). The UK government must ensure that any penalties imposed for breach of the EU credit rights are 'effective, proportionate and dissuasive' (Art. 23, CCD).

---

[83] Article 5.6: 'Member States shall ensure that creditors and, where applicable, credit intermediaries provide adequate explanations to the consumer, in order to place the consumer in a position of enabling him to assess whether the proposed credit agreement is adapted to his needs and to his financial situation . . .'.

[84] Article 3(j)–(k): '. . . the interest rate expressed as a fixed or variable percentage applied on an annual basis to the amount of the credit drawn down.'

[85] On APR calculation, see Art. 19 and Annex I, and, on early rebate allowances, Art. 16. Both Articles seem to leave great flexibility to Member States (BERR, 2009, Chapter 12).

The compatibility of national implementation of the CCD will no doubt take years to be fully litigated before the Court of Justice of the European Union.[86]

8.6   Consumer credit licensing

A central plank of the consumer credit regime is the licensing system administered by the Office of Fair Trading,[87] designed to ensure that only 'fit and proper' persons carry on consumer credit businesses.[88] Two key points to note at the outset is that trading without a licence is a criminal offence and any credit agreement entered into by an unlicensed trader may be civilly unenforceable by the creditor. The CCD merely states in Art. 20 that: 'Member States shall ensure that creditors are supervised by a body or authority independent from financial institutions, or regulated.'

Clearly the threat of refusal or withdrawal of a licence (leading to loss of livelihood) is an extremely strong sanction. Unfortunately, unlicensed criminal activity has remained stubbornly resistant to the actions of the authorities and weeding out unlicensed moneylending has proved extremely difficult, partly as consumers are often reluctant to give evidence because of the fear of violent reprisals and also they realise that the source of funds, albeit illegal, is probably the only way they can obtain credit.[89] Consequently, illegal money-lending units have been set up, working through local trading standards authorities, to target this problem more effectively.[90] Reforms introduced by the Consumer Credit Act 2006 are

---

[86] An interesting example of the interaction of consumer credit law, the Unfair Contract Terms Directive and the Unfair Commercial Practices Directive was the case of *Perenicova* v *SOS finance spol s.r.o* [2012] CMLR 28 where the APR was incorrectly stated as 48.63 per cent when it was in fact 58.76 per cent, within the terms of Consumer Credit Directive 87/102 (repealed by the CCD but applying to this contract as entered into before May 12 2010). The Spanish court held that this was an unfair term within the Unfair Contract Terms Directive 93/13 and set aside the whole contract. A reference was made to the CJEU on the question of if only partial rescission of the specific unfair term should have been ordered. The Court ruled that, as the consequences of the breach of the Directive had not been subject to harmonisation, a state was permitted to order total avoidance of the contract and not merely the removal of the specifically disadvantageous terms if they felt that the contract as a whole was disadvantageous to the consumer. The false statement of the APR infringed Directive 2005/29 on Unfair Commercial Practices but this had no direct effect on the assessment of the unfairness of the term under Unfair Contract Terms Directive and the remedy in contract law.

[87] Section 6A, CCA allows the OFT to charge differential fees.

[88] Section 189(1), that is a business so 'far as it comprises or relates' to the licensed activity. Section 189(2) states that: 'A person is not to be treated as carrying on a particular type of business merely because occasionally he enters into transactions belonging to a business of that type.' The odd social loan to a friend does not mean you are carrying on a consumer credit business. In order to cover the increasing practice of the disposal of credit agreement portfolios to third parties, the definition of consumer credit business has been widened by s. 23(a) of the CCA 2006 to cover a person who does not provide the credit but is otherwise a creditor under a regulated consumer credit agreement. A case at the very margin is *Khodari* v *Tamini* [2008] EWHC 3065, 10/12/08, where a bank employee regularly lent money to the defendant gambler on short-term loans, imposing a 10 per cent charge; no proper records were kept. Blair J permitted the recovery of some £240,500, holding that this was not an unlicensed moneylending business.

[89] The OFT carried out a sweep of websites which revealed a considerable amount of unlicensed trading by so-called 'lead generation' businesses – who source information from people looking for credit and sell this data on to other businesses – in particular targeting people with disabilities, limited access to credit and military personnel. Some 19 such sites were closed down – 'OFT shuts unlicensed websites to protect borrowers', OFT PN 54/11, 8 April 2011.

[90] See BIS' Illegal Money Lending Project (at: http://webarchive.nationalarchives.gov.uk/+/http://www.bis.gov.uk/policies/consumer-issues/consumer-credit-and-dest/real-help-now-for-those-in-difficulty/illegal-money-lending-and-loan-sharks/illegal-money-lending-project) and see 'Tackling Loan Sharks – and More', DTI Consultation Paper No CCP/007/03, 2003.

also intended to try and address this problem by more focused and targeted enforcement by the Office of Fair Trading and local trading standards authorities.[91]

DEBATE BOX

How do we deal effectively with the persistently stubborn problem of unlicensed illegal moneylending? In 2006 it was estimated that 165,000 households in the UK used illegal moneylenders, with about half of these in deprived areas, which represented 0.44 per cent of the adult UK population – 3 per cent of low-income households and 6 per cent of households in the most deprived areas. This can be contrasted with 2.3 million users of high-cost but licensed home credit lenders – 6.15 per cent of the UK adult population. On deprived estates 50 per cent of households have used these legal but high-cost lenders within the last five years.[92]

Should there be harsher penalties for the illegal lenders or more accessible credit for the poor through the government-funded Social Fund or development of local self-help credit cooperatives (known as credit unions)?[93]

Licensing will also cover the carrying on of an ancillary credit business which will include – credit brokerage, debt adjusting,[94] debt counselling, debt collecting, debt administration, the provision of credit information services and the operation of a credit reference agency.[95] Part III of the CCA 1974 (ss. 21–42) sets out the licensing regime. As a general rule all persons carrying on a consumer credit or consumer hire business or ancillary credit business will need a standard licence.[96]

8.6.1 Types of licences

Licences are divided into two categories – standard and group. The latter is intended to cover situations where the OFT consider that it is in the public interest to issue a licence to a

---

[91] Considerable efforts and finance are being put into the illegal loan shark problem and people are being encouraged to report loan sharks. For reporting details see: https://www.gov.uk/report-loan-shark. An example of a successful prosecution, and indeed increase of his sentence on appeal, by the Attorney-General against an unduly lenient sentence is *AG's Ref (No 57/2007): R v Lee Reece Walker* [2007] EWCA Crim 2435.

[92] A. Ellison, S. Collard and R. Forster, 'Illegal Lending in the UK', Research Report by policis and PfRC (November 2006, URN 06/1883) accessible on BIS website at www.berr.gov.uk/files/file35171.pdf.

[93] A good overview is set out in the Executive Summary of 'Illegal Lending in the UK', *op. cit.*

[94] During the financial crisis and recession following it, the so-called 'credit crunch', firms offering debt management services and often making unjustified and exaggerated claims and 'cold-calling' prospective clients have become a problem (see 'OFT Warns Debt Management Businesses over Cold Calling', OFT Press Release 69/09, 25 May 2009 and 'Debt Management (and credit administration) Guidelines, OFT 366 March 2012).

[95] Section 145(1), CCA 1974.

[96] Licences are not required by local authorities and certain statutory corporations even though they entered into agreements which are regulated by other parts of the Act (s. 21(2)–(3)).

relevant group rather than requiring individual members of the group to seek a licence.[97] The key issues are if the group and its members would normally be fit persons within the meaning of s. 25 of the CCA 1974 and if the group has in place the mechanisms for assessing and monitoring the fitness of the members of the group for the duration of the licence.[98] The presumption is that a group licence will be for a fixed period unless OFT feels there is good reason for it to be indefinite.[99]

The vast majority of businesses will require a standard licence and they will have to specify which category or categories of regulated activity they wish to carry on and any limitations on their licence.[100] The applicant is free to apply for a licence covering all regulated categories and, subject to any specific exclusions included in the licence, to carry on business covering all lawful activities done in the course of that business.[101] Over the history of the Act, licence periods have varied, most recently having been five years. However, to allow the OFT to focus their resources on problems such as criminal unlicensed moneylending and free up resources from bureaucratic renewal procedures, the CCA 2006 introduced the power to grant indefinite licences.[102]

In future all licences will be for an indefinite period unless the applicant requests a limited licence or the OFT feels that there is a good reason why the licence should be for a limited period – perhaps in the case of a business where issues have been raised as to their probity or business practice and they are in effect on probation.

Licences are not generally assignable or transmissible.[103] A licence held by an individual will terminate if the licensee dies, becomes bankrupt or becomes a patient affected by mental illness or is deemed to lack mental capacity, though in such cases regulations may provide for the termination of the licence to be deferred for a period of up to 12 months and the business carried on by someone else, such as the personal representative of the deceased to enable an orderly wind down or sale or transfer of the business.[104]

---

[97] Section 23(5)–(8): such a licence may be limited to certain activities, may exclude named persons from the group, and a person covered by one can apply for a standard licence in respect of regulated activities not covered by the group licence. Two main groups benefit from group licences: professions already adequately regulated under other legislation and where the credit-regulated activities are essentially ancillary, such as solicitors making bridging loans to clients to acquire property, etc., and charities such as the National Association of Citizens Advice Bureaux or Help the Aged in respect of debt counselling. See the full list on the OFT website (at: http://www.oft.gov.uk/OFTwork/credit-licensing/group-licenses).

[98] See OFT, 'Group Licensing Regime: Guidance for Consumer Credit Group Licence Holders and Applicants' (OFT990, April 2008). Registered solicitors benefit from a group licence issued to the Law Society of England and Wales, No G900001, covering consumer credit, credit brokerage, debt adjusting and debt counselling, debt collecting, debt administration and provision of credit information (including credit repair).

[99] Section 22(1D), CCA 1974.

[100] Section 24A, CCA 1974: within each general type of business, such as, consumer credit, the OFT can specify descriptions of business activity which can be set out in an application and an applicant can choose to exclude certain descriptions of business from his application (s. 24(A)(5)–(6)).

[101] Section 22(1), CCA 1974: however, if an applicant wishes to sell goods and services off trade premises, the canvassing of D-C-S agreements off trade premises, this must be specifically authorised in the licence (s. 23(3)) and the OFT can, by general notice, specify other specific activities within a regulated class which must be specifically authorised by an express term in the licence (s. 23(4)).

[102] Section 22(1A)–(E), CCA 1974.

[103] Section 22(2), CCA 1974.

[104] Section 37, CCA 1974 and the Consumer Credit (Termination of Licences) Regulations 1976, SI 1976/1002, allowing termination to be deferred for 12 months in favour of the specified person who must give the OFT specified information about themselves. The Secretary of State can specify other events which are deemed to automatically terminate a licence.

8.6.2 Powers and duties of the OFT when dealing with licences

The OFT has wide-ranging powers under s. 6 of the CCA 1974 to specify by general notice the type of information to be given in an application and to require further specific information in dealing with a specific application. It is an offence under s. 7 to knowingly or recklessly give false information to the OFT or an officer of the OFT information which is, in a material particular, false or misleading. It is also important to note an obligation to notify the OFT within 21 days of any material changes that occur in the registered particulars of a licence during the currency of the licence, for example, any changes in the officers of a body corporate or the identity of a controller of a body corporate, etc.[105] The OFT is given extensive enforcement powers to require information, to observe the licensed business in operation, to search and seize documents, to secure search warrants and to apply for court orders requiring information to be provided to ensure that licensed activity is carried on lawfully.[106]

Under the licensing procedure an applicant has the right to submit written representations and to make oral representations either in person or via a legal representative.[107]

The central core of the licensing provisions is that licences should only be granted to a *'fit person'* operating under a name that is not misleading or undesirable.[108] The onus of proof is on the applicant and the grant of a licence is a privilege not a right.[109] The OFT has persistently rejected the notion that it is subjecting the applicant to double punishment if they have already been punished for an earlier offence but this is again taken into account in assessing whether or not they should be granted a licence. This view was confirmed by the Consumer Credit Appeals Tribunal:

> . . . a grant of a licence is a privilege and not a right, and to take away a privilege is not a penalty. Mr Cooper is therefore not being penalised twice for this offence [clocking car mileometers contrary to Trade Descriptions Act 1968].[110]

---

[105] Section 36: also, if the OFT issues a general notice under s. 6 requiring further information to be given, an existing licensee must supply that information to the OFT within a specified period.

[106] Section 36(B)–(E): the actual enforcement will generally be undertaken by trading standards officers of local trading standards departments on behalf of the OFT (s. 36(F)).

[107] Section 34, CCA 1974.

[108] See 'Misleading or Otherwise Undesirable Names: Consumer Credit Act 1974', OFT1378, April 2012, and OFT PN 34/12, 20 April 2012. One issue has been names suggesting a link to the government or a charity where none exists. In December 2010, the OFT refused an application from Baker Evans Limited to use the trading names 'The Bankruptcy Helpline' and 'The Insolvency Helpline'. In October 2011, the OFT also stopped Money Advice Direct Limited (MADL) using its former existing trading name, 'The UK Insolvency Helpline' and proposed domain names including the word 'helpline', because they failed to make the commercial nature of the business clear to consumers, see 'OFT Acts Against Debt Management Businesses' (OFT PN 109/11, 10 October 2011).

[109] Section 25(1): the fitness will be determined either generally or in relation to the specified type and description of business set out in the licence.

[110] See *Mark Cooper* v *The Office of Fair Trading*, 12 March 2009, Decision 03 Consumer Credit Appeals Tribunal (at: www.consumercreditappeals.tribunals.gov.uk/decisions.htm). This confirms the view of the court in *North Wales Motor Auctions* v *Secretary of State for Trade* [1981] CCLR 1, when the court upheld rejection of a licence application where the trader had served two years in prison for tax evasion, rejecting the double jeopardy argument and ingenious argument that, while he had defrauded the Revenue, there was no evidence he had ever defrauded individual consumers.

The OFT may decide that, instead of an unlimited licence, the licence should be limited to specified types and descriptions of business.[111]

The OFT must consider 'all matters appearing to them relevant', including evidence tending to show that they have:

(a) committed any offence involving fraud or other dishonesty or violence;

(b) contravened the CCA 1974 or Part 16 of the Financial Services and Markets Act 2000 or any other enactment relating to the provision of credit to individuals or other transactions with individuals;

(c) contravened any provision equivalent to those set out in (b) in any other European Economic Area State;

(d) practised discrimination on grounds of sex, colour, race or ethnic or national origin in or in connection with the carrying on of any business;[112] or

(e) engaged in any business practices appearing to the OFT to be deceitful or oppressive or otherwise unfair or improper (whether unlawful or not) – this importantly includes engaging in what the OFT considers to be irresponsible lending.[113]

It is important to note that in assessing the applicant's fitness the conduct of the applicant's employees, agents, associates (whether past or present) or business controller of the applicant can be taken into account. This extends the net very wide and prevents abuses of the legislation, for example, an application by the spouse of a moneylender who has engaged in violence or fraud and had their licence revoked, for a licence to, in effect, continue the old business as a front for the banned spouse who might then be 'employed' in the new business.[114]

One of the problems with the licensing regime set out in the 1974 Act was that, providing a person had not infringed the law, they would almost certainly get a licence when in reality they had neither the business experience or compliance regime in place to operate a consumer credit business. This lacuna was closed by the CCA 2006 inserting a new s. 25(2) into the 1974 Act allowing the OFT to take account of:

(a) the applicant's skills, knowledge and experience in relation to the relevant business;

(b) the skills, knowledge and experience of other business participants, such as account managers, credit controllers, etc.; and

(c) the practices and procedures that the applicant proposes to implement in connection with the carrying on of the business.

---

[111] Section 25(1A), CCA 1974: the Financial Services Authority and OFT can liaise on whether a licence should be granted to someone who is an authorised deposit taker or carrying certain specified listed activities under the Financial Services and Markets Act 2000 and related European legislation (ss. 25(1B)–(1C)). The FSA could tell the OFT that, in its view, the applicant should not be granted a licence.

[112] It is important to note of course that refusal to grant credit on discriminatory grounds such as sex or race can give rise to independent civil legal action by the victim. See *Quinn v Williams* [1981] ICR 328 (CA) where an employed married woman wanted to buy a suite of furniture and was asked to provide a guarantor but was told if her husband was the principal debtor, no guarantor would be needed. A successful action for damages was brought for breach of ss. 1 and 29 of the Sex Discrimination Act 1975. However, such conduct could also lead to the revocation of the trader's licence as well.

[113] Section 25(2A)–(2B), CCA.

[114] 'Associate' has a broad definition in s. 184, CCA 1974 and also includes business associates (s. 25(3)).

To help guide applicants through the complex procedures, the OFT is required to prepare and publish statutory guidance.[115] Breach of these guidelines may well lead to OFT action against the licence holder – two recent examples of such guidelines in areas that have given rise to concerns were those on 'Debt Management'[116] and 'Credit brokers'.[117]

The Secretary of State can supplement the licensing procedures by mandating conduct of business rules under s. 26 CCA 1974. If the OFT intends to refuse an application, it issues a 'minded to refuse notice' with reasons and invites the applicant to submit representations before making a final decision.[118]

It is important to note that if the licence holder infringes the licensing provisions during the currency of a licence, the OFT has the power to compulsorily vary,[119] suspend or revoke a licence.[120] This could involve either the complete cessation of a business by revocation of the licence or compulsorily varying it, for example, by removing the right of a business to collect debts but allowing it to continue to conduct a consumer credit business or by suspending the licence for a period while the business gets its house in order. An indefinite licence could be converted into a limited duration licence confined to certain limited types or descriptions of business.[121]

The power of revocation in particular is the 'nuclear option' and, particularly in the case of a large business, may not be appropriate so the CCA 2006 introduced an intermediate power to impose *'requirements'*, the breach of which would be subject to civil penalties of up to £50,000 for each infringement.[122]

This new power is extraordinarily wide-ranging in the sense that to issue a requirements direction the OFT only has to be *'dissatisfied'* (undefined in the legislation) with any matter in connection with:

(a) a business being carried on or which has been carried on by the licensee or by an associate or former associate of the licensee;

---

[115] Section 25(A), CCA: an example of how lack of competence, compliance, proper systems and training could lead to a loss of a licence is the Financial Services Authority Final Notice banning a London mortgage broker from operating. He had in effect allowed a system where fraud and false applications were prevalent in applications for mortgages: 'Final Notice to Akin Johnson' FRN 303931, 9/6/09 at www.fsa.gov.uk/pubs/final/akin_johnson.pdf.

[116] See 'Debt Management (and Credit Repair Services) Guidance', OFT366 rev (March 2012).

[117] See 'Credit Brokers and Intermediaries', OFT1388, Nov 2011.

[118] Section 27 and the Consumer Credit Licensing (Appeals) Regulations 196 (as amended); the OFT can take account of evidence which would not be admissible in a court of law.

[119] Section 31, CCA 1974.

[120] Sections 32–33, CCA 1974. Post 'credit crunch' the era of 'light touch' regulation has gone and regulatory authorities, including the OFT, are taking a harder regulatory stance about breaches of consumer protection financial services law and this has been reflected in a more proactive stance on licensing matters. See the decision to revoke the licence of 'Yes Loans' one of the UK's largest brokers of unsecured credit and its associated companies – 'OFT Acts to Revoke Yes Loans' Licence'. OFT PN15/12, 8/3/12 – for using high pressure sales tactics, deducting fees without making clear fees were payable, offering different products to those initially sought and treating customers poorly by not providing refunds in a timely manner. See also a similar decision in SAS Fire & Security Systems Ltd, 'OFT Takes Action Against Security Firm Over Aggressive Sales Tactics' OFT PN 84/11, 22 July 2011.

[121] The licensee has of course the right to make oral and written representations as to why the OFT should not suspend, vary or revoke under s. 34 and the OFT is given expansive powers to issue directions as to the running down of a business in such cases in s. 34A, essentially to allow the transfer or winding up of the now unlicensed business to someone other than the original licensee if necessary. Section 108 of the Financial Services Act 2012 has introduced a new 12 month suspension procedure for urgent cases demanding immediate action.

[122] Sections 39A–C, CCA: complying with s. 39(C) the OFT have issued guidance on how they intend to operate the penalties system – 'Consumer Credit Licensing – Statement of Policy on Civil Penalties', January 2008 OFT971.

(b) a proposal to carry on a business which has been made by the licensee or by an associate or a former associate of a licensee; or

(c) any conduct not included in (a) or (b) of a licensee or of an associate or a former associate of a licensee.[123]

It is important to note that this is not merely concerned with the business of the licensee who is the subject of a notice. If an associate of the licensee who has a history of violence sets up an unregulated business, for example, a taxi firm, and it is agreed that he will drive the firm's debt collectors to the homes of debtors, presumably a notice could be issued directing the licensee to use alternative means of transport? The notice could require the licensee to dismiss or not employ a named person.[124] An illustration of such a notice is seen in the OFT's case relating to CIM Technologies Ltd, trading as Tooth Fairy Finance, a payday lender which typically lent amounts of £100–£300 to students on a short-term basis via telephone or SMS.

The OFT imposed requirements on Tooth Fairy Finance, which set out that it should not:

- vary the repayment date or amount payable in respect of the loan, unless that was specifically agreed in advance with the debtor;

- trade using names other than those permitted by its credit licence;

- levy debt collection charges that are disproportionate to the amount owed.

The company should also appoint a suitably qualified person to advise on, and administer as necessary, legal and regulatory compliance.[125]

The notice will require the licensee to address the matters of concern and to ensure that matters of the *same or similar* kind do not arise again in the future (s. 33A(2) CCA, 1974). It is important to note that these notices are purely regulatory in nature and cannot require the business to compensate people who have suffered loss or damage as a result of the unsatisfactory conduct.[126] The licensee has the right to receive advance notice of any proposed determination and to make representations and, if unhappy with the ruling, can appeal to the First Tier Tribunal (formerly the Consumer Credit Appeals Tribunal).[127] To pacify concerns in the industry about these very wide-ranging discretionary powers the OFT has had to issue statutory guidance on how it intends to exercise the powers.[128] There may be several separate 'requirements' relating to different and separate parts of the businesses' behaviour and the £50,000 penalty relates to each separate requirement and can be imposed in relation to each separate infringement. One of the first requirements notices issued was against a firm of debt collectors, Mackenzie Hall, requiring some of its debt-collecting practices to match its written standards, which were on paper satisfactory, for example, not pursuing a debt where it had

---

[123] Section 33A. See P. Stokes, 'New OFT Powers in Credit Clamp Down' (2005) *NLJ* 236.

[124] Such persons can apply to have the notice varied or revoked, s. 33C(5)–(7).

[125] 'OFT Acts to Improve Lending Practices', OFT PN Notice 116/10, 9, November 2010 and see 'OFT Requires Wonga to Ensure Improved Debt Collection Practices', OFT PN 40/12, 22 May 2012, and text of notice issued (at: www.oft.gov.uk/shared_oft/press_release_attachments/wonga/wonga.pdf).

[126] Section 33C(3).

[127] Section 33D and 41 and, on a point of law from the Consumer Credit Appeals Tribunal to the Court of Appeal in England and Wales or Northern Ireland or Court of Session in Scotland, s. 42, CCA.

[128] Section 33E and see *Consumer Credit Licensing: Statement on Civil Penalties*, January 2008, OFT971. Among issues taken into account will be consistency of OFT decisions, seriousness and nature of non-compliance, staff involvement, preventive steps, cooperation, acceptance of responsibility, awareness of senior management, negligence, compliance procedures, duration of conduct, detriment to consumers, financial benefit gained and disproportionate impact on vulnerable consumers.

been notified in writing it was statute-barred or where there was reasonable cause to believe that the debt was in dispute.[129]

It is important to note that these notices can also be issued in respect of the carrying on of an ancillary business – a number have been issued in relation to debt management companies seeking to exploit the business opportunities thrown up by over-indebtedness and the fall-out of the 'credit crunch' – induced recession.[130]

Operating a regulated business without a valid licence or under a different name from the authorised business name is a strict liability criminal offence under s. 39(1) CCA 1974.[131]

Any agreement entered into by an unlicensed business is *prima facie* civilly unenforceable by the business – though it is enforceable by the consumer. For example, if the consumer buys a car on hire purchase from an unlicensed finance company and does not pay the instalments, the creditor cannot sue the consumer debtor for any outstanding instalments, but if the car is not of satisfactory quality the consumer buyer can sue the finance company for breach of contract.[132] The same principle applies to any ancillary credit business entered into while the business is unlicensed. It is also important to note that if an agreement is entered into by a creditor as a result of an introduction by an unlicensed credit broker then both the credit brokerage agreement and the principal credit agreement are unenforceable even though the creditor is properly licensed.[133]

Unenforceability can apply at two stages: (a) if the business was not licensed at the time it entered into the relevant agreement and (b) if it is not licensed at the time it is seeking to enforce the agreement.[134]

The restriction of civil enforcement is capable of operating harshly if the lack of a licence is owing to a genuine error by the business or an administrative oversight, as opposed to deliberate and culpable ignoring of the law. The Act therefore permits the OFT to grant retrospective validation orders, in effect deeming the business to have been licensed at the relevant time when it entered into the agreement. However, it is important to note that this validation procedure does not operate if at the time the business seeks to enforce the agreement it is not licensed to enforce the agreement. Here there is no dispensing power and the agreement cannot be enforced until the business has secured a licence. It is also important to note that such validation orders cover specific periods as opposed to specified agreements. In particular the OFT will take into account if any debtors have been prejudiced by the conduct of the business and whether or not, if the business had applied at the correct time, the OFT would have been minded to grant the application. The business has the right to make written and oral representations.[135]

---

[129] See OFT Press Release 44/09, 21 April 2009, and OFT Press Release 45/09, 23 April 2009. Requirements imposed on Citifinancial Europe to stop misleading credit card holders about their rights under s. 75, CCA 1974, in particular falsely telling them they had no rights when they used their cards abroad if the goods or services acquired were unsatisfactory. This involved them in informing past and present customers that they had such rights.

[130] See OFT Press Release 20/09, issued in respect of 1st Credit (re. debt-collection practices), 25/2/09 and 'OFT Accepts Undertakings from Debt Management Firms to Improve Practices', OFT Press Release 31/09, 13/3/09.

[131] Subject to a statutory due diligence defence in s. 168, CCA 1974.

[132] Section 40, CCA. It is important to note 'unenforceable' does not mean void or voidable, simply that the business cannot use the court to enforce the agreement, so if the debtor pays all the instalments without query, these cannot be recovered; the agreement will have been properly carried out.

[133] Sections 148–149.

[134] See s. 40(1) and s. 40(1A).

[135] See ss. 40(2), (4) CCA. If the OFT refuses to grant a validation order, there is a right of appeal to the First Tier Tribunal (Consumer Credit), s. 41 and, further, with leave – to the Upper Tier Tribunal.

8.6.3 **Right of appeal to the Tribunal**

The Consumer Credit Act 2006 created a wholly independent appeal tribunal to deal with matters relating to licensing – so if the OFT refuses to grant a licence; revokes, suspends or varies a licence; issues a requirements notice or refuses to grant a validation order allowing an unlicensed agreement to be enforced, a dissatisfied applicant or business could appeal to the Consumer Credit Appeals Tribunal.[136] The Tribunal had very wide-ranging powers and the appeal was a full rehearing of the merits, plus the Tribunal could consider new evidence not before the OFT.[137] The Tribunal might confirm, quash, vary or remit the matter back to the OFT, but it could not increase an OFT penalty.[138] If the business was unhappy with the decision of the Tribunal it could appeal, but only with leave and on a point of law to the Court of Appeal of England and Wales or Northern Ireland or the Court of Session in Scotland.[139]

After a very brief life the Consumer Credit Appeals Tribunal has been abolished and its powers transferred to the what is called a First Tier Tribunal[140] under the new unified tribunal system set up by the Tribunals, Courts and Enforcement Act 2007. The new system consists of a First Tier Tribunal, divided into a series of Chambers with rights of appeal to an Upper Tribunal and, on a point of law,[141] with leave, to the Court of Appeal (Civil Division) (and equivalent appeal courts in Scotland and Northern Ireland). The Transfer of Functions of the Consumer Credit Appeals Tribunal Order 2009[142] abolished the Consumer Credit Appeals Tribunal and transferred its functions to the Grand Regulatory Chamber of the First Tier Tribunal from 1 September 2009.

Appeals to the First Tier Tribunal are by way of rehearing and s. 41ZB(2) CCA 1974 states that the First Tier Tribunal may confirm an OFT determination, quash it, vary it, remit the matter to the OFT in accordance with any direction given by the Tribunal and give the OFT directions for the purpose of giving effect to the Tribunal's decision. However, the First Tier

---

[136] CCA, ss. 55–58 and Sch. 1. Decisions can be accessed on its website (at: www.consumercreditappeals.tribunals. gov.uk/decisions.htm).

[137] CCA, Sch. 1, para. 9.

[138] CCA, Sch. 1, para. 12. See the First Tier Tribunal (Consumer Credit) decision in European Environmental Controls Ltd (EEC), CCA/2009/002, 23 November 2009 (at: www.consumercreditappeals.tribunals.gov.uk/ Documents/decisions/0002_GRCdecisionPrelimIssues23Nov09_EECLtd_v_OFTDirections_NCN_dec09. pdf). The tribunal upheld the decision by the OFT to revoke the licence of a company which sold security systems. The company was guilty of inappropriately dealing with elderly or otherwise vulnerable customers by making repeated visits, not giving clear reasons for visits, selling unsuitable or unnecessary products, staying in homes an unreasonable period of time, installing products within the cancellation period and imposing unfair terms etc. (OFT PN 75/10, 7 July 2010).

[139] Section 41A, CCA 1974.

[140] See First Tier Tribunal (Consumer Credit) website (at: www.justice.gov.uk/tribunals/consumer-credit), which is now incorporated into the general website of the Ministry of Justice.

[141] See *Log Books Loans* v *OFT* [2011] UKUT 280 and [2012] AACR 12. One of the issues the OFT considered in revoking the appellant's licence was whether or not an employee could validly act as a witness and attest a bill of sale (chattel mortgage) under s. 10, Bills of Sale (1978) Amendment Act 1882. If the bill of sale had not been validly witnessed, it would have been void.

[142] SI 2009/1835: consequently, the following provisions of the 1974 Act are repealed: s. 40A, s. 41 1A–1D, s. 41A and Sch. A1. Section 41ZA is inserted: 'In case of appeals to the First Tier Tribunal, Tribunal Procedure Rules may make provision for the suspension of determinations of the OFT.' Under Sch. 4 to the Regulations all current proceedings are transferred to the First Tier Tribunal and any existing orders and directions will be treated as if made by the First Tier Tribunal. Any appeals will be treated as appeals from the First Tier Tribunal.

Tribunal may not increase a penalty (s. 41ZB(3) CCA 1974). The Tribunal Procedure (First Tier Tribunal) (General Regulatory Chamber) Rules 2009[143] set out the procedures for conducting hearings.[144]

There is a right to appeal to the Upper Tier Tribunal with the leave of either the First Tier or Upper Tier Tribunal, which may uphold the decision, re-make it or remit the matter back to the First Tier Tribunal.[145] There is a right of further appeal to the relevant appellate court (in England and Wales, the Court of Appeal, Civil Division) on a point of law with the leave of the appellate court or the Upper Tier Tribunal.[146] The Upper Tier Tribunal also has 'judicial review' jurisdiction and, in so far as the First Tier Tribunal were to exceed its powers or act in a procedurally unfair way, etc., the decision could be challenged. The Upper Tier Tribunal has powers to issue mandatory orders, prohibitory orders, quashing orders, declarations and injunctions.[147]

8.6.4 Businesses based in other European Economic Area countries – the EEA passport

Under EU single market policies, credit businesses based in other EU and EEA countries may well wish to provide loans and other credit facilities in the UK and the question arises as to whether or not they need to be licensed. The basic principle adopted is country of origin regulation and a 'passport procedure' operates which is set out in Sch. 3 of the Financial Services and Markets Act (FSMA) 2000. A firm authorised by its 'home authority' which has raised no objection to the carrying on of the regulated activity in the UK will be deemed to be licensed in the UK provided it has satisfied what are called the 'establishment conditions'.[148] The OFT under s. 27A(1) must refuse the application, but if the firm wishes to carry out non-permitted activities which are not covered by the EEA passport, it must obtain a licence and prove itself a 'fit and proper person' in relation to the non-permitted activities.[149]

If, once in the UK, the EEA firm acts in a way that would have been a breach of a standard licence under s. 25(2A)(a)–(e) (it has not acted as fit and proper person) if it held one, then the OFT can intervene and impose an absolute or conditional prohibition on the firm in respect of its credit business activities under ss. 203 and 204 FSMA 2000. Such a prohibition can be limited by reference to a specified period, the occurrence of a specified event or the satisfaction of specified conditions. Instead of a prohibition, the OFT can give

---

[143] SI 2009/1976.

[144] The overriding objective set out in SI 2009/1976, reg. 2 should be noted, in particular the requirements of avoiding unnecessary formality, seeking flexibility with cases being dealt with in ways which are proportionate to the importance of the case, the complexity of the issues, the anticipated costs and the resources of the parties. Regulation 3 encourages the use and facilitation of alternative dispute resolution procedures.

[145] Sections 11 and 12, Tribunals, Courts and Enforcement Act 2007 (TCEA 2007).

[146] Sections 13 and 14, TCEA 2007. However, by virtue of the Appeals from the Upper Tribunal to the Court of Appeal Order 2008, SI 2008/2834, such an appeal can only be made where the Upper Tribunal refuses permission, the relevant appellate court considers that '(a) the proposed appeal would raise some important point of principle or practice; or (b) there is some other compelling reason for the relevant appellate court to hear the appeal'.

[147] Sections 15–21, TECA 2007. There is power for such issues to be transferred from the High Court (and equivalent courts in Scotland and Northern Ireland) to the Upper Tier Tribunal.

[148] FSMA 2000, Sch. 3, paras 12–16.

[149] Section 27(2)–(3). A 'permitted activity' is defined in FSMA 2000, Sch. 3, para. 15.

directions which impose 'restrictions' on the firm and limit the firm from carrying on its business except in line with the restrictions.[150]

If the OFT is aware of any problems with the firm before it seeks to start up business in the UK, the OFT can request the Financial Services Authority to exercise its powers under Part XIII of the FSMA 2000 to prevent the firm from operating in the UK or liaising with the home authority to rectify the matter. It is important to note, the FSA can only act if the home authority has failed to deal with the problem or unreasonably refused to take action.[151] In this way the OFT can act to protect the interests of UK consumers adversely affected by the malpractices of firms based in other EEA countries.

8.7 Seeking business and making agreements

Part IV of the Consumer Credit Act 1974 deals with the seeking of business.

8.7.1 Advertising

An advertisement is generally within the scope of Part IV if it is advertising consumer credit, consumer hire or generally an ancillary credit business[152] and the advertiser is *indicating that he is willing* to provide the relevant service.[153] Both the concepts of an advertisement and an advertiser have broad definitions. An advertisement includes:

> every form of advertising, whether in a publication, by television or radio, by display of notices, signs, labels, showcards or goods, by distribution of samples. Circulars, catalogues, price lists or other material, by exhibition of pictures, models or films, or in any other way . . .

An advertiser 'means any person indicated by the advertisement as willing to enter into transactions to which the advertisement relates.'[154] It follows from the definition of advertiser that if a credit broker indicates that X Bank is willing to provide credit at certain rates and this was false, X Bank could be prosecuted under ss. 47 and 167(2), even if this information was placed in the advertisement by the broker without its authority, but presumably, all other things being equal, they could rely on the due diligence defence set out in s. 167.[155]

Certain categories of advertising are exempt from these controls:

- the advertiser does not carry on a consumer credit business;
- the advertisement indicates the advertiser is not willing to enter into a consumer hire agreement;

---

[150] Section 204, FSMA 2000. These directions can be withdrawn or varied by written notice and breach of them constitutes a criminal offence.

[151] FSMA 2000, ss. 194(2)–(3) as amended by the Financial Services Act 2012.

[152] Sections 43 and 151, CCA.

[153] This requires a reasonably specific factual indication rather than merely suggesting by using a corporate logo. See *Jenkins* v *Lombard North Central* [1984] 1 WLR 307, in which a finance company supplied price stickers to be placed on windscreens of cars. In one section of the sticker was the corporate logo – the name with the L in the form of a stylised £ sign. This was held not to be an advertisement within Part IV, CCA.

[154] Section 189, CCA.

[155] See section 8.14.2.

- the advertiser does not carry on a business in the course of which it provides credit to individuals secured on land;

- the advertiser does not carry on a business which comprises or relates to unregulated agreements which are governed by the law of a country outside the UK, but which would be regulated were they to be governed by the law of part of the UK;

- credit is only available to a body corporate;

- invitations or inducements in relation to investment activity within s. 21 FSMA 2000 other than a generic advertisement;

- any other category specifically exempted by the Secretary of State by statutory instrument, for example, advertisements that indicate that the credit or hire is available for business purposes, only here the advertisements are exempt from the advertising regulations made under s. 44 CCA, but not from s. 46 CCA prior to its repeal (however, they could still be caught and open to criminal prosecution under the Business Protection from Misleading Marketing Regulations 2008,[156] regs 3, 6 and 11[157]).

8.7.1.1 False and misleading credit advertising

One of the key principles of the 1974 Act was to promote what the Americans call 'truth-in-lending'. This was to be achieved firstly by the prevention of false and misleading advertising by the creation of a general offence in s. 46 CCA:

> If an advertisement to which this Part applies conveys information which in any material respect is false or misleading the advertiser commits an offence.

A typical case is *R v Metsoja v H Norman Pitt Co Ltd.*[158] A garage advertised a car for sale with '0% APR'. However, what was not disclosed was that if buyers were prepared to pay cash, they got £1,000 more trade-in allowance on their part exchanged old car than if they wished to purchase on credit terms. The court held that while '0% APR' was literally true it was misleading in that the difference between the two levels of part exchange allowance amounted to a disguised interest charge.[159]

Section 46 has now been repealed and the general control of false and misleading credit advertisements subsumed under the Consumer Protection from Unfair Trading Regulations

---

[156] SI 2008/1276.
[157] *Croydon LBC v Hogarth* [2011] EWHC 1126 (QB). It is important to note that, as well as criminal prosecutions, a number of successful enforcement orders, or voluntary undertakings in lieu of an enforcement order, have been secured under Part 8 of the Enterprise Act 2002 and the predecessor 'Stop Now' Regulations. See OFT Press Releases PR57/02 (action against misleading interest free advertising), 46/01, 10/02, 20/02, 73/04 and 98/04 which can be accessed in the Press Release section of the OFT's website (at: www.oft.gov.uk/news-and-updates/press/#.USIVBKX7XG).
[158] [1990] CCLR 12.
[159] Information implying an intention on the advertiser's part which he did not have would also constitute an offence (s. 46(2)). See *Home Insulation v Wadsley* [1988] 10 CL 48, where a booklet contained a table indicating that a specified rebate would be payable if the debtor paid off the debt early. In fact the creditor only intended to allow the lower statutory rebate set out in the Consumer Credit (Rebate on Early Settlement) Regulations 1983. The false intention would have to be shown at the time of the publication of the advertisement; merely changing one's mind later would not be an offence.

2008[160] (see section 7.8).[161] It is of course important to note that in many instances complaints about misleading advertisements will be made to the industry's self-regulatory body, the Advertising Standards Authority, which can require withdrawal of misleading or unsubstantiated credit advertisements.[162] The Financial Services Authority has order powers in relation to credit advanced by way of first mortgage lending.[163]

To permit consumers to make valid comparisons it was a criminal offence to advertise restricted use credit to acquire goods and services unless the advertiser also offered the relevant items for cash (s. 45 CCA).[164]

8.7.1.2 Positive disclosure – form and content of credit advertising

Under s. 44 of the CCA, the Secretary of State can make regulations governing the form and content of credit advertising, with the intention of ensuring that such advertisements 'convey a fair and reasonably comprehensive indication of the nature of the credit or hire facilities offered by the advertiser and of their true cost to the persons using them' (s. 44(1)). In addition he can require specified information to be included in the prescribed manner and other specified material to be excluded and also enforce rules about the relevant prominence of specified items (s. 44(2)).

The detailed Regulations are complex and it has been argued that in fact advertising and accompanying disclosure regulations do not achieve a great deal because of information overkill and the majority of consumers neither reading nor properly absorbing the information.[165]

The underlying philosophy of the regulations is that a creditor need not advertise but, if he does, the greater the information given, in effect, the greater the degree of statutorily defined disclosure. So, under the original regulations advertisements were divided into simple, intermediate and full, and an advertiser could content himself by publishing a simple advertisement merely giving name, type of business and address.[166]

The original scheme was deemed to be overly prescriptive and complex and a new 'simplified' regime was introduced by the Consumer Credit (Advertisement) Regulations 2004.[167]

---

[160] SI 1008/1277.

[161] It is suggested that if *Metsoja* had come before the court in 2009, it would have been found guilty of a misleading omission in reg. 6(1)(a) or (b) which 'causes or is likely to cause the average consumer to take a transactional decision he would not have taken otherwise' and strictly liable for criminal prosecution under reg. 10. On regulations generally, see *Tiscali UK Ltd* v *British Telecommunications PLC* [2008] EWHC 3129 (QB).

[162] See ASA Adjudication of WageDayAdvance Ltd, 16 May 2012, upholding a complaint in particular of not giving sufficient prominence to the annual percentage rate. The representative example required did not include an APR more prominent than any other information relating to the cost of credit in the credit advertisement under the Consumer Credit (Advertisement) Regulations 2010, SI 2010/1970 (at: www.asa.org.uk/ASA-action/Adjudications/2012/5/WageDayAdvance-Ltd/SHP_ADJ_186237.aspx).

[163] Final Notice in respect of Mortgageland Ltd, 21 May 2008. The misdemeanours were the firm's failure to ensure that the financial promotion was clear and not misleading, and to give appropriate prominence to the APR (at: www.fsa.gov.uk/pubs/final/Mortgageland.pdf).

[164] Under s. 182(3) the Secretary of State can also statutorily define the meaning of certain terms, for example, what is a typical credit transaction or what does 'interest free' mean?

[165] 'Warning: Too Much Information Can Harm', Better Regulation Executive/National Consumer Council, November 2007 07/1553 (at: www.berr.gov.uk/files/file44588.pdf).

[166] There were problems and gaps. A difficulty was the advertising of initial interest rate discounts when the APR would go to a higher level when the introductory period was over. See *Carrrington Carr* v *Leicester CC* (1993) 158 JP 570.

[167] SI 2004/1484 as amended. See also, *Credit Advertising*, OFT, September 2005 and *Consumer Credit (Advertisement) Regulations 2004: Frequently Asked Questions*, OFT 746, September 2005.

The 2004 Regulations remain in force but only in relation to consumer credit agreements secured on land and a further set of Regulations, the Consumer Credit (Advertisements) Regulations 2010, have introduced further changes to implement changes required under the EU CCD (see section 8.5.2).[168]

Under the 2004 scheme, displaying certain financial information in credit or hire advertisements will trigger the requirement to display other key information.

In addition, the Regulations, when combined with the Regulations defining the annual percentage rate, or APR, allowed advertisers (particularly credit card companies) considerable leeway in expressing their APRs, creating confusion and preventing genuine interest rate comparisons.

The reform orders made in 2004 reflected four key objectives:

1. to make the regime less complex and easier to use for the industry and more easily understood by consumers by less prescription as to the precise information that has to be supplied;

2. a resolution of the confusion over the use of Annual Percentage Rates on credit cards and other credit agreements by providing for a single set of assumptions in calculating them;[169]

3. revision of the rules on prominence for key mandatory information; and

4. to ease the use of bona fide and honest comparisons with like for like products.[170]

Key requirements for a compliant advertisement under the 2004 Regulations as amended are:

- all advertisements must use plain and intelligible language and must be easily legible;

- certain financial information must be shown together (for example, in credit advertisements if any of the following are displayed they must be presented together as a whole – amount of credit, any deposit on account, cash price, any advance payment, frequency and number of repayments and any other payments or charges) and such information must be capable of being read as a whole and no one item must be given greater prominence than the others;

- the Annual Percentage Rate and security warnings enjoy special prominence, thus the APR must have greater prominence than other interest rates which might be displayed;

- flexibility is allowed by the display of a 'typical APR' – which generally must represent at least 66 per cent of all credit agreements covered by the advertisement that the advertiser reasonably expects that he will enter into as a result of the advertisement – and if the advertising campaign is to run for a period of time then that assessment must be made at reasonable intervals to check if the assumption is still reasonably correct.

---

[168] Consumer Credit (Advertisements) Regulations 2010, SI 2010/1970.

[169] There has been major criticism that the fluidity of the previous Regulations permitted up to at least 12 different ways of calculating the APR in relation to credit cards. This prompted the Consumers' Association to make a super-complaint on the 'fast-track' procedure in s. 11 Enterprise Act 2002 (see *Interest Calculation Methods*, Consumers' Association, April 2007, *Response to the Super-complaint on Credit Card Interest Calculation Methods*, April 2007 and the result, *Credit Card Comparisons*, OFT 987, February 2008).

[170] For a good overview of the 2004 regime, see M. Griffiths, 'Consumer Credit Advertising: Transparent at Last?' (2006) 11(3) *Comms L* 75–84.

EXAMPLE

(Outside scope of EU CCD regime)
Compliant advertisement

Bloggs Double Glazing Company

2 Railway Cuttings, Coketown CAD E56

WINDOWS INSTALLED IN FOUR WEEKS
01234 567 890
8 uPVC windows
£1900 (inc VAT)

INTEREST-FREE CREDIT AVAILABLE

subject to status

0% APR Typical
(other rates may apply)

Comment

'Interest free' can only be used to describe credit agreements where the total amount payable does not exceed the cash price.

The phrase can also be regarded as an incentive which triggers the requirement to display a typical APR, which is displayed – it can also be regarded as stating a zero rate interest rate which also triggers the need for a typical APR.

The APR displayed is more prominent than 'other rates may apply' – the assumption being that at least 66 per cent of credit purchasers of the windows will be eligible for the zero rate.

The requirement, 'Other rates may apply', is not mandatory but its inclusion will prevent the advertisement being misleading.

EXAMPLE

(Outside scope of EU CCD regime)
Non-compliant advertisement

Need a loan? We can help

£61,000–£65,000	13.1% APR typical
£65,000–£75,000	8.1% APR typical
£75,000–£80,000	5.8% APR typical

Loans for any purpose

Call us now on 0800 45 67 890

A.N. OTHER BROKER

> ## Comment
>
> As this can be regarded as a single advertisement, it should only have one typical APR based on a reasonable assumption of the rate charged to the totality of borrowers, whatever the band the amount of the loan fell into. Neither can an individual APR be displayed without also specifying the typical APR as an APR is a rate of charge.
>
> As well as triggering the need to display a typical APR, this advertisement will also trigger the need to show 'from' and 'to' APRs, in particular the 'from APR' must be the APR which the advertiser reasonably expects, at the date on which the advertisement is published, will be the lowest APR at which the credit will be provided under not less than 10 per cent of the agreements resulting from the advertisement. The 'to' APR must be the APR which the advertiser reasonably expects, at the date, will be the highest APR at which credit will be provided under any of the agreements resulting from the advertisement.
>
> These 'from' and 'to' advertisements must be of equal prominence (but less prominent than the typical APR). While the particular words 'from' and 'to' are not required it is advisable to display them to avoid confusion.[171]

The advertising regulations statutorily define certain terms and restrict the use of certain terminology such as 'interest free', for example, which means that that phrase or any similar phrase can only be used where customers buying on credit are liable to pay no more than cash buyers, except where the total amount payable does not exceed the cash price. This means that interest-bearing credit terms that waive interest charges if the cash price is paid within a certain period cannot be advertised because, of course, if the cash is not paid, usually strictly according to the conditions of the offer, the debtor *may* retrospectively become liable for interest charges. Similarly, so-called 'nothing to pay for X years' offers, again, if the terms of the offer are not strictly complied with, require retrospective payment of interest.

The regulations require warnings to be issued in certain cases, such as where the loan is secured by a mortgage or charge on the borrowers' home:

YOUR HOME MAY BE REPOSSESSED IF YOU DO NOT KEEP UP REPAYMENTS ON A MORTGAGE OR ANY OTHER DEBT SECURED ON IT.

Again, the regulations require warnings in relation to the controversial equity release schemes whereby borrowers wish to access money tied up in the value of their homes without having to pay any interest until they cease to occupy the house as their main residence (often the death of the elderly people who most commonly use this type of arrangement):

CHECK THAT THIS MORTGAGE WILL MEET YOUR NEEDS IF YOU WANT TO MOVE OR SELL YOUR HOME OR YOU WANT YOUR FAMILY TO INHERIT IT. IF YOU ARE IN ANY DOUBT, SEEK INDEPENDENT ADVICE.

A breach of the Advertising Regulations constitutes a strict liability criminal offence[172] but no additional civil sanction such as rescission or unenforceability is provided for in relation to any subsequent credit agreement entered into. Under the general law of contract and tort, however, remedies may be available for misrepresentation and/or breach of contract if the advertising

---

[171] For more useful examples and an illustrative flow chart showing what item of information triggers what required statutory information, see Annexe to *Credit Advertising Booklet*, OFT016a (March 2006).

[172] Subject to a due diligence and reasonable precautions defence in s. 168 covering mistaken or inadvertent breaches, the onus on proving the defence lies on the advertiser.

is deemed to constitute a promise made with contractual intention. The OFT can issue requirements notices requiring firms to comply with the advertising regulations and avoid misleading claims.[173]

If an advertiser commits an offence under the Act or would have been deemed to commit an offence but for successful reliance on the due diligence and reasonable precautions defence in s. 168 CCA, certain third parties may also be held to be liable:

(a) the publisher of the advertisement;[174]

(b) any person who, in the course of a business carried on by him, devised the advertisement or any part of it relevant to the offence (for example, an advertising agency); and

(c) the person who procured the publication of the advertisement, where it was not the advertiser who did so (for example, a creditor procuring the publication of an advertisement by a credit broker but not named as providing credit in the advertisement).[175]

It is important to note that the advertising of ancillary credit businesses is also controlled subject to prosecution.[176]

Section 52 of the Act provides for the giving of quotations but these are no longer mandatory (this requirement being removed in a previous 'deregulation' exercise in 1997), but if given on a voluntary basis they must comply with the Consumer Credit (Content of Quotation) Regulations 1999 (as amended).[177]

8.7.1.3 Advertising regulation under the EU Consumer Credit Directive

Article 4(1) of the CCD requires any advertising concerning credit agreements which indicates any interest rate or any figures relating to the cost of the credit to include standard information set out in the Article.[178] This standard information shall be set out in a 'clear, concise and prominent way by means of a representative example'.[179] The standard items are:

(a) the borrowing rate, fixed, variable or both, together with the particulars of any charges, included in the total cost of the credit to the consumer;

(b) the total amount of the credit;

(c) the APR;

(d) if applicable, the duration of the credit agreement;

(e) in the case of credit in the form of deferred payment for a specific good or service, the cash price and the amount of any advance payment; and

(f) if applicable, the total amount payable by the consumer and the amount of the instalments (Art. 4(2), CCD).

---

[173] 'OFT imposes requirements on Reset Finance over credit brokerage adverts', OFT PN 21/10, 26 February 2010, and Requirement Notice (at: www.oft.gov.uk/shared_oft/press_release_attachments/Signed-Reset-Requirements.pdf).

[174] Publishers such as newspapers and broadcasters have an 'innocent publication' defence in s. 47(2), CCA.

[175] Section 47(1), CCA.

[176] Section 151, CCA.

[177] SI 1999/2725. Section 53 provides for regulations to be made requiring specific information to be displayed in a prescribed manner at the creditor's premises but no regulations have been made under this section.

[178] Subject to the proviso that if national legislation merely requires an indication of the APR and no other interest rates or any figures relating to any cost of the credit, this obligation shall not apply.

[179] The UK government intends to interpret this as: the terms of the offer (or better) should be provided under at least 50 per cent of agreements entered into as a result of the advertisement (BERR, 2009, para. 2.24).

The non-credit aspects of any regulated consumer credit advertisement will be regulated by the Unfair Business to Consumer Commercial Practices Directive 2005/29/EC and the UK government also takes the view that Recital 18 permits it to continue to regulate aspects of the advertising that do not relate to the cost of the credit. There was a detailed reappraisal of the specifics of the UK Consumer Credit Advertisement Regulations to bring them into line (see the approach of the UK government in BERR, 2009, paras 2.16–2.29).[180] The new EU-compliant regime was introduced by the Consumer Credit (Advertisement) Regulations 2010, which will apply to all regulated advertisements other than those secured on land. A person who causes a credit advertisement to be published has to ensure that the advertisement complies with the Regulations (reg. 2). A key requirement, in many cases, will be the publication of a 'representative APR', defined in reg. 1 as:

> 'the representative APR' is an APR at or below which the advertiser reasonably expects, at the date on which the credit advertisement is published, that credit would be provided under at least 51 per cent of the consumer credit agreements which will be entered into as a result of the advertisement.

Where a credit advertisement includes a rate of interest or an amount relating to the cost of credit, whether expressed as a sum of money or a proportion of a specified amount, it will need to include the standard information set out in a representative example (reg. 4(1)), which is defined in reg. 5.[181]

LEGISLATIVE PROVISION

5. Representative Example

(1) Subject to paragraph (5), the representative example referred to in regulation 4(1)(a) shall comprise the following items of information:

(a) the rate of interest, whether fixed, variable or both;

(b) the nature and amount of any other charge included in the total charge for credit;

(c) the total amount of credit;

(d) the representative APR;

(e) in the case of credit in the form of a deferred payment for specific goods, services, land or other things, the cash price and the amount of any advance payment; and

(f) except where the consumer credit agreement is an open-end agreement:

    (i) the duration of the agreement; and

    (ii) the total amount payable by the debtor and the amount of each repayment of credit.

---

[180] Article 4(3) of the CCD states that, if compulsory ancillary contracts such as insurance are required to be entered into to obtain the terms of the credit and the cost is not known in advance, the obligation to enter the contract shall be stated in a clear, concise and prominent way, together with the APR of the cost of the ancillary charge if taken on credit.

[181] Under reg. 6, a representative APR will have to be given with greater prominence than other interest rates if the advertisement is aimed at persons who might consider their access to credit restricted or suggests more favourable terms than corresponding credit or provides an incentive to apply for credit.

(2) For the purposes of the representative example, the information referred to in sub-paragraphs (a) to (c), (e) and (f) of paragraph (1) shall be that which the advertiser reasonably expects at the date on which the credit advertisement is published to be representative of consumer credit agreements to which the representative APR applies and which are expected to be entered into as a result of the advertisement. For these purposes in the case of a credit advertisement which falls within section 151(1) of the Act, 'advertiser' means the person carrying on the business of credit brokerage.

(3) For the purposes of paragraph (2), 'agreements to which the representative APR applies' in the case of paragraph (1)(e) means agreements providing credit for the purchase of specific goods, services, land or other things to which the representative APR applies.

(4) For the purposes of paragraph (1)(a), where the consumer credit agreement provides different ways of draw down with different rates of interest, the rate of interest shall be assumed to be the highest rate applied to the most common draw down mechanism for the product to which the agreement relates.

(5) Paragraphs (1)(d) and (2) shall not apply to a credit advertisement relating to an authorised non-business overdraft agreement.

(6) The standard information contained in the representative example shall be:

(a) specified in a clear and concise way;

(b) accompanied by the words 'representative example';

(c) presented together with each item of information being given equal prominence; and

(d) given greater prominence than:

    1. (i) any other information relating to the cost of the credit in the credit advertisement except for any statement relating to an obligation to enter into a contract for an ancillary service referred to in regulation 8(1); and

    2. (ii) any indication or incentive of a kind referred to in regulation 6(1).

(7) In this regulation a reference to a rate of interest is a reference to the interest rate expressed as a fixed or variable percentage applied on an annual basis to the amount of credit drawn down.

Under reg. 8 a clear and concise statement must be provided about any obligation to an ancillary contract where this is compulsory to obtain the credit or to obtain it on the advertised terms (for example, compulsory payment protection insurance) and the cost of that ancillary service cannot be determined in advance. This must be no less prominent than the standard information and presented together with the representative APR.[182] Under reg. 9 any security and its nature must be stated, but, unlike the 2004 Regulations, no warnings are required about loss of the debtor's home, etc. Certain defined expressions must not be used except under defined circumstances (reg. 10), for example the expression

---

[182] An 'ancillary service' is defined in reg. 1 as a service that relates to the provision of credit under the consumer credit agreement and includes in particular an insurance or insurance payment. This is yet another definition to enter the equation in an already complex regime.

'loan guaranteed' or 'pre-approved' or any similar expression cannot be used unless the agreement is free of any conditions regarding the credit status of the debtor, plus 'weekly equivalent' cannot be used unless provision is made for weekly payments.

8.7.1.4 Credit intermediaries

It is important to note that, under Art. 21 of the CCD, credit intermediaries[183] will have to indicate in advertising and contractual documentation whether they are truly independent or tied to one or more creditors. Any fee must be in writing and properly disclosed before the conclusion of the principal credit agreement and such fee communicated to the creditor for correct assessment of the total APR. This article has been implemented in s. 160A, which defines a credit intermediary as a person who carries on the following activities:

(a) recommending or making available prospective regulated consumer credit agreements, other than agreements secured on land, to individuals;

(b) assisting individuals by undertaking other preparatory work in relation to such agreements; or

(c) entering into regulated consumer credit agreements, other than agreements secured on land, with individuals on behalf of creditors.[184]

The credit intermediary must indicate the extent of his independence and whether or not he works for the creditor exclusively, as well as disclose any fee payable by the debtor to the debtor before the regulated agreement is concluded. Failure to do this constitutes an offence (s. 160A(6)).[185]

8.7.1.5 Other forms of marketing: canvassing

Under s. 49 of the Act it is an offence to canvass D-C agreements off trade premises,[186] which covers the making of oral representations during a visit made for that purpose (so not covering representations made at a chance social encounter).[187] There is no offence, however, as long as the visit is made in response to a signed request.[188] This section does not apply to D-C-S agreements, which can be canvassed off trade premises (without any signed request) as long as the trader is licensed and the licence specifically authorises the activity.[189]

---

[183] Defined in Art. 3(f) and not entirely analogous to the notion of a credit broker in s. 145, CCA.

[184] Section 160A(2) – not to be confused with the existing domestic concept of a 'credit broker'.

[185] Under s. 38 of the Regulatory Enforcement and Sanctions Act 2008, regulations can provide for civil penalties for breach of the section. The level of any commission payable to the credit intermediary by the creditor does not have to be disclosed, which is regrettable.

[186] Generally, this means that the canvassing (to be legal) must be at the premises of the creditor, the supplier or an employer of the canvasser and certainly not at the home of the prospective customer. 'Trade premises' includes a business run by the prospective customer (s. 48(2)), however, so it is legal to canvass at such premises. It should be noted that this only covers physical canvassing; telephone canvassing is not covered but could be by s. 54 of the CCA (power to make conduct of business regulations in relation to seeking business). However, unsolicited calls to consumers' homes without prior consent may be caught by the Privacy and Electronic Communications (EC Directive) Regulations 2003, SI 2003/2426, regs 19–26, which also deal with canvassing via e-mail, fax and the use of automated calling systems.

[187] However, it is legal to canvass an overdraft off trade premises if the customer already has an account with the creditor (OFT determination, June 1977).

[188] See R v Chadda [1999] Goode's CCLR 595: oral request is insufficient.

[189] Section 23(3), CCA.

8.7.2 Circulars and credit information to minors

It is an offence to send to a minor a document inviting him to borrow money, obtain goods or services on credit or goods on hire or apply for information or advice on any of these things.[190] There is a defence where the sender did not know, and had no reasonable cause to suspect, that the addressee was a minor.[191]

8.7.3 Unsolicited credit tokens

At the time that consumer credit law reform was being considered by the Crowther Committee, the domestic rivals of Barclays Bank PLC, trying to secure market share from the then-dominant Barclaycard, jointly mass-mailed Access credit cards to their customers. This caused outrage in some circles and consequently, to avoid a future repetition of such an event, s. 51 makes it an offence to distribute unsolicited credit tokens[192] on either a mass or individual basis, unless is it is either done under a small D-C-S agreement or is for use in a credit token agreement already made or a renewal or replacement card.[193] Credit and store card firms have now agreed with the Department for Business, Innovation and Skills not to unilaterally raise the credit limit on cards and give cardholders the right to reject such increases (see 'A Better Deal for Consumers: Review of the Regulation of Credit and Store Cards', BIS, March 2010, paras 18–23). Provisions restricting the use of the controversial unsolicited credit card cheque other than for predominantly business purposes has not been activated the government, which has instead relied on industry self-regulation to prevent abuses.[194] Credit card cheques are used like personal cheques, but because they are linked to a credit card rather than a current account, any spend attracts interest. This is usually far higher than the credit card's APR and there are no interest-free periods. There are also handling fees for using a credit card cheque, often as much as 2 per cent of the transaction cost. The OFT estimated that credit card cheques cost people £57m in interest each year. The 2009 White Paper 'A Better Deal for Consumers' had proposed banning unsolicited credit card cheques, which it warned could 'tempt' consumers unaware of the high interest rate charges.

---

[190] Section 50(1) and see *Alliance and Leicester BS* v *Babbs* (1993) 157 JP 906, which ruled it was no offence when a brochure was sent to a minor but contained the statement, 'Loans not available to persons under the age of 18'. The company had a computer program designed to exclude loans to minors and general policy not to lend to minors.

[191] Section 50(2).

[192] A credit token, which includes credit cards, is defined in s. 14 of the CCA and has been held to include the sending of facsimile tokens which in fact require some other action, such as opening a repayment direct debit or standing order (see *Elliott* v *Director General of Fair Trading* [1080] 1 WLR 977).

[193] Firms have run foul of this provision by automatically 'upgrading customers' when they have changed the firms' cards from dedicated store cards to credit cards which can be used anywhere. See 'Clearer Card Choice for Consumers: M&S Agree to Amend Conversion of Store Cards to Credit Cards', Office of Fair Trading Press Release, 128/03 (at: www.oft.gov.uk/news/press/2003/pn_128-03).

[194] Section 51A and s. 51B of the CCA, inserted by s. 15, Financial Services Act 2010.

8.8 Precontract disclosure

One of the major problems with the provision of credit is the lack of understanding of credit conditions and the high levels of financial ignorance among UK consumers. One way to tackle this is to supplement advertising controls with specific precontract disclosure. This was first activated as part of the 2004 'mini-reform package' by the activation of s. 55 of the CCA, which had previously lain dormant, to make regulations governing the disclosure of information in the prescribed manner to the prospective debtor before the agreement is made. This was done by means of the Consumer Credit (Disclosure of Information) Regulations 2004.[195] Failure to comply with the precontract disclosure renders the subsequent credit agreement 'improperly executed' under s. 65 and *prima facie* unenforceable without either the free and informed consent of the debtor or an enforcement order under s. 127 of the CCA (see section 8.11.4). These Regulations are now confined in operation to consumer credit agreements secured on land (except those to which a precontract reflection period under s. 58 applied), consumer hire agreements, consumer credit agreements under which the creditor provides the debtor with credit which exceeds £60,260, regulated agreements for wholly or predominantly for the purpose of business carried on, or intended to be carried on, by them and small D-C-S agreements, except to the extent that the Consumer Credit (Disclosure of Information) Regulations 2010 apply to them.

8.8.1 Content of disclosure document (outside scope of EU CCD)

Key points to note about the format and giving of the disclosure document are that it must:

(i)   be separate from and precede the credit agreement;

(ii) be presented separately and as a self-contained document;

(iii) be on paper or other durable medium that the consumer can take away;

(iv) be easily legible;

(v)   not be interspersed with other information; and

(vi) give equal prominence to the precontractual information and any other information.

Key content includes the type of the agreement, the address of the creditor and debtor, the description of any goods to be acquired, the cash price, any advance payments, the amount of the credit, the timing and amount of repayments, the APR, the description of any security required, any default charges, whether or not any guarantee fund is provided and if any ADR services, and their identification, are to be provided.

Clearly in some cases all these things may not be precisely known so the Regulations permit the provision of 'estimated information' which is based on such 'assumptions as he may reasonably make in all the circumstances of the case'.

---

[195] SI 2004/1481. These Regulations do not govern distance contracts and contracts secured by land mortgages under s. 58 of the CCA.

What is problematic about this regulation is that it does not specify any minimum gap between the delivery of the disclosure document and the signing of the full contract, perhaps reducing it in some cases to a mindless formality – 'Sorry to detain you, sir, but can you just scan this document?'

DEBATE BOX

Are we suffering from information overkill? Do consumers actually make much effective use of information in advertisements and precontractual disclosure documents?

See the FSA's Discussion Paper 08/05, 'Consumer Responsibility', December 2008 (at: www.fsa.gov.uk/pubs/discussion/dp08_05.pdf).

8.8.1.1 Precontract disclosure under the EU CCD regime

Article 5 of the CCD provides for the provision of precontract disclosure, setting out a range of information which must be given on paper or another durable medium in the form of the *Standard European Credit Information* form (SECI), which is set out in Annex II.[196]

The objective of Art. 5 is much the same as the 2004 UK precontract disclosure requirements and, again, it was a case of technical adjustments being made to bring UK law into line with the EU. However, two key points need to made:

(a) Article 5(1) requires provision *'in good time'* of supply of the document, so this should lead to a period of reflection to allow the information to be absorbed before signing the contract;

(b) Article 5.6 requires the provision of *'adequate explanations'* by creditors and credit intermediaries to allow the consumer 'to assess whether the proposed credit agreement is adapted to his needs and to his financial situation, where appropriate by explaining the precontractual information . . . the essential characteristics of the products proposed and the specific effects they may have on the consumer, including the consequences of default in payment by the consumer'.

This seems to be moving towards the 'know your customer' and 'treat your customer fairly' notions that are prevalent in investment and insurance law, though current UK thoughts seem more minimalist (see BERR, 2009, paras 4.1–4.18).

The Consumer Credit (Disclosure of Information) Regulations[197] implement Arts 5.1 to 5.5 of the CCD. Importantly, the 2010 Regulations provide for the issuing of the Standard European Consumer Credit Information and, in the case of overdrafts, the European Consumer Credit Information, which provide the prospective debtor with key information about the proposed contract. Key will be the Standard European Consumer Credit Information Sheet.

---

[196] Subject to exceptions and modifications set out in Art. 6 and also in relation to distance marketing in Art. 5.
[197] Consumer Credit (Disclosure of Information) Regulations 2010, SI 2010/1013.

LEGISLATIVE PROVISION

Section 55A of the CCA sets out specific precontractual explanation requirements.

(1) Before a regulated consumer credit agreement, other than an excluded agreement, is made, the creditor must:

(a) provide the debtor with an adequate explanation of the matters referred to in subsection (2) in order to place him in a position enabling him to assess whether the agreement is adapted to his needs and his financial situation;

(b) advise the debtor:

(i) to consider the information which is required to be disclosed under section 55(1); and

(ii) where this information is disclosed in person to the debtor, that the debtor is able to take it away;

(c) provide the debtor with an opportunity to ask questions about the agreement; and

(d) advise the debtor how to ask the creditor for further information and explanation.

(2) The matters referred to in subsection (1)(a) are:

(a) the features of the agreement which may make the credit to be provided under the agreement unsuitable for particular types of use;

(b) how much the debtor will have to pay periodically and, where the amount can be determined, in total under the agreement;

(c) the features of the agreement which may operate in a manner which would have a significant adverse effect on the debtor in a way which the debtor is unlikely to foresee;

(d) the principal consequences for the debtor arising from a failure to make payments under the agreement at the times required by the agreement including legal proceedings and, where this is a possibility, repossession of the debtor's home; and

(e) the effect of the exercise of any right to withdraw from the agreement and how and when this right may be exercised.

(3) The advice and explanation may be given orally or in writing except as provided in subsection (4).

It is important to note that this advice may be oral and there is no set time to elapse between delivery of the information and the conclusion of the contract, which may lead to a box-ticking approach, with the information being rapidly given and then consumer moving swiftly on to conclude the contract in the shop.

In light of the concerns regarding a growing trend of overindebtedness, an important pre-contractual duty introduced in s. 55B that the creditor must undertake an assessment of the creditworthiness of the debtor and in any subsequent transactions significantly increasing the amount of credit under an existing agreement or an existing credit limit. This information must be obtained from the debtor and, where necessary, credit reference agencies.[198] If requested, the creditor must give the debtor a copy of the prospective agreement or at least such terms as have at that time been reduced to writing if the creditor is willing to proceed with the agreement. Again, perhaps the need for a request is limiting in the case of an unsure or insecure consumer (s. 55C).

For business loans and loans exceeding £60,260 or secured over land, the pre-February 2011 rules continue to apply, though lenders can choose to comply with the new rules if they prefer. This obligation to provide adequate explanations does not apply to loans above £60,260.

8.9   Form and content of agreements

Again, provision of information was the key philosophy behind the agreement Regulations and the companion provisions requiring copies. Once more, it must be questioned how many consumers actually read, if they do read, and fully understand what are often complex Regulations.

Section 60 of the CCA provides for the Secretary of State to issue form and content regulations, in particular to ensure that the debtor or hirer is made aware of:

(a) the rights and duties conferred on him by the agreement;

(b) the amount and rate of the total charge for credit (in the case of regulated consumer credit agreements);

(c) the protection and remedies available to the debtor/hirer under the Act; and

(d) any other matters which, in the opinion of the Secretary of State it is desirable for him to know about in connection with the agreement.[199]

An agreement properly complying with the Regulations has to be executed by the consumer and failure to do so will mean that the agreement is improperly executed. This in turn means that the agreement cannot be enforced without a court order or the free and informed consent of the debtor/hirer given at the time that enforcement action is required (see section 8.11.4). Some relief has been provided to creditors in that the mandatory grounds for refusing an enforcement order under s. 127(3)–(5) have been repealed by s. 15 of the CCA 2006, giving the court a discretion in all cases to permit an improperly executed agreement to be enforced if the debtor/hirer has not suffered any prejudice (section 8.11.4).

---

[198] This issue was considered by the government in its Consumer Credit and Personal Insolvency Review: Formal Response on Consumer Credit, BIS, November 2011. 'The Government believes that additional data sharing could lead to better-quality lending decisions to some extent. Given the concerns expressed and the differing views about how best data can be shared in this market, the Government has decided to discuss with key stakeholders how to ensure that any increase in data sharing would be to the benefit of consumers' (para. 33). The problem with this is that it involves complex issues of privacy and data protection if the individual prospective debtor is reluctant to cooperate.

[199] The OFT can by order waive compliance with the requirements if it is impracticable to do so and such a waiver would not prejudice consumers (s. 60(3)–(4), CCA).

8.9.1 **Proper execution**

For an agreement to be properly executed, certain steps must be followed:

(a) a document in the prescribed form, containing all the prescribed terms and conforming to the Agreement Regulations, must be signed in the prescribed manner by the debtor or hirer or on behalf of the creditor or owner;

(b) the document must embody[200] all the terms of the agreement – other than the implied terms (for implied terms in hire purchase and conditional sale agreements and service contracts; see Chapter 4);[201]

(c) the document when presented to the debtor or hirer for signature is in such a state that all the terms are legible.

8.9.2 **Content of the agreement**

Key elements of the agreement that need to be focused on:

(i) inclusion of the prescribed terms – these are certain core terms, such as, where relevant, the amount of credit supplied or credit limit in running account agreements, the APR and the number, amount, frequency and timing of repayments;[202]

(ii) informational requirements, such as names and addresses of the parties, if goods are involved, their description and cash price, amounts of any advance payments and description of any security to be provided;

(iii) the relevant order of headings and contents must be followed to help achieve transparency and comprehensibility;

(iv) proper layout of the document in relation to lettering, etc., which must be easily legible and in a colour distinguishable from the background colour of any paper on which the credit agreement is printed;

(v) relevant signature boxes included with any prescribed statements, for example, regarding cancellation rights;

(vi) required statements of protections and remedies; and

(vii) required statutory warnings, for example, 'MISSING PAYMENTS COULD HAVE SEVERE CONSEQUENCES AND MAKE THE OBTAINING OF CREDIT MORE DIFFICULT'.

As it may not be practicable to have fixed every aspect of the agreement in advance, then a creditor may make 'such assumptions as the creditor may reasonably make in all the

---

[200] Under s. 189(4), 'embody' can include in the principal credit agreement itself or by cross-reference to another document referred to in the principal credit agreement.

[201] For arguments concerning the scope of common law implied terms relating to the credit aspect of the agreement, and rejecting the implication of a term that an interest must be adjusted in relation to the rise and fall of the base rate or market rates more generally, but accepting a more limited term, that interest rate variation would not be operated capriciously or dishonestly. See *Nash* v *Paragon Finance* [2001] 2 All ER (Comm) 1025 and *Paragon Finance* v *Plender* [2005] EWCA Civ 760.

[202] See Sch. 6 CCAR 1983 (as amended). Prescribed terms have lost some of their nuisance value to creditors now that s. 127(3) has been repealed which required mandatory unenforceability if all the prescribed terms were not included in the agreement.

circumstances of the case' – providing what assumptions have been made are set out in the agreement.

An example of litigation in relation to the expression of terms is the case of *Lombard Tricity Finance* v *Paton*. A credit agreement stipulated that:

> Interest is payable on the credit balance. Subject to variation by the creditor from time to time on notification as required by law.

The debtor contended that the agreement was improperly executed because it did not set out all the circumstances in which the creditor might vary the interest rate and was contrary to Sch. 1 para. 19 of the Agreement Regulations 1983 which stated:

> A statement indicating the circumstances in which any variation referred to in para. 18 above may occur . . .

The Court of Appeal concluded it was sufficient to indicate a unilateral power to vary from time to time on giving of the prescribed notice and it was not necessary, even if possible, to set out every commercial factual circumstance which might give rise to a revision of the interest rate.

Of course an agreement often contains a power to vary a term (for example, raise or lower the interest rate) during its currency. Such a variation will not take effect until notified to the debtor or hirer in the prescribed manner (s. 82(1), CCA).

Provision is also made for the regulation of so-called 'modifying agreements' under s. 82, where, in effect, a revised agreement is being entered into by varying or modifying the original agreement. The modifying agreement will be taken to have revoked the earlier agreement and contained, subject to certain exceptions, provisions reproducing the combined effect of the two agreements and pre-existing obligations under the original agreement will be taken to be outstanding under the modified agreement (s. 82(2), CCA 1974).

Problems can arise if the creditor makes a temporary concession, payment waiver or interest holiday. Does this amount to a formal modification of the agreement to which s. 82 applies or merely an *ex gratia* concession? The issue arose in *Broadwick Financial Services* v *Spencer*[203] where the creditor was seeking possession of the debtor's home. The debtor had entered into a loan secured by a mortgage with lender A. By virtue of a separate concession letter, A had agreed to a reduction in the amount of the repayment instalments. A subsequently transferred the benefit of the mortgage to B. B had a commercial policy of not reducing interest rates even when prevailing market rates dropped. The debtor fell into arrears with the mortgage repayments and B sought to enforce their mortgagee rights. The debtor argued that the concession letter contained terms and that therefore the agreement was not properly executed under s. 61 of the CCA and the Consumer Credit (Agreement) Regulations (failure to state the prescribed terms correctly) and therefore (at that time) permanently unenforceable under s. 127(3) of the CCA. The Court held that the concession letter was merely an *ex gratia* concession and was not a variation, revision or modification of the agreement and therefore the principal agreement was properly executed.[204]

---

[203] [2002] EWCA Civ 35, [2002] 1 All ER (Comm) 446. Note H. Johnson, 'Non-status Borrowers and the Consumer Credit Act 1974' (April 2002) *F&CL* 3–5.

[204] Neither was the agreement an extortionate credit bargain under ss. 137–142. While such a policy could in principle be regarded as grossly extortionate, it was not and the debtor had adduced no evidence that they would not have proceeded with the bargain even if they had known of the policy.

One of the key issues is that the agreement must contain all the 'prescribed terms' (s. 61(1)(a)). These requirements are quite technical and fairly easily broken. This was the issue in *HSBC Bank* v *Patrick Brophy*.[205] The Court of Appeal held that a credit card agreement did comply with the regulations and was properly executed. In particular, a notification that the debtor's credit card limit would be an amount from time to time determined by the credit card company complied with the requirement to notify him how much credit would be available and then notify the debtor. The debtor's further argument, that the application form was not a contractual document or merely an agreement to enter a prospective agreement and void under s. 59, CCA of the was rejected by the court.[206]

Adjustments have needed to be made to the detail of UK agreement regulations to bring them into line with Arts 10–13 (BERR, 2009, chapters 7–9). The CCD's requirements are less extensive but more prescriptive than current UK ones so there is room for some latitude for the UK in implementation. The new agreement requirements are set out in the Consumer Credit (Agreement) Regulations 2010.[207]

It should also be noted that the consumer is entitled to certain information in relation to any payment services provided in connection with the credit agreement, such as direct debits, standing orders and credit transfers, etc., under Part 5 of the Payment Services Regulations 2009 (PSR, 2009).[208] To avoid overlaps and confusion between the payment services regime and the consumer credit regime, reg. 34 of the Payment Services Regulations 2005 disapplies a considerable amount of the information requirements of the payment service Regulations in relation to so-called 'framework contracts', for example not a single transaction, but where a series of payment services are envisaged, such as a series of direct debit payments under a regulated consumer credit agreement requiring the repaying of the credit by instalments.[209] However, creditors will need to be wary of failing to comply with PSR 2009, particularly where cross-border transactions and payments in different currencies are involved.

8.9.3 Special cases

It is important to realise that there may be restrictions on marketing; informational requirements imposed by other legislation on either the principal credit agreement or a linked transaction. Two examples are set out below where there have been major problems in connection with the selling and marketing of credit-related products.

---

[205] [2011] EWCA Civ 87; [2011] ECC 14.

[206] See also *Sternlight* v *Barclays Bank* [2010] EWHC 1865 (QB), Wakesman QC.

[207] SI 2010/2014, as amended.

[208] SI 2009/209. For an overview of these Regulations, see section 6.5, regulation of payment services.

[209] Disapplied are regs 41, 42 and 43, reg. 40 (save para. 3(b), Sch. 4) and 45 (save para. 2(d)), but certain information must be given in addition to any required under the consumer credit regime. Under para. 3(b), where relevant, details of the interest and exchange rates to be applied or, if reference interest and exchange rates are to be used, the method of calculating the actual interest and the relevant date and index or base for determining such reference interest or exchange rates. Also, under reg. 45, para. 2(d), where applicable, the exchange rate used in the payment transaction by the payer's payment service provider and the amount of the payment transaction after that currency conversion.

8.9.4 **PPI – Payment Protection Policies**

A hugely profitable market for banks and other financial businesses has been the selling of Payment Protection Policies (PPI), designed, at least in principle, to insure the debtor in respect of the repayment of a loan if some unexpected event such as illness, unemployment or other specified event occurs. A major misselling scandal has arisen as unsuitable products have been sold to often ignorant consumers who find, when they actually seek to claim on the policies, they do not cover the events in question. As the policies themselves are insurance policies, the companies are principally regulated by the Financial Services Authority (FSA) and action taken in the area has been undertaken jointly by them, the OFT and the Competition Commission.

The charity Citizens Action (National Association of Citizens Advice Bureaux) made a super-complaint[210] under s. 11 of the Enterprise Act 2002, which led to a market study by the OFT and a market investigation reference to the Competition Commission under Part IV, Enterprise Act 2002. There was considerable controversy and dispute over proposals of the remedy to abuses. The Competition Commission issued its final report, 'Market Investigation into Payment Protection Insurance', in January 2009.[211]

In outline they proposed to use their legislative power under the Act to:

(a) impose a prohibition on distributors and intermediaries from selling PPI to their customers within seven days of a credit sale unless the customer had proactively returned to the seller at least 24 hours after the credit sale;

(b) impose a prohibition on selling single-premium PPI policies (where the premium is paid in one upfront payment, generally by adding the premium to the credit borrowed);

(c) impose a requirement on retail PPI distributors to offer retail PPI separately when they also offer retail PPI bundled with merchandise cover; and

(d) to aid transparency and to impose comprehensibility in marketing materials, at the point of sale and in PPI policy documents and each year after the PPI policy has entered into force.[212]

Ultimately the outcome was the Payment Protection Insurance Market Investigation Order 2011, made under ss. 161 and 165 of and Sch. 10 to the Enterprise Act 2002,[213] which implemented the above with a mixture of point-of-sale restrictions, informational requirements and with compliance requirements, including the conduct of a mystery shopping exercise by providers of PPI in excess of gross premium income of £60m per year. The structure of the exercise has to be approved by the OFT (reg. 13).

---

[210] See 'Protection Racket', Citizens Advice, 13 September 2005 (at: www.citizensadvice.org.uk/index/campaigns/policy_campaign_publications/evidence_reports/er_consumerandebt/protection_racket).

[211] See www.competition-commission.org.uk/rep_pub/reports/2009/fulltext/542.pdf

[212] The whole protracted saga can be followed on the competition website (at: www.competition-commission.org.uk/ourwork/directory-of-all-inquiries/ppi-market-investigation-and-remittal). Barclays Bank PLC challenged the point of sale ban and the reasoning underlying it before the Competition Appeal Tribunal. In *Barclays Bank PLC v Competition Commission* [2009] CAT 27 [2009] Comp AR 381, 16 October 2009, the Competition Appeal Tribunal quashed a finding by the Competition Commission banning the sale of PPI at the same time as entry into the principal credit agreement, on the grounds of proportionality and failure by the CC to take into account sufficiently the loss of customer convenience this might involve. The finding was remitted to the CC for reconsideration of the matter.

[213] www.competition-commission.org.uk/assets/competitioncommission/docs/2011/disclosures/ppi_order.pdf

At the same time parallel action was being taken by the Financial Services Authority for misselling. A not untypical example was a fine of £7m (reduced by 30 per cent from £10m for early settlement) imposed on the bank Alliance & Leicester for serious failings in telephone sales to customers who had taken out unsecured loans with the bank – 210,000 policies were involved. While the insurance was optional, staff were pressurised to sell, with the implication that at times it was suggested as compulsory, there was a lack of information about costs and in breach of FSA 'know your customer' *and* 'treat your customer fairly' requirements unsuitable products were being sold to customers.[214] The FSA has a webpage advising consumers on making claims.[215]

The FSA has also launched a comparison website to give customers information.[216] One sector of the market that has caused particular concern is the single premium PPI market and in February 2009 the FSA wrote to regulated firms requesting that they stop selling this type of product.[217] In the end the banks have given up the fight and are setting aside huge provisions to meet the estimated costs of compensation for misselling abuses after an unsuccessful challenge to the Financial Services Authority's policy statement setting out how it expected regulated firms to deal with claims and compensation.[218] The vast number of complaints has proved a major challenge for the Financial Ombudsman Service (see section 8.18).

8.9.5 Home credit selling

Doorstep selling of credit has historically been a problem. Aimed often at the poorer sub-prime market, while the amount of the loans are often relatively small, interest rates are high and there have been alleged abuses with such things as 'rollover loans'. This prompted the National Consumer Council (now part of Consumer Focus) to make a super-complaint under s. 11 of the Enterprise Act 2002 highlighting problems such as information asymmetries, high market concentration of lenders, barriers to entry for new suppliers, high prices, little evidence of mobility by debtors and significant switching costs.[219] This led to an OFT market investigation and a market investigation reference under Part IV of the Enterprise Act 2002 to the Competition Commission and ultimately an order by them to attempt to rectify some of the deficiencies of the market.[220] The outcome was the Home Credit Market Investigations Order 2007 – a mixture of informational and marketing requirements, strengthening rules about

---

[214] See FSA Press Notice PN/115/2008, 7/10/08 (at: www.fsa.gov.uk/pages/Library/Communication/PR/2008/115.shtml full text of notice at www.fsa.gov.uk/pubs/final/alliance_leicester.pdf).

[215] www.fsa.gov.uk/consumerinformation/product_news/insurance/payment_protection_insurance_/claim-back-ppi

[216] See www.fsa.gov.uk/tables/bespoke/PPI and FSA Press Notices PN/012/09, 20/1/09 and PN/112/2008, 30/9/08.

[217] See text of FSA letter of 23 February 2009 (at: www.fsa.gov.uk/pubs/ceo/loan_ppi.pdf).

[218] *R (on the application of British Bankers Association)* v *Financial Services Authority* [2011] EWHC 999 (Admin), [2011] Bus LR 1531.

[219] See C. Whyley and S. Brooker, 'Home Credit: An Investigation into the UK Home Credit Market' PD25/04, June 2004, and 'The NCC Lodges Super-complaint on Home Credit and Calls for More Low-income Credit Choices', NCC Press Release, 14/6/04 (at: http://collections.europarchive.org/tna/20080804145057/http://www.ncc.org.uk/news_press/pr.php?recordID=161).

[220] See Competition Commission's website on home credit (at: www.competition-commission.org.uk/inquiries/current/homecredit/index.htm).

rebates for early settlement, provision of clear, regular statements and an information website to encourage debtors to look at costs and shop around.[221]

8.9.6 Store cards

There were also problems for consumers with the way that the dedicated £4.8bn store card market was operating – in particular problems of market dominance, market penetration, high interest costs compared with typical credit cards, consumer ignorance, pressure sales tactics, not letting consumers take away agreements to consult but seeking to get them to sign at the point of sale, etc.

After a market investigation by the OFT the matter was again referred to the Competition Commission which held that certain aspects of the market were operating contrary to the public and consumer interest, which led to the Store Cards Market Investigation Order 2006 (largely warnings and information – particularly a bold statement of APR when 25 per cent higher than the defined market rate, ability to pay by direct debit, warnings about minimum payments and separate selling of Payment Protection Insurance).[222] Despite these reforms, there remained concerns about the high cost and other problems associated with store cards (as well as similar problems with credit cards). The Labour government initiated a review of credit and store cards in 2009[223] and the outcome was a decision to pursue, at least initially, a self-regulatory approach and the various industry bodies agreed to give consumers five new 'rights' which it was argued would give them more control over the way in which they could choose and use their credit cards:

The five new rights are as follows.

1. **Right to repay:** consumers' repayments will always be put against the highest rate debt first. For consumers opening new accounts the minimum payment will always cover at least interest, fees and charges, plus 1 per cent of the principal to encourage better repayment practice.

2. **Right to control:** consumers will have the right to choose not to receive credit limit increases in future and the right to reduce their limit at any time. Consumers will also have better automated payment options. Consumers will be able to do both of these online.

3. **Right to reject:** consumers will be given more time to reject increases in their interest rate or their credit limit.

4. **Right to information:** consumers at risk of financial difficulties will be given guidance on the consequences of paying back too little and all consumers will be given clear information on increases in their interest rate or their credit limit, including the right to reject.

5. **Right to compare:** consumers will have an annual statement that allows for easy cost comparison with other providers.

---

[221] See independent comparison website (at: www.lenderscompared.org.uk).

[222] See Competition Commission's website on store cards (at: www.competition-commission.org.uk/inquiries/completed/2006/storecard/index.htm).

[223] 'A Better Deal for Consumers: Review of the Regulation of Credit and Store Cards: A Consultation', October 2009 (at: http://webarchive.nationalarchives.gov.uk/+/http://www.bis.gov.uk/assets/biscore/corporate/docs/c/credit-card-consultation.pdf).

In addition, consumers who are at risk of financial difficulties will be protected through a ban on increases in their credit limit as well as the ban on increases in their interest rate and card companies will work with debt advice agencies to agree new ways they will provide targeted support to consumers at risk to help improve their situation before they are in too deep.[224]

The Coalition government then initiated a review, 'Managing Borrowing and Dealing with Debt',[225] the outcome of which in this connection has been further restrictions in relation to store cards,[226] in agreement with the industry, involving three core features:

1. a ban on direct commission to sales staff;

2. a good practice training scheme; and

3. a seven-day ban on retail incentives when a consumer takes out a store card.

The ban means that stores will not be able to offer discounts, free gifts or similar incentives to encourage consumers to take out store cards at the point of sale or for the first seven days. It is hoped this will decouples the decision to take out a credit card from related bargain opportunities. However, the government decided that rate caps would do more harm than good and is not pursuing them.[227]

8.9.7 Copies

The form and content regulations would be of little use if the creditor could whisk away the original agreement as soon as it was signed and give the debtor no time to read it or look at it again if a subsequent dispute arose with the creditor. Therefore, ss. 62–64 of the CCA provide for the giving of copies to the debtor – which in most cases will mean the debtor ends up with two copies.

Copies that do not comply with the regulations, for example, by stating incorrect figures or interest rates, are deemed not to have been given and, consequently, the agreement is not properly executed (s. 180(2) CCA).[228] It is also important to note that the right copy should be given including, where necessary, appropriate notice of cancellation rights (s. 64). In most situations under UK domestic law the debtor would end up with two copies – one of the unexecuted agreement and one of the executed agreement (for example, after the contract has been made).

---

[224] 'A Better Deal for Consumers: Review of the Regulation of Credit and Store Cards: Government Response to Consultation', March 2010 (at: http://webarchive.nationalarchives.gov.uk/+/http://www.bis.gov.uk/assets/biscore/corporate/docs/c/10-768-consumer-credit-card-consultation-response.pdf).

[225] www.gov.uk/government/uploads/system/uploads/attachment_data/file/31892/10-1185-managing-borrowing-call-for-evidence.pdf 15 October 2010

[226] 'Consumer Credit and Personal Insolvency Review: Formal Response on Consumer Credit', November 2011 (at: www.gov.uk/government/uploads/system/uploads/attachment_data/file/31453/11-1341-consumer-credit-and-insolvency-response-on-credit.pdf).

[227] *Ibid.*, at para. 16.

[228] *Keith Harrison* v *Link Financial Ltd* [2011] ECC 26 – unenforceability due to serial failures by the creditor. There, the creditor had failed to send terms and conditions with a credit card, in breach of s. 61(1), to provide a copy of the original agreement during the currency of the agreement, contrary to s. 78, and to give 14 days' notice to remedy breaches, contrary to s. 88. It was also guilty of excessive harassment of the debtor. All this led to cancellation of the debt – an object lesson in non-compliance.

EXAMPLE

Outside scope of EU CCD[229]

A consumer approaches a garage with a view to buying a car on hire purchase for £70,000, of which £65,000 is advanced on credit. The garage has an arrangement with a finance company and will sell the car to it and it will then contract to let the car on hire purchase to the consumer. The garage has a stock of preprinted contract forms and, by signing it, the prospective debtor will be deemed to be an offeror and it will be the finance company that 'makes' and executes the contract by accepting that offer. In the interim it will make appropriate credit reference checks to see that the prospective debtor is creditworthy. By virtue of s. 62(1) the prospective debtor must then and there be presented with a copy of the agreement plus any other documents referred to therein.[230]

Under s. 63(2) within seven days of the making the agreement, a second copy must be sent to the debtor.[231]

It is important to note that, in cases of cancellable agreements (see section 8.8.1), a notice in the prescribed form must be given in every copy, indicating:

(i)   the right of the debtor or hirer to cancel the agreement;

(ii) how and when the right is exercisable; and

(iii) the name and address of a person to whom the notice of cancellation may be given (s. 64, CCA).

The copy requirement provisions have been revised to incorporate the requirements of the CCD and are now set out in s. 61A and s. 61B (overdraft agreements).

Under s. 61A the creditor must give the debtor a copy of the executed agreement and any other document referred to in it unless he has already been given a copy of the unexecuted agreement and document referred to it and the unexecuted agreement is in identical terms to the executed agreement (s. 61A(1)–(2)). However, in the second case the creditor has to further inform the debtor in writing that the agreement has been executed and is identical to the unexecuted agreement, but the debtor still has the right to ask for a copy of the executed agreement (s. 61A(3)) within 14 days after the relevant date set out in s. 66A(3). This copy must be supplied 'without delay' (s. 61A(4)).

---

[229] An excluded agreement is defined under s. 61A(6) and, in effect, means those that are excluded from the new EU CCD regime but were within the scope of the previous domestic UK law.

[230] Under the Consumer Credit (Cancellation Notices and Copies of Documents) Regulations 1983, SI 1983/1557 (as amended), the Secretary of State has power by regulation to authorise 'the omission from a copy of certain material or its issue in a condensed form'.

[231] The methods and manner of serving documents is set out in ss. 176 and 176A (electronic transmission). Documents must be sent in by 'an appropriate method' which means by post or transmission in the form of an electronic communication in accordance with ss. 176A(1)–(3).

8.10 Currency of the credit agreement

The CCA provides that the consumer can access copies of the original agreement and the current state of their indebtedness[232] and failure to facilitate this means that the creditor is unable to enforce the agreement while the failure continues and there is no dispensing power in cases where the courts consider that the debtor has suffered no real prejudice by the breach (ss. 77–79, CCA). Complying with these requests has often proved a headache for creditors because copies of original agreements had been lost, destroyed or never existed in the first place. This, along with claims that the agreements were improperly executed in the first place and so unenforceable without a court order, has led to the growth of an industry of firms claiming to rescue consumers from their debts often for a substantial fee regardless of the success of the outcome.[233] The problem for creditors is illustrated in the case of *Phoenix Recoveries (UK) Ltd Sarl* v *Devendra Kotechna*,[234] where, after a merger of the original creditor bank with another bank and some 10 years later, the debtor requested a copy of the agreement and alleged that the one sent was not the original one because of material discrepancies in interest rates on balance transfers and cash advances. The Court of Appeal agreed that there was a strong inference that this was not a copy of the original agreement and refused to grant an enforcement order. The case indicates strongly that on mergers, reorganisations, relocations and installation of new computer systems, banks need to keep a tight grip on their document recording. This case was one of several thousand cases where consumer debtors have taken up this issue to avoid repayment orders.[235] However, it has been held that the obligation under s. 78 can be satisfied by delivering a 'reconstituted' agreement from sources other than the original signed document.[236] It is also important to note that, if the creditor assigns his rights to a third party during the currency of the agreement, the assignee must arrange for notice of assignment either as soon as reasonably possible or before the first occasion on which the arrangements for servicing the debt take place – unless the agreement is secured on land where these requirements do not apply (s. 82A).

8.11 Customer rights to end the agreement

8.11.1 Cancellation and withdrawal

Once an otherwise valid contract has been made, a customer (debtor or hirer) has a number of cancellation rights depending on the situation in which the contract is entered into (by a

---

[232] There is a duty on the debtor to inform the creditor within seven days of the whereabouts of any goods that he is under a duty to keep in his possession or control (s. 80, CCA).

[233] See Advertising Standards Authority's upholding of a complaint against Individual Credit Solutions Ltd t/a Unfair Credit Direct, 19 May 2010, not making clear that a fee would be charged for the service and being unable to substantiate a claim that up to 70 per cent of credit agreements might be unenforceable (at: www.asa.org.uk/Rulings/Adjudications/2010/5/Individual-Credit-Solutions-Ltd/TF_ADJ_48495.aspx).

[234] [2011] EWCA Civ 105; [2011] ECC 13.

[235] Failure to comply with documentation can go into the fairness equation under s.140A – *Keith Harrison* v *Link Financial Ltd* [2011] ECC 26.

[236] *Carey* v *HSBC Bank PLC* [2009] EWHC 3417 (QB); [2010] Bus LR 1142.

visit to the consumer's home, via the Internet or other form of distance selling) or the subject matter of the contract (whether it involves credit, investments or insurance, etc.) which are dealt with in the general section on cancellation rights (see section 7.2).

8.11.1.1 Revocation of the offer

Of course, on general contractual principles, a customer would not be bound at all until there was a valid contract.[237] So, the customer can revoke his offer at any point before accepting it. Section 59 of the CCA strengthens the position of the customer in such a scenario by providing that any agreement binding a customer to enter an agreement (that is, not to revoke his offer) is void.

To exercise the right to withdraw prior to acceptance of the offer, the customer must give notice to the credit broker or supplier or anyone acting on behalf of the customer in negotiations, for example, his solicitor.[238] The effect of withdrawal is to terminate also all linked transactions (unless they have been exempted from automatic cancellation) and to make all payments (for example, deposits) recoverable.

8.11.1.2 Secured loans – precontract reflection period

A postcontractual cancellation period is not really appropriate for secured mortgage transactions, involving as it does a statutory registration system for interests in land. Consequently the Act provides for a precontract reflection period which enables the prospective debtor to be untroubled by sales pressure from the creditor to consider the implications of the transaction and to seek, if they wish, independent advice.

The prospective debtor must be sent a copy of the unexecuted agreement which must contain a notice indicating the prospective debtor can withdraw from the prospective transaction and then there must be no communication for at least a period of seven days when a further copy of the unexecuted agreement can be sent for signature. In the interim period there must be no communication with the prospective debtor by the prospective creditor or anyone acting on his behalf – if there is, the resulting agreement is improperly executed. Contact can only be made in response to a specific request from the prospective debtor and contact includes both personal and telephone or an electronic communication. Even the inadvertent sending of an acknowledgment slip by a junior member of the creditor's office staff could trigger improper execution.

8.11.1.3 Postcontract cooling off period and right to cancel

The CCA was concerned with one type of situation: credit agreements entered into off trade premises – the stereotypical situation is the bored housewife being seduced by the glib salesman into buying white goods such as washing machines or vacuum cleaners that she did not want and facing the wrath of her husband on return from work – so cancellation rights have been around since the Hire Purchase Act 1938. As stated above other parallel regimes deal with distance selling of goods and services on credit.

---

[237] See *Financings Ltd* v *Stimson* [1962] 1 WLR 1184 and *Campbell Discount* v *Gall* [1961] 1 QB 431, CA.
[238] Section 57.

A complex regime is set out in ss. 67–74 of the CCA and any business sensibly advised would try and keep away from being tangled in it. The regime has been considerably narrowed now because it will not apply where the new general right of cancellation introduced by s. 66A of the CCA applies (s. 67(2)). The old regime does not apply to agreements secured on land or is restricted use credit agreement to finance the purchase of land or is an agreement for a bridging loan in connection with the purchase of land (s. 67(1) CCA).

An agreement is cancellable if the *'antecedent negotiations'* (defined in s. 56 CCA):

(a) include oral representations made when in the presence of the debtor (not necessarily to the debtor or off trade premises) by an individual acting as, or on behalf of, the negotiator (the requirement of physical presence rules out telephone canvassing); and

(b) the agreement is signed off the permanent or temporary trade premises of the creditor, the negotiator or any party to a linked transaction.[239]

In such circumstances the consumer has a unilateral and unfettered right to cancel the contract, provided he acts within the statutory cooling off period. The length of this period will either be:

(a) the end of the fifth day, from the day following the receipt of the second statutory copy or relevant cancellation notice; or

(b) more rarely, if the sending of a prescribed cancellation notice has been dispensed with, 14 days from the day following the day on which the unexecuted agreement was signed by the debtor.[240]

The debtor is not required to use the statutory form provided; any form of words indicating an intention to cancel will be sufficient. Oral communication is, however, not an effective statutory cancellation. Such a notice can be sent electronically by e-mail or text message. The notice is deemed to be valid when sent even if never received by the creditor.[241] The effect is to unravel the transaction and any linked transaction that is not exempt from the effect of cancellation of the principal agreement (such as certain insurance policies).

Any goods, with certain minor exceptions, must be handed back to the creditor, though the debtor is under no obligation to physically return them but simply to allow the creditor reasonable access to collect them. The debtor has a statutory lien (or right to retain physical possession of the goods) until any deposits or advance payments, etc. have been returned.

---

[239] Section 56(1)(a)–(c), CCA 1974. At one time the National Coal Board (when the coalmines were in public ownership) used to sell solid fuel central heating systems by sending out salesmen in a caravan. They would call at homes and invite householders to come to the caravan to see pictures, etc. of the system and sign installation contracts involving credit in the caravan. These agreements were not cancellable as the agreements were signed on the trade premises of the NCB.

[240] Section 68, CCA.

[241] Section 69(7), the notice can be served on other connected parties, such as a credit broker who acted as a negotiator (s. 69(6)).

EXAMPLE

Outside scope of EU CCD

D is approached by X, a salesman for Y Electricals, who is selling white goods such as fridge freezers on a door-to-door basis. D invites X into his home where he is watching television with his wife. X gets out his brochure and talks to the wife about them getting a new, bigger fridge freezer. D does not listen as he is watching a UEFA Champions League football match on television. The wife decides to buy on credit a particular model and asks her husband D to sign the draft contract, which he does on 1 May. D pays a £100 deposit. The fridge freezer is delivered the next day. On 5 May a second statutory copy of the agreement arrives at D's home by post. In the fridge freezer is a special offer of some family meals which D and his family eat. On 8 May they decide they do not really like the model and overtime at D's work has been reduced because of the effects of the credit crunch and they do not feel they can afford it. D posts the prescribed cancellation notice to Y Electricals on 10 May but it never arrives. On 15 May there is a fire in their kitchen which completely destroys the fridge freezer.

Advice

The agreement is cancellable as there have been 'antecedent negotiations' made in the presence of the debtor, if not to him, and the agreement has been signed off trade premises (ss. 56 and 67). The second statutory copy has been served within 7 days (s. 63).[242] A valid cancellation notice has been sent – even though it is never received, it is effective on posting (s. 69). A statutory 21-day bailment kicks in and D is under a statutory duty to take reasonable care of the goods – after that it appears that the debtor is now treated merely as an involuntary bailee whose only duty is not to wilfully damage the goods (s. 72). Here it appears the creditor has not returned the £100 deposit so the debtor has a statutory lien, a right to retain possession, until that money is refunded (s. 70(2)). D does not have to physically re-deliver the item, merely to respond to a written request from the creditor and give the creditor reasonable access to collect it (s. 72). In this case, though the product was destroyed, unless the fire was the result of the negligence of D, then he is not liable for the value of the product to the creditor – the risk of accidental loss or 'an act of God' is on the creditor. The fact that the family has eaten the food sent with the product is not relevant as they are not liable for its value under s. 72(9)(a) or (b). This is an anti-avoidance provision designed to ensure that consumers are not afraid to exercise their cancellation rights because they have made use of a free product such as this supplied by the creditor with the main product.

A similar, complex procedure exists for repayment of straight money loans, which will not be discussed here.[243]

8.11.1.4 EU CCD general cancellation right

In this area the CCD has had quite a radical impact by virtue of Art. 14. A 14-day cooling off period will be introduced, commencing normally with the conclusion of the credit

---

[242] It seems that the agreement might be permanently cancellable if the second copy is not served within seven days because it is not then capable of being a statutory copy. The cancellation period within s. 68(1) can never end because no second statutory copy can ever be legally served.

[243] See s. 71.

agreement – this probably works out at roughly the same length of time as currently operates under the CCA 1974. This is a universal right and not limited to off trade premises agreements. Ancillary agreements made as a result of 'an agreement' between the creditor and the third party will also be cancelled (Art. 14(4)). As in other areas, the UK government has retained the 'old domestic cancellation right' for those areas not within the scope of the right introduced by Art. 14. The new right is implemented in domestic law by s. 66A which states that a debtor under a regulated consumer credit agreement (but not hire agreement), other than an excluded agreement, may withdraw from the agreement without giving any reason (s. 66A(1)). However, the right does not apply to:

(a) an agreement for credit exceeding £60,260;

(b) an agreement secured on land;

(c) a restricted use credit agreement to finance the purchase of land; or

(d) an agreement for a bridging loan in connection with the purchase of land.

Oral or written notice must be given to the creditor before the end of 14 days, beginning with the day after the relevant day (s. 66(2)).[244] Any oral notice must be given in the manner specified in the agreement (s. 66A(4)). E-mail or fax notice is permitted, provided it is sent to the number or electronic address explicitly specified in the agreement. If sent by post it is regarded as having been received by the creditor at time of posting (s. 66A(6)). The effect is to treat the principal credit agreement or any ancillary agreement[245] (either with the creditor or third party) as never having been entered into (s. 66A(7), (8)). The debtor will have to repay any credit extended with accrued interest but no other charges within 30 days, beginning with the day after the day on which the notice of withdrawal was given and, if not repaid within that period, is recoverable by the creditor as a debt (ss. 66A(9) and (10). Where the agreement is a hire purchase, conditional sale or credit sale agreement and the debtor repays in full any credit advanced within the 30-day period, the title to the goods purchased or supplied under the agreement is to pass to the debtor on the same terms as would have applied had the debtor not withdrawn from the agreement (s. 66A(11)). The section does not specify what is to happen if the amount is not repaid, in particular any duties in respect of looking after the goods, etc. pending their repossession by the finance company. The assumption must be that ss. 72 and 73 apply as they do not distinguish the *type* of cancellation right being exercised in relation to an agreement concerning goods.

8.11.2 Rescission and termination at common Law

As with any other contract, the customer has a right to rescind where a vitiating factor such as duress, undue influence or misrepresentation exists. In addition, the consumer is entitled to terminate the contract where the other party commits a breach of a condition or a sufficiently serious breach of an innominate term.

[244] The relevant day varies and is the latest of a series of days set out in s. 66A(3), starting with the date on which the agreement is made or the creditor is required to inform the debtor of the credit limit under the agreement and the day on which the creditor first does so or the supply of a copy of the executed agreement either under s. 61A or s. 63.

[245] Section 66A(13) provides that an ancillary service means a service that relates to the provision of credit under the agreement and includes in particular an insurance or payment protection policy.

8.11.3 **Termination under the Act**

In non-default cases the creditor must give the debtor at least seven days' notice of termination in the statutorily prescribed form.[246] A debtor is entitled to terminate an 'open-ended' consumer credit agreement by giving one month's notice and the creditor by giving two months' notice, beginning on the day when the notice is served.[247] An open-ended credit agreement means an agreement of no fixed duration (s. 189). Where an open-ended credit agreement provides for termination or suspension of the debtor's right to withdraw credit, the creditor must serve a notice on the debtor before such termination or suspension or immediately afterwards with objectively justified reasons being required.[248] An objectively justifiable reason for immediate suspension of access to credit would be unauthorised or fraudulent use of a credit card or a significantly increased risk of the debtor being unable to fulfil his obligation to repay the credit.

Sections 99 and 100 allow debtors to terminate hire purchase and conditional sale agreements at any point before the last instalment is due by giving notice to whoever is entitled to receive payment. However, these rights are not available where title has passed to the buyer in a conditional sale agreement for land or where, again under a conditional sale, property has passed to the buyer and then on to a third party.

On termination, the customer must pay all sums already accrued that are due.[249] Obviously, early termination may leave the creditor with goods that have depreciated in value. As such (in addition to paying sums already accrued due, as just mentioned), the debtor must pay any additional sum (if any) required to bring the total paid up to one half of the total price;[250] although, if this total price includes installation of goods, the customer must pay the installation charge in full and then half of the remaining balance.[251] If the court is satisfied that a smaller sum is sufficient to compensate the trader for the depreciation, then it can order that such smaller sum be paid.[252] At the same time, the customer is liable in damages for breach of any obligation to take reasonable care of the goods.[253]

EXAMPLE

D buys a home entertainment system for his downstairs living room for £1,500 and a wide-screen television for his bedroom for £600 under a single conditional sale agreement with C Co. He has paid £700 when he is declared redundant and finds he cannot make any more payments and he has no payment protection insurance. He writes to C. Co stating, 'I want to end the agreement as I cannot pay any more.'

[246] Consumer Credit (Enforcement, Default and Termination Notices) Regulations 1983, SI 1983/1561 (as amended).
[247] Sections 98 and 98A. The concept of an open-ended agreement introduced by the CCD is defined in s 189 CCA.
[248] Section 98A(4)–(6). Notice is not required where it would prejudice the detection of crime or administration of justice. It should be noted exceeding an authorised overdraft is not covered by this provision, nor an agreement secured on land (s. 98A(8)).
[249] Section 99(2).
[250] Section 100(1).
[251] Section 100(2).
[252] Section 100(3).
[253] Section 100(4).

Advice

First, before any action is taken – assuming voluntary discussions, if any, on rescheduling payments, etc. fail – C. Co is to serve a default notice compliant with the provisions of ss. 87–89 CCA. This will give D a 14-day breathing space to consider his situation and see if he can arrange a way out of his problems. It is important to note that, as he has paid one-third of the total hire purchase price, the goods cannot be taken back without his free and voluntary consent given at the time C. Co wish to take them. His letter will be treated as a repudiation of the contract and C. Co, by seeking the goods, as terminating the contract. They should be very careful about seizure otherwise they may find under s. 91 they have to refund the £700 D has paid and not have any claim for future instalments.

D could seek to exercise his statutory right of termination under ss. 99 and 100 of the CCA, which would mean that his maximum liability would be £1,050 or such lesser figure that the court might fix (s. 100(3) CCA). If 50 per cent, then he would have an additional sum of £350 to pay.

Alternatively, D might seek a 'split order' or 'return and transfer order' under s. 133 of the CCA. However, unfortunately, he has not made sufficient payments for such an order to be made. He would have had to pay an amount equal to the value of the television set, which he has done but not an additional amount equal to one-third of the unpaid balance (which would be $^1/_3 \times £1,400 = £466.67p$, but he has only paid £100 above the value of the television).

Section 101 gives the hirer under a hire agreement the right to terminate, but only 18 months after making the agreement, unless there is contractual provision for a shorter period. The period of notice is the lesser of one instalment period or three months. So, for instance, if payments are due monthly, termination can be effected by a month's notice at the end of the 17th month. However, there is no right to terminate where the total hire payments (disregarding sums payable on breach) exceed £1,500 in any one year, where the goods are hired for the hirer's business and are selected by the hirer and (at the hirer's request) acquired from a third party or where the hirer requires the goods to rehire them, in the course of a business, to another party.

The debtor under a regulated agreement may choose to complete the agreement early (early settlement) by giving notice to the creditor and paying all sums due, minus any statutory rebate of the charge for credit.[254] (Obviously, in hire purchase or conditional sales cases, such early settlement will mean that the debtor becomes the owner of the goods at this point.) Rebates are calculated according to the Consumer Credit (Early Settlement) Regulations 2004 (as amended).[255] The rules have been revised by the CCD to include partial repayments under s. 95.[256] The creditor must be given notice of the amount payable by the debtor as far as is practicable to do so and cannot enforce the agreement while the failure to give the prescribed notice continues.[257]

---

[254] Section 94.

[255] SI 2004/1483 (replacing the Consumer Credit (Rebate on Early Settlement) Regulations 1983, SI 1983/1562).

[256] Section 95A provides for payment to the creditor of 'fair, objectively justified' compensatory payment which must not exceed the upper limit set out in the section in relation to a fixed interest period loan. Section 96 discharges non-excluded linked transactions on early termination.

[257] Section 97 and, in relation to partial payment, s. 97A.

8.11.4 **Unenforceability**

Where the creditor does not comply with various information and formality requirements (see sections 8.8–8.9), the agreement may become unenforceable under s. 127 of the CCA. The rules on this are set out in Part V of the CCA, which deals with actual information and formality requirements as well.

Because breach of the informational and copy requirements render an agreement '*improperly executed*' under s. 65 of the CCA, such an agreement is civilly unenforceable in the courts by the creditor (but enforceable by the debtor) unless the debtor either gives his voluntary and informed consent at the time enforcement is sought (s. 173(3), CCA) or an enforcement order granted by the court under s. 127. Major problems revolved around the fact that, in certain cases involving the omission or misstating of any of the 'prescribed terms' or failure to serve proper cancellation notices, the court had no option but to refuse an enforcement order, regardless of whether or not the debtor had actually suffered any prejudice, and this gave rise to people seeking to take advantage of technical breaches. It has been estimated that one in four agreements is vulnerable to challenge and some consumers have revelled in their prowess at running up huge debts and avoiding paying them.[258] The Internet is replete with advertisements and websites offering to rescue distressed debtors from their problems.[259]

Matters were brought to a head in *Wilson v First County Trust (No 1)*, where the debtor entered into a loan agreement for £35,000. In addition to the interest and other charges, there was a document fee of £250, which was added to the amount of the loan. The Court of Appeal held that it was in fact part of the total charge for credit, even though time was given to pay it under s. 9(4) of the CCA. The result was that the amount of credit was overstated by £250 and thus the credit figure was incorrect and deemed therefore not to have been given. Unfortunately, the amount of credit was a core 'prescribed term' under Sch. 6 to the Consumer Credit Agreement Regulations 1983 (as amended). The result was that the agreement was permanently unenforceable under s. 127(3) of the CCA and the security given in relation to the car (the deposit of the debtor's car) also unenforceable. The bank challenged this in *Wilson v First County Trust (No 2)*, arguing that the automatic unenforceability contravened Art. 6 of the European Convention on Human Rights 1950 (right to free and fair trial of the dispute) and Art. 1 of Protocol 1 (seizure of property without just compensation). The

---

[258] This was vividly illustrated in a *Panorama* programme, 'Can't Pay, Won't Pay', 10 November 2008, in which a couple from the Midlands claimed to have avoided paying over £100,000 in debts on technical grounds. They overreached themselves and went to court to dispute one claim and ended up with a bill of nearly £100,000 for costs! The programme is accessible to watch again via the BBC *Panorama* website via BBC iPlayer. Some relief to creditors has been provided by permitting delivery of reconstituted copies of original agreements – see *Carey* v *HSBC Bank PLC* [2009] EWHC 34/7 (QB) 24/12/09.

[259] Tony Levene, 'Can You Really Dodge Your Debts?' *The Guardian*, 29 November 2008 (at: www.guardian. co.uk/money/2008/nov/29/debt-creditcards). Some legal firms make a speciality of dealing in such claims – a whole new industry of 'claims handlers' has grown up. See Bournes Debt Solutions website (at: www. bournesdebtsolutions.com). It must be stressed that no impropriety is being suggested here; merely taking advantage of overly complex law, Bournes assert, 'In our opinion the vast majority of credit agreements are unenforceable because they fail to comply with the prescribed terms.' Information overload and complexity under the CCA is savagely attacked by Richard Mawrey QC in 'Rewrite, Revise, Redraft' (2008) 152(40) *Sol Jo* 21/10/08. Apparently, reference of a debtor legally refusing to pay under an unenforceable agreement to a credit reference agency does not constitute enforcement. See *McGuffick* v *Royal Bank of Scotland* [2010] 1 All ER 634, in relation to failure of a bank to provide a statement under s. 77 of the CCA.

House of Lords held that Art. 6 was not engaged as the creditor never had a right to have the matter litigated in the first place and, while Art. 1 of the Protocol was engaged in the circumstances, given the historic abuse of debtors by unscrupulous creditors and the dictates of adequate consumer protection, the provision was justified.

Under pressure from the industry and the many clearly unjustified cases relying on technical breaches, s. 15 of the CCA 2006 repealed s. 127(3)–(5), so for the future at least there are no longer any grounds for automatic unenforceability and in all cases the court will have a general discretion under s. 127(1)–(2) to grant an enforcement order.[260]

In the future, in the event that an agreement is *prima facie* unenforceable, the court will dismiss an application only if it considers just to do so regarding:

(a) the prejudice caused to any person by the contravention and the degree of culpability for it;

(b) the power conferred on the court by s. 127(2) to reduce or discharge any sum payable by the debtor or hirer, or any surety, so as to compensate him for prejudice suffered as a result of the contravention in question; and

(c) the power conferred on the court by s. 135 (the power to impose conditions, or suspend the operation of, terms of an order) and s. 136 (power to vary agreements and related securities).

Therefore, a case such as *Wilson v Robertsons (London) Ltd*[261] would now not even be disputed as it is suggested no real prejudice was suffered by the debtor. In this case the automatic and immediate deduction of an £8 document fee from a pawn loan agreement for £400 resulted in the debtor only getting £392 and the agreement being permanently unenforceable as the credit was incorrectly stated and the document fee was wrongly classified as part of the credit instead of the total charge for credit.[262]

8.12 Creditor liability for dealer actions – connected lender liability

8.12.1 Section 56 – statutory agency

Section 56 imposes responsibility on certain creditors for misrepresentations and contractual promises made by those who have conducted the negotiations which have brought about the credit agreement – known as 'antecedent negotiations' – including both oral and written statements, the contents of advertisements and brochures, labels and marking on packaging.[263] This applies in D-C-S agreements, both the two-party and the three-party situations described above. It will be recalled that the two-party situation is one in which the creditor

---

[260] However, the problem will remain for creditors for a while as the repeal does not affect improperly executed agreements entered into before the commencement of the repeal. See CCA 2006, Sch. 3, para. 11.

[261] [2006] 1 WLR 1248.

[262] See *HSBC Bank* v *Brophy* [2011] EWCA Civ 67; [2011] ECC 14.

[263] Section 56(4), CCA. Basically any form of communication between the debtor and negotiator.

and the supplier are the same person, for example, where the goods are supplied by a retailer under a hire purchase or conditional sale agreement financed by the retailer or where the goods are supplied by a finance company on some such basis, having been sold to the finance company by the retailer. The three-party situation is where the creditor and supplier are different persons but have an arrangement, for example, where retail sellers or suppliers agree to accept certain credit cards to finance purchases from their shops or where they have an arrangement with a finance company that the finance company will extend credit to finance purchases from the retailers' shops.

In such cases, s. 56(2) of the CCA says that a person other than the creditor who conducts 'antecedent negotiations' leading to the making of an agreement is deemed to do so as agent of the creditor as well as in his own capacity.

This means that the creditor will be responsible for misrepresentations and contractual statements made by the party conducting the antecedent negotiations. So if the person conducting these negotiations has made a pre-contractual statement which is a misrepresentation or which would generate contractual responsibility, the creditor will be responsible along with the party who conducted the negotiations, for example, if an employee of a garage owner said to the prospective debtor that a secondhand car being acquired on hire purchase was safe and it had defective brakes, the finance company could be sued.[264]

EXAMPLE

Suppose, then, that a retailer has conducted negotiations with a buyer, which have resulted in the retailer selling goods to a finance company and the latter supplying them to the buyer on hire purchase or conditional sale terms. The retailer may have made a statement which is a misrepresentation or which would make the retailer responsible under a contract which would be collateral to the contract between the finance company and the consumer. The effect of s. 56(2) is that the finance company will also be responsible for any such misrepresentation[265] or fulfilment of the relevant contractual obligation. Another scenario is where a retailer has conducted negotiations which lead to the buyer entering into a contract to buy goods from him (the retailer) but financed by a party with whom he has an arrangement (for example, a credit card company). Here the credit card company will be responsible for misrepresentations and contractual obligations which are brought about by the retailer's statements.

In these cases the imposition of responsibility upon the party supplying credit can be justified on the basis that this party benefits from the buyer being persuaded to enter into the transaction, and if this party is held responsible along with the retailer the consumer stands a much better chance in practice of obtaining a remedy (for example, in cases where the retailer is insolvent or is based some distance away).

The 'statutory agency' created by s. 56 does not apply where a retailer initiates a hire or leasing contract through a finance company as this is not an agreement involving credit or

---

[264] Section 56(1)(b), (2) and (3), assuming that by introducing the consumer buyer to the source of the credit, the finance company, the garage owner was deemed to be acting as a credit broker. See *Brookes* v *Retail Credit Cards* (1986) 150 JP 131.

[265] See, for example, *Forthright Finance Ltd* v *Ingate (Carlyle Finance Ltd, third party)* [1997] 4 All ER 90, CA.

other financial accommodation as is required under s. 56.[266] In such circumstances the finance company will only be liable for the retailer's statements where it can be established at common law that the retailer was his agent. There is no presumption of an agency in such circumstances, although it may be established on the facts of the case.[267]

Section 56 illustrates also that the very precise way parts of the Act are drafted facilitates possible evasion of protections, which was illustrated in the case of *Black Horse Ltd* v *Langford*. In this case a car dealer agreed to accept the buyer's car under a part-exchange agreement in relation to the purchase of a new car on hire purchase from the appellant finance company. The car dealer promised to discharge the amount outstanding on the existing hire purchase agreement on the traded-in car. The car dealer, instead of dealing with a finance company direct, approached an intermediary dealer who bought the new car and arranged a hire purchase agreement with the appellant finance company, which, by coincidence, was also the finance company in respect of the traded-in car – the resale to the finance company was at the same price the garage had sold it to the intermediary broker. The car dealer did not honour the promise to pay off the balance on the existing hire purchase agreement in relation to the traded-in car, which the consumer had to pay. The consumer then sued the finance company under s. 56(1)(b), arguing that there was a statutory agency and they were liable for the car dealer's promise because it was 'in relation' to the hire purchase of the new car. Gray J held that there was no liability because s. 56(1)(b) did not apply. It would only have applied if the car dealer had sold the car directly to the finance company, the creditor, which had then entered into a hire purchase agreement with the consumer. Here the car was not sold to the creditor but to a broker intermediary who had made no promise about paying off the earlier hire purchase agreement. Further, at common law there was no evidence that the car dealer was acting as agent of the finance company when the promise was made.[268]

8.12.2 Section 75 – connected lender liability

One of the most successful provisions of the Act is the connected lender liability provision in s. 75 – stemming from the view that the supplier and the creditor were engaged in a 'joint venture' and should share both the profits and losses so, if goods purchased using a credit card with an authorised dealer were defective, a claim could be made against the creditor, who would have made a profit out of the initial sale involving its credit card. The section does not apply where debit cards, charge cards or cheques are used. The credit industry has campaigned arduously over the years to have the section repealed or limited only to the amount of credit they had advanced, but unsuccessfully.[269] It has proved a very useful protection where suppliers have gone into liquidation – particularly in areas like travel and holidays, where travel companies are prone to insolvency, often quite abruptly leaving holidaymakers

---

[266] *Moorgate Mercantile Leasing* v *Gell & Ugolini* [1988] CCLR 1.

[267] See *Mercantile Credit Co Ltd* v *Hamblin* [1965] 2 QB 242, CA, *Branwhite* v *Worcester Works Finance Ltd* [1969] 1 AC 552, HL and *Purnell Secretarial Services Ltd* v *Lease Management Services Ltd* [1994] CCLR 127.

[268] See H. Johnson, 'Credit Intermediary Problems' (Aug/Sep 2007) *F&CL* 1–4, and 'Carte Blanche for Hire Purchase Sharks' (2007) *NLJ* 734–735.

[269] C. Bisping, 'The case against s.75 of the Consumer Credit Act 1974 in credit card transactions' (2011) 5 *JBL* 457–474.

stranded abroad. Section 75 applies to a three-party and four-party[270] D-C-S agreement, that is, where the creditor and supplier are different persons but have an arrangement, for example, where purchases from a shop are financed (under arrangements) by credit cards or by finance companies that give other credit to finance purchases. It is important to note that the section does not apply where the creditor and supplier are the same person, as in the case of hire purchase agreements where the supplier sells the goods to a specialist finance company who enters into a hire purchase agreement with the consumer. Here, if there is a breach of contract in respect of either the goods or services element or the credit element, the consumer will sue the finance company directly.[271] The section does not apply when you use a credit card to get cash from an ATM machine and take the cash to the shop to buy goods, even if the shop would have accepted the card directly as payment. Neither does the section apply to charge cards such as American Express, debit cards (at least when the current account is in credit) or payments by cheque with or without a cheque guarantee card.[272]

It is also important to note that the liability of creditors under s. 75 is not limited to the amount of credit they advance and they face liability for all non-remote damages. For example, if a consumer buys a television with defective wiring, for £200, from a supplier under a regulated credit card agreement and the wiring causes a fire, burning down the consumer's house, seriously damaging his furniture and causing him physical injury, which means he is off work for a year and loses his sex drive, then damages under all these headings would normally be recoverable from the credit card company and could easily amount to over £1m.

In such cases s. 75(1) says that, 'if the debtor . . . has . . . any claim against the supplier in respect of a misrepresentation or breach of contract he shall have a like claim against the creditor, who, with the supplier, shall accordingly be jointly and severally liable to the debtor'.

For this to apply, the cash price (as opposed to the credit price) must be for more than £100 and no more than £30,000. The effect of s. 75 is that (subject to the financial limits) where a seller or supplier is liable to the buyer for misrepresentation, for breach of an express term or for breach of one of the implied terms as to description, quality or fitness, the buyer will, in addition, have a 'like claim' against the creditor. Of course, there may also be a claim under s. 56, which (as we have just seen) will make the creditor liable for misrepresentations and express promises made by the supplier. Indeed, s. 56 will often be more useful – first, because it also applies to two-party D-C-S cases (which s. 75 does not) and, second, because, even in the three-party cases where s. 75 does apply, this is subject to the upper and lower

---

[270] A four-party agreement will involve the debtor, the credit card company, the supplier and a merchant acquirer. The latter, usually a bank, signs people up to the respective networks such as Visa and MasterCard and also deals with suppliers, in processing vouchers, etc., and arranging payment less a commission to the supplier and passing payments to the credit card company, again less a commission or interchange fee. An attempt to argue that s. 75 did not apply because there were no direct 'arrangements' between the supplier and the credit card company was rejected by the Court of Appeal in *Office of Fair Trading* v *Lloyds TSB Bank PLC* [2007] QB 1 and H. Johnson, 'Credit Cards and Connected Lender Liability: Round Two to the Consumers' (May, 2006) *F&CL* 1–4, and the issue was not pursued when the case went to the House of Lords. The position of the merchant acquirer is considered in *NSB Ltd* v *Worldpay* [2012] EWHC 927 and *Lancore Services Ltd* v *Barclays Bank PLC* [2010] 2 All ER (Comm) 273. Essentially a series of contractual relationships between them, the suppliers and credit card companies was operating within the overall interchange arrangements operated by bodies such as MasterCard and Visa.

[271] The judge got this aspect wrong and misapplied the section in *Porter* v *General Guarantee Corp* [1982] RTR 384. Complex terminology can easily lead judges and counsel astray.

[272] Section 187 of the CCA defines 'arrangements'. Also excluded are the electronic transfer of funds from a current account, for example, using a debit card such as Barclays Connect Card.

financial limits mentioned just above and these do not apply under s. 56. However, s. 75 extends beyond s. 56 in applying (unlike s. 56) to the implied terms as to description, quality and fitness as mentioned above. As with s. 56, s. 75 therefore means that consumers have a better chance of obtaining a remedy (for example, in cases where the retailer is insolvent or is based some distance away).[273]

If the buyer chooses to exercise his claim against the creditor, the creditor is entitled to join the seller as a party to the claim and to claim an indemnity from him.[274]

Unlike many of the systems in mainland Europe the consumer does not have to exhaust any remedies they have against the supplier first – they can sue the creditor directly, usually because they are seen as having the deeper pocket.[275]

8.12.3 Secondary liability of the creditor under the CCD

The UK has successfully preserved s. 75 in the reform of EU consumer credit law.[276] However, the Directive is in some respects more wide-ranging than s. 75, for example, it applies to all 'linked credit agreements' of more than €200 and less than €75,000 (£60,260 at date of UK implementation of the CCD) and the government inserted an additional provision which would reflect the Directive. So, in the first instance, the consumer would look to s. 75 the CCA. If that were not available he could then look to the new provision but here this would only kick in if the consumer had failed to obtain satisfaction from the supplier – it is a form of 'secondary liability'.[277]

Section 75A provides for this form of 'secondary liability' – where the debtor under a linked credit agreement'[278] can pursue a claim but only where the claim against the supplier has failed. He can use the section where the supplier cannot be traced, the supplier does not respond to the debtor, the supplier is insolvent or the debtor has taken reasonable steps to pursue his claim against the supplier but has not obtained satisfaction for his claim (s. 75A(2)). However, reasonable steps do not have to include litigation. Satisfaction can include where the debtor has accepted a replacement product or service. This is slightly

---

[273] See H. McQueen, 'Faulty Goods, Rejection and Connected Lender Liability' (2011) 15(1) *Edin LR* 111–115, discussing the Scottish cases of *Douglas* v *Glenvarigill Co Ltd* [2010] CSOH 14 (OH) and *Durkin* v *DSG Retail Ltd* [2010] CSIH 49 (IH (1 Div)).

[274] Sections 75(2) and (5).

[275] Article 11 Directive 87/102. As a minimum requirements directive, the UK could have stricter rules in s. 75 for credit companies under UK jurisdiction. See Case C-429/05 *Rampion* v *Franfinance SA* [2008] BusLR 715 (ECJ) and H. Johnson, 'Article 11 Consumer Credit Directive: Joint Liability: Continental Style' (Jan 2008) *F&CL* 1–3.

[276] Article 15(3), Directive 2008/48/EC.

[277] Article 15(2), Directive 2008/48/EC, and BERR (2009), paras 11.11–11.17.

[278] A 'linked agreement' is defined in s. 75(5): 'In this section "linked credit agreement" means a regulated consumer credit agreement which serves exclusively to finance an agreement for the supply of specific goods or the provision of a specific service and where:

(a) the creditor uses the services of the supplier in connection with the preparation or making of the credit agreement; or

(b) the specific goods or provision of a specific service are explicitly specified in the credit agreement.'

Note that this is different from the definition of a 'linked transaction' in s. 19 of the CCA 1974. This will require the courts to analyse the impact of the section where a credit card is used – will it be the case that the credit card forms a master agreement and each time it is used to buy an item that separate use will form a separate contract independent of the master agreement? Again this is only likely to impact very rarely because few credit cards would cover purchases in excess of £30,000.

ambiguous in the sense he may have other claims despite the claim to a replacement product. The key point is however that this section will only apply where the cash value of the product exceeds £30,000 or the linked credit agreement does not exceed £60,260 or the linked credit agreement is entered into by the debtor 'wholly or predominantly' for the purpose of a business carried on, or intended to be carried on, by him (s. 75A(6)). Section 75A will not apply if the credit agreement is secured on land (s. 75A(8)). In practice therefore the new form of 'secondary liability' will have a fairly limited effect and largely be used in the luxury goods and services market.

DEBATE BOX

In Scotland, the 'like claim' which the buyer has against the creditor has been held to go beyond the right to claim damages and to extend to the right to terminate the credit agreement.[279] This decision has been criticised and the view advanced that the buyer is only entitled to terminate the *supply* contract giving a right to a refund, as against the supplier. He may also have a damages claim against the supplier. The argument runs that the consumer may then withhold payments due under the credit agreement as a means of enforcing the right to a refund or to damages which exists against the supplier, but that there is no right to terminate the credit agreement as such.[280] This view may now have support from the decision of the Court of Appeal in *Jarrett* v *Barclays Bank PLC*,[281] where it was held that a 'like claim' means a 'like cause of action' and that this does not necessarily mean exactly the same remedy. On the facts of the case, it was held that the specific performance remedy available against the supplier was not available against the creditor.

Another question is if s. 75 applies to transactions made outside of the UK or containing some foreign element. However, it has now been made clear by the House of Lords that it does.[282]

ISSUE BOX

Mr Buyer holds a credit card issued by Card Issuer PLC. Mrs Seller is selling an item on the eBay Internet auction site. Mr Buyer makes a successful bid for the item being sold by Mrs Seller. Payment is made through PayPal (an FSA-regulated electronic money institution). Mr Buyer opens an account with PayPal and credits that account with a payment from his credit card, issued by Card Issuer PLC. PayPal transfers the payment to Mrs Seller's PayPal account and she withdraws it. Mrs Seller does not send the paid-for item to Mr Buyer and Mr Buyer is unable to recover his payment from either PayPal or eBay. Mr Buyer claims reimbursement from Card Issuer PLC.

Can he do so?

---

[279] *United Dominions Trust Ltd* v *Taylor* 1980 SLT 28. For a good overview, see C. Hare, 'Credit cards and connected lender liability' (2008) 3 *LMCLQ* 333–352.
[280] See R. Bradgate, *Commercial Law* (4th edn, Butterworths, London, 2009) p. 590 and see Davidson 'The Missing Link Transaction' (1980) 96 *LQR* 343.
[281] [1997] 2 All ER 484.
[282] *Office of Fair Trading* v *Lloyds TSB Bank PLC* [2007] 3 WLR 733.

8.12.4 **Unauthorised use of credit card**

The provisions of the Consumer Credit Act 1974 have now to be considered alongside the Payment Services Regulations 2009 (PSR 2009)[283] which implement the EU Payment Services Directive[284] in the UK.[285] These regulations will include a range of transactions which may be part of or connected with credit agreements (both regulated and unregulated) – including the use of credit cards, direct debits, standing orders and other forms of credit transfer.[286] Part VI of the PSR 2009 deals with the respective rights and obligations of parties in relation to the provision of payment services.[287] The consumers' rights are not waivable or excludable.[288] The Consumer Credit Act 1974 continues to apply to contracts which involved the provision of payment services which are also regulated agreements in relation to certain specified regulations in PSR:

(a) sending out of unsolicited credit tokens (s. 51, CCA 1974) applies instead of reg. 58(1)(b);[289]

(b) acceptance of credit tokens (s. 66, CCA 1974) and misuse of credit tokens (s. 84, CCA 1974) apply instead of regs 59, 61 and 62 PSR 2009;

(c) liability for misuse of credit facilities (s. 83, CCA 1974) applies instead of regs 59, 61 and 62, PSR 2009;

(d) duty to give notice before taking action for non-breach events (s. 76, CCA 1974);

(e) need for issuing a default notice (ss. 87–89, CCA 1974) in respect of the grounds set out in reg. 56(2)[290] disapplies reg. 56(3)–(6) PSR 2009.

The combined effect of ss. 66, 83 and 84 of the CCA 1974 will be that, in most cases, the consumer cardholder will not be liable for any unauthorised transactions carried out by a third party with the card. However, if the consumer has authorised the third party to have possession of the card, it may face unlimited liability for its misuse but can restrict that liability by giving the appropriate written notice or oral notice, confirmed within seven days in

---

[283] SI 2009/209.

[284] Payment Services Directive, 2007/64/EC, 13 November 2007.

[285] For an overview of this Directive, see section 6.5, Regulation of payment services.

[286] See PSR 2009, Sch. I, Part I (on the scope of services covered).

[287] Regulation PSR 2009, 51, provides that the Regulations will apply where the payment services are provided from an establishment maintained by a payment service provider or its agent in the UK, payment service providers of both the payer and payee are located within the EEA or where the payment services are carried out in euros or currency of an EEA state that has not adopted the euro. Regulation 53 disapplies most of the regulations in relation to small accounts and transactions.

[288] Regulation 51(3). To complicate matters the PSR apply to a narrower range of parties than the CCA 1974. In reg. 2 a consumer is defined as 'an individual who, in contracts for payment services to which these Regulations apply, is acting for purposes other than a trade, business or profession'.

[289] The regulation will therefore apply to unregulated credit token agreements and states that the payment service provider should 'not send an unsolicited payment instrument, except where a payment instrument already issued to a payment service user is to be replaced'.

[290] Regulation 56(2) provides 'A framework contract may provide for the payment service provider to have the right to stop the use of a payment instrument on reasonable grounds relating to: (a) the security of the payment instrument; (b) the suspected unauthorised or fraudulent use of the payment instrument; or (c) in the case of a payment instrument with a credit line, a significantly increased risk that the payer may be unable to fulfil its liability to pay.' In these situations ss. 76 and 87 of the CCA 1974 will apply instead of the PSR 2009.

writing to the creditor. There will be no further liability from the point that the creditor has been given notice for any more unauthorised transactions.[291] If the cardholder loses the card, he may face a maximum liability of £50 but, again, can limit this liability by giving prompt notice of the loss to the creditor so he will not be responsible for any unauthorised transactions after the required notice has been given.[292]

The other aspects of the PSR 2009 are discussed in Chapter 6, s. 6.3.1, but some key points to be noted in relation to credit cards are:

(a) any charges in relation to the use of the card can be fixed by agreement, but such charges must 'reasonably correspond to the payment service provider's actual costs – this will of course include such things as late payment penalties which must be reasonable and proportionate to costs involved in the administration, etc. of the late payment (reg. 54(1));

(b) consent to credit card transactions will only be taken to have been authorised if the payer has given consent and consent can be withdrawn before the payment can no longer be revoked (see regs 55 and 67);

(c) the cardholder must use the instrument in accordance with the terms and conditions governing its issue and notify the payment service provider in the agreed manner and without undue delay on becoming aware of the loss, theft, misappropriation or unauthorised use of the payment instrument (reg. 57(1)(a) and (b));

(d) the payment service user must, on receiving a payment instrument, take all reasonable steps to keep its personalised security features safe (reg. 57(2));

(e) the payment service provider must ensure that the personalised security features of the payment instrument are not accessible to persons other than the payment service user to whom the payment instrument has been issued – the payment service provider bears the risk of a payment instrument or any of its personalised security features to the payment service user (reg. 58(1));

(f) the onus is on the payment service provider to prove that the payment transaction was authenticated, accurately recorded, entered into the payment service provider's accounts and not affected by a technical breakdown or some other deficiency (reg. 60);

(g) if the payment service provider refuses to execute a payment order, it must notify the cardholder of the refusal, if possible the reasons for the refusal and the procedure for rectifying any factual errors that led to the refusal.[293]

A consumer who suffers loss as a result of a breach of the PSR may bring a civil action under reg. 120. In addition, supervision and enforcement is carried out by the FSA, which includes the right to impose financial penalties (reg. 85), injunctions (reg. 87) and a power to seek orders for restitution to consumers who have suffered loss (regs 88–90).

---

[291] Section 84(2)–(8) of the CCA 1974, even that liability will not apply if the consumer has not been given the statutorily required details of how to contact the creditor.

[292] Section 84(10) of the CCA 1974. However, provisions on giving of authorised possession and loss do not apply to distance contracts and distance finance contracts. See s. 84(3A)–(3C) and Chapter 7, section 7.2 on distance selling contracts.

[293] The time limits for giving such notice are set out in reg. 7. Notice need not be given if it would be unlawful, for example, suspected money laundering or terrorist financing (reg. 66(4)).

8.13 Consumer default and protection

First of all, if the consumer is in default, he might be able to escape or limit his liability on the basis that there is a claim for breach of contract or misrepresentation against the creditor or that the agreement is cancellable[294] or is unenforceable because of failure to follow formalities or provide required information.[295]

Apart from these possibilities, there are various other protections for consumers in default.

8.13.1 Information about default in general

Sections 9–11 of the 2006 Act inserted new provisions in the 1974 Act requiring notice of default to be served by the creditor within 14 days of the debtor being at least two payments in arrears, including 'arrears information sheets' to help the debtor understand his position.[296] If this is not done the agreement cannot be enforced and interest cannot be claimed during the period of non-compliance.[297]

Requirements in relation to default information will have to be modified under Art. 18 of the CCD. Where there is a *'significant overrunning'*, exceeding a period of a month, the consumer must be informed of the overrunning, the amount involved, of the borrowing rate and of any penalties, charges or interest on arrears applicable (see BERR, 2009, chapter 17).

8.13.2 Default notices in relation to particular action

In cases of debtor default, the agreement will often allow creditors to take such action as terminating the contract, demanding early payment, recovering possession of goods or land, enforcing a security or terminating, restricting or deferring any rights of the debtor. Such provisions are only enforceable if the creditor serves a default notice which specifies the breach[298] and how (and by when)[299] to remedy it or, if it cannot be remedied, what compensation must be paid; the consequences of non-compliance; a default information sheet; and, where relevant, restrictions on the right to repossess 'protected goods'.[300] If the debtor

---

[294] See *Forthright Finance Ltd* v *Ingate & Caryle Finance* [1997] 4 All ER 90, and note the extension of liability for misrepresentation by the deemed agency under s. 56 of the CCA 1974.

[295] See *Broadwick Financial Services Ltd* v *Spencer* [2002] 1 All ER (Comm) 446 and *Black Horse Ltd* v *Hanson* [2009] EWCA Civ 73.

[296] Sections 86A, 86B and 86C, 1974 Act. See also the rules on notice of default sums and interest under s. 86E.

[297] Section 86D, 1974 Act.

[298] Overstatement of the amount owing (unless *de minimis*) invalidates the notice: *Woodchester Lease Management Services Ltd* v *Swain* [1999] CCLR 8.

[299] The time allowed for compliance must be at least 14 days from service of the notice (changed from 7 days by s. 14(1) of the 2006 Act). See J. MacDonald, S. Phipps and K. Holderness, 'Brandon v American Express Services Ltd [2011] EWCA Civ 1187, [2012] ECC 2 and Compliance with s. 88(2) of the Consumer Credit Act 1974' (2012) 27(1) BJIB&FL 58–59.

[300] Sections 87 and 88, the latter as amended by s. 14 of the 2006 Act; and see the Consumer Credit (Enforcement Default and Termination Notices) Regulations 1983, SI 1983/1561.

complies with the notice, the breach is treated as never having occurred.[301] If he does not comply, the creditor is free to pursue any of the above remedies, so long as they are otherwise provided for under the agreement.

Although there is no statutory sanction for a failure to serve a compliant default notice, a debtor can rely on non-compliance with s. 87 and/or 88 as a defence if the creditor seeks judicial enforcement of its claims. A non-compliant default notice might, therefore, have serious consequences for a creditor's claim. However, it might well be possible for a creditor to remedy a bad default notice by serving a 'good' default notice.[302]

8.13.3 Special protection in hire purchase and conditional sale

In these contracts the creditor cannot enter premises to repossess goods without a court order[303] and, where land is the subject of a conditional sale, the creditor cannot repossess the land without an order.[304]

In cases where the seller remains the owner of the goods and the consumer has paid at least a third of the price and is in breach but has not terminated the agreement under s. 99, the goods are 'protected' and there can be no recovery without either the free and voluntary consent of the debtor or a court order.[305] If the goods are recovered in contravention of this rule, the agreement is ended, the consumer is released from all further liability and able to recover all previous sums paid.[306]

A further protection is available in equity, that is, the court has a general power to protect against forfeiture of a proprietary or possessory right, although only in exceptional circumstances.[307]

The court also has powers to order the consumer to return the goods to the creditor (a 'return order') or to return some of them, while vesting the creditor's title to the remainder in the debtor (a 'transfer order').[308]

8.13.4 Special protection in hire

Where the owner recovers possession other than through court action, the hirer can apply for an order extinguishing (in whole or part) future liability to pay (possibly applicable where either has terminated or the consumer defaulted) or requiring repayment (in whole or part) of sums paid by the hirer[309] (again, where the agreement is terminated or the consumer has defaulted, but, say, a large deposit has been paid).

---

[301] Section 89, 1974 Act.
[302] This was suggested by HHJ Chambers QC (sitting as a judge of the High Court) in *Harrison* v *Link Financial* [2011] ECC 26, and it is also advocated by some practitioner texts.
[303] Section 92(1).
[304] Section 92(2).
[305] Section 90.
[306] Section 91.
[307] *Transag Haulage Ltd* v *Leyland Daf* (1994) 13 Tr LR 361.
[308] Section 133.
[309] Section 132.

8.13.5 **Time orders**

If the consumer is in default, he can apply for a 'time order' when he has been served with a default notice,[310] when proceedings have been brought against him[311] or where, 14 days after having been given a notice of sums in arrears, they have notified the creditor or owner of an intention to apply for a time order and made a proposal for payment.[312] Various guidelines have been laid down by the Court of Appeal as to time orders.[313] Principally, that whether or not it is just to make the order is dependent on consideration of all the circumstances and the position of both parties, that any order should normally be for a stipulated period, appropriate instalments should be considered in the light of amount, timing, impact on payment period and interest[314] and, on granting an order, any possession order should be suspended.[315] Courts have been reminded that it is not only the interests of the debtor or hirer that must be considered but also the legitimate interests of the creditor.[316] Time orders have not been that effective and the insertion of s. 129(1)(b) into the Act, which allows a debtor or hirer to apply for a time order following a notice of receipt of a notice of arrears under s. 86B or s. 86C of the Act, is to encourage greater and more effective use of them. However, to avoid this simply being used as a delaying tactic by the debtor or hirer, under s. 129A such an application can only be made if (a) the debtor has given the creditor or owner a notice indicating his intention to make an application, (b) indicating that he wants to make a proposal to the creditor and owner in relation to the making of payments under the agreement, (c) giving details of the proposal and (d) a period of 14 days has elapsed since the notice was given to the creditor.[317] For small amounts of consumer debt of under £15,000, subject to certain conditions, a debt relief order may be the most appropriate way forward because after 12 months the debts may be written off.[318]

The central point of a time order is that, whilst it is in force and being complied with, the creditor's right to terminate the agreement, demand early payment of any sum, recover possession of any goods or land, enforce any security, etc. – in effect, the creditor's rights – are put on hold and, if the breach is remedied by meeting the payments under the time order, the breach is deemed never to have taken place.[319] A good step-by-step guide to using the

---

[310] Count Court (Amendment) Rules 1985, SI 1985/566, Ord. 49, reg. 4(5).

[311] Section 129.

[312] Section 129A, inserted by s. 16 of the 2006 Act.

[313] *Southern and District Finance* v *Barnes* [1995] CCLR 62, CA. It is worth noting that the courts have indicated that, in making time orders, adjustments or variations to the credit agreement can be made, such as reduction of the interest rate using their powers under ss. 135 and 136 of the CCA.

[314] See also s. 136 on the power to vary terms, including interest.

[315] In relation to hire purchase and conditional sale agreements, orders can be made both to instalments already accrued and in arrears but future instalments not yet payable (s. 130(2), CCA). In relation to other agreements the order only relates to 'any sum owed', but of course if a debtor defaults on any one instalment, acceleration clauses kick in, triggering a requirement to pay the balance of the debt immediately, so here the court could make an order covering the total sum. See A. Dunn, '"Footprints on the Sands of Time": Sections 129 and 136 Consumer Credit Act 1974' (1996) *Conv* 209.

[316] *First National Bank* v *Syed* [1991] 2 All ER 250. So, if there is no realistic prospect of the debtor paying off the loan, even with a time order perhaps allowing instalments to be made at half the agreed rate over twice the period, if even this cannot realistically be met, no order should be made.

[317] Orders can require the remedying of non-monetary breaches, such as repairing the goods (s. 129(2)(b)).

[318] See s. 108, Tribunals, Courts and Enforcement Act 2007, and National Debtline website (at: www.national-debtline.co.uk/england_wales/factsheet.php?page=37_debt_relief_orders).

[319] Section 130(5), CCA. The order may be varied or revoked by an application of an 'affected person' to the court (s. 130(6), CCA).

procedure is to be found on the National Debtline website.[320] A system of approved debt management schemes which, in effect, lead to the writing off of a specified debt and restrictions on enforcement action by creditors, subject to a right of appeal by a creditor, is provided for in Chapter 4 (ss. 109–133) of the Tribunals, Courts and Enforcement Act 2007, but these provisions have not yet been brought into force.[321]

The CCD does not touch on the issue of consumer debt and any restrictions on the creditor's rights to enforce a validly owed debt.

8.13.6 Unfair relationships

Prior to the 2006 Act, there were powers to protect consumers by setting aside 'extortionate credit bargains'.[322] However, the focus just being on a 'bargain', only unfairness of the actual terms (and not of performance and enforcement issues) was covered. In addition, the courts tended to focus only on interest rates and not other terms and the requirement for 'gross' contravention of fair dealing meant that only the most extreme cases of high rates tended to be viewed as covered by the courts.[323] The jurisdiction was a form of statutory equity and the courts would look at the behaviour of both the creditor and of the debtor.[324] In practice, as the provisions relied on individual consumers taking the initiative and many of the problems related to high-interest sub-prime loans to disadvantaged and financially vulnerable consumers, they were either unable or unwilling to be involved in the legal process.

ISSUE BOX

The 2006 Act sought to address these problems. It created a new s. 140A and B of the 1974 Act, containing the concept of an 'unfair relationship'.[325] There may be such an unfair relationship based on the terms of the contract.[326] This overlaps with the regimes on fairness of terms but extends beyond these in catching the interest rate (a term that would be a core

---

[320] www.nationaldebtline.co.uk/england_wales/factsheet.php?page=06_time_orders

[321] The National Debtline offers to organise a 'voluntary' debt management scheme but creditors are not compelled to sign up to it (at: www.nationaldebtline.co.uk/england_wales/factsheet.php?page=29_debt_management_plan).

[322] Sections 137–140 of the CCA 1974. These provisions were repealed by the CCA 2006, but it is important to note that the new provisions can be used to reopen existing credit agreements made before the new regime came into force and which were not completed within a 12-month transitional period to allow businesses to adjust to the new regime. During this transitional period the old extortionate credit bargain provisions could be relied on. See Sch. 3, paras 14–15 and *Barnes v Black Horse Ltd* [2011] 2 All ER (Comm) 1130. An excellent critique of the earlier regime, which remained valid until its repeal, is G. Howells and L. Bentley, 'Loansharks and Extortionate Credit Bargains' (1989) *Conv* 164 (Part I) and 234 (Part II).

[323] See, for example, the comments of Dyson LJ in *Broadwick Financial Services Ltd v Spencer* [2002] 1 All ER (Comm) 446 and *Paragon Finance v Pender* [2005] 1 WLR 3412, plus the White Paper, *Fair, Clear and Competitive Markets – the Consumer Credit Market in the 21st Century*, 2003.

[324] See *Ketley v Scott* [1981] ICR 241. A loan to buy property was arranged at extremely short notice to experienced property buyers by a moneylender of last resort, with some false answers to questions by borrowers. The court refused to reopen the bargain and upheld a 48 per cent interest rate.

[325] On the new test, see *Patel v Patel* [2009] EWCH 3264, 10/12/09, *Shaw v Nine Regions Ltd* [2009] EWCH 3514, 18/12/09 and *MBNA Europe Ltd v Lynne Thorius*, Lawted, 4/1/2010.

[326] Section 140(1)(a).

term under the Unfair Terms in Consumer Contracts Regulations). However, there can also be an unfair relationship based on (1) the way the lender has exercised or enforced his rights or (2) anything done or not done by the lender before or after the agreement.[327]

Both categories (1) and (2) seem to have the potential to catch virtually any type of pre- or postcontractual unfairness (that is, misleading or aggressive practices leading to a transactional decision or wholly unilateral unfairness by the creditor). So, for example, there might be tactics to pressure the consumer to pay what the lender claims is owed, which tactics might be argued to be unfair, for example, giving a misleading impression as to the amounts owed, not giving clear breakdowns as to what is owed so as to deter the consumer from making a calm assessment of the position, refusing to cooperate with consumer attempts to resolve the issue.

The issue is whether this newer, more expansive, protection will deal with the problem of excessive interest rates and harsh enforcement of credit agreements more effectively.

Consumers can raise the issue of an unfair relationship by applying to the county court or by raising it in the context of enforcement by the trader or any other relevant proceedings. It is important to note that the jurisdiction is very wide-ranging and can apply to agreements between individuals which are, in most other respects, transactions that would be exempt from most of the provisions of the rest of the Act, for example, a business loan between individuals in excess of £25,000.[328] The onus of proof lies on the party seeking to uphold the arrangements to show that they were fair and reasonable.[329] In addition, acting contrary to the new standard could well amount to a 'domestic infringement', allowing the OFT to seek an enforcement order against the trader.[330] It is important to note that the issue can also be considered by the Financial Ombudsman Service (see section 8–18).[331] The concept of unfairness is extremely broad and only over time will the extent and scope of the concept become clearer. The OFT has issued guidance on the concept and its use of its powers under Part 8 of the Enterprise Act 2002 to seek civil enforcement orders restraining unfair credit practices.[332] On rates and charges the guidance states the following.

EXAMPLE

Rates and charges

3.17 The interest rate under a credit agreement, or other charges falling within the total charge for credit, would normally be core terms and so, if clearly expressed, would not themselves be subject to an assessment of fairness under the UTCCRs. This would not, however, preclude the court from taking such terms into account in deciding if the

---

[327] Section 140(1)(b) and (c) respectively.

[328] A failed attempt to challenge a business loan in relation to a property deal is illustrated in *Shafik Rahman* v *HSBC Bank* [2012] EWHC 11 (Ch) Judge Behrens, 17/1/2012. The court found that the transaction was a large-scale commercial loan with parties of equal bargaining power and there was no evidence that the terms were unfair or inconsistent with industry practice.

[329] *Bevin* v *Datum Finance Ltd* [2011] EWHC 3542 (Ch), 15 December 2011.

[330] See below, section 8.14.1.

[331] Dispute resolution by this means is discussed there.

[332] 'Unfair Relationships: Enforcement Action under Part 8 of the Enterprise Act 2002' (revised August 2011) OFT854Rev (at: www.oft.gov.uk/shared_oft/business_leaflets/enterprise_act/oft854Rev.pdf).

relationship is unfair to the borrower. Equally, the OFT or another enforcer would be entitled to have regard to such terms in deciding whether to take Part 8 action.

3.18 A term providing for variations in the interest rate would not, in the OFT's view, constitute a core term within the meaning of the UTCCRs as it does not relate to the adequacy of the initial price. A variation term which confers excessive discretion on the creditor either to vary rates and charges or not to vary them, in line with changes in the market, may be considered unfair under the UTCCRs and may also be a relevant factor in considering whether or not there is an unfair relationship.

3.19 The unfair relationships test in s. 140A of the Act does not refer expressly to rates or payments, in contrast to the previous extortionate credit bargains provisions. Section 138 of the Act provided that, amongst other things, a credit bargain was extortionate if it required the borrower to make payments which were grossly exorbitant, having regard to interest rates and other relevant considerations.

3.20 Nevertheless, in the OFT's view, there is scope for the court, at its discretion, to find that a credit relationship is unfair on the grounds that it involves excessive costs for the borrower. Section 140A (2) of the Act states that the court shall have regard to all matters it thinks relevant. This could include, for example, the cost of the credit agreement or any related agreement. This appears to be endorsed by Ministerial statements in Parliament during the passage of the 2006 Act.

3.21 For example, the rate of interest charged under a credit agreement, or the rate or amount of other fees or charges, may be so much higher than those applicable generally in the particular market sector, or payable by borrowers in similar situations, as to make the relationship as a whole unfair to the borrower. They may also, in the particular circumstances, be oppressive or exploitative of the individual borrower even if they are in line with rates prevailing in the particular sector.

3.22 In some cases, excessive prices may be accompanied by other unfair terms or practices which may contribute to an unfair relationship as well as being susceptible to possible Part 8 action in their own right. For example, the borrower may be unaware that a fee would be charged in a particular case or of the level of the fee or how this might impact on the debt. He may also be unaware that rates might increase in particular circumstances or were unlikely to reduce in line with changes in the market. The creditor (or a broker or other intermediary) may have failed to disclose relevant information or may have done so in a false or misleading manner, misrepresenting key elements. The information may have been unclear or ambiguous and so may not have been readily comprehensible.

Where there is found to be an unfair relationship, the court has an extensive variety of powers (much more so than under the old regime) including ordering repayment of money by the creditor; requiring the creditor to do (or cease to do) anything in connection with the agreement; reducing or discharging money owed by the debtor or a surety; requiring the return of property to a surety; setting aside any duty owed by the debtor or a surety under this or a related agreement; altering the terms of the agreement; or directing accounts to be taken.[333]

[333] Section 140(b)(1).

A case involving alleged misselling of PPI was *Harrison* v *Black Horse Ltd.*[334] In this case the consumers had been sold a PPI policy in connection with a loan from the defendants. The lender had not disclosed to the borrower that it would receive from the insurer a handsome commission upon the sale of the PPI – no less than 87 per cent of the premium. Indeed, the policy also represented fairly poor value for money and in fact only lasted for the first 5 years of a 23-year loan repayment period. It was also alleged that, as the lender did not explain this to the borrower, the lender had breached the then Insurance Conduct of Business Rules promulgated by the Financial Services Authority. It was suggested that that amounted to a serious conflict of interest and possible breach of a fiduciary duty. While the Court of Appeal was of the view that many might regard the lender's conduct as unacceptable, it declined to hold the transaction to be unfair. The proper sales procedure had been gone through and the borrower was aware of the overall price of the PPI premium and it would be, in the Court of Appeal's view, anomalous if a lender was obliged to disclose receipt of a commission in order to escape a finding of unfairness under s. 140A of the CCA, but yet not obliged to disclose it pursuant to the statutorily imposed regulatory requirement under which it operated. Neither did they consider the size of the premium affected the objectivity of the lender about the desirability of such a policy being taken out. The lender was then under no obligation to advise that cheaper products might be available elsewhere.[335]

At the moment the notion of a general express interest rate cap beyond which any interest rate would be deemed to be unfair has been rejected despite attempts to amend the Financial Services Act 2012 during its passage. The government, however, took the view that, in respect of specific products, the new Financial Conduct Authority being introduced by the Financial Services Act 2012 would have power to ban specific consumer credit products if it considered them to be detrimental to the consumer interest and, in considering such detriment, the cost of the product could be taken into account.[336] The OFT has also concluded that such price controls would be complex, expensive and difficult to administer.[337]

The CCD does not touch on the issue of unfair terms in credit contracts.

---

[334] [2011] EWCA Civ 1128; [2012] ECC 7, discussed in J. Bruce, D. McDonald and M. McGarrigle, 'Unfairness as Justice' (2011) 40 *CoLJ* 14–17.

[335] For a list of cases and summaries of outcomes see OFT's webpage 'Unfair relationships cases' (at: www.oft. gov.uk/about-the-oft/legal-powers/legal/cca/CCA2006/unfair/unfair-rel-full) and see *Tew* v *BOS (Shared Appreciation Mortgages) (No. 1)* [2011] EWHC 203 (Ch), Mann J, where the judge, in relation to a challenge to terms of so-called 'shared appreciation mortgages', refused to frame the issues under a Group Litigation Order, so excluding consideration of the borrowers' individual circumstances from an assessment of fairness. The claimants had wanted a selection of lead cases to determine the fairness of the schemes in the abstract, regardless of individual positions of the debtors.

[336] See *Hansard*, Vol 543, No 292, House of Commons, Official Report, 23 April 2012, cols 712–730, and S. Brown, 'Using the Law as Usury Law: Definitions of Usury and Recent Developments in the Regulation of Unfair Charges in Consumer Credit Transactions' (2011) 1 *JBL* 91–118.

[337] 'Review of High-cost Credit: Final Report', June 2010, OFT1232, Executive Summary.

ISSUE BOX

Of course, a key question in relation to this new fairness principle is as to just how unfair the relationship needs to be. Certainly, the intention does seem to be to increase the level of protection from the old 'extortionate bargain' rule, so there is at least some suggestion that the provisions are aimed at more routine unfairness. However, we shall need to await court decisions in order to see just how protective the new unfairness test is interpreted to be by the courts.

8.14 Security agreements

The general nature of security in a commercial law context is discussed in Chapter 2. As well as protecting the principal debtor or hirer, the CCA also seeks to provide protections for any third party that provides a real or personal security, such as a guarantor.[338] Provision of security, except by the debtor, must be set out in writing in the prescribed form.[339] A parallel set of provisions concerns improper execution of security agreements if they are not concluded in the prescribed form and the prescribed copies are not provided.[340] The points to note are:

(i) a security instrument will not be properly executed if, where the security is provided after or at the time the principal regulated agreement is executed, the surety is not given a copy of that agreement and other documents referred to in it;

(ii) if the security instrument is provided before the regulated agreement is concluded then within seven days of the principal credit agreement being made, the surety must receive a copy of the regulated agreement;

(iii) if the security agreement is improperly executed and an enforcement order is refused in respect of that security then, unless such an order is dismissed on technical grounds, the security will be ineffective and any security provided will be treated as never having existed and any property must be returned or any money received by the creditor or owner in respect of the ineffective security must be repaid to the surety (s. 106, CCA);

(iv) sections 107–109 give the surety rights to receive information about the position under the principal credit agreement and failure to do means that the creditor or owner cannot enforce the agreement until the omission is rectified and, similarly, copies of default notices, acceleration notices and non-default termination notices under ss. 87, 98 and 76 of the CCA must be given to the surety and failure to do so means that the security agreement is unenforceable without a court order of the free and voluntary consent of the surety given at the time enforcement is sought (ss. 111 and 173(3), CCA).

---

[338] Security for these purposes includes a 'mortgage, charge, pledge, bond, debenture, indemnity, guarantee, bill, note or other right provided by the debtor or hirer, or at his request (express or implied) to secure the carrying out of the obligations of the debtor or hirer under the agreement' (s. 189, CCA). Importantly this does not cover securities provided by a dealer not at the request of the debtor, such as indemnities given by the dealer under a recourse agreement.

[339] See Consumer Credit (Guarantees and Indemnities) Regulations 1983, SI 1983/1356 (as amended).

[340] Section 105.

8.14.1 Use of securities as evasion devices

It would of course be easy for a creditor to get around the protections provided for the principal debtor by seeking to recover the value of an unenforceable loan by enforcing a third-party guarantee or security which naturally could be achieved by inserting a clause into the principal agreement stating that no impediment to enforcing the principal agreement should prevent enforcement of the security. To prevent this scenario there is an anti-evasion provision in the CCA 1974 (s. 113).

The key provision is s. 113(1), which states that a security agreement cannot be enforced to benefit the creditor or owner, directly or indirectly, to any greater extent than would be the case if the security were not provided, for example, if a debtor under a hire purchase agreement had exercised his statutory right of termination under ss. 99–100 of the CCA and was therefore only liable for a maximum of 50 per cent of the total price, the creditor could not enforce any security agreement to recover the other 50 per cent of the hire purchase price. The same rule applies in respect of any actual or prospective linked transaction (s. 113(8)).

Similarly, if the principal regulated agreement is only enforceable on an order of a court or the OFT, any related security is only enforceable either with the informed and voluntary consent of the surety given at the time enforcement is sought or where such an enforcement order has been granted (s. 113(2)).

If the principal credit agreement is cancelled, then any requirement on the debtor or hirer to repay the credit and interest and to restore any goods will not be enforceable until the creditor or owner has in effect cancelled the security and returned any goods deposited as a security – the steps required by s. 106 of the CCA. However, where a guarantee is given in relation to a debt of a minor, it can be enforced as if the minor had been an adult when he had entered the agreement (s. 133(7)).

A security will also become ineffective and subject to s. 106:

(a) if a regulated agreement is cancelled under s. 69;

(b) if a regulated agreement is terminated under s. 91 (wrongful seizure of protected goods held under a hire purchase or conditional sale agreement);

(c) enforcement or validation orders are refused under ss. 40(2), 65(1), 124(1) or 149(2) – except where the application is refused on 'technical grounds' (undefined); or

(d) a declaration is made by the court under s. 142(1) (refusal of an enforcement order).[341]

An illustration of the operation of these provisions is the case of *Wilson v Robertsons (London) Ltd*. In the case, W, the debtor, had pawned a number of items with a pawnbroker for a series of loans – a pawn being a depository security where the goods can be redeemed on repayment of the loan and interest.[342] The pawn agreements were improperly executed and held to

---

[341] Savings are made for bona fide purchasers of value of registered charges, etc. under s. 177 of the CCA, but if a land mortgage is enforced against the debtor by the third party, the debtor has a right of indemnity against the original creditor (s. 177(4), CCA).

[342] Prior to the advent of the welfare state before the Second World War, pawnbrokers were a common sight in most major cities and often the only sources of credit for what we might now call sub-prime borrowers. The sector was one of the earliest to be regulated, in the early 17th century. There is a special regime set out in ss. 114–122 of the CCA, which will not be discussed here. Though now an insignificant part of the credit industry, the sector has experienced growth in recent years, with discreet shops lending to the middle classes on security of jewellery, electrical equipment, etc.

be unenforceable under s. 127 of the Act and so, under ss. 113 and 106, the pawnbroker's securities were ineffective and six of the seven deposited items were returned to the debtor who also, of course, retained the value of the loans and had to pay no interest. A seventh item, a gold signet ring with a special engraving, had been sold for its gold value and could not be returned. The price realised for the gold value of the ring was less than its replacement value for the debtor.

The debtor sought to bring a claim for conversion for the full value of the ring but the pawnbroker argued she was limited to her right under s. 106(d) of the CCA to be repaid the amount realised on the sale of the security and that s. 170 of the CCA prevented any additional claim.[343] This argument succeeded at first instance but the Court of Appeal ruled that s. 170 was not inconsistent with a parallel common law remedy for conversion of her property – she could rely on her ordinary property right.

8.15 Negotiable instruments

8.15.1 The problem

The freestanding nature of negotiable instruments is a problem in relation to consumer credit agreements because, if they are negotiated to a bona fide purchaser for value ('a holder in due course'), they can be enforced by the third party regardless of any problems with the underlying transaction. In commercial law, negotiable instruments give rise to autonomous obligations, for example, if a builder takes a bill of exchange in his favour representing the price, interest and charges for the installation of a central heating system, if the system proves faulty or is not properly completed, a third party to whom the builder has endorsed the bill of exchange can enforce it against the consumer debtor regardless of any separate contractual claim the consumer debtor may have for breach of the contract to install the central heating system. The problem is reduced now cheques (a form of negotiable instrument) are made out to the payee only and not as historically 'or order', so they cannot be endorsed to a third party (for a general discussion of negotiable instruments, see section 6.6).

8.15.2 The solution

As a result, s. 123 of the CCA 1974 imposes certain restrictions on the use of negotiable instruments (which simply means that title to a document and the money it represents can be transferred by signing (endorsement) and delivery to the third party):

---

[343] Section 170(1) states in effect that no additional civil or criminal remedy shall be provided for a breach of the Act beyond that expressly stated in the relevant provision, save that the OFT can take account of breaches of the Act in relation to such things as its licensing decisions, even if the Act provides no remedy for the breach of a specific provision. Also, under s. 170(3), remedies for judicial review and injunctions for persistent breaches of the Act are unaffected.

(i)   a negotiable instrument (other than a banknote or a cheque where the latter is nego-
      tiable) may not be taken in discharge of any sum payable by a debtor or hirer under a
      regulated agreement;

(ii) a negotiable cheque which is taken in discharge of any sum payable can only be nego-
      tiated through a banker, which in practice will normally take as the collecting agent
      for the creditor;

(iii) no negotiable instrument may (other than in relation to non-commercial agreements
      and some hire agreements) be taken by a creditor or owner as security for the discharge
      of any sum payable by a debtor, hirer or surety;

(iv) if s. 123 is contravened, then the regulated agreement or security instrument can only
      be enforced with a court order (s. 124, CCA);

(v)   a person other than a bona fide purchaser for value (holder in due course of the instru-
      ment) cannot enforce the negotiable instrument (s. 125, CCA);

(vi) if the debtor has to pay the value of the instrument to a holder in due course, he
      is entitled to be indemnified by the creditor or owner in respect of that liability
      (s. 125(3), CCA).

8.16   Land mortgages

Under s. 126 of the CCA, any land mortgage securing a regulated agreement is enforceable
(so far as provided in relation to the agreement) on an order of court only, so that if the
creditor wishes to exercise a right to take possession and sell a property, he will require an
order of court. No sanction is provided, however, for failure to comply with this provision
and the exact scope of the section is somewhat uncertain, as are the consequences of non-
compliance for all parties including a third-party purchaser with notice.[344]

8.17   Enforcement of the Act

The UK government was satisfied that the current range of penalties provided for in the CCA
1974 meet the requirements of Art. 23 of the CCD to provide penalties that are *'effective,
proportionate and dissuasive'* and intend to retain the existing regime (BERR, 2009, para. 18.5).
The government was also satisfied that s. 173 of the CCA meets the need to provide for
contracting out bans in Art. 22 of the CCD (BERR, 2009, para. 18.3).

---

[344] J. E. Adams 'Mortgages and the Consumer Credit Act' (1975) *Conv* 94 and S. Brown 'The Consumer Credit
Act 2006: Real Additional Mortgagor Protection?' (2007) *Conv* 316. Major reform of the sale and marketing
of mortgage credit is being undertaken by the European Commission, with its proposal for a Directive on
credit agreements relating to residential property' (COM (2011) 142 Final, 31.3.2011). See the FSA's
response, 'The Mortgage Credit Directive (MCD): Key Considerations' (at: www.fsa.gov.uk/about/what/
international/mortgages/priorities).

8.17.1 **Administrative controls**

Regulatory enforcement of the Act has traditionally been criminal (see section 8.17.2 below) but local authorities do not have unlimited budgets, the burden of proof is heavy – beyond all reasonable doubt – and some judges or magistrates often imposed derisory penalties not reflective of the profits to be made by criminal conduct. The Enterprise Act 2002 (EA 2002) provides for civil enforcement via an administrative enforcement procedure by way of Part 8 orders (formerly known as 'Stop Now' orders) in ss. 210–236 of the EA 2002. Under Part 8 of the EA 2002 certain designated enforcers can seek voluntary undertakings or, if that fails, interim[345] or final enforcement orders to prohibit persons from committing breaches of both domestic and EU consumer protection legislation, including the consumer credit legislation.[346] If a business breaches such an order it can face penalties for contempt of court, which can include up to two years in prison, a fine without upper limit and sequestration of the company's assets. The procedure is not designed to provide individual compensation for debtors and will only be used where the 'collective interests' of consumers are involved. Designated enforcers include the OFT, local trading standards authorities, regulators of privatised industries such as the Office of Communications (Ofcom) in relation to telecoms, Internet service providers, radio and television services,[347] and one private-sector body – the Consumers' Association, the publishers of *Which?* magazine. Other private and public interest bodies can be added as designated enforcers if they satisfy the criteria.[348] Reflecting the increasing number of consumer transactions across borders on the Internet in the case of 'Community infringements' (that is, infringements of EU consumer law), designated 'Community enforcers' can seek undertakings and court orders in the UK, in so far as activities, say, on UK websites, aimed at their consumers, adversely affect the interests of those consumers. In the same way the OFT and other designated UK Community enforcers can seek similar undertakings and orders in other EU countries if the collective interests of UK consumers are being affected.[349] An example of the use of the procedure in relation to the credit area is the voluntary undertaking given by the car supermarket firm Carcraft to make clearer to customers the terms of motor finance, such as the level of repayments or that the consumer was signing more than one finance agreement.[350] The firm agreed to inform consumers in a

---

[345] For an example of an interim order, see the *Momentum Network Ltd* decision in Birmingham County Court in relation to unfair commercial practices and making of misleading claims by a 'debt sale' firm claiming to make debtors 'debt free' in two weeks (OFT PN PN 43/10, 26 April 2010).

[346] The OFT has issued guidance: *Enforcement of Consumer Protection Legislation: Guidance on Part 8 of the Enterprise Act 2002* (OFT, 2003). The legislation covered is regularly updated by statutory instrument (see Enterprise Act 2002 (Part 8) (Domestic Infringements) Order 2003, SI 2003/1593, and Enterprise Act 2002 (Part 8) (Community Infringements: Specified UK Laws) Order 2003, SI 2003/1374).

[347] See H. Johnson, 'The Communications Industry and Unfair Contract Terms: Tightening Control' (2009) 14(2) *Comms Law* 57–60.

[348] See the Enterprise Act 2002 (Part 8 Designated Enforcers; Criteria for Designation, Designation of Public Bodies as Designated Enforcers, etc.) Order 2003, SI 2003/1399 (as amended) and The Enterprise Act 2002 (Part 8) (Designation of the Consumers' Association) Order 2005, SI 2005/917.

[349] This is the impact of the EU Injunctions Directive, Directive 98/27/EC, 19 May 1998, on injunctions for the protection of consumers' interests. See OFT's Press Release 63/04, 'First Ever Cross-border Action by OFT Court', setting out action in Belgium against a company sending misleading mailings to UK consumers (at: www.oft.gov.uk/news-and-updates/press/2004/63-04#.USo3aaX7XKQ).

[350] See 'OFT takes action against used car supermarket over sales practices', OFT PN 121/11, 9 November 2011 and full text of the undertaking (at: www.oft.gov.uk/OFTwork/consumer-enforcement/consumer-enforcement-completed/cc-automotive#.USo41qX7XKQ).

clear and timely manner prior to the sale of the terms of any finance agreements and ancillary products and to ensure that effective audits were regularly undertaken of the sale of consumer finance and that ongoing training on the sale of consumer finance was provided to relevant staff.[351]

The impact of the court orders is wide in that a person can be ordered not to engage in, or desist from engaging in, the relevant conduct either in his own or another's business. A person can also be ordered not to consent or connive at the carrying on of such conduct by a body corporate with which he has a relationship. The court can order the publication of corrective statements to eliminate the continuing impact or effects of any prohibited conduct.[352]

8.17.2 **Criminal offences**

In addition to civil litigation and administrative enforcement the Act creates a number of criminal offences for breach of the Act's provisions and any regulations made under ss. 44, 52, 53, 112, 26 and 54. These are set out in Sch. 1 to the Act with the modes of trial and financial penalties, for example, it was a criminal offence under s. 45 to advertise credit where the same goods are not available for cash and is an offence to send circulars advertising credit to minors, under s. 50.

These are strict liability regulatory offences subject to a statutory due diligence defence, thus the prosecution will have to prove the offence beyond all reasonable doubt and the burden will then pass to the business to show, on the balance of probabilities, that they come within the scope of the due diligence defence.[353] Enforcement and prosecution will usually be carried out by the local trading standards authorities[354] which have extensive enforcement powers set out in ss. 161–166 of the CCA.[355] In practice, modern enforcement focuses more on warnings, advice and voluntary correction, with prosecution tending to be a last resort and often used in cases of overt fraud as opposed to merely careless infringement.[356] A good

---

[351] See, ibid., OFT's website.

[352] Examples of Part 8 and previous Stop Now orders can be found in, for example, *Allied Carpets*, OFT Press Release 46/01, 13/11/2001, stopping infringing 'interest-free credit' advertisements. For a list of actions taken, see OFT's website (at: www.oft.gov.uk/about-the-oft/legal-powers/legal/enterprise-act/part8/action/#.USo61aX7XKQ).

[353] Where an offence is committed by a body corporate and a member of the senior management, such as a director, manager, company secretary, etc., then if they have 'consented or connived at the commission of the offence' they may also be prosecuted, under s. 169.

[354] A study by the OFT, *Trading Standards Impact* (OFT June 1085 and OFT PN 65/09, June 2009) showed, over the whole area of consumer law, TSA's saved consumers £347m a year.

[355] These are the standard powers available in connection with enforcement of regulatory offences, such as powers of entry and inspection (s. 162), powers to make test purchases (s. 164). To wilfully obstruct or without reasonable cause fail to give the enforcement officer such assistance as he may reasonably require is a criminal offence (s. 165).

[356] This trend is reinforced by the provisions of the Regulatory Enforcement and Sanctions Act 2008 and the creation of a Local Better Regulation Office (LBRO, at: how the Better Regular Delivery Office – http://www.bis.gov.uk/brdo) with greater reliance on regulatory enforcement codes and a more flexible range of penalties. See 'Regulators Compliance Code Briefing' 30/5/08 (at: www.lbro.org.uk/FileUploads/2008530_Regulators'_20Compliance_20Code_20briefing._pdf) and 'Statutory Primary Authority Guidance' 2/4/09, setting out arrangements for what will be a lead local authority in conducting enforcement measures (at: www.lbro.org.uk/FileUploads/200942_Primary_Authority_Guidance._pdf). Further reforms are in the pipeline, in particular to seek greater coordination and consistency at both national and local levels. See 'Empowering and protecting consumers: Consultation on institutional changes for provision of consumer information, advice, education, advocacy and enforcement', BIS, June 2011, which among other things envisages the creation of a new National Trading Standards Board.

example of the enforcement work done by local authorities is the month-long survey, carried out in February 2012, into the operation of payday lenders in Northern Ireland by the Northern Ireland Trading Standards Service, which revealed that many lenders failed to carry out credit checks, adequately explain the borrowing costs involved. Some lenders were also found inappropriately to offer to rollover loans so that the credit charges escalated substantially. Enforcement action was threatened if the lenders did not put their houses in order.[357]

While the offences are strict liability in not requiring any *mens rea* on the part of the business, there is a statutory due diligence defence. There are two prongs to the defence: first, the defendant must show that his act or omission was due to a mistake, or to reliance on information supplied to him, or to an act or omission by another person or to an accident or to some other cause beyond his control and, secondly, that he took all reasonable precautions and exercised all due diligence to avoid the commission of the offence.[358] Controversially, a corporate body is allowed to plead the acts of its junior employees as a defence, provided they have taken reasonable precautions to avoid employees committing offences, for example, by training, monitoring, systems compliance and following up complaints.[359] Clearly if offences are persistently committed by junior employees, then that would tend to show inefficient systems and compliance and, therefore, a lack of taking reasonable precautions. A business cannot rely on the defence when the offence is committed by a senior employee or 'part of the managing mind' of the company such as a managing director because their acts will be identified with those of the company.

An illustration of the operation of the defence is the case of *Coventry CC* v *Lazarus*. A garage, arranging or entering into conditional sale or hire purchase agreements in relation to used cars, was prosecuted for breach of the Consumer Credit Advertisement Regulations 1989, made under s. 44 of the CCA. The firm had been advised by enforcement officers in the past about infringing the Act and had taken advice and received written information from a trade association. The problem was that some of that advice was incorrect. When prosecuted, the firm argued that it had relied on information supplied by another, for example, the trade association, and had taken all reasonable precautions to avoid the commission of the offence by relying on that information. The court held the first limb of the defence was satisfied – advice could constitute information – but the defence failed on the second limb in that they company had failed to take the simple precaution of running the advertisement past the enforcement officers to get their views on its compliance, given past problems.[360] In straight-forward cases, the criminal courts can make 'compensation orders' to compensate consumers for the loss and damage they have suffered as a result of the commission of offences under the Act and its associated statutory instruments.[361]

---

[357] www.tradingstandards.gov.uk/extra/news-item.cfm/newsid/852, 16 March 2012.

[358] If relying on the fact that the information was supplied by another or due to an act or omission of a third party, then the identity of that person must be supplied to the prosecution at least seven clear days before the hearing (s. 68(2), CCA).

[359] See a case on a similar defence in s. 24 of the Trade Descriptions Act 1968, *Tesco Supermarkets* v *Nattrass* [1972] AC 153 (HL).

[360] See also *R* v *Mumford* (1994) 159 JP 395.

[361] Under s. 130 of the Powers of Criminal Courts (Sentencing) Act 2000. See *R* v *Ben Stapylton* [2012] EWCA Crim 728.

8.18 Dispute resolution – role of the Financial Ombudsman Service

Historically, a major problem in relation to the effectiveness of consumer protection legislation generally, and consumer credit legislation in particular, has been the reluctance of consumers to take legal action to enforce their rights. The reasons for this range from expense, ignorance, technicalities, delays and reluctance to be involved in personal hearings to general suspicion and fear of the operation of the legal system. The CCA 2006 introduced a new alternative dispute resolution procedure, building on the existing jurisdiction of the Financial Ombudsman Service (FOS),[362] created by the Financial Services and Markets Act 2000. The FOS acquired a new 'consumer credit jurisdiction'.[363] The statutory framework was fleshed out by consumer credit rules laid down by the FOS and approved by the FSA.[364]

Under the rules, claims must be made within appropriate time limits and the complainant must give the creditor a chance to resolve the complaint through his internal complaints system.[365] Licensees will be required to establish appropriate internal complaints systems. The key advantage to the consumer is that access to the system is free and will be funded by levies on the industry.[366] However, complainants may be required to make a contribution to 'the costs in favour of the scheme operator (not the specific creditor), if, in the opinion of the ombudsman the complaint's conduct was "improper or unreasonable" or the complainant was responsible for "an unreasonable delay"'.[367] Under the statutory scheme an upper limit will be imposed on the amount of compensation payable.[368] The initial upper limit was set at £100,000, but this was raised to £150,000 in January 2012, with a further streamlining of the complaints procedure.[369]

The FOS will determine a complaint by reference to what is 'fair and reasonable in all the circumstances of the case', supported by a written statement of reasons for the

---

[362] See its website (at: www.financial-ombudsman.org.uk/default.htm).

[363] Section 59 of and Sch. 2 to the CCA 2006 inserting a new s. 226A and Sch. 17, Part 3A into the FSMA 2000. For the operation of the Scheme generally, see Part XVI and Sch. 17 to the FSMA 2000. The work of the FOS was reviewed by Lord Hunt of Wirral MBE, *Opening Up, Reaching Out and Aiming High: An Agenda for Accessibility and Excellence in the Financial Ombudsman Service* (April 2008). For a useful overview, see P. E. Morris, 'The Financial Ombudsman Service and the Hunt Review: Continuing Evolution in Dispute Resolution' (2008) 8 *JBL* 785 (also on Westlaw).

[364] In addition, the type of business in question must be specified in an order by the Secretary of State, with the approval of the Treasury: see s. 59 of the CCA 06, inserting s. 226A(2)(e) and (5) into the FSMA 2000. So that the current system was not overwhelmed, there was a staged introduction of the scheme.

[365] See FSMA 2000, Sch. 17, Part 3A, para. 16B(1), inserted by Sch. 2 to the CCA 2006. It is important to note that a complaint can relate to a principal consumer credit activity but also any ancillary matter related to such an activity, including any advice given to the consumer. The detailed rules are laid out in the FSA Handbook (at: http://fsahandbook.info/FSA/html/handbook/DISP).

[366] Section 60 of the CCA 2006, inserting s. 234A in the FSMA 2000. Licences granted by the OFT will stipulate that licensees must make the necessary contributions. Differential fees can be charged to different groups of licensees.

[367] FSMA 2000, s. 230(4).

[368] Section 61(5), CCA 2006, inserting a new s. 229(4A) into the FSMA 2000.

[369] See 'Consumer Complaints: The Ombudsman Award Limit and Changes to the Complaints-handling Rules' (FOS/FSA CP11/10, May 2011, at: www.fsa.gov.uk/pubs/cp/cp11_10.pdf).

determination.[370] The procedure is highly flexible and is not designed to ape court proceedings[371] so the Ombudsman can consider evidence that would be inadmissible in court or refuse to hear evidence that would be admissible in court.[372] The defendant creditor is bound by the final decision, subject to a right of judicial review,[373] but the complainant has the option to reject the outcome and pursue the matter in the courts. The Ombudsman has extensive powers:

(i)   he can grant *'fair compensation'* – monetary awards which can cover both financial and non-financial loss, such as distress and aggravation;[374]

(ii) he can *'recommend'* that the business pay the complainant a sum above the statutory maximum, if this is necessary to achieve 'fair compensation'; and

(iii) he can direct the firm to take such steps in relation to the complainant as he considers *'just and appropriate'*.

It is important to note that these steps can include ones which a court could not order, for example, the Ombudsman could direct the adjustment of a contractual interest rate if he considered it *'unfair'*.[375] However, the FOS does not deal with questions of improper execution as currently it has no powers to declare an improperly executed agreement unenforceable. That has to be done by a court.

---

[370] FSMA 2000, s. 228. It is important to note that the Ombudsman has a very wide-ranging jurisdiction and is not confined to following strict legal precedent – see *R (on application of IFG Financial Services Ltd) v Financial Ombudsman Service Ltd* [2005] EWHC 1153 (Admin), [2005] All ER (D) 301 (May) and P. Aiker, 'A Balancing Act' (2006) *NLJ* 974. Claims that refusal of a request for an oral hearing by a creditor contravened Art. 6 of the European Convention on Human Rights 1950 were rejected by the Court of Appeal in *R (on application of Heather Moor & Edgecomb Ltd) v Financial Ombudsman Service* [2009] 1 All ER 328. There was no unfairness in a completely written procedure, given the desirability of speedy decisions at minimum cost and minimum formality. The safeguard for creditors was the right to apply for a judicial review of the decision which might be quashed if the decision was arbitrary and unpredictable, including an unreasoned and unjustified failure to treat like cases alike. A challenge to this decision was declared inadmissible by the European Court of Human Rights in *Heather Moor & Edgecomb Ltd v United Kingdom* (2011) 53 EHRR SE 18. See A. Ibrahim and P. Johnson, 'Is FOS Above the Law'? (2008) 23(8) *BJIB&FL* 423.

[371] The intervention of claims management companies soliciting business from consumers with potential claims for misselling of payment protection insurance (PPI) belatedly led to a concordat between the banks, the claims management regulator (the Ministry of Justice), the FSA and FOS pointing out the complaints procedure was simple and straightforward and free and did not need the intervention of third-party complaint handlers. See 'Claims Management Companies and Financial Services Complaints' July 2011, Ministry of Justice (at: www.justice.gov.uk/downloads/claims-regulation/note-about-claims-management-companies.pdf).
    A summit of interested parties was held on 23 April 2012 with a view to simplifing and raising awareness of how to claim in relation to missold PPI policies. See Press Release by British Bankers', Association 'Commitment to Help Consumers Agreed at PPI Summit' (at: www.bba.org.uk/customer/article/commitment-to-help-consumers-agreed-at-ppi-summit).

[372] See FSA Handbook DISP 3.5.9 (at: http://fsahandbook.info/FSA/html/handbook/DISP/3/5).

[373] See *R (on the application of Green) v FOS Ltd* [2012] EWHC 1253 (Admin), Collins J, 18/5/12. An independent assessor reviews annually how complaints are dealt with but this system does not constitute a review of the merits of any complaint. See 2008/09 Annual Review, pp. 96–102, 265. Cases were referred to the Independent Assessor and he upheld in whole or part 83 against the FOS and awarded compensation of between £50 and £600 for administrative and other failings. The vast majority of cases are resolved by preliminary mediation and recommended settlements and provisional adjudication – in 2008/09, 105,275 with only 8,674 final determinations by the team of Ombudsmen.

[374] The current statutory maximum which can be awarded is £150,000, losses in excess of maximum can be pursued in the courts see: *Clark v Focus Asset Management and Tax Solutions* [2012] EWHC 3669, Cranston J, 19/12/12.

[375] FSMA 2000, s. 229.

The business is bound by a monetary award made by the Ombudsman and the award can be enforced by county court execution procedures and any related directions to take steps can be enforced by an injunction.[376] To help decide a case, the Ombudsman can order the business to produce any specified information if it is *'necessary for the determination of the complaint'*. A business which fails to comply with any such requirement without reasonable cause may be found guilty of contempt by the High Court.[377] Information received by the FOS in dealing with complaints can be disclosed to the OFT in relation to the carrying out of its prescribed functions under the CCA 2006, for example, the licensing procedures.[378] If a complaint raises important or novel legal issues, the Ombudsman can dismiss a complaint and refer the matter to the courts. Generally the business must agree to pay the complainant's reasonable legal costs on an indemnity basis, including the costs involved in any appeals, even if the business wins the case.[379]

This avenue for complaints has already been well used by consumers and, in the first year of the operation of the consumer credit jurisdiction, the FOS received around 2,000 complaints.[380] In fact a succession of financial scandals, including most recently the misselling of payment protection insurance, has threatened to overwhelm the FOS. In the case of PPI, tens of thousands of complaints have been received and there have been delays while the recalcitrant banks challenged the wideranging compensation procedures laid down by the FSA.[381] In addition the unsolicited intervention of unscrupulous claims management companies offering to handle complaints without properly disclosing the fee they would charge has muddied the picture and also stimulated a significant number of fraudulent claims from consumers who have never taken out PPI at all![382] A good overview of its work can be seen in the 2011/2012 Annual Review, stating it had dealt with 1,268,798 initial enquiries, which turned into 264,375 formal disputes, of which 60 per cent were in connection with PPI – totaling so far 157,716 complaints – the largest number ever received in a year about a single financial product.[383]

The FOS Ombudsman system seems to meet the requirement of the CCD for Member States to 'ensure that adequate and effective out-of-court dispute resolution procedures for

---

[376] Section 229(8)–(9), and see Sch. 17, Part 3A, para. 16D to the FSMA, inserted by Sch. 2 to the CCA 2006.

[377] FSMA, ss. 231, 232.

[378] Section 61(9), CCA 2006, inserting a new s. 353(1) into the FSMA 2000.

[379] FSA Handbook DISP 3.3.5 (at: http://fsahandbook.info/FSA/html/handbook/DISP/3/3). In 2007 the FOS suspended dealing with thousands of complaints concerning charges levied by banks in relation to 'unauthorised' overdrafts. See OFT v *Abbey National PLC* [2009] 2 CMLR 30 and FSA/PN/090/2007, 27 July 2007, and related notice by the FOS (at: www.financial-ombudsman.org.uk/faq/bank-charges.html).

[380] See *Ombudsman News*, 68 March/April 2008. Only complaints about events occurring after the operative date of 5 April 2007 could be considered. One early concern was failure of companies to highlight the mandatory internal complaints procedure they should have in place. See a selection of case studies in *Ombudsman News* 75, January/February 2009, largely featuring bad debt-collecting practices. Complaints often involve the overlapping powers of several regulatory bodies and the FSA, OFT and FOS collaborate on dealing with cases which raise 'of general public interest' involving a large number of consumers or businesses (see the joint website at: www.wider-implications.info/default.htm). In 2008/09, there were 18,590 new cases involving credit cards, 4,242 (largely late payment default charges) unsecured loans, 762 hire purchase, 407 debt collecting, 372 store cards and 31,066 PPI (p. 323, *FOS Annual Review 2008/09*).

[381] See R (on the application of the British Bankers Association) v Financial Services Authority [2011] Bus LR 1531.

[382] Banks have made provisions of billions in their accounts for compensation. In the first 6 months of 2011 the FSA estimated that £557m had been paid out in compensation.

[383] www.financial-ombudsman.org.uk/publications/ar12/index.html

the settlement of disputes concerning consumer credit agreements are in place, using existing bodies where appropriate' (Art. 24(1), CCD).[384]

8.19 Reform of law – EU Consumer Credit Directive and future changes

The UK had to implement the CCD by 20 May 2010 (Art. 27). The implementation approach was to retain as much of the current domestic legislation as possible and bolt on new provisions where UK law did not extend as far as that in the Directive and by further statutory instruments, for example, see s. 75 (original UK connected lender liability) and s. 75A (EU-based secondary liability where cash price of item exceeds £30,000). Therefore there have been some modifications to the CCA but the main thrust of protection will remain the same.[385] Thankfully from a business point of view the CCD will not be retrospective and will not apply to agreements entered into before the national implementing measures enter into force (Art. 30, CCD).[386] Further reform is on the way in respect of credit extended in relation to the sale, advertising and marketing of mortgage lending in a draft directive working its way through the EU legislative process.[387]

8.20 Conclusion

Consumer credit law is a complex area but more effectively designed licensing and enforcement mechanisms focusing on problem areas, better provision of information, development of policies on responsible lending, public enforcement of the legislation by bodies such as the OFT under Part 8 of the Enterprise Act 2002, wide-ranging provisions to act against unfair credit transactions and the introduction of a free at point of use Ombudsman system should ensure that the law protects consumers more effectively than in the past. However, while levels of financial ignorance remain high, much of the effect of these reforms may be wasted as people buy unsuitable products and fail to fully appreciate the nature of the financial commitments they are entering into. As far as further reforms were concerned, the thinking of the Brown Labour government was set out in *A Better Deal For Consumers: Delivering Real Help Now and Change for the Future*, Cm 7669, July 2009, Chapter 2. These issues included high interest rates

---

[384] The FOS is moving to fuller transparency in relation to the publication in full, including names of parties, of an Ombudsman's formal adjudications and provision for this is being made in the Financial Services Bill 2012 (see 'Transparency and the Financial Ombudsman Service' FOS, September 2011, at: www.financial-ombudsman.org.uk/publications/policy-statements/publishing-decisions-sep11.pdf). In addition, complaints data in relation to the main regulated firms can be accessed on the FOS' website (at: www.ombudsman-complaints-data.org.uk).

[385] The main problem is not the broad thrust but the complex detail. A good example is seen in the two sets of advertising regulations – the Consumer Credit (Advertisement) Regulations 2004, SI 2004/1484, which apply to credit advertisements secured on land based on the previous domestic law (such agreements being outside the CCD) and the newer Consumer Credit (Advertisement) Regulations 2010, SI 2010/1970, which implement the changes required by the CCD into all other regulated credit advertisements. Reconciling the differences of detail between the two will prove challenging.

[386] Though Arts 11, 12, 13, 17, 18(2) will apply to so-called existing open-ended credit agreements.

[387] Draft Directive 'Credit agreements relating to residential property', COM (2011) 142 Final, 31/3/11.

on credit cards, information, expansion of independent credit comparison websites, problems relating to consumer debt and one eye-catching marketing restriction, a proposed ban on the sending of consumer credit card cheques. The latter are controversial because they are sent unsolicited, which is said to encourage irresponsible borrowing; there is no interest-free period as with normal cards (s. 75 connected lender liability does not apply) and there are often little-understood handling fees for the consumer.[388] There was a suggestion that a further Consumer Credit Bill might be in the offing, but the Coalition government, elected in 2010, dropped the idea of a new Bill and, instead, is proceeding by means of a mixture of voluntary codes and a proposed major rejigging of consumer credit regulation by handing responsibility to a newly created Financial Conduct Authority (see section 8.2), with greater reliance on use of rulebooks containing core principles and conduct of business rules, and the possibility of abolishing some parts of the Consumer Credit Act 1974 with a view to producing a more simplified and proportionate regulatory regime. It remains to be seen if that ambition can be realised in what is a complex and fast-moving industry. It is proposed that this new regime will come into force in April 2014.

Further reading

Goode, R., (ed.), *Consumer Credit Law and Practice* (Butterworths, London, 1999).

Kelsall, R., *Consumer Credit Law: Practice and Precedents* (Law Society Publishing, London, 2012).

Lomnicka, E. (ed.), *Encyclopedia of Consumer Credit Law* (Looseleaf, Sweet and Maxwell, London, 1975).

Mawrey, R. and Riley-Smith, T., *Blackstone's Guide to the Consumer Credit Act 2006* (Oxford University Press, Oxford, 2006).

Philpott, F., *et al.*, *The Law of Consumer Credit and Hire* (Oxford University Press, Oxford, 2009).

Rosenthal, D., *A Guide to Consumer Credit Law and Practice* (3rd edn, Tottel Publishing, London, 2008).

Smith, J. and McCalla, S., *Consumer Credit Act 2006: A Guide to the New Act* (The Law Society, London, 2006).

Companion Website

For open-access **student resources** specifically written to complement this textbook and support your learning, please visit **www.pearsoned.co.uk/legalupdates**

ON THE WEBSITE

---

[388] See 'A Better Deal for Consumers: Review of the Regulation of Store Cards: Government Response to Consultation (March 2010, at: www.bis.gov.uk/assets/biscore/corporate/docs/c/10-768-consumer-credit-card-consulation-response.pdf). The Coalition government has preferred, at least initially, to proceed via an industry self-regulatory code to deal with most of these problems (see section 8.3) and 'A New Approach to Financial Regulation: Consultation on Reforming the Consumer Credit Regime' (BIS/HM Treasury, Consultation Document, December 2010, at: www.hm-treasury.gov.uk/d/consult_consumer_credit211210.pdf). Reform proposals now published, see FSA consultation Paper CP13/7, March 2013 at weblink.

Commercial mediation, conciliation and arbitration

By Jason Chuah

9.1 Introduction to alternative dispute resolution

Litigation is expensive and can be lengthy despite much progress having been made in recent times to make it more affordable and accessible. Non-consumer commercial litigation is even more prohibitive with huge legal fees involved. Businesses also may not like the sort of publicity litigation might generate and there have been complaints in the past that specialist disputes deserve resolution by experts, not generalist judges.[1] Hence, alternative dispute resolution methods are particularly needed. Alternative dispute resolution methods are also based on consensus. The parties must agree to use these methods. That consensus, it is envisaged, would promote settlement of the dispute. Litigation on the other hand is not voluntary; if the court deems itself to have jurisdiction, the defendant will be subject to the court's process whether he agrees to it or not.

POINT OF INTEREST

The Centre for Effective Dispute Resolution and the Chartered Institute of Public Relations carried out a survey of 160 executives and the following graph shows the attitudes of business towards dispute resolution or conflict management:

[1] In England and Wales, this criticism is less persuasive because the judicial system has become far more specialist than before. There are specialist courts to deal with commercial, admiralty, employment, land, technology, probate, etc. matters (see www.judiciary.gov.uk).

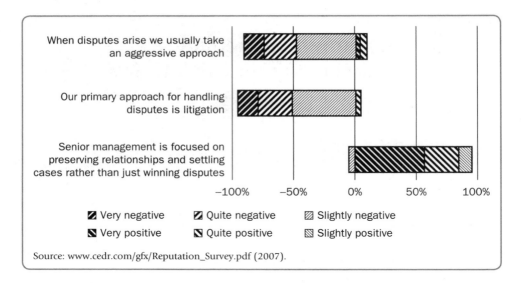

Source: www.cedr.com/gfx/Reputation_Survey.pdf (2007).

9.2 Mediation and conciliation

9.2.1 Concept of mediation

Mediation usually involves a neutral third party who will try to encourage the contentious parties to arrive at a compromise. He will normally hold separate discussions with the parties and apply his goodwill to suggest the parties clarify their demands and concerns. He may try to mediate if and when negotiations between the parties become heated. However, the parties remain in control of the decision to settle and terms of the settlement. In the event that the parties agree to a compromise, that settlement may be reduced to a binding contract. The main advantages are cost and publicity. The proceedings are conducted in private and confidence; no report will be made public.

A mediation may be encouraged or ordered by the court in exercise of its case management powers[2] and parties who refuse to mediate or arbitrate when it is reasonable to do so may be punished when costs of the litigation are ordered.[3] In *Dunnett* v *Railtrack*[4] the claimant had sued unsuccessfully for compensation for the death of her horses which were struck near Bridgend by an express train travelling from Swansea to London. Usually, the costs of the litigation would be borne by the losing side, namely the claimant. However, the Court of Appeal held that as Railtrack had refused to contemplate mediation at a stage when the costs of the appeal began to flow, the court refused to make an order for costs.[5] Railtrack therefore had to bear the costs of the appeal themselves. Brooke LJ had this to say:

[2] Rule 1.4(2), CPR 1998: See also *Hurst* v *Leeming* [2001] EWHC 1051 (Ch), *Dunnett* v *Railtrack* [2002] 2 All ER 850 and *Burchell* v *Bullard* [2005] EWCA Civ 358.
[3] Rule 44.5(3)(a) CPR 1998.
[4] [2002] 2 All ER 850.
[5] See also *Halsey* v *Milton Keynes General NHS Trust* [2004] EWCA Civ 576.

It is to be hoped that any publicity given to this . . . judgment . . . will draw the attention of lawyers to their duties to further the overriding objective in the way that is set out in CPR Pt 1 and to the possibility that, if they turn down out of hand the chance of alternative dispute resolution when suggested by the court, as happened on this occasion, they may have to face uncomfortable costs consequences.[6]

Rule 1.4 of the Civil Procedure Rules 1998 provides that the court must further the overriding objective by actively managing cases. Rule 1.4(2) stresses that active case management includes 'encouraging the parties to use an alternative dispute resolution procedure if the court considers that appropriate and facilitating the use of such procedure'.

Similarly, in *Ghaith* v *Indesit*[7] the Court of Appeal was concerned that although the defendant was encouraged to seek mediation when permission to appeal was given, the company did not do so. Lord Justices Ward and Longmore both thought the fact that costs had already exceeded the amount claimed was an inadequate reason to refuse to use mediation since a full day in the Court of Appeal would have resulted in an even more substantial increase in costs. The company's reaction however was all too frequent and the courts were strove to change corporate culture when it came to litigation. Lord Justice Longmore reminded the parties that since April 2012,[8] it was decided by the Court of Appeal that any claim for less than £100,000 will be the subject of compulsory mediation. Lord Justice Ward went on to say that it was not enough merely for the lawyers to attempt to settle the case by correspondence. His Lordship said:

The opening bids in a mediation are likely to remain as belligerently far apart as they were in correspondence but no one should underestimate the new dynamic that an experienced mediator brings to the round table. He has a canny knack of transforming the intractable into the possible. That is the art of good mediation and that is why mediation should not be spurned when it is offered.

There are six factors which the court will usually take into account when deciding whether or not a party unreasonably spurned mediation or ADR as an option.[9]

1. **The nature of the dispute.** For example where the parties wish the court to determine issues of law or construction of contracts which may be essential to the future trading relations of the parties, as under an ongoing long-term contract or where the issues are generally important for those participating in a particular trade or market. Where allegations of fraud or other commercially disreputable conduct are made against an individual or group, such disputes are probably best taken to court rather than mediation. So too when a party needs injunctive relief which a mediator would not be able to give.

---

[6] At para. 15.
[7] [2012] EWCA Civ 642.
[8] The Court of Appeal has a mediation scheme for non-family disputes administered by the Centre for Effective Dispute Resolution (CEDR). In 2012, a new pilot was introduced. The pilot applies to all personal injury and contract claims up to the value of £100,000 for which permission to appeal is sought and obtained (or adjourned). Unless a judge, exceptionally, directs otherwise, the parties in such cases will be informed that case papers are automatically recommended for mediation to CEDR. If the parties agree to mediate, a panel of accredited CAMS mediators will be nominated by CEDR. The selected mediator will bring the parties together to try to reach a settlement. If there is a settlement, the case will not go back to the Court of Appeal. For more information, see www.justice.gov.uk/courts/rcj-rolls-building/court-of-appeal/civil-division/mediation
[9] See *Halsey* v *Milton Keynes General NHS Trust* [2004] EWCA Civ 576 and *PGF II SA* v *OMFS Co* [2012] EWHC 83 (TCC).

2. **The merits of the case.** Depending on the strength of one side's case, mediation may not be suitable. For example, the courts will try to prevent a manipulative claimant from using the threat of a cost sanction against, usually, a large organisation or public body, to extract a settlement even though they do not have a strong claim.

3. **The extent to which other settlement methods have been attempted.** The fact that a settlement offer has been rejected may be relevant to show how convinced a litigant is as to the merit of his case.

4. **If the costs of the ADR would be disproportionately high.**

5. **If any delay in setting up and attending the ADR would have been prejudicial.**

6. **If the ADR had a reasonable prospect of success.** This is not always easily as certained as, in some cases, the prospect of success depends on the willingness of the parties to come to a resolution. Where one party is intransigent, the prospect of success will diminish. Is his refusal to accept any reasonable resolution unreasonable or is it based on his genuine belief that the other side is acting in bad faith or that his case is meritorious? The court therefore has a difficult task if it relies on this factor. As such, this factor cannot be determinative of the cost issue.

Indeed, none of the factors above will be solely decisive and they should not be regarded as an exhaustive checklist.

Mediation is particularly useful where strong feelings have arisen. Skilled mediators can achieve results satisfactory to both parties in many cases which are quite beyond the power of lawyers and courts to achieve. Minor personal injury and property damage cases can often involve very passionate and angry accusations and counter-accusations. These are not always best resolved by the judicial system. A mediator can often provide solutions which the court is unable to offer. In some cases, an apology may be all that the claimant is really seeking and the money side simply falls away.

POINT OF INTEREST

The EU is keen to encourage mediation across the single market. Below is an excerpt from the Commission's press release of 23 April 2008 (IP/08/628), which heralded the publishing of Directive 2008/52/EC (21 May 2008) on certain aspects of mediation in civil and commercial matters:

"A Directive on certain aspects of mediation in civil and commercial matters was adopted today 23 April 2008. The purpose of the Directive is to facilitate access to cross-border dispute resolution and to promote the amicable settlement of disputes by encouraging the use of mediation and by ensuring a sound relationship between mediation and judicial proceedings. The Directive is one of the follow-up actions to the Green Paper on alternative dispute resolution presented by the Commission in 2002, the other being the European Code of Conduct for Mediators established by a group of stakeholders with the assistance of the Commission and launched in July 2004.

The key components of the Directive are as follows:

● The Directive obliges Member States to *encourage* the *training of mediators* and the development of, and adherence to, *voluntary codes of conduct* and other *effective quality control mechanisms* concerning the provision of mediation services.

- The Directive gives every Judge in the Community, at any stage of the proceedings, the right to suggest that the parties attend an information meeting on mediation and, if the Judge deems it appropriate, to *invite the parties to have recourse to mediation.*

- The Directive enables parties to give *an agreement concluded following mediation* a status similar to that of a Court judgment by rendering it *enforceable.* This can be achieved, for example, by way of judicial approval or notarial certification, thereby allowing such agreements to be enforceable in the Member States under existing Community rules.

- The Directive ensures that mediation takes place in an atmosphere of *confidentiality* and that information given or submissions made by any party during mediation cannot be used against that party in subsequent judicial proceedings if the mediation fails. This provision is essential to give parties confidence in, and to encourage them to make use of, mediation. To this end, the Directive provides that the mediator cannot be compelled to give evidence about what took place during mediation in subsequent judicial proceedings between the parties.

- The provision of the Directive on *periods* of *limitation and prescription* will ensure that parties that have recourse to mediation will not be prevented from going to court as a result of the time spent on mediation. The Directive thus preserves the parties' access to justice should mediation not succeed."

As far as England and Wales are concerned, the existing legal framework on mediation would, it seems, cover much of what the directive is aimed at achieving. On two aspects of the new directive, some legislative change is required. The Civil Procedure (Amendment) Rules 2011 have now been enacted and came into force on 6 April 2011. The Rules provide for the (i) judicial enforceability of agreements resulting from a mediation (see Art. 6 of the Directive) held in the UK or elsewhere in the EEA and (ii) confidentiality of mediation (Art. 7 of the Directive). There are also new rules governing disclosure and inspection of mediation evidence in a mediator's of mediation administrator's control (CPR 78.26).

9.2.2 Concept of conciliation

Conciliation requires the neutral third party to give a reasoned opinion on the dispute. That opinion will be used by the parties to achieve a settlement. Thus, unlike the mediation process, here the parties do not control the substance of the dispute. It might be interesting to note the definition of conciliation given by the Institute of International Law:

A method of settlement of international disputes of any nature according to which a Commission set up by the Parties, either on a permanent basis or an *ad hoc* basis, to deal with a dispute attempts to define the terms of a settlement susceptible of being accepted by them or affording the Parties, with a view to its settlement, such aid as they may have requested.[10]

The key feature of conciliation is the work or opinion of the expert third party.

---

[10] Art. I, Regulations on the Procedure of International Conciliation.

9.3 Arbitration

Arbitration is akin to judicial settlement. The parties appoint a third party who will hear arguments from both sides and make an award. That award will be binding on the parties and can be enforced by a court of law. There are however several important differences from judicial settlement:

(a) the arbitrator may take into account principles (whether legal or not) which the parties may have pre-agreed for their arbitration (*Channel Tunnel Group* v *Balfour Beatty*);[11]

(b) the legal basis of arbitration is the arbitration agreement;

(c) the arbitrator and the arbitration procedures are controlled by the parties;

(d) the arbitration process is more informal than court;

(e) it can be quicker than court proceedings;[12]

(f) proceedings are almost always in private.

Arbitration may be conducted on an *ad hoc* basis or an institutional basis. The former can be more cumbersome as the parties need to agree as to the entire arbitration process and set-up. Alternatively, some commercial parties may agree to be subject to a pre-established arbitration system, such as a national body with expertise in conducting arbitration (such as the London Court of International Arbitration) or a tribunal administered by a relevant trade body (such as the International Chamber of Commerce). The advantage of an institutional arbitration is that the process is more certain and the onus on the parties to set up the arbitration from scratch is relieved.

Arbitration may be wholly domestic in nature[13] or it may contain an international element. In the latter, issues relating to the recognition of international arbitral awards in England and enforcement of an English award abroad can arise.

9.3.1 The arbitration agreement

The arbitration agreement may be made in anticipation of disputes arising or after the dispute has arisen.[14] The arbitration agreement will bind the parties to refer their disputes falling

---

[11] [1993] AC 334. In that case, the contract stipulated: 'The construction, validity and performance of the contract shall in all respects be governed by and interpreted in accordance with the principles common to both English law and French law, and in the absence of such common principles by such general principles of international trade law as have been applied by national and international tribunals. Subject in all cases, with respect to the works to be respectively performed in the French and in the English part of the site, to the respective French or English public policy (*ordre public*) provisions.' See also s. 46(1)(b), Arbitration Act 1996.

[12] That said, in some areas such as construction arbitration, the judicial process can actually be just as swift. This is because the court's case management powers under the CPR and the factual circumstances lend themselves to speedy trials.

[13] Section 85(2) defines a domestic arbitration agreement as an arbitration agreement to which none of the parties is (a) an individual who is a national of, or habitually resident in, a state other than the UK, or (b) a body corporate which is incorporated in, or whose central control and management is exercised in, a state other than the UK, and under which the seat of the arbitration is in the UK.

[14] Section 6, Arbitration Act 1996. The arbitration agreement must naturally have been properly incorporated into the parties' contract. In *Midgulf International* v *Groupe Chimiche Tunisien* [2009] EWHC 1684 (Comm), for example, it was found that there was no agreement to refer disputes to London arbitration because the fax in which one party claimed to have accepted the offer (which referred to London arbitration) was not an acceptance but a counter-offer.

within the scope of the agreement to arbitration before taking the matter to court. Section 9 of the Arbitration Act 1996 lays down the fundamental principle that a court of law will prevent a party from commencing judicial proceedings in breach of the arbitration agreement. It will stay its own proceedings if those proceedings had been instituted in breach of the arbitration agreement. The main exception is where the arbitration clause is null and void, inoperative or incapable of being performed (s. 9(4)). It should however be noted that s. 9(4)'s reference to incapability does not extend to the incapability of the parties. In *Janos Paczy* v *Haendler Natermann GmbH*,[15] J argued that he had no money to go to arbitration, but if he was allowed to proceed in court, he could rely on legal aid. The court rejected his application to proceed in defiance of the arbitration agreement. The court held that practical difficulty on the part of one of the parties is irrelevant to the effect of the arbitration agreement. However, if there is clear evidence that the arbitration agreement had been forged or made without proper and ostensible authority, s. 9(4) will apply but the court will only act in clear and exceptional circumstances.[16]

It must also be noted that s. 9(4) does not apply to domestic arbitration agreements. Instead, s. 86(2) provides that a court shall grant a stay of proceedings unless satisfied:

(a) that the arbitration agreement is null and void, inoperative or incapable of being performed; or

(b) that there are other sufficient grounds for not requiring the parties to abide by the arbitration agreement.

It is immediately obvious that para. (b) is the main difference between s. 86(2) and s. 9(4). Section 86(2) allows the court to look to other circumstances for proceeding despite the presence of the arbitration agreement.

Prior to the Arbitration Act 1996, parties used what is called a '*Scott* v *Avery*'[17] clause to make arbitration a precondition to litigation. If a party were to breach the clause, the court could be asked to stay proceedings to allow the arbitration to take place first.

A court will also make interim orders for the protection of assets or evidence pending the constitution of the arbitration (*Belair* v *Basel LLC*)[18] (s. 44). Section 44(3) makes it possible for the court to act quickly and simply on the application of one party in urgent cases. As Morison J put it in *Econet Wireless Ltd* v *VEE Networks Ltd*:

> the powers of the court under s. 44 are plainly intended to cover over the crack between the moment of the application and the time when the arbitral tribunal can be formed and take its own decisions about preserving the status quo.[19]

The court is only concerned with whether or not there is an arguable case. It will not express any views as to the substance of the case. In non-urgent cases, the court will act only with the permission of the tribunal or the agreement of the other party (s. 44(4)). In both urgent and non-urgent cases, there is also an overriding duty on the court not to interfere if the tribunal is able to act effectively (s. 44(5)).[20]

---

[15] [1981] 1 Lloyd's Rep 30.
[16] *Albon* v *Naza Motor Trading Sdn Bhd (No 3)* [2007] 2 Lloyd's Rep 1 EWHC 327 (Ch).
[17] (1856) 10 ER 1121.
[18] [2009] EWHC 725 (Comm).
[19] [2006] EWHC 1568 (Comm) at para. 14; see also *Cetelem SA* v *Roust Holdings Ltd* [2005] 1 WLR 3555.
[20] Paragraph 215, Report of the Departmental Advisory Committee on Arbitration Law.

It is important to remember that the arbitration agreement is separate from the main agreement. Section 7 states that the arbitration agreement forming part of another agreement shall not be regarded as invalid, non-existent or ineffective simply because that other agreement is invalid or did not come into existence or has become ineffective.[21] That does not mean, however, that the arbitration agreement could never be tainted by the invalidity of the main contract. Section 7 simply states that any assessment of the arbitration agreement should be made on its own merits. In general, if a person signing the underlying contract does not have the authority to do so, the arbitration clause is likely also to be have been made without authority.[22] However, where the person signing the underlying agreement (such as an agent) had merely exceeded his authority, that is not necessarily an attack on the arbitration agreement. It would have to be shown that whatever the terms of the main agreement or the reasons for which the agent concluded it, he would have had no authority to enter into an arbitration agreement.[23]

CASE

Nurdin Jivraj v Sadruddin Hashwani[24]

The arbitration agreement contained in a joint venture investment contract required that the arbitrator should be appointed from the Ismaili community. The Ismaili community formed part of the Shia branch of Islam and was headed by the Aga Khan. H claimed that that requirement was unlawful because it constituted religious discrimination contrary to the Employment Equality (Religion or Belief) Regulations 2003 (now replaced by the Equality Act 2010), the Human Rights Act 1998 and public policy.

At the High Court, David Steel J held that the 2003 Regulations were not applicable to the selection, engagement or appointment of arbitrators.[25] Although the appointment of an arbitrator was contractual, the contract involved was not a contract of employment. Even if the role or status of an arbitrator could be classified as akin to that of an independent contractor, the employer could not give instructions as to how he was to work or what outcome he was to achieve. The arbitrator was entirely independent and had no client. In the alternative, the exception in reg. 7(3) would apply since the parties shared an ethos based on religion and belief and, having regard to that ethos and to the function of an arbitrator under the joint venture agreement, the appointment of an arbitrator being of the same religion and belief was a genuine occupational requirement which it was proportionate to apply.

The Court of Appeal, however, reversed that decision holding an arbitrator appointment was a contract for provision of services and 'a contract personally to do any work' which satisfied the definition of 'employment' in reg. 2(3), and that a party appointing an arbitrator was an 'employer' under reg. 6(1). Thus, it was contrary to reg. 6(1)(a)(c) to restrict the choice of arbitrator to the Ismaili community. The exception in reg. 7 could

[21] The common law equivalent is found in *Harbour Assurance v Kansa General International Insurance* [1993] QB 701.

[22] *Vee Networks v Econet Wireless* [2004] EWHC 2909.

[23] See Lord Hoffmann's speech in *Fiona Trust v Privalov* [2007] UKHL 40; [2008] 1 Lloyd's Rep 254.

[24] [2011] UKSC 40.

[25] [2009] EWHC 1364 (Comm).

not apply because being Ismaili was not a necessary quality of an arbitrator's role. The arbitrator's appointment clause could not be severed from the arbitration agreement; as such, the entire agreement was void and unenforceable.

At the Supreme Court, Lord Clarke held that an arbitrator's position could not fall under the 2003 Regulations (now the EA 2010, especially, s. 13). In the light of Directive 2000/78, and the jurisprudence of the Court of Justice of the EU, a distinction must be made between those who work for a wage in a subordinate position and those independent providers of services who are remunerated for their services. An arbitrator was not subordinate and was not even, under a contract personally to do work. The agreement was therefore enforceable. The court added that the religious qualification for the arbitrators could, if necessary, have been justified as falling within the exception for genuine occupational requirements.

9.3.2 Construing the arbitration agreement

Most arbitration agreements will usually say something like this:

Any dispute arising out of this contract will be referred to . . . arbitration.

The clause thus provides the scope the for arbitration. For some time there was some confusion[26] as to whether or not there are significant differences between the following:

- 'disputes arising out of . . .';
- 'disputes arising under . . .';
- 'disputes in connection with . . .';
- 'disputes arising from . . .'.

It has now been confirmed by the Supreme Court in *Fiona Trust* v *Privalov*[27] that fine distinctions should not be made between such phrases. Lord Hoffmann said:

In my opinion the construction of an arbitration clause should start from the assumption that the parties, as rational businessmen, are likely to have intended any dispute arising out of the relationship into which they have entered or purported to enter to be decided by the same tribunal. The clause should be construed in accordance with this presumption unless the language makes it clear that certain questions were intended to be excluded from the arbitrator's jurisdiction.

The arbitration clause would thus be construed in an inclusionary manner.

An arbitration agreement does not even need to use the word 'arbitration' as long as it is clear from the agreement that arbitration was intended. In *David Wilson Homes* v *Survey Services*,[28] the arbitration agreement read:

any dispute or difference arising . . . between the assured and the insurers shall be referred to a Queen's Counsel . . . to be mutually agreed . . . or in the event of disagreement, by the Chairman of the Bar Council.

---

[26] *Heyman v Darwins Ltd* [1942] AC 356; *Overseas Union Insurance Ltd* v *AA Mutual International Insurance Co Ltd* [1988] 2 Lloyd's Rep 63; *Fillite (Runcorn) Ltd* v *Aqua-Lift* (1989) 45 BLR 27; *Mackender, Hill and White* v *Feldia AG* [1966] 2 Lloyd's Rep 449.

[27] [2007] UKHL 40 (sub nom *Premium NAFTA* v *Fili Shipping*).

[28] [2001] EWCA Civ 34.

The defendants had argued that the clause did not refer to an arbitration, only a non-binding settlement of the dispute by a neutral third party (as in conciliation, for example). The Technology and Construction Court agreed with the defendants. However, the Court of Appeal disagreed and held that, although no reference was made to 'arbitration', an arbitration was intended. The test is that laid down by Lord Esher MR in *Re Carus-Wilson v Green*:

> The question here is whether the umpire was merely a valuer substituted for the valuers originally appointed by the parties in a certain event, or arbitrator. If it appears from the terms of the agreement by which a matter is submitted to a person's decision, that the intention of the parties was that he should hold an inquiry in the nature of a judicial inquiry, and hear the respective cases of the parties, and decide upon evidence laid before him, then the case is one of an arbitration. The intention in such cases is that there shall be a judicial inquiry worked out in a judicial manner. On the other hand, there are cases in which a person is appointed to ascertain some matter for the purpose of preventing differences from arising, not of settling them when they have arisen, and where the case is not one of arbitration but of a mere valuation. There may be cases of an intermediate kind, where, though a person is appointed to settle disputes that have arisen, still it is not intended that he shall be bound to hear evidence or arguments. In such cases it may be often difficult to say whether he is intended to be an arbitrator or to exercise some function other than that of an arbitrator. Such cases must be determined each according to its particular circumstances.[29]

It also follows that the arbitration agreement does not need to spell out that the arbitral award will be final and conclusive because the finality of the award is made quite explicit by s. 58(1), Arbitration Act 1996.

9.3.3 Binding on third parties?

The arbitration agreement is also binding on third parties who claim under or through the original contracting parties (*Astra SA Insurance and Reinsurance* v *Yasuda Fire and Marine Insurance*).[30] In *Sun Life Assurance* v *The Lincoln National Life Insurance Co*,[31] L underwrote certain reinsurance risks for S's benefit. C had also offered similar cover to S on related risks. Disputes had arisen between S and C and between S and L. An arbitral award was made in arbitration involving S and C. The arbitrator found that C was entitled to refuse payment because there had been misrepresentation and non-disclosure by S. As to if L could rely on these findings in their arbitration with S, the lower court held that it was possible because 'the modern tendency when tackling serial litigation involving a common issue [is] to move away from technical rules towards a broader consideration of what was fair'.[32] The Court of Appeal, however, disagreed and overturned the decision. It held that the principle of mutuality required that someone who was not a party, such as L, could not take advantage of a decision in proceedings made when he was not there. Although the Court of Appeal's decision is preferable to that of the lower court's, identifying the parties who were sufficiently close to the arbitration proceedings in question is not always straightforward in serial arbitration/litigation.

---

[29] (1887) 18 QBD 7 at 9.
[30] [1999] CLC 950. In *Footness valve Recovery Fund v Bike Sky Special Opportunities Fund* [2012] EWHC 1486 (Comm), it was held that if the third party had not avail themselves of a substance term in the main contract, they could not enforce the arbitsation clause in that contract. See also 5.8 contract (Rights of Third Parties) Act 1999.
[31] [2004] EWCA Civ 1660.
[32] Paragraph 9.

9.3.4 **The duty of the tribunal**

Section 33 requires the tribunal to:

(a) act fairly and impartially as between the parties, giving each party a reasonable opportunity to present his case and defend himself; and

(b) adopt procedures suitable to the circumstances of the case, avoiding unnecessary delay or expense, so as to provide a fair means for the resolution of the matters falling to be determined.

The arbitrator shall decide all procedural and evidential matters, subject to the parties' right to agree on these matters (s. 34(1)).

There is much discretion given to the arbitrator in the conduct of the arbitration. The London Court of International Arbitration Rules, for example, provides that:

the tribunal may:

● conduct such enquiries as are necessary and expedient to ascertain the relevant facts;

● order any party to make any property, site or thing under its control and relating to the subject matter of the arbitration available for inspection;

● order any party to produce any relevant document or classes of document for inspection; and

● decide whether or not to apply strict rules of evidence as to admissibility, relevance or weight of any factual or expert material.[33]

There is currently a debate as to how proactive arbitrators should be. An officious arbitrator who antagonises the parties does not help with the resolution of the dispute. On the other hand, a proactive arbitrator who prescribes to the parties as to how the arguments are to be presented could very well save time and expense. That is especially the case where the arbitrator is experienced and highly qualified.

If the arbitrator fails to comply with the duties in s. 33, s. 24 provides that he could be removed. The detailed grounds for removal in s. 24 are where:

● there are circumstances giving rise to justifiable doubt as to his impartiality;

● there is clear evidence that he does not possess the qualifications required by the arbitration agreement;

● he is physically or mentally incapable of conducting the arbitration;

● he has refused or failed properly to conduct the proceedings or to use all reasonable despatch to conduct the proceedings or make the award and that substantial injustice has been or will be caused.

Naturally, these provisions should not be abused by a disgruntled party. The Departmental Advisory Committee in its report on the Arbitration Act 1996 stated:

We trust that the Courts will not allow [this provision] to be abused by those intent on disrupting the arbitral process . . . We have every confidence that the Courts will carry through the intent of this Part of the [Act], which is that it should only be available where the conduct of

---

[33] Article 22.1.

the arbitrator is such as to go so beyond anything that could reasonably be defended that sub-stantial injustice has resulted or will result. The provision is not intended to allow the Court to substitute its own view as to how the arbitral proceedings should be conducted.

The approach should therefore be guided by the need to prevent *substantial* injustice. In cases where bias is claimed, this spirit should not be forgotten. In *Rustal Trading Ltd v Duffus*[34] it was argued that the arbitrator should be removed because he had expressed animosity towards the claimant and was in fact involved in a dispute with the claimant two years previously. Moore-Bick J held that as the parties had chosen to have their disputes resolved by people who are active traders and so have direct and relevant knowledge of the trade, they must be presumed to have had that fact in mind when the arbitration agreement was made. The court would therefore be slow to remove an expert trade arbitrator simply because he had been involved in a previous dispute with one of the parties.[35]

It should also be stressed that if one of the parties is concerned about the arbitrator's ability to conduct the proceedings, he should seek his removal as soon as practicable. Failure to do so may be deemed to be a waiver.[36]

9.3.5 Challenging an arbitral award

Where the arbitral proceedings are governed by English law, the award may be challenged on any of the following grounds:

(a) failure of substantive jurisdiction (s. 67);

(b) serious irregularity (s. 68);

(c) error of law (s. 69).

The court, in dealing with the challenge, may confirm the award, vary the award or set aside the award in part or in whole. However, consistent with the objective to encourage arbitration, the law stresses that the parties should always exhaust every remedy of appeal or review as provided for in the arbitration agreement before challenging the award in court (s. 70(2)). The application or appeal must be brought within 28 days of the date of the award (s. 70(3)).

9.3.5.1 Failure of substantive jurisdiction

The *failure of substantive jurisdiction* is described in s. 67 as the absence of a valid arbitration agreement or that the arbitration agreement does not cover the dispute in question or that the arbitrators have not been properly appointed. Where it is claimed that an underlying contract (containing the arbitration clause) has not come into existence because certain conditions have not been met, a distinction should be made between cases of a contingent condition precedent and cases of a promissory condition precedent. In the former, a contract is not binding until the specified event occurs. In the latter, the contract is binding, albeit that the performance of the condition by one party will be a condition precedent to the *liability* of

---

[34] [2000] 1 Lloyd's Rep 14.
[35] See also *ASM Shipping Ltd* v *Harris* [2007] EWHC 1513.
[36] Section 73(1), Arbitration Act 1996.

the other.[37] In *UR Power GmbH v Kuok Oils and Grains PTE Ltd*[38] one party had failed to open a letter of credit under the contract. That failure meant the other party was freed from the liability to deliver the goods. It does not however mean that his failure to open the letter of credit prevented the contract (and the arbitration clause contained in it) from coming into existence.

Under s. 30, the arbitrator himself will decide on these issues of competency (s. 30). This is called the *kompetenz-kompetenz* doctrine. That, however, does not mean that his decision on his own competency is not open to review by the courts. If he makes a decision about his competency which is not objected to by the parties, s. 73 will deem the parties as having waived their right to object and, hence, may not be able to rely on s. 67 to challenge the award.

9.3.5.2 Serious irregularity

As far as a claim of *serious irregularity* is concerned, s. 68(2) refers to instances where the arbitrator had acted unfairly but always subject to the test of substantial injustice (that is to say, mere unfairness which does not lead to substantial injustice would not be relevant). Those instances are:

(a) failure by the tribunal to comply with s. 33 (general duty of tribunal);

(b) the tribunal exceeding its powers (otherwise than by exceeding its substantive jurisdiction: see s. 67);

(c) failure by the tribunal to conduct the proceedings in accordance with the procedure agreed by the parties;

(d) failure by the tribunal to deal with all the issues that were put to it;

(e) any arbitral or other institution or person vested by the parties with powers in relation to the proceedings or the award exceeding its powers;

(f) uncertainty or ambiguity as to the effect of the award;

(g) the award being obtained by fraud[39] or the award or the way in which it was procured being contrary to public policy;

(h) failure to comply with the requirements as to the form of the award; or

(i) any irregularity in the conduct of the proceedings or in the award which is admitted by the tribunal or by any arbitral or other institution or person vested by the parties with powers in relation to the proceedings or the award.[40]

In addressing a challenge based on s. 68, the court will not try the material issue to ascertain if substantial injustice has been caused. In *Vee Networks Ltd v Econet Wireless*

---

[37] *UR Power GmbH v Kuok Oils and Grains PTE Ltd* [2009] EWHC 1940 (Comm).

[38] *Ibid.*

[39] The fraud must have been perpetrated by the party to the arbitration, not a mere third party (*Elektrim SA v Vivendi Universal SA* [2007] EWHC 11 (Comm), [2007] 2 All ER (Comm) 365). See also *Nestor Maritime v Sea Anchor Shipping Co Ltd* [2012] EWHC 996 (Comm). In *Chantiers de l'Atlantique SA v Gaztransport & Technigaz Sas* [2011] EWHC 3383 (Comm) it should also be shown that the fraud did lead to substantial injustice. That is to say, if, despite the fraud, the arbitrators would have decided in exactly the same way on the other evidence, the award would not be set aside.

[40] Section 68(2).

International Ltd,[41] V submitted that the arbitral award should be set aside because the tribunal had relied on an argument, demonstrably wrong, that was not advanced by either party, giving no warning or opportunity to make further submissions. The other side argued that the fact that the tribunal had considered irrelevant materials would not have led to a different result. The court was effectively invited to consider the merits of the arguments. The court declined and held that the tribunal had acted unfairly because it had not given the parties a reasonable opportunity to deal with those additional materials. Colman J said:

> The element of serious injustice in the context of s. 68 does not in such a case depend on the arbitrator having come to the wrong conclusion as a matter of law or fact but whether he was caused by adopting inappropriate means to reach one conclusion whereas had he adopted appropriate means he might well have reached another conclusion favourable to the applicant. Thus, where there has been an irregularity of procedure, it is enough if it is shown that it caused the arbitrator to reach a conclusion unfavourable to the applicant which, but for the irregularity, he might well never have reached, provided always that the opposite conclusion is at least reasonably arguable. Above all it is not normally appropriate for the court to try the material issue in order to ascertain whether substantial injustice has been caused. To do so would be an entirely inappropriate inroad into the autonomy of the arbitral process.[42]

In determining if there had been substantial injustice the court was not required to decide for itself what would have happened in the arbitration had there been no irregularity.[43] In *Van der Giessen de-noord Shipbuilding Division BV v Imtech Marine and Offshore BV*[44] it was asserted by the party that the tribunal had not addressed itself to each and every one of the points submitted in the arbitration. The court held that whilst a failure to deal with the essential issues may constitute serious irregularity, the arbitrator is entitled to deal with those issues collectively and concisely provided it afforded the parties the opportunity to respond and address those issues. A failure to deal with an issue was not the same as a failure to set out the reasoning for rejecting a particular argument.[45] The latter can be cured by s. 70(4). Moreover, the arbitral decision and reasons should not be subject to minute textual analysis; a fair and reasonable reading is called for (*Pace Shipping* v *Churchgate Nigeria*).[46]

The court will be slow to intervene in the arbitrator's discretion to conduct the proceedings as he sees fit. Serious irregularity would only be found where there is actual misconduct. In *Fletamentos Maritimos SA v Effjohn International BV*,[47] for example, an umpire sitting with the arbitrators had intervened far more frequently than is usual but the Court of Appeal held that he had not overstepped the mark. His frequent interruptions did not, as far as the evidence disclosed, lead to the usurpation of the arbitrator's role. There is also no serious irregularity for an arbitrator to omit to consider the views of his fellow dissenting arbitrators.[48] However,

---

[41] [2004] EWHC 2909 (Comm).

[42] At para. 90.

[43] *London Underground Ltd* v *Citylink Telecommunications Ltd* [2007] BLR 391.

[44] [2009] 1 Lloyd's Rep 273.

[45] In *Buyuk Camlica Shipping* v *Progress Bulk Carriers Ltd* [2010] EWHC (Comm) 442, for instance, there had been a failure by the arbitral tribunal to deal with an issue put to it within the Arbitration Act 1996 s. 68(2)(b), but that irregularity had not caused substantial injustice because the point was not arguable on the merits. It was necessary to establish that the arbitrator had failed to deal at all with a fundamental issue which was essential to the decision (*Fidelity Management SA* v *Myriad International Holdings BV* [2005] EWHC 1193 (Comm); [2005] 2 All ER (Comm) 312).

[46] [2009] EWHC 1975 (Comm).

[47] [1997] 2 Lloyd's Rep 302.

[48] *Ispat Industries* v *Western Bulk* [2011] EWHC 93 (Comm).

where the arbitrator acts contrary to the powers conferred on him by the arbitration agreement, the court will find serious irregularity. In *Omnibridge Consulting Ltd* v *Clear Springs (Management) Ltd*[49] the arbitrator, by refusing to accept the common position agreed to between the parties and proceeding on his own opinion, was held to be guilty of serious irregularity.

POINT OF INTEREST

Serious irregularity is likely to pose problems for online and paper only arbitration, a phenomenon which is on the rise and is, indeed, often promoted and encouraged by the EU. In such an arbitration where the parties are not physically present, the arbitrator must make sure that he does not introduce into the arbitration matters not specifically referred to in the documentation. As Colman J said in *Pacol Ltd* v *Joint Stock Co Rossakhar*:

> In a paper arbitration the temptation to arrive at a conclusion which might not have been envisaged by either party by reference to matters upon which the parties have not had the opportunity of adducing further evidence, may be a particular temptation which arbitrators should be careful to avoid. It is important for the continuation of the standing and quality of international commercial arbitrations in London, particularly in the commodity fields, that arbitrators should have the problem very clearly in mind . . .[50]

The duty to allow both sides the opportunity to present their case and defence is central to the conduct of arbitration. In *ED & F Man Sugar Ltd* v *Belmont Shipping Ltd*[51] it was clear that the arbitrators appreciated from the papers that one of the parties was not aware of a particular legal argument. The question arose as to whether or not, under s. 33, the arbitrators are required to alert that party to the legal point. Had there been an oral hearing, the matter would obviously have been raised and no serious irregularity would have arisen.

It might be useful to look at s. 33:

(1) The tribunal shall:

(a)   act fairly and impartially as between the parties, giving each party a reasonable opportunity of putting his case and dealing with that of his opponent.

The court held that the tribunal's failure to alert that party of the legal point which might have afforded them an opportunity to put their case in a different way was not covered by the duty to give the party a reasonable opportunity to put its case. There was no case of serious irregularity. However, that case does demonstrate the risks with paper arbitrations.

9.3.5.3   Error of law

Section 69 provides for the right of a party to appeal to the court on a *point of law*. Permission must, however, first be granted before the substantive matter will be heard by the court. Section 69(3) states that leave to appeal shall be given only if the court is satisfied:

---

[49] [2004] EWHC 2276 (Comm).
[50] [2000] 1 Lloyd's Rep 109 at 115.
[51] [2011] EWHC 2992 (Comm).

(a) that the determination of the question will substantially affect the rights of one or more of the parties;

(b) that the question is one which the tribunal was asked to determine;

(c) that, on the basis of the findings of fact in the award;

    (i) the decision of the tribunal on the question is obviously wrong; or

    (ii) the question is one of general public importance and the decision of the tribunal is at least open to serious doubt; and

(d) that, despite the agreement of the parties to resolve the matter by arbitration, it is just and proper in all the circumstances for the court to determine the question.

It does not need restating that the court will be very slow to interfere. Indeed, at common law, the House of Lords made clear in *The Nema*[52] that in so-called 'one-off' cases (meaning cases which are not of public significance), leave to appeal should not be granted. In other cases, leave to appeal should be subject to the court's satisfaction that a strong *prima facie* case has been made out that the arbitrator was wrong and the appeal should provide clarity and certainty in the law.

Section 69(3)(c)(ii), whilst following the principle of finality of awards in *The Nema*, is expressed slightly differently in substance. The main criteria are that the question should be one of general importance and that the arbitrator's decision should at least be open to serious doubt. The threshold is still therefore very high; the intention behind s 69 was to curtail factual challenges being disguised as legal submissions.[53]

What is a question of law for the purposes of s. 69? Section 82(1) states: '(a) for a court in England and Wales, a question of the law of England and Wales; and (b) for a court in Northern Ireland, a question of the law of Northern Ireland'.[54] This is deliberately narrow and excludes questions of foreign law even though the seat of the arbitration is in England. In *Sanghi Polyesters Ltd v The International Investors (KCFC) (Kuwait)*[55] the arbitration agreement referred to the applicable law as 'the laws of England except to the extent it may conflict with Islamic Shari'a which shall prevail'. The point of law her was if there was a conflict with Shari'a. The court rightly refused to give leave to appeal under s. 69 because there was no question of [English] law in dispute.

ISSUE BOX

What are the commercial and legal implications the narrow approach espoused in *Sanghi Polyester*?

Consider for example an arbitration which involves international law or the *lex mercatoria*.

When dealing with a challenge, the court may require the arbitrator to give reasons for his award or clarify the reasons for his award (s. 70(4)). These may be given to the court in confidence so that the privacy the parties had sought in the arbitration would be preserved.[56]

---

[52] [1982] AC 724.

[53] *House of Fraser Ltd v Scottish Widows PLC* [2011] EWHC 2800 (Comm).

[54] The Arbitration Act 1996 does not apply to Scotland. Scotland however has adopted the UNCITRAL Convention on International Arbitration and is in the process of considering the introduction of a Scottish Arbitration Act.

[55] [2000] 1 Lloyd's Rep 480.

[56] *President of India v Jadranska Slobodna Plovidba* [1992] 2 Lloyd's Rep 274.

DEBATE BOX

There was some belief that allowing English awards to be reviewed on the basis of an error of law might inhibit the use of English law clauses in international commercial contracts. The guidelines in *The Nema* and s. 69, Arbitration Act 1996 go some way to preventing this. It might be said that the approach in s. 69(3) therefore represents a careful balance – reflecting the significance of England as an arbitral forum and the importance of English law as the applicable law of international commercial contracts. The following point is made by a commentator about the then draft Scottish Arbitration Bill 2009 (now Arbitration (Scotland) Act 2010):

> It is suggested that Scotland has no need to seek to strike that balance. Scotland is not a favoured forum for international arbitration. Nor is Scots law likely to be chosen to govern international commercial contracts, while no key decision in Scots commercial law has ever come from an appeal against an arbitral award. In short, none of the conditions which underpin the particular form to s. 69(3) apply in Scotland.
>
> Accordingly, Scotland can start by asking the simple question: should parties have the right to challenge an award on the basis of an error of law? If the answer is yes, a general right of appeal might be created. While under English common law an award could be challenged on the basis that it contained an error of law, the position under Scots common law is summed up by Lord Jeffrey in *Mitchell* v *Cable* ((1848) 10 D. 1297 at 1309):
>
>> On every matter touching the merits of the case, the judgment of the arbiter is beyond question . . . He may overlook and flagrantly misapply the most ordinary principles of law, and there is no appeal for those who have chosen to subject themselves to his despotic power.
>
> Davidson, 'Some Thoughts on the Draft Arbitration (Scotland) Bill' (2009) *JBL* 44.

Do you agree? Are there any other considerations behind s. 69(3)?

Can the right to appeal be contracted out of? In s. 69(1) the words 'unless otherwise agreed by the parties' are used. Hence, the answer is yes. In *Shell Egypt West Manzala GmbH v Dana Gas Egypt Ltd (formerly Centurion Petroleum Corporation)*,[57] however, Gloster J stressed that the arbitration clause which read 'the decision of the majority of the arbitrators . . . shall be final, conclusive and binding on the parties' could not be construed as such an agreement.

By the same token, s. 69(1) suggests that the parties can, by contract, improve or modify their statutory right to appeal. For example, the parties may provide that an appeal based on something less than an error of law (such as an error of foreign law) might be appealable.

9.3.6 Recognition and enforcement of arbitral awards

An award made in England and Wales may be enforced by leave of court in the same manner as a court judgment (s. 66(1)). Leave to enforce will not be given where it is shown that the tribunal lacked the substantive jurisdiction to make an award. This right may be lost at a late

---

[57] [2009] EWHC 2097 (Comm); see also *Essex County Council v Premier Recycling Ltd* [2006] EWHC 3594.

stage because the disgruntled party who did not challenge the award promptly would be deemed to have waived his right of objection (s. 73).

As far as foreign awards are concerned, ss. 100–104 of the Arbitration Act 1996 will apply. Those provisions enact into English law the New York Convention on the Recognition and Enforcement of Foreign Arbitral Awards 1958, to which the UK is a signatory. The Convention has been ratified by over 130 countries. This means the UK is required by the principle of reciprocity to recognise and enforce arbitral awards made in any of these contracting states. Section 101(2) states that a New York Convention award may, by leave of the court, be enforced in the same manner as a judgment of the court to the same effect. Section 103(2) provides that:

> recognition or enforcement of the award *may* be refused if the person against whom it is invoked proves:
>
> (a) that a party to the arbitration agreement was (under the law applicable to him) under some incapacity;[58]
>
> (b) that the arbitration agreement was not valid under the law to which the parties subjected it or, failing any indication thereon, under the law of the country where the award was made;
>
> (c) that he was not given proper notice of the appointment of the arbitrator or of the arbitration proceedings or was otherwise unable to present his case;
>
> (d) that the award deals with a difference not contemplated by or not falling within the terms of the submission to arbitration or contains decisions on matters beyond the scope of the submission to arbitration;
>
> (e) that the composition of the arbitral tribunal or the arbitral procedure was not in accordance with the agreement of the parties or, failing such agreement, with the law of the country in which the arbitration took place;
>
> (f) that the award has not yet become binding on the parties, or has been set aside or suspended by a competent authority of the country in which, or under the law of which, it was made. [Emphasis added.]

The word 'may' means that the court has discretion;[59] it does not have to withhold recognition and enforcement simply because one of the above grounds is proved.

A contracting state also retains a residual jurisdiction not to recognise or enforce arbitral awards which are contrary to its public policy. It may also decline to recognise and enforce an award which it finds to be incapable of being settled by arbitration. These residual provisions in s. 103(3) may appear quite capacious but the English courts have always attempted to apply them very narrowly.[60] Examples where an award was refused recognition on s. 103(3) may be where recognition would result in a breach of the UK's EU obligations[61] or facilitating illegality or fraud in the underlying transaction.[62]

---

[58] The party's illness during arbitration, for example, was considered to fall within the provision in *Kanoria v Guinness* [2006] EWCA Civ 222.

[59] *Dardana Ltd v Yukos Oil* [2002] EWCA Civ 543; also *Dallah Real Estate and Tourism Holding Co v Pakistan* [2009] EWCA Civ 755.

[60] *Westacre Investments Inc v Jugoimport SDPR Holding Co* [1998] 2 Lloyd's Rep 111.

[61] Case C-126/97 *Eco Swiss China Time Ltd v Benetton International NV* [1999] CLR 183.

[62] *Soleimany v Soleimany* [1998] 3 WLR 811.

Further reading

Blackaby, N. and Partasides, C., Redfern, A. and Hunter, M., *Law and Practice of International Commercial Arbitration* (5th edn, Sweet and Maxwell, London, 2004).

Bühring-Uhle, C., Kirchhoff, L. and Scherer, G., *Arbitration and Mediation in International Business* (2nd edn, Kluwer Law International, The Netherlands, 2006).

Merkin, R. M. and Flannery, L., *Arbitration Act 1996* (4th edn, Informa Law, London, 2008).

Moses, M. L., *The Principles and Practice of International Commercial Arbitration* (Cambridge University Press, Cambridge, 2008).

St John Sutton, D., Gill, J. and Gearing, M., *Russell on Arbitration* (23rd edn, Sweet and Maxwell, London, 2007).

Tweeddale, A. and Tweeddale, K., *Arbitration of Commercial Disputes: International and English Law and Practice* (Oxford University Press, Oxford, 2007).

Companion Website

ON THE WEBSITE

For open-access **student resources** specifically written to complement this textbook and support your learning, please visit **www.pearsoned.co.uk/legalupdates**

Commercial conflict of laws

By Louise Merrett

Chapter outline

➤ 10.1   Introduction

➤ 10.2   Jurisdiction

➤ 10.3   Choice of law

➤ 10.4   Enforcement of foreign judgments

➤ Further reading

10.1 Introduction

POINT OF INTEREST

- In 2004–2005, the number of claims in the English Commercial Court where at least one claimant *and* one defendant originated from outside the UK constituted about 50 per cent of all claims issued.[1]

- Over the same period, the number of claims where at least one claimant *or* one defendant emanated from outside the jurisdiction constituted 80 per cent of all claims.

- In 2005–2006 the number of claims where at least one claimant *or* one defendant emanated from outside the jurisdiction continued to constitute about 80 per cent of all claims.[2]

A typical commercial contract will very often have international elements: the parties may come from different countries; goods might be shipped from one country to another; an insurer, guarantor or bank involved in the transaction might be situated in a different country.

---

[1] Report of the Commercial Court 2004–2005.

[2] Report of the Commercial Court 2005–2006. Of the 1,259 actions issued in 2009, 951 or 75.5 per cent involved a foreign party (*The Times*, 2 September 2011).

The transnational nature of commercial transactions is reflected in the international nature of litigation in the English Commercial Court. If a dispute arises in relation to such a contract, the court will need to apply conflict of law rules (also referred to as rules of private international law) to deal with the international aspects of the transaction. Conflict of laws rules apply to determine three separate issues: jurisdiction, choice of law and enforcement.

For example, A Ltd, an English company, agrees to sell B Ltd, a French company, with a branch in London, a printing press. When the press is delivered, B Ltd says that it does not print to the quality or at the speed agreed in the contract and refuses to pay. A Ltd is considering commencing proceedings for payment of the price: it says that the press is perfectly suitable for the purposes B Ltd said it was needed for.

If A Ltd decides that legal proceedings are its only option, it will first need to decide where to commence proceedings. Commercial considerations, such as, how much proceedings will cost and where A Ltd's assets are situated, will clearly be important. The legal question of which court or courts will be entitled to hear the case is answered by the conflict of laws rules on *jurisdiction*. Very commonly, in commercial transactions, the parties might have agreed in advance that all claims relating to the contract must be brought before a certain court. The effect of such an agreement will also be determined by the rules relating to jurisdiction.

The merits of the dispute itself may well depend on what law is applied to the contract. For example, under English sale of goods law, the contract might include an implied term as to fitness for particular purposes. Under French sale of goods law there might be no such term. The question of which law the court hearing the dispute should apply is determined by the conflict of laws rules on *choice of law*.

Before A Ltd starts expensive legal proceedings it will also want to be sure that it can enforce any judgment it obtains against B Ltd's assets. This question will be determined by the conflict of law rules relating to *enforcement*.

In this chapter, the rules currently applied by English courts in typical commercial disputes in relation to jurisdiction, choice of law and enforcement will be outlined.

10.2 Jurisdiction

10.2.1 Introduction to the jurisdiction regimes

In order to decide whether or not it has jurisdiction, the English court must decide which rules to apply. Essentially, jurisdiction is governed by two, mutually exclusive, regimes: the Brussels I Regulation[3] and, residually, by the common law or traditional rules.[4]

---

[3] Council Regulation (EC) No 44/2001 of 22 December 2000, on jurisdiction and the recognition and enforcement of judgments in civil and commercial cases. The Brussels I Regulation, which came into force on 1 March 2002, replaced the Brussels Convention, which was first negotiated between the original six Member States and to which new Member States acceded on entry into the Community. As a directly effective piece of Community legislation, the Brussels I Regulation applies automatically to all Member States (except Denmark) as and when they join the Community. Under the EC/Denmark agreement (OJ 2005 L 299/61) the provisions of the Regulation, with minor modifications, apply between the Community and Denmark.

[4] A modified version of the Brussels regime applies to allocate jurisdiction within the UK and also between European States and the EFTA states – Iceland, Norway and Switzerland (the Lugano Convention).

The court must first decide if the European rules apply. The crucial provisions are Arts 1 and 4 of the Brussels I Regulation.

LEGISLATIVE PROVISION

Article 1

(1) This Regulation shall apply in civil and commercial matters whatever the nature of the court or tribunal. It shall not extend, in particular, to revenue, customs or administrative matters.

(2) The Regulation shall not apply to:

(a) the status or legal capacity of natural persons, rights in property arising out of a matrimonial relationship, wills and succession;

(b) bankruptcy, proceedings relating to the winding-up of insolvent companies or other legal persons, judicial arrangements, compositions and analogous proceedings;

(c) social security;

(d) arbitration.

Article 4

(1) If the defendant is not domiciled in a Member State, the jurisdiction of the courts of each Member State shall, subject to Articles 22 and 23, be determined by the law of that Member State.[5]

Article 1 sets out the *material scope* of the Regulation: most commercial cases will be 'civil and commercial matters'. Even cases involving public authorities may be included unless the authority was acting in the exercise of its public authority powers,[6] that is, powers going beyond those existing under the rules applicable to the relationships between private individuals.[7] Furthermore, the exclusions set out in Art. 1(2) do not normally apply in commercial cases. The important exception to this is Art. 1(2)(d). Where the main purpose of the proceedings is arbitration, the Regulation will not apply, but the scope of this exception is controversial (see below).

In cases falling within the material scope of the Regulation, the Regulation rules on jurisdiction will engage, according to Art. 4, when:

1. the defendant is domiciled in a Member State; or

2. a Member State has exclusive jurisdiction by virtue of Art. 22 (most relevant in general commercial cases is the provision that, in 'proceedings which have as their object rights *in rem* in immovable property or tenancies of immovable property, the courts of the

---

[5] Brussels I Regulation, Arts 1 and 4.
[6] *Sonntag* v *Waidmann* Case C-172/91 [1993] ECR I-1963 [20].
[7] Case C-266/01 *Préservatrice Foncière TIARD SA* v *Netherlands State* [2003] ECR I-4867 and Case C-265/02 *Frahuil SA* v *Assitalia SpA* [2004] ECR I-1543.

Member State in which the property is situated shall have exclusive jurisdiction, regardless of domicile') (Art. 22(1));[8] or

3. there is a jurisdiction agreement in favour of a Member State which satisfies the requirements of Art. 23.

As will be described in section 10.2.3 below, the Regulation also sets out rules governing parallel proceedings (Arts 27 and 28) which engage whenever there are competing claims in Member States, regardless of the basis on which jurisdiction was taken in each of those states.

The crucial touchstone for the application of the Brussels I Regulation rules on jurisdiction is, accordingly, whether or not the defendant is domiciled in a Member State.[9] The way in which domicile is determined for these purposes depends on whether the defendant is an individual or a company.

LEGISLATIVE PROVISION

Article 59

(1) In order to determine whether a party is domiciled in the Member State whose courts are seised of a matter, the court shall apply its internal law.

(2) If a party is not domiciled in the Member State whose courts are seised of the matter, then, in order to determine whether the party is domiciled in another Member State, the courts shall apply the law of that Member State.

Article 60

(1) For the purposes of this Regulation, a company or other legal person or association of natural or legal persons is domiciled at the place where it has its:

(a) statutory seat; or

(b) central administration; or

(c) principal place of business.

(2) For the purposes of the United Kingdom and Ireland 'statutory seat' means the registered office or, where there is no such office anywhere, the place of incorporation, or, where there is no such place anywhere, the place under the law of which the formation took place.[10]

In the case of individuals, the court will apply the national law of the alleged domicile. Thus, the court will first determine whether or not the defendant is domiciled in England by applying

---

[8] Exclusive jurisdiction also exists in relation to company proceedings (Art. 22(2)) and proceedings concerned with patents and trademarks (Art. 22(4)).

[9] In the original proposal for a recast BIR published on 14.12.10 (COM 2010 748 final), Art. 4 of BIR would have been removed and a modified version of the Regulations rules would have applied to all defendants whether from a Member State or not. However, in the new Regulation itself (No 1215/2012) published on 12 December 2012 the rules of jurisdiction generally do not apply. The BIR recast will apply from 10 January 2015 (Art. 81).

[10] Brussels I Regulation, Arts 59 and 60.

English law.[11] If the defendant is not domiciled in England, the court will determine if he is domiciled in another Member State by applying the law of that Member State.

The position in relation to companies is more straightforward because Art. 60 of the Regulation sets out a Community-wide definition for determining the domicile of a company. The following points should be noted about this definition.

1. A company may be domiciled in more than one Member State, pursuant to Art. 60(1)(a), (b) and (c).

2. The statutory seat of a company is easily ascertained, but Art. 60 extends the domicile of a company beyond the country where it is incorporated. A company is also domiciled under Arts 60(1)(b) and (c) – where it is managed or run.

3. It has been suggested[12] that 'principal' place of business does not mean 'main' but 'most important'; in other words, it refers not simply to the volume of business at that office but also to the importance of that office to the conduct of the business. The 'principal place of business' is the centre from which instructions are given when necessary and ultimate control exercised.[13]

4. Whilst 'principal place of business' suggests the executive control of the business, 'central administration' has something of 'the back office' about it and is likely to be where the operational rather than executive functions are concentrated.[14]

5. The location of important personnel in the company is also important.[15]

According to Art. 60, a company will therefore be domiciled in a Member State – and, thus, the Regulation rules on jurisdiction will engage – where either it is incorporated *or* has its statutory seat in a Member State *or* its executive centre is in a Member State *or* its operational functions are concentrated in a Member State.

If the Brussels I Regulation rules are *not* engaged, Art. 4 allows the court to apply its traditional rules on jurisdiction (which will be outlined in section 10.2.4 below).

10.2.2 The Brussels I Regulation rules on jurisdiction

10.2.2.1 Article 2: the defendant's domicile

Once the English court has established that the Brussels I Regulation rules on jurisdiction are engaged, the starting point and primary rule under the Regulation is that 'persons domiciled

---

[11] To do so, it will apply the Civil Jurisdiction and Judgments Order 2001, SI 2001/3929, Sch. 1, para. 9, which provides that, for the purposes of the Regulation, a person is domiciled in the UK or in a particular part thereof if and only if (a) he is resident in the UK and (b) the nature and circumstances of his residence indicate that he has a substantial connection with the UK. It is further provided that, in the case of an individual who is resident in the UK and has been so resident for the last three months or more, the requirements of sub-para. (b) shall be presumed to be fulfilled unless the contrary in proved (sub-para. 9(6)). For a recent example, see *Yugraneft* v *Abramovich* [2008] EWHC 2613.

[12] *The Rewia* [1991] 2 Lloyd's Rep 325.

[13] *Ministry of Defence and Support of the Armed Forces for the Islamic Republic of Iran* v *FAZ Aviation Ltd* [2007] EWHC 1042 (Comm); [2007] ILPr 42.

[14] *King* v *Crown Energy Trading AG* [2003] EWHC 163 (Comm), at [12], and [2003] ILPr 28.

[15] *Alberta Inc* v *Katanga Mining Ltd* [2009] 1 BCLC 189.

in a Member State shall, whatever their nationality, be sued in the courts of that Member State' (Art. 2). This rule applies regardless of the nature of the claim and where the cause of action arose.

The primary rule in Art. 2 is subject to two overriding rules. First, that the court will not have jurisdiction if the parties have entered into a jurisdiction agreement, which complies with Art. 23 of the Brussels I Regulation, in favour of a different Member State. Secondly, if another court has exclusive jurisdiction by virtue of Art. 22, that court and no other will have jurisdiction. Articles 22 and 23, if they apply, oust the jurisdiction of the court of the defendant's domicile.

The effect of the rules considered so far on the example set out at the beginning of this chapter is that, because B Ltd is a French company (and domiciled in France under Art. 60) and the matter is a civil and commercial matter, the Brussels I Regulation rules engage (Arts 1 and 4). Furthermore, B Ltd must be sued in France under Art. 2, unless it can also be said to be domiciled in England because its executive centre is in England *or* its operational functions are centred in England (Art. 60 and Art. 2).

That is not the end of the matter, as the Regulation also contains a series of provisions for additional or special heads of jurisdiction, which may, in limited circumstances, give another Member State's courts' jurisdiction in addition to that provided for in Art. 2. In commercial cases, two of these special heads are of particular importance: jurisdiction in matters relating to contract (Art. 5(1)); jurisdiction in relation to the operations of a branch in another Member State (Art. 5(5)).[16] Unlike the provisions which give exclusive jurisdiction, these provisions add further grounds of jurisdiction and do not oust the court of the defendant's domicile. Where the claimant can satisfy the requirements for one of these special heads of jurisdiction, *he may choose* whether to bring the claim in that court *or* the court of the defendant's domicile. The special heads are themselves also subject to Art. 23 and Art. 22, however. Thus, the hierarchy between the various rules of jurisdiction in the Brussels I Regulation can be illustrated as follows:

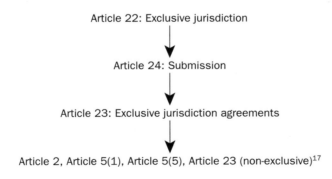

Article 22: Exclusive jurisdiction

Article 24: Submission

Article 23: Exclusive jurisdiction agreements

Article 2, Article 5(1), Article 5(5), Article 23 (non-exclusive)[17]

---

[16] Special jurisdiction is also provided for in matters relating to tort (Art. 5(3)) and for claims against co-defendants (Art. 6(1)), third parties (Art. 6(2)) and in relation to counterclaims (Art. 6(3)). Special rules apply to matters relating to insurance (s. 3), to consumer contracts (s. 4) and in relation to jurisdiction over individual contracts of employment (s. 5).

[17] A non-exclusive jurisdiction agreement under Art. 23 will give the chosen court jurisdiction *in addition to* any other court which may have jurisdiction under another rule (not instead of).

10.2.2.2 Article 5(1): jurisdiction in matters relating to contract

---

LEGISLATIVE PROVISION

A person domiciled in a Member State may, in another Member State, be sued:

1. (a) in matters relating to a contract, in the courts for the place of performance of the obligation in question;

   (b) for the purpose of this provision and unless otherwise agreed, the place of performance of the obligation in question shall be:

   – in the case of the sale of goods, the place in a Member State where, under the contract, the goods were delivered or should have been delivered;

   – in the case of the provision of services, the place in a Member State where, under the contract, the services were provided or should have been provided.

   (c) if sub-paragraph (b) does not apply then sub-paragraph (a) applies.[18]

Article 5(1) applies 'in matters relating to contract'. This is an autonomous Community concept, not dependent on the law of the forum or the law applicable to the contract.[19] This Community notion of a contract assumes 'an undertaking freely assumed by one party towards another'.[20]

If it is a matter relating to contract, the court must then determine:

1. what is the obligation in question; and

2. what is the place of performance of that obligation?

The special rules in Art. 5(1)(b) applicable to contracts for the sale of goods or the provision of services were added by the Brussels I Regulation when it came into force in 2002. In cases not covered by these special provisions[21] the approach is that established under the Brussels Convention. In such cases, the obligation in question 'refers to the contractual obligation forming the basis of the legal proceedings . . . The obligation to be taken into account is that which corresponds to the contractual right on which the plaintiff's action is based'.[22] Thus, in the case of a contract for the sale of shares, if the seller is suing the buyer for payment of the price, the obligation to pay is the obligation in question, whereas if the buyer is suing the seller for damages for failing to deliver, the obligation to deliver the shares is the obligation in question.

The basic approach is clear, but difficult questions can arise when more than one obligation is sued on. In such cases, the first question is if it is possible to identify a *principal*

---

[18] Brussels I Regulation, Art. 5(1).

[19] Confirmed, in the context of Art. 5(1), in *Martin Peters* v *Zuid* Case C-34/82 [1983] ECR I-987.

[20] *Handte* v *TMCS* Case C-26/91 [1992] ECR I-3967. In *Martin Peters* v *Zuid* Case C-34/82 [1983] ECR I-987, obligations owed by an association to a member were contractual for Art. 5(1) purposes, even though not under the applicable law.

[21] Possible examples include reinsurance contracts; a joint venture agreement; an undertaking not to do something in a certain country; sales of land or intangibles and licensing agreements. In *Falco Privatstiftung* v *Weller-Lindhorst* (C-533/07) [2010] Bus LR 210; [2009] ECR 3327, it was held that a contract to license intellectual property rights was not a contract for services within Art. 5(1)(b). Contracts of individual employment are dealt with separately in section 5 of the Regulation.

[22] *De Bloos* v *Bouyer* Case C-14/76 [1976] ECR I-1479 at [10], [13].

obligation. If so, the principal and any accessory obligations can all be sued for in place of performance of the principal obligation.[23]

However, if it is not possible to identify a principal obligation, each of the obligations in question can only be sued for in the place of performance of that specific obligation.[24] The result will be that the Art. 5(1) may allocate jurisdiction to different Member States (a result sometimes referred to as fragmentation).[25]

Once the obligation in question has been identified, the court must then determine the place for performance of that obligation. The ECJ in *Tessili v Dunlop*[26] held that the applicable law under the conflicts rules of the forum will determine where that obligation is to be performed.[27] For example, if the seller is suing for payment of the price, it is necessary to determine where the price was to be paid. In the absence of an express agreement as to place of payment, different legal systems have different rules as to where the consideration for a contract is to be paid. According to English contract law, the promisor must seek out the promisee and perform the contract there. To put it another way, the debtor must seek out the creditor. Under other legal systems the opposite is the case. According to the *Tessili* doctrine, the court must first apply its choice of law rules in order to determine what law governs the contract. It will then apply the rule which is relevant according to that governing law. If the contract is governed by English law, the place of performance will be the habitual residence of the creditor or seller. If the contract was governed by a different law, the opposite might be the case. This process is complex and creates uncertainty and a new rule was therefore introduced by the Brussels I Regulation for contracts for the sale of goods and the provision of services.

Under Art. 5(1)(b) of the Brussels I Regulation, it is now provided that, in the case of the sale of goods and provision of services, the place of performance of the obligation in question is where the goods were to be delivered or the services to be provided (subject to a different agreement by the parties). Rather than having to apply the proper law of the contract, Art. 5(1)(b):

> now gives an autonomous definition of the place for performance of 'the obligation in question' in two specific situations . . . This pragmatic determination of the place of performance applies regardless of the obligation in question, even where this obligation is the payment of the financial consideration for the contract. It also applies where the claim relates to several obligations. The rule may, however, be 'displaced' by an explicit agreement on the place of performance.[28]

Returning once more to the example set out at the beginning of the chapter, because this is a contract for the sale of goods, Art. 5(1)(b) would apply. Because A Ltd is suing for the

---

[23] *Shenevai v Kreischer* Case C-266/85 [1987] ECR I-239 at [19].
[24] *Leathertex v Bodetex* Case C-420/97 [1999] ECR I-6747. Furthermore, Art. 5(1) requires that the obligation in question must have only one place for performance. If there can be no one place for performance (for example, an obligation not to compete with or supply anyone else anywhere in the world) the consequence is that Art. 5(1) does not apply (*Besix v WABAG* Case C-256/00 [2002] ECR I-1699).
[25] Although the claimant will, of course, be able to sue for all the claims in the court of the defendant's domicile under Art. 2 if he wishes to avoid that result.
[26] Case C-12/76 [1976] ECR 1473.
[27] *Tessili v Dunlop AG* Case C-12/76 [1976] ECR 1473.
[28] Proposal for a council regulation on jurisdiction and the recognition and enforcement of judgments in civil and commercial matters, 99/0154 (CNS), p. 14.

price, the obligation in question is the obligation to pay. If the parties have agreed where payment is to be made, that court will have jurisdiction. If not, the courts of the place where the press should have been delivered will be the courts identified by Art. 5(1).

In *Car Trim GmBH v KeySafety Systems Srl*[29] the CJEU held that a contract for the manufacture of goods to the buyer's specification was a contract for the sale of goods not services. Where the sale involves the carriage of goods, the place where the goods were to be delivered was to be determined on the basis of the provisions of the contract, failing which, that place was likely to be the place of physical transfer of the goods to the buyer at the final destination.[30]

Difficulties can arise when an obligation or obligations are to be performed in different places or jurisdictions. In *Color Drack GmBH v Lexx International Vertriebs GmBH*,[31] the CJEU held that where goods were to be delivered to different places within a single Member State, the court must identify the principal place of delivery based on economic criteria. If none could be identified, the claimant must choose one place and bring the whole of the claim in that place. In *Rehder v Air Baltic*,[32] the CJEU applied an analogous approach to a contract for the provision of services (in other words, an indivisible obligation) in different Member States. The court held that it was impossible to distinguish between the obligations relating to take-off and landing and the claimant could therefore chose to bring the claim in either jurisdiction. In *Wood Floor Solutions v Silva Trade SA*,[33] which concerned a contract for services to be performed under an agency agreement in more than one Member State, the court again said that the first stage was to identify the main provision of services. If that was not possible on the basis of economic criteria, that place would be presumed to be the domicile of the characteristic performer (here the agent).

All of these provisions only apply unless otherwise agreed. It seems, therefore that if the parties have expressly provided for the place of performances and the obligation in question is the obligation to pay, that obligation is to be performed where agreed.[34]

A final point to note is that any 'agreement otherwise' under Art. 5(1) must be a genuine agreement. In *MSG v Les Gravieres*,[35] the parties agreed that the place for performance was Germany, although, in fact, performance (chartering a barge for service in French waterways) had little or nothing to do with Germany. The ECJ held that:

> to specify a place of performance which has no actual connection with the real subject-matter of the real contract becomes fictitious and has as its sole purpose the determination of the place of the courts having jurisdiction. Such agreements conferring jurisdiction are governed by Art. 17 of the Convention [now Art. 23 of the Brussels I Regulation] and are therefore subject to specific requirements as to form.[36]

It is clear that a defendant cannot defeat Art. 5(1) jurisdiction simply by denying that a contract was entered into.[37] Similarly, where a claimant alleges that he is entitled to set aside a contract because of breach of contract by the defendant, that is also a matter relating to

---

[29] Case C-381/08.
[30] Cf *Scottish & Newcastle International v Othon Ghalanos Ltd* [2008] UKHL 11.
[31] Case C-386/05.
[32] Case C-204/08.
[33] Case C-19/09.
[34] Although it is unclear if the parties also have to say that this is the place of performance for jurisdictional purposes. See *Continuity Promotions Ltd v O'Connor's Nenagh Shopping Centre* [2005] EWHC 3462.
[35] Case C-106/95 [1997] ECR I-911.
[36] At para. [33].
[37] *Effer v Kantner* Case C-38/81 [1982] ECR I-825.

contract under Art. 5(1),[38] as is a case where the defendant seeks to avoid a claim or contract for non-disclosure or misrepresentation.[39]

Whether or not all claims which might be brought arising from a contractual relationship fall within the scope of Art. 5(1) is a more difficult question. If both parties accept that the alleged 'contract' was void, it seems that the Article cannot apply. In *Kleinwort Benson* v *Glasgow*[40] the claimant sought to recover sums paid to the defendant under swap transactions later held *ultra vires* and void. A majority of the House of Lords held that, where there was no issue that the contract was void, the dispute could not be a matter relating to a contract within Art. 5(1).[41]

Another problem is, what if it is *the claimant* who alleges that no contract was made? In *Boss Group* v *Boss France*,[42] the claimant sought a declaration that it had not made a distributorship contract. The Court of Appeal held that Art. 5(1) applied. The court looked at the claim by the *defendant* that there was a contract and concluded that the defendant could not at the same time maintain there was a contract and that the matter did not relate to a contract. However, this seems inconsistent with the approach of the ECJ that the obligation in question must be the obligation in the contract on which the claimant bases his claim.[43]

10.2.2.3 Article 5(5): jurisdiction by virtue of a branch or agency

LEGISLATIVE PROVISION

A person domiciled in a Member State may, in another Member State, be sued:

as regards a dispute arising out of the operations of a branch, agency or other establishment, in the courts for the place in which the branch, agency or other establishment is situated.[44]

Article 5(5) sets out two criteria which must be satisfied:[45]

1. the defendant must have a 'branch, agency or other establishment' in that Member State; and

2. the dispute must have arisen 'out of the operations' of that branch.

In relation to the first requirement, a company can operate in another Member State directly by opening an office there (a 'branch'). This must be a place of business with an appearance of permanence with a local management which is materially equipped to negotiate business

---

[38] *De Bloos* v *Bouyer* Case C-14/76 [1976] ECR I-1479.

[39] *Agnew* v *Länsförsäkringsbolagens* A13 [2001] 1 AC 223.

[40] [1999] 1 AC 153.

[41] It is not clear that the same arguments would apply in other restitution cases, such as a claim for return of sums paid for a total failure of consideration.

[42] [1997] 1 WLR 351.

[43] In *Agnew* v *Länsförsäkringsbolagens* [2001] 1 AC 223, Lord Millett described the approach in *Boss Group* as 'doubtful' (at p. 246).

[44] Brussels I Regulation, Art. 5(5).

[45] As with almost all questions of construction under the Regulation, the need for legal certainty and uniformity means that the provisions must be given an independent interpretation common to all the Member States. This was confirmed in the context of Art. 5(5) in *Somafer* v *Saar-Ferngas* Case C-33/78 [1978] ECR I-2182 at [8].

with third parties.[46] Alternatively, it may operate indirectly through an agent in that Member State (an 'agency'), but one of the essential characteristics of the concepts of branch, agency or other establishment is that the entity must be subject to the 'direction and control of the parent body'.[47] A company can have an 'establishment' in another Member State if the entity in question, even if not formally a branch or agency, acts as such in its dealings with third parties.[48]

Secondly, the dispute must also have arisen out of the operations of that branch, agency or other establishment. Where the claim relates to a contract, the connection can be derived *either* from the fact that the operations themselves took place in that country (that is, the contract was performed at or by the establishment) *or* from the negotiations between the claimant and the branch.[49]

Going back again to the example considered above, the English court will thus have jurisdiction under Art. 5(5) of the Brussels I Regulation by virtue of B Ltd's branch in London if either the contract was entered into through B Ltd's London branch or if the London branch was responsible for the performance of the contract.

10.2.2.4 Article 22: exclusive jurisdiction

Article 22 of the Brussels I Regulation does not apply very often in general commercial cases, but when it does it is of crucial importance. Under Art. 22, certain courts are given exclusive jurisdiction to hear certain disputes. The jurisdiction given is exclusive in that it overrides any other provisions of the Regulation, including Arts 23 and 24. Exclusive jurisdiction applies in proceedings concerning the constitution of companies (Art. 22(2));[50] proceedings which have as their object the validity of entries in public registers (Art. 22(3)); proceedings concerned with registration or validity of patents (Art. 22(4)); and proceedings concerned with the enforcement of judgments (Art. 22(5)). The provision most likely to be relevant in general commercial cases is Art. 22(1) which provides that: 'in proceedings which have as their object rights *in rem* in immoveable property or tenancies of immovable property, the courts of the Member State in which the property is situated' shall have exclusive jurisdiction regardless of domicile.

Article 22(1) encompasses claims directly concerning rights or ownership in land. It does not cover *in personam* claims, for example, claims brought on a contract dealing with land or a claim for a declaration that land is held on trust.[51]

---

[46] *Somafer* v *Saar-Ferngas* Case C-33/78 [1978] ECR I-2182 at [12].

[47] *De Bloos* v *Bouyer* Case C-14/76 [1976] ECR I-1479 at [21].

[48] *Schotte* v *Parfums Rothschild* Case C-218/86 [1987] ECR I-4905.

[49] *Anton Durbeck GmbH* v *Den Norske Bank ASA* [2003] 2 WLR 1296. In *Somafer* v *Saar-Ferngas* Case C-33/78 [1978] ECR I-2182, the ECJ had indicated *obiter* that the concept of operations comprised only undertakings which were entered into at the place of business *and* which were to be performed in the Member State where the place of business was established. However, this very narrow reading of Art. 5(5) was rejected by the ECJ in *Lloyd's Register* v *Campenon Bernard* Case C-439/93 [1995] ECR I-961.

[50] In *Berliner Verkehrsbetriebe (BVG)* v *JP Morgan* Chase Bank NA, Frankfurt Branch (C-144/10) [2011] All ER (D) 192, the CJEU held that Art. 22(2) only engages if the principal object of the proceedings is the validity of a corporation's decisions. In the case of a contractual dispute (here a claim under a loan agreement) where the principal object was the intrinsic validity, interpretation and enforceability of the contract, the legitimacy of the decision to contract which was alleged to be *ultra vires* the corporation, was merely ancillary and Art. 22 did not engage.

[51] *Webb* v *Webb* Case C-294/92 [1994] ECR I-1717.

10.2.3 Declining jurisdiction under the Brussels I Regulation: *lis alibi pendens*

In many cases, various courts could potentially have jurisdiction under the Brussels I Regulation. Different states may have jurisdiction under Art. 2, Art. 5(1) or Art. 5(5) for example. In such cases, there is the possibility that proceedings dealing with the same or similar issues could take place in more than one Member State. This possibility brings with it the risk of irreconcilable or at least inconsistent decisions on those issues.

Articles 27 and 28 of the Brussels I Regulation (which deal with parallel proceedings in different Member States) are:

> designed to preclude, in so far as possible *and from the outset*, the possibility of a situation arising such as that referred to in Art. [34],[52] that is to say the non-recognition on account of its irreconcilability with a judgment given in proceedings between the same parties in the State in which recognition is sought.[53] [Emphasis added.]

LEGISLATIVE PROVISION

Article 27

(1) Where proceedings involving the same cause of action and between the same parties are brought in the courts of different Member States, any court other than the court first seised shall of its own motion stay its proceedings until such time as the jurisdiction of the court first seised is established.

(2) Where the jurisdiction of the court first seised is established, any court other than the court first seised shall decline jurisdiction in favour of that court.

Article 28

(1) Where related actions are pending in the courts of different Member States, any court other than the court first seised may stay its proceedings.

(2) Where these actions are pending at first instance, any court other than the court first seised may also, on the application of one of the parties, decline jurisdiction if the court first seised has jurisdiction over the actions in question and its law permits the consolidation thereof.

(3) For the purposes of this Article, actions are deemed to be related where they are so closely connected that it is expedient to hear and determine them together to avoid the risk of irreconcilable judgments resulting from separate proceedings.

Article 30

For the purposes of this Section, a court shall be deemed to be seised:

➡

---

[52] Article 34 provides that a judgment shall not be recognised if it is irreconcilable with a judgment given in a dispute between the same parties in that Member State (Art. 34(3)) or with an earlier judgment given in another Member State (Art. 34(4)).

[53] *Overseas Union Insurance Ltd v New Hampshire Insurance Co* Case C-351/89 [1991] ECR I-3317 [16].

(1) at the time when the document instituting the proceedings or an equivalent document is lodged with the court, provided that the plaintiff has not subsequently failed to take the steps he was required to take to have service effected on the defendant; or

(2) if the document has to be served before being lodged with the court, at the time when it is received by the authority responsible for service, provided that the plaintiff has not subsequently failed to take the steps he was required to take to have the document lodged with the court.[54]

Article 27 attempts to deal with the specific problem of irreconcilable judgments. It applies when proceedings are commenced in different Member States which deal with the same cause of action and between the same parties. Where Art. 27 engages, all proceedings *must* be stayed in favour of the court first seised. Article 28 is a more wide-ranging provision which enables courts to deal with the problem of related actions. When it engages, all other courts have *a discretion* to stay in favour of the court first seised.

The application of both Arts 27 and 28 depend on determining which court is first seised. Article 30 of the Brussels I Regulation sets out a new Community-wide definition of when a court is seised. Whether para. 1 or 2 applies depends on the national procedural rules of the state concerned. In England, para. 1 will apply. Thus, an English court is seised for these purposes when the claim form is lodged with the court.

10.2.3.1 Article 27: proceedings between the same parties involving the same cause of action

The requirement that the proceedings involve the same cause of action encompasses two related requirements: the two sets of proceedings must have the same 'object' and the same 'cause'.[55]

The 'object' of an action is its legal purpose or 'the end the action has in view'.[56]

The 'cause' of the action means the juridical basis of the claim and 'comprises the facts and the rules of law relied on as the basis of the action'.[57]

For example, proceedings in one Member State for damages and proceedings in another for a declaration that the defendant in the other legal proceedings was not liable in damages have the same subject matter. The legal objective in both actions is to establish the defendant's liability in damages.

Similarly, proceedings to enforce a contract in one Member State and proceedings to annul it in another have a common object. The legal objective of both is to establish the enforceability of the contract.[58]

---

[54] Brussels I Regulation, Arts 27, 28 and 30.
[55] In the French version of the text, the same *'objet and cause'*.
[56] *The owners of the cargo lately laden on board the ship Tatry* v *The owners of the ship Maciej Rataj (The Tatry)* Case C-406/92 [1992] ECR I-5474 [41].
[57] *The Tatry* Case C-406/92 [1992] ECR I-5474 [39].
[58] *Gubisch Maschinefabrik KG* v *Giulio Palumbo* Case C-144/86 [1987] ECR 4861.

10.2.3.2 Article 28: related proceedings

Article 28 is intended to apply more widely than Art. 27. Proceedings will be 'related' when the same legal issue arises in two actions involving different parties. For example, in *The Tatry*,[59] proceedings brought by two different groups of cargo owners against a shipowner under different but identical contracts for the carriage of goods which formed part of the same cargo were related proceedings. Proceedings are also 'related' when connected but not identical issues arise between the same parties, for example, an action for damages in one court and proceedings to limit any liability that might arise in another.[60]

Clearly, Art. 28, unlike Art. 27, envisages that if the court has a discretion, it may choose to stay related proceedings in favour of the court first seised but is not bound to do so. It remains unclear, however, how that discretion should be exercised and on what basis. It seems that there may well be a presumption in favour of a stay.[61] It has been suggested that a stay should be refused if the basis of the second court's jurisdiction is Art. 23.[62]

10.2.4 Traditional or common law rules on jurisdiction

If the Brussels I Regulation rules on jurisdiction are not engaged, the court can apply its common law or traditional rules on jurisdiction. There are two key features to the common law rules on jurisdiction. First, jurisdiction depends on *service* of the claim form. Thus 'whoever is served with the King's writ, and can be compelled consequently to submit to the decree made, is a person over whom the Court has jurisdiction.'[63] Secondly, whilst the ground of jurisdiction is service, the *exercise* of the court's jurisdiction is always discretionary. Even if the claim *prima facie* falls within the jurisdiction of the English court, the defendant can apply for a stay of the proceedings and the jurisdiction will not be exercised if England is not the appropriate forum, or, '*forum conveniens*'.[64] In both respects, the traditional rules are very different from those in the Brussels I Regulation outlined above. As has been described, the jurisdictional rules set out in the Brussels I Regulation are rigid and certain – either the provisions of Art. 2, Art. 5(1) or 5(5) are satisfied or they are not and, if they are, the court can and will hear the case, if not, it cannot. Furthermore, the court will first consider whether or not there is a good ground of jurisdiction and, if there is, proceedings can be served, if not, they cannot.

---

[59] *The Tatry* Case C-406/92 [1992] ECR I-5474.

[60] *Mærsk Olie & Gas A/S v Firma M. de Haan en W Boer* Case C-39/02 [2004] ECR I 9657.

[61] Jenard Report on the Brussels Convention, p. 41, Advocate General Lenz in *Owens Bank Ltd v Fulvio Bracco Industria Chemica SPA* Case C-129/92 [1994] ECR I-117. Cf *FKI Engineering Ltd v Stribog Ltd* [2011] EWCA Civ 622 per Rix LJ at [131].

[62] *JP Morgan Ltd v Primacom AG* [2005] EWHC 508 (Comm); *Nordea Bank Norge ASA v Unicredit Corporate Banking SPA* [2011] EWHC 30 (Comm).

[63] *Russell & Co v Cayzer, Irvine Ltd* [1916] 2 AC 298, 302 (Lord Haldane).

[64] This approach has been subject to criticism. First, the defendant who is *prima facie* subject to the jurisdiction of the court is forced to come to England to argue that the court should not exercise its discretion. Secondly, because the exercise of jurisdiction is discretionary, it could be said to be uncertain and, indeed, it has been argued that the approach might be incompatible with access to justice guaranteed in Art. 6 ECHR (see AG Leger in *Owusu v Jackson* Case C-281 [2005] ECR I-1383 para. [270].).

10.2.4.1 Common law rules on service of proceedings: service as of right

At common law, proceedings can be served in two ways: first, service as of right on a defendant *within* the jurisdiction; and, secondly, service can also be made, with the permission of the court, on a defendant *outside* the jurisdiction.

(a) Service as of right: individuals

Proceedings can be served on a defendant who is present in the jurisdiction. For an individual, temporary presence is enough and there is no requirement that the claim itself has to have anything to do with this jurisdiction. The breadth of this rule is illustrated by the well-known case of *Maharanee of Baroda* v *Wildenstein*.[65] The claimant, an Indian princess resident in France, bought a painting in France from the defendant, a French citizen and world famous art expert. It was subsequently discovered that the painting was not by the famous artist it was claimed to be and the claimant issued proceedings in England. The proceedings were eventually served on the defendant at Ascot racecourse when he was in England for a couple of days to watch the races. The Court of Appeal confirmed that he had been properly served, albeit he was in England on a short visit which had nothing to do with the claim. In that case, the proceedings were served personally on the defendant. The methods of service are now set out in the Civil Procedure Rules, r. 6.3 which provides that a document may also be served by first-class post, by leaving it at a specified place or, in certain circumstances, by fax or other means of electronic communication.[66]

(b) Service on a company within the jurisdiction

Service on companies is subject to the same principles as service on an individual. Again the main question is whether or not the company is present in England.

If the company is incorporated in England, there is no problem, proceedings can be served at its registered office in England. Foreign companies can also be served in England under CPR 6.9(7) by service at:

1. any place within the jurisdiction where the corporation carries on its activities; or

2. any place of business of the company within the jurisdiction.

The width of this rule can be seen from the case of *Dunlop Pneumatic Tyre Co* v *Cudell & Co*.[67] The defendant was a foreign corporation which manufactured motor cars. It had hired a stand at a nine-day exhibition at Crystal Palace. It was held that, during the continuance of the show, the defendant was carrying on business so as to be resident at a place within the jurisdiction and therefore could be served with proceedings. Thus, even temporary business activities are sufficient. Furthermore, there is no requirement that the claim itself resulted from those activities within the jurisdiction. In both respects, the rule is more wide-ranging than that in

---

[65] [1972] 2 QB 283.

[66] Generally speaking, if the defendant is not present, he cannot be served without the permission of the court, but there are three other ways in which proceedings can be served as of right: first, where a contract is made in England, through an agent of the defendant in England, a claim relating to that contract may be served on the defendant's agent (CPR 6.12); secondly, a claim form will also be deemed to be served on a defendant if it is served by a method specified in a contract (CPR 6.11); and, thirdly, a solicitor might be authorised to accept service in particular proceedings (CPR 6.7).

[67] [1902] 1 KB 342.

Art. 5(5) of the Brussels Regulation and the other statutory methods of service on companies which have now been largely superseded by the Civil Procedure Rules.[68]

Service with permission outside the jurisdiction

If the defendant is not present in England, the claimant will have to apply for permission to serve the proceedings outside the jurisdiction. An application must be made in accordance with CPR 6.37, which sets out three requirements the claimant must satisfy:

1. the grounds on which the application is made;

2. that he believes that his claim has a reasonable prospect of success; and

3. that England and Wales is the proper place to bring the claim.

The standard of proof in relation to each of these requirements was considered in *Seaconsar Far East Ltd v Bank Markazi Iran*.[69] In relation, first, to the ground relied on, the claimant must satisfy the court that there is a *good arguable case*. This standard falls short of the usual civil standard of proof on the balance of probabilities. That is because of the limitations inherent in interlocutory proceedings: the hearing will be short, there will be little opportunity to test the evidence and in particular, there will be no cross-examination of witnesses. Furthermore, the court does not wish to prejudge issues which are for the eventual substantive trial of the action, but the claimant must show a better argument on the material than the defendant and the court must be satisfied, given the limitations inherent in the nature of the proceedings, that jurisdiction is established.[70]

On the second requirement, the merits of the case, the claimant has a lesser standard to meet.[71] He need only show that there is *reasonable prospect of success* on the merits (CPR 6.37).[72] This means that 'on the written evidence there was a serious issue to be tried i.e. a substantial question of fact or law, or both, which the claimant bona fide desires to have tried.'[73]

The third, and often most important, requirement – that England is the appropriate forum for the action – will be considered in detail below.

Grounds for service out of jurisdiction

The grounds on which an application for service out of the jurisdiction can be based are set out in a Practice Direction accompanying CPR 6.36. The most relevant in commercial cases are likely to be those relating to claims in contract (PD 6B 3.1(6)–(8)) and property (PD 6B 3.1(11)).[74]

---

[68] The alternative jurisdiction taken over foreign companies under the Companies Act 2006 is now less important because these rules, which in some respects are stricter than those under the Civil Procedure Rules, need not be complied with if service is permissible under CPR 6.9 (*Saab v Saudi American Bank* [1999] 1 WLR 1861 and *Sea Assets Ltd v Garuda* [2000] 4 All ER 371).

[69] [1994] 1 AC 438.

[70] *Canada Trust Co v Stolzenberg* (No 2) [1998] 1 WLR 547 approved [2002] 1 AC 1.

[71] The threshold is the same as if the claimant was resisting an application for summary judgment on the grounds that he has no real prospect of succeeding on the claim (*Carvill America Inc v Camperdown UK Ltd* [2005] EWCA 645).

[72] This is likely to be equivalent to the test set out in *Seaconsar Far East Ltd v Bank Markazi Iran* [1994] 1 AC 438, namely, that there was a serious issue to be tried.

[73] *Ophthalmic Innovations International (UK) Ltd v Ophthalmic Innovations International Incorporated* [2004] EWHC 2984.

[74] Additional grounds include those which relate to necessary and proper parties (PD 6B 3.1(3)), claims in tort (PD 6B 3.1(9)), claims about trusts (PD 6B 3.1(12)–(16)) and admiralty claims (PD 6B 3.1(19)).

LEGISLATIVE PROVISION

The claimant may serve a claim form out of the jurisdiction with the permission of the court under rule 6.36 where:

(6) A claim is made in respect of a contract where the contract:

(a) was made within the jurisdiction;

(b) was made by or through an agent trading or residing within the jurisdiction;

(c) is governed by English law; or

(d) contains a term to the effect that the court shall have jurisdiction to determine any claim in respect of the contract.

(7) A claim is made in respect of a breach of contract committed within the jurisdiction.

(8) a claim is made for a declaration that no contract exists where, if the contract was found to exist, it would comply with the conditions set out in para. (6).

. . .

(11) the whole subject matter of a claim relates to property located within the jurisdiction.[75]

To some extent, these grounds mirror the special heads of jurisdiction under the Brussels I Regulation.[76] For example, the rule in sub-para. (7), breach of contract within the jurisdiction, is similar to Art. 5(1), and that in sub-para. (11), claims relating to property, mirrors Art. 22, but in some significant respects the grounds are more wide-ranging, in particular, the fact that the contract is governed by English law or was made in England (rules (6)(a) and (c)). In such cases, which might be said to provide exorbitant jurisdiction due to their apparent breadth, the fact that the claimant must also show that England is the appropriate forum becomes crucial. The discretion of the court to decide if England is the appropriate forum to hear the case forms part of the doctrine of *forum conveniens*.

10.2.4.3 The court's adjudicatory discretion: *forum conveniens*

The court's adjudicatory discretion arises in two distinct situations:

1. where proceedings have been served on a defendant in the jurisdiction, as of right he can still apply for a *stay* of proceedings validly commenced in England;

2. if the defendant cannot be served in the jurisdiction, the claimant may apply for permission to serve out of the jurisdiction under CPR 6.36, but even if the claimant shows a good ground for service out, and satisfies the test on the merits, he will not get permission unless he can also show that England and Wales is the *proper place in which to bring the claim* (CPR 6.37(3)).

---

[75] CPR PD 6B 3.1.

[76] Note that if there is an agreement as to service within the jurisdiction, as is often the case in commercial contracts, then proceedings can be served as of right (CPR 6.11). Otherwise, unless the defendant is present in the jurisdiction and can be served as of right, the fact that there is a jurisdiction agreement in favour of the English courts does not, without more, give the English courts jurisdiction. Under CPR PD 6B 3.1(6)(d) the 'problem' is solved by allowing the fact that there is a jurisdiction agreement to provide a ground for service on the defendant outside the jurisdiction.

Together, these cases are known as the doctrine of *forum conveniens*. The considerations on an application to serve out are essentially the obverse of those on a submission of *forum non conveniens* for the purposes of a stay. In both cases, the court must identify the court where the case may be tried most suitably for the interests of both parties and the interests of justice.

The test to be applied in both situations was considered by the House of Lords in the very important case of *The Spiliada*.

CASE

Spiliada v *Cansulex*[77]

A Liberian-owned vessel was chartered to carry a cargo of sulphur from Vancouver to India. The shipowners alleged that the cargo was wet when loaded and, as a result, caused severe corrosion to the vessel. They obtained permission to serve proceedings on the basis that the contract was governed by English law, but also had to show that England was the appropriate forum. Lord Goff set out the proper approach to be taken to that question, both in the case of service out and also in cases where the applicant sought a stay of proceedings validly commenced in England. In both cases, he said, the question at bottom, is to identify the forum in which the case can be suitably tried for the interests of all the parties and for the ends of justice.

In summary, in the case of a *stay*, the following apply.

1. 'The basic principle is that a stay will only be granted on the ground of *forum non conveniens* where the court is satisfied that there is some other available forum, having competent jurisdiction, which is the appropriate forum for the trial of the action, i.e. in which the case may be tried more suitably for the interests of all the parties and the ends of justice.'[78]

2. The burden on the defendant is to show that there is 'another available forum which is clearly or distinctly more appropriate than the English forum'[79] (*stage 1*). At stage 1, the court is essentially weighing *convenience factors* in assessing which is the most appropriate forum.

3. If the court is not satisfied that there is another available forum which is more appropriate that is usually the end of the matter; the stay will be refused.

4. Once the court is satisfied that there is another available forum which is *prima facie* the appropriate forum for trial the burden shifts to *the claimant* to show that there are special circumstances by reason of which justice requires that the trial should take place in England[80] (*stage 2*). At stage 2, the court can consider wider *justice* and *legitimate juridical advantages* to the parties.

---

[77] [1987] 1 AC 460.
[78] [1987] 1 AC 460 at 476.
[79] *Ibid.*, at 477.
[80] *Ibid.*, at 478.

In summary, in the case of *permission to serve out* of the jurisdiction, the following apply.

1. The basic principle is that permission will only be granted if *the claimant* establishes that England is the most appropriate forum, that is, in which the claimant's claim may be tried suitably in the interests of the parties and the ends of justice. The *convenience factors* which will be relevant at this stage will be the same as those which are assessed at *stage 1* of a stay application.

2. If the court concludes that England is clearly the appropriate forum it will ordinarily give permission to serve out. However, there may be circumstances by reason of which justice requires that permission should nevertheless be granted even if England is not on the face of it the most convenient forum (*stage 2*). The court will consider all the circumstances going beyond the connecting factors between the dispute and the rival forums (that is, *justice and juridical advantages*).

Thus, in the case of permission to serve out, the claimant effectively gets another bite at the cherry. Permission will be granted if England is the most appropriate forum for the claim *or* there are reasons of justice why the claim should be heard in England.

The overriding aim at the first stage is to identify the forum with which the action has its most real and substantial connection. The connecting factors identified by Lord Goff included factors affecting convenience and expense (particularly, the location of witnesses, factual and legal), but also other factors such as the law governing the relevant transaction and the places where the parties respectively reside or carry on business.

As to stage 2, Lord Goff recognised that it would not normally be enough for the claimant to show that there was some advantage to him in proceeding in England – what was an advantage to one party was likely to be a disadvantage to the other. The key was to have in mind the underlying fundamental principle, that is, where the case may be tried 'suitably for the interests of all the parties and the ends of justice'.[81]

The factor which was crucial on the facts of the *Spiliada* case itself has since come to be referred to as the 'Cambridgeshire factor'. At the same time as the original proceedings in the *Spiliada*, a very similar action was proceeding against the same defendants before the English courts. The action concerned a different ship, the *Cambridgeshire*, owned by an English company, which was also claiming damages allegedly caused by a cargo of sulphur shipped by the same defendant. The trial had commenced and had been due to last for six months. The claimant shipowners were different, but they were represented by the same solicitors and counsel. The trial judge had seen this as a crucial factor and his decision was upheld by the House of Lords. Given the work that had already been undertaken as part of that trial, the learning curve of the lawyers and experts involved, it made sense for the *Spiliada* trial also to take place in England.

Factors to be taken into account in establishing *forum conveniens* (stage 1 factors)

The factors which the court is entitled to take into account in considering whether one forum is more appropriate than another, and the weight to be given to each factor, vary from case to case. The court will consider the location of the parties, the likely location of the evidence

[81] *Ibid.*, at 482.

(for example, documents and factual and legal witnesses). Three factors which very often assume particular importance are:

(a) the existence of parallel proceedings;

(b) questions concerning applicable law; and

(c) most importantly, the existence of a jurisdiction agreement, which completely changes the picture.

Parallel proceedings, also referred to as *lis alibi pendens*, occur where proceedings are taking place in two jurisdictions relating to the same matter between the same parties. As has been seen, the Brussels I Regulation takes a strict and mechanistic approach to the existence of parallel proceedings: any court other than that first seised must stay its proceedings. At common law, the existence of parallel proceedings might be a reason for allowing a stay or refusing permission to serve out because:

> Where a suit about a particular subject matter between a plaintiff and a defendant is already pending in a foreign court which is a natural and appropriate forum for the resolution of the dispute between them, and the defendant in the foreign suit seeks to institute as plaintiff an action in England about the same matter to which the person who is plaintiff in the foreign suit is made defendant, then the additional inconvenience and expense which must result from allowing two sets of legal proceedings to be pursued concurrently in two different countries where the same facts will be in issue and the testimony of the same witnesses required, can only be justified if the would-be plaintiff can establish objectively by cogent evidence that there is some personal or judicial advantage that would be available to him only in the English action that is of such importance that it would cause injustice to him to deprive him of it.
>
> Quite apart from the additional inconvenience and expense, if the two actions are allowed to proceed concurrently in the two jurisdictions the Courts of the two countries may reach conflicting decisions . . . an unseemly race to be the first to obtain judgment . . . might well ensue . . . Comity demands that such a situation should not be permitted to occur as between courts of two civilized and friendly states. It is a recipe for confusion and injustice.[82]

However, the approach at common law is ultimately more flexible than that under the Brussels I Regulation, and the weight given to existence of parallel proceedings will depend on various factors, for example, how long proceedings have been underway, the reason the proceedings were started, etc. In some cases, the existence of parallel foreign proceedings 'may be of no relevance at all, for example, if one party has commenced the proceedings for the purpose of demonstrating the existence of a competing jurisdiction, or the proceedings have not passed beyond the stage of the initiating process'.[83]

In contractual cases, the question of which law governs the contract will almost always be relevant to the question of *forum conveniens*, but, again, the weight of this factor varies. Where issues of public policy are involved this is always likely to be an important factor.[84]

In other cases, the court may view it is as important that an English court deals with issues of English law or *vice versa* that issues of foreign law should be dealt with by the foreign court.[85] Three distinct reasons have been given:

---

[82] *The Abidin Daver* [1984] AC 398, 411–412, *per* Lord Diplock.
[83] *De Dampierre* v *De Dampierre* [1988] AC 92, 108, *per* Lord Goff.
[84] *Dupont* v *Agnew* [1987] 2 Lloyd's Rep 585, 594.
[85] *Seashell* v *Mutualidad de Seguros* [1989] 1 Lloyd's Rep 47, 51, Parker LJ. See also *Assicurazione* v *Sigorta* [2002] 1 Lloyd's Rep 480 at 486, where Colman J expressed a preference for an English court to deal with a complex English contract law in the technical field of reinsurance.

1. efficiency, in that it avoids the delay, inconvenience and expense of establishing foreign law;

2. the courts of one country may lack the legal and cultural qualifications to establish and apply foreign law accurately;

3. the issues of foreign law involved might be of such a type that the courts whose law is applicable have an overwhelming interest in resolving them.[86]

In such cases, the weight given to these factors will vary depending on, for example, whether the case turns primarily on factual or legal issues and the nature of the other law and the legal issue involved.[87] For example, in *Amin Rasheed* v *Kuwait*,[88] although the insurance policy at issue was governed by English law, the central issue in the case was the factual question of whether or not the vessel was engaged in smuggling when detained; if so, the loss was excluded. The local court in Kuwait was far better suited to deciding that than the English court. Furthermore, although there were questions of English law, the evidence was that the Kuwaiti court would apply English law and there was no reason to think the Kuwaiti court could not deal with those issues. Accordingly permission to serve out of the jurisdiction was set aside.

The single most important factor which changes completely the nature of the *forum conveniens* exercise is the existence of a jurisdiction agreement. Because jurisdiction agreements are so important in commercial cases, they are considered separately in section 10.2.5 below.

The proper approach at stage 2 of the *Spiliada*

Even though the court might have determined the *prima facie* appropriate and most suitable forum for the trial, that forum can be displaced on justice grounds. At stage 2, the fundamental question is where the proceedings may be tried suitably for the interests of the parties and the ends of justice. For that reason, the mere fact that one of the parties has an advantage in proceedings in a particular jurisdiction cannot be decisive. In particular:

1. what is an advantage to one party is likely to be a disadvantage to the other; and

2. judicial comity prohibits a comparison of the system of law in one country with that in another.[89]

This means that:

> the plaintiff will not ordinarily discharge the burden lying upon him by showing that he will enjoy procedural advantages, or a higher scale of damages or more generous rules of limitation if he sues in England; generally speaking, the plaintiff must take a foreign forum as he finds it, even if it is in some respects less advantageous to him than the English forum . . . It is only if the plaintiff can establish that substantial justice will not be done in the appropriate forum that a stay will be refused.[90]

---

[86] Questions of public policy are an obvious example.

[87] Problems are less likely to arise when the construction of legislation is involved and when the laws of another common law jurisdiction are involved (for example, *AG of NZ* v *Ortiz* [1984] 1 AC 41, interpretation of a New Zealand statute by the English court without resort to expert evidence; *cf. The Nile Rhapsody* [1992] 2 Lloyd's Rep 399, difficult questions of Egyptian law were better dealt with by the Egyptian court).

[88] [1984] 1 AC 50.

[89] *Amin Rasheed* v *Kuwait Insurance* [1984] AC 50, 67, 72; *The Abidin Daver* [1984] AC 398, 410; *The Bergen* [1997] 2 Lloyd's Rep 710, 715.

[90] *Lubbe* v *Cape* [2000] 2 Lloyd's Rep 383, 390, *per* Lord Bingham.

One of the clearest cases of injustice is where the defendant would not obtain a fair trial or cannot bring proceedings in the other jurisdiction. For example, in *Oppenheimer* v *Louis Rosenthal*,[91] a German Jew would not have received a fair trial in Germany.[92] Sometimes, the fact that the law applied by the foreign court means that the claimant would be bound to fail in that jurisdiction also amounts to a denial of justice if he is not permitted to continue English proceedings.[93]

Although differences in the procedures in the foreign court should not, without more, be enough, there are cases where a stay has been refused on the grounds of, for example: excessive delay in the foreign jurisdiction;[94] differences in the amount of damages recoverable;[95] or other procedural advantages.[96]

If a party would be time-barred in the foreign jurisdiction that may swing the balance away from an otherwise appropriate foreign jurisdiction in favour of granting permission to pursue or continue proceedings in England, which would not be time-barred, *provided* that the claimant acted reasonably in commencing proceedings in England and not unreasonably in allowing the foreign limitation period to pass.[97] Again much will depend on the facts of the case and, in some 'extreme cases', the fact that proceedings have become time-barred in the appropriate forum should be irrelevant, for example, if the claimant had deliberately allowed time to expire simply to take advantage of a more generous time bar in England or obviously should have filed protective proceedings but did not.[98] Even in cases where a time bar is *prima facie* relevant, the appropriate action in such a case might be to allow a stay if the time bar is waived.[99]

---

[91] [1937] 1 All ER 23.

[92] In *Mohammed* v *Bank of Kuwait and Middle East KSC* [1996] 1 WLR 1483, an Iraqi citizen could not travel to Kuwait to bring a claim and would face great difficulties in instructing lawyers there. In this case this was treated as a stage 1 consideration, that is, that Kuwait was not an 'available' alternative forum. However, in *Askin* v *Absa Bank* [1999] ILPr 471, the Court of Appeal indicated that they would have preferred to treat such considerations under stage 2. However, on the facts, there was no cogent evidence that it was not safe for the defendant to return to South Africa and the risk of arrest was, in any event, essentially self-induced. On allegedly inopportune overseas forums, see further *Deripaska* v *Cherney* [2010] 2 All ER (Comm) 456 and *AK Investment CJSC* v *Kyrgyz Mobile Tel Ltd* [2011] UKPC 7.

[93] *Banco Atlantico* v *British Bank of Middle East* [1990] 2 Lloyd's Rep 504.

[94] *The Vishva Ajay* [1989] 2 Lloyd's Rep 558, a delay of six to ten years in Indian proceedings would lead to injustice because witnesses would not remember events. *Cf. Radhakrishna Hospitality Service Private Ltd* v *EIH Ltd* [1999] 2 Lloyd's Rep 249, substantial justice could be done in India even if it took longer.

[95] See *The Vishva Abha* [1990] 2 Lloyd's Rep 312, where the court said that, where the difference between damages that could be recovered was very considerable, it would amount to an injustice to require the claim to be pursued abroad (damages were limited to £367,500 under South African law compared to a potential liability of £1.5 million under English law). *Cf. Herceg Novi* v *Ming Galaxy* [1998] 4 All ER 238, in which the different damage limitation levels under two different treaty regimes were not a ground for refusing a stay where neither Convention was more just than the other.

[96] See, for example, *Roneleigh Ltd* v *MII Exports Inc* [1989] 1 WLR 619, a case in which New Jersey was plainly the more closely connected forum, but the Court of Appeal upheld the judge's decision to allow service out of the jurisdiction on the basis that the law of New Jersey does not allow a successful claimant to recover costs, so that substantial justice would not be done in that forum. See also *International Credit and Investment* v *Sheikh Kamal Adham* [1999] ILPr 302, where the fact that an English judgment (enforceable under the Brussels regime) was more easily enforceable than a foreign judgment meant it may be unjust to deprive the claimant of the ability to sue in England.

[97] See, for a recent example, *Citi-March* v *Neptune Orient Lines Ltd* [1996] 1 WLR 1376.

[98] Lord Goff, *Spiliada* v *Cansulex* [1987] 1 AC 460, at p. 483.

[99] Possible advantage or disadvantage can often be 'neutralised' through undertakings offered by the parties. For example, in *Lubbe* v *Cape* [2000] 2 Lloyd's Rep 383, the claimant undertook to sue only in relation to injury caused by that particular party, which negated any disadvantage of not being able to join a third party in England.

Another factor which has been of crucial importance in two important recent decisions is the availability of legal aid or conditional fee arrangements.

In *Connelly* v *RTZ Corporation*,[100] the claimants, who worked in uranium mines in Namibia, claimed they had contracted cancer as a result. They brought proceedings against the parent company in England. The claimants were impecunious and could get legal aid in England, but Namibia was the jurisdiction with which the case had the most real and substantial connection. The House of Lords held that where a plainly more appropriate forum had been identified, in general, the plaintiff would have to take that forum as he found it, but that the nature and complexity of the case was such that it could not be tried at all without the benefit of financial assistance and that of expert scientific evidence. Thus, the availability of legal aid in England was the crucial factor in refusing to stay the English proceedings.

In *Lubbe* v *Cape*[101] it was again accepted that England was not the most convenient forum – in this case it was South Africa (the claim arose out of asbestos mining in South Africa) – but again a stay was refused. The evidence was that the South African Legal Aid Board had excluded personal injury claims from the scheme. There was also evidence that no firm would take the case on a contingency fee basis. By contrast, the claimants had legal aid for their action in England. According to Lord Bingham, 'In the special and unusual circumstances of these proceedings, lack of the means, in South Africa, to prosecute these claims to a conclusion provides a compelling ground, at the second stage of the *Spiliada* test, for refusing to stay the proceedings here.'[102] By contrast, the absence of established procedures in South Africa for handling group actions did not fall into the 'exceptional' category and, standing alone, it involved 'the kind of procedural comparison which the English court should be careful to eschew'.[103]

10.2.5 Jurisdiction agreements

In commercial cases, the jurisdiction of the English court is very often consensual, that is, it is founded on an agreement between the parties that the English court should have jurisdiction.

Jurisdiction agreements can be exclusive or non-exclusive. By a non-exclusive jurisdiction clause, the parties seek to give a particular court jurisdiction when that court would not otherwise have jurisdiction. They are enabling clauses and do not prevent the parties from suing elsewhere. Exclusive jurisdiction clauses could have an enabling element themselves, but the essence of an exclusive jurisdiction clause is that it also seeks to prescribe the parties' conduct by requiring them to sue in a particular forum; there is an *obligation* not to sue elsewhere.

10.2.5.1 Jurisdiction agreements under the Brussels I Regulation

In the Brussels I Regulation, exclusive and non-exclusive jurisdictions are dealt with in Art. 23.

---

[100] [1998] AC 854.
[101] [2000] 2 Lloyd's Rep 383.
[102] *Ibid.*, at 393.
[103] *Ibid.*, at 393. Although the absence of established group action procedures reinforced the submissions made on the funding issues.

LEGISLATIVE PROVISION

Article 23

(1) If the parties, one or more of whom is domiciled in a Member State, have agreed that a court or the courts of a Member State are to have jurisdiction to settle any disputes which have arisen or which may arise in connection with a particular legal relationship, that court or those courts shall have jurisdiction. Such jurisdiction shall be exclusive unless the parties have agreed otherwise. Such an agreement conferring jurisdiction shall be either:

(a) in writing or evidenced in writing; or

(b) in a form which accords with practices which the parties have established between themselves; or

(c) in international trade or commerce, in a form which accords with a usage of which the parties are or ought to have been aware and which in such trade or commerce is widely known to, and regularly observed by, parties to contracts of the type involved in the particular trade or commerce concerned.

(2) Any communication by electronic means which provides a durable record of the agreement shall be equivalent to 'writing'.

(3) Where such an agreement is concluded by parties, none of whom is domiciled in a Member State, the courts of other Member States shall have no jurisdiction over their disputes unless the court or courts chosen have declined jurisdiction.[104]

By Art. 23(1), where parties *one or more of whom is domiciled in a Member State* agree that the courts *of a Member State* shall have jurisdiction, that court will have jurisdiction to hear the case (provided the formalities in Art. 23 are complied with). Article 23 therefore allows the parties to submit to a court other than a court which would have jurisdiction by virtue of, for example, Arts 2, 5(1) or 5(5). If it is an exclusive jurisdiction agreement (which will be assumed to be the case) it also has a negative effect in that it precludes proceedings in any other Member State (except where that other court has exclusive jurisdiction under Art. 22 or the parties submit under Art. 24).

If parties *none of whom is domiciled in a Member State* agree to confer jurisdiction on the courts of *a Member State* although Art. 23(1) cannot apply, such a jurisdiction agreement does still have a limited effect. Although Art. 23(3) does not have any positive effect in that it cannot confer jurisdiction on the chosen court, it has a negative effect in that courts of other Member States must decline jurisdiction in favour of the chosen court.

Article 23 provides, in effect, a comprehensive code for the enforcement of jurisdiction agreements which come within the scope of the Brussels regime. This has a number of important consequences.

Formal validity is governed exclusively by the conditions specified in Art. 23 without reference to any national rules regulating form.[105] The agreement must satisfy one of the three requirements set out in Art. 23 of the Regulation in that it must be:

---

[104] Brussels I Regulation, Art. 23.
[105] *Elefanten Shuh GmbH v Jacqmain* Case C-150/80 [1980] ECR 1671.

1. in writing or evidenced in writing;

2. in a form which accords with practices between the parties;[106] or

3. in a form which accords with international trade usage.[107]

It appears that *essential validity* is also to be governed exclusively by the provisions and requirements of Art. 23. Once the formal requirements set out in Art. 23 are complied with the validity of the agreement is presumed.[108] The enforcement of jurisdiction agreements is a matter of procedure, not contract. In other words, the validity of the agreement is tested by applying Art. 23, not by reference to the law applicable to the underlying contract or indeed the law applicable to the jurisdiction agreement itself. 'A jurisdiction clause, which serves a procedural purpose, is governed by the provisions [of the Brussels I Regulation] whose aim is to establish uniform rules of international jurisdiction.'[109]

This could be problematic. What if it is alleged that the jurisdiction agreement was procured by duress, undue influence or through misrepresentation? Must the alleged wrongful conduct of one of the parties in procuring the agreement be ignored provided the formal requirements are satisfied, for example, the alleged agreement is in writing? This appears to be the result of treating Art. 23 as providing a comprehensive code for the validity of such agreements. One answer which has been suggested is that, in extreme cases, the agreement would be unenforceable, although compliant with Art. 23, for infringing the community concept of good faith.[110] It is also important to remember that jurisdiction agreements are severable: the agreement as to jurisdiction is separate from the 'host' agreement in which it is found. This means that even if the substantive obligations of the contract are void or voidable, that does not *of itself* destroy the agreement as to jurisdiction.[111] Thus, even if it is alleged that the underlying contract was procured by duress, mistake or misrepresentation, that does not necessarily impact on the separate jurisdiction agreement contained in that contract.

The *construction* of an Art. 23 jurisdiction agreement remains a matter for national law, namely the law applicable to the clause.[112] Such questions of interpretation include whether a particular dispute falls within the scope of the clause and whether the clause is exclusive or non-exclusive.[113]

---

[106] This relaxation was agreed as part of the Lugano Convention.

[107] This relaxation was first introduced when the UK became a party to the Brussels Convention and was intended to deal, in particular, with clauses contained in a bill of lading (see, for example, *Transporti Castelletti Spedizioni Internazionali SpA v Hugo Trumpy SpA* Case C-159/97 [1999] ECR 1597).

[108] *Transporti Castelletti SpA v Trumpy SpA* Case C-159/97 [1999] ECR 1597, paras [46]–[52].

[109] *Benincasa v Dentalkit* Case C-269/95 [1997] ECR I-3767, 3797.

[110] *F Berghoefer v ASA SA* Case C-221/84 [1985] ECR 2699. See, further, A. Briggs and P. Rees (eds), *Civil Jurisdiction and Judgments* (5th edn, Informa Law, Abingdon, 2009) at 2.115, A. Briggs, *Agreements on Jurisdiction and Choice of Law* (Oxford University Press, Oxford, 2008) at 7.12 and L. Collins (general ed.), *Dicey, Morris and Collins: The Conflict of Laws* (14th edn, Sweet and Maxwell, London, 2006), pp. 12–108.

[111] *Benincasa v Dentalkit* Case 269/95 [1997] ECR I-3767; *Deutsche Bank v Asia Pacific Broadband Wireless* [2008] EWCA 1091 at [24].

[112] Although the jurisdiction agreement forms an agreement which is separate from the underlying host contract, capable therefore of having its own applicable law, in practice, as a matter of English conflict of law rules, jurisdiction agreements are almost always governed by the same law as that which governs the underlying contract.

[113] This is apparently subject to the provision in Art. 23(1) that 'such jurisdiction shall be exclusive unless the parties have agreed otherwise'. How that 'presumption' should operate is far from clear.

10.2.5.2 Jurisdiction agreements at common law

At common law, jurisdiction agreements are crucially relevant to the exercise of the court's adjudicatory discretion.

First, the court must determine, as a matter of construction, whether the agreement is exclusive or non-exclusive and if it covers the dispute in question.[114]

The basic principle is that the existence of an *exclusive* jurisdiction agreement *in favour of England* will create a 'strong *prima facie* case' that England is the appropriate forum: permission to serve out will usually be granted and a stay refused. Similarly, if there is an *exclusive* jurisdiction agreement in favour of *another jurisdiction*, the court will require a strong reason as to why permission should nevertheless be granted (or a stay declined).[115]

Thus:

> an agreement to submit disputes to the courts of a particular country is a powerful factor when the court comes to exercising its discretion in matters of this kind. It is rare that the court will permit a party to maintain an action in England in breach of an exclusive jurisdiction clause or refuse to exercise its jurisdiction over a defendant if there is an exclusive jurisdiction agreement in favour of the courts of this country.[116]

Unlike the position under the Brussels I Regulation, however, the court ultimately retains a discretion. One important situation in which the court may give permission to serve out, even though there is a jurisdiction agreement in favour of another jurisdiction, is where there are related proceedings involving a number of parties, only some of whom are bound by the jurisdiction agreement.[117]

Thus, the English courts do not traditionally take a simple contractual approach to jurisdiction agreements. If they did, one would expect an exclusive jurisdiction agreement to be enforced by way of right. Rather, the existence of a jurisdiction agreement is seen as a factor (albeit usually a crucially important factor) in the *Spiliada* exercise. This 'estoppel'-based approach can also be seen in the approach to non-exclusive jurisdiction clauses. Even though the parties have not, as a matter of contract, promised not to sue anywhere else, if they have agreed to the non-exclusive jurisdiction of the English courts:

> it simply should not be open to [the defendant] to start arguing about the relative merits of fighting an action in [another jurisdiction] as compared with fighting an action in London, where the factors relied on would have been eminently foreseeable at the time that they entered into the contract . . . Surely they must point to some factor which they could not have foreseen on which they can rely for displacing the bargain which they made i.e. that they would not object to the jurisdiction of the English Court.[118]

---

[114] The leading case on the construction of jurisdiction agreements under English law is *British Aerospace PLC* v *Dee Howard Co* [1993] 1 Lloyd's Rep 368.

[115] See *The Pioneer Container* [1994] 1 AC 324 and *Aratra Potato Co Ltd* v *Egyptian Navigation Co* [1981] 2 Lloyd's Rep 119.

[116] *Burrows* v *Jamaica* [2002] 1 Lloyd's Rep IR 466 at 470, Moore-Bick J; *Marubeni* v *Mongolian Government* [2002] 2 All ER 873 at 890–1 and the cases there cited; *Donohue* v *Armco* [2002] 1 Lloyd's Rep 425 at 433, in the context of a stay application.

[117] *Donohue* v *Armco* [2002] 1 Lloyd's Rep 425 at 433–434. See also *Carvalho* v *Hull, Blyth (Angola) Ltd* [1979] 1 WLR 1228, where the plaintiff, who had fled Angola shortly after the start of the civil war, was able to sue the defendant in England even though the parties' contract (which had been concluded before the civil war) referred disputes to the Angolan courts. The court refused to grant a stay, not only because the post-revolution court was completely different but also because there was a question as to whether or not he would be treated fairly by the court.

[118] *British Aerospace* v *Dee Howard* [1993] 1 Lloyd's Rep 368, 376 and see *BP* v *Aon* [2006] 1 Lloyd's Rep 549.

Again, there is a strong *prima facie* presumption that the jurisdiction referred to in the non-exclusive jurisdiction agreement is an appropriate one. The usual *Spiliada* factors, such as, the cost of proceedings, the whereabouts of parties or the location of documents are less powerful because of the agreement of the parties. Indeed, in a case which has little connection with England it may be that the parties are taken to have agreed on a neutral forum for the resolution of disputes.[119] However, there remains a difference between exclusive and non-exclusive clauses: although the parties are taken to have agreed that England is *an* appropriate forum, they have not agreed that England is *the* appropriate forum. A non-exclusive jurisdiction agreement:

> does not go as far as saying that it is agreed that in all circumstances that may in future arise the designated court will necessarily be the court where the case may most suitably be tried for the interests of all parties and the ends of justice. If that were so, the effect of such a clause would be indistinguishable from that of an exclusive jurisdiction clause. The *forum non conveniens* test would be deployed not as a flexible comparative exercise but so as to impose an inflexible constraint analogous to that imposed by a contract . . . It is sufficient for it to be shown that although Illinois is an appropriate forum, there is a clear balance of justice and fairness as between the parties in favour of London. By a clear balance I mean one which substantially relies on considerations which would not have been obvious to the parties at the time when they entered into the [contract] and a balance which while not overwhelming, is substantially more than a fine balance.[120]

10.2.6 Party autonomy and Articles 27 and 28 of the Brussels I Regulation

As has been seen, the Brussels I Regulation sets out strict rules which govern parallel proceedings. Any court other than that first seised must stay its proceedings in favour of that court. Questions arise as to the relationship between these provisions and Art. 23. Those issues were addressed by the ECJ in the very important case of *Erich Gasser*.

CASE

Erich Gasser GmbH v MISAT Srl[121]

The claimant was an Austrian company which had sold children's clothing to the defendant Italian company. The defendant brought an action against the claimant in Italy seeking a declaration that the contract between them had terminated. Subsequently, the claimant brought an action in Austria for payment of outstanding invoices. The claimant contended that the Austrian court had jurisdiction, *inter alia*, by virtue of an agreement conferring jurisdiction which it said satisfied the requirements of what is now Art. 23 of

---

[119] See, for example, *The Rothnie* [1996] 2 Lloyd's Rep 206. A non-exclusive jurisdiction agreement in favour of Gibraltar created a presumption that was the appropriate forum and that was not displaced, for example, by delays there, particularly as the defendant offered undertakings as to certain procedural time limits. See also for a recent application of these principles *Antec International Ltd v Biosafety USA Inc* [2006] EWHC 47.

[120] *BP v Aon* [2006] 1 Lloyd's Rep 549 J. See also *Highland Crusader Offshore Partners v Deutsche Bank* [2009] EWCA Civ 725 [2009] 2 Lloyd's Rep 617 and section 10.2.7.2 below.

[121] Case C-116/02 [2005] QBI; [2003] ECR I-14693.

the Brussels I Regulation. The claimant further alleged that its rights had been adversely affected by the excessive length of proceedings in Italy.

The Austrian court referred a number of questions about the operation of what is now Art. 27 of the Brussels I Regulation to the ECJ for a preliminary ruling. Most importantly it asked the following.

1. May a court other than the court first seised, within the meaning of the first paragraph of Art. 27, review the jurisdiction of the court first seised if the second court has exclusive jurisdiction pursuant to an agreement conferring jurisdiction under Art. 23 of the Brussels I Regulation or must the agreed second court proceed in accordance with Art. 27, notwithstanding the agreement conferring jurisdiction?

2. Can the fact that court proceedings in a Member State take an unjustifiably long time (for reasons largely unconnected with the conduct of the parties), so that material detriment may be caused to one party, have the consequence that the court other than the court first seised within the meaning of Art. 27, is allowed to proceed?

The first of these questions essentially asked if there was an exception to the court first seised rule where there was a jurisdiction agreement in favour of another Member State. The Advocate General, Advocate General Léger, thought that there should be. He drew an analogy with the position in relation to what is now Art. 22[122] and said that any other result would undermine the effectiveness of Art. 23 and the legal certainty that attaches to it. He also said that the risk of irreconcilable decisions can be significantly reduced, because the court first seised will in any event eventually have to decline jurisdiction (particularly as the courts must assess the validity of the contested agreement conferring jurisdiction in accordance with the same principles and the same conditions by applying Art. 23 of the Regulation).[123] His suggested solution was that the court second seised should be authorised to derogate from the requirements of Art. 27 only when it has made absolutely sure that it does have exclusive jurisdiction under an agreement conferring jurisdiction. If there were any doubts as to the validity of the agreement, or its scope, the court second seised would have to stay its proceedings.[124]

As to the second question, he refused to allow a derogation from Art. 27 on the basis of delay, primarily, because that would breach the principles of trust and certainty on which the Brussels regime is based.[125]

The ECJ agreed with the Advocate General on the second question and confirmed that delay in the court first seised could not constitute a ground for derogating from Art. 27. Like the Advocate General, the ECJ stressed that 'the [Brussels I Regulation] is necessarily based on the trust which the Member States accord to each other's legal systems and judicial institutions' and that the Regulation 'thereby seeks to ensure legal certainty by allowing individuals to foresee with sufficient certainty which court will have jurisdiction'.[126]

---

[122] In *Overseas Union Insurance Ltd* v *New Hampshire Insurance Co* Case C-351/89 [1991] ECR I-3317, the ECJ had indicated that the requirements of Art. 27 may be derogated from where the court second seised has exclusive jurisdiction to hear the case under Art. 22.

[123] Paragraph [77].

[124] Paragraph [81].

[125] Paragraphs [88]–[89].

[126] Paragraph [72].

> Crucially, however, the court disagreed in relation to the Art. 23 argument and held that there was no exception to the court first seised rule where there was an exclusive jurisdiction agreement in favour of another Member State. The ECJ said that Art. 22 holds a unique position in the Regulation and, whatever the position in relation to Art. 22, there could be no exception for Art. 23. The court also said that Art. 27 had to be applied widely because the court second seised is never in a better position than the court first seised to determine if the latter has jurisdiction. That jurisdiction is determined directly by the rules of the Brussels I Regulation, which are common to both courts and may be interpreted and applied with the same authority by each of them.[127]
>
> Finally, 'the difficulties of the kind referred to by the United Kingdom Government, stemming from delaying tactics by parties who, with the intention of delaying settlement of the substantive dispute, commence proceedings before a court which they know to lack jurisdiction by reason of the existence of a jurisdiction clause are not such as to call into question the interpretation of any provision of the [Brussels Regulation], as deduced from its wording and purpose.'[128]

The result of the decision in *Erich Gasser* is that, once proceedings have been commenced in a Member State, all other courts must decline in favour of that court, even if there is an exclusive jurisdiction agreement in favour of another Member State. The decision raises two problems. The first is practical. The effect of the decision is to allow a party who wishes to avoid an exclusive jurisdiction agreement to stall proceedings in the chosen state by commencing proceedings elsewhere, for example, for a negative declaration that they are not liable (and in particular in a jurisdiction where it will take the court a long time to rule on jurisdiction). It thus condones the use of the so-called 'Italian torpedo'.[129] Secondly, as a matter of principle, it arguably frustrates the parties' agreement and expectation that all matters in dispute, including the applicability of the jurisdiction agreement, will be determined by the chosen court.

ISSUE BOX

Has the decision in *Erich Gasser* fatally undermined party autonomy in Brussels regime cases?

Both the Advocate General and, to a lesser extent, the ECJ itself in *Erich Gasser*, recognised that the effect of applying Art. 27 even in cases where there is an Art. 23 jurisdiction agreement might be to encourage delaying tactics and undermine the effectiveness of the jurisdiction agreement.

An example of the way in which such tactics could perhaps be used can be seen in the facts of the case of *JP Morgan Ltd* v *Primacom AG*.[130] Several banks, acting through JP Morgan as agent, had lent substantial sums to Primacom, a German company. The loan

---

[127] Paragraph [48].
[128] Paragraph [53].
[129] A term apparently first used by an Italian *avvocato*, Mario Franzosi, and since widely adopted (see T. C. Hartley, 'The European Union and the Systematic Dismantling of the Common Law of the Conflict of Laws' [2005] *ICLQ* 813 at 817).
[130] [2005] EWHC 508 (Comm).

agreement provided unambiguously that any disputes were to be submitted to the exclusive jurisdiction of the English courts. Having failed to make two payments, Primacom initiated proceedings in Germany for a negative declaration that it owed no interest. JP Morgan responded by suing in England pursuant to the jurisdiction agreement. The judge in the English proceedings, Clarke J, applying the decision in *Erich Gasser*, had to stay the English proceedings pursuant to Art. 27 pending the decision of the German court on its jurisdiction.

Whether or not the decision in *Erich Gasser* is correct in principle, it certainly has serious practical implications. The banks in *JP Morgan* were placed in a difficult position. All the parties had clearly agreed that the English courts were to have exclusive jurisdiction, yet the proceedings were delayed for several months whilst the German court decided that was the case and stayed proceedings in favour of the English courts. Even then, the banks were arguably deprived of their right to have the effect of the jurisdiction agreement tested in the agreed forum.

A number of possible solutions to the *Erich Gasser* problem have been suggested.

Most radically, the Brussels I Regulation could be amended to allow the court second seised to proceed if there is a *prima facie* valid Art. 23 agreement.[131] This would effectively reverse the decision in *Erich Gasser*.

Other changes to the Regulation which might indirectly improve the situation would be that judgments in breach of an Art. 23 agreement should be unenforceable and that the court should raise Art. 23 of its own motion (in other words that the provisions in Art. 35(1) and Art. 25 should be extended to include Art. 23 as well as Art. 22).[132]

Another possibility is that, if Member States were required to have a preliminary procedure for determining jurisdiction, this would reduce the practical effect of the Italian torpedo by ensuring that the court first seised hears the case quickly.[133]

In the meantime, commercial parties are likely to explore other solutions, including the use of hybrid arbitration clauses and/or claims for damages as a means of indirectly enforcing jurisdiction agreements.[134]

A solution might also eventually be provided by the Hague Convention on choice of court agreements.[135] On 1 April 2009, the European Community signed the Convention. The USA and Mexico have also signed, although to date only Mexico has acceded to the Convention.

---

[131] In the Report on the Application of the Brussels I Regulation published in September 2007 by B. Hess, Pfeiffer and T. Schlosser (Study JLS/C4/2005/03 – referred to as the Heidelberg Report), it was accepted, as a policy decision, that it might be appropriate to release the court designated by a standard form jurisdiction agreement but second seised from its obligations under Art. 27 (para. 453), with the possibility of extending this to all choice of forum agreements in a future revision. In the recast Regulation No (1215/2002) Art. 31(2) reverses the decision in Eric Gasses.

[132] Under the new Art. 28 of the recast Regulation, where a dependant domiciled in a Member State does not enter a approval, the court shall declare of its own motion that it has no jurisdiction unless its jurisdiction is derived from the provisions of the Regulation.

[133] In the original proposal of a recast Regulation, the operation of Art. 27 is improved by stipulating a time limit within which the court first seised must determine its jurisdiction, save in exceptional circumstances. This provision is not found in the final version.

[134] See, further, R. Fentiman, '*Erich Gasser GmbH v MISAT Srl*' (2005) CMLR 241; R. Fentiman 'Jurisdiction Agreements and Forum Shopping in Europe' (2006) *JIBFL* 304; J. Mance, 'Exclusive Jurisdiction Agreements and European Ideals' (2004) 120 *LQR* 357 and L. Merrett, 'The Enforcement of Jurisdiction Agreements within the Brussels Regime' (2006) 55 *ICLQ* 315. On the proposed changes to the BIR, see R. Fentiman, 'Brusseks I and Third States: Future Imperfect?' [2010–2011] 13 CYELS 65.

[135] Hague Convention on Choice of Court Agreements, 30 June 2005.

One more ratification is required before the Convention can enter into force. Through the Convention, states will agree to recognise or enforce the judgments of other state parties when those judgments follow a valid choice of court agreement. Choice of court agreements are also defined and regulated. Under the Convention, any court other than the agreed court must decline jurisdiction (Art. 6) and the chosen court shall not decline in favour of another state (Art. 5(2)). Thus, there is no equivalent to Art. 27 of the Brussels I Regulation and no exception where another court is first seised. However, the Convention will only engage if one party is domiciled in a non-Member State, not if both are EU domiciled (Art. 26(6)(a)).

10.2.7 Anti-suit injunctions

One of the ways in which parallel proceedings are dealt with at common law is through the use of anti-suit injunctions.[136]

An anti-suit injunction is an injunction granted by the English court against a defendant (the respondent to the injunction) to prevent the defendant (the claimant in foreign proceedings) from commencing or maintaining proceedings abroad.

The order is directed at the defendant, not the foreign court, and is enforced against the defendant personally. If the defendant breaches the order he will be in contempt of court and accordingly risk a number of possible consequences:

1. the court has the power to make an unlimited fine or imprison a defendant in contempt of court; it can also seize the defendant's assets in England;

2. if the defendant is a party to proceedings in England, he may be prevented from appearing to defend those proceedings;[137]

3. any judgment obtained by the defendant abroad will be unenforceable in England as a matter of English public policy.[138]

The legal basis for an anti-suit injunction is the court's general equitable power to prevent injustice, now enshrined in s. 37, Supreme Court Act 1981, which provides:

1. the High Court may by order (whether interlocutory or final) grant an injunction or appoint a receiver in all cases in which it appears to the court to be just and convenient to do so;

2. any such order may be made either unconditionally or on such terms and conditions as the court thinks just.

Because an anti-suit injunction is an *in personam* order, aimed at the defendant, the English court must have personal jurisdiction over the defendant (in other words, it must be possible to serve proceedings on the defendant). Following the decision of the House of Lords in

---

[136] For a recent example, see *RBS v Hicks and Gillett* [2010] EWHC 2579 (Ch).

[137] In *Motorola Credit Corporation v Uzan* [2004] WLR 113, the Court of Appeal considered the discretion of the court to refuse to hear a person in contempt of court. The court must in each case decide whether in all the circumstances the interests of justice are served by hearing the party or not. The ECJ in *Marco Gambazzi v Daimler-Chrysler Canada Inc* Case C-394/07 said that a court asked to enforce an order given without the defendant being heard could refuse to enforce such an order on the grounds of public policy, but only if the exclusion measure constituted a manifest and disproportionate infringement of the defendant's right to be heard.

[138] *Philip Alexander Securities Ltd v Bamberger* [1997] ILPr 73 at 115.

Airbus Industrie CIE v *Patel*,[139] there is also a further jurisdictional requirement, namely, that the English court has a connection with, or an interest in, the substantive dispute between the parties. In that case, the defendants, who were British citizens, were passengers or representatives of passengers who were injured or killed in an air crash in Bangalore. They had brought proceedings in India against the employers of the pilot and the airport authorities, which had been settled. They subsequently commenced proceedings in Texas against a number of other parties, including the applicant, who had designed and manufactured the aircraft. The applicant sought an injunction from the English court restraining the defendants from continuing with the Texas action. It was clear that the choice of jurisdictions was really Texas or India. In those circumstances, the House of Lords held that there was no jurisdiction to grant the injunction since, as a general rule, it was contrary to the doctrine of comity for an English court to grant an anti-suit injunction unless the English forum had a sufficient interest in, or connection with, the matter in question to justify such interference.

The connection will be clearest where the defendant is a party in parallel, related English proceedings, but it is not always necessary that England is the natural forum or even that it is a possible forum for the dispute. In *Midland Bank* v *Laker Airways*,[140] the liquidator of the defendant companies caused proceedings to be commenced in the USA against the applicants under USA anti-trust legislation. The applicants were UK-based bankers and they had no business in the USA. The Court of Appeal granted the anti-suit injunction, holding that the bringing of proceedings in the USA was unconscionable given that the applicant had no relevant presence in the USA, the proceedings related to activities which were part of its business in England and which were intended to be governed by English law. The fact that the dispute was uniquely connected with England meant that the English court had jurisdiction to intervene even though the defendant had no cause of action, let alone similar relief available in England. The important point seems to have been that the defendant was acting in bad faith, which in itself was a sufficient reason for the English court to intervene.

Having established that it has jurisdiction to grant the injunction, the court will consider whether or not there are grounds for the granting of relief.

10.2.7.1 Grounds for the grant of an anti-suit injunction

The injunction will be granted wherever *justice* requires it.[141] It is *not* enough that there are concurrent proceedings and England is the *forum conveniens*.[142] The clearest case is where the foreign proceedings are brought in breach of contract (usually because there is an exclusive jurisdiction agreement in favour of the English court).

10.2.7.2 Enforcing contractual rights

These cases are relatively straightforward. It is inherently unjust to infringe an applicant's contractual rights. Thus, where the foreign proceedings are in breach of either an arbitration agreement or an exclusive jurisdiction agreement, an anti-suit injunction will usually be

---

[139] [1999] 1 AC 119.
[140] [1986] QB 689.
[141] It was suggested in *Masri* v *Consolidated Contractors International Company Sal* [2008] EWCA Civ 625 that an injunction might also be granted in the public interest.
[142] *Aerospatiale* v *Lee Kui Jak* [1987] AC 871.

granted to prevent the defendant from carrying on proceedings in breach of that agreement.[143] In such cases, the burden is effectively reversed and is on the defendant to show why relief should not be granted.

10.2.7.3 Unconscionable claims

Where there is no breach of contract, the respondent's conduct must be unconscionable.[144] In a number of cases, the courts have also referred to the fact that the claim is vexatious or oppressive, but it is not always clear how these terms interrelate. The clearest case is where the defendant's conduct is fraudulent or in bad faith. A good example is provided by the facts in *Turner* v *Grovit*.[145] The applicant had brought proceedings in England for constructive unfair dismissal. The defendant, who was one of the defendants in those proceedings, commenced proceedings against the applicant in Spain claiming damages for breach of contract. The Court of Appeal held that:

> On the question of abuse of process, it is to my mind plain beyond the possibility of argument that the Spanish proceedings were launched in bad faith in order to vex the plaintiff in his pursuit of the application before the employment tribunal here . . . The documents lead to the ineluctable conclusion that, as I have said, the Spanish proceedings were intended and intended only to oppress the plaintiff and as such fall to be condemned as abusive as a matter of elementary principle.[146]

Other, perhaps less clear cut, examples of foreign proceedings which have been found to be an abuse of process and thus restrained by injunction, include:

1. foreign proceedings which penalise the legitimate conduct of a party in English proceedings, for example, in *Bank of Tokyo* v *Karoon*[147] an English court restrained New York proceedings for breach of confidence brought against a bank which had supplied evidence concerning its customer's business in the course of English proceedings;

2. cases where the respondent has invoked an exorbitant jurisdiction – this was one of the several grounds relied on in *Midland Bank* v *Laker Airways*;[148]

3. foreign claims which are bound to fail – this was again a suggestion made in *Midland Bank* v *Laker Airways* and also in *SIPC* v *Coral Oil Co Ltd*[149] where relief was granted because the foreign claim was 'utterly absurd'; similarly, an attempt to relitigate abroad a case where judgment has been obtained in England can amount to vexation and oppression;[150]

---

[143] See *Donohue* v *Armco Inc* [2002] 1 Lloyd's Rep 425: 'If contracting parties agree to give a particular court exclusive jurisdiction to rule on claims between those parties, and a claim falling within the scope of the agreement is made in proceedings in a forum other than that which the parties have agreed, the English Court will ordinarily exercise its discretion (whether by granting a stay of proceedings in England, or by restraining the prosecution of proceedings in the non-contractual forum abroad, or by such other procedural order as is appropriate in the circumstances) to secure compliance with the contractual bargain, unless the party suing in the non-contractual forum (the burden being on him) can show strong reasons for suing in that forum' (*per* Lord Bingham at [24]). An example of such a strong reason can be seen from the facts of *Donohue* v *Armco* itself, that is, where the interests of third parties not bound by the agreement would be prejudiced. On non-exclusive jurisdiction agreements see *Highland Crusader Offshore Partners LP* v *Deutsche Bank AG* [2009] EWCA Civ 725.

[144] See Lord Hobhouse in *Turner* v *Grovit* [2002] 1 WLR 107 at para. [25].

[145] [2002] 1 WLR 107.

[146] [2000] QB 345 at 362.

[147] [1986] 3 WLR 414.

[148] [1986] QB 689.

[149] [1999] 2 Lloyd's Rep 606 at 609.

[150] *Masri* v *Consolidated Contractors International Company Sal* [2008] EWCA Civ 625. *Cf. Star Reefers Pool Inc* v *JFC Group Co Ltd* [2012] EWCA Civ 14.

4. cases where the foreign claim has no legitimate purpose, for example, in *Glencore Internation AG v Exter Shipping Ltd*[151] the defendants had embarked on parallel proceedings in the US state of Georgia, involving issues pending in English proceedings, so the Court asked two questions, first, if the same issues involved in both proceedings, so as to 'raise *prima facie* a case of vexatious conduct', and, secondly, if so, if the foreign proceedings nonetheless have a 'legitimate purpose' and, in the absence of any credible explanation for the proceedings the court drew the inference that they were simply part of a deliberate strategy of harassment and vexation designed to wear down the applicant by making it litigate on several fronts.

10.2.7.4 Unjust prejudice: protecting the applicant's legitimate advantage

In other cases, although the defendant's conduct is not inherently wrongful (or unconscionable *per se*), an injunction has been granted to prevent unjust prejudice to the applicant. The clearest example of an injunction being granted on this ground is *SNI Aerospatiale* v *Lee Kui Jak*.[152] The case arose out of a helicopter crash in Brunei. The defendant was the widow of one of the passengers killed in the accident. The applicant was the French manufacturer of the helicopter. The defendant had brought proceedings in several jurisdictions, including a claim against the defendant in Texas. The applicant sought an order restraining the Texas proceedings. The applicant had served a contribution notice on the Malaysian company which had been responsible for maintenance of the helicopter. That Malaysian company had intimated that it would submit to the courts of Brunei but not Texas. Here Brunei not Texas was the natural forum but that was not in itself enough. Even though there was arguably nothing inherently wrongful or unconscionable in bringing proceedings in Texas, it was oppressive for the defendant to continue those proceedings because of the serious injustice to the applicant in not being able to claim an indemnity in those proceedings. Since undertakings issued by the applicant were sufficient to ensure that any advantage to proceedings in Texas would also be available in Brunei, no injustice would be caused to the defendants by requiring them to litigate in Brunei.[153]

Because the injunction is a form of equitable relief, even if grounds exist for granting relief, a court may decline relief in its discretion, for example, if the application was not timely or if the applicant does not come to the court with clean hands. Even if it is shown that the court has jurisdiction to grant relief, and even if a ground for granting relief is established, the courts retain a discretion not to issue an injunction.[154] The court can also take into account the interests of third parties[155] and other interests of the respondent.[156]

---

[151] [2002] EWCA 524.

[152] [1987] AC 871 (PC). For a recent example, see *Elektrim SA v Vivendi Holdings Corp* [2008] EWCA Civ 1178.

[153] This case demonstrates that there is often an overlap between the categories because it could also be seen as a case where the foreign proceedings became an abuse of process because the respondent had no legitimate interest in pursuing them. This might also be an explanation for Lord Hobhouse's comments in *Turner* v *Grovit* [2002] 1 WLR 107 where he seems to suggest that wrongful conduct is always required. It is unclear if he meant anything more than unconscionable (which can of course be satisfied in a case where even if the defendant's conduct is not inherently wrongful, it is treated as such if it produces unjust consequences).

[154] *Oceanconnect UK Ltd v Angara Maritime Ltd* [2010] EWCA Civ 1050, following *Deutsch Bank AG v Highland Crusader Partners Lp* [2009] EWCA Civ 925. See also *Star Reefers Pool Inc v JFC Group Co Ltd* [2012] EWCA Civ 14.

[155] As in *Donohue* v *Armco* [2002] 1 All ER 749.

[156] As in *Welex AG v Rosa Maritime* [2003] EWCA Civ 938. There the court held that relief would be denied if it would be unjust to the defendant, for example, because it would be deprived of security if prevented from suing in the foreign court because a vessel has been arrested in the foreign court's jurisdiction as security for the claim.

10.2.7.5 Comity and access to justice

The granting of an anti-suit injunction raises two further issues: compliance with the access to justice requirements in Art. 6 ECHR and comity.

Article 6 confers a right to access to justice. Can a respondent who is ordered not to continue with proceedings in another jurisdiction argue that that right is infringed? This issue was considered in *The Kribi*.[157] The judge (Aikens J) held that, although a party is guaranteed a fair trial, Art. 6 ECHR does not provide that a person must also have a free choice of tribunal in which to pursue or defend his civil rights. In other words, Art. 6 does not deal with *where* rights are to be exercised, the crucial point is that they must be exercised *somewhere*. On the facts, the parties had agreed to the exclusive jurisdiction of the English court and it would not deprive them of their Art. 6 right to prevent them from continuing proceedings in Antwerp.

However, that reasoning – that is, that it does not matter where a trial takes place, provided it takes place somewhere – raises an issue which has already been touched on, that is, to what extent is it a requirement that proceedings must be possible in England? It seems from cases like *Aerospatiale* v *Lee Kui Jak*[158] that in cases where the object is to prevent the unjust consequences of litigation (and where the defendant's conduct is not inherently wrongful), the English court should be the natural forum for the claim, but this may not be required in cases of 'wrongful conduct'.[159]

As well as access to justice implications, anti-suit injunctions, which restrain, albeit indirectly, proceedings in another court, clearly also raise issues of comity.[160] In particular, the English court must be satisfied that it is right to interfere rather than leave the foreign court itself to decide, for example, whether another court has jurisdiction under an exclusive jurisdiction agreement or the case is bound to fail.[161] In recent cases, English courts have taken a broader view of comity as deference to the fact that the foreign judge is the best person to decide whether an action in his or her own court should proceed.[162] These difficulties are particularly acute in Brussels I Regulation cases, as explained by the ECJ in its decision in *Turner* v *Grovit*.

---

[157] [2001] 1 Lloyd's Rep 76 at [42].

[158] [1987] AC 871.

[159] As in *Midland Bank* v *Laker Airways* [1986] QB 689. *Cf.* Lord Hobhouse in *Turner* v *Grovit* [2002] 1 WLR 107. In *Ocenconnect UK Ltd* v *Angara Maritime Ltd* [2010] EWCA Civ 1050 the Court of Appeal discharged an injunction on the basis that the judge had overlooked the importance of being able to seek a remedy in Louisiana which was not available in English proceedings.

[160] Comity has been described by the supreme Court of Canada (*Mourguard Investments Ltd* v *De Savoye* [1990] 3 SCR 1077 citing a famous US decision in *Hilton* v *Guyot* 159 US 113 (1895)) in the following terms: 'Comity is the recognition which one nation allows within its territory to the legislative, executive or judicial acts of another nation, having due regard both to international duty and convenience, and to the rights of its own citizens or of other persons who are under the protection of its law.'

[161] *Cf.* the approach taken by the Supreme Court of Canada in the famous case of *Achem Products Inc* v *Workers' Compensation Board* (1993) 102 DLR (4th) 97. There Sopinka J, having referred to the principle of comity, said: 'The result of the application of these principles is that when a foreign court assumes jurisdiction on a basis that generally conforms to our rule of private international law relating to *forum non conveniens*, that decision will be respected and a Canadian court will not purport to make the decision for the foreign court. If, however, a foreign court assumes jurisdiction on a basis that is inconsistent with our rules of private international law and an injustice results to a litigant or 'would-be' litigant in our courts, then the assumption of jurisdiction is inequitable and the party invoking the foreign jurisdiction can be restrained. The foreign court, not having itself observed the rules of comity, cannot expect its decision to be respected on the basis of comity.'

[162] See *Deutsch Bank AG* v *Highland Crusader Partners Lp* [2009] EWCA Civ 925 and *Star Reefers Pool Inc* v *JFC Group Co Ltd* [2012] EWCA Civ 14.

10.2.8 Compatibility of anti-suit injunctions with the Brussels I Regulation

CASE

Turner v Grovit[163]

The claimant applied to the English court for an anti-suit injunction preventing the defendant from pursuing proceedings in Spain. The injunction was granted by the Court of Appeal, which, as has been described above, stated in its judgment that the proceedings in Spain had been brought in bad faith, for the purpose of obstructing the English proceedings. On appeal by the defendant, the House of Lords referred the following question to the ECJ: 'Is it inconsistent with the [Brussels Convention] to grant restraining orders against defendants who are threatening to commence or continue legal proceedings in another Convention country when those defendants are acting in bad faith with the intent and purpose of frustrating or obstructing proceedings properly brought before the English courts?'

The ECJ noted first that 'the Convention is necessarily based on the trust which the Contracting States accord to one another's legal systems and judicial institutions.' The court continued that it is inherent in that principle of mutual trust that the rules on jurisdiction laid down by the Convention may be interpreted and applied equally by the courts of each Contracting State. Furthermore, the Convention does not permit the jurisdiction of a court to be reviewed by a court in another state.[164]

The ECJ rejected the argument that the *in personam* nature of the anti-suit injunction means that it does not involve any assessment of the jurisdiction of the foreign court, holding that an anti-suit injunction does undermine the court's jurisdiction to determine the dispute and is therefore incompatible with the Convention.[165]

The decision of the ECJ in *Turner* v *Grovit*, together with the decision in *Erich Gasser*, discussed above, emphasise that it is always for the court first seised to decide on its own jurisdiction. Together, these decisions appear to give sole control of cases to the court first seised and clearly place a very significant restriction on the ability of the English court to grant anti-suit injunctions to prevent proceedings in another Member State.[166] One important question remained. Could an anti-suit injunction be granted against proceedings in another Member State commenced in breach of an arbitration agreement? This was the issue raised in the *West Tankers* case.

---

[163] [2005] 1 AC 101.

[164] At paras [24]–[26].

[165] At para. [27].

[166] *Turner v Grovit* seems to apply only where the courts of another Member State have jurisdiction under the Brussels I Regulation, not under national law, and only in relation to proceedings in other Member States: *cf.* C. Knight, '*Owusu* and *Turner*: The Shark in the Water' [2007] 66 *CLJ* 288.

CASE

Allianz SpA and Generalo Assicurazoni Generali SpA v West Tankers Inc[167]

This case concerned a charter party expressed to be governed by English law and containing a clause providing for arbitration in London. Arbitration proceedings were commenced in London, but the defendants subsequently commenced proceedings in the courts in Italy. It was accepted that, but for the arbitration agreement, the Italian court would have had jurisdiction under Art. 5(3) of the Brussels I Regulation. The claimant in the arbitration sought a declaration from the English court that the Italian proceedings were in breach of the arbitration agreement and also sought an anti-suit injunction to prevent those proceedings.

When the proceedings reached the House of Lords, their Lordships referred the following question to the ECJ:

> Is it consistent with [the Brussels I Regulation] for a court of a Member State to make an order to restrain a person from commencing or continuing proceedings in another Member State on the ground that such proceedings are in breach of an arbitration agreement?

Any such injunction faced two significant hurdles in the shape of two ECJ cases, *Erich Gasser* and *Turner* v *Grovit*, which have already been discussed. Both decisions were based on the proposition that the Regulation provides a complete set of uniform rules for the allocation of jurisdiction between Member States and that the courts of each Member State have to trust the courts of other Member States to apply those rules correctly. Furthermore, the decision in *Turner* v *Grovit* forbidding the grant of an anti-suit injunction against the courts of another Member State would seem, on the face of it, to be directly applicable: the anti-suit injunction sought was against proceedings commenced in Italy under Art. 5(3) of the Brussels I Regulation. As the court made clear in *Erich Gasser*, as the Italian court was always best placed to consider its own jurisdiction, it was for the Italian court therefore to decide whether or not the arbitration clause applied.

The case accordingly turned on the scope of the arbitration exclusion in Art. 1(2)(d) of the Brussels I Regulation. The opinion of the House of Lords was that, as the proceedings for the anti-suit injunction fell within the exclusion and therefore entirely outside the scope of the Regulation, the English court effectively escaped the constraints of the ECJ case law on the Brussels I Regulation (particularly, *Erich Gasser* and *Turner* v *Grovit*).

The ECJ held first that the English proceedings did not come within the scope of the Regulation,[168] but, despite that, and contrary to the view of the House of Lords, that did not mean they escaped from the Regulation entirely. Although not themselves within the scope of the Brussels I Regulation, the ECJ held that the proceedings had consequences which undermine the Regulation's effectiveness (namely, by preventing the attainment of the objectives of unification of the jurisdiction rules in Member States by preventing another Member State's courts from exercising jurisdiction conferred on

---

[167] Case C-185/07.
[168] Paragraph [23].

it by the Regulation).[169] Because the Italian court had jurisdiction under Art. 5(3) of the Regulation it was for that court to rule on its jurisdiction, including the application of any arbitration exception. Such an order would, the ECJ said, also run counter to the principle of mutual trust which supported the decisions in *Erich Gasser* and *Turner* v *Grovit*.[170] The ECJ was not moved by the argument that because, unlike the position in *Turner* v *Grovit* and *Erich Gasser*, there were no parallel proceedings in Member States, the whole basis of those decisions, that is, preventing irreconcilable judgments, falls away. As will be seen, a similar argument was rejected by the ECJ in *Owusu* v *Jackson*.[171] Both decisions reflect a move towards a wider justification for regulating jurisdiction, namely, the overriding interest of securing a free market by having uniform rules in all Member States.

The ECJ has therefore confirmed that it is not possible to grant an anti-suit injunction against the courts of another Member State, even in support of an arbitration agreement.[172] As discussed above in the context of *Erich Gasser*, this may have important commercial and practical implications. Again it could be argued that the decision undermines the effectiveness of the arbitration agreement. Although in arbitration the effect is less clear cut because the arbitration can continue in parallel, the party with the benefit of an arbitration agreement might still be put to additional expense and delay by having to appear in the courts of another Member State. Furthermore, the expectation that by choosing to arbitrate the parties are contracting out of the constraints of the Brussels I Regulation will arguably be frustrated.[173]

10.2.9 Relationship between the Brussels I Regulation and the common law

The previous sections have outlined the way in which the Brussels I Regulation regulates the existence of jurisdiction, either directly, by setting out grounds of jurisdiction, for example, under Art. 2 or Art. 5, or indirectly, by allowing Member States to apply their traditional rules under Art. 4. We have also seen how the Brussels I Regulation regulates declining jurisdiction where another Member State has exclusive jurisdiction under Arts 22 and 23 or where there are parallel proceedings in another Member State under Arts 27 and 28. The question considered in this section is the extent to which the Brussels I Regulation regulates declining jurisdiction in favour of a *non*-Member State where jurisdiction is derived from the Regulation. This was the issue in the very important case of *Owusu* v *Jackson*.

[169] This argument reflects the *effet utile* principle similar to that relied on by the ECJ in the *Lugano* opinion (Opinion 1/03, request for an opinion pursuant to Art. 300(6) EC made on 5 March 2003 by the Council of the European Union), that is, the objective of unification of the rules of conflicts of jurisdiction for furtherance of the free market.

[170] Paragraphs [24]–[30].

[171] Case C-281/02 [2005] ECR I-1383.

[172] However, relief is possible where an injunction is sought to restrain arbitral proceedings in another Member State because such arbitral proceedings are outside the material scope of the Regulation (see *Claxton Engineering Ltd* v *TXMRTF* [2011] EWHC 345 (Comm)) and where the dispute relates to succession (see *Morris* v *Davies* [2011] EWHC 1272).

[173] In the Wadi Sur [2009] EWCA Civ 1397 [2010] 2 All ER (Comm) 1243 the Court of Appeal held that the judgement of a Spanish Court on the incorporation of an arbitration agreement was binding under the Regulation. This decision seems to have been reversed by Recital 12 to the recast Regulation but the scope and effect of that Revital remains unclear.

CASE

Owusu v Jackson[174]

The claimant, who was domiciled in the UK, had hired a holiday villa in Jamaica from the first defendant, also domiciled in the UK. The claimant suffered severe injuries when he dived from a private beach, accessed via the villa, onto a submerged sandbank. He brought an action in England for damages. The English court had jurisdiction under Art. 2 of the Brussels I Regulation as the defendant was domiciled in England. The defendant invited the judge to decline jurisdiction in favour of the courts of Jamaica on the basis of the doctrine of *forum non conveniens*.

Previously, the Court of Appeal in *Re Harrods (Buenos Aires) Ltd*[175] had famously allowed a stay in similar circumstances. The Court of Appeal there had held that the granting of a stay in such a case does not in any way impair the object of the Convention (expressed in Art. 220 of the Treaty) of securing the enforcement of judgments, since *ex hypothesi* if the English court refuses jurisdiction there will be no judgment of the English court to be enforced in the other Member States.[176] Furthermore, the Court of Appeal held that the Member States were setting up an intra-Community mandatory system of jurisdiction; they were not regulating relations with non-Member States.[177]

However, the Court of Appeal in Owusu decided that the matter was not clear and referred the following two questions to the ECJ:

> (1) Is it inconsistent with the Brussels Convention, where a claimant contends that jurisdiction is founded on Art. 2, for a court of a contracting state to exercise a discretionary power, available under its national law, to decline to hear proceedings brought against a person domiciled in that state in favour of the courts of a non-contracting state, (a) if the jurisdiction of no other contracting state under the 1968 Convention is in issue, (b) if the proceedings have no connecting factors to any other contracting state?
>
> (2) If the answer to question 1(a) or (b) is yes, is it inconsistent in all circumstances or only in some and if so which?

The first question was directed at a stay on 'pure' *forum conveniens* grounds. The second question hinted at other situations where a stay was sought on additional grounds, in particular, that there was a jurisdiction agreement in favour of a non-Member State, where proceedings had already been commenced in favour of a non-Member State (*lis alibi pendens*) or cases where proceedings concerned, for example, land in a non-Member State.

The ECJ began by confirming that Art. 2 engaged on the facts, but the real issue was whether the question of declining Art. 2 jurisdiction in favour of a non-Member State is also within the scope of the uniform rules of the Regulation or not. Although the issue was not clearly addressed in these terms, it is clear from the ECJ's reasoning on Art. 2 that it felt that this issue also fell within the scope of the Regulation. In particular, the ECJ ➡

---

[174] Case C-281/02 [2005] ECR I-1383.
[175] [1992] Ch 72.
[176] *Per* Dillon LJ at p. 97.
[177] *Per* Bingham LJ (adopting the conclusions of Lawrence Collins writing in the *LQR* at (1990) 106 *LQR* 535), at p. 103.

referred to the argument that the Brussels I Regulation was all about the enforcement of judgments between Member States and said:

> The purpose of the fourth indent of Art. 220 of the EC Treaty (now the fourth indent of Art. 293 EC), on the basis of which the member states concluded the Brussels Convention, is to facilitate the working of the common market through the adoption of rules of jurisdiction for disputes relating thereto and through the elimination, as far as is possible, of difficulties concerning the recognition and enforcement of judgments in the territory of the contracting states . . . However, the uniform rules of jurisdiction contained in the Brussels Convention are not intended to apply only to situations in which there is a real and sufficient link with the working of the internal market, by definition involving a number of member states. Suffice it to observe in that regard that the consolidation as such of the rules on conflict of jurisdiction and on the recognition and enforcement of judgments, effected by the Brussels Convention in respect of cases with an international element, is without doubt intended to eliminate obstacles to the functioning of the internal market which may derive from disparities between national legal systems on the subject.[178]

The ECJ concluded that: 'Art. 2 of the Brussels Convention is mandatory in nature, and according to its terms there can be no derogation from the principle it lays down except in the cases expressly provided for by the Convention.'[179] Thus, the ECJ held that there could be no declining jurisdiction derived under Art. 2 of the Convention in favour of a non-Member State because the result would be that the rules of jurisdiction would be applied differently in different Member States. However, the ECJ's decision was limited to the specific facts of the case itself (in other words, stays on 'pure' *forum non conveniens* grounds) because the court declined to answer the second question. This leaves two problems. First, it means that the ECJ did not deal with one of the main grounds relied on by the Court of Appeal in its contrary decision in *Re Harrods* that relations with a non-Member State were obviously not within the contemplated scope of the Brussels I Regulation at all.[180]

It also leaves the problem of what to do in these alternative situations.

In *Owusu*, as has been described, the ECJ held that the English court could not grant a stay on 'pure' *forum conveniens* grounds where it had jurisdiction over the defendant under Art. 2 of the Brussels I Regulation.

However, the implications of this decision remain unclear in two important respects.

First, what if jurisdiction is taken not on the basis of Art. 2, but on some other Regulation ground?

Secondly, what if a stay is sought not on 'pure' *forum conveniens* grounds, but on the basis of an additional factor such as a jurisdiction agreement or *lis alibi pendens*?

Turning to the first of these issues, the question is whether the decision (or at least reasoning) in *Owusu* applies if the court has jurisdiction under another Brussels I Regulation ground, for

---

[178] At paras [33]–[34]. Stating the purposes behind the Regulation in such broad terms, again hints at the *effet utile* justification and at the approach also taken in the *Lugano* opinion referred to above.

[179] At para. [37].

[180] Namely, that the reason there is no reference to declining jurisdiction where, for example, there is a jurisdiction agreement in favour of a non-Member State, is because relations with non-Member States generally were not included within the scope of the Regulation.

example, because the contractual obligation in question was to be performed in England (Art. 5(1)), the defendant domiciled in another Member State has a branch in England (Art. 5(5)) or there is a jurisdiction agreement in favour of England (Art. 23). Is it only Art. 2 which imposes mandatory jurisdiction or will a stay now be prevented in any of these cases?[181] Although the ECJ expressly referred to the 'terms' of Art. 2 being mandatory, it seems likely that the reasoning adopted in *Owusu* will lead to the same result in these cases and that a stay will not be permissible because:

1. the need to apply the Brussels I Regulation heads of jurisdiction uniformly throughout the EU is the same whatever head of jurisdiction is being relied on; and

2. once a claimant has chosen to rely on, say, Art. 5(1), it becomes as mandatory as Art. 2.[182]

The second uncertainty created by the decision in *Owusu* relates to cases where the stay is sought on some additional ground. It is useful to start with cases where there is a jurisdiction agreement in favour of a non-Member State and, in particular, the obiter remarks of Colman J on this very point in *Konkola Copper Mines v Coromin*.[183] In that case, the English court had jurisdiction over English reinsurers on the basis of Art. 2. It was accordingly submitted that the decision in *Owusu* prevented the court from staying those proceedings in order to give effect to a Zambian exclusive jurisdiction clause. Colman J started by noting that, unlike cases where a stay is granted on purely discretionary grounds, there may be a difference where there is an exclusive jurisdiction agreement because Art. 23 of the Regulation reflects an underlying policy to give effect to such jurisdiction agreements. Thus the question becomes why Art. 2 should not yield to an analogous rule where it is a non-Member State which is chosen.

The judge then referred to the decision of the ECJ in *Coreck Maritime Gmbh v Handelsveem BV*.[184] There the ECJ held that a court situated in a Member State must, if it is seised notwithstanding such a jurisdiction clause, assess the validity of the clause according to the applicable law, including conflict of laws rules, where it sits. The ECJ referred to the *Schlosser Report* where it was said that if, when these tests are applied, the agreement is found to be invalid then the jurisdictional provisions of the Brussels Convention become applicable.[185]

---

[181] Some argue that taken to its conclusion, it could be argued that even if the English court has applied its traditional rules of jurisdiction because the defendant was not domiciled in a Member State (that is, the English court 'has jurisdiction' under Art. 4) – because this is jurisdiction 'under' the Brussels I Regulation, a stay is excluded here as well. This point was said by Collins J in *Barros Mattos Junior v Macdaniels* [2005] EWHC 1323 at para. [127] to be an open question.

[182] An exception to this might be jurisdiction founded on a non-exclusive jurisdiction agreement. In *Antec Intl Ltd v Biosafety USA Inc* [2006] EWHC 47 (Comm) the English court had jurisdiction under Art. 23 on the basis of a non-exclusive jurisdiction clause in favour of England. The judge, Gloster J, held that there were in fact no grounds for a stay and that it was therefore not necessary to give a decision on the question of whether or not *Owusu* would apply. However, the judge noted that it could be argued different considerations apply in relation to Art. 23, which is not expressed in the mandatory terms of Art. 2, and that Art. 23 does not impose any requirement upon the court which is identified in the non-exclusive jurisdiction clause to exercise such jurisdiction. See cases based on Art. 5, such as *Gomez ROB v Encarnacion Gomez–Monche Viver* [2008] 3 WLR 309. In the case of exclusive jurisdiction agreements, see *Equitas Ltd v Allstate Insurance Co* [2000] EWHC 1671 and *Skype Technologies SA v Joltid Ltd* [2009] EWHC 2783.

[183] [2005] EWHC 896 (Comm).

[184] Case C-387/98 [2000] ECR I-9337.

[185] Report by Professor Schlosser on the Convention of 9 October 1978 on the Accession of the Kingdom of Denmark, Ireland and the United Kingdom of Great Britain and Northern Ireland to the Convention on Jurisdiction and the enforcement of judgments in Civil and Commercial matters and to the Protocol on its interpretation by the Court of Justice, OJ 1979 C 59, p. 71, para. 176.

Colman J continued that:

> This characteristic of cases involving foreign jurisdiction clauses is, in my judgment, an important feature of such cases which distinguishes them from *forum non conveniens* cases. The Convention by Art. 17 recognises that character of certainty and party autonomy by superimposing it on the domicile rule. The *Schlosser Report* contemplates that the Convention will continue to apply unless the effect of the conflicts rules of the court seised leads to the application of a jurisdiction agreement relating to a non-Member State. However, it does not suggest that the methodology of the local conflicts rules for deciding whether to give effect to the jurisdiction agreement must have any particular characteristic. In particular, there is nothing in *Schlosser* which suggests that it is necessary to evaluate the intrinsic quality of those rules by reference to certainty or predictability of application or to the general objectives of the Convention. It may be that Professor Schlosser had not directed his mind to the fact that under English conflicts rules there was residual discretion whether to enforce perfectly valid and binding jurisdiction agreements . . . by reference to considerations in some respects similar to those applicable to the *forum non conveniens* doctrine. Nevertheless, I do not consider that it is now open either to the English courts or to the ECJ to rewrite *Schlosser* so as to import ground rules analogous to the considerations in *Owusu* which should govern the methodology of the conflicts rules of the court seised. In as much as the Convention is to be interpreted in accordance with the *Schlosser Report*, it is by reference to that construction alone that the English courts need be concerned.[186]

In other words, Colman J indicated that the English court was entitled to apply its own conflicts rules (in England discretionary *forum conveniens* stays) to give effect to a jurisdiction clause in favour of a non-Member State. This is different from the pure *effet réflexe* argument which has been proposed as another solution to the *Owusu* problem. According to that argument, one should read into Art. 23 an equivalent rule for non-Member States. The result is that the regime applies but allows a stay or dismissal under Community law in cases equivalent to those in which a stay or dismissal is permitted between Member States. Practically this could lead to a very different result from that in *Konkola* as the court would apply the Art. 23 rules directly, for example, if the formal requirements are met, and only if, a stay *must* be granted, whereas under the *Konkola* approach, it is for the national conflict of laws rules, whatever they may be, to give effect to the jurisdiction agreement.

It is unclear whether similar arguments will apply to cases analogous to Arts 27 and 28 and Art. 22 of the Brussels I Regulation. It could be argued, by analogy with the approach in *Konkola*, that in such cases, because the Brussels I Regulation itself reflects an underlying policy to cede jurisdiction, when a non-Member State is concerned, Member States can apply national law to produce analogous rules. Alternatively, a full *effet réflexe* argument might again be advocated, that is, to apply Arts 22, 27 and 28 directly as though it were a Member State involved. In *Ferrexpo v Gilson Investments Ltd*[187] Andrew Smith J applied a partial reflexive effect to both Arts 22 and 28, but Art. 27, in particular, may well raise different considerations.[188]

---

[186] Paragraph [99]. See, further, *Masri v Consolidated Contractors International (UK) Ltd* [2008] EWCA Civ 303 [2008] 1 CLC 657 and *Winnetka Trading Corpo v Julius Baer International Ltd* [2009] Bus LR 109.

[187] [2012] EWHC 721 (Comm).

[188] Before *Owusu*, the English courts had suggested that a case involving parallel proceedings abroad was distinguishable from one involving a jurisdiction agreement (see *Arkwright Mutual Insurance v Bryanston Insurance Co Ltd* [1990] 2 Lloyd's Rep 705 at 721). See *Catalyst Investment Group Ltd v Max Lewinsolm* [2009] EWHC 1964 (Ch), where a stay was said to be impossible. *Cf. Lucasfilm Ltd v Ainsworth* [2009] EWCA Civ 1328, *JKN v JCN* [2010] EWHC 843 (Fam) and *Ferrexpo v Gilson Investments Limited* [2012] EWHC 721 (Comm).

The Brussels I Regulation rules about parallel proceedings must be seen against the background of the fact that the Regulation also regulates jurisdiction, which means that all of the Member States have the same jurisdiction rules which they are bound to apply in the same way. When a non-Member State is involved, which is not therefore bound by those same rules, the situation may well be different and it is unlikely that Member States would wish to be bound by an equivalent to Art. 27.[189]

10.3 Choice of law

The conflict of law rules outlined above relating to jurisdiction determine which court can hear a claim. When that court begins to hear the merits of the dispute between the parties, it will need to decide which substantive law it will apply to determine the case. To do so it will need to apply the conflict of law rules relating to choice of law.[190]

The application of choice of law rules involves three stages:[191]

1. It is necessary to characterise the issue that is before the court, for example, is it a matter relating to contract, tort or property?

2. The court must identify the 'connecting factor' for the issue in question. The connecting factor is the rule of (English) conflict of laws that ties the issue before the court to a particular legal system.

3. Having identified the connecting factor, the court must apply it so as to identify the applicable legal system.

10.3.1 Choice of law in contract – the Rome Regulation

If the court characterises the issue as being one in contract (at stage 1 above) it will apply the choice of law rules for contract.

---

[189] It might be possible to deal with Art. 22-type situations in a different way. In particular, in proceedings concerning land in a non-Member State, the English court would not have jurisdiction in any event, this being traditionally an exclusionary rule of jurisdiction not part of *forum non conveniens*. See, further, *Lucasfilm Ltd v Ainsworth* [2009] EWCA 1328 (an appeal to the Supreme Court was decided on different grounds [2011] UKSC 39). In the recast Regulation, Art. 33 provides limited grounds for staying proceedings where an action is pending in a non-member state, but the stay is indiscretionary.

[190] Although the issues sometimes overlap as choice of law questions also often arise in the context of jurisdiction: (i) in some cases the identity of the applicable law is significant, such as, under CPR, 6PD 3.1 (6)(c), as a ground for service out where a claim is made in respect of a contract where the contract 'is governed by English law' (for example, *Bank of Baroda v Vysya Bank Ltd* [1994] 2 Lloyd's Rep 87); and (ii) the content of the applicable law may also be significant – the applicable law may be relevant in determining the validity, interpretation and effect of a jurisdiction agreement or if a claimant has a reasonable prospect of success for the purposes of CPR 6.36 (for example, *Seaconsar Far East Ltd v Bank Markazi Iran* [1994] 1 AC 438); (iii) whether the English court or another court is the *forum conveniens* may also turn on the applicable law; and (iv) it might also be necessary to determine the proper law of a contract for the purposes of ascertaining place of performance under Brussels I Regulation Art. 5(1) (the doctrine *Tessili*).

[191] *MacMillan Inc v Bishopsgate Investment Trust PLC (No 3)* [1996] 1 WLR 387 at 391–392 (*per* Staughton LJ).

First, the court will have to determine which regime applies. There are three choices:

1. the Rome I Regulation which applies from 17 December 2009 to contracts entered into after that date;[192]

2. the Rome Convention on the Law Applicable to Contractual Obligations ('the Rome Convention') concluded in 1980 by the Member States of the European Community and implemented in the UK by the Contracts (Applicable Law) Act 1990, which came into force on 1 April 1991;

3. if neither of those apply, the common law.

The Rome I Regulation is now in force and so this section will concentrate on the rules in that Regulation. The Rome Convention will continue to apply to contracts entered into before 17 December 2009. The common law applies where neither regime is applicable.

The Rome I Regulation applies 'in situations involving a conflict of laws, to contractual obligations in civil and commercial matters' (Art. 1(1)).[193] A broad European approach must be taken to the meaning of 'contractual obligations' and will include some situations which do not give rise to enforceable contractual obligations according to English domestic law, such as gifts.[194]

The Rome I Regulation applies whenever the English court is faced with a question involving choice of law in contract and irrespective of whether or not the law specified is the law of a Member State (Art. 2).

In order to determine what law applies, first, the court must consider if the parties themselves have chosen what law should govern. If they have not, the court must identify with which law the contract is objectively most closely connected.[195]

10.3.1.1 Article 3: express or implied choice

Under the Rome I Regulation, first the court will consider Art. 3, which provides that:

> A contract shall be governed by the law chosen by the parties. The choice shall be made expressly or clearly demonstrated by the terms of the contract or the circumstances of the case.

---

[192] On 17 June 2008, the European Parliament and Council adopted Regulation (EC) No 593/2008 on the law applicable to contractual obligations (Rome I). The UK notified the Commission by a letter dated 24 July 2008, received by the Commission on 30 July 2008, of its intention to accept and participate in the Regulation. On 11 November 2008, the Commission gave a positive opinion to the Council on the request from the UK and on 22 December 2008, the Commission published its decision.

[193] Certain matters are excluded. For example, obligations arising out of family relationships, questions governed by the law of companies, the constitution of trusts and, importantly, arbitration agreements and agreements on choice of court (Art. 1(2)).

[194] *Re Bonacina* [1912] 2 Ch 394.

[195] A similar approach was taken under the Rome Convention and at common law. At common law, the starting point was that every contract was governed by its 'proper law'. When the parties had expressed their intention as to what law should govern, that intention, in general, determined the proper law. When there was no express selection, an intention could be inferred from the terms and nature of the contract and from the general circumstances of the case. Otherwise, the contract was governed by the system of law with which the transaction had its closest and most real connection, in other words through the application of an 'objective test' (*John Lavington Bonython* v *Commonwealth of Australia* [1951] AC 201).

Thus, the parties can and often do *expressly* choose what law will govern the contract and, if they do, the courts will give effect to that choice.[196] For example, the parties might provide that 'this contract shall be governed by English law' or that 'any dispute arising out of this contract shall be decided according to English law'. The parties can also agree to subject the contract to a law other than that which previously governed it (Art. 3(2)) and can select the law applicable to the whole or part only of the contract (Art. 3(1) – referred to as depeçage). Art. 3 goes further than expressing choice, however, and recognises that there may be situations where it can be *implied* that the parties chose a particular law to govern.

10.3.1.2 Examples of implied choice of law

The Giuliano-Lagarde Report, which accompanied the Rome Convention,[197] gave three examples of the sort of factual situations in which a choice of law might be implied:

(a) standard form contracts;

(b) jurisdiction and arbitration clauses;

(c) course of dealing between the parties.

(a) Standard form contracts

The first example given is where the contract is in a standard form which is known to be governed by a particular system of law, even though there is no express statement to this effect. The Report gives as an example a Lloyd's policy of marine insurance.[198] A choice of law is often implied in insurance and reinsurance cases on this basis.[199]

(b) Jurisdiction and arbitration clauses

A choice of jurisdiction is not the same as a choice of law. It is perfectly possible for the parties to provide that the English courts shall have exclusive jurisdiction to hear disputes under a contract, which they also expressly provide is to be governed by French law. The English court would simply apply French law proved as a fact through expert evidence.[200] Similarly,

---

[196] However, the choice must be of a municipal legal system, rather than, for example, a religious law, legal code or the *lex mercatoria*. At common law the parties could not select a 'floating' choice of law (*The Mariannina* [1983] 1 Lloyd's Rep 12 and *Star Shipping AS v China National Foreign Trade Transportation Corp 'The Star Texas'* [1993] 2 Lloyd's Rep 445), although it is unclear whether or not this is permissible under the Regulation.

[197] OJ 1980 C/282/1. The 1990 Act provides that the court may consider the Report when applying the Convention (s. 3(1)(c)). The test under Art. 3 of the Rome I Regulation appears to be stricter in that the choice must be 'clearly demonstrated' (as opposed to 'demonstrated with reasonable certainty') but, provided these strict words are complied with, it is likely that implied choice will be found in the same kinds of cases under the Regulation and that the Report will continue to provide useful guidance.

[198] Note, the parties may simply have intended to incorporate a particular legal provision into the contract, rather than apply the law to the contract as a whole. See, for example, *DR Insurance Co v Central National Insurance Co of Omaha* [1996] 1 Lloyd's Rep 74, where a clause referring to s. 315 of the New York insurance law, was said to be 'indicative of an intention to incorporate the provisions of that section into the contract rather than to render the contract as a whole subject to New York law'. The crucial difference is that if all the parties have done is incorporate a particular provision of law into the contract, that provision becomes a term of the contract and will not change even if the law itself does.

[199] See, at common law, *Amin Rasheed Shipping Corp v Kuwait Insurance Co*, [1984] AC 50, where a marine insurance policy was based on the Lloyd's standard form of marine policy. Also, under Art. 3 of the Rome Convention, *Gan Insurance Co Ltd v Tai Ping Insurance Co Ltd* [1999] ILPr 729, *Kiernan v The Amgen Insurance Co Ltd* [2000] ILPr 517 and *Gard Marine and Energy Ltd v Tunnicliffe* [2010] EWCA Civ 1052.

[200] On the proof of foreign law in English proceedings, see, generally, R. Fentiman, *Foreign Law in English Courts: Pleading, Proof and Choice of Law* (Oxford University Press, Oxford, 1998).

the parties can provide that arbitration occur in London but intend that the contract be governed by a different law, the arbitrator applying that law to determine the merits of the dispute.

However, at common law, one of the strongest indications of an implied choice of law is a choice of forum clause. Assuming that the parties have not provided otherwise, the courts at common law readily assume that the parties must have had in mind that the chosen court or arbitrator would apply its own law.[201]

The Giuliano-Lagarde Report confirms that in some cases the choice of a particular forum may show, in no uncertain manner, that the parties intend the contract to be governed by the law of that forum, albeit that this must always be subject to the other terms of the contract and circumstances of the case. The Report also refers to the possibility that the choice of a place where disputes are to be settled by arbitration may also indicate that the arbitrator should apply the law of that place.[202] The strength of that inference is affected by a number of factors, for example, the presumption is strongest where England has been chosen as a 'neutral' forum; in arbitration cases, the inference will be stronger where, not just the place of arbitration is chosen, but where there is also provision for an English arbitrator or someone familiar with English law or practice or where the parties also provide for arbitration in accordance with the English Arbitration Acts. The presumption will be weaker if the clause applies only to a narrow category of disputes.[203]

A similar inference is likely to be drawn under the Rome I Regulation. Recital 12 states:

> An agreement between the parties to confer on one or more courts or tribunals of a Member State exclusive jurisdiction to determine disputes under the contract should be one of the factors to be taken into account in determining whether a choice of law has been clearly demonstrated.

(c) Course of dealing between the parties

The Giuliano-Lagarde Report refers to two situations where a course of dealing between the parties might be relevant. First, a previous course of dealing between the parties under contracts containing an express choice of law may leave the court in no doubt that the contract in question is to be governed by the law previously chosen, where the choice of law clause has been omitted in circumstances which do not indicate a deliberate change of policy by the parties.[204] Secondly, the Report notes that an express choice of law in related transactions between the *same* parties might lead to an implied choice of law.[205]

10.3.1.3 Other factors not considered in the Giuliano-Lagarde Report

English courts have sometimes drawn an inference as to choice of law from other factors such as the currency and place of payment and from the supposed intention of the parties to create

---

[201] See, for example, *The Komninos S* [1991] 1 Lloyd's Rep 37 and, in relation to arbitration, *Compagnie Tunisienne de Navigation SA* v *Compagnie d'Armament Maritime SA* [1971] AC 572.

[202] The similarity of the Convention test to the common law approach was confirmed in *Egon Odendorff* v *Libera Corp* [1996] 1 Lloyd's Rep 380.

[203] See Jonathan Hurst QC (sitting as a judge of the High Court) in *Travellers' Casualty and Surety Company of Europe Ltd* v *Sun Life Assurance Company of Canada (UK) Ltd* [2004] Lloyd's Rep IR 846.

[204] For example, *Marubeni Hong Kong and South China Ltd* v *Mongolia* [2002] 2 All ER (Comm) 873.

[205] *Attock Cement Co Ltd* v *Romanian Bank* [1989] 1 Lloyd's Rep 572; *Wahda Bank* v *Arab Bank* [1996] 1 Lloyd's Rep 470. See also *Star Reefers Pool* v *JFC* [2010] EWHC 3003 related contracts between very closely connected parties.

or include a valid contract or term (the inference *in favorem negotii*).[206] These sorts of factors are likely to be insufficient (at least on their own) to show a real choice, particularly under the stricter test in the Rome I Regulation, but might support an implication on the grounds discussed above.

10.3.1.4 Article 4: applicable law in the absence of choice

LEGISLATIVE PROVISION

Article 4

(1) To the extent that the law applicable to the contract has not been chosen in accordance with Art. 3 and without prejudice to Arts 5 to 8,[207] the law governing the contract shall be determined as follows:

(a) a contract for the sale of goods shall be governed by the law of the country where the service provider has his habitual residence;

(b) a contract for the provision of services shall be governed by the law of the country where the service provider has his habitual residence . . .

(2) Where the contract is not covered by para. 1 or where the elements of the contract would be covered by more than one of the points (a) to (h) of para. 1, the contract shall be governed by the law of the country where the party required to effect the characteristic performance of the contract has his habitual residence.

(3) Where it is clear from all the circumstances of the case that the contract is manifestly more closely connected with a country other than that indicated in para. 1 or 2, the law of that country shall apply.

(4) Where the law applicable cannot be determined pursuant to paras 1 or 2, the contract shall be governed by the law of the country with which it is most closely connected.

Article 19

(1) For the purposes of this Regulation, the habitual residence of companies and other bodies, corporate or unincorporated, shall be the place of central administration.

The habitual residence of a natural person acting in the course of his business activity shall be his principal place of business.

(2) Where the contract is concluded in the course of the operations of a branch, agency, or other establishment, or if, under the contract, performance is the responsibility of such a branch, agency or establishment, the place where the branch, agency or other establishment is located shall be treated as the place of habitual residence.[208]

The general approach set out in Art. 4 of the Rome I Regulation is similar to that under the Rome Convention: first the court applies the rules set out in Art. 4 to see what law is presumed

---

[206] For example, in the case of contracts of insurance connected with states in which such contracts might be invalid by Muslim law the courts will be ready to infer that the parties would not have intended the contract to have been governed by that system of law (see *Islamic Arab Ins Co v Saudi Egyptian American Reinsurance Co* [1987] 1 Lloyd's Rep 315 at 320).

[207] Special rules apply to contracts of carriage (Art. 5), consumer contracts (Art. 6), insurance contracts (Art. 7) and individual employment contracts (Art. 8).

[208] Rome I Regulation, Arts 4 and 19.

to apply to the contract. Article 4(1) contains a series of presumptions, intended to identify the law with which the contract is most closely connected. Different presumptions apply to different contracts. These presumptions are, however, not conclusive. They can be displaced or disregarded in favour of another more closely connected law (Art. 4(3)).

Under the Rome Convention, the court started with a general presumption in Art. 4(2): it shall be presumed that the contract is most closely connected with the country where the party who is to effect the performance which is characteristic of the contract has, at the time of conclusion of the contract, his habitual residence or, in the case of a body corporate or unincorporated, its central administration. However, if the contract is entered into in the course of that party's trade or profession, that country shall be the country in which the principal place of business is situated or, where, under the terms of the contract, performance is to be effected through a place of business other than the principal place of business, the country in which that other place of business is situated.

Article 4(2) of the Rome Convention envisages a three-stage process:

1. identify the performance which is characteristic of the contract;
2. identify the party who is to effect that performance (that is, the characteristic performer);
3. find the relevant territorial connection for that party.

The presumptions applying to the specific contracts set out in Art. 4(1) of the Rome I Regulation in general reflect the same characteristic performance approach. Thus, the end result will, in most cases, be the same as that reached under the Rome I Convention. The Regulation contains specific rules for a number of different sorts of contract, in particular sales of goods and services, and applies the place of habitual residence of the seller. The seller would also have been the characteristic performer under Art. 4(2)[209] of the Convention and the rules about habitual residence set out in Art. 19 are likely to lead to the same results as the territorial connection applied under Art. 4(2) of the Rome Convention.[210]

10.3.1.5 Disregarding the presumption

It will usually be relatively straightforward to apply the presumptions set out in Art. 4 to arrive at a presumed applicable law. Indeed, the whole point of having presumptions is that they are easy to apply and result in a clear and predictable answer.[211] However, the presumption

---

[209] In a bilateral contract, where the counter-performance takes the form of money, the characteristic performance is that for which the payment is due. The notion of characteristic performance was adopted from Swiss law. Where there are two performances involving the payment of money, the characteristic performer is the party carrying the greater risk (see D'Oliveira *Characteristic Obligation* in the Draft EEC Obligation Convention (1977) 25 *Am J Comp L*, as discussed in C. M. V. Clarkson and J. Hill, *Jaffey on the Conflict of Laws* (3rd edn, Oxford University Press, Oxford, 2006) pp. 215–216).

[210] Although the Regulation refers to the central administration rather than principle place at business, some uncertainty exists as to when the provision relating to branches applies. A relatively clear example is that, in a dispute concerning a bank, the relevant place will be the branch where the account is held (*Sierra Leone Telecommunications Co Ltd v Barclays Bank PLC* [1998] 2 All ER 820 and *Bank of Baroda v Vysya Bank Ltd* [1994] 2 Lloyd's Rep 87). In other cases, however, it was unclear if 'to be effected through' (the test under the Rome Convention) should be construed narrowly as requiring a contractual obligation (see *Ennstone Building Products Ltd v Stanger Ltd* [2002] EWCA Civ 916) *cf. Iran Continental Shelf Oil Co 7 Ors v IRI International Corporation* [2002] EWCA Civ 1024). Under the Rome I Regulation the contract must have been concluded through the branch or performance must be 'the responsibility of' the branch, but again it is unclear whether this means in practice or as a matter of contractual obligation.

[211] One of the early drafts of the Rome I Regulation involved a proposal by the Commission to 'enhance certainty as to the law by converting mere presumptions into fixed rules and abolishing the exception clause'. Thus the presumptions in Art. 4 became rules and there was no way of displacing that rule, but that was very controversial and, in the Rome I Regulation itself, the rules became presumptions again.

can be rebutted under Art. 4(3) in appropriate cases and it is the question of *when* the presumption can be rebutted which is likely to lead to the most difficult problems. Under the Rome Convention, a similar provision applied in Art. 4(5) allowed the court to displace the law of the place of the characteristic performer. This became an area of considerable controversy under the Rome Convention and it is useful to start by considering that debate.

DEBATE BOX

When can the Art. 4 presumptions be displaced in favour of another law?

Essentially, there are three alternative tests. First, and at one extreme, the Art. 4(2) presumption could be given the greatest possible weight, so that it can only be disregarded if the law identified has no real significance as a connecting factor. This was the approach adopted by the Dutch court in *Société Nouvelle des Papeteries de l'Aa SA* v *BV Machine-fabriek BOA*.[212]

Alternatively, and at the other extreme, the court could look at all the factors connecting the contract to various systems of law and, if more point to another country than the country selected under Art. 4(2), then the presumption can be displaced. The presumption thus operates only as a tie-breaker when the laws of two countries are otherwise equally connected.[213]

There are problems with both of the extreme positions. The first test – which gives the presumption the greatest possible weight – serves to deprive the exception of virtually any effect. It will only apply in the most extreme of cases.

By contrast, the second option – which elevates the Art. 4(5) test to one of almost equal standing with the Art. 4(2) presumption – deprives the presumption of almost all effect, so that in every case it will be necessary to consider all the factors in the case and balance those against the law selected by the Art. 4(2) presumption.

Although there is some authority to support both of the extreme positions, a halfway house is likely to be the solution. An approach is needed which accepts that Art. 4(2) will provide the usual rule (thereby giving the presumption some clear role), but that the exception has a greater role to play then merely when the Art. 4(2)-selected law has no real connection with the dispute.

Under the Rome Convention, the English courts did indeed adopt an intermediate model: their approach was that the Art. 4(2) presumption will be applied unless the evidence clearly demonstrates either a preponderance[214] or (more likely) a *clear* preponderance[215] of factors in favour of another country.

The Rome I Regulation also seems to adopt a variation of the intermediate model. Article 4(3) requires that the contract is 'manifestly more closely connected' with another

---

[212] 1992 Nederlands Jurisprudentie 750, noted and discussed by T. H. D. Struycken, 'Some Dutch Reflections on the Rome Convention, Article 4(5)' [1996] *LMCLQ* 18, and J. Hill, 'Choice of Law in Contract under the Rome Convention' [1994] *ICLQ* 325. The strong model was considered by the ECJ in its first case under the Rome Convention, *Intercontainer Interfrigo (ICF)* v *Balhenende* Case C-133/08 [2010] All ER (EC) 1.

[213] See the comments of Hobhouse LJ in *Crédit Lyonnais* v *New Hampshire Insurance Co Ltd* [1997] 2 Lloyd's Rep 1.

[214] *Samcrete Egyptian Engineer and Contractors SAE* v *Land Rover Exports Ltd* [2002] CLC 533.

[215] See *Definitely Maybe (Touring) Ltd* v *Marek Lieberberg Konzertagentur GmbH (No 2)* [2001] 1 WLR 1745, *Caledonia Subsea Ltd* v *Microperi, SRL* 2001 SC 716 (OH), 2003 SC 70 (at paras [36]–[41]) and *Waldwoese Stiftung* v *Lewis* [2004] EWHC 2589.

country. If it had been intended to adopt the strong model, it would have done so explicitly, but it also rejects a weak model and makes it clear that the contract must be *manifestly* more closely connected with another country. One particular situation were the English courts have tended to displace the presumption is where related contracts are governed by a different law.[216] This situation is now expressly recognised in Recital 20 to the Rome I Regulation:

> Where the contract is manifestly more closely connected with a country other than that indicated in Art. 4(1) or (2), an escape clause should provide that the law of that other country is to apply. In order to determine that country, account should be taken, *inter alia*, of whether the contract in question has a very close relationship with another contract or contracts.

10.3.1.6 Scope of the applicable law

Once the court has determined the law applicable to the contract, it will govern most[217] of the substantive questions which arise under the contract. Thus, the existence and validity of a contract, or of any term of a contract, shall be determined by the law which would govern it if the contract or term were valid (Art. 10).[218] The applicable law will therefore govern questions concerning whether or not the parties have reached an agreement at all regarding the existence of a contract. Questions regarding the validity of a contract will include if consideration is required and if there was an intention to create legal relations. It seems that invalidating factors, for instance, whether a contract is void for mistake or voidable for misrepresentation or non-disclosure, will also fall within the scope of Art. 10.[219] Formal validity[220] is also tested according to the applicable law, in that a contract is valid if it satisfies the formal requirements of the applicable law. However, it will also be valid if it satisfies the requirements of the law where it was concluded or where either of the parties was when it was concluded (Arts 11(1) and (2)).

---

[216] For example, in *Samcrete Egypt Engineers and Contractors SAE* v *Land Rover Exports Ltd* [2002] CLC 533 in relation to a guarantee and the underlying contract and in relation to letters of credit in *Marconi Communications Int* v *PT Pan Indonesian Bank Ltd* [2005] EWCA Civ 422, where there was a 'valid reason and commercial logic' why Art. 4(5) should be applied.

[217] Capacity is generally excluded from the scope of the Rome I Regulation (Art. 1(2)(a)). The exception is the rule contained in Art. 13: 'In a contract concluded between persons who are in the same country, a natural person who would have had capacity under the law of that country may invoke his incapacity resulting from the law of another country only if the other party to the contract was aware of that incapacity at the time of the conclusion of the contract or was not aware thereof as a result of negligence.'

[218] There is a proviso contained in Art. 10(2): '. . . a party may rely upon the law of the country in which he has his habitual residence to establish that he did not consent if it appears from the circumstances that it would not be reasonable to determine the effect of his conduct in accordance with the law specified in the preceding paragraph.' See, for an example, *The Egon Oldendorff* v *Liberia Corp* [1995] 2 Lloyd's Rep 64.

[219] See T. M. Yeo, *Choice of Law for Equitable Doctrines* (Oxford University Press, Oxford, 2004) and *Mackender* v *Feldia AG* [1967] 2 QB 590, where the claimant was seeking a declaration that an insurance contract was voidable for non-disclosure because of a failure to disclose alleged smuggling activities. It was held that the question of whether the insurer was entitled to repudiate must be determined by the proper law of the policy. The reasoning in *Gan Insurance Company Ltd* v *Tai Ping Insurance Company Ltd* [1999] ILPr 729 is also consistent with the question of duty of disclosure being governed by the proper law of the contract.

[220] Formal validity, according to the Giuliano-Lagarde Report, includes 'every external manifestation required on the part of a person expressing the will to be legally bound, and in the absence of which such expression of will would not be regarded as fully effective'.

According to Art. 12 of the Rome I Regulation, the applicable law shall also govern:

(a) interpretation;

(b) performance;[221]

(c) within the limits of the powers conferred on the court by its procedural law, the consequences of a total or partial breach of obligations, including the assessment of damages in so far as it is governed by rules of law;

(d) the various ways of extinguishing obligations,[222] and prescription and limitation of actions;[223] and

(e) the consequences of nullity of the contract.[224]

Article 1(3) provides that the Regulation does not apply to evidence and procedure.[225] This is because questions of procedure are governed by the *lex fori*. The difficult question is where to draw the line between procedure and substance.

In *Harding* v *Wealands*,[226] the Court of Appeal had to consider (in the context of a claim in tort) this distinction between questions of substance and procedure. Although there was some support traditionally for a distinction between heads of damage (substance) and assessment of damages (procedure), the majority adopted a narrower view of procedure, that is, that procedure is concerned with matters as to the mode and conduct of the trial. On that basis, the majority in the Court of Appeal held that various statutory provisions of New South Wales law were substantive, including a cap on recovery, limits on recovery for gratuitous care as well as a discount rate and provisions relating to payment of interest and credit for insurance recoveries. The Court gave as examples of areas which would be classified as procedural whether matters were to be assessed by a jury and whether damages can be paid in instalments or in foreign currency. In the House of Lords,[227] however, their Lordships held that the wording of the Private International Law (Miscellaneous Provisions) Act 1995, under which

---

[221] Questions such as where payments are to be made and any time limit within which a claim must be made will all be determined by the applicable law. Other matters covered are the diligence with which the obligation must be performed, the extent to which the obligation can be performed by another person, conditions of performance of the obligation in the case of joint and several or alternative obligations (see the Giuliano Lagarde Report commentary on Art. 12 para. 2). Once again, there is a gloss to this rule. Article 10(2) provides: 'in relation to the manner of performance and the steps to be taken in the event of defective performance regard shall be had to the laws of the country in which performance takes place.' This provision was intended to cover minor details of performance, such as the currency of payment, the rules governing public holidays, the manner in which goods are to be examined and the steps to be taken if they are refused (commentary to Art. 10 para. 3).

[222] The applicable law therefore governs frustration, termination for breach and termination for any other reason, for example, insolvency.

[223] At common law, limitation periods had been seen as procedural and thus applied to all claims brought in English courts, but the Foreign Limitation Periods Act 1984 adopts a general rule that the limitation rules of the governing law are to be applied subject to a public policy-based exception. The same result is achieved in contractual cases by Art. 12(1)(d).

[224] The UK exercised its opt out in relation to this provision in the Rome Convention.

[225] Without prejudice to Art. 18, which provides: '(1) The law governing a contractual obligation under this Regulation shall apply to the extent that, in matters of contractual obligations, it contains rules which raise presumptions of law or determine the burden of proof; (2) a contract or an act intended to have legal effect may be proved by any mode of proof recognised by the law of the forum or by any of the laws referred to in Article 11 under which that contract or act is formally valid, provided that such mode of proof can be administered by the forum.'

[226] [2005] 1 All ER 415.

[227] [2007] 2 AC 1.

the case was decided, codified the old common law distinction between heads of damage and assessment of damage and that only Parliament could change that test. On the basis of that traditional distinction, their Lordships found that all of the rules of New South Wales law went to the assessment of damages and were therefore procedural.

In contract cases, the court will not be bound by the decision of the House of Lords in *Harding* v *Wealands*, which was based on the wording of the 1995 Act (which applies only in tort). Furthermore, under the Rome I Regulation it is clear from Art. 12(1)(c) that the assessment of damages is a matter for the applicable law. Thus it is likely that procedure will be given a very much narrower role than at common law and will be limited to the sort of issues identified by the Court of Appeal in *Harding* v *Wealands*.

10.3.1.7 Displacement of the applicable law: mandatory rules and public policy

The applicable law selected by Arts 3 and 4 may be displaced or supplemented by mandatory rules and/or rules of public policy. The application of mandatory rules is essentially positive in effect, as they will be applied regardless of the law applicable to the contract. By contrast, the use of the doctrine of public policy is essentially negative, as the application of the applicable law may be refused if it is incompatible with public policy.

(a) Mandatory rules

Rules can be mandatory in two different ways. Some rules of law cannot be derogated from by agreement. Because Art. 3 provides an unfettered choice of law, the parties to a contract may use that freedom to escape provisions in the law that would otherwise apply under Art. 4. Generally speaking, they will be permitted to do so, but this type of mandatory rule prevents the parties from excluding their operation in this way because the parties are not permitted (whether by an express choice of law or otherwise), to derogate from that rule.[228] These rules are often referred to as 'non-excludable' mandatory rules.

The second type of mandatory rule goes further and applies to a contract irrespective of the applicable law. In other words, even if the parties have chosen a law other than English law pursuant to Art. 3 *and* English law would *not* be the 'default' law pursuant to Art. 4, the mandatory rule still applies.[229] These rules are often referred to as 'overriding' mandatory rules.

---

[228] An example in English law is the Landlord and Tenant Act 1985, which provides that, in a lease of residential premises for a term of less than seven years, there is an implied statutory covenant to keep the structure and exterior in repair. The Act provides that an agreement which purports to exclude or limit this obligation is void. A choice of law provision is one such exclusion or limitation. In effect, the provisions of the Landlord and Tenant Act will apply if the contract would otherwise be governed by English law, but for an express choice of another law.

[229] An example in English law is the Employment Rights Act 1996, which provides in s. 204(1) that, 'for the purposes of this Act it is immaterial whether the law which (apart from this Act) governs any person's employment is the law of the United Kingdom, or if a part of the United Kingdom, or not'. Another example of an overriding rule, according to the ECJ, is to be found in the Commercial Agents Regulations. In *Ingmar GB Ltd* v *Eaton Leonard Technologies Inc* Case C-381/98 [2000] ECR I-9305, the ECJ, disagreeing with the English High Court, held that the Commercial Agents (Council Directive) Regulations applied to an agency contract entered into between a Californian company and an English agent despite the fact that there was an express choice of Californian law. The ECJ held that the Regulations, the purpose of which is to guarantee certain rights to commercial agents, apply regardless of the law applicable to the contract, where the commercial agent carries on his activity in a Member State.

The two types of mandatory rule are dealt with in different parts of the Rome I Regulation. Article 3(3) deals with non-excludable mandatory rules and provides that, even if the parties have made a valid choice of law:

> Where all the other elements relevant to the situation at the time of the choice are located in a country other than the country whose law has been chosen, the choice of the parties shall not prejudice the application of provisions of the law of that other country which cannot be derogated from by agreement.[230]

Article 3(3) only applies where *all* the elements relevant to the situation at the time of the choice (apart from party choice of law and party choice of jurisdiction) are connected with *one* country only. This is a stringent test, because the presence of a single element pointing to another country will render Art. 3(3) inapplicable.

Under the Rome I Regulation, the parties' choice is also now subject to the new Art. 3(4), which allows for the application of Community law and this cannot be derogated from by contract when all other elements are located in one or more Member States.[231]

Overriding mandatory rules are dealt with in Art. 9.[232] According to Art. 9(2):

> Nothing in this Regulation shall restrict the application of the overriding mandatory provisions of the law of the forum.

Article 9(2) allows the court to apply any rules of its own national law which constitute 'overriding mandatory provisions' (and mirrors a similar provision in Art. 7(2) of the Rome Convention). The Regulation also gives a new definition of 'overriding mandatory provisions' in Art. 9(1):

> Overriding mandatory provisions are provisions the respect for which is regarded as crucial by a country for safeguarding its public interests, such as its political, social or economic organisations, to such an extent that they are applicable to any situation falling within their scope, irrespective of the law otherwise applicable to the contract under this Regulation.

This provision explicitly draws on the decision in *Arblade*[233] where the ECJ applied what seems to be a narrow definition in order to decide if the relevant national legislation could be classified as public order legislation.[234] The question now is if the relevant national law provision is 'crucial for safeguarding the public interest'.[235]

As has been described, Art. 9(2) allows for the application of mandatory rules of *the forum*. Article 9(3) gives limited effect to mandatory rules of *third states*. Article 9(3) provides that:

---

[230] This provision mirrors an almost identical provision in Art. 3(3) of the Rome Convention.

[231] This provision reflects the decision of the ECJ in *Ingmar GB Ltd* v *Eaton Leonard Technologies Inc* Case 381/98 [2000] ECR 9305.

[232] Which replaces the old Art. 7 of the Rome Convention.

[233] Case 369/96 [1998] ECR 8453, para. 31. See the Commission's Explanatory Memorandum (COM (2005) 650, 7.

[234] Under the Rome Convention, it seems to have been assumed that internationally mandatory rules will always be capable of application since in their very nature they represent 'crystallised rules of public policy' of the forum (*Collins, Dicey, Morris and Collins: The Conflict of Laws, op. cit.*, at para. 1–60). *Cf.* R. M. Merkin and A. Rodger, *EC Insurance Law* (Longman, Harlow, 1997), p. 143: mandatory rules constitute a derogation from the principle of free movement of services contained in Art. 59 of the EEC treaty. It would therefore appear that a Member State may designate a rule as mandatory only where this is justified on the grounds either of public policy or the general good.

[235] The decision of the ECJ in *Commission* v *Luxembourg* Case C-319–96 [2008] ECR I-4323, seems to confirm a narrow reading of Arts 9(1) and (2) in this context.

Effect may be given to the overriding mandatory provisions of the law of the country where the obligations arising out of the contract have to be or have been performed, in so far as those overriding mandatory provisions render the performance of the contract unlawful. In considering whether to give effect to those provisions, regard shall be had to their nature and purpose and to the consequences of their application or non-application.

Like the old Art. 7(1) of the Rome Convention this provision envisages the application of a third state's mandatory rules (although in more limited circumstances).[236] This rule, to some extent, reflects the principle in English common law (applied in cases like *Foster* v *Driscoll*[237] and *Regazzoni* v *KC Sethia*)[238] that the court will not enforce a contract which is illegal according to its place of performance. The court is now permitted (but not required) to give direct effect to that foreign law (such as an exchange control law or tax law) which renders performance illegal. In practice, the cases when Art. 9(3) could even potentially apply are likely to be rare.[239]

(b) Public policy

Article 21 of the Rome I Regulation states:

> The application of a provision of the law of any country specified by this Regulation may be refused only if such application is manifestly incompatible with the public policy (*'ordre public'*) of the forum.

This Article allows the English court to disregard a rule of foreign law that would otherwise be applicable, by virtue of Arts 3 or 4, where to apply it would be manifestly incompatible with English public policy. The use of the word 'manifestly' stresses that the exception can only be applied in exceptional circumstances.

A good example is *Royal Boskalis Westminster NV* v *Mountain*.[240] The claimants, five Dutch companies, owned and operated a dredging fleet which was insured against war risks by the defendant insurers. The insurance policy was expressly governed by English law. Two of the claimants formed a joint venture with the Iraqi authorities, that agreement being governed by Iraqi law and providing for arbitration in France. When war broke out the claimants were forced (by threats to use their personnel as part of a 'human shield') to enter into a finalisation agreement in order to secure release of the fleet and its personnel and, as part of that agreement, waived all claims under the joint venture contract. The Court of Appeal held that the finalisation agreement was valid according to Iraqi law, but it would still be open to the arbitrators as a matter of French public policy to refuse to give effect to the finalisation agreement. In the absence of evidence to the contrary it was assumed that English public policy was the same as French public policy in this regard and it was not seriously disputed that the English court would not as a matter of public policy give effect to the agreement. Thus, even though the contract was valid according to its governing Iraqi law, it would be contrary to English public policy to enforce a contract entered into in those circumstances.

---

[236] Article 7(1) did not form a part of English law. The UK, along with Germany, Austria, Luxembourg, Portugal, Latvia, Slovenia and Ireland made use of a reservation to Art. 7(1). The transformation of the Convention into a Regulation does away with reservations.

[237] [1929] 1 KB 470.

[238] [1958] AC 301. These cases are discussed in detail in F. Reynolds, 'Contracts Illegal by the *lex loci solutionis*' (1992) 108 *LQR* 553.

[239] The authors in a recent article noted that, since the Rome Convention came into force, they were aware of no reported cases in which a European court has invoked Art. 7(1) of the Rome Convention (see O. Lando and P. Nielsen, 'The Rome I Regulation' [2008] *CMLR* 1687, 1722).

[240] [1999] QB 674.

Another area where considerations of public policy often arise is that of exchange control, which may render payment under a policy illegal in a particular jurisdiction. If payment is illegal from the outset, this is often referred to as 'initial illegality'. Alternatively, the payment might have been legal when the contract was entered into, but rendered illegal some time later, either when new regulations were made or due to a change in factual circumstances, for example, a change in the exchange rate. This is often referred to as 'supervening illegality'. In the first situation, initial illegality, there is no problem if the contract is governed by the law under which it is illegal; it will not be enforced. Greater difficulties arise if the contract is governed by another law, where no restrictions exist. At common law, the courts refused to enforce such contracts.[241] One explanation is that the courts refused to apply the applicable law of the contract, under which performance was allowed, on the grounds of public policy based on comity and respect for the laws of the place of performance.[242]

Supervening illegality raises rather different questions. Again, if the contract is governed by the law under which it is now illegal, the situation is clear, but if the contract is governed by another law, the answer may well depend on the law of the particular country. In English law, the contract may well have been frustrated, as in the well-known case of *Ralli Bros* v *Compania Naviera Sota y Aznar*.[243] The Court of Appeal held that the charterparty was an English contract but that, as part of the contract dealing with the obligation to pay freight had to be performed in Spain, and as, by the law of Spain, the payment was illegal, that part of the contract was invalid and could not be enforced against the charterers. However, the case is sometimes referred to as a further example of the rule of public policy that the court will not enforce a contract illegal by its place of performance, that is, as being analogous to the comity cases discussed above.[244]

10.3.2 **Choice of law in tort**

If the court characterises the issue in the case as being one in tort, it will need to apply the choice of law rules for tort. Again there is a choice of three regimes:

1. the Rome II Regulation;[245]

2. the Private International Law (Miscellaneous Provisions) Act 1995; and

3. the common law – if neither of the statutory regimes applies, the court will apply the common law and, in particular, defamation is excluded from both regimes and will be governed by the common law.[246]

---

[241] For example, in *Foster* v *Driscoll* [1929] 1 KB 470, a contract for the supply and sale of whisky, which it was intended should be smuggled into the USA in violation of the prohibition laws, was not enforced and, in *Regazzoni* v *KC Sethia (1944) Ltd* [1958] AC 301, a seller in India agreed to sell jute bags to a Swiss buyer, knowing that the buyer intended to redeliver them to South Africa, which would have been an offence under Indian law, so the contract was not enforced.

[242] However, this could also be seen as giving effect to a mandatory law of the place of performance which is now expressly allowed under Art. 9(3) of the Rome I Regulation. The problem under the Rome Convention was that Art. 7(1) did not form a part of English law.

[243] [1920] 2 KB 287.

[244] Again this situation would now also potentially be covered by Art. 9(3) of the Rome I Regulation, under which courts are permitted to apply the mandatory rules of the country of performance.

[245] Regulation No 864/2007 on the law applicable to non-contractual obligations.

[246] Defamation will therefore continue to be governed by the double actionability rule, which means it must be actionable according to English law and the law of the place of the tort (*Phillips* v *Eyre* (1870) LR 6 QB 1). In

The Rome II Regulation came into effect 11 January 2009.[247] It applies in situations involving a conflict of laws in relation to non-contractual obligations (Art. 1). The Regulation applies regardless of whether the law specified is the law of a Member State (Art. 3) or not, and, accordingly, sets out choice of law rules in all non-contractual cases. As in the case of the Rome I Regulation, the definition of non-contractual matters must be given a community meaning. By Art. 2(1) the Regulation extends to 'tort/delict, unjust enrichment, *negotiorum gestio* or *culpa contrahendo*'.[248]

10.3.2.1 The general rule

The general rule is set out in Art. 4.[249]

LEGISLATIVE PROVISION

Article 4

(1) Unless otherwise provided for in this Regulation, the law applicable to a non-contractual obligation arising out of a tort/delict shall be the law of the country in which the damage occurs irrespective of the country in which the event giving rise to the damage occurred and irrespective of the country or countries in which the indirect consequences of that event occur.

(2) However, where the person claimed to be liable and the person sustaining damage both have their habitual residence in the same country at the time when the damage occurs, the law of that country shall apply.

(3) Where it is clear from all the circumstances of the case that the tort/delict is manifestly more closely connected with a country other than that indicated in paras 1 or 2, the law of that other country shall apply. A manifestly closer connection with another country might be based in particular on a pre-existing relationship between the parties, such as a contract, that is closely connected with the tort/delict in question.[250]

As under the Rome I Regulation in relation to contract, the court carries out a two stage process. First it applies a presumption. The tort will be presumed to be governed by the law of the country where the damage occurred (Art. 4(1)), or, in certain circumstances, where the parties have their habitual residence (Art. 4(2)). Secondly, however, in appropriate cases, that law can be displaced in favour of a more closely connected country (Art. 4(3)).

---

defamation cases, that means it must be actionable according to English law and the law of the place where publication occurs (*Bata* v *Bata* [1948] WN 366 and *Church of Scientology* v *Metropolitan Police Commissioner* (1976) 120 Sol J 690), unless the double actionability rule can be displaced (*Red Sea Insurance Co* v *Bouygues SA* [1994] 3 WLR 926).

[247] There was a dispute as to whether it applies to events occurring on or after 20 August 2007 or only after 11 January 2009 when the Regulation came into force. In *Homawoo* v *GMF Assurances* Case C-412/10, the CJEU ruled that the date of application is 11 January 2009, with the consequence that the Regulation applies to events giving rise to damage occurring from that date.

[248] The latter concerns pre-contractual obligations, which the Rome II Regulation deals with in Art. 12.

[249] The Regulation provides special rules for product liability (Art. 5); unfair competition (Art. 6); environmental damages (Art. 7); infringement of intellectual property rights (Art. 8) and industrial action (Art. 9).

[250] Rome II Regulation, Art. 4.

Again, the difficulty is likely to arise in deciding if the presumption can be displaced under Art. 4(3). Again it might be useful to start by considering the approach under the 1995 Act. A similar two-stage approach was set out in the 1995 Act: the tort was presumed to be governed by the law of the country in which the most significant element or elements of the tort occurred (s. 11(2)),[251] but that law could be displaced under s. 12 if it 'appeared from a comparison of the significance of the factors which connected the tort with each country that it was substantially more appropriate that another law should apply to *that issue*' (emphasis added).[252] Various factors assumed particular importance. First, if the place where the tort occurs is fortuitous, it is likely to be easier to displace the presumption, for example, if two friends go on holiday abroad and are injured in an accident there.[253] Similarly, the Rome II Regulation gives one example of when the closer connection might be found, namely where there is a pre-existing relationship between the parties.[254]

Conversely, according to the Court of Appeal in *Harding v Wealands*,[255] it is very unlikely that the general rule would be displaced where it was also the national law of one of the parties. In such a case, it is also unlikely that the tort could be manifestly more closely connected with another country for the purposes of Art. 4(3) of the Rome II Regulation.

At common law, the courts sometimes adopted a version of the US state interests approach,[256] asking if the relevant countries had an interest in their law being applied.[257] It is unclear whether such an analysis was permitted under the Act or would be appropriate under the Rome II Regulation.

According to Art. 14 of the Rome II Regulation, the parties may agree to submit non-contractual obligations to a law of their choice. Neither the common law nor the 1995 Act envisaged such an express or implied choice of law.

10.3.2.2 Scope of the applicable law

By Art. 15, the applicable law governs the following matters:

(a) the basis and extent of liability, including the determination of persons who may be held liable for acts performed by them; (b) the grounds for exemption from liability; any limitation of liability and any division of liability; (c) the existence, the nature and the assessment of damage or the remedy claimed; (d) within the limits of powers conferred on the court by its procedural law, the measures which a court may take to prevent or terminate injury or damage or to ensure the provision of compensation; (e) the question whether a right to claim damages

---

[251] The most significant element was usually that of where the damage occurred – as in *Morin v Bonhams Ltd* [2003] EWCA 1802, where the most significant element of the tort of misrepresentation was where the claimant relied on the representation by bidding for a car in an auction.

[252] Under the 1995 Act, different laws could apply to different issues (see *Smith v Skanska Construction Services Ltd* [2008] EWHC 1776). Article 4 of the Rome II Regulation refers to tort as a whole, although one issue is dealt with separately in Art. 17 in that in assessing a defendant's conduct, regard shall be had to 'rules of safety and conduct' in force where the event causing damage occurred.

[253] As in *Edmunds v Simmonds* [2001] 1 WLR 1003.

[254] Although where the two parties are from the same country (whether or not they have a pre-existing relationship) that law, in any event, will govern rather than the place where the damage occurred under Art. 4(2). It is unclear how Art. 4(2) applies where the claimant shares a country of residence with some but not all of a number of defendants (see, for example, *Alliance Bank JSC v Aguanta Corporation* [2011] EWHC 3281 (Comm)).

[255] [2004] EWCA 1735, *per* Waller LJ.

[256] Set out in the US Restatement Second, Conflict of Laws, ss. 6 and 148.

[257] A good example is *Johnson v Coventry Churchill* [1992] 3 All ER 14.

or a remedy may be transferred, including by inheritance; (f) persons entitled to compensation for damage sustained personally; (g) liability for the acts of another person; (h) the manner in which an obligation may be extinguished and rules of prescription and limitation, including rules relating to the commencement, interruption and suspension of a period of prescription or limitation.

Again the role for procedure will be more limited than that at common law because Art. 15 refers expressly to the assessment of damages as being a matter for the applicable law.[258]

Again the applicable law can be overridden by the forum's mandatory rules (Art. 16) or on grounds of public policy (Art. 26).

10.3.3 **Choice of law in property**

For the purposes of the conflict of laws, property is divided into immoveable and moveable property.[259] Property can also be tangible (land and chattels, for example) or intangible (for example, choses in action such as debts, intellectual property rights or company shares).

The choice of law rule in relation to tangible property, whether moveable or immoveable, is clear. Title to tangible property is determined according to the *lex situs* (the law of the country where the property is situated).[260] Even if property is transferred under a contract, for example, a contract for the sale of goods, the proprietary aspects of the transaction are governed by the *lex situs*, not the law applicable to the contract.

There are a number of reasons for this rule.[261]

1. It reflects the practical realities of the situation. Only the *lex situs* can actually control the way in which property is held. In particular, in the case of land, it is the country where the land is situated which will control the use of the land.

2. Again in the case of land, the rule reflects the sovereignty a country has over its own territory.

3. Application of the *lex situs*, unlike, for example, the law applicable to any underlying contract, will often accord with the expectations of commercial parties and will increase the security of international transactions. Proprietary questions inevitably affect the rights of third parties. It will usually be clear where the goods are situated and there will be no need to investigate the provenance of goods.[262]

4. The *lex situs*, unlike, for example, the law of the domicile of the parties, will also usually point to a single system of law.[263]

---

[258] Which means that it is almost certain that *Harding* v *Wealands* [2007] 2 AC 1 would be decided differently under the Rome II Regulation (*Maher* v *Groupama Grand EST* [2009] EWHC 38 (QB) and *Bacon* v *Nacional Suiza Cia SA* [2010] EWHC 2017 (QB)).

[259] Unlike domestic English law where the division is between personalty and realty.

[260] See, in the case of land, *Nelson* v *Bridport* (1845) 8 Beav 527, and, in the case of moveable tangible property, *Cammell* v *Sewell* (1860) 5 H&N 728 and *Glencore* v *Metro Trading* [2001] 2 Lloyd's Rep 283. Whether the *lex situs* rule is qualified by the doctrine of *renvoi* was considered by Beatson J in *Blue Sky One Ltd* v *Mahan Air* [2010] EWHC 631. It was held that *renvoi* did not apply in cases concerning title to tangible moveable assets.

[261] These justifications are discussed in *Glencore* v *Metro Trading* [2001] 2 Lloyd's Rep 283.

[262] See *Macmillan Inc* v *Bishopsgate Investments PLC* [1996] 1 WLR 387, 400.

[263] This may not be the case where goods are in transit and, for that reason, there is an exception for goods in transit (*Winkworth* v *Christie Manson & Woods* [1980] 1 Ch 496).

As in cases of contract and tort, in exceptional cases, the court might apply the mandatory rules of the forum or may refuse to apply the *lex situs* for reasons of public policy,[264] but otherwise the *lex situs* rule will apply to determine all proprietary questions.[265]

Intangible property poses more difficulties. The *lex situs* will inevitably be a more artificial concept in such cases as intangible property cannot readily be said to have a geographical location. One alternative is to apply the law of the place where enforcement is possible (for example, the law of the debtor's residence), another is to apply the law which creates the interest (for example, the law governing the contract which creates a debt). In the case of rights which can be registered (for example, company shares or trademarks) it is normal to apply the law of the place of the register.

One particular type of transaction, namely the assignment of contractual debts, is dealt with in the Rome I Regulation.

LEGISLATIVE PROVISION

Article 14

(1) The relationship between assignor and assignee[266] under a voluntary assignment or contractual subrogation of a claim against another person (the debtor) shall be governed by the law that applies to the contract between the assignor and assignee under this Regulation.

(2) The law governing the assigned or subrogated claim shall determine its assignability, the relationship between the assignee and the debtor, the conditions under which the assignment or subrogation can be invoked against the debtor and whether the debtor's obligations have been discharged.

(3) The concept of assignment in this Article includes outright transfers of claims, transfers of claims by way of security and pledges or other security rights over claims.[267]

Certain issues are expressly governed by Art. 14. Others, however, are not expressly referred to. For example, the question of perfection of the assignment, that is, the legal requirements which must be satisfied if the assignee is to acquire rights under the assignment. Typically the question is whether, and in what form, notice must be given. This was the issue in *Raiffeisen*

---

[264] See, for example, *Kuwait Airways* v *Iraqi Airways* [2001] 3 WLR 1137.

[265] It has been suggested that there should also be an exception if *lex situs* does not require good faith, but the court in *Glencore* v *Metro Trading* [2001] 2 Lloyd's Rep 282 at 295 doubted that there should be a separate requirement of good faith and preferred to see good faith as being an element of public policy if relevant at all.

[266] Article 12 of the Rome Convention referred to 'the mutual obligations of assignor and assignee'.

[267] Rome I Regulation, Art. 14. Recital 38 provides further that, 'In the context of voluntary assignment, the term "relationship" should make it clear that Article 14(1) also applies to the property aspects of an assignment, as between assignor and assignee, in legal orders where such aspects are treated separately from the aspects under the law of obligations. However, the term "relationship" should not be understood as relating to any relationship that may exist between assignor and assignee. In particular, it should not cover preliminary questions as regards a voluntary assignment or a contractual subrogation. The term should be strictly limited to the aspects which are directly relevant to the voluntary assignment or contractual subrogation in question.'

Zentralbank AG v *Five Star General Trading (The Mount I).*[268] The Court of Appeal held, first, that it was irrelevant whether English lawyers would regard this issue as proprietary (and therefore outside the scope of the Rome I Regulation entirely) or contractual. The characterisation of the issue was an autonomous Community matter. The Court of Appeal then held that, applying that autonomous Community definition, the natural meaning of what is now Art. 14(2) was that it covered the effect of the assignment and therefore the perfection of the assignment. Thus, the question of whether or not notice had to be given was governed by the law of the underlying contract.[269] It remains uncertain if Art. 14 also regulates the issue of priority between competing assignments. The issue was left open in *Raiffeisen* but it is arguable that the same reasoning can be applied. In particular, it should be irrelevant if this issue would be classified as propriety according to national law if, according to its natural meaning (even if not express words), Art. 14 covers the issue. Arguably, questions of priority concern not the relationship between successive assignees but the question in each case of whether or not the debtor should pay a particular assignee. Hence, priority is not a 'separate' issue; rather, it depends on whether or not an assignment has been perfected between debtor and each assignee and is thus also covered by Art. 14(2).[270] Whatever the answer under the current form of Art. 14(2), the whole issue of choice of law in assignment is to be reviewed by the Commission under Art. 27(2) of the Rome I Regulation.[271]

10.4 Enforcement of foreign judgments

If, how and to what extent a judgment of a foreign court will be recognised[272] or enforced[273] by the English court depends on the country where the judgment comes from. There are three broad categories.

1. The easiest to enforce are judgments covered by the *Brussels regime*, that is, judgments from other parts of the UK, other Brussels Regulation states and EFTA states covered by the Lugano Convention.

2. At the other extreme are judgments which are still covered entirely by the *common law*.

---

[268] [2001] 1 Lloyd's Rep 596.

[269] *Cf.* the Supreme Court of the Netherlands in *Brandsma q.q.* v *Hansa Chemie AG, Hoge Raad* Struycken [1998] LMCLQ 345, where it was held that what is now Art. 14(1) governs the proprietary aspects of an assignment.

[270] It seems that Art. 14(1) would not be a possibility in this case as each assignment might be governed by a different law.

[271] The Commission was due to submit a report on Art. 14 by 17 June 2010 but has not yet done so. One issue which might well require consideration is if a different rule is needed in the case of the bulk assignment of debts where it would be impractical if the effect of each assignment was governed by a different law.

[272] Recognition means treating the claim which was adjudicated as having been determined once and for all. A defendant who is successful in foreign proceedings may wish to rely on a foreign judgment as a defence to English proceedings involving the same issue or cause of action. Alternatively, a defendant may seek to rely on a foreign judgment given in the claimant's favour. S. 34 of the Civil Jurisdiction and Judgments Act 1982 provides that no proceedings may be brought by a person in England on a cause of action in respect of which a judgment has been given in his favour in proceedings between the same parties in a foreign court (for example, *Black* v *Yates* [1992] QB 526). The principle of *res judicata* operates in relation to entire causes of action as well as on discrete issues which arise (see, for example, *Carl Zeiss Stiftung* v *Rayner & Keeler Ltd (No 2)* [1967] 1 AC 853).

[273] Not every foreign judgment which is recognised in England can be enforced. To be enforced a foreign judgment must first be recognised. Enforcement of a judgment means actually obtaining the relief awarded.

3. Between those two are judgments from a small number of states which are party to a *bilateral treaty* with the UK, for which the statutory conditions for recognition and enforcement reflect the common law, but which benefit from a simplified procedure for enforcement.

10.4.1 Recognition and enforcement of judgments at common law

A judgment will be recognised at common law if it is:

1. a final and conclusive judgment;[274]

2. for a fixed sum;

3. not being a tax or penalty;[275]

4. of a 'court' which;

5. had 'international jurisdiction' and;

6. as long as there is no defence to its recognition.

The burden in relation to the first five of these requirements is on the party seeking enforcement. If the judgment creditor can satisfy the court that these criteria are met, the foreign judgment is *prima facie* entitled to enforcement. The burden then shifts to the judgment debtor to establish a defence.

Once the judgment creditor has satisfied the court that the judgment is of a kind which is capable of being recognised at common law (the requirements at 1 to 4 above) it must then be shown that the foreign court had jurisdiction over the judgment debtor in the required international sense.

Jurisdiction in the required international sense for the purposes of enforcement can be established on one of two bases:

1. presence/residence of the defendant in that jurisdiction; or

2. submission to the jurisdiction of the judgment court.

10.4.1.1 Sufficient territorial connection

The foreign court will have had jurisdiction in the required sense if, at the time the proceedings were served on the defendant, he was resident[276] and/or present[277] in that jurisdiction. In

---

[274] The fact that a judgment is subject to appeal does not mean it is not final and conclusive, although, in such a case, the English court might stay enforcement proceedings pending the outcome of the appeal (*Colt Industries Inc* v *Sarlie (No 2)* [1966] 3 All ER 85).

[275] For example, in *USA* v *Inkley* [1989] QB 255, the Court of Appeal refused to enforce a judgment granted in Florida relating to a bail appearance bond where the purpose of the enforcement action was the execution of a foreign public law/penal process. A sum is not a penalty in the eyes of English law, even though the foreign law under which it is imposed regards or even describes it as such, if it is payable to a private individual (see *Huntington* v *Atrill* [1893] AC 150 and *SA Consortium General Textiles* v *Sun and Sand* [1978] QB 279. See also *United States Securities and Exchange Commission* v *Manterfield* [2009] EWCA Civ 27, where it was held that part of a judgment in an action brought by US regulatory authorities could be enforced as it sought to return disgorged funds to injured investors.

[276] The question of whether or not residence without presence is enough was expressly left open by the Court of Appeal in *Adams* v *Cape* [1990] Ch 433.

[277] The Court of Appeal in *Adams* v *Cape Industries* [1990] Ch 433 expressed the view that voluntary presence in the jurisdiction would be enough.

the case of a company, rather than looking for mere economic presence, the Court of Appeal in *Adams* v *Cape* set out a test based on physical presence through a place of business.[278] The first defendant, Cape, an English company, presided over a group of subsidiary companies engaged in mining in South Africa and marketing of asbestos. Default judgment was eventually given against the defendant by a court in Texas and the claimants sought to enforce that judgment in England. They argued, *inter alia*, that the Texas court was entitled to take jurisdiction over the defendant by reason of its presence in Illinois through a marketing subsidiary in Illinois when the actions were commenced.[279]

The Court of Appeal held that a corporation was likely to be treated by the English court as present in another country for the purposes of enforcement only where either:

1. such a corporation had established and maintained at its own expense in that other country a fixed place of business and, for more than a minimal period of time, had carried on its own business at or from such premises (a branch office case); or

2. a representative of the overseas corporation had, for more than a minimal period of time, been carrying on the overseas corporation's business in the other country at or from some fixed place of business.

The court further held that, in order to ascertain if a representative had carried on the corporation's business or his own, it would be necessary to investigate his functions and relationship with the overseas corporation and that the following points are likely to be relevant:

1. if the fixed place of business was originally acquired for the purpose of enabling him to act on behalf of the corporation;

2. if the corporation has directly reimbursed him for:

    (a) the cost of his accommodation; or

    (b) the cost of his staff;

3. what other contributions, if any, the corporation makes to the financing of the business carried on by the representative;

4. if the representative is remunerated by reference to transactions, for example, by commission, or by fixed regular payments or some other way;

5. what degree of control the overseas corporation exercises over the running of the business conducted by the representative;

6. whether the representative reserves:

    (a) part of his accommodation; or

    (b) part of his staff

    for conducting business related to the corporation;

---

[278] [1990] Ch 433. See also *Lucasfilm* v *Ainsworth* [2009] EWCA Civ 1328, Reversed in part [2011] UKSC 39, [2012] AC 208, where the Court of Appeal confirmed that it was not sufficient that the defendant was doing Internet business, advertising and making sales in the relevant state.

[279] The debate proceeded on the basis that presence in Illinois would have been enough, even though the judgment court was in Texas. That rested on the fact that the proceedings themselves were federal proceedings. It was accepted that if proceedings had been in a local Texas court, presence in Texas would have been necessary.

7. if the representative displays the corporation's name at his premises or on his stationery and, if so, he does so in such a way as to indicate that he is a representative of the overseas corporation;

8. what business, if any, the representative transacts as principal exclusively on his own behalf;

9. if the representative makes contracts with customers or other third parties in the name of the corporation or otherwise in such a manner as to bind it;

10. if so, whether or not the representative requires specific authority before binding the overseas corporation to contractual obligations.[280]

On the facts of the case itself, the claimants were relying on indirect presence. The question was whether or not the defendant, Cape, was indirectly present in the USA through its subsidiary US marketing company. It was held that, since a substantial part of the subsidiary's business was in every sense its own business, it did not act as an agent of the Cape group. In any event, since it had no general authority to enter into contracts binding Cape and third parties and no such transactions were ever entered into, the defendants were not present in the USA through any subsidiary. In other words, the relationship of principal and agent must be made out and does not exist solely because of the parent–subsidiary nexus. On the facts, the marketing company was carrying on its own rather than the defendant's business.

10.4.1.2 Submission

Submission can take one of three forms.

1. The defendant voluntarily participates in the foreign proceedings. Section 33(1) of the Civil Jurisdiction and Judgments Act 1982 provides:

   (1) for the purposes of determining whether a judgment given by a court of an overseas country should be recognised or enforced in England and Wales or Northern Ireland, the person against whom the judgment was given shall not be regarded as having submitted to the jurisdiction of the court by reason only of the fact that he has appeared (conditionally or otherwise) in the proceedings for all or any one or more of the following purposes, namely:

   (a) to contest the jurisdiction of the court;

   (b) to ask the court to dismiss or stay the proceedings on the ground that the dispute in question should be submitted to arbitration or to the determination of the courts of another country;[281]

   (c) to protect or obtain the release of property seized or threatened with seizure in the proceedings.[282]

---

[280] Although the court made it clear that the list was not exhaustive and that no one single factor is decisive, whether or not the representative is able to contract on behalf of the company is of particular significance, (for example, *Vogel* v *R & A Kohnstamm Ltd* [1973] QB 133).

[281] This overrules the decision in *Henry* v *Geoprosco International* [1976] QB 726 in relation to a stay in favour of arbitration.

[282] This provision safeguards a defendant who is sued in a foreign country whose courts exercise jurisdiction on the ground of the presence of the defendant's property in that country. Such a defendant may enter an appearance to protect his property, but, since this is not regarded as a voluntary appearance, any judgment obtained will not be enforceable in England by virtue of the defendant's participation.

Thus, the defendant will not be held to have submitted,[283] even if he argues the merits of the case, provided that is not inconsistent with also challenging the jurisdiction of the court.[284]

2. The judgment debtor will be held to have submitted to the jurisdiction of a foreign court if he took part in the proceedings as claimant.[285]

3. If the judgment debtor consented to the jurisdiction of the forum in which the judgment was obtained, usually through a jurisdiction agreement.

One of these two heads, presence or submission, must be satisfied. It is not enough, for example, that the foreign court had jurisdiction according to its own rules;[286] that the foreign court exercised a jurisdiction which mirrors that which English law would exercise itself;[287] that the foreign court was the natural forum for the trial; that the debtor was a national of or was domiciled in the relevant country; nor that the cause of action arose in the country of origin.[288]

10.4.1.3 Defences to recognition and enforcement at common law

There are a number of possible defences to enforcement at common law. They can be summarised as follows.

(a) *Natural justice*: the defendant must have had notice of the proceedings and a proper opportunity to present his case.[289]

(b) *Substantial justice*: in *Adams* v *Cape*,[290] the trial judge in the Texas proceedings simply directed that the average award for each claimant should be $75,000 and counsel placed the claimants in four bands according to the seriousness of their injuries. The Court of Appeal indicated that the foreign proceedings offended against English views of 'substantial justice'. In cases involving a claim for unliquidated damages for a tortious wrong, the notion of substantial justice requires the amount of compensation to be assessed objectively by an independent judge, rather than subjectively by or on behalf of the claimant.

(c) *Fraud*: often divided broadly into two categories:

   (i) *fraud on the merits* – for example, that the judgment was obtained by the presentation of evidence which the other party knew to be false; or that the litigant was deprived of the opportunity to take part through trick or threats; or

   (ii) *fraud on the court* – for example, the court has accepted a bribe.

---

[283] In principle, if the foreign court does not characterise the defendant's participation as amounting to an appearance, an English court should not do so either (*Adams* v *Cape Industries* [1990] Ch 433, 461; *The Eastern Trader* [1996] 2 Lloyd's Rep 585). Conversely, it is not sufficient that the judgment debtor submitted in the eyes of the foreign court; it must be shown that the judgement debtor took part in the foreign proceedings in a way accepted by English law as amounting to a voluntary appearance (*Desert Sun Loan Corp* v *Hill* [1996] 2 All ER 847 and *Akande* v *Balfour Beatty Construction Ltd* [1998] ILPr 110).

[284] *Marc Rich & Co AG* v *Società Italiana Impanti PA (No 2)* [1992] 1 Lloyd's Rep 624.

[285] Whether a claimant is taken to submit to any and every counterclaim or not will depend on whether the counterclaim arises out of the same facts or transaction as his claim or out of facts which are reasonably connected. A test of broad common sense applies (*Murthy* v *Sivajothi* [1999] 1 WLR 467).

[286] *Buchanan* v *Rucker* (1808) 9 East 192.

[287] *Schisbsby* v *Westenholz* (1870) LR 6 QB 155.

[288] *Sirdar Gurdyal Singh* v *Rajah of Faridkote* [1894] AC 670.

[289] Cf. *Feyerick* v *Hubbard* (1902) 71 LJKB 509; *Scarpetta* v *Lowenfield* (1911) 27 TLS 509.

[290] [1990] Ch 433.

By way of exception to general principle,[291] the defendant is normally entitled to raise fraud even if the allegations of fraud:

(i) were considered and rejected by the foreign court; or

(ii) could have been raised before the foreign court but were not.[292]

However, fraud cannot be raised again if a finding was made in separate proceedings[293] or where to do so would constitute an abuse of process.[294]

(d) *Public policy*: it might be against public policy to enforce a judgment obtained in breach of an English anti-suit injunction[295] or which was obtained in flagrant breach of the European Convention on Human Rights.[296] It is unlikely, however, that a judgment for punitive damages would be refused recognition on this basis.[297]

(e) *Conflicting judgments*: a prior *English* judgment is a defence not only to subsequent English proceedings but also to the recognition or enforcement of a subsequent foreign judgment. If there are two conflicting *foreign* judgments – both of which satisfy the conditions for recognition and enforcement – the earlier judgment will prevail unless the circumstances are such that the party wishing to rely on the earlier judgment is estopped from doing so.[298]

(f) *Nullity*: if a judgment is invalid under foreign law, in the sense of being a nullity even without its having been set aside by the court, it cannot be recognised or enforced. However, if the judgment is merely voidable it will be recognised and enforced unless and until it is set aside.[299]

(g) *Breach of an agreement*: a judgment obtained in breach of a jurisdiction or arbitration agreement will not be enforced because of s. 32 of the Civil Jurisdiction and Judgments Act 1982.

(1) Subject to the following provisions of this section, a judgment given by a court of an overseas country in any proceedings shall not be recognised or enforced in the United Kingdom if:

(a) the bringing of those proceedings in that court was contrary to an agreement under which the dispute in question was to be settled otherwise than by proceedings in the courts of that country; and

---

[291] The general rule is illustrated by *Israel Discount Bank of New York* v *Hadjipateras* [1983] 3 All ER 129. The defendant sought to resist enforcement of a New York judgment on the basis of undue influence. The Court of Appeal rejected the defence on the ground that the defendant, having failed to raise the issue of undue influence in the New York proceedings, was unable to raise the matter in the English enforcement proceedings.

[292] See *Abouloff* v *Oppenheimer* (1882) 10 QBD 295; *Jet Holdings Inc* v *Patel* [1990] 1 QB 335 and *Owens Bank* v *Bracco* [1992] 2 AC 443. In *Syal* v *Heyward* [1948] 2 KB 443, the Court of Appeal took matters even further by allowing retrial in England notwithstanding that the claimant deliberately refrained from raising in the original trial the facts upon which the allegation of fraud was based.

[293] As in *House of Spring Gardens* v *Waite* [1990] 2 All ER 990.

[294] *Owens Bank* v *Etoile* [1995] 1 WLR 44.

[295] *Philip Alexander Securities* v *Bamberger* [1997] ILPr 73.

[296] *USA* v *Montgomery (No 2)* [2004] 1 WLR 2241. *Cf.* the decision of the Ect HR in *Pelligrini* v *Italy* 20 July 2001, which held that, before an Italian court could recognise a decree annulling a marriage, it was under a duty to satisfy itself that the proceedings before the ecclesiastical courts granting the decree fulfilled the requirements of Art. 6.

[297] See *SA Consortium General Textiles* v *Sun and Sand Agencies* [1978] QB 279.

[298] See *Showlag* v *Mansour* [1995] 1 AC 431.

[299] *SA Consortium General Textiles* v *Sun and Sand Agencies Ltd* [1978] QB 279.

(b) those proceedings were not brought in that court by, or with the agreement of, the person against whom the judgment was given; and

(c) that person did not counterclaim in the proceedings or otherwise submit to the jurisdiction of the court . . .

(2) Subsection (1) does not apply where the agreement referred to in para. (a) of that subsection was illegal, void or unenforceable or was incapable of being performed for reasons not attributable to the fault of the party bringing the proceedings in which the judgment was given.

(3) . . . a court in the United Kingdom shall not be bound by any decision of the overseas court relating to any of the matters mentioned in sub-section (1) and (2).

Thus, if the claimant sues in a foreign court on a contract which contains a provision that the courts of some other country shall have jurisdiction, or that the dispute shall be submitted to arbitration (whether in England or abroad), the ensuing judgment shall normally be refused recognition and enforcement.[300]

(h) *Multiple damages*: the Protection of Trading Interests Act 1980 applies to any judgment given by a court of an overseas country being a judgment for multiple damages (that is, a judgment for an amount arrived at by doubling, trebling, or otherwise multiplying a sum assessed as compensation for the loss or damage sustained by the person in whose favour the judgment is given); or based on a provision or rule of law specified in an order made under the Act. Such judgments shall not by enforced by any court in the UK.[301]

It is *not* a defence to recognition or enforcement that the judgment was wrong on the merits, whether on the facts or the law. It is even immaterial that the foreign court misapplied English law in reaching its decision.[302]

10.4.2 Enforcement under one of the reciprocal statutory regimes

At common law, if the judgment creditor wishes to enforce the judgment he will need to bring an action on the judgment. The action is founded on the judgment and not on the underlying cause of action,[303] but some countries' judgments can be registered and then enforced directly. The Administration of Justice Act 1920, applies to many colonial and Commonwealth territories, for example, Malaysia, Singapore and New Zealand. Provided the judgment can be recognised at common law, a claimant may apply to register the judgment

[300] *Tracomin SA v Sudan Oil Seeds Co Ltd* [1983] 1 WLR 1026.
[301] Clearly the 'multiple damages' part cannot be enforced (s. 5), but it is unclear if the compensatory part of the award can be enforced. The Court of Appeal in *Lewis v Eliades* [2003] EWCA Civ 1758 held that the fact a money judgment was in the form of a single composite judgment should not prevent enforcement of any unexceptional parts which could be readily distinguished, but left open if this principle could be applied to the compensatory part of a multiplied award. The Court of Appeal in *Lucasfilm v Ainsworth* [2009] EWCA Civ 1328 confirmed that the Act only bars the enforcement of the element arising out of the multiplication – the compensatory part remained recoverable.
[302] *Godard v Gray* (1870) LR 6 QB 139.
[303] Section 34, Civil Jurisdiction and Judgments Act 1982.

under the Act. The Foreign Judgments (Reciprocal Enforcement) Act 1933, which superseded the 1920 Act, applies to judgments from Australia and Canada, also Guernsey, Jersey, India and Pakistan. The terms of the Act are very close to the common law, as this stood at the date of enactment, so, in substance, recognition will be according to the rules of the common law. These two statutes allow the applicant to register the judgment for enforcement, it being then of the same force and effect as if it had been an English judgment.

10.4.3 Recognition and enforcement under the Brussels I Regulation

The Brussels I Regulation rules[304] for the enforcement of judgments apply where:

1. the judgment has been given by the courts of a Member State; and
2. it falls within the material scope of the Brussels regime (that is, 'civil and commercial matters') as defined by Art. 1.[305]

It is *not* a requirement that the judgment court took jurisdiction under the Brussels I Regulation provided it is a judgment of a Member State.

Article 33 of the Brussels I Regulation provides that:

A judgment given in a Member State shall be recognised in the other Member States without any special procedure being required.[306]

Article 38 provides that:

(1) A judgment given in a Member State and enforceable in that State shall be enforced in another Member State when, on the application of any interested party, it has been declared enforceable there.

There is no requirement that the judgment should be final and conclusive or for a fixed sum of money.

Chapter II of the Regulation contains a detailed series of provisions regulating the procedure whereby enforcement is to be obtained.[307] In general terms, the procedure can be broken down into a series of elements:

1. the claimant makes an application to the High Court;
2. the court orders enforcement without considering any defences;

---

[304] Similar rules apply under the Lugano Convention to judgments from EFTA states, and the rules also apply to judgments from other parts of the UK.

[305] Although there is no express exclusion of enforcement of penal revenue or other public laws, where payment accrues to the State, rather than to an individual, the likelihood is that the judgment will concern public law questions rather than 'civil or commercial matters' and will therefore fall outside the scope of the Brussels regime altogether. Cf *Realchemie Nederland* v *Bayer* Case C-406/09.

[306] It would seem that judgments so recognised can create both cause of action and issue estoppels. See *Hoffman* v *Krieg* Case C-145/86 [1988] ECR 645, where the ECJ confirmed that a foreign judgment which has been recognised by virtue of the Convention must in principle have the same effects in the state in which enforcement is sought as it does in the state in which judgment was given.

[307] Articles 38–52 and Annexes II–IV. In the recast BIR, this declaratory procedure, often referred to as the exequatur procedure, would be abolished.

3. the enforcement order is served on the judgment debtor who may appeal; and

4. finally, either party may appeal to the Court of Appeal on a point of law.

The grounds on which recognition may be refused are also the grounds for refusing enforcement.[308]

10.4.3.1 Automatic enforcement under the Brussels regime

One of the most important differences from the rules on enforcement at common law is that it is for the original court to ensure that it had jurisdiction, whether according to the bases of jurisdiction laid down in the Regulation itself or according to its traditional rules if the case fell within Art. 4. Article 35(3) of the Brussels I Regulation provides that, 'subject to para. 1, the jurisdiction of the court of the Member State of origin may not be reviewed. The test of public policy referred to in point 1 of Art. 34 may not be applied to the rules relating to jurisdiction.'

The only exception is provided by Art. 35(1) which states that, 'a judgment shall not be recognised if it conflicts with sections 3 [on insurance], 4 [consumer contracts] or 6 [Art. 22 exclusive jurisdiction][309] of Chapter II, or in a case provided for in Art. 72.'

Thus, there is no need to establish the jurisdiction of the judgment court, indeed the enforcing court is usually prevented from even considering that issue. Recognition is automatic unless one of the defences can be established.

10.4.3.2 Defences under the Brussels I Regulation

The defences to enforcement under the Brussels I Regulation are set out in Art. 34.[310]

> **LEGISLATIVE PROVISION**
>
> **Article 34**
>
> A judgment shall not be recognised:
>
> (1) if such recognition is manifestly contrary to public policy in the Member State in which recognition is sought;
>
> (2) where it was given in default of appearance, if the defendant was not served with the document which instituted the proceedings or with an equivalent document in sufficient time and in such a way as to enable him to arrange for his defence, unless the defendant failed to commence proceedings to challenge the judgment when it was possible for him to do so;

---

[308] Article 45 provides that: '(1) the court with which an appeal is lodged . . . shall refuse or revoke a declaration of enforceability only on one of the grounds specified in Articles 34 and 35 . . . (2) Under no circumstances may the foreign judgment be reviewed as to its substance.'

[309] These are the provisions relating to insurance, consumer contracts and Art. 22 exclusive jurisdiction.

[310] In certain respects they are significantly narrower than the defences to enforcement at common law. In particular, there is no equivalent to s. 32 of the Civil Jurisdiction and Judgments Act 1982, where a judgment is obtained in breach of an agreement. Declarations of enforceability can only be challenged on grounds provided by BIR: *Prism Investments v Jaap Anne van der Meer* Case C-139/190.

(3) if it is irreconcilable with a judgment given in a dispute between the same parties in the Member State in which recognition is sought;

(4) if it is irreconcilable with an earlier judgment given in another Member State or in a third state involving the same cause of action and between the same parties, provided that the earlier judgment fulfils the conditions necessary for its recognition in the Member State addressed.[311]

Public policy

A judgment will not be enforced by the English court if it conflicts with English public policy. For example, a judgment will not be enforced where the judgment debtor's right to be defended has been infringed. The test is strict as enforcement will only be prevented if it would be at variance to such a degree with the legal order in the state of enforcement to constitute a manifest breach of public policy.[312]

Although there is no separate defence of fraud under Art. 34, it is generally accepted that, in certain circumstances, a foreign judgment which has been obtained by fraud may be refused recognition or enforcement on the grounds of public policy. However, the defence is likely to be significantly narrower than at common law. In particular, unlike at common law, the issue cannot be raised again if it has already been raised in the foreign proceedings.[313] Where, in support of the case of fraud, the defendant seeks to raise a fresh case or to rely on evidence that was not before the foreign court, the normal approach should be that:

(i) the English court should first consider if a remedy lies in the foreign jurisdiction in question and, if so, it will normally be appropriate to leave the defendant to pursue his remedy in that jurisdiction;

(ii) if not, the English court should not normally entertain a challenge in circumstances where it would not permit a challenge to an English judgment.[314]

Natural justice

Article 34(2) provides for a form of natural justice defence. The following points should be noted about this defence.

(i)   A defendant may rely on Art. 34(2) notwithstanding the fact that the issues which are relevant – service and sufficiency of time – have already been considered by the original

---

[311] Brussels I Regulation, Art. 34. Under the proposal for a recast BIR published on 14.12.10, the public policy defence would be abolished.

[312] *Krombach* v *Bamberski* Case C-7/98 [2000] ECR I-395. A breach of Art. 6 of the ECHR was a valid reason for not enforcing the judgment in *Maronier* v *Larmer* [2003] QB 620 applied in *Merchant International Co Ltd* v *Natsionalna* [2011] EWHC 1820. *Cf. Renault* v *Maxicar* 38/98. In this case the allegation was that the state of origin had erred in applying Community law. The ECJ held that the fact that the alleged error concerns rules of Community law does not alter the position. As the error of law alleged did not constitute a manifest breach of a rule of law regarded as essential in the legal order, the judgment debtor could not rely on public policy as a reason for not enforcing the judgment.

[313] *Interdesco* v *Nullifire* [1992] 1 Lloyd's Rep 180.

[314] The approach of Phillips J in *Interdesco* was approved by the Court of Appeal in *Société d'Informatique Service Réalisation Organisation* v *Ampersand Software BV* [1994] ILPr 55.

court. Even if the original court concludes that the defendant was served in sufficient time, this conclusion is not binding on the court of the country in which recognition and enforcement is sought.

(ii) The defence is available only if the judgment was given 'in default of appearance'. If a defendant appears, even to contest jurisdiction or ask for a postponement, the judgment will not have been given in default of appearance.

(iii) The order may lose its original default character if a subsequent application is made to set it aside but this is dismissed.

(iv) The question of whether or not the defendant had time to prepare his defence is primarily one of fact, not law.

(v) A defendant will lose the defence provided by Art. 34(2) if he fails to take the opportunity to challenge the judgment in the country of origin.[315]

Inconsistent judgments

Article 34(3) applies where recognition of the foreign judgment produces consequences which are incompatible with an *English* judgment in a dispute between the same parties, whether this is handed down earlier or later than the foreign one.[316]

Article 34(4) applies when the English court is faced by conflicting judgments of foreign courts, for example, one granted by a court in New York and the other by the court of a Member State, such as an Italian court. In order to determine if the Italian judgment is entitled to recognition under Chapter III, the court must consider the effect of the New York judgment under the common law and the Italian judgment under the Regulation itself. If both judgments satisfy the conditions for recognition and enforcement under the relevant regime, the English court must give priority to the earlier judgment.

If an 'ordinary appeal' is pending against the judgment in the state of its origin, Art. 37 of the Brussels I Regulation permits, though does not oblige, the recognising court to stay any proceedings in which the issue of recognition will arise. No doubt it will be necessary to make some form of assessment of how likely it is that the judgment will be reversed and the degree of prejudice likely to be suffered if the application is or is not stayed.[317]

---

[315] See *Debaecker* v *Bouwman* Case C-49/84 [1985] ECR 1779; *Denilauler* v *SNC Couchet Frères* Case C-125/79; *Hendrikman* v *Magenta Druck* [1997] QB 426. *Cf. Sonntag* v *Waidmann* Case C-172/91 [1993] ECR I-1963. See also *Marco Gambazzi* v *Daimler Chrysler Canada Inc* Case C-394/07 and *Apostolides* v *Orams* Case C-420/07 [2009] ECR I 3571.

[316] For example, a judgment that a contract was lawfully rescinded is irreconcilable with an order that damages be paid for its breach (*Gubisch Maschinenfabrik* v *Palumbo* Case C-144/86 [1987] ECR 4861). However, a decision that a seller is liable for breach of warranty of quality may not be irreconcilable with a judgment that the buyer was liable to pay the price of goods. See also *Italian Leather* v *Weco* [2000] ILPr 668. The legal concept of irreconcilability must be interpreted independently and this includes the question of whether or not any difference between the two judgments in question affects an area of law which, by virtue of its importance, can justify the application of the provision at all. Thus the court in the enforcing state should be authorised to refrain from applying the provision on the ground that the difference is not serious enough.

[317] See *SISRO* v *Ampersand* [1994] ILPr 55.

Further reading

Briggs, A., *The Conflict of Laws* (2nd edn, Oxford University Press, Oxford, 2008).

Clarkson, C. M. V. and Hill, J., *Jaffeyon The Conflict of Laws* (3rd edn, Oxford University Press, Oxford, 2006).

Fawcett, J., Carruthers, J. and North, P., *Cheshire, North and Fawcett: Private International Law* (14th edn, Oxford University Press, Oxford, 2008).

Hartley, T., *International Commercial Litigation: Text, Cases and Materials on Private International Law* (Cambridge University Press, Cambridge, 2009).

McClean, D. and Beevers, K., *Morris: The Conflict of Laws* (6th edn, Sweet and Maxwell, London, 2005).

For reference

Collins, L. (general ed.), *Dicey, Morris and Collins: The Conflict of Laws* (14th rev. edn, Sweet and Maxwell, London, 2008).

Layton, A. and Mercer, H. *European Civil Practice* (2nd rev. edn, Sweet and Maxwell, London, 2004).

Fentiman, R., *International Commercial Litigation* (Oxford University Press, Oxford, 2010).

Companion Website

For open-access **student resources** specifically written to complement this textbook and support your learning, please visit **www.pearsoned.co.uk/legalupdates**

ON THE WEBSITE

11 Insurance

By Michael Furmston

11.1 Nature of insurance

Most owners of buildings insure them against fire. In such a contract the owner of the building (the insured) agrees to pay a sum of money (the premium) to the insurer who agrees to pay the insured if the building is damaged or destroyed by fire. Contracts of this kind are usually made for a year (though the premium may well be paid monthly), but in many cases they will be renewed year after year. This contract has a number of unusual features. The most obvious is that both insurer and insured hope that the event upon which payment is due (the risk) will never happen and indeed in the majority of cases that is so. A second is that for this to be a sensible business for the insurer he needs to insure a lot of buildings. If he has a big enough pool of risk, some of the buildings will be damaged by fire but if he has set the premium right the payments out will be less than the payments in. Furthermore as the fires are unlikely to all take place at the beginning of the year he will have the use of the money during the year. Normally the insurer will be much better informed than the insured about the risks of fires but some forms of insurance, such as car insurance, are highly competitive which tends to drive premiums down.

11.2 Types of insurance

Broadly speaking nearly every kind of risk can be insured but some particularly important types are worth a brief discussion.

11.2.1 Marine insurance

Historically the insurance of ships and the cargoes carried on them came very early and is still very important. The law relating to marine insurance was codified in the Marine Insurance Act 1906. The rest of insurance law is still common law with some statutory modifications. Marine insurance was important in the development of Lloyd's, still an important player in the insurance industry.

11.2.2 Life insurance

This is also an old form. In straight life insurance the risk is not of course death, which is certain, but how long it will be postponed, which is not. In modern practice there are a is very wide range of possibilities. So for instance a 30-year-old man taking out a 25-year mortgage on his house might insure against his dying during the term. Since he will get nothing if he lives to 55, which is much the most likely possibility, the premium will be small and his family will be covered against the danger of his dying before the mortgage is paid off.

11.2.3 Liability insurance

The examples we have given so far are of loss insurance, where the risk is a loss which the insured will suffer, but in modern practice much insurance is designed to cover liabilities which the insured may incur to other people (what is often called third-party risk). Many policies contain both loss and liability elements. An obvious example is the standard car policy, which typically covers both damage to the car and the driver's potential liability to someone injured by his negligent driving. Nearly all professionals have professional negligence policies to cover them against the risk of being sued for negligence by clients.

11.2.4 Reinsurance

Some of the risks insured are very large. One way to handle this is for several insurers to take shares in the risk. Another is for the insurer itself to reinsure its risk. There are a number of companies which specialise in reinsurance.

11.3 Insurable interest

Suppose A and B agree that A will pay B £10 a month until the Queen dies and that B will pay A £1,000 on the death of the Queen. This would be, in effect, a gamble on how long the Queen would live. In the early 18th century such contracts were common and came to be thought undesirable. Two steps were taken. One was a series of statutes aimed against gambling (the Gaming Acts of 1710, 1738, 1845 and 1892) and the other was the enactment of the Life Assurance Act 1774. The result has been the development of a complex body of rules under which the insured needs to show an interest in the subject matter of the policy. The doctrine operates in different ways in relation to different types of insurance.

11.3.1 Life insurance

In *Dalby* v *India and London Life Assurance Co*[1] the claimant was director of a company which had insured the life of the Duke of Cambridge and which reinsured the risk with the defendant. The original policies were cancelled but the claimant continued to pay the premiums on the reinsurance policy until the death of the Duke. The Court of Exchequer Chamber held both ss 1 and 3 of the 1774 Act were satisfied as the claimant had an interest at the time of taking out the policy. He did not have to show an interest at the date of loss.

A life assured does not have to show an interest in his own life. An interest is presumed in the case of a spouse or of a registered civil partner of the same sex. Probably in modern conditions the same should be said of couples living together.

Outside this area it is necessary to show a pecuniary interest in the life insured. A creditor can, for instance, insure the life of a debtor but only for the amount of the debt. It seems very likely that in practice a good many marginal contracts are made and performed. An important modern decision is *Feasey* v *Sun Life Assurance Corporation of Canada*.[2] A P&I club assured members of the club in respect of their liabilities for personal injury or death suffered by employers of members and others on board their vessels. Originally the club reinsured their liabilities with a Lloyd's syndicate. In 1995 the position was changed and the syndicate agreed to pay a fixed sum to the club in respect of relevant injuries and death. It was held that the club still had an insurable interest.

11.3.2 Property insurance

In *Lucena* v *Craufurd*[3] the Crown Commissioners insured a number of enemy ships which had been captured by British ships but were still on the high seas. A number of the ships were lost before they reached British ports. The House of Lords held, after consulting the judges, that as the relevant statute only gave the commissioners power to take charge of ships when they reached British ports, the commissioners had no interest. A mere expectation was not enough.

[1] (1854) 15 CB 365.
[2] [2003] EWCA Civ 885; [2003] Lloyds Rep 1R 637.
[3] (1806) 2 B&PNR 269.

In *Macaura* v *Northern Assurance Co Ltd*[4] the insured took out a policy on timber, which belonged to a company of which he was the sole shareholder and which was substantially indebted to him. The timber was effectively the only asset of the company. When the timber was destroyed by fire it was held that he had no insurable interest. Obviously he could and should have taken out the policy in the name of the company but the result shows how strict the requirement of a proprietary interest in the property insured is.

11.3.3 Limited interests in property

Someone who has a limited interest in property can certainly insure the limited interest but there are commonly occurring situations where it would be convenient if they could insure the whole interest. In *Hepburn* v *ATomlinson (Hauliers) Ltd*,[5] carriers of goods took out a goods in transit policy, insuring the full value of the goods while they were in transit. The owners of the goods were expressly named. The carriers were clearly entitled to insure their potential liabilities to the owners, but the goods had been stolen without any liability on the carriers. The House of Lords held that the carriers could recover the full value of the goods.

This decision is certainly commercially convenient since it will often be easier for the carrier to insure than the owner. It is not clear how far it goes. In *Petrofina (UK) Ltd* v *Magnaload Ltd*,[6] Lloyd J held that an insurance policy covering work on an extension to an oil refinery taken out by the owner and main contractors to cover all the sub-contractors involved was effective. This is regarded as very convenient by construction lawyers since, if all parties involved are insured by the same insurer, this greatly reduces the scope for disputes, which are endemic in the construction industry, but some insurance lawyers have had doubts.

11.4 Formation

The general rules about formation of contracts apply to insurance contracts. In practice only the rules of offer and acceptance are likely to cause trouble. Insurers often invite the insured to complete a proposal form. The form will usually be an offer and a contract will come into existence when the insurer does something which amounts to an acceptance. The proposal form will usually contain a clause incorporating the insurer's standard conditions for this type of policy. The policy itself will usually come a good deal later.

Policies are often negotiated with the use of intermediaries who may be treated as the agent of the insurer or insured. Intermediaries are not often given authority to bind the insurer to issue a policy but, in certain areas, particularly motor insurance, they are often empowered to issue cover notes, which may well be binding on the insurer. In general, if the insurer, as he often will, gives blank cover notes to an intermediary he gives him apparent authority (*Mackie* v *European Assurance Society*).[7]

---

[4] [1925] AC 619.
[5] [1966] AC 451.
[6] [1984] 1 QB 127.
[7] (1869) 21 LT 102.

The length of the policy must be a matter of construction on the normal principles. The normal expectation will be that a life policy is a single contract for the full term of the policy. Other policies will be for a limited term – most commonly a year, even though there is an expectation of renewal. This is very important because a renewed policy is a new contract with fresh duties of disclosure as discussed below (11.5).

11.5 Non-disclosure

One of the major factors in deciding the premium will be information provided by the insured. In assessing the premium for car insurance for instance, the type of car, the age and gender of the driver and the driving record of the driver all affect the chances of accidents or the costs of repairs after accidents. The insurer will often ask the insured questions for instance by getting him to complete a proposal form. In the case of life insurance, insurers often require the insured to have a medical examination. For this process the normal rules of the law of contract apply. Inaccurate answers may amount to misrepresentation or, if deliberately untruthful, fraud. The proposal form will usually contain provisions as to whether or not statements made by the insured are terms of the contract and, if so, whether or not they are to be treated as conditions. Quite often insurers ask questions which are ambiguous. It appears that if the insured gives a truthful answer to one possible meaning of the question this is sufficient.[8]

However, insurance law has a further doctrine which is not generally applicable to contracts. Insurance is treated as a contract *uberrimae fidei*, of the utmost good faith, imposing on the parties a duty to disclose to the other material facts known to them. This was stated by Lord Mansfield in *Carter* v *Boehm*,[9] where he said:

> Insurance is a contract of speculation. The special facts upon which the contingent chance is to be computed lie most commonly in the knowledge of the assured only; the underwriter trusts to his representation, and proceeds upon confidence that he does not keep back any circumstances in his knowledge to mislead that underwriter into a belief that the circumstance does not exist. The keeping back such circumstance is a fraud, and therefore the policy is void. Although the suppression should happen through mistake, without any fraudulent intention, yet still the underwriter is deceived and the policy is void; because the risqué run is really different from the risqué understood and intended to be run at the time of the agreement . . . The policy would be equally void against the underwriter if he concealed . . . Good faith forbids either party, by concealing what he privately knows, to draw the other into a bargain from the ignorance of the fact, and his believing the contrary.

In principle the duty falls on both parties (see below section 11.5.2), but in practice it falls principally on the insured. Failure to disclose what should have been disclosed makes the contract voidable. This means that if the insured makes a claim and the insurer discovers that there has been failure to disclose, he can simply refuse to pay the claim. Because of the nature of the insurance as a contract, the insurer hardly ever needs to make a claim for damages. The duty of good faith permeates the contract but it is particularly important in relation to

---

[8] See the Authorities usefully collected in *R&R Developments Ltd* v *AXA Insurance UK PLC* [2009] EWHC 2429 (Ch); [2010] 2 All ER (Comm) 527.
[9] (1766) 3 Burr 1905, 1909–1910.

pre-contract disclosure. We shall consider the insured's pre-contract duty of disclosure first, then discuss the duty of the insurer and, finally, consider the position after the contract has been formed.

11.5.1 The insured's duty of disclosure

The duty relates to the period until the contract is formed, but, in contracts with annual renewals, there is a new contract with each renewal. This means that with each renewal there is a need to consider whether or not to disclose events which happened since the last renewal. So, in a car policy where the driver had an accident and did not report it to the insurer because there was no claim, he needs to consider whether or not to disclose it. The insured is obliged to disclose all material facts known to him at the time of entering the contract.

11.5.1.1 The test of materiality

The leading decision is that of the House of Lords in *Pan Atlantic Insurance Co* v *Pine Top Insurance Co Ltd*.[10] A fact is material if it would influence the judgement of a reasonable insurer as to whether or not to accept the risk or what premium to charge or to impose particular terms (for example, an excess – that is, a provision the insured meet the first £X of the claim himself). This test has been long established, but before *Pan Atlantic*, there were different views as to whether or not it was necessary to show that the fact would be decisive or merely that it was something which the reasonable insurer would like to know. The House of Lords decided by 3 to 2 in favour of the latter view. The decision qualified the practical effect of this, however, by requiring it to be shown that the non-disclosure had actually induced the insurer to enter into the contract.

11.5.1.2 Inducement

The potential importance of the inducement test is illustrated by *Drake Insurance PLC* v *Provident Insurance PLC*.[11] This was in fact a dispute between two insurers, both of whom had issued policies, one covering the wife and the other covering the husband's car when driven by the wife. Provident sought to deny liability on the ground that it had not been told of a speeding conviction of the wife. It was accepted that this was material, but, since Provident had a wholly mechanical points system for fixing premiums, it was possible to show that telling them would have made no difference.

Expert evidence by other insurers as to materiality is admissible and in difficult cases is often offered. There are suggestions in *Pan Atlantic* that normally if materiality is established, inducement can be presumed. If this is right, in some cases the insurer may be able to avoid giving evidence on inducement. The insured only has to disclose material facts which he knows and, provided he does not wilfully close his eyes, does not have to disclose what he might have discovered.[12]

---

[10] [1994] 3 All ER 581.
[11] [2003] EWCA Civ 1834; [2004] Lloyds Rep IR 227.
[12] *Joel* v *Law Union and Crown Insurance Company* [1908] 2 KB 863; *Economides* v *Commercial Union Assurance PLC* [1997] 3 All ER 636.

11.5.2 **The Insurer's duty of good faith**

In *Banque Financière de la Cité SA* v *Westgate Insurance Co*[13] the House of Lords held that there was a duty of disclosure on the insurer but that, even if the duty was broken, the only remedy would be avoidance of the insurance policy. This was on the facts, as would usually be the case, a rather unhelpful remedy. It is worth noting that Steyn J, at first instance, had been willing to go much further and find a remedy in damages.

11.5.3 **The continuing duty of good faith**

It is clear that the duty of disclosure comes to an end when the contract is made but it appears that there is some continuing duty of good faith between the parties after the contract is complete. This was stated by the House of Lords in the leading case of *Manifest Shipping Ltd* v *Uni-Polaris Insurance Co. Ltd (The Star Sea)*.[14] The content of this duty is far from clear.

11.5.4 **Reform**

It has been thought for over 50 years that the practical operation of the law on non-disclosure was unsatisfactory. The Law Reform Committee recommended reform in 1957 as did the English Law Commission in 1980 and the National Consumer Council in 1997.[15] In December 2009 the English and Scottish Law Commissions proposed legislation in relation to Consumer Insurance Law. Basically this would give legislative effect to the current practice under the Financial Ombudsman Service and require insurers dealing with consumers to ask clearly for the information they require and not rely on non-disclosure.

11.6 **Subrogation**

Suppose A, the owner of Blackacre, has a fire insurance policy with XYZ insurers. One day B, the owner of Whiteacre, an adjoining property, starts a bonfire in his garden which gets out of hand and burns down A's house. On these facts, A has a claim to recover the value of Blackacre both from XYZ and from B. What happens? The basic principle here is that a policy of fire insurance is one of indemnity, that is, the insured should recover his loss and no more. In practice, in such a case, A is likely to be paid pretty quickly by XYZ and very slowly if at all by B, who will have put the case in the hands of his lawyers or insurers. Once they have paid A, XYZ can claim to be subrogated to A's claim against B – that is, to have control of the action and be entitled to keep the proceeds. The contract of insurance may well contain express powers, but the right of subrogation (unless abandoned) arises from the fact situation.

---

[13] [1991] 2 AC 249.
[14] [2001] UKHL 1; [2001] 2 WLR 170.
[15] See the report of the English and Scottish Law Commission (Law Com 319, Scot Law Com, 21 December 2009).

The operation of the principle is well illustrated by two classic cases. In *Rayner* v *Preston*,[16] P contracted to sell property to R. After the contract had been made but before the conveyance had been completed, the property was destroyed by fire. P insisted on the rule that the risk was on the purchaser from the date of contract and that therefore he could insist on the conveyance being completed and be paid in full. P was also paid by the insurers. R bought a claim for the insurance moneys, but the Court of Appeal held by a majority that R had no right to the money.

In the later case of *Castellain* v *Preston*,[17] it was held that the insurers were entitled to recover the insurance money from P. This result is clearly right as between insurer and insured. No doubt R felt aggrieved, but his solicitor should have advised him to insure from the moment the contracts were exchanged.

These cases exemplify the two general principles that the insured should not make a profit and the insurer should be put in the insured's shoes, but the facts may be more difficult, as is shown by *Lord Napier and Ettrick* v *Hunter*.[18] Here the facts were treated for the purposes of discussion in the House of Lords as being as follows. The claimant was a Lloyd's Name who suffered a net underwriting loss of £160,000 and had stop loss insurance of £100,000 with an excess of £25,000. The stop loss insurer paid the Name £100,000. Subsequently the Name recovered £130,000. The House of Lords held that the key determining factor was that the Name had agreed to bear the first £25,000 himself and that he should therefore pay £95,000, that is $(100,000 + 130,000) - 160,000 + 25,000$.

Insurers may and quite often do, agree to waive their subrogation rights. So the members of the British Insurance Association and Lloyd's who write employer's liability insurance have agreed not to pursue claims in an employer's name against a negligent employee arising out of a claim by a fellow employee, thus reversing in practice the decision of the House of Lords in *Lister* v *Romford Ice & Cold Storage Co. Ltd.*[19]

Further reading

Birds, J., *Birds' Modern Insurance Law* (7th edn, Sweet and Maxwell, London, 2007).

Lowry, J., Rawlings, P. and Merkin, R., *Insurance Law: Doctrines and Principles* (Hart Publishing, Oxford, 2011).

Brooke, H., 'Materiality in Insurance Contracts' [1985] *LMCLQ* 437.

Clarke, M., *Policies and Perceptions of Insurance Law in the Twenty-first Century* (Oxford University Press, Oxford, 2005).

Fleming, J. G., 'Insurer's Breach of Good Faith: A New Tort?' (1992) 108 *LQR* 357.

[16] (1881) 18 Ch D 1.
[17] (1883) 11 QBD 380.
[18] [1993] AC 713.
[19] [1978] AC 18.

Hasson, R. A., 'The Doctrine of Uberrima Fides in Insurance Law: A Critical Evaluation' (1969) 32 *MLR* 615.

Hasson, R. A., 'Misrepresentation and Non-disclosure in Life Insurance: Some Steps Forward' (1975) 38 *MLR* 89.

Hasson, R. A., 'Subrogation in Insurance Law: A Critical Evaluation' (1985) 5 *OJLS* 416.

Kelly, D., 'The Insured's Rights in Relation to the Provision of Information by the Insurer' (1989) 2 *Ins LJ* 45.

McMeel, G., 'The FSA's Insurance Conduct of Business Regime: A Revolution in (Consumer) Insurance Law?' [2005] *LMCLQ* 186.

Yeo, H. Y., 'Of Reciprocity and Remedies: Duty of Disclosure in Insurance Contracts' (1991) 11 *LS* 131.

Companion Website

For open-access **student resources** specifically written to complement this textbook and support your learning, please visit **www.pearsoned.co.uk/legalupdates**

References

Adams, J. E., 'Mortgages and the Consumer Credit Act' (1975) *Conv.* 94.

Adams, J. and MacQueen, H., *Atiyah's Sale of Goods* (12th edn, Pearson Longman, Harlow, 2010).

Ademuni-Odeke, *Law of International Trade* (Blackstone Press, London, 1999).

Aiker, P., 'A Balancing Act' (2006) *NLJ* 974.

Andrews, G. M. and Millett, R., *The Law of Guarantees* (4th edn, Sweet and Maxwell, London, 2005).

Atiyah, P. S., 'Economic Duress and the Overborne Will' (1982) 98 *LQR* 197.

Atiyah, P. S., Adams, J. and MacQueen, H., *The Sale of Goods* (11th edn, Longman, Harlow, 2005).

Atwood, B., Thompson, K. and Willet, C., *Food Law* (Bloomsbury Professional, London, 2009).

Baker, J. H., *An Introduction to Legal History* (3rd edn, Butterworths, London, 1990).

Bamforth, N., 'Unconscionability as a Vitiating Factor' [1987] *LMCLQ* 538.

Barton, C., 'The Enforcement of Hard Bargains' (1987) 103 *MLR* 118.

Bateson, H. D., 'Forms of Mercantile Contracts' [1895] *LQR* 266.

Battersby, G. and Preston, A. D., 'The Concepts of "Property", "Title" and "Owner" Used in the Sale of Goods Act 1893' (1972) 35 *MLR* 268.

Beale, H., 'Legislative Control of Fairness: The Directive on Unfair Terms in Consumer Contracts', in J. Beatson and D. Friedmann (eds), *Good Faith and Fault in Contract Law* (Clarendon Press, Oxford, 1995).

Beale, H., 'The Draft Directive on Consumer Rights and UK Consumer Law: Where Now?', in G. Howells and R. Schultze (eds) *Modernising and Harmonising Consumer Contract Law* (Sellier European Law Publishers, Munich, 2009).

Beale, H., *Chitty on Contracts* (Vol. 2, 30th edn, Sweet and Maxwell, London, 2010).

Beale, H., Bridge, M., Gullifer, L. and Lomnicka, E., *The Law of Security and Title-based Financing* (Oxford University Press, Oxford, 2012).

Beatson, J., 'Duress as a Vitiating Factor in Contract' [1974] *CLJ* 97.

Bell, A. P., *Modern Law of Personal Property in England and Ireland* (Butterworths, London, 1989).

Bennion, F., 'Multiple Agreements under the Consumer Credit Act 1974', in F. Bennion and P. Dobson, *Consumer Credit Encyclopedia*, Doc 1999. 004 Release 49 (at: www.francisbennion.com).

Benson, J., *The Rise of Consumer Society in Britain 1880–1980* (Longman, London, 1994).

Bernitz, U. and Weatherill, S. (eds), *The Regulation of Unfair Commercial Practices Under EC Directive 2005/29: New Rules and New Techniques* (Clarendon Press, Oxford, 2007).

Bigwood, R., 'Undue Influence: "Impaired Consent" or "Wicked Exploitation"' (1996) 16 *OJLS* 503.

Bigwood, R., *Exploitative Contracts* (Oxford University Press, Oxford, 2003).

Birds, J., *Birds' Modern Insurance Law* (7th edn, Sweet and Maxwell, London, 2007).

Birks, P., 'Undue Influence as Wrongful Exploitation' (2004) 120 *LQR* 34.

Birks, P. and Chin, Y., 'On the Nature of Undue Influence', in J. Beatson and D. Friedmann (eds), *Good Faith and Fault in Contract Law* (Clarendon, Oxford, 1995).

Bisping, C., 'The Case Against s. 75 of the Consumer Credit Act 1974 in Credit Card Transactions' (2011) 5 *JBL* 457–474.

Blackaby, N., Partasides, C., Redfern, A. and Hunter, M., *Law and Practice of International Commercial Arbitration* (5th edn, Sweet and Maxwell, London, 2004).

Bradgate, R., *Commercial Law* (3rd edn, Butterworths, London, 2000, p. 510, and 4th edn, Butterworths, London, 2009, p. 590).

Bradgate, R. and Twigg-Flesner, C., *Blackstone's Guide to Consumer Sales and Associated Guarantees* (Oxford University Press, Oxford, 2003).

Bradgate, R. and White, F., 'Sale of Goods Forming Part of a Bulk: Proposals for Reform' [1994] *LMCLQ* 315.

Bridge, M. G., 'The Evolution of Modern Sales Law' [1991] *LMCLQ* 52.

Bridge, M., *Personal Property Law* (3rd edn, Oxford University Press, Oxford, 2002).

Bridge, M., *The International Sale of Goods: Law and Practice* (2nd edn, Oxford University Press, Oxford, 2007).

Bridge, M., 'Reardon Smith Lines Ltd v Yngvar Hansen-Tangen, The Diana Prosperity (1976)', in C. Mitchell and P. Mitchell (eds), *Landmark Cases in the Law of Contract* (Hart Publishing, Oxford, 2008).

Bridge, M., *Sale of Goods* (2nd edn, Oxford University Press, Oxford, 2009).

Briggs, A., *Agreements on Jurisdiction and Choice of Law* (Oxford University Press, Oxford, 2008).

Briggs, A., *The Conflicts of Laws* (2nd edn, Oxford University Press, Oxford, 2008).

Briggs, A. and Rees, P. (eds), *Civil Jurisdiction and Judgments* (5th edn, Informa Law, Abingdon, 2005).

Bright, S., 'Winning the Battle Against Unfair Contract Terms' (2000) 20 *LS* 331.

Brindle, M. and Cox, R. W., *Law of Bank Payments* (4th edn, Sweet and Maxwell, London, 2010).

Britton, W. E., *Handbook on the Law of Bills and Notes* (1943).

Brown, I., *Commercial Law* (Butterworths, Oxford, 2001) pp. 302–304.

Brown, S., 'The Consumer Credit Act 2006: Real Additional Mortgagor Protection?' (2007) *Conv.* 316.

Brown, S., 'Using the Law as Usury Law: Definitions of Usury and Recent Developments in the Regulation of Unfair Charges in Consumer Credit Transactions' (2011) 1 *JBL* 91–118.

Brownsword, R., *Contract Law: Themes for the Twenty-first Century* (2nd edn, Oxford University Press, Oxford, 2006).

Bruce, J., McDonald, D. and McGarrigle, M., 'Unfairness as Justice' (2011) 40 *ColJ* 14–17.

Brooke, H., 'Materiality in Insurance Contracts' [1985] *LMCLQ* 437.

Buhring-Uhle, C., Kirchhorff, L. and Scherer, G., *Arbitration and Mediation in International Business* (2nd edn, Kluwer Law International, The Netherlands, 2006).

Burns, T., 'Better Late than Never: The Reform of the Law on the Sale of Goods Forming Part of a Bulk' [1996] MLR 260.

Capper, D., 'Unconscionable Bargains and Unconscionable Gifts' [1996] 60 *Conv.* 308.

Capper, D., 'Undue Influence and Unconscionability: A Rationalisation' (1998) 114 *LQR* 479.

Carter, R., 'Statutory Interpretation Using Legislated Examples: Bennion on Multiple Consumer Agreements' (2011) 32(2) *Stat LR* 86–115.

Cartwright, J., *Unequal Bargaining: A Study of Vitiating Factors in the Formation of Contracts* (Clarendon Press, Oxford, 1991).

Cartwright, J., 'An Unconscionable Bargain' (1993) 109 *LQR* 530.

Chandler, A., Devenney, J. and Poole, J., 'Common Mistake: Theoretical Justification and Remedial Inflexibility' [2004] *JBL* 34.

Chen-Wishart, M., *Unconscionable Bargains* (Butterworths, Sydney, 1989).

Chen-Wishart, M., 'The O'Brien Principle and Substantive Unfairness' [1997] *CLJ* 60.

Chen-Wishart, M., 'Undue Influence: Beyond Impaired Consent and Wrongdoing Towards a Relational Analysis', in A. Burrows and A. Rodger (eds), *Mapping the Law: Essays in Memory of Peter Birks* (Oxford University Press, Oxford, 2006) p. 208.

Chuah, J., 'Documentary Credits and Illegality in the Underlying, Transaction [2003] 9 *JIML* 518.

Chuah, J., *Law of International Trade: Cross-border Commercial Transactions* (4th edn, Sweet and Maxwell, London, 2009).

Chuah, J., 'Third-party Processing in Credit Card Arrangements' (2009) *F&CL* 4–6.

Clarke, M., *Policies and Perceptions of Insurance Law in the Twenty-first Century* (Oxford University Press, Oxford, 2005).

Clarkson, C. M. V. and Hill, J., *Jaffey on The Conflict of Laws* (3rd edn, Oxford University Press, Oxford, 2006).

Collins, H. (ed.), *The Forthcoming EC Directive on Unfair Commercial Practices: Contract, Consumer and Competition Law Implications* (Kluwer Law International, Oxford, 2004).

Collins, L. (general ed.), *Dicey, Morris and Collins: The Conflict of Laws* (14th edn, Sweet and Maxwell, London, 2006).

Colombi Ciacchi, A., 'Non-legislative Harmonisation of Private Law under the European Constitution: The Case of Unfair Suretyships' (2005) 13 *ERPL* 297.

Cope, M., *Duress, Undue Influence and Unconscientious Bargains* (The Law Book Company Ltd, Sydney, 1985).

Cresswees, Blain Hill, Wood et al., Encyclopaedia of Banking Law, (lonelay from 1996) Butterworths, Lexisneres, London).

Dale, R., Controlling Foreign Settlement Risks' (1999) 14 *BFLR* 329.

Daniel, J. W., A Treatise on the Law of Negotiable Instruments (1933).

Davidson, F., 'Some Thoughts on the Draft Arbitration (Scotland) Bill' (2009) *JBL* 44.

Davidson 'The Missing Link Transaction' (1980) 96 *LQR* 343.

Davies, I., *Effective Retention of Title* (Fourmat Publishing, London, 1991).

Dawson, J. P., 'Economic Duress: An Essay in Perspective' (1947) 45 *Michigan Law Review* 253.

Debattista, C., 'Legislative Techniques in International Trade: Madness of Method?' [2002] *JBL* 626.

Devenney, J., 'A Pack of Unruly Dogs: Unconscionable Bargains, Lawful Act (Economic) Duress and Clogs on the Equity of Redemption' [2002] *JBL* 539.

Devenney, J., 'An Analytical Deconstruction of the Unconscionable Bargain Doetrine in England and Wales' (University of Wales Unpublished PhD thesis, Cardiff, 2003) pp. 1–7.

Devenney, J. and Chandler, A., 'Unconscionability and the Taxonomy of Undue Influence' [2007] *JBL* 541.

Devenney, J. and Kenny, M., 'Unfair Terms, Surety Transactions and European Harmonisation: A Crucible of Europeanised Private Law?' [2009] *Conv.* 295.

Devenney, J. and Kenny, M. *Consumer Credit, Debt and Investment in Europe* (Cambridge University Press, Cambridge, 2012).

Devenney, J. and Ryder, N. 'The Cartography of the Concept of "Total Charge for Credit" under the Consumer Credit Act 1974' [2006] *Conv.* 475.

Devenney, J., Fox O'Mahony, L. and Kenny, M., 'Standing Surety in England and Wales: The Sphinx of Procedural Protection' (2008) *LMCLQ* 527.

Devenney, J., Kenny, M. and Fox O'Mahoney, L., 'England and Wales', in A. Columbi-Ciacchi and S. Weatherill (eds), *Regulating Unfair Banking Practices in Europe: The Case of Personal Suretyships* (Oxford University Press, Oxford, 2010).

Devlin, P., 'Relation Between Commercial Law and Commercial Practice' [1951] *MLR* 249.

Diamond, A. L., *A Review of Security Interests in Property* (DTI, London, 1989).

Disney, R., Bridges, S. and Gathergood, J., *Drivers of Over-indebtedness* (Centre for Policy Evaluation, University of Nottingham, October 2008).

Dobson, P. 'The Consumer's Right to Reject: A Sacred Cow?' (2009) SLR 57(1).

Donnelly, K. 'Nothing for Nothing: A Nullity Exception in Letters of Credit' [2008] *JBL* 316.

Draffin, N., *An Introduction to Bunkering* (Petrospot Adderbury, 2008).

Dwnn, A., '"Footprints on the Sands of Time": Sections 129 and 136 Consumer Credit Act 1974' (1996) *Conv* 209.

Ellinger, E. P., 'Travellers' Cheques and the Law' (1969) 19 *Univ of Toronto LJ* 132.

Ellinger, E. P., Lomnicka, E. and Hare, C., *Ellinger's Modern Banking Law* (5th edn, Oxford University Press, Oxford, 2010).

Elliott, N., Odgers, R. and Phillips, J. M., *Byles on Bills of Exchange and Cheques* (28th edn, Sweet and Maxwell, London, 2007).

Emery, C. T., 'The Date Fixed for Completion' [1978] *Conv* 144.

Enonchong, N., *Duress, Undue Influence and Unconscionable Dealing* (Sweet and Maxwell, London, 2006).

Enonchong, N., *The Independence Principle of Letters of Credit and Demand Guarantees* (Oxford University Press, Oxford, 2011).

Fawcett, J., Carruthers, J. and North, P., *Cheshire, North and Fawcett: Private International Law* (14th edn, Oxford University Press, Oxford, 2008).

Fehlberg, B., 'The Husband, the Bank, the Wife and Her Signature – The Sequel' (1996) 59 *MLR* 675.

Fehlberg, B., *Sexually Transmitted Debt* (Clarendon Press, Oxford, 1997).

Fentiman, R., *Foreign Law in English Courts: Pleading, Proof and Choice of Law* (Oxford University Press, Oxford, 1998).

Fentiman, R., '*Erich Gasser GmbH v MISAT Srl*' (2005) *CMLR* 241.

Fentiman, R., 'Jurisdiction Agreements and Forum Shopping in Europe' (2006) *JIBFL* 304.

Fentiman, R., *International Commercial Litigation* (Oxford University Press, Oxford, 2010).

Fentiman, R., 'Brussels I and Third States: Future Imperfeet?' [2010–2011] 13 CYELS 65.

Finlay, A., 'Can We See the Chancellor's Footprint?' (1999) 14 *JCL* 265.

Fleming, J. G., 'Insurers' Breach of Faith: A New Port?' (1992) 108 *LQR* 357.

Fox, D., *Property Rights in Money* (Oxford University Press, Oxford, 2008).

Fox O'Mahony, L., *Conceptualising Home: Theories, Laws and Policies* (Hart Publishing, Oxford, 2006).

Fox O'Mahony, L. and Devenney, J., 'The Elderly, Their Homes and the Unconscionable Bargain Doctrine', in M. Dixon (ed.), *Modern Studies in Property Law* (Vol. 5, Hart Publishing, Oxford, 2009).

Frohlich 'Travellers' Cheque and the Law in Australia', (1980) 54 *ALJ* 388.

Fuller, L. L. and Purdue Jr, W. R., 'The Reliance Interest in Contract Damages' (1936) 46 *Yate LJ* 52.

Furmston, M. P., *The Law of Contract* (4th edn, Butterworths, London, 2010).

Furmston, M. P., *Cheshire, Fifoot and Furmston's Law of Contract* (16th edn, Oxford University Press, Oxford, 2012).

Goode, R. M., 'Ownership and Obligation in Commercial Transactions' (1987) 103 *LQR* 433.

Goode, R., *Commercial Law in the Next Millennium* (Sweet and Maxwell, London, 1998).

Goode, R. (ed.), *Consumer Credit Law and Practice* (Butterworths, London, 1999).

Goode, R. M., 'Removing the Obstacles to Commercial Law Reform' (2007) 123 *LQR* 602.

Goode, R., *Commercial Law* (3rd edn, Penguin, London, 2004; 4th edn, Penguin, London, 2010).

Goldberg, R. 'Paying for Bad Blood: Strict Product Liability after the Hepatitis C Litigation' (2002) *MLR* 165.

Grant, D. and Mason, S., *Holiday Law: The Law Relating to Travel and Tourism* (4th edn, Sweet and Maxwell, London, 2007).

Grant and Urbanowicz, 'Tour Operators, Package Holiday Contracts and Strict Liability' (2001) *JBL* 253.

Griffiths, M., 'Consumer Credit Advertising: Transparent At Last?' (2006) 11(3) *Comms L* 75–84.

Guest, A. G. (gen. ed.), Benjamin's Sale of Goods (7th rev. edn, Sweet and Maxwell, 2006).

Guest, A. G., *Chalmers and Guest on Bills of Exchange, Cheques and Promissory Notes* (17th edn, Sweet and Maxwell, London, 2009).

Guest, A. G., *Chitty on Contracts* (30th edn, Sweet and Maxwell, London, 2009).

Hardingham, I. J., 'The High Court of Australia and Unconscionable Dealing' (1984) 4 *OJLS* 275.

Hare, C., 'Credit Cards and Connected Lender Liability' (2008) 3 *LMCLQ* 333–352.

Hartley, T. C., 'The European Union and the Systematic Dismantling of the Common Law of the Conflict of Laws' [2005] *ICLQ* 813.

Hartley, T., *International Commercial Litigation: Text, Cases and Materials on Private International Law* (Cambridge University Press, Cambridge, 2009).

Hasson, R. A., 'The Doctrine of Uberrima Fides in Insurance Law: A Critical Evaluation' (1969) 32 *MLR* 615.

Hasson, R. A., 'Misrepresentation and Non-disclosure in Life Insurance: Some Steps Forward' (1975) 38 *MLR* 89.

Hasson, R. A., 'Subrogation in Insurance Law: A Critical Evaluation' (1985) 5 *OJLS* 416.

Hedley, W., *Bills of Exchange and Bankers' Documentary Credits* (4th edn, LLP, London, 2001).

Hill, J., 'Choice of Law in Contract under the Rome Convention' [1994] *ICLQ* 325.

Honoré, A. M., 'Ownership', in Guest, A. G., (ed.), *Oxford Essays in Jurisprudence: A Collaborative Work* (Oxford University Press, Oxford, 1961).

Honoré, A. M., 'A Theory of Coercion' (1990) 10 *OJLS* 94.

Hooley, R. J. A., 'Frand and Letters of Credit' [2002] *CLJ* 379.

Hooley, R. and O' Sullivan, J., 'Undue Influence and Unconscionable Bargains' [1997] *LMCLQ* 17.

Howard, M., Masefield, R. and Chuah, J. (eds), *Butterworths' Banking Law Guide* (Butterworths, London, 2006).

Howells, G., 'Social Fund Budgeting Loans: Social and Civil Justice?' (1990) *CJQ* 118.

Howells, G., *Comparative Product Liability* (Dartmouth Publishing Company, Dartmouth, 1993).

Howells, G., 'The Potential and Limits of Consumer Empowerment by Information' (2005) 32(3) *JLS* 2349–2370.

Howells, G., 'Data Protection, Confidentiality, Unfair Contract Terms, Consumer Protection and Credit Reference Agencies (1995) *JBL* 343–359.

Howells, G., 'Strict Liability' in G. Howells (ed.), *The Law of Product Liability* (2nd edn, Butterworths, London, 2007).

Howells, G., 'The Consumer Credit Litigation Explosion' (2010) 126 *LQR* 617–644.

Howells, G. and Bentley, L., 'Loansharks and Extortionate Credit Bargains' (1989) *Conv* 164 (Part I) and 234 (Part II).

Howells, G. and Weatherill, S., *Consumer Protection Law* (2nd edn, Ashgate Publishing, Surrey, 2005).

Howells, G., Micklitz, H. and Wilhelmsson, T., *European Fair Trading Law: The Unfair Commercial Practices Directive* (Ashgate Publishing, Surrey, 2006).

Ibbetson, D., '*Coggs v Bernard*', in C. Mitchell and P. Mitchell (eds), *Landmark Cases in the Law of Contract* (Hart Publishing, Oxford, 2008) Chapter 1.

Ibrahim, A. and Johnson, P., 'Is FOS Above the Law?' (2008) 23(8) *BJIB&FL* 423.

Johnson, H., 'Non-status Borrowers and the Consumer Credit Act 1974' (April 2002) *F&CL* 3–5.

Johnson, H., 'The Concept of Credit' (2004) *F&CL* 4–5.

Johnson, H., 'Credit Cards and Connected Lender Liability: Round Two to the Consumers' (May 2006) *F&CL*.

Johnson, H., 'Credit Intermediary Problems' (Aug/Sept 2007) *F&CL* 1–4.

Johnson, H., 'Carte Blanche for Hire Purchase Sharks' (2007) *NLJ* 734–735.

Johnson, H., 'Article 11 Consumer Credit Directive: Joint Liability: Continental Style' (Jan 2008) *F&CL* 1–3.

Johnson, H., 'The Communications Industry and Unfair Contract Terms: Tightening Control' (2009) 14(2) *Comms Law* 57–60.

Johnson, H., 'Consumer Chattel Mortgages: To Ban or Nor to Ban – Opportunity or Problem' (2011) *Durham Law Review*, 26 November.

Kelly, D., 'The Insured's Rights in Relation to the Provision of Information by the Insurer' (1989) 2 *Ins LJ* 45.

Kelsall, R., *Consumer Credit Law: Practice and Precedents* (Law Society Publishing, London, 2012).

Kenny, M., 'Standing Surety in Europe: Common Core or Tower of Babel' (2007) *MLR* 175.

Kenny, M. and Devenney, J., 'The Fallacy of the Common Core: Polycontextualism in Surety Protection: A Hard Case in Harmonisation Discourse' in M. Andenæs and C. Andersen (eds), *The Theory and Practice of Harmonisation* (Edward Elgar Publishing, Cheltenham, 2012).

Knight, C., 'Owusu and Turner: The Shark in the Water' [2007] 66 *CLJ* 288.

Kenny, M., Devenney, J. and Fox-O'Mahony, L. *Unconscionability in European Private Law Financial Transactions* (Cambridge University Press, Cambridge, 2010).

Kornhauser, L. A., 'Unconscionability in Standard Forms' (1976) 64(5) Sept. *California Law Review* 1152.

Lando, O. and Nielsen, P., 'The Rome I Regulation' [2008] *CMLR* 1687, 1722.

Law Commission, *Implied Terms in Contracts for the Supply of Services* (Law Com No 156, 1986).

Law Commission, *Rights of Suit: Carriage of Goods by Sea* (Law Com No 196, 1991).

Law Commission, *Restitution: Mistakes of Law and* Ultra Vires *Public Authority Receipts and Payments* (Law Com No 227, 1994).

Law Commission (No 292), *Unfair Terms in Contracts* (HMSO, London, 2005).

Law Commission, *Company Security Interests* (Law Com No 295, 2005).

Law Commission, *A Private Right of Redress for Unfair Commercial Practices* (Law Commission, London, 2008).

Lawson, F. H., 'The Passing of Property and Risk in Sale of Goods: A Comparative Study' (1949) 65 *LQR* 352.

Low Commissions, 'Consumer Remedies for Faulty Goods' (2008) (Law Com Consultation Paper 188 and Scot Law Com Discussion Paper No 139).

Law Commissions, 'Consumer remedies for Faully Goods: A Summary of Responses to Consultation' (May 2009).

Layton, A. and Mercer, H., *European Civil Practice* (2nd rev. edn, Sweet and Maxwell, London, 2004).

Leff, A. A., 'Contract as a Thing' (2006) 19 *American University Law Review* 131–157.

Lomnicka, E. (ed.), *Encyclopedios of Consumer Credit Law* (Looseleaf, Sweet and Maxwell, London, 1975).

Loos, M., 'Rights of Withdrawal', in G. Howells and R. Schultze, *Modernising and Harmonising Consumer Contract Law* (Sellier European Law Publishers, Munich, 2009).

Lorenzon, F., 'International Trade and Shipping Documents', in Y. Baatz, *Maritime Law* (formerly Sonthampton on Shipping Law (Sweet and Maxwell, London, 2011).

Lowry, J., Rawlings, P. and Merkin, R., *Insurance Law: Doctrines and Principles* (Hart Publishing, Oxford, 2011).

Lumsden, J., 'Contracts (Rights of Third Parties) Act 1999: Its Impact on Financiers' Assignments of Contracts' [2000] *JIBL* 160.

Macdonald, E., 'Unifying Unfair Terms Legislation' (2004) 67 *MLR* 69.

Macdonald, E., 'Bank Charges and the Core Exemption' (2008) 71 *MLR* 987.

MacDonald, J., Phipps, S. and Holderness, K., '*Brandon v American Express Services Ltd* [2011] EWCA Civ 1187, [2012] ECC 2 and Compliance with s. 88(2) of the Consumer Credit Act 1974' (2012) 27(1) *BJIB&FL* 58–59.

MacDonald, I., 'What's the Story with Multiple Agreements?' (1999) *NLJ* 962.

MacLeod, J., *Consumer Sales Law: The Law Relating to Consumer Sales and Financing of Goods* (2nd edn, Routledge-Cavendish, Oxford, 2007).

Malcolm, C. A., *The Bank of Scotland 1695–1945* (1948).

Malek, A. and Quest, D., *Jack on Documentary Credits* (4th edn, Tottel, London, 2009).

Mance, J., 'Exclusive Jurisdiction Agreements and European Ideals' (2004) 120 *LQR* 357.

Mawrey, R. and Riley-Smith, T., *Blackstone's Guide to the Consumer Credit Act 2006* (Oxford University Press, Oxford, 2006).

Mayson, S., French, D. and Ryan, C., *Company Law* (28th edn, Oxford University Press, Oxford, 2011).

McBain, G., 'Modernising and Codifying the Law of Bailment' [2008] *JBL* 1.

McBarnet, D. and Whelan, C., 'The Elusive Spirit of the Law: Formalism and the Struggle for Legal Control' [1991] *MLR* 848.

McCormack, G., *Reservation of Title* (Sweet and Maxwell, London, 1990).

McCormack, G., 'Reservation of Title in England and New Zealand' (1992) 12 *LS* 195.

McCormack, G., 'Protection of Surety Guarantors in England: Prophylactics and Procedure', in A. Colombi Ciacchi (ed.), *Protection of Non-professional Sureties in Europe: Formal and Substantive Disparity* (Nomos, Germany, 2007).

McGrath, P., 'The Nature of Modern Guarantees' (2009) *CRI* 10.

McKendrick, E. (ed.), *Force Majeure and Frustration of Contract* (2nd edn, LLP, London, 1995).

McKendrick, E., *Goode on Commercial Law* (4th edn, Butterworths, London, 2010).

McLean, D. and Beevers, K., *Morris: The Conflict of Laws* (6th edn, Sweet and Maxwell, London, 2005).

McMeel, G., 'The FSA's Insurance Conduct of Business Regime: A Revolution in (Consumer) Insurance Law?' [2005] *LMCLQ* 186.

McMurtry, L., 'Unconscionability and Undue Influence: An Interaction?' [2000] 64 *Conv* 573.

McQneen, H., 'Faulty Goods, Rejection and Connected Lender Liability' (2011) 15(1) *Edin LR* 111–115.

Mee, J., 'Undue influence and Bank Guarantees' [2002] 37 *Irish Jurist* 292.

Merkin, R. M. and Flannery, L., *Arbitration Act 1996* (4th edn, Informa Law, London, 2008).

Merkin, R. M. and Rodger, A., *EC Insurance Law* (Longman, Harlow, 1997).

Merrett, L., 'The Enforcement of Jurisdiction Agreements within the Brussels Regime' (2006) 55 *ICLQ* 315.

Micklitz, H., 'La Loi Allemand Relative au Régime Fundique des Conditions Générales des Contrats du 9 Decembre 1976' (1989) *Rev. Int. Droit Comparé* 101.

Mitchell, C. and Mitchell, P. (eds), *Landmark Cases in the Law of Contract* (Hart Publishing, Oxford, 2008).

Morgan-Taylor, M. and Naidoo, A., 'The Draft Regulations to Adopf the Directive on Certain Aspects of the Sale of Consumer Goods and Associated Guarantees: Problems of the Time of Conformity for the Quality Obligation' [2002] 3 *WebJCLI*.

Morgan-Taylor, M., 'Preventing Distribution of Promotions to Consumers Involving Unfair Practices: OFT Application for Order Under Euterprise Act 2002: OFT v Purely Creative Ltd et al.', *Communications Law* 16(3) 2011, 115–117.

Morris, D., 'Surety Wives in the House of Lords: Time for Solicitors to "Get Real"?' (2003) 11 *Feminist LS* 57.

Morris, P. E., 'The Financial Ombudsman Service and the Hunt Review: Continuing Evolution in Dispute Resolution' (2008) 8 *JBL* 785.

Moses, M. L., *The Principles and Practice of International Commercial Arbitration* (Cambridge University Press, Cambridge, 2008).

Munro, N., *The History of the Royal Bank of Scotland 1727–1927* (1927).

Murray, C., Holloway, D. and Timson-Hunt, D., *Schmitthoff's Export Trade: The Law and Practice of International Trade* (11th edn, Sweet and Maxwell, London, 2007).

Murray, C., Dixon, G., Holloway, D. and Timson-Hunt, D. *Schmitthoff's Export Trade: The Law and Practice of International Trade* (11th edn, Sweet and Maxwell, London, 2007).

Nebbia, P., *Unfair Contract Terms in European Law* (Hart Publishing, Oxford, 2007).

Newdick, C., 'The Development Risk Defence of the Consumer Protection Act 1987' (1988) 47 *CLJ* 455.

Nordhausen Scholes, A., 'Information Requirements', in G. Howells and R. Schultze (eds) *Modernising and Harmonising Consumer Contract Law* (Sellier European Law Publishers, Munich, 2009).

O'Callaghan, P., 'Protection from Unfair Suretyships in Ireland' in A. Colombi Ciacchi (ed.), *Protection of Non-Professional Sureties in Europe: Formal and Substantive Disparity* (Nomos, Germany, 2007).

O'Donovan, J. and Phillips, J., *The Modern Contract of Guarantee* (Sweet and Maxwell, London, 2003).

Offer, A., *The Challenge of Affluence: Self-control and Well-being in the United States and Britain since 1950* (Oxford University Press, Oxford, 2007).

OFT, *Extended Warranties on Domestic Electrical Goods*, 2002b, OFT, para. 4.31.

OFT, *Doorstep Selling: A Report on the Market Study*, 2004, OFT 716.

OFT, *Trading Standards Impact*, 2009, OFT June 1085 and OFT PN 65/09, June 2009.

Oldham, M., ' "Neither Borrower Nor Lender Be": the Life of O'Brien' (1995) *Child and Family Law Quarterly* 104.

O'Sullivan, J., 'Undue Influence and Misrepresentation after O'Brien: Making Security Secure', F. in Rose (ed.) *Restitution and Banking Law* (Mansfield Press, Oxford, 1998).

Palmer, N., 'Reservation of Title' (1992) 5 *JCL* 175.

Palmer, N. and Yates, D., 'The Application of Consumer Credit Act 1974 to Consumer Hire Agreements' (1979) 38 *CLJ* 180.

Parris, J., *Effective Retention of Title Clauses* (WileyBlackwell, Oxford, 1986).

Parry, D., 'Judicial Approaches to Due Diligence' (1995) *CLR* 695.

Parry, R., 'The Position of Family Sureties within the Framework of Protection for Consumer Debtors in European Member States' (2005) 13 *ERPL* 357.

Pawlowski, M. and Brown, J., *Undue Influence and the Family Home* (Cavendish, London, 2001).

Phang, A., 'Undue Influence Methodology, Sources and Linkages' [1995] *JBL* 552.

Phillips, J., 'Equitable Liens: A Search for a Unifying Principle', in N. Palmer and E. McKendrick (eds), *Interests in Goods* (2nd edn, LLP, London, 1998).

Philpott, F. *et al.*, *The Law of Consumer Credit and Hire* (Oxford University Press, Oxford, 2009).

Poole, J. and Keyser, A., 'Justifying Partial Rescission in English Law' (2005) 121 *LQR* 273.

Price, N. S., 'Undue Influence: *Finis Litium*' (1999) 115 *LQR* 8.

Proctor, C., *Mann on the Legal Aspect of Money* (6th edn, Oxford University Press, Oxford, 2005).

Proctor, C., *Goode on Payment Obligations in Commercial and Financial Transactions* (2nd rev. edn, Sweet and Maxwell, London, 2009).

Rakoff, T. D., 'Contracts of Adhesion: An Essay in Reconstruction', 96 *Harvard Law Review* 1176.

Ramsay, I., *Consumer Law and Policy: Text and Materials on Regulating Consumer Markets* (2nd edn, Hart Publishing, Oxford, 2007).

Reich, N., 'Crisis or Future of European Consumer Law', in D. Parry, A. Nordhausen, G. Howells and C. Twigg-Flesner (eds), *The Yearbook of Consumer Law 2009* (Ashgate Surrey, 2008).

Reynolds, F., 'Contracts Illegal by the *lex loci solutionis*' (1992) 108 *LQR* 553.

Rosenthal, D., *A Guide to Consumer Credit Law and Practice* (3rd edn, Tottel Publishing, London, 2008).

Ryder, N. and Devenney, J. P., 'The Labour Government and Access to Affordable Credit: More Spin than Action?' (2005) 27(3–4) *Journal of Social Welfare and Family Law* 395.

Ryder, N., Devenney, N. P. and Howells, G., 'The Credit Crunch: The Right Time for Credit Unions to Strike?' (2009) 29(1) *LS* 75–98.

Saggerson, A., *Travel: Law and Litigation* (3rd edn, XPL Publishing, St Albans, 2004).

Saldov, D. and Cunnington, R. (eds), *Contract Damages: Domestic and International Perspectives* (Hart Publishing, Oxford, 2008).

Salinger, F. R., Davidson, N., Mills, S. and Ruddy, N., *Salinger on Factoring: The Law and Practice of Invoice Finance* (4th edn, Sweet and Maxwell, London, 2005).

Sassoon, D. M., 'The Origin of FOB and CIF Terms and the Factors Influencing their Choice' [1967] *JBL* 32.

Schmitthoff, C. M., 'The Concept of Economic Law in England' [1966] *JBL* 309.

Schmitthoff, C. M., *Commercial Law in a Changing Economic Climate* (2nd edn, Sweet and Maxwell, London, 1981).

Schmitthoff, C. M., *Select Essays on International Trade Law* (Nijhoff, Graham and Trotman, London, 1988).

Schulte-Nölke, H., *EC Consumer Law Compendium – Comparative Analysis* (2008) (at: http://ec.europa.eu/consumers/rights/does/consumer_law_compendium_comparitive_analysis_en_final.pdf).

Sealy, L. S., 'Risk in the Law of Sale' [1972B] *CLJ* 225.

Sealy, L. S. and Hooley, R. J. A., *Commercial Law: Text, Cases and Materials* (4th edn, Oxford University Press, Oxford, 2008).

Sheehan, D., *The Principles of Personal Property Law* (Hart Publishing, Oxford, 2011).

Sheridan, L. A. and Keeton, G. W., *Fraud and Unconscionable Bargains* (Barry Rose, Chichester, 1985).

Simpson, B., Chapter 1 in, M. P. Furmston, *Cheshire, Fifoot and Furmston's Law of Contract* (16th edn, Oxford University Press, Oxford, 2012).

Skene, L., 'Proprietary Rights in Human Bodies, Body Parts and Tissue: Regulatory Contexts and Proposals for New Laws' (2002) 22 *LS* 102.

Smith, J. and McCalla, S., *Consumer Credit Act 2006: A Guide to the New Act* (The Law Society, London, 2006).

Smith, S., 'In Defence of Substantive Fairness' (1996) 112 *LQR* 138.

Smith, L., 'Threeparty . . . for Mistake of Law (*Kleinwort Benson* v *Lincoln CC*)' [1999] *RLR* 148.

Smith, S. and Atiyah, P. S., *Atiyah's Introduction to the Law of Contract* (6th edn, Clarendon, Oxford, 2002).

St John Sutton, D., Gill, J. and Gearing, M., *Russell on Arbitration* (23rd edn, Sweet and Maxwell, London, 2007).

Stapleton, J., *Product Liability* (Butterworths, London, 1994).

Stassen, J. C., (1978) 95 *South African Law Journal* 180.

Stearns, P., 'Stages of Consumerism: Recent Work on the Issues of Periodization' (1997) 69 *Journal of Modern History* 102.

Steyn, 'Contract Law: Fulfilling the Expectations of Honest Men' [1997] *LQR* 433.

Stokes, P., 'New OFT Powers in Credit Clamp Down' (2005) *NLJ* 236.

Struycken, T. H. D., 'Some Dutch Reflections on the Rome Convention, Article 4(5)' [1996] *LMCLQ* 18.

Stuyck, J., 'Unfair Terms', in G. Howells and R. Schultze (eds) *Modernising and Harmonising Consumer Contract Law* (Sellier European Law Publishers, Munich, 2009).

Sydenham, A., 'Unreasonable Delay: Something of a Long-stop on the Failure of a Notice to Complete?' (1980) 44 *Conv* 19.

Takahashi, K., 'Right to Terminate (Avoid) International Sales of Commodities' [2003] *JBL* 102.

Tijo, H., 'O'Brien and Unconscionability' (1997) 113 *LQR* 129.

Todd, P., *Cases and Materials on International Trade Law* (Thomson Sweet and Maxwell, London, 2003).

Todd, P. [2008], 'Non-genuine Shipping Documents and Nullities' *LMCLQ* 547.

Trackman, L. E., 'The Evolution of the Law Merchaut: Our Commercial Heritage' [1980] 12(1) *JML&C* 1.

Treitel, G. H., 'Specific Performance in the Sale of Goods' [1966] *JBL* 21, at 215.

Treitel, G. H., *Frustration and Force Majeure* (Sweet and Maxwell, London, 2004).

Tweeddale, A. and Tweeddale, K., *Arbitration of Commercial Disputes: International and English Law and Practice* (Oxford University Press, Oxford, 2007).

Twigg-Flesner, C., *Consumer Product Guarantees* (Ashgate, Surrey, 2003).

Twigg-Flesner, C., Parry, D., Howells, G. and Nordhausen, A., *An Analysis of the Application and Scope of the UCP Directive* (DTI, London, 2005).

Twigg-Flesner, C., 'Fit for Purpose?: The Proposals on Sales', in G. Howells and R. Schultze (eds) *Modernising and Harmonising Consumer Contract Law* (Sellier European Law Publishers, Munich, 2009).

Tyler, E. L. G. and Palmer, N. E., *Crossley Vaines' Personal Property* (5th edn, Butterworths, London, 1973).

Von Bar, C. and Clive, E., *Principles, Definitions and Model Rules of European Private Law: Draft Common Frame of Reference* (OUP/Sellier, Oxford, 2010).

Verrill, J., 'Unlocking Capital: Factoring and Invoice Discounting' (1997) 8(2) *PLC* 31.

Waddams, S. M., 'Protection of Wealeer Parties in English Law', in M. Kenny, J. Devenney and L. Fox O'Mahony, *Unconscionability in European Private Law Financial Transactions* (Cambridge University Press, Cambridge, 2010).

Walters, A., 'Priority of the Floating Charge in Corporate Insolvency: *Griffiths* v *Yorkshire Bank PLC*' (1995) 16 *Co Law* 291.

Watts, G., *Bowstead and Reynolds on Agency* (18th edn and 2nd supp., Sweet and Maxwell, London, 2009).

Weatherill, S., 'Who is the Average Consumer?' in Bernitz, U. and Weatherill, S. (eds), *The Regulation of Unfair Commercial Practices Under EC Directive 2005/29: New Rules and New Techniques* (Hart Publishing, Oxford, 2007).

Wheeler, S., *Reservation of Title Clauses: Impact and Implications* (Oxford University Press, Oxford, 1991).

Whittaker, S., 'A Framework of Principle for European Contract Law' (2009) 125 *LQR* 616.

Wilhelmsson, T. and Willett, C., 'Unfair Terms and Standard Form Contracts', in G. Howells, I. Ramsay and T. Wilhelmsson (eds), *Handbook of Research on International Consumer Law* (Edward Elgar Publishing, Cheltenham, 2010).

Willett, C., 'Implementation of the Unfair Terms Directive in the UK' (1997) *ERPL* 223.

Willett, C., 'The Functions of Transparency in Regulating Contract Terms: UK and Australian Approaches' (2001) 60 *ICLQ* 355–385.

Willett, C., 'Direct Producer Liability', in G. Howells and R. Schultze (eds), *Modernising and Harmonising Consumer Contract Law* (Sellier European Law Publishers, Munich, 2009).

Willett, C., *Fairness in Consumer Contracts: The Case of Unfair Terms* (Ashgate, Surrey, 2007).

Willett, C., 'The Role of Contract Law in Product Liability', in G. Howells (ed.), *The Law of Product Liability* (2nd edn, Butterworths, London, 2007).

Willett, C. and Oughton, D., 'Liability for Incorrect Installation and Other Services Associated with Consumer Goods', in G. Howells, A. Nordhausen, D. Parry and C. Twigg-Flesner (eds), *The Yearbook of Consumer Law 2007* (Ashgate, Surrey, 2007).

Willett, C., 'Unfairness under the Consumer Protection from Unfair Trading Regulations', in J. Devenney, L. Fox-O'Mahoney and M. Kenny (eds), *Unconscionability in European Financial Transactions* (Cambridge University Press, Cambridge, 2010).

Willett, C., 'Fairness and Consumer Decision Making Under the Unfair Commercial Practices Directive' (2010) 33 *Journal of Consumer Policy* 247–273.

Willett, C., 'The Functions of Transparency in Regulating Contract Terms: UK and Australian Approaches' (2011) 60 *ICLQ* 355–385.

Willett, C., 'General Clanses and Competing Ethics of European Consumer Law in the UK' (2012) 71(2) *CLJ* 412–440.

Willett, C. and Morgan-Taylor, M., 'Recognising the Limits of Transparency in EU Consumer Law', in J. Devenney and M. Kenny (eds) *European Consumer Protection, Theory and Practice* (Cambridge University Press, Cambridge, 2012).

Willett, C., Naidoo, A. and Morgan-Taylor, M., 'The Sale and Supply of Goods to Consumers Regulations' (2004) *JBL* 94.

Worthington, S., 'Floating Charges: An Alternative Theory' [1994] *CLJ* 81.

Worthington, S., *Personal Property Law: Text, Cases and Materials* (Hart Publishing, Oxford, 2000).

Worthington, S., *Equity* (2nd edn, Oxford University Press, Oxford, 2006).

Yeo, T. M., *Choice of Law for Equitable Doctrines* (Oxford University Press, Oxford, 2004).

Yeo, H. Y., 'Of Reciprocity and Remedies: Dnty of Disclosure in Insurance Contracts' (1991) 11 *LS* 131.

Index